Hana Chockler · Georg Weissenbacher (Eds.)

Computer Aided Verification

30th International Conference, CAV 2018
Held as Part of the Federated Logic Conference, FloC 2018
Oxford, UK, July 14–17, 2018
Proceedings, Part I

Editors
Hana Chockler
King's College
London
UK

Georg Weissenbacher
TU Wien
Vienna
Austria

https://doi.org/10.1007/978-3-319-96145-3

LNCS Sublibrary: SL1 – Theoretical Computer Science and General Issues

Preface

It was our privilege to serve as the program chairs for CAV 2018, the 30th International Conference on Computer-Aided Verification. CAV is an annual conference dedicated to the advancement of the theory and practice of computer-aided formal analysis methods for hardware and software systems. CAV 2018 was held in Oxford, UK, July 14–17, 2018, with the tutorials day on July 13.

This year, CAV was held as part of the Federated Logic Conference (FLoC) event and was collocated with many other conferences in logic. The primary focus of CAV is to spur advances in hardware and software verification while expanding to new domains such as learning, autonomous systems, and computer security. CAV is at the cutting edge of research in formal methods, as reflected in this year's program.

CAV 2018 covered a wide spectrum of subjects, from theoretical results to concrete applications, including papers on application of formal methods in large-scale industrial settings. It has always been one of the primary interests of CAV to include papers that describe practical verification tools and solutions and techniques that ensure a high practical appeal of the results. The proceedings of the conference are published in Springer's *Lecture Notes in Computer Science* series. A selection of papers were invited to a special issue of *Formal Methods in System Design* and the *Journal of the ACM*.

This is the first year that the CAV proceedings are published under an Open Access license, thus giving access to CAV proceedings to a broad audience. We hope that this decision will increase the scope of practical applications of formal methods and will attract even more interest from industry.

CAV received a very high number of submissions this year—215 overall—resulting in a highly competitive selection process. We accepted 13 tool papers and 52 regular papers, which amounts to an acceptance rate of roughly 30% (for both regular papers and tool papers). The high number of excellent submissions in combination with the scheduling constraints of FLoC forced us to reduce the length of the talks to 15 minutes, giving equal exposure and weight to regular papers and tool papers.

The accepted papers cover a wide range of topics and techniques, from algorithmic and logical foundations of verification to practical applications in distributed, networked, cyber-physical, and autonomous systems. Other notable topics are synthesis, learning, security, and concurrency in the context of formal methods. The proceedings are organized according to the sessions in the conference.

The program featured two invited talks by Eran Yahav (Technion), on using deep learning for programming, and by Somesh Jha (University of Wisconsin Madison) on adversarial deep learning. The invited talks this year reflect the growing interest of the CAV community in deep learning and its connection to formal methods. The tutorial day of CAV featured two invited tutorials, by Shaz Qadeer on verification of concurrent programs and by Matteo Maffei on static analysis of smart contracts. The subjects of the tutorials reflect the increasing volume of research on verification of concurrent software and, as of recently, the question of correctness of smart contracts. As every year, one of the winners of the CAV award also contributed a presentation. The tutorial day featured a workshop in memoriam of Mike Gordon, titled "Three Research Vignettes in Memory of Mike Gordon," organized by Tom Melham and jointly supported by CAV and ITP communities.

Moreover, we continued the tradition of organizing a LogicLounge. Initiated by the late Helmut Veith at the Vienna Summer of Logic 2014, the LogicLounge is a series of discussions on computer science topics targeting a general audience and has become a regular highlight at CAV. This year's LogicLounge took place at the Oxford Union and was on the topic of "Ethics and Morality of Robotics," moderated by Judy Wajcman and featuring a panel of experts on the topic: Luciano Floridi, Ben Kuipers, Francesca Rossi, Matthias Scheutz, Sandra Wachter, and Jeannette Wing. We thank May Chan, Katherine Fletcher, and Marta Kwiatkowska for organizing this event, and the Vienna Center of Logic and Algorithms for their support.

In addition, CAV attendees enjoyed a number of FLoC plenary talks and events targeting the broad FLoC community.

In addition to the main conference, CAV hosted the Verification Mentoring Workshop for junior scientists entering the field and a high number of pre- and post-conference technical workshops: the Workshop on Formal Reasoning in Distributed Algorithms (FRIDA), the workshop on Runtime Verification for Rigorous Systems Engineering (RV4RISE), the 5th Workshop on Horn Clauses for Verification and Synthesis (HCVS), the 7th Workshop on Synthesis (SYNT), the First International Workshop on Parallel Logical Reasoning (PLR), the 10th Working Conference on Verified Software: Theories, Tools and Experiments (VSTTE), the Workshop on Machine Learning for Programming (MLP), the 11th International Workshop on Numerical Software Verification (NSV), the Workshop on Verification of Engineered Molecular Devices and Programs (VEMDP), the Third Workshop on Fun With Formal Methods (FWFM), the Workshop on Robots, Morality, and Trust through the Verification Lens, and the IFAC Conference on Analysis and Design of Hybrid Systems (ADHS).

The Program Committee (PC) for CAV consisted of 80 members; we kept the number large to ensure each PC member would have a reasonable number of papers to review and be able to provide thorough reviews. As the review process for CAV is double-blind, we kept the number of external reviewers to a minimum, to avoid accidental disclosures and conflicts of interest. Altogether, the reviewers drafted over 860 reviews and made an enormous effort to ensure a high-quality program. Following the tradition of CAV in recent years, the artifact evaluation was mandatory for tool submissions and optional but encouraged for regular submissions. We used an Artifact Evaluation Committee of 25 members. Our goal for artifact evaluation was to provide friendly "beta-testing" to tool developers; we recognize that developing a stable tool on a cutting-edge research topic is certainly not easy and we hope the constructive comments provided by the Artifact Evaluation Committee (AEC) were of help to the developers. As a result of the evaluation, the AEC accepted 25 of 31 artifacts accompanying regular papers; moreover, all 13 accepted tool papers passed the evaluation. We are grateful to the reviewers for their outstanding efforts in making sure each paper was fairly assessed. We would like to thank our artifact evaluation chair,

Igor Konnov, and the AEC for evaluating all artifacts submitted with tool papers as well as optional artifacts submitted with regular papers.

Of course, without the tremendous effort put into the review process by our PC members this conference would not have been possible. We would like to thank the PC members for their effort and thorough reviews.

We would like to thank the FLoC chairs, Moshe Vardi, Daniel Kroening, and Marta Kwiatkowska, for the support provided, Thanh Hai Tran for maintaining the CAV website, and the always helpful Steering Committee members Orna Grumberg, Aarti Gupta, Daniel Kroening, and Kenneth McMillan. Finally, we would like to thank the team at the University of Oxford, who took care of the administration and organization of FLoC, thus making our jobs as CAV chairs much easier.

July 2018

Hana Chockler
Georg Weissenbacher

Organization

Program Committee

Aws Albarghouthi	University of Wisconsin-Madison, USA
Christel Baier	TU Dresden, Germany
Clark Barrett	Stanford University, USA
Ezio Bartocci	TU Wien, Austria
Dirk Beyer	LMU Munich, Germany
Per Bjesse	Synopsys Inc., USA
Jasmin Christian Blanchette	Vrije Universiteit Amsterdam, Netherlands
Roderick Bloem	Graz University of Technology, Austria
Ahmed Bouajjani	IRIF, University Paris Diderot, France
Pavol Cerny	University of Colorado Boulder, USA
Rohit Chadha	University of Missouri, USA
Swarat Chaudhuri	Rice University, USA
Wei-Ngan Chin	National University of Singapore, Singapore
Hana Chockler	King's College London, UK
Alessandro Cimatti	Fondazione Bruno Kessler, Italy
Loris D'Antoni	University of Wisconsin-Madison, USA
Vijay D'Silva	Google, USA
Cristina David	University of Cambridge, UK
Jyotirmoy Deshmukh	University of Southern California, USA
Isil Dillig	The University of Texas at Austin, USA
Cezara Dragoi	Inria Paris, ENS, France
Kerstin Eder	University of Bristol, UK
Michael Emmi	Nokia Bell Labs, USA
Georgios Fainekos	Arizona State University, USA
Dana Fisman	University of Pennsylvania, USA
Vijay Ganesh	University of Waterloo, Canada
Sicun Gao	University of California San Diego, USA
Alberto Griggio	Fondazione Bruno Kessler, Italy
Orna Grumberg	Technion - Israel Institute of Technology, Israel
Arie Gurfinkel	University of Waterloo, Canada
William Harrison	Department of CS, University of Missouri, Columbia, USA
Gerard Holzmann	Nimble Research, USA
Alan J. Hu	The University of British Columbia, Canada
Franjo Ivancic	Google, USA
Alexander Ivrii	IBM, Israel
Himanshu Jain	Synopsys, USA
Somesh Jha	University of Wisconsin-Madison, USA

Susmit Jha	SRI International, USA
Ranjit Jhala	University of California San Diego, USA
Barbara Jobstmann	EPFL and Cadence Design Systems, Switzerland
Stefan Kiefer	University of Oxford, UK
Zachary Kincaid	Princeton University, USA
Laura Kovacs	TU Wien, Austria
Viktor Kuncak	Ecole Polytechnique Fédérale de Lausanne, Switzerland
Orna Kupferman	Hebrew University, Israel
Shuvendu Lahiri	Microsoft, USA
Rupak Majumdar	MPI-SWS, Germany
Ken McMillan	Microsoft, USA
Alexander Nadel	Intel, Israel
Mayur Naik	Intel, USA
Kedar Namjoshi	Nokia Bell Labs, USA
Dejan Nickovic	Austrian Institute of Technology AIT, Austria
Corina Pasareanu	CMU/NASA Ames Research Center, USA
Nir Piterman	University of Leicester, UK
Pavithra Prabhakar	Kansas State University, USA
Mitra Purandare	IBM Research Laboratory Zurich, Switzerland
Shaz Qadeer	Microsoft, USA
Arjun Radhakrishna	Microsoft, USA
Noam Rinetzky	Tel Aviv University, Israel
Philipp Ruemmer	Uppsala University, Sweden
Roopsha Samanta	Purdue University, USA
Sriram Sankaranarayanan	University of Colorado, Boulder, USA
Martina Seidl	Johannes Kepler University Linz, Austria
Koushik Sen	University of California, Berkeley, USA
Sanjit A. Seshia	University of California, Berkeley, USA
Natasha Sharygina	Università della Svizzera Italiana, Lugano, Switzerland
Sharon Shoham	Tel Aviv University, Israel
Anna Slobodova	Centaur Technology, USA
Armando Solar-Lezama	MIT, USA
Ofer Strichman	Technion, Israel
Serdar Tasiran	Amazon Web Services, USA
Caterina Urban	ETH Zurich, Switzerland
Yakir Vizel	Technion, Israel
Tomas Vojnar	Brno University of Technology, Czechia
Thomas Wahl	Northeastern University, USA
Bow-Yaw Wang	Academia Sinica, Taiwan
Georg Weissenbacher	TU Wien, Austria
Thomas Wies	New York University, USA
Karen Yorav	IBM Research Laboratory Haifa, Israel
Lenore Zuck	University of Illinois in Chicago, USA
Damien Zufferey	MPI-SWS, Germany
Florian Zuleger	TU Wien, Austria

Artifact Evaluation Committee

Thibaut Balabonski	Université Paris-Sud, France
Sergiy Bogomolov	The Australian National University, Australia
Simon Cruanes	Aesthetic Integration, USA
Matthias Dangl	LMU Munich, Germany
Eva Darulova	Max Planck Institute for Software Systems, Germany
Ramiro Demasi	Universidad Nacional de Córdoba, Argentina
Grigory Fedyukovich	Princeton University, USA
Johannes Hölzl	Vrije Universiteit Amsterdam, The Netherlands
Jochen Hoenicke	University of Freiburg, Germany
Antti Hyvärinen	Università della Svizzera Italiana, Lugano, Switzerland
Swen Jacobs	Saarland University, Germany
Saurabh Joshi	IIT Hyderabad, India
Dejan Jovanovic	SRI International, USA
Ayrat Khalimov	The Hebrew University, Israel
Igor Konnov (Chair)	Inria Nancy (LORIA), France
Jan Kretínský	Technical University of Munich, Germany
Alfons Laarman	Leiden University, The Netherlands
Ravichandhran Kandhadai Madhavan	Ecole Polytechnique Fédérale de Lausanne, Switzerland
Andrea Micheli	Fondazione Bruno Kessler, Italy
Sergio Mover	University of Colorado Boulder, USA
Aina Niemetz	Stanford University, USA
Burcu Kulahcioglu Ozkan	MPI-SWS, Germany
Markus N. Rabe	University of California, Berkeley, USA
Andrew Reynolds	University of Iowa, USA
Martin Suda	TU Wien, Austria
Mitra Tabaei	TU Wien, Austria

Additional Reviewers

Alpernas, Kalev
Asadi, Sepideh
Athanasiou, Konstantinos
Bauer, Matthew
Bavishi, Rohan
Bayless, Sam
Berzish, Murphy
Blicha, Martin
Bui, Phi Diep
Cauderlier, Raphaël
Cauli, Claudia
Ceska, Milan
Cohen, Ernie
Costea, Andreea
Dangl, Matthias
Doko, Marko
Drachsler Cohen, Dana
Dreossi, Tommaso
Dutra, Rafael
Ebrahimi, Masoud
Eisner, Cindy
Fedyukovich, Grigory
Fremont, Daniel
Freund, Stephen
Friedberger, Karlheinz
Ghorbani, Soudeh
Ghosh, Shromona
Goel, Shilpi
Gong, Liang
Govind, Hari
Gu, Yijia
Habermehl, Peter
Hamza, Jad
He, Paul
Heo, Kihong
Holik, Lukas

Humenberger, Andreas
Hyvärinen, Antti
Hölzl, Johannes
Iusupov, Rinat
Jacobs, Swen
Jain, Mitesh
Jaroschek, Maximilian
Jha, Sumit Kumar
Keidar-Barner, Sharon
Khalimov, Ayrat
Kiesl, Benjamin
Koenighofer, Bettina
Krstic, Srdjan
Laeufer, Kevin
Lee, Woosuk
Lemberger, Thomas
Lemieux, Caroline
Lewis, Robert
Liang, Jia
Liang, Jimmy
Liu, Peizun
Lång, Magnus
Maffei, Matteo
Marescotti, Matteo
Mathur, Umang
Miné, Antoine
Mora, Federico
Nevo, Ziv
Ochoa, Martin
Orni, Avigail
Ouaknine, Joel
Padhye, Rohan
Padon, Oded
Partush, Nimrod
Pavlinovic, Zvonimir
Pavlogiannis, Andreas
Peled, Doron
Pendharkar, Ishan
Peng, Yan
Petri, Gustavo
Polozov, Oleksandr
Popescu, Andrei
Potomkin, Kostiantyn
Raghothaman, Mukund
Reynolds, Andrew
Reynolds, Thomas
Ritirc, Daniela
Rogalewicz, Adam
Scott, Joe
Shacham, Ohad
Song, Yahui
Sosnovich, Adi
Sousa, Marcelo
Subramanian, Kausik
Sumners, Rob
Swords, Sol
Ta, Quang Trung
Tautschnig, Michael
Traytel, Dmitriy
Trivedi, Ashutosh
Udupa, Abhishek
van Dijk, Tom
Wendler, Philipp
Zdancewic, Steve
Zulkoski, Ed

Contents – Part I

Invited Papers

Tutorials

Model Checking

Program Analysis Using Polyhedra

Synthesis

Learning

Runtime Verification, Hybrid and Timed Systems

Tools

Probabilistic Systems

Contents – Part II

Invited Papers

Semantic Adversarial Deep Learning

Tommaso Dreossi[1], Somesh Jha[2(✉)], and Sanjit A. Seshia[1]

[1] University of California at Berkeley, Berkeley, USA
{dreossi,sseshia}@berkeley.edu
[2] University of Wisconsin, Madison, Madison, USA
jha@cs.wisc.edu

Abstract. Fueled by massive amounts of data, models produced by machine-learning (ML) algorithms, especially deep neural networks, are being used in diverse domains where trustworthiness is a concern, including automotive systems, finance, health care, natural language processing, and malware detection. Of particular concern is the use of ML algorithms in cyber-physical systems (CPS), such as self-driving cars and aviation, where an adversary can cause serious consequences.

However, existing approaches to generating adversarial examples and devising robust ML algorithms mostly ignore the *semantics* and *context* of the overall system containing the ML component. For example, in an autonomous vehicle using deep learning for perception, not every adversarial example for the neural network might lead to a harmful consequence. Moreover, one may want to prioritize the search for adversarial examples towards those that significantly modify the desired semantics of the overall system. Along the same lines, existing algorithms for constructing robust ML algorithms ignore the specification of the overall system. In this paper, we argue that the semantics and specification of the overall system has a crucial role to play in this line of research. We present preliminary research results that support this claim.

1 Introduction

Machine learning (ML) algorithms, fueled by massive amounts of data, are increasingly being utilized in several domains, including healthcare, finance, and transportation. Models produced by ML algorithms, especially *deep neural networks* (DNNs), are being deployed in domains where trustworthiness is a big concern, such as automotive systems [35], finance [25], health care [2], computer vision [28], speech recognition [17], natural language processing [38], and cyber-security [8,42]. Of particular concern is the use of ML (including deep learning) in *cyber-physical systems* (CPS) [29], where the presence of an adversary can cause serious consequences. For example, much of the technology behind autonomous and driver-less vehicle development is "powered" by machine learning [4,14]. DNNs have also been used in airborne collision avoidance systems for unmanned aircraft (ACAS Xu) [22]. However, *in designing and deploying these algorithms in critical cyber-physical systems, the presence of an active adversary is often ignored.*

H. Chockler and G. Weissenbacher (Eds.): CAV 2018, LNCS 10981, pp. 3–26, 2018.
https://doi.org/10.1007/978-3-319-96145-3_1

Adversarial machine learning (AML) is a field concerned with the analysis of ML algorithms to adversarial attacks, and the use of such analysis in making ML algorithms robust to attacks. It is part of the broader agenda for safe and verified ML-based systems [39,41]. In this paper, we first give a brief survey of the field of AML, with a particular focus on deep learning. We focus mainly on attacks on outputs or models that are produced by ML algorithms that occur *after training* or "external attacks", which are especially relevant to cyber-physical systems (e.g., for a driverless car the ML algorithm used for navigation has been already trained by the manufacturer once the "car is on the road"). These attacks are more realistic and are distinct from other type of attacks on ML models, such as attacks that poison the training data (see the paper [18] for a survey of such attacks). We survey attacks caused by *adversarial examples*, which are inputs crafted by adding small, often imperceptible, perturbations to force a trained ML model to misclassify.

We contend that the work on adversarial ML, while important and useful, is not enough. In particular, we advocate for the increased use of *semantics* in adversarial analysis and design of ML algorithms. *Semantic adversarial learning* explores a space of semantic modifications to the data, uses system-level semantic specifications in the analysis, utilizes semantic adversarial examples in training, and produces not just output labels but also additional semantic information. Focusing on deep learning, we explore these ideas and provide initial experimental data to support them.

Roadmap. Section 2 provides the relevant background. A brief survey of adversarial analysis is given in Sect. 3. Our proposal for semantic adversarial learning is given in Sect. 4.

2 Background

Background on Machine Learning. Next we describe some general concepts in machine learning (ML). We will consider the supervised learning setting. Consider a sample space Z of the form $X \times Y$, and an ordered training set $S = ((x_i, y_i))_{i=1}^m$ (x_i is the data and y_i is the corresponding label). Let H be a hypothesis space (e.g., weights corresponding to a logistic-regression model). There is a loss function $\ell : H \times Z \mapsto \mathbb{R}$ so that given a hypothesis $w \in H$ and a sample $(x, y) \in Z$, we obtain a loss $\ell(w, (x, y))$. We consider the case where we want to minimize the loss over the training set S,

$$L_S(w) = \frac{1}{m} \sum_{i=1}^{m} \ell(w, (x_i, y_i)) + \lambda \mathcal{R}(w).$$

In the equation given above, $\lambda > 0$ and the term $\mathcal{R}(w)$ is called the *regularizer* and enforces "simplicity" in w. Since S is fixed, we sometimes denote $\ell_i(w) = \ell(w, (x_i, y_i))$ as a function only of w. We wish to find a w that minimizes $L_S(w)$ or we wish to solve the following optimization problem:

$$\min_{w \in H} L_S(w)$$

Example: We will consider the example of logistic regression. In this case $X = \mathbb{R}^n$, $Y = \{+1, -1\}$, $H = \mathbb{R}^n$, and the loss function $\ell(w, (x, y))$ is as follows ($\cdot$ represents the dot product of two vectors):

$$\log\left(1 + e^{-y(w^T \cdot x)}\right)$$

If we use the L_2 regularizer (i.e. $\mathcal{R}(w) = \|w\|_2$), then $L_S(w)$ becomes:

$$\frac{1}{m}\sum_{i=1}^{m} \log\left(1 + e^{-y_i(w^T \cdot x_i)}\right) + \lambda \|w\|_2$$

Stochastic Gradient Descent. *Stochastic Gradient Descent (SGD)* is a popular method for solving optimization tasks (such as the optimization problem $\min_{w \in H} L_S(w)$ we considered before). In a nutshell, SGD performs a series of updates where each update is a gradient descent update with respect to a small set of points sampled from the training set. Specifically, suppose that we perform SGD T times. There are two typical forms of SGD: in the first form, which we call Sample-SGD, we uniformly and randomly sample $i_t \sim [m]$ at time t, and perform a gradient descent based on the i_t-th sample (x_{i_t}, y_{i_t}):

$$w_{t+1} = G_{\ell_t, \eta_t}(w_t) = w_t - \eta_t \ell'_{i_t}(w_t) \tag{1}$$

where w_t is the hypothesis at time t, η_t is a parameter called the *learning rate*, and $\ell'_{i_t}(w_t)$ denotes the derivative of $\ell_{i_t}(w)$ evaluated at w_t. We will denote G_{ℓ_t, η_t} as G_t. In the second form, which we call Perm-SGD, we first perform a random permutation of S, and then apply Eq. 1 T times by cycling through S according to the order of the permutation. The process of SGD can be summarized as a diagram:

$$w_0 \xrightarrow{G_1} w_1 \xrightarrow{G_2} \cdots \xrightarrow{G_t} w_t \xrightarrow{G_{t+1}} \cdots \xrightarrow{G_T} w_T$$

Classifiers. The output of the learning algorithm gives us a *classifier*, which is a function from $\Re^n$ to $\mathcal{C}$, where $\Re$ denotes the set of reals and $\mathcal{C}$ is the set of class labels. To emphasize that a classifier depends on a hypothesis $w \in H$, which is the output of the learning algorithm described earlier, we will write it as F_w (if w is clear from the context, we will sometimes simply write F). For example, after training in the case of logistic regression we obtain a function from $\Re^n$ to $\{-1, +1\}$. Vectors will be denoted in boldface, and the r-th component of a vector $\mathbf{x}$ is denoted by $\mathbf{x}[r]$.

Throughout the paper, we refer to the function $s(F_w)$ as the *softmax layer* corresponding to the classifier F_w. In the case of logistic regression, $s(F_w)(\mathbf{x})$ is the following tuple (the first element is the probability of -1 and the second one is the probability of $+1$):

$$\langle \frac{1}{1 + e^{w^T \cdot \mathbf{x}}}, \frac{1}{1 + e^{-w^T \cdot \mathbf{x}}} \rangle$$

Formally, let $c = |\mathcal{C}|$ and F_w be a classifier, we let $s(F_w)$ be the function that maps $\mathbb{R}^n$ to $\mathbb{R}^c_+$ such that $\|s(F_w)(\mathbf{x})\|_1 = 1$ for any $\mathbf{x}$ (i.e., $s(F_w)$ computes a probability vector). We denote $s(F_w)(\mathbf{x})[l]$ to be the probability of $s(F_w)(\mathbf{x})$ at label l. Recall that the softmax function from $\mathbb{R}^k$ to a probability distribution over $\{1, \cdots, k\} = [k]$ such that the probability of $j \in [k]$ for a vector $\mathbf{x} \in \mathbb{R}^k$ is

$$\frac{e^{\mathbf{x}[j]}}{\sum_{r=1}^{k} e^{\mathbf{x}[r]}}$$

Some classifiers $F_w(\mathbf{x})$ are of the form $\arg\max_l s(F_w)(\mathbf{x})[l]$ (i.e., the classifier F_w outputs the label with the maximum probability according to the "softmax layer"). For example, in several deep-neural network (DNN) architectures the last layer is the *softmax* layer. We are assuming that the reader is a familiar with basics of deep-neural networks (DNNs). For readers not familiar with DNNs we can refer to the excellent book by Goodfellow et al. [15].

Background on Logic. Temporal logics are commonly used for specifying desired and undesired properties of systems. For cyber-physical systems, it is common to use temporal logics that can specify properties of real-valued signals over real time, such as *signal temporal logic* (STL) [30] or *metric temporal logic* (MTL) [27].

A *signal* is a function $s : D \to S$, with $D \subseteq \mathbb{R}_{\geq 0}$ an interval and either $S \subseteq \mathbb{B}$ or $S \subseteq \mathbb{R}$, where $\mathbb{B} = \{\top, \bot\}$ and $\mathbb{R}$ is the set of reals. Signals defined on $\mathbb{B}$ are called *booleans*, while those on $\mathbb{R}$ are said *real-valued*. A *trace* $w = \{s_1, \ldots, s_n\}$ is a finite set of real-valued signals defined over the same interval D. We use variables x_i to denote the value of a real-valued signal at a particular time instant.

Let $\Sigma = \{\sigma_1, \ldots, \sigma_k\}$ be a finite set of predicates $\sigma_i : \mathbb{R}^n \to \mathbb{B}$, with $\sigma_i \equiv p_i(x_1, \ldots, x_n) \lhd 0$, $\lhd \in \{<, \leq\}$, and $p_i : \mathbb{R}^n \to \mathbb{R}$ a function in the variables $x_1, \ldots, x_n$. An STL formula is defined by the following grammar:

$$\varphi := \sigma \,|\, \neg\varphi \,|\, \varphi \wedge \varphi \,|\, \varphi \,\mathtt{U}_I\, \varphi \tag{2}$$

where $\sigma \in \Sigma$ is a predicate and $I \subset \mathbb{R}_{\geq 0}$ is a closed non-singular interval. Other common temporal operators can be defined as syntactic abbreviations in the usual way, like for instance $\varphi_1 \vee \varphi_2 := \neg(\neg\varphi_1 \wedge \varphi_2)$, $\mathtt{F}_I\, \varphi := \top \,\mathtt{U}_I\, \varphi$, or $\mathtt{G}_I\, \varphi := \neg\mathtt{F}_I\, \neg\varphi$. Given a $t \in \mathbb{R}_{\geq 0}$, a shifted interval I is defined as $t+I = \{t+t' \mid t' \in I\}$. The qualitative (or Boolean) semantics of STL is given in the usual way:

Definition 1 (Qualitative semantics). *Let w be a trace, $t \in \mathbb{R}_{\geq 0}$, and φ be an STL formula. The* qualitative semantics *of φ is inductively defined as follows:*

$$\begin{aligned}
w, t &\models \sigma \text{ iff } \sigma(w(t)) \text{ is true}\\
w, t &\models \neg\varphi \text{ iff } w, t \not\models \varphi\\
w, t &\models \varphi_1 \wedge \varphi_2 \text{ iff } w, t \models \varphi_1 \text{ and } w, t \models \varphi_2\\
w, t &\models \varphi_1 \mathtt{U}_I \varphi_2 \text{ iff } \exists t' \in t+I \text{ s.t. } w, t' \models \varphi_2 \text{ and } \forall t'' \in [t, t'], w, t'' \models \varphi_1
\end{aligned} \tag{3}$$

A trace w satisfies a formula φ if and only if $w, 0 \models \varphi$, in short $w \models \varphi$. STL also admits a quantitative or robust semantics, which we omit for brevity. This provides quantitative information on the formula, telling how strongly the specification is satisfied or violated for a given trace.

3 Attacks

There are several types of attacks on ML algorithms. For excellent material on various attacks on ML algorithms we refer the reader to [3,18]. For example, in *training time* attacks an adversary wishes to poison a data set so that a "bad" hypothesis is learned by an ML-algorithm. This attack can be modeled as a game between the algorithm ML and an adversary A as follows:

- ML picks an ordered training set $S = ((x_i, y_i))_{i=1}^m$.
- A picks an ordered training set $\widehat{S} = ((\hat{x_i}, \hat{y_i}))_{i=1}^r$, where r is $\lfloor \epsilon m \rfloor$.
- ML learns on $S \cup \widehat{S}$ by essentially minimizing

$$\min_{w \in H} L_{S \cup \widehat{S}}(w).$$

The attacker wants to maximize the above quantity and thus chooses $\widehat{S}$ such that $\min_{w \in H} L_{S \cup \widehat{S}}(w)$ is maximized. For a recent paper on certified defenses for such attacks we refer the reader to [44]. In *model extraction* attacks an adversary with black-box access to a classifier, but no prior knowledge of the parameters of a ML algorithm or training data, aims to duplicate the functionality of (i.e., steal) the classifier by querying it on well chosen data points. For an example, model-extraction attacks see [45].

In this paper, we consider *test-time attacks*. We assume that the classifier F_w has been trained without any interference from the attacker (i.e. no training time attacks). Roughly speaking, an attacker has an image $\mathbf{x}$ (e.g. an image of stop sign) and wants to craft a perturbation δ so that the label of $\mathbf{x} + \delta$ is what the attacker desires (e.g. yield sign). The next sub-section describes test-time attacks in detail. We will sometimes refer to F_w as simply F, but the hypothesis w is lurking in the background (i.e., whenever we refer to w, it corresponds to the classifier F).

3.1 Test-Time Attacks

The adversarial goal is to take any input vector $\mathbf{x} \in \Re^n$ and produce a minimally altered version of $\mathbf{x}$, *adversarial sample* denoted by $\mathbf{x}^\star$, that has the property of being misclassified by a classifier $F : \Re^n \rightarrow \mathcal{C}$. Formally speaking, an adversary wishes to solve the following optimization problem:

$$\begin{array}{rr} \min_{\delta \in \Re^n} & \mu(\delta) \\ \text{such that } & F(\mathbf{x} + \delta) \in T \\ & \delta \cdot \mathbf{M} = 0 \end{array}$$

The various terms in the formulation are μ is a metric on $\Re^n$, $T \subseteq \mathcal{C}$ is a subset of the labels (the reader should think of T as the target labels for the attacker), and $\mathbf{M}$ (called the *mask*) is a n-dimensional 0–1 vector of size n. The objective function minimizes the metric μ on the perturbation δ. Next we describe various constraints in the formulation.

- $F(\mathbf{x} + \delta) \in T$
  The set T constrains the perturbed vector $\mathbf{x} + \delta$[1] to have the label (according to F) in the set T. For *mis-classification* problems the label of $\mathbf{x}$ and $\mathbf{x} + \delta$ are different, so we have $T = \mathcal{C} - \{F(\mathbf{x})\}$. For *targeted mis-classification* we have $T = \{t\}$ (for $t \in \mathcal{C}$), where t is the target that an attacker wants (e.g., the attacker wants t to correspond to a yield sign).
- $\delta \cdot \mathbf{M} = 0$
  The vector M can be considered as a mask (i.e., an attacker can only perturb a dimension i if $M[i] = 0$), i.e., if $M[i] = 1$ then $\delta[i]$ is forced to be 0. Essentially the attacker can only perturb dimension i if the i-th component of M is 0, which means that δ lies in k-dimensional space where k is the number of non-zero entries in Δ. This constraint is important if an attacker wants to target a certain area of the image (e.g., glasses of in a picture of person) to perturb.
- *Convexity*
  Notice that even if the metric μ is convex (e.g., μ is the L_2 norm), because of the constraint involving F, the optimization problem is *not convex* (the constraint $\delta \cdot \mathbf{M} = 0$ is convex). In general, solving convex optimization problems is more tractable non-convex optimization [34].

Note that the constraint $\delta \cdot \mathbf{M} = 0$ essentially constrains the vector to be in a lower-dimensional space and does add additional complexity to the optimization problem. Therefore, for the rest of the section we will ignore that constraint and work with the following formulation:

$$\begin{array}{ll} \min_{\delta \in \Re^n} & \mu(\delta) \\ \text{such that } F(\mathbf{x} + \delta) \in T & \end{array}$$

FGSM Mis-classification Attack - This algorithm is also known as the *fast gradient sign method (FGSM)* [16]. The adversary crafts an adversarial sample $\mathbf{x}^\star = \mathbf{x} + \delta$ for a given legitimate sample $\mathbf{x}$ by computing the following perturbation:

$$\delta = \varepsilon \ \text{sign}(\nabla_{\mathbf{x}} L_F(\mathbf{x})) \tag{4}$$

The function $L_F(\mathbf{x})$ is a shorthand for $\ell(w, \mathbf{x}, l(\mathbf{x}))$, where w is the hypothesis corresponding to the classifier F, $\mathbf{x}$ is the data point and $l(\mathbf{x})$ is the label of $\mathbf{x}$ (essentially we evaluate the loss function at the hypothesis corresponding to the classifier). The gradient of the function L_F is computed with respect to

[1] The vectors are added component wise.

$\mathbf{x}$ using sample $\mathbf{x}$ and label $y = l(\mathbf{x})$ as inputs. Note that $\nabla_{\mathbf{x}} L_F(\mathbf{x})$ is an n-dimensional vector and $\text{sign}(\nabla_{\mathbf{x}} L_F(\mathbf{x}))$ is a n-dimensional vector whose i-th element is the sign of the $\nabla_{\mathbf{x}} L_F(\mathbf{x}))[i]$. The value of the *input variation parameter* ε factoring the sign matrix controls the perturbation's amplitude. Increasing its value increases the likelihood of $\mathbf{x}^\star$ being misclassified by the classifier F but on the contrary makes adversarial samples easier to detect by humans. The key idea is that FGSM takes a step *in the direction of the gradient of the loss function* and thus tries to maximize it. Recall that SGD takes a step in the direction that is opposite to the gradient of the loss function because it is trying to minimize the loss function.

JSMA Targeted Mis-classification Attack - This algorithm is suitable for targeted misclassification [37]. We refer to this attack as JSMA throughout the rest of the paper. To craft the perturbation δ, components are sorted by decreasing *adversarial saliency value.* The adversarial saliency value $S(\mathbf{x},t)[i]$ of component i for an adversarial target class t is defined as:

$$S(\mathbf{x},t)[i] = \begin{cases} 0 \text{ if } \frac{\partial s(F)[t](\mathbf{x})}{\partial \mathbf{x}[i]} < 0 \text{ or } \sum_{j \neq t} \frac{\partial s(F)[j](\mathbf{x})}{\partial \mathbf{x}[i]} > 0 \\ \frac{\partial s(F)[t](\mathbf{x})}{\partial \mathbf{x}[i]} \left| \sum_{j \neq t} \frac{\partial s(F)[j](\mathbf{x})}{\partial \mathbf{x}[i]} \right| \text{ otherwise} \end{cases} \tag{5}$$

where matrix $J_F = \left[\frac{\partial s(F)[j](\mathbf{x})}{\partial \mathbf{x}[i]} \right]_{ij}$ is the Jacobian matrix for the output of the softmax layer $s(F)(\mathbf{x})$. Since $\sum_{k \in C} s(F)[k](\mathbf{x}) = 1$, we have the following equation:

$$\frac{\partial s(F)[t](\mathbf{x})}{\partial \mathbf{x}[i]} = - \sum_{j \neq t} \frac{\partial s(F)[j](\mathbf{x})}{\partial \mathbf{x}[i]}$$

The first case corresponds to the scenario if changing the i-th component of $\mathbf{x}$ takes us further away from the target label t. Intuitively, $S(\mathbf{x},t)[i]$ indicates how likely is changing the i-th component of $\mathbf{x}$ going to "move towards" the target label t. Input components i are added to perturbation δ in order of decreasing adversarial saliency value $S(\mathbf{x},t)[i]$ until the resulting adversarial sample $\mathbf{x}^\star = \mathbf{x} + \delta$ achieves the target label t. The perturbation introduced for each selected input component can vary. Greater individual variations tend to reduce the number of components perturbed to achieve misclassification.

CW Targeted Mis-classification Attack. The CW-attack [5] is widely believed to be one of the most "powerful" attacks. The reason is that CW cast their problem as an unconstrained optimization problem, and then use state-of-the art solver (i.e. Adam [24]). In other words, they leverage the advances in optimization for the purposes of generating adversarial examples.

In their paper Carlini-Wagner consider a wide variety of formulations, but we present the one that performs best according to their evaluation. The optimization problem corresponding to CW is as follows:

$$\begin{array}{ll} \min_{\delta \in \Re^n} & \mu(\delta) \\ \text{such that } F(\mathbf{x} + \delta) = t & \end{array}$$

CW use an existing solver (Adam [24]) and thus need to make sure that each component of $\mathbf{x} + \delta$ is between 0 and 1 (i.e. valid pixel values). Note that the other methods did not face this issue because they control the "internals" of the algorithm (i.e., CW used a solver in a "black box" manner). We introduce a new vector $\mathbf{w}$ whose i-th component is defined according to the following equation:

$$\delta[i] = \frac{1}{2}(\tanh(\mathbf{w}[i]) + 1) - \mathbf{x}[i]$$

Since $-1 \leq \tanh(\mathbf{w}[i]) \leq 1$, it follows that $0 \leq \mathbf{x}[i] + \delta[i] \leq 1$. In terms of this new variable the optimization problem becomes:

$$\begin{array}{l} \min_{\mathbf{w} \in \Re^n} \ \mu(\frac{1}{2}(\tanh(\mathbf{w}) + 1) - \mathbf{x}) \\ \text{such that } F(\frac{1}{2}(\tanh(\mathbf{w}) + 1)) = t \end{array}$$

Next they approximate the constraint $(F(\mathbf{x}) = \mathbf{t})$ with the following function:

$$g(\mathbf{x}) = \max\left(\max_{i \neq t} Z(F)(\mathbf{x})[i] - Z(F)(\mathbf{x})[t], -\kappa\right)$$

In the equation given above $Z(F)$ is the input of the DNN to the softmax layer (i.e. $s(F)(\mathbf{x}) = \text{softmax}(Z(F)(\mathbf{x}))$) and κ is a confidence parameter (higher κ encourages the solver to find adversarial examples with higher confidence). The new optimization formulation is as follows:

$$\begin{array}{l} \min_{\mathbf{w} \in \Re^n} \ \mu(\frac{1}{2}(\tanh(\mathbf{w}) + 1) - \mathbf{x}) \\ \text{such that } g(\frac{1}{2}(\tanh(\mathbf{w}) + 1)) \ \leq 0 \end{array}$$

Next we incorporate the constraint into the objective function as follows:

$$\min_{\mathbf{w} \in \Re^n} \ \mu(\tfrac{1}{2}(\tanh(\mathbf{w}) + 1) - \mathbf{x}) + c\, g(\tfrac{1}{2}(\tanh(\mathbf{w}) + 1))$$

In the objective given above, the "Lagrangian variable" $c > 0$ is a suitably chosen constant (from the optimization literature we know that there exists $c > 0$ such that the optimal solutions of the last two formulations are the same).

3.2 Adversarial Training

Once an attacker finds an adversarial example, then the algorithm can be retrained using this example. Researchers have found that retraining the model with adversarial examples produces a more robust model. For this section, we will work with attack algorithms that have a target label t (i.e. we are in the targeted mis-classification case, such as JSMA or CW). Let $\mathcal{A}(w, \mathbf{x}, t)$ be the attack algorithm, where its inputs are as follows: $w \in H$ is the current hypothesis, $\mathbf{x}$ is the data point, and $t \in C$ is the target label. The output of $\mathcal{A}(w, \mathbf{x}, t)$ is a perturbation δ such that $F(\mathbf{x} + \delta) = t$. If the attack algorithm is simply a mis-classification algorithm (e.g. FGSM or Deepfool) we will drop the last parameter t.

An *adversarial training* algorithm $\mathcal{R}_{\mathcal{A}}(w, \mathbf{x}, t)$ is parameterized by an attack algorithm $\mathcal{A}$ and outputs a new hypothesis $w' \in H$. Adversarial training works by taking a datapoint $\mathbf{x}$ and an attack algorithm $\mathcal{A}(w, \mathbf{x}, t)$ as its input and then retraining the model using a specially designed loss function (essentially one performs a single step of the SGD using the new loss function). The question arises: what loss function to use during the training? Different methods use different loss functions.

Next, we discuss some adversarial training algorithms proposed in the literature. At a high level, an important point is that the more sophisticated an adversarial perturbation algorithm is, harder it is to turn it into adversarial training. The reason is that it is hard to "encode" the adversarial perturbation algorithm as an objective function and optimize it. We will see this below, especially for the virtual adversarial training (VAT) proposed by Miyato et al. [32].

Retraining for FGSM. We discussed the FGSM attack method earlier. In this case $\mathcal{A}$ = FGSM. The loss function used by the retraining algorithm $\mathcal{R}_{\text{FGSM}}(w, \mathbf{x}, t)$ is as follows:

$$\ell_{\text{FGSM}}(w, \mathbf{x}_i, y_i) = \ell(w, \mathbf{x}_i, y_i) + \lambda \ell\left(w, \mathbf{x}_i + \text{FGSM}(w, \mathbf{x}_i), y_i\right)$$

Recall that $\text{FGSM}(w, \mathbf{x})$ was defined earlier, and λ is a regularization parameter. The simplicity of $\text{FGSM}(w, \mathbf{x}_i)$ allows taking its gradient, but this objective function requires label y_i because we are reusing the same loss function ℓ used to train the original model. Further, $\text{FGSM}(w, \mathbf{x}_i)$ may not be very good because it may not produce good adversarial perturbation direction (i.e. taking a bigger step in this direction might produce a distorted image). The retraining algorithm is simply as follows: *take one step in the SGD using the loss function* ℓ_{FGSM} *at the data point* $\mathbf{x}_i$.

A caveat is needed for taking gradient during the SGD step. At iteration t suppose we have model parameters w_t, and we need to compute the gradient of the objective. Note that $\text{FGSM}(w, \mathbf{x})$ depends on w so by chain rule we need to compute $\partial \text{FGSM}(w, \mathbf{x}) / \partial w|_{w=w_t}$. However, this gradient is volatile[2], and so instead Goodfellow et al. only compute:

$$\left.\frac{\partial \ell\left(w, \mathbf{x}_i + \text{FGSM}(w_t, \mathbf{x}_i), y_i\right)}{\partial w}\right|_{w=w_t}$$

Essentially they treat $\text{FGSM}(w_t, \mathbf{x}_i)$ as a constant while taking the derivative.

Virtual Adversarial Training (VAT). Miyato et al. [32] observed the drawback of requiring label y_i for the adversarial example. Their intuition is that one wants the classifier to behave "similarly" on $\mathbf{x}$ and $\mathbf{x}+\delta$, where δ is the adversarial perturbation. Specifically, the distance of the distribution corresponding to the output of the softmax layer F_w on $\mathbf{x}$ and $\mathbf{x}+\delta$ is small. VAT uses *KullbackLeibler*

[2] In general, second-order derivatives of a classifier corresponding to a DNN vanish at several points because several layers are piece-wise linear.

(KL) *divergence* as the measure of the distance between two distributions. Recall that KL divergence of two distributions P and Q over the same finite domain D is given by the following equation:

$$\mathrm{KL}(P, Q) = \sum_{i \in D} P(i) \log \left(\frac{P(i)}{Q(i)} \right)$$

Therefore, they propose that, instead of reusing ℓ, they propose to use the following for the regularizer,

$$\Delta(r, \mathbf{x}, w) = \mathrm{KL}\left(s(F_w)(\mathbf{x})[y], s(F_w)(\mathbf{x}+r)[y]\right)$$

for some r such that $\|r\| \leq \delta$. As a result, the label y_i is *no longer* required. The question is: what r to use? Miyato et al. [32] propose that in theory we should use the "best" one as

$$\max_{r:\|r\|\leq\delta} \ \mathrm{KL}\left(s(F_w)(\mathbf{x})[y], s(F_w)(\mathbf{x}+r)[y]\right)$$

This thus gives rise to the following loss function to use during retraining:

$$\ell_{\mathrm{VAT}}(w, \mathbf{x}_i, y_i) = \ell(w, \mathbf{x}_i, y_i) + \lambda \max_{r:\|r\|\leq\delta} \Delta(r, \mathbf{x}_i, w)$$

However, one cannot easily compute the gradient for the regularizer. Hence the authors perform an approximation as follows:

1. Compute the Taylor expansion of $\Delta(r, \mathbf{x}_i, w)$ at $r = 0$, so $\Delta(r, \mathbf{x}_i, w) = r^T H(\mathbf{x}_i, w)\, r$ where $H(\mathbf{x}_i, w)$ is the Hessian matrix of $\Delta(r, \mathbf{x}_i, w)$ with respect to r at $r = 0$.
2. Thus $\max_{\|r\|\leq\delta} \Delta(r, \mathbf{x}_i, w) = \max_{\|r\|\leq\delta} \left(r^T H(\mathbf{x}_i, w)\, r\right)$. By variational characterization of the symmetric matrix ($H(\mathbf{x}_i, w)$ is symmetric), $r^* = \delta\bar{v}$ where $\bar{v} = \overline{v(\mathbf{x}_i, w)}$ is the unit eigenvector of $H(\mathbf{x}_i, w)$ corresponding to its largest eigenvalue. Note that r^* depends on $\mathbf{x}_i$ and w. Therefore the loss function becomes:

$$\ell_{\mathrm{VAT}}(\theta, \mathbf{x}_i, y_i) = \ell(\theta, \mathbf{x}_i, y_i) + \lambda\Delta(r^*, \mathbf{x}_i, w)$$

3. Now suppose in the process of SGD we are at iteration t with model parameters w_t, and we need to compute $\partial\ell_{\mathrm{VAT}}/\partial w|_{w=w_t}$. By chain rule we need to compute $\partial r^*/\partial w|_{w=w_t}$. However the authors find that such gradients are volatile, so they instead fix r^* as a constant at the point θ_t, and compute

$$\left.\frac{\partial \mathrm{KL}\left(s(F_w)(\mathbf{x})[y], s(F_w)(\mathbf{x}+r)[y]\right)}{\partial w}\right|_{w=w_t}$$

3.3 Black Box Attacks

Recall that earlier attacks (e.g. FGSM and JSMA) needed white-box access to the classifier F (essentially because these attacks require first order information about the classifier). In this section, we present black-box attacks. In this case, an attacker can *only* ask for the labels $F(\mathbf{x})$ for certain data points. Our presentation is based on [36], but is more general.

Let $\mathcal{A}(w, \mathbf{x}, t)$ be the attack algorithm, where its inputs are: $w \in H$ is the current hypothesis, $\mathbf{x}$ is the data point, and $t \in \mathcal{C}$ is the target label. The output of $\mathcal{A}(w, \mathbf{x}, t)$ is a perturbation δ such that $F(\mathbf{x}+\delta) = t$. If the attack algorithm is simply a mis-classification algorithm (e.g. FGSM or Deepfool) we will drop the last parameter t (recall that in this case the attack algorithm returns a δ such that $F(\mathbf{x}+\delta) \neq F(\mathbf{x})$). An *adversarial training* algorithm $\mathcal{R}_{\mathcal{A}}(w, \mathbf{x}, t)$ is parameterized by an attack algorithm $\mathcal{A}$ and outputs a new hypothesis $w' \in H$ (this was discussed in the previous subsection).

Initialization: We pick a substitute classifier G and an initial seed data set S_0 and train G. For simplicity, we will assume that the sample space $Z = X \times Y$ and the hypothesis space H for G is same as that of F (the classifier under attack). However, this is not crucial to the algorithm. We will call G the *substitute classifier* and F the *target classifier.* Let $S = S_0$ be the initial data set, which will be updated as we iterate.

Iteration: Run the attack algorithm $\mathcal{A}(w, \mathbf{x}, t)$ on G and obtain a δ. If $F(\mathbf{x}+\delta) = t$, then **stop** we are done. If $F(\mathbf{x}+\delta) = t'$ but not equal to t, we augment the data set S as follows:

$$S = S \cup (\mathbf{x}+\delta, t')$$

We now retrain G on this new data set, which essentially means running the SGD on the new data point $(\mathbf{x}+\delta, t')$. Notice that we can also use adversarial training $\mathcal{R}_{\mathcal{A}}(w, \mathbf{x}, t)$ to update G (to our knowledge this has been not tried out in the literature).

3.4 Defenses

Defenses with formal guarantees against test-time attacks have proven elusive. For example, Carlini and Wagner [6] have a recent paper that breaks *ten recent defense proposals.* However, defenses that are based on robust-optimization objectives have demonstrated promise [26,33,43]. Several techniques for verifying properties of a DNN (in isolation) have appeared recently (e.g., [12,13,19,23]). Due to space limitations we will not give a detailed account of all these defenses.

4 Semantic Adversarial Analysis and Training

A central tenet of this paper is that the analysis of deep neural networks (and machine learning components, in general) must be more *semantic.* In particular, we advocate for the increased use of semantics in several aspects of adversarial analysis and training, including the following:

- *Semantic Modification Space:* Recall that the goal of adversarial attacks is to modify an input vector $\mathbf{x}$ with an adversarial modification δ so as to achieve a target misclassification. Such modifications typically do not incorporate the application-level semantics or the context within which the neural network is deployed. We argue that it is essential to incorporate more application-level, contextual semantics into the modification space. Such *semantic modifications* correspond to modifications that may arise more naturally within the context of the target application. We view this not as ignoring arbitrary modifications (which are indeed worth considering with a security mind set), but as prioritizing the design and analysis of DNNs towards semantic adversarial modifications. Sect. 4.1 discusses this point in more detail.
- *System-Level Specifications:* The goal of much of the work in adversarial attacks has been to generate misclassifications. However, not all misclassifications are made equal. We contend that it is important to find misclassifications that lead to violations of desired properties of the system within which the DNN is used. Therefore, one must identify such *system-level specifications* and devise analysis methods to verify whether an erroneous behavior of the DNN component can lead to the violation of a system-level specification. System-level counterexamples can be valuable aids to repair and re-design machine learning models. See Sect. 4.1 for a more detailed discussion of this point.
- *Semantic (Re-)Training:* Most machine learning models are trained with the main goal of reducing misclassifications as measured by a suitably crafted loss function. We contend that it is also important to train the model to avoid undesirable behaviors at the system level. For this, we advocate using methods for *semantic training*, where system-level specifications, counterexamples, and other artifacts are used to improve the semantic quality of the ML model. Sect. 4.2 explores a few ideas.
- *Confidence-Based Analysis and Decision Making:* Deep neural networks (and other ML models) often produce not just an output label, but also an associated confidence level. We argue that *confidence levels* must be used within the design of ML-based systems. They provide a way of exposing more information from the DNN to the surrounding system that uses its decisions. Such confidence levels can also be useful to prioritize analysis towards cases that are more egregious failures of the DNN. More generally, any *explanations* and *auxiliary information* generated by the DNN that accompany its main output decisions can be valuable aids in their design and analysis.

4.1 Compositional Falsification

We discuss the problem of performing system-level analysis of a deep learning component, using recent work by the authors [9,10] to illustrate the main points. The material in this section is mainly based on [40].

We begin with some basic notation. Let S denote the model of the full system S under verification, E denote a model of its environment, and Φ denote the specification to be verified. C is an ML model (e.g. DNN) that is part of S. As in Sect. 3, let $\mathbf{x}$ be an input to C. We assume that Φ is a trace property – a set of behaviors of the closed system obtained by composing S with E, denoted $S\|E$. The goal of falsification is to find one or more counterexamples showing how the composite system $S\|E$ violates Φ. In this context, *semantic analysis of C is about finding a modification δ from a space of semantic modifications Δ such that C, on $\mathbf{x}+\delta$, produces a misclassification that causes $S\|E$ to violate Φ.*

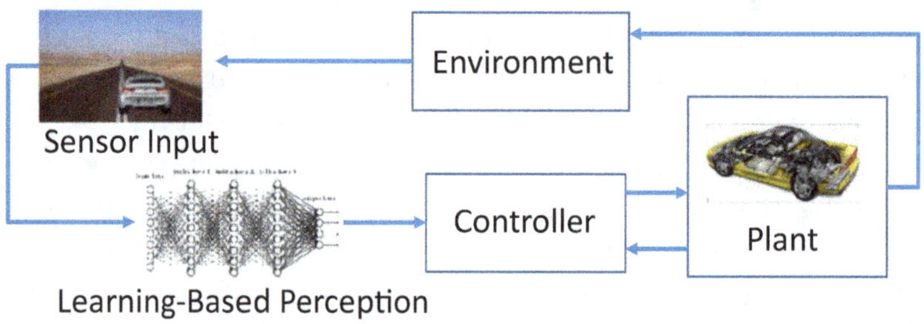

Fig. 1. Automatic Emergency Braking System (AEBS) in closed loop. An image classifier based on deep neural networks is used to perceive objects in the ego vehicle's frame of view.

Example Problem. As an illustrative example, consider a simple model of an Automatic Emergency Braking System (AEBS), that attempts to detect objects in front of a vehicle and actuate the brakes when needed to avert a collision. Figure 1 shows the AEBS as a system composed of a controller (automatic braking), a plant (vehicle sub-system under control, including transmission), and an advanced sensor (camera along with an obstacle detector based on deep learning). The AEBS, when combined with the vehicle's environment, forms a closed loop control system. The controller regulates the acceleration and braking of the plant using the velocity of the subject (ego) vehicle and the distance between it and an obstacle. The sensor used to detect the obstacle includes a camera along with an image classifier based on DNNs. In general, this sensor can provide noisy measurements due to incorrect image classifications which in turn can affect the correctness of the overall system.

Suppose we want to verify whether the distance between the ego vehicle and a preceding obstacle is always larger than 2 m. In STL, this requirement Φ can be written as $\mathtt{G}_{0,T}(\|\mathbf{x}_{\text{ego}}-\mathbf{x}_{\text{obs}}\|_2 \geq 2)$. Such verification requires the exploration of a very large input space comprising of the control inputs (e.g., acceleration and braking pedal angles) and the machine learning (ML) component's feature space (e.g., all the possible pictures observable by the camera). The latter space is particularly large—for example, note that the feature space of RGB images of dimension 1000×600 px (for an image classifier) contains $256^{1000\times600\times3}$ elements.

In the above example, $S\|E$ is the closed loop system in Fig. 1 where S comprises the DNN and the controller, and E comprises everything else. C is the DNN used for object detection and classification.

This case study has been implemented in Matlab/Simulink[3] in two versions that use two different Convolutional Neural Networks (CNNs): the Caffe [20] version of AlexNet [28] and the Inception-v3 model created with Tensorflow [31], both trained on the ImageNet database [1]. Further details about this example can be obtained from [9].

Approach. A key idea in our approach is to have a *system-level verifier* that abstracts away the component C while verifying Φ on the resulting abstraction. This system-level verifier communicates with a component-level analyzer that searches for semantic modifications δ to the input $\mathbf{x}$ of C that could lead to violations of the system-level specification Φ. Figure 2 illustrates this approach.

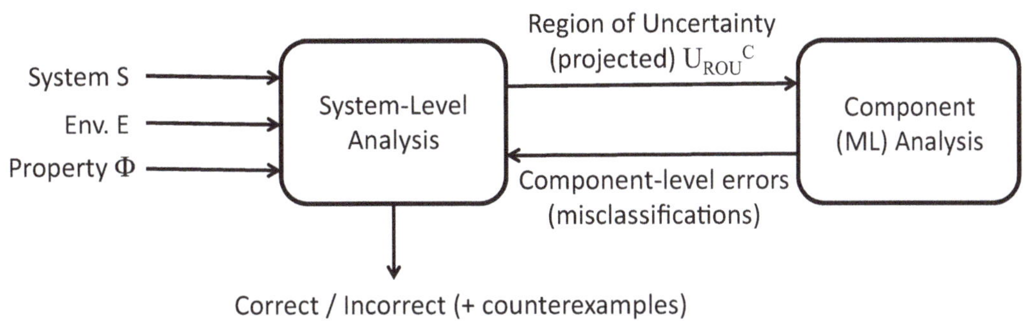

Fig. 2. Compositional verification approach. A system-level verifier cooperates with a component-level analysis procedure (e.g., adversarial analysis of a machine learning component to find misclassifications).

We formalize this approach while trying to emphasize the intuition. Let T denote the set of all possible traces of the composition of the system with its environment, $S \| E$. Given a specification Φ, let T_Φ denote the set of traces in T satisfying Φ. Let U_Φ denote the projection of these traces onto the state and interface variables of the environment E. U_Φ is termed as the *validity domain* of Φ, i.e., the set of environment behaviors for which Φ is satisfied. Similarly, the complement set $U_{\neg\Phi}$ is the set of environment behaviors for which Φ is violated.

Our approach works as follows:

1. The System-level Verifier initially performs two analyses with two extreme abstractions of the ML component. First, it performs an *optimistic* analysis, wherein the ML component is assumed to be a "perfect classifier", i.e., all feature vectors are correctly classified. In situations where ML is used for perception/sensing, this abstraction assumes perfect perception/sensing. Using this abstraction, we compute the validity domain for this abstract model of the system, denoted U^+_Φ. Next, it performs a *pessimistic* analysis where the ML component is abstracted by a "completely-wrong classifier", i.e., all feature vectors are misclassified. Denote the resulting validity domain as U^-_Φ. It is expected that $U^+_\Phi \supseteq U^-_\Phi$.

[3] https://github.com/dreossi/analyzeNN.

Abstraction permits the System-level Verifier to operate on a lower-dimensional search space and identify a region in this space that may be affected by the malfunctioning of component C—a so-called "region of uncertainty" (ROU). This region, U^C_{ROU} is computed as $U^+_\Phi \setminus U^-_\Phi$. In other words, it comprises all environment behaviors that could lead to a system-level failure when component C malfunctions. This region U^C_{ROU}, projected onto the inputs of C, is communicated to the ML Analyzer. (Concretely, in the context of our example of Sect. 4.1, this corresponds to finding a subspace of images that corresponds to U^C_{ROU}.)

2. The Component-level Analyzer, also termed as a Machine Learning (ML) Analyzer, performs a detailed analysis of the projected ROU U^C_{ROU}. A key aspect of the ML analyzer is to explore the *semantic modification space* efficiently. Several options are available for such an analysis, including the various adversarial analysis techniques surveyed earlier (applied to the semantic space), as well as systematic sampling methods [9]. Even though a component-level formal specification may not be available, each of these adversarial analyses has an implicit notion of "misclassification." We will refer to these as *component-level errors*. The working of the ML analyzer from [9] is shown in Fig. 3.
3. When the Component-level (ML) Analyzer finds component-level errors (e.g., those that trigger misclassifications of inputs whose labels are easily inferred), it communicates that information back to the System-level Verifier, which checks whether the ML misclassification can lead to a violation of the system-level property Φ. If yes, we have found a system-level counterexample. If no component-level errors are found, and the system-level verification can prove the absence of counterexamples, then it can conclude that Φ is satisfied. Otherwise, if the ML misclassification cannot be extended to a system-level counterexample, the ROU is updated and the revised ROU passed back to the Component-level Analyzer.

The communication between the System-level Verifier and the Component-level (ML) Analyzer continues thus, until we either prove/disprove Φ, or we run out of resources.

Sample Results. We have applied the above approach to the problem of *compositional falsification* of cyber-physical systems (CPS) with machine learning components [9]. For this class of CPS, including those with highly non-linear dynamics and even black-box components, simulation-based falsification of temporal logic properties is an approach that has proven effective in industrial practice (e.g., [21,46]). We present here a sample of results on the AEBS example from [9], referring the reader to more detailed descriptions in the other papers on the topic [9,10].

In Fig. 4 we show one result of our analysis for the Inception-v3 deep neural network. This figure shows both correctly classified and misclassified images on a range of synthesized images where (i) the environment vehicle is moved away from or towards the ego vehicle (along z-axis), (ii) it is moved sideways along

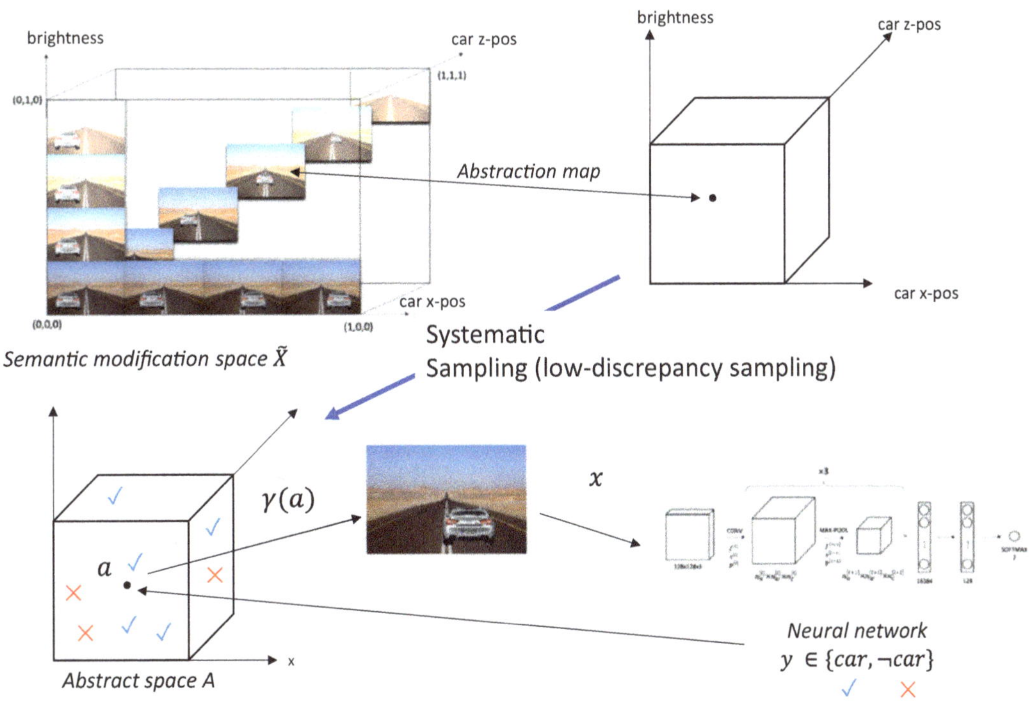

Fig. 3. Machine Learning Analyzer: Searching the Semantic Modification Space. A concrete semantic modification space (top left) is mapped into a discrete abstract space. Systematic sampling, using low-discrepancy methods, yields points in the abstract space. These points are concretized and the NN is evaluated on them to ascertain if they are correctly or wrongly classified. The misclassifications are fed back for system-level analysis.

the road (along x-axis), or (iii) the brightness of the image is modified. These modifications constitute the 3 axes of the figure. Our approach finds misclassifications that do not lead to system-level property violations and also misclassifications that do lead to such violations. For example, Fig. 4 shows two misclassified images, one with an environment vehicle that is too far away to be a safety hazard, as well as another image showing an environment vehicle driving slightly on the wrong side of the road, which is close enough to potentially cause a violation of the system-level safety property (of maintaining a safe distance from the ego vehicle).

For further details about this and other results with our approach, we refer the reader to [9,10].

4.2 Semantic Training

In this section we discuss two ideas for *semantic training and retraining* of deep neural networks. We first discuss the use of *hinge loss* as a way of incorporating confidence levels into the training process. Next, we discuss how system-level counterexamples and associated misclassifications can be used in the retraining process to both improve the accuracy of ML models and also to gain more assurance in the overall system containing the ML component. A more detailed study

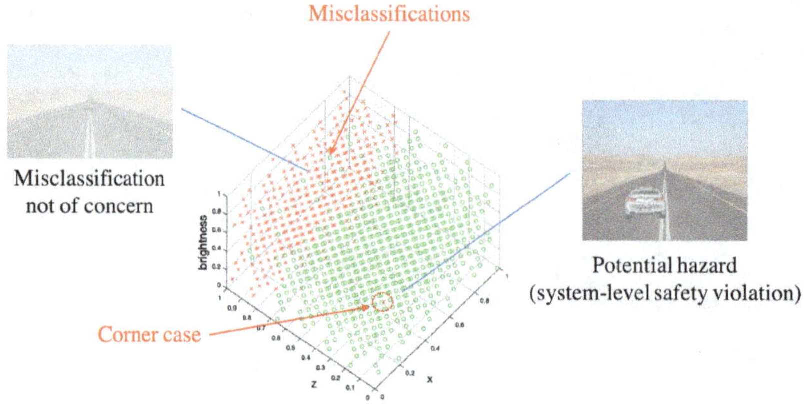

Fig. 4. Misclassified images for Inception-v3 neural network (trained on ImageNet with TensorFlow). Red crosses are misclassified images and green circles are correctly classified. Our system-level analysis finds a corner-case image that could lead to a system-level safety violation. (Color figure online)

of using misclassifications (ML component-level counterexamples) to improve the accuracy of the neural network is presented in [11]; this approach is termed *counterexample-guided data augmentation*, inspired by counterexample-guided abstraction refinement (CEGAR) [7] and similar paradigms.

Experimental Setup. As in the preceding section, we consider an Automatic Emergency Braking System (AEBS) using a DNN-based object detector. However, in these experiments we use an AEBS deployed within Udacity's self-driving car simulator, as reported in our previous work [10].[4] We modified the Udacity simulator to focus exclusively on braking. In our case studies, the car follows some predefined way-points, while accelerating and braking are controlled by the AEBS connected to a convolutional neural network (CNN). In particular, whenever the CNN detects an obstacle in the images provided by the onboard camera, the AEBS triggers a braking action that slows the vehicle down and avoids the collision against the obstacle.

We designed and implemented a CNN to predict the presence of a cow on the road. Given an image taken by the onboard camera, the CNN classifies the picture in either "cow" or "not cow" category. The CNN architecture is shown in Fig. 5. It consists of eight layers: the first six are alternations of convolutions and max-pools with ReLU activations, the last two are a fully connected layer and a softmax that outputs the network prediction (confidence level for each label).

We generated a data set of 1000 road images with and without cows. We split the data set into 80% training and 20% validation data. Our model was implemented and trained using the Tensorflow library with cross-entropy cost function and the Adam algorithm optimizer (learning rate 10^{-4}). The model

[4] Udacity's self-driving car simulator: https://github.com/udacity/self-driving-car-sim.

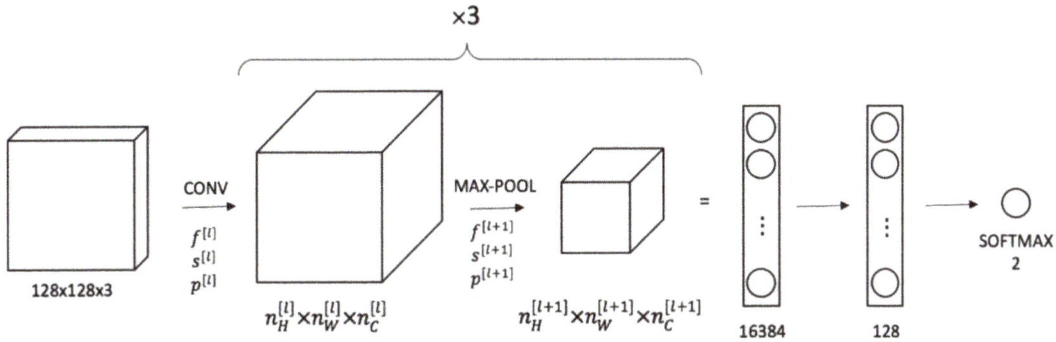

Fig. 5. CNN architecture.

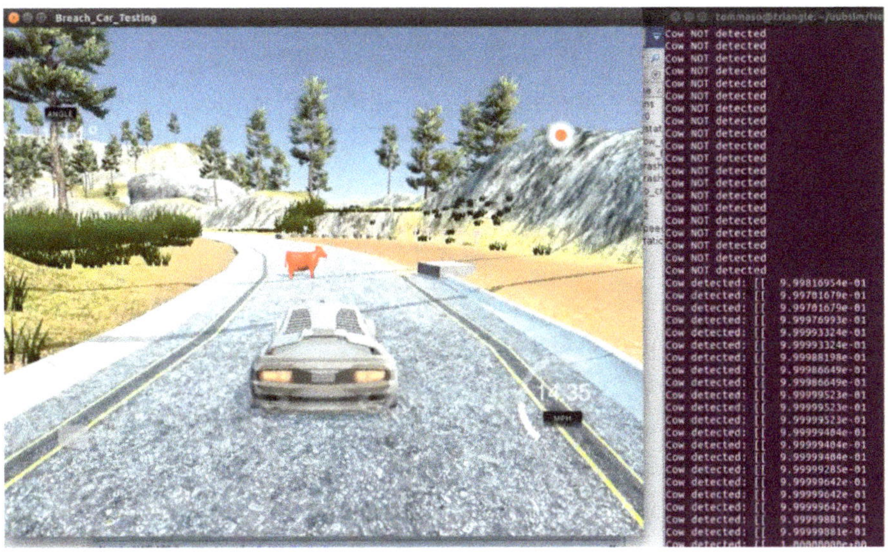

Fig. 6. Udacity simulator with a CNN-based AEBS in action.

reached 95% accuracy on the test set. Finally, the resulting CNN is connected to the Unity simulator via Socket.IO protocol.[5] Figure 6 depicts a screenshot of the simulator with the AEBS in action in proximity of a cow.

Hinge Loss. In this section, we investigate the relationship between multiclass hinge loss functions and adversarial examples. *Hinge loss* is defined as follows:

$$l(\hat{y}) = \max(0, k + \max_{i \neq l}(\hat{y}_i) - \hat{y}_l) \tag{6}$$

where (x, y) is a training sample, $\hat{y} = F(x)$ is a prediction, and l is the *ground truth* label of x. For this section, the output $\hat{y}$ is a numerical value indicating the *confidence level* of the network for each class. For example, $\hat{y}$ can be the output of a softmax layer as described in Sect. 2.

[5] Socket.IO protocol: https://github.com/socketio.

Consider what happens as we vary k. Suppose there is an $i \neq l$ s.t. $\hat{y}_i > \hat{y}_l$. Pick the largest such i, call it i^*. For $k = 0$, we will incur a loss of $\hat{y}_{i^*} - \hat{y}_l$ for the example (x, y). However, as we make k more negative, we increase the tolerance for "misclassifications" produced by the DNN F. Specifically, we incur no penalty for a misclassification as long as the associated confidence level deviates from that of the ground truth label by no more than $|k|$. Larger the absolute value of k, the greater the tolerance. Intuitively, this biases the training process towards avoiding "high confidence misclassifications".

In this experiment, we investigate the role of k and explore different parameter values. At training time, we want to minimize the mean hinge loss across all training samples. We trained the CNN described above with different values of k and evaluated its precision on both the original test set and a set of counterexamples generated for the original model, i.e., the network trained with cross-entropy loss.

Table 1 reports accuracy and log loss for different values of k on both original and counterexamples test sets ($T_{original}$ and $T_{countex}$, respectively).

Table 1. Hinge loss with different k values.

k	$T_{original}$		$T_{countex}$	
	Acc	Log-loss	Acc	Log-loss
0	0.69	0.68	0.11	0.70
−0.01	0.77	0.69	0.00	0.70
−0.05	0.52	0.70	0.67	0.69
−0.1	0.50	0.70	0.89	0.68
−0.25	0.51	0.70	0.77	0.68

Table 1 shows interesting results. We note that a negative k increases the accuracy of the model on counterexamples. In other words, biasing the training process by penalizing high-confidence misclassifications improves accuracy on counterexamples! However, the price to pay is a reduction of accuracy on the original test set. This is still a very preliminary result and further experimentation and analysis is necessary.

System-Level Counterexamples. By using the composition falsification framework presented in Sect. 4.1, we identify orientations, displacements on the x-axis, and color of an obstacle that leads to a collision of the vehicle with the obstacle. Figure 7 depicts configurations of the obstacle that lead to specification violations, and hence, to collisions.

In an experiment, we augment the original training set with the elements of $T_{countex}$, i.e., images of the original test set $T_{original}$ that are misclassified by the original model (see Sect. 4.2).

We trained the model with both cross-entropy and hinge loss for 20 epochs. Both models achieve a high accuracy on the validation set (≈92%). However,

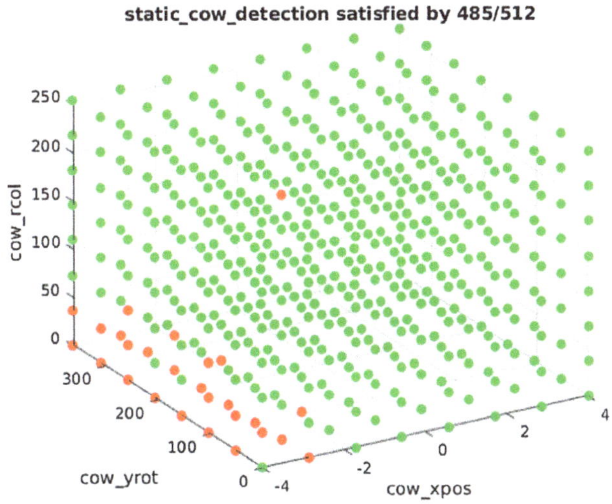

Fig. 7. Semantic counterexamples: obstacle configurations leading to property violations (in red). (Color figure online)

when plugged into the AEBS, neither of these models prevents the vehicle from colliding against the obstacle with an adversarial configuration. This seems to indicate that simply retraining with some semantic (system-level) counterexamples generated by analyzing the system containing the ML model may not be sufficient to eliminate all semantic counterexamples.

Interestingly, though, it appears that in both cases the impact of the vehicle with the obstacle happens at a slower speed than the one with the original model. In other words, the AEBS system starts detecting the obstacle earlier than with the original model, and therefore starts braking earlier as well. This means that despite the specification violations, the counterexample retraining procedure seems to help with limiting the damage in case of a collision. Coupled with a run-time assurance framework (see [41]), semantic retraining could help mitigate the impact of misclassifications on the system-level behavior.

5 Conclusion

In this paper, we surveyed the field of adversarial machine learning with a special focus on deep learning and on test-time attacks. We then introduced the idea of *semantic adversarial machine (deep) learning*, where adversarial analysis and training of ML models is performed using the semantics and context of the overall system within which the ML models are utilized. We identified several ideas for integrating semantics into adversarial learning, including using a semantic modification space, system-level formal specifications, training using semantic counterexamples, and utilizing more detailed information about the outputs produced by the ML model, including confidence levels, in the modules that use these outputs to make decisions. Preliminary experiments show the promise of these ideas, but also indicate that much remains to be done. We believe the field of semantic adversarial learning will be a rich domain for research at the intersection of machine learning, formal methods, and related areas.

Acknowledgments. The first and third author were supported in part by NSF grant 1646208, the DARPA BRASS program under agreement number FA8750-16-C0043, the DARPA Assured Autonomy program, and Berkeley Deep Drive.

References

1. Imagenet. http://image-net.org/
2. Alipanahi, B., Delong, A., Weirauch, M.T., Frey, B.J.: Predicting the sequence specificities of DNA-and RNA-binding proteins by deep learning. Nat. Biotechnol. **33**, 831–838 (2015)
3. Barreno, M., Nelson, B., Joseph, A.D., Tygar, J.D.: The security of machine learning. Mach. Learn. **81**(2), 121–148 (2010)
4. Bojarski, M., Del Testa, D., Dworakowski, D., Firner, B., Flepp, B., Goyal, P., Jackel, L., Monfort, M., Muller, U., Zhang, J., Zhang, X., Zhao, J., Zieba, K.: End to end learning for self-driving cars. Technical report (2016). CoRR, abs/1604.07316. http://arxiv.org/abs/1604.07316
5. Carlini, N., Wagner, D.: Towards evaluating the robustness of neural networks. In: IEEE Symposium on Security and Privacy (2017)
6. Carlini, N., Wagner, D.: Adversarial examples are not easily detected: bypassing ten detection methods. In: ACM Workshop on Artificial Intelligence and Security (2017)
7. Clarke, E., Grumberg, O., Jha, S., Lu, Y., Veith, H.: Counterexample-guided abstraction refinement. In: Emerson, E.A., Sistla, A.P. (eds.) CAV 2000. LNCS, vol. 1855, pp. 154–169. Springer, Heidelberg (2000). https://doi.org/10.1007/10722167_15
8. Dahl, G.E., Stokes, J.W., Deng, L., Yu, D.: Large-scale malware classification using random projections and neural networks. In: Proceedings of the IEEE International Conference on Acoustics, Speech and Signal Processing (ICASSP), pp. 3422–3426. IEEE (2013)
9. Dreossi, T., Donzé, A., Seshia, S.A.: Compositional falsification of cyber-physical systems with machine learning components. In: Barrett, C., Davies, M., Kahsai, T. (eds.) NFM 2017. LNCS, vol. 10227, pp. 357–372. Springer, Cham (2017). https://doi.org/10.1007/978-3-319-57288-8_26
10. Dreossi, T., Donzé, A., Seshia, S.A.: Compositional falsification of cyber-physical systems with machine learning components. CoRR, abs/1703.00978 (2017)
11. Dreossi, T., Ghosh, S., Yue, X., Keutzer, K., Sangiovanni-Vincentelli, A., Seshia, S.A.: Counterexample-guided data augmentation. In: International Joint Conference on Artificial Intelligence (IJCAI), July 2018
12. Dutta, S., Jha, S., Sankaranarayanan, S., Tiwari, A.: Output range analysis for deep neural networks (2018, to appear)
13. Dvijotham, K., Stanforth, R., Gowal, S., Mann, T., Kohli, P.: A Dual Approach to Scalable Verification of Deep Networks. ArXiv e-prints, March 2018
14. Eddy, N.: AI, machine learning drive autonomous vehicle development (2016). http://www.informationweek.com/big-data/big-data-analytics/ai-machine-learning-drive-autonomous-vehicle-development/d/d-id/1325906
15. Goodfellow, I., Bengio, Y., Courville, A.: Deep Learning. MIT Press (2016). http://www.deeplearningbook.org

16. Goodfellow, I.J., Shlens, J., Szegedy, C.: Explaining and harnessing adversarial examples. In: Proceedings of the 2015 International Conference on Learning Representations. Computational and Biological Learning Society (2015)
17. Hinton, G., Deng, L., Dong, Y., Dahl, G.E., Mohamed, A., Jaitly, N., Senior, A., Vanhoucke, V., Nguyen, P., Sainath, T.N., et al.: Deep neural networks for acoustic modeling in speech recognition: the shared views of four research groups. IEEE Signal Process. Mag. **29**(6), 82–97 (2012)
18. Huang, L., Joseph, A.D., Nelson, B., Rubinstein, B.I.P., Tygar, J.D.: Adversarial machine learning. In: Proceedings of the 4th ACM Workshop on Security and Artificial Intelligence, pp. 43–58. ACM (2011)
19. Huang, X., Kwiatkowska, M., Wang, S., Wu, M.: Safety verification of deep neural networks. In: Majumdar, R., Kunčak, V. (eds.) CAV 2017. LNCS, vol. 10426, pp. 3–29. Springer, Cham (2017). https://doi.org/10.1007/978-3-319-63387-9_1
20. Jia, Y., Shelhamer, E., Donahue, J., Karayev, S., Long, J., Girshick, R., Guadarrama, S., Darrell, T.: Caffe: convolutional architecture for fast feature embedding. In: ACM Multimedia Conference, ACMMM, pp. 675–678 (2014)
21. Jin, X., Donzé, A., Deshmukh, J., Seshia, S.A.: Mining requirements from closed-loop control models. IEEE Trans. Comput.-Aided Des. Circuits Syst. **34**(11), 1704–1717 (2015)
22. Julian, K., Lopez, J., Brush, J., Owen, M., Kochenderfer, M.: Policy compression for aircraft collision avoidance systems. In: Proceedings of the 35th Digital Avionics Systems Conference (DASC) (2016)
23. Katz, G., Barrett, C., Dill, D.L., Julian, K., Kochenderfer, M.J.: Reluplex: an Efficient SMT solver for verifying deep neural networks. In: Majumdar, R., Kunčak, V. (eds.) CAV 2017. LNCS, vol. 10426, pp. 97–117. Springer, Cham (2017). https://doi.org/10.1007/978-3-319-63387-9_5
24. Kingma, D.P., Ba, J.: Adam: a method for stochastic optimization (2017). https://arxiv.org/abs/1412.6980
25. Knorr, E.: How PayPal beats the bad guys with machine learning (2015). http://www.infoworld.com/article/2907877/machine-learning/how-paypal-reduces-fraud-with-machine-learning.html
26. Kolter, J.Z., Wong, E.: Provable defenses against adversarial examples via the convex outer adversarial polytope. CoRR, abs/1711.00851 (2017)
27. Koymans, R.: Specifying real-time properties with metric temporal logic. Real-Time Syst. **2**(4), 255–299 (1990)
28. Krizhevsky, A., Sutskever, I., Hinton, G.E.: Imagenet classification with deep convolutional neural networks. In: Advances in Neural Information Processing Systems, pp. 1097–1105 (2012)
29. Lee, E.A., Seshia, S.A.: Introduction to Embedded Systems: A Cyber-Physical Systems Approach, 2nd edn. MIT Press, Cambridge (2016)
30. Maler, O., Nickovic, D.: Monitoring temporal properties of continuous signals. In: Lakhnech, Y., Yovine, S. (eds.) FORMATS/FTRTFT - 2004. LNCS, vol. 3253, pp. 152–166. Springer, Heidelberg (2004). https://doi.org/10.1007/978-3-540-30206-3_12
31. Martín Abadi et al. TensorFlow: large-scale machine learning on heterogeneous systems (2015). Software: tensorflow.org
32. Miyato, T., Maeda, S., Koyama, M., Nakae, K., Ishii, S.: Distributional smoothing by virtual adversarial examples. CoRR, abs/1507.00677 (2015)
33. Mdry, A., Makelov, A., Schmidt, L., Tsipras, D., Vladu, A.: Towards deep learning models resistant to adversarial attacks. In: ICLR (2018)

34. Nocedal, J., Wright, S.: Numerical Optimization. Springer, New York (2006). https://doi.org/10.1007/978-0-387-40065-5
35. NVIDIA: Nvidia Tegra Drive PX: Self-driving Car Computer (2015)
36. Papernot, N., McDaniel, P., Goodfellow, I., Jha, S., Celik, Z.B., Swami, A.: Practical black-box attacks against machine learning. In: Proceedings of the 2017 ACM Asia Conference on Computer and Communications Security (AsiaCCS), April 2017
37. Papernot, N., McDaniel, P., Jha, S., Fredrikson, M., Celik, Z.B., Swami, A.: The limitations of deep learning in adversarial settings. In: Proceedings of the 1st IEEE European Symposium on Security and Privacy. arXiv preprint arXiv:1511.07528 (2016)
38. Pennington, J., Socher, R., Manning, C.D.: Glove: global vectors for word representation. In: Proceedings of the Empirical Methods in Natural Language Processing (EMNLP 2014), vol. 12, pp. 1532–1543 (2014)
39. Russell, S., Dietterich, T., Horvitz, E., Selman, B., Rossi, F., Hassabis, D., Legg, S., Suleyman, M., George, D., Phoenix, S.: Letter to the editor: research priorities for robust and beneficial artificial intelligence: an open letter. AI Mag. **36**(4), 3–4 (2015)
40. Seshia, S.A.: Compositional verification without compositional specification for learning-based systems. Technical report UCB/EECS-2017-164, EECS Department, University of California, Berkeley, November 2017
41. Seshia, S.A., Sadigh, D., Sastry, S.S.: Towards Verified Artificial Intelligence. ArXiv e-prints, July 2016
42. Shin, E.C.R., Song, D., Moazzezi, R.: Recognizing functions in binaries with neural networks. In: 24th USENIX Security Symposium (USENIX Security 2015), pp. 611–626 (2015)
43. Sinha, A., Namkoong, H., Duchi, J.: Certifiable distributional robustness with principled adversarial training. In: ICLR (2018)
44. Steinhardt, J., Koh, P.W., Liang, P.: Certified defenses for data poisoning attacks. In: Advances in Neural Information Processing Systems (NIPS) (2017)
45. Tramer, F., Zhang, F., Juels, A., Reiter, M., Ristenpart, T.: Stealing machine learning models via prediction APIs. In: USENIX Security (2016)
46. Yamaguchi, T., Kaga, T., Donzé, A., Seshia, S.A.: Combining requirement mining, software model checking, and simulation-based verification for industrial automotive systems. In: Proceedings of the IEEE International Conference on Formal Methods in Computer-Aided Design (FMCAD), October 2016

From Programs to Interpretable Deep Models and Back

Eran Yahav(✉)

Technion, Haifa, Israel
yahave@cs.technion.ac.il

Abstract. We demonstrate how deep learning over programs is used to provide (preliminary) augmented programmer intelligence. In the first part, we show how to tackle tasks like code completion, code summarization, and captioning. We describe a general path-based representation of source code that can be used across programming languages and learning tasks, and discuss how this representation enables different learning algorithms. In the second part, we describe techniques for extracting interpretable representations from deep models, shedding light on what has actually been learned in various tasks.

1 Introduction

We describe a journey from programs to interpretable deep models, and back. First, we show how to apply neural networks to learn interesting facts about programs, and build (interpretable) models for several programming-related tasks. Then, we show how to extract finite-state automata from a given recurrent neural network, providing some insight on what a network has actually learned.

1.1 Motivating Tasks

Semantic Labeling of Code Snippets. Consider the code snippet of Figure 1. This snippet only contains low-level assignments to arrays, but a human reading the code may (correctly) label it as performing the *reverse* operation. Our goal is to be able to predict such labels automatically. The right hand side of Fig. 1 shows the labels predicted automatically using our approach. The most likely prediction (77.34%) is *reverseArray*. Alon et al. [3] provide additional examples.

Intuitively, this problem is hard because it requires *learning a correspondence* between the *entire content of a code snippet* and a semantic label. That is, it requires aggregating possibly hundreds of expressions and statements from the snippet into a single, descriptive label.

E. Yahav—Joint work with Uri Alon, Yoav Goldberg, Omer Levy, Gail Weiss, and Meital Zilberstein.

H. Chockler and G. Weissenbacher (Eds.): CAV 2018, LNCS 10981, pp. 27–37, 2018.
https://doi.org/10.1007/978-3-319-96145-3_2

```
String[] f(final String[] array) {
 final String[] newArray = new String[array.length];
 for (int index = 0; index < array.length; index++) {
  newArray[array.length - index - 1] = array[index];
 }
 return newArray;
}
```

Fig. 1. A code snippet and its predicted labels as computed by our model.

```
iTextSharp.text.pdf.PdfReader reader = new iTextSharp.text.pdf.PdfReader(
    new iTextSharp.text.pdf.RandomAccessFileOrArray(@"C:\PDFFile.pdf"), null);
```

Prediction: *get the text of a pdf file in C#*

Fig. 2. A code snippet and its predicted caption as computed by our model.

Captioning Code Snippets. Consider the short code snippet of Fig. 2. The goal of *code captioning* is to assign a natural language caption that captures the task performed by the snippet. For the example of Fig. 2 our approach automatically predicts the caption *"get the text of a pdf file in C#"*. Intuitively, this task is harder than semantic labeling, as it requires the generation of a natural language sentence in addition to capturing (something about) the meaning of the code snippet.

```
OkHttpClient ok = new OkHttpClient();
Request request = new Request.Builder().url("programming.ai").build();
Response response =
```

Prediction: `ok.newCall(request).execute()`

Fig. 3. A code snippet and its predicted completion as computed by our model.

Code Completion. Consider the code of Fig. 3. Our code completion automatically predicts the next steps in the code: `ok.newCall(request).execute()`. This task requires prediction of the missing part of the code based on a given context. Technically, this can be expressed as predicting a completion of a partial abstract syntax tree.

In the next section, we show how techniques based on neural networks address all of these tasks, as well as other programming-related tasks.

2 From Programs to Deep Models

2.1 Representation

Leveraging machine learning models for predicting program properties such as variable names, method names, and expression types is a topic of much recent interest [1,2,6,8,9]. These techniques are based on learning a statistical model from a large amount of code and using the model to make predictions in new programs. A major challenge in these techniques is how to represent instances of the input space to facilitate learning [10]. Designing a program representation that enables effective learning is a critical task that is *often done manually for each task and programming language.*

Our Approach. We present a program representation for learning from programs. Our approach uses different *path-based abstractions of the program's abstract syntax tree.* This family of path-based representations is natural, general, fully automatic, and works well across different tasks and programming languages.

```
while (!d) {
  if (someCondition()) {
    d = true;
  }
}
```

(a) A simple JavaScript program.

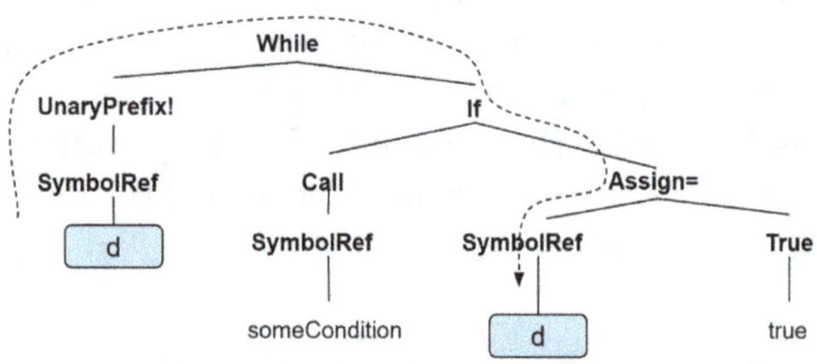

(b) The program's AST, and a path.

Fig. 4. A JavaScript program and its AST, along with an example of one of the paths.

AST Paths. We define AST paths as paths between nodes in a program's abstract syntax tree (AST). To automatically generate paths, we first parse the program to produce an AST, and then extract paths between nodes in the tree. We represent a path in the AST as a sequence of nodes connected by up and down movements, and represent a program element as the set of paths that its occurrences participate in. Figure 4a shows an example JavaScript program. Figure 4b shows its AST, and one of the extracted paths. The path from the first occurrence of the variable `d` to its second occurrence can be represented as:

$$\text{SymbolRef} \uparrow \text{UnaryPrefix!} \uparrow \text{While} \downarrow \text{If} \downarrow \text{Assign=} \downarrow \text{SymbolRef}$$

This is an example of a pairwise path between leaves in the AST, but in general the family of path-based representations contains n-wise paths, which do not necessarily span between leaves and do not necessarily contain all the nodes in between. We consider several choices of subsets of this family in [4].

Using a path-based representation has several major advantages:

1. Paths are generated automatically: there is no need for manual design of features aiming to capture potentially interesting relationships between program elements. This approach extracts unexpectedly useful paths, without the need for an expert to design features. The user is required only to choose a subset of our proposed family of path-based representations.
2. This representation is useful for any programming language, without the need to identify common patterns and nuances in each language.
3. The same representation is useful for a variety of prediction tasks, by using it with off-the-shelf learning algorithms or by simply replacing the representation of program elements in existing models (as we show in [4]).
4. AST paths are purely syntactic, and do not require any semantic analysis.

2.2 Code2vec: Learning Code Embeddings

In [3], we present a framework for predicting program properties using neural networks. The main idea is a neural network that learns *code embeddings* - continuous distributed vector representations for code. The code embeddings allow us to model correspondence between code snippet and labels in a natural and effective manner. By learning code embeddings, our long term goal is to enable the application of neural techniques to a wide-range of programming-languages tasks. A live demo of the framework is available at https://code2vec.org.

Our neural network architecture uses a representation of code snippets that *leverages the structured nature of source code*, and learns to aggregate multiple syntactic paths into a single vector. This ability is fundamental for the application of deep learning in programming languages. By analogy, word embeddings in natural language processing (NLP) started a revolution of application of deep learning for NLP tasks.

The input to our model is a code snippet and a corresponding tag, label, caption, or name. This tag expresses the semantic property that we wish the network to model, for example: a tag, name that should be assigned to the snippet, or the name of the method, class, or project that the snippet was taken from. Let $\mathcal{C}$ be the code snippet and $\mathcal{L}$ be the corresponding label or tag. Our underlying hypothesis is that *the distribution of labels can be inferred from syntactic paths in* $\mathcal{C}$. Our model therefore attempts to learn the tag distribution, conditioned on the code: $P(\mathcal{L}|\mathcal{C})$.

Model. For the full details of the model, see [3]. At a high-level, the key point is that a code snippet is composed of a bag of contexts, and each context is represented by a vector that its values are learned. The values of this vector capture two distinct goals: (i) the semantic meaning of this context, and (ii) the amount of attention this context should get.

The problem is as follows: given an arbitrarily large number of context vectors, we need to aggregate them into a single vector. Two trivial approaches would be to learn the most important one of them, or to use them all by vector-averaging them. These alternatives are shown to yield poor results (see [3]).

Our main observation is that *all* context vectors need to be used, but the model should learn how much focus to give each vector. This is done by learning how to average context vectors in a weighted manner. The weighted average is obtained by weighting each vector by its dot product with another global attention vector. The vector of each context and the attention vector are trained and learned *simultaneously*, using the standard neural approach of backpropagation.

Interpreting Attention. Despite the "black-box" reputation of neural networks, our model is partially interpretable thanks to the attention mechanism, which allows us to visualize the distribution of weights over the bag of path-contexts. Figures 5 and 6 illustrates a few predictions, along with the path-contexts that were given the most attention in each method. The width of each of the visualized paths is proportional to the attention weight that it was allocated. We note that in these figures the path is represented only as a connecting line between tokens, while in fact it contains rich syntactic information which is not expressed properly in the figures.

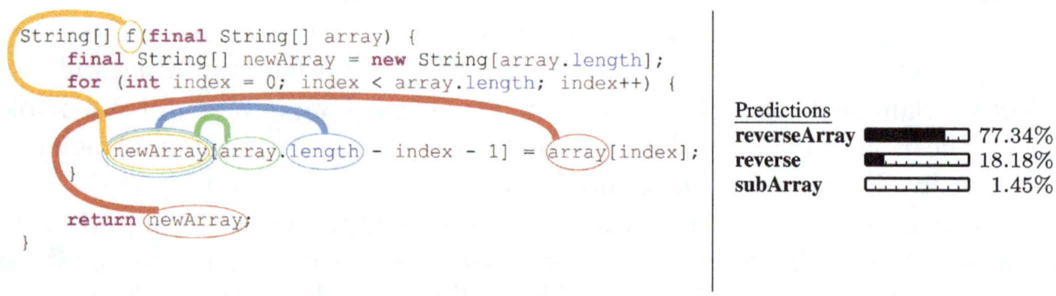

Fig. 5. Predictions and attention paths for the program of Fig. 1. The width of a path is proportional to its attention.

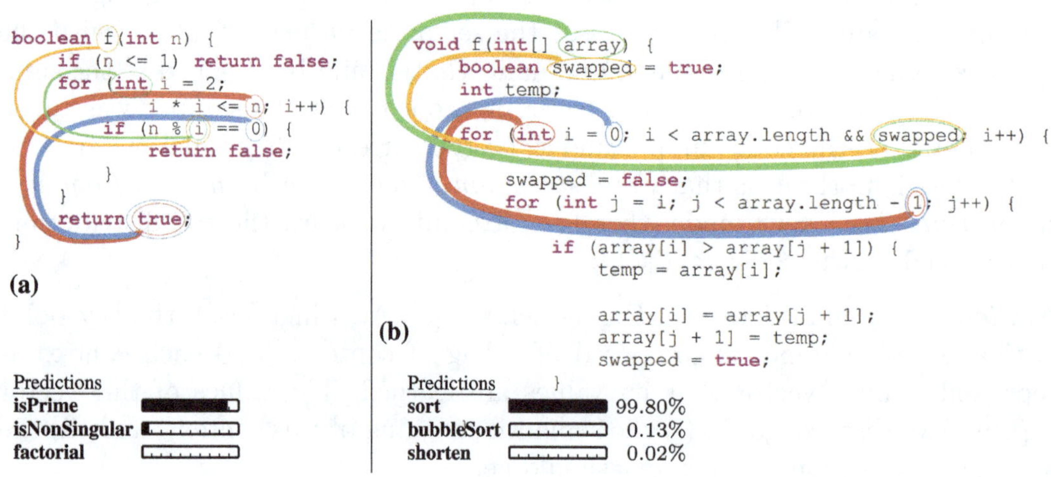

Fig. 6. Example predictions from our model. The width of a path is proportional to its attention.

The examples of Figs. 5 and 6 are interesting since the top names are accurate and descriptive (`reverseArray` and `reverse`; `isPrime`; `sort` and `bubbleSort`) but do not appear explicitly in the code snippets. The code snippets, and specifically the most attended path-contexts describe lower-level operations. Suggesting a descriptive name for each of these methods is difficult and might take time even for a trained human programmer.

2.3 Code2seq: Generating Sequences from Structured Representations of Code

In contrast to classical (and widespread) seq2seq models for translation, we introduce a new model that performs encoding over source code, and decoding to natural language.

Following [3,4], we introduce an approach for encoding source code that leverages the unique syntactic structure of programming languages. We represent a given code snippet as a set of paths over its abstract syntax tree (AST), where each path is compressed to a fixed-length vector. During decoding, code2seq attends over a different weighted sum of the path-vectors to produce each output token, much like NMT models attend over contextualized token representations in the source sentence. A live demo of the framework is available at https://code2seq.org.

3 From Deep Models to Automata

In this section, we focus on extraction of finite-state automata from recurrent neural networks (RNNs). In recent years, there has been significant interest in the use of recurrent neural networks (RNNs), for learning languages. Like other supervised machine learning techniques, RNNs are trained based on a large set of examples of the target concept. While neural networks can reasonably approximate a variety of languages, and even precisely represent a regular language [5], they are in practice unlikely to generalize exactly to the concept being trained, and *what they eventually learn in actuality is unclear* [7]. Our goal in this work is to provide some insight into what a given trained network has actually learned, without requiring changes to the network architecture, or access to the original training data.

Recurrent Neural Networks. Recurrent neural networks (RNNs) are a class of neural networks which are used to process sequences of arbitrary lengths. When operating over sequences of discrete alphabets, the input sequence is fed into the RNN on a symbol-by-symbol basis. For each input symbol the RNN outputs a *state vector* representing the sequence up to that point. A state vector and an input symbol are combined for producing the next state vector. The RNN is essentially a parameterized mathematical function that takes as input a state vector and an input vector, and produces a new state vector. The state vectors can be passed to a classification component that is used to produce a binary or multi-class classification decision. The RNN is trainable, and, when trained together with the classification component, the training procedure drives the state vectors to provide a representation of the prefix which is informative for the classification task being trained. We call a combination of an RNN and a classification component an *RNN-acceptor.*

A trained RNN-acceptor can be seen as a state machine in which the states are high-dimensional vectors: it has an initial state, a well defined transition function between internal states, and a well defined classification for each internal state.

Problem Definition. Given an RNN-acceptor R trained to accept or reject sequences over an alphabet Σ, our goal is to extract a deterministic finite-state automaton (DFA) A that mimics the behavior of R. That is, our goal is to extract a DFA A such that the language $L \subseteq \Sigma^*$ of sequences accepted by A is observably equivalent to that accepted by R. Intuitively, we would like to obtain a DFA that accepts *exactly* the same language as the network, but this is generally practically impossible as we do not know in advance any bound on the maximum sample length necessary in order to observe all of its behavior.

Extraction Using Queries and Counterexamples. In [11], we present a framework for extracting a finite state automaton from a given RNN. The main idea is to use the L^* learning algorithm to learn an automaton while using the RNN as the teacher.

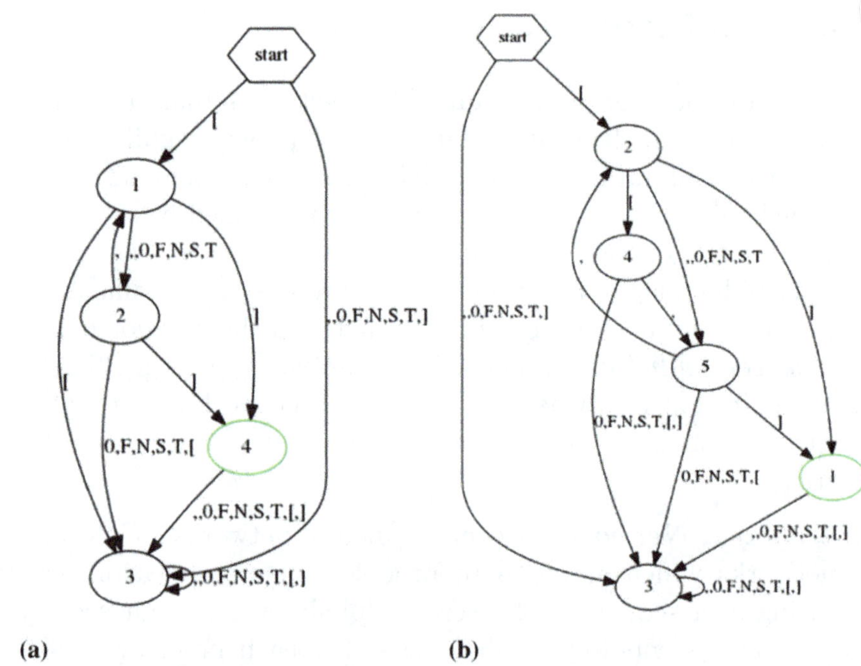

Fig. 7. Two DFAs resembling, but not perfectly, the correct DFA for the regular language of tokenised JSON lists, (\[\])|(\[[SONTF](, [SONTF])∗ \])$. DFA (a) is almost correct, but accepts also list-like sequences in which the last item is missing, i.e. there is a comma followed by a closing bracket. DFA (b) is returned by L* after the teacher (network) rejects (a), but is also not a correct representation of the target language—treating the sequence `[,` as a legitimate list item equivalent to the characters `S`, `0`, `N`, `T`, `F`.

3.1 What Has a Network Learned?

Tokenized JSON Lists. We trained a GRU network with 2 layers and hidden size 100 on the regular language representing a simple tokenized JSON list with no nesting,

$$(\backslash[\backslash])|(\backslash[[S0NTF](,[S0NTF])*\backslash])\$$$

over the 8-letter alphabet { `[`, `]`, `S`, `0`, `N`, `T`, `F`, `,` }, to accuracy 100% on a training set of size 20000 and a test set of size 2000, both evenly split between positive and negative examples. As before, we extracted from this network using our method.

Within 2 counterexamples (1 provided and 1 generated), our method extracted the automaton shown in Fig. 7a, which is almost but not quite representative of the target language. A few seconds later it returned a counterexample to this DFA which pushed L* to refine further and return the DFA shown in Fig. 7b, which is also almost but not quite representative of zero-nesting tokenized JSON lists.

Ultimately after 400 s, our method extracted (but did not reach equivalence on) an automaton of size 441, returning the counterexamples listed in Table 1 and achieving 100% accuracy against the network on both its train set and all

Table 1. Counterexamples returned to the equivalence queries made by L* during extraction of a DFA from a network trained to 100% accuracy on both train and test sets on the regular language $(\backslash[\backslash])|(\backslash[[S0NTF](,[S0NTF])*\backslash])\$$ over the 8-letter alphabet { `[`, `]`, `S`, `0`, `N`, `T`, `F`, `,` }. Counterexamples highlighting the discrepancies between the network behaviour and the target behaviour are shown in bold.

Counterexample generation for the non-nested tokenized JSON-lists language			
Counterexample	Generation time (seconds)	Network classification	Target classification
[]	provided	True	True
[SS]	3.49	False	False
[[,]	7.12	True	False
[S,,	8.61	True	False
[0, F	8.38	True	False
[N, 0,	8.07	False	False
[S, N, 0,	9.43	True	False
[T, S,	9.56	False	False
[S, S, T, []	15.15	False	False
[F, T, [	3.23	False	False
[N, F, S, 0	10.04	True	False
[S, N, [,,,,	27.79	True	False
[T, 0, T,	28.06	True	False
[S, T, 0,],	26.63	True	False

sampled sequence lengths. As before, we note that each state split by the method is justified by concrete inputs to the network, and so the extraction of a large DFA is a sign of the inherent complexity of the learned network behavior.

3.2 Counterexamples

For many RNN-acceptors that train to 100% accuracy and exhibit perfect test set behavior on large test sets, our method was able to find many simple examples which the network misclassifies.

For instance, for a network trained to classify simple email addresses over the 38-letter alphabet {`a`,`b`, ...,`z`,`0`,`1`, ...,`9`,`@`,`.`} as defined by the regular expression

[a-z][a-z0-9]*@[a-z0-9]+.(com|net|co.[a-z][a-z])$

with 100% accuracy on a 40,000 sample train set and 100% accuracy on a 2,000 sample test set (i.e., a seemingly perfect network), the refinement-based L* extraction quickly returned several counterexamples, showing words that the network classifies incorrectly (e.g., the network accepted the non-email sequence `25.net`). While we could not extract a representative DFA from the network in the allotted time frame, our method did show that the network learned a far more elaborate (and incorrect) function than needed.

Beyond demonstrating the counterexample generation capabilities of our extraction method, these results also highlight the brittleness in generalization of trained RNN networks, and suggests that evidence based on test-set performance should be taken with extreme caution.

4 Conclusion

We provide a brief description of a journey from programs to (somewhat) interpretable deep models that work well across different tasks and different programming languages. As we gained experience with these models, the question of *what have they actually learned* became more important (and subtle). Attention over AST paths provides some insight on what drives the predictions performed by (some of) the models, but a different approach is required for RNN-based models. This motivated the second part of our journey, trying to extract an interpretable model from a given RNN acceptor. This also motivated future work on classifying what can and cannot be learned by different kinds of RNNs [12].

References

1. Allamanis, M., Barr, E.T., Bird, C., Sutton, C.: Suggesting accurate method and class names. In: Proceedings of the 2015 10th Joint Meeting on Foundations of Software Engineering, ESEC/FSE 2015, pp. 38–49. ACM, New York (2015). http://doi.acm.org/10.1145/2786805.2786849

2. Allamanis, M., Peng, H., Sutton, C.A.: A convolutional attention network for extreme summarization of source code. In: Proceedings of the 33nd International Conference on Machine Learning, ICML 2016, New York City, NY, USA, 19–24 June 2016, pp. 2091–2100 (2016). http://jmlr.org/proceedings/papers/v48/allamanis16.html
3. Alon, U., Zilberstein, M., Levy, O., Yahav, E.: code2vec: learning distributed representations of code. arXiv preprint arXiv:1803.09473 (2018)
4. Alon, U., Zilberstein, M., Levy, O., Yahav, E.: A general path-based representation for predicting program properties. In: Proceedings of the ACM SIGPLAN Conference on Programming Language Design and Implementation, PLDI 2018 (2018)
5. Casey, M.: Correction to proof that recurrent neural networks can robustly recognize only regular languages. Neural Comput. **10**(5), 1067–1069 (1998). https://doi.org/10.1162/089976698300017340
6. Maddison, C.J., Tarlow, D.: Structured generative models of natural source code. In: Proceedings of the International Conference on Machine Learning, ICML 2014, vol. 32, pp. II-649–II-657. JMLR.org (2014). http://dl.acm.org/citation.cfm?id=3044805.3044965
7. Omlin, C.W., Giles, C.L.: Symbolic knowledge representation in recurrent neural networks: insights from theoretical models of computation. In: Cloete, I., Zurada, J.M. (eds.) Knowledge-Based Neurocomputing, pp. 63–116. MIT Press, Cambridge (2000). http://dl.acm.org/citation.cfm?id=337224.337236
8. Raychev, V., Bielik, P., Vechev, M.: Probabilistic model for code with decision trees. In: Proceedings of the 2016 ACM SIGPLAN International Conference on Object-Oriented Programming, Systems, Languages, and Applications, OOPSLA 2016, pp. 731–747. ACM, New York (2016). http://doi.acm.org/10.1145/2983990.2984041
9. Raychev, V., Vechev, M., Krause, A.: Predicting program properties from "big code". In: Proceedings of the 42nd Annual ACM SIGPLAN-SIGACT Symposium on Principles of Programming Languages, POPL 2015, pp. 111–124. ACM, New York (2015). http://doi.acm.org/10.1145/2676726.2677009
10. Shalev-Shwartz, S., Ben-David, S.: Understanding Machine Learning: From Theory to Algorithms. Cambridge University Press, New York (2014)
11. Weiss, G., Goldberg, Y., Yahav, E.: Extracting automata from recurrent neural networks using queries and counterexamples (2017). http://arxiv.org/abs/1711.09576
12. Weiss, G., Goldberg, Y., Yahav, E.: On the practical computational power of finite precision RNNs for language recognition. In: 56th Annual Meeting of the Association for Computational Linguistics, ACL 2018 (2018)

Formal Reasoning About the Security of Amazon Web Services

Byron Cook[1,2](✉)

[1] Amazon Web Services, Seattle, USA
byron@amazon.com
[2] University College London, London, UK

Abstract. We report on the development and use of formal verification tools within Amazon Web Services (AWS) to increase the security assurance of its cloud infrastructure and to help customers secure themselves. We also discuss some remaining challenges that could inspire future research in the community.

1 Introduction

Amazon Web Services (AWS) is a provider of *cloud services*, meaning on-demand access to IT resources via the Internet. AWS adoption is widespread, with over a million active customers in 190 countries, and $5.1 billion in revenue during the last quarter of 2017. Adoption is also rapidly growing, with revenue regularly increasing between 40–45% year-over-year.

The challenge for AWS in the coming years will be to accelerate the development of its functionality while simultaneously increasing the level of security offered to customers. In 2011, AWS released over 80 significant services and features. In 2012, the number was nearly 160; in 2013, 280; in 2014, 516; in 2015, 722; in 2016, 1,017. Last year the number was 1,430. At the same time, AWS is increasingly being used for a broad range of security-critical computational workloads.

Formal automated reasoning is one of the investments that AWS is making in order to facilitate continued simultaneous growth in both functionality and security. The goal of this paper is to convey information to the formal verification research community about this industrial application of the community's results. Toward that goal we describe work within AWS that uses formal verification to raise the level of security assurance of its products. We also discuss the use of formal reasoning tools by externally-facing products that help customers secure themselves. We close with a discussion about areas where we see that future research could contribute further impact.

Related Work. In this work we discuss efforts to make formal verification applicable to use-cases related to cloud security at AWS. For information on previous work within AWS to show functional correctness of some key distributed algorithms, see [43]. Other providers of cloud services also use formal verification to establish security properties, *e.g.* [23,34].

H. Chockler and G. Weissenbacher (Eds.): CAV 2018, LNCS 10981, pp. 38–47, 2018.
https://doi.org/10.1007/978-3-319-96145-3_3

Our overall strategy on the application of formal verification has been heavily influenced by the success of previous applied formal verification teams in industrial settings that worked as closely with domain experts as possible, *e.g.* work at Intel [33,50], NASA [31,42], Rockwell Collins [25], the Static Driver Verifier project [20], Facebook [45], and the success of Prover AB in the domain of railway switching [11].

External tools that we use include Boogie [1], Coq [4], CBMC [2], CVC4 [5], Dafny [6], HOL-light [8], Infer [9], OpenJML [10], SAW [13], SMACK [14], Souffle [37], TLA+ [15], VCC [16], and Z3 [17]. We have also collaborated with many organizations and individuals, *e.g.* Galois, Trail of Bits, the University of Sydney, and the University of Waterloo. Finally, many PhD student interns have applied their prototype tools to our problems during their internships.

2 Security of the Cloud

Amazon and AWS aim to innovate quickly while simultaneously improving on security. An original tenet from the founding of the AWS security team is to never be the organization that says *"no"*, but instead to be the organization that answers difficult security challenges with *"here's how"*. Toward this goal, the AWS security team works closely with product service teams to quickly identify and mitigate potential security concerns as early as possible while simultaneously not slowing the development teams down with bureaucracy. The security team also works with service teams early to facilitate the certification of compliance with industry standards.

The AWS security team performs formal security reviews of all features/services, *e.g.* 1,430 services/features in 2017, a 41% year-over-year increase from 2016. Mitigations to security risks that are developed during these security reviews are documented as a part of the security review process. Another important activity within AWS is ensuring that the cloud infrastructure *stays* secure after launch, especially as the system is modified incrementally by developers.

Where Formal Reasoning Fits In. The application security review process used within AWS increasingly involves the use of deductive theorem proving and/or symbolic model checking to establish important temporal properties of the software. For example, in 2017 alone the security team used deductive theorem provers or model checking tools to reason about cryptographic protocols/systems (*e.g.* [24]), hypervisors, boot-loaders/BIOS/firmware (*e.g.* [27]), garbage collectors, and network designs. Overall, formal verification engagements within the AWS security team increased 76% year-over-year in 2017, and found 45% more pre-launch security findings year-over-year in 2017.

To support our needs we have modified a number of open-source projects and contributed those changes back. For example, changes to CBMC [2] facilitate its application to C-based systems at the bottom of the compute stack used in AWS data centers [27]. Changes to SAW [13] add support for the Java programming language. Contributions to SMACK [14] implement automata-theoretic constructions that facilitate automatic proofs that s2n [12] correctly implements the *code balancing* mitigation for side-channel timing attacks. Source-code contributions to OpenJML [10] add support for Java 8 features needed to prove the correctness of code implementing a secure streaming protocol used throughout AWS.

In many cases we use formal verification tools *continuously* to ensure that security is implemented as designed, *e.g.* [24]. In this scenario, whenever changes and updates to the service/feature are developed, the verification tool is re-executed automatically prior to the deployment of the new version.

The security operations team also uses automated formal reasoning tools in its effort to identify security vulnerabilities found in internal systems and determine their potential impact on demand. For example, an SMT-based semantic-level policy reasoning tool is used to find misconfigured resource policies.

In general we have found that the internal use of formal reasoning tools provides good value for the investment made. Formal reasoning provides higher levels of assurance than testing for the properties established, as it provides clear information about what has and has not been secured. Furthermore, formal verification of systems can begin long before code is written, as we can prove the correctness of the high-level algorithms and protocols, and use under-constrained symbolic models for unwritten code or hardware that has not been fabricated yet.

3 Securing Customers *in* the Cloud

AWS offers a set of cloud-based services designed to help customers be secure *in* the cloud. Some examples include AWS Config, which provides customers with information about the configurations of their AWS resources; Amazon Inspector, which provides automated security assessments of customer-authored AWS-based applications; Amazon GuardDuty, which monitors AWS accounts looking for unusual account usage on behalf of customers; Amazon Macie, which helps customers discover and classify sensitive data at risk of being leaked; and AWS Trusted Advisor, which automatically makes optimization and security recommendations to customers.

In addition to automatic cloud-based security services, AWS provides people to help customers: *Solutions Architects* from different disciplines work with customers to ensure that they are making the best use of available AWS services; *Technical Account Managers* are assigned to customers and work with them when security or operational events arise; the *Professional Services* team can be hired by customers to work on bespoke cloud-based solutions.

Where Formal Reasoning Fits In. Automated formal reasoning tools today provide functionality to customers through the AWS services Config, Inspector, GuardDuty, Macie, Trusted Advisor, and the storage service S3. As an example, customers using the S3 web-based console receiving alerts—via SMT-based reasoning—when their S3 bucket policies are possibly misconfigured. AWS Macie uses the same engine to find possible data exfiltration routes. Another application is the use of high-performance datalog constraint solvers (*e.g.* [37]) to reason about questions of reachability in complex virtual networks built using AWS EC2 networking primitives. The theorem proving service behind this functionality regularly receives 10s of millions of calls daily.

In addition to the automated services that use formal techniques, some members of the AWS Solutions Architects, Technical Account Managers and Professional Services teams are applying and/or deploying formal verification directly with customers. In particular, in certain security-sensitive sectors (*e.g.* financial services), the Professional Services organization are working directly with customers to deploy formal reasoning into their AWS environments.

The customer reaction to features based on formal reasoning tools has been overwhelmingly positive, both anecdotally as well as quantitatively. Calls by AWS services to the automated reasoning tools increased by four orders of magnitude in 2017. With the formal verification tools providing the semantic foundation, customers can make stronger universal statements about their policies and networks and be confident that their assumptions are not violated.

4 Challenges

At AWS we have successfully applied existing or bespoke formal verification tools to both raise the level of security assurance *of* the cloud as well as help customers protect themselves *in* the cloud. We now know that formal verification provides value to applications in cloud security. There are, however, many problems yet to be solved and many applications of formal verification techniques yet to be discovered and/or applied. In the future we are hoping to solve the problems we face in partnership with the formal verification research community. In this section we outline some of those challenges. Note that in many cases existing teams in the research community will already be working on topics related to these problems, too many to cite comprehensively. Our comments are intended to encourage and inspire more work in this space.

Reasoning About Risk and Feasibility. A security engineer spends the majority of their time informally reasoning about risk. The same is true for any corporate Chief Information Security Officer (CISO). We (the formal verification community) potentially have a lot to contribute in this space by developing systems that help reason more formally about the consequences of combinations of events and their relationships to bugs found in systems. Furthermore, our community has a lot to offer by bridging between our concept of a counterexample and the security community's notion of a *proof of concept* (PoC), which is a constructive realization of a security finding in order to demonstrate its feasibility. Often security engineers will develop partial PoCs, meaning that they combine reasoning about risk and the finding of constructive witnesses in order to increase their confidence in the importance of a finding. There are valuable results yet to be discovered by our community at the intersection of reasoning about and synthesis of threat models, environment models, risk/probabilities, counterexamples, and PoCs. A few examples of current work on this topic include [18,28,30,44,48].

Fixes Not Findings. Industrial users of formal verification technology need to make systems more secure, not merely find security vulnerabilities. This is true both for securing the cloud, as well as helping customers be secure in the cloud. If there are security findings, the primary objective is to find them *and* fix them quickly. In practice a lot of work is ahead for an organization once a security finding has been identified. As a community, anything we can do to reduce the friction for users trying to triage and fix vulnerabilities, the better. Tools that report false findings are quickly ignored by developers, thus as a community we should focus on improving the fidelity of our tools. Counterexamples can be downplayed by optimistic developers: any assistance in helping users understand the bugs found and/or their consequences is helpful. Security vulnerabilities that require fixes that are hard to build or hard to deploy are an especially important challenge: our community has a lot to offer here via the development of more powerful synthesis/repair methods (*e.g.* [22,32,39]) that take into account threat models, environment models, probabilities, counterexamples.

Auditable Proof Artifacts for Compliance. Proof is actually two activities: *searching* for a candidate proof, and *checking* the candidate proof's validity. The searching is the art form, often involving a combination of heuristics that attempt to work around the undecidable. The checking of a proof is (in principle) the boring yet rigorous part, usually decidable, often linear in the size of the proof. Proof artifacts that can be re-checked have value, especially in applications related to compliance certification, *e.g.* DO-333 [26], CENENLEC EN 50128 SIL 4 [11], EAL7 MILS [51]. Non-trivial parts of the various compliance and conformance standards can be checked via mechanical proof, *e.g.* parts of PCI and FIPS 140. Found proofs of compliance controls that can be shared and checked/re-checked have the possibility to reduce the cost of compliance certification, as well as reduce the time-to-market for organizations who require certification before using systems.

Tracking Casual or Unrealistic Assumptions. Practical formal verification efforts often make unrealistic assumptions that are later forgotten. As an example, most tools assume that the systems we are analyzing are immune to *single-event upsets*, *e.g.* ionizing particles striking the microprocessor or semiconductor memory. We sometimes assume compilers and runtime garbage collectors are correct. In some cases (*e.g.* [20]) the environment models used by formal verification tools do not capture all possible real-world scenarios. As formal verification tools become more powerful and useful we will increasingly need to reason about what has been proved and what has not been proved, in order to avoid misunderstandings that could lead to security vulnerabilities. In applications of security this reasoning about assumptions made will need to interact with the treatment of risk and how risk is modified by various mitigations, *e.g.* some mitigations for single-event upsets make the events so unlikely they they are not a viable security risk, but still not impossible. This topic has been the focus of some attention over the years, *e.g.* CLINC stack [41], CompCert [3], and DeepSpec [7]. We believe that this will become an increasingly important problem in the future.

Distributed Formal Verification in the Cloud. Formal verification tools do not take enough advantage of modern data centers via distributing coordinated processes. Some examples of work in the right direction include [21,35,36,38,40,47]. Especially in the area of program verification and analysis, our community still focuses on procedures that work on single computers, or perhaps *portfolio* solvers that try different problem encodings or solvers in parallel. Today large formal verification problems are often decomposed manually, and then solved in parallel. There has not been much research in methods for automatically introducing and managing the reasoning about the decompositions automatically in cloud-based distributed systems. This is in part perhaps due to the rules at various annual competitions such as SV-COMP, SMT-COMP, and CASC. We encourage the participants and organizers of competitions to move to cloud-based competitions where solvers have the freedom to use cloud-scale distributed computing to solve formal verification problems. Tool developers could build AMIs or CloudFormation templates that allow cloud distribution. Perhaps future contestants might even make Internet endpoints available with APIs supporting SMTLIB or TPTP such that the competition is simply a series of remote API calls to each competitor's implementation. In this case competitors that embrace the full power of the cloud will have an advantage, and we will see dramatic improvements in the computational power of our formal verification tools.

Continuous Formal Verification. As discussed previously, we have found that it is important to focus on *continuous verification*: it is not enough to simply prove the correctness of a protocol or system once, what we need is to *continuously* prove the desired property during the lifetime of the system [24]. This matches reports from elsewhere in industry where formal verification is being applied, *e.g.* [45]. An interesting consequence of our focus on continuous formal verification is that the time and effort spent finding an initial proof before a system is deployed is not as expensive as the time spent maintaining the proof later, as the up-front human cost of the pre-launch proof is amortized over the lifetime of the system. It would be especially interesting to see approaches developed that synthesize new proofs of modified code based on existing proofs of unmodified code.

The Known Problems are Still Problems. Many of the problems that we face in AWS are well known to the formal verification community. For example, we need better tools for formal reasoning about languages such as Ruby, Python, and Javascript, *e.g.* [29,49]. Proofs about security-oriented properties of many large open source systems remain an open problem, *e.g.* Angular, Linux, OpenJDK, React, NGINX, Xen. Many formal verification tools are hard to use. Many tools are brittle prototypes only developed for the purposes of publication. Better understanding of ISAs and memory models (*e.g.* [19,46]) are also key to prove the correctness of code operating on low-level devices. Practical and scalable methods for proving the correctness of distributed and/or concurrent systems remains an open problem. Improvements to the performance and scalability of formal verification tools are needed to prove the correctness of larger modules without manual decomposition. Abstraction refinement continues to be a problem, as false bugs are expensive to triage in an industrial setting. Buggy (and thus unsound) proof-based tools lose trust in formal verification with the users who are trying to deploy them.

5 Conclusion

In this paper we have discussed how formal verification contributes to the ability of AWS to quickly develop and deploy new features while simultaneously increasing the security of the AWS cloud infrastructure. We also discussed how formal verification techniques contribute to customer-facing AWS services. In this paper we have outlined some challenges we face. We actively seek solutions to these problems and are happy to collaborate with partners in this pursuit. We look forward to more partnerships, more tools, more collaboration, and more sharing of information as we try to bring affordable, efficient and secure computation to all.

References

1. Boogie program prover. https://github.com/boogie-org/boogie
2. CBMC model checker. https://github.com/diffblue/cbmc
3. CompCert project. http://compcert.inria.fr
4. Coq theorem prover. https://github.com/coq/coq
5. CVC4 decision procedure. http://cvc4.cs.stanford.edu
6. Dafny theorem prover. https://github.com/Microsoft/dafny
7. DeepSpec project. https://deepspec.org
8. HOL-light theorem prover. https://github.com/jrh13/hol-light
9. Infer program analysis. https://github.com/facebook/infer
10. OpenJML program prover. https://github.com/OpenJML
11. Prover Certifier. https://www.prover.com/software-solutions-rail-control/prover-certifier
12. s2n TLS/SSL implementation. https://github.com/awslabs/s2n
13. SAW program prover. https://github.com/GaloisInc/saw-script
14. SMACK software verifier. http://smackers.github.io/
15. TLA+ theorem prover. https://github.com/tlaplus
16. VCC program prover. https://vcc.codeplex.com
17. Z3 decision procedure. https://github.com/Z3Prover/z3
18. Aldini, A., Seigneur, J.M., Ballester Lafuente, C., Titi, X., Guislain, J.: Design and validation of a trust-based opportunity-enabled risk management system. Inf. Comput. Secur. **25**(2), 2–25 (2017)
19. Alglave, J., Cousot, P.: Ogre and Pythia: an invariance proof method for weak consistency models. In: POPL (2017)
20. Ball, T., Bounimova, E., Cook, B., Levin, V., Lichtenberg, J., McGarvey, C., Ondrusek, B., Rajamani, S.K., Ustuner, A.: Thorough static analysis of device drivers. In: EuroSys, pp. 73–85 (2006)
21. Beyer, D., Dangl, M., Dietsch, D., Heizmann, M.: Correctness witnesses: exchanging verification results between verifiers (2016)

22. Griesmayer, A., Bloem, R., Cook, B.: Repair of Boolean programs with an application to C. In: Ball, T., Jones, R.B. (eds.) CAV 2006. LNCS, vol. 4144, pp. 358–371. Springer, Heidelberg (2006). https://doi.org/10.1007/11817963_33
23. Bouchenak, S., Chockler, G., Chockler, H., Gheorghe, G., Santos, N., Shraer, A.: Verifying cloud services: present and future. ACM SIGOPS Oper. Syst. Rev. **47**(2), 6–19 (2013)
24. Chudnov, A., Collins, N., Cook, B., Dodds, J., Huffman, B., Magill, S., MacCarthaigh, C., Mertens, E., Mullen, E., Tasiran, S., Tomb, A., Westbrook, E.: Continuous formal verification of Amazon S2N. In: CAV (2018)
25. Cofer, D., Gacek, A., Miller, S., Whalen, M.W., LaValley, B., Sha, L.: Compositional verification of architectural models. In: Goodloe, A.E., Person, S. (eds.) NFM 2012. LNCS, vol. 7226, pp. 126–140. Springer, Heidelberg (2012). https://doi.org/10.1007/978-3-642-28891-3_13
26. Cofer, D., Miller, S.: DO-333 certification case studies. In: Badger, J.M., Rozier, K.Y. (eds.) NFM 2014. LNCS, vol. 8430, pp. 1–15. Springer, Cham (2014). https://doi.org/10.1007/978-3-319-06200-6_1
27. Cook, B., Khazem, K., Kroening, D., Tasiran, S., Tautschnig, M., Tuttle, M.R.: Model checking boot code from AWS data centers. In: CAV (2018)
28. Dullien, T.F.: Weird machines, exploitability, and provable unexploitability. IEEE Trans. Emerg. Top. Comput. **PP**(99) (2017)
29. Eilers, M., Müller, P.: Nagini: a static verifier for Python. In: CAV (2018)
30. Ganesh, V., Banescu, S. and Ochoa, M.: The meaning of attack-resistant programs. In: International Workshop on Progamming Languages and Security (2015)
31. Goodloe, A.E., Muñoz, C., Kirchner, F., Correnson, L.: Verification of numerical programs: from real numbers to floating point numbers. In: Brat, G., Rungta, N., Venet, A. (eds.) NFM 2013. LNCS, vol. 7871, pp. 441–446. Springer, Heidelberg (2013). https://doi.org/10.1007/978-3-642-38088-4_31
32. Gulwani, S., Polozov, O., Singh, R.: Program synthesis. In: Foundations and Trends in Programming Languages, vol. 4 (2017)
33. Harrison, J.: Formal verification of IA-64 division algorithms. In: TPHOLs (2000)
34. Hawblitzel, C., Howell, J., Kapritsos, M., Lorch, J.R., Parno, B., Roberts, M.L., Setty, S., Zill, B.: IronFleet: proving practical distributed systems correct. In: SOSP (2015)
35. Heule, M.J.H., Kullmann, O., Marek, V.W.: Solving and verifying the Boolean Pythagorean triples problem via cube-and-conquer. In: Creignou, N., Le Berre, D. (eds.) SAT 2016. LNCS, vol. 9710, pp. 228–245. Springer, Cham (2016). https://doi.org/10.1007/978-3-319-40970-2_15
36. Holzmann, G.J., Joshi, R., Groce, A.: Tackling large verification problems with the swarm tool. In: Havelund, K., Majumdar, R., Palsberg, J. (eds.) SPIN 2008. LNCS, vol. 5156, pp. 134–143. Springer, Heidelberg (2008). https://doi.org/10.1007/978-3-540-85114-1_11
37. Jordan, H., Scholz, B., Subotic, P.: Towards proof synthesis by neural machine translation. In: CAV (2016)
38. Kumar, R., Ball, T., Lichtenberg, J., Deisinger, N., Upreti, A., Bansal, C.: CloudSDV enabling static driver verifier using Microsoft azure. In: Ábrahám, E., Huisman, M. (eds.) IFM 2016. LNCS, vol. 9681, pp. 523–536. Springer, Cham (2016). https://doi.org/10.1007/978-3-319-33693-0_33
39. Le Goues, C., Forrest, S., Weimer, W.: Current challenges in automatic software repair. Softw. Qual. J. **21**, 421–443 (2013)

40. Lopes, N.P., Rybalchenko, A.: Distributed and predictable software model checking. In: Jhala, R., Schmidt, D. (eds.) VMCAI 2011. LNCS, vol. 6538, pp. 340–355. Springer, Heidelberg (2011). https://doi.org/10.1007/978-3-642-18275-4_24
41. Moore, J.S.: Machines reasoning about machines: 2015. In: Finkbeiner, B., Pu, G., Zhang, L. (eds.) ATVA 2015. LNCS, vol. 9364, pp. 4–13. Springer, Cham (2015). https://doi.org/10.1007/978-3-319-24953-7_2
42. Narkawicz, A., Muñoz, C.A.: Formal verification of conflict detection algorithms for arbitrary trajectories. Reliab. Comput. **17**, 209–237 (2012)
43. Newcombe, C., Rath, T., Zhang, F., Munteanu, B., Brooker, M., Deardeuff, M.: How Amazon web services uses formal methods. Commun. ACM **58**(4), 66–73 (2004)
44. Ochoa, M., Banescu, S., Disenfeld, C., Barthe, G., Ganesh, V.: Reasoning about probabilistic defense mechanisms against remote attacks. In: IEEE European Symposium on Security and Privacy (2017)
45. O'Hearn, P.: Continuous reasoning: scaling the impact of formal methods. In: LICS (2018)
46. Reid, A., Chen, R., Deligiannis, A., Gilday, D., Hoyes, D., Keen, W., Pathirane, A., Shepherd, O., Vrabel, P., Zaidi, A.: End-to-end verification of processors with ISA-formal. In: Chaudhuri, S., Farzan, A. (eds.) CAV 2016. LNCS, vol. 9780, pp. 42–58. Springer, Cham (2016). https://doi.org/10.1007/978-3-319-41540-6_3
47. Rozier, K.Y., Vardi, M.Y.: A Multi-encoding approach for LTL symbolic satisfiability checking. In: Butler, M., Schulte, W. (eds.) FM 2011. LNCS, vol. 6664, pp. 417–431. Springer, Heidelberg (2011). https://doi.org/10.1007/978-3-642-21437-0_31
48. Rushby, J.: Software verification and system assurance. In: IEEE International Conference on Software Engineering and Formal Methods, pp. 3–10 (2009)
49. Santos, J.F., Maksimović, P., Naudžiūnienė, D., Wood, T., Gardner, P.: JaVerT: JavaScript verification toolchain. In: POPL (2017)
50. Seger, C.-J.H., Jones, R.B., O'Leary, J.W., Melham, T., Aagaard, M.D., Barrett, C., Syme, D.: An industrially effective environment for formal hardware verification. IEEE Trans. Comput. Aided Des. Integr. Circuits Syst. **24**(9), 1381–1405 (2005)
51. Wilding, M.M., Greve, D.A., Richards, R.J., Hardin, D.S.: Formal verification of partition management for the AAMP7G microprocessor. In: Hardin, D. (ed.) Design and Verification of Microprocessor Systems for High-Assurance Applications. Springer, Boston (2010). https://doi.org/10.1007/978-1-4419-1539-9_6

Tutorials

Foundations and Tools for the Static Analysis of Ethereum Smart Contracts

Ilya Grishchenko(✉), Matteo Maffei(✉), and Clara Schneidewind(✉)

TU Wien, Vienna, Austria
{ilya.grishchenko,matteo.maffei,clara.schneidewind}@tuwien.ac.at

Abstract. The recent growth of the blockchain technology market puts its main cryptocurrencies in the spotlight. Among them, Ethereum stands out due to its virtual machine (EVM) supporting smart contracts, i.e., distributed programs that control the flow of the digital currency Ether. Being written in a Turing complete language, Ethereum smart contracts allow for expressing a broad spectrum of financial applications. The price for this expressiveness, however, is a significant semantic complexity, which increases the risk of programming errors. Recent attacks exploiting bugs in smart contract implementations call for the design of formal verification techniques for smart contracts. This, however, requires rigorous semantic foundations, a formal characterization of the expected security properties, and dedicated abstraction techniques tailored to the specific EVM semantics. This work will overview the state-of-the-art in smart contract verification, covering formal semantics, security definitions, and verification tools. We will then focus on EtherTrust [1], a framework for the static analysis of Ethereum smart contracts which includes the first complete small-step semantics of EVM bytecode, the first formal characterization of a large class of security properties for smart contracts, and the first static analysis for EVM bytecode that comes with a proof of soundness.

1 Introduction

Blockchain technologies promise secure distributed computations even in absence of trusted third parties. The core of this technology is a distributed ledger that keeps track of previous transactions and the state of each account, and whose functionality and security is ensured by a careful combination of incentives and cryptography. Within this framework, software developers can implement sophisticated distributed, transaction-based computations by leveraging the scripting language offered by the underlying cryptocurrency. While many of these cryptocurrencies have an intentionally limited scripting language (e.g., Bitcoin [2]), Ethereum was designed from the ground up with a quasi Turing-complete language[1]. Ethereum programs, called *smart contracts*, have thus found a variety of

[1] While the language itself is Turing complete, computations are associated with a bounded computational budget (called gas), which gets consumed by each instruction thereby enforcing termination.

H. Chockler and G. Weissenbacher (Eds.): CAV 2018, LNCS 10981, pp. 51–78, 2018.
https://doi.org/10.1007/978-3-319-96145-3_4

appealing use cases, such as auctions [3], data management systems [4], financial contracts [5], elections [6], trading platforms [7,8], permission management [9] and verifiable cloud computing [10], just to mention a few. Given their financial nature, bugs and vulnerabilities in smart contracts may lead to catastrophic consequences. For instance, the infamous DAO vulnerability [11] recently led to a 60M$ financial loss and similar vulnerabilities occur on a regular basis [12,13]. Furthermore, many smart contracts in the wild are intentionally fraudulent, as highlighted in a recent survey [14].

A rigorous security analysis of smart contracts is thus crucial for the trust of the society in blockchain technologies and their widespread deployment. Unfortunately, this task is quite challenging for various reasons. First, Ethereum smart contracts are developed in an ad-hoc language, called Solidity, which resembles JavaScript but features specific transaction-oriented mechanisms and a number of non-standard semantic behaviours, as further described in this paper. Second, smart contracts are uploaded on the blockchain in the form of Ethereum Virtual Machine (EVM) bytecode, a stack-based low-level code featuring dynamic code creation and invocation and, in general, very little static information, which makes it extremely difficult to analyze.

Our Contributions. This work overviews the existing approaches taken towards formal verification of Ethereum smart contracts and discusses EtherTrust, the first sound static analysis tool for EVM bytecode. Specifically, our contributions are

- A survey on recent theories and tools for formal verification of Ethereum smart contracts including a systematization of existing work with an overview of the open problems and future challenges in the smart contract realm.
- An illustrative presentation of the small-step semantics presented by [15] with special focus on the semantics of the bytecode instructions that allow for the initiation of internal transactions. The subtleties in the semantics of these transactions have shown to form an integral part of the attack surface in the context of Ethereum smart contracts.
- A review of an abstraction based on Horn clauses for soundly over-approximating the small-step executions of Ethereum bytecode [1].
- A demonstration of how relevant security properties can be over-approximated and automatically verified using the static analyzer EtherTrust [1] by the example of the single-entrancy property defined in [15].

Outline. The remainder of this paper is organized as follows. Section 2 briefly overviews the Ethereum architecture, Sect. 3 reviews the state of the art in formal verification of Ethereum smart contracts, Sect. 4 revisits the Ethereum small-step semantics introduced by [15], Sect. 5 presents the single-entrancy property for smart contracts as defined by [15], Sect. 6 discusses the key ideas of the first sound static analysis for Ethereum bytecode as implemented in EtherTrust [1], Sect. 7 shows how reachability properties can automatically be checked using EtherTrust, and Sect. 8 concludes summarizing the key points of the paper.

2 Background on Ethereum

In the following we will shortly overview the mechanics of the cryptocurrency Ethereum and its built-in scripting language EVM bytecode.

2.1 Ethereum

Ethereum is a cryptographic currency system built on top of a blockchain. Similar to Bitcoin, network participants publish transactions to the network that are then grouped into blocks by distinct nodes (the so called *miners*) and appended to the blockchain using a proof of work (PoW) consensus mechanism. The state of the system – that we will also refer to as *global state* – consists of the state of the different accounts populating it. An account can either be an external account (belonging to a user of the system) that carries information on its current balance or it can be a contract account that additionally obtains persistent storage and the contract's code. The account's balances are given in the subunit *wei* of the virtual currency *Ether*.[2]

Transactions can alter the state of the system by either creating new contract accounts or by calling an existing account. Calls to external accounts can only transfer Ether to this account, but calls to contract accounts additionally execute the code associated to the contract. The contract execution might alter the storage of the account or might again perform transactions – in this case we talk about *internal transactions.*

The execution model underlying the execution of contract code is described by a virtual state machine, the *Ethereum Virtual Machine* (EVM). This is *quasi Turing complete* as the otherwise Turing complete execution is restricted by the upfront defined resource *gas* that effectively limits the number of execution steps. The originator of the transaction can specify the maximal gas that should be spent for the contract execution and also determines the gas price (the amount of wei to pay for a unit of gas). Upfront, the originator pays for the gas limit according to the gas price and in case of successful contract execution that did not spend the whole amount of gas dedicated to it, the originator gets reimbursed with gas that is left. The remaining wei paid for the used gas are given as a fee to a beneficiary address specified by the miner.

2.2 EVM Bytecode

Contracts are delivered and executed in *EVM bytecode* format – an Assembler like bytecode language. As the core of the EVM is a stack-based machine, the set of instructions in EVM bytecode consists mainly of standard instructions for stack operations, arithmetics, jumps and local memory access. The classical set of instructions is enriched with an opcode for the SHA3 hash and several opcodes for accessing the environment that the contract was called in. In addition, there are opcodes for accessing and modifying the storage of the account

[2] One Ether is equivalent to 10^{18} wei.

currently running the code and distinct opcodes for performing internal call and create transactions. Another instruction particular to the blockchain setting is the SELFDESTRUCT code that deletes the currently executed contract - but only after the successful execution of the external transaction.

The execution of each instruction consumes a positive amount of *gas*. The sender of the transaction specifies a gas limit and exceeding it results in an exception that reverts the effects of the current transaction on the global state. In the case of nested transactions, the occurrence of an exception only reverts its own effects, but not those of the calling transaction. Instead, the failure of an internal transaction is only indicated by writing zero to the caller's stack.

3 Overview on Formal Verification Approaches

In the following we give an overview on the approaches taken so far in the direction of securing (Ethereum) smart contracts. We distinguish between verification approaches and design approaches. According to our terminology, the goal of verification approaches is to check smart contracts written in existing languages (such as Solidity) for their compliance with a security policy or specification. In contrast, design approaches aim at facilitating the creation of secure smart contracts by providing frameworks for their development: These approaches encompass new languages which are more amenable to verification, provide a clear and simple semantics that is understandable by smart contract developers or allow for a direct encoding of desired security policies. In addition, we count works that aim at providing design patterns for secure smart contracts to this category.

3.1 Verification

In the field of smart contract verification we categorize the existing approaches along the following dimensions: target language (bytecode vs high level language), point of verification (static vs. dynamic analysis methods), provided guarantees (bug-finding vs. formal soundness guarantees), checked properties (generic contract properties vs. contract specific properties), degree of automation (automated verification vs. assisted analysis vs. manual inspection). From the current spectrum of analysis tools, we can find solutions in the following clusters:

Static Analysis Tools for Automated Bug-Finding. Oyente [16] is a state-of-the-art static analysis tool for EVM bytecode that relies on symbolic execution. Oyente supports a variety of pre-defined security properties, such as transaction order dependency, time-stamp dependency, and reentrancy that can be checked automatically. However, Oyente is not striving for soundness nor completeness. This is on the one hand due to the simplified semantics that serves as foundation of the analysis [15]. On the other hand, the security properties are rather syntactic or pattern based and are lacking a semantic characterization. Recently, Zhou et al. proposed the static analysis tool SASC [17] that extends

Oyente by additional patterns and provides a visualization of detected risks in the topology diagram of the original Solidity code.

Majan [18] extends the approach taken in Oyente to trace properties that consider multiple invocations of one smart contract. As Oyente, it relies on symbolic execution that follows a simplified version of the semantics used in Oyente and uses a pattern-based approach for defining the concrete properties to be checked. The tool covers safety properties (such as prodigality and suicidality) and liveness properties (greediness). As for Oyente, the authors do not make any security claims, but consider their tool a 'bug catching approach'.

Static Analysis Tools for Automated Verification of Generic Properties. In contrast to the aforementioned class of tools, this line of research aims at providing formal guarantees for the analysis results.

A recently published work is the static analysis tool ZEUS [19] that analyzes smart contracts written in Solidity using symbolic model checking. The analysis proceeds by translating Solidity code to an abstract intermediate language that again is translated to LLVM bitcode. Finally, existing symbolic model checking tools for LLVM bitcode are leveraged for checking generic security properties. ZEUS consequently only allows for analyzing contracts whose Solidity source code is made available. In addition, the semantics of the intermediate language cannot easily be reconciled with the actual Solidity semantics that is determined by its translation to EVM bytecode. This is as the semantics of the intermediate language by design does not allow for the revocation of the global system state in the case of a failed call – which however is fundamental feature of Ethereum smart contract execution.

Other tools proposed in the realm of automated static analysis for generic properties are Securify [20], Mythril [21] and Manticore [22] (for analysing bytecode) and SmartCheck [23] and Solgraph [24] (for analyzing Solidity code). These tools however are not accompanied by any academic paper so that the concrete analysis goals stay unspecified.

Frameworks for Semi-automated Proofs for Contract Specific Properties. Hirai [25] formalizes the EVM semantics in the proof assistant Isabelle/HOL and uses it for manually proving safety properties for concrete contracts. This semantics, however, constitutes a sound over-approximation of the original semantics [26]. Building on top of this work, Amani et al. propose a sound program logic for EVM bytecode based on separation logics [27]. This logic allows for semi-automatically reasoning about correctness properties of EVM bytecode using the proof assistant Isabelle/HOL.

Hildebrandt et al. [28] define the EVM semantics in the $\mathbb{K}$ framework [29] – a language independent verification framework based on reachability logics. The authors leverage the power of the $\mathbb{K}$ framework in order to automatically derive analysis tools for the specified semantics, presenting as an example a gas analysis tool, a semantic debugger, and a program verifier based on reachability logics. The derived program verifier still requires the user to manually specify loop invariants on the bytecode level.

Bhargavan et al. [30] introduce a framework to analyze Ethereum contracts by translation into F*, a functional programming language aimed at program verification and equipped with an interactive proof assistant. The translation supports only a fragment of the EVM bytecode and does not come with a justifying semantic argument.

Dynamic Monitoring for Predefined Security Properties. Grossman et al. [31] propose the notion of effectively callback free executions and identify the absence of this property in smart contract executions as the source of common bugs such as reentrancy. They propose an efficient online algorithm for discovering executions violating effectively callback freeness. Implementing a corresponding monitor in the EVM would guarantee the absence of the potentially dangerous smart contract executions, but is not compatible with the current Ethereum version and would require a hard fork.

A dynamic monitoring solution compatible with Ethereum is offered by the tool DappGuard [32]. The tool actively monitors the incoming transactions to a smart contract and leverages the tool Oyente [16], an own analysis engine and a simulation of the transaction on the testnet for judging whether the incoming transaction might cause a (generic) security violation (such as transaction order dependency). If a transaction is considered harmful, a counter transaction (killing the contract or performing some other fixes) is made. The authors claim that this transaction will be mined with high probability before the problematic one. Due to this uncertainty and the bug-finding tools used for evaluation of incoming transactions, this approach does not provide any guarantees.

3.2 Design

The current research on secure smart contract design focuses on the following four areas: high-level programming languages, intermediate languages (for verification), security patterns for existing languages and visual tools for designing smart contracts.

High-Level Languages. One line of research on high-level smart contract languages concentrates on the facilitation of secure smart contract design by limiting the language expressiveness and enforcing strong static typing discipline. Simplicity [33] is a typed functional programming language for smart contracts that disallows loops and recursion. It is a general purpose language for smart contracts and not tailored to the Ethereum setting. Simplicity comes with a denotational semantics specified in Coq that allows for reasoning formally about Simplicity contracts. As there is no (verified) compiler to EVM bytecode so far, such results don't carry over to Ethereum smart contracts. In the same realm, Pettersson and Edström [34], propose a library for the programming language Idris that allows for the development of secure smart contracts using dependent and polymorphic types. They extend the existing Idris compiler with a generator for Serpent code (a Python-like high-level language for Ethereum smart contracts). This compiler is a proof of concept and fails in compiling more advanced contracts (as it cannot handle recursion). In a preliminary work, Coblenz [35] propose Obsidian, an object-oriented programming language that pursues the goal of preventing common bugs in smart contracts such as reentrancy. To this end, Obsidian makes states explicit and uses a linear type system for quantities of money.

Another line of research focuses on designing languages that allow for encoding security policies that are dynamically enforced at runtime. A first step in this direction is sketched in the preliminary work on Flint [36], a type-safe, capabilities-secure, contract-oriented programming language for smart contracts that gets compiled to EVM bytecode. Flint allows for defining caller capabilities restricting the access to security sensitive functions. These capabilities shall be enforced by the EVM bytecode created during compilation. But so far, there is only an extended abstract available.

In addition to these approaches from academia, the Ethereum foundation currently develops the high-level languages Viper [37] and Bamboo [38]. Furthermore, the Solidity compiler used to support a limited export functionality to the intermediate language WhyML [39] allowing for a pre/post condition style reasoning on Solidity code by leveraging the deductive program verification platform Why3 [40].

Intermediate Languages. The intermediate language Scilla [41] comes with a semantics formalized in the proof assistant Coq and therefore allows for a mechanized verification of Scilla contracts. In addition, Scilla makes some interesting design choices that might inspire the development of future high level languages for smart contracts: Scilla provides a strict separation not only between computation and communication, but also between pure and effectful computations.

Security Patterns. Wöhrer [42] describes programming patterns in Solidity that should be adapted by smart contract programmers for avoiding common bugs. These patterns encompass best coding practices such as performing calls at the end of a function, but also off-the-self solutions for common security bugs such as locking a contract for avoiding reentrancy or the integration of a mechanism that allows the contract owner to disable sensitive functionalities in the case of a bug.

Tools. Mavridou and Laszka [43] introduce a framework for designing smart contracts in terms of finite state machines. They provide a tool with a graphical editor for defining contract specifications as automata and give a translation of the constructed finite state machines to Solidity. In addition, they present some security extensions and patterns that can be used as off-the-shelf solutions for preventing reentrancy and implementing common security challenges such as time constraints and authorization. The approach however is lacking formal foundations as neither the correctness of the translation is proven correct, nor are the security patterns shown to meet the desired security goals.

3.3 Open Challenges

Even though the previous section highlights the wide range of steps taken towards the analysis of Ethereum smart contracts, there are still a lot of open challenges left.

Secure Compilation of High-Level Languages. Even though there are several proposals made for new high-level languages that facilitate the design of secure smart contracts and that are more amenable to verification, none of them comes so far with a verified compiler to EVM bytecode. Such a secure compilation however is the requirement for the results shown on high-level language programs to carry over to the actual smart contracts published on the blockchain.

Specification Languages for Smart Contracts. So far, all approaches to verifying contract specific properties focus on either ad-hoc specifications in the used verification framework [25,27,28,30] or the insertion of assertions into existing contract code [39]. For leveraging the power of existing model checking techniques for program verification, the design of a general-purpose contract specification language would be needed.

Study of Security Policies. There has been no fundamental research made so far on the classes of security policies that might be interesting to enforce in the setting of smart contracts. In particular, it would be compelling to characterize the class of security policies that can be enforced by smart contracts within the existing EVM.

Compositional Reasoning About Smart Contracts. Most research on smart contract verification focuses on reasoning about individual contracts or at most a bunch of contracts whose bytecode is fully available. Even though there has been work observing the similarities between smart contracts and concurrent programs [44], there has been no rigorous study on compositional reasoning for smart contracts so far.

4 Semantics

Recently, Grishchenko et al. [15] introduced the first complete small-step semantics for EVM bytecode. As this semantics serves as a basis for the static analyzer EtherTrust, we will in the following shortly review the general layout and the most important features of the semantics.

4.1 Execution Configurations

Before discussing the small-step rules of the semantics, we first introduce the general shape of execution configurations.

Global State. The global state of the Ethereum blockchain is represented as a (partial) mapping from account addresses to accounts. In the case that an account does not exist, we assume it to map to $\bot$. Accounts are composed of a nonce n that is incremented with every other account that the account creates, a balance b, a persistent unbounded storage *stor* and the account's code. External accounts carry an empty code which makes their storage inaccessible and hence irrelevant.

Small-Step Relation. The semantics is formalized by a small-step relation $\Gamma \vDash S \rightarrow S'$ that specifies how a call stack S representing the state of the execution evolves within one step under the transaction environment Γ. We call the pair (Γ, S) a *configuration.*

Transaction Environments. The transaction environment represents the static information of the block that the transaction is executed in and the immutable parameters given to the transaction as the gas prize or the gas limit. These parameters can be accessed by distinct bytecode instructions and consequently influence the transaction execution.

Call Stacks. A call stack S is a stack of execution states which represents the state of the overall execution of the initial external transaction. The individual execution states of the stack represent the states of the uncompleted internal transactions performed during the execution. Formally, a call stack is a stack of regular execution states of the form (μ, ι, σ) that can optionally be topped with a halting state $HALT(\sigma, gas, d)$ or an exception state EXC. Semantically, halting states indicate regular halting of an internal transaction, exception states indicate exceptional halting, and regular execution states describe the state of internal transactions in progress. Halting and exception states can only occur as top elements of the call stack as they represent terminated internal transactions. Halting states carry the information affecting the callee state such as the global state σ that the internal execution halted in, the unspent gas *gas* from the internal transaction execution and the return data d.

The state of a non-terminated internal transaction is described by a regular execution state of the form (μ, ι, σ). The state is determined by the current global state σ of the system as well as the execution environment ι that specifies the parameters of the current transaction (including inputs and the code to be executed) and the local state μ of the stack machine.

Table 1. Semantic rules for ADD

$$\text{ADD}\quad \frac{\mu.\mathsf{s} = a :: b :: s \qquad \mu.\mathsf{gas} \geq 3 \qquad \begin{array}{c}\iota.code\,[\mu.\mathsf{pc}] = \mathsf{ADD} \\ \mu' = \mu[\mathsf{s} \to (a+b) :: s][\mathsf{pc} \mathrel{+}= 1][\mathsf{gas} \mathrel{-}= 3]\end{array}}{\Gamma \vDash (\mu, \iota, \sigma) :: S \to (\mu', \iota, \sigma) :: S}$$

$$\text{ADD-FAIL}\quad \frac{\iota.code\,[\mu.\mathsf{pc}] = \mathsf{ADD} \qquad (|\mu.\mathsf{s}| < 2 \vee \mu.\mathsf{gas} < 3)}{\Gamma \vDash (\mu, \iota, \sigma) :: S \to \mathit{EXC} :: S}$$

Execution Environment. The execution environment ι of an internal transaction is a tuple of static parameters $(actor, input, sender, value, code)$ to the transaction that, i.a., determine the code to be executed and the account in whose context the code will be executed. The execution environment incorporates the following components: the active account *actor* that is the account that is currently executing and whose account will be affected when instructions for storage modification or money transfer are performed; the input data *input* given to the transaction; the address *sender* of the account that initiated the transaction; the amount of wei *value* transferred with the transaction; the code *code* that is executed by the transaction. The execution environment is determined upon initialization of an internal transaction execution, and it can be accessed, but not altered during the execution.

Machine State. The local machine state μ represents the state of the underlying stack machine used for execution. Formally it is represented by a tuple (gas, pc, m, aw, s) holding the amount of gas *gas* available for execution, the program counter *pc*, the local memory *m*, the number of active words in memory *aw*, and the machine stack *s*.

The execution of each internal transaction starts in a fresh machine state, with an empty stack, memory initialized to all zeros, and program counter and active words in memory set to zero. Only the gas is instantiated with the gas value available for the execution. We call execution states with machine states of this form *initial*.

4.2 Small-Step Rules

In the following, we will present a selection of interesting small-step rules in order to illustrate the most important features of the semantics.

Local Instructions. For demonstrating the overall design of the semantics, we start with the example of the arithmetic expression ADD performing addition of two values on the machine stack. The small-step rules for ADD are shown in Table 1. We use a dot notation, in order to access components of the different state parameters. We name the components with the variable names introduced for these components in the last section written in sans-serif-style. In addition, we use the usual notation for updating components: $t[\mathsf{c} \rightarrow v]$ denotes that the component c of tuple t is updated with value v. For expressing incremental updates in a simpler way, we additionally use the notation $t[\mathsf{c} \mathrel{+}= v]$ to denote that the (numerical) component of c is incremented by v and similarly $t[\mathsf{c} \mathrel{-}= v]$ for decrementing a component c of t.

The execution of the arithmetic instruction ADD only performs local changes in the machine state affecting the local stack, the program counter, and the gas budget. For deciding upon the correct instruction to execute, the currently executed code (that is part of the execution environment) is accessed at the position of the current program counter. The cost of an ADD instruction consists always of three units of gas that get subtracted from the gas budget in the machine state. As every other instruction, ADD can fail due to lacking gas or due to underflows on the machine stack. In this case, the exception state is entered and the execution of the current internal transaction is terminated. For better readability, we use here the slightly sloppy $\vee$ notation for combining the two error cases in one inference rule.

Transaction Initiating Instructions. A class of instructions with a more involved semantics are those instructions initiating internal transactions. This class incorporates instructions for calling another contract (CALL, CALLCODE and DELEGATECALL) and for creating a new contract (CREATE). We will explain the semantics of those instructions in an intuitive way omitting technical details.

The call instructions initiate a new internal call transaction whose parameters are specified on the machine stack – including the recipient (callee) and the amount of money to be transferred (in the case of CALL and CALLCODE). In addition, the input to the call is specified by providing the corresponding local memory fragment and analogously a memory fragment for the return value.

When executing a call instruction, the specified amount of wei is transferred to the callee and the code of the callee is executed. The different call types diverge in the environment that the callee code is executed in. In the case of a CALL instruction, while executing the callee code (only) the account of the callee can be accessed and modified. So intuitively, the control is completely handed to the callee as its code is executed in its own context. In contrast, in the case of CALLCODE, the executed callee code can (only) access and modify the account of the caller. So the callee's code is executed in the caller's context which might be useful for using library functionalities implemented in a separate library contract that e.g., transfer money on behalf of the caller.

This idea is pushed even further in the DELEGATECALL instruction. This call type does not allow for transferring money and executes the callee's code not only in the caller's context, but even preserves part of the execution environment of the previous call (in particular the call value and the sender information). Intuitively, this instruction resembles adding the callee's code to the caller as

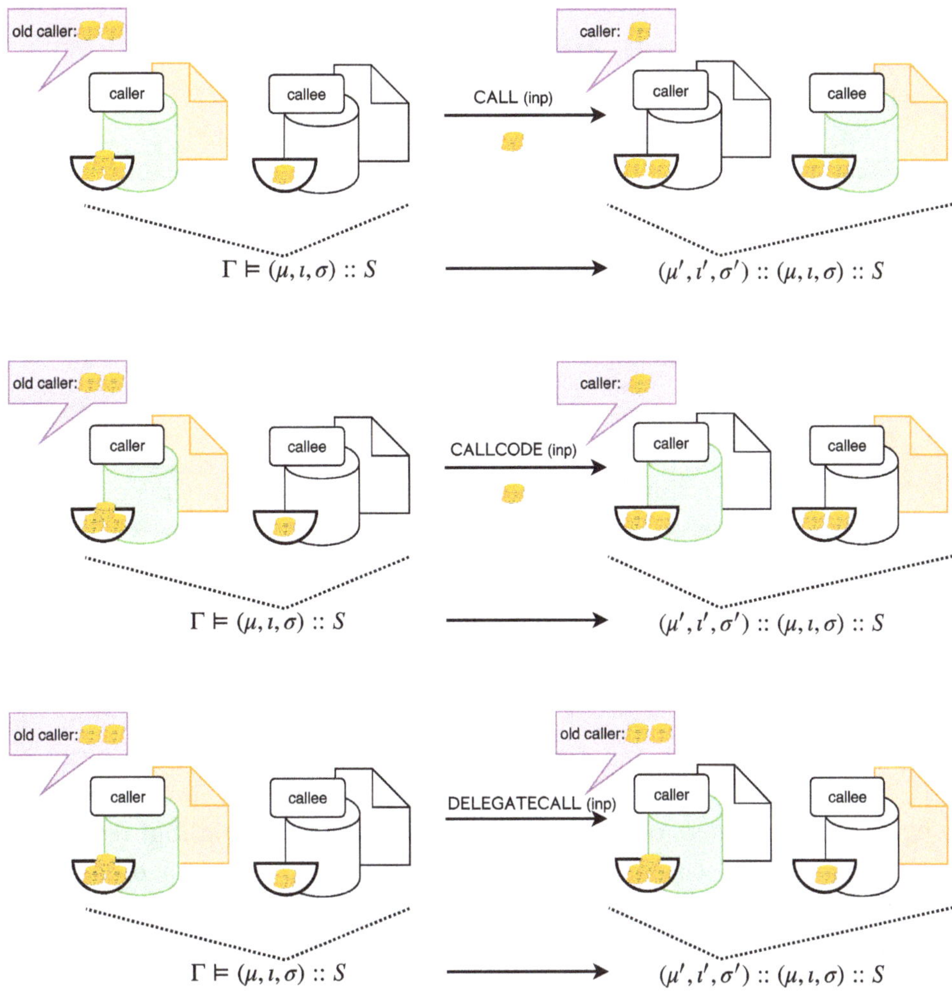

Fig. 1. Illustration of the semantics of different call types

an internal function so that calling it does not cause a new internal transaction (even though it formally does).

Figure 1 summarizes the behavior of the different call instructions in EVM bytecode. The executed code of the respective account is highlighted in orange while the accessible account state is depicted in green. The remaining internal transaction information (as specified in the execution environment) on the sender of the internal transaction and the transferred value are marked in violet. In addition, the picture relates the corresponding changes to the small-step semantics: the execution of a call transaction adds a new execution state to the call stack while preserving the old one. The new global state σ' records the changes in the accounts' balances, while the new execution environment ι' determines the accessible account (by setting the actor of the internal transaction correspondingly), the code to be executed (by setting code) and further accessible transaction information as the sender, value and input (by setting sender, value and input respectively).

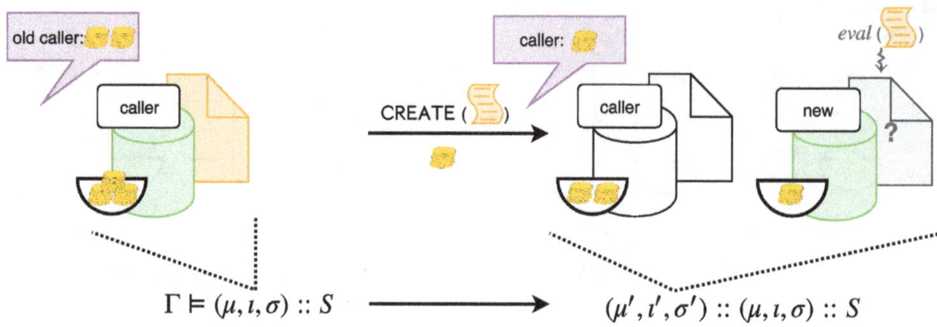

Fig. 2. Illustration of the semantics of the CREATE instruction (Color figure online)

The CREATE instruction initiates an internal transaction that creates a new account. The semantics of this instruction is similar to the one of CALL, with the exception that a fresh account is created, which gets the specified value transferred, and that the input provided to this internal transaction, which is again specified in the local memory, is interpreted as the initialization code to be executed in order to produce the newly created account's code as output. Figure 2 depicts the semantics of the CREATE instruction in a similar fashion as it is done for the call instructions before. It is notable that the input to the CREATE instruction is interpreted as code and executed (therefore highlighted in orange) in the context of the newly created contract (highlighted in green). During this execution the newly created contract does not have any contract code itself (therefore depicted in gray), but only after completing the internal transaction the return value of the transaction will be set as code for the freshly created contract.

5 Security Properties

Grishchenko et al. [15] propose generic security definitions for smart contracts that rule out certain classes of potentially harmful contract behavior. These properties constitute trace properties (more precisely, safety properties) as well as hyper properties (in particular, value independence properties). In this work, we revisit one of these safety properties called *single-entrancy* and use this property as a case study for showing how safety properties of smart contracts (that can be over-approximated by pure reachability properties) can be automatically checked by static analysis. For checking value independence properties, in [1] the reviewed analysis technique is extended with a simple dependency analysis that we will not discuss further in this work.

5.1 Preliminary Notations

Formally, contracts are represented as tuples of the form $(a, code)$ where a denotes the address of the contract and *code* denotes the contract's code.

In order to give concise security definitions, we further introduce, and assume all through the paper, an annotation to the small step semantics in order to highlight the contract c that is currently executed. In the case of initialization code being executed, we use $\perp$. We write $S + +S'$ for the concatenation of call stacks S and S'. Finally, for arguing about EVM bytecode executions, we are only interested in those initial configurations that might result from a valid external transaction in a valid block. In the following, we will call these configurations *reachable* and refer to [15] for a detailed definition.

5.2 Single-Entrancy

For motivating the definition of single-entrancy, we introduce a class of bugs in Ethereum smart contracts called *reentrancy bugs* [14,16].

The most famous representative of this class is the so-called DAO bug that led to a loss of 60 million dollars in June 2016 [11]. In an attack exploiting this bug, the affected contract was drained out of money by subsequently reentering it and performing transactions to the attacker on behalf of the contract.

The cause of such bugs mostly roots in the developer's misunderstanding of the semantics of Solidity's call primitives. In general, calling a contract can invoke two kinds of actions: Transferring Ether to the contract's account or Executing (parts of) a contracts code. In particular, Solidity's `call` construct (being translated to a CALL instruction in EVM bytecode) invokes the execution of a fraction of the callee's code – specified in the so called *fallback function*. A contract's fallback function is written as a function without names or argument as depicted in the `Mallory` contract in Fig. 3b.

Consequently, when using the `call` construct the developer may expect an atomic value transfer where potentially another contract's code is executed. For illustrating how to exploit this sort of bug, we consider the contracts in Fig. 3.

```
contract Bob{
  bool sent = false;
  function ping( address c){
    if (!sent) { c.call.value(2)();
                 sent = true; }}}
```

(a) Smart contract with reentrancy bug

```
contract Mallory{
  function(){
    Bob(msg.sender).ping(this);}}
```

(b) Smart contract exploiting reentrancy bug

Fig. 3. Reentrancy attack

The function `ping` of contract `Bob` sends an amount of 2 *wei* to the address specified in the argument. However, this should only be possible once, which is potentially ensured by the `sent` variable that is set after the successful money transfer. Instead, it turns out that invoking the `call.value` function on a contract's address invokes the contract's fallback function as well.

Given a second contract `Mallory`, it is possible to transfer more money than the intended 2 *wei* to the account of `Mallory`. By invoking `Bob`'s function `ping` with the address of `Mallory`'s account, 2 *wei* are transferred to `Mallory`'s account and additionally the fallback function of `Mallory` is invoked. As the fallback function again calls the `ping` function with `Mallory`'s address another 2 *wei* are transferred before the variable `sent` of contract `Bob` was set. This looping goes on until all gas of the initial call is consumed or the callstack limit is reached. In this case, only the last transfer of *wei* is reverted and the effects of all former calls stay in place. Consequently the intended restriction on contract `Bob`'s `ping` function (namely to only transfer 2 *wei* once) is circumvented.

Motivated by these kinds of attacks, the notion of single-entrancy was introduced. Intuitively, a contract is single-entrant if it cannot perform any more calls once it has been reentered. Formally this property can be expressed in terms of the small-steps semantics as follows:

Definition 1 (Single-entrancy [15]). *A contract c is single-entrant if for all reachable configurations $(\Gamma, s_c :: S)$, it holds for all s', s'', S' that*

$$\begin{aligned} &\Gamma \vDash s_c :: S \rightarrow^* {s'}_c :: S' ++ s_c :: S \\ \implies \neg\exists s'' \in \mathcal{S}, c' \in \mathcal{C}_\bot . \, &\Gamma \vDash {s'}_c :: S' ++ s_c :: S \rightarrow^* {s''}_{c'} :: {s'}_c :: S' ++ s_c :: S \end{aligned}$$

This property constitutes a safety property. We will show in Sect. 7 how it can be appropriately abstracted for being expressed in the EtherTrust analysis framework.

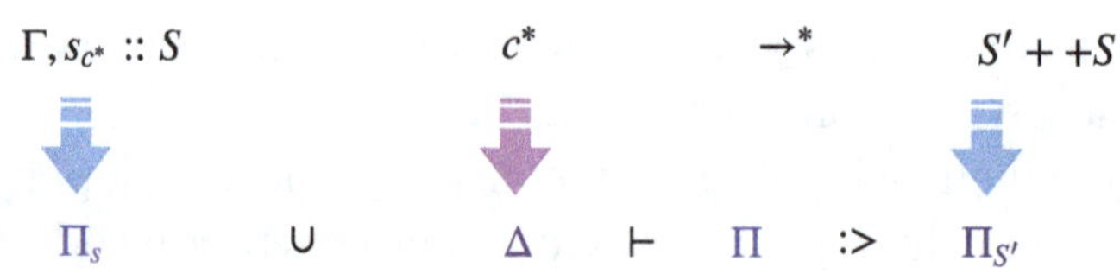

Fig. 4. Simplified soundness statement

6 Verification

Grishchenko et al. [1] developed a static analysis framework for analyzing reachability properties of EVM smart contracts. This framework relies on an abstract semantics for EVM bytecode soundly over-approximating the semantics presented in Sect. 4.

In the following we will review the abstractions performed on the small-step configurations and execution rules using the example of the abstract execution rule for the ADD instruction. Afterwards, we will discuss shortly how call instructions are over-approximated.

6.1 Abstract Semantics

Figure 4 gives an overview on the relation between the small-step and the abstract semantics. For the analysis, we will consider a particular contract c^* under analysis whose code is known. An over-approximation of the behavior of this smart contract will be encoded in *Horn clauses*(Δ). These describe how an abstract configuration (represented by a set of abstract state predicates) evolves within the execution of the contract's instructions. Abstract configurations are obtained by translating small-step configurations to a set Π of facts over state predicates that characterize (an over-approximation of) the original configuration. This transformation is performed with respect to the contract c^* as only all local behavior of this particular contract will be over-approximated and consequently only those elements on the callstack representing executions of c^* are translated. Finally, we will show that no matter how the contract c^* is called (so for every arbitrary reachable configuration $\Gamma, s_{c^*} :: S$), every sequence of execution steps that is performed while executing it can be mimicked by a derivation of the abstract configuration Π_s (obtained from translating the execution state s) using the horn clauses Δ (that model the abstract semantics of the contract c^*). More precisely, this means that from the set of facts $\Pi_s \cup \Delta$ a set Π can be derived that is a coarser abstraction ($<:$) than $\Pi_{S'}$ which is the translation of the execution's intermediate call stack S'. A corresponding formal soundness statement is proven in [1].

6.2 Abstract Configurations

Table 2 shows the analysis facts used for describing the abstract semantics. These consist of (instances of) state predicates that represent partial abstract configurations. Accordingly, abstract configurations are sets of facts not containing any variables as arguments. We will refer to such facts as *closed facts*. Finally, abstract contracts are characterized as sets of Horn clauses over the state predicates (facts) that describe the state changes induced by the instructions at the different program positions. Here only those state predicates are depicted that are needed for describing the abstract semantics of the ADD instruction.

The state predicates are parametrized by a program point *pp* that is a tuple of the form (id^*, pc) with id^* being a contract identifier for contract c^* and *pc* being the program counter at which the abstract state holds.[3] The parametrization by the contract identifier helps to make the analysis consider a set of contracts whose code is known (such as e.g., library code that is known to be used by the contract). In this work however we focus on the case where c^* represented by identifier id^* is the only known contract. In addition, the predicates carry the relative call depth *cd* as argument. The relative call depth is the size of the call stack built up on the execution of c^* (Cf. call stack S' in Fig. 4) and serves as abstraction for the (relative) call stack that contract c^* is currently executed on.

[3] Making the program counter a parameter instead of an argument is a design choice made in order to minimize the number of recursive horn clauses simplifying automated verification.

Table 2. Analysis Facts. All arguments in the analysis facts marked with a hat $(\hat{\cdot})$ range over $\hat{D} \cup Vars$ where $\hat{D}$ is the abstract domain and *Vars* is the set of variables. All other arguments of analysis facts range over $\mathbb{N}$ with exception of *sa* that ranges over $(\mathbb{N} \to \hat{D}) \cup Vars$. Closed facts *cf* are assumed to be facts with arguments not coming from *Vars*.

Facts	f :=	
Abs. machine state	|	$\mathsf{MState}_{pp}\,((size, sa), \hat{aw}, \hat{gas}, cd)$
Abs. memory	|	$\mathsf{Mem}_{pp}\,(\hat{pos}, \hat{va}, cd)$
Abs. exception state	|	$\mathsf{Exc}_{id^*}\,(cd)$
...	|	...
Abs. configurations	Π :=	$\{cf_1, \ldots, cf_n\}$
Horn clauses	H :=	$\forall x^*. \bigwedge_i f_i \implies f$
Abs. contracts	Δ :=	$\{H_1, \ldots, H_n\}$

The relative call depth helps to distinguish different recursive executions of c^* and thereby improves the precision of the analysis.

As the ADD instruction only operates on the local machine state, we focus on the abstract representation of the machine state μ: The state predicates representing μ are MState_{pp} and Mem_{pp}. The fact $\mathsf{MState}_{pp}\,((size, sa), \hat{aw}, \hat{gas}, cd)$ says that at program point *pp* and relative call depth *cd* the machine stack is of size *size* and its current configuration is described by the mapping *sa* which maps stack positions to abstract values, $\hat{aw}$ represents the number of active words in memory, and $\hat{gas}$ is the remaining gas. Similarly, the fact $\mathsf{Mem}_{pp}\,(\hat{pos}, \hat{v}, cd)$ states that at program point *pp* and relative call depth *cd* at memory address $\hat{pos}$ there is the (abstract) value $\hat{v}$. The values on the stack and in local memory range over an abstract domain. Concretely, we define the abstract domain $\hat{D}$ to be the set $\{\bot, \top, a^*\} \cup \mathbb{N}$ which constitutes a bounded lattice $(\hat{D}, \sqsubseteq, \sqcup, \sqcap, \top, \bot)$ satisfying $\bot \sqsubset a^* \sqsubset \top$ and $\bot \sqsubset n \sqsubset \top$ for all $n \in \mathbb{N}$. Intuitively, in our analysis $\top$ will represent unknown (symbolic) values and a^* will represent the unknown (symbolic) address of contract c^*.

Treating the address of the contract under analysis in a symbolic fashion is crucial for obtaining a meaningful analysis, as the address of this account on the blockchain can not easily be assumed to be known upfront. Although discussing this peculiarity is beyond the scope of this paper, a broader presentation of the symbolic address paradigm can be found in the technical report [1].

For performing operations and comparisons on values from the abstract domain, we will assume versions of the unary, binary and comparison operators on the values from $\hat{D}$. We will mark abstract operators with a hat $(\widehat{\cdot})$ and e.g., write $\widehat{+}$ for abstract addition or $\widehat{=}$ for abstract equality. The operators will treat $\top$ and a^* as arbitrary values so that e.g., $\top \widehat{+} n$ evaluates to $\top$ and $\top \widehat{=} n$ evaluates to *true* and *false* for all $n \in \mathbb{N}$.

Formally, we establish the relation between a concrete machine state μ and its abstraction by an abstraction function that translates machine states to a set of closed analysis facts. Figure 3 shows the abstraction function α_μ that maps a local machine state into an abstract state consisting of a set of analysis facts. The abstraction is defined with respect to the relative call depth *cd* of the execution and a value abstraction function $\mathring{\cdot}$ that maps concrete values into values from the abstract domain. The function $\mathring{\cdot}$ thereby maps all concrete values to the corresponding (concrete) values in the abstract domain, but those values that can potentially represent the address of contract c^*, hence, they are translated to a^* and therefore over-approximated. This treatment might introduce spurious counterexamples with respect to the concrete execution of the real contract on the blockchain (where it is assigned a concrete address). On the one hand, this is due to the fact that by this abstraction the concrete value of the address is assumed to be arbitrary. On the other hand, abstract computations with α always result in $\top$ and therefore possible constraints on these results are lost. However, the first source of imprecision should not be considered an imprecision per se, as the c^*'s address is not assumed to be known statically, thus, the goal of the abstraction is to over-approximate the executions with all possible addresses.

The translation proceeds by creating a set of instances of the machine state predicates. For creating instances of the MState_{pp} predicate, the concrete values aw and gas are over-approximated by $\mathring{aw}$ and $\mathring{gas}$ respectively, and the stack is translated to an abstract array representation using the function $\mathsf{stackToArray}$. The instances of the memory predicate are created by translating the memory mapping m to a relational representation with abstract locations and values.[4]

Table 3. Abstraction function for the local machine state μ

$$\alpha_\mu\left((gas, pc, m, aw, s), cd\right) := \{\mathsf{MState}_{(id^*,\, pc)}\left(\mathsf{stackToArray}\left(s\right), \mathring{aw}, \mathring{gas}, cd\right)\}$$
$$\cup \{\mathsf{Mem}_{(id^*,\, pc)}\left(\mathring{pos}, \mathring{v}, cd\right) \mid m\,[pos] = v \wedge pos \leq 2^{256}\}$$

$$\mathsf{stackToArray}\left(\epsilon\right) := (0, \lambda x.\, 0)$$
$$\mathsf{stackToArray}\left(x :: s\right) := \mathit{let}\ (size, sa) = \mathsf{stackToArray}\left(s\right)\ \mathit{in}\ (size + 1, sa_{\mathring{x}}^{size})$$

6.3 Abstract Execution Rules

As all state predicates are parametrized by their program points, the abstract semantics needs to be formulated with respect to program points as well. More precisely this means that for each program counter of contract c^* a set of Horn clauses is created that describes the semantics of the instruction at this program counter. Formally, a function $(\!|\cdot|\!)_{pp}^{\{c^*\}}$ is defined that creates the required set of rules given that the instruction *inst* is at position *pc* of contract c^*'s code.

[4] The reason for using a separate predicate for representing local memory instead of encoding it as an argument of array type in the main machine state predicate is purely technical: for modeling memory usage correctly we would need a rich set of array operations that are however not supported by the fixedpoint engines of modern SMT solvers.

Table 4 shows a part of the definition (excerpt of the rules) of $(\!|\cdot|\!)_{pp}^{\{c^*\}}$ for the ADD instruction. The main functionality of the rule is described by the Horn clause 1 that describes how the machine stack and the gas evolve when executing ADD. First the precondition is checked whether the sufficient amount of gas and stack elements are available. Then the two (abstract) top elements $\hat{x}$ and $\hat{y}$ are extracted from the stack and their sum is written to the top of the stack while reducing the overall stack size by 1. In addition, the local gas value is reduced by 3 in an abstract fashion. In the memory rule (Horn clause 2), again the preconditions are checked and then (as memory is not affected by the ADD instruction) the memory is propagated. This propagation is needed due to the memory predicate's parametrization with the program counter: For making the memory accessible in the next execution step, its values need to be written into the corresponding predicate for the next program counter. Finally, Horn clauses 3 and 4 characterize the exception cases: an exception while executing the ADD instruction can occur either because of a stack underflow or as the execution runs out of gas. In both cases the exception state is entered which is indicated by recording the relative call depth of the exception in the predicate $\mathsf{Exc}_{id^*}(cd)$.

By allowing gas values to come from the abstract domain, we enable symbolic treatment of gas. In particular this means that when starting the analysis with gas value $\top$, all gas calculations will directly result in $\top$ again (and could therefore be omitted) and in particular all checks on the gas will result in *true* and *false* and consequently always both paths (regular execution via Horn clauses 1 and 2 and exception via Horn clause 4) will be triggered in the analysis.

For over-approximating the semantics of call instructions, more involved abstractions are needed. We will illustrate these abstractions in the following in an intuitive way and refer to [1] for the technical details. Note that in the following we will assume CALL instructions to be the only kind of transaction initiating instructions that are contained in the contracts that we consider for analysis. A generalization of the analysis that allows for incorporating also other call types is presented in [1].

As we are considering c^* the only contract to be known, whenever a call is performed that is not a self-call, we need to assume that an arbitrary contract $c^?$ gets executed. The general idea for over-approximating calls to an unknown contract $c^?$ is that only those execution states that represent executions of contract c^* will be over-approximated. Consequently, when a call is performed, all possible effects on future executions of c^* that might be caused by the execution of $c^?$ (including the initiation of further initial transactions that might cause reentering c^*) need to be captured. For doing this as accurate as possible, we use the following observations:

1. Given that c^* only executes plain CALL instructions the persistent storage of contract c^* can only be altered during executions of c^*.
2. Contracts have a single entry point: their execution always starts in a fresh machine state at program counter zero.

In general, we can soundly capture the possibility of contract c^* being reentered during the execution of $c^?$ by assuming to reenter c^* at every higher call

Table 4. Excerpt of the abstract rules for ADD

$$
\begin{aligned}
(\!|\mathsf{ADD}|\!)^{\{c^*\}}_{(id*,pc)} = \{ & \mathsf{MState}_{(id^*,\,pc)}\left((\mathit{size}, \mathit{sa}), \hat{aw}, \hat{gas}, \mathit{cd}\right) \land \mathit{size} > 1 \land \hat{gas} \mathrel{\hat{\geq}} 3 \\
& \land \hat{x} = \mathit{sa}[\mathit{size}-1] \land \hat{y} = \mathit{sa}[\mathit{size}-2] \\
& \Rightarrow \mathsf{MState}_{(id^*,\,pc+1)}\left((\mathit{size}-1, \mathit{sa}^{\mathit{size}-2}_{\hat{x} \,\hat{+}\, \hat{y}}), \hat{aw}, \hat{gas} \mathrel{\hat{-}} 3, \mathit{cd}\right), & (1) \\
& \mathsf{Mem}_{(id^*,\,pc)}\left(\hat{pos}, \hat{va}, \mathit{cd}\right) \land \mathsf{MState}_{(id^*,\,pc)}\left((\mathit{size}, \mathit{sa}), \hat{gas}, \hat{aw}, \mathit{cd}\right) \\
& \land \mathit{size} > 1 \land \hat{gas} \mathrel{\hat{\geq}} 3 \Rightarrow \mathsf{Mem}_{(id^*,\,pc+1)}\left(\hat{pos}, \hat{va}, \mathit{cd}\right), & (2) \\
& \mathsf{MState}_{(id^*,\,pc)}\left((\mathit{size}, \mathit{sa}), \hat{gas}, \hat{aw}, \mathit{cd}\right) \land \mathit{size} < 2 \Rightarrow \mathsf{Exc}_{id*}\left(\mathit{cd}\right), & (3) \\
& \mathsf{MState}_{(id^*,\,pc)}\left((\mathit{size}, \mathit{sa}), \hat{gas}, \hat{aw}, \mathit{cd}\right) \land \hat{gas} \mathrel{\hat{<}} 3 \Rightarrow \mathsf{Exc}_{id*}\left(\mathit{cd}\right) \ldots \} & (4)
\end{aligned}
$$

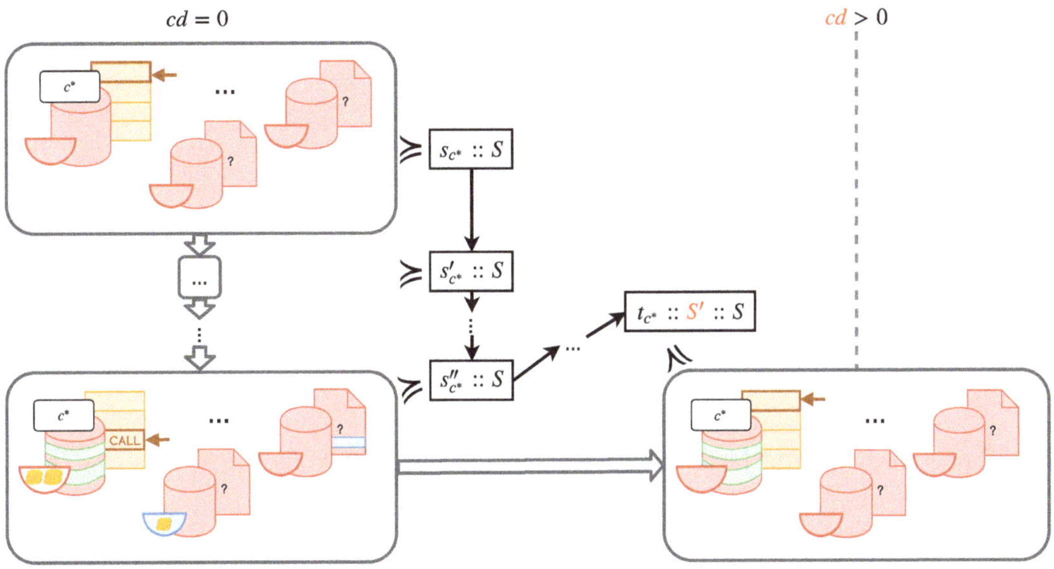

Fig. 5. Illustration of the abstraction of the semantics for the CALL instruction.

level. For keeping the desired precision, we can use the previously made observations for imposing restrictions on the reenterings of c^*: First, we assume the persistent storage of c^* to be the same as at the point of calling (observation 1.). Second, we know that execution starts at program counter 0 in a fresh machine state (observation 2.). This allows us to initialize the machine state predicates presented in Table 2 accordingly at program counter zero. All other parts of the global state and the execution environment need to be considered unknown at the point of reentering as they might have potentially been changed during the execution of $c^?$. This in particular also applies to the balance of contract c^*.

Figure 5 illustrates how the abstract configurations over-approximating the concrete execution states of c^* evolve within the execution of the abstract semantics. We write $\Pi \succcurlyeq S$ for denoting that an abstract configuration Π (here graphically depicted in gray frames) is an over-approximation of call stack S. The depicted execution starts in the initial execution state s_{c^*} of c^*. This is state is over-approximated by assuming the storage and balance of c^* as well as all other information on the global state to be unknown and therefore initialized to $\top$ in the corresponding state predicates of the abstract configuration (denoted in the picture by marking the corresponding state components in red). The execution steps representing the executions of local instructions are mimicked step-wise by corresponding abstract execution steps. During these steps a more refined knowledge about the state of c^* and its environment might be gained (e.g., the value of some storage cells where information is written, or some restrictions on the account's balances, marked in green or blue, respectively). When finally a CALL instruction is executed, every potential reentering of contract c^* (here exemplified by execution state t_{c^*}) is over-approximated by abstract configurations for every call depths $cd > 0$ that consider all global state and environmental information to be arbitrary, but the parts modeling the persistent storage of c^* to be as at the point of calling. In Sect. 7 we will show how this abstraction will help us to automatically check smart contracts for single-entrancy in a sound and precise manner. In addition to these over-approximations that capture the effects on c^* during the execution of an unknown contract, for over-approximating CALL instructions some other abstractions need to be performed that model the semantics of returning:

- For returning it is always assumed that potentially the call failed or returned with arbitrary return values.
- After returning the global state is assumed to be altered arbitrarily by the call and therefore its components are set to $\top$.

For a complete account and formal description of the abstractions, we refer to the full specification of the abstract semantics spelled out in the technical report [1].

7 Verifying Security Properties

In this section, we will show how the previously presented analysis can be used for proving reachability properties of Ethereum smart contracts in an automated fashion.

To this end, we review EtherTrust [1], the first sound static analyzer for EVM bytecode. EtherTrust proceeds by translating contract code provided in the bytecode format into an internal Horn clause representation. This Horn clause representation, together with facts over-approximating all potential initial configurations are handed to the SMT solver Z3 [45] via an API. For showing that the analyzed contract satisfies a reachability property, the unsatisfiability of the corresponding analysis queries needs to be verified using Z3's fixedpoint engine SPACER [46]. If all analysis queries are deemed unsatisfiable then the contract under analysis is guaranteed to satisfy the original reachability query due to the soundness of the underlying analysis.

In the following we will discuss the analysis queries used for verifying single-entrancy and illustrate how these queries allow for capturing contracts that are vulnerable to reentrancy such as the example presented in Sect. 5.

7.1 Over-Approximating Single-Entrancy

For being able to automatically check for single-entrancy, we need to simplify the original property in order to obtain a description that is expressible in terms of the analysis framework described in Sect. 6. To this end, a strictly stronger property named *call unreachability* is presented that is proven to imply single-entrancy:

Definition 2 (Call unreachability [1]). *A contract c is call unreachable if for all initial execution states (μ, ι, σ) such that $(\mu, \iota, \sigma)_c$ is well formed, it holds that for all transaction environments Γ and all call stacks S*

$$\neg\exists s, S'.\, \Gamma \vDash (\mu, \iota, \sigma)_c :: S \rightarrow^* s_c :: S' ++ S \\ \wedge\ |S'| > 0\ \wedge\ code(c)\,[s.\mu.pc] \in Inst_{call}$$

With $Inst_{call} = \{\mathit{CALL}, \mathit{CALLCODE}, \mathit{DELEGATECALL}, \mathit{CREATE}\}$

Intuitively, this property states that it should not be possible to reach a call instruction of c^* after reentering. As we are excluding all transaction initiating instructions but CALL from the analysis, it is sufficient to query for the reachability of a CALL instruction of c^* on a higher call depth. More precisely, we end up with the following set of queries:

$$\{\mathsf{MState}_{(id,\ pc)}\,((size, sa), aw, gas, cd) \wedge cd > 0 \mid code(c^*)\,[pc] = \mathsf{CALL}\} \quad (5)$$

As the MState_{pp} predicate tracks the state of the machine state at all program points, it can be used as indicator for reachability of the program point as such. Consequently, by querying the $\mathsf{MState}_{(id*,\ pc)}$ for all program counters pc where c^* has a CALL instruction and along with that requiring a call depth exceeding zero, we can check whether a call instruction is reachable in some reentering execution.

7.2 Examples

We will use examples for showing how the analysis detects, and proves the absence of reentrancy bugs, respectively. To this end, we revisit the contract `Bob` presented in Sect. 5, and introduce a contract `Alice` that fixes the reentrancy bug that is present in `Bob`. The two contracts are shown in Figure 6.

Detecting Reentrancy Bugs. We illustrate how the analysis detects reentrancy bugs using the example in Figure 6a. To this end we give a graphical description of the over-approximations performed when analyzing contract `Bob` which is depicted in Figure 7. For the sake of presentation, we give the contract code in Solidity instead of bytecode and argue about it on this level even though the analysis is carried out on bytecode level.

As discussed in Sect. 6.3, the analysis considers the execution of contract `Bob` to start in an unknown environment, which implies that also the value of the

```
1 contract Bob{
2   bool sent = false;
3   function ping( address c){
4     if (!sent) { c.call.value(2)();
5                  sent = true; }}}
```

(a) Smart contract with reentrancy bug

```
1 contract Alice{
2   bool sent = false;
3   function ping( address c){
4     if (!sent) { sent = true;
5                  c.call.value(2)(); }}}
```

(b) Smart contract with fixed reentrancy bug

Fig. 6. Examples for contracts showing and being robust against the reentrancy bug.

contract's `sent` variable is unknown and hence initialized to $\top$. As a consequence, the equality check in line 4 is considered to evaluate to both *true* and *false* in the abstract setting (as $\top$ needs to be considered to potentially equal every concrete value). Accordingly, the analysis needs to consider the `then`-branch of the conditional and consequently the call in line 4. This call is over-approximated as discussed in Sect. 6.3, and therefore considers reentering contract `Bob` in an arbitrary call depth. In this situation, the `sent` variable is still over-approximated to have value $\top$ wherefore the call at line 4 can be reached again which satisfies the reachability query in Eq. 5.

Proving Single-Entrancy. We consider the contract `Alice` shown in Figure 6b. In contrast to contract `Bob`, this contract does not have the reentrancy vulnerability, as the guard `sent` that should prevent the call instruction in line 5 from being executed more than once is set before performing the call. As a consequence, when reentering the contract, the guard is already set and stops any further calls. We show that the analysis presented in Sect. 6 is precise enough for proving this contract to be single-entrant. Intuitively, the abstraction is precise as it considers that the contract's persistent storage can be assumed to be unchanged at the point of reentering. Consequently, the `then`-branch of the conditional can be excluded from the analysis when reentering and the contract can be proven to be single-entrant. A graphic description of this argument is provided in Figure 8. As for contract `Bob`, the analysis starts in an abstract configuration that assigns the `sent` variable value $\top$, which forces the analysis to consider the `then` as well as the `else`-branch of the conditional in line 4. When taking the `else`-branch, the contract execution terminates without reaching a state satisfying the reachability query. Therefore, it is sufficient to only consider the `then`-branch for proving the impossibility of re-reaching the call instruction. When executing the `call` in the `then`-branch, according to the abstract call semantics, the analysis needs to take all abstract configurations representing executions of `Alice` at higher call depths into account. However, in each of these abstract configurations it can be assumed that the state of the persistent storage (including the `sent` variable, highlighted in green) is the same as at the point of calling. As at this point `sent` was already initialized to the concrete value `true`, the `then`-branch of the conditional can be excluded from the analysis at any call depth $cd > 0$ and consequently the unreachability of the query in Eq. 5 is proven.

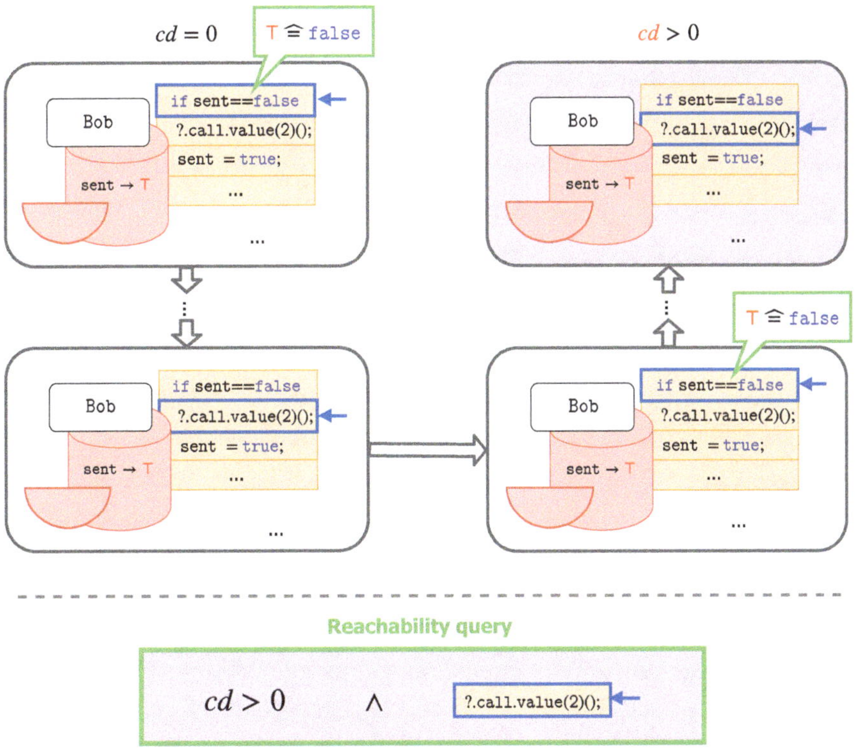

Fig. 7. Illustration of the attack detection in contract `Bob` by the static analysis.

7.3 Discussion

In this section, we illustrated how the static analysis underlying EtherTrust [1] in principle is capable not only of detecting re-entrancy bugs, but also of proving smart contracts single-entrant. In practice, EtherTrust manages to analyze real-world contracts from the blockchain within several seconds, as detailed in the experimental evaluation presented in [1]. Even though EtherTrust produces false positives due to the performed over-approximations, it still shows better precision on a benchmark than the state-of-the art bug-finding tool Oyente [16] – despite being sound. Similar results are shown when using EtherTrust for checking a simple value independency property.

In general, EtherTrust could be easily extended to support more properties on contract execution – given that those properties or over-approximations of them are expressible as reachability or simple value independency properties. By contrast, checking more involved hyper properties, or properties that span more than one execution of the external transaction execution is currently out of the scope for EtherTrust.

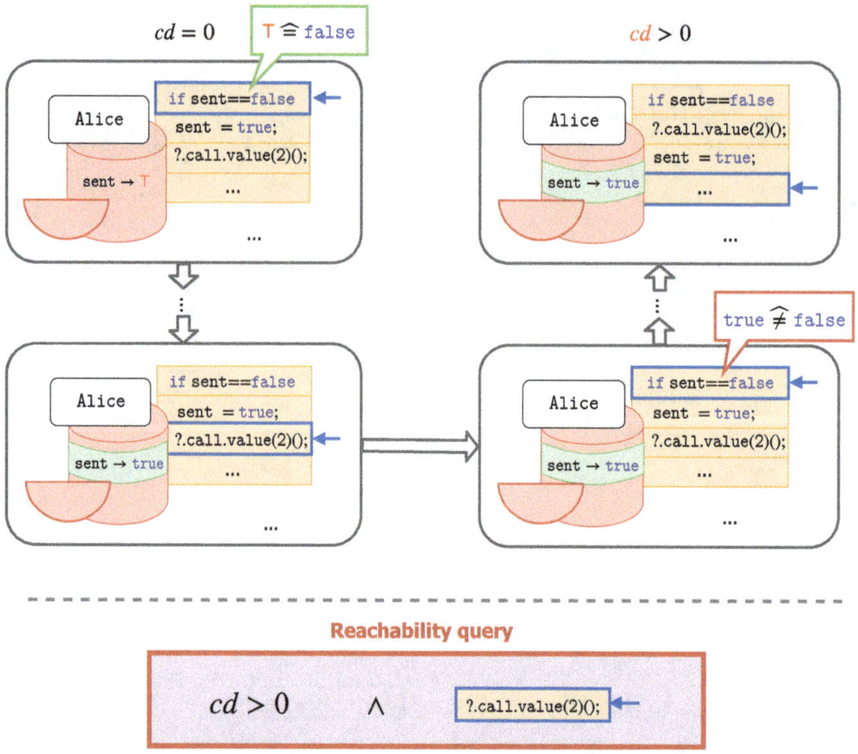

Fig. 8. Illustration of proving single-entrancy of contract `Alice` by the static analysis.

8 Conclusion

We presented a systematization of the state-of-the-art in Ethereum smart contract verification and outlined the open challenges in this field. Also we discussed in detail the foundations of EtherTrust [1], the first sound static analyzer for EVM bytecode. In particular, we reviewed how the small-step semantics presented in [15] is abstracted into a set of Horn clauses. Also we presented how single-entrancy – a relevant smart contract security property – is expressed in terms of queries, which can be then automatically solved leveraging the power of an SMT solver.

Acknowledgments. This work has been partially supported by the European Research Council (ERC) under the European Union's Horizon 2020 research (grant agreement No 771527-BROWSEC), by Netidee through the project EtherTrust (grant agreement 2158), by the Austrian Research Promotion Agency through the Bridge-1 project PR4DLT (grant agreement 13808694) and COMET K1 SBA.

References

1. EtherTrust: Technical report. https://www.netidee.at/ethertrust
2. Nakamoto, S.: Bitcoin: a peer-to-peer electronic cash system (2008). http://bitcoin.org/bitcoin.pdf

3. Hahn, A., Singh, R., Liu, C.C., Chen, S.: Smart contract-based campus demonstration of decentralized transactive energy auctions. In: 2017 IEEE Power & Energy Society Innovative Smart Grid Technologies Conference (ISGT), pp. 1–5. IEEE (2017)
4. Adhikari, C.: Secure framework for healthcare data management using ethereum-based blockchain technology (2017)
5. Biryukov, A., Khovratovich, D., Tikhomirov, S.: Findel: secure derivative contracts for ethereum. In: Brenner, M., Rohloff, K., Bonneau, J., Miller, A., Ryan, P.Y.A., Teague, V., Bracciali, A., Sala, M., Pintore, F., Jakobsson, M. (eds.) FC 2017. LNCS, vol. 10323, pp. 453–467. Springer, Cham (2017). https://doi.org/10.1007/978-3-319-70278-0_28
6. McCorry, P., Shahandashti, S.F., Hao, F.: A smart contract for boardroom voting with maximum voter privacy. In: Kiayias, A. (ed.) FC 2017. LNCS, vol. 10322, pp. 357–375. Springer, Cham (2017). https://doi.org/10.1007/978-3-319-70972-7_20
7. Notheisen, B., Gödde, M., Weinhardt, C.: Trading stocks on blocks - engineering decentralized markets. In: Maedche, A., vom Brocke, J., Hevner, A. (eds.) DESRIST 2017. LNCS, vol. 10243, pp. 474–478. Springer, Cham (2017). https://doi.org/10.1007/978-3-319-59144-5_34
8. Mathieu, F., Mathee, R.: Blocktix: decentralized event hosting and ticket distribution network (2017). https://blocktix.io/public/doc/blocktix-wp-draft.pdf
9. Azaria, A., Ekblaw, A., Vieira, T., Lippman, A.: MedRec: using blockchain for medical data access and permission management. In: International Conference on Open and Big Data (OBD), pp. 25–30. IEEE (2016)
10. Dong, C., Wang, Y., Aldweesh, A., McCorry, P., van Moorsel, A.: Betrayal, distrust, and rationality: Smart counter-collusion contracts for verifiable cloud computing (2017)
11. The DAO smart contract (2016). http://etherscan.io/address/0xbb9bc244d798123fde783fcc1c72d3bb8c189413#code
12. The parity wallet breach (2017). https://www.coindesk.com/30-million-ether-reported-stolen-parity-wallet-breach/
13. The parity wallet vulnerability (2017). https://paritytech.io/blog/security-alert.html
14. Atzei, N., Bartoletti, M., Cimoli, T.: A survey of attacks on Ethereum smart contracts (SoK). In: Maffei, M., Ryan, M. (eds.) POST 2017. LNCS, vol. 10204, pp. 164–186. Springer, Heidelberg (2017). https://doi.org/10.1007/978-3-662-54455-6_8
15. Grishchenko, I., Maffei, M., Schneidewind, C.: A semantic framework for the security analysis of Ethereum smart contracts. In: Bauer, L., Küsters, R. (eds.) POST 2018. LNCS, vol. 10804, pp. 243–269. Springer, Cham (2018). https://doi.org/10.1007/978-3-319-89722-6_10
16. Luu, L., Chu, D.H., Olickel, H., Saxena, P., Hobor, A.: Making smart contracts smarter. In: Proceedings of the 2016 ACM SIGSAC Conference on Computer and Communications Security, pp. 254–269. ACM (2016)
17. Zhou, E., Hua, S., Pi, B., Sun, J., Nomura, Y., Yamashita, K., Kurihara, H.: Security assurance for smart contract. In: 2018 9th IFIP International Conference on New Technologies, Mobility and Security (NTMS), pp. 1–5. IEEE (2018)
18. Nikolic, I., Kolluri, A., Sergey, I., Saxena, P., Hobor, A.: Finding the greedy, prodigal, and suicidal contracts at scale. arXiv preprint arXiv:1802.06038 (2018)
19. Kalra, S., Goel, S., Dhawan, M., Sharma, S.: ZEUS: analyzing safety of smart contracts. In: NDSS (2018)

20. Buenzli, F., Dan, A., Drachsler-Cohen, D., Gervais, A., Tsankov, P., Vechev, M.: Securify (2017). http://securify.ch
21. Mythril. https://github.com/ConsenSys/mythril
22. Manticore. https://github.com/trailofbits/manticore
23. SmartDec: Smartcheck. https://github.com/smartdec/smartcheck
24. Solgraph. https://github.com/raineorshine/solgraph
25. Hirai, Y.: Defining the Ethereum virtual machine for interactive theorem provers. In: Brenner, M., Rohloff, K., Bonneau, J., Miller, A., Ryan, P.Y.A., Teague, V., Bracciali, A., Sala, M., Pintore, F., Jakobsson, M. (eds.) FC 2017. LNCS, vol. 10323, pp. 520–535. Springer, Cham (2017). https://doi.org/10.1007/978-3-319-70278-0_33
26. Wood, G.: Ethereum: a secure decentralised generalised transaction ledger. Ethereum Proj. Yellow Pap. **151**, 1–32 (2014)
27. Amani, S., Bégel, M., Bortin, M., Staples, M.: Towards verifying Ethereum smart contract bytecode in Isabelle/HOL. In: CPP. ACM (2018, to appear)
28. Hildenbrandt, E., Saxena, M., Zhu, X., Rodrigues, N., Daian, P., Guth, D., Rosu, G.: Kevm: A complete semantics of the Ethereum virtual machine. Technical report (2017)
29. Roşu, G., Şerbnut, T.F.: An overview of the K semantic framework. J. Log. Algebraic Program. **79**(6), 397–434 (2010)
30. Bhargavan, K., Delignat-Lavaud, A., Fournet, C., Gollamudi, A., Gonthier, G., Kobeissi, N., Kulatova, N., Rastogi, A., Sibut-Pinote, T., Swamy, N., et al.: Formal verification of smart contracts: short paper. In: Proceedings of the 2016 ACM Workshop on Programming Languages and Analysis for Security, pp. 91–96. ACM (2016)
31. Grossman, S., Abraham, I., Golan-Gueta, G., Michalevsky, Y., Rinetzky, N., Sagiv, M., Zohar, Y.: Online detection of effectively callback free objects with applications to smart contracts. Proc. ACM Program. Lang. **2**(POPL), 48 (2017)
32. Cook, T., Latham, A., Lee, J.H.: Dappguard: active monitoring and defense for solidity smart contracts (2017)
33. O'Connor, R.: Simplicity: a new language for blockchains. arXiv preprint arXiv:1711.03028 (2017)
34. Pettersson, J., Edström, R.: Safer smart contracts through type-driven development. Master's thesis (2016)
35. Coblenz, M.: Obsidian: a safer blockchain programming language. In: 2017 IEEE/ACM 39th International Conference on Software Engineering Companion (ICSE-C), pp. 97–99. IEEE (2017)
36. Schrans, F., Eisenbach, S., Drossopoulou, S.: Writing safe smart contracts in flint (2018)
37. Vyper. https://github.com/ethereum/vyper
38. Bamboo. https://github.com/pirapira/bamboo
39. Formal verification for solidity contracts. https://forum.ethereum.org/discussion/3779/formal-verification-for-solidity-contracts
40. Filliâtre, J.-C., Paskevich, A.: Why3—where programs meet provers. In: Felleisen, M., Gardner, P. (eds.) ESOP 2013. LNCS, vol. 7792, pp. 125–128. Springer, Heidelberg (2013). https://doi.org/10.1007/978-3-642-37036-6_8
41. Sergey, I., Kumar, A., Hobor, A.: Scilla: a smart contract intermediate-level language. arXiv preprint arXiv:1801.00687 (2018)
42. Wöhrer, M., Zdun, U.: Smart contracts: security patterns in the Ethereum ecosystem and solidity (2018)

43. Mavridou, A., Laszka, A.: Designing secure Ethereum smart contracts: a finite state machine based approach. arXiv preprint arXiv:1711.09327 (2017)
44. Sergey, I., Hobor, A.: A concurrent perspective on smart contracts. arXiv preprint arXiv:1702.05511 (2017)
45. de Moura, L., Bjørner, N.: Z3: an efficient SMT solver. In: Ramakrishnan, C.R., Rehof, J. (eds.) TACAS 2008. LNCS, vol. 4963, pp. 337–340. Springer, Heidelberg (2008). https://doi.org/10.1007/978-3-540-78800-3_24
46. Komuravelli, A., Gurfinkel, A., Chaki, S.: Smt-based model checking for recursive programs. Form. Methods Syst. Des. **48**(3), 175–205 (2016)

Layered Concurrent Programs

Bernhard Kragl[1(✉)] and Shaz Qadeer[2]

[1] IST Austria, Klosterneuburg, Austria
bkragl@ist.ac.at
[2] Microsoft Research, Redmond, USA

Abstract. We present layered concurrent programs, a compact and expressive notation for specifying refinement proofs of concurrent programs. A layered concurrent program specifies a sequence of connected concurrent programs, from most concrete to most abstract, such that common parts of different programs are written exactly once. These programs are expressed in the ordinary syntax of imperative concurrent programs using gated atomic actions, sequencing, choice, and (recursive) procedure calls. Each concurrent program is automatically extracted from the layered program. We reduce refinement to the safety of a sequence of concurrent checker programs, one each to justify the connection between every two consecutive concurrent programs. These checker programs are also automatically extracted from the layered program. Layered concurrent programs have been implemented in the CIVL verifier which has been successfully used for the verification of several complex concurrent programs.

1 Introduction

Refinement is an approach to program correctness in which a program is expressed at multiple levels of abstraction. For example, we could have a sequence of programs $\mathcal{P}_1, \ldots, \mathcal{P}_h, \mathcal{P}_{h+1}$ where $\mathcal{P}_1$ is the most concrete and the $\mathcal{P}_{h+1}$ is the most abstract. Program $\mathcal{P}_1$ can be compiled and executed efficiently, $\mathcal{P}_{h+1}$ is obviously correct, and the correctness of $\mathcal{P}_i$ is guaranteed by the correctness of $\mathcal{P}_{i+1}$ for all $i \in [1, h]$. These three properties together ensure that $\mathcal{P}_1$ is both efficient and correct. To use the refinement approach, the programmer must come up with each version $\mathcal{P}_i$ of the program and a proof that the correctness of $\mathcal{P}_{i+1}$ implies the correctness of $\mathcal{P}_i$. This proof typically establishes a connection from every behavior of $\mathcal{P}_i$ to some behavior of $\mathcal{P}_{i+1}$.

Refinement is an attractive approach to the verified construction of complex programs for a number of reasons. First, instead of constructing a single monolithic proof of $\mathcal{P}_1$, the programmer constructs a collection of localized proofs establishing the connection between $\mathcal{P}_i$ and $\mathcal{P}_{i+1}$ for each $i \in [1, h]$. Each localized proof is considerably simpler than the overall proof because it only needs to reason about the (relatively small) difference between adjacent programs. Second, different localized proofs can be performed using different reasoning methods, e.g., interactive deduction, automated testing, or even informal reasoning.

H. Chockler and G. Weissenbacher (Eds.): CAV 2018, LNCS 10981, pp. 79–102, 2018.
https://doi.org/10.1007/978-3-319-96145-3_5

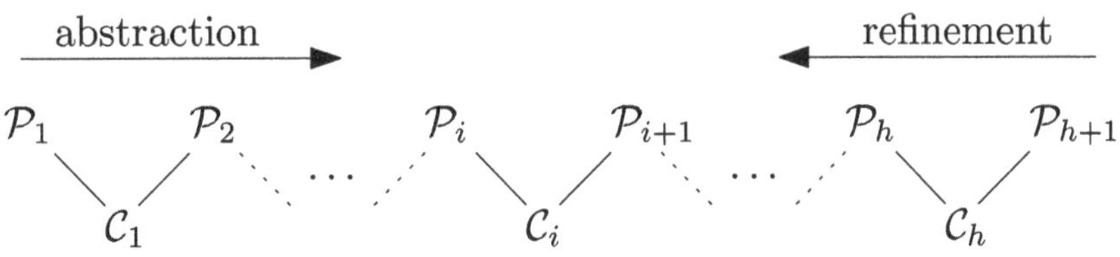

Fig. 1. Concurrent programs $\mathcal{P}_i$ and connecting checker programs $\mathcal{C}_i$ represented by a layered concurrent program $\mathcal{LP}$.

Finally, refinement naturally supports a bidirectional approach to correctness—bottom-up verification of a concrete program via successive abstraction or top-down derivation from an abstract program via successive concretization.

This paper explores the use of refinement to reason about concurrent programs. Most refinement-oriented approaches model a concurrent program as a flat transition system, a representation that is useful for abstract programs but becomes increasingly cumbersome for a concrete implementation. To realize the goal of verified construction of efficient and implementable concurrent programs, we must be able to uniformly and compactly represent both highly-detailed and highly-abstract concurrent programs. This paper introduces layered concurrent programs as such a representation.

A layered concurrent program $\mathcal{LP}$ represents a sequence $\mathcal{P}_1, \ldots, \mathcal{P}_h, \mathcal{P}_{h+1}$ of concurrent programs such that common parts of different programs are written exactly once. These programs are expressed not as flat transition systems but in the ordinary syntax of imperative concurrent programs using gated atomic actions [4], sequencing, choice, and (recursive) procedure calls. Our programming language is accompanied by a type system that allows each $\mathcal{P}_i$ to be automatically extracted from $\mathcal{LP}$. Finally, refinement between $\mathcal{P}_i$ and $\mathcal{P}_{i+1}$ is encoded as the safety of a checker program $\mathcal{C}_i$ which is also automatically extracted from $\mathcal{LP}$. Thus, the verification of $\mathcal{P}_1$ is split into the verification of h concurrent checker programs $\mathcal{C}_1, \ldots, \mathcal{C}_h$ such that $\mathcal{C}_i$ connects $\mathcal{P}_i$ and $\mathcal{P}_{i+1}$ (Fig. 1).

We highlight two crucial aspects of our approach. First, while the programs $\mathcal{P}_i$ have an interleaved (i.e., preemptive) semantics, we verify the checker programs $\mathcal{C}_i$ under a cooperative semantics in which preemptions occur only at procedure calls. Our type system [5] based on the theory of right and left movers [10] ensures that the cooperative behaviors of $\mathcal{C}_i$ cover all preemptive behaviors of $\mathcal{P}_i$. Second, establishing the safety of checker programs is not tied to any particular verification technique. Any applicable technique can be used. In particular, different layers can be verified using different techniques, allowing for great flexibility in verification options.

1.1 Related Work

This paper formalizes, clarifies, and extends the most important aspect of the design of CIVL [6], a deductive verifier for layered concurrent programs. Hawblitzel et al. [7] present a partial explanation of CIVL by formalizing the connection between two concurrent programs as sound program transformations. In this paper, we provide the first formal account for layered concurrent programs to represent all concurrent programs in a multi-layered refinement proof, thereby establishing a new foundation for the verified construction of concurrent programs.

CIVL is the successor to the QED [4] verifier which combined a type system for mover types with logical reasoning based on verification conditions. QED enabled the specification of a layered proof but required each layer to be expressed in a separate file leading to code duplication. Layered programs reduce redundant work in a layered proof by enabling each piece of code to be written exactly once. QED also introduced the idea of abstracting an atomic action to enable attaching a stronger mover type to it. This idea is incorporated naturally in layered programs by allowing a concrete atomic action to be wrapped in a procedure whose specification is a more abstract atomic action with a more precise mover type.

Event-B [1] is a modeling language that supports refinement of systems expressed as interleaved composition of events, each specified as a top-level transition relation. Verification of Event-B specifications is supported by the Rodin [2] toolset which has been used to model and verify several systems of industrial significance. TLA+ [9] also specifies systems as a flat transition system, enables refinement proofs, and is more general because it supports liveness specifications. Our approach to refinement is different from Event-B and TLA+ for several reasons. First, Event-B and TLA+ model different versions of the program as separate flat transition systems whereas our work models them as different layers of a single layered concurrent program, exploiting the standard structuring mechanisms of imperative programs. Second, Event-B and TLA+ connect the concrete program to the abstract program via an explicitly specified refinement mapping. Thus, the guarantee provided by the refinement proof is contingent upon trusting both the abstract program and the refinement mapping. In our approach, once the abstract program is proved to be free of failures, the trusted part of the specification is confined to the gates of atomic actions in the concrete program. Furthermore, the programmer never explicitly specifies a refinement mapping and is only engaged in proving the correctness of checker programs.

The methodology of refinement mappings has been used for compositional verification of hardware designs [11,12]. The focus in this work is to decompose a large refinement proof connecting two versions of a hardware design into a collection of smaller proofs. A variety of techniques including compositional reasoning (converting a large problem to several small problems) and customized abstractions (for converting infinite-state to finite-state problems) are used to create small and finite-state verification problems for a model checker. This work is mostly orthogonal to our contribution of layered programs. Rather, it could be considered an approach to decompose the verification of each (potentially large) checker program encoded by a layered concurrent program.

2 Concurrent Programs

In this section we introduce a concurrent programming language. The syntax of our programming language is summarized in Fig. 2.

$$
\begin{array}{rll}
 & \mathit{Val} & \supseteq \mathbb{B} \\
v \in & \mathit{Var} & = \mathit{GVar} \cup \mathit{LVar} \\
I, O, L \subseteq & \mathit{LVar} & \\
\sigma \in & \mathit{Store} & = \mathit{Var} \to \mathit{Val} \\
e \in & \mathit{Expr} & = \mathit{Store} \to \mathit{Val} \\
t \in & \mathit{Trans} & = 2^{\mathit{Store} \times \mathit{Store}} \\
A \in & \mathit{Action} & \\
P, Q \in & \mathit{Proc} & \\
\iota, o \in & \mathit{IOMap} & = \mathit{LVar} \rightharpoonup \mathit{LVar}
\end{array}
\qquad
\begin{array}{l}
gs \in 2^{\mathit{GVar}} \\
as \in A \mapsto (I, O, e, t) \\
ps \in P \mapsto (I, O, L, s) \\
m \in \mathit{Proc} \cup \mathit{Action} \\
\mathcal{I} \in 2^{\mathit{Store}} \\
\\
\mathcal{P} \in \mathit{Prog} ::= (gs, as, ps, m, \mathcal{I})
\end{array}
$$

$$
s \in \mathit{Stmt} ::= \texttt{skip} \mid s \,;\, s \mid \texttt{if}\ e\ \texttt{then}\ s\ \texttt{else}\ s \mid \texttt{pcall}\ \overline{(A, \iota, o)}\ \overline{(P, \iota, o)}\ \overline{(A, \iota, o)}
$$

Fig. 2. Concurrent programs

Preliminaries. Let *Val* be a set of *values* containing the Booleans. The set of *variables Var* is partitioned into *global variables GVar* and *local variables LVar*. A *store* σ is a mapping from variables to values, an *expression* e is a mapping from stores to values, and a *transition* t is a binary relation between stores.

Atomic Actions. A fundamental notion in our approach is that of an atomic action. An atomic action captures an indivisible operation on the program state together with its precondition, providing a universal representation for both low-level machine operations (e.g., reading a variable from memory) and high-level abstractions (e.g., atomic procedure summaries). Most importantly for reasoning purposes, our programming language confines all accesses to global variables to atomic actions. Formally, an *atomic action* is a tuple (I, O, e, t). The semantics of an atomic action in an execution is to first evaluate the expression e, called the *gate*, in the current state. If the gate evaluates to *false* the execution *fails*, otherwise the program state is updated according to the transition t. *Input variables* in I can be read by e and t, and *output variables* in O can be written by t.

Remark 1. Atomic actions subsume many standard statements. In particular, (nondeterministic) assignments, assertions, and assumptions. The following table shows some examples for programs over variables x and y.

Command	e	t
$x := x + y$	*true*	$x' = x + y \wedge y' = y$
havoc x	*true*	$y' = y$
assert $x < y$	$x < y$	$x' = x \wedge y' = y$
assume $x < y$	*true*	$x < y \wedge x' = x \wedge y' = y$

Procedures. A *procedure* is a tuple (I, O, L, s) where I, O, L are the *input*, *output*, and *local variables* of the procedure, and s is a *statement* composed from skip, sequencing, if, and parallel call statements. Since only atomic actions can refer to global variables, the variables accessed in if conditions are restricted to the inputs, outputs, and locals of the enclosing procedure. The meaning of skip, sequencing, and if is as expected and we focus on parallel calls.

Pcalls. A *parallel call* (*pcall*, for short) pcall $\overline{(A, \iota, o)}\ \overline{(P, \iota, o)}\ \overline{(A, \iota, o)}$ consists of a sequence of invocations of atomic actions and procedures. We refer to the invocations as the *arms* of the pcall. In particular (A, ι, o) is an *atomic-action arm* and (P, ι, o) is a *procedure arm*. An atomic-action arm executes the called atomic action, and a procedure arm creates a child thread that executes the statement of the called procedure. The parent thread is blocked until all arms of the pcall finish. In the standard semantics the order of arms does not matter, but our verification technique will allow us to consider the atomic action arms before and after the procedure arms to execute in the specified order. Parameter passing is expressed using partial mappings ι, o between local variables; ι maps formal inputs of the callee to actual inputs of the caller, and o maps actual outputs of the caller to formal outputs of the callee. Since we do not want to introduce races on local variables, the outputs of all arms must be disjoint and the output of one arm cannot be an input to another arm. Finally, notice that our general notion of a pcall subsumes sequential statements (single atomic-action arm), synchronous procedure calls (single procedure arm), and unbounded thread creation (recursive procedure arm).

Concurrent Programs. A *concurrent program* $\mathcal{P}$ is a tuple $(gs, as, ps, m, \mathcal{I})$, where gs is a finite set of global variables used by the program, as is a finite mapping from *action names* A to atomic actions, ps is a finite mapping from *procedure names* P to procedures, m is either a procedure or action name that denotes the entry point for program executions, and $\mathcal{I}$ is a set of initial stores. For convenience we will liberally use action and procedure names to refer to the corresponding atomic actions and procedures.

Semantics. Let $\mathcal{P} = (gs, as, ps, m, \mathcal{I})$ be a fixed concurrent program. A *state* consists of a global store assigning values to the global variables and a pool of *threads*, each consisting of a local store assigning values to local variables and a statement that remains to be executed. An *execution* is a sequence of states, where from each state to the next some thread is selected to execute one step. Every step that switches the executing thread is called a *preemption* (also called a context switch). We distinguish between two semantics that differ in (1) preemption points, and (2) the order of executing the arms of a pcall.

In *preemptive semantics*, a preemption is allowed anywhere and the arms of a pcall are arbitrarily interleaved. In *cooperative semantics*, a preemption is allowed only at the call and return of a procedure, and the arms of a pcall are executed as follows. First, the leading atomic-action arms are executed from left to right without preemption, then all procedure arms are executed arbitrarily interleaved, and finally the trailing atomic-action arms are executed, again from left to right without preemption. In other words, a preemption is only allowed when a procedure arm of a pcall creates a new thread and when a thread terminates.

For $\mathcal{P}$ we only consider executions that start with a single thread that execute m from a store in $\mathcal{I}$. $\mathcal{P}$ is called *safe* if there is no failing execution, i.e., an execution that executes an atomic action whose gate evaluates to *false*. We write *Safe*($\mathcal{P}$) if $\mathcal{P}$ is safe under preemptive semantics, and *CSafe*($\mathcal{P}$) if $\mathcal{P}$ is safe under cooperative semantics.

2.1 Running Example

In this section, we introduce a sequence of three concurrent programs (Fig. 3) to illustrate features of our concurrent programming language and the layered approach to program correctness. Consider the program $\mathcal{P}_1^{lock}$ in Fig. 3(a). The program uses a single global Boolean variable `b` which is accessed by the two atomic actions `CAS` and `RESET`. The compare-and-swap action `CAS` atomically reads the current value of `b` and either sets `b` from *false* to *true* and returns *true*, or leaves `b` *true* and returns *false*. The `RESET` action sets `b` to *false* and has a gate (represented as an assertion) that states that the action must only be called when `b` is *true*. Using these actions, the procedures `Enter` and `Leave` implement a spinlock as follows. `Enter` calls the `CAS` action and retries (through recursion on itself) until it succeeds to set `b` from *false* to *true*. `Leave` just calls the `RESET` action which sets `b` back to *false* and thus allows another thread executing `Enter` to stop spinning. Finally, the procedures `Main` and `Worker` serve as a simple client. `Main` uses a pcall inside a nondeterministic if statement to create an unbounded number of concurrent worker threads, which just acquire the lock by calling `Enter` and then release the lock again by calling `Leave`. The call to the empty procedure `Alloc` is an artifact of our extraction from a layered concurrent program and can be removed as an optimization.

Proving $\mathcal{P}_1^{lock}$ safe amounts to showing that `RESET` is never called with `b` set to *false*, which expresses that $\mathcal{P}_1^{lock}$ follows a locking discipline of releasing only previously acquired locks. Doing this proof directly on $\mathcal{P}_1^{lock}$ has two drawbacks. First, the proof must relate the possible values of `b` with the program counters of all running threads. In general, this approach requires sound introduction of ghost code and results in complicated case distinctions in program invariants. Second, the proof is not reusable across different lock implementations. The correctness of the client does not specifically depend on using a spinlock over a Boolean variable, and thus the proof should not as well. We show how our refinement-based approach addresses both problems.

Program $\mathcal{P}_2^{lock}$ in Fig. 3(b) is an abstraction of $\mathcal{P}_1^{lock}$ that introduces an abstract lock specification. The global variable `b` is replaced by `lock` which ranges over integer thread identifiers (`0` is a dedicated value indicating that the lock is available). The procedures `Alloc`, `Enter` and `Leave` are replaced by the atomic actions `ALLOC`, `ACQUIRE` and `RELEASE`, respectively. `ALLOC` allocates unique and non-zero thread identifiers using a set of integers `slot` to store the identifiers not allocated so far. `ACQUIRE` blocks executions where the lock is not

(a) $\mathcal{P}_1^{lock}$

```
var b : bool

proc Main()
  if (*)
    pcall Worker(), Main()

proc Worker()

  pcall Alloc()
  pcall Enter()
  pcall Leave()

proc Alloc() : ()
  skip


proc Enter()
  var success : bool
  pcall success := CAS()
  if (success)
    skip
  else
    pcall Enter()

proc Leave()
  pcall RESET()
  skip

atomic CAS() : (success : bool)
  if (b) success := false
  else   success, b := true, true

atomic RESET()
  assert b
  b := false
```

(b) $\mathcal{P}_2^{lock}$

```
var lock : int
var linear slots : set<int>

proc Main()
  if (*)
    pcall Worker(), Main()

proc Worker()
  var linear tid : int
  pcall tid := ALLOC()
  pcall ACQUIRE(tid)
  pcall RELEASE(tid)

right ALLOC() : (linear tid : int)
  assume tid != 0 && tid ∈ slots
  slots := slots - tid

right ACQUIRE(linear tid : int)
  assert tid != 0
  assume lock == 0
  lock := tid




left RELEASE(linear tid : int)
  assert tid != 0 && lock == tid
  lock := 0
```

(c) $\mathcal{P}_3^{lock}$

```
both SKIP()
  skip
```

Fig. 3. Lock example

available (`assume lock == 0`) and sets `lock` to the identifier of the acquiring thread. `RELEASE` asserts that the releasing thread holds the lock and sets `lock` to `0`. Thus, the connection between $\mathcal{P}_1^{lock}$ and $\mathcal{P}_2^{lock}$ is given by the invariant `b <==> lock != 0` which justifies that `Enter` refines `ACQUIRE` and `Leave` refines `RELEASE`. The potential safety violation in $\mathcal{P}_1^{lock}$ by the gate of `RESET` is preserved in $\mathcal{P}_2^{lock}$ by the gate of `RELEASE`. In fact, the safety of $\mathcal{P}_2^{lock}$ expresses the stronger locking discipline that the lock can only be released by the thread that acquired it.

Reasoning in terms of `ACQUIRE` and `RELEASE` instead of `Enter` and `Leave` is more general, but it is also simpler! Figure 3(b) declares atomic actions with a *mover type* [5], `right` for *right mover*, and `left` for *left mover*. A right mover executed by a thread commutes to the right of any action executed by a different thread. Similarly, a left mover executed by thread commutes to the left of any action executed by a different thread. A sequence of right movers followed by at most one non-mover followed by a sequence of left movers in a thread can be considered atomic [10]. The reason is that any interleaved execution can be rearranged (by commuting atomic actions), such that these actions execute consecutively. For $\mathcal{P}_2^{lock}$ this means that `Worker` is atomic and thus the gate of `RELEASE` can be discharged by pure sequential reasoning; `ALLOC` guarantees `tid != 0` and after executing `ACQUIRE` we have `lock == tid`. As a result, we finally obtain that the atomic action `SKIP` in $\mathcal{P}_3^{lock}$ (Fig. 3(c)) is a sound abstraction of procedure `Main` in $\mathcal{P}_2^{lock}$. Hence, we showed that program $\mathcal{P}_1^{lock}$ is safe by soundly abstracting it to $\mathcal{P}_3^{lock}$, a program that is trivially safe.

The correctness of `right` and `left` annotations on `ACQUIRE` and `RELEASE`, respectively, depends on pair-wise commutativity checks among atomic actions in $\mathcal{P}_2^{lock}$. These commutativity checks will fail unless we exploit the fact that every thread identifier allocated by `Worker` using the `ALLOC` action is unique. For instance, to show that `ACQUIRE` executed by a thread commutes to the right of `RELEASE` executed by a different thread, it must be known that the parameters `tid` to these actions are distinct from each other. The *`linear`* annotation on the local variables named `tid` and the global variable `slots` (which is a set of integers) is used to communicate this information.

The overall invariant encoded by the *`linear`* annotation is that the set of values stored in `slots` and in local linear variables of active stack frames across all threads are pairwise disjoint. This invariant is guaranteed by a combination of a linear type system [14] and logical reasoning on the code of all atomic actions. The linear type system ensures using a flow analysis that a value stored in a linear variable in an active stack frame is not copied into another linear variable via an assignment. Each atomic action must ensure that its state update preserves the disjointness invariant for linear variables. For actions `ACQUIRE` and `RELEASE`, which do not modify any linear variables, this reasoning is trivial. However, action `ALLOC` modifies `slots` and updates the linear output parameter `tid`. Its correctness depends on the (semantic) fact that the value put into `tid` is removed from `slots`; this reasoning can be done using automated theorem provers.

3 Layered Concurrent Programs

A layered concurrent program represents a sequence of concurrent programs that are connected to each other. That is, the programs derived from a layered concurrent program share syntactic structure, but differ in the granularity of the atomic actions and the set of variables they are expressed over. In a layered concurrent program, we associate layer numbers and layer ranges with variables (both global and local), atomic actions, and procedures. These layer numbers control the introduction and hiding of program variables and the summarization of compound operations into atomic actions, and thus provide the scaffolding of a refinement relation. Concretely, this section shows how the concurrent programs $\mathcal{P}_1^{lock}$, $\mathcal{P}_2^{lock}$, and $\mathcal{P}_3^{lock}$ (Fig. 3) and their connections can all be expressed in a single layered concurrent program. In Sect. 4, we discuss how to check refinement between the successive concurrent programs encoded in a layered concurrent program.

Syntax. The syntax of layered concurrent programs is summarized in Fig. 4. Let $\mathbb{N}$ be the set of non-negative integers and $\mathbb{I}$ the set of nonempty *intervals* $[a, b]$.

$$[a,b] = \{x \mid a,b,x \in \mathbb{N} \land a \leq x \leq b\}$$

$$n, \alpha \in \mathbb{N}$$
$$r \in \mathbb{I} = \{[a,b] \mid a \leq b\}$$
$$ns \in LVar \rightharpoonup \mathbb{N}$$

$$\begin{aligned} GS &\in GVar \rightharpoonup \mathbb{I} \\ AS &\in A \mapsto (I, O, e, t, r) \\ IS &\in A \mapsto (I, O, e, t, n) \\ PS &\in P \mapsto (I, O, L, s, n, ns, A) \\ m &\in Proc \\ \mathcal{I} &\in 2^{Store} \end{aligned}$$

$$\mathcal{LP} \in LayeredProg ::= (GS, AS, IS, PS, m, \mathcal{I})$$

$$s \in Stmt ::= \cdots \mid \texttt{icall}\ (A, \iota, o) \mid \texttt{pcall}_\alpha\ \overline{(P_i, \iota_i, o_i)}_{i \in [1,k]} \quad (\alpha \in \{\varepsilon\} \cup [1,k])$$

Fig. 4. Layered concurrent programs

We refer to integers as *layer numbers* and intervals as *layer ranges*. A *layered concurrent program* $\mathcal{LP}$ is a tuple $(GS, AS, IS, PS, m, \mathcal{I})$ which, similarly to concurrent programs, consists of global variables, atomic actions, and procedures, with the following differences.

1. GS maps global variables to layer ranges. For $GS(v) = [a,b]$ we say that v is introduced at layer a and available up to layer b.
2. AS assigns a layer range r to atomic actions denoting the layers at which an action exists.
3. IS (with a disjoint domain from AS) distinguishes a special type of atomic actions called *introduction actions*. Introduction actions have a single layer number n and are responsible for assigning meaning to the variables introduced at layer n. Correspondingly, statements in layered concurrent programs are extended with an `icall` statement for calling introduction actions.
4. PS assigns a layer number n, a layer number mapping for local variables ns, and an atomic action A to procedures. We call n the *disappearing layer* and A the *refined atomic action*. For every local variable v, $ns(v)$ is the *introduction layer* of v.
   The $\texttt{pcall}_\alpha$ statement in a layered concurrent program differs from the `pcall` statement in concurrent programs in two ways. First, it can only have procedure arms. Second, it has a parameter α which is either ε (*unannotated pcall*) or the index of one of its arms (*annotated pcall*). We usually omit writing ε in unannotated pcalls.
5. m is a procedure name.

The *top layer* h of a layered concurrent program is the disappearing layer of m.

Intuition Behind Layer Numbers. Recall that a layered concurrent program $\mathcal{LP}$ should represent a sequence of $h+1$ concurrent programs $\mathcal{P}_1, \cdots, \mathcal{P}_{h+1}$ that are connected by a sequence of h checker programs $\mathcal{C}_1, \cdots, \mathcal{C}_h$ (cf. Fig. 1). Before we provide formal definitions, let us get some intuition on two core mechanisms: global variable introduction and procedure abstraction/refinement.

Let v be a global variable with layer range $[a,b]$. The meaning of this layer range is that the "first" program that contains v is $\mathcal{C}_a$, the checker program connecting $\mathcal{P}_a$ and $\mathcal{P}_{a+1}$. In particular, v is not yet part of $\mathcal{P}_a$. In $\mathcal{C}_a$ the introduction actions at layer a can modify v and thus assign its meaning in terms of all other available variables. Then v is part of $\mathcal{P}_{a+1}$ and all programs up to and including $\mathcal{P}_b$. The "last" program containing v is $\mathcal{C}_b$. In other words, when going from a program $\mathcal{P}_i$ to $\mathcal{P}_{i+1}$ the variables with upper bound i disappear and the variables with lower bound i are introduced; the checker program $\mathcal{C}_i$ has access to both and establishes their relationship.

Let P be a procedure with disappearing layer n and refined atomic action A. The meaning of the disappearing layer is that P exists in all programs from $\mathcal{P}_1$ up to and including $\mathcal{P}_n$. In $\mathcal{P}_{n+1}$ and above every invocation of P is replaced by an invocation of A. To ensure that this replacement is sound, the checker program $\mathcal{C}_n$ performs a refinement check that ensures that every execution of P behaves like A. Observe that the body of procedure P itself changes from $\mathcal{P}_1$ to $\mathcal{P}_n$ according to the disappearing layer of the procedures it calls.

With the above intuition in mind it is clear that the layer annotations in a layered concurrent program cannot be arbitrary. For example, if procedure P calls a procedure Q, then Q cannot have a higher disappearing layer than P, for Q could introduce further behaviors into the program after P was replaced by A, and those behaviors are not captured by A.

3.1 Type Checker

We describe the constraints that need to be satisfied for a layered concurrent program to be well-formed. A full formalization as a type checker with top-level judgment $\vdash \mathcal{LP}$ is given in Fig. 5. For completeness, the type checker includes standard constraints (e.g., variable scoping, parameter passing, etc.) that we are not going to discuss.

(Atomic Action)/(Introduction Action). Global variables can only be accessed by atomic actions and introduction actions. For a global variable v with layer range $[a, b]$, introduction actions with layer number a are allowed to modify v (for sound variable introduction), and atomic actions with a layer range contained in $[a+1, b]$ have access to v. Introduction actions must be nonblocking, which means that every state that satisfies the gate must have a possible transition to take. This ensures that introduction actions only assign meaning to introduced variables but do not exclude any program behavior.

(If). Procedure bodies change from layer to layer because calls to procedures become calls to atomic actions. But the control-flow structure within a procedure is preserved across layers. Therefore (local) variables accessed in an if condition must be available on all layers to ensure that the if statement is well-defined on every layer.

(Introduction Call). Let A be an introduction action with layer number n. Since A modifies global variables introduced at layer n, icalls to A are only allowed from procedures with disappearing layer n. Similarly, the formal output parameters of an icall to A must have introduction layer n. The icall is only preserved in $\mathcal{C}_n$.

(Program)

$$\frac{\begin{array}{l} dom(AS) \cap dom(IS) = \varnothing \\ PS(m) = (\_,\_,\_,\_,h,\_,A_m) \\ AS(A_m) = (\_,\_,\_,\_,r) \\ h+1 \in r \\ \forall\, A \in dom(AS) : (GS, AS) \vdash A \\ \forall\, A \in dom(IS) : (GS, IS) \vdash A \\ \forall\, P \in dom(PS) : (AS, IS, PS) \vdash P \end{array}}{\vdash (GS, AS, IS, PS, m, \mathcal{I})}$$

(Atomic action)

$$\frac{\begin{array}{l} AS(A) = (I, O, e, t, r) \\ Disjoint(I, O) \\ \forall\, v \in ReadVars(e,t) : v \in I \vee r \subseteq \widehat{GS}(v) \\ \forall\, v \in WriteVars(t) : v \in O \vee r \subseteq \widehat{GS}(v) \end{array}}{(GS, AS) \vdash A}$$

(Introduction action)

$$\frac{\begin{array}{l} IS(A) = (I, O, e, t, n) \\ Disjoint(I, O) \\ \forall\, v \in ReadVars(e,t) : v \in I \vee n \in GS(v) \\ \forall\, v \in WriteVars(t) : v \in O \vee GS(v) = [n, \_] \\ Nonblocking(e, t) \end{array}}{(GS, IS) \vdash A}$$

(Procedure)

$$\frac{\begin{array}{l} PS(P) = (I, O, L, s, n, ns, A) \\ AS(A) = (I, O, \_, \_, \_) \\ Disjoint(I, O, L) \\ \forall\, v \in I \cup O \cup L : ns(v) \leq n \\ (AS, IS, PS), P \vdash s \end{array}}{(AS, IS, PS) \vdash P}$$

(Skip)

$$\frac{}{(AS, IS, PS), P \vdash \texttt{skip}}$$

(Sequence)

$$\frac{(AS, IS, PS), P \vdash s_1 \quad (AS, IS, PS), P \vdash s_2}{(AS, IS, PS), P \vdash s_1 \; ; \; s_2}$$

(If)

$$\frac{\begin{array}{l} PS(P) = (I, \_, L, \_, \_, ns, \_) \\ \forall\, x \in ReadVars(e) : x \in I \cup L \wedge ns(x) = 0 \\ (AS, IS, PS), P \vdash s_1 \quad (AS, IS, PS), P \vdash s_2 \end{array}}{(AS, IS, PS), P \vdash \texttt{if}\ e\ \texttt{then}\ s_1\ \texttt{else}\ s_2}$$

(Parameter passing)

$$\frac{\begin{array}{ll} dom(\iota) = I' & dom(o) \subseteq O \cup L \\ img(\iota) \subseteq I \cup O \cup L & img(o) \subseteq O' \end{array}}{ValidIO(\iota, o, I, O, L, I', O')}$$

(Introduction call)

$$\frac{\begin{array}{l} PS(P) = (I_P, O_P, L_P, \_, n_P, ns_P, \_) \\ IS(A) = (I_A, O_A, \_, t, n_A) \\ ValidIO(\iota, o, I_P, O_P, L_P, I_A, O_A) \\ n_A = n_P \\ \forall\, v \in dom(o) : ns_P(v) = n_P \end{array}}{(AS, IS, PS), P \vdash \texttt{icall}\ (A, \iota, o)}$$

(Parallel call)

$$\frac{\begin{array}{l} \forall\, i \neq j : dom(o_i) \cap dom(o_j) = \varnothing \\ \qquad\qquad dom(o_i) \cap img(\iota_j) = \varnothing \\ \forall\, i : PS(P) = (I_P, O_P, L_P, \_, n_P, ns_P, \_) \\ \quad PS(Q_i) = (I_i, O_i, \_, \_, n_i, ns_i, A_i) \\ \quad AS(A_i) = (\_,\_,\_,\_,r_i) \\ \quad ValidIO(\iota_i, o_i, I_P, O_P, L_P, I_i, O_i) \\ \quad \forall\, v \in dom(\iota_i) : ns_P(\iota_i(v)) \leq ns_i(v) \\ \quad \forall\, v \in dom(o_i) : ns_i(o_i(v)) \leq ns_P(v) \\ \quad n_i \leq n_P \qquad [n_i + 1, n_P] \subseteq r_i \\ \quad i = \alpha \implies n_i = n_P \wedge O_P \subseteq dom(o_i) \\ \quad i \neq \alpha \wedge n_i = n_P \implies dom(o_i) \subseteq L_i \\ \exists\, i : n_1 \leq \cdots \leq n_i \geq \cdots \geq n_k \end{array}}{(AS, IS, PS), P \vdash \texttt{pcall}_\alpha\ (Q_i, \iota_i, o_i)_{i \in [1,k]}}$$

$$\begin{array}{l} \widehat{GS}(v) = [a+1, b] \text{ for } GS(v) = [a, b] \\ ReadVars(e) = \{v \mid \exists\, \sigma, a : e(\sigma) \neq e(\sigma[v \mapsto a])\} \cup \\ ReadVars(t) = \{v \mid \exists\, \sigma, \sigma', a : (\sigma, \sigma') \in t \wedge (\sigma[v \mapsto a], \sigma') \notin t\} \\ ReadVars(e,t) = ReadVars(e) \cup ReadVars(t) \\ WriteVars(t) = \{v \mid \exists\, \sigma, \sigma' : (\sigma, \sigma') \in t \wedge \sigma(v) \neq \sigma'(v)\} \\ Nonblocking(e,t) = \forall\, \sigma \in e : \exists\, \sigma' : (\sigma, \sigma') \in t \end{array}$$

Fig. 5. Type checking rules for layered concurrent programs

(Parallel Call). All arms in a pcall must be procedure arms invoking a procedure with a disappearing layer less than or equal to the disappearing layer of the caller. Furthermore, above the disappearing layer of the callee its refined atomic action must be available up to the disappearing layer of the caller. Parameter passing can only be well-defined if the actual inputs exist before the formal inputs, and the formal outputs exist before the actual outputs. The sequence of disappearing layers of the procedures in a pcall must be monotonically increasing and then decreasing, such that the resulting pcall in the extracted programs consists of procedure arms surrounded by atomic-action arms on every layer.

Annotated pcalls are only used for invocations to procedures with the same disappearing layer n as the caller. In particular, during refinement checking in $\mathcal{C}_n$ only the arm with index α is allowed to modify the global state, which must be according to the refined atomic action of the caller. The remaining arms must leave the global state unchanged.

3.2 Concurrent Program Extraction

Let $\mathcal{LP} = (GS, AS, IS, PS, m, \mathcal{I})$ be a layered concurrent program such that $PS(m) = (\_, \_, \_, \_, h, \_, A_m)$. We show how to extract the programs $\mathcal{P}_1, \cdots, \mathcal{P}_{h+1}$ by defining a function $\Gamma_\ell(\mathcal{LP})$ such that $\mathcal{P}_\ell = \Gamma_\ell(\mathcal{LP})$ for every $\ell \in [1, h+1]$. For a local variable layer mapping ns we define the set of local variables with layer number less then ℓ as $ns|_\ell = \{v \mid ns(v) < \ell\}$. Now the extraction function Γ_ℓ is defined as

$$\Gamma_\ell(\mathcal{LP}) = (gs, as, ps, m', \mathcal{I}),$$

where

$$\begin{aligned}
gs &= \{v \mid GS(v) = [a,b] \wedge \ell \in [a+1, b]\},\\
as &= \{A \mapsto (I, O, e, t) \mid AS(A) = (I, O, e, t, r) \wedge \ell \in r\},\\
ps &= \{P \mapsto (I \cap ns|_\ell, O \cap ns|_\ell, L \cap ns|_\ell, \Gamma_\ell^P(s)) \mid PS(P) = (I, O, L, s, n, ns, _) \wedge \ell \le n\},\\
m' &= \begin{cases} m & \text{if } \ell \in [1, h] \\ A_m & \text{if } \ell = h+1 \end{cases},
\end{aligned}$$

and the extraction of a statement in the body of procedure P is given by

$$\begin{aligned}
&\Gamma_\ell^P(\texttt{skip}) &&= \texttt{skip},\\
&\Gamma_\ell^P(s_1 \texttt{ ; } s_2) &&= \Gamma_\ell^P(s_1) \texttt{ ; } \Gamma_\ell^P(s_2),\\
&\Gamma_\ell^P(\texttt{if } e \texttt{ then } s_1 \texttt{ else } s_2) &&= \texttt{if } e \texttt{ then } \Gamma_\ell^P(s_1) \texttt{ else } \Gamma_\ell^P(s_2),\\
&\Gamma_\ell^P(\texttt{icall } (A, \iota, o)) &&= \texttt{skip},\\
&\Gamma_\ell^P(\texttt{pcall}_\alpha\ \overline{(Q, \iota, o)}) &&= \texttt{pcall}\ \overline{(X, \iota|_{ns_Q|_\ell}, o|_{ns_P|_\ell})},\\
& &&\quad \text{for } \begin{matrix} PS(P) = (_, _, _, _, _, ns_P, _) \\ PS(Q) = (_, _, _, _, n, ns_Q, A) \end{matrix} \text{ and } X = \begin{cases} Q \text{ if } \ell \le n \\ A \text{ if } \ell > n \end{cases}.
\end{aligned}$$

Thus $\mathcal{P}_\ell$ includes the global and local variables that were introduced before ℓ and the atomic actions with ℓ in their layer range. Furthermore, it does not contain introduction actions and correspondingly all icall statements are removed. Every arm of a pcall statement, depending on the disappearing layer n of the called procedure Q, either remains a procedure arm to Q, or is replaced by an atomic-action arm to A, the atomic action refined by Q. The input and output mappings are restricted to the local variables at layer ℓ. The set of initial stores of $\mathcal{P}_\ell$ is the same as for $\mathcal{LP}$, since stores range over all program variables.

In our programming language, loops are subsumed by the more general mechanism of recursive procedure calls. Observe that $\mathcal{P}_\ell$ can indeed have recursive procedure calls, because our type checking rules (Fig. 5) allow a pcall to invoke a procedure with the same disappearing layer as the caller.

3.3 Running Example

We return to our lock example from Sect. 2.1. Figure 6 shows its implementation as the layered concurrent program $\mathcal{LP}^{lock}$. Layer annotations are indicated using an `@` symbol. For example, the global variable `b` has layer range $[0, 1]$, all occurrences of local variable `tid` have introduction layer 1, the atomic action `ACQUIRE` has layer range $[2, 2]$, and the introduction action `iSetLock` has layer number 1.

First, observe that $\mathcal{LP}^{lock}$ is well-formed, i.e., $\vdash \mathcal{LP}^{lock}$. Then it is an easy exercise to verify that $\Gamma_\ell(\mathcal{LP}^{lock}) = \mathcal{P}_\ell^{lock}$ for $\ell \in [1, 3]$. Let us focus on procedure `Worker`. In $\mathcal{P}_1^{lock}$ (Fig. 3(a)) `tid` does not exist, and correspondingly `Alloc`, `Enter`, and `Leave` do not have input respectively output parameters. Furthermore, the icall in the body of `Alloc` is replaced with `skip`. In $\mathcal{P}_2^{lock}$ (Fig. 3(b)) we have `tid` and the calls to `Alloc`, `Enter`, and `Leave` are replaced with their respective refined atomic actions `ALLOC`, `ACQUIRE`, and `RELEASE`. The only annotated pcall in $\mathcal{LP}^{lock}$ is the recursive call to `Enter`.

In addition to representing the concurrent programs in Fig. 3, the program $\mathcal{LP}^{lock}$ also encodes the connection between them via introduction actions and calls. The introduction action `iSetLock` updates `lock` to maintain the relationship between `lock` and `b`, expressed by the predicate `InvLock`. It is called in `Enter` in case the CAS operation successfully set `b` to *true*, and in `Leave` when `b` is set to *false*. The introduction action `iIncr` implements linear thread identifiers using the integer variables `pos` which points to the next value that can be allocated. For every allocation, the current value of `pos` is returned as the new thread identifier and `pos` is incremented.

The variable `slots` is introduced at layer 1 to represent the set of unallocated identifiers. It contains all integers no less than `pos`, an invariant that is expressed by the predicate `InvAlloc` and maintained by the code of `iIncr`. The purpose of `slots` is to encode linear allocation of thread identifiers in a way that the body of `iIncr` can be locally shown to preserve the disjointness invariant for linear variables; `slots` plays a similar role in the specification of the atomic action `ALLOC` in $\mathcal{P}_2$. The variable `pos` is both introduced and hidden at layer 1 so that it exists neither in $\mathcal{P}_1^{lock}$ nor $\mathcal{P}_2^{lock}$. However, `pos` is present in the checker program $\mathcal{C}_1$ that connects $\mathcal{P}_1^{lock}$ and $\mathcal{P}_2^{lock}$.

$\mathcal{LP}^{lock}$

```
var b@[0,1] : bool
var lock@[1,2] : int
var pos@[1,1] : int
var linear slots@[1,2] : set<int>

predicate InvLock
  b <==> lock != 0

predicate InvAlloc
  pos > 0 && slots == [pos,∞)

init InvLock && InvAlloc

both SKIP@3 ()
  skip

proc Main@2()
refines SKIP
  if (*)
    pcall Worker(), Main()

proc Worker@2()
refines SKIP
  var linear tid@1 : int
  pcall tid := Alloc()
  pcall Enter(tid)
  pcall Leave(tid)

right ALLOC@[2,2]() : (linear tid : int)
  assume tid != 0 && tid ∈ slots
  slots := slots - tid

proc Alloc@1() : (linear tid@1 : int)
refines ALLOC
  icall tid := iIncr()

iaction iIncr@1() : (linear tid : int)
  assert InvAlloc
  tid := pos
  pos := pos + 1
  slots := slots - tid
```

```
right ACQUIRE@[2,2](linear tid : int)
  assert tid != 0
  assume lock == 0
  lock := tid

left RELEASE@[2,2](linear tid : int)
  assert tid != 0 && lock == tid
  lock := 0

proc Enter@1(linear tid@1 : int)
refines ACQUIRE
  var success@0 : bool
  pcall success := Cas()
  if (success)
    icall iSetLock(tid)
  else
    pcall_1 Enter(tid)

proc Leave@1(linear tid@1 : int)
refines RELEASE
  pcall Reset()
  icall iSetLock(0)

iaction iSetLock@1(v : int)
  lock := v

atomic CAS@[1,1]() : (success : bool)
  if (b) success := false
  else   success, b := true, true

atomic RESET@[1,1]()
  assert b
  b := false

proc Cas@0() : (success@0 : bool)
refines CAS

proc Reset@0()
refines RESET
```

Fig. 6. Lock example (layered concurrent program)

The bodies of procedures `Cas` and `Reset` are not shown in Fig. 6 because they are not needed. They disappear at layer 0 and are replaced by the atomic actions `CAS` and `RESET`, respectively, in $\mathcal{P}_1^{lock}$.

The degree of compactness afforded by layered programs (as in Fig. 6) over separate specification of each concurrent program (as in Fig. 3) increases rapidly with the size of the program and the maximum depth of procedure calls. In our experience, for realistic programs such as a concurrent garbage collector [7] or a data-race detector [15], the saving in code duplication is significant.

4 Refinement Checking

Section 3 described how a layered concurrent program $\mathcal{LP}$ encodes a sequence $\mathcal{P}_1, \ldots, \mathcal{P}_h, \mathcal{P}_{h+1}$ of concurrent programs. In this section, we show how the safety of any concurrent program in the sequence is implied by the safety of its successor, ultimately allowing the safety of $\mathcal{P}_1$ to be established by the safety of $\mathcal{P}_{h+1}$.

There are three ingredients to connecting $\mathcal{P}_\ell$ to $\mathcal{P}_{\ell+1}$ for any $\ell \in [1, h]$—reduction, projection, and abstraction. Reduction allows us to conclude the safety of a concurrent program under preemptive semantics by proving safety only under cooperative semantics.

Theorem 1 (Reduction). *Let $\mathcal{P}$ be a concurrent program. If MSafe($\mathcal{P}$) and CSafe($\mathcal{P}$), then Safe($\mathcal{P}$).*

The judgment *MSafe*($\mathcal{P}$) uses logical commutativity reasoning and mover types to ensure that cooperative safety is sufficient for preemptive safety (Sect. 4.1). We use this theorem to justify reasoning about *CSafe*($\mathcal{P}_\ell$) rather than *Safe*($\mathcal{P}_\ell$).

The next step in connecting $\mathcal{P}_\ell$ to $\mathcal{P}_{\ell+1}$ is to introduce computation introduced at layer ℓ into the cooperative semantics of $\mathcal{P}_\ell$. This computation comprises global and local variables together with introduction actions and calls to them. We refer to the resulting program at layer ℓ as $\widetilde{\mathcal{P}}_\ell$.

Theorem 2 (Projection). *Let $\mathcal{LP}$ be a layered concurrent program with top layer h and $\ell \in [1, h]$. If CSafe($\widetilde{\mathcal{P}}_\ell$), then CSafe($\mathcal{P}_\ell$).*

Since introduction actions are nonblocking and $\widetilde{\mathcal{P}}_\ell$ is safe under cooperative semantics, every cooperative execution of $\mathcal{P}_\ell$ can be obtained by projecting away the computation introduced at layer ℓ. This observation allows us to conclude that every cooperative execution of $\mathcal{P}_\ell$ is also safe.

Finally, we check that the safety of the cooperative semantics of $\widetilde{\mathcal{P}}_\ell$ is ensured by the safety of the preemptive semantics of the next concurrent program $\mathcal{P}_{\ell+1}$. This connection is established by reasoning about the cooperative semantics of a concurrent checker program $\mathcal{C}_\ell$ that is automatically constructed from $\mathcal{LP}$.

Theorem 3 (Abstraction). *Let $\mathcal{LP}$ be a layered concurrent program with top layer h and $\ell \in [1, h]$. If CSafe($\mathcal{C}_\ell$) and Safe($\mathcal{P}_{\ell+1}$), then CSafe($\widetilde{\mathcal{P}}_\ell$).*

The checker program $\mathcal{C}_\ell$ is obtained by instrumenting the code of $\widetilde{\mathcal{P}}_\ell$ with extra variables and procedures that enable checking that procedures disappearing at layer ℓ refine their atomic action specifications (Sect. 4.2).

Our refinement check between two consecutive layers is summarized by the following corollary of Theorems 1–3.

Corollary 1. *Let $\mathcal{LP}$ be a layered concurrent program with top layer h and $\ell \in [1, h]$. If MSafe($\mathcal{P}_\ell$), CSafe($\mathcal{C}_\ell$) and Safe($\mathcal{P}_{\ell+1}$), then Safe($\mathcal{P}_\ell$).*

The soundness of our refinement checking methodology for layered concurrent programs is obtained by repeated application of Corollary 1.

Corollary 2. *Let $\mathcal{LP}$ be a layered concurrent program with top layer h. If MSafe($\mathcal{P}_\ell$) and CSafe($\mathcal{C}_\ell$) for all $\ell \in [1, h]$ and Safe($\mathcal{P}_{h+1}$), then Safe($\mathcal{P}_1$).*

4.1 From Preemptive to Cooperative Semantics

We present the judgment *MSafe*($\mathcal{P}$) that allows us to reason about a concurrent program $\mathcal{P}$ under cooperative semantics instead of preemptive semantics. Intuitively, we want to use the commutativity of individual atomic actions to rearrange the steps of any execution under preemptive semantics in such a way that it corresponds to an execution under cooperative semantics. We consider mappings $M \in Action \rightarrow \{\mathrm{N}, \mathrm{R}, \mathrm{L}, \mathrm{B}\}$ that assign mover types to atomic actions; N for non-mover, R for right mover, L for left mover, and B for both mover. The judgment *MSafe*($\mathcal{P}$) requires a mapping M that satisfies two conditions.

First, the atomic actions in $\mathcal{P}$ must satisfy the following logical commutativity conditions [7], which can be discharged by a theorem prover.

- *Commutativity:* If A_1 is a right mover or A_2 is a left mover, then the effect of A_1 followed by A_2 can also be achieved by A_2 followed by A_1.
- *Forward preservation:* If A_1 is a right mover or A_2 is a left mover, then the failure of A_2 after A_1 implies that A_2 must also fail before A_1.
- *Backward preservation:* If A_2 is a left mover (and A_1 is an arbitrary), then the failure of A_1 before A_2 implies that A_1 must also fail after A_2.
- *Nonblocking:* If A is a left mover, then A cannot block.

Second, the sequence of atomic actions in preemptive executions of $\mathcal{P}$ must be such that the desired rearrangement into cooperative executions is possible. Given a preemptive execution, consider, for each thread individually, a labeling of execution steps where atomic action steps are labeled with their mover type and procedure calls and returns are labeled with Y (for yield). The nondeterministic *atomicity automaton* $\mathcal{A}$ on the right defines all allowed sequences. Intuitively, when we map the execution steps of a thread to a run in the automaton, the state RM denotes that we are in the right mover phase in which we can stay until the occurrence of a non-right mover (L or N). Then we can stay in the left mover phase (state LM) by executing left movers, until a preemption point (Y) takes us back to RM. Let $\mathcal{E}$ be the mapping from edge labels to the set of edges that contain the label, e.g., $\mathcal{E}(\mathrm{R}) = \{\mathrm{RM} \rightarrow \mathrm{RM}, \mathrm{RM} \rightarrow \mathrm{LM}\}$. Thus we have a representation of mover types as sets of edges in $\mathcal{A}$, and we define $\mathcal{E}(A) = \mathcal{E}(M(A))$. Notice that the set representation is closed under relation composition $\circ$ and intersection, and behaves as expected, e.g., $\mathcal{E}(\mathrm{R}) \circ \mathcal{E}(\mathrm{L}) = \mathcal{E}(\mathrm{N})$.

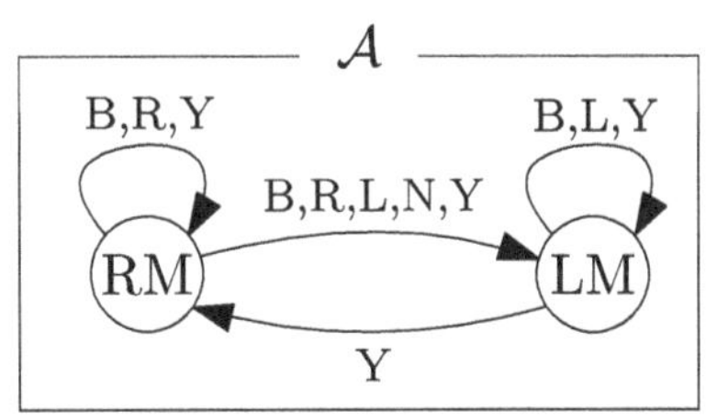

Now we define an intraprocedural control flow analysis that lifts $\mathcal{E}$ to a mapping $\widehat{\mathcal{E}}$ on statements. Intuitively, $x \rightarrow y \in \widehat{\mathcal{E}}(s)$ means that every execution of the statement s has a run in $\mathcal{A}$ from x to y. Our analysis does not have to be interprocedural, since procedure calls and returns are labeled with Y, allowing every possible state transition in $\mathcal{A}$. *MSafe*($\mathcal{P}$) requires $\widehat{\mathcal{E}}(s) \neq \varnothing$ for every procedure body s in $\mathcal{P}$, where $\widehat{\mathcal{E}}$ is defined as follows:

$$\widehat{\mathcal{E}}(\texttt{skip}) = \mathcal{E}(\text{B}) \quad \widehat{\mathcal{E}}(s_1 \texttt{ ; } s_2) = \widehat{\mathcal{E}}(s_1) \circ \widehat{\mathcal{E}}(s_2) \quad \widehat{\mathcal{E}}(\texttt{if } e \texttt{ then } s_1 \texttt{ else } s_2) = \widehat{\mathcal{E}}(s_1) \cap \widehat{\mathcal{E}}(s_2)$$

$$\widehat{\mathcal{E}}(\texttt{pcall } \overline{A}_1 \overline{P}\, \overline{A}_2) = \begin{cases} \mathcal{E}^*(\overline{A}_1 \overline{A}_2) & \text{if } \overline{P} = \varepsilon \\ \mathcal{E}(\text{L}) \circ \mathcal{E}^*(\overline{A}_1) \circ \mathcal{E}(\text{Y}) \circ \mathcal{E}^*(\overline{A}_2) \circ \mathcal{E}(\text{R}) & \text{if } \overline{P} \neq \varepsilon \end{cases}$$

Skip is a both mover, sequencing composes edges, and if takes the edges possible in both branches. In the arms of a pcall we omit writing the input and output maps because they are irrelevant to the analysis. Let us first focus on the case $\overline{P} = \varepsilon$ with no procedure arms. In the preemptive semantics all arms are arbitrarily interleaved and correspondingly we define the function

$$\mathcal{E}^*(A_1 \cdots A_n) = \bigcap_{\tau \in S_n} \mathcal{E}(A_{\tau(1)}) \circ \cdots \circ \mathcal{E}(A_{\tau(n)})$$

to consider all possible permutations (τ ranges over the symmetric group S_n) and take the edges possible in all permutations. Observe that $\mathcal{E}^*$ evaluates to non-empty in exactly four cases: $\mathcal{E}(\text{N})$ for $\{\text{B}\}^*\text{N}\{\text{B}\}^*$, $\mathcal{E}(\text{B})$ for $\{\text{B}\}^*$, $\mathcal{E}(\text{R})$ for $\{\text{R},\text{B}\}^* \setminus \{\text{B}\}^*$, and $\mathcal{E}(\text{L})$ for $\{\text{L},\text{B}\}^* \setminus \{\text{B}\}^*$. These are the mover-type sequences for which an arbitrary permutation (coming from a preemptive execution) can be rearranged to the order given by the pcall (corresponding to cooperative execution).

In the case $\overline{P} \neq \varepsilon$ there is a preemption point under cooperative semantics between $\overline{A}_1$ and $\overline{A}_2$, the actions in $\overline{A}_1$ are executed in order before the preemption, and the actions in $\overline{A}_2$ are executed in order after the preemption. To ensure that the cooperative execution can simulate an arbitrarily interleaved preemptive execution of the pcall, we must be able to move actions in $\overline{A}_1$ to the left and actions in $\overline{A}_2$ to the right of the preemption point. We enforce this condition by requiring that $\overline{A}_1$ is all left (or both) movers and $\overline{A}_2$ all right (or both) movers, expressed by the leading $\mathcal{E}(\text{L})$ and trailing $\mathcal{E}(\text{R})$ in the edge composition.

4.2 Refinement Checker Programs

In this section, we describe the construction of checker programs that justify the formal connection between successive concurrent programs in a layered concurrent program. The description is done by example. In particular, we show the checker program $\mathcal{C}_1^{lock}$ that establishes the connection between $\mathcal{P}_1^{lock}$ and $\mathcal{P}_2^{lock}$ (Fig. 3) of our running example.

Overview. Cooperative semantics splits any execution of $\mathcal{P}_1^{lock}$ into a sequence of preemption-free execution fragments separated by preemptions. Verification of $\mathcal{C}_1^{lock}$ must ensure that for all such executions, the set of procedures that disappear at layer 1 behave like their atomic action specifications. That is, the procedures `Enter` and `Leave` must behave like their specifications `ACQUIRE` and `RELEASE`, respectively. It is important to note that this goal of checking refinement is easier than verifying that $\mathcal{P}_1^{lock}$ is safe. Refinement checking may succeed even though $\mathcal{P}_1^{lock}$ fails; the guarantee of refinement is that such a failure can be simulated by a failure in $\mathcal{P}_2^{lock}$. The construction of $\mathcal{C}_1^{lock}$ can be understood in two steps. First, the program $\widetilde{\mathcal{P}}_1^{lock}$ shown in Fig. 7 extends $\mathcal{P}_1^{lock}$ (Fig. 3(a)) with the variables introduced at layer 1 (globals `lock`, `pos`, `slots` and locals `tid`) and the corresponding introduction actions (`iIncr` and `iSetLock`). Second, $\mathcal{C}_1^{lock}$ is obtained from $\widetilde{\mathcal{P}}_1^{lock}$ by instrumenting the procedures to encode the refinement check, described in the remainder of this section.

$\widetilde{\mathcal{P}}_1^{lock}$

```
var b : bool
var lock : int
var pos : int
var linear slots : set<int>

proc Main()
  if (*)
    pcall Worker(), Main()

proc Worker()
  var linear tid : int
  pcall tid := Alloc()
  pcall Enter(tid)
  pcall Leave(tid)

proc Alloc() : (linear tid : int)
  icall tid := iIncr()

iaction iIncr() : (tid : int)
  assert InvAlloc
  tid := pos
  pos := pos + 1
  slots := slots - tid

proc Enter(linear tid : int)
  var success : bool
  pcall success := CAS()
  if (success)
    icall iSetLock(tid)
  else
    pcall Enter(tid)

proc Leave(linear tid : int)
  pcall RESET()
  icall iSetLock(0)

iaction iSetLock(v : int)
  lock := v

atomic CAS() : (success : bool)
  if (b) success := false
  else   success, b := true, true

atomic RESET()
  assert b
  b := false
```

Fig. 7. Lock example (variable introduction at layer 1)

Context for Refinement. There are two kinds of procedures, those that continue to exist at layer 2 (such as `Main` and `Worker`) and those that disappear at layer 1 (such as `Enter` and `Leave`). $\mathcal{C}_1^{lock}$ does not need to verify anything about the first kind. These procedures only provide the context for refinement checking and thus all invocation of an atomic action (I, O, e, t) in any atomic-action arm of a pcall is converted into the invocation of a fresh atomic action $(I, O, \mathit{true}, e \wedge t)$. In other words, the assertions in procedures that continue to exist at layer 2 are converted into assumptions for the refinement checking at layer 1; these assertions are verified during the refinement checking on a higher layer. In our example, `Main` and `Worker` do not have atomic-action arms, although this is possible in general.

Refinement Instrumentation. We illustrate the instrumentation of procedures `Enter` and `Leave` in Fig. 8. The core idea is to track updates by preemption-free execution fragments to the shared variables that continue to exist at layer 2. There are two such variables—`lock` and `slots`. We capture snapshots of `lock` and `slots` in the local variables `_lock` and `_slots` and use these snapshots to check that the updates to `lock` and `slots` behave according to the refined atomic action. In general, any path from the start to the end of the body of a

$\mathcal{C}_1^{lock}$

```
macro *CHANGED* is !(lock == _lock && slots == _slots)
macro *RELEASE* is lock == 0 && slots == _slots
macro *ACQUIRE* is _lock == 0 && lock == tid && slots == _slots

proc Leave(linear tid)                       # Leave must behave like RELEASE
  var _lock, _slots, pc, done
  pc, done := false, false                   # initialize pc and done
  _lock, _slots := lock, slots               # take snapshot of global variables
  assume pc || (tid != 0 && lock == tid)     # assume gate of RELEASE

  pcall RESET()
  icall iSetLock(0)

  assert *CHANGED* ==> (!pc && *RELEASE*)    # state change must be the first and like RELEASE
  pc := pc || *CHANGED*                      # track if state changed
  done := done || *RELEASE*                  # track if RELEASE happened

  assert done                                # check that RELEASE happened

proc Enter(linear tid)                       # Enter must behave like ACQUIRE
  var success, _lock, _slots, pc, done
  pc, done := false, false                   # initialize pc and done
  _lock, _slots := lock, slots               # take snapshot of global variables
  assume pc || tid != 0                      # assume gate of ACQUIRE

  pcall success := CAS()
  if (success)
    icall iSetLock(tid)
  else
    assert *CHANGED* ==> (!pc && *ACQUIRE*)  # state change must be the first and like ACQUIRE
    pc := pc || *CHANGED*                    # track if state changed
    done := done || *ACQUIRE*                # track if ACQUIRE happened

    if (*)                                   # then: check refinement of caller
      pcall pc := Check_Enter_Enter(tid,     #   check annotated procedure arm
                                  tid, pc)   #     in fresh procedure (defined below)
      done := true                           #   above call ensures that ACQUIRE happened
    else                                     # else: check refinement of callee
      pcall Enter(tid)                       #   explore behavior of callee
      assume false                           #   block after return (only then is relevant below)

    _lock, _slots := lock, slots             # take snapshot of global variables
    assume pc || tid != 0                    # assume gate of ACQUIRE

  assert *CHANGED* ==> (!pc && *ACQUIRE*)    # state change must be the first and like ACQUIRE
  pc := pc || *CHANGED*                      # track if state changed
  done := done || *ACQUIRE*                  # track if ACQUIRE happened

  assert done                                # check that ACQUIRE happened

proc Check_Enter_Enter(tid, x, pc) : (pc')   # check annotated pcall from Enter to Enter
  var _lock, _slots
  _lock, _slots := lock, slots               # take snapshot of global variables
  assume pc || tid != 0                      # assume gate of ACQUIRE

  pcall ACQUIRE(x)                           # use ACQUIRE to "simulate" call to Enter

  assert *ACQUIRE*                           # check that ACQUIRE happened
  assert *CHANGED* ==> !pc                   # state change must be the first
  pc' := pc || *CHANGED*                     # track if state changed
```

Fig. 8. Instrumented procedures `Enter` and `Leave` (layer 1 checker program) procedure may comprise many preemption-free execution fragments. The checker program must ensure that exactly one of these fragments behaves like the specified atomic action; all other fragments must leave `lock` and `slot` unchanged. To track whether the atomic action has already happened, we use two local Boolean variables—`pc` and `done`. Both variables are initialized to *false*, get updated to *true* during the execution, and remain at *true* thereafter. The variable `pc` is set to *true* at the end of the first preemption-free execution fragment that modifies the tracked state, which is expressed by the macro `*CHANGED*` on line 1. The variable `done` is set to *true* at the end of the first preemption-free execution fragment that behaves like the refined atomic action. For that, the macros `*RELEASE*` and `*ACQUIRE*` on lines 2 and 3 express the transition relations of `RELEASE` and `ACQUIRE`, respectively. Observe that we have the invariant `pc ==> done`. The reason we need both `pc` and `done` is to handle the case where the refined atomic action may stutter (i.e., leave the state unchanged).

Instrumenting `Leave`. We first look at the instrumentation of `Leave`. Line 8 initializes the snapshot variables. Recall that a preemption inside the code of a procedure is introduced only at a pcall containing a procedure arm. Consequently, the body of `Leave` is preemption-free and we need to check refinement across a single execution fragment. This checking is done by lines 14–16. The assertion on line 14 checks that if any tracked variable has changed since the last snapshot, (1) such a change happens for the first time (`!pc`), and (2) the current value is related to the snapshot value according to the specification of `RELEASE`. Line 15 updates `pc` to track whether any change to the tracked variables has happened so far. Line 16 updates `done` to track whether `RELEASE` has happened so far. The assertion at line 18 checks that `RELEASE` has indeed happened before `Leave` returns. The assumption at line 9 blocks those executions which can be simulated by the failure of `RELEASE`. It achieves this effect by assuming the gate of `RELEASE` in states where `pc` is still *false* (i.e., `RELEASE` has not yet happened). The assumption yields the constraint `lock != 0` which together with the invariant `InvLock` (Fig. 6) proves that the gate of `RESET` does not fail.

The verification of `Leave` illustrates an important principle of our approach to refinement. The gates of atomic actions invoked by a procedure P disappearing at layer ℓ are verified using a combination of invariants established on $\mathcal{C}_\ell$ and pending assertions at layer $\ell + 1$ encoded as the gate of the atomic action refined by P. For `Leave` specifically, `assert b` in `RESET` is propagated to `assert tid != nil && lock == tid` in `RELEASE`. The latter assertion is verified in the checker program $\mathcal{C}_2^{lock}$ when `Worker`, the caller of `RELEASE`, is shown to refine the action `SKIP` which is guaranteed not to fail since its gate is *true*.

Instrumenting `Enter`. The most sophisticated feature in a concurrent program is a pcall. The instrumentation of `Leave` explains the instrumentation of the simplest kind of pcall with only atomic-action arms. We now illustrate the instrumentation of a pcall containing a procedure arm using the procedure `Enter` which refines the atomic action `ACQUIRE` and contains a pcall to `Enter` itself. The instrumentation of this pcall is contained in lines 30–43.

A pcall with a procedure arm is challenging for two reasons. First, the callee disappears at the same layer as the caller so the checker program must reason about refinement for both the caller and the callee. This challenge is addressed by the code in lines 34–40. At line 34, we introduce a nondeterministic choice between two code paths—`then` branch to check refinement of the caller and `else` branch to check refinement of the callee. An explanation for this nondeterministic choice is given in the next two paragraphs. Second, a pcall with a procedure arm introduces a preemption creating multiple preemption-free execution fragments. This challenge is addressed by two pieces of code. First, we check that `lock` and `slots` are updated correctly (lines 30–32) by the preemption-free execution fragment ending before the pcall. Second, we update the snapshot variables (line 42) to enable the verification of the preemption-free execution fragment beginning after the pcall.

Lines 35–37 in the `then` branch check refinement against the atomic action specification of the caller, exploiting the atomic action specification of the callee. The actual verification is performed in a fresh procedure `Check_Enter_Enter` invoked on line 35. Notice that this procedure depends on both the caller and the callee (indicated in colors), and that it preserves a necessary preemption point. The procedure has input parameters `tid` to receive the input of the caller (for refinement checking) and `x` to receive the input of the callee (to generate the behavior of the callee). Furthermore, `pc` may be updated in `Check_Enter_Enter` and thus passed as both an input and output parameter. In the body of the procedure, the invocation of action `ACQUIRE` on line 56 overapproximates the behavior of the callee. In the layered concurrent program (Fig. 6), the (recursive) pcall to `Enter` in the body of `Enter` is annotated with 1. This annotation indicates that for any execution passing through this pcall, `ACQUIRE` is deemed to occur during the execution of its unique arm. This is reflected in the checker program by updating `done` to *true* on line 37; the update is justified because of the assertion in `Check_Enter_Enter` at line 58. If the pcall being translated was instead unannotated, line 37 would be omitted.

Lines 39–40 in the `else` branch ensure that using the atomic action specification of the callee on line 56 is justified. Allowing the execution to continue to the callee ensures that the called procedure is invoked in all states allowed by $\mathcal{P}_1$. However, the execution is blocked once the call returns to ensure that downstream code sees the side-effect on `pc` and the snapshot variables.

To summarize, the crux of our instrumentation of procedure arms is to combine refinement checking of caller and callee. We explore the behaviors of the callee to check its refinement. At the same time, we exploit the atomic action specification of the callee to check refinement of the caller.

Instrumenting Unannotated Procedure Arms. Procedure `Enter` illustrates the instrumentation of an annotated procedure arm. The instrumentation of an unannotated procedure arm (both in an annotated or unannotated pcall) is simpler, because we only need to check that the tracked state is not modified. For such an arm to a procedure refining atomic action `Action`, we introduce a procedure `Check_Action` (which is independent of the caller) comprising three instructions: take snapshots, `pcall A`, and `assert !*CHANGED*`.

Pcalls with Multiple Arms. Our examples show the instrumentation of pcalls with a single arm. Handling multiple arms is straightforward, since each arm is translated independently. Atomic action arms stay unmodified, annotated procedure arms are replaced with the corresponding `Check_Caller_Callee` procedure, and unannotated procedure arms are replaced with the corresponding `Check_Action` procedure.

Output Parameters. Our examples illustrate refinement checking for atomic actions that have no output parameters. In general, a procedure and its atomic action specification may return values in output parameters. We handle this generalization but lack of space does not allow us to present the technical details.

5 Conclusion

In this paper, we presented layered concurrent programs, a programming notation to succinctly capture a multi-layered refinement proof capable of connecting a deeply-detailed implementation to a highly-abstract specification. We presented an algorithm to extract from the concurrent layered program the individual concurrent programs, from the most concrete to the most abstract. We also presented an algorithm to extract a collection of refinement checker programs that establish the connection among the sequence of concurrent programs encoded by the layered concurrent program. The cooperative safety of the checker programs and the preemptive safety of the most abstract concurrent program suffices to prove the preemptive safety of the most concrete concurrent program.

Layered programs have been implemented in CIVL, a deductive verifier for concurrent programs, implemented as a conservative extension to the Boogie verifier [3]. CIVL has been used to verify a complex concurrent garbage collector [6] and a state-of-the-art data-race detection algorithm [15]. In addition to these two large benchmarks, around fifty smaller programs (including a ticket lock and a lock-free stack) are available at https://github.com/boogie-org/boogie.

There are several directions for future work. We did not discuss how to verify an individual checker program. CIVL uses the Owicki-Gries method [13] and rely-guarantee reasoning [8] to verify checker programs. But researchers are exploring many different techniques for verification of concurrent programs. It would be interesting to investigate whether heterogeneous techniques could be brought to bear on checker programs at different layers.

In this paper, we focused exclusively on verification and did not discuss code generation, an essential aspect of any programming system targeting the construction of verified programs. There is a lot of work to be done in connecting the most concrete program in a concurrent layered program to executable code. Most likely, different execution platforms will impose different obligations on the most concrete program and the general idea of layered concurrent programs would be specialized for different target platforms.

Scalable verification is a challenge as the size of programs being verified increases. Traditionally, scalability has been addressed using modular verification techniques but only for single-layer programs. It would be interesting to explore modularity techniques for concurrent layered programs in the context of a refinement-oriented proof system.

Layered concurrent programs bring new challenges and opportunities to the design of programming languages and development environments. Integrating layers into a programming language requires intuitive syntax to specify layer information and atomic actions. For example, ordered layer names can be more readable and easier to refactor than layer numbers. An integrated development environment could provide different views of the layered concurrent program. For example, it could show the concurrent program, the checker program, and the introduced code at a particular layer. Any updates made in these views should be automatically reflected back into the layered concurrent program.

Acknowledgements. We thank Hana Chockler, Stephen Freund, Thomas A. Henzinger, Viktor Toman, and James R. Wilcox for comments that improved this paper. This research was supported in part by the Austrian Science Fund (FWF) under grants S11402-N23 (RiSE/SHiNE) and Z211-N23 (Wittgenstein Award).

References

1. Abrial, J.-R.: The B-Book - Assigning Programs to Meanings. Cambridge University Press, Cambridge (2005)
2. Abrial, J.-R., Butler, M.J., Hallerstede, S., Hoang, T.S., Mehta, F., Voisin, L.: Rodin: an open toolset for modelling and reasoning in Event-B. STTT **12**(6), 447–466 (2010). https://doi.org/10.1007/s10009-010-0145-y
3. Barnett, M., Chang, B.-Y.E., DeLine, R., Jacobs, B., Leino, K.R.M.: Boogie: a modular reusable verifier for object-oriented programs. In: de Boer, F.S., Bonsangue, M.M., Graf, S., de Roever, W.-P. (eds.) FMCO 2005. LNCS, vol. 4111, pp. 364–387. Springer, Heidelberg (2006). https://doi.org/10.1007/11804192_17
4. Elmas, T., Qadeer, S., Tasiran, S.: A calculus of atomic actions. In: Shao, Z., Pierce, B.C. (eds.) POPL 2009, pp. 2–15. ACM (2009). https://doi.org/10.1145/1480881.1480885
5. Flanagan, C., Qadeer, S.: A type and effect system for atomicity. In: Cytron, R., Gupta, R. (eds.) PLDI 2003, pp. 338–349. ACM (2003). https://doi.org/10.1145/781131.781169
6. Hawblitzel, C., Petrank, E., Qadeer, S., Tasiran, S.: Automated and modular refinement reasoning for concurrent programs. In: Kroening, D., Păsăreanu, C.S. (eds.) CAV 2015. LNCS, vol. 9207, pp. 449–465. Springer, Cham (2015). https://doi.org/10.1007/978-3-319-21668-3_26
7. Hawblitzel, C., Petrank, E., Qadeer, S., Tasiran, S.: Automated and modular refinement reasoning for concurrent programs. Technical report MSR-TR-2015-8, Microsoft Research, February 2015. https://www.microsoft.com/en-us/research/publication/automated-and-modular-refinement-reasoning-for-concurrent-programs/
8. Jones, C.B.: Specification and design of (parallel) programs. In: IFIP Congress (1983)

9. Lamport, L.: Specifying Systems: The TLA+ Language and Tools for Hardware and Software Engineers. Addison-Wesley, Boston (2002)
10. Lipton, R.J.: Reduction: a method of proving properties of parallel programs. Commun. ACM **18**(12), 717–721 (1975). https://doi.org/10.1145/361227.361234
11. McMillan, K.L.: A compositional rule for hardware design refinement. In: Grumberg, O. (ed.) CAV 1997. LNCS, vol. 1254, pp. 24–35. Springer, Heidelberg (1997). https://doi.org/10.1007/3-540-63166-6_6
12. McMillan, K.L.: Verification of an implementation of Tomasulo's algorithm by compositional model checking. In: Hu, A.J., Vardi, M.Y. (eds.) CAV 1998. LNCS, vol. 1427, pp. 110–121. Springer, Heidelberg (1998). https://doi.org/10.1007/BFb0028738
13. Owicki, S.S., Gries, D.: Verifying properties of parallel programs: an axiomatic approach. Commun. ACM **19**(5), 279–285 (1976). https://doi.org/10.1145/360051.360224
14. Wadler, P.: Linear types can change the world! In: Programming Concepts and Methods (1990)
15. Wilcox, J.R., Flanagan, C., Freund, S.N.: VerifiedFT: a verified, high-performance precise dynamic race detector. In: Krall, A., Gross, T.R. (eds.) PPoPP 2018, pp. 354–367. ACM (2018). https://doi.org/10.1145/3178487.3178514

Model Checking

Propositional Dynamic Logic for Higher-Order Functional Programs

Yuki Satake(✉) and Hiroshi Unno

University of Tsukuba, Tsukuba, Japan
{satake,uhiro}@logic.cs.tsukuba.ac.jp

Abstract. We present an extension of propositional dynamic logic called HOT-PDL for specifying temporal properties of higher-order functional programs. The semantics of HOT-PDL is defined over Higher-Order Traces (HOTs) that model execution traces of higher-order programs. A HOT is a sequence of events such as function calls and returns, equipped with two kinds of pointers inspired by the notion of justification pointers from game semantics: one for capturing the correspondence between call and return events, and the other for capturing higher-order control flow involving a function that is passed to or returned by a higher-order function. To allow traversal of the new kinds of pointers, HOT-PDL extends PDL with new path expressions. The extension enables HOT-PDL to specify interesting properties of higher-order programs, including stack-based access control properties and those definable using dependent refinement types. We show that HOT-PDL model checking of higher-order functional programs over bounded integers is decidable via a reduction to modal μ-calculus model checking of higher-order recursion schemes.

1 Introduction

Temporal verification of higher-order programs has been an emerging research topic [12,14,18,22–24,26,27,31,34]. The specification languages used there are (ω-)regular word languages (that subsume LTL) [12,18,26] and modal μ-calculus (that subsumes CTL) [14,24,31], which are interpreted over sequences or trees consisting of events. (Extended) dependent refinement types are also used to specify temporal [23,27] and branching properties [34]. These specification languages, however, cannot sufficiently express specifications of control flow involving (higher-order) functions. For example, let us consider the following simple higher-order program $D_{\texttt{tw}}$ (in OCaml syntax):

```
let tw f x = f (f x) in let inc x = x + 1 in let r = * in tw inc r
```

Here, $*$ denotes a non-deterministic integer, and the higher-order function $\texttt{tw} : (\texttt{int} \to \texttt{int}) \to \texttt{int} \to \texttt{int}$ applies its function argument $\texttt{f} : \texttt{int} \to \texttt{int}$ to the integer argument $\texttt{x}$ twice. For example, for $\texttt{r} = 0$, the program $D_{\texttt{tw}}$ exhibits the following call-by-value reduction sequence (with the redexes underlined).

$$\underline{\texttt{tw inc}}\ 0 \longrightarrow \underline{(\lambda x.\texttt{inc}\ (\texttt{inc}\ x))\ 0} \longrightarrow \texttt{inc}\ (\underline{\texttt{inc}\ 0}) \longrightarrow^* \underline{\texttt{inc}\ 1} \longrightarrow^* 2$$

H. Chockler and G. Weissenbacher (Eds.): CAV 2018, LNCS 10981, pp. 105–123, 2018.
https://doi.org/10.1007/978-3-319-96145-3_6

Example properties of the program $D_{\mathtt{tw}}$ that cannot be expressed by the previous specification languages are:

Prop.1. If the function returned by a partial application of `tw` to some function (e.g., $\lambda x.$`inc` (`inc` x) in the above sequence) is called with some integer n, the function argument passed to `tw` (i.e., `inc`) is eventually called with n.

Prop.2. If the function returned by a partial application of `tw` to some function is never called, then the function argument passed to `tw` is never called.

To remedy the limitation, we introduce a notion of Higher-Order Trace (HOT) that captures the control flow of higher-order programs and propose a dynamic logic over HOTs called Higher-Order Trace Propositional Dynamic Logic (HOT-PDL) for specifying temporal properties of higher-order programs.

Intuitively, a HOT models a program execution trace which is a possibly infinite sequence of events such as function calls and returns with information about actual arguments and return values. Furthermore, HOTs are equipped with two kinds of pointers to enable precise specification of control flow: one for capturing the correspondence between call and return events, and the other for capturing higher-order control flow involving a function that is passed to or returned by a higher-order function. The two kinds of pointers are inspired by the notion of justification pointers from the game semantics of PCF [1,2,19,20].

For the higher-order program $D_{\mathtt{tw}}$, for $\mathtt{r} = 0$, we get the following HOT $G_{\mathtt{tw}}$:[1]

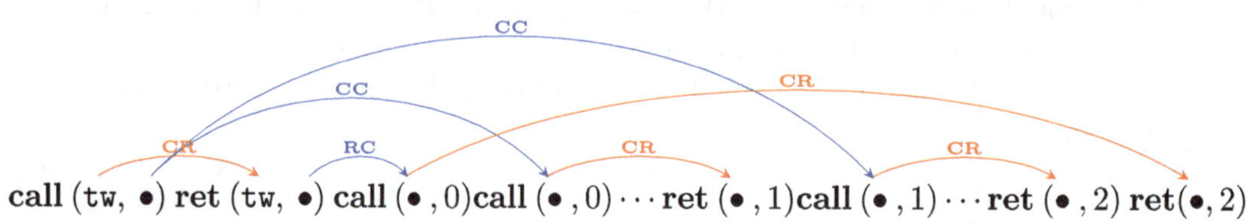

Here, • represents some function value, **call**(f, v) represents a call event of the function f with the argument v, and **ret**(f, v) represents a return event of the function f with the return value v. This trace corresponds to the previous reduction sequence: the call events **call**(`tw`, •), **call**(•, 0), **call**(•, 0), and **call**(•, 1) that occur in the trace in this order correspond respectively to the redexes `tw inc`, ($\lambda x.$`inc` (`inc` x)) 0, `inc` 0, and `inc` 1. The three important points here are that (1) the call events have pointers labeled with CR to the corresponding return events **ret**(`tw`, •), **ret**(•, 2), **ret**(•, 1), and **ret**(•, 2), (2) the call event **call**(`tw`, •) has two pointers labeled with CC, where • represents the function argument `f` of `tw` and the pointed call events **call**(•, 0) and **call**(•, 1) represent the two calls to `f` in `tw`, and (3) the return event **ret**(`tw`, •) has a pointer labeled with RC, where • represents the partially-applied function $\lambda x.$`inc` (`inc` x) and the pointed call event **call**(•, 0) represents the call to the function.

To allow traversal of the pointers, HOT-PDL extends propositional dynamic logic with new path expressions (see Sect. 3 for details). The extension enables

---

[1] The symbol ··· indicates the omission of a subsequence. The two omitted subsequences are **call**(`inc`, 0) $\overset{\text{CR}}{\frown}$ **ret**(`inc`, 1) and **call**(`inc`, 1) $\overset{\text{CR}}{\frown}$ **ret**(`inc`, 2) in this order.

HOT-PDL to specify interesting properties of higher-order programs, including stack-based access control properties and those definable using dependent refinement types. Here, stack-based access control is a security mechanism implemented in runtimes like JVM for ensuring secure execution of programs that have components with different levels of trust: the mechanism ensures that a *security-critical* function (e.g., file access) is invoked only if all the (immediate and indirect) callers in the current call stack are *trusted*, or one of the callers is a *privileged* function and its callees are all *trusted*. We introduce a new variant of stack-based access control properties for higher-order programs, formalized in HOT-PDL from the point of view of interactions among callers and callees.

Compared to the previous specification languages with respect to the expressiveness, HOT-PDL subsumes (ω-)regular languages because PDL interpreted over words is already as expressive as them [15]. Temporal logics over nested words [6] such as CaRet [5] and NWTL [4] can capture the correspondence between call and return events (i.e., pointers labeled with **CR**) but cannot capture higher-order control flow (i.e., pointers labeled with **CC** and **RC**). Branching properties (expressible in, e.g., CTL), however, are out of the scope of the present paper, and such an extension of HOT-PDL remains an interesting future direction. Dependent refinement types are often used to specify properties of higher-order programs for partial- and total-correctness verification [29,33,39,40]. For example, the following properties of the program $D_{\mathtt{tw}}$ are expressible:

Prop.3. The function yielded by applying `tw` to a strictly increasing function is strictly increasing.

Prop.4. The function yielded by applying `tw` to a terminating function is terminating.

This paper shows that HOT-PDL can encode such dependent refinement types.

We also study HOT-PDL model checking: given a higher-order program D over bounded integers and a HOT-PDL formula ϕ, the problem is to decide whether ϕ is satisfied by all the execution traces of D modeled as HOTs. We show the decidability of HOT-PDL model checking via a reduction to modal μ-calculus model checking of higher-order recursion schemes [21,28].

The rest of the paper is organized as follows. Section 2 formalizes HOTs and explains how to use them to model execution traces of higher-order functional programs. Section 3 defines the syntax and the semantics of HOT-PDL and Sect. 4 shows how to encode stack-based access control properties and dependent refinement types in HOT-PDL. Section 5 discusses HOT-PDL model checking. We compare HOT-PDL with related work in Sect. 6 and conclude the paper with remarks on future work in Sect. 7. Omitted proofs are given in the extended version of this paper [30].

2 Higher-Order Traces

This section defines the notion of Higher-Order Trace (HOT), which is used to model execution traces of higher-order programs. To this end, we first define *(Σ, Γ)-labeled directed graphs* and *DAGs*.

Definition 1 ((Σ, Γ)-labeled directed graphs). *Let Σ be a finite set of node labels and Γ be a finite set of edge labels. A (Σ, Γ)-*labeled directed graph* is defined as a triple (V, λ, ν), where V is a countable set of nodes, $\lambda : V \to \Sigma$ is a node labeling function, and $\nu : V \times V \to 2^{\Gamma}$ is an edge labeling function. We call a (Σ, Γ)-labeled directed graph that has no directed cycle (Σ, Γ)-labeled DAG.*

Note that an edge may have multiple labels. For nodes $u, u' \in V$, $\nu(u, u') = \emptyset$ means that there is no edge from u to u'. We use σ and γ as meta-variables ranging respectively over Σ and Γ. We write V_σ for the set $\{u \in V \mid \sigma = \lambda(u)\}$ of all the nodes labeled with σ. We also write V_Σ for the set $\bigcup_{\sigma \in \Sigma} V_\sigma$. For $u, u' \in V$, we write $u \prec_\gamma u'$ if $\gamma \in \nu(u, u')$. A binary relation $\prec_\gamma^+$ (resp. $\prec_\gamma^*$) denotes the transitive (resp. reflexive and transitive) closure of $\prec_\gamma$.

Definition 2 (HOTs). *A HOT is a (Σ, Γ)-DAG, $G = (V, \lambda, \nu)$ that satisfies:*

1. *$V \neq \emptyset$, $\Gamma = \{\mathbf{N}, \mathbf{CR}, \mathbf{CC}, \mathbf{RC}\}$, $\Sigma = \Sigma_{\mathbf{call}} \uplus \Sigma_{\mathbf{ret}}$, and $\Sigma_{\mathbf{call}} = \Sigma_{\mathbf{call}}^T \uplus \Sigma_{\mathbf{call}}^A$*
2. *$\prec_{\mathbf{CR}} \subseteq (V_{\Sigma_{\mathbf{call}}} \times V_{\Sigma_{\mathbf{ret}}})$, $\prec_{\mathbf{CC}} \subseteq (V_{\Sigma_{\mathbf{call}}} \times V_{\Sigma_{\mathbf{call}}^A})$, and $\prec_{\mathbf{RC}} \subseteq (V_{\Sigma_{\mathbf{ret}}} \times V_{\Sigma_{\mathbf{call}}^A})$.*
3. *The elements of V are linearly ordered by $\prec_{\mathbf{N}}$*
4. *If $u \prec_{\mathbf{CR}} u'$ and $u \prec_{\mathbf{CR}} u''$, then $u' = u''$.*
5. *For all $u' \in V_{\Sigma_{\mathbf{ret}}}$, there uniquely exists $u \in V_{\Sigma_{\mathbf{call}}}$ such that $u \prec_{\mathbf{CR}} u'$ holds.*
6. *For all $u' \in V_{\Sigma_{\mathbf{call}}^A}$, there uniquely exists $u \in V$ such that $u \prec_{\mathbf{CC}} u'$ or $u \prec_{\mathbf{RC}} u'$ holds.*

Intuitively, $\Sigma_{\mathbf{call}}$ (resp. $\Sigma_{\mathbf{ret}}$) represents a set of call (resp. return) events. $\Sigma_{\mathbf{call}}^T$ (resp. $\Sigma_{\mathbf{call}}^A$) represents a set of call events of top-level functions (resp. functions that are returned by or passed to (higher-order) functions). $u \prec_{\mathbf{N}} u'$ means that u' is the next event of u in the trace. $u \prec_{\mathbf{CR}} u'$ indicates that u' is the return event corresponding to the call event u. $u \prec_{\mathbf{CC}} u'$ represents that u' is a call event of the function argument passed at the call event u. $u \prec_{\mathbf{RC}} u'$ means that u' is a call event of the partially-applied function returned at the return event u. We call the minimum node of a HOT G with respect to $\prec_{\mathbf{N}}$ the *root node*, denoted by 0_G. For HOTs G_1 and G_2, we say G_1 is a *prefix* of G_2 and write $G_1 \preceq G_2$, if G_1 is a sub-graph of G_2 such that $0_{G_1} = 0_{G_2}$. Note that the HOT $G_{\mathtt{tw}}$ in Sect. 1, where $\mathbf{N}$-labeled edges are omitted, satisfies the above conditions, with $\{\mathbf{call}(\mathtt{tw}, \bullet), \mathbf{call}(\mathtt{inc}, 0), \mathbf{call}(\mathtt{inc}, 1)\} \subseteq \Sigma_{\mathbf{call}}^T$, $\{\mathbf{call}(\bullet, 0), \mathbf{call}(\bullet, 1)\} \subseteq \Sigma_{\mathbf{call}}^A$, and $\{\mathbf{ret}(\mathtt{tw}, \bullet), \mathbf{ret}(\mathtt{inc}, 1), \mathbf{ret}(\mathtt{inc}, 2), \mathbf{ret}(\bullet, 1), \mathbf{ret}(\bullet, 2)\} \subseteq \Sigma_{\mathbf{ret}}$.

2.1 Trace Semantics for Higher-Order Functional Programs

We now formalize our target language $\mathcal{L}$, which is an ML-like typed call-by-value higher-order functional language. The syntax is defined by

$$\begin{array}{rl}
\text{(programs)} & D ::= \{f_1 \mapsto \lambda x.e_1, \dots, f_m \mapsto \lambda x.e_m\} \\
\text{(expressions)} & e ::= x \mid f \mid \lambda x.e \mid e_1\ e_2 \mid n \mid \mathtt{op}(e_1, e_2) \mid \mathtt{ifz}\ e_1\ e_2\ e_3 \\
\text{(values)} & v ::= f \mid \lambda x.e \mid n \\
\text{(types)} & \tau ::= \mathtt{int} \mid \tau_1 \to \tau_2
\end{array}$$

Here, x and f are meta-variables ranging respectively over term variables and names of top-level functions. The meta-variable n ranges over the set of bounded integers $\mathbb{Z}_b = \{n_{\mathbf{min}}, \cdots, n_{\mathbf{max}}\} \subset \mathbb{Z}$. For simplicity of presentation, $\mathcal{L}$ has the type `int` of bounded integers as the only base type. `op` represents binary operators such as $+$, $-$, $\times$, $=$, and $>$. The binary relations $=$ and $>$ return an integer that encodes a boolean value (e.g., 1 for `true` and 0 for `false`). A program D maps each top-level function name f_i to its definition $\lambda x.e_i$. We write $\mathrm{dom}(D)$ for $\{f_1, \ldots, f_m\}$. We assume that D has the main function `main` of the type $\mathtt{int} \to \mathtt{int}$. The functions in D can be mutually recursive. Expressions e comprise variables x, function names f, lambda abstractions $\lambda x.e$, function applications $e_1\ e_2$, bounded integers n, binary operations $\mathtt{op}(v_1, v_2)$, and conditional branches $\mathtt{ifz}\ e_1\ e_2\ e_3$. We assume that expressions are simply-typed. As usual, the simple type system guarantees that an evaluation of a typed expression never causes a runtime type mismatch like $1 + \lambda x.x$. An expression $\mathtt{ifz}\ e_1\ e_2\ e_3$ evaluates to e_2 (resp. e_3) if e_1 evaluates to 0 (resp. a non-zero integer). For example, the program $D_{\mathtt{tw}}$ in Sect. 1 is defined in $\mathcal{L}$ as follows:

$$D_{\mathtt{tw}} \triangleq \{\mathtt{tw} \mapsto \lambda f.\lambda x.f\ (f\ x), \mathtt{inc} \mapsto \lambda x.x + 1, \mathtt{main} \mapsto \lambda r.\mathtt{tw}\ \mathtt{inc}\ r\}$$

Domains

$$\begin{array}{rl}
\text{(configurations)} & C ::= (I, E[e]) \\
\text{(eval. contexts)} & E ::= [\,] \mid E\ e \mid v\ E \mid \mathtt{op}(E, e) \mid \mathtt{op}(v, E) \mid \mathtt{ifz}\ E\ e_1\ e_2 \mid \mathtt{ret}(h, i, E) \\
\text{(interfaces)} & I ::= \left\{h_1 \stackrel{i_1}{\mapsto} v_1, \ldots, h_m \stackrel{i_m}{\mapsto} v_m\right\} \\
\text{(handles)} & h ::= n \mid f \mid \lfloor h \rfloor_i \mid \lceil h \rceil_i \\
\text{(events)} & \alpha ::= \mathbf{call}(h_1, i, h_2) \mid \mathbf{ret}(h_1, i, h_2)
\end{array}$$

Derivation Rules

$$(I, E[(\lambda x.e)\ v]) \xrightarrow{\epsilon} (I, E[[v/x]e]) \quad (\textsc{App})$$

$$\frac{n = [\![\mathsf{op}]\!](n_1, n_2)}{(I, E[\mathsf{op}(n_1, n_2)]) \xrightarrow{\epsilon} (I, E[n])} \quad (\textsc{Op})$$

$$(I, E[\mathtt{ifz}\ 0\ e_1\ e_2]) \xrightarrow{\epsilon} (I, E[e_1]) \quad (\textsc{IfZ})$$

$$\frac{n \neq 0}{(I, E[\mathtt{ifz}\ n\ e_1\ e_2]) \xrightarrow{\epsilon} (I, E[e_2])} \quad (\textsc{IfN})$$

$$C \stackrel{\epsilon}{\Rightarrow} C \quad (\textsc{Refl})$$

$$\frac{C \xrightarrow{\varpi_1} C'' \qquad C'' \xRightarrow{\varpi_2} C'}{C \xRightarrow{\varpi_1 \cdot \varpi_2} C'} \quad (\textsc{Tran})$$

$$\frac{C \xrightarrow{\varpi} C' \qquad C' \stackrel{\pi}{\Rightarrow} \bot}{C \xRightarrow{\varpi \cdot \pi} \bot} \quad (\textsc{Tran}\omega)$$

$$\frac{(h \stackrel{i}{\mapsto} v) \in I \qquad \alpha = \mathbf{call}(h, i, n) \qquad I' = I\left\{h \stackrel{i+1}{\mapsto} v\right\}}{(I, E[h\ n]) \xrightarrow{\alpha} (I', E[\mathtt{ret}(h, i, v\ n)])} \quad (\textsc{CInt})$$

$$\frac{v \text{ is a function} \qquad (h \stackrel{i}{\mapsto} v') \in I \qquad \alpha = \mathbf{call}(h, i, \lfloor h \rfloor_i) \qquad I' = I\left\{h \stackrel{i+1}{\mapsto} v', \lfloor h \rfloor_i \stackrel{0}{\mapsto} v\right\}}{(I, E[h\ v]) \xrightarrow{\alpha} (I', E[\mathtt{ret}(h, i, v'\ \lfloor h \rfloor_i)])} \quad (\textsc{CFun})$$

$$\frac{\alpha = \mathbf{ret}(h, i, n)}{(I, E[\mathtt{ret}(h, i, n)]) \xrightarrow{\alpha} (I, E[n])} \quad (\textsc{RInt})$$

$$\frac{v \text{ is a function} \qquad \alpha = \mathbf{ret}(h, i, \lceil h \rceil_i) \qquad I' = I\left\{\lceil h \rceil_i \stackrel{0}{\mapsto} v\right\}}{(I, E[\mathtt{ret}(h, i, v)]) \xrightarrow{\alpha} (I', E[\lceil h \rceil_i])} \quad (\textsc{RFun})$$

Fig. 1. Labeled transition relations ($\stackrel{\varpi}{\Rightarrow}$) and ($\stackrel{\pi}{\Rightarrow}$) for $\mathcal{L}$

$$
\begin{array}{rl|l}
 & (I_1, \mathtt{main}\ 0) & I_1 \triangleq \left\{ \begin{array}{c} \mathtt{tw} \overset{0}{\mapsto} e_{\mathtt{tw}}, \\ \mathtt{inc} \overset{0}{\mapsto} \lambda x.x+1, \\ \mathtt{main} \overset{0}{\mapsto} \lambda r.\mathtt{tw}\ \mathtt{inc}\ r \end{array} \right\} \\
\xrightarrow{\mathtt{call}(\mathtt{main},0,0)} & (I_2, E_{\mathtt{main}}[(\lambda r.\mathtt{tw}\ \mathtt{inc}\ r)\ 0]) & I_2 \triangleq I_1 \left\{ \mathtt{main} \overset{1}{\mapsto} \lambda r.\mathtt{tw}\ \mathtt{inc}\ r \right\} \\
\longrightarrow & (I_2, E_{\mathtt{main}}[\mathtt{tw}\ \mathtt{inc}\ 0]) & \\
\xrightarrow{\mathtt{call}(\mathtt{tw},0,\lfloor\mathtt{tw}\rfloor_0)} & (I_3, E_{\mathtt{tw}}[(\lambda f.\lambda x.f\ (f\ x))\ \lfloor\mathtt{tw}\rfloor_0]) & I_3 \triangleq I_2 \left\{ \mathtt{tw} \overset{1}{\mapsto} e_{\mathtt{tw}}, \lfloor\mathtt{tw}\rfloor_0 \overset{0}{\mapsto} \mathtt{inc} \right\} \\
\longrightarrow & (I_3, E_{\mathtt{tw}}[\lambda x.\ \lfloor\mathtt{tw}\rfloor_0\ (\lfloor\mathtt{tw}\rfloor_0\ x)]) & \\
\xrightarrow{\mathtt{ret}(\mathtt{tw},0,\lceil\mathtt{tw}\rceil_0)} & (I_4, E_{\mathtt{main}}[\lceil\mathtt{tw}\rceil_0\ 0]) & I_4 \triangleq I_3 \left\{ \lceil\mathtt{tw}\rceil_0 \overset{0}{\mapsto} e'_{\mathtt{tw}} \right\} \\
\xrightarrow{\mathtt{call}(\lceil\mathtt{tw}\rceil_0,0,0)} & (I_5, E_{\lceil\mathtt{tw}\rceil_0}[(\lambda x.\ \lfloor\mathtt{tw}\rfloor_0\ (\lfloor\mathtt{tw}\rfloor_0\ x))\ 0]) & I_5 \triangleq I_4 \left\{ \lceil\mathtt{tw}\rceil_0 \overset{1}{\mapsto} e'_{\mathtt{tw}} \right\} \\
\longrightarrow & (I_5, E_{\lceil\mathtt{tw}\rceil_0}[\lfloor\mathtt{tw}\rfloor_0\ (\lfloor\mathtt{tw}\rfloor_0\ 0)]) & \\
\xrightarrow{\mathtt{call}(\lfloor\mathtt{tw}\rfloor_0,0,0)} & (I_6, E_{\lfloor\mathtt{tw}\rfloor_0}[\mathtt{inc}\ 0]) & I_6 \triangleq I_5 \left\{ \lfloor\mathtt{tw}\rfloor_0 \overset{1}{\mapsto} \mathtt{inc} \right\} \\
\xrightarrow{\mathtt{call}(\mathtt{inc},0,0)} & (I_7, E_{\mathtt{inc}}[(\lambda x.x+1)\ 0]) & I_7 \triangleq I_6 \left\{ \mathtt{inc} \overset{1}{\mapsto} \lambda x.x+1 \right\} \\
\Longrightarrow & (I_7, E_{\mathtt{inc}}[1]) & \\
\xRightarrow{\mathtt{ret}(\mathtt{inc},0,1)\cdot\mathtt{ret}(\lfloor\mathtt{tw}\rfloor_0,0,1)} & (I_7, E_{\lceil\mathtt{tw}\rceil_0}[\lfloor\mathtt{tw}\rfloor_0\ 1]) & \\
\xrightarrow{\mathtt{call}(\lfloor\mathtt{tw}\rfloor_0,1,1)} & (I_8, E_{\lfloor\mathtt{tw}\rfloor'_0}[\mathtt{inc}\ 1]) & I_8 \triangleq I_7 \left\{ \lfloor\mathtt{tw}\rfloor_0 \overset{2}{\mapsto} \mathtt{inc} \right\} \\
\xrightarrow{\mathtt{call}(\mathtt{inc},1,1)} & (I_9, E_{\mathtt{inc}'}[(\lambda x.x+1)\ 1]) & I_9 \triangleq I_8 \left\{ \mathtt{inc} \overset{2}{\mapsto} \lambda x.x+1 \right\} \\
\Longrightarrow & (I_9, E_{\mathtt{inc}'}[2]) & \\
\xRightarrow{\mathtt{ret}(\mathtt{inc},1,2)\cdot\mathtt{ret}(\lfloor\mathtt{tw}\rfloor_0,1,2)\cdot\mathtt{ret}(\lceil\mathtt{tw}\rceil_0,0,2)\cdot\mathtt{ret}(\mathtt{main},0,2)} & (I_9, 2) &
\end{array}
$$

$$
\begin{array}{llll}
e_{\mathtt{tw}} & \triangleq \lambda f.\lambda x.f\ (f\ x) & e'_{\mathtt{tw}} & \triangleq \lambda x.\ \lfloor\mathtt{tw}\rfloor_0\ (\lfloor\mathtt{tw}\rfloor_0\ x) \\
E_{\mathtt{main}} & \triangleq \mathtt{ret}(\mathtt{main}, 0, [\,]) & E_{\mathtt{tw}} & \triangleq E_{\mathtt{main}}[\mathtt{ret}(\mathtt{tw}, 0, [\,])\ 0] \\
E_{\lceil\mathtt{tw}\rceil_0} & \triangleq E_{\mathtt{main}}[\mathtt{ret}(\lceil\mathtt{tw}\rceil_0, 0, [\,])] & E_{\lfloor\mathtt{tw}\rfloor_0} & \triangleq E_{\lceil\mathtt{tw}\rceil_0}[\lfloor\mathtt{tw}\rfloor_0\ \mathtt{ret}(\lfloor\mathtt{tw}\rfloor_0, 0, [\,])] \\
E_{\mathtt{inc}} & \triangleq E_{\lfloor\mathtt{tw}\rfloor_0}[\mathtt{ret}(\mathtt{inc}, 0, [\,])] & E_{\lfloor\mathtt{tw}\rfloor'_0} & \triangleq E_{\lceil\mathtt{tw}\rceil_0}[\mathtt{ret}(\lfloor\mathtt{tw}\rfloor_0, 1, [\,])] \\
E_{\mathtt{inc}'} & \triangleq E_{\lfloor\mathtt{tw}\rfloor'_0}[\mathtt{ret}(\mathtt{inc}, 1, [\,])] & &
\end{array}
$$

Fig. 2. Example trace of $D_{\mathtt{tw}}$

We now introduce a trace semantics of the language $\mathcal{L}$, which will be used in Sect. 5 to define our model checking problems of higher-order programs. In the trace semantics, a program execution trace is represented by a sequence of function call and return events without an explicit representation of pointers but with enough information to construct them. We will explain how to model traces of $\mathcal{L}$ as HOTs by presenting a translation.

The trace semantics $[\![D]\!]$ of the language $\mathcal{L}$ is defined as $[\![D]\!]_{\mathtt{fin}} \cup [\![D]\!]_{\mathtt{inf}}$ where $[\![D]\!]_{\mathtt{fin}} = \left\{ \varpi \,\middle|\, (I, \mathtt{main}\ n) \overset{\varpi}{\Rrightarrow} C \right\}$ and $[\![D]\!]_{\mathtt{inf}} = \left\{ \pi \,\middle|\, (I, \mathtt{main}\ n) \overset{\pi}{\Rrightarrow} \bot \right\}$ are respectively the sets of *finite* and *infinite* execution traces obtained by evaluating $\mathtt{main}\ n$ for some integer n using *trace-labeled* multi-step reduction relations $\overset{\varpi}{\Rrightarrow}$ and $\overset{\pi}{\Rrightarrow}$, which are presented in Fig. 1, under the program $I = \left\{ f \overset{0}{\mapsto} v \,\middle|\, (f \mapsto v) \in D \right\}$ annotated with the number of calls to each function occurred so far (i.e., initialized to 0). There, we use ϖ (resp. π) as a meta-variable ranging over finite sequences $\alpha_1 \cdots \alpha_m$ (resp. infinite sequences $\alpha_1 \cdot \alpha_2 \cdots$) of events α_i. We write ϵ for the empty sequence, $\varpi_1 \cdot \varpi_2$ for the concatenation of the sequences ϖ_1 and ϖ_2, and $|\varpi|$ for the length of ϖ. An *event* α is either of the form $\mathbf{call}(h_1, i, h_2)$ or $\mathbf{ret}(h_1, i, h_2)$, where a *handle* h represents a top-level function or a runtime value exchanged among functions. An event $\mathbf{call}(h_1, i, h_2)$ represents the $(i+1)^{\text{th}}$ call to the function h_1 with the argument h_2. On the other hand, an event $\mathbf{ret}(h_1, i, h_2)$ represents the return of the $(i+1)^{\text{th}}$ call to the function h_1 with the return value h_2. We thus equip call and return events of h_1 with the information about (1) the number i of the calls to h_1 occurred so far and (2) the runtime value h_2 passed to or returned by h_1, so that we can construct pointers (see Definition 3 for details). Note here that handles h are also equipped with meta-information necessary for constructing pointers. More specifically, h is any of the following: a bounded integer n, a top-level function name $f \in \mathrm{dom}(D)$, the special identifier $\lfloor h \rfloor_i$ for the function argument of the $(i+1)^{\text{th}}$ call to the higher-order function h, or the special identifier $\lceil h \rceil_i$ for the partially-applied function returned by the $(i+1)^{\text{th}}$ call to h. We thus use handles to track for each function value where it is constructed and how many times it is called. We shall assume that the syntax of expressions e and values v is also extended with handles h. As we have seen, the finite traces $[\![D]\!]_{\mathtt{fin}}$ of a program D are collected using the *terminating* trace-labeled multi-step reduction relation $\stackrel{\varpi}{\Rrightarrow}$ on configurations. A *configuration* $(I, E[e])$ is a pair of an interface I and an expression $E[e]$ consisting of an evaluation context E and a sub-expression e under evaluation. A special evaluation context $\mathtt{ret}(h, i, E)$ represents the calling context of the $(i+1)^{\text{th}}$ call to h that waits for the return value computed by E. An *interface* I is defined to be $\left\{h_1 \stackrel{i_1}{\mapsto} v_1, \ldots, h_m \stackrel{i_m}{\mapsto} v_m\right\}$ that maps each function handle h_j to its definition v_j, where i_j records the number of calls to the function h_j occurred so far. In the derivation rules for $\stackrel{\varpi}{\longrightarrow}$, $[\![\mathtt{op}]\!]$ represents the integer function denoted by $\mathtt{op}$, and $I\left\{h \stackrel{i}{\mapsto} v\right\}$ represents the interface obtained from I by adding (or replacing existing assignment to h with) the assignment $h \stackrel{i}{\mapsto} v$. In the rule CINT (resp. RINT) for function calls (resp. returns) with an integer n, the reduction relation is labeled with $\mathbf{call}(h, i, n)$ (resp. $\mathbf{ret}(h, i, n)$). By contrast, in the rule CFUN (resp. RFUN) for function calls (resp. returns) with a function value v, the special identifier $\lfloor h \rfloor_i$ (resp. $\lceil h \rceil_i$) for v is used in the label $\mathbf{call}(h, i, \lfloor h \rfloor_i)$ (resp. $\mathbf{ret}(h, i, \lceil h \rceil_i)$) of the reduction relation, and v in the expression is replaced by the identifier. For example, as shown in Fig. 2, the following finite trace $\varpi_{\mathtt{tw}}$ is generated from the program $D_{\mathtt{tw}}$:

$$\begin{aligned}
&\mathbf{call}(\mathtt{main}, 0, 0) \cdot \mathbf{call}(\mathtt{tw}, 0, \lfloor \mathtt{tw} \rfloor_0) \cdot \mathbf{ret}(\mathtt{tw}, 0, \lceil \mathtt{tw} \rceil_0) \cdot \mathbf{call}(\lceil \mathtt{tw} \rceil_0, 0, 0) \cdot \\
&\mathbf{call}(\lfloor \mathtt{tw} \rfloor_0, 0, 0) \cdot \mathbf{call}(\mathtt{inc}, 0, 0) \cdot \mathbf{ret}(\mathtt{inc}, 0, 1) \cdot \mathbf{ret}(\lfloor \mathtt{tw} \rfloor_0, 0, 1) \cdot \mathbf{call}(\lfloor \mathtt{tw} \rfloor_0, 1, 1) \cdot \\
&\mathbf{call}(\mathtt{inc}, 1, 1) \cdot \mathbf{ret}(\mathtt{inc}, 1, 2) \cdot \mathbf{ret}(\lfloor \mathtt{tw} \rfloor_0, 1, 2) \cdot \mathbf{ret}(\lceil \mathtt{tw} \rceil_0, 0, 2) \cdot \mathbf{ret}(\mathtt{main}, 0, 2)
\end{aligned}$$

Similarly, the infinite traces $[\![D]\!]_{\mathtt{inf}}$ of a program D are collected using the *non-terminating* trace-labeled reduction relation $C \stackrel{\pi}{\Rrightarrow} \bot$ on configurations. Intuitively, $C \stackrel{\pi}{\Rrightarrow} \bot$ means that an execution from the configuration C diverges, producing an infinite event sequence π. In the rule TRANω, the double horizontal line represents that the rule is interpreted co-inductively.

We now define the translation from traces $[\![D]\!]_{\mathtt{fin}}$ to HOTs with $\Sigma^T_{\mathbf{call}} = \{\mathbf{call}(f, n), \mathbf{call}(f, \bullet) \mid f \in \mathrm{dom}(D), n \in \mathbb{Z}_b\}$, $\Sigma^A_{\mathbf{call}} = \{\mathbf{call}(\bullet, n), \mathbf{call}(\bullet, \bullet) \mid n \in \mathbb{Z}_b\}$, and $\Sigma_{\mathbf{ret}} = \{\mathbf{ret}(f, n), \mathbf{ret}(f, \bullet), \mathbf{ret}(\bullet, n), \mathbf{ret}(\bullet, \bullet) \mid f \in \mathrm{dom}(D), n \in \mathbb{Z}_b\}$. We shall write $\Sigma(D)$ for $\Sigma^T_{\mathbf{call}} \cup \Sigma^A_{\mathbf{call}} \cup \Sigma_{\mathbf{ret}}$. Note that $\Sigma(D)$ is finite because $\mathrm{dom}(D)$ and $\mathbb{Z}_b$ are finite. We write $|\alpha|$ for the element of $\Sigma(D)$ obtained from the event α by dropping the second argument and replacing $\lfloor h \rfloor_i$ and $\lceil h \rceil_i$ by $\bullet$. For example, we get $|\mathbf{call}(\mathtt{tw}, 0, \lfloor \mathtt{tw} \rfloor_0)| = \mathbf{call}(\mathtt{tw}, \bullet)$.

Definition 3 (Finite Traces to HOTs). *Given a finite trace $\varpi = \alpha_1 \cdots \alpha_m \in [\![D]\!]_{\mathtt{fin}}$ with $m > 0$, the corresponding HOT $G_\varpi = (V_\varpi, \lambda_\varpi, \nu_\varpi)$ is defined by:*

- $V_\varpi = \{1, \ldots, m\}$,
- $\lambda_\varpi = \{j \mapsto |\alpha_j| \mid j \in V_\varpi\}$, *and*
- ν_ϖ *is the smallest relation that satisfies: for any* $j_1, j_2 \in V_\varpi$,
  - $j_1 \prec_{\mathbf{N}} j_2$ *if* $j_2 = j_1 + 1$,
  - $j_1 \prec_{\mathbf{CR}} j_2$ *if* $\exists h, h', h'', i.\ \alpha_{j_1} = \mathbf{call}(h, i, h') \wedge \alpha_{j_2} = \mathbf{ret}(h, i, h'')$,
  - $j_1 \prec_{\mathbf{CC}} j_2$ *if* $\exists h, h', h'', i, i'.\ \alpha_{j_1} = \mathbf{call}(h', i, h) \wedge \alpha_{j_2} = \mathbf{call}(h, i', h'')$,
  - $j_1 \prec_{\mathbf{RC}} j_2$ *if* $\exists h, h', h'', i, i'.\ \alpha_{j_1} = \mathbf{ret}(h', i, h) \wedge \alpha_{j_2} = \mathbf{call}(h, i', h'')$.

For example, the HOT $G_{\mathtt{tw}}$ in Sect. 1 is translated from the finite trace $\varpi_{\mathtt{tw}}$ defined above (with the call and return events of `main` omitted).

For an infinite trace $\pi = \alpha_1 \cdot \alpha_2 \cdots \in [\![D]\!]_{\mathtt{inf}}$, the HOT $G_\pi = (V_\pi, \lambda_\pi, \nu_\pi)$ is defined similarly for $V_\pi = \{j \in \mathbb{N} \mid j \geq 1\}$ and $\lambda_\pi = \{j \mapsto |\alpha_j| \mid j \in V_\pi\}$.

3 Propositional Dynamic Logic over Higher-Order Traces

This section presents HOT-PDL, a propositional dynamic logic (PDL) defined over HOTs (see [16] for a general exposition of PDL). HOT-PDL extends path expressions of PDL with $\rightarrow_{\mathbf{ret}}$ and $\rightarrow_{\mathbf{call}}$ for traversing edges of HOTs labeled respectively with **CR** and **CC**/**RC**. The syntax is defined by:

$$\begin{aligned} &(\text{formulas})\ \phi ::= p \mid \phi_1 \wedge \phi_2 \mid \neg \phi \mid [\pi]\,\phi \\ &(\text{path expressions})\ \pi ::= \rightarrow \mid \rightarrow_{\mathbf{call}} \mid \rightarrow_{\mathbf{ret}} \mid \{\phi\}? \mid \pi_1 \cdot \pi_2 \mid \pi_1 + \pi_2 \mid \pi^* \end{aligned}$$

Here, p is a meta-variable ranging over atomic propositions $\mathcal{AP}$. Let $\top$ and $\bot$ denote tautology and contradiction, respectively. Path expressions π are defined using a syntax based on regular expressions: we have concatenation $\pi_1 \cdot \pi_2$, alternation $\pi_1 + \pi_2$, and Kleene star π^*. We write π^+ for $\pi \cdot \pi^*$. Path expressions $\rightarrow$, $\rightarrow_{\mathbf{ret}}$, and $\rightarrow_{\mathbf{call}}$ are for traversing edges labeled with **N**, **CR**, and **CC** or **RC**, respectively. A path expression $\{\phi\}?$ is for testing if ϕ holds at the current node. A formula $[\pi]\,\phi$ means that ϕ always holds if one moves along any path represented by the path expression π. The dual formula $\langle \pi \rangle\,\phi$ is defined by $\neg\,[\pi]\,\neg\phi$ and means that there is a path represented by π such that ϕ holds if one moves along the path. $\langle \pi \rangle$ and $[\pi]$ have the same priority as $\neg$.

We now define the semantics of HOT-PDL. For a given HOT $G = (V, \lambda, \nu)$ with $\Sigma = \mathcal{AP}$, $\lambda(u)$ represents the atomic proposition satisfied at the node $u \in V$. We define the semantics $[\![\phi]\!]_G$ of a formula ϕ as the set of all nodes $u \in V$

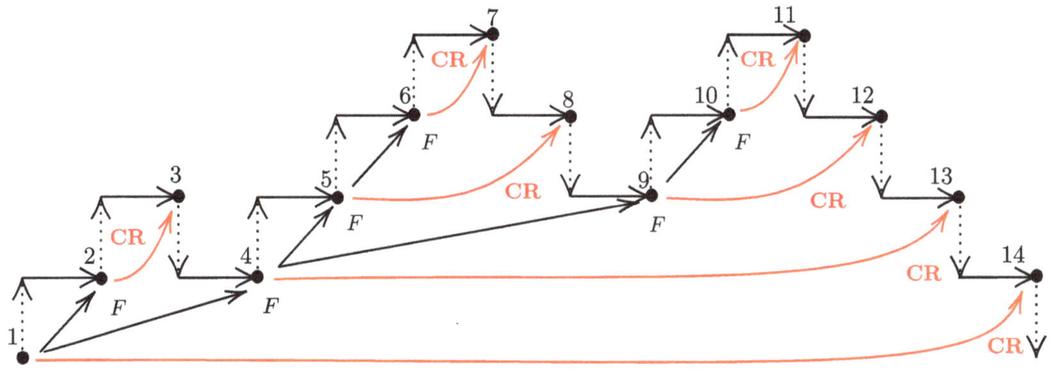

$1 : \mathbf{call}(\mathtt{main}, 0), 2 : \mathbf{call}(\mathtt{tw}, \bullet), 3 : \mathbf{ret}(\mathtt{tw}, \bullet), 4 : \mathbf{call}(\bullet, 0), 5 : \mathbf{call}(\bullet, 0),$
$6 : \mathbf{call}(\mathtt{inc}, 0), 7 : \mathbf{ret}(\mathtt{inc}, 1), 8 : \mathbf{ret}(\bullet, 1), 9 : \mathbf{call}(\bullet, 1), 10 : \mathbf{call}(\mathtt{inc}, 1),$
$11 : \mathbf{ret}(\mathtt{inc}, 2), 12 : \mathbf{ret}(\bullet, 2), 13 : \mathbf{ret}(\bullet, 2), 14 : \mathbf{ret}(\mathtt{main}, 2)$

Fig. 3. The pairs of nodes in $G_{\mathtt{tw}}$ related by CR or $\nearrow_F$

where ϕ is satisfied, and the semantics $[\![\pi]\!]_G$ of a path expression π as the set of all pairs $(u_1, u_2) \in V \times V$ such that one can move along π from u_1 to u_2.

$$[\![p]\!]_G = \{u \in V \mid p = \lambda(u)\} \quad [\![\phi_1 \wedge \phi_2]\!]_G = [\![\phi_1]\!]_G \cap [\![\phi_2]\!]_G \quad [\![\neg\phi]\!]_G = V \setminus [\![\phi]\!]_G$$
$$[\![[\pi]\,\phi]\!]_G = \{u \in V \mid \forall u'. ((u, u') \in [\![\pi]\!]_G \Rightarrow u' \in [\![\phi]\!]_G)\}$$
$$[\![\rightarrow]\!]_G = \prec_{\mathbf{N}} \qquad [\![\rightarrow_{\mathbf{ret}}]\!]_G = \prec_{\mathbf{CR}} \qquad [\![\rightarrow_{\mathbf{call}}]\!]_G = \prec_{\mathbf{CC}} \cup \prec_{\mathbf{RC}}$$
$$[\![\{\phi\}?]\!]_G = \{(u, u) \in V \times V \mid u \in [\![\phi]\!]_G\}$$
$$[\![\pi_1 \cdot \pi_2]\!]_G = \{(u_1, u_3) \in V \times V \mid \exists u_2 \in V.\ (u_1, u_2) \in [\![\pi_1]\!]_G \wedge (u_2, u_3) \in [\![\pi_2]\!]_G\}$$
$$[\![\pi_1 + \pi_2]\!]_G = [\![\pi_1]\!]_G \cup [\![\pi_2]\!]_G \qquad [\![\pi^*]\!]_G = \bigcup_{m \geq 0} [\![\pi]\!]_G^m$$

Here, for a binary relation R, R^m denotes the m-th power of R. Note that this semantics can interpret a given HOT-PDL formula over both finite and infinite HOTs. $[\![p]\!]_G$ consists of all nodes labeled by p. $[\![[\pi]\,\phi]\!]_G$ contains all nodes from which we always reach to a node in $[\![\phi]\!]_G$ if we take a path represented by π. $[\![\rightarrow]\!]_G$, $[\![\rightarrow_{\mathbf{ret}}]\!]_G$, and $[\![\rightarrow_{\mathbf{call}}]\!]_G$ contain the pairs of nodes linked by an edge labeled by **N**, **CR**, and **CC** or **RC**, respectively. We write $G \models \phi$ if $0_G \in [\![\phi]\!]_G$. For example, let us consider the HOT $G_{\mathtt{tw}}$ and $\mathcal{AP} = \Sigma(D_{\mathtt{tw}})$. Then, $[\![\langle\rightarrow\rangle\, \mathbf{ret}(\mathtt{tw}, \bullet)]\!]_{G_{\mathtt{tw}}}$ consists of the node labeled by $\mathbf{call}(\mathtt{tw}, \bullet)$. $[\![\langle\rightarrow_{\mathbf{ret}}\rangle\, \mathbf{ret}(\bullet, 2)]\!]_{G_{\mathtt{tw}}}$ consists of a node labeled by $\mathbf{call}(\bullet, 0)$ and the node labeled by $\mathbf{call}(\bullet, 1)$. $[\![\langle\rightarrow_{\mathbf{call}}\rangle\, \mathbf{call}(\bullet, 0)]\!]_{G_{\mathtt{tw}}}$ consists of the two nodes respectively labeled by $\mathbf{call}(\mathtt{tw}, \bullet)$ and $\mathbf{ret}(\mathtt{tw}, \bullet)$. The example properties of $D_{\mathtt{tw}}$ discussed in Sect. 1 can be expressed as follows:

Prop.1.: $[\rightarrow^*] \bigwedge_{x \in \mathbb{Z}_b} ((\mathbf{call}(\mathtt{tw}, \bullet) \wedge \langle\rightarrow_{\mathbf{ret}} \cdot \rightarrow_{\mathbf{call}}\rangle\, \mathbf{call}(\bullet, x)) \Rightarrow \langle\rightarrow_{\mathbf{call}}\rangle\, \mathbf{call}(\bullet, x))$
Prop.2.: $[\rightarrow^*] ((\mathbf{call}(\mathtt{tw}, \bullet) \wedge \neg \langle\rightarrow_{\mathbf{ret}} \cdot \rightarrow_{\mathbf{call}}\rangle \top) \Rightarrow \neg \langle\rightarrow_{\mathbf{call}}\rangle \top)$

Here, $\bigwedge_{x \in \mathbb{Z}_b} \phi$ abbreviates $[n_{\mathbf{min}}/x]\,\phi \wedge \cdots \wedge [n_{\mathbf{max}}/x]\,\phi$.

In Sect. 4, we show further examples that express interesting properties of higher-order programs, including stack based access control properties and those

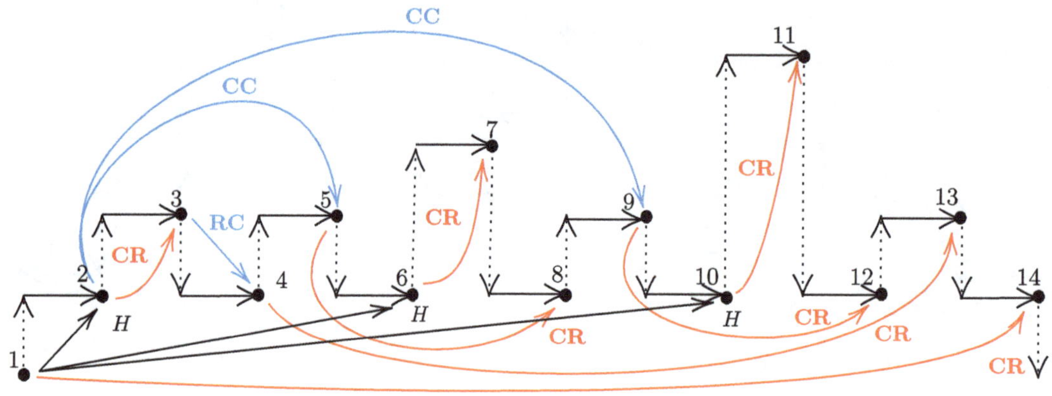

$1 : \textbf{call}(\texttt{main}, 0), 2 : \textbf{call}(\texttt{tw}, \bullet), 3 : \textbf{ret}(\texttt{tw}, \bullet), 4 : \textbf{call}(\bullet, 0), 5 : \textbf{call}(\bullet, 0),$
$6 : \textbf{call}(\texttt{inc}, 0), 7 : \textbf{ret}(\texttt{inc}, 1), 8 : \textbf{ret}(\bullet, 1), 9 : \textbf{call}(\bullet, 1), 10 : \textbf{call}(\texttt{inc}, 1),$
$11 : \textbf{ret}(\texttt{inc}, 2), 12 : \textbf{ret}(\bullet, 2), 13 : \textbf{ret}(\bullet, 2), 14 : \textbf{ret}(\texttt{main}, 2)$

Fig. 4. The pairs of nodes in $G_{\texttt{tw}}$ related by **CR**, **CC**, **RC**, or $\nearrow_H$

definable using dependent refinement types. We here prepare notations used there. First, we overload the symbols $\Sigma_{\textbf{call}}$, $\Sigma_{\textbf{ret}}$, and $\Sigma^T_{\textbf{call}}$ to denote the path expressions $\{\bigvee \Sigma_{\textbf{call}}\}?$, $\{\bigvee \Sigma_{\textbf{ret}}\}?$, and $\{\bigvee \Sigma^T_{\textbf{call}}\}?$, respectively. We write $\rightarrow_F$ for the path expression $\rightarrow_{\textbf{ret}} \cdot \rightarrow$, which is used to move from a call event to the next event of the caller (by skipping to the next event of the corresponding return event). We also write $\nearrow_F$ for the path expression $\Sigma_{\textbf{call}} \cdot \rightarrow \cdot \rightarrow_F^* \cdot \Sigma_{\textbf{call}}$, which is used to move from a call event to any call event invoked by the callee. Figure 3 illustrates the pairs of nodes in $G_{\texttt{tw}}$ related by $\nearrow_F$. To capture control flow of higher-order programs, where function callers and callees may exchange functions as values, we need to use **CC**- and **RC**-labeled edges. For example, an event raised by the function argument f_{arg} of a higher-order function f could be regarded as an event of the caller g of f, because f_{arg} is constructed by g. Similarly, an event raised by the (partially-applied) function f_{ret} returned by a function f could be regarded as an event of f. To formalize the idea, we introduce variants $\rightarrow_H$ and $\nearrow_H$ of $\rightarrow_F$ and $\nearrow_F$ with higher-order control flow taken into consideration: $\rightarrow_H$ denotes $(\rightarrow_{\textbf{ret}} \cdot \rightarrow) + (\rightarrow_{\textbf{call}} \cdot \rightarrow)$ and $\nearrow_F$ denotes $\Sigma^T_{\textbf{call}} \cdot \rightarrow \cdot \rightarrow_H^* \cdot \Sigma^T_{\textbf{call}}$. Note that the source and the target of $\nearrow_H$ are restricted to call events of top-level functions. Figure 4 illustrates the pairs of nodes in $G_{\texttt{tw}}$ related by $\nearrow_H$, where nodes labeled with events of the same function (in the sense discussed above) are arranged in the same horizontal line.

4 Applications of HOT-PDL

We show how to encode dependent refinement types and stack-based access control properties using HOT-PDL.

4.1 Dependent Refinement Types

HOT-PDL can specify pre- and post-conditions of higher-order functions, by encoding dependent refinement types τ for partial [29,33,40] and total [23,27,34,36,39] correctness verification, defined as: $\tau ::= \{\nu \mid \psi\} \mid (x:\tau_1) \to \tau_2^Q$. Here, Q is either $\forall$ or $\exists$. An integer refinement type $\{\nu \mid \psi\}$ is the type of bounded integers ν that satisfy the refinement formula ψ over bounded integers. A dependent function type $(x:\tau_1) \to \tau_2^\forall$ is the type of functions that, for any argument x conforming to the type τ_1, *if terminating*, return a value conforming to the type τ_2. By contrast, $(x:\tau_1) \to \tau_2^\exists$ is the type of functions that, for any argument x conforming to τ_1, *always terminate* and return a value conforming to τ_2. For example, Prop.3 and Prop.4 of $D_{\mathtt{tw}}$ are expressed by the following types of `tw`:

$$\text{Prop.3.:}\ \left(f:(x:\mathtt{int}) \to \{\nu \mid \nu > x\}^\forall\right) \to \left((x:\mathtt{int}) \to \{\nu \mid \nu > x\}^\forall\right)^\forall$$

$$\text{Prop.4.:}\ \left(f:(x:\mathtt{int}) \to \mathtt{int}^\exists\right) \to \left((x:\mathtt{int}) \to \mathtt{int}^\exists\right)^\forall$$

We here write `int` for $\{\nu \mid \top\}$. These types can be encoded in HOT-PDL as:

$$\text{Prop.3.:}\ \mathbf{call}(\mathtt{tw},\bullet) \Rightarrow ([\to_{\mathbf{call}}]\,\mathtt{incr}(\bullet)) \wedge [\to_{\mathbf{ret}}]\left(\mathbf{ret}(\mathtt{tw},\bullet) \Rightarrow [\to_{\mathbf{call}}]\,\mathtt{incr}(\bullet)\right)$$
$$\text{Prop.4.:}\ \mathbf{call}(\mathtt{tw},\bullet) \Rightarrow ([\to_{\mathbf{call}}]\,\mathtt{term}(\bullet)) \wedge [\to_{\mathbf{ret}}]\left(\mathbf{ret}(\mathtt{tw},\bullet) \Rightarrow [\to_{\mathbf{call}}]\,\mathtt{term}(\bullet)\right)$$

Here, $\mathtt{incr}(g) = \bigwedge_{x \in \mathbb{Z}_b} \mathbf{call}(g,x) \Rightarrow [\to_{\mathbf{ret}}] \bigwedge_{y \in \mathbb{Z}_b} (\mathbf{ret}(g,y) \Rightarrow y > x)$ and $\mathtt{term}(g) = \bigwedge_{x \in \mathbb{Z}_b} (\mathbf{call}(g,x) \Rightarrow \langle \to_{\mathbf{ret}} \rangle \top)$ for $g \in \{\bullet\} \cup \{f \mid f \in \mathrm{dom}(D)\}$. We now define a translation F from types to HOT-PDL formulas as follows:

$$F(g,(x:\tau_1) \to \tau_2^Q) = \bigwedge_{x \in |\tau_1|} \left(\mathbf{call}(g,x) \Rightarrow F_{arg}(x,\tau_1) \wedge F_{ret}(g,\tau_2^Q)\right)$$

$$|(x:\tau_1) \to \tau_2^Q| = \{\bullet\} \qquad |\{x \mid \psi\}| = \mathbb{Z}_b$$

$$F_{arg}(\bullet,\tau) = [\to_{\mathbf{call}}]\,F(\bullet,\tau) \qquad F_{arg}(n,\{x \mid \psi\}) = \begin{cases} \top & (\text{if } \models [n/x]\psi) \\ \bot & (\text{if } \not\models [n/x]\psi) \end{cases}$$

$$F_{ret}(g,\tau^\forall) = [\to_{\mathbf{ret}}] \bigwedge_{x \in |\tau|} (\mathbf{ret}(g,x) \Rightarrow F(x,\tau))$$

$$F_{ret}(g,\tau^\exists) = (\langle \to_{\mathbf{ret}} \rangle \top) \wedge F_{ret}(g,\tau^\forall)$$

4.2 Stack-Based Access Control Properties

As briefly summarized in Sect. 1, stack-based access control [13] ensures that a *security-critical* function (e.g., file access) is invoked only if all the (immediate and indirect) callers in the current call stack are *trusted*, or one of the callers is a *privileged* function and its callees are all *trusted*. We here use HOT-PDL to specify stack-based access control properties for higher-order programs. Let **Critical**, **Trusted**, and **Priv** be HOT-PDL formulas that tell whether the current node is labeled with a call event of security-critical, trusted, and privileged functions, respectively. We assume that **Critical**, **Priv**, and ¬**Trusted** do not overlap each other, and a function in **Priv** can be directly called only from a function in **Trusted**. Then, one may think we can express the specification as:

$$\neg \langle \nearrow_F^* \cdot \{\neg\mathbf{Trusted}\}? \cdot (\nearrow_F \cdot \{\neg\mathbf{Priv}\}?)^+ \rangle\, \mathbf{Critical}$$

Here, the path expression $\nearrow_F$ introduced in Sect. 3 is used to traverse the call stack bottom-up. The above formula says that an invalid call stack never occurs, where a call stack is called *invalid* if it contains a call to an untrusted function (represented by the part $\nearrow_F^* \{\neg\mathbf{Trusted}\}?$), followed by a call to a critical function (represented by **Critical**), with no intervening call to a privileged function (represented by $(\nearrow_F \cdot \{\neg\mathbf{Priv}\}?)^+$).

This definition, however, is not sufficient for our higher-order language. Let us consider the following program D_{pa}, which involves a partial application:

$$\begin{aligned}&\texttt{let untrusted } () = \lambda u.\texttt{critical } u\\&\texttt{let main } () = \texttt{untrusted } ()\ ()\end{aligned}$$

Here, untrusted $\notin$ **Trusted** and critical $\in$ **Critical**. Intuitively, D_{pa} should be regarded as *unsafe* because critical in the body of untrusted is called. However, D_{pa} satisfies the specification above (under the assumption that anonymous functions are in **Trusted**), because the partial application untrusted () never causes a call to critical but just returns the anonymous (and trusted) function $\lambda u.\texttt{critical}\ u$. The following higher-order program D_{ho} is yet another unsafe example that satisfies the specification:

$$\begin{aligned}&\texttt{let privileged } f = f\ ()\\&\texttt{let trusted } f = \texttt{if test } ()\texttt{ then privileged } f \texttt{ else } ()\\&\texttt{let untrusted } () = \texttt{trusted } (\lambda x.\texttt{crash } (); \texttt{critical } ())\\&\texttt{let main } () = \texttt{untrusted } ()\end{aligned}$$

Here, privileged $\in$ **Priv**, trusted $\in$ **Trusted**, untrusted $\notin$ **Trusted**, and critical $\in$ **Critical**. Note that critical in the body of untrusted is called as follows: the anonymous function $\lambda x.\texttt{crash}\ (); \texttt{critical}\ ()$ is first passed to trusted and then to privileged (if test () returns true), and is finally called by privileged, causing a call to critical.

To remedy the limitation, we introduce a new refined variant of stack-based access control properties for higher-order programs, formalized in HOT-PDL from the point of view of interactions among callers and callees as follows:

$$\neg \langle \nearrow_H^* \cdot \{\neg\mathbf{Trusted}\}? \cdot (\nearrow_H \cdot \{\neg\mathbf{Priv}\}?)^+ \rangle\, \mathbf{Critical}$$

Note that this is obtained from the previous version by just replacing $\nearrow_F$ with $\nearrow_H$, which takes into account which function constructed each function value exchanged among functions. The refined version rejects the unsafe D_{pa} and D_{ho} as intended: D_{pa} (resp. D_{ho}) is rejected because the call event of $\lambda u.\texttt{critical}\ u$ (resp. $\lambda x.\texttt{crash}\ (); \texttt{critical}\ ()$) is regarded as an event of untrusted.

Fournet and Gordon [13] have studied variants of stack-based access control properties for a call-by-value higher-order language. We conclude this section by comparing ours with one of theirs called "stack inspection with frame capture".[2] The ideas behind the two are similar but what follows illustrates the difference:

```
let untrusted f = crash (); f ()
  let trusted x = untrusted (λx.if test () then critical () else ())
    let main () = trusted ()
```

This program satisfies ours but violates theirs. Note that ours allows a function originally constructed by a trusted function to invoke a critical function even if the function is passed around by an untrusted function. By contrast, in their definition, a trusted function value gets "contaminated" (i.e., disabled to invoke a critical function) once it is passed to or returned by an untrusted function. In some cases, their conservative policy is useful, but we believe ours would be more semantically robust (e.g., even works well with the CPS transformation).

5 HOT-PDL Model Checking

In this section, we define HOT-PDL model checking problems for higher-order functional programs over bounded integers and sketch a proof of the decidability.

Definition 4 (HOT-PDL model checking). *Given a program D and a HOT-PDL formula ϕ with $\mathcal{AP} = \Sigma(D)$, HOT-PDL model checking is the problem of deciding whether $G_\varpi \models \phi$ and $G_\pi \models \phi$ for all $\varpi \in [\![D]\!]_{\mathtt{fin}}$ and $\pi \in [\![D]\!]_{\mathtt{inf}}$.*

Theorem 1 (Decidability). *HOT-PDL model checking is decidable.*

We show this by a reduction to modal μ-calculus (μ-ML) model checking of higher-order recursion schemes (HORSs), which is known decidable [21,28]. A HORS is a grammar for generating a (possibly infinite) ranked tree, and HORSs are essentially simply-typed lambda calculus with general recursion, tree constructors, and finite data domains such as booleans and bounded integers.

In the reduction, we encode the set of HOTs that are generated from the given program D as a single tree (generated by a HORS). For example, Fig. 5 shows such a tree that encodes the HOTs of $D_{\mathtt{tw}}$.[3] There, a node labeled with `end` represents the termination of the program. Note that the branching at the root node is due to the input to the function `main`. The subtree with the root node labeled with **call**(`main`, 0) is obtained from the HOT $G_{\mathtt{tw}}$ by appending a special node labeled with `end`, adding, for each edge with the label $\gamma \in \{\mathbf{N}, \mathbf{CR}, \mathbf{CC}, \mathbf{RC}\}$, a new node labeled with γ, and expanding the resulting DAG into a tree. Thus, the edge labels of $G_{\mathtt{tw}}$ are turned into node labels of the tree.

[2] We do not compare with the other variants in [13] because they are too syntactic to be preserved by simple program transformations like inlining.

[3] There, for simplicity, we illustrate an *unranked* tree and omit the label of branching nodes. In the formalization, we express an unranked tree as a binary tree using a special node label **br** of the arity 2 representing a binary branching.

It is also worth mentioning here that we are allowed to expand DAGs into trees because the truth value of a HOT-PDL formula is not affected by node-sharing in the given HOT. This nice property is lost if we extend the path expressions of HOT-PDL, for example, with intersections. Thus, the decidability of model checking for extensions of HOT-PDL is an open problem.

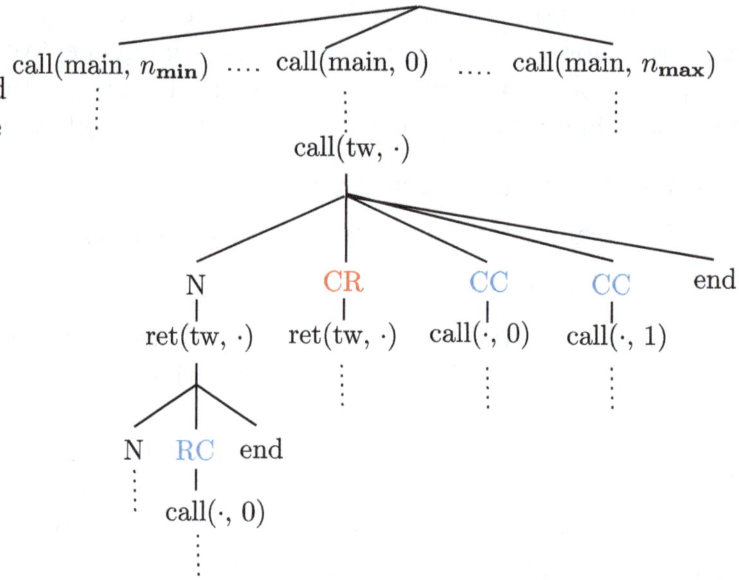

Fig. 5. A tree encoding the HOTs generated from $D_{\mathtt{tw}}$

We next explain our translation from a HOT-PDL formula into a μ-ML formula interpreted over trees that encode HOTs. Our translation is based on an existing one for ordinary PDL [11]. The syntax of μ-ML is defined as follows:

$$\varphi ::= X \mid p \mid \neg\varphi \mid \varphi \wedge \varphi \mid \Box\varphi \mid \nu X.\varphi \mid \mu X.\varphi$$

Here, X represents a propositional variable and p represents an atomic proposition. A formula $\Box\varphi$ means that φ holds for any child of the current node. A formula $\mu X.\varphi$ (resp. $\nu X.\varphi$) represents the least (resp. greatest) fixpoint of the function $\lambda X.\varphi$. Here, we assume X occurs only positively in φ. For example, the HOT-PDL formulas $[\rightarrow]p$, $[\rightarrow_{\mathbf{ret}}]p$, and $[\rightarrow_{\mathbf{call}}]p$ are respectively translated to μ-ML formulas: $\Box(\nu X.(\mathbf{N} \Rightarrow \Box p) \wedge (\mathbf{br} \Rightarrow \Box X))$, $\Box(\nu X.(\mathbf{CR} \Rightarrow \Box p) \wedge (\mathbf{br} \Rightarrow \Box X))$, and $\Box(\nu X.((\mathbf{CC} \vee \mathbf{RC}) \Rightarrow \Box p) \wedge (\mathbf{br} \Rightarrow \Box X))$, where the greatest fixpoints are used to skip the branching nodes labeled with **br** (that may repeat infinitely).

Finally, we explain how to obtain a HORS for generating a tree that encodes the set of HOTs generated from the given program D. We here need to simulate pointer traversals of HOT-PDL by using purely functional features of HORSs because μ-ML does not support pointers. Intuitively, we obtain the desired HORS from D by embedding an event monitor and an event handler. Whenever the monitor detects a function call or return event during the execution of D, the handler creates a new node labeled with the event or ignores the event until a certain event is detected by the monitor, depending on the current mode of the handler. The handler has the following three modes:

$m_{\mathbf{N}}$: The handler always creates and links two new nodes $u_{\mathbf{N}}$ and u_α labeled respectively with **N** and the event α observed. The handler then continues as follows, depending on the form of the event α:

call(g, n): Spawns a new handler with the mode $m_{\mathbf{ret}}$. Then, the two handlers of the modes $m_{\mathbf{N}}$ and $m_{\mathbf{ret}}$ continue to create subtrees of u_α.

call$(g, \bullet)$: Spawns two new handlers with the modes $m_{\mathbf{ret}}$ and $m_{\mathbf{call}}$. The three handlers of $m_{\mathbf{N}}$, $m_{\mathbf{ret}}$, and $m_{\mathbf{call}}$ continue to create subtrees of u_α.

ret(g, n): The handler of the mode $m_{\mathbf{N}}$ continues to create a subtree of u_α.

ret$(g, \bullet)$: Spawns a new handler with the mode $m_{\mathbf{call}}$. Then, the two handlers of the modes $m_{\mathbf{N}}$ and $m_{\mathbf{call}}$ continue to create subtrees of u_α.

$m_{\mathbf{ret}}$: The handler ignores all events but the return event corresponding to the call event that caused the spawn of the handler. If not ignored, the handler creates and links new nodes $u_{\mathbf{CR}}$ and u_α labeled with **CR** and the event α. The handler changes its mode to $m_{\mathbf{N}}$ and continues creating a subtree of u_α.

$m_{\mathbf{call}}$: The handler ignores all events but the call event of the function passed to or returned by the call or return event that caused the spawn of the handler. If not ignored, the handler creates and links new nodes u and u_α labeled respectively with **CC** or **RC** and the event α, duplicates itself, and changes the mode of the original to $m_{\mathbf{N}}$. The handler of the mode $m_{\mathbf{N}}$ (resp. $m_{\mathbf{call}}$) continues to create a subtree of u_α (resp. the parent of u).

For simplicity of the construction, we assume that D is in the Continuation-Passing Style (CPS). This does not lose generality because we can enforce this form by the CPS transformation. Because CPS explicates the order of function call and return events, it simplifies event monitoring, handling, and tracking of the current mode of the monitors, which often changes as monitoring proceeds.

6 Related Work

HOT-PDL can specify temporal trace properties of higher-order programs. An extension for specifying branching properties, however, remains a future work.

There have been proposed logics and formal languages on richer structures than words. Regular languages of nested words, or equivalently, Visibly Pushdown Languages (VPLs) have been introduced by Alur and Madhusudan [7]. An (ω-)nested word is a (possibly infinite) word with additional well-nested pointers from call events to the corresponding return events. Compared to temporal logics CaRet [5] and NWTL [4] over (ω-)nested words, HOT-PDL is defined over HOTs that have richer structures. Recall that a HOT is equipped with two kinds of pointers: one kind with the label **CR**, which is the same as the pointers of nested words, and the other kind with the label **CC** or **RC**, which is newly introduced to capture higher-order control flow. Bollig et al. proposed nested traces as a generalization of nested words for modeling traces of concurrent (first-order) recursive programs, and presented temporal logics over nested traces [8]. Nested traces, however, cannot model traces of higher-order programs. We expect a combination of our work with theirs enables us to specify temporal trace properties of concurrent and higher-order recursive programs. Cyriac et al. have recently introduced an extension of PDL defined over traces of *order-2* collapsible pushdown systems (CPDS) [3]. Interestingly, their traces are also equipped with two kinds of pointers: one kind of pointers captures the correspondence between ordinary push and pop stack operations, and the other captures the correspondence between order-2 push and pop operations for second-order stacks. Our work deals with higher-order programs that correspond to order-n CPDS for arbitrary n.

Finally, we compare HOT-PDL with existing logics defined over words. It is well known that LTL is less expressive than ω-regular languages [38]. To remedy the limitation of LTL, Wolper introduced ETL [38] that allows users to define new temporal operators using right-linear grammars. Henriksen and Thiagarajan proposed DLTL [17] that generalizes the until operator of LTL using regular expressions. Leucker and Sánchez proposed RLTL [25] that combines LTL and regular expressions. Vardi and Giacomo have introduced Linear Dynamic Logic (LDL), a variant of PDL interpreted over infinite words [15,35]. LDL_f, a variant of PDL interpreted over finite words, has also been studied in [15]. ETL, DLTL, RLTL, and LDL are as expressive as ω-regular languages. Note that HOT-PDL subsumes (ω-)regular languages because LDL and LDL_f can be naturally embedded in HOT-PDL. (ω-)VPLs strictly subsume (ω-)regular languages. Though CaRet [5] and NWTL [4] are defined over nested words, they do not capture the full class of VPLs [10]. To remedy the limitation, VLTL [10] combines LTL and VRE [9] in the style of RLTL, where VRE is a generalization of regular expressions for VPLs. VLDL [37] extends LDL by replacing the path expressions with VPLs over finite words. VLTL and VLDL exactly characterize ω-VPLs. Because VPLs and HOT-PDL are incomparable, it remains future work to extend HOT-PDL to subsume (ω-)VPLs.

7 Conclusion and Future Work

We have presented HOT-PDL, an extension of PDL defined over HOTs that model execution traces of call-by-value and higher-order programs. HOT-PDL enables a precise specification of temporal trace properties of higher-order programs and consequently provides a foundation for specification in various application domains including stack-based access control and dependent refinement types. We have also studied HOT-PDL model checking and presented a reduction method to modal μ-calculus model checking of higher-order recursion schemes.

To further widen the scope of our approach, it is worth investigating how to adapt HOTs and HOT-PDL to call-by-name and/or effectful languages. To this end, it is natural to incorporate more ideas from achievements of game semantics [1,20,32] and extend HOTs with new kinds of events and pointers for capturing call-by-name and/or effectful computations.

Acknowledgments. We would like to thank anonymous referees for their useful comments. This work was supported by JSPS KAKENHI Grant Numbers 15H05706, 16H05856, 17H01720, and 17H01723.

References

1. Abramsky, S., Jagadeesan, R., Malacaria, P.: Full abstraction for PCF. Inf. Comput. **163**, 409–470 (2000)
2. Abramsky, S., McCusker, G.: Call-by-value games. In: Nielsen, M., Thomas, W. (eds.) CSL 1997. LNCS, vol. 1414, pp. 1–17. Springer, Heidelberg (1998). https://doi.org/10.1007/BFb0028004
3. Aiswarya, C., Gastin, P., Saivasan, P.: Nested words for order-2 pushdown systems. arXiv:1609.06290 (2016)
4. Alur, R., Arenas, M., Barcelo, P., Etessami, K., Immerman, N., Libkin, L.: First-order and temporal logics for nested words. Log. Methods Comput. Sci. **4**(4), 1–44 (2008)
5. Alur, R., Etessami, K., Madhusudan, P.: A temporal logic of nested calls and returns. In: Jensen, K., Podelski, A. (eds.) TACAS 2004. LNCS, vol. 2988, pp. 467–481. Springer, Heidelberg (2004). https://doi.org/10.1007/978-3-540-24730-2_35
6. Alur, R., Madhusudan, P.: Visibly pushdown languages. In: STOC 2004, pp. 202–211. ACM (2004)
7. Alur, R., Madhusudan, P.: Adding nesting structure to words. J. ACM **56**(3), 16:1–16:43 (2009)
8. Bollig, B., Cyriac, A., Gastin, P., Zeitoun, M.: Temporal logics for concurrent recursive programs: satisfiability and model checking. J. Appl. Log. **12**(4), 395–416 (2014)
9. Bozzelli, L., Sánchez, C.: Visibly rational expressions. In: FSTTCS 2012. LIPIcs, vol. 18, pp. 211–223. Schloss Dagstuhl-Leibniz-Zentrum fuer Informatik (2012)
10. Bozzelli, L., Sánchez, C.: Visibly linear temporal logic. In: Demri, S., Kapur, D., Weidenbach, C. (eds.) IJCAR 2014. LNCS (LNAI), vol. 8562, pp. 418–433. Springer, Cham (2014). https://doi.org/10.1007/978-3-319-08587-6_33
11. Carreiro, F., Venema, Y.: PDL inside the μ-calculus: a syntactic and an automata-theoretic characterization. Adv. Modal Log. **10**, 74–93 (2014)
12. Disney, T., Flanagan, C., McCarthy, J.: Temporal higher-order contracts. In: ICFP 2011, pp. 176–188. ACM (2011)
13. Fournet, C., Gordon, A.D.: Stack inspection: theory and variants. In: POPL 2002, pp. 307–318. ACM (2002)
14. Fujima, K., Ito, S., Kobayashi, N.: Practical alternating parity tree automata model checking of higher-order recursion schemes. In: Shan, C. (ed.) APLAS 2013. LNCS, vol. 8301, pp. 17–32. Springer, Cham (2013). https://doi.org/10.1007/978-3-319-03542-0_2
15. Giacomo, G.D., Vardi, M.Y.: Linear temporal logic and linear dynamic logic on finite traces. In: IJCAI 2013, pp. 854–860. AAAI Press (2013)
16. Harel, D., Tiuryn, J., Kozen, D.: Dynamic Logic. MIT Press, Cambridge (2000)
17. Henriksen, J.G., Thiagarajan, P.: Dynamic linear time temporal logic. Ann. Pure Appl. Log. **96**(1), 187–207 (1999)
18. Hofmann, M., Chen, W.: Abstract interpretation from Büchi automata. In: CSL-LICS 2014, pp. 51:1–51:10. ACM (2014)
19. Honda, K., Yoshida, N.: Game theoretic analysis of call-by-value computation. In: Degano, P., Gorrieri, R., Marchetti-Spaccamela, A. (eds.) ICALP 1997. LNCS, vol. 1256, pp. 225–236. Springer, Heidelberg (1997). https://doi.org/10.1007/3-540-63165-8_180

20. Hyland, J.M.E., Ong, C.H.L.: On full abstraction for PCF: I, II, and III. Inf. Comput. **163**, 285–408 (2000)
21. Kobayashi, N., Ong, C.H.L.: A type system equivalent to the modal Mu-calculus model checking of higher-order recursion schemes. In: LICS 2009, pp. 179–188. IEEE (2009)
22. Kobayashi, N., Tsukada, T., Watanabe, K.: Higher-order program verification via HFL model checking. In: Ahmed, A. (ed.) ESOP 2018. LNCS, vol. 10801, pp. 711–738. Springer, Cham (2018). https://doi.org/10.1007/978-3-319-89884-1_25
23. Koskinen, E., Terauchi, T.: Local temporal reasoning. In: CSL-LICS 2014, pp. 59:1–59:10. ACM (2014)
24. Lester, M.M., Neatherway, R.P., Ong, C.H.L., Ramsay, S.J.: Model checking liveness properties of higher-order functional programs (2011). http://mjolnir.comlab.ox.ac.uk/papers/thors.pdf
25. Leucker, M., Sánchez, C.: Regular linear temporal logic. In: Jones, C.B., Liu, Z., Woodcock, J. (eds.) ICTAC 2007. LNCS, vol. 4711, pp. 291–305. Springer, Heidelberg (2007). https://doi.org/10.1007/978-3-540-75292-9_20
26. Murase, A., Terauchi, T., Kobayashi, N., Sato, R., Unno, H.: Temporal verification of higher-order functional programs. In: POPL 2016, pp. 57–68. ACM (2016)
27. Nanjo, Y., Unno, H., Koskinen, E., Terauchi, T.: A fixpoint logic and dependent effects for temporal property verification. In: LICS 2018. ACM (2018)
28. Ong, C.H.L.: On model-checking trees generated by higher-order recursion schemes. In: LICS 2006, pp. 81–90. IEEE (2006)
29. Rondon, P., Kawaguchi, M., Jhala, R.: Liquid types. In: PLDI 2008, pp. 159–169. ACM (2008)
30. Satake, Y., Unno, H.: Propositional dynamic logic for higher-order functional programs (2018). http://www.cs.tsukuba.ac.jp/~uhiro/
31. Suzuki, R., Fujima, K., Kobayashi, N., Tsukada, T.: Streett automata model checking of higher-order recursion schemes. In: FSCD 2017. LIPIcs, vol. 84, pp. 32:1–32:18. Schloss Dagstuhl-Leibniz-Zentrum fuer Informatik (2017)
32. Tzevelekos, N.: Nominal game semantics. Ph.D. thesis, University of Oxford (2008)
33. Unno, H., Kobayashi, N.: Dependent type inference with interpolants. In: PPDP 2009, pp. 277–288. ACM (2009)
34. Unno, H., Satake, Y., Terauchi, T.: Relatively complete refinement type system for verification of higher-order non-deterministic programs. Proc. ACM Program. Lang. **2**(POPL), 12:1–12:29 (2017)
35. Vardi, M.Y.: The rise and fall of LTL. GandALF (2011)
36. Vazou, N., Seidel, E.L., Jhala, R., Vytiniotis, D., Peyton Jones, S.L.: Refinement types for Haskell. In: ICFP 2014, pp. 269–282. ACM (2014)
37. Weinert, A., Zimmermann, M.: Visibly linear dynamic logic. In: FSTTCS 2016. LIPIcs, vol. 65, pp. 28:1–28:14. Schloss Dagstuhl-Leibniz-Zentrum fuer Informatik (2016)
38. Wolper, P.: Temporal logic can be more expressive. Inf. Control **56**(1), 72–99 (1983)
39. Xi, H.: Dependent types for program termination verification. In: LICS 2001, pp. 231–242. IEEE (2001)
40. Xi, H., Pfenning, F.: Dependent types in practical programming. In: POPL 1999, pp. 214–227. ACM (1999)

Syntax-Guided Termination Analysis

Grigory Fedyukovich(✉), Yueling Zhang, and Aarti Gupta

Princeton University, Princeton, USA
{grigoryf,yuelingz,aartig}@cs.princeton.edu

Abstract. We present new algorithms for proving program termination and non-termination using syntax-guided synthesis. They exploit the symbolic encoding of programs and automatically construct a formal grammar for symbolic constraints that are used to synthesize either a termination argument or a non-terminating program refinement. The constraints are then added back to the program encoding, and an off-the-shelf constraint solver decides on their fitness and on the progress of the algorithms. The evaluation of our implementation, called FreqTerm, shows that although the formal grammar is limited to the syntax of the program, in the majority of cases our algorithms are effective and fast. Importantly, FreqTerm is competitive with state-of-the-art on a wide range of terminating and non-terminating benchmarks, and it significantly outperforms state-of-the-art on proving non-termination of a class of programs arising from large-scale Event-Condition-Action systems.

1 Introduction

Originated from the field of program synthesis, an approach of syntax-guided synthesis (SyGuS) [2] has recently been applied [14,16] to verification of program safety. In general, a SyGuS-based method walks through a set of candidates, restricted by a formal grammar, and searches for a candidate that meets the predetermined specification. The distinguishing insight of [14,16], in which SyGuS discovers inductive invariants, is that a formal grammar need not necessarily be provided by the user (as in applications to program synthesis), but instead it could be automatically constructed on the fly from the symbolic encoding of the program being analyzed. Despite being incomplete, the approach shows remarkable practical success due to its ability to discover various facts about program behaviors whose syntactic representations are compact and look similar to the actual program statements.

Problems of proving and disproving program termination have a known connection to safety verification, e.g., [7,19,28,39,40]. In particular, to prove termination, a program could be augmented by a counter (or a set of counters) that is

This work was supported in part by NSF Grant 1525936.

Y. Zhang—Visiting Student Research Collaborator from East China Normal University, China.

H. Chockler and G. Weissenbacher (Eds.): CAV 2018, LNCS 10981, pp. 124–143, 2018.
https://doi.org/10.1007/978-3-319-96145-3_7

initially assigned a reasonably large value and monotonically decreases at each iteration [38]. It remains to solve a safety verification task: to prove that the counter never goes negative. On the other hand, to prove that a program has only infinite traces, one could prove that the negation of a loop guard is never reachable, which boils down to another safety verification task. This knowledge motivates us not only to exploit safety verification as a subroutine in our techniques, but also to adapt successful methods across application domains.

We present a set of SyGuS-based algorithms for proving and disproving termination. For the former, our algorithm LinRank adds a decrementing counter to a loop, iteratively guesses lower bounds on its initial value (using the syntactic patterns obtained from the code), which lead to the safety verification tasks to be solved by an off-the-shelf Horn solver. Existence of an inductive invariant guarantees termination, and the algorithm converges. Otherwise LinRank proceeds to strengthening the lower bounds by adding another guess. Similarly, our algorithm LexRank deals with a system of extra counters ordered lexicographically and thus enables termination analysis for a wider class of programs.

For proving non-termination, we present a novel algorithm NontermRef that iteratively searches for a restriction on the loop guard, that *might lead* to infinite traces. Since safety verification cannot in general answer such queries, we build NontermRef on top of a solver for the validity of $\forall\exists$-formulas. In particular, we prove that if at the beginning of any iteration the desired restriction is fulfilled, then there exists a sequence of states from the beginning to the end of that iteration, and the desired restriction is fulfilled at the end of that iteration as well. Recent symbolic techniques [15] to handle quantifier alternation enabled us to prove non-termination of a large class of programs for which a reduction to safety verification is not effective.

These three algorithms are independent of each other, but they all rely on a generator of constraints that are further applied in different contexts. This distinguishes our work from most of the related approaches [7,18,20,23,30,32, 36,39,40]. The key insight, adapted from [14,16], is that the syntactical structures that appear in the program give rise to a formal grammar, from which many candidates could be sampled. Because the grammar is composed from a finite number of numeric constants, operators, and variable combinations, the number of sampled constraints is always finite. Furthermore, since our samples are syntactically close to the actual constructs which appear in the code, they often provide a practical guidance towards the proof of the task. Thus in the majority of cases, the algorithms converge with the successful result.

We have implemented our algorithms in a tool called FreqTerm, which utilizes solvers for Satisfiability Modulo Theory (SMT) [11,15] and satisfiability of constrained Horn clauses [16,24,26]. These automatic provers become more robust and powerful every day, which affects performance of FreqTerm only positively. We have evaluated FreqTerm on a range of terminating and nonterminating programs taken from SVCOMP[1] and on large-scale benchmarks

[1] Software Verification Competition, http://sv-comp.sosy-lab.org/.

arising from Event-Condition-Action systems[2] (ECA). Compared to state-of-the-art termination analyzers [18,22,30], FREQTERM exhibits a competitive runtime, and achieves several orders of magnitude performance improvement while proving non-termination of ECAs.

In the rest of the paper, we give background on automated verification (Sect. 2) and on SyGuS (Sect. 3); then we describe the application of SyGuS for proving termination (Sect. 4) and non-termination (Sect. 5). Finally, after reporting experimental results (Sect. 6), we overview related work (Sect. 7) and conclude the paper (Sect. 8).

2 Background and Notation

In this work, we formulate tasks arising in automated program analysis by encoding them to instances of the SMT problem [12]: for a given first-order formula φ and a background theory to decide whether there is an assignment m of values from the theory to variables in φ that makes φ true (denoted $m \models \varphi$). If every assignment to φ is also an assignment to some formula ψ, we write $\varphi \implies \psi$.

Definition 1. *A* transition system *P is a tuple $\langle V \cup V', \mathit{Init}, \mathit{Tr} \rangle$, where V is a vector of variables; V' is its primed copy; formulas Init and Tr encode the* initial states *and the* transition relation *respectively.*

We view *programs* as *transition systems* and throughout the paper use both terms interchangeably. An assignment s of values to all variables in V (or any copy of V such as V') is called a *state*. A trace is a (possibly infinite) sequence of states $s, s', \ldots$, such that (1) $s \models \mathit{Init}$, and (2) for each i, $s^{(i)}, s^{(i+1)} \models \mathit{Tr}$.

We assume, without loss of generality, that the transition-relation formula $\mathit{Tr}(V, V')$ is in Conjunctive Normal Form, and we split $\mathit{Tr}(V, V')$ to a conjunction $\mathit{Guard}(V) \wedge \mathit{Body}(V, V')$, where $\mathit{Guard}(V)$ is the maximal subset of conjuncts of Tr expressed over variables just from V, and every conjunct of $\mathit{Body}(V, V')$ can have appearances of variables from V and V'.

Intuitively, formula $\mathit{Guard}(V)$ encodes a loop guard of the program, whose loop body is encoded in $\mathit{Body}(V, V')$. For example, for a program shown in Fig. 1a, $V = \{x, y, K\}$, the $\mathit{Guard} = y < K \vee y > K$, and the entire encoding of the transition relation is shown in Fig. 1b.

Definition 2. *If each program trace contains a state s, such that $s \models \neg \mathit{Guard}$, then the program is called* terminating *(otherwise, it is called* non-terminating*).*

Tasks of proving termination and non-termination are often reduced to tasks of proving program safety. A *safety verification task* is a pair $\langle P, \mathit{Err} \rangle$, where $P = \langle V \cup V', \mathit{Init}, \mathit{Tr} \rangle$ is a program, and Err is an encoding of the *error states*. It has a solution if there exists a formula, called a *safe inductive invariant*, that implies Init, is closed under Tr, and is inconsistent with Err.

---

[2] Provided at http://rers-challenge.org/2012/index.php?page=problems.

```
while (y != K) {
  x = (x > K) ? x - 1 :
      (x < K) ? x + 1 : x;
  y = (y > x) ? y - 1 :
      (y < x) ? y + 1 : y; }
```

(a)

$$Tr(x, x', y, y', K, K') =$$
$$\boxed{(y < K \vee y > K)} \wedge K' = K \wedge$$
$$x' = \texttt{ite}\ (x > K, x - 1, \texttt{ite}\ (x < K, x + 1, x)) \wedge$$
$$y' = \texttt{ite}\ (y > x', y - 1, \texttt{ite}\ (y < x', y + 1, y))$$

(b)

$$\begin{cases} 1 \cdot y + (-1) \cdot K > 0 \\ (-1) \cdot y + 1 \cdot K > 0 \\ 1 \cdot x + (-1) \cdot K > 0 \\ (-1) \cdot x + 1 \cdot K > 0 \end{cases}$$

(c)

$$\begin{aligned} \text{CONST} &::= 0 \\ \text{COEF} &::= 1 \mid -1 \\ \text{VAR} &::= x \mid y \mid K \\ \text{SUM} &::= \text{COEF} \cdot \text{VAR} + \text{COEF} \cdot \text{VAR} + \text{CONST} \\ \text{INEQ} &::= \text{SUM} > 0 \end{aligned}$$

(d)

Fig. 1. (a): C-code; (b): transition relation *Tr* (in the framebox – *Guard*); (c): formulas S extracted from *Tr* and normalized; (d): grammar that generalizes S.

Definition 3. *Let* $P = \langle V \cup V', Init, Tr \rangle$; *a formula Inv is a* safe inductive invariant *if the following conditions hold:* (1) $Init(V) \implies Inv(V)$, (2) $Inv(V) \wedge Tr(V, V') \implies Inv(V')$, *and* (3) $Inv(V) \wedge Err(V) \implies \bot$.

If there exists a trace c (called a *counterexample*) that contains a state s, such that $s \models Err$, then the safety verification task does not have a solution.

3 Exploiting Program Syntax

The key driver of our termination and non-termination provers is a generator of constraints which help to analyze the given program in different ways. The source code often gives useful information, e.g., of occurrences of variables, constants, arithmetic and comparison operators, that could bootstrap the formula generator. We rely on the SyGuS-based algorithm [16] introduced for verifying program safety. It automatically constructs the grammar G based on the fixed set of formulas S obtained by traversing parse trees of *Init*, *Tr*, and *Err*. In our case, *Err* is not given, so G is based only on *Init* and *Tr*.

For simplicity, we require formulas in S to have the form of inequalities composed from a linear combination over either V or V' and a constant (e.g., $x' < y' + 1$ is included, but $x' = x + 1$ is excluded). Then, if needed, variables are deprimed (e.g., $x' < y' + 1$ is replaced by $x < y + 1$), and formulas are normalized, such that all terms are moved to the left side (e.g., $x < y + 1$ is replaced by $x - y - 1 < 0$), the subtraction is rewritten as addition, $<$ is rewritten as $>$, and respectively $\leq$ as $\geq$ (e.g., $x - y - 1 < 0$ is replaced by $(-1) \cdot x + y + 1 > 0$).

The entire process of creation of G is exemplified in Fig. 1. Production rules of G are constructed as follows: (1) the production rule for normalized inequalities

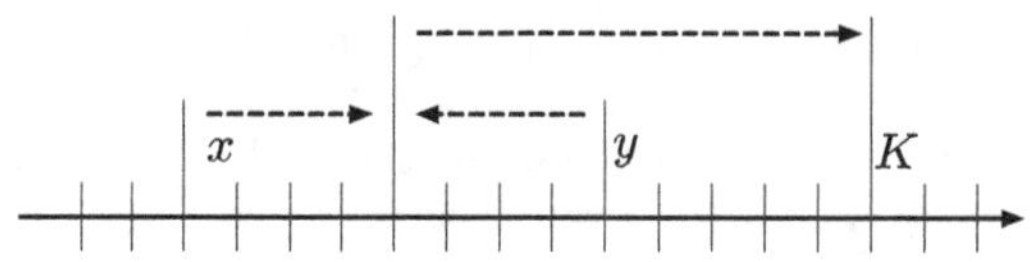

(a)

$$\text{①}\ i > \boxed{x-K} \land i > \boxed{K-x} \land i > \boxed{y-K} \land$$
$$i > \boxed{K-y} \land i > \boxed{x-y} \land i > \boxed{y-x} \Longrightarrow \boldsymbol{Inv}(x,y,i,K)$$

$$\text{②}\ \boldsymbol{Inv}(x,y,i,K) \land (y < K \lor y > K) \land K' = K \land i' = i-1 \land$$
$$x' = \texttt{ite}\ (x > K, x-1, \texttt{ite}\ (x < K, x+1, x)) \land$$
$$y' = \texttt{ite}\ (y > x', y-1, \texttt{ite}\ (y < x', y+1, y)) \Longrightarrow \boldsymbol{Inv}(x', y', i', K')$$

$$\text{③}\ \boldsymbol{Inv}(x,y,i,K) \land (y < K \lor y > K) \land i < 0 \Longrightarrow \bot$$

(b)

Fig. 2. (a): The worst-case dynamics of program from Fig. 1a; (b): the termination-argument validity check (in the frameboxes – lower bounds $\{\ell_j\}$ for i).

(denoted INEQ) consists of choices corresponding to distinct types of inequalities in S, (2) the production rule for linear combinations (denoted SUM) consists of choices corresponding to distinct arities of inequalities in S, (3) production rules for variables, coefficients, and constants (denoted respectively VAR, COEF, and CONST) consist of choices corresponding respectively to distinct variables, coefficients, and constants that occur in inequalities in S. Note that the method of creation of G naturally extends to considering disjunctions and nonlinear arithmetic [16].

Choices in production rules of grammar G can be further assigned probabilities based on frequencies of certain syntactic features (e.g., frequencies of particular constants or combinations of variables) that belong to the program's symbolic encoding. In the interest of saving space, we do not discuss it here and refer the reader to [16]. The generation of formulas from G is performed recursively by sampling from probability distributions assigned to rules. Note that the choice of distributions affects only the order in which formulas are sampled and does not affect which formulas *can* or *cannot* be sampled in principle (because the grammar is fixed). Thus, without loss of generality, it is sound to assume that all distributions are uniform. In the context of termination analysis, we are interested in formulas produced by rules INEQ and SUM.

4 Proving Termination

We start this section with a motivating example and then proceed to presenting the general-purpose algorithms for proving program termination.

Example 1. The program shown in Fig. 1a terminates. It operates on three integer variables, x, y, and K: in each iteration y gets closer to x, and x gets closer

Algorithm 1. LinRank(P): proving termination with linear termination argument

Input: $P = \langle V \cup V', \mathit{Init}, \mathit{Tr} \rangle$ where $\mathit{Tr} = \mathit{Guard} \wedge \mathit{Body}$
Output: $\mathit{res} \in \langle$TERMINATES, UNKNOWN$\rangle$

$V \leftarrow V \cup \{i\}$; $V' \leftarrow V' \cup \{i'\}$;
$\mathit{Tr} \leftarrow \mathit{Tr} \wedge i' = i - 1$; $\mathit{Err} \leftarrow \mathit{Guard} \wedge i < 0$;
$G \leftarrow$ getGrammarAndDistributions(Init, Tr);
while canSample(G) **do**
  $\mathit{cand} \leftarrow$ sample(G, sum);
  $G \leftarrow$ adjust(G, cand);
  if $\mathit{Init} \implies i > \mathit{cand}$ **then continue**;
  $\mathit{Init} \leftarrow \mathit{Init} \wedge i > \mathit{cand}$;
  if isSafe(Init, Tr, Err) **then return** TERMINATES;
return UNKNOWN;

to K. Thus, the total number of values taken by y before it equals K is no bigger than the maximal distance among x, y, and K (in the following, denoted Max). The worst-case dynamics happens when initially $x < y < K$ (shown in Fig. 2a), in other cases the program terminates even faster. To formally prove this, the program could be augmented by a so-called *termination argument*. For this example, it is simply a fresh variable i which is initially assigned Max (or any other value greater than Max) and which gets decremented by one in each iteration. The goal now is to prove that i never gets negative. Fig. 2b shows the encoding of this safety verification task (recall Definition 3). The existence of a solution to this task guarantees the safety of the augmented program, and thus, the termination of the original program. Most state-of-the-art Horn solvers are able to find a solution immediately. □

The main challenge in preparing the termination-argument validity check is the generation of lower bounds $\{\ell_j\}$ for i in Init (e.g., conjunctions of the form $i > \ell_j$ in ① in Fig. 2b). We build on the insight that each ℓ_j could be constructed independently from the others, and then an inequality $i > \ell_j$ could be conjoined with Init, thus giving rise to a new safety verification task. For a generation of candidate inequalities, we utilize the algorithm from Sect. 3: all $\{\ell_j\}$ can be sampled from grammar G which is obtained in advance from Init and Tr.

For example, all six formulas in ① in Fig. 2b: $x - K, K - x, y - K, K - y, x - y$, and $y - x$ belong to the grammar shown in Fig. 1d. Note that for proving termination it is not necessary to have the most precise lower bounds. Intuitively, the larger the initial value of i, the more iterations it will stay positive. Thus, it is sound to try formulas which are not even related to actual lower bounds at all and keep them conjoined with Init.

4.1 Synthesizing Linear Termination Arguments

Algorithm 1 shows an "*enumerate-and-try*" procedure to search for a linear termination argument that proves termination of a program P. To initialize this search, the algorithm introduces an extra counter variable i and adds it to V (respectively, its primed copy i' gets added to V') (line 1).[3] Then the transition-relation formula *Tr* gets augmented by $i' = i-1$, the decrement of the counter in the loop body. To specify a set of error states, Algorithm 1 introduces a formula *Err* (line 2): whenever the loop guard is satisfied and the value of counter i is negative. Algorithm 1 then starts searching for large enough lower bounds for i (i.e., a set of constraints over $V \cup \{i\}$ to be added to *Init*), such that no error state is ever reachable.

Before the main loop of our synthesis procedure starts, various formulas are extracted from the symbolic encoding of P and generalized to a formal grammar (line 3). The grammar is used for an iterative probabilistic sampling of candidate formulas (line 5) that are further added to the validity check of the current termination argument (line 8). In particular, each new constraint over i has the form $i > cand$, where *cand* is produced by the SUM production rule described in Sect. 3. Once *Init* is strengthened by this constraint, a new safety verification condition is compiled and checked (line 9) by an off-the-shelf Horn solver.

As a result of each safety check, either a formula satisfying Definition 3 or a counterexample *cex* witnessing reachability of an error state is generated. Existence of an inductive invariant guarantees that the conjunction of all synthesized lower bounds for i is large enough to prove termination, and thus Algorithm 1 converges. Otherwise, if grammar G still contains a formula that has not been considered yet, the synthesis loop iterates.

For the progress of the algorithm, it must keep track of the strength of each new candidate *cand*. That is, *cand* should add more restrictions on i in *Init*. Otherwise, the outcome of the validity check (line 9) would be the same as in the previous iteration. For this reason, Algorithm 1 includes an important routine [16]: after each sampled candidate *cand*, it adjusts the probability distributions associated with the grammar, such that *cand* could not be sampled again in the future iterations (line 6). Additionally, it checks (line 7) if a new constraint adds some value over the already accepted constraints. Consequently, our algorithm does not require explicit handing of counterexamples: if in each iteration *Init* gets only stronger then current *cex* is invalidated. While in principle the algorithm could explicitly store *cex* and check its consistency with each new *cand*, however in our experiments it did not lead to significant performance gains.

Theorem 1. *If Algorithm 1 returns* TERMINATES *for program P, then P terminates.*

Indeed, the verification condition, which is proven safe in the last iteration of Algorithm 1, corresponds to some program P' that differs from P by the presence of variable i. The set of traces of P has a one-to-one correspondence with the

[3] Assume that initially set V does not contain i.

Algorithm 2. LexRank(P): proving termination with lexicographic termination argument

Input: $P = \langle V \cup V', Init, Tr \rangle$ where $Tr = Guard \wedge Body$
Output: $res \in \langle$TERMINATES, UNKNOWN$\rangle$

$V \leftarrow V \cup \{i, j\}$; $\quad V' \leftarrow V' \cup \{i', j'\}$;
$Err \leftarrow Guard \wedge i < 0$; $\quad jBounds \leftarrow \varnothing$;
$G, G', G'' \leftarrow$ getGrammarAndDistributions($Init$, Tr);
while canSample(G) **or** canSample(G') **or** canSample(G'') **do**
    if nondet() **then**
        $cand \leftarrow$ sample(G, sum); $G \leftarrow$ adjust(G, $cand$);
        $Init \leftarrow Init \wedge i > cand$;
    if nondet() **then**
        $cand \leftarrow$ sample(G', sum); $G' \leftarrow$ adjust(G', $cand$);
        $Init \leftarrow Init \wedge j > cand$;
    if nondet() **then**
        $cand \leftarrow$ sample(G'', sum); $G'' \leftarrow$ adjust(G'', $cand$);
        $jBounds \leftarrow jBounds \cup \{j > cand\}$;
    $Tr' \leftarrow Tr \wedge ite(j > 0, i' = i \wedge j' = j - 1, i' = i - 1 \wedge \bigwedge_{b \in jBounds} b)$;
    if isSafe($Init$, Tr', Err) **then return** TERMINATES;
return UNKNOWN;

set of traces of P', such that each state reachable in P could be extended by a valuation of i to become a reachable state in P'. That is, P terminates iff P' terminates, and P' terminates by construction: i is initially assigned a reasonably large value, monotonically decreases at each iteration, and never goes negative.

We note that the loop in Algorithm 1 always executes only a finite number of iterations since G is constructed from the finite number of components, and in each iteration it gets adjusted to avoid re-sampling of the same candidates. However, an off-the-shelf Horn solver that checks validity of each candidate might not converge because the safety verification task is undecidable in general. To mitigate this obstacle, our implementation supports several state-of-the-art solvers and provides a flexibility to specify one to use.

4.2 Synthesizing Lexicographic Termination Arguments

There is a wide class of terminating programs for which no linear termination argument exists. A commonly used approach to handle them is via a search for a so-called lexicographic termination argument that requires introducing two or more extra counters. A SyGuS-based instantiation of such a procedure for two counters is shown in Algorithm 2 (more counters could be handled similarly). Algorithm 2 has a similar structure to Algorithm 1: the initial program gets augmented by counters, formula Err is introduced, lower bounds for counters are iteratively sampled and added to *Init* and *Tr*, and the verification condition is checked for safety.

The differences in Algorithm 2 are in how it handles two counters i and j, between which an implicit order is fixed. In particular, *Err* is still expressed over i only, but i gets decremented by one only when j equals zero (line 14). At the same time, j gets updated in each iteration: if it was equal to zero, it gets assigned a value satisfying the conjunction of constraints in an auxiliary set *jBounds*; otherwise it gets decremented by one. Algorithm 2 synthesizes *jBounds* as well as lower bounds for initial conditions over i and j. The sampling proceeds separately from three different grammars (lines 6, 9, and 12), and the samples are used in three different contexts (lines 7, 10, and 13 respectively). Optionally, Algorithm 2 could be parametrized by a synthesis strategy that gives interpretations for each of the NONDET() calls (lines 5, 8, and 11 respectively). In the simplest case, each NONDET() call is replaced by $\top$, which means that in each iteration Algorithm 2 needs to sample from all three grammars. Alternatively, NONDET() could be replaced by a method to identify only one grammar per iteration to be sampled from.

Theorem 2. *If Algorithm 2 returns* TERMINATES *for program P, then P terminates.*

The proof sketch for Theorem 2 is similar to the one for Theorem 1: an augmented program P' terminates by construction (due to a mapping of values of $\langle i, j \rangle$ into ordinals), and its set of traces has a one-to-one correspondence with the set of traces of P.

5 Proving Non-termination

In this section, we aim at solving the opposite task to the one in Sect. 4, i.e., we wish to witness infinite program traces and thus, to prove program non-termination. However, in contrast to a traditional search for a single infinite trace, it is often easier to search for groups of infinite traces.

Lemma 1. *Program $P = \langle V \cup V', Init, Tr \rangle$ where $Tr = Guard \wedge Body$ does not terminate if:*

1. *there exists a state s, such that $s \models Init$ and $s \models Guard$,*
2. *for every state s, such that $s \models Guard$, there exists a state s', such that $s, s' \models Tr$ and $s' \models Guard$.*

The lemma distinguishes a class of programs, for which the following holds. First, the loop guard is reachable from the set of initial states. Second, whenever the loop guard is satisfied, there exists a transition to a state in which the loop guard is satisfied again. Therefore, each initial state s, from which the loop guard is reachable, gives rise to at least one infinite trace that starts with s.

Note that for programs with deterministic transition relations (like, e.g., in Fig. 1a), the check of the second condition of Lemma 1 reduces to deciding the

```
while (y != K) {
  x = (x > K) ? x - 1 :
      ( * ) ? x + 1 : x;
  y = (y > x) ? y - 1 :
      (y < x) ? y + 1 : y; }
```

(a)

$$\forall x, y, K \,.\, \boxed{x < K \wedge y < K \wedge (y < K \vee y > K)} \implies$$
$$\exists x', y', K' \,.\, K' = K \wedge$$
$$x' = \texttt{ite}\ (x > K, x - 1, x + 1 \vee x)) \wedge$$
$$y' = \texttt{ite}\ (y > x', y - 1, \texttt{ite}\ (y < x', y + 1, y)) \wedge$$
$$\boxed{x' < K' \wedge y' < K' \wedge (y' < K' \vee y' > K')}$$

(b)

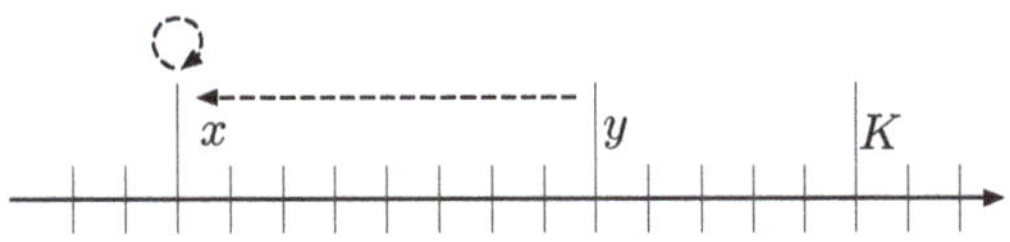

(c)

Fig. 3. (a): A variant of program from Fig. 1a; (b): the valid ∀∃-formula for its non-terminating refinement (in frameboxes – refined *Guard*-s); (c): an example of a non-terminating dynamics, when value of `x` (and eventually, `y`) never gets changed.

satisfiability of a quantifier-free formula since each state can be transitioned to exactly one state. But if the transition relation is non-deterministic, the check reduces to deciding validity of a ∀∃-formula. Although handling quantifiers is in general hard, some recent approaches [15] are particularly tailored to solve this type of queries efficiently.

In practice, the conditions of Lemma 1 are too strict to be fulfilled for an arbitrary program. However, to prove non-termination, it is sufficient to constrain the transition relation as long as it preserves at least one original transition and only then to apply Lemma 1.

Definition 4. *Given programs* $P = \langle V \cup V', Init, Tr \rangle$, *and* $P' = \langle V \cup V', Init, Tr' \rangle$, *we say that* P' *is a* refinement *of* P *if* $Tr' \implies Tr$.

Intuitively, Definition 4 requires P and P' to operate over the same sets of variables and to start from the same initial states. Furthermore, each transition allowed by Tr' is also allowed by Tr. One way to refine P is to restrict $Tr = Guard \wedge Body$ by conjoining either *Guard*, or *Body*, or both with some extra constraints (called *refinement constraints*). In this work, we propose to sample them from our automatically constructed formal grammar (recall Sect. 3).

Example 2. Consider a program shown in Fig. 3a. It differs from the one shown in Fig. 1a by a non-deterministic choice in the second `ite`-statement. That is, y still moves towards x; but x moves towards K only when $x > K$, and otherwise x may always keep the initial value. The formal grammar generated for this program is the same as shown in Fig. 1d, and it contains constraints $x < K$ and $y < K$. Lemma 1 does not apply for the program as is, but it does after refining *Guard* with those constraints. In particular, the ∀∃-formula in Fig. 3b is valid, and a witness to its validity is depicted in Fig. 3c: eventually both x and

Algorithm 3. NONTERMREF(P): proving non-termination

Input: $P = \langle V \cup V', \mathit{Init}, \mathit{Tr}\rangle$ where $\mathit{Tr} = \mathit{Guard} \wedge \mathit{Body}$
Output: $\mathit{res} \in \langle$TERMINATES, DOES NOT TERMINATE, UNKNOWN$\rangle$

1 **if** $\mathit{Init}(V) \wedge \mathit{Guard}(V) \implies \bot$ **then return** TERMINATES;
2 $\mathit{Tr} \leftarrow \mathit{Tr} \wedge$ GETINVS($\mathit{Init}, \mathit{Tr}$);
3 $G \leftarrow$ GETGRAMMARANDDISTRIBUTIONS($\mathit{Init}, \mathit{Tr}$);
4 $\mathit{Refs} \leftarrow \varnothing$; $\mathit{Gramms} \leftarrow \varnothing$; Gramms.PUSH(G);
5 **while** *true* **do**
6   **if** $\forall V \,.\, \mathit{Guard}(V) \wedge \bigwedge_{r \in \mathit{Refs}} r(V) \implies \exists V' \,.\, \mathit{Body}(V, V') \wedge \mathit{Guard}(V') \wedge \bigwedge_{r \in \mathit{Refs}} r(V')$ **then**
7   **return** DOES NOT TERMINATE;
8     $\mathit{cand} \leftarrow \top$;
9   **while** $\mathit{Guard}(V) \wedge \bigwedge_{r \in \mathit{Refs}} r(V) \implies \mathit{cand}(V)$ **or** $\mathit{Init}(V) \wedge \mathit{Guard}(V) \wedge \mathit{cand}(V) \wedge \bigwedge_{r \in \mathit{Refs}} r(V) \implies \bot$ **do**
10   **if** $\mathit{Refs} = \varnothing$ **and** $\neg$CANSAMPLE(G) **then return** UNKNOWN;
11   **if** $\mathit{Refs} \neq \varnothing$ **and** $\neg$CANSAMPLE(G) **then**
12   Refs.POP();
13   Gramms.POP();
14             $\mathit{cand} \leftarrow \top$; $G \leftarrow \mathit{Gramms}$.TOP();
15   **continue**;
16         $\mathit{cand} \leftarrow$ SAMPLE(G, INEQ);
17         $G \leftarrow$ ADJUST(G, cand);
18   Refs.PUSH(cand);
19   Gramms.PUSH(G);

y become equal and always remain smaller than K. Thus, the program does not terminate. □

5.1 Synthesizing Non-terminating Refinements

The algorithm for proving program's non-termination is shown in Algorithm 3. It starts with a simple satisfiability check (line 1) which filters out programs that never reach the loop body (thus they immediately terminate). Then, the transition relation *Tr* gets strengthened by auxiliary inductive invariants obtained with the help of the initial states *Init* (line 2). The algorithm does not impose any specific requirements on the invariants (and it is sound even for a trivial invariant $\top$) and on a method that detects them. In many cases, auxiliary invariants make the algorithm converge faster. Similar to Algorithms 1–2, Algorithm 3 splits *Init* and *Tr* to a set of formulas and generalizes them to a grammar. The difference lies in the type of formulas sampled from the grammar (INEQ vs SUM) and their use in the synthesis loop: Algorithm 3 treats sampled candidates as *refinement constraints* and attempts to apply Lemma 1 (line 6).

The algorithm maintains a stack of refinement constraints *Refs*. At the first iteration, *Refs* is empty, and thus the algorithm tries to apply Lemma 1 to the original program. For that application, a ∀∃-formula is constructed and checked for validity. Intuitively the formula expresses the ability of *Body* to transition each state which satisfies *Guard* to a state which satisfies *Guard* as well. If the validity of ∀∃-formula is proven, the algorithm converges (line 7). Otherwise, a refinement of P needs to be guessed. Thus, the algorithm samples a new formula (line 16) using the production rule INEQ, which is described in Sect. 3, pushes it to *Refs*, and iterates. Note that G permits formulas over V only (i.e., to restrict *Guard*), however, in principle it can be extended for sampling formulas over $V \cup V'$ (thus, to restrict *Body* as well).

For the progress of the algorithm, it must keep track of how each new candidate *cand* corresponds to constraints already belonging to *Refs*. That is, *cand* should not be implied by $\mathit{Guard} \wedge \bigwedge_{r \in \mathit{Refs}} r$ since otherwise the ∀∃-formula in the next iteration would not change. Also, *cand* should not over-constrain the loop guard, and thus it is important to check that after adding *cand* to constraints from *Guard* and *Refs*, the loop guard is still reachable from the initial states. Both these checks are performed before the sampling (line 9). After the sampling, necessary adjustments on the probability distributions, assigned to the production rules of the grammar [16], are applied to ensure the same refinement candidates are not re-sampled again (line 17).

Because by construction G cannot generate conjunctions of constraints, the algorithm handles conjunctions externally. It is useful in case when a single constraint is not enough for application of Lemma 1, and it should be strengthened by another constraint. On the other hand, it also might be needed to withdraw some sampled candidates before converging. For this reason, Algorithm 3 maintains a stack *Gramms* of grammars and handles it synchronously with stack *Refs* (lines 12–14 and 18–19). When all candidates from a grammar were considered and were unsuccessful, the algorithm pops the latest candidate from *Refs* and rolls back to the grammar used in the previous iteration. Additionally, a maximum size of *Refs* can be specified to avoid considering too deep refinements.

Theorem 3. *If Algorithm 3 returns* DOES NOT TERMINATE *for program P, then P does not terminate.*

Indeed, constraints that belong to *Refs* in the last iteration of the algorithm give rise to a refinement P' of P, such that $P' = \langle V \cup V', \mathit{Init}, \mathit{Tr} \wedge \bigwedge_{r \in \mathit{Refs}} r \rangle$. The satisfiability check (line 9) and the validity check (line 6) passed, which correspond to the conditions of Lemma 1. Thus, P' does not terminate, and consequently it has an infinite trace. Finally, since P' refines P then all traces (including infinite ones) of P' belong to P, and P does not terminate as well.

5.2 Integrating Algorithms Together

With a few exceptions [30,39], existing algorithms address either the task of proving, or the task of disproving termination. The goal of this paper is to show that both tasks benefit from syntax-guided techniques. While an algorithmic integration of several orthogonal techniques is itself a challenging problem, it is not the focus of our paper. Still, we use a straightforward idea here. Since each presented algorithm has one big loop, an iteration of Algorithm 1 could be followed by an iteration of Algorithm 2 and in turn, by an iteration of Algorithm 3 (i.e., in a lockstep fashion). A positive result obtained by any algorithm forces all remaining algorithms to terminate. Based on our experiments, provided in detail in Sect. 6, the majority of benchmarks were proven either terminating or non-terminating by one of the algorithms within seconds. This justifies why the lockstep execution of all algorithms in practice would not bring a significant overhead.

6 Evaluation

We have implemented algorithms for proving termination and non-termination in a tool called FreqTerm[4]. It is developed on top of FreqHorn [16], uses it for Horn solving, and supports other Horn solvers, Spacer3 [26] and μZ [24], as well. To solve ∀∃-formulas, FreqTerm uses the AE-VAL tool [15]. All the symbolic reasoning in the end is performed by the Z3 SMT solver [11].

FreqTerm takes as input a program encoded as a system of linear constrained Horn clauses (CHC). It supports any programming language, as long as a translator from it to CHCs exists. For encoding benchmarks to CHCs, we used SeaHorn v.0.1.0-rc3. To the best of our knowledge, FreqTerm is the only (non)-termination prover that supports a selection of Horn solvers in the backend. This allows the prover to leverage advancements in Horn solving easily.

We have compared FreqTerm against AProVE rev. c181f40 [18], Ultimate Automizer v.0.1.23 [22], and HipTNT+ v.1.0 [30]. The rest of the section summarizes three sets of experiments. Sections 6.1 and 6.2 discuss the comparison on small but tricky programs, respectively terminating and non-terminating, which shows that our approach is applicable to a wide range of conceptually challenging problems. In Sect. 6.3, we target several large-scale benchmarks and show that FreqTerm is capable of significant pushing the boundaries of termination and non-termination proving. In total, we considered 856 benchmarks of various size and complexity. All experiments were conducted on a Linux SMP machine, Intel(R) Xeon(R) CPU E5-2680 v4 @ 2.40 GHz, 56 CPUs, 377 GB RAM.

6.1 Performance on Terminating Benchmarks

We considered **171** terminating programs[5] from the Termination category of SVCOMP and programs crafted by ourselves. Altogether, four tools in our experiment were able to prove termination of 168 of them within a timeout of 60 s and

[4] The source code of the tool is publicly available at https://goo.gl/HecBWc.

[5] These benchmarks are available at https://goo.gl/MPimXE.

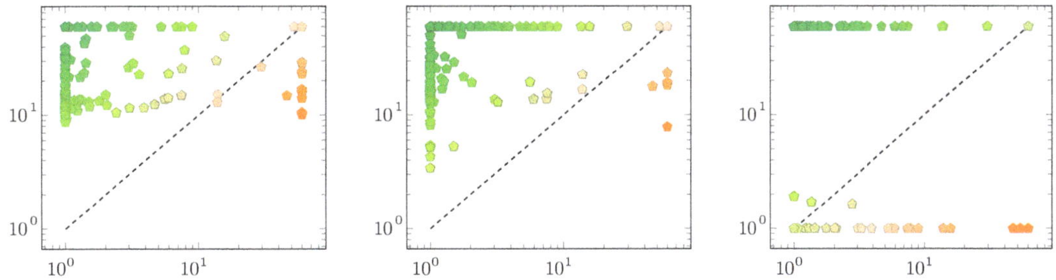

(a) terminating examples (171)

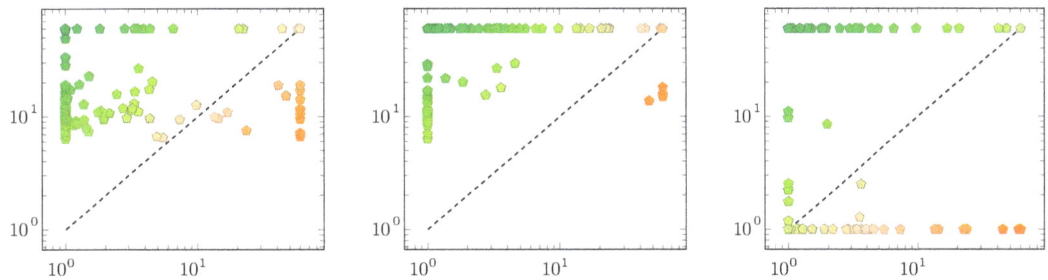

(b) non-terminating examples (176)

Fig. 4. FreqTerm vs respectively Ultimate Automizer, AProVE, and HipTNT+.

left only three programs without a verdict. AProVE verified 76 benchmarks, HipTNT+ 90 (including 3 that no other tool solved), Ultimate Automizer 105 (including 4 that no other tool solved). FreqTerm, implementing Algorithms 1–2 and relying on different solvers verified in total **155** (including **30** that no other tool solved). In particular, Algorithm 1 instantiated with Spacer3, proved termination of 88 programs, with μZ 79, and with FreqHorn 80. Algorithm 2 instantiated with Spacer3, proved termination of 92 programs, with μZ 109, and with FreqHorn 74.

A scatterplot with logarithmic scale on the axes in Fig. 4(a) shows comparisons of best running times of FreqTerm vs the running times of competing tools. Each point in a plot represents a pair of the FreqTerm run (x-axis) and the competing tool run (y-axis). Intuitively, green points represent cases when FreqTerm outperforms the competitor. On average, for programs solved by both FreqTerm and Ultimate Automizer, FreqTerm is 29 times faster (speedup calculated as a ratio of geometric means of the corresponding runs). In a similar setting, FreqTerm is 32 times faster than AProVE. However, FreqTerm is 2 times slower than HipTNT+. The evaluation further revealed (in Sect. 6.3) that the latter tool is efficient only on small programs (around 10 lines of code each), and for large-scale benchmarks it exceeds the timeout.

6.2 Performance on Non-terminating Benchmarks

We considered **176** terminating programs[6] from the Termination category of SVCOMP and programs crafted by ourselves. Altogether, four tools proved non-termination of 172 of them: APROVE 35, HIPTNT+ 92, ULTIMATE AUTOMIZER 123, and Algorithm 3 implemented in FREQTERM **152**. Additionally, we evaluated the effect of $\forall\exists$-solving in FREQTERM. For that reason, we implemented a version of Algorithm 3 in which non-termination is reduced to safety, but the conceptual SyGuS-based refinement generator remained the same. This implementation used SPACER3 for proving that the candidate refinement *can never* exit the loop. Among 176 benchmarks, such routine solved only 105, which is 30% fewer than Algorithm 3. However, it managed to verify 8 benchmarks that Algorithm 3 could not verify (we believe, because SPACER3 was able to add an auxiliary inductive invariant).

Logarithmic scatterplot in Fig. 4(b) shows comparisons of FREQTERM vs the running times of competing tools. On average, FREQTERM is 41 times faster than ULTIMATE AUTOMIZER, 73 times faster than APROVE, and exhibits roughly similar runtimes to HIPTNT+ (again, here we considered only programs solved by both tools). Based on these experiments, we conclude that currently FREQTERM is more effective and more efficient at synthesizing non-terminating program refinements than at synthesizing terminating arguments.

6.3 Large-Scale Benchmarks

We considered some large-scale benchmarks for evaluation arising from Event-Condition-Action (ECA) systems that describe reactive behavior [1]. We considered various modifications of five challenging ECAs[7]. Each ECA consists of one large loop, where each iteration reads an input and modifies its internal state. If an unexpected input is read, the ECA terminates.

In our first case study, we aimed to prove non-termination of the given ECAs, i.e., that for any reachable internal state there exists an input value that would keep the ECA alive. The main challenge appeared to be in the size of benchmarks (up to 10000 lines of C code per loop) and reliance on an auxiliary inductive invariant. With the extra support of SPACER3 to provide the invariant, FREQTERM was able to prove non-termination of a wide range of programs. Among all the competing tools, only ULTIMATE AUTOMIZER was able to handle these benchmarks, but it verified only a small fraction of them within a 2 h timeout. In contrast, FREQTERM solved 301 out of 302 tasks and outperformed ULTIMATE AUTOMIZER by up to several orders of magnitude (i.e., from seconds to hours). Table 1 contains a brief summary of our experimental evaluation.[8]

In our second case study, we instrumented the ECAs by adding extra conditions to the loop guards, thus imposing an implicit upper bound on the number

[6] These benchmarks are available at https://goo.gl/bZbuA2.

[7] These benchmarks are available at https://goo.gl/7mc2Ww.

[8] To calculate average timings, we excluded cases when the tool exceeded timeout.

Table 1. FreqTerm vs Ultimate Automizer on non-terminating ECAs (302).

Benchmarks			FreqTerm		Ultimate Automizer	
Class	# of tasks	Avg # of LoC	# solved	Avg time	# solved	Avg time
1 & 2	122	500	122	5 sec	3	27 min
3	60	1600	60	56 sec	0	∞
4	60	4700	60	9 min	6	82 min
5	60	10000	59	52 min	0	∞

Table 2. FreqTerm vs Ultimate Automizer on terminating ECAs (207).

Benchmarks			FreqTerm		Ultimate Automizer	
Class	# of tasks	Avg # of LoC	# solved	Avg time	# solved	Avg time
1 & 2	97	500	97	8 sec	96	73 sec
3	40	1600	40	3 min	12	56 min
4	35	4700	35	10 min	27	19 min
5	35	10000	34	65 min	19	99 min

of loop iterations, and applied tools to prove termination[9] (shown in Table 2). Again, only Ultimate Automizer was able to compete with FreqTerm, and interestingly it was more successful here than in the first case study. Encouragingly, FreqTerm solved all but one instance and was consistently faster.

7 Related Work

Proving Termination. A wide range of state-of-the-art methods are based on iterative reasoning driven by counterexamples [4,5,9,10,19,21,23,27,29,36] whose goal is to show that transitions cannot be executed forever. These approaches typically combine termination arguments, proven independently, but none of them leverages the syntax of programs during the analysis.

A minor range of tools of termination analyzers are based on various types of learning. In particular, [39] discovers a terminating argument from attempts to prove that no program state is terminating; [34] exploits information derived from tests, [37] guesses and checks transition invariants (over-approximations to the reachable transitive closure of the transition relation) from libraries of templates. The closest to our approach, [31] guesses and checks transition invariants using loop guards and branch conditions. In contrast, our algorithms guess lower bounds for auxiliary program counters and extensively use all available source code for guessing candidates.

[9] The task of adding interesting guards appeared to be non-trivial, so we were able to instrument only a part of all non-terminating benchmarks.

Proving Non-termination. Traditional algorithms, e.g. [3,6,8,20,22], are based on a search for lasso-shaped traces and a discovery of *recurrence sets*, i.e., states that are visited infinitely often. For instance, [32] searches for a geometric series in lasso-shaped traces. Our algorithm discovers *existential* recurrence sets and does not deal with traces at all: it handles their abstraction via a $\forall\exists$-formula.

A reduction to safety attracts significant attention here as well. In particular, [40] relies only on invariant generation to show that the loop guard is also satisfied, [19] infers weakest preconditions over inputs, under which program is non-terminating; and [7,28] iteratively eliminate terminating traces through a loop by adding extra assumptions. In contrast, our approach does not reduce to safety, and thus does not necessarily require invariants. However, we observed that if provided, in practice they often accelerate our verification process.

Syntax-Guided Synthesis. SyGuS [2] is applied to various tasks related to program synthesis, e.g., [13,17,25,33,35,41]. However, the formal grammar in those applications is typically given or constructed from user-provided examples. To the best of our knowledge, the only application of SyGuS to automatic program analysis was proposed by [14,16], and it inspired our approach. Originally, the formal grammar, constructed from the verification condition, was iteratively used to guess and check only inductive invariants. In this paper, we showed that a similar reasoning is practical and easily transferable across applications.

8 Conclusion

We have presented new algorithms for synthesis of termination arguments and non-terminating program refinements. Driven by SyGuS, they iteratively generate candidate formulas which tend to follow syntactic patterns obtained from the source code. By construction, the number of possible candidates is always finite, thus the search space is always relatively small. The algorithms rely on recent advances in constraint solving, they do not depend on a particular backend engine, and thus performance of checking validity of a candidate can be improved by advancements in solvers. Our implementation FreqTerm is evaluated on a wide range of terminating and non-terminating benchmarks. It is competitive with state-of-the-art and it significantly outperforms other tools when proving non-termination of large-scale Event-Condition-Action systems.

In future work, it would be interesting to investigate synergetic ways of integrating the proposed algorithms together, as well as exploiting strengths of different backend Horn solvers for different verification tasks.

References

1. Almeida, E.E., Luntz, J.E., Tilbury, D.M.: Event-condition-action systems for reconfigurable logic control. IEEE Trans. Autom. Sci. Eng. **4**(2), 167–181 (2007)
2. Alur, R., Bodík, R., Juniwal, G., Martin, M.M.K., Raghothaman, M., Seshia, S.A., Singh, R., Solar-Lezama, A., Torlak, E., Udupa, A.: Syntax-guided synthesis. In: FMCAD, pp. 1–17. IEEE (2013)

3. Bakhirkin, A., Piterman, N.: Finding recurrent sets with backward analysis and trace partitioning. In: Chechik, M., Raskin, J.-F. (eds.) TACAS 2016. LNCS, vol. 9636, pp. 17–35. Springer, Heidelberg (2016). https://doi.org/10.1007/978-3-662-49674-9_2
4. Balaban, I., Pnueli, A., Zuck, L.D.: Ranking abstraction as companion to predicate abstraction. In: Wang, F. (ed.) FORTE 2005. LNCS, vol. 3731, pp. 1–12. Springer, Heidelberg (2005). https://doi.org/10.1007/11562436_1
5. Brockschmidt, M., Cook, B., Fuhs, C.: Better termination proving through cooperation. In: Sharygina, N., Veith, H. (eds.) CAV 2013. LNCS, vol. 8044, pp. 413–429. Springer, Heidelberg (2013). https://doi.org/10.1007/978-3-642-39799-8_28
6. Brockschmidt, M., Ströder, T., Otto, C., Giesl, J.: Automated detection of non-termination and NullPointerExceptions for Java Bytecode. In: Beckert, B., Damiani, F., Gurov, D. (eds.) FoVeOOS 2011. LNCS, vol. 7421, pp. 123–141. Springer, Heidelberg (2012). https://doi.org/10.1007/978-3-642-31762-0_9
7. Chen, H.-Y., Cook, B., Fuhs, C., Nimkar, K., O'Hearn, P.: Proving nontermination via safety. In: Ábrahám, E., Havelund, K. (eds.) TACAS 2014. LNCS, vol. 8413, pp. 156–171. Springer, Heidelberg (2014). https://doi.org/10.1007/978-3-642-54862-8_11
8. Cook, B., Fuhs, C., Nimkar, K., O'Hearn, P.W.: Disproving termination with overapproximation. In: FMCAD, pp. 67–74. IEEE (2014)
9. Cook, B., Podelski, A., Rybalchenko, A.: Termination proofs for systems code. In: PLDI, pp. 415–426. ACM (2006)
10. Cook, B., See, A., Zuleger, F.: Ramsey vs. lexicographic termination proving. In: Piterman, N., Smolka, S.A. (eds.) TACAS 2013. LNCS, vol. 7795, pp. 47–61. Springer, Heidelberg (2013). https://doi.org/10.1007/978-3-642-36742-7_4
11. de Moura, L.M., Bjørner, N.: Z3: an efficient SMT solver. In: Ramakrishnan, C.R., Rehof, J. (eds.) TACAS 2008. LNCS, vol. 4963, pp. 337–340. Springer, Heidelberg (2008). https://doi.org/10.1007/978-3-540-78800-3_24
12. Detlefs, D., Nelson, G., Saxe, J.B.: Simplify: a theorem prover for program checking. J. ACM **52**(3), 365–473 (2005)
13. Fedyukovich, G., Ahmad, M.B.S., Bodík, R.: Gradual synthesis for static parallelization of single-pass array-processing programs. In: PLDI, pp. 572–585. ACM (2017)
14. Fedyukovich, G., Bodík, R.: Accelerating syntax-guided invariant synthesis. In: Beyer, D., Huisman, M. (eds.) TACAS 2018. LNCS, vol. 10805, pp. 251–269. Springer, Cham (2018). https://doi.org/10.1007/978-3-319-89960-2_14
15. Fedyukovich, G., Gurfinkel, A., Sharygina, N.: Automated discovery of simulation between programs. In: Davis, M., Fehnker, A., McIver, A., Voronkov, A. (eds.) LPAR 2015. LNCS, vol. 9450, pp. 606–621. Springer, Heidelberg (2015). https://doi.org/10.1007/978-3-662-48899-7_42
16. Fedyukovich, G., Kaufman, S., Bodík, R.: Sampling invariants from frequency distributions. In: FMCAD, pp. 100–107. IEEE (2017)
17. Galenson, J., Reames, P., Bodík, R., Hartmann, B., Sen, K.: CodeHint: dynamic and interactive synthesis of code snippets. In: ICSE, pp. 653–663. ACM (2014)
18. Giesl, J., et al.: Proving termination of programs automatically with AProVE. In: Demri, S., Kapur, D., Weidenbach, C. (eds.) IJCAR 2014. LNCS (LNAI), vol. 8562, pp. 184–191. Springer, Cham (2014). https://doi.org/10.1007/978-3-319-08587-6_13
19. Gulwani, S., Srivastava, S., Venkatesan, R.: Program analysis as constraint solving. In: PLDI, pp. 281–292. ACM (2008)

20. Gupta, A., Henzinger, T.A., Majumdar, R., Rybalchenko, A., Xu, R.: Proving non-termination. In: POPL, pp. 147–158. ACM (2008)
21. Harris, W.R., Lal, A., Nori, A.V., Rajamani, S.K.: Alternation for termination. In: Cousot, R., Martel, M. (eds.) SAS 2010. LNCS, vol. 6337, pp. 304–319. Springer, Heidelberg (2010). https://doi.org/10.1007/978-3-642-15769-1_19
22. Heizmann, M., et al.: Ultimate automizer with an on-demand construction of floyd-hoare automata. In: Legay, A., Margaria, T. (eds.) TACAS 2017. LNCS, vol. 10206, pp. 394–398. Springer, Heidelberg (2017). https://doi.org/10.1007/978-3-662-54580-5_30
23. Heizmann, M., Hoenicke, J., Podelski, A.: Termination analysis by learning terminating programs. In: Biere, A., Bloem, R. (eds.) CAV 2014. LNCS, vol. 8559, pp. 797–813. Springer, Cham (2014). https://doi.org/10.1007/978-3-319-08867-9_53
24. Hoder, K., Bjørner, N.: Generalized property directed reachability. In: Cimatti, A., Sebastiani, R. (eds.) SAT 2012. LNCS, vol. 7317, pp. 157–171. Springer, Heidelberg (2012). https://doi.org/10.1007/978-3-642-31612-8_13
25. Jha, S., Gulwani, S., Seshia, S.A., Tiwari, A.: Oracle-guided component-based program synthesis. In: ICSE, pp. 215–224. ACM (2010)
26. Komuravelli, A., Gurfinkel, A., Chaki, S.: SMT-based model checking for recursive programs. In: Biere, A., Bloem, R. (eds.) CAV 2014. LNCS, vol. 8559, pp. 17–34. Springer, Cham (2014). https://doi.org/10.1007/978-3-319-08867-9_2
27. Kroening, D., Sharygina, N., Tsitovich, A., Wintersteiger, C.M.: Termination analysis with compositional transition invariants. In: Touili, T., Cook, B., Jackson, P. (eds.) CAV 2010. LNCS, vol. 6174, pp. 89–103. Springer, Heidelberg (2010). https://doi.org/10.1007/978-3-642-14295-6_9
28. Larraz, D., Nimkar, K., Oliveras, A., Rodríguez-Carbonell, E., Rubio, A.: Proving non-termination using Max-SMT. In: Biere, A., Bloem, R. (eds.) CAV 2014. LNCS, vol. 8559, pp. 779–796. Springer, Cham (2014). https://doi.org/10.1007/978-3-319-08867-9_52
29. Larraz, D., Oliveras, A., Rodríguez-Carbonell, E., Rubio, A.: Proving termination of imperative programs using Max-SMT. In: FMCAD, pp. 218–225. IEEE (2013)
30. Le, T.C., Qin, S., Chin, W.: Termination and non-termination specification inference. In: PLDI, pp. 489–498. ACM (2015)
31. Lee, W., Wang, B.-Y., Yi, K.: Termination analysis with algorithmic learning. In: Madhusudan, P., Seshia, S.A. (eds.) CAV 2012. LNCS, vol. 7358, pp. 88–104. Springer, Heidelberg (2012). https://doi.org/10.1007/978-3-642-31424-7_12
32. Leike, J., Heizmann, M.: Geometric nontermination arguments. In: Beyer, D., Huisman, M. (eds.) TACAS 2018. LNCS, vol. 10806, pp. 266–283. Springer, Cham (2018). https://doi.org/10.1007/978-3-319-89963-3_16
33. Miltner, A., Fisher, K., Pierce, B.C., Walker, D., Zdancewic, S.: Synthesizing bijective lenses. PACMPL **2**(POPL), 1:1–1:30 (2018)
34. Nori, A.V., Sharma, R.: Termination proofs from tests. In: ESEC/FSE, pp. 246–256. ACM (2013)
35. Panchekha, P., Torlak, E.: Automated reasoning for web page layout. In: OOPSLA, pp. 181–194. ACM (2016)
36. Podelski, A., Rybalchenko, A.: Transition invariants and transition predicate abstraction for program termination. In: Abdulla, P.A., Leino, K.R.M. (eds.) TACAS 2011. LNCS, vol. 6605, pp. 3–10. Springer, Heidelberg (2011). https://doi.org/10.1007/978-3-642-19835-9_2
37. Tsitovich, A., Sharygina, N., Wintersteiger, C.M., Kroening, D.: Loop summarization and termination analysis. In: Abdulla, P.A., Leino, K.R.M. (eds.) TACAS

2011. LNCS, vol. 6605, pp. 81–95. Springer, Heidelberg (2011). https://doi.org/10.1007/978-3-642-19835-9_9
38. Turing, A.M.: Checking a large routine. In: Report of a Conference on High Speed Automatic Calculating Machines (1949)
39. Urban, C., Gurfinkel, A., Kahsai, T.: Synthesizing ranking functions from bits and pieces. In: Chechik, M., Raskin, J.-F. (eds.) TACAS 2016. LNCS, vol. 9636, pp. 54–70. Springer, Heidelberg (2016). https://doi.org/10.1007/978-3-662-49674-9_4
40. Velroyen, H., Rümmer, P.: Non-termination checking for imperative programs. In: Beckert, B., Hähnle, R. (eds.) TAP 2008. LNCS, vol. 4966, pp. 154–170. Springer, Heidelberg (2008). https://doi.org/10.1007/978-3-540-79124-9_11
41. Wang, X., Dillig, I., Singh, R.: Program synthesis using abstraction refinement. PACMPL **2**, 63:1–63:30 (2018)

Model Checking Quantitative Hyperproperties

Bernd Finkbeiner, Christopher Hahn, and Hazem Torfah(✉)

Reactive Systems Group, Saarland University, Saarbrücken, Germany
{finkbeiner,hahn,torfah}@react.uni-saarland.de

Abstract. Hyperproperties are properties of sets of computation traces. In this paper, we study quantitative hyperproperties, which we define as hyperproperties that express a bound on the number of traces that may appear in a certain relation. For example, quantitative non-interference limits the amount of information about certain secret inputs that is leaked through the observable outputs of a system. Quantitative non-interference thus bounds the number of traces that have the same observable input but different observable output. We study quantitative hyperproperties in the setting of HyperLTL, a temporal logic for hyperproperties. We show that, while quantitative hyperproperties can be expressed in HyperLTL, the running time of the HyperLTL model checking algorithm is, depending on the type of property, exponential or even doubly exponential in the quantitative bound. We improve this complexity with a new model checking algorithm based on model-counting. The new algorithm needs only logarithmic space in the bound and therefore improves, depending on the property, exponentially or even doubly exponentially over the model checking algorithm of HyperLTL. In the worst case, the new algorithm needs polynomial space in the size of the system. Our Max#Sat-based prototype implementation demonstrates, however, that the counting approach is viable on systems with nontrivial quantitative information flow requirements such as a passcode checker.

1 Introduction

Model checking algorithms [17] are the cornerstone of computer-aided verification. As their input consists of both the system under verification and a logical formula that describes the property to be verified, they uniformly solve a wide range of verification problems, such as all verification problems expressible in linear-time temporal logic (LTL), computation-tree logic (CTL), or the modal μ-calculus. Recently, there has been a lot of interest in extending model checking from standard trace and tree properties to *information flow* policies like observational determinism or quantitative information flow. Such policies are called

This work was partly supported by the ERC Grant 683300 (OSARES) and by the German Research Foundation (DFG) in the Collaborative Research Center 1223.

H. Chockler and G. Weissenbacher (Eds.): CAV 2018, LNCS 10981, pp. 144–163, 2018.
https://doi.org/10.1007/978-3-319-96145-3_8

hyperproperties [21] and can be expressed in HyperLTL [18], an extension of LTL with trace quantifiers and trace variables. For example, *observational determinism* [47], the requirement that any pair of traces that have the same observable input also have the same observable output, can be expressed as the following HyperLTL formula: $\forall \pi . \forall \pi' . (\Box \pi =_I \pi') \rightarrow (\Box \pi =_O \pi')$ For many information flow policies of interest, including observational determinism, there is no longer a need for property-specific algorithms: it has been shown that the standard HyperLTL model checking algorithm [26] performs just as well as a specialized algorithm for the respective property.

The class of hyperproperties studied in this paper is one where, by contrast, the standard model checking algorithm performes badly. We are interested in *quantitative hyperproperties*, i.e., hyperproperties that express a bound on the number of traces that may appear in a certain relation. A prominent example of this class of properties is *quantitative non-interference* [43,45], where we allow some flow of information but, at the same time, limit the amount of information that may be leaked. Such properties are used, for example, to describe the correct behavior of a password check, where some information flow is unavoidable ("the password was incorrect"), and perhaps some extra information flow is acceptable ("the password must contain a special character"), but the information should not suffice to guess the actual password. In HyperLTL, quantitative non-interference can be expressed [18] as the formula $\forall \pi_0 .\ \forall \pi_1 \ldots \forall \pi_{2^c} . \left(\bigwedge_i \Box(\pi_i =_I \pi_0)\right) \rightarrow \left(\bigvee_{i \neq j} \Box(\pi_i =_O \pi_j)\right)$. The formula states that there do not exist $2^c + 1$ traces (corresponding to more than c bits of information) with the same observable input but different observable output. The bad performance of the standard model checking algorithm is a consequence of the fact that the $2^c + 1$ traces are tracked simultaneously. For this purpose, the model checking algorithm builds and analyzes a $(2^c + 1)$-fold self-composition of the system.

We present a new model checking algorithm for quantitative hyperproperties that avoids the construction of the huge self-composition. The key idea of our approach is to use *counting* rather than *checking* as the basic operation. Instead of building the self-composition and then *checking* the satisfaction of the formula, we add new atomic propositions and then *count* the number of sequences of evaluations of the new atomic propositions that satisfy the specification. Quantitative hyperproperties are expressions of the following form:

$$\forall \pi_1 . \ldots \forall \pi_k . \varphi \rightarrow (\#\sigma : X . \psi \lhd n),$$

where $\lhd \in \{\leq, <, \geq, >, =\}$. The universal quantifiers introduce a set of reference traces against which other traces can be compared. The formulas φ and ψ are HyperLTL formulas. The counting quantifier $\#\sigma : X . \psi$ counts the number of paths σ with different valuations of the atomic propositions X that satisfy ψ. The requirement that no more than c bits of information are leaked is the following quantitative hyperproperty:

$$\forall \pi . \#\sigma\colon O . \Box(\pi =_I \sigma) \leq 2^c$$

As we show in the paper, such expressions do not change the expressiveness of the logic; however, they allow us to express quantitative hyperproperties in exponentially more concise form. The counting-based model checking algorithm then maintains this advantage with a logarithmic counter, resulting in exponentially better performance in both time and space.

The viability of our counting-based model checking algorithm is demonstrated on a SAT-based prototype implementation. For quantitative hyperproperties of intrest, such as bounded leakage of a password checker, our algorithm shows promising results, as it significantly outperforms existing model checking approaches.

1.1 Related Work

Quantitative information-flow has been studied extensively in the literature. See, for example, the following selection of contributions on this topic: [1,14,19,32, 34,43]. Multiple verification methods for quantitative information-flow were proposed for sequential systems. For example, with static analysis techniques [15], approximation methods [35], equivalence relations [3,22], and randomized methods [35]. Quantitative information-flow for multi-threaded programs was considered in [11].

The study of quantitative information-flow in a reactive setting gained a lot of attention recently after the introduction of hyperproperties [21] and the idea of verifying the self-composition of a reactive system [6] in order to relate traces to each other. There are several possibilities to measure the amount of leakage, such as Shannon entropy [15,24,37], guessing entropy [3,34], and min-entropy [43]. A classification of quantitative information-flow policies as safety and liveness hyperproperties was given in [46]. While several verification techniques for hyperproperties exists [5,31,38,42], the literature was missing general approaches to quantitative information-flow control. SecLTL [25] was introduced as first general approach to model check (quantitative) hyperproperties, before HyperLTL [18], and its corresponding model checker [26], was introduced as a temporal logic for hyperproperties, which subsumes the previous approaches.

Using counting to compute the number of solutions of a given formula is studied in the literature as well and includes many probabilistic inference problems, such as Bayesian net reasoning [36], and planning problems, such as computing robustness of plans in incomplete domains [40]. State-of-the-art tools for propositional model counting are `Relsat` [33] and `c2d` [23]. Algorithms for counting models of temporal logics and automata over infinite words have been introduced in [27,28,44]. The counting of projected models, i.e., when some parts of the models are irrelevant, was studied in [2], for which tools such as `#CLASP` [2] and `DSharp_P` [2,41] exist. Our SAT-based prototype implementation is based on a reduction to a Max#SAT [29] instance, for which a corresponding tool exists.

Among the already existing tools for computing the amount of information leakage, for example, `QUAIL` [8], which analyzes programs written in a specific while-language and `LeakWatch` [12], which estimates the amount of leakage in

Java programs, Moped-QLeak [9] is closest to our approach. However, their approach of computing a symbolic summary as an Algebraic Decision Diagram is, in contrast to our approach, solely based on model counting, not maximum model counting.

2 Preliminaries

2.1 HyperLTL

HyperLTL [18] extends linear-time temporal logic (LTL) with trace variables and trace quantifiers. Let AP be a set of *atomic propositions*. A *trace* t is an infinite sequence over subsets of the atomic propositions. We define the set of traces $TR := (2^{AP})^\omega$. A subset $T \subseteq TR$ is called a *trace property* and a subset $H \subseteq 2^{TR}$ is called a *hyperproperty*. We use the following notation to manipulate traces: let $t \in TR$ be a trace and $i \in \mathbb{N}$ be a natural number. $t[i]$ denotes the i-th element of t. Therefore, $t[0]$ represents the starting element of the trace. Let $j \in \mathbb{N}$ and $j \geq i$. $t[i, j]$ denotes the sequence $t[i]\ t[i+1] \ldots t[j-1]\ t[j]$. $t[i, \infty]$ denotes the infinite suffix of t starting at position i.

HyperLTL Syntax. Let $\mathcal{V}$ be an infinite supply of trace variables. The syntax of HyperLTL is given by the following grammar:

$$\begin{aligned} \psi &::= \exists \pi.\psi \mid \forall \pi.\psi \mid \varphi \\ \varphi &::= a_\pi \mid \neg\varphi \mid \varphi \vee \varphi \mid \bigcirc\varphi \mid \varphi\, \mathcal{U}\, \varphi \end{aligned}$$

where $a \in AP$ is an atomic proposition and $\pi \in \mathcal{V}$ is a trace variable. Note that atomic propositions are indexed by trace variables. The quantification over traces makes it possible to express properties like "on all traces ψ must hold", which is expressed by $\forall \pi.\ \psi$. Dually, one can express that "there exists a trace such that ψ holds", which is denoted by $\exists \pi.\ \psi$. The derived operators $\Diamond$, $\Box$, and $\mathcal{W}$ are defined as for LTL. We abbreviate the formula $\bigwedge_{x \in X}(x_\pi \leftrightarrow x_{\pi'})$, expressing that the traces π and π' are equal with respect to a set $X \subseteq AP$ of atomic propositions, by $\pi =_X \pi'$. Furthermore, we call a trace variable π free in a HyperLTL formula if there is no quantification over π and we call a HyperLTL formula φ closed if there exists no free trace variable in φ.

HyperLTL Semantics. A HyperLTL formula defines a *hyperproperty*, i.e., a set of sets of traces. A set T of traces satisfies the hyperproperty if it is an element of this set of sets. Formally, the semantics of HyperLTL formulas is given with respect to a *trace assignment* Π from $\mathcal{V}$ to TR, i.e., a partial function mapping trace variables to actual traces. $\Pi[\pi \mapsto t]$ denotes that π is mapped to t, with everything else mapped according to Π. $\Pi[i, \infty]$ denotes the trace assignment that is equal to $\Pi(\pi)[i, \infty]$ for all π.

$\Pi \models_T \exists\pi.\psi$	iff	there exists $t \in T : \Pi[\pi \mapsto t] \models_T \psi$
$\Pi \models_T \forall\pi.\psi$	iff	for all $t \in T : \Pi[\pi \mapsto t] \models_T \psi$
$\Pi \models_T a_\pi$	iff	$a \in \Pi(\pi)[0]$
$\Pi \models_T \neg\psi$	iff	$\Pi \not\models_T \psi$
$\Pi \models_T \psi_1 \vee \psi_2$	iff	$\Pi \models_T \psi_1$ or $\Pi \models_T \psi_2$
$\Pi \models_T \bigcirc\psi$	iff	$\Pi[1,\infty] \models_T \psi$
$\Pi \models_T \psi_1 \mathcal{U} \psi_2$	iff	there exists $i \geq 0 : \Pi[i,\infty] \models_T \psi_2$ and for all $0 \leq j < i$ we have $\Pi[j,\infty] \models_T \psi_1$

We say a set of traces T *satisfies* a HyperLTL formula φ if $\Pi \models_T \varphi$, where Π is the empty trace assignment.

2.2 System Model

A *Kripke structure* is a tuple $K = (S, s_0, \delta, AP, L)$ consisting of a set of states S, an initial state $s_0 \in S$, a transition function $\delta : S \to 2^S$, a set of *atomic propositions* AP, and a *labeling function* $L : S \to 2^{AP}$, which labels every state with a set of atomic propositions. We assume that each state has a successor, i.e., $\delta(s) \neq \emptyset$. This ensures that every run on a Kripke structure can always be extended to an infinite run. We define a *path* of a Kripke structure as an infinite sequence of states $s_0 s_1 \cdots \in S^\omega$ such that s_0 is the initial state of K and $s_{i+1} \in \delta(s_i)$ for every $i \in \mathbb{N}$. We denote the set of all paths of K that start in a state s with $\mathit{Paths}(K, s)$. Furthermore, $\mathit{Paths}^*(K, s)$ denotes the set of all path prefixes and $\mathit{Paths}^\omega(K, s)$ the set of all path suffixes. A *trace* of a Kripke structure is an infinite sequence of sets of atomic propositions $L(s_0), L(s_1), \cdots \in (2^{AP})^\omega$, such that s_0 is the initial state of K and $s_{i+1} \in \delta(s_i)$ for every $i \in \mathbb{N}$. We denote the set of all traces of K that start in a state s with $TR(K, s)$. We say that a Kripke structure K *satisfies* a HyperLTL formula φ if its set of traces satisfies φ, i.e., if $\Pi \models_{TR(K,s_0)} \varphi$, where Π is the empty trace assignment.

2.3 Automata over Infinite Words

In our construction we use automata over infinite words. A *Büchi automaton* is a tuple $\mathcal{B} = (Q, Q_0, \delta, \Sigma, F)$, where Q is a set of states, Q_0 is a set of initial states, $\delta : Q \times \Sigma \to 2^Q$ is a transition relation, and $F \subset Q$ are the accepting states. A run of $\mathcal{B}$ on an infinite word $w = \alpha_1\alpha_2 \cdots \in \Sigma^\omega$ is an infinite sequence $r = q_0 q_1 \cdots \in Q^\omega$ of states, where $q_0 \in Q_0$ and for each $i \geq 0$, $q_{i+1} = \delta(q_i, \alpha_{i+1})$. We define $\mathbf{Inf}(r) = \{q \in Q \mid \forall i \exists j > i.\ r_j = q\}$. A run r is called accepting if $\mathbf{Inf}(r) \cap F \neq \emptyset$. A word w is accepted by $\mathcal{B}$ and called a *model* of $\mathcal{B}$ if there is an accepting run of $\mathcal{B}$ on w.

Furthermore, an *alternating automaton*, whose runs generalize from sequences to trees, is a tuple $\mathcal{A} = (Q, Q_0, \delta, \Sigma, F)$. Q, Q_0, Σ, and F are defined as above and $\delta : Q \times \Sigma \to \mathbb{B}^+ Q$ being a transition function, which maps a state and a symbol into a Boolean combination of states. Thus, a run(-tree) of an alternating Büchi automaton $\mathcal{A}$ on an infinite word w is a Q-labeled tree. A word w is accepted by $\mathcal{A}$ and called a *model* if there exists a run-tree T such that all paths p trough T are accepting, i.e., $\mathbf{Inf}(p) \cap F \neq \emptyset$.

A strongly connected component (SCC) in $\mathcal{A}$ is a maximal strongly connected component of the graph induced by the automaton. An SCC is called *accepting* if one of its states is an accepting state in $\mathcal{A}$.

3 Quantitative Hyperproperties

Quantitative Hyperproperties are properties of sets of computation traces that express a bound on the number of traces that may appear in a certain relation. In the following, we study quantitative hyperproperties that are specified in terms of HyperLTL formulas. We consider expressions of the following general form:

$$\forall \pi_1, \ldots, \pi_k.\ \varphi \rightarrow (\#\sigma : A.\ \psi \triangleleft n)$$

Both the universally quantified variables $\pi_1, \ldots, \pi_k$ and the variable σ after the *counting* operator $\#$ are trace variables; φ is a HyperLTL formula over atomic propositions AP and free trace variables $\pi_1 \ldots \pi_k$; $A \subseteq AP$ is a set of atomic propositions; ψ is a HyperLTL formula over atomic propositions AP and free trace variables $\pi_1 \ldots \pi_k$ and, additionally σ. The operator $\triangleleft \in \{<, \leq, =, >, \geq\}$ is a comparison operator; and $n \in \mathbb{N}$ is a natural number.

For a given set of traces T and a valuation of the trace variables $\pi_1, \ldots, \pi_k$, the term $\#\sigma : A.\ \psi$ computes the number of traces σ in T that differ in their valuation of the atomic propositions in A and satisfy ψ. The expression $\#\sigma : A.\ \psi \triangleleft n$ is *true* iff the resulting number satisfies the comparison with n. Finally, the complete expression $\forall \pi_1, \ldots, \pi_k.\ \varphi \rightarrow (\#\sigma : A.\ \psi \triangleleft n)$ is *true* iff for all combinations $\pi_1, \ldots, \pi_k$ of traces in T that satisfy φ, the comparison $\#\sigma : A.\ \psi \triangleleft n$ is satisfied.

Example 1 (Quantitative non-interference). Quantitative information-flow policies [13,20,30,34] allow the flow of a bounded amount of information. One way to measure leakage is with *min-entropy* [43], which quantifies the amount of information an attacker can gain given the answer to a single guess about the secret. The *bounding problem* [45] for min-entropy is to determine whether that amount is bounded from above by a constant 2^c, corresponding to c bits. We assume that the program whose leakage is being quantified is deterministic, and assume that the secret input to that program is uniformly distributed. The bounding problem then reduces to determining that there is no tuple of $2^c + 1$ distinguishable traces [43,45]. Let $O \subseteq AP$ be the set of observable outputs. A simple quantitative information flow policy is then the following quantitative hyperproperty, which bounds the number of distinguishable outputs to 2^c, corresponding to a bound of c bits of information:

$$\#\sigma : O.\ \mathit{true} \leq 2^c$$

A slightly more complicated information flow policy is quantitative non-interference. In quantitative non-interference, the bound must be satisfied for every individual input. Let $I \subseteq AP$ be the observable inputs to the system. Quantitative non-interference is the following quantitative hyperproperty[1]:

$$\forall \pi.\, \#\sigma\colon O.\, (\Box(\pi =_I \sigma)) \leq 2^c$$

For each trace π in the system, the property checks whether there are more than 2^c traces σ that have the same observable input as π but different observable output.

Example 2 (Deniability). A program satisfies *deniability* (see, for example, [7, 10]) when there is no proof that a certain input occurred from simply observing the output, i.e., given an output of a program one cannot derive the input that lead to this output. A deterministic program satisfies deniability when each output can be mapped to at least two inputs. A quantitative variant of deniability is when we require that the number of corresponding inputs is larger than a given threshold. Quantitative deniability can be specified as the following quantitative Hyperproperty:

$$\forall \pi.\, \#\sigma\colon I.\, (\Box(\pi =_O \sigma)) > n$$

For all traces π of the system we count the number of sequences σ in the system with different input sequences and the same output sequence of π, i.e., for the fixed output sequence given by π we count the number of input sequences that lead to this output.

4 Model Checking Quantitative Hyperproperties

We present a model checking algorithm for quantitative hyperproperties based on model counting. The advantage of the algorithm is that its runtime complexity is independent of the bound n and thus avoids the n-fold self-composition necessary for any encoding of the quantitative hyperproperty in HYPERLTL.

Before introducing our novel counting-based algorithm, we start by a translation of quantitative hyperproperties into formulas in HYPERLTL and establishing an exponential lower bound for its representation.

4.1 Standard Model Checking Algorithm: Encoding Quantitative Hyperproperties in HyperLTL

The idea of the reduction is to check a lower bound of n traces by existentially quantifying over n traces, and to check an upper bound of n traces by *universally* quantifying over $n+1$ traces. The resulting HyperLTL formula can be verified using the standard model checking algorithm for HyperLTL [18].

[1] We write $\pi =_A \pi'$ short for $\pi_A = \pi'_A$ where π_A is the A-projection of π.

Theorem 1. *Every quantitative hyperproperty* $\forall \pi_1, \ldots, \pi_k.\ \psi_\iota \rightarrow (\#\sigma : A.\ \psi \lhd n)$ *can be expressed as a HyperLTL formula. For* $\lhd \in \{\leq\}(\{<\})$*, the HyperLTL formula has* $n + k + 1$*(resp.* $n + k$*) universal trace quantifiers in addition to the quantifiers in* ψ_ι *and* ψ*. For* $\lhd \in \{\geq\}(\{>\})$*, the HyperLTL formula has* k *universal trace quantifiers and* n *(resp.* $n + 1$*) existential trace quantifiers in addition to the quantifiers in* ψ_ι *and* ψ*. For* $\lhd \in \{=\}$*, the HyperLTL formula has* $k + n + 1$ *universal trace quantifiers and* n *existential trace quantifiers in addition to the quantifiers in* ψ_ι *and* ψ*.*

Proof. For $\lhd \in \{\leq\}$, we encode the quantitative hyperproperty $\forall \pi_1, \ldots, \pi_k.\ \psi_\iota \rightarrow (\#\sigma : A.\ \psi \lhd n)$ as the following HyperLTL formula:

$$\forall \pi_1, \ldots, \pi_k.\ \forall \pi'_1, \ldots, \pi'_{n+1}.\ \left(\psi_\iota \wedge \bigwedge_{i \neq j} \Diamond(\pi'_i \neq_A \pi'_j)\right) \rightarrow \left(\bigvee_i \neg\psi[\sigma \mapsto \pi'_i]\right)$$

where $\psi[\sigma \mapsto \pi'_i]$ is the HyperLTL formula ψ with all occurrences of σ replaced by π'_i. The formula states that there is no tuple of $n + 1$ traces $\pi'_1, \ldots, \pi'_{n+1}$ different in the evaluation of A, that satisfy ψ. In other words, for every $n + 1$ tuple of traces $\pi'_1, \ldots, \pi'_{n+1}$ that differ in the evaluation of A, one of the paths must violate ψ. For $\lhd \in \{<\}$, we use the same formula, with $\forall \pi'_1, \ldots, \pi'_n$ instead of $\forall \pi'_1, \ldots, \pi'_{n+1}$.

For $\lhd \in \{\geq\}$, we encode the quantitative hyperproperty analogously as the HyperLTL formula

$$\forall \pi_1, \ldots, \pi_k.\ \exists \pi'_1, \ldots, \pi'_n.\ \psi_\iota \rightarrow \left(\bigwedge_{i \neq j} \Diamond(\pi'_i \neq_A \pi'_j)\right) \wedge \left(\bigwedge_i \psi[\sigma \mapsto \pi'_i]\right)$$

The formula states that there exist paths $\pi'_1, \ldots, \pi'_n$ that differ in the evaluation of A and that all satisfy ψ. For $\lhd \in \{>\}$, we use the same formula, with $\exists \pi'_1, \ldots, \pi'_{n+1}$ instead of $\forall \pi'_1, \ldots, \pi'_n$. Lastly, for $\lhd \in \{=\}$, we encode the quantitative hyperproperty as a conjunction of the encodings for $\leq$ and for $\geq$.

Example 3 (Quantitative non-interference in HyperLTL). As discussed in Example 1, quantitative non-interference is the quantitative hyperproperty

$$\forall \pi.\ \#\sigma : O.\ \square(\pi =_I \sigma) \leq 2^c,$$

where we measure the amount of leakage with min-entropy [43]. The bounding problem for min-entropy asks whether the amount of information leaked by a system is bounded by a constant 2^c where c is the number of bits. This is encoded in HyperLTL as the requirement that there are no $2^c + 1$ traces distinguishable in their output:

$$\forall \pi_0.\ \forall \pi_1 \ldots \forall \pi_{2^c}.\ \left(\bigwedge_i \square(\pi_i =_I \pi_0)\right) \rightarrow \left(\bigvee_{i \neq j} \square(\pi_i =_O \pi_j)\right).$$

This formula is equivalent to the formalization of quantitative non-interference given in [26].

Model checking quantitative hyperproperties via the reduction to HyperLTL is very expensive. In the best case, when $\triangleleft \in \{\leq, <\}$, ψ_ι does not contain existential quantifiers, and ψ does not contain universal quantifiers, we obtain an HyperLTL formula without quantifier alternations, where the number of quantifiers grows linearly with the bound n. For m quantifiers, the HyperLTL model checking algorithm [26] constructs and analyzes the m-fold self-composition of the Kripke structure. The running time of the model checking algorithm is thus exponential in the bound. If $\triangleleft \in \{\geq, >, =\}$, the encoding additionally introduces a quantifier alternation. The model checking algorithm checks quantifier alternations via a complementation of Büchi automata, which adds another exponent, resulting in an overall doubly exponential running time.

The model checking algorithm we introduce in the next section avoids the n-fold self-composition needed in the model checking algorithm of HyperLTL and its complexity is independent of the bound n.

4.2 Counting-Based Model Checking Algorithm

A Kripke structure $K = (S, s_0, \tau, AP, L)$ violates a quantitative hyperproperty

$$\varphi = \forall \pi_1, \ldots, \pi_k.\ \psi_\iota \rightarrow (\#\sigma : A.\psi \triangleleft n)$$

if there is a k-tuple $t = (\pi_1, \ldots, \pi_k)$ of traces $\pi_i \in TR(K)$ that satisfies the formula

$$\exists \pi_1, \ldots, \pi_k.\ \psi_\iota \wedge (\#\sigma : A.\ \psi \overline{\triangleleft} n)$$

where $\overline{\triangleleft}$ is the negation of the comparison operator $\triangleleft$. The tuple t then satisfies the property ψ_ι and the number of $(k+1)$-tuples $t' = (\pi_1, \ldots, \pi_k, \sigma)$ for $\sigma \in TR(K)$ that satisfy ψ and differ pairwise in the A-projection of σ satisfies the comparison $\overline{\triangleleft}\ n$ (The A-projection of a sequence σ is defined as the sequence $\sigma_A \in (2^A)^\omega$, such that for every position i and every $a \in A$ it holds that $a \in \sigma_A[i]$ if and only if $a \in \sigma[i]$). The tuples t' can be captured by the automaton composed of the product of an automaton $A_{\psi_\iota \wedge \psi}$ that accepts all $k+1$ of traces that satisfy both ψ_ι and ψ and a $k+1$-self composition of K. Each accepting run of the product automaton presents $k+1$ traces of K that satisfy $\psi_\iota \wedge \psi$. On top of the product automaton, we apply a special counting algorithm which we explain in detail in Sect. 4.4 and check if the result satisfies the comparison $\overline{\triangleleft}\ n$.

Algorithm 1 gives a general picture of our model checking algorithm. The algorithm has two parts. The first part applies if the relation $\overline{\triangleleft}$ is one of $\{\geq, >\}$. In this case, the algorithm checks whether a sequence over AP_ψ (propositions in ψ) corresponds to infinitely many sequences over A. This is done by checking whether the product automaton B has a so-called *doubly pumped lasso*(DPL), a subgraph with two connected lassos, with a unique sequence over AP_ψ and different sequences over A. Such a doubly pumped lasso matches the same sequence over AP_ψ with infinitely many sequences over A (more in Sect. 4.4). If no doubly pumped lasso is found, a projected model counting algorithm is applied in the second part of the algorithm in order to compute either the maximum or the minimum value, corresponding to the comparison operator $\overline{\triangleleft}$. In the next subsections, we explain the individual parts of the algorithm in detail.

Algorithm 1. Counting-based Model Checking of Quantitative Hyperproperties

Input: Quantitative Hyperproperty $\varphi = \forall \pi_1 \ldots \pi_k.\ \psi_\iota \rightarrow (\#\sigma : A.\psi \lhd n)$, Kripke Structure $K = (S, s_0, \tau, AP, L)$
Output: $K \models \varphi$

```
B = QHLTL2BA(K, π_1, ..., π_k, ψ_ι ∧ ψ)
/*Check Infinity*/
if ⩤ ∈ {≥, >} then
    ce = DPL(B)
    if ce ≠ ⊥ then
        return ce
/*Apply Projected Counting Algorithm*/
if ⩤ ∈ {≥, >} then
    ce = MaxCount(B, n, ⩤)
else
    ce = MinCount(B, n, ⩤)
return ce
```

4.3 Büchi Automata for Quantitative Hyperproperties

For a quantitative hyperproperty $\varphi = \forall \pi_1 \ldots \pi_k.\ \psi_\iota \rightarrow (\#\sigma : A.\psi \lhd n)$ and a Kripke structure $K = (S, s_0, \tau, AP, L)$, we first construct an alternating automaton $A_{\psi_\iota \wedge \psi}$ for the HyperLTL property $\psi_\iota \wedge \psi$. Let $A_{\psi_1} = (Q_1, q_{0,1}, \Sigma_2, \delta_1, F_1)$ and $A_{\psi_2} = (Q_2, q_{0,2}, \Sigma_2, \delta_2, F_2)$ be alternating automata for subformulas ψ_1 and ψ_2. Let $\Sigma = 2^{AP_\varphi}$ where AP_φ are all indexed atomic propositions that appear in φ. $A_{\psi_\iota \wedge \psi}$ is constructed using following rules[2]:

$\varphi = a_\pi$	$A_\varphi = (\{q_0\}, q_0, \Sigma, \delta, \emptyset)$ where $\delta(q_0, \alpha) = (a_\pi \in \alpha)$
$\varphi = \neg a_\pi$	$A_\varphi = (\{q_0\}, q_0, \Sigma, \delta, \emptyset)$ where $\delta(q_0, \alpha) = (a_\pi \notin \alpha)$
$\varphi = \psi_1 \wedge \psi_2$	$A_\varphi = (Q_1 \uplus Q_2 \uplus \{q_0\}, q_0, \Sigma, \delta, F_1 \uplus F_2)$ where $\delta(q, \alpha) = \delta_1(q_{0,1}, \alpha) \wedge \delta_2(q_{0,2}, \alpha)$ and $\delta(q, \alpha) = \delta_i(q, \alpha)$ when $q \in Q_i$ for $i \in \{1, 2\}$
$\varphi = \psi_1 \vee \psi_2$	$A_\varphi = (Q_1 \uplus Q_2 \uplus \{q_0\}, q_0, \Sigma, \delta, F_1 \uplus F_2)$ where $\delta(q, \alpha) = \delta_1(q_{0,1}, \alpha) \vee \delta_2(q_{0,2}, \alpha)$ and $\delta(q, \alpha) = \delta_i(q, \alpha)$ when $q \in Q_i$ for $i \in \{1, 2\}$
$\varphi = \bigcirc \psi_1$	$A_\varphi = (Q_1 \uplus \{q_0\}, q_0, \Sigma, \delta, F_1)$ where $\delta(q, \alpha) = q_{0,1}$ and $\delta(q, \alpha) = \delta_1(q, \alpha)$ for $q \in Q_1$
$\varphi = \psi_1 \mathcal{U} \psi_2$	$A_\varphi = (Q_1 \uplus Q_2 \uplus \{q_0\}, q_0, \Sigma, \delta, F_1 \uplus F_2)$ where $\delta(q_0, \alpha) = \delta_2(q_{0,2}, \alpha) \vee (\delta_1(q_{0,1}, \alpha) \wedge q_0)$ and $\delta(q, \alpha) = \delta_i(q, \alpha)$ when $q \in Q_i$ for $i \in \{1, 2\}$
$\varphi = \psi_1 \mathcal{R} \psi_2$	$A_\varphi = (Q_1 \uplus Q_2 \uplus \{q_0\}, q_0, \Sigma, \delta, F_1 \uplus F_2 \uplus \{q_0\})$ where $\delta(q_0, \alpha) = \delta_2(q_{0,2}, \alpha) \wedge (\delta_1(q_{0,1}, \alpha) \vee q_0)$ and $\delta(q, \alpha) = \delta_i(q, \alpha)$ when $q \in Q_i$ for $i \in \{1, 2\}$

For a quantified formula $\varphi = \exists \pi.\psi_1$, we construct the product automaton of the Kripke structure K and the Büchi automaton of ψ_1. Here we reduce the alphabet of the automaton by projecting all atomic proposition in AP_π away:

[2] The construction follows the one presented in [26] with a slight modification on the labeling of transitions. Labeling over atomic proposition instead of the states of the Kripke structure suffices, as any nondeterminism in the Kripke structure is inherently resolved, because we quantify over trace not paths.

$\varphi = \exists\pi.\psi_1$	$A_\varphi = (Q_1 \times S \uplus \{q_0\}, \Sigma \setminus AP_\pi, \delta, F_1 \times S)$ where $\delta(q_0, \alpha) = \{(q', s') \mid q' \in \delta_1(q_{0,1}, \alpha \cup \alpha'), s' \in \tau(s_0), (L(s_0))_\pi =_{AP_\pi} \alpha'\}$ and $\delta((q, s), \alpha) = \{(q', s') \mid q' \in \delta_1(q, \alpha \cup \alpha'), s' \in \tau(s), (L(s))_\pi =_{AP_\pi} \alpha'\}$

Given the Büchi automaton for the hyperproperty $\psi_\iota \wedge \psi$ it remains to construct the product with the $k+1$-self composition of K. The transitions of the automaton are defined over labels from $\Sigma = 2^{AP^*}$ where $AP^* = AP_\sigma \cup \bigcup_i AP_{\pi_i}$. $A_{\psi_\iota \wedge \psi}$. This is necessary to identify which transition was taken in each copy of K, thus, mirroring a tuple of traces in K. For each of the variables $\pi_1, \ldots \pi_k$ and σ we use following rule:

$\varphi = \exists\pi.\psi_1$	$A_\varphi = (Q_1 \times S \uplus \{q_0\}, \Sigma, \delta, F_1 \times S)$ where $\delta(q_0, \alpha) = \{(q', s') \mid q' \in \delta_1(q_{0,1}, \alpha), s' \in \tau(s_0), (L(s_0))_\pi =_{AP_\pi}\}$ and $\delta((q, s), \alpha) = \{(q', s') \mid q' \in \delta_1(q, \alpha), s' \in \tau(s), (L(s))_\pi =_{AP_\pi}\}$

Finally, we transform the resulting alternating automaton to an equivalent Büchi automaton following the construction of Miyano and Hayashi [39].

4.4 Counting Models of ω-Automata

Computing the number of words accepted by a Büchi automaton can be done by examining its accepting lassos. Consider, for example, the Büchi automata over the alphabet $2^{\{a\}}$ in Fig. 1. The automaton on the left has one accepting lasso $(q_0)^\omega$ and thus has only one model, namely $\{a\}^\omega$. The automaton on the right has infinitely many accepting lassos $(q_0\{\})^i\{a\}(q_1(\{\} \vee \{a\}))^\omega$ that accept infinitely many different words all of the from $\{\}^*\{a\}(\{\} \vee \{a\})^\omega$. Computing the models of a Büchi automaton is insufficient for model checking quantitative hyperproperties as we are not interested in the total number of models. We rather *maximize*, respectively *minimize*, over sequences of subsets of atomic propositions *the number of projected models* of the Büchi automaton. For instance, consider the automaton given in Fig. 2. The automaton has infinitely many models. However, the maximum number of sequences $\sigma_b \in 2^{\{b\}}$ that correspond to accepting lassos in the automaton with a unique sequence $\sigma_a \in 2^{\{a\}}$ is two: For example, let n be a natural number. For any model of the automaton and for each sequence $\sigma_a := \{\}^n\{a\}(\{\})^\omega$ the automaton accepts the following two sequences: $\{b\}^n\{\}\{b\}^\omega$ and $\{b\}^\omega$. Formally, given a Büchi automaton $\mathcal{B}$ over AP and a set A, such that $A \subseteq AP$, an *A-projected model* (or projected model over A) is defined as a sequence $\sigma_A \in (2^A)^\omega$ that results in the A-projection of an accepting sequence $\sigma \in (2^{AP})^\omega$.

Fig. 1. Büchi automata with one model (left) and infinitely many models (right).

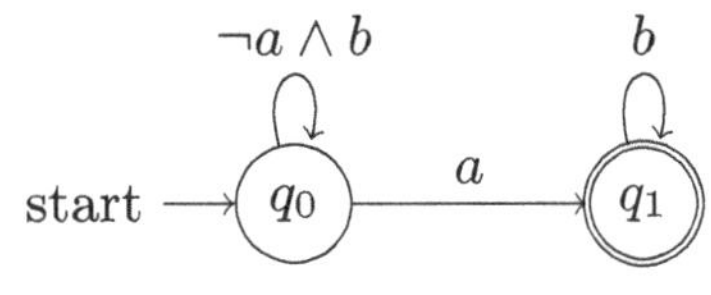

Fig. 2. A two-state Büchi automaton, such that there exist exactly two $\{b\}$-projected models for each $\{a\}$-projected sequence.

In the following, we define the maximum model counting problem over automata and give an algorithm for solving the problem. We show how to use the algorithm for model checking quantitative hyperproperties.

Definition 1 (Maximum Model Counting over Automata (MMCA)). *Given a Büchi automaton B over an alphabet 2^{AP} for some set of atomic propositions AP and sets $X, Y, Z \subseteq AP$ the maximum model counting problem is to compute*

$$\max_{\sigma_Y \in (2^Y)^\omega} |\{\sigma_X \in (2^X)^\omega \mid \exists \sigma_Z \in (2^Z)^\omega.\ \sigma_X \cup \sigma_Y \cup \sigma_Z \in L(B)\}|$$

where $\sigma \cup \sigma'$ is the point-wise union of σ and σ'.

As a first step in our algorithm, we show how to check whether the maximum model count is equal to infinity.

Definition 2 (Doubly Pumped Lasso). *For a graph G, a doubly pumped lasso in G is a subgraph that entails a cycles C_1 and another different cycle C_2 that is reachable from C_1.*

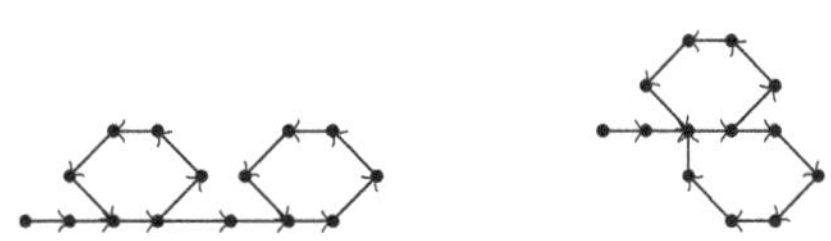

Fig. 3. Forms of doubly pumped lassos.

In general, we distinguish between two types of doubly pumped lassos as shown in Fig. 3. We call the lassos with periods C_1 and C_2 the lassos of the doubly pumped lasso. A doubly pumped lasso of a Büchi automaton B is one in the graph structure of B. The doubly pumped lasso is called accepting when C_2 has an accepting state. A more generalized formalization of this idea is given in the following theorem.

Theorem 2. *Let $B = (Q, q_0, \delta, 2^{AP}, F)$ be a Büchi automaton for some set of atomic propositions $AP = X \cup Y \cup Z$ and let $\sigma' \in (2^Y)^\omega$. The automaton B has infinitely many $X \cup Y$-projected models σ with $\sigma =_Y \sigma'$ if and only if B has an accepting doubly pumped lasso with lassos ρ and ρ' such that: (1) ρ is an accepting lasso (2) $tr(\rho) =_Y tr(\rho') =_Y \sigma'$ (3) The period of ρ' shares at least one state with ρ and (4) $tr(\rho) \neq_X tr(\rho')$.*

To check whether there is a sequence $\sigma' \in (2^Y)^\omega$ such that the number of $X \cup Y$-projected models σ of B with $\sigma =_Y \sigma'$ is infinite, we search for a doubly pumped lasso satisfying the constraints given in Theorem 2. This can be done by applying the following procedure:

Given a Büchi automaton $B = (Q, q_0, 2^{AP}, \delta, F)$ and sets $X, Y, Z \subseteq AP$, we construct the following product automaton $B_\times = (Q_\times, q_{\times,0}, 2^{AP} \times 2^{AP}, \delta_\times, F_\times)$ where: $Q_\times = Q \times Q$, $q_{\times,0} = (q_0, q_0)$, $\delta_\times = \{(s_1, s_2) \xrightarrow{(\alpha,\alpha')} (s'_1, s'_2) \mid s_1 \xrightarrow{\alpha} s_2, s'_1 \xrightarrow{\alpha'} s'_2, \alpha =_Y \alpha'\}$ and $F_\times = Q \times F$. The automaton B has infinitely many models σ' if there is an accepting lasso $\rho = (q_0, q_0)(\alpha_1, \alpha'_1) \ldots ((q_j, q'_j)(\alpha_{j+1}, \alpha'_{j+1}) \ldots (q_k, q'_k)(\alpha_{k+1}, \alpha'_{k+1}))$ in $B_\times$ such that: $\exists h \leq j.\ q'_h = q_j$, i.e., B has lassos ρ_1 and ρ_2 that share a state in the period of ρ_1 and $\exists h > j.\ \alpha_h \neq_X \alpha'_h$, i.e., the lassos differ in the evaluation of X in a position after the shared state and thus allows infinitely many different sequence over X for the a sequence over Y. The lasso ρ simulates a doubly pumped lasso in B satisfying the constraints of Theorem 2.

Theorem 3. *Given an alternating Büchi automaton $A = (Q, q_0, \delta, 2^{AP}, F)$ for a set of atomic propositions $AP = X \cup Y \cup Z$, the problem of checking whether there is a sequence $\sigma' \in (2^Y)^\omega$ such that A has infinitely many $X \cup Y$-projected models σ with $\sigma =_Y \sigma'$ is* PSPACE*-complete.*

The lower and upper bound for the problem can be given by a reduction from and to the satisfiability problem of LTL [4]. Due to the finite structure of Büchi automata, if the number of models of the automaton exceed the exponential bound $2^{|Q|}$, where Q is the set of states, then the automaton has infinitely many models.

Lemma 1. *For any Büchi automaton B, the number of models of B is less or equal to $2^{|Q|}$ otherwise it is ∞.*

Proof. Assume the number of models is larger than $2^{|Q|}$ then there are more than $2^{|Q|}$ accepting lassos in B. By the pigeonhole principle, two of them share the same $2^{|Q|}$-prefix. Thus, either they are equal or we found doubly pumped lasso in B.

Corollary 1. *Let a Büchi automaton B over a set of atomic propositions AP and sets $X, Y \subseteq AP$. For each sequence $\sigma_Y \in (2^Y)^\omega$ the number of $X \cup Y$-projected models σ with $\sigma =_Y \sigma_Y$ is less or equal than $2^{|Q|}$ otherwise it is ∞.*

From Corollary 1, we know that if no sequence $\sigma_Y \in (2^Y)^\omega$ matches to infinitely many $X \cup Y$-projected models then the number of such models is bound by $2^{|Q|}$. Each of these models has a run in B which ends in an accepting strongly connected component. Also from Corollary 1, we know that every model has a lasso run of length $|Q|$. For each finite sequence w_Y of length $|w_Y| = |Q|$ that reaches an accepting strongly connected component, we count the number $X \cup Y$-projected words w of length $|Q|$ with $w =_Y w_Y$ and that end in an accepting

Algorithm 2 Maximum Model Counting

Input: $B = (Q, q_0, 2^{AP}, \delta, F)$, disjoint $X, Y, Z \subseteq AP$, $n \in \mathbb{N}$
Output: $\#_{X,Y,Z}(B) > n$

$SCC = acceptingSCC(B)$
$i = 1$
$W = \bigcup_{S \in SCC} S$
while $i \leq |Q|$ **do**
  $i = i + 1$
  for $q \in W$ **do**
    for (q', α, q) **do**
      $W' = W' \cup \{q'\}$
      for $\sigma \in \Pi(q)$ **do**
        $\Pi'(q') = \Pi'(q') \cup \{\alpha_{Y \cup X} \cdot \sigma\}$
  $W = W'$
  $W' = \emptyset$
  for $q \in W$ **do**
    $\Pi'(q) = \emptyset$
return $\max_{X,Y,Z} \Pi(q_0) \geq n$

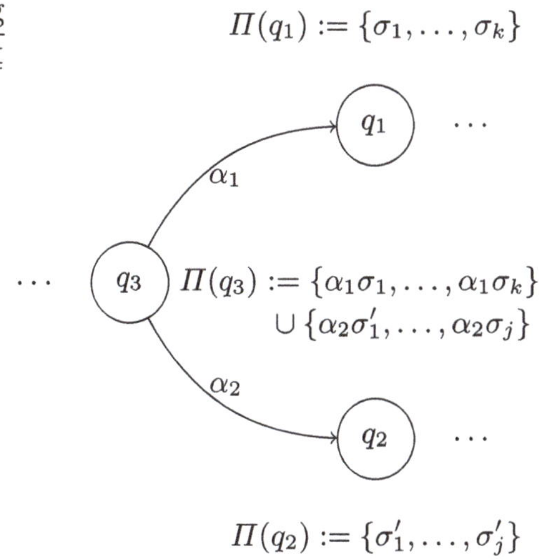

Fig. 4. Maximum Model Counting Algorithm (left) and a Sketch of a step in this algorithm (right): Current elements of our working set are $q_1, q_2 \in W$ and $q_3 \in W'$. If $i = 0$, i.e., we are in the first step of the algorithm, then q_1 and q_2 are states of accepting SCCs.

strongly connected component. This number is equal to the maximum model counting number.

Algorithm 2 describes the procedure. An algorithm for the minimum model counting problem is defined in similar way. The algorithm works in a backwards fashion starting with states of accepting strongly connected components. In each iteration i, the algorithm maps each state of the automaton with $X \cup Y$-projected words of length i that reach an accepting strongly connected component. After $|Q|$ iterations, the algorithm determines from the mapping of initial state q_0 a Y-projected word of length $|Q|$ with the maximum number of matching $X \cup Y$-projected words (Fig. 4).

Theorem 4. *The decisional version of the maximum model counting problem over automata (MMCA), i.e. the question whether the maximum is greater than a given natural number n, is in $NP^{\#P}$.*

Proof. Let a Büchi automaton over an alphabet 2^{AP} for a set of atomic propositions AP and sets $AP_X, AP_Y, AP_Z \subseteq AP$ and a natural number n be given. We construct a nondeterministic Turing Machine M with access to a $\#P$-oracle as follows: M guesses a sequence $\sigma_Y \in 2^{AP_Y}$. It then queries the oracle, to compute a number c, such that $c = |\{\sigma_X \in (2^{AP_X})^\omega \mid \exists \sigma_Z \in (2^{AP_Z})^\omega.\ \sigma_X \cup \sigma_Y \cup \sigma_Z \in L(B)\}|$, which is a $\#P$ problem [27]. It remains to check whether $n > c$. If so, M accepts.

The following theorem summarizes the main findings of this section, which establish, depending on the property, an exponentially or even doubly exponentially better algorithm (in the quantitative bound) over the existing model checking algorithm for HyperLTL.

Theorem 5. *Given a Kripke structure K and a quantitative hyperproperty φ with bound n, the problem whether $K \models \varphi$ can be decided in logarithmic space in the quantitative bound n and in polynomial space in the size of K.*

5 A Max#Sat-Based Approach

For existential HyperLTL formulas ψ_ι and ψ, we give a more practical model checking approach by encoding the automaton-based construction presented in Sect. 4 into a propositional formula.

Given a Kripke structure $K = (S, s_0, \tau, AP_K, L)$ and a quantitative hyperproperty $\varphi = \forall\pi_1, \ldots, \pi_k.\ \psi_\iota \rightarrow (\#\sigma : A.\ \psi) \triangleleft n$ over a set of atomic propositions $AP_\varphi \subseteq AP_K$ and bound μ, our algorithm constructs a propositional formula ϕ such that, every satisfying assignment of ϕ uniquely encodes a tuple of lassos $(\pi_1, \ldots, \pi_k, \sigma)$ of length μ in K, where $(\pi_1, \ldots, \pi_k)$ satisfies ψ_ι and $(\pi_1, \ldots, \pi_k, \sigma)$ satisfies ψ. To compute the values $\max\limits_{(\pi_1,\ldots,\pi_k)} |\{\sigma_A \mid (\pi_1, \ldots, \pi_k, \sigma) \models \psi_\iota \wedge \psi\}|$ (in case $\triangleleft \in \{\leq, <\}$) or $\min\limits_{(\pi_1,\ldots,\pi_k)} |\{\sigma_A \mid (\pi_1, \ldots, \pi_k, \sigma) \models \psi_\iota \wedge \psi\}|$ (in case $\triangleleft \in \{\geq, >\}$), we pass ϕ to a maximum model counter, respectively, to a minimum model counter with the appropriate sets of counting and maximization, respectively, minimization propositions. From Lemma 1 we know that it is enough to consider lasso of length exponential in the size of φ. The size of ϕ is thus exponential in the size of φ and polynomial in the size of K.

The construction resembles the encoding of the bounded model checking approach for LTL [16]. Let $\psi_\iota = \exists\pi'_1 \ldots \pi'_{k'}.\ \psi'_\iota$ and $\psi = \exists\pi''_1 \ldots \pi''_{k''}.\ \psi''$ and let AP_{ψ_ι} and AP_ψ be the sets of atomic propositions that appear in ψ_ι and ψ respectively. The propositional formula ϕ is given as a conjunction of the following propositional formulas: $\phi = \bigwedge_{i \leq k} [\![K]\!]^\mu_{\pi_i} \wedge [\![K]\!]^\mu_\sigma \wedge [\![\psi_\iota]\!]^0_\mu \wedge [\![\psi]\!]^0_\mu$ where:

- μ is length of considered lassos and is equal to $\mu = 2^{|\psi'_\iota \wedge \psi''|} * |S|^{k+k'+k''+1} + 1$ which is one plus the size of the product automaton constructed from the $k + k' + k'' + 1$ self-composition and the automaton for $\psi_\iota \wedge \psi$. The "plus one" is to additionally check whether the number of models is infinite.
- $[\![K]\!]^k_\pi$ is the encoding of the transition relation of the copy of K where atomic propositions are indexed with π and up to an unrolling of length k. Each state of K can be encoded as an evaluation of a vector of $\log |S|$ unique propositional variables. The encoding is given by the propositional formula $I(\vec{v}^\pi_0) \wedge \bigwedge_{i=0}^{k-1} \tau(\vec{v}^\pi_i, \vec{v}^\pi_{i+1})$ which encodes all paths of K of length k. The formula $I(\vec{v}^\pi_0)$ defines the assignment of the initial state. The formulas $\tau(\vec{v}^\pi_i, \vec{v}^\pi_{i+1})$ define valid transitions in K from the ith to the $(i + 1)$st state of a path.
- $[\![\psi_\iota]\!]^0_k$ and $[\![\psi]\!]^0_k$ are constructed using the following rules[3]:

[3] We omitted the rules for boolean operators for the lack of space.

	$i < k$	$i = k$
$[\![a_\pi]\!]_k^i$	a_π^i	$\bigvee_{j=0}^{k-1}(l_j \wedge a_\pi^j)$
$[\![\neg a_\pi]\!]_k^i$	$\neg a_\pi^i$	$\bigvee_{j=0}^{k-1}(l_j \wedge \neg a_\pi^j)$
$[\![\bigcirc \varphi_1]\!]_k^i$	$[\![\varphi_1]\!]_k^{i+1}$	$\bigvee_{j=0}^{k-1}(l_j \wedge [\![\varphi_1]\!]_k^j)$
$[\![\varphi_1 \mathcal{U} \varphi_2]\!]_k^i$	$[\![\varphi_2]\!]_k^i \vee ([\![\varphi_1]\!]_k^i \wedge [\![\varphi_1 \mathcal{U} \varphi]\!]_k^{i+1})$	$\bigvee_{j=0}^{k-1}(l_j \wedge \langle \varphi_1 \mathcal{U} \varphi_2 \rangle_k^j)$
$\langle \varphi_1 \mathcal{U} \varphi_2 \rangle_k^i$	$[\![\varphi_2]\!]_k^i \vee ([\![\varphi_1]\!]_k^i \wedge \langle \varphi_1 \mathcal{U} \varphi \rangle_k^{i+1})$	false
$[\![\varphi_1 \mathcal{R} \varphi_2]\!]_k^i$	$[\![\varphi_2]\!]_k^i \wedge ([\![\varphi_1]\!]_k^i \vee [\![\varphi_1 \mathcal{R} \varphi]\!]_k^{i+1})$	$\bigvee_{j=0}^{k-1}(l_j \wedge \langle \varphi_1 \mathcal{R} \varphi_2 \rangle_k^j)$
$\langle \varphi_1 \mathcal{R} \varphi_2 \rangle_k^i$	$[\![\varphi_2]\!]_k^i \wedge ([\![\varphi_1]\!]_k^i \vee \langle \varphi_1 \mathcal{R} \varphi \rangle_k^{i+1})$	true

in case of an existential quantifier over a trace variable π, we add a copy of the encoding of K with new variables distinguished by π:

$[\![\exists \pi . \varphi_1]\!]_k^i$	$[\![K]\!]_\pi^k \wedge [\![\varphi_1]\!]_k^i$

We define sets $X = \{a_\sigma^i \mid a \in A, i \leq k\}$, $Y = \{a^i \mid a \in AP_\psi \setminus A, i \leq k\}$ and $Z = P \setminus X \cup Y$, where P is the set of all propositions in ϕ. The maximum model counting problem is then $MMC(\phi, X, Y, Z)$.

5.1 Experiments

We have implemented the Max#Sat-based model checking approach from the last section. We compare the Max#Sat-based approach to the expansion-based approach using HyperLTL [26]. Our implementation uses the MaxCount tool [29]. We use the option in MaxCount that enumerates, rather than approximates, the number of assignments for the counting variables. We furthermore instrumented the tool so that it terminates as soon as a sample is found that exceeds the given bound. If no sample is found after one hour, we report a timeout.

Table 1 shows the results on a parameterized benchmark obtained from the implementation of an 8bit passcode checker. The parameter of the benchmark is

Table 1. Comparison between the expansion-based approach (MCHyper) and the Max#Sat-based approach (MCQHyper). #max is the number of maximization variables (set Y). #count is the number of the counting variables (set X). TO indicates a time-out after 1 h.

Benchmark	Specification	MCHyper			MCQHyper			
		#Latches	#Gates	Time(sec)	#var	#max	#count	Time(sec)
Pwd_8bit	1bit_leak	9	55	0.3	97	16	2	1
	2bit_leak			0.4	176	32	4	1
	3bit_leak			1.3	336	64	8	2
	4bit_leak			97	656	128	16	4
	5bit_leak			TO	1296	256	32	8
	6bit_leak			TO	2576	512	64	335
	8bit_leak			TO	10256	2048	256	TO

the bound on the number of bits that is leaked to an adversary, who might, for example, enter passcodes in a brute-force manner. In all instances, a violation is found. The results show that the Max#Sat-based approach scales significantly better than the expansion-based approach.

6 Conclusion

We have studied quantitative hyperproperties of the form $\forall \pi_1, \ldots, \pi_k.\, \varphi \rightarrow (\#\sigma : A.\ \psi \lhd n)$, where φ and ψ are HyperLTL formulas, and $\#\sigma : A.\varphi \lhd n$ compares the number of traces that differ in the atomic propositions A and satisfy ψ to a threshold n. Many quantitative information flow policies of practical interest, such as quantitative non-interference and deniability, belong to this class of properties. Our new counting-based model checking algorithm for quantitative hyperproperties performs at least exponentially better in both time and space in the bound n than a reduction to standard HyperLTL model checking. The new counting operator makes the specifications exponentially more concise in the bound, and our model checking algorithm solves the concise specifications efficiently.

We also showed that the model checking problem for quantitative hyperproperties can be solved with a practical Max#SAT-based algorithm. The SAT-based approach outperforms the expansion-based approach significantly for this class of properties. An additional advantage of the new approach is that it can handle properties like deniability, which cannot be checked by MCHyper because of the quantifier alternation.

References

1. Alvim, M.S., Andrés, M.E., Palamidessi, C.: Quantitative information flow in interactive systems. J. Comput. Secur. **20**(1), 3–50 (2012)
2. Aziz, R.A., Chu, G., Muise, C.J., Stuckey, P.J.: #∃sat: projected model counting. In: Proceedings of the 18th International Conference on Theory and Applications of Satisfiability Testing - SAT 2015, Austin, TX, USA, 24–27 September 2015, pp. 121–137 (2015)
3. Backes, M., Köpf, B., Rybalchenko, A.: Automatic discovery and quantification of information leaks. In: 30th IEEE Symposium on Security and Privacy (S&P 2009), Oakland, California, USA, 17–20 May 2009, pp. 141–153 (2009)
4. Baier, C., Katoen, J.-P.: Principles of Model Checking (Representation and Mind Series). The MIT Press, Cambridge (2008)
5. Banerjee, A., Naumann, D.A.: Stack-based access control and secure information flow. J. Funct. Program. **15**(2), 131–177 (2005)
6. Barthe, G., D'Argenio, P.R., Rezk, T.: Secure information flow by self-composition. Math. Struct. Comput. Sci. **21**(6), 1207–1252 (2011)
7. Bindschaedler, V., Shokri, R., Gunter, C.A.: Plausible deniability for privacy-preserving data synthesis. PVLDB **10**(5), 481–492 (2017)
8. Biondi, F., Legay, A., Traonouez, L.-M., Wąsowski, A.: QUAIL: a quantitative security analyzer for imperative code. In: Sharygina, N., Veith, H. (eds.) CAV 2013. LNCS, vol. 8044, pp. 702–707. Springer, Heidelberg (2013). https://doi.org/10.1007/978-3-642-39799-8_49

9. Chadha, R., Mathur, U., Schwoon, S.: Computing information flow using symbolic model-checking. In: 34th International Conference on Foundation of Software Technology and Theoretical Computer Science, FSTTCS 2014, New Delhi, India, 15–17 December 2014, pp. 505–516 (2014)
10. Chakraborti, A., Chen, C., Sion, R.: Datalair: efficient block storage with plausible deniability against multi-snapshot adversaries. PoPETs **2017**(3), 179 (2017)
11. Chen, H., Malacaria, P.: Quantitative analysis of leakage for multi-threaded programs. In: Proceedings of the 2007 Workshop on Programming Languages and Analysis for Security, PLAS 2007, San Diego, California, USA, 14 June 2007, pp. 31–40 (2007)
12. Chothia, T., Kawamoto, Y., Novakovic, C.: LeakWatch: estimating information leakage from Java programs. In: Kutyłowski, M., Vaidya, J. (eds.) ESORICS 2014. LNCS, vol. 8713, pp. 219–236. Springer, Cham (2014). https://doi.org/10.1007/978-3-319-11212-1_13
13. Clark, D., Hunt, S., Malacaria, P.: Quantified interference for a while language. Electr. Notes Theor. Comput. Sci. **112**, 149–166 (2005)
14. Clark, D., Hunt, S., Malacaria, P.: Quantitative information flow, relations and polymorphic types. J. Log. Comput. **15**(2), 181–199 (2005)
15. Clark, D., Hunt, S., Malacaria, P.: A static analysis for quantifying information flow in a simple imperative language. J. Comput. Secur. **15**(3), 321–371 (2007)
16. Clarke, E., Biere, A., Raimi, R., Zhu, Y.: Bounded model checking using satisfiability solving. Form. Methods Syst. Des. **19**(1), 7–34 (2001)
17. Clarke, E.M., Emerson, E.A.: Design and synthesis of synchronization skeletons using branching time temporal logic. In: Kozen, D. (ed.) Logic of Programs 1981. LNCS, vol. 131, pp. 52–71. Springer, Heidelberg (1982). https://doi.org/10.1007/BFb0025774
18. Clarkson, M.R., Finkbeiner, B., Koleini, M., Micinski, K.K., Rabe, M.N., Sánchez, C.: Temporal logics for hyperproperties. In: Abadi, M., Kremer, S. (eds.) POST 2014. LNCS, vol. 8414, pp. 265–284. Springer, Heidelberg (2014). https://doi.org/10.1007/978-3-642-54792-8_15
19. Clarkson, M.R., Myers, A.C., Schneider, F.B.: Belief in information flow. In: 18th IEEE Computer Security Foundations Workshop, (CSFW-18 2005), Aix-en-Provence, France, 20–22 June 2005, pp. 31–45 (2005)
20. Clarkson, M.R., Myers, A.C., Schneider, F.B.: Quantifying information flow with beliefs. J. Comput. Secur. **17**(5), 655–701 (2009)
21. Clarkson, M.R., Schneider, F.B.: Hyperproperties. J. Comput. Secur. **18**(6), 1157–1210 (2010)
22. Cohen, E.S.: Information transmission in sequential programs. In: Foundations of Secure Computation, pp. 297–335 (1978)
23. Darwiche, A.: New advances in compiling CNF into decomposable negation normal form. In: Proceedings of the 16th European Conference on Artificial Intelligence, ECAI 2004, including Prestigious Applicants of Intelligent Systems, PAIS 2004, Valencia, Spain, 22–27 August 2004, pp. 328–332 (2004)
24. Denning, D.E.: Cryptography and Data Security. Addison-Wesley, Boston (1982)
25. Dimitrova, R., Finkbeiner, B., Kovács, M., Rabe, M.N., Seidl, H.: Model checking information flow in reactive systems. In: Kuncak, V., Rybalchenko, A. (eds.) VMCAI 2012. LNCS, vol. 7148, pp. 169–185. Springer, Heidelberg (2012). https://doi.org/10.1007/978-3-642-27940-9_12

26. Finkbeiner, B., Rabe, M.N., Sánchez, C.: Algorithms for model checking HyperLTL and HyperCTL*. In: Kroening, D., Păsăreanu, C.S. (eds.) CAV 2015. LNCS, vol. 9206, pp. 30–48. Springer, Cham (2015). https://doi.org/10.1007/978-3-319-21690-4_3
27. Finkbeiner, B., Torfah, H.: Counting models of linear-time temporal logic. In: Dediu, A.-H., Martín-Vide, C., Sierra-Rodríguez, J.-L., Truthe, B. (eds.) LATA 2014. LNCS, vol. 8370, pp. 360–371. Springer, Cham (2014). https://doi.org/10.1007/978-3-319-04921-2_29
28. Finkbeiner, B., Torfah, H.: The density of linear-time properties. In: D'Souza, D., Narayan Kumar, K. (eds.) ATVA 2017. LNCS, vol. 10482, pp. 139–155. Springer, Cham (2017). https://doi.org/10.1007/978-3-319-68167-2_10
29. Fremont, D.J., Rabe, M.N., Seshia, S.A.: Maximum model counting. In: Proceedings of the Thirty-First AAAI Conference on Artificial Intelligence, San Francisco, California, USA, 4–9 February 2017, pp. 3885–3892 (2017)
30. Gray III, J.W.: Toward a mathematical foundation for information flow security. In: Proceedings of the IEEE Symposium on Security and Privacy, pp. 210–234, May 1991
31. Hammer, C., Snelting, G.: Flow-sensitive, context-sensitive, and object-sensitive information flow control based on program dependence graphs. Int. J. Inf. Secur. **8**(6), 399–422 (2009)
32. Gray III, J.W.: Toward a mathematical foundation for information flow security. In: IEEE Symposium on Security and Privacy, pp. 21–35 (1991)
33. Bayardo Jr., R.J., Schrag, R.: Using CSP look-back techniques to solve real-world SAT instances. In: Proceedings of the Fourteenth National Conference on Artificial Intelligence and Ninth Innovative Applications of Artificial Intelligence Conference, AAAI 1997, Providence, Rhode Island, 27–31 July 1997, pp. 203–208 (1997)
34. Köpf, B., Basin, D.A.: An information-theoretic model for adaptive side-channel attacks. In: Proceedings of the 2007 ACM Conference on Computer and Communications Security, CCS 2007, Alexandria, Virginia, USA, 28–31 October 2007, pp. 286–296 (2007)
35. Köpf, B., Rybalchenko, A.: Approximation and randomization for quantitative information-flow analysis. In: Proceedings of the 23rd IEEE Computer Security Foundations Symposium, CSF 2010, Edinburgh, United Kingdom, 17–19 July 2010, pp. 3–14 (2010)
36. Littman, M.L., Majercik, S.M., Pitassi, T.: Stochastic boolean satisfiability. J. Autom. Reason. **27**(3), 251–296 (2001)
37. Malacaria, P.: Assessing security threats of looping constructs. In: Proceedings of the 34th ACM SIGPLAN-SIGACT Symposium on Principles of Programming Languages, POPL 2007, Nice, France, 17–19 January 2007, pp. 225–235 (2007)
38. Milushev, D., Clarke, D.: Incremental hyperproperty model checking via games. In: Riis Nielson, H., Gollmann, D. (eds.) NordSec 2013. LNCS, vol. 8208, pp. 247–262. Springer, Heidelberg (2013). https://doi.org/10.1007/978-3-642-41488-6_17
39. Miyano, S., Hayashi, T.: Alternating finite automata on ω-words. Theoret. Comput. Sci. **32**(3), 321–330 (1984)
40. Morwood, D., Bryce, D.: Evaluating temporal plans in incomplete domains. In: Proceedings of the Twenty-Sixth AAAI Conference on Artificial Intelligence, 22–26 July 2012, Toronto, Ontario, Canada (2012)
41. Muise, C.J., McIlraith, S.A., Beck, J.C., Hsu, E.I.: DSHARP: fast d-DNNF compilation with sharpSAT. In: Kosseim, L., Inkpen, D. (eds.) AI 2012. LNCS (LNAI), vol. 7310, pp. 356–361. Springer, Heidelberg (2012). https://doi.org/10.1007/978-3-642-30353-1_36

42. Myers, A.C.: JFlow: practical mostly-static information flow control. In: Proceedings of the 26th ACM SIGPLAN-SIGACT Symposium on Principles of Programming Languages, POPL 1999, San Antonio, TX, USA, 20–22 January 1999, pp. 228–241 (1999)
43. Smith, G.: On the foundations of quantitative information flow. In: de Alfaro, L. (ed.) FoSSaCS 2009. LNCS, vol. 5504, pp. 288–302. Springer, Heidelberg (2009). https://doi.org/10.1007/978-3-642-00596-1_21
44. Torfah, H., Zimmermann, M.: The complexity of counting models of linear-time temporal logic. Acta Informatica **55**(3), 191–212 (2016)
45. Yasuoka, H., Terauchi, T.: On bounding problems of quantitative information flow. In: Gritzalis, D., Preneel, B., Theoharidou, M. (eds.) ESORICS 2010. LNCS, vol. 6345, pp. 357–372. Springer, Heidelberg (2010). https://doi.org/10.1007/978-3-642-15497-3_22
46. Yasuoka, H., Terauchi, T.: Quantitative information flow as safety and liveness hyperproperties. Theor. Comput. Sci. **538**, 167–182 (2014)
47. Zdancewic, S., Myers, A.C.: Observational determinism for concurrent program security. In: Proceedings of CSF, p. 29. IEEE Computer Society (2003)

Exploiting Synchrony and Symmetry in Relational Verification

Lauren Pick(✉), Grigory Fedyukovich, and Aarti Gupta

Princeton University, Princeton, USA
{lpick,grigoryf,aartig}@cs.princeton.edu

Abstract. Relational safety specifications describe multiple runs of the same program or relate the behaviors of multiple programs. Approaches to automatic relational verification often compose the programs and analyze the result for safety, but a naively composed program can lead to difficult verification problems. We propose to exploit relational specifications for simplifying the generated verification subtasks. First, we maximize opportunities for synchronizing code fragments. Second, we compute symmetries in the specifications to reveal and avoid redundant subtasks. We have implemented these enhancements in a prototype for verifying k-safety properties on Java programs. Our evaluation confirms that our approach leads to a consistent performance speedup on a range of benchmarks.

1 Introduction

The verification of relational program specifications is of wide interest, having many applications. Relational specifications can describe multiple runs of the same program or relate the behaviors of multiple programs. An example of the former is the verification of security properties such as non-interference, where different executions of the same program are compared to check whether there is a leak of sensitive information. The latter is useful for checking equivalence or refinement relationships between programs after applying some transformations or during iterative development of different software versions.

There is a rich history of work on the relational verification of programs. Representative efforts include those that target general analysis using relational program logics and frameworks [4,5,8,27,31] or specific applications such as security verification [1,7,9], compiler validation [16,32], and differential program analysis [17,19,21–23]. These efforts are supported by tools that range from automatic verifiers to interactive theorem-provers. In particular, many automatic verifiers are based on constructing a *composition* over the programs under consideration, where the relational property over multiple runs (of the same or different programs) is translated into a functional property over a single run of a composed program. This has the benefit that standard techniques and tools for program verification can then be applied.

However, it is also well known that a naively composed program can lead to difficult verification problems for automatic verifiers. For example, a *sequential*

H. Chockler and G. Weissenbacher (Eds.): CAV 2018, LNCS 10981, pp. 164–182, 2018.
https://doi.org/10.1007/978-3-319-96145-3_9

composition of two loops would require effective techniques for generating loop invariants. In contrast, a *parallel* composition would provide potential for aligning the loop bodies, where relational invariants may be easier to establish than a functional loop invariant. Examples of techniques that exploit opportunities for such alignment include use of type-based analysis with self-composition [29], allowing flexibility in composition to be a mix of sequential and parallel [6], exploiting structurally equivalent programs for compiler validation [32], lockstep execution of loops in reasoning using Cartesian Hoare Logic [27], and merging Horn clause rules for relational verification [13,24].

In this paper, we present a compositional framework that leverages relational specifications to further simplify the generated verification tasks on the composed program. Our framework is motivated by two main strategies. The first strategy, similar to the efforts mentioned above, is to exploit opportunities for *synchrony*, i.e., aligning code fragments across which relational invariants are easy to derive, perhaps due to functional similarity or due to similar code structure, etc. Specifically, we choose to *synchronize* the programs at conditional blocks as well as at loops. Similar to closely related efforts [6,27], we would like to execute loops in lockstep so that relational invariants can be derived over corresponding iterations over the loop bodies. Specifically, we propose a novel technique that analyzes the relational specifications to infer, under reasonable assumptions, *maximal sets of loops* that can be executed in lockstep. Synchronizing at conditional blocks in addition to loops enables simplification due to relational specifications and conditional guards that might result in infeasible or redundant subtasks. Pruning of such infeasible subtasks has been performed and noted as important in existing work [27], and synchronizing at conditional blocks allows us to prune eagerly. More importantly, aligning different programs at conditional statements sets up our next strategy.

Our second strategy is the exploitation of symmetry in relational specifications. Due to control flow divergences or non-lockstep executions of loops, even different copies of the same program may proceed along different code fragments. However, some of the resulting verification subtasks may be indistinguishable from each other due to underlying symmetries among related fragments. We analyze the relational specifications, expressed as formulas in first-order theories (e.g., linear integer arithmetic) with multi-index variables, to discover symmetries and exploit them to prune away redundant subtasks. Prior works on use of symmetry in model checking [11,14,15,20] are typically based on symmetric states satisfying the same set of indexed atomic propositions, and do not consider symmetries among different indices in specifications. To the best of our knowledge, ours is the first work to *extract* such symmetries in relational specifications, and to *use* them for pruning redundant subtasks during relational verification. For extracting these symmetries, we have lifted core ideas from symmetry-discovery and symmetry-breaking in SAT formulas [12] to richer formulas in first-order theories.

The strategies we propose for exploiting synchrony and symmetry via relational specifications are fairly general in that they can be employed in vari-

```
if (yj > 20) {
  while (ij < 10) {
    xj *= ij;
    ij++;
  }
} else {
  while (ij < 10) {
    xj++;
    ij++;
  }
}
```

$y_1 > 20 \wedge y_2 > 20 \wedge y_3 > 20$
$y_1 > 20 \wedge y_2 > 20 \wedge y_3 \leq 20$
$y_1 > 20 \wedge y_2 \leq 20 \wedge y_3 > 20$
$y_1 > 20 \wedge y_2 \leq 20 \wedge y_3 \leq 20$
$y_1 \leq 20 \wedge y_2 > 20 \wedge y_3 > 20$
$y_1 \leq 20 \wedge y_2 > 20 \wedge y_3 \leq 20$
$y_1 \leq 20 \wedge y_2 \leq 20 \wedge y_3 > 20$
$y_1 \leq 20 \wedge y_2 \leq 20 \wedge y_3 \leq 20$

Fig. 1. Example program (left), and eight possible control-flow decisions (right).

ous verification methods. We provide a generic logic-based description of these strategies at a high level (Sect. 4), and also describe a specific instantiation in a verification algorithm based on forward analysis that computes strongest-postconditions (Sect. 5). We have implemented our approach in a prototype tool called SYNONYM built on top of the DESCARTES tool [27]. Our experimental evaluation (Sect. 6) shows the effectiveness of our approach in improving the performance of verification in many examples (and a marginal overhead in smaller examples). In particular, exploiting symmetry is crucial in enabling verification to complete for some properties, without which DESCARTES exceeds a timeout on all benchmark examples.

2 Motivating Example

Consider three C-like integer programs $\{P_j\}$ of the form shown in Fig. 1 (left). They are identical modulo renaming, and we use indices $j \in \{1, 2, 3\}$ as subscripts to denote variables in the different copies. We assume that each variable initially takes a nondeterministic value in each program.

A *relational verification problem* (RVP) is a tuple consisting of programs $\{P_j\}$, a relational precondition *pre*, and a relational postcondition *post*. In the example RVPs below, we consider the three conditionals, which in turn lead to eight possible control-flow decisions (Fig. 1, right) in a composed program. Each RVP reduces to subproblems for proving that *post* can be derived from *pre* for each of these control-flow decisions. In the rest of the section, we demonstrate the underlying ideas behind our approach to solve these subproblems efficiently.

Maximizing Lockstep Execution. Given an RVP (referred to as RVP_1) with precondition $x_1 < x_3 \wedge x_1 > 0 \wedge i_1 > 0 \wedge i_2 \geq i_1 \wedge i_1 = i_3$ (*pre*) and postcondition $(x_1 < x_3 \vee y_1 \neq y_3) \wedge i_1 > 0 \wedge i_2 \geq i_1 \wedge i_1 = i_3$ (*post*), consider a control-flow decision $y_1 > 20 \wedge y_2 > 20 \wedge y_3 > 20$. This leads to another RVP, consisting of three programs of the following form:

```
assume(yj > 20); while (ij < 10) {xj *= ij; ij++;}
```

where $j \in \{1, 2, 3\}$, and the aforementioned *pre* and *post*. From *pre*, it follows that $i_1 = i_3$ and $i_2 \geq i_1$. We can thus infer that the first and third loops are always executed the same number of times, while the second loop may be executed for fewer iterations. This knowledge lets us infer a single relational invariant for the first and third loops and handle the second loop separately. Clearly, the relational invariant $x_1 < x_3 \wedge i_1 = i_3 \wedge i_1 \leq 10$ and the non-relational invariant $i_2 \leq 10$ are enough to derive *post*. If we were to handle the first and third loop separately, we would need complex nonlinear invariants such as $x_1 = \frac{x_{1,init} \times i_1!}{i_{1,init}!}$ and $x_3 = \frac{x_{3,init} \times i_3!}{i_{3,init}!}$, which involve auxiliary variables $x_{j,init}$ and $i_{j,init}$ denoting the initial values of x_j and i_j respectively.

Symmetry-Breaking. For the same program, and an RVP (referred to as RVP_2) with precondition $i_1 > 0 \wedge i_2 \geq i_1 \wedge i_1 = i_3$ and postcondition $i_1 > 0 \wedge i_2 \geq i_1 \wedge i_1 = i_3$, consider a control-flow decision $y_1 > 20 \wedge y_2 > 20 \wedge y_3 \leq 20$. We generate another RVP involving the following set of programs:

```
assume(y1 > 20); while (i1 < 10) {x1 *= i1; i1++;}
assume(y2 > 20); while (i2 < 10) {x2 *= i2; i2++;}
assume(y3 ≤ 20); while (i3 < 10) {x3++; i3++;}
```

Similarly, decision $y_1 \leq 20 \wedge y_2 > 20 \wedge y_3 > 20$ generates yet another RVP over the following:

```
assume(y1 ≤ 20); while (i1 < 10) {x1++; i1++;}
assume(y2 > 20); while (i2 < 10) {x2 *= i2; i2++;}
assume(y3 > 20); while (i3 < 10) {x3 *= i3; i3++;}
```

Both RVPs have the same precondition and postcondition as RVP_2. We can see that both RVPs differ only in their subscripts; by taking one and swapping the subscripts 1 and 3 due to symmetry, we arrive at the other. Thus, knowing the verification result for either RVP allows us to skip verifying the other one, by discovering and exploiting such symmetries.

3 Background and Notation

Given a loop-free program over input variables $\vec{x}$ and output variables $\vec{y}$ (such that $\vec{x}$ and $\vec{y}$ are disjoint), let $Tr(\vec{x}, \vec{y})$ denote its symbolic encoding.

Proposition 1. *Given two loop-free programs, $Tr_1(\vec{x}_1, \vec{y}_1)$ and $Tr_2(\vec{x}_2, \vec{y}_2)$, a precondition $pre(\vec{x}_1, \vec{x}_2)$, and a postcondition $post(\vec{y}_1, \vec{y}_2)$, the task of relational verification is reduced to checking validity of the following formula.*

$$pre(\vec{x}_1, \vec{x}_2) \wedge Tr_1(\vec{x}_1, \vec{y}_1) \wedge Tr_2(\vec{x}_2, \vec{y}_2) \Longrightarrow post(\vec{y}_1, \vec{y}_2)$$

Given a program with one loop (i.e., a transition system) over input variables $\vec{x}$ and output variables $\vec{y}$, let $Init(\vec{x}, \vec{u})$ denote a symbolic encoding of the block of code before the loop, $Guard(\vec{u})$ denote the loop guard, and $Tr(\vec{u}, \vec{y})$ encode the loop body. Here, $\vec{u}$ is the vector of local variables that are live at the loop guard. For example, consider the program from our motivating example:

```
assume(y1 > 20); while (i1 < 10) {x1 *= i1; i1++;}
```

In its encoding, $\vec{x} = \vec{u} = (i_1, x_1, y_1)$, $\vec{y} = (i_1', x_1')$, $Init(\vec{x}, \vec{u}) = y_1 > 20$, $Guard(\vec{u}) = i_1' < 10$, and $Tr(\vec{u}, \vec{y}) = x_1' = x_1 \times i_1 \wedge i_1' = i_1 + 1$.

Proposition 2 (Naive parallel composition). *Given two loopy programs, $\langle Init(\vec{x}_1, \vec{u}_1), Guard(\vec{u}_1), Tr(\vec{u}_1, \vec{y}_1)\rangle$ and $\langle Init(\vec{x}_2, \vec{u}_2), Guard(\vec{u}_2), Tr(\vec{u}_2, \vec{y}_2)\rangle$, a precondition $pre(\vec{x}_1, \vec{x}_2)$, and a postcondition $post(\vec{y}_1, \vec{y}_2)$, the task of relational verification is reduced to the task of finding (individual) inductive invariants $\boldsymbol{I_1}$ and $\boldsymbol{I_2}$:*

$$\begin{aligned} pre(\vec{x}_1, \vec{x}_2) \wedge Init(\vec{x}_1, \vec{u}_1) &\Longrightarrow \boldsymbol{I_1}(\vec{u}_1) \\ pre(\vec{x}_1, \vec{x}_2) \wedge Init(\vec{x}_2, \vec{u}_2) &\Longrightarrow \boldsymbol{I_2}(\vec{u}_2) \\ \boldsymbol{I_1}(\vec{u}_1) \wedge Guard_1(\vec{u}_1) \wedge Tr_1(\vec{u}_1, \vec{y}_1) &\Longrightarrow \boldsymbol{I_1}(\vec{y}_1) \\ \boldsymbol{I_2}(\vec{u}_1) \wedge Guard_2(\vec{u}_2) \wedge Tr_2(\vec{u}_2, \vec{y}_2) &\Longrightarrow \boldsymbol{I_2}(\vec{y}_2) \\ \boldsymbol{I_1}(\vec{y}_1) \wedge \boldsymbol{I_2}(\vec{y}_2) \wedge \neg Guard_1(\vec{y}_1) \wedge \neg Guard_2(\vec{y}_2) &\Longrightarrow post(\vec{y}_1, \vec{y}_2) \end{aligned}$$

Note that the method of naive composition requires handling of multiple invariants, which is known to be difficult. Furthermore, it might lose some important relational information specified in $pre(\vec{x}_1, \vec{x}_2)$. One way to avoid this is to exploit the fact that loops could be executed in lockstep.

Proposition 3 (Lockstep composition). *Given two loopy programs, $\langle Init(\vec{x}_1, \vec{u}_1), Guard(\vec{u}_1), Tr(\vec{u}_1, \vec{y}_1)\rangle$ and $\langle Init(\vec{x}_2, \vec{u}_2), Guard(\vec{u}_2), Tr(\vec{u}_2, \vec{y}_2)\rangle$, a precondition $pre(\vec{x}_1, \vec{x}_2)$, and a postcondition $post(\vec{y}_1, \vec{y}_2)$. Let* ***both loops iterate exactly the same number of times,*** *then the task of relational verification is reduced to the task of finding one (relational) inductive invariant $\boldsymbol{I}$:*

$$\begin{aligned} pre(\vec{x}_1, \vec{x}_2) \wedge Init(\vec{x}_1, \vec{u}_1) \wedge Init(\vec{x}_2, \vec{u}_2) &\Longrightarrow \boldsymbol{I}(\vec{u}_1, \vec{u}_2) \\ \boldsymbol{I}(\vec{u}_1, \vec{u}_2) \wedge Guard_1(\vec{u}_1) \wedge Tr_1(\vec{u}_1, \vec{y}_1) \wedge Guard_2(\vec{u}_2) \wedge Tr_2(\vec{u}_2, \vec{y}_2) &\Longrightarrow \boldsymbol{I}(\vec{y}_1, \vec{y}_2) \\ \boldsymbol{I}(\vec{y}_1, \vec{y}_2) \wedge \neg Guard_1(\vec{y}_1) \wedge \neg Guard_2(\vec{y}_2) &\Longrightarrow post(\vec{y}_1, \vec{y}_2) \end{aligned}$$

In this paper, we do not focus on a specific method for deriving these invariants – a plethora of suitable methods have been proposed in the literature, and any of these could be used.

4 Leveraging Relational Specifications

In this section, we describe the main components of our compositional framework where we leverage relational specifications to simplify the verification subtasks. We first describe our novel algorithm for inferring maximal sets of loops that can be executed in lockstep (Sect. 4.1). Next, we describe our technique for handling conditionals (Sect. 4.2). While this is similar to other prior work, the main purpose here is to set the stage for our novel methods for exploiting symmetry (Sect. 4.3).

4.1 Synchronizing Loops

Given a set of loopy programs, we would like to determine which ones can be executed in lockstep. As mentioned earlier, relational invariants over lockstep loops are often easier to derive than loop invariants over a single copy.

Our algorithm CHECKLOCKSTEP takes as input a set of loopy programs $\{P_1, \ldots, P_k\}$ and outputs a set of *maximal* classes of programs that can be executed in lockstep. The algorithm partitions its input set of programs and recursively calls CHECKLOCKSTEP on the partitions.

First, CHECKLOCKSTEP infers a relational inductive invariant over the loop bodies, synthesizing $\boldsymbol{I}(\vec{u}_1, \ldots, \vec{u}_k)$ in the following:

$$pre(\vec{x}_1, \ldots, \vec{x}_k) \wedge \bigwedge_{i=1}^{k} Init(\vec{x}_i, \vec{u}_i) \implies \boldsymbol{I}(\vec{u}_1, \ldots, \vec{u}_k)$$

$$\boldsymbol{I}(\vec{u}_1, \ldots, \vec{u}_k) \wedge \bigwedge_{i=1}^{k} Guard_i(\vec{u}_i) \wedge Tr_i(\vec{u}_i, \vec{y}_i) \implies \boldsymbol{I}(\vec{y}_1, \ldots, \vec{y}_k)$$

CHECKLOCKSTEP then poses the following query:

$$\neg\left(\left(\boldsymbol{I}(\vec{u}_1, \ldots, \vec{u}_k) \wedge \bigvee_{i=1}^{k} \neg Guard(\vec{u}_i)\right) \implies \bigwedge_{i=1}^{k} \neg Guard(\vec{u}_i)\right) \qquad (1)$$

The left-hand side of the implication holds whenever one of the loops has terminated (the relational invariant holds, and at least one of the loop conditions must be false), and the right-hand side holds only if all of the loops have terminated. If the formula is unsatisfiable, then the termination of one loop implies the termination of all loops, and all loops can be executed simultaneously [27]. In this case, the entire set of input programs is one maximal class, and the set containing the set of all input programs is returned.

Otherwise, CHECKLOCKSTEP gets a satisfying assignment and partitions the input programs into a set *Terminated* and a set *Unfinished*. The *Terminated* set contains all programs P_i whose guards $Guard(\vec{u}_i)$ are false in the model for the formula, and the *Unfinished* set contains the remaining programs. The CHECKLOCKSTEP algorithm is then called recursively on both *Terminated* and *Unfinished*, with its final result being the union of the two sets returned by these recursive calls.

The following theorem assumes that any relational invariant $\boldsymbol{I}(\vec{u}_1, \ldots, \vec{u}_k)$, generated externally and used by the algorithm, is stronger than any relational invariant $\boldsymbol{I}(\vec{u}_1, \ldots, \vec{u}_{i-1}, \vec{u}_{i+1}, \ldots, \vec{u}_k)$ that could be synthesized over the same set of k loops with the ith loop removed.

Theorem 1. *For any call to* CHECKLOCKSTEP, *it always partitions its set of input programs such that for all $P_i \in$ Terminated and $P_j \in$ Unfinished, P_i and P_j cannot be executed in lockstep.*

Proof. Assume that CHECKLOCKSTEP has partitioned its set of programs into the *Terminated* and *Unfinished* sets. Let $P_i \in Terminated, P_j \in Unfinished$ be arbitrary programs. Based on how the partitioning is performed, we know that there is a model for Eq. 1 such that $Guard(\vec{u}_i)$ does not hold and $Guard(\vec{u}_j)$ does. We can thus conclude that the following formula is satisfiable:

$$\neg\Big(\boldsymbol{I}(\vec{u}_1, \ldots, \vec{u}_k) \wedge \neg Guard(\vec{u}_i) \implies \neg Guard(\vec{u}_j)\Big)$$

From the assumption on our invariant synthesizer, we conclude that the following is also satisfiable, indicating that P_i and P_j cannot be executed in lockstep:

$$\neg\Big(\boldsymbol{I}(\vec{u}_i, \vec{u}_j) \wedge \neg Guard(\vec{u}_i) \implies \neg Guard(\vec{u}_j)\Big)$$

where $\boldsymbol{I}(\vec{u}_i, \vec{u}_j)$ is the relational invariant for P_i and P_j that our invariant synthesizer infers. □

4.2 Synchronizing Conditionals

Let two programs have forms `if` $\mathtt{Q}_i$ `then` $\mathtt{R}_i$ `else` $\mathtt{S}_i$, where $i \in \{1, 2\}$ and $\mathtt{R}_i$ and $\mathtt{S}_i$ are arbitrary blocks of code and could possibly have loops. Let them be a part of some RVP, which reduces to applying Propositions 1, 2, or 3, depending on the content of each block of code, to four pairs of programs. As we have seen in previous sections, each of the four verification tasks could be expensive. In order to reduce the number of verification tasks where possible, we use the relational preconditions to filter out pairs of programs for which verification conclusions can be derived trivially.

For k programs of the form `if` $\mathtt{Q}_i$ `then` $\mathtt{R}_i$ `else` $\mathtt{S}_i$ for $i \in \{1, \ldots, k\}$ and precondition $pre(\vec{x}_1, \ldots, \vec{x}_k)$, we can simultaneously generate all possible combinations of decisions by querying a solver for all truth assignments to the $\mathtt{Q}_i$s:

$$pre(\vec{x}_1, \ldots, \vec{x}_k) \wedge \bigwedge_{i=1}^{k} Q_i \tag{2}$$

We can then use the result of this All-SAT query to generate sets of programs in subtasks. For each assignment j, where each Q_i is assigned a Boolean value v_i, the following set is generated: $\{$`assume (`$\mathtt{V}_1$`);` $\mathtt{U}_1, \ldots,$ `assume (`$\mathtt{V}_k$`);` $\mathtt{U}_k\}$ where for each $i \in \{1, \ldots, k\}$, if $v_i = true$, then $\mathtt{V}_i = \mathtt{Q}_i$ and $\mathtt{U}_i = \mathtt{R}_i$, else $\mathtt{V}_i = \neg\mathtt{Q}_i$ and $\mathtt{U}_i = \mathtt{S}_i$. We need to apply our verification algorithm on only the resulting sets of programs. For example, in our above RVP, if $\mathtt{Q}_1$ is equivalent to $\mathtt{Q}_2$ in all solutions, then the RVP reduces to verification of just two pairs of programs:

`assume (`$\mathtt{Q}_1$`);` $\mathtt{R}_1$ and `assume (`$\mathtt{Q}_2$`);` $\mathtt{R}_2$

`assume (`$\neg\mathtt{Q}_1$`);` $\mathtt{S}_1$ and `assume (`$\neg\mathtt{Q}_2$`);` $\mathtt{S}_2$

Algorithm 1. Algorithm for constructing a graph to find symmetries.

procedure MAKEGRAPH(F)
  $(V, E) \leftarrow (\{v_1^{Id}, \dots, v_k^{Id}\}, \varnothing)$ where each v_i^{Id} has $color(v_i^{Id}) = Id$
  for $d \in$ CLAUSES(F) **do** $(V, E) \leftarrow$ MAKECOLOREDAST(d) $\cup (V, E)$
  for $v \in V$ with $x_i \in vars(color(v))$ **do**
    $V \leftarrow (V \setminus \{v\}) \cup \{$RECOLOR$(v, v[x_i \mapsto x])\}$
    $E \leftarrow E \cup \{(v, v_i^{Id})\}$

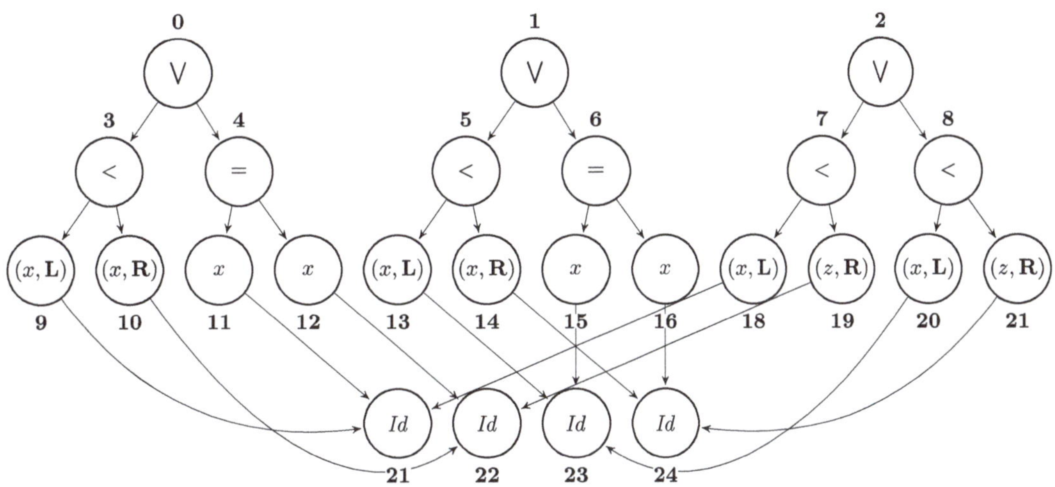

Fig. 2. Graph with vertex names (outside the vertices) and colors (inside the vertices).

4.3 Discovering and Exploiting Symmetries

Using the All-SAT query from Eq. 2 allows us to prune trivial RVPs. However, as we have seen in Sect. 2, some of the remaining RVPs could be regarded as equivalent due to symmetry. First, we discuss how to identify symmetries in formulas syntactically, and then we show how to use such symmetries.

4.3.1 Identifying Symmetries in Formulas

Formally, symmetries in formulas are defined as permutations. Note that any permutation π of set $\{1, \dots, k\}$ can be lifted to be a permutation of set $\{\vec{x}_1, \dots, \vec{x}_k\}$.

Definition 1 (Symmetry). *Let $\vec{x}_1, \dots, \vec{x}_k$ be vectors of the same size over disjoint sets of variables. A* symmetry *π of a formula $F(\vec{x}_1, \dots, \vec{x}_k)$ is a permutation of set $\{\vec{x}_i \mid 1 \leq i \leq k\}$ such that $F(\vec{x}_1, \dots, \vec{x}_k) \iff F(\pi(\vec{x}_1), \dots, \pi(\vec{x}_k))$.*

The task of finding symmetries within a set of formulas can be performed syntactically by first canonicalizing the formulas, converting the formulas into a graph representation of their syntax, and then using a graph automorphism algorithm to find the symmetries of the graph. We demonstrate how this can be done for a formula φ over Linear Integer Arithmetic with the following example.

Let $\varphi = (x_1 \leq x_2 \wedge x_3 \leq x_4) \wedge (x_1 < z_2 \vee x_3 < z_4)$. Note that this formula is symmetric under a permutation of the subscripts that simultaneously swaps

1 with 3 and 2 with 4. Let $\{(x_1, z_1), (x_2, z_2), (x_3, z_3), (x_4, z_4)\}$ be the vectors of variables. We identify a vector by its subscript (e.g., we identify (x_1, z_1) by 1).

Our algorithm starts with canonicalizing the formula: $\varphi = (x_1 < x_2 \lor x_1 = x_2) \land (x_3 < x_4 \lor x_3 = x_4) \land (x_1 < z_2 \lor x_3 < z_4)$. It then constructs a colored graph for the canonicalized formula with the procedure in Algorithm 1. The algorithm initializes a graph by the set of k vertices $v_1^{Id}, \ldots, v_k^{Id}$ with color *Id* (vertices 21–24 in Fig. 2), where k is the number of identifiers. It then (Line 3) adds to the graph the union of the abstract syntax trees (AST) for the formula's conjuncts, where each vertex has a color corresponding to the type of its AST node. If a parent vertex has a color of an ordering-sensitive operation or predicate, then the children should have colors that include a tag to indicate their ordering (e.g., vertices 9 and 10 in Fig. 2 have colors with tags because their parent has color $<$, but vertices 11 and 12 do not have tags because their parent has color $=$). Next (Line 4), the algorithm performs an appropriate renaming of vertex colors so that each indexed variable name x_i is replaced with a non-indexed version x, while simultaneously adding edges from each vertex with a renamed color to v_i^{Id}. The resulting graph for φ is shown in Fig. 2. Finally, the algorithm applies a graph automorphism finder to get the following automorphism (in addition to the identity automorphism), which is shown here in a cyclic notation where $(x\ y)$ means that $x \mapsto y$ and $y \mapsto x$ (vertices that map to themselves are omitted):

$$(0\ 1)(3\ 5)(4\ 6)(7\ 8)(9\ 13)(10\ 14)(11\ 15)(12\ 16)(17\ 19)(18\ 20)(21\ 23)(22\ 24)$$

We are only interested in permutations of the vectors, so we project out the relevant parts of the permutation (21 23)(22 24) and map them back to our vector identifiers to get the following permutation on the identifiers:

$$\pi = \{1 \mapsto 3, 2 \mapsto 4, 3 \mapsto 1, 4 \mapsto 2\}$$

4.3.2 Exploiting Symmetries

We now define the notion of symmetric RVPs and application of symmetry-breaking to generate a single representative per equivalence class of RVPs.

Definition 2 (Symmetric RVPs). *Two RVPs:* $\langle Ps, pre(\vec{x}_1, \ldots, \vec{x}_k), post(\vec{y}_1, \ldots, \vec{y}_k)\rangle$ *and* $\langle Ps', pre(\vec{x}_1, \ldots, \vec{x}_k), post(\vec{y}_1, \ldots, \vec{y}_k)\rangle$, *where* $Ps = \{P_1, \ldots, P_k\}$, *and* $Ps' = \{P'_1, \ldots, P'_k\}$, *are called* symmetric *under a permutation* π *iff*

1. π *is a symmetry of formula* $pre(\vec{x}_1, \ldots, \vec{x}_k) \land post(\vec{y}_1, \ldots, \vec{y}_k)$
2. *for every* $P_i \in Ps$ *and* $P_j \in Ps'$, *if* $\pi(i) = j$, *then* P_i *and* P_j *have the same number of inputs and outputs and have logically equivalent encodings for the same set of input variables* $\vec{x}_i$ *and output variables* $\vec{y}_i$

As we have seen in Sect. 4.3.1, identification of symmetries could be made purely on the syntactic level of the relational preconditions and postconditions. For each detected symmetry, it remains to check equivalence between the corresponding programs' encodings, which can be formulated as an SMT problem.

To exploit symmetries, we propose a simple but intuitive approach. First, we identify the set of symmetries using $pre \wedge post$. Then, we solve the All-SAT query from Eq. 2 and get a *reduced* set R of RVPs (i.e., one without all trivial problems). For each $RVP_i \in R$, we perform the relational verification only if no symmetric $RVP_j \in R$ has already been verified. Thus, the most expensive part of the routine, checking equivalence of RVPs, is performed on demand and only on a subset of all possible pairs $\langle RVP_i, RVP_j \rangle$.

Alternatively, in some cases (e.g., for parallelizing the algorithm) it might help to identify all symmetric RVPs prior to solving the All-SAT query from Eq. 2. From this set, we can generate symmetry-breaking predicates (SBPs) [12] and conjoin them to Eq. 2. Constrained with SBPs, this query will have fewer models, and will contain a single representative per equivalence class of RVPs. We describe how to construct SBPs in more detail in the next section.

4.3.3 Generating Symmetry-Breaking Predicates (SBPs)

SBPs have previously been applied in pruning the search space explored by SAT solvers. Traditionally, techniques construct SBPs based on symmetries in truth assignments to the literals in the formula, but SBP-construction can be adapted to be based on symmetries in truth assignments to conditionals, allowing us to break symmetries in our setting.

We can construct an SBP by treating each condition the way a literal is treated in existing SBP constructions. In particular, we can construct the common Lex-Leader SBP used for predicate logic [12], which in our case will force a solver to choose the lexicographically least representative per equivalence class for a particular ordering of the conditions. For the ordering of conditions where $\mathtt{Q}_i \leq \mathtt{Q}_j$ iff $i \leq j$ and a set of symmetries S over $\{1, \ldots, k\}$, we can construct a Lex-Leader SBP $SBP(S) = \bigwedge_{\pi \in S} PP(\pi)$ with the more efficient predicate chaining construction [2], where we have that

$$PP(\pi) = p_{\min(I)} \wedge \bigwedge_{i \in I} p_i \implies g_{prev(i,I)} \implies l_i \wedge p_{next(i,I)}$$

and that I is the support of π with the last condition for each cycle removed, $\min(I)$ is the minimal element of I, $prev(i, I)$ is the maximal element of I still less than i or 0 if there is none, $next(i, I)$ is the minimal element of I still greater than i or 0 if there is none, $p_0 = g_0 = true$, p_i is a fresh predicate for $i \neq 0$, $g_i = \mathtt{Q}_{\pi(i)} \implies \mathtt{Q}_i$ for $i \neq 0$, and $l_i = \mathtt{Q}_i \implies \mathtt{Q}_{\pi(i)}$.

After constructing the SBP, we conjoin it to the All-SAT query in Eq. 2. Our solver now generates sets of programs that, when combined with the relational precondition and postcondition, form a set of irredundant RVPs.

Example. Let us consider how SBPs can be applied to RVP_2 from Sect. 2 to avoid generating two of the eight RVPs we would otherwise generate.

First, we see that our three programs are all copies the same program and are at the same program point, so they will have the same encoding. Next, we find the set of permutations S over $\{1, 2, 3\}$ such that for each $\pi \in S$, we have that $i_1 > 0 \land i_2 \geq i_1 \land i_1 = i_3$ iff $i_{\pi(1)} > 0 \land i_{\pi(2)} \geq i_{\pi(1)} \land i_{\pi(1)} = i_{\pi(3)}$. In this case, we have that S is the set of permutations $\{\{1 \mapsto 1, 2 \mapsto 2, 3 \mapsto 3\}, \{1 \mapsto 3, 2 \mapsto 2, 3 \mapsto 3\}\}$. Now, we construct a Lex-Leader SBP (using the predicate chaining construction described above):

$$p_1 \land (p_1 \implies ((y_1 > 20) \implies (y_2 > 20)))$$

where p_1 is a fresh predicate. Conjoining this SBP to Eq. 2, leads to the RVPs arising from the control-flow decisions $y_1 > 20 \land y_2 > 20 \land y_3 \leq 20$ and $y_1 > 20 \land y_2 \leq 20 \land y_3 \leq 20$ no longer being generated.

5 Instantiation of Strategies in Forward Analysis

We now describe an instantiation of our proposed strategies in a verification algorithm based on forward analysis using a strongest-postcondition computation. Other instantiations, e.g., on top of a Horn solver based on Property-Directed Reachability [24] are possible, but outside the scope of this work.

```
procedure VERIFY(pre, Current, Ifs, Loops, post)
    while Current ≠ ∅ do
        if PROCESSSTATEMENT(pre, P_i, Ifs, Loops, post) = safe then return safe
    if Loops ≠ ∅ then HANDLELOOPS(pre, Loops, post)
    else if Ifs ≠ ∅ then HANDLEIFS(pre, Ifs, Loops, post)
    else return unsafe
```

Given an RVP in the form of a Hoare triple $\{Pre\}\ P_1||\cdots||P_k\ \{Post\}$, where $||$ denotes parallel composition, the top-level VERIFY procedure takes as input the relational specification $pre = Pre$ and $post = Post$, the set of input programs $Current = \{P_1, \ldots, P_k\}$, and empty sets *Loops* and *Ifs*. It uses a strongest-postcondition computation to compute the next Hoare triple at each step until it can conclude the validity of the original Hoare triple.

Synchronization. Throughout verification, the algorithm maintains three disjoint sets of programs: one for programs that are currently being processed (*Current*), one for programs that have been processed up until a loop (*Loops*), and one for programs that have been processed up until a conditional statement (*Ifs*). The algorithm processes statements in each program independently, with PROCESSSTATEMENT choosing an arbitrary interleaving of statements from the programs in *Current*. When the algorithm encounters the end of a program in its call to PROCESSSTATEMENT, it removes this program from the *Current* set. At this point, the algorithm returns safe if the current Hoare triple is proven valid. When a program has reached a point of control-flow divergence and is processed by PROCESSSTATEMENT, it is removed from *Current* and added to the appropriate set (*Loops* or *Ifs*).

Handling Loops. Once all programs are in the *Loops* or *Ifs* sets (i.e. *Current* = ∅), the algorithm handles the programs in the *Loops* set if it is nonempty. HandleLoops behaves like CheckLockstep but computes postconditions where possible; when a set of loops are able to be executed in lockstep, HandleLoops computes their postconditions before placing the programs into the *Terminated* set. After all loops have been placed in the *Terminated* set and a new precondition pre' has been computed, rather than returning *Terminated*, HandleLoops invokes Verify(pre', *Terminated*, *Ifs*, ∅, *post*).

Handling Conditionals. When *Current* = *Loops* = ∅, Verify handles conditional statements. HandleIfs exploits symmetries by using the All-SAT query with Lex-Leader SBPs as described in Sect. 4 and calls Verify on each generated verification problem.

6 Implementation and Evaluation

To evaluate the effectiveness of increased lockstep execution of loops and symmetry-breaking, we implemented our algorithm from Sect. 5 on top of the Descartes tool for verifying k-safety properties, i.e., RVPs over k identical Java programs. We implemented two variants: Syn uses only synchrony (i.e., no symmetry is used), while Synonym uses both. All implementations (including Descartes) use the same guess-and-check invariant generator (the same originally used by Descartes, but modified to generate more candidate invariants). In Synonym, we compute symmetries in preconditions and postconditions only when all program copies are the same. For our examples, it sufficed to compute symmetries simply by checking if each possible permutation leads to equivalent formulas[1]. We compare the performance of our prototype implementations to Descartes[2]. We use two metrics for comparison: the time taken and the number of Hoare triples processed by the verification procedure. All experiments were conducted on a MacBook Pro, with a 2.7 GHz Intel Core i5 processor and 8 GB RAM.

6.1 Stackoverflow Benchmarks

The first set of benchmarks we consider are the Stackoverflow benchmarks originally used to evaluate Descartes. These implement (correctly or incorrectly) the Java `Comparator` or `Comparable` interface, and check whether or not their *compare* functions satisfy the following properties:

1 Our implementation includes the syntactic symmetry-finding algorithm from Sect. 4.3.1, though we do not use it for evaluation here due to its high overhead in using an external tool for finding graph automorphisms.

2 While there are several tools for relational verification (e.g. Rosette/Unbound [25], VeriMapRel [13], Reve [17], MoCHi [17], SymDiff [22]), most of these do not handle Java programs, and to the best of our knowledge, none of these tools has support for k-safety verification for k greater than 2.

P1: $\forall x, y.sgn(compare(x, y)) = -sgn(compare(y, x))$
P2: $\forall x, y, z.(compare(x, y) > 0 \wedge compare(y, z) > 0) \implies compare(x, z) > 0$
P3: $\forall x, y, z.(compare(x, y) = 0) \implies (sgn(compare(x, z)) = sgn(compare(y, z)))$

(One of the original 34 Stackoverflow examples is excluded from our evaluation here because of the inability of the invariant generator to produce a suitable invariant.) We compare the results of running SYN and SYNONYM vs. DESCARTES for each property in Table 1. (Expanded versions and plots of these results are available in an extended version of the paper [26].)

Because property P1 contains a symmetry, we notice an improvement in terms of number of Hoare triples with the use of symmetry for this property; however, the overhead of computing symmetries leads to SYNONYM performing more slowly than SYN even for some examples that exhibit reduced Hoare triple counts. Property P1 is also the easiest to prove (all implementations can verify each example in under 0.3 s), so the overheads contribute more significantly to the runtime. For examples on which our implementations do not perform as well as DESCARTES, we perform reasonably closely to DESCARTES. These examples are typically smaller, and again overheads play a larger role in our poorer performance.

Table 1. Stackoverflow Benchmarks. Total times (in seconds) and Hoare triple counts (HTC) for Stackoverflow benchmarks, where for each property, the results for SYN and SYNONYM are divided into those for examples where they exhibit a factor of improvement over DESCARTES that is greater or equal to 1 (top) and those for which they do not (bottom). *Improv* reports the factor of improvement over DESCARTES, where the number of examples is given in parentheses.

Prop	DESCARTES		SYN				SYNONYM			
	Time	HTC	Time	Improv	HTC	Improv	Time	Improv	HTC	Improv
P1	3.11	4422	1.91	1.39 (27)	2255	1.69 (27)	1.82	1.32 (25)	2401	1.82 (32)
			0.57	0.789 (6)	752	0.809 (6)	0.87	0.816 (8)	48	0.979 (1)
P2	24.6	13434	7.83	2.62 (20)	3285	3.081 (16)	7.31	2.80 (19)	3224	3.140 (16)
			4.98	0.823 (13)	4638	0.714 (17)	5.1	0.816 (14)	4638	0.714 (17)
P3	18.85	10938	5.22	2.92 (20)	1565	4.36 (16)	5.22	2.91 (19)	1537	4.74 (16)
			6.18	0.584 (13)	6600	0.623 (17)	6.16	0.594 (14)	6600	0.623 (17)

6.2 Modified Stackoverflow Benchmarks

The original Stackoverflow examples are fairly small, with all implementations taking under 6 s to verify any example. To assess how we perform on larger examples, we modified several of the larger Stackoverflow comparator examples to be longer, take more arguments, and contain more control-flow decisions. The resulting functions take three arguments and pick the "largest" object's id, where comparison among objects is performed based on the original Stackoverflow example code. (Ties are broken by choosing the least id.) We check whether these *pick* functions satisfy the following properties that allow reordering input arguments:

P13: $\forall x, y, z.pick(x, y, z) = pick(y, x, z)$
P14: $\forall x, y, z.pick(x, y, z) = pick(y, x, z) \wedge pick(x, y, z) = pick(z, y, x)$

Note that P13 allows swapping the first two input arguments, while P14 allows any permutation of inputs, a useful hyperproperty.

The results from running property P13 are shown in Table 2. We see here that for these larger examples, Hoare triple counts are more reliably correlated with the time taken to perform verification. SYN outperforms DESCARTES on 14 of the 16 examples, and SYNONYM outperforms both DESCARTES and SYN on all 16 examples.

The results from running property P14 are shown in Table 3. For this property, note thatDESCARTES is unable to verify any of the examples within a one-hour timeout. Meanwhile, SYN is able to verify 10 of the 16 examples without exceeding the timeout. Exploiting symmetries here exhibits an obvious improvement, with SYNONYM not only being able to verify the same examples as SYN, with consistently faster performance on the larger examples, but also being able to verify an additional example within an hour.

Table 2. Verifying P13 for modified Stackoverflow examples. Times (in seconds) and Hoare triple counts (HTC).

Example	DESCARTES		SYN		SYNONYM	
	Time	HTC	Time	HTC	Time	HTC
ArrayInt-pick3-false-simple	1.71	2573	1	1355	0.64	682
ArrayInt-pick3-false	1.55	2591	1.06	1439	0.8	724
ArrayInt-pick3-true-simple	1.71	2573	1.03	1355	0.65	682
ArrayInt-pick3-true	1.55	2591	1.08	1439	0.81	724
Chromosome-pick3-false-simple	0.9	1115	0.9	883	0.53	446
Chromosome-pick3-false	2.51	2891	2.94	3019	1.59	1514
Chromosome-pick3-true-simple	0.9	1115	0.9	883	0.53	446
Chromosome-pick3-true	2.51	2891	2.96	3019	1.59	1514
PokerHand-pick3-false-part1	5.87	5825	0.42	359	0.46	359
PokerHand-pick3-false-part2	9.74	10589	0.85	323	0.86	323
PokerHand-pick3-false	16.91	16475	0.73	159	0.79	159
PokerHand-pick3-true-part1	5.83	5825	3.98	3503	2.4	1756
PokerHand-pick3-true-part2	9.8	10565	7.36	5933	4.53	2971
PokerHand-pick3-true	17.25	16475	12.1	9293	7.34	4651
Solution-pick3-false	76.4	99910	25.05	20645	20.42	10327
Solution-pick3-true	64.5	99910	19.66	20645	15.21	10327
Total	219.64	283914	82.02	74252	59.15	37605
Improvement	1	1	2.68	3.8237	3.713	7.5499

Table 3. Verifying P14 for modified Stackoverflow examples. Times (in seconds) and Hoare triple counts (HTC). - indicates that no sufficient invariant could be inferred.

Example	DESCARTES		SYN		SYNONYM	
	Time	HTC	Time	HTC	Time	HTC
ArrayInt-pick3-false-simple	TO	TO	4.12	1938	4.66	1734
ArrayInt-pick3-false	TO	TO	4.92	2017	6.03	1500
ArrayInt-pick3-true-simple	TO	TO	321.15	140593	170.43	58586
ArrayInt-pick3-true	TO	TO	366.98	149125	240.25	62141
Chromosome-pick3-false-simple	TO	TO	47.8	14097	1.67	834
Chromosome-pick3-false	TO	TO	264.21	93052	4.91	3043
Chromosome-pick3-true-simple	TO	TO	299.51	79613	135.56	33179
Chromosome-pick3-true	TO	TO	TO	TO	848.22	225044
PokerHand-pick3-false-part1	TO	TO	0.57	391	0.73	391
PokerHand-pick3-false-part2	TO	TO	0.81	228	0.81	228
PokerHand-pick3-false	-	-	-	-	-	-
PokerHand-pick3-true-part1	TO	TO	2277.03	819553	1272.58	341486
PokerHand-pick3-true-part2	TO	TO	-	-	-	-
PokerHand-pick3-true	-	-	-	-	-	-
Solution-pick3-false	TO	TO	TO	TO	TO	TO
Solution-pick3-false	TO	TO	TO	TO	TO	TO

Summary of Experimental Results. Our experiments indicate that our performance improvements are consistent: on all DESCARTES benchmarks (in Table 1, which are all small) our techniques either have low overhead or show some improvement despite the overhead; and on modified (bigger) programs they lead to significant improvements. In particular, we report (Table 2) speedups up to 21.4x (on an example where the property doesn't hold) and 4.2x (on an example where it does). More importantly, we report (Table 3) that DESCARTES times out on 14 examples, where of these SYNONYM times out for 2 and cannot infer an invariant for one example.

7 Related Work

The work most closely related to ours is by Sousa and Dillig [27], which proposed Cartesian Hoare Logic (CHL) for proving k-safety properties and the tool DESCARTES for automated reasoning in CHL. In addition to the core program logic, CHL includes additional proof rules for loops, referred to as Cartesian Loop Logic (CLL). A generalization of CHL, called Quantitative Cartesian Hoare Logic was subsequently used by Chen et al. [10] to detect side-channel vulnerabilities in cryptographic implementations.

In terms of comparison, neither CHL nor CLL force alignment at conditional statements or take advantage of symmetries. We believe our algorithm for identifying a maximal set of lockstep loops is also novel and can be used in other methods that do not rely on CHL/CLL. On the other hand, CLL proof rules allow not only fully lockstep loops, but also *partially* lockstep loops. Although we did not consider it here, our maximal lockstep-loop detection algorithm can be combined with their partial lockstep execution to further improve the efficiency of verification. For example, applying the Fusion 2 rule from CLL to our example while loops generated from RVP_1 (Sect. 2) would result in *three* subproblems and require reasoning twice about the second copy's loop finishing later. When combined with maximal lockstep-loop detection, we could generate just *two* subproblems: one where the first and third loops terminate first, and another where the second loop terminates first.

Other automatic efforts for relational verification typically use some kind of product programs [6,13,17,21,22,24,28], with a possible reduction to Horn solving [13,17,21,24]. Similarly to our strategy for synchrony, most of them attempt to leverage similarity (structural or functional) in programs to ease verification. However, we have seen less focus on leveraging relational specifications themselves to simplify verification tasks, although this varies according to the verification method used. Some efforts do not reason over product programs at all, relying on techniques based on decomposition [3] or customized theories with theorem proving [4,30] instead. To the best of our knowledge, none of these efforts exploit symmetry in programs or in relational specifications.

On the other hand, symmetry has been used very successfully in model checking parametric finite state systems [11,15,20] and concurrent programs [14]. Our work differs from these efforts in two main respects. First, the parametric systems considered in these efforts have components that interact with each other or share variables. Second, the correctness specifications are also parametric, usually single-index or double-index properties in a propositional (temporal) logic. In contrast, in our RVPs, the individual programs are independent and do not share any common variables. The only interaction between them is via relational specifications. Furthermore, we discover symmetries in these relational specifications over multi-index variables, expressed as formulas in first-order theories (e.g., linear integer arithmetic). We then exploit these symmetries to prune redundant RVPs during verification.

There are also some similarities between relational verification and verification of concurrent/parallel programs. In the latter, a typical verifier [18] would use *visible* operations (i.e., synchronization operations or communication on shared state) as synchronizing points in the composed program. In our work, this selection is made based on the structure of the component programs and the ease of utilizing or deriving relational assertions for the code fragments. Furthermore, one does not need to consider different orderings in interleavings of programs in the RVPs. Since these fragments are independent, it suffices to explore any one ordering. Instead, we exploit symmetries in the relational assertions to prune away redundant RVPs.

Finally, specific applications may impose additional synchrony requirements pertaining to visibility. For example, one may want to check for information leaks from private inputs to public outputs not only at the end of a program but at other specified intermediate points, or information leakage models for side-channel attacks may check for leaks based on given observer models [1]. Such requirements can be viewed as relational specifications at selected synchronizing points in the composed program. Again, we can leverage these relational specifications to simplify the resulting verification subproblems.

8 Conclusions and Future Work

We have proposed novel techniques for improving relational verification, which has several applications including security verification, program equivalence checking, and regression verification. Our two key ideas are maximizing the amount of code that can be synchronized and identifying symmetries in relational specifications to avoid redundant subtasks. Our prototype implementation on top of the DESCARTES verification tool leads to consistent improvements on a range of benchmarks. In the future, we would be interested in implementing these ideas on top of a Horn-based relational verifier (e.g., [25]) and extending it to work with recursive data structures. We are also interested in developing an algorithm for finding symmetries in formulas that does not rely on an external graph automorphism tool.

Acknowledgements. We gratefully acknowledge the help from Marcelo Sousa and Işil Dillig on their DESCARTES tool, which provides the base for our prototype development and experimental comparison. This work was supported in part by NSF Grant 1525936.

References

1. Almeida, J.B., Barbosa, M., Barthe, G., Dupressoir, F., Emmi, M.: Verifying constant-time implementations. In: USENIX, pp. 53–70. USENIX Association (2016)
2. Aloul, F.A., Sakallah, K.A., Markov, I.L.: Efficient symmetry breaking for Boolean satisfiability. IEEE Trans. Comput. **55**(5), 549–558 (2006)
3. Antonopoulos, T., Gazzillo, P., Hicks, M., Koskinen, E., Terauchi, T., Wei, S.: Decomposition instead of self-composition for proving the absence of timing channels. In: PLDI, pp. 362–375 (2017)
4. Asada, K., Sato, R., Kobayashi, N.: Verifying relational properties of functional programs by first-order refinement. Sci. Comput. Program. **137**, 2–62 (2017)
5. Banerjee, A., Naumann, D.A., Nikouei, M.: Relational logic with framing and hypotheses. In: IARCS. LIPIcs, vol. 65, pp. 11:1–11:16. Schloss Dagstuhl - Leibniz-Zentrum fuer Informatik (2016)
6. Barthe, G., Crespo, J.M., Kunz, C.: Relational verification using product programs. In: Butler, M., Schulte, W. (eds.) FM 2011. LNCS, vol. 6664, pp. 200–214. Springer, Heidelberg (2011). https://doi.org/10.1007/978-3-642-21437-0_17
7. Barthe, G., D'Argenio, P.R., Rezk, T.: Secure information flow by self-composition. In: CSFW, pp. 100–114. IEEE (2004)
8. Benton, N.: Simple relational correctness proofs for static analyses and program transformations. In: POPL, pp. 14–25 (2004)

9. Beringer, L., Hofmann, M.: Secure information flow and program logics. In: CSF, pp. 233–248. IEEE Computer Society (2007)
10. Chen, J., Feng, Y., Dillig, I.: Precise detection of side-channel vulnerabilities using quantitative Cartesian hoare logic. In: Proceedings of the 2017 ACM SIGSAC Conference on Computer and Communications Security, CCS 2017, pp. 875–890 (2017)
11. Clarke, E.M., Filkorn, T., Jha, S.: Exploiting symmetry in temporal logic model checking. In: Courcoubetis, C. (ed.) CAV 1993. LNCS, vol. 697, pp. 450–462. Springer, Heidelberg (1993). https://doi.org/10.1007/3-540-56922-7_37
12. Crawford, J.M., Ginsberg, M.L., Luks, E.M., Roy, A.: Symmetry-breaking predicates for search problems. In: KR, pp. 148–159 (1996)
13. De Angelis, E., Fioravanti, F., Pettorossi, A., Proietti, M.: Relational verification through horn clause transformation. In: Rival, X. (ed.) SAS 2016. LNCS, vol. 9837, pp. 147–169. Springer, Heidelberg (2016). https://doi.org/10.1007/978-3-662-53413-7_8
14. Donaldson, A., Kaiser, A., Kroening, D., Wahl, T.: Symmetry-aware predicate abstraction for shared-variable concurrent programs. In: Gopalakrishnan, G., Qadeer, S. (eds.) CAV 2011. LNCS, vol. 6806, pp. 356–371. Springer, Heidelberg (2011). https://doi.org/10.1007/978-3-642-22110-1_28
15. Emerson, E.A., Sistla, A.P.: Symmetry and model checking. In: Courcoubetis, C. (ed.) CAV 1993. LNCS, vol. 697, pp. 463–478. Springer, Heidelberg (1993). https://doi.org/10.1007/3-540-56922-7_38
16. Fedyukovich, G., Gurfinkel, A., Sharygina, N.: Property directed equivalence via abstract simulation. In: Chaudhuri, S., Farzan, A. (eds.) CAV 2016. LNCS, vol. 9780, pp. 433–453. Springer, Cham (2016). https://doi.org/10.1007/978-3-319-41540-6_24
17. Felsing, D., Grebing, S., Klebanov, V., Rümmer, P., Ulbrich, M.: Automating regression verification. In: ASE, pp. 349–360. ACM (2014)
18. Godefroid, P.: VeriSoft: a tool for the automatic analysis of concurrent reactive software. In: Grumberg, O. (ed.) CAV 1997. LNCS, vol. 1254, pp. 476–479. Springer, Heidelberg (1997). https://doi.org/10.1007/3-540-63166-6_52
19. Godlin, B., Strichman, O.: Regression verification. In: DAC, pp. 466–471. ACM (2009)
20. Ip, C.N., Dill, D.L.: Verifying systems with replicated components in murϕ. In: Alur, R., Henzinger, T.A. (eds.) CAV 1996. LNCS, vol. 1102, pp. 147–158. Springer, Heidelberg (1996). https://doi.org/10.1007/3-540-61474-5_65
21. Kiefer, M., Klebanov, V., Ulbrich, M.: Relational program reasoning using compiler IR. In: Blazy, S., Chechik, M. (eds.) VSTTE 2016. LNCS, vol. 9971, pp. 149–165. Springer, Cham (2016). https://doi.org/10.1007/978-3-319-48869-1_12
22. Lahiri, S.K., McMillan, K.L., Sharma, R., Hawblitzel, C.: Differential assertion checking. In: FSE, pp. 345–355. ACM (2013)
23. Logozzo, F., Lahiri, S.K., Fähndrich, M., Blackshear, S.: Verification modulo versions: towards usable verification. In: PLDI, p. 32. ACM (2014)
24. Mordvinov, D., Fedyukovich, G.: Synchronizing constrained horn clauses. In: LPAR. EPiC Series in Computing, vol. 46, pp. 338–355. EasyChair (2017)
25. Mordvinov, D., Fedyukovich, G.: Verifying safety of functional programs with rosette/unbound. CoRR, abs/1704.04558 (2017). https://github.com/dvvrd/rosette
26. Pick, L., Fedyukovich, G., Gupta, A.: Exploiting synchrony and symmetry in relational verification (extended version of CAV 2018 paper). https://cs.princeton.edu/%7Eaartig/papers/synonym-cav18.pdf

27. Sousa, M., Dillig, I.: Cartesian hoare logic for verifying k-safety properties. In: PLDI, pp. 57–69. ACM (2016)
28. Strichman, O., Veitsman, M.: Regression verification for unbalanced recursive functions. In: Fitzgerald, J., Heitmeyer, C., Gnesi, S., Philippou, A. (eds.) FM 2016. LNCS, vol. 9995, pp. 645–658. Springer, Cham (2016). https://doi.org/10.1007/978-3-319-48989-6_39
29. Terauchi, T., Aiken, A.: Secure information flow as a safety problem. In: Hankin, C., Siveroni, I. (eds.) SAS 2005. LNCS, vol. 3672, pp. 352–367. Springer, Heidelberg (2005). https://doi.org/10.1007/11547662_24
30. Unno, H., Torii, S., Sakamoto, H.: Automating induction for solving horn clauses. In: Majumdar, R., Kunčak, V. (eds.) CAV 2017. LNCS, vol. 10427, pp. 571–591. Springer, Cham (2017). https://doi.org/10.1007/978-3-319-63390-9_30
31. Yang, H.: Relational separation logic. Theoret. Comput. Sci. **375**(1–3), 308–334 (2007)
32. Zaks, A., Pnueli, A.: CoVaC: compiler validation by program analysis of the cross-product. In: Cuellar, J., Maibaum, T., Sere, K. (eds.) FM 2008. LNCS, vol. 5014, pp. 35–51. Springer, Heidelberg (2008). https://doi.org/10.1007/978-3-540-68237-0_5

JBMC: A Bounded Model Checking Tool for Verifying Java Bytecode

Lucas Cordeiro[1,2(✉)], Pascal Kesseli[1], Daniel Kroening[1,2], Peter Schrammel[1,3], and Marek Trtik[1]

[1] Diffblue Ltd., Oxford, UK
[2] University of Oxford, Oxford, UK
lucas.cordeiro@manchester.ac.uk
[3] University of Sussex, Brighton, UK

Abstract. We present a bounded model checking tool for verifying Java bytecode, which is built on top of the CPROVER framework, named *Java Bounded Model Checker* (JBMC). JBMC processes Java bytecode together with a model of the standard Java libraries and checks a set of desired properties. Experimental results show that JBMC can correctly verify a set of Java benchmarks from the literature and that it is competitive with two state-of-the-art Java verifiers.

1 Introduction

The Java Programming Language is a general-purpose, concurrent, strongly typed, object-oriented language [13]. Applications written in Java are compiled to the bytecode instruction set and binary format as defined in the Java Virtual Machine (JVM) specification. This compiled Java bytecode can run on all platforms on top of a JVM without the need for recompilation. However, Java programs may have bugs, which may result in array bound violations, unintended arithmetic overflows, and other kinds of functional and runtime errors. In addition, Java allows multi-threading, and thus, problems such as race conditions and deadlocks can occur.

To detect such issues, we developed an extension to the C Bounded Model Checker (CBMC) [6], named JBMC,[1] that verifies Java bytecode. JBMC consists of a frontend for parsing Java bytecode and a Java operational model (JOM), which is an exact but verification-friendly model of the standard Java libraries. A distinct feature of JBMC, when compared with other approaches [2,7,9], is the use of Bounded Model Checking (BMC) [4] in combination with Boolean Satisfiability and Satisfiability Modulo Theories (SMT) [3] and full symbolic state-space exploration, which allows us to perform a bit-accurate verification

Support by ERC project 280053 CPROVER and the H2020 FET OPEN 712689 SC^2.

[1] Available at https://www.cprover.org/jbmc/.

H. Chockler and G. Weissenbacher (Eds.): CAV 2018, LNCS 10981, pp. 183–190, 2018.
https://doi.org/10.1007/978-3-319-96145-3_10

of Java programs. Apart from JBMC, there are other Java verifiers, which use different verification approaches.

Existing Java Verifiers. *JayHorn* is a verifier for Java bytecode [9] that uses the Java optimization framework Soot [14] as a front-end and then produces a set of constrained Horn clauses to encode the verification condition (VC). *Java Path Finder* (JPF) is an explicit-state and symbolic software model checker for Java bytecode [2]. JPF is used to find and explain defects, collect runtime information as coverage metrics, deduce test vectors, and create corresponding test drivers for Java programs. JPF checks for property violations such as deadlocks or unhandled exceptions along all potential execution paths as well as user-specified assertions. *ESC/Java* is a compile-time extended static checker, which detects common programming errors (e.g., null dereference, array bounds errors, and type cast errors) [7]. It uses an automatic theorem prover to catch bugs that go beyond the abilities of the Java type checker, including runtime errors and synchronization errors in concurrent programs.

2 JBMC: A Bounded Model Checker for Java Bytecode

2.1 Architecture and Implementation

Our front-end integrates a class loader, which accepts Java bytecode *class* files and *jar* archives (Fig. 1). The parse trees for the classes are translated into the CPROVER CFG representation, which is called a *GOTO* program [6].

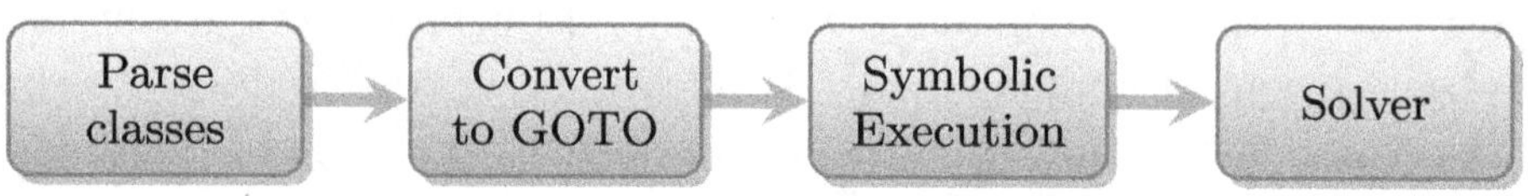

Fig. 1. JBMC verification process

To handle polymorphism, JBMC encodes virtual method dispatch into a *switch* over the runtime type information attached to the object in order to select the correct method to be called. Similarly, the complex control flow arising from exceptions is encoded into conditional branches. We record the exception thrown in a global variable, which is then used to propagate the exception up the call stack until a matching *catch* statement (if any) to handle the error is reached. JBMC can detect when the JVM would abort due to an exception that is not caught within the program.

The resulting *GOTO* program is then passed to the bounded model checking algorithm for finding bugs. The BMC algorithm symbolically executes the program, unwinding loops and unfolding recursive function calls up to a given bound. The resulting bit-vector formula is then passed on to the configured SAT or SMT solver [6].

2.2 Java Operational Model

The Java language relies on compiler-generated functions and classes as well as a large standard library. In order to correctly support Java functionality, we developed an abstract representation of the standard Java libraries, called the operational model (OM). The use of OMs is commonplace in analysers for Java; for instance, a similar approach was previously proposed for the formal verification of Android applications [12]. Currently, our OM consists of models of the most common classes from *java.lang* and a few from *java.util*. Our Java OM simplifies the implementation of the standard Java library by removing verification-irrelevant performance optimizations (e.g., in the implementation of container classes), exploiting declarative specifications (using *assume*) and functions that are built into the CPROVER framework (e.g., for array and string manipulation). We are continuously extending our OM to speed up verification by replacing the original standard Java library classes by our models.

Java has an `assert(`c`)` statement for specifying safety properties. In addition, we provide API classes that allow users to define non-deterministic verification harnesses and stub functions. The API contains such methods for primitive types (e.g., `int nondetInt()`) and *generic* methods (i.e., parametrised by a type `T`) as `<T> T nondetWithNull()` and `<T> T nondetWithoutNull()` to non-deterministically initialize object references that may or may not be `null`. The API also provides an `assume(`c`)` method, which advises JBMC to ignore paths that do not satisfy a user-specified condition c.

Currently, JBMC handles neither the Java Native Interface, which allows Java code to interface native libraries, nor reflection, which allows the program to inspect and manipulate itself at runtime. We are currently extending JBMC to support generics and lambdas; and to verify multi-threaded Java programs (that use *java.lang.Thread*), exploiting the partial order encoding technique of [1].

2.3 String Solver

One of the biggest challenges in verifying Java programs is the widespread use of character strings, which makes verification problems resulting from Java programs highly complex. Solving such constraints is an active area of research [5,8,11]. JBMC implements a solver for strings to determine the satisfiability of a set of constraints involving string operations. Our string solver supports the most common basic accesses (e.g., obtain the length of a string and a character at a given position); comparisons (e.g., lexicographic comparison and equality); transformations (e.g., insertion, concatenation, replacement, and removal); and conversions (e.g., conversion of the primitive data types into a string and parsing them from a string). The axioms for these operations use quantified constraints. For instance, a Java expression `s.substring(5)` is translated into a predicate $substring(res, s, 5)$, where res, s are pairs $(length, charArray)$, representing the resulting and the input string `s`, respectively; and *substring* is axiomatized by the formula $\forall i.(0 \leq i \wedge i < s.length - 5) \rightarrow (res.length = s.length - 5) \wedge (res.charArray[i] = s.charArray[i + 5])$. The universal quantifiers are handled using quantifier elimination [10].

2.4 JBMC Usage

Runtime errors in Java (e.g., illegal memory access) are detected by the JVM and an appropriate exception is thrown (e.g., `NullPointerException`, `ArrayIndexOutOfBoundsException`). An `AssertionError` is thrown on violation of a condition specified by the programmer using the `assert` keyword. JBMC analyzes the program and verifies whether such error conditions occur.

JBMC can be used to analyze a single class file:[2] `jbmc C.class --unwind` k or a Java archive (jar) file: `jbmc file.jar --main-class class --unwind` k. In both cases the entry point for the analysis of the program is the `static void main` method of the specified main class. k is a positive integer limiting the number of times loops are unwound and recursions are unfolded. If no bug is found, up to a k-depth unwinding, then JBMC reports `VERIFICATION SUCCESSFUL`; otherwise, it reports `VERIFICATION FAILED` along with a counterexample in the form of an execution trace (`--trace`), which contains the full variable assignment in each program state with file, method, and line information. Note that if the Java bytecode is compiled with debug information, then JBMC can also provide the original program variable names in the counterexample, rather than just bytecode variable slots. Further JBMC options can be retrieved via `jbmc --help`.

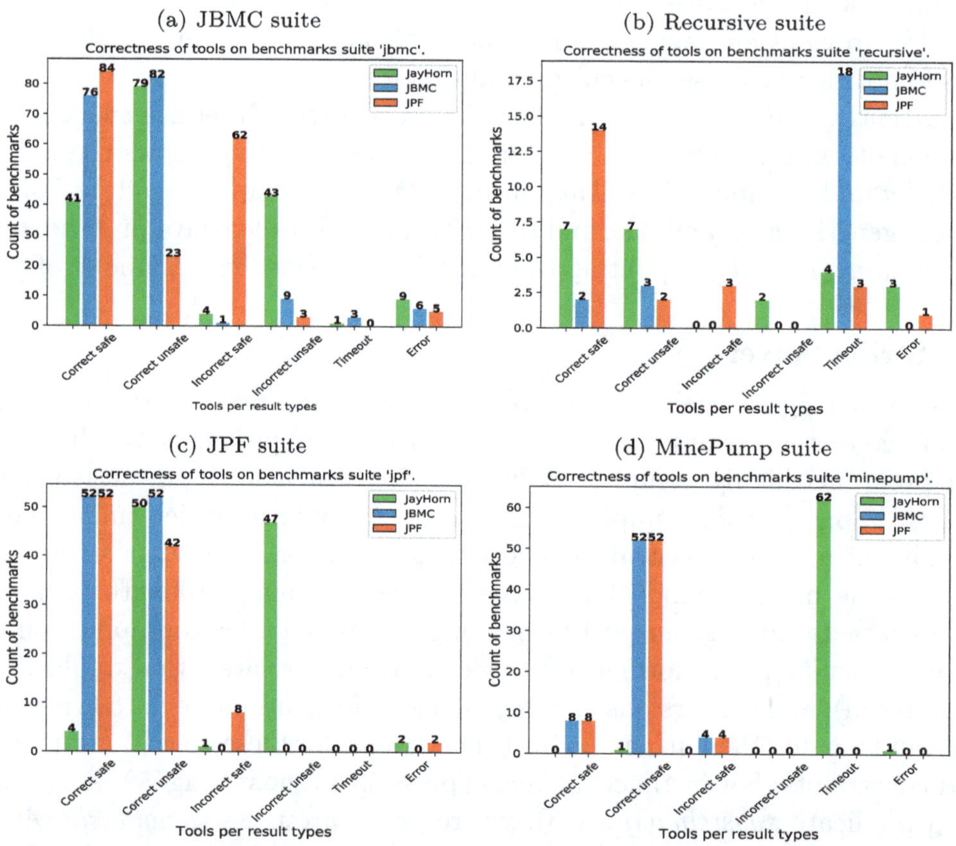

Fig. 2. Verification results for JayHorn, JBMC and JPF

[2] If a class `C` is in a package `x.y`, then compile it to *some-dir*/`x/y/C.class`, and in *some-dir* execute *jbmc-installation-dir*/`jbmc x/y/C.class --unwind` k.

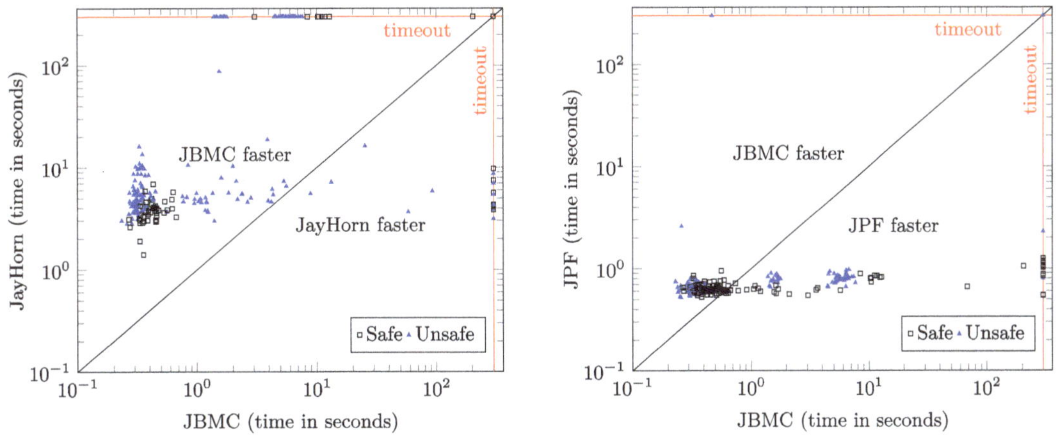

Fig. 3. Runtime comparison of JBMC to JayHorn and JPF

3 Experimental Evaluation

There is no standard benchmark suite for Java verification. Therefore, we took our entire regression test suite consisting of 177 benchmarks (including known bugs and hard benchmarks that JBMC cannot yet handle); these benchmarks (denoted as "jbmc") test common Java features (e.g., polymorphism, exceptions, arrays, and strings). We also used 23 recursive benchmarks (denoted as "recursive") taken from the JayHorn repository [9], and 64 minepump benchmarks (denoted as "minepump") from the SV-COMP repository. Additionally, we have extracted 104 benchmarks from the JPF regression test suite [2]. The following table summarizes the characteristics of the benchmark sets:[3]

Benchmark set	Total	Safe	Unsafe	Avg. LOC
jbmc	177	89	88	25
jpf	104	52	52	52
recursive	23	14	9	35
minepump	64	8	56	62
total	368	163	205	40

3.1 Objectives and Setup

Our experiments aim at answering two research questions: [RQ1] **(correctness)** How accurate is JBMC when verifying the chosen benchmarks? [RQ2] **(performance)** How does JBMC performance compare to other existing verifiers? To answer both questions, we analyze all benchmarks with three Java verifiers

[3] Benchmarks and detailed results are available at https://www.cprover.org/jbmc.

(JBMC v5.8-cav18, JayHorn v0.5.1, and JPF v32) on an Intel Core i7-6700 CPU 8×3.40 GHz, with 32 GB of RAM, running Ubuntu 16.04 LTS. We restrict CPU time and memory to 300 s and 15 GB, respectively. JBMC uses a stepwise approach to unwinding loops (to prove unbounded safety) and runs with MiniSat2 as its SAT backend.

3.2 Results

Figure 2 gives an overview of the experimental results for the four benchmark suites. *Correct safe* means that the program was analyzed to be free of errors, *correct unsafe* means that the error in the program was found, *incorrect safe* means that the program had an error but the verifier did not find it, *incorrect unsafe* means that an error is reported for a program that fulfills the specification, *timeout* indicates that the verifier has exceeded the time limit, and *error* represents an internal failure in the verifier or exhaustion of available memory. The following table summarizes the overall results:

	Correct			Incorrect				
	Total	Safe	Unsafe	Total	Safe	Unsafe	Timeout	Error
JayHorn	189	52	137	97	**5**	92	67	15
JBMC	**327**	138	**189**	**14**	**5**	9	21	**6**
JPF	277	**158**	119	80	77	**3**	**3**	8

The experimental results show that JBMC reached a successful verification rate of approximately 89% while JayHorn reported 51% and JPF 75%, which positively answers RQ1. JayHorn and JPF currently produce 6 times more *incorrect* results (i.e., bugs in the tool) than JBMC. To answer RQ2, Fig. 3 compares the analysis times for the benchmarks where the tools return correct results. None of the three tools is consistently better than the other two. JBMC is faster than JPF on 176 benchmarks, JPF is faster than JBMC on 93. JBMC is faster than JayHorn on 222 benchmarks, whereas JayHorn is faster than JBMC on 25. In comparison to JayHorn, JBMC deals poorly with recursion, as its analysis led to timeout for 69% of the recursive benchmarks, whereas JayHorn could only solve a single benchmark from the minepump benchmark suite. In summary, we observed that JBMC's scalability depends mainly on the complexity of string operations, loops, recursion and (floating-point) arithmetic.

4 Conclusions and Future Work

Despite more than 15 years of research in BMC and Java verification, JBMC is the first BMC-based Java verifier. To achieve this, we based our implementation on an industrial-strength verification framework, and developed a Java

OM, removing verification-irrelevant optimizations and exploiting declarative specifications and built-in functions. Because of the prevalent use of character strings in Java programs, we have also developed a string solver using an efficient quantifier elimination scheme. We compare JBMC to JayHorn and JPF, which are state-of-the-art verifiers for Java bytecode based on constrained Horn clauses and path-based symbolic execution, respectively. Experimental results show that JBMC achieves a successful verification rate of 89% compared to 51% of JayHorn and 75% of JPF. For future work, the Java OM will be extended to support more Java classes, with the goal of speeding up verification of larger Java applications. In addition, we are currently extending JBMC to verify multi-threaded programs.

Acknowledgments. We thank P. Rümmer and W. Visser for helpful discussions about JayHorn and JPF, respectively.

References

1. Alglave, J., Kroening, D., Tautschnig, M.: Partial orders for efficient bounded model checking of concurrent software. In: Sharygina, N., Veith, H. (eds.) CAV 2013. LNCS, vol. 8044, pp. 141–157. Springer, Heidelberg (2013). https://doi.org/10.1007/978-3-642-39799-8_9
2. Anand, S., Păsăreanu, C.S., Visser, W.: JPF–SE: a symbolic execution extension to Java PathFinder. In: Grumberg, O., Huth, M. (eds.) TACAS 2007. LNCS, vol. 4424, pp. 134–138. Springer, Heidelberg (2007). https://doi.org/10.1007/978-3-540-71209-1_12
3. Barrett, C., Sebastiani, R., Seshia, S.A., Tinelli, C.: Satisfiability modulo theories. In: Frontiers in Artificial Intelligence and Applications, vol. 185, chap. 26, pp. 825–885. IOS Press, February 2009
4. Biere, A., Heule, M., van Maaren, H., Walsh, T. (eds.): Handbook of Satisfiability. Frontiers in Artificial Intelligence and Applications, vol. 185. IOS Press, Amsterdam (2009)
5. Chen, T., Chen, Y., Hague, M., Lin, A.W., Wu, Z.: What is decidable about string constraints with the ReplaceAll function. PACMPL **2**(POPL), 3:1–3:29 (2018). https://doi.org/10.1145/3158091
6. Clarke, E., Kroening, D., Lerda, F.: A tool for checking ANSI-C programs. In: Jensen, K., Podelski, A. (eds.) TACAS 2004. LNCS, vol. 2988, pp. 168–176. Springer, Heidelberg (2004). https://doi.org/10.1007/978-3-540-24730-2_15
7. Flanagan, C., Leino, K.R.M., Lillibridge, M., Nelson, G., Saxe, J.B., Stata, R.: PLDI 2002: extended static checking for Java. SIGPLAN Not. **48**(4S), 22–33 (2013). https://doi.org/10.1145/2502508.2502520
8. Holík, L., Janku, P., Lin, A.W., Rümmer, P., Vojnar, T.: String constraints with concatenation and transducers solved efficiently. PACMPL **2**(POPL), 4:1–4:32 (2018). https://doi.org/10.1145/3158092
9. Kahsai, T., Rümmer, P., Sanchez, H., Schäf, M.: JayHorn: a framework for verifying Java programs. In: Chaudhuri, S., Farzan, A. (eds.) CAV 2016. LNCS, vol. 9779, pp. 352–358. Springer, Cham (2016). https://doi.org/10.1007/978-3-319-41528-4_19
10. Li, G., Ghosh, I.: PASS: string solving with parameterized array and interval automaton. In: Bertacco, V., Legay, A. (eds.) HVC 2013. LNCS, vol. 8244, pp. 15–31. Springer, Cham (2013). https://doi.org/10.1007/978-3-319-03077-7_2

11. Liang, T., Reynolds, A., Tsiskaridze, N., Tinelli, C., Barrett, C., Deters, M.: An efficient SMT solver for string constraints. Formal Methods Syst. Des. **48**(3), 206–234 (2016). https://doi.org/10.1007/s10703-016-0247-6
12. van der Merwe, H., Tkachuk, O., van der Merwe, B., Visser, W.: Generation of library models for verification of Android applications. ACM SIGSOFT Softw. Eng. Notes **40**(1), 1–5 (2015). https://doi.org/10.1145/2693208.2693247
13. Oracle: Java^{TM} programming language. https://docs.oracle.com/javase/8/docs/technotes/guides/language/index.html (2017), accessed: 31–01-2018
14. Vallée-Rai, R., Co, P., Gagnon, E., Hendren, L., Lam, P., Sundaresan, V.: Soot - a Java bytecode optimization framework. In: CASCON, p. 13. IBM Press (1999)

Eager Abstraction for Symbolic Model Checking

Kenneth L. McMillan(✉)

Microsoft Research, Redmond, USA
kenmcmil@microsoft.com

Abstract. We introduce a method of abstraction from infinite-state to finite-state model checking based on eager theory explication and evaluate the method in a collection of case studies.

1 Introduction

In constructing decision procedures for arithmetic formulas and other theories, a successful approach has been to separate propositional reasoning and theory reasoning in a modular way. This approach is usually called Satisfiability Modulo Theories, or SMT [1]. There are two primary approaches to SMT: *eager* and *lazy* theory explication. Both approaches abstract the formula in question by constructing its propositional skeleton, that is, converting each atomic predicate to a corresponding free Boolean variable. Obviously, propositional abstraction loses a great deal of information. The eager approach compensates for this by conjoining tautologies of the theory to the formula before propositional abstraction. In abstract interpretation terms, we can think of this as a *semantic reduction*: it makes the formula more explicit without changing its semantics. The lazy approach, on the other hand, performs the propositional abstraction first, then retroactively adds tautologies of the theory to rule out infeasible propositional models.

In this paper, we will consider applying the same concepts to the symbolic model checking problem (SMC). In this problem, we are given a Kripke model M that is expressed implicitly using logical formulas, and a temporal formula ϕ, and we wish to determine whether $M \models \phi$. The states of the Kripke model are structures of a logic L over a given vocabulary, while the set of initial states I and the set of transitions T are expressed, respectively, by one- and two-vocabulary formulas. The atomic propositions in ϕ are also presumed to be expressed in L.

In the case where L is propositional logic, the Kripke model is finite-state, the SMC problem is PSPACE-complete, and many well-developed techniques are available to solve it in a heuristically efficient way. On the other hand, if L is a richer logic (say, Presburger arithmetic) SMC is usually undecidable. Here, we propose to solve instances of this problem by separating propositional reasoning and theory reasoning in a modular way, as in SMT. Given an SMC problem (I, T, ϕ), we will form its propositional abstraction by computing the

H. Chockler and G. Weissenbacher (Eds.): CAV 2018, LNCS 10981, pp. 191–208, 2018.
https://doi.org/10.1007/978-3-319-96145-3_11

propositional skeletons of I, T and ϕ. This abstraction is sound, and allows us to apply well-developed tools for propositional SMC, however it loses a great deal of information. To compensate for this loss, we will use incomplete eager theory explication. By controlling theory explication, the user controls the abstraction. We will call this general approach *eager symbolic model checking*, or ESMC.

Related Work. Because of the propositional abstraction, ESMC may at first seem to be a form of predicate abstraction [9]. This is not the case, however. Predicate abstraction uses a vocabulary of predicates to abstract the state, but does not abstract the theory itself. As a result, a decision procedure for the theory is needed to compute the best abstract transformer. This is problematic if the logic is undecidable, and in any event requires an exponential number of decision procedure calls in the worst case. In ESMC, the abstraction is performed in a purely syntactic way. One controls the abstraction by giving a set of axiom schemata to be instantiated and by introducing prophecy variables, as opposed to giving abstraction predicates. One effect of this is that the abstraction may depend on the precise syntactic expression of the transition relation.

The technique of "datatype reductions" [18] is also closely related. This method has been used to verify various parameterized protocols and microarchitectures using finite-state model checking [5,6,12,19,20]. The technique also abstracts an infinite-state SMC problem to a finite-state one syntactically. Though it does not do this by explicating the theory, we will see that the abstraction it produces can be simulated by ESMC. Compared to this method, ESMC is user-extensible and allows both a simpler theoretical account and a simpler implementation. Moreover, it uses a smaller trusted computing base, since the tautologies it introduces can be mechanically checked.

The methods of Invisible Invariants [25] and Indexed Predicate Abstraction [14] use different methods to compute the least fixed point in a finite abstract domain of quantified formulas. This requires decidability and incurs a relatively high cost for computing an extremal fixed point, limiting scalability (though IPA can approximate the best transformer in the undecidable case). The abstractions are also difficult to refine in practice.

Road Map. After preliminaries in the next section, we introduce our schema-based class of abstractions in Sect. 3. The next section gives some useful instantiations of this class. Section 5 describes a methodology for exploiting the abstraction in proofs of infinite-state systems, as implemented in the IVy tool. In Sect. 5, we evaluate the approach using case studies.

2 Preliminaries

Let $FO_{=}(\mathbb{S}, \Sigma)$ be standard sorted first-order logic with equality, where $\mathbb{S}$ is a collection of first-order sorts and Σ is a vocabulary of sorted non-logical symbols. We assume a special sort $\mathbb{B} \in \mathbb{S}$ that is the sort of propositions. Each symbol

$f^S \in \Sigma$ has an associated sort S of the form $D_1 \times \cdots \times D_n \rightarrow R$, where $D_i, R \in \mathbb{S}$ and $n \geq 0$ is the *arity* of the symbol. If $n = 0$, we say f^S is a *constant*, and if $R = \mathbb{B}$ it is a *relation*. We write vocab(t) for the set of non-logical symbols occurring in term t.

Given a set of sorts $\mathbb{S}$, a *universe* U maps each sort in $\mathbb{S}$ to a non-empty set (with $U(\mathbb{B}) = \{\top, \bot\}$). An *interpretation* of a vocabulary Σ over universe U maps each symbol $f^{D_1 \times \cdots \times D_n \rightarrow R}$ in Σ to a function in $U(D_1) \times \cdots \times U(D_n) \rightarrow U(R)$. A Σ-structure is a pair $\mathcal{M} = (U, \mathcal{I})$ where U is a universe and $\mathcal{I}$ is an interpretation of Σ over U. The structure is a *model* of a proposition ϕ in $FO_=(\mathbb{S}, \Sigma)$ if ϕ evaluates to $\top$ under $\mathcal{I}$ according to the standard semantics of first-order logic. In this case, we write $\mathcal{M} \models \phi$. Given an interpretation $\mathcal{J}$ with domain disjoint from $\mathcal{I}$, we write $\mathcal{M}, \mathcal{J}$ to abbreviate the structure $(U, \mathcal{I} \cup \mathcal{J})$.

In the sequel, we take the vocabulary Σ to be a disjoint union of four sets: Σ_S, the *state* symbols, Σ'_S the *primed* symbols, Σ_T the *temporary* symbols, and Σ_B, the *background* symbols. We take $(\cdot)'$ to be a bijection $\Sigma_S \rightarrow \Sigma'_S$ and extend it in the expected way to terms and interpretations. We write unprime(t) for the term u such that $u' = t$, if u exists.

A *transition system* is a pair (I, T) where I is a proposition over $\Sigma_S \cup \Sigma_B$ and T is a proposition over Σ. Let $\mathcal{M}_B = (U, \mathcal{I}_B)$ be a Σ_B-structure (that is, fix the universe and the interpretation of the background symbols). A *U-state* of the system is an interpretation of Σ_S (the state symbols) over U. A $\mathcal{M}_B$*-run* of the system is an infinite sequence $s_0, s_1, \ldots$ of U-states such that:

- $\mathcal{M}_B, s_0 \models I$, and
- for all $0 \leq i$, there exists and interpretation $\mathcal{I}_T$ of Σ_T over U such that $\mathcal{M}_B, s_i, \mathcal{I}_T, s'_{i+1} \models T$.

That is, under the background interpretation, the initial state must satisfy the initial condition, and for every successive pair of states, there must be an interpretation of the temporary symbols such that the transition condition is satisfied. The temporary symbols are used, for example, to model local variables of procedures, and may also be Skolem symbols. Because they can have second-order sort, we cannot existentially quantify them within the logic, so instead we quantify them implicitly in the transition system semantics. Given a background theory $\mathcal{T}$ over Σ_B, a $\mathcal{T}$*-run* is any $\mathcal{M}_B$-run such that $\mathcal{M}_B \models \mathcal{T}$.

A *linear temporal formula* over Σ applies the operators of $FO_=(\mathbb{S}, \Sigma)$ plus the standard strict until operator $\mathcal{U}$ and strict since operator $\mathcal{S}$. We define $\bigcirc\phi = \bot\mathcal{U}\phi$, $\Box\phi = \phi \wedge \neg(\top\mathcal{U}\neg\phi)$ and also $\mathcal{H}\phi = \phi\mathcal{S}\bot$, meaning "always ϕ in the strict past". We fix $\mathcal{T}$ and say $(I, T) \models \phi$ if every $\mathcal{T}$-run of (I, T) satisfies ϕ under the standard LTL semantics. The symbolic model checking problem SMC is to determine whether $(I, T) \models \phi$.

3 A Schema-Based Abstraction Class

An *atom* is a proposition in which every instance of $\{\wedge, \vee, \neg, \mathcal{U}, \mathcal{S}\}$ occurs under a quantifier. The *propositional skeleton* of a proposition ϕ is obtained by replacing each atom in ϕ by a corresponding propositional constant. The propositional skeleton is an abstraction, in the sense that for every model M of ϕ we can construct a model of its propositional skeleton from the truth values of each atomic proposition in M. We will use propositional skeletons here to convert an infinite-state model checking problem to a finite-state one.

We assume that each vocabulary Σ_B, Σ_S and Σ_T contains a countably infinite set of propositional constants. This allows us to construct injections $\mathcal{A}_B$, $\mathcal{A}_S$, $\mathcal{A}_T$ from atomic propositions of the logic to propositional constants in Σ_B, Σ_S and Σ_T respectively.

In defining the propositional skeleton of a transition formula we must consider atomic propositions containing symbols from more than one vocabulary. To which vocabulary should we map such an atom in the propositional skeleton? Here, we take a simple solution that is sound, though it may lose some state information. That is, for any atomic proposition ϕ, we say

- if $\text{vocab}(\phi) \subseteq \Sigma_B$, then $\mathcal{A}(\phi) = \mathcal{A}_B(\phi)$,
- else if $\text{vocab}(\phi) \subseteq \Sigma_B \cup \Sigma_S$ then $\mathcal{A}(\phi) = \mathcal{A}_S(\phi)$
- else if $\text{vocab}(\phi) \subseteq \Sigma_B \cup \Sigma'_S$ then $\mathcal{A}(\phi) = \mathcal{A}_S(\text{unprime}(\phi))'$
- else $\mathcal{A}(\phi) = \mathcal{A}_T(\phi)$

That is, pure background propositions are abstracted to background symbols, state propositions are abstracted to state symbols and next-state propositions are abstracted to the primed version of the corresponding state proposition. Everything else is abstracted to a temporary symbol (which is existentially quantified in the abstract transition relation).

We then extend $\mathcal{A}$ to non-atomic formulas in the obvious way, such that $\mathcal{A}(\phi \wedge \psi) = \mathcal{A}(\phi) \wedge \mathcal{A}(\psi)$, $\mathcal{A}(\bigcirc\phi) = \bigcirc\mathcal{A}(\phi)$ and so on. The following theorem shows that we can use propositional skeletons to convert infinite-state to finite-state model checking problems in a sound (but incomplete) way:

Theorem 1. *For any symbolic transition system (I,T) and linear temporal formula ϕ, if $(\mathcal{A}(I), \mathcal{A}(T)) \models \mathcal{A}(\phi)$ then $(I,T) \models \phi$.*

Intuitively, this holds because we can convert every concrete counterexample to an abstract one by simply extracting the truth values of the atomic propositions.

Theory Explication. While propositional skeletons are sound, they lose a great deal of information. For example, suppose our transition relation is $y' = x$. Given a predicate p, we would like to infer that $p(x) \Rightarrow \bigcirc p(y)$. However, in the propositional skeleton, the transition relation $\mathcal{A}(T)$ is just $\mathcal{A}_T(y' = x)$. In other words, it is just a free propositional symbol with no relation to any other proposition. Thus, we cannot prove the abstracted property $\mathcal{A}(p(x)) \Rightarrow \bigcirc\mathcal{A}(p(y))$.

To mitigate this loss of information, we use *theory explication*. That is, before abstracting T, we conjoin to it tautologies of the logic or the background theory. This doesn't change the semantics of T, and thus the set of runs of the transition system remains unchanged. It does, however, change the propositional skeleton.

For example, $y' = x \wedge p(x) \Rightarrow p(y')$ is a tautology of the theory of equality. If we conjoin this formula to T in the above example, the abstract transition relation becomes $\mathcal{A}_T(y' = x) \wedge (\mathcal{A}_T(y' = x) \wedge \mathcal{A}_S(p(x)) \Rightarrow \mathcal{A}_S(p(y))')$ which is strong enough to prove the abstracted property.

In general, theory explication adds predicates to the abstraction. This is the only mechanism we will use to add predicates; we will not supply them manually, or obtain them automatically from counterexamples. The following theorem justifies model checking with eager theory explication:

Theorem 2. *For any symbolic transition system (I, T), linear temporal formula ϕ, $\Sigma_B \cup \Sigma_S$ formula ψ_I and Σ formula ψ_T, if $\mathcal{T} \models \psi_I \wedge \psi_T$ then $(I \wedge \psi_I, T \wedge \psi_T) \models \phi$ iff $(I, T) \models \phi$.*

The question, of course, is how to choose the tautologies in ψ_I and ψ_T. This is not just a question of capturing the transition relation semantics, since theory explication also determines the FO predicates representing state of the finite abstraction. Thus, complete theory explication is at least as hard as predicate discovery in predicate abstraction. Our goal is not to solve this problem, but to find an effective incomplete strategy that is useful in practice. It is important that the resulting finite-state model checking problems be easily resolved by a modern model checker, and that in case the strategy fails, a human can use the resulting counterexample and effectively refine the abstraction.

Schema-Based Theory Explication. The basic approach we will use to controlling theory explication is a restricted case of the pattern-based quantifier instantiation method introduced in the Simplify prover [8]. That is, we are given a set of axioms, and for each axiom a set of triggers. A trigger is a term (or terms) containing all of the free variables in the axiom. The trigger is matched against all ground subterms in the formula being explicated. Each match induces an instance of the axiom.

In our example above, suppose we have the axiom $Y = X \wedge p(X) \Rightarrow p(Y)$ with a trigger $Y = X$ (here and in the sequel, capital letters will stand for free variables). The trigger $Y = X$ matches the ground term $y' = x$ in T which generates the ground instance $y' = x \wedge p(x) \Rightarrow p(y')$. Since we match modulo the symmetry of equality, we also get $x = y' \wedge p(y') \Rightarrow p(x)$.

A risk of trigger-based instantiation is the matching loop. For example, if we have the axiom $f(X) > X + 1$ with a trigger $f(X)$, then we can generate an infinite sequence of instantiations: $f(y) > y + 1$, $f(f(y)) > f(y) + 1$ and so on. A simple approach to prevent this is to bound the number of generations of matching. In practice, we will use just one generation and expand the set axioms in cases where more than one generation is needed. This has the benefit of keeping the number of generated terms small, which limits the size of the SMC problem and also makes it easier for users to understand counterexamples.

To avoid having to write a large number of axioms, we specify the axioms using general schemata. A schema is a parameterized axiom. It takes a list of sorts and symbols as parameters and yields an axiom. In the sequel we will use s

and t to stand for sort parameters. As an example, here is a general congruence schema that can be used in place of our axiom above:

$$\frac{f : s \to t}{X = Y \Rightarrow f(X) = f(Y)\ \{X = Y\}}$$

The trigger is in curly braces. We first instantiate the axiom schemata for all possible parameter valuations using the sorts and symbols of the concrete system. Then we ground the resulting axioms using pattern-based instantiation.

One further technique is needed, however, to ground the quantifiers occurring in the formula being explicated. Quantifiers usually occur in the transition relations of parameterized systems either in the guards of guarded commands or in state updates. As an example, suppose a given command sets the state of process p to 'ready'. This would appear in the transition formula as a constraint such as the following:

$$\forall x.\ \text{state}'(x) = \text{ready if } x = p \text{ else state}(x)$$

If this quantifier is not instantiated, then all information about process state will be lost. To avoid this, we would like to apply the following schema:

$$\frac{y : s,\ p : s \to \mathbb{B}}{(\forall X.\ p(X)) \Rightarrow p(y)\ \{\forall X.\ p(X)\}}$$

Here we intend that p should match *any* predicate with one free variable and not just a predicate symbol (including non-temporal sub-formulas of the property to be proved). However, rather than implement a general second-order matching scheme, it is simpler to build this particular schema into the theory explication process. There is some question as to which ground terms to supply for the parameter y. As with other schemata, only constants are used in the current implementation. This appears to be adequate, but it might also be useful to allow the user to supply explicit triggers for quantifiers in the transition system or property.

The theory explication process thus has three steps:

1. Instantiate quantifiers in the formulas using the quantifier schema above.
2. Generate axioms from the user axiom schemata, supplying symbols from the formulas as parameters.
3. Instantiate the axioms using triggers for one generation.

Notice this is a slight departure from the policy of one generation of matching, since terms generated in step 1 can be used to match axioms in step 3. This is important in practice since without grounding the quantifiers there may be no ground terms to match in step 3.

4 Example Abstractions in the Class

A typical approach to verifying parameterized protocols with finite-state model checking is to track the state of a representative fixed collection of processes and abstract away the state of the remaining processes. In this approach, introduced in [17], a small collection background constants (typically two or three) is used to identify the tracked processes. For each process identifier in the system, the abstraction records whether it is equal to each of the tracked ids, but carries no further information. For each function f over process ids, the abstraction maintains the value of $f(x)$ only if x is equal to one of the background constants. This approach has been used, for example, to verify processor microarchitectures [12,16,17] and cache coherence protocols [5,6,19].

This abstraction can be implemented using schema-based instantiation. The high-level idea is to create a set of schemata that make it possible to abstractly evaluate terms in a bottom-up manner.

For example, consider an occurrence $t = u$ of the equality operator where t and u are terms of sort s. The abstract value of this term is $\top$ if t and u are both equal to some background constant c, $\bot$ if $t = c$ and $u \neq c$, and otherwise is unknown. To implement this abstraction, we use the following schemata:

$$\frac{c : s}{X = c \wedge Y = c \Rightarrow X = Y \ \{X = Y\}} \quad \frac{c : s}{X = c \wedge Y \neq c \Rightarrow X \neq Y \ \{X = Y\}}$$

The triggers of these two schemata cause them to be applied to every occurrence of an equality operator in the formula being abstracted.

For an application $f(t)$ of a function symbol, the abstract value is the abstraction of $f(c)$ if t is equal to background constant c, and is otherwise unknown. This fact could be captured by chaining the congruence schema above with the above two equality schemata. That is, matching the congruence schema, we obtain $t = c \Rightarrow f(t) = f(c)$. Then matching the equality operator schemata with this result, we obtain (in the contrapositive) $f(t) = f(c) \wedge f(c) = d \Rightarrow f(t) = d$ and $f(t) = f(c) \wedge f(c) \neq d \Rightarrow f(t) \neq d$ (for any background constants c, d). Recall, however, that we allow only one generation of matching, so this second matching step will not occur. Instead, we write the above two facts explicitly as a schema:

$$\frac{c : s, \ d : t, \ f : s \rightarrow t}{X = c \Rightarrow (f(X) = d \Leftrightarrow f(c) = d) \ \{f(X)\}}$$

This schema is matched for every application of a symbol of arity one in the formula. We also specify similar schemata for arities greater than one. Notice that this schema also applies to relation symbols if we treat $\top$ and $\bot$ as background constants of sort $\mathbb{B}$. However, for relations and functions to finitely enumerated sorts, it is more efficient to use the congruence schema, since it produces fewer instances.

Finally, we need one additional schema to guarantee that the abstract values are consistent with the equality relation on the background constants:

$$\frac{c : s, \ d : s}{X = c \Rightarrow (X = d \Leftrightarrow c = d) \ \{X\}}$$

Notice that this axiom is instantiated for every term in the formula (though in practice not for propositions). Though it doesn't affect satisfiability of formulas, it is also helpful to add reflexivity, symmetry and transitivity over the background constants as it makes the resulting counterexamples easier to understand.

These schemata produce an abstraction of the formula that is at least as strong as the datatype reduction for scalarset types described in [18]. In fact, this is true if we restrict the application of the schemata to constants c and d in the set of background constants, which we do in practice. The cost of the abstraction is moderate, since the number of axiom instances is directly proportional to the size of the formula and to the number of background constants.

An advantage of the schema-based explication approach is that we can use it to construct abstractions for various datatypes and even use different abstractions of the same datatype for different applications. As an example, consider an abstraction for totally ordered datatypes such as the integers. We want the abstraction to track, for any term t of this sort, whether it is equal to, less than or greater than each background constant. The abstract value of a term t is captured by the values of the predicates $t < c$ and $t = c$ for background constants c. We begin with the abstract semantics of equality given above. The abstract semantics of the $<$ relation can be given by the following schemata (where $t \leq c$ is an abbreviation for $t < c \vee t = c$):

$$\frac{c : s}{X \leq c \wedge c < Y \Rightarrow X < Y \; \{X < Y\}} \quad \frac{c : s}{X < c \wedge c \leq Y \Rightarrow X < Y \; \{X < Y\}}$$

$$\frac{c : s}{Y \leq c \wedge \neg(X < c) \Rightarrow \neg(X < Y) \; \{X < Y\}}$$

By chaining the congruence schema with these, we can obtain the abstract semantics of function application, but again we wish to limit the number of matching generations to one. Thus, as with equality, we write an explicit schema combining the two steps:

$$\frac{c : s,\; d : t,\; f : s \rightarrow t}{X = c \Rightarrow (f(X) < d \Leftrightarrow f(c) < d) \; \{f(X)\}}$$

We also require that the abstract value of every term be consistent with the interpretation of $=$ and $<$ over the background constants. This gives us:

$$\frac{c : s}{\neg(X = c \wedge X < c) \; \{X\}} \quad \frac{c : s,\; d : t}{X \leq d \wedge \neg(X < c) \Rightarrow c \leq d \; \{X\}}$$

With the equality schemata, these imply that the background constants are totally ordered. As an extension, if the totally ordered sort has a least element 0, we can add it as a background constant along with the axiom $\neg(X < 0)$.

This abstraction is a bit weaker than the "ordset" abstraction used, for example, in [20]. We can simulate that abstraction by adding schemata that interpret the $+$ operator, and facts about numeric constants such as $0 < 1$. In general, for a given datatype, we can tailor an abstraction that captures just the properties of that type needed to prove a given system property. This extensibility makes the schema-based approach more flexible and possibly more efficient than the built-in abstractions of [18]. The above schemata have been verified by Z3.

5 Proof Methodology

In the previous sections, we developed an approach to produce a sound finite-state abstraction of an infinite-state system using eager theory explication and propositional skeletons. Now we consider how to construct proofs of systems using this approach. This section is essentially a summary of some results in [18].

The first question that arises is how to obtain the set of background constants that determine the abstraction. Generally speaking these arise as prophecy variables. For example, suppose we wish to prove a mutual exclusion property of the form $\Box\forall x, y.\ p(x) \wedge p(y) \Rightarrow x = y$. To do this, we replace the bound variables x and y with fresh background constants a and b, to obtain the quantifier-free property $\Box p(a) \wedge p(b) \Rightarrow a = b$. In effect a and b are immutable prophecy variables that predict the values of x and y for which the property will fail. By introducing prophecy variables, we refine the abstraction so that it tracks the state of the pair of processes that ostensibly cause the mutual exclusion property to fail. We hope, of course, to prove that there are no such processes. We apply the following theorem to introduce prophecy variables soundly:

Theorem 3. *Let (I, T) be a symbolic transition system, $x{:}s$ a variable, $\phi(x)$ a temporal formula and $v{:}s$ a background symbol not occurring in I, T, ϕ. Then $(I, T) \models \Box\forall x.\ \phi(x)$ iff $(I, T) \models \Box\phi(v)$.*

This theorem can be applied as many times as needed to eliminate universal quantifiers from an invariance property. Further refinement can be obtained if needed by manually adding prophesy variables. For example, suppose that each process x has a ticket number $t(x)$, and we wish to track the ticket number held by process a at the time of the failure. To do this, we replace our property with the property $\Box\ c = t(a) \Rightarrow (p(a) \wedge p(b) \Rightarrow a = b)$ where c is a fresh background constant. In general, we can introduce additional prophecy variables using this theorem:

Theorem 4. *Let (I, T) be a transition system, ϕ a temporal formula and t a term. Then $(I, T) \models \Box\phi$ iff $(I, T) \models \Box\forall x.\ x = t \Rightarrow \phi$, where x is not free in ϕ.*

The theorem can be applied repeatedly to introduce as many prophecy variables as needed to refine the abstraction. The introduced quantifiers can be converted to background symbols by the preceding theorem.

Since our abstraction tracks the state of only processes a and b, a protocol step in which an untracked process sends a message to a or b is likely to produce an incorrect result in the abstraction. To mitigate this problem, we assume by induction over time that our universally quantified invariant property ϕ has always held in the strict past. This makes use of the following theorem:

Theorem 5. *Let (I, T) be a symbolic transition system, and ϕ a temporal formula. Then $(I, T) \models \Box\phi$ iff $(I, T) \models \Box\ (\mathcal{H}\phi) \Rightarrow \phi$.*

The quantifiers in ϕ will be instantiated with ground terms in T. Thus, in our mutual exclusion example, we can rely on the fact that the sender of a past message (identified by some temporary symbol) is not in its critical section if either a or b are. Using induction in this way can mitigate the loss of information in the finite abstraction. Note we can pull quantifiers out of the above implication in order to apply Theorem 3. That is, $(\mathcal{H}\forall x.\ \phi) \Rightarrow \forall x.\phi$ is equivalent to $\forall x.\ (\mathcal{H}\forall x.\ \phi) \Rightarrow \phi$.

If the above tactics fail to prove an invariant property because the abstraction loses too much information, we can strengthen the invariant by adding conjuncts to it. These conjuncts have been called "non-interference lemmas", since they serve to reduce the interference with the tracked processes that is caused by loss of information about the untracked processes. We use the following theorem:

Theorem 6. *Let (I,T) be a symbolic transition system, and ϕ, ψ temporal formulas. Then if $(I,T) \models \Box\phi \wedge \psi$ then $(I,T) \models \Box\phi$.*

The general proof approach has the following steps:

1. Strengthen the invariant property (manually) with Theorem 6.
2. Apply temporal induction with Theorem 5.
3. Add quantifiers to the invariant with Theorem 4.
4. Convert the invariant quantifiers to background symbols with Theorem 3.
5. Add tautologies to the system using Theorem 2 and specified schemata.
6. Abstract to a finite-state SMC problem using Theorem 1.
7. Apply a finite-state symbolic model checker to check the property.

Implementation in IVy. This approach has been implemented in the IVy tool [15]. In IVy, the state of the model is expressed in terms of mutable functions and relations over primitive sorts. The language is procedural, and allows the expression of protocol models as interleavings of atomic guarded commands, the semantics of which is expressible in first-order logic.

To implement the approach, IVy's language was augmented with a syntax for expressing schemata. The schemata of Sect. 4 were added to the tool's standard library. Syntax is also provided to decorate invariant assertions with terms to be used as prophecy variables. IVy extends the above theory slightly by allowing invariant properties to be asserted not only between commands, but also in the middle of sequential commands. This can be convenient, since it allows invariants to reference local variables inside the commands.

With this input, the tool applies the six transformation steps detailed above to produce a purely propositional SMC problem. This problem is then converted to the AIGER format [2], a standard for hardware model checking. At present, the system only handles safety properties of the form $\Box(\mathcal{H}\phi) \Rightarrow \phi$, where ϕ is non-temporal. The AIGER format does support liveness, however, and this is planned as a future extension.

The resulting AIGER file is passed to the tool ABC [4] which uses its implementation of property driven reachability [10] to check the property. The counterexample, if any, is converted back to a run of the abstract transition system. The propositional symbols in this run are converted back to the corresponding atoms by inverting the abstraction mapping $\mathcal{A}$. This yields an *abstract counterexample*: a sequence of predicate valuations that correspond to both the state and temporary symbols in the abstraction.

The abstract counterexample may be spurious in the sense that it corresponds to no run of the concrete transition system. In this case, the user must analyze the trace to determine where necessary information was lost and either modify the invariant or refine the abstraction by adding a prophecy variable.

6 Case Studies

In this section, we consider the proof of safety properties of four parameterized algorithms and protocols. We wish to address three main questions. First, is the abstraction approach efficient? That is, if we construct an abstract model using schema-based theory explication, can the resulting finite-state problem be solved using a modern symbolic model checker? Second, is the methodology usable? That is, can a human user construct a proof using the methodology by analyzing the abstract counterexamples? Third, when is it more effective than the current best alternative, which is to write an inductive invariant manually and check it using an SMT solver, as in [11]? We will call this approach "invariant checking". We note that predicate abstraction is not suitable to these examples because the invariants require complex quantified formulas while current methods that synthesize quantified invariants for parameterized systems are unreliable in practice and do not scale well.

The last question in particular has not been well addressed in prior work on model checking approaches to parameterized verification. In most cases, either no comparison was made, or comparison was made to proofs using general-purpose proof assistants, which tend to be extremely laborious and do not make use of current state-of-the art proof automation techniques. To make a reasonably direct comparison, we construct proofs of each model using both methodologies, using the same language and tool, using the state-of-the art tools ABC [4] for model checking and Z3 [7] for invariant checking.

To apply the invariant checking method, some of the protocol models have been slightly re-encoded. In particular, it is helpful in some cases to use relations rather than functions in modeling the protocol state, as this can prevent the prover from diverging in a "matching loop" [8]. This re-encoding adds negligibly to the proof effort and is arguably harmless, since it does not appear in practice to affect the difficulty of refining the model to a concrete implementation.

Our four example models are:

1. **Tomasulo:** a parameterized model of Tomasulo's algorithm for out-or-order instruction execution, taken from [17].
2. **German:** a model of a simple directory-based cache coherence protocol from [6].
3. **FLASH:** a model of a more complex and realistic cache coherence protocol from [19,23], based on the Stanford FLASH multiprocessor [13].
4. **VS-Paxos:** a model of Virtually Synchronous Paxos [3], a distributed consensus algorithm, from [21].

Table 1. Comparison of proofs using two methodologies.

Model	Size	Model checking					Invariant checking			
		|Inv|	HVars	PVars	|Pf|	Time	|Inv|	HVars	|Pf|	Time
Tomasulo	1245	100	6	11	248	0.39	318	5	398	2.4
German	754	23	1	0	29	0.60	234	1	240	1.8
FLASH	2427	81	3	2	122	69	1235	1	1255	9.1
VS-Paxos	1442	224	8	34	512	23	1022	2	1101	59

A comparison of the proofs obtained using the two methodologies is shown in Table 1. The column "size" shows the textual size of the model plus property in lexical tokens. The columns labeled |Inv| give the size of the auxiliary invariants used in the proofs, expressed in the number of lexical tokens not including the property to be proved. Since both methods require the user to supply auxiliary invariants and discovering this invariant is the largest part of the effort in both cases, this number provides a fairly direct comparison of the complexity of the proofs. In both methodologies, the user also defines history or "ghost" variables that help in expressing the invariant. The number of these variables is shown in the columns labeled HVars. In the model checking approach, the user also refines the abstraction by defining prophecy variables. These were not used in the invariant checking proofs. The closest analogy in invariant checking proofs to this type of information would be quantifier instantiations or triggers provided by the user. This was not needed, however, since the methodology of [22] was applied to ensure that all verification conditions reside in a decidable fragment of the logic. For the model checking methodology, the number of distinct terms supplied by the user as prophecy variables is shown in the column labeled PVars. The time columns show the total time in seconds for model checking or invariant checking for the completed proofs on a 2.6 GHz Intel Xeon CPU using one core. Times to produce counterexamples were generally faster.

When measuring the overall complexity of the proofs, it is unclear how to weight the three kinds of information supplied by the user. In a sense, prophecy variables are the easiest to handle, since their behavior is monotone. That is, adding a prophecy variable only increases precision so it cannot cause passing invariants to fail. Ghost variables are more conceptually difficult to introduce, since the invariants depend on them. If a ghost variable definition is changed to repair a failing invariant, this may cause a different invariant to fail. Similarly if we strengthen a passing invariant, it may fail to be proved and if we weaken a failing one it may cause other formerly passing invariants to fail. This instability can cause the manual proof search to fail to converge and is the chief cause of conceptual difficulty in constructing proofs in both methodologies. Having said this, for lack of a principled way to weight the different aspects of the proof effort, we will measure the proof size as simply the sum of the number of lexical tokens in the auxiliary invariant, the history variable definitions, and all terms used as prophecy variables. The total proof size is shown in the columns labeled |Pf|.

These numbers should be taken as unreliable for several reasons that are common to any attempt to measure the effectiveness of a proof methodology. First, the size of the proof (or any other measure of the proof difficulty, such as expended time) can depend on the proficiency of the user in the particular methodology. Even if the same user produces both proofs, the user's proficiency in the two methodologies may differ, and knowledge gained in the first proof will effect the second one. Since resources were not available to train and test a statistically significant population users in both methodologies (assuming such could be found) the numbers presented here should not be considered a direct comparison of the methods. Rather, they are presented to support some observations made below about the specific case studies and proofs.

Case Study: Tomasulo's Algorithm. This is a simple abstract model of a processor microarchitecture that executes instructions concurrently out of order. The model state consists of a register file, a set of reservation stations (RS) and a set of execution units (EU) and is parameterized on the size of each of these, as well as the data word size. The machine's instructions are register-to-register and are modeled abstractly by an uninterpreted function. Each register has a flag that records whether it is the destination of a pending instruction. If so, its tag indicates which RS is holding that instruction. Each RS stores the tags of its instruction arguments, and waits for these to be computed before issuing the instruction to an EU.

Both proofs are based on history variables that record the correct values of arguments and result for each RS. The principal invariant of both states that the arguments obtained by all RS's are correct. In the model checking case, the abstraction is refined by making the tags of these arguments and chosen EU into prophecy variables. This allows the model checker to track enough state information to prove the main invariant, though one additional "non-interference" lemma is needed to guarantee that other EU's do not interfere by producing an incorrect tag. An interesting aspect of the invariant is that it does not refer to the states of the register file or EU's. The necessary invariants of these structures can be inferred by the model checker. On the other hand, this information must be supplied explicitly in the manual invariant. As the table shows, the resulting invariant is more complex.

Case Study: German's Cache Protocol. This simple distributed directory-based cache coherence protocol allows the caches to communicate directly only with the directory. The property proved is coherence, in effect that exclusive copies are exclusive. In the model checking proof, there is one non-interference lemma, stating that no cache produces a spurious invalidation acknowledgment message. No extra prophecy variables are need, as tracking the state of just the two caches that produce the coherence failure suffices. The manual invariant on the other hand is much more detailed, in fact about an order of magnitude larger. This is because it must relate the state of all the various types of messages in the network to the cache and directory states. These relationships were inferred automatically by the model checker, resulting in a much simpler proof.

Case Study: FLASH Cache Coherence Protocol. This is a much more complex (and realistic) distributed cache coherence protocol model. The increased protocol complexity derives from the fact that information can be transferred directly from one cache to another. In a typical transaction, a cache sends a request to the directory for (say) an exclusive copy of a cache line. The directory forwards the request to the current owner of the line, which then sends a copy to the original requester, as well as a response to the directory confirming the ownership transfer. Handling various race conditions in this scheme makes both the protocol and its proof complex. Again the property proved is coherence. The model checking proof is similar to [19], though there data correctness and liveness were proved.

In this case, three non-interference lemmas are used in the model checking proof, ruling out three types of spurious messages. Also two additional prophecy variables are needed. For example, one of these identifies the cache that sent an exclusive copy. This allows the abstraction to track the state of the third participant in the triangular transaction described above. Generally, protocols with more complex communication patterns require more prophecy variables to refine the abstraction.

As with German's protocol, and for the same reason, the manual invariant is an order of magnitude larger. In this case, the additional protocol complexity makes it quite challenging to converge to an invariant and a large number of strengthenings and weakenings were needed.

Case Study: Virtually Synchronous Paxos. This is a high-level model of a distributed consensus protocol, designed to allow a collection of processes to agree on a sequence of decisions, despite process and network failures. This model was previous proved by a manual invariant to be consistent, meaning that two decisions for a given index never disagree [21].

The protocol operates in a sequence of epochs, each of which has a leader process. The leader proposes decision values and any proposal that receives votes of a majority of processes becomes a decision. When the leader fails the protocol must move on to a new epoch. For consistency, any decisions that are possibly made in the old epoch must be preserved in the new. This is accomplished by choosing a majority of processes to start the new epoch and preserving all of their votes. Any decision having a majority of votes in the old epoch must have one voter in the new epoch's starting majority and thus must be preserved. The choice of an epoch's starting majority is itself a single-decree consensus problem. This is solved in a sequence of rounds called "stakes". A stake can be created by a majority of processes and proposes the votes of some majority to be carried to the next epoch. Each process in the stake promises not accept any lesser stake with differing votes. If a majority accepts the stake, then the votes of that stake can be passed to the next epoch.

The important auxiliary invariants of the model checking proof are these:

- At each epoch, the votes of the majority that ends the epoch are known to the leaders of all future epochs, and
- When a stake is created, every lesser stake with different votes is "dead" in the sense that a majority of nodes has promised not to accept it, and
- In any epoch, any two accepted stakes agree on their votes.

Perhaps not surprisingly, the manual invariant is much larger. The model checking proof, however, requires many extra prophecy variables. This is mainly accounted for by the fact that the model has seven unbounded sorts: process id's, decision indices, decision values, epochs, stakes, vote sets and process sets. Typically each invariant (including the one to be proved) requires one or two prophecy variables of each sort to refine the abstraction (though some of these may not be unique).

An additional complication is dealing with sets and majorities. Sets of processes are represented by an abstract data type. This type provides a predicate called 'majority' that indicates that a set contains more than half of the process id's. A function 'common' returns a common element between two sets if both are majorities (and is otherwise undefined). For example, to prove that we cannot have two conflicting decisions, we use the majorities that voted for each decision and declare the common process between these majorities as a prophecy variable. It then suffices to show that this particular process cannot have voted for both decisions (which requires the auxiliary invariants above). Since majorities are used in several places in the protocol, this tactic is applied several times.

Because of the larger number of prophecy variables, our (admittedly arbitrary) measure of overall proof complexity does not show as much advantage for model checking in this protocol as it does for the cache protocols. In fact, getting the details right in this proof was much more difficult subjectively than for FLASH.

This difficulty may be related to the two sorts in the model that are totally ordered: epochs and stakes. For these sorts we use the schemata for totally ordered sets detailed in Sect. 4. The ordering of these sorts introduces some difficulty in the proof, requiring more detailed invariants. For example, suppose we want to show that the first invariant above holds at the moment when a given process leaves one epoch and enters the next. The votes received at the epoch depend on all the previous epochs. We cannot however, make all of the unboundedly many lesser epochs concrete by adding a finite number of prophecy variables. This means our property must be inductive over epochs, that is, it holds now if it held in the past at the start of some *particular* epoch we can identify (perhaps the previous one). The need to write invariants that are inductive over ordered datatypes may account for the fact that the VS-Paxos invariant is more complex than that of the more complex FLASH protocol.

Discussion. We can make several general observations about these case studies. First, the performance of the finite-state model checker was never problematic. It always produced results in a reasonable amount of time and was not the bottleneck in constructing any of the proofs. Rather the most time-consuming task was usually analyzing the abstract counterexamples. This task proved tractable in practice, allowing the proof search process to converge.

Second, the invariants used in the model checking approach are generally much smaller than the manual ones because of the model checker's ability to infer state invariants.

This advantage may be somewhat offset by the need to provide prophecy variables to refine the abstraction, especially in the case where there are many unbounded sorts. Moreover, the need to write properties that are inductive over ordered sorts may lessen the advantage of model checking in invariant complexity. This was evident in the case of VS-Paxos and to some extent in Tomasulo as well, because of the implicit induction over the instruction stream. These criteria may be helpful in deciding which approach to take to a given proof problem.

Finally, it is interesting to note that the schemata presented in Sect. 4 proved adequate in all cases. That is, in no case was it necessary to add a schema to refine the abstraction of the transition relation. This indicates there is no need in practice to restrict to decidable logics or pay the cost of computing best transformers.

7 Conclusion

We have presented a method of abstracting parameterized or infinite-state SMC problems to finite-state problems based on propositional skeletons and eager theory explication. The method is extensible in the sense that users can add abstractions (or refine existing abstractions) by providing axiom schemata. It generalizes the 'datatype reduction' approach of [18] while giving both a simpler theoretical account and allowing a simpler implementation. Compared to predicate abstraction, it has the advantage that it can be applied to undecidable logics and does not require a costly decision procedure in the loop. The approach has been implemented in the IVy tool. Based on some case studies, we found that the approach is practical and requires substantially less complex auxiliary invariants than inductive invariant checking. We identified some conditions under which the approach is likely to be most effective.

Conceivably some of the tasks performed here by a human could be automated. However, the resulting system would be liable to fail unpredictably and opaquely. The present approach is an attempt to create a usable trade-off between human input and reliability.

The next step is to implement liveness. Recent work has constructed liveness proofs in IVy by an infinite-state liveness-to-safety reduction, but the proofs are complex [21]. It would interesting to compare this to an approach that leverages a finite-state model checker's ability to prove liveness.

References

1. Barrett, C., Sebastiani, R., Seshia, S.A., Tinelli, C.: Satisfiability modulo theories. In: Biere, A., Heule, M., van Maaren, H., Walsch, T. (eds.) Handbook of Satisfiability, chap. 12, pp. 737–797. IOS Press (2008)
2. Biere, A., Heljanko, K., Wieringa, S.: AIGER 1.9 and beyond. Technical report 11/2, Institute for Formal Models and Verification, Johannes Kepler University, July 2011
3. Birman, K., Malkhi, D., van Renesse, R.: Virtually synchronous methodology for dynamic service replication. Technical report MSR-TR-2010-151, Microsoft Research, November 2010
4. Brayton, R., Mishchenko, A.: ABC: an academic industrial-strength verification tool. In: Touili, T., Cook, B., Jackson, P. (eds.) CAV 2010. LNCS, vol. 6174, pp. 24–40. Springer, Heidelberg (2010). https://doi.org/10.1007/978-3-642-14295-6_5
5. Chen, X., Yang, Y., Gopalakrishnan, G., Chou, C.-T.: Reducing verification complexity of a multicore coherence protocol using assume/guarantee. In: Proceedings of the 6th International Conference on Formal Methods in Computer-Aided Design, FMCAD 2006, San Jose, California, USA, 12–16 November 2006, pp. 81–88. IEEE Computer Society (2006)
6. Chou, C.-T., Mannava, P.K., Park, S.: A simple method for parameterized verification of cache coherence protocols. In: Hu, A.J., Martin, A.K. (eds.) FMCAD 2004. LNCS, vol. 3312, pp. 382–398. Springer, Heidelberg (2004). https://doi.org/10.1007/978-3-540-30494-4_27
7. de Moura, L., Bjørner, N.: Z3: an efficient SMT solver. In: Ramakrishnan, C.R., Rehof, J. (eds.) TACAS 2008. LNCS, vol. 4963, pp. 337–340. Springer, Heidelberg (2008). https://doi.org/10.1007/978-3-540-78800-3_24
8. Detlefs, D., Nelson, G., Saxe, J.B.: Simplify: a theorem prover for program checking. J. ACM **52**(3), 365–473 (2005)
9. Graf, S., Saidi, H.: Construction of abstract state graphs with PVS. In: Grumberg, O. (ed.) CAV 1997. LNCS, vol. 1254, pp. 72–83. Springer, Heidelberg (1997). https://doi.org/10.1007/3-540-63166-6_10
10. Hassan, Z., Bradley, A.R., Somenzi, F.: Better generalization in IC3. In: Formal Methods in Computer-Aided Design, FMCAD 2013, Portland, OR, USA, 20–23 October 2013, pp. 157–164. IEEE (2013)
11. Hawblitzel, C., Howell, J., Kapritsos, M., Lorch, J.R., Parno, B., Roberts, M.L., Setty, S.T.V., Zill, B.: IronFleet: proving practical distributed systems correct. In: Miller, E.L., Hand, S. (eds.) Proceedings of the 25th Symposium on Operating Systems Principles, SOSP 2015, Monterey, CA, USA, 4–7 October 2015, pp. 1–17. ACM (2015)
12. Jhala, R., McMillan, K.L.: Microarchitecture verification by compositional model checking. In: Berry, G., Comon, H., Finkel, A. (eds.) CAV 2001. LNCS, vol. 2102, pp. 396–410. Springer, Heidelberg (2001). https://doi.org/10.1007/3-540-44585-4_40
13. Kuskin, J., Ofelt, D., Heinrich, M., Heinlein, J., Simoni, R., Gharachorloo, K., Chapin, J., Nakahira, D., Baxter, J., Horowitz, M., Gupta, A., Rosenblum, M., Hennessy, J.L.: The stanford FLASH multiprocessor. In: Patterson, D.A. (ed.) Proceedings of the 21st Annual International Symposium on Computer Architecture, Chicago, IL, USA, April 1994, pp. 302–313. IEEE Computer Society (1994)
14. Lahiri, S.K., Bryant, R.E.: Constructing quantified invariants via predicate abstraction. In: Steffen, B., Levi, G. (eds.) VMCAI 2004. LNCS, vol. 2937, pp. 267–281. Springer, Heidelberg (2004). https://doi.org/10.1007/978-3-540-24622-0_22

15. McMillan, K.L.: IVy. http://microsoft.github.io/ivy/. Accessed 28 Jan 2018
16. McMillan, K.L.: Circular compositional reasoning about liveness. In: Pierre and Kropf [24], pp. 342–345
17. McMillan, K.L.: Verification of infinite state systems by compositional model checking. In: Pierre and Kropf [24], pp. 219–234
18. McMillan, K.L.: A methodology for hardware verification using compositional model checking. Sci. Comput. Program. **37**(1–3), 279–309 (2000)
19. McMillan, K.L.: Parameterized verification of the FLASH cache coherence protocol by compositional model checking. In: Margaria, T., Melham, T. (eds.) CHARME 2001. LNCS, vol. 2144, pp. 179–195. Springer, Heidelberg (2001). https://doi.org/10.1007/3-540-44798-9_17
20. McMillan, K.L., Qadeer, S., Saxe, J.B.: Induction in compositional model checking. In: Emerson, E.A., Sistla, A.P. (eds.) CAV 2000. LNCS, vol. 1855, pp. 312–327. Springer, Heidelberg (2000). https://doi.org/10.1007/10722167_25
21. Padon, O., Losa, G., Sagiv, M., Shoham, S.: Paxos made EPR: decidable reasoning about distributed protocols. PACMPL **1**(OOPSLA), 108:1–108:31 (2017)
22. Padon, O., McMillan, K.L., Panda, A., Sagiv, M., Shoham, S.: Ivy: safety verification by interactive generalization. In: Krintz, C., Berger, E. (eds.) Proceedings of the 37th ACM SIGPLAN Conference on Programming Language Design and Implementation, PLDI 2016, Santa Barbara, CA, USA, 13–17 June 2016, pp. 614–630. ACM (2016)
23. Park, S., Dill, D.L.: Verification of FLASH cache coherence protocol by aggregation of distributed transactions. In: SPAA, pp. 288–296 (1996)
24. Pierre, L., Kropf, T. (eds.): CHARME 1999. LNCS, vol. 1703. Springer, Heidelberg (1999). https://doi.org/10.1007/3-540-48153-2
25. Pnueli, A., Ruah, S., Zuck, L.: Automatic deductive verification with invisible invariants. In: Margaria, T., Yi, W. (eds.) TACAS 2001. LNCS, vol. 2031, pp. 82–97. Springer, Heidelberg (2001). https://doi.org/10.1007/3-540-45319-9_7

Program Analysis Using Polyhedra

Fast Numerical Program Analysis with Reinforcement Learning

Gagandeep Singh(✉), Markus Püschel, and Martin Vechev

Department of Computer Science, ETH Zürich, Zürich, Switzerland
{gsingh,pueschel,martin.vechev}@inf.ethz.ch

Abstract. We show how to leverage reinforcement learning (RL) in order to speed up static program analysis. The key insight is to establish a correspondence between concepts in RL and those in analysis: a state in RL maps to an abstract program state in analysis, an action maps to an abstract transformer, and at every state, we have a set of sound transformers (actions) that represent different trade-offs between precision and performance. At each iteration, the agent (analysis) uses a policy learned offline by RL to decide on the transformer which minimizes loss of precision at fixpoint while improving analysis performance. Our approach leverages the idea of online decomposition (applicable to popular numerical abstract domains) to define a space of new approximate transformers with varying degrees of precision and performance. Using a suitably designed set of features that capture key properties of abstract program states and available actions, we then apply Q-learning with linear function approximation to compute an optimized context-sensitive policy that chooses transformers during analysis. We implemented our approach for the notoriously expensive Polyhedra domain and evaluated it on a set of Linux device drivers that are expensive to analyze. The results show that our approach can yield massive speedups of up to two orders of magnitude while maintaining precision at fixpoint.

1 Introduction

Static analyzers that scale to real-world programs yet maintain high precision are difficult to design. Recent approaches to attacking this problem have focused on two complementary methods. On one hand is work that designs clever algorithms that exploits the special structure of particular abstract domains to speed up analysis [5,10,15,16,20,21]. These works tackle specific types of analyses but the gains in performance can be substantial. On the other hand are approaches that introduce creative mechanisms to trade off precision loss for gains in speed [9,12,18,19]. While promising, these methods typically do not take into account the particular abstract states arising during analysis which determine the precision of abstract transformers (e.g., join), resulting in suboptimal analysis precision or performance. A key challenge then is coming up with effective and general

H. Chockler and G. Weissenbacher (Eds.): CAV 2018, LNCS 10981, pp. 211–229, 2018.
https://doi.org/10.1007/978-3-319-96145-3_12

approaches that can decide where and how to lose precision *during analysis* for best tradeoff between performance and precision.

Our Work. We address the above challenge by offering a new approach for dynamically losing precision based on reinforcement learning (RL) [24]. The key idea is to learn a policy that determines when and how the analyzer should lose the least precision at an abstract state to achieve best performance gains. Towards that, we establish a correspondence between concepts in static analysis and RL, which demonstrates that RL is a viable approach for handling choices in the inner workings of a static analyzer.

To illustrate the basic idea, imagine that a static analyzer has at each program state two available abstract transformers: the precise but slow T_p and the fast but less precise T_f. Ideally, the analyzer would decide adaptively at each step on the best choice that maximizes speed while producing a final result of sufficient precision. Such a policy is difficult to craft by hand and hence we propose to leverage RL to discover the policy automatically.

To explain the connection with RL intuitively, we think of abstract states and transformers as analogous to states of a Go board and moves made by the Go player, respectively. In Go, the goal is to learn a policy that at each state decides on the next player action (transformer to use) which maximizes the chances of eventually winning the game (obtaining a precise fixpoint while improving performance in our case). Note that the reward to be maximized in Go is long-term and not an immediate gain in position, which is similar to iterative static analysis. To learn the policy with RL, one typically extracts a set of features ϕ from a given state and action, and uses those features to define a so-called Q-function, which is then learned, determining the desired policy.

In the example above, a learned policy would determine at each step whether to choose action T_p or T_f. To do that, for a given state and action, the analyzer computes the value of the Q-function using the features ϕ. Querying the Q-function returns the suggested action from that state. Eventually, such a policy would ideally lead to a fixpoint of sufficient precision but be computed quicker.

While the overall connection between static analysis and reinforcement learning is conceptually clean, the details of making it work in practice pose significant challenges. The first is the design of suitable approximations to actually be able to gain performance when precision is lost. The second is the design of features ϕ that are cheap to compute yet expressive enough to capture key properties of abstract states. Finally, a suitable reward function combining both precision and performance is needed. We show how to solve these challenges for Polyhedra analysis.

Main Contributions. Our main contributions are:

- A space of sound, approximate Polyhedra transformers spanning different precision/performance trade-offs. The new transformers combine online decomposition with different constraint removal and merge strategies for approximations (Sect. 3).

- A set of feature functions which capture key properties of abstract states and transformers, yet are efficient to extract (Sect. 4).
- A complete instantiation of RL for Polyhedra analysis based on Q-learning with linear function approximation (i.e., actions, reward function, Q-function).
- An end-to-end implementation and evaluation of our approach. Given a training dataset of programs, we first learn a policy (based on the Q-function) over analysis runs of these programs. We then use the resulting policy during analysis of new, unseen programs. The experimental results on a set of realistic programs (e.g., Linux device drivers) show that our RL-based Polyhedra analysis achieves substantial speed-ups (up to 515x) over a heavily optimized state-of-the-art Polyhedra library.

We believe the reinforcement learning based approach outlined in this work can be applied to speed up other program analyzers (beyond Polyhedra).

2 Reinforcement Learning for Static Analysis

In this section we first introduce the general framework of reinforcement learning and then discuss its instantiation for static analysis.

2.1 Reinforcement Learning

Reinforcement learning (RL) [24] involves an *agent* learning to achieve a goal by interacting with its *environment*. The agent starts from an initial representation of its environment in the form of an initial state $s_0 \in \mathcal{S}$ where $\mathcal{S}$ is the set of possible states. Then, at each time step $t = 0, 1, 2, \ldots$, the agent performs an action $a_t \in \mathcal{A}$ in state s_t ($\mathcal{A}$ is the set of possible actions) and moves to the next state s_{t+1}. The agent receives a numerical reward $r(s_t, a_t, s_{t+1}) \in \mathbb{R}$ for moving from the state s_t to s_{t+1} through action a_t. The agent repeats this process until it reaches a final state. Each sequence of states and actions from an initial state to the final state is called an *episode*.

In RL, state transitions typically satisfy the Markov property: the next state s_{t+1} depends only on the current state s_t and the action a_t taken from s_t. A *policy* $p\colon \mathcal{S} \to \mathcal{A}$ is a mapping from states to actions: it specifies the action $a_t = p(s_t)$ that the agent will take when in state s_t. The agent's goal is to learn a policy that maximizes not an immediate but a cumulative reward for its actions in the long term. The agent does this by selecting the action with the highest expected long-term reward in a given state. The quality function (Q-function) $Q\colon \mathcal{S} \times \mathcal{A} \to \mathbb{R}$ specifies the long term cumulative reward associated with choosing an action a_t in state s_t. Learning this function, which is not available a priori, is essential for determining the best policy and is explained next.

Algorithm 1. Q-learning algorithm

function Q-LEARN($\mathcal{S}, \mathcal{A}, r, \gamma, \alpha, \phi$)
  Input:
    $\mathcal{S} \leftarrow$ set of states, $\mathcal{A} \leftarrow$ set of actions, $r \leftarrow$ reward function
    $\gamma \leftarrow$ discount factor, $\alpha \leftarrow$ learning rate
    $\phi \leftarrow$ set of feature functions over $\mathcal{S}$ and $\mathcal{A}$
  Output: parameters θ
  $\theta =$ Initialize arbitrarily (which also initializes Q)
  for each episode **do**
    Start with an initial state $s_0 \in \mathcal{S}$
    for $t = 0, 1, 2, \ldots, length(episode)$ **do**
      Take action a_t, observe next state s_{t+1} and $r(s_t, a_t, s_{t+1})$
      $\theta := \theta + \alpha \cdot (r(s_t, a_t, s_{t+1}) + \gamma \cdot \mathtt{max}_{a_{t+1}} Q(s_{t+1}, a_{t+1}) - Q(s_t, a_t)) \cdot \phi(s_t, a_t)$
  return θ

Q-learning and Approximating the Q-function. Q-learning [25] can be used to learn the Q-function over state-action pairs. Typically the size of the state space is so large that it is not feasible to explicitly compute the Q-function for each state-action pair and thus the function is approximated. In this paper, we consider a *linear* function approximation of the Q-function for three reasons: (i) *effectiveness*: the approach is efficient, can handle large state spaces, and works well in practice [6]; (ii) *it leverages our application domain*: in our setting, it is possible to choose meaningful features (e.g., approximation of volume and cost of transformer) that relate to precision and performance of the static analysis and thus it is not necessary to uncover them automatically (as done, e.g., by training a neural net); and (iii) *interpretability of policy*: once the Q-function and associated policy are learned they can be inspected and interpreted.

The Q-function is described as a linear combination of ℓ basis functions $\phi_i \colon \mathcal{S} \times \mathcal{A} \to \mathbb{R}$, $i = 1, \ldots, \ell$. Each ϕ_i is a feature that assigns a value to a (state, action) pair and ℓ is the total number of chosen features. The choice of features is important and depends on the application domain. We collect the feature functions into a vector $\phi(s, a) = (\phi_1(s, a), \phi_2(s, a), \ldots, \phi_\ell(s, a))$; doing so, the Q-function has the form:

$$Q(s, a) = \sum_{j=1}^{\ell} \theta_j \cdot \phi_j(s, a) = \phi(s, a) \cdot \theta^T, \tag{1}$$

where $\theta = (\theta_1, \theta_2, \ldots, \theta_\ell)$ is the parameter vector. The goal of Q-learning with linear function approximation is thus to estimate (learn) θ.

Algorithm 1 shows the Q-learning procedure. In the algorithm, $0 \leq \gamma < 1$ is the *discount factor* which represents the difference in importance between immediate and future rewards. $\gamma = 0$ makes the agent only consider immediate rewards while $\gamma \approx 1$ gives more importance to future rewards. The parameter $0 < \alpha \leq 1$ is the *learning rate* that determines the extent to which the newly acquired information overrides the old information. The algorithm first initializes θ randomly. Then, for each step t in an episode, the agent takes an action a_t,

Table 1. Mapping of RL concepts to Static analysis concepts.

RL concept	Static analysis concept
Agent	Static analyzer
State $s \in \mathcal{S}$	Features of abstract state
Action $a \in \mathcal{A}$	Abstract transformer
Reward function r	Transformer precision and runtime
Feature	Value associated with abstract state features and transformer

moves to the next state s_{t+1} and receives a reward $r(s_t, a_t, s_{t+1})$. Line 12 in the algorithm shows the equation for updating the parameters θ. Notice that Q-learning is an off-policy learning algorithm as the update in the equation assumes that the agent follows a greedy policy (from state s_{t+1}) while the action (a_t) taken by the agent (in s_t) need not be greedy.

Once the Q-function is learned, a policy p^* for maximizing the agent's cumulative reward is obtained as:

$$p^*(s) = \texttt{argmax}_{a \in \mathcal{A}} Q(s, a). \tag{2}$$

In the application, p^* is computed on the fly at each stage s by computing Q for each action a and choosing the one with maximal $Q(s, a)$. Since the number of actions is typically small, this incurs little overhead.

2.2 Instantiation of RL to Static Analysis

We now discuss a general recipe for instantiating the RL framework described above to the domain of static analysis. The precise formal instantiation to the specific numerical (Polyhedra) analysis is provided later.

In Table 1, we show a mapping between RL and program analysis concepts. Here, the analyzer is the agent that observes its environment, which is the abstract program state (e.g., polyhedron) arising at every iteration of the analysis. In general, the number of possible abstract states can be very large (or infinite) and thus, to enable RL in this setting, we abstract the state through a set of features (Table 2). An example of a feature could be the number of bounded program variables or the volume of a polyhedron. The challenge is to define the features to be fast to evaluate, yet sufficiently representative so the policy derived through learning generalizes well to unseen abstract program states.

Further, at every abstract state, the analyzer should have the choice between different actions corresponding to different abstract transformers. The transformers should range from expensive and precise to cheap and approximate. The reward function r is thus composed of a measure of precision and speed and should encourage approximations that are both precise and fast.

The goal of our agent is to then learn an approximation policy that at each step selects an action that tries to minimize the loss of analysis precision at fixpoint, while gaining overall performance. Learning such a policy is typically done offline using a given dataset $\mathcal{D}$ of programs (discussed in evaluation). However, this is computationally challenging because the dataset $\mathcal{D}$ can contain many programs and each program will need to be analyzed many times over during training: even a single run of the analysis can contain many (e.g., thousands) calls to abstract transformers. Thus, a good heuristic may be a complicated function of the chosen features. Hence, to improve the efficiency of learning in practice, one would typically exercise the choice for multiple transformers/actions only at certain program points. A good choice, and one we employ, are join points, where the most expensive transformer in numerical domains usually occurs.

Another key challenge lies in defining a suitable space of transformers. As we will see later, we accomplish this by leveraging recent advances in online decomposition for numerical domains [20–22]. We show how to do that for the notoriously expensive Polyhedra analysis; however, the approach is easily extendable to other popular numerical domains, which all benefit from decomposition.

3 Polyhedra Analysis and Approximate Transformers

In this section we first provide brief background on polyhedra analysis and online decomposition, a recent technique to speed up analysis *without losing precision* and applicable to all popular numerical domains [22]. Then we leverage online decomposition to define a flexible approximation framework that *loses precision* in a way that directly translates into performance gains. This framework forms the basis for our RL approach discussed in Sect. 4.

3.1 Polyhedra Analysis

Let $\mathcal{X} = \{x_1, x_2, \ldots, x_n\}$ be the set of n (numerical) program variables where each variable $x_i \in \mathbb{Q}$ takes a rational value. An abstract element $P \subseteq \mathbb{Q}^n$ in the Polyhedra domain is a conjunction of linear constraints $\sum_{i=1}^{n} a_i x_i \leq c$ between the program variables where $a_i \in \mathbb{Z}, c \in \mathbb{Q}$. This is called the *constraint* representation of the polyhedron.

Constraints and Generator Representation. For efficiency, it is common to maintain besides the constraint representations also the *generator* representation, which encodes a polyhedron as the convex hull of a finite set of vertices, rays, and lines. Rays and lines are represented by their direction. Thus, by abuse of prior notation we write $P = (\mathcal{C}_P, \mathcal{G}_P)$ where $\mathcal{C}_P$ is the constraints representation (before just called P) and $\mathcal{G}_P$ is the generator representation.

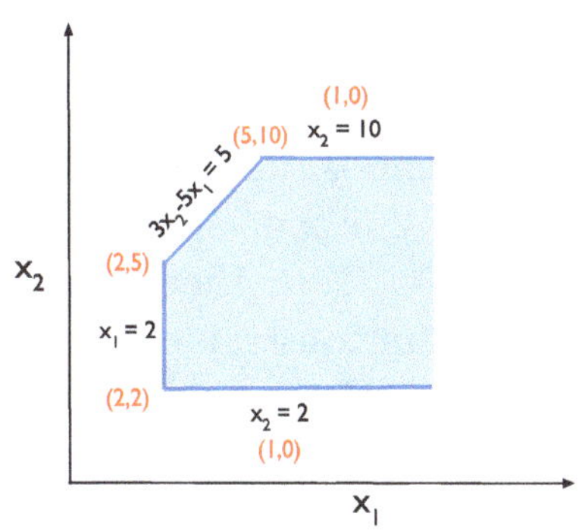

Fig. 1. Two representations of polyhedron P: As conjunction of 4 constraints $\mathcal{C}_P$, and as convex hull of 3 vertices and 2 rays $\mathcal{G}_P$.

Example 1. *Figure 1 shows an example of the two representations of an abstract element P in the Polyhedra domain. $\mathcal{C}_P$ is the intersection of 4 linear constraints:*

$$\mathcal{C}_P = \{-x_1 \leq -2, -x_2 \leq -2, x_2 \leq 10, 3x_2 - 5x_1 \leq 5\}.$$

$\mathcal{G}_P$ is the convex hull of 3 vertices and 2 rays:

$$\mathcal{G}_P = \{vertices,\ rays,\ lines\} = \{\{(2,2),(2,5),(5,10)\},\{(1,0),(1,0)\},\emptyset\}.$$

Notice that $\mathcal{G}_P$ contains two rays in the same direction $(1,0)$; thus one of them could be removed without changing the set of points in P.

During analysis, the abstract elements are manipulated with abstract transformers that model the effect of statements and control flow in the program such as assignment, conditional, join, and others. Upon termination of the analysis, each program statement has an associated subsequent P containing all possible variable values after this statement. The main bottleneck for the Polyhedra analysis is the join transformer ($\sqcup$), and thus it is the focus for our approximations.

Recently, Polyhedra domain analysis was sped up by orders of magnitude, without approximation, using the idea of online decomposition [21]. The basic idea is to dynamically decompose the occurring abstract elements into independent components (in essence abstract elements on smaller variable sets) based on the connectivity between variables in the constraints, and to maintain this (permanently changing) decomposition during analysis. The finer the decomposition, the faster the analysis.

Our approximation framework builds on online decomposition. The basic idea is simple: we approximate by dropping constraints to reduce connectivity among constraints and thus to yield finer decompositions of abstract elements. These directly translate into speedup. We consider various options of such approximation; reinforcement learning (in Sect. 4) will then learn a proper, context-sensitive strategy that stipulates when and which approximation option to apply.

Next, we provide brief background on the ingredients of online decomposition and explain our mechanisms for soundly approximating the join transformer.

3.2 Online Decomposition

Online decomposition is based on the observation that during analysis, the set of variables $\mathcal{X}$ in a given polyhedron P can be partitioned as $\pi_P = \{\mathcal{X}_1, \ldots, \mathcal{X}_r\}$ into *blocks* $\mathcal{X}_t$, such that constraints exist only between variables in the same block. Each unconstrained variable $x_i \in \mathcal{X}$ yields a singleton block $\{x_i\}$. Using this partition, P can be decomposed into a set of smaller Polyhedra $P(\mathcal{X}_t)$ called *factors*. As a consequence, the abstract transformer can now be applied only on the small subset of factors relevant to the program statement, which translates into better performance.

Example 2. *Consider the set $\mathcal{X} = \{x_1, x_2, x_3, x_4, x_5, x_6\}$ and the polyhedron:*

$$P = \{2x_1 - 3x_2 + x_3 + x_4 \leq 0, x_5 = 0\}.$$

Here, $\pi_P = \{\{x_1, x_2, x_3, x_4\}, \{x_5\}, \{x_6\}\}$ *is a possible partition of* $\mathcal{X}$ *with factors*

$$P(\mathcal{X}_1) = \{2x_1 - 3x_2 + x_3 + x_4 \leq 0\},\ P(\mathcal{X}_2) = \{x_5 = 0\},\ P(\mathcal{X}_3) = \emptyset.$$

The set of partitions of $\mathcal{X}$ forms a lattice with the ordering $\pi \sqsubseteq \pi'$ iff every block of π is a subset of a block of π'. Upper and lower bound of two partitions π_1, π_2, i.e., $\pi_1 \sqcup \pi_2$ and $\pi_1 \sqcap \pi_2$ are defined accordingly.

The optimal (finest) partition for an element P is denoted with π_P. Ideally, one would always determine and maintain this finest partition for each output Z of a transformer but it may be too expensive to compute. Thus, the online decomposition in [20,21] often computes a (cheaply computable) *permissible* partition $\overline{\pi}_Z \sqsupseteq \pi_Z$. Note that making the output partition coarser (while keeping the same constraints) does not change the precision of the abstract transformer.

3.3 Approximating the Polyhedra Join

Let $\overline{\pi}_{\text{com}} = \overline{\pi}_{P_1} \sqcup \overline{\pi}_{P_2}$ be a common permissible partition for the inputs P_1, P_2 of the join transformer. Then, from [21], a permissible partition for the (not approximated) output is obtained by keeping all blocks $\mathcal{X}_t \in \overline{\pi}_{\text{com}}$ for which $P_1(\mathcal{X}_t) = P_2(\mathcal{X}_t)$ in the output partition $\overline{\pi}_Z$, and fusing all remaining blocks into one. Formally, $\overline{\pi}_Z = \{\mathcal{N}\} \cup \mathcal{U}$, where

$$\mathcal{N} = \bigcup \{\mathcal{X}_k \in \overline{\pi}_{\text{com}} : P_1(\mathcal{X}_k) \neq P_2(\mathcal{X}_k)\}, \quad \mathcal{U} = \{\mathcal{X}_k \in \overline{\pi}_{\text{com}} : P_1(\mathcal{X}_k) = P_2(\mathcal{X}_k)\}.$$

The join transformer computes the generators $\mathcal{G}_Z$ for the output Z as $\mathcal{G}_Z = \mathcal{G}_{P_1(\mathcal{X} \setminus \mathcal{N})} \times (\mathcal{G}_{P_1(\mathcal{N})} \cup \mathcal{G}_{P_2(\mathcal{N})})$ where $\times$ is the Cartesian product. The constraint representation $\mathcal{C}_Z$ is computed as $\mathcal{C}_Z = \mathcal{C}_{P_1(\mathcal{X} \setminus \mathcal{N})} \cup \texttt{conversion}(\mathcal{G}_{P_1(\mathcal{N})} \cup \mathcal{G}_{P_2(\mathcal{N})})$. The conversion algorithm has worst-case exponential complexity and is the most expensive step of the join. Note that the decomposed join applies it only on the generators $\mathcal{G}_{P_1(\mathcal{N})} \cup \mathcal{G}_{P_2(\mathcal{N})}$ corresponding to the block $\mathcal{N}$.

The cost of the decomposed join transformer depends on the size of the block $\mathcal{N}$. Thus, it is desirable to bound this size by a *threshold* $\in \mathbb{N}$. Let $\mathcal{B} = \{\mathcal{X}_k \in \overline{\pi}_{\text{com}} : \mathcal{X}_k \cap \mathcal{N} \neq \emptyset\}$ be the set of blocks that merge into $\mathcal{N}$ in the output $\overline{\pi}_Z$ and $\mathcal{B}_t = \{\mathcal{X}_k \in \mathcal{B} : |\mathcal{X}_k| > \textit{threshold}\}$ be the set of blocks in $\mathcal{B}$ with size $>$ *threshold*.

Splitting of Large Blocks. For each block $\mathcal{X}_t \in \mathcal{B}_t$, we apply the join on the associated factors: $Z(\mathcal{X}_t) = P_1(\mathcal{X}_t) \sqcup P_2(\mathcal{X}_t)$. We then remove constraints from $Z(\mathcal{X}_t)$ until it decomposes into blocks of sizes $\leq$ *threshold*. Since we only remove constraints from $Z(\mathcal{X}_t)$, the resulting transformer remains sound. There are many choices for removing constraints as shown in the next example.

Example 3. *Consider the following polyhedron and threshold* $= 4$

$$\begin{aligned} \mathcal{X}_t &= \{x_1, x_2, x_3, x_4, x_5, x_6\}, \\ Z(\mathcal{X}_t) &= \{x_1 - x_2 + x_3 \leq 0, x_2 + x_3 + x_4 \leq 0, x_2 + x_3 \leq 0, \\ &\qquad x_3 + x_4 \leq 0, x_4 - x_5 \leq 0, x_4 - x_6 \leq 0\}. \end{aligned}$$

We can remove $\mathcal{M} = \{x_4 - x_5 \leq 0, x_4 - x_6 \leq 0\}$ *from* $Z(\mathcal{X}_t)$ *to obtain the constraint set* $\{x_1 - x_2 + x_3 \leq 0, x_2 + x_3 + x_4 \leq 0, x_2 + x_3 \leq 0, x_3 + x_4 \leq 0\}$ *with partition* $\{\{x_1, x_2, x_3, x_4\}, \{x_5\}, \{x_6\}\}$*, which obeys the threshold.*

We could also remove $\mathcal{M}' = \{x_2 + x_3 + x_4 \leq 0, x_3 + x_4 \leq 0\}$ *from* $Z(\mathcal{X}_t)$ *to get the constraint set* $\{x_1 - x_2 + x_3 \leq 0, x_2 + x_3 \leq 0, x_4 - x_5 \leq 0, x_4 - x_6 \leq 0\}$ *with partition* $\{\{x_1, x_2, x_3\}, \{x_4, x_5, x_6\}\}$*, which also obeys the threshold.*

We next discuss our choices for the constraint removal algorithm.

Stoer-Wagner min-cut. The first basic idea is to remove a minimal number of constraints in $Z(\mathcal{X}_t)$ that decomposes the block $\mathcal{X}_t$ into two blocks. To do so, we associate with $Z(\mathcal{X}_t)$ a weighted undirected graph $G = (\mathcal{V}, \mathcal{E})$, where $\mathcal{V} = \mathcal{X}_t$. Further, there is an edge between x_i and x_j, if there is a constraint containing both; its weight m_{ij} is the number of such constraints. We then apply the standard Stoer-Wagner min-cut algorithm [23] to obtain a partition of $\mathcal{X}_t$ into $\mathcal{X}'_t$ and $\mathcal{X}''_t$. $\mathcal{M}$ collects all constraints that need to be removed, i.e., those that contain at least one variable from both $\mathcal{X}'_t$ and $\mathcal{X}''_t$.

Example 4. *Figure 2 shows the graph G for* $Z(\mathcal{X}_t)$ *in Example 3. Applying the Stoer-Wagner min-cut on G once will cut off* x_5 *or* x_6 *by removing the constraint* $x_4 - x_5$ *or* $x_4 - x_6$*, respectively. In either case a block of size 5 remains, exceeding the threshold of 4. After two applications, both constraints have been removed and the resulting block structure is given by* $\{\{x_1, x_2, x_3, x_4\}, \{x_5\}, \{x_6\}\}$*. The associated factors are* $\{x_1 - x_2 + x_3 \leq 0, x_2 + x_3 + x_4 \leq 0, x_2 + x_3 \leq 0, x_3 + x_4 \leq 0\}$ *and* x_5, x_6 *become unconstrained.*

Weighted Constraint Removal. Our second approach for constraints removal does not associate weights with edges but with constraints. It then removes greedily edges with high weights. Specifically, we consider the following two choices of constraint weights, yielding two different constraint removal policies:

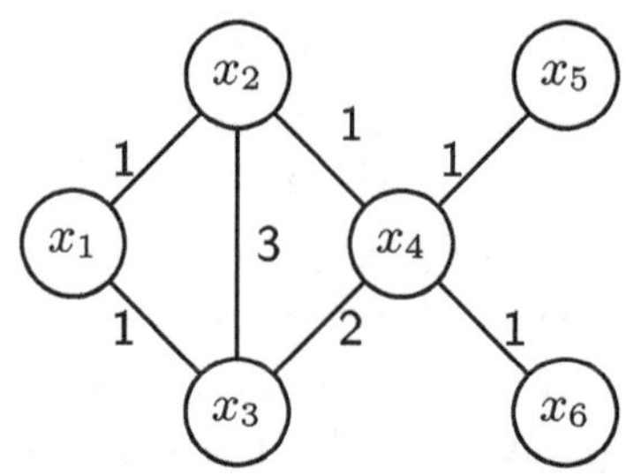

Fig. 2. Graph G for $Z(\mathcal{X}_t)$ in Example 3

- For each variable $x_i \in \mathcal{X}_t$, we first compute the number n_i of constraints containing x_i. The weight of a constraint is then the sum of the n_i over all variables occurring in the constraint.
- For each pair of variables $x_i, x_j \in \mathcal{X}_t$, we first compute the number n_{ij} of constraints containing both x_i and x_j. The weight of a constraint is then the sum of the n_{ij} over all pairs x_i, x_j occurring in the constraint.

Once the weights are computed, we remove the constraint with maximum weight. The intuition is that variables in this constraint most likely occur in other constraints in $Z(\mathcal{X}_t)$ and thus they do not become unconstrained upon constraint removal. This reduces the loss of information.

Example 5. *Applying the first definition of weights in Example 3, we get* $n_1 = 1, n_2 = 3, n_3 = 4, n_4 = 4, n_5 = 1, n_6 = 1$. *The constraint* $x_2 + x_3 + x_4 \leq 0$ *has the maximum weight of* $n_2 + n_3 + n_4 = 11$ *and thus is chosen for removal. Removing this constraint from* $Z(\mathcal{X}_t)$ *does not yet yield a decomposition; thus we have to repeat. Doing so* $\{x_3 + x_4 \leq 0\}$ *is chosen. Now,* $Z(\mathcal{X}_t) \setminus \mathcal{M} = \{x_1 - x_2 + x_3 \leq 0, x_2 + x_3 \leq 0, x_4 - x_5 \leq 0, x_4 - x_6 \leq 0\}$ *which can be decomposed into two factors* $\{x_1 - x_2 + x_3 \leq 0, x_2 + x_3 \leq 0\}$ *and* $\{x_4 - x_5 \leq 0, x_4 - x_6 \leq 0\}$ *corresponding to blocks* $\{x_1, x_2, x_3\}$ *and* $\{x_4, x_5, x_6\}$*, respectively, each of size* $\leq$ *threshold.*

Merging Blocks. The sizes of all blocks in $\mathcal{B} \setminus \mathcal{B}_t$ are $\leq$ *threshold* and we can apply merging to obtain larger blocks $\mathcal{X}_m \leq$ *threshold* to increase the precision of the subsequent join. The join is then applied on the factors $P_1(\mathcal{X}_m), P_2(\mathcal{X}_m)$ and the result is added to the output Z. We consider the following three merging strategies. To simplify the explanation, we assume that the blocks in $\mathcal{B} \setminus \mathcal{B}_t$ are ordered by ascending size:

1. *No merge:* None of the blocks are merged.
2. *Merge smallest first:* We start merging the smallest blocks as long as the size stays below the threshold. These blocks are then removed and the procedure is repeated on the remaining set.
3. *Merge large with small:* We start to merge the largest block with the smallest blocks as long as the size stays below the threshold. These blocks are then removed and the procedure is repeated on the remaining set.

Example 6. *Consider threshold* $= 5$ *and* $\mathcal{B} \setminus \mathcal{B}_t$ *with block sizes* $\{1, 1, 2, 2, 2, 2, 3, 5, 7, 10\}$. *Merging smallest first yields blocks* $1 + 1 + 2$, $2 + 2$, $2 + 3$ *leaving the rest unchanged. The resulting sizes are* $\{4, 4, 5, 5, 7, 10\}$. *Merging large with small leaves* $10, 7, 5$ *unchanged and merges* $3 + 1 + 1$, $2 + 2$, *and* $2 + 2$. *The resulting sizes are also* $\{4, 4, 5, 5, 7, 10\}$ *but the associated factors are different (since different blocks are merged), which will yield different results in following transformations.*

Need for RL. Algorithm 2 shows how to approximate the join transformer. Different choices of threshold, splitting, and merge strategies yield a range of transformers with different performance and precision depending on the inputs. All of the transformers are non-monotonic, however the analysis always converges to a fixpoint when combined with widening [2]. Determining the suitability of a given choice on an input is highly non-trivial and thus we use RL to learn it.

Algorithm 2. Approximation algorithm for Polyhedra join

function APPROXIMATE_JOIN$((\overline{\pi}_{P_1}, P_1), (\overline{\pi}_{P_2}, P_2), threshold)$
  Input:
    $(\overline{\pi}_{P_1}, P_1), (\overline{\pi}_{P_2}, P_2) \leftarrow$ decomposed inputs to the join
    threshold $\leftarrow$ Upper bound on size of $\mathcal{N}$
  Output: decomposed output $(\overline{\pi}_Z, Z)$ of the join
  $Z := \bigcup\{P_1(\mathcal{X}_k) : P_1(\mathcal{X}_k) = P_2(\mathcal{X}_k)\}, \overline{\pi}_Z := \mathcal{U}$ ▷ *initialize output*
  $\mathcal{B} := \{\mathcal{X}_k \in \overline{\pi}_{P_1} \sqcup \overline{\pi}_{P_2} : \mathcal{X}_k \cap \mathcal{N} \neq \emptyset\}$, $\mathcal{B}_t := \{\mathcal{X}_t \in \mathcal{B} : |\mathcal{X}_t| > threshold\}$
  ▷ *join factors for blocks in* $\mathcal{B}_t$ *and split the outputs via a split algorithm*
  for $\mathcal{X}_t \in \mathcal{B}_t$ ***do***
    $P' := P_1(\mathcal{X}_t) \sqcup P_2(\mathcal{X}_t)$
    $s\_algo :=$ `split_alg`$(\mathcal{X}_t, \mathcal{C}_{P'}), (\mathcal{C}, \overline{\pi}) :=$ `split`$(\mathcal{X}_t, \mathcal{C}_{P'}, threshold, s\_algo)$
    for $\mathcal{X}_{t'} \in \overline{\pi}$ ***do***
      $\mathcal{G}(\mathcal{X}_{t'}) :=$ `conversion`$(\mathcal{C}(\mathcal{X}_{t'}))$, $Z := Z \cup (\mathcal{C}(\mathcal{X}_{t'}), \mathcal{G}(\mathcal{X}_{t'}))$
    $\overline{\pi}_Z := \overline{\pi}_Z \cup \overline{\pi}$
  ▷ *merge blocks* $\in \mathcal{B} \setminus \mathcal{B}_t$ *via a merge algorithm and apply join*
  $m\_algo :=$ `merge_alg`$(\mathcal{B} \setminus \mathcal{B}_t)$, $\mathcal{B}_m :=$ `merge`$(\mathcal{B} \setminus \mathcal{B}_t, threshold, m\_algo)$
  for $\mathcal{X}_m \in \mathcal{B}_m$ ***do***
    $Z := Z \cup (P_1(\mathcal{X}_m) \sqcup P_2(\mathcal{X}_m))$, $\overline{\pi}_Z := \overline{\pi}_Z \cup \{\mathcal{X}_m\}$
  return $(\overline{\pi}_Z, Z)$

Table 2. Features for describing RL state s ($m \in \{1,2\}, 0 \leq j \leq 8, 0 \leq h \leq 3$).

Feature ψ_i	Extraction complexity	Typical range	n_i	Buckets for feature ψ_i
$\lvert\mathcal{B}\rvert$	$O(1)$	1–10	10	$\{[j+1, j+1]\} \cup \{[10, \infty)\}$
$\mathtt{min}(\lvert\mathcal{X}_k\rvert : \mathcal{X}_k \in \mathcal{B})$	$O(\lvert\mathcal{B}\rvert)$	1–100	10	$\{[10 \cdot j+1, 10 \cdot (j+1)]\} \cup \{[91, \infty)\}$
$\mathtt{max}(\lvert\mathcal{X}_k\rvert : \mathcal{X}_k \in \mathcal{B})$	$O(\lvert\mathcal{B}\rvert)$	1–100	10	$\{[10 \cdot j+1, 10 \cdot (j+1)]\} \cup \{[91, \infty)\}$
$\mathtt{avg}(\lvert\mathcal{X}_k\rvert : \mathcal{X}_k \in \mathcal{B})$	$O(\lvert\mathcal{B}\rvert)$	1–100	10	$\{[10 \cdot j+1, 10 \cdot (j+1)]\} \cup \{[91, \infty)\}$
$\mathtt{min}(\lvert\bigcup \mathcal{G}_{P_m(\mathcal{X}_k)}\rvert : \mathcal{X}_k \in \mathcal{B})$	$O(\lvert\mathcal{B}\rvert)$	1–1000	10	$\{[100 \cdot j+1, 100 \cdot (j+1)]\} \cup \{[901, \infty)\}$
$\mathtt{max}(\lvert\bigcup \mathcal{G}_{P_m(\mathcal{X}_k)}\rvert : \mathcal{X}_k \in \mathcal{B})$	$O(\lvert\mathcal{B}\rvert)$	1–1000	10	$\{[100 \cdot j+1, 100 \cdot (j+1)]\} \cup \{[901, \infty)\}$
$\mathtt{avg}(\lvert\bigcup \mathcal{G}_{P_m(\mathcal{X}_k)}\rvert : \mathcal{X}_k \in \mathcal{B})$	$O(\lvert\mathcal{B}\rvert)$	1–1000	10	$\{[100 \cdot j+1, 100 \cdot (j+1)]\} \cup \{[901, \infty)\}$
$\lvert\{x_i \in \mathcal{X} : x_i \in [l_m, u_m] \text{ in } P_m\}\rvert$	$O(ng)$	1–25	5	$\{[5 \cdot h+1, 5 \cdot (h+1)]\} \cup \{[21, \infty)\}$
$\lvert\{x_i \in \mathcal{X} : x_i \in [l_m, \infty) \text{ in } P_m\}\rvert + \lvert\{x_i \in \mathcal{X} : x_i \in (-\infty, u_m] \text{ in } P_m\}\rvert$	$O(ng)$	1–25	5	$\{[5 \cdot h+1, 5 \cdot (h+1)]\} \cup \{[21, \infty)\}$

4 Reinforcement Learning for Polyhedra Analysis

We now describe how to instantiate reinforcement learning for approximating Polyhedra domain analysis. The instantiation consists of the following steps:

- Extracting the RL state s from the abstract program state numerically using a set of features.
- Defining actions a as the choices among the threshold, merge and split methods defined in the previous section.
- Defining a reward function r favoring both high precision and fast execution.
- Defining the feature functions $\phi(s, a)$ to enable Q-learning.

States. We consider nine features for defining a state s for RL. The features ψ_i, their extraction complexity and their typical range on our benchmarks are shown in Table 2. The first seven features capture the asymptotic complexity of the join [21] on the input polyhedra P_1 and P_2. These are the number of blocks, the distribution (using maximum, minimum and average) of their sizes, and the number of generators. The precision of the inputs is captured by considering the number of variables $x_i \in \mathcal{X}$ with finite upper and lower bound, and the number of those with only a finite upper or lower bound in both P_1 and P_2.

As shown in Table 2, each state feature ψ_i returns a natural number, however, its range can be rather large, resulting in a massive state space. To ensure scalability and generalization of learning, we use bucketing to reduce the state space size by clustering states with similar precision and expected join cost. The number n_i of buckets for each ψ_i and their definition are shown in the last two columns of Table 2. Using bucketing, the RL state s is then a 9-tuple consisting of the indices of buckets where each index indicates the bucket that ψ_i's return value falls into.

Actions. An action a is a 3-tuple (th, r_algo, m_algo) consisting of:

- $th \in \{1, 2, 3, 4\}$ depending on *threshold* $\in [5, 9]$, $[10, 14]$, $[15, 19]$, or $[20, \infty)$.
- $r\_algo \in \{1, 2, 3\}$: the choice of a constraint removal, i.e., splitting method.
- $m\_algo \in \{1, 2, 3\}$: the choice of merge algorithm.

All three of these have been discussed in detail in Sect. 3. The *threshold* values were chosen based on performance characterization on our benchmarks. With the above, we have 36 possible actions per state.

Reward. After applying the (approximated join transformer) according to action a_t in state s_t, we compute the precision of the output polyhedron $P_1 \sqcup P_2$ by first computing the smallest (often unbounded) box[1] covering $P_1 \sqcup P_2$ which has complexity $O(ng)$. We then compute the following quantities from this box:

- n_s: number of variables x_i with singleton interval, i.e., $x_i \in [l, u], l = u$.
- n_b: number of variables x_i with finite upper and lower bounds, i.e., $x_i \in [l, u], l \neq u$.
- n_{hb}: number of variables x_i with either finite upper or finite lower bounds, i.e., $x_i \in (-\infty, u]$ or $x_i \in [l, \infty)$.

Further, we measure the runtime in CPU cycles cyc for the approximate join transformer. The reward is then defined by

$$r(s_t, a_t, s_{t+1}) = 3 \cdot n_s + 2n_b + n_{hb} - \log_{10}(cyc). \tag{3}$$

As the order of precision for different types of intervals is: singleton > bounded > half bounded interval, the reward function in (3) weighs their numbers by 3, 2, 1. The reward function in (3) favors both high performance and

[1] A natural measure of precision is the volume of $P_1 \sqcup P_2$. However, calculating it is very expensive and $P_1 \sqcup P_2$ is often unbounded.

Table 3. Instantiation of Q-learning to Polyhedra static analysis.

RL concept	Polyhedra analysis instantiation
Agent	Polyhedra analysis
State $s \in \mathcal{S}$	As described in Table 2
Action $a \in \mathcal{A}$	Tuple $(th,\ r\_algo,\ m\_algo)$
Reward function r	Shown in (3)
Feature ϕ	Defined in (4)
Q-function	Q-function from (5)

precision. It also ensures that the precision part $(3 \cdot n_s + 2n_b + n_{hb})$ has a similar magnitude range as the performance part $(\log_{10}(cyc))^2$.

Q-function. As mentioned before, we approximate the Q-function by a linear function (1). We define binary feature functions ϕ_{ijk} for each (state, action) pair. $\phi_{ijk}(s, a) = 1$ if the tuple $s(i)$ lies in j-th bucket and action $a = a_k$

$$\phi_{ijk}(s, a) = 1 \iff s(i) = j \text{ and } a = a_k \tag{4}$$

The Q-function is a linear combination of state action features ϕ_{ijk}

$$Q(s, a) = \sum_{i=1}^{9} \sum_{j=1}^{n_i} \sum_{k=1}^{36} \theta_{ijk} \cdot \phi_{ijk}(s, a). \tag{5}$$

Q-learning. During the training phase, we are given a dataset of programs $\mathcal{D}$ and we use `Q-LEARN` from Algorithm 1 on each program in $\mathcal{D}$ to perform Q-learning. Q-learning is performed with input parameters instantiated as explained above and summarized in Table 3. Each episode consists of a run of Polyhedra analysis on a benchmark in $\mathcal{D}$. We run the analysis multiple times on each program in $\mathcal{D}$ and update the Q-function after each join by calling `Q-LEARN`.

A Q-function is typically learned using an ϵ-greedy policy [24] where the agent takes greedy actions by exploiting the current Q-estimates while also exploring randomly. The policy requires initial random exploration to learn good Q-estimates that can be later exploited. This is infeasible for the Polyhedra analysis as a typical episode contains thousands of join calls. Therefore, we generate actions for Q-learning by exploiting the optimal policy for precision (which always selects the precise join) and explore performance by choosing a random approximate join: both with a probability of 0.5[3].

[2] The log is used since the join has exponential complexity.

[3] We also tried exploitation probabilities of 0.7 and 0.9, however the resulting policies had suboptimal performance during testing due to limited exploration.

Formally, the action $a_t := p(s_t)$ selected in state s_t during learning is given by $a_t = (th,\, r\_algo,\, m\_algo)$ where

$$th = \begin{cases} \texttt{rand() \% 4+1} \text{ with probability } 0.5 \\ \texttt{min}(4, (\sum_{i=1}^{|\mathcal{B}|} |\mathcal{X}_k|)/5) \text{ with probability } 0.5 \end{cases}, \qquad (6)$$
$$r\_algo = \texttt{rand}()\ \%\ 3 + 1, m\_algo = \texttt{rand}()\ \%\ 3 + 1.$$

Obtaining the Learned Policy. After learning over the dataset $\mathcal{D}$, the learned approximating join transformer in state s_t chooses an action according to (2) by selecting the maximal value over all actions. The value of $th = 1, 2, 3, 4$ is decoded as *threshold* $= 5, 10, 15, 20$ respectively.

5 Experimental Evaluation

We implemented our approach in the form of a C-library for Polyhedra analysis, called Poly-RL. We compare the performance and precision of Poly-RL against the state-of-the-art ELINA [1], which uses online decomposition for Polyhedra analysis without losing precision. In addition, we implemented two Polyhedra analysis approximations (baselines) based on the following heuristics:

- Poly-Fixed: uses a *fixed* strategy based on the results of Q-learning. Namely, we selected the threshold, split and merge algorithm most frequently chosen by our (adaptive) learned policy during testing.
- Poly-Init: uses an approximate join with probability 0.5 based on (6).

All Polyhedra implementations use 64-bit integers to encode rational numbers. In the case of overflow, the corresponding polyhedron is set to top.

Experimental Setup. All our experiments including learning the parameters θ for the Q-function and the evaluation of the learned policy on unseen benchmarks were carried out on a 2.13 GHz Intel Xeon E7- 4830 Haswell CPU with 24 MB L3 cache and 256 GB memory. All Polyhedra implementations were compiled with gcc 5.4.0 using the flags `-O3 -m64 -march=native`.

Analyzer. For both learning and evaluation, we used the *crab-llvm* analyzer for C-programs, part of the larger SeaHorn [7] verification framework. The analyzer performs intra-procedural analysis of llvm-bitcode to generate Polyhedra invariants which can be used for verifying assertions using an SMT solver [11].

Benchmarks. SVCOMP [3] contains thousands of challenging benchmarks in different categories suited for different kinds of analysis. We chose the Linux Device Drivers (LD) category, known to be challenging for Polyhedra analysis [21] as to prove properties in these programs one requires Polyhedra invariants (and not say Octagon invariants which are weaker).

Training Dataset. We chose 70 large benchmarks for Q-learning. We ran each benchmark a thousand times over a period of three days to generate sample traces of Polyhedra analysis containing thousands of calls to the join transformer. We set a timeout of 5 minutes per run and discarded incomplete traces in case of a timeout. In total, we performed Q-learning over 110811 traces.

Evaluation Method. For evaluating the effectiveness of our learned policy, we then chose benchmarks based on the following criteria:

- No overfitting: the benchmark was not used for learning the policy.
- Challenging: ELINA takes ≥ 5 s on the benchmark.
- Fair: there is no integer overflow in the expensive functions in the benchmark. Because in the case of an overflow, the polyhedron is set to top resulting in a trivial fixpoint at no cost and thus in a speedup that is due to overflow.

Based on these criteria, we found 11 benchmarks on which we present our results. We used a timeout of 1 h and memory limit of 100 GB for our experiments.

Inspecting the Learned Policy. Our learned policy chooses in the majority of cases *threshold*=20, the binary weighted constraint removal algorithm for splitting, and the merge smallest first algorithm for merging. Poly-Fixed always uses these values for defining an approximate transformer, i.e., it follows a fixed strategy. Our experimental results show that following this fixed strategy results in suboptimal performance compared to our learned policy that makes adaptive, context-sensitive decisions to improve performance.

Results. We measure the precision as a fraction of program points at which the Polyhedra invariants generated by approximate analysis are semantically the same or stronger than the ones generated by ELINA. This is a less biased and more challenging measure than the number of discharged assertions [4,18,19] where one can write weak assertions that even a weaker domain can prove.

Table 4 shows the number of program points[4], timings (in seconds), and the precision (in %) of Poly-RL, Poly-Fixed, and Poly-Init w.r.t. ELINA on all 11 benchmarks. In the table, the entry `TO` (`MO`) means that the analysis did not finish within 1 h (exceeded the memory limit). For an incomplete analysis, we compute the precision by comparing program points for which the incomplete analysis can produce invariants.

Poly-RL vs ELINA. In Table 4, Poly-RL obtains > 7x speed-up over ELINA on 6 of the 11 benchmarks with a maximum of 515x speedup for the `mfd_sm501` benchmark. It also obtains the same or stronger invariants on $\geq 87\%$ of program

[4] The benchmarks contain up to 50K LOC but SeaHorn encodes each basic block as one program point, thus the number of points in Table 4 is significantly reduced.

Table 4. Timings (seconds) and precision of approximations (%) w.r.t. ELINA.

Benchmark	#Program Points	ELINA Time	Poly-RL Time	Poly-RL Precision	Poly-Fixed Time	Poly-Fixed Precision	Poly-Init Time	Poly-Init Precision
wireless_airo	2372	877	6.6	100	6.7	100	5.2	74
net_ppp	680	2220	9.1	87	TO	34	7.7	55
mfd_sm501	369	1596	3.1	97	1421	97	2	64
ideapad_laptop	461	172	2.9	100	157	100	MO	41
pata_legacy	262	41	2.8	41	2.5	41	MO	27
usb_ohci	1520	22	2.9	100	34	100	MO	50
usb_gadget	1843	66	37	60	35	60	TO	40
wireless_b43	3226	19	13	66	TO	28	83	34
lustre_llite	211	5.7	4.9	98	5.4	98	6.1	54
usb_cx231xx	4752	7.3	3.9	≈100	3.7	≈100	3.9	94
netfilter_ipvs	5238	20	17	≈100	9.8	≈100	11	94

points on 8 benchmarks. Note that Poly-RL obtains both large speedups and the same invariants at all program points on 3 benchmarks.

The widening transformer removes many constraints produced by the precise join transformer from ELINA which allows Poly-RL to obtain the same invariants as ELINA despite the loss of precision during join in most cases. Poly-RL produces large number of non-comparable fixpoints on 3 benchmarks in Table 4 due to non-monotonic join transformers.

We also tested Poly-RL on 17 benchmarks from the product lines category. ELINA did not finish within an hour on any of these benchmarks whereas Poly-RL finished within 1 s. Poly-RL had 100% precision on the subset of program points at which ELINA produces invariants. With Poly-RL, SeaHorn successfully discharged the assertions. We did not include these results in Table 4 as the precision w.r.t. ELINA cannot be completely compared.

Poly-RL vs Poly-Fixed. Poly-Fixed is never significantly more precise than Poly-RL in Table 4. Poly-Fixed is faster than Poly-RL on 4 benchmarks, however the speedups are small. Poly-Fixed is slower than ELINA on 3 benchmarks and times out on 2 of these. This is due to the overhead of the binary weight constraints removal algorithm and the exponential number of generators in the output.

Poly-RL vs Poly-Init. From (6), Poly-Init takes random actions and thus the quality of its result varies depending on the run. Table 4 shows the results on a sample run. Poly-RL is more precise than Poly-Init on all benchmarks in Table 4. Poly-Init also does not finish on 4 benchmarks.

6 Related Work

Our work can be seen as part of the general research direction on parametric program analysis [4,9,14,18,19], where one tunes the precision and cost of the analysis by adapting it to the analyzed program. The main difference is that prior approaches fix the learning parameters for a given program while our method is adaptive and can select parameters dynamically based on the abstract states encountered during analysis, yielding better cost/precision tradeoffs. Further, prior work measures precision by the number of assertions proved whereas we target the stronger notion of fixpoint equivalence.

The work of [20,21] improve the performance of Octagon and Polyhedra domain analysis respectively based on online decomposition without losing precision. We compared against [21] in this paper. As our results suggest, the performance of Polyhedra analysis can be significantly improved with RL. We believe that our approach can be easily extended to the Octagon domain for achieving speedups over the work of [20] as the idea of online decomposition applies to all sub-polyhedra domains [22].

Reinforcement learning based on linear function approximation of the Q-function has been applied to learn branching rules for SAT solvers in [13]. The learned policies achieve performance similar to those of the best branching rules. We believe that more powerful techniques for RL such as deep Q-networks (DQN) [17] or double Q-learning [8] can be investigated to potentially improve the quality of results produced by our approach.

7 Conclusion

Polyhedra analysis is notoriously expensive and has worst-case exponential complexity. We showed how to gain significant speedups by adaptively trading precision for performance during analysis, using an automatically learned policy. Two key insights underlie our approach. First, we identify reinforcement learning as a conceptual match to the learning problem at hand: deciding which transformers to select at each analysis step so to achieve the eventual goal of high precision and fast convergence to fixpoint. Second, we build on the concept of online decomposition, and offer an effective method to directly translate precision loss into significant speed-ups. Our work focused on polyhedra analysis for which we provide a complete implementation and evaluation. We believe the approach can be instantiated to other forms of static analysis in future work.

Acknowledgments. We would like to thank Afra Amini for her help in implementing the approximate transformers. We would also like to thank the anonymous reviewers for their constructive feedback. This research was supported by the Swiss National Science Foundation (SNF) grant number 163117.

References

1. ELINA: ETH Library for Numerical Analysis. http://elina.ethz.ch
2. Bagnara, R., Hill, P.M., Ricci, E., Zaffanella, E.: Precise widening operators for convex polyhedra. In: Cousot, R. (ed.) SAS 2003. LNCS, vol. 2694, pp. 337–354. Springer, Heidelberg (2003). https://doi.org/10.1007/3-540-44898-5_19
3. Beyer, D.: Reliable and reproducible competition results with benchexec and witnesses (Report on SV-COMP 2016). In: Chechik, M., Raskin, J.-F. (eds.) TACAS 2016. LNCS, vol. 9636, pp. 887–904. Springer, Heidelberg (2016). https://doi.org/10.1007/978-3-662-49674-9_55
4. Chae, K., Oh, H., Heo, K., Yang, H.: Automatically generating features for learning program analysis heuristics for C-like languages. Proc. ACM Program. Lang. **1**(OOPSLA), 101:1–101:25 (2017)
5. Gange, G., Navas, J.A., Schachte, P., Søndergaard, H., Stuckey, P.J.: Exploiting sparsity in difference-bound matrices. In: Rival, X. (ed.) SAS 2016. LNCS, vol. 9837, pp. 189–211. Springer, Heidelberg (2016). https://doi.org/10.1007/978-3-662-53413-7_10
6. Geramifard, A., Walsh, T.J., Tellex, S.: A Tutorial on Linear Function Approximators for Dynamic Programming and Reinforcement Learning. Now Publishers Inc., Hanover (2013)
7. Gurfinkel, A., Kahsai, T., Komuravelli, A., Navas, J.A.: The seahorn verification framework. In: Kroening, D., Păsăreanu, C.S. (eds.) CAV 2015. LNCS, vol. 9206, pp. 343–361. Springer, Cham (2015). https://doi.org/10.1007/978-3-319-21690-4_20
8. Hasselt, H.V.: Double Q-learning. In: Lafferty, J.D., Williams, C.K.I., Shawe-Taylor, J., Zemel, R.S., Culotta, A. (eds.) Neural Information Processing Systems (NIPS), pp. 2613–2621 (2010)
9. Heo, K., Oh, H., Yang, H.: Learning a variable-clustering strategy for octagon from labeled data generated by a static analysis. In: Rival, X. (ed.) SAS 2016. LNCS, vol. 9837, pp. 237–256. Springer, Heidelberg (2016). https://doi.org/10.1007/978-3-662-53413-7_12
10. Jourdan, J.-H.: Sparsity preserving algorithms for octagons. Electron. Notes Theor. Comput. Sci. **331**, 57–70 (2017). Workshop on Numerical and Symbolic Abstract Domains (NSAD)
11. Komuravelli, A., Gurfinkel, A., Chaki, S.: SMT-based model checking for recursive programs. In: Biere, A., Bloem, R. (eds.) CAV 2014. LNCS, vol. 8559, pp. 17–34. Springer, Cham (2014). https://doi.org/10.1007/978-3-319-08867-9_2
12. Kulkarni, S., Mangal, R., Zhang, X., Naik, M.: Accelerating program analyses by cross-program training. In: Proceedings of Object-Oriented Programming, Systems, Languages, and Applications (OOPSLA), pp. 359–377 (2016)
13. Lagoudakis, M.G., Littman, M.L.: Learning to select branching rules in the DPLL procedure for satisfiability. Electron. Notes Discret. Math. **9**, 344–359 (2001)
14. Liang, P., Tripp, O., Naik, M.: Learning minimal abstractions. In: Proceedings Symposium on Principles of Programming Languages (POPL), pp. 31–42 (2011)
15. Maréchal, A., Monniaux, D., Périn, M.: Scalable minimizing-operators on polyhedra via parametric linear programming. In: Ranzato, F. (ed.) SAS 2017. LNCS, vol. 10422, pp. 212–231. Springer, Cham (2017). https://doi.org/10.1007/978-3-319-66706-5_11
16. Maréchal, A., Périn, M.: Efficient elimination of redundancies in polyhedra by raytracing. In: Bouajjani, A., Monniaux, D. (eds.) VMCAI 2017. LNCS, vol. 10145, pp. 367–385. Springer, Cham (2017). https://doi.org/10.1007/978-3-319-52234-0_20

17. Mnih, V., Kavukcuoglu, K., Silver, D., Rusu, A.A., Veness, J., Bellemare, M.G., Graves, A., Riedmiller, M., Fidjeland, A.K., Ostrovski, G., Petersen, S., Beattie, C., Sadik, A., Antonoglou, I., King, H., Kumaran, D., Wierstra, D., Legg, S., Hassabis, D.: Human-level control through deep reinforcement learning. Nature **518**(7540), 529–533 (2015)
18. Oh, H., Lee, W., Heo, K., Yang, H., Yi, K.: Selective context-sensitivity guided by impact pre-analysis. In: Proceedings of Programming Language Design and Implementation (PLDI), pp. 475–484 (2014)
19. Oh, H., Yang, H., Yi, K.: Learning a strategy for adapting a program analysis via Bayesian optimisation. In: Proceedings of Object-Oriented Programming, Systems, Languages, and Applications (OOPSLA), pp. 572–588 (2015)
20. Singh, G., Püschel, M., Vechev, M.: Making numerical program analysis fast. In: Proceedings of Programming Language Design and Implementation (PLDI), pp. 303–313 (2015)
21. Singh, G., Püschel, M., Vechev, M.: Fast polyhedra abstract domain. In: Proceedings of Principles of Programming Languages (POPL), pp. 46–59 (2017)
22. Singh, G., Püschel, M., Vechev, M.: A practical construction for decomposing numerical abstract domains. Proc. ACM Program. Lang. **2**(POPL), 55:1–55:28 (2017)
23. Stoer, M., Wagner, F.: A simple min-cut algorithm. J. ACM **44**(4), 585–591 (1997)
24. Sutton, R.S., Barto, A.G.: Introduction to Reinforcement Learning, 1st edn. MIT Press, Cambridge (1998)
25. Watkins, C.J.C.H., Dayan, P.: Q-learning. Mach. Learn. **8**(3), 279–292 (1992)

A Direct Encoding for NNC Polyhedra

Anna Becchi and Enea Zaffanella(✉)

Department of Mathematical, Physical and Computer Sciences,
University of Parma, Parma, Italy
anna.becchi@studenti.unipr.it, enea.zaffanella@unipr.it

Abstract. We present an alternative Double Description representation for the domain of NNC (not necessarily closed) polyhedra, together with the corresponding Chernikova-like conversion procedure. The representation uses no slack variable at all and provides a solution to a few technical issues caused by the encoding of an NNC polyhedron as a closed polyhedron in a higher dimension space. A preliminary experimental evaluation shows that the new conversion algorithm is able to achieve significant efficiency improvements.

1 Introduction

The Double Description (DD) method [28] allows for the representation and manipulation of convex polyhedra by using two different geometric representations: one based on a finite collection of *constraints*, the other based on a finite collection of *generators*. Starting from any one of these representations, the other can be derived by application of a conversion procedure [10–12], thereby obtaining a DD pair. The procedure is incremental, capitalizing on the work already done when new constraints and/or generators need to be added to an input DD pair.

The DD method lies at the foundation of many software libraries and tools[1] which are used, either directly or indirectly, in research fields as diverse as bioinformatics [31,32], computational geometry [1,2], analysis of analog and hybrid systems [8,18,22,23], automatic parallelization [6,29], scheduling [16], static analysis of software [4,13,15,17,21,24].

In the classical setting, the DD method is meant to compute geometric representations for *topologically closed* polyhedra in an n-dimensional vector space. However, there are applications requiring the ability to also deal with linear *strict* inequality constraints, leading to the definition of *not necessarily closed* (NNC) polyhedra. For example, this is the case for some of the analysis tools developed for the verification of hybrid systems [8,18,22,23], static analysis tools such as Pagai [24], and tools for the automatic discovery of ranking functions [13].

The few DD method implementations providing support for NNC polyhedra (Apron and PPL) are all based on an *indirect* representation. The approach, proposed in [22,23] and studied in more detail in [3,5], encodes the strict inequality

[1] An incomplete list of available implementations includes cdd [19], PolyLib [27], Apron [25], PPL [4], 4ti2 [1], Skeleton [33], Addibit [20], ELINA [30].

H. Chockler and G. Weissenbacher (Eds.): CAV 2018, LNCS 10981, pp. 230–248, 2018.
https://doi.org/10.1007/978-3-319-96145-3_13

constraints by means of an additional space dimension, playing the role of a *slack variable*; the new space dimension, usually denoted as ϵ, needs to be non-negative and bounded from above, i.e., the constraints $0 \leq \epsilon \leq 1$ are added to the topologically closed representation $\mathcal{R}$ (called ϵ-representation) of the NNC polyhedron $\mathcal{P}$. The main advantage of this approach is the possibility of reusing, almost unchanged, all of the well-studied algorithms and optimizations that have been developed for the classical case of closed polyhedra. However, the addition of a slack variable carries with itself a few technical issues.

- At the implementation level, more work is needed to make the ϵ dimension *transparent* to the end user.
- The ϵ-representation causes an *intrinsic overhead*: in any generator system for an ϵ-polyhedron, most of the "proper" points (those having a positive ϵ coordinate) need to be paired with the corresponding "closure" point (having a zero ϵ coordinate), almost doubling the number of generators.
- The DD pair in minimal form computed for an ϵ-representation $\mathcal{R}$, when reinterpreted as encoding the NNC polyhedron $\mathcal{P}$, typically includes many redundant constraints and/or generators, leading to inefficiencies. To avoid this problem, *strong minimization procedures* were defined in [3,5] that are able to detect and remove those redundancies. Even though effective, these procedures are not fully integrated into the DD conversion: they can only be applied *after* the conversion, since they interfere with incrementality. Hence, during the iterations of the conversion the ϵ-redundancies are not removed, causing the computation of bigger intermediate results.

In this paper, we pursue a different approach for the handling of NNC polyhedra in the DD method. Namely, we specify a *direct* representation, dispensing with the need of the slack variable. The main insight of this new approach is the separation of the (constraints or generators) geometric representation into two components, the skeleton and the non-skeleton of the representation, playing quite different roles: while keeping a geometric encoding for the skeleton component, we will adopt a combinatorial encoding for the non-skeleton one. For this new representation, we propose the corresponding variant of the Chernikova's conversion procedure, where both components are handled by respective processing phases, so as to take advantage of their peculiarities. In particular, we develop *ad hoc* functions and procedures for the combinatorial non-skeleton part.

The new representation and conversion procedure, in principle, can be integrated into any of the available implementations of the DD method. Our experimental evaluation is conducted in the context of the PPL and shows that the new algorithm, while computing the correct results for all of the considered tests, achieves impressive efficiency improvements with respect to the implementation based on the slack variable.

The paper is structured as follows. Section 2 briefly introduces the required notation, terminology and background concepts. Section 3 proposes the new representation for NNC polyhedra; the proofs of the stated results are in [7]. The extension of the Chernikova's conversion algorithm to this new representation is presented in Sect. 4. Section 5 reports the results obtained by the experimental evaluation. We conclude in Sect. 6.

2 Preliminaries

We assume some familiarity with the basic notions of lattice theory [9]. For a lattice $\langle L, \sqsubseteq, \bot, \top, \sqcap, \sqcup \rangle$, an element $a \in L$ is an *atom* if $\bot \sqsubset a$ and there exists no element $b \in L$ such that $\bot \sqsubset b \sqsubset a$. For $S \subseteq L$, the *upward closure* of S is defined as $\uparrow S \stackrel{\text{def}}{=} \{ x \in L \mid \exists s \in S \,.\, s \sqsubseteq x \}$. The set $S \subseteq L$ is *upward closed* if $S = \uparrow S$; we denote by $\wp_{\uparrow}(L)$ the set of all the upward closed subsets of L. For $x \in L$, $\uparrow x$ is a shorthand for $\uparrow\{x\}$. The notation for *downward closure* is similar. Given two posets $\langle L, \sqsubseteq \rangle$ and $\langle L^\sharp, \sqsubseteq^\sharp \rangle$ and two monotonic functions $\alpha \colon L \to L^\sharp$ and $\gamma \colon L^\sharp \to L$, the pair (α, γ) is a *Galois connection* [14] between L and $L^\sharp$ if $\forall x \in L, x^\sharp \in L^\sharp : \alpha(x) \sqsubseteq^\sharp x^\sharp \Leftrightarrow x \sqsubseteq \gamma(x^\sharp)$.

We write $\mathbb{R}^n$ to denote the Euclidean topological space of dimension $n > 0$ and $\mathbb{R}_+$ for the set of non-negative reals; for $S \subseteq \mathbb{R}^n$, $\mathrm{cl}(S)$ and $\mathrm{relint}(S)$ denote the topological closure and the relative interior of S, respectively. A topologically closed convex polyhedron (for short, closed polyhedron) is defined as the set of solutions of a finite system $\mathcal{C}$ of linear non-strict inequality and linear equality constraints; namely, $\mathcal{P} = \mathrm{con}(\mathcal{C})$ where

$$\mathrm{con}(\mathcal{C}) \stackrel{\text{def}}{=} \bigl\{ \boldsymbol{p} \in \mathbb{R}^n \bigm| \forall \beta = (\boldsymbol{a}^{\mathrm{T}} \boldsymbol{x} \bowtie b) \in \mathcal{C}, \bowtie \in \{\geq, =\} \,.\, \boldsymbol{a}^{\mathrm{T}} \boldsymbol{p} \bowtie b \bigr\}.$$

A vector $\boldsymbol{r} \in \mathbb{R}^n$ such that $\boldsymbol{r} \neq \boldsymbol{0}$ is a *ray* of a non-empty polyhedron $\mathcal{P} \subseteq \mathbb{R}^n$ if, $\forall \boldsymbol{p} \in \mathcal{P}$ and $\forall \rho \in \mathbb{R}_+$, it holds $\boldsymbol{p} + \rho \boldsymbol{r} \in \mathcal{P}$. The empty polyhedron has no rays. If both $\boldsymbol{r}$ and $-\boldsymbol{r}$ are rays of $\mathcal{P}$, then $\boldsymbol{r}$ is a *line* of $\mathcal{P}$. The set $\mathcal{P} \subseteq \mathbb{R}^n$ is a closed polyhedron if there exist finite sets $L, R, P \subseteq \mathbb{R}^n$ such that $\boldsymbol{0} \notin (L \cup R)$ and $\mathcal{P} = \mathrm{gen}\bigl(\langle L, R, P \rangle\bigr)$, where

$$\mathrm{gen}\bigl(\langle L, R, P \rangle\bigr) \stackrel{\text{def}}{=} \bigl\{ L\boldsymbol{\lambda} + R\boldsymbol{\rho} + P\boldsymbol{\pi} \in \mathbb{R}^n \bigm| \boldsymbol{\lambda} \in \mathbb{R}^\ell, \boldsymbol{\rho} \in \mathbb{R}^r_+, \boldsymbol{\pi} \in \mathbb{R}^p_+, \textstyle\sum_{i=1}^p \pi_i = 1 \bigr\}.$$

When $\mathcal{P} \neq \emptyset$, we say that $\mathcal{P}$ is described by the *generator system* $\mathcal{G} = \langle L, R, P \rangle$. In the following, we will abuse notation by adopting the usual set operator and relation symbols to denote the corresponding component-wise extensions on systems. For instance, for $\mathcal{G} = \langle L, R, P \rangle$ and $\mathcal{G}' = \langle L', R', P' \rangle$, we will write $\mathcal{G} \subseteq \mathcal{G}'$ to mean $L \subseteq L'$, $R \subseteq R'$ and $P \subseteq P'$.

The DD method due to Motzkin et al. [28] allows combining the constraints and the generators of a polyhedron $\mathcal{P}$ into a DD pair $(\mathcal{C}, \mathcal{G})$: a *conversion* procedure [10–12] is used to obtain each description starting from the other one, also removing the redundant elements. For presentation purposes, we focus on the conversion from constraints to generators; the opposite conversion works in the same way, using duality to switch the roles of constraints and generators. We do not describe lower level details such as the *homogenization* process, mapping the polyhedron into a polyhedral cone, or the *simplification* step, needed for computing DD pairs in minimal form.

The conversion procedure starts from a DD pair $(\mathcal{C}_0, \mathcal{G}_0)$ representing the whole vector space and adds, one at a time, the elements of the input constraint system $\mathcal{C} = \{\beta_0, \dots, \beta_m\}$, producing a sequence of DD pairs $\{(\mathcal{C}_k, \mathcal{G}_k)\}_{0 \leq k \leq m+1}$ representing the polyhedra

$$\mathbb{R}^n = \mathcal{P}_0 \xrightarrow{\beta_0} \dots \xrightarrow{\beta_{k-1}} \mathcal{P}_k \xrightarrow{\beta_k} \mathcal{P}_{k+1} \xrightarrow{\beta_{k+1}} \dots \xrightarrow{\beta_m} \mathcal{P}_{m+1} = \mathcal{P}.$$

At each iteration, when adding the constraint β_k to polyhedron $\mathcal{P}_k = \mathrm{gen}(\mathcal{G}_k)$, the generator system $\mathcal{G}_k$ is partitioned into the three components $\mathcal{G}_k^+$, $\mathcal{G}_k^0$, $\mathcal{G}_k^-$, according to the sign of the scalar products of the generators with β_k (those in $\mathcal{G}_k^0$ are the *saturators* of β_k); the new generator system for polyhedron $\mathcal{P}_{k+1}$ is computed as $\mathcal{G}_{k+1} \stackrel{\mathrm{def}}{=} \mathcal{G}_k^+ \cup \mathcal{G}_k^0 \cup \mathcal{G}_k^\star$, where $\mathcal{G}_k^\star = \mathrm{comb\_adj}_{\beta_k}(\mathcal{G}_k^+, \mathcal{G}_k^-)$ and

$$\mathrm{comb\_adj}_{\beta_k}(\mathcal{G}_k^+, \mathcal{G}_k^-) \stackrel{\mathrm{def}}{=} \{\, \mathrm{comb}_{\beta_k}(g^+, g^-) \mid g^+ \in \mathcal{G}_k^+, g^- \in \mathcal{G}_k^-, \mathrm{adj}_{\mathcal{P}_k}(g^+, g^-) \,\}.$$

Function 'comb_{β_k}' computes a linear combination of its arguments, yielding a generator that saturates the constraint β_k; predicate '$\mathrm{adj}_{\mathcal{P}_k}$' is used to select only those pairs of generators that are *adjacent* in $\mathcal{P}_k$.

The set $\mathbb{CP}_n$ of all closed polyhedra on the vector space $\mathbb{R}^n$, partially ordered by set inclusion, is a lattice $\langle \mathbb{CP}_n, \subseteq, \emptyset, \mathbb{R}^n, \cap, \uplus \rangle$, where the empty set and $\mathbb{R}^n$ are the bottom and top elements, the binary meet operator is set intersection and the binary join operator '$\uplus$' is the convex polyhedral hull. A constraint $\beta = (\boldsymbol{a}^{\mathrm{T}}\boldsymbol{x} \bowtie b)$ is said to be *valid* for $\mathcal{P} \in \mathbb{CP}_n$ if all the points in $\mathcal{P}$ satisfy β; for each such β, the subset $F = \{\, \boldsymbol{p} \in \mathcal{P} \mid \boldsymbol{a}^{\mathrm{T}}\boldsymbol{p} = b \,\}$ is a *face* of $\mathcal{P}$. We write $\mathit{cFaces}_{\mathcal{P}}$ (possibly omitting the subscript) to denote the finite set of faces of $\mathcal{P} \in \mathbb{CP}_n$. This is a meet sublattice of $\mathbb{CP}_n$ and $\mathcal{P} = \bigcup \{\, \mathrm{relint}(F) \mid F \in \mathit{cFaces}_{\mathcal{P}} \,\}$.

When $\mathcal{C}$ is extended to allow for *strict* inequalities, $\mathcal{P} = \mathrm{con}(\mathcal{C})$ is an NNC (not necessarily closed) polyhedron. The set $\mathbb{P}_n$ of all NNC polyhedra on $\mathbb{R}^n$ is a lattice $\langle \mathbb{P}_n, \subseteq, \emptyset, \mathbb{R}^n, \cap, \uplus \rangle$ and $\mathbb{CP}_n$ is a sublattice of $\mathbb{P}_n$. As shown in [3, Theorem 4.4], a description of an NNC polyhedron $\mathcal{P} \in \mathbb{P}_n$ can be obtained by extending the generator system with a finite set C of *closure points*. Namely, for $\mathcal{G} = \langle L, R, C, P \rangle$, we define $\mathcal{P} = \mathrm{gen}(\mathcal{G})$, where

$$\mathrm{gen}\bigl(\langle L, R, C, P \rangle\bigr) \stackrel{\mathrm{def}}{=} \left\{ L\boldsymbol{\lambda} + R\boldsymbol{\rho} + C\boldsymbol{\gamma} + P\boldsymbol{\pi} \in \mathbb{R}^n \;\middle|\; \begin{array}{l} \boldsymbol{\lambda} \in \mathbb{R}^\ell, \boldsymbol{\rho} \in \mathbb{R}_+^r, \\ \boldsymbol{\gamma} \in \mathbb{R}_+^c, \boldsymbol{\pi} \in \mathbb{R}_+^p, \boldsymbol{\pi} \neq \mathbf{0}, \\ \sum_{i=1}^c \gamma_i + \sum_{i=1}^p \pi_i = 1 \end{array} \right\}.$$

For an NNC polyhedron $\mathcal{P} \in \mathbb{P}_n$, the finite set $\mathit{nncFaces}_{\mathcal{P}}$ of its faces is a meet sublattice of $\mathbb{P}_n$ and $\mathcal{P} = \bigcup \{\, \mathrm{relint}(F) \mid F \in \mathit{nncFaces}_{\mathcal{P}} \,\}$. Letting $\mathcal{Q} = \mathrm{cl}(\mathcal{P})$, the closure operator $\mathrm{cl} \colon \mathit{nncFaces}_{\mathcal{P}} \to \mathit{cFaces}_{\mathcal{Q}}$ maps each NNC face of $\mathcal{P}$ into a face of $\mathcal{Q}$. The image $\mathrm{cl}(\mathit{nncFaces}_{\mathcal{P}})$ is a join sublattice of $\mathit{cFaces}_{\mathcal{Q}}$ and its nonempty elements form an *upward closed subset*, which can be described by recording the minimal elements only (i.e., the atoms of the $\mathit{nncFaces}_{\mathcal{P}}$ lattice).

3 Direct Representations for NNC Polyhedra

An NNC polyhedron can be described by using an extended constraint system $\mathcal{C} = \langle C_=, C_\geq, C_> \rangle$ and/or an extended generator system $\mathcal{G} = \langle L, R, C, P \rangle$. These representations are said to be *geometric*, meaning that they provide a precise description of the position of their elements. For a closed polyhedron $\mathcal{P} \in \mathbb{CP}_n$, the use of completely geometric representations is an adequate choice. In the case of an NNC polyhedron $\mathcal{P} \in \mathbb{P}_n$ such a choice is questionable, since the precise geometric position of some of the elements is not really needed.

Example 1. Consider the NNC polyhedron $\mathcal{P} \in \mathbb{P}_2$ in the next figure, where the (strict) inequality constraints are denoted by (dashed) lines and the (closure) points are denoted by (unfilled) circles.

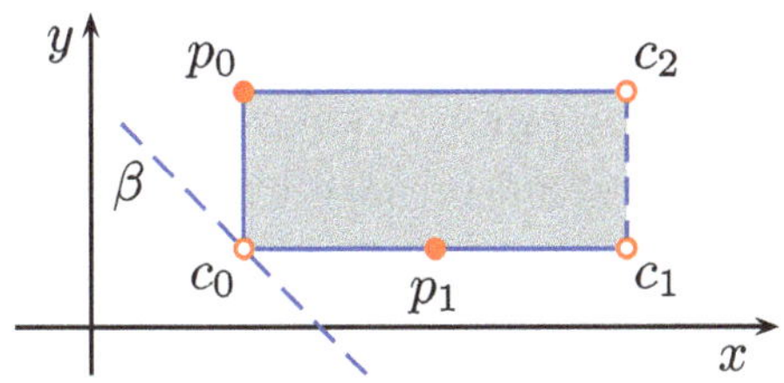

$\mathcal{P}$ is described by $\mathcal{G} = \langle L, R, C, P \rangle$, where $L = R = \emptyset$, $C = \{c_0, c_1, c_2\}$ and $P = \{p_0, p_1\}$. However, there is no need to know the position of point p_1, since it can be replaced by any other point on the open segment (c_0, c_1). Similarly, when considering the constraint representation, there is no need to know the exact slope of the strict inequality constraint β.

We now show that $\mathcal{P} \in \mathbb{P}_n$ can be more appropriately represented by integrating a geometric description of $\mathcal{Q} = \mathrm{cl}(\mathcal{P}) \in \mathbb{CP}_n$ (the *skeleton*) with a combinatorial description of $nncFaces_{\mathcal{P}}$ (the *non-skeleton*). We consider here the generator system representation; the extension to constraints will be briefly outlined in a later section.

Definition 1 (Skeleton of a generator system). *Let $\mathcal{G} = \langle L, R, C, P \rangle$ be a generator system in minimal form, $\mathcal{P} = \mathrm{gen}(\mathcal{G})$ and $\mathcal{Q} = \mathrm{cl}(\mathcal{P})$. The* skeleton *of $\mathcal{G}$ is $\mathcal{SK}_{\mathcal{Q}} = \mathrm{skel}(\mathcal{G}) \stackrel{\mathrm{def}}{=} \langle L, R, C \cup SP, \emptyset \rangle$, where $SP \subseteq P$ holds the points that can not be obtained by combining the other generators in $\mathcal{G}$.*

Note that the skeleton has no points at all, so that $\mathrm{gen}(\mathcal{SK}_{\mathcal{Q}}) = \emptyset$. However, we can define a variant function $\overline{\mathrm{gen}}\big(\langle L, R, C, P \rangle\big) \stackrel{\mathrm{def}}{=} \mathrm{gen}\big(\langle L, R, \emptyset, C \cup P \rangle\big)$, showing that the skeleton of an NNC polyhedron provides a non-redundant representation of its topological closure.

Proposition 1. *If $\mathcal{P} = \mathrm{gen}(\mathcal{G})$ and $\mathcal{Q} = \mathrm{cl}(\mathcal{P})$, then $\overline{\mathrm{gen}}(\mathcal{G}) = \overline{\mathrm{gen}}(\mathcal{SK}_{\mathcal{Q}}) = \mathcal{Q}$. Also, there does not exist $\mathcal{G}' \subset \mathcal{SK}_{\mathcal{Q}}$ such that $\overline{\mathrm{gen}}(\mathcal{G}') = \mathcal{Q}$.*

The elements of $SP \subseteq P$ are called *skeleton points*; the non-skeleton points in $P \setminus SP$ are redundant when representing the topological closure; these *non-skeleton points* are the elements in $\mathcal{G}$ that need not be represented geometrically.

Consider a point $\boldsymbol{p} \in \mathcal{Q} = \text{cl}(\mathcal{P})$ (not necessarily in P). There exists a single face $F \in cFaces_{\mathcal{Q}}$ such that $\boldsymbol{p} \in \text{relint}(F)$. By definition of function 'gen', point $\boldsymbol{p}$ behaves as a *filler* for $\text{relint}(F)$ meaning that, when combined with the skeleton, it generates $\text{relint}(F)$. Note that $\boldsymbol{p}$ also behaves as a filler for the relative interiors of all the faces in the set $\uparrow F$. The choice of $\boldsymbol{p} \in \text{relint}(F)$ is actually arbitrary: any other point of $\text{relint}(F)$ would be equivalent as a filler. A less arbitrary representation for $\text{relint}(F)$ is thus provided by its own skeleton $\mathcal{SK}_F \subseteq \mathcal{SK}_{\mathcal{Q}}$; we say that $\mathcal{SK}_F$ is the *support* for the points in $\text{relint}(F)$ and that any point $\boldsymbol{p}' \in \text{relint}\big(\overline{\text{gen}}(\mathcal{SK}_F)\big) = \text{relint}(F)$ is a *materialization* of $\mathcal{SK}_F$.

In the following we will sometimes omit subscripts when clear from context.

Definition 2 (Support sets for a skeleton). *Let $\mathcal{SK}$ be the skeleton of an NNC polyhedron and let $\mathcal{Q} = \overline{\text{gen}}(\mathcal{SK}) \in \mathbb{CP}_n$. The set of all supports for $\mathcal{SK}$ is defined as $\mathbb{NS}_{\mathcal{SK}} \stackrel{\text{def}}{=} \{\, \mathcal{SK}_F \subseteq \mathcal{SK} \mid F \in cFaces_{\mathcal{Q}} \,\}$.*

We now define functions mapping a subset of the (geometric) points of an NNC polyhedron into the set of supports filled by these points, and vice versa.

Definition 3 (Filled supports). *Let $\mathcal{SK}$ be the skeleton of the polyhedron $\mathcal{P} \in \mathbb{P}_n$, $\mathcal{Q} = \text{cl}(\mathcal{P})$ and $\mathbb{NS}$ be the corresponding set of supports. The abstraction function $\alpha_{\mathcal{SK}} \colon \wp(\mathcal{Q}) \to \wp_{\uparrow}(\mathbb{NS})$ is defined, for each $S \subseteq \mathcal{Q}$, as*

$$\alpha_{\mathcal{SK}}(S) \stackrel{\text{def}}{=} \bigcup \{\, \uparrow \mathcal{SK}_F \mid \exists \boldsymbol{p} \in S, F \in cFaces \,.\, \boldsymbol{p} \in \text{relint}(F) \,\}.$$

The concretization function $\gamma_{\mathcal{SK}} \colon \wp_{\uparrow}(\mathbb{NS}) \to \wp(\mathcal{Q})$, for each $NS \in \wp_{\uparrow}(\mathbb{NS})$, is defined as

$$\gamma_{\mathcal{SK}}(NS) \stackrel{\text{def}}{=} \bigcup \Big\{\, \text{relint}\big(\overline{\text{gen}}(ns)\big) \;\Big|\; ns \in NS \,\Big\}.$$

Proposition 2. *The pair of functions $(\alpha_{\mathcal{SK}}, \gamma_{\mathcal{SK}})$ is a Galois connection. If $\mathcal{P} = \text{gen}\big(\langle L, R, C, P\rangle\big) \in \mathbb{P}_n$ and $\mathcal{SK}$ is its skeleton, then $\mathcal{P} = (\gamma_{\mathcal{SK}} \circ \alpha_{\mathcal{SK}})(P)$.*

The non-skeleton component of a geometric generator system can be abstracted by '$\alpha_{\mathcal{SK}}$' and described as a combination of skeleton generators.

Definition 4 (Non-skeleton of a generator system). *Let $\mathcal{P} \in \mathbb{P}_n$ be defined by generator system $\mathcal{G} = \langle L, R, C, P\rangle$ and let $\mathcal{SK}$ be the corresponding skeleton component. The* non-skeleton *component of $\mathcal{G}$ is defined as $NS_{\mathcal{G}} \stackrel{\text{def}}{=} \alpha_{\mathcal{SK}}(P)$.*

Example 2. Consider the generator system $\mathcal{G}$ of polyhedron $\mathcal{P}$ from Example 1. Its skeleton is $\mathcal{SK} = \big\langle \emptyset, \emptyset, \{c_0, c_1, c_2, p_0\}, \emptyset \big\rangle$, so that p_1 is not a skeleton point. By Definition 3, $NS_{\mathcal{G}} = \alpha_{\mathcal{SK}}\big(\{p_0, p_1\}\big) = \uparrow\{p_0\} \cup \uparrow\{c_0, c_1\}$[2] The minimal elements in $NS_{\mathcal{G}}$ can be seen to describe the atoms of $nncFaces_{\mathcal{P}}$, i.e., the 0-dimension face $\{p_0\}$ and the 1-dimension open segment (c_0, c_1).

The new representation is semantically equivalent to the fully geometric one.

[2] Since there are no rays and no lines, we adopt a simplified notation, identifying each support with the set of its closure points. Also note that $\text{relint}(\{p_0\}) = \{p_0\}$.

Corollary 1. *For a polyhedron $\mathcal{P} = \text{gen}(\mathcal{G}) \in \mathbb{P}_n$, let $\langle \mathcal{SK}, \mathit{NS} \rangle$ be the skeleton and non-skeleton components for $\mathcal{G}$. Then $\mathcal{P} = \gamma_{\mathcal{SK}}(\mathit{NS})$.*

4 The New Conversion Algorithm

The CONVERSION function in Pseudocode 1 incrementally processes each of the input constraints $\beta \in \mathcal{C}_{in}$ keeping the generator system $\langle \mathcal{SK}, \mathit{NS} \rangle$ up-to-date. The distinction between the skeleton and non-skeleton allows for a corresponding separation in the conversion procedure. Moreover, a few minor adaptations to their representation, discussed below, allow for efficiency improvements.

First, observe that every support $ns \in \mathit{NS}$ always includes all of the lines in the L skeleton component; hence, these lines can be left *implicit* in the representation of the supports in NS. Note that, even after removing the lines, each $ns \in \mathit{NS}$ is still a non-empty set, since it includes at least one closure point.

When lines are implicit, those supports $ns \in \mathit{NS}$ that happen to be singletons[3] can be seen to play a special role: they correspond to the combinatorial encoding of the skeleton points in SP (see Definition 1). These points are not going to benefit from the combinatorial representation, hence we move them from the non-skeleton to the skeleton component; namely, $\mathcal{SK} = \langle L, R, C \cup \mathit{SP}, \emptyset \rangle$ is represented as $\mathcal{SK} = \langle L, R, C, \mathit{SP} \rangle$. The formalization presented in Sect. 3 is still valid, replacing '$\gamma_{\mathcal{SK}}$' with $\gamma'_{\mathcal{SK}}(\mathit{NS}) \stackrel{\text{def}}{=} \text{gen}(\mathcal{SK}) \cup \gamma_{\mathcal{SK}}(\mathit{NS})$.

At the implementation level, each support $ns \in \mathit{NS}$ can be encoded by using a *set of indices* on the data structure representing the skeleton component $\mathcal{SK}$. Since NS is a finite upward closed set, the representation only needs to record its minimal elements. A support $ns \in \mathit{NS}$ is *redundant in* $\langle \mathcal{SK}, \mathit{NS} \rangle$ if there exists $ns' \in \mathit{NS}$ such that $ns' \subset ns$ or if $ns \cap \mathit{SP} \neq \emptyset$, where $\mathcal{SK} = \langle L, R, C, \mathit{SP} \rangle$. We write $\mathit{NS}_1 \oplus \mathit{NS}_2$ to denote the non-redundant union of $\mathit{NS}_1, \mathit{NS}_2 \subseteq \mathbb{NS}_{\mathcal{SK}}$.

4.1 Processing the Skeleton

Line 3 of CONVERSION partitions the skeleton $\mathcal{SK}$ into $\mathcal{SK}^+$, $\mathcal{SK}^0$ and $\mathcal{SK}^-$, according to the signs of the scalar products with constraint β. Note that the partition information is *logically* computed (no copies are performed) and it is stored in the $\mathcal{SK}$ component itself; therefore, any update to $\mathcal{SK}^+$, $\mathcal{SK}^0$ and $\mathcal{SK}^-$ directly propagates to $\mathcal{SK}$. In line 7 the generators in $\mathcal{SK}^+$ and $\mathcal{SK}^-$ are combined to produce $\mathcal{SK}^\star$, which is merged into $\mathcal{SK}^0$. These steps are similar to the ones for closed polyhedra, except that we now have to consider more kinds of combinations: the systematic case analysis is presented in Table 1. For instance, when processing a non-strict inequality $\beta_\geq$, if we combine a closure point in $\mathcal{SK}^+$ with a ray in $\mathcal{SK}^-$ we obtain a closure point in $\mathcal{SK}^\star$ (row 3, column 6). Since it is restricted to work on the skeleton component, this combination phase can safely apply the adjacency tests to quickly get rid of redundant elements.

---

[3] By 'singleton' here we mean a system $ns = \langle \emptyset, \emptyset, \{\boldsymbol{p}\}, \emptyset \rangle$.

Pseudocode 1. Incremental conversion from constraints to generators.

```
    function CONVERSION(𝒞_in, ⟨𝒮𝒦, NS⟩)
2:      for all β ∈ 𝒞_in do
            skel_partition(β, 𝒮𝒦);
4:          nonskel_partition(⟨𝒮𝒦, NS⟩);
            if line l ∈ 𝒮𝒦⁺ ∪ 𝒮𝒦⁻ then VIOLATING-LINE(β, l, ⟨𝒮𝒦, NS⟩);
6:          else
                𝒮𝒦* ← comb_adj_β(𝒮𝒦⁺, 𝒮𝒦⁻); 𝒮𝒦⁰ ← 𝒮𝒦⁰ ∪ 𝒮𝒦*;
8:              NS* ← MOVE-NS(β, ⟨𝒮𝒦, NS⟩);
                NS* ← NS* ∪ CREATE-NS(β, ⟨𝒮𝒦, NS⟩);
10:             if is_equality(β) then ⟨𝒮𝒦, NS⟩ ← ⟨𝒮𝒦⁰, NS⁰ ⊕ NS*⟩;
                else if is_strict_ineq(β) then
12:                 𝒮𝒦⁰ ← points_become_closure_points(𝒮𝒦⁰);
                    ⟨𝒮𝒦, NS⟩ ← ⟨𝒮𝒦⁺ ∪ 𝒮𝒦⁰, NS⁺ ⊕ NS*⟩;
14:             else ⟨𝒮𝒦, NS⟩ ← ⟨𝒮𝒦⁺ ∪ 𝒮𝒦⁰, (NS⁺ ∪ NS⁰) ⊕ NS*⟩;
                PROMOTE-SINGLETONS(⟨𝒮𝒦, NS⟩);
16:     return ⟨𝒮𝒦, NS⟩;
```

Table 1. Case analysis for function 'comb$_\beta$' when adding an equality ($\beta_=$), a non-strict ($\beta_\geq$) or a strict ($\beta_>$) inequality constraint to a pair of generators from $\mathcal{SK}^+$ and $\mathcal{SK}^-$ (R = ray, C = closure point, SP = skeleton point).

	$\mathcal{SK}^+$	R	R	R	C	C	C	SP	SP	SP
	$\mathcal{SK}^-$	R	C	SP	R	C	SP	R	C	SP
$\beta_=$ or $\beta_\geq$	$\mathcal{SK}^\star$	R	C	SP	C	C	SP	SP	SP	SP
$\beta_>$	$\mathcal{SK}^\star$	R	C	C	C	C	C	C	C	C

4.2 Processing the Non-skeleton

Line 4 partitions the supports in NS by exploiting the partition information for the skeleton $\mathcal{SK}$, so that no additional scalar product is computed. Namely, each support $ns \in \mathit{NS}$ is classified as follows:

$$
\begin{aligned}
ns \in \mathit{NS}^+ &\iff ns \subseteq (\mathcal{SK}^+ \cup \mathcal{SK}^0) \wedge ns \cap \mathcal{SK}^+ \neq \emptyset;\\
ns \in \mathit{NS}^0 &\iff ns \subseteq \mathcal{SK}^0;\\
ns \in \mathit{NS}^- &\iff ns \subseteq (\mathcal{SK}^- \cup \mathcal{SK}^0) \wedge ns \cap \mathcal{SK}^- \neq \emptyset;\\
ns \in \mathit{NS}^\pm &\iff ns \cap \mathcal{SK}^+ \neq \emptyset \wedge ns \cap \mathcal{SK}^- \neq \emptyset.
\end{aligned}
$$

This partitioning is consistent with the previous one. For instance, if $ns \in \mathit{NS}^+$, then for every possible materialization $\boldsymbol{p} \in \mathrm{relint}(\overline{\mathrm{gen}}(ns))$ the scalar product of $\boldsymbol{p}$ and β is strictly positive. The supports in $\mathit{NS}^\pm$ are those whose materializations can satisfy, saturate and violate the constraint β (i.e., the corresponding face *crosses* the constraint hyperplane).

In lines 8 and 9, we find the calls to the two main functions processing the non-skeleton component. A set $NS^{\star}$ of new supports is built as the union of the contributes provided by functions MOVE-NS and CREATE-NS.

Moving Supports. The MOVE-NS function, shown in Pseudocode 2, processes the supports in $NS^{\pm}$: this function "moves" the fillers of the faces that are crossed by the new constraint, making sure they lie on the correct side.

Let $ns \in NS^{\pm}$ and $F = \mathrm{relint}(\overline{\mathrm{gen}}(ns))$. Note that $ns = \mathcal{SK}_F$ *before* the addition of the new constraint β; at this point, the elements in $\mathcal{SK}^{\star}$ have been added to $\mathcal{SK}^0$, but this change still has to be propagated to the non-skeleton component NS. Therefore, we compute the *support closure* 'supp.cl$_{\mathcal{SK}}(ns)$' according to the updated skeleton $\mathcal{SK}$. Intuitively, $\mathrm{supp.cl}_{\mathcal{SK}}(ns) \subseteq \mathcal{SK}$ is the subset of all the skeleton elements that are included in face F.

At the implementation level, support closures can be efficiently computed by exploiting the same *saturation information* used for the adjacency tests. Namely, for constraints $\mathcal{C}$ and generators $\mathcal{G}$, we can define

$$\mathrm{sat.inter}_{\mathcal{C}}(\mathcal{G}) \stackrel{\mathrm{def}}{=} \{\, \beta' \in \mathcal{C} \mid \forall g \in \mathcal{G} : g \text{ saturates } \beta' \,\},$$

$$\mathrm{sat.inter}_{\mathcal{G}}(\mathcal{C}) \stackrel{\mathrm{def}}{=} \{\, g \in \mathcal{G} \mid \forall \beta' \in \mathcal{C} : g \text{ saturates } \beta' \,\}.$$

Then, if $\mathcal{C}$ and $\mathcal{SK} = \langle L, R, C, SP \rangle$ are the constraint system and the skeleton generator system for the polyhedron, for each $ns \in NS$ we can compute [26]:

$$\mathrm{supp.cl}_{\mathcal{SK}}(ns) \stackrel{\mathrm{def}}{=} \mathrm{sat.inter}_{\mathcal{SK}}\big(\mathrm{sat.inter}_{\mathcal{C}}(ns)\big) \setminus L.$$

Face F is split by constraint β into F^+, F^0 and F^-. When β is a strict inequality, only F^+ shall be kept in the polyhedron; when the new constraint is a non-strict inequality, both F^+ and F^0 shall be kept. A minimal non-skeleton representation for these subsets can be obtained by *projecting* the support:

$$\mathrm{proj}^{\beta}_{\mathcal{SK}}(ns) \stackrel{\mathrm{def}}{=} \begin{cases} ns \setminus \mathcal{SK}^-, & \text{if } \beta \text{ is a strict inequality;} \\ ns \cap \mathcal{SK}^0, & \text{otherwise.} \end{cases}$$

To summarize, by composing support closure and projection in line 3 of MOVE-NS, each support in $NS^{\pm}$ is moved to the correct side of β.

Example 3. Consider $\mathcal{P} \in \mathbb{P}_2$ in the left hand side of the next figure.

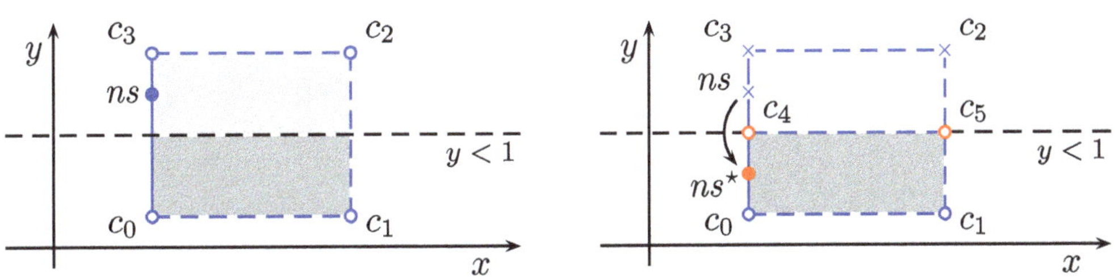

The skeleton $\mathcal{SK} = \langle \emptyset, \emptyset, C, \emptyset \rangle$ contains the closure points in $C = \{c_0, c_1, c_2, c_3\}$; the non-skeleton $NS = \{ns\}$ contains a single support $ns = \{c_0, c_3\}$, which makes sure that the open segment (c_0, c_3) is included in $\mathcal{P}$; the figure shows a single materialization for ns.

When processing $\beta = (y < 1)$, we obtain the polyhedron in the right hand side of the figure. In the skeleton phase of the CONVERSION function the adjacent skeleton generators are combined: c_4 (from $c_0 \in \mathcal{SK}^+$ and $c_3 \in \mathcal{SK}^-$) and c_5 (from $c_1 \in \mathcal{SK}^+$ and $c_2 \in \mathcal{SK}^-$) are added to $\mathcal{SK}^0$. Since the non-skeleton support ns belongs to $NS^{\pm}$, it is processed in the MOVE-NS function:

$$ns^* = \mathrm{proj}^{\beta}_{\mathcal{SK}}(\mathrm{supp.cl}_{\mathcal{SK}}(ns)) = \mathrm{proj}^{\beta}_{\mathcal{SK}}(\{c_0, c_3, c_4\}) = \{c_0, c_4\}.$$

In contrast, if we were processing the non-strict inequality $\beta' = (y \leq 1)$, we would have obtained $ns' = \mathrm{proj}^{\beta'}_{\mathcal{SK}}(\mathrm{supp.cl}_{\mathcal{SK}}(ns)) = \{c_4\}$. Since ns' is a singleton, it is upgraded to become a skeleton point by procedure PROMOTE-SINGLETONS. Hence, in this case the new skeleton is $\mathcal{SK} = \langle \emptyset, \emptyset, C, SP \rangle$, where $C = \{c_0, c_1, c_5\}$ and $SP = \{c_4\}$, while the non-skeleton component is empty.

Creating New Supports. Consider the case of a support $ns \in NS^-$ violating a non-strict inequality constraint β: this support has to be removed from NS. However, the upward closed set NS is represented by its minimal elements only so that, by removing ns, we are also implicitly removing other supports from the set $\uparrow ns$, including some that do not belong to NS^- and hence should be kept. Therefore, we have to explore the set of faces and detect those that are going to lose their filler: their minimal supports will be added to $NS^{\star}$. Similarly, when processing a non-strict inequality constraint, we need to consider the new faces introduced by the constraint: the corresponding supports can be found by projecting on the constraint hyperplane those faces that are possibly filled by an element in SP^+ or NS^+.

This is the task of the CREATE-NS function, shown in Pseudocode 2. It uses ENUMERATE-FACES as a helper:[4] the latter provides an enumeration of all the (higher dimensional) faces that contain the initial support ns. The new faces are obtained by adding to ns a new generator g and then composing the support closure and projection functions, as done in MOVE-NS. For efficiency purposes, a case analysis is performed so as to restrict the search area of the enumeration phase, by considering only the faces crossing the constraint.

Example 4. Consider $\mathcal{P} \in \mathbb{P}_2$ in the left hand side of the next figure, described by skeleton $\mathcal{SK} = \langle \emptyset, \emptyset, \{c_0, c_1, c_2\}, \{p\} \rangle$ and non-skeleton $NS = \emptyset$.

[4] This enumeration phase is inspired by the algorithm in [26].

Pseudocode 2. Helper functions for moving and creating supports.

function MOVE-NS(β, $\langle \mathcal{SK}, \mathcal{NS} \rangle$)
  $\mathcal{NS}^\star \leftarrow \emptyset$;
  for all $ns \in \mathcal{NS}^\pm$ **do** $\mathcal{NS}^\star \leftarrow \mathcal{NS}^\star \cup \{\mathrm{proj}^\beta_{\mathcal{SK}}(\mathrm{supp.cl}_{\mathcal{SK}}(ns))\}$;
  return $\mathcal{NS}^\star$;
function CREATE-NS(β, $\langle \mathcal{SK}, \mathcal{NS} \rangle$)
  $\mathcal{NS}^\star \leftarrow \emptyset$;
  let $\mathcal{SK} = \langle L, R, C, SP \rangle$;
  for all $ns \in \mathcal{NS}^- \cup \{\{\boldsymbol{p}\} \mid \boldsymbol{p} \in SP^-\}$ **do**
    $\mathcal{NS}^\star \leftarrow \mathcal{NS}^\star \cup$ ENUMERATE-FACES(β, ns, $\mathcal{SK}^+$, $\mathcal{SK}$);
  if is_strict_ineq(β) **then**
    for all $ns \in \mathcal{NS}^0 \cup \{\{\boldsymbol{p}\} \mid \boldsymbol{p} \in SP^0\}$ **do**
      $\mathcal{NS}^\star \leftarrow \mathcal{NS}^\star \cup$ ENUMERATE-FACES(β, ns, $\mathcal{SK}^+$, $\mathcal{SK}$);
  else
    for all $ns \in \mathcal{NS}^+ \cup \{\{\boldsymbol{p}\} \mid \boldsymbol{p} \in SP^+\}$ **do**
      $\mathcal{NS}^\star \leftarrow \mathcal{NS}^\star \cup$ ENUMERATE-FACES(β, ns, $\mathcal{SK}^-$, $\mathcal{SK}$);
  return $\mathcal{NS}^\star$;
function ENUMERATE-FACES(β, ns, $\mathcal{SK}'$, $\mathcal{SK}$)
  $\mathcal{NS}^\star \leftarrow \emptyset$; let $\mathcal{SK}' = \langle L', R', C', SP' \rangle$;
  for all $g \in (R' \cup C')$ **do** $\mathcal{NS}^\star \leftarrow \mathcal{NS}^\star \cup \{\mathrm{proj}^\beta_{\mathcal{SK}}(\mathrm{supp.cl}_{\mathcal{SK}}(ns \cup \{g\}))\}$;
  return $\mathcal{NS}^\star$;
procedure PROMOTE-SINGLETONS($\langle \mathcal{SK}, \mathcal{NS} \rangle$)
  let $\mathcal{SK} = \langle L, R, C, SP \rangle$;
  for all $ns \in \mathcal{NS}$ such that $ns = \langle \emptyset, \emptyset, \{\boldsymbol{c}\}, \emptyset \rangle$ **do**
    $\mathcal{NS} \leftarrow \mathcal{NS} \setminus \{ns\}$; $C \leftarrow C \setminus \{\boldsymbol{c}\}$; $SP \leftarrow SP \cup \{\boldsymbol{c}\}$;

Pseudocode 3. Processing a line violating constraint β.

procedure VIOLATING-LINE(β, $\boldsymbol{l}$, $\langle \mathcal{SK}, \mathcal{NS} \rangle$)
  split $\boldsymbol{l}$ into rays $\boldsymbol{r}^+$ satisfying β and $\boldsymbol{r}^-$ violating β;
  $\boldsymbol{l} \leftarrow \boldsymbol{r}^+$;
  for all $g \in \mathcal{SK}$ **do** $g \leftarrow \mathrm{comb}_\beta(g, \boldsymbol{l})$;
  if is_equality(β) **then** $\mathcal{SK} \leftarrow \mathcal{SK}^0$;
  if is_strict_ineq(β) **then** STRICT-ON-EQ-POINTS(β, $\langle \mathcal{SK}, \mathcal{NS} \rangle$);
procedure STRICT-ON-EQ-POINTS(β, $\langle \mathcal{SK}, \mathcal{NS} \rangle$)
  $\mathcal{NS}^\star \leftarrow \emptyset$; let $\mathcal{SK}^0 = \langle L^0, R^0, C^0, SP^0 \rangle$;
  for all $ns \in \mathcal{NS}^0 \cup \{\{\boldsymbol{p}\} \mid \boldsymbol{p} \in SP^0\}$ **do**
    $\mathcal{NS}^\star \leftarrow \mathcal{NS}^\star \cup$ ENUMERATE-FACES(β, ns, $\mathcal{SK}^+$, $\mathcal{SK}$);
  $\mathcal{SK}^0 \leftarrow$ points-become-closure-points($\mathcal{SK}^0$);
  $\langle \mathcal{SK}, \mathcal{NS} \rangle \leftarrow \langle \mathcal{SK}^+ \cup \mathcal{SK}^0, \mathcal{NS}^+ \oplus \mathcal{NS}^\star \rangle$;

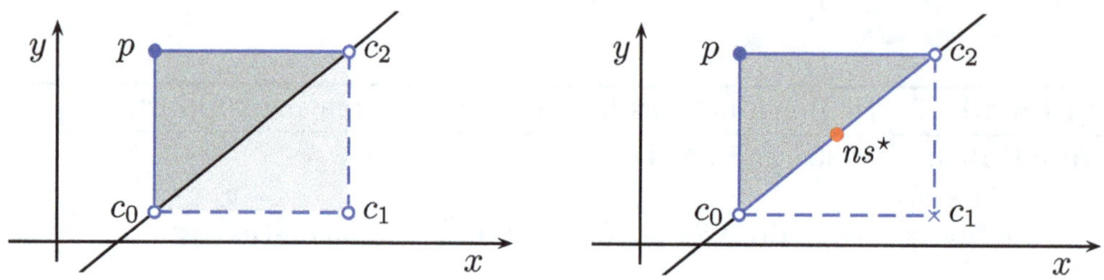

The partition for $\mathcal{SK}$ induced by the non-strict inequality is as follows:

$$\mathcal{SK}^+ = \langle \emptyset, \emptyset, \emptyset, \{p\} \rangle, \quad \mathcal{SK}^0 = \langle \emptyset, \emptyset, \{c_0, c_2\}, \emptyset \rangle, \quad \mathcal{SK}^- = \langle \emptyset, \emptyset, \{c_1\}, \emptyset \rangle.$$

There are no adjacent generators in $\mathcal{SK}^+$ and $\mathcal{SK}^-$, so that $\mathcal{SK}^\star$ is empty. When processing the non-skeleton component, the skeleton point in $\mathcal{SK}^+$ will be considered in line 15 of function CREATE-NS. The corresponding call to function ENUMERATE-FACES computes

$$ns^\star = \mathrm{proj}^{\beta}_{\mathcal{SK}}\big(\mathrm{supp.cl}_{\mathcal{SK}}(\{p\} \cup \{c_1\})\big) = \mathrm{proj}^{\beta}_{\mathcal{SK}}\big(\{c_0, c_1, c_2, p\}\big) = \{c_0, c_2\},$$

thereby producing the filler for the open segment (c_0, c_2). The resulting polyhedron, shown in the right hand side of the figure, is thus described by the skeleton $\mathcal{SK} = \langle \emptyset, \emptyset, \{c_0, c_2\}, \{p\} \rangle$ and the non-skeleton $\mathit{NS} = \{ns^\star\}$.

It is worth noting that, when handling Example 4 adopting an entirely geometric representation, closure point c_1 needs to be combined with point p even if the two generators are *not* adjacent: this leads to a significant efficiency penalty. Similarly, an implementation based on the ϵ-representation will have to combine closure point c_1 with point p (and/or with some other ϵ-redundant points), because the addition of the slack variable makes them adjacent. Therefore, an implementation based on the new approach obtains a twofold benefit: first, the distinction between skeleton and non-skeleton allows for restricting the handling of non-adjacent combinations to the non-skeleton phase; second, thanks to the combinatorial representation, the non-skeleton component can be processed by using set index operations only, i.e., computing no linear combination at all.

Preparing for Next Iteration. In lines 10 to 15 of CONVERSION the generator system is updated for the next iteration. The new supports in $\mathit{NS}^\star$ are merged (using '$\oplus$' to remove redundancies) into the appropriate portions of the non-skeleton component. In particular, when processing a strict inequality, in line 12 the helper function

$$\text{points\_become\_closure\_points}\big(\langle L, R, C, \mathit{SP} \rangle\big) \stackrel{\text{def}}{=} \langle L, R, C \cup \mathit{SP}, \emptyset \rangle$$

is applied to $\mathcal{SK}^0$, making sure that all of the skeleton points saturating β are transformed into closure points having the same position. The final processing step (line 15) calls helper procedure PROMOTE-SINGLETONS (see Pseudocode 2), making sure that all singleton supports get promoted to skeleton points.

Note that line 5 of CONVERSION, by calling procedure VIOLATING-LINE (see Pseudocode 3) handles the special case of a line violating β. This is just an optimization: the helper procedure STRICT-ON-EQ-POINTS can be seen as a tailored version of CREATE-NS, also including the final updating of $\mathcal{SK}$ and NS.

4.3 Duality

The definitions given in Sect. 3 for a geometric generator system have their dual versions working on a geometric *constraint* system. We provide a brief overview of these correspondences, which are summarized in Table 2.

Table 2. Correspondences between generator and constraint concepts.

	Generators	Constraints
Geometric skeleton		
singular	line	equality
non-singular	ray or closure point	non-strict inequality
semantics	$\mathrm{gen}(\mathcal{SK}) = \emptyset$	$\mathrm{con}(\mathcal{SK}) = \mathrm{cl}(\mathcal{P})$
Combinatorial non-skeleton		
abstracts	point	strict inequality
element role	face filler	face cutter
represents	upward closed set	downward closed set
encoding	minimal support	minimal support
singleton	skeleton point	skeleton strict inequality

For a non-empty $\mathcal{P} = \mathrm{con}(\mathcal{C}) \in \mathbb{P}_n$, the skeleton of $\mathcal{C} = \langle C_=, C_\geq, C_> \rangle$ includes the non-redundant constraints defining $\mathcal{Q} = \mathrm{cl}(\mathcal{P})$. Denoting by $SC_>$ the *skeleton strict inequalities* (i.e., those whose corresponding non-strict inequality is not redundant for $\mathcal{Q}$), we have $\mathcal{SK}_\mathcal{Q} \stackrel{\mathrm{def}}{=} \langle C_=, C_\geq \cup SC_>, \emptyset \rangle$, so that $\mathcal{Q} = \mathrm{con}(\mathcal{SK}_\mathcal{Q})$. The *ghost* faces of $\mathcal{P}$ are the faces of the closure $\mathcal{Q}$ that do not intersect $\mathcal{P}$: $\mathit{gFaces}_\mathcal{P} \stackrel{\mathrm{def}}{=} \{ F \in \mathit{cFaces}_\mathcal{Q} \mid F \cap \mathcal{P} = \emptyset \}$; thus, $\mathcal{P} = \mathrm{con}(\mathcal{SK}_\mathcal{Q}) \setminus \bigcup \mathit{gFaces}_\mathcal{P}$. The set $\mathit{gFaces}' \stackrel{\mathrm{def}}{=} \mathit{gFaces} \cup \{\mathcal{Q}\}$ is a meet sublattice of *cFaces*; also, *gFaces* is downward closed and can be represented by its *maximal* elements.

The skeleton support $\mathcal{SK}_F$ of a face $F \in \mathit{cFaces}_\mathcal{Q}$ is defined as the set of all the skeleton constraints that are saturated by all the points in F. Each face $F \in \mathit{gFaces}$ saturates a strict inequality $\beta_> \in C_>$: we can represent such a face using its skeleton support $\mathcal{SK}_F$ of which $\beta_>$ is a possible materialization. A constraint system non-skeleton component $\mathit{NS} \subseteq \mathbb{NS}$ is thus a combinatorial representation of the *strict inequalities* of the polyhedron.

Hence, the non-skeleton components for generators and constraints have a complementary role: in the case of generators they are face *fillers*, marking the minimal faces that are *included* in *nncFaces*; in the case of constraints they are face *cutters*, marking the maximal faces that are *excluded* from *nncFaces*. Note that the non-redundant cutters in *gFaces* are those having a *minimal* skeleton support, as is the case for the fillers.

As it happens with lines, all the equalities in $C_=$ are included in all the supports $\mathit{ns} \in \mathit{NS}$ so that, for efficiency, they are not represented explicitly.

After removing the equalities, a singleton $ns \in NS$ stands for a *skeleton strict inequality* constraint, which is better represented in the skeleton component, thereby obtaining $\mathcal{SK} = \langle C_{=}, C_{\geq}, SC_{>} \rangle$. Hence, a support $ns \in NS$ is redundant if there exists $ns' \in NS$ such that $ns' \subset ns$ or if $ns \cap SC_{>} \neq \emptyset$.

When the concepts underlying the skeleton and non-skeleton representation are reinterpreted as discussed above, it is possible to define a conversion procedure mapping a generator representation into a constraint representation which is very similar to the one from constraints to generators.

5 Experimental Evaluation

The new representation and conversion algorithms for NNC polyhedra have been implemented and tested in the context of the PPL (Parma Polyhedra Library). A full integration in the PPL domain of NNC polyhedra is not possible, since the latter assumes the presence of the slack variable ϵ. The approach, summarized by the diagram in Fig. 1, is to intercept each call to the PPL's conversion (working on ϵ-representations in $\mathbb{CP}_{n+1}$) and pair it with a corresponding call to the new algorithm (working on the new representations in $\mathbb{P}_n$).

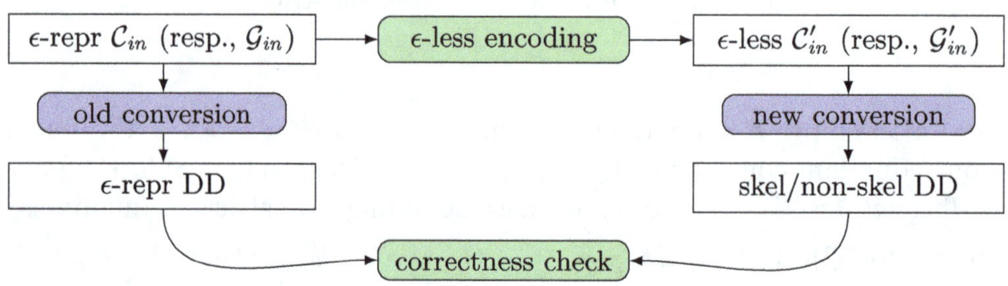

Fig. 1. High level diagram for the experimental evaluation (non-incremental case).

On the left hand side of the diagram we see the application of the standard PPL conversion procedure: the input ϵ-representation is processed by 'old conversion' so as to produce the output ϵ-representation DD pair. The 'ϵ-less encoding' phase produces a copy of the input without the slack variable; this is processed by 'new conversion' to produce the output DD pair, based on the new skeleton/non-skeleton representation. After the two conversions are completed, the outputs are checked for both semantic equivalence and non-redundancy. This final checking phase was successful on all the experiments performed, which include all of the tests in the PPL. In order to assess efficiency, additional code was added to measure the time spent inside the old and new conversion procedures, disregarding the input encoding and output checking phases. It is worth stressing that several experimental evaluations, including recent ones [2], confirm that the PPL is a state-of-the-art implementation of the DD method for a wide spectrum of application contexts.

The first experiment[5] on efficiency is meant to evaluate the *overhead* incurred by the new representation and algorithm for NNC polyhedra when processing topologically closed polyhedra, so as to compare it with the corresponding overhead incurred by the ϵ-representation. To this end, we considered the `ppl_lcdd` demo application of the PPL, which solves the *vertex/facet enumeration problem*. In Table 3 we report the results obtained on a selection of the test benchmarks[6] when using: the conversion algorithm for closed polyhedra (columns 2–3); the conversion algorithm for the ϵ-representation of NNC polyhedra (columns 4–5); and the new conversion algorithm for the new representation of NNC polyhedra (columns 6–7). Columns 'time' report the number of milliseconds spent; columns 'sat' report the number of saturation (i.e., bit vector) operations, in millions.

The results in Table 3 show that the use of the ϵ-representation for closed polyhedra incurs a significant overhead. In contrast, the new representation and algorithm go beyond all expectations: in almost all of the tests there is no overhead at all (that is, any overhead incurred is so small to be masked by the improvements obtained in other parts of the algorithm).

Table 3. Overhead of conversion for C polyhedra. Units: time (ms), sat (M).

test	closed poly		ϵ-repr		$\langle \mathcal{SK}, \mathcal{NS} \rangle$	
	time	sat	time	sat	time	sat
cp6.ext	21	1.1	47	5.3	13	1.1
cross12.ine	157	17.1	215	18.1	180	17.2
in7.ine	47	1.7	149	6.1	27	0.9
kkd38_6.ine	498	28.3	1870	113.2	218	14.2
kq20_11_m.ine	42	1.7	153	6.1	27	0.9
metric80_16.ine	39	2.3	76	5.4	25	2.0
mit31-20.ine	1109	88.7	35629	702.2	816	60.1
mp6.ine	86	6.4	215	17.9	72	8.0
reg600-5_m.ext	906	24.7	3062	119.1	723	14.0
sampleh8.ine	5916	307.4	42339	1420.7	3309	154.1
trunc10.ine	1274	91.7	5212	396.6	803	89.9

The second experiment is meant to evaluate the efficiency gains obtained in a more appropriate context, i.e., when processing polyhedra that are *not* topologically closed. To this end, we consider the same benchmark discussed in [3, Table 2],[7] which highlights the efficiency improvement resulting from the adoption of an *enhanced* evaluation strategy (where a knowledgeable user of the

[5] All experiments have been performed on a laptop with an Intel Core i7-3632QM CPU, 16 GB of RAM and running GNU/Linux 4.13.0-25.

[6] We only show the tests where PPL time on closed polyhedra is above 20 ms.

[7] The test `dualhypercubes.cc` is distributed with the source code of the PPL.

library explicitly invokes, when appropriate, the strong minimization procedures for ϵ-representations) with respect to the *standard* evaluation strategy (where the user simply performs the required computation, leaving the burden of optimization to the library developers). In Table 4 we report the results obtained for the most expensive test among those described in [3, Table 2], comparing the standard and enhanced evaluation strategies for the ϵ-representation (rows 1 and 2) with the new algorithm (row 3). For each algorithm we show in column 2 the total number of iterations of the conversion procedures and, in the next two columns, the median and maximum sizes of the representations computed at each iteration (i.e., the size of the intermediate results); in columns from 5 to 8 we show the numbers of incremental and non-incremental calls to the conversion procedures, together with the corresponding time spent (in milliseconds); in column 9 we show the time spent in strong minimization of ϵ-representations; in the final column, we show the overall time ratio, computed with respect to the time spent by the new algorithm.

Table 4. Comparing ϵ-representation based (standard and enhanced) computations for NNC polyhedra with the new conversion procedures.

algorithm	# iter	iter sizes		full conv		incr conv		ϵ-min	time
		median	max	num	time	num	time	time	ratio
ϵ-repr standard	1142	3706	7259	4	11	3	30336	27	1460.9
ϵ-repr enhanced	525	109	1661	7	204	0	—	29	11.2
$\langle \mathcal{SK}, \mathcal{NS} \rangle$ standard	314	62	180	4	6	3	15	—	1.0

Even though adopting the standard computation strategy (requiring no clever guess by the end user), the new algorithm obtains impressive time improvements, outperforming not only the standard, but also the enhanced computation strategy for the ϵ-representation. The reason for the latter efficiency improvement is that the enhanced computation strategy, when invoking the strong minimization procedures, interferes with incrementality: the figures in Table 4 confirm that the new algorithm performs three of the seven required conversions in an incremental way, while in the enhanced case they are all non-incremental. Moreover, a comparison of the iteration counts and the sizes of the intermediate results provides further evidence that the new algorithm is able to maintain a non-redundant description even *during* the iterations of a conversion.

6 Conclusion

We have presented a new approach for the representation of NNC polyhedra in the Double Description framework, avoiding the use of slack variables and distinguishing between the skeleton component, encoded geometrically, and the non-skeleton component, provided with a combinatorial encoding. We have proposed and implemented a variant of the Chernikova conversion procedure achieving significant efficiency improvements with respect to a state-of-the-art implementation of the domain of NNC polyhedra, thereby providing a solution to all the issues affecting the ϵ-representation approach. As future work, we plan to develop a full implementation of the domain of NNC polyhedra based on this new representation. To this end, we will have to reconsider each semantic operator already implemented by the existing libraries (which are based on the addition of a slack variable), so as to propose, implement and experimentally evaluate a corresponding correct specification based on the new approach.

References

1. 4ti2 team: 4ti2—a software package for algebraic, geometric and combinatorial problems on linear spaces. www.4ti2.de
2. Assarf, B., Gawrilow, E., Herr, K., Joswig, M., Lorenz, B., Paffenholz, A., Rehn, T.: Computing convex hulls and counting integer points with polymake. Math. Program. Comput. **9**(1), 1–38 (2017)
3. Bagnara, R., Hill, P.M., Zaffanella, E.: Not necessarily closed convex polyhedra and the double description method. Form. Asp. Comput. **17**(2), 222–257 (2005)
4. Bagnara, R., Hill, P.M., Zaffanella, E.: Applications of polyhedral computations to the analysis and verification of hardware and software systems. Theor. Comput. Sci. **410**(46), 4672–4691 (2009)
5. Bagnara, R., Ricci, E., Zaffanella, E., Hill, P.M.: Possibly not closed convex polyhedra and the Parma polyhedra library. In: Hermenegildo, M.V., Puebla, G. (eds.) SAS 2002. LNCS, vol. 2477, pp. 213–229. Springer, Heidelberg (2002). https://doi.org/10.1007/3-540-45789-5_17
6. Bastoul, C.: Code generation in the polyhedral model is easier than you think. In: Proceedings of the 13th International Conference on Parallel Architectures and Compilation Techniques (PACT 2004), Antibes Juan-les-Pins, France, pp. 7–16. IEEE Computer Society (2004)
7. Becchi, A., Zaffanella, E.: A conversion procedure for NNC polyhedra. CoRR, abs/1711.09593 (2017)
8. Benerecetti, M., Faella, M., Minopoli, S.: Automatic synthesis of switching controllers for linear hybrid systems: safety control. Theor. Comput. Sci. **493**, 116–138 (2013)
9. Birkhoff, G.: Lattice Theory. 3rd edn. Volume XXV of Colloquium Publications. American Mathematical Society, Providence (1967)
10. Chernikova, N.V.: Algorithm for finding a general formula for the non-negative solutions of system of linear equations. U.S.S.R. Comput. Math. Math. Phys. **4**(4), 151–158 (1964)
11. Chernikova, N.V.: Algorithm for finding a general formula for the non-negative solutions of system of linear inequalities. U.S.S.R. Comput. Math. Math. Phys. **5**(2), 228–233 (1965)
12. Chernikova, N.V.: Algorithm for discovering the set of all solutions of a linear programming problem. U.S.S.R. Comput. Math. Math. Phys. **8**(6), 282–293 (1968)
13. Colón, M.A., Sipma, H.B.: Synthesis of linear ranking functions. In: Margaria, T., Yi, W. (eds.) TACAS 2001. LNCS, vol. 2031, pp. 67–81. Springer, Heidelberg (2001). https://doi.org/10.1007/3-540-45319-9_6

14. Cousot, P., Cousot, R.: Systematic design of program analysis frameworks. In: Proceedings of the Sixth Annual ACM Symposium on Principles of Programming Languages, San Antonio, TX, USA, pp. 269–282 (1979)
15. Cousot, P., Halbwachs, N.: Automatic discovery of linear restraints among variables of a program. In: Conference Record of the Fifth Annual ACM Symposium on Principles of Programming Languages, Tucson, Arizona, pp. 84–96 (1978)
16. Doose, D., Mammeri, Z.: Polyhedra-based approach for incremental validation of real-time systems. In: Yang, L.T., Amamiya, M., Liu, Z., Guo, M., Rammig, F.J. (eds.) EUC 2005. LNCS, vol. 3824, pp. 184–193. Springer, Heidelberg (2005). https://doi.org/10.1007/11596356_21
17. Ellenbogen, R.: Fully automatic verification of absence of errors via interprocedural integer analysis. Master's thesis, School of Computer Science, Tel-Aviv University, Tel-Aviv, Israel, December 2004
18. Frehse, G.: PHAVer: algorithmic verification of hybrid systems past HyTech. Softw. Tools Technol. Transf. **10**(3), 263–279 (2008)
19. Fukuda, K., Prodon, A.: Double description method revisited. In: Deza, M., Euler, R., Manoussakis, I. (eds.) CCS 1995. LNCS, vol. 1120, pp. 91–111. Springer, Heidelberg (1996). https://doi.org/10.1007/3-540-61576-8_77
20. Genov, B.: The Convex Hull Problem in Practice: Improving the Running Time of the Double Description Method. Ph.D. thesis, University of Bremen, Germany (2014)
21. Gopan, D.: Numeric Program Analysis Techniques with Applications to Array Analysis and Library Summarization. Ph.D. thesis, University of Wisconsin, Madison, Wisconsin, USA, August 2007
22. Halbwachs, N., Proy, Y.-E., Raymond, P.: Verification of linear hybrid systems by means of convex approximations. In: Le Charlier, B. (ed.) SAS 1994. LNCS, vol. 864, pp. 223–237. Springer, Heidelberg (1994). https://doi.org/10.1007/3-540-58485-4_43
23. Halbwachs, N., Proy, Y.-E., Roumanoff, P.: Verification of real-time systems using linear relation analysis. Form. Methods Syst. Des. **11**(2), 157–185 (1997)
24. Henry, J., Monniaux, D., Moy, M.: PAGAI: a path sensitive static analyser. Electr. Notes Theor. Comput. Sci. **289**, 15–25 (2012)
25. Jeannet, B., Miné, A.: APRON: a library of numerical abstract domains for static analysis. In: Bouajjani, A., Maler, O. (eds.) CAV 2009. LNCS, vol. 5643, pp. 661–667. Springer, Heidelberg (2009). https://doi.org/10.1007/978-3-642-02658-4_52
26. Kaibel, V., Pfetsch, M.E.: Computing the face lattice of a polytope from its vertex-facet incidences. Comput. Geom. **23**(3), 281–290 (2002)
27. Loechner, V.: PolyLib: a library for manipulating parameterized polyhedra (1999). http://icps.u-strasbg.fr/PolyLib/
28. Motzkin, T.S., Raiffa, H., Thompson, G.L., Thrall, R.M.: The double description method. In: Contributions to the Theory of Games - Volume II, number 28 in Annals of Mathematics Studies, pp. 51–73. Princeton University Press, Princeton (1953)
29. Pop, S., Silber, G.-A., Cohen, A., Bastoul, C., Girbal, S., Vasilache, N.: GRAPHITE: Polyhedral analyses and optimizations for GCC. Technical Report A/378/CRI, Centre de Recherche en Informatique, École des Mines de Paris, Fontainebleau, France (2006)
30. Singh, G., Püschel, M., Vechev, M.T.: Fast polyhedra abstract domain. In: Proceedings of the 44th ACM SIGPLAN Symposium on Principles of Programming Languages, POPL 2017, Paris, France, pp. 46–59 (2017)

31. Terzer, M., Stelling, J.: Large-scale computation of elementary flux modes with bit pattern trees. Bioinformatics **24**(19), 2229–2235 (2008)
32. Terzer, M., Stelling, J.: Parallel extreme ray and pathway computation. In: Wyrzykowski, R., Dongarra, J., Karczewski, K., Wasniewski, J. (eds.) PPAM 2009. LNCS, vol. 6068, pp. 300–309. Springer, Heidelberg (2010). https://doi.org/10.1007/978-3-642-14403-5_32
33. Zolotykh, N.Y.: New modification of the double description method for constructing the skeleton of a polyhedral cone. Comput. Math. Math. Phys. **52**(1), 146–156 (2012)

Synthesis

What's Hard About Boolean Functional Synthesis?

S. Akshay(✉), Supratik Chakraborty, Shubham Goel, Sumith Kulal, and Shetal Shah

Indian Institute of Technology Bombay, Mumbai, India
akshayss@cse.iitb.ac.in

Abstract. Given a relational specification between Boolean inputs and outputs, the goal of Boolean functional synthesis is to synthesize each output as a function of the inputs such that the specification is met. In this paper, we first show that unless some hard conjectures in complexity theory are falsified, Boolean functional synthesis must generate large Skolem functions in the worst-case. Given this inherent hardness, what does one do to solve the problem? We present a two-phase algorithm, where the first phase is efficient both in terms of time and size of synthesized functions, and solves a large fraction of benchmarks. To explain this surprisingly good performance, we provide a sufficient condition under which the first phase must produce correct answers. When this condition fails, the second phase builds upon the result of the first phase, possibly requiring exponential time and generating exponential-sized functions in the worst-case. Detailed experimental evaluation shows our algorithm to perform better than other techniques for a large number of benchmarks.

Keywords: Skolem functions · Synthesis · SAT solvers
CEGAR based approach

1 Introduction

The algorithmic synthesis of Boolean functions satisfying relational specifications has long been of interest to logicians and computer scientists. Informally, given a Boolean relation between input and outupt variables denoting the specification, our goal is to synthesize each output as a function of the inputs such that the relational specification is satisfied. Such functions have also been called *Skolem functions* in the literature [23,29]. Boole [8] and Lowenheim [27] studied variants of this problem in the context of finding most general unifiers. While these studies are theoretically elegant, implementations of the underlying techniques have been found to scale poorly beyond small problem instances [28]. More recently, synthesis of Boolean functions has found important applications in a wide range of contexts including reactive strategy synthesis [4,19,40], certified QBF-SAT solving [7,21,31,34], automated program synthesis [35,37], circuit

H. Chockler and G. Weissenbacher (Eds.): CAV 2018, LNCS 10981, pp. 251–269, 2018.
https://doi.org/10.1007/978-3-319-96145-3_14

repair and debugging [22], disjunctive decomposition of symbolic transition relations [39] and the like. This has spurred recent interest in developing practically efficient Boolean function synthesis algorithms. The resulting new generation of tools [3,17,23,29,33,34,38] have enabled synthesis of Boolean functions from much larger and more complex relational specifications than those that could be handled by earlier techniques, viz. [20,21,28].

In this paper, we re-examine the Boolean functional synthesis problem from both theoretical and practical perspectives. Our investigation shows that unless some hard conjectures in complexity theory are falsified, Boolean functional synthesis must necessarily generate super-polynomial sized Skolem functions, thereby requiring super-polynomial time, in the worst-case. Therefore, it is unlikely that an efficient algorithm exists for solving all instances of Boolean functional synthesis. There are two ways to address this hardness in practice: (i) design algorithms that are provably efficient but may give "approximate" Skolem functions that are correct on only a fraction of all possible input assignments, or (ii) design a phased algorithm, wherein the initial phase(s) is/are provably efficient and solve a subset of problem instances, and subsequent phase(s) have worst-case exponential behaviour and solve all remaining problem instances. In this paper, we combine the two approaches while giving heavy emphasis on efficient instances. We also provide a sufficient condition for our algorithm to be efficient, which indeed is borne out by our experiments.

The primary contributions of this paper can be summarized as follows.

1. We start by showing that unless $\mathsf{P} = \mathsf{NP}$, there exist problem instances where Boolean functional synthesis must take super-polynomial time. Moreover, if the non-uniform exponential time hypothesis [14] holds, there exist problem instances where Boolean functional synthesis must generate exponential sized Skolem functions, thereby also requiring at least exponential time.
2. We present a new two-phase algorithm for Boolean functional synthesis.
   (a) Phase 1 of our algorithm generates candidate Skolem functions of size polynomial in the input specification. This phase makes polynomially many calls to an NP oracle (SAT solver in practice). Hence it directly benefits from the progess made by the SAT solving community, and is efficient in practice. Our experiments indicate that Phase 1 suffices to solve a large majority of publicly available benchmarks.
   (b) However, there are indeed cases where the first phase is not enough (our theoretical results imply that such cases likely exist). In such cases, the first phase provides good candidate Skolem functions as starting points for the second phase. Phase 2 of our algorithm starts from these candidate Skolem functions, and uses a CEGAR-based approach to produce correct Skolem functions whose size may indeed be exponential in the input specification.
3. We analyze the surprisingly good performance of the first phase (especially in light of the theoretical hardness results) and show a sufficient condition on the structure of the input representation that guarantees correctness of the first phase. Interestingly, popular representations like ROBDDs [11] give

rise to input structures that satisfy this condition. The goodness of Skolem functions generated in this phase of the algorithm can also be quantified with high confidence by invoking an approximate model counter [13], whose complexity lies in $\mathsf{BPP}^{\mathsf{NP}}$.

4. We conduct an extensive set of experiments over a variety of benchmarks, and show that our algorithm performs favourably vis-a-vis state-of-the-art algorithms for Boolean functional synthesis.

Related Work. The literature contains several early theoretical studies on variants of Boolean functional synthesis [6,8,9,16,27,30]. More recently, researchers have tried to build practically efficient synthesis tools that scale to medium or large problem instances. In [29], Skolem functions for $\mathbf{X}$ are extracted from a proof of validity of $\forall \mathbf{Y} \exists \mathbf{X} \, F(\mathbf{X}, \mathbf{Y})$. Unfortunately, this doesn't work when $\forall \mathbf{Y} \exists \mathbf{X} \, F(\mathbf{X}, \mathbf{Y})$ is not valid, despite this class of problems being important, as discussed in [3,17]. Inspired by the spectacular effectiveness of CDCL-based SAT solvers, an incremental determinization technique for Skolem function synthesis was proposed in [33]. In [20,39], a synthesis approach based on iterated compositions was proposed. Unfortunately, as has been noted in [17,23], this does not scale to large benchmarks. A recent work [17] adapts the composition-based approach to work with ROBDDs. For factored specifications, ideas from symbolic model checking using implicitly conjoined ROBDDs have been used to enhance the scalability of the technique further in [38]. In the genre of CEGAR-based techniques, [23] showed how CEGAR can be used to synthesize Skolem functions from factored specifications. Subsequently, a compositional and parallel technique for Skolem function synthesis from arbitrary specifications represented using AIGs was presented in [3]. The second phase of our algorithm builds on some of this work. In addition to the above techniques, template-based [37] or sketch-based [36] approaches have been found to be effective for synthesis when we have information about the set of candidate solutions. A framework for functional synthesis that reasons about some unbounded domains such as integer arithmetic, was proposed in [25].

2 Notations and Problem Statement

A Boolean formula $F(z_1, \ldots z_p)$ on p variables is a mapping $F : \{0,1\}^p \rightarrow \{0,1\}$. The set of variables $\{z_1, \ldots z_p\}$ is called the *support* of the formula, and denoted $\mathsf{sup}(F)$. A *literal* is either a variable or its complement. We use $F|_{z_i=0}$ (resp. $F|_{z_i=1}$) to denote the positive (resp. negative) cofactor of F with respect to z_i. A *satisfying assignment* or *model* of F is a mapping of variables in $\mathsf{sup}(F)$ to $\{0,1\}$ such that F evaluates to 1 under this assignment. If π is a model of F, we write $\pi \models F$ and use $\pi(z_i)$ to denote the value assigned to $z_i \in \mathsf{sup}(F)$ by π. Let $\mathbf{Z} = (z_{i_1}, z_{i_2}, \ldots z_{i_j})$ be a sequence of variables in $\mathsf{sup}(F)$. We use $\pi{\downarrow}\mathbf{Z}$ to denote the projection of π on $\mathbf{Z}$, i.e. the sequence $(\pi(z_{i_1}), \pi(z_{i_2}), \ldots \pi(z_{i_j}))$.

A Boolean formula is in *negation normal form (NNF)* if (i) the only operators used in the formula are conjunction ($\wedge$), disjunction ($\vee$) and negation ($\neg$), and (ii) negation is applied only to variables. Every Boolean formula can be converted to a semantically equivalent formula in NNF. We assume an NNF formula is represented by a rooted directed acyclic graph (DAG), where internal nodes are labeled by $\wedge$ and $\vee$, and leaves are labeled by literals. In this paper, we use AIGs [24] as the initial representation of specifications. Given an AIG with t nodes, an equivalent NNF formula of size $\mathcal{O}(t)$ can be constructed in $\mathcal{O}(t)$ time. We use $|F|$ to denote the number of nodes in a DAG representation of F.

Let α be the subformula represented by an internal node N (labeled by $\wedge$ or $\vee$) in a DAG representation of an NNF formula. We use $lits(\alpha)$ to denote the set of literals labeling leaves that have a path to the node N representing α in the DAG. A formula is said to be in *weak decomposable NNF*, or wDNNF, if it is in NNF and if for every $\wedge$-labeled node in the DAG, the following holds: let $\alpha = \alpha_1 \wedge \ldots \wedge \alpha_k$ be the subformula represented by the internal node. Then, there is no literal l and distinct indices $i, j \in \{1, \ldots k\}$ such that $l \in lits(\alpha_i)$ and $\neg l \in lits(\alpha_j)$. Note that wDNNF is a weaker structural requirement on the NNF representation vis-a-vis the well-studied DNNF representation, which has elegant properties [15]. Specifically, every DNNF formula is also a wDNNF formula.

We say a *literal* l is *pure* in F iff the NNF representation of F has a leaf labeled l, but no leaf labeled $\neg l$. F is said to be *positive unate* in $z_i \in \mathsf{sup}(F)$ iff $F|_{z_i=0} \Rightarrow F|_{z_i=1}$. Similarly, F is said to be *negative unate* in z_i iff $F|_{z_i=1} \Rightarrow F|_{z_i=0}$. Finally, F is *unate* in z_i if F is either positive unate or negative unate in z_i. A function that is not unate in $z_i \in \mathsf{sup}(F)$ is said to be *binate* in z_i.

We also use $\mathbf{X} = (x_1, \ldots x_n)$ to denote a sequence of Boolean outputs, and $\mathbf{Y} = (y_1, \ldots y_m)$ to denote a sequence of Boolean inputs. The *Boolean functional synthesis* problem, henceforth denoted BFnS, asks: given a Boolean formula $F(\mathbf{X}, \mathbf{Y})$ specifying a relation between inputs $\mathbf{Y} = (y_1, \ldots y_m)$ and outputs $\mathbf{X} = (x_1, \ldots x_n)$, determine functions $\mathbf{\Psi} = (\psi_1(\mathbf{Y}), \ldots \psi_n(\mathbf{Y}))$ such that $F(\mathbf{\Psi}, \mathbf{Y})$ holds whenever $\exists \mathbf{X} F(\mathbf{X}, \mathbf{Y})$ holds. Thus, $\forall \mathbf{Y} (\exists \mathbf{X}\, F(\mathbf{X}, \mathbf{Y})) \Leftrightarrow F(\psi, \mathbf{Y})$ must be rendered valid. The function ψ_i is called a *Skolem function* for x_i in F, and $\mathbf{\Psi} = (\psi_1, \ldots \psi_n)$ is called a *Skolem function vector* for $\mathbf{X}$ in F.

For $1 \le i \le j \le n$, let $\mathbf{X}_i^j$ denote the subsequence $(x_i, x_{i+1}, \ldots x_j)$ and let $F^{(i-1)}(\mathbf{X}_i^n, \mathbf{Y})$ denote $\exists \mathbf{X}_1^{i-1} F(\mathbf{X}_1^{i-1}, \mathbf{X}_i^n, \mathbf{Y})$. It has been argued in [3,17,20,23] that given a relational specification $F(\mathbf{X}, \mathbf{Y})$, the BFnS problem can be solved by first ordering the outputs, say as $x_1 \prec x_2 \cdots \prec x_n$, and then synthesizing a function $\psi_i(\mathbf{X}_{i+1}^n, \mathbf{Y})$ for each x_i such that $F^{(i-1)}(\psi_i, \mathbf{X}_{i+1}^n, \mathbf{Y}) \Leftrightarrow \exists x_i F^{(i-1)}(x_i, \mathbf{X}_{i+1}^n, \mathbf{Y})$. Once all such ψ_i are obtained, one can substitute ψ_{i+1} through ψ_n for x_{i+1} through x_n respectively, in ψ_i to obtain a Skolem function for x_i as a function of only $\mathbf{Y}$. We adopt this approach, and therefore focus on obtaining ψ_i in terms of $\mathbf{X}_{i+1}^n$ and $\mathbf{Y}$. Furthermore, we know from [20,23] that a function ψ_i is a Skolem function for x_i iff it satisfies $\Delta_i{}^F \Rightarrow \psi_i \Rightarrow \neg \Gamma_i{}^F$, where $\Delta_i{}^F \equiv \neg \exists \mathbf{X}_1^{i-1}\; F(\mathbf{X}_1^{i-1}, 0, \mathbf{X}_{i+1}^n, \mathbf{Y})$, and $\Gamma_i{}^F \equiv \neg \exists \mathbf{X}_1^{i-1} F(\mathbf{X}_1^{i-1}, 1, \mathbf{X}_{i+1}^n, \mathbf{Y})$. When F is clear from the context, we often omit it and write Δ_i and Γ_i. It is easy to see that both Δ_i and $\neg \Gamma_i$ serve as Skolem functions for x_i in F.

3 Complexity-Theoretical Limits

In this section, we investigate the computational complexity of BFnS. It is easy to see that BFnS can be solved in EXPTIME. Indeed a naive solution would be to enumerate all possible values of inputs $\mathbf{Y}$ and invoke a SAT solver to find values of $\mathbf{X}$ corresponding to each valuation of $\mathbf{Y}$ that makes $F(\mathbf{X}, \mathbf{Y})$ true. This requires worst-case time exponential in the number of inputs and outputs, and may produce an exponential-sized circuit. Given this, one can ask if we can develop a better algorithm that works faster and synthesizes "small" Skolem functions in all cases? Our first result shows that existence of such small Skolem functions would violate hard complexity-theoretic conjectures.

Theorem 1. *1. Unless* $\mathsf{P} = \mathsf{NP}$*, there exist problem instances where any algorithm for* BFnS *must take super-polynomial time*[1]*.*

2. Unless the non-uniform exponential-time hypothesis (or $\mathsf{ETH_{nu}}$) *fails, there exist problem instances where any algorithm for* BFnS *must generate Skolem functions of size exponential in the input size.*

A consequence of the second statement is that, under the same hypothesis, there must exist an instance of BFnS for which any algorithm must take EXPTIME time. The exponential-time hypothesis ETH and its strengthened version, the non-uniform exponential-time hypothesis $\mathsf{ETH_{nu}}$, are unproven computational hardness assumptions (see [14,18]), which have been used to show that several classical decision, functional and parametrized NP-complete problems (such as p-Clique) are unlikely to have sub-exponential algorithms. $\mathsf{ETH_{nu}}$ states that there is no family of algorithms (one for each family of inputs of size n) that can solve 3-SAT in subexponential time. In [14] it is shown that if $\mathsf{ETH_{nu}}$ holds, then *p-Clique, the parametrized clique problem,* cannot be solved in sub-exponential time, i.e., for all $d \in \mathbb{N}$, and sufficiently large fixed k, determining whether a graph G has a clique of size k is not in $\mathsf{DTIME}(n^d)$.

Proof. We describe a reduction from p-Clique to BFnS. Given an undirected graph $G = (V, E)$ on n-vertices and a number k (encoded in binary), we want to check if G has a clique of size k. We encode the graph as follows: each vertex $v \in V$ is identified by a unique number in $\{1, \ldots n\}$, and for every $(i, j) \in V \times V$, we introduce an input variable $y_{i,j}$ that is set to 1 iff $(i, j) \in E$. We call the resulting vector of input variables $\boldsymbol{y}$. We also have additional input variables $\boldsymbol{z} = z_1, \ldots z_m$, which represent the binary encoding of k ($m = \lceil \log_2 k \rceil$). Finally, we introduce output variables x_v for each $v \in V$, whose values determine which vertices are present in the clique. Let $\boldsymbol{x}$ denote the vector of x_v variables.

Given inputs $\mathbf{Y} = \{\boldsymbol{y}, \boldsymbol{z}\}$, and outputs $\mathbf{X} = \{\boldsymbol{x}\}$, our specification is represented by a circuit F over $\mathbf{X}, \mathbf{Y}$ that verifies whether the vertices encoded by $\mathbf{X}$ indeed form a k-clique of the graph G. The circuit F is constructed as follows:

[1] Since the submission of this paper, we have obtained a sharper complexity result. Details of this can be found in [2].

1. For every i, j such that $1 \leq i < j \leq n$, we construct a sub-circuit implementing $x_i \wedge x_j \Rightarrow y_{i,j}$. The outputs of all such subcircuits are conjoined to give an intermediate output, say $\mathsf{EdgesOK}$. Clearly, all the subcircuits taken together have size $\mathcal{O}(n^2)$.
2. We have a tree of binary adders implementing $x_1 + x_2 + \ldots x_n$. Let the $\lceil \log_2 n \rceil$-bit output of the adder be denoted $\mathsf{CliqueSz}$. The size of this adder is clearly $\mathcal{O}(n)$.
3. We have an equality checker that checks if $\mathsf{CliqueSz} = k$. Clearly, this sub-circuit has size $\lceil \log_2 n \rceil$. Let the output of this equality checker be called SizeOK.
4. The output of the specification circuit F is $\mathsf{EdgesOK} \wedge \mathsf{SizeOK}$.

Given an instance $\mathbf{Y} = \{\boldsymbol{y}, \boldsymbol{z}\}$ of p-Clique, we now consider the specification $F(\mathbf{X}, \mathbf{Y})$ as constructed above and feed it as input to any algorithm A for solving BFnS. Let $\boldsymbol{\Psi}$ be the Skolem function vector output by A. For each $i \in \{1, \ldots n\}$, we now feed ψ_i to the input y_i of the circuit F. This effectively constructs a circuit for $F(\boldsymbol{\Psi}, \mathbf{Y})$. It is easy to see from the definition of Skolem functions that for every valuation of $\mathbf{Y}$, the function $F(\boldsymbol{\Psi}, \mathbf{Y})$ evaluates to 1 iff the graph encoded by $\mathbf{Y}$ contains a clique of size k.

Using this reduction, we can complete the proofs of both our statements:

1. If the circuits for the Skolem functions $\boldsymbol{\Psi}$ are super-polynomial sized, then of course any algorithm generating $\boldsymbol{\Psi}$ must take super-polynomial time. On the other hand, if the circuits for the Skolem functions $\boldsymbol{\Psi}$ are always poly-sized, then $F(\boldsymbol{\Psi}, \mathbf{Y})$ is polynomial-sized, and evaluating it takes time that is polynomial in the input size. Thus, if A is a polynomial-time algorithm, we also get an algorithm for solving p-Clique in polynomial time, which implies that $\mathsf{P} = \mathsf{NP}$.
2. If the circuits for the Skolem functions $\boldsymbol{\Psi}$ are sub-exponential sized in the input n, then $F(\boldsymbol{\Psi}, \mathbf{Y})$ is also sub-exponential sized and can be evaluated in sub-exponential time. It then follows that we can solve any instance p-Clique of input length n in sub-exponential time – a violation of $\mathsf{ETH}_{\mathsf{nu}}$. Note that since our circuits can be different for different input lengths, we may have different algorithms for different n. Hence we have to appeal to the non-uniform variant of ETH. □

Theorem 1 implies that efficient algorithms for BFnS are unlikely. We therefore propose a two-phase algorithm to solve BFnS in practice. The first phase runs in polynomial time relative to an NP-oracle and generates polynomial-sized "approximate" Skolem functions. We show that under certain structural restrictions on the NNF representation of F, the first phase always returns exact Skolem functions. However, these structural restrictions may not always be met. An NP-oracle can be used to check if the functions computed by the first phase are indeed exact Skolem functions. In case they aren't, we proceed to the second phase of our algorithm that runs in worst-case exponential time. Below, we discuss the first phase in detail. The second phase is an adaptation of an existing CEGAR-based technique and is described briefly later.

4 Phase 1: Efficient Polynomial-Sized Synthesis

An easy consequence of the definition of unateness is the following.

Proposition 1. *If $F(\mathbf{X}, \mathbf{Y})$ is positive (resp. negative) unate in x_i, then $\psi_i = 1$ (resp. $\psi_i = 0$) is a correct Skolem function for x_i.*

All omitted proofs, including that of the above, may be found in [2]. The above result gives us a way to identify outputs x_i for which a Skolem function can be easily computed. Note that if x_i (resp. $\neg x_i$) is a pure literal in F, then F is positive (resp. negative) unate in x_i. However, the converse is not necessarily true. In general, a semantic check is necessary for unateness. In fact, it follows from the definition of unateness that F is positive (resp. negative) unate in x_i, iff the formula η_i^+ (resp. η_i^-) defined below is unsatisfiable.

$$\eta_i^+ = F(\mathbf{X}_1^{i-1}, 0, \mathbf{X}_{i+1}^n, \mathbf{Y}) \wedge \neg F(\mathbf{X}_1^{i-1}, 1, \mathbf{X}_{i+1}^n, \mathbf{Y}). \tag{1}$$

$$\eta_i^- = F(\mathbf{X}_1^{i-1}, 1, \mathbf{X}_{i+1}^n, \mathbf{Y}) \wedge \neg F(\mathbf{X}_1^{i-1}, 0, \mathbf{X}_{i+1}^n, \mathbf{Y}). \tag{2}$$

Note that each such check involves a single invocation of an NP-oracle, and a variant of this method is described in [5].

If F is binate in an output x_i, Proposition 1 doesn't help in synthesizing ψ_i. Towards synthesizing Skolem functions for such outputs, recall the definitions of Δ_i and Γ_i from Sect. 2. Clearly, if we can compute these functions, we can solve BFnS. While computing Δ_i and Γ_i *exactly* for all x_i is unlikely to be efficient in general (in light of Theorem 1), we show that polynomial-sized "good" approximations of Δ_i and Γ_i can be computed efficiently. As our experiments show, these approximations are good enough to solve BFnS for several benchmarks. Furthermore, with access to an NP-oracle, we can also check when these approximations are indeed good enough.

Given a relational specification $F(\mathbf{X}, \mathbf{Y})$, we use $\widehat{F}(\mathbf{X}, \overline{\mathbf{X}}, \mathbf{Y})$ to denote the formula obtained by first converting F to NNF, and then replacing every occurrence of $\neg x_i$ ($x_i \in \mathbf{X}$) in the NNF formula with a fresh variable $\overline{x_i}$. As an example, suppose $F(\mathbf{X}, \mathbf{Y}) = (x_1 \vee \neg(x_2 \vee y_1)) \vee \neg(x_2 \vee \neg(y_2 \wedge \neg y_1))$. Then $\widehat{F}(\mathbf{X}, \overline{\mathbf{X}}, \mathbf{Y}) = (x_1 \vee (\overline{x_2} \wedge \neg y_1)) \vee (\overline{x_2} \wedge y_2 \wedge \neg y_1)$. The following are easy to see.

Proposition 2. *(a) $\widehat{F}(\mathbf{X}, \overline{\mathbf{X}}, \mathbf{Y})$ is positive unate in both $\mathbf{X}$ and $\overline{\mathbf{X}}$.*
(b) Let $\neg\mathbf{X}$ denote $(\neg x_1, \ldots \neg x_n)$. Then $F(\mathbf{X}, \mathbf{Y}) \Leftrightarrow \widehat{F}(\mathbf{X}, \neg\mathbf{X}, \mathbf{Y})$.

For every $i \in \{1, \ldots n\}$, we can split $\mathbf{X} = (x_1, \ldots x_n)$ into two parts, $\mathbf{X}_1^i$ and $\mathbf{X}_{i+1}^n$, and represent $\widehat{F}(\mathbf{X}, \overline{\mathbf{X}}, \mathbf{Y})$ as $\widehat{F}(\mathbf{X}_1^i, \mathbf{X}_{i+1}^n, \overline{\mathbf{X}}_1^i, \overline{\mathbf{X}}_{i+1}^n, \mathbf{Y})$. We use these representations of $\widehat{F}$ interchangeably, depending on the context. For $b, c \in \{0, 1\}$, let $\mathbf{b}^i$ (resp. $\mathbf{c}^i$) denote a vector of i b's (resp. c's). For notational convenience, we use $\widehat{F}(\mathbf{b}^i, \mathbf{X}_{i+1}^n, \mathbf{c}^i, \overline{\mathbf{X}}_{i+1}^n, \mathbf{Y})$ to denote $\widehat{F}(\mathbf{X}_1^i, \mathbf{X}_{i+1}^n, \overline{\mathbf{X}}_1^i, \overline{\mathbf{X}}_{i+1}^n, \mathbf{Y})|_{\mathbf{X}_1^i=\mathbf{b}^i, \overline{\mathbf{X}}_1^i=\mathbf{c}^i}$ in the subsequent discussion. The following is an easy consequence of Proposition 2.

Proposition 3. *For every $i \in \{1, \ldots n\}$, the following holds:*
$\widehat{F}(\mathbf{0}^i, \mathbf{X}_{i+1}^n, \mathbf{0}^i, \neg\mathbf{X}_{i+1}^n, \mathbf{Y}) \Rightarrow \exists \mathbf{X}_1^i F(\mathbf{X}, \mathbf{Y}) \Rightarrow \widehat{F}(\mathbf{1}^i, \mathbf{X}_{i+1}^n, \mathbf{1}^i, \neg\mathbf{X}_{i+1}^n, \mathbf{Y})$

Proposition 3 allows us to bound Δ_i and Γ_i as follows.

Lemma 1. *For every $x_i \in \mathbf{X}$, we have:*

(a) $\neg\widehat{F}(\mathbf{1}^{i-1}0, \mathbf{X}_{i+1}^n, \mathbf{1}^i, \neg\mathbf{X}_{i+1}^n, \mathbf{Y}) \Rightarrow \Delta_i \Rightarrow \neg\widehat{F}(\mathbf{0}^i, \mathbf{X}_{i+1}^n, \mathbf{0}^{i-1}1, \neg\mathbf{X}_{i+1}^n, \mathbf{Y})$
(b) $\neg\widehat{F}(\mathbf{1}^i, \mathbf{X}_{i+1}^n, \mathbf{1}^{i-1}0, \neg\mathbf{X}_{i+1}^n, \mathbf{Y}) \Rightarrow \Gamma_i \Rightarrow \neg\widehat{F}(\mathbf{0}^{i-1}1, \mathbf{X}_{i+1}^n, \mathbf{0}^i, \neg\mathbf{X}_{i+1}^n, \mathbf{Y})$

In the remainder of the paper, we only use under-approximations of Δ_i and Γ_i, and use δ_i and γ_i respectively, to denote them. Recall from Sect. 2 that both Δ_i and $\neg\Gamma_i$ suffice as Skolem functions for x_i. Therefore, we propose to use either δ_i or $\neg\gamma_i$ (depending on which has a smaller AIG) obtained from Lemma 1 as our approximation of ψ_i. Specifically,

$$\delta_i = \neg\widehat{F}(\mathbf{1}^{i-1}0, \mathbf{X}_{i+1}^n, \mathbf{1}^i, \neg\mathbf{X}_{i+1}^n, \mathbf{Y}),\ \gamma_i = \neg\widehat{F}(\mathbf{1}^i, \mathbf{X}_{i+1}^n, \mathbf{1}^{i-1}0, \neg\mathbf{X}_{i+1}^n, \mathbf{Y})$$
$$\psi_i = \delta_i \text{ or } \neg\gamma_i, \text{ depending on which has a smaller AIG} \quad (3)$$

Example 1. Consider the specification $\mathbf{X} = \mathbf{Y}$, expressed in NNF as $F(\mathbf{X}, \mathbf{Y}) \equiv \bigwedge_{i=1}^n ((x_i \wedge y_i) \vee (\neg x_i \wedge \neg y_i))$. As noted in [33], this is a difficult example for CEGAR-based QBF solvers, when n is large.

From Eq. 3, $\delta_i = \neg(\neg y_i \wedge \bigwedge_{j=i+1}^n (x_j \Leftrightarrow y_j)) = y_i \vee \bigvee_{j=i+1}^n (x_j \Leftrightarrow \neg y_j)$, and $\gamma_i = \neg(y_i \wedge \bigwedge_{j=i+1}^n (x_j \Leftrightarrow y_j)) = \neg y_i \vee \bigvee_{j=i+1}^n (x_j \Leftrightarrow \neg y_j)$. With δ_i as the choice of ψ_i, we obtain $\psi_i = y_i \vee \bigvee_{j=i+1}^n (x_j \Leftrightarrow \neg y_j)$. Clearly, $\psi_n = y_n$. On reverse-substituting, we get $\psi_{n-1} = y_{n-1} \vee (\psi_n \Leftrightarrow \neg y_n) = y_{n-1} \vee 0 = y_{n-1}$. Continuing in this way, we get $\psi_i = y_i$ for all $i \in \{1, \ldots n\}$. The same result is obtained regardless of whether we choose δ_i or $\neg\gamma_i$ for each ψ_i. Thus, our approximation is good enough to solve this problem. In fact, it can be shown that $\delta_i = \Delta_i$ and $\gamma_i = \Gamma_i$ for all $i \in \{1, \ldots n\}$ in this example. □

Note that the approximations of Skolem functions, as given in Eq. (3), are efficiently computable for all $i \in \{1, \ldots n\}$, as they involve evaluating $\widehat{F}$ with a subset of inputs set to constants. This takes no more than $\mathcal{O}(|F|)$ time and space. As illustrated by Example 1, these approximations also often suffice to solve BFnS. The following lemma partially explains this.

Theorem 2. *(a) For $i \in \{1, \ldots n\}$, suppose the following holds:*

$$\forall j \in \{1, \ldots i\}\ \ \widehat{F}(\mathbf{1}^j, \mathbf{X}_{j+1}^n, \mathbf{1}^j, \overline{\mathbf{X}}_{j+1}^n, \mathbf{Y}) \Rightarrow \widehat{F}(\mathbf{1}^{j-1}0, \mathbf{X}_{j+1}^n, \mathbf{1}^{j-1}1, \overline{\mathbf{X}}_{j+1}^n, \mathbf{Y})$$
$$\vee\ \widehat{F}(\mathbf{1}^{j-1}1, \mathbf{X}_{j+1}^n, \mathbf{1}^{j-1}0, \overline{\mathbf{X}}_{j+1}^n, \mathbf{Y})$$

Then $\exists \mathbf{X}_1^i F(\mathbf{X}, \mathbf{Y}) \Leftrightarrow \widehat{F}(\mathbf{1}^i, \mathbf{X}_{i+1}^n, \mathbf{1}^i, \neg\mathbf{X}_{i+1}^n, \mathbf{Y})$.
(b) If $\widehat{F}(\mathbf{X}, \neg\mathbf{X}, \mathbf{Y})$ is in wDNNF, then $\delta_i = \Delta_i$ and $\gamma_i = \Gamma_i$ for every $i \in \{1, \ldots n\}$.

Proof. To prove part (a), we use induction on i. The base case corresponds to $i = 1$. Recall that $\exists \mathbf{X}_1^1 F(\mathbf{X}, \mathbf{Y}) \Leftrightarrow \widehat{F}(1, \mathbf{X}_2^n, 0, \neg\mathbf{X}_2^n, \mathbf{Y}) \vee F(0, \mathbf{X}_2^n, 1, \neg\mathbf{X}_2^n, \mathbf{Y})$ by definition. Proposition 3 already asserts that $\exists \mathbf{X}_1^1 F(\mathbf{X}, \mathbf{Y}) \Rightarrow \widehat{F}(1, \mathbf{X}_2^n, 1, \neg\mathbf{X}_2^n, \mathbf{Y})$. Therefore, if the condition in Theorem 2(a) holds for $i = 1$, we then have

$\widehat{F}(1, \mathbf{X}_2^n, 1, \neg\mathbf{X}_2^n, \mathbf{Y}) \Leftrightarrow \widehat{F}(1, \mathbf{X}_2^n, 0, \neg\mathbf{X}_2^n, \mathbf{Y}) \vee F(0, \mathbf{X}_2^n, 1, \neg\mathbf{X}_2^n, \mathbf{Y})$, which in turn is equivalent to $\exists \mathbf{X}_1^1 F(\mathbf{X}, \mathbf{Y})$. This proves the base case.

Let us now assume (inductive hypothesis) that the statement of Theorem 2(a) holds for $1 \leq i < n$. We prove below that the same statement holds for $i+1$ as well. Clearly, $\exists \mathbf{X}_1^{i+1} F(\mathbf{X}, \mathbf{Y}) \Leftrightarrow \exists x_{i+1} \left(\exists \mathbf{X}_1^i F(\mathbf{X}, \mathbf{Y})\right)$. By the inductive hypothesis, this is equivalent to $\exists x_{i+1} \widehat{F}(\mathbf{1}^i, \mathbf{X}_{i+1}^n, \mathbf{1}^i, \neg\mathbf{X}_{i+1}^n, \mathbf{Y})$. By definition of existential quantification, this is equivalent to $\widehat{F}(\mathbf{1}^{i+1}, \mathbf{X}_{i+2}^n, \mathbf{1}^i 0, \neg\mathbf{X}_{i+2}^n, \mathbf{Y}) \vee \widehat{F}(\mathbf{1}^i 0, \mathbf{X}_{i+2}^n, \mathbf{1}^{i+1}, \neg\mathbf{X}_{i+2}^n, \mathbf{Y})$. From the condition in Theorem 2(a), we also have

$$\widehat{F}(\mathbf{1}^{i+1}, \mathbf{X}_{i+2}^n, \mathbf{1}^{i+1}, \overline{\mathbf{X}}_{i+2}^n, \mathbf{Y}) \Rightarrow \widehat{F}(\mathbf{1}^i 0, \mathbf{X}_{i+2}^n, \mathbf{1}^{i+1}, \overline{\mathbf{X}}_{i+2}^n, \mathbf{Y}) \\ \vee \widehat{F}(\mathbf{1}^{i+1}, \mathbf{X}_{i+2}^n, \mathbf{1}^i 0, \overline{\mathbf{X}}_{i+2}^n, \mathbf{Y})$$

The implication in the reverse direction follows from Proposition 2(a). Thus we have a bi-implication above, which we have already seen is equivalent to $\exists \mathbf{X}_1^{i+1} F(\mathbf{X}, \mathbf{Y})$. This proves the inductive case.

To prove part (b), we first show that if $\widehat{F}(\mathbf{X}, \neg\mathbf{X}, \mathbf{Y})$ is in wDNNF, then the condition in Theorem 2(a) must hold for all $j \in \{1, \ldots n\}$. Theorem 2(b) then follows from the definitions of Δ_i and Γ_i (see Sect. 2), from the statement of Theorem 2(a) and from the definitions of δ_i and γ_i (see Eq. 3).

For $j \in \{1, \ldots n\}$, let $\zeta(\mathbf{X}_{j+1}^n, \overline{\mathbf{X}}_{j+1}^n, \mathbf{Y})$ denote the formula $\widehat{F}(\mathbf{1}^j, \mathbf{X}_{j+1}^n, \mathbf{1}^j, \overline{\mathbf{X}}_{j+1}^n, \mathbf{Y}) \wedge \neg \left(\widehat{F}(\mathbf{1}^{j-1}0, \mathbf{X}_{j+1}^n, \mathbf{1}^{j-1}1, \overline{\mathbf{X}}_{j+1}^n, \mathbf{Y}) \vee \widehat{F}(\mathbf{1}^{j-1}1, \mathbf{X}_{j+1}^n, \mathbf{1}^{j-1}0, \overline{\mathbf{X}}_{j+1}^n, \mathbf{Y})\right)$. Suppose, if possible, $\widehat{F}(\mathbf{X}, \neg\mathbf{X}, \mathbf{Y})$ is in wDNNF but there exists j $(1 \leq j \leq n)$ such that $\zeta(\mathbf{X}_{j+1}^n, \overline{\mathbf{X}}_{j+1}^n, \mathbf{Y})$ is satisfiable. Let $\mathbf{X}_{j+1}^n = \sigma$, $\overline{\mathbf{X}}_{j+1}^n = \kappa$ and $\mathbf{Y} = \theta$ be a satisfying assignment of ζ. We now consider the simplified circuit obtained by substituting $\mathbf{1}^{j-1}$ for $\mathbf{X}_1^{j-1}$ as well as for $\overline{\mathbf{X}}_1^{j-1}$, σ for $\mathbf{X}_{j+1}^n$, κ for $\overline{\mathbf{X}}_{j+1}^n$ and θ for $\mathbf{Y}$ in the AIG for $\widehat{F}$. This simplification replaces the output of every internal node with a constant (0 or 1), if the node evaluates to a constant under the above assignment. Note that the resulting circuit can have only x_j and $\overline{x}_j$ as its inputs. Furthermore, since the assignment satisfies ζ, it follows that the simplified circuit evaluates to 1 if both x_j and $\overline{x}_j$ are set to 1, and it evaluates to 0 if any one of x_j or $\overline{x}_j$ is set to 0. This can only happen if there is a node labeled $\wedge$ in the AIG representing $\widehat{F}(\mathbf{X}, \neg\mathbf{X}, \mathbf{Y})$ with a path leading from the leaf labeled x_j, and another path leading from the leaf labeled $\neg x_j$. This is a contradiction, since $\widehat{F}(\mathbf{X}, \neg\mathbf{X}, \mathbf{Y})$ is in wDNNF. Therefore, there is no $j \in \{1, \ldots n\}$ such that the condition of Theorem 2(a) is violated. □

In general, the candidate Skolem functions generated from the approximations discussed above may not always be correct. Indeed, the conditions discussed above are only sufficient, but not necessary, for the approximations to be exact. Hence, we need a separate check to see if our candidate Skolem functions are correct. To do this, we use an *error formula* $\varepsilon_{\mathbf{\Psi}}(\mathbf{X}', \mathbf{X}, \mathbf{Y}) \equiv F(\mathbf{X}', \mathbf{Y}) \wedge \bigwedge_{i=1}^n (x_i \leftrightarrow \psi_i) \wedge \neg F(\mathbf{X}, \mathbf{Y})$, as described in [23], and check its satisfiability. The correctness of this check depends on the following result from [23].

Theorem 3 ([23]). *ε_{Ψ} is unsatisfiable iff Ψ is a correct Skolem function vector.*

Algorithm 1. BFSS

Input: $\widehat{F}(\mathbf{X}, \mathbf{Y})$ in NNF (or wDNNF) with inputs $|\mathbf{Y}| = m$, outputs $|\mathbf{X}| = n$,
Output: Candidate Skolem Functions $\Psi = (\psi_1, \ldots, \psi_n)$
1 **Initialize**: Fix sets $U_0 = U_1 = \emptyset$;
2 **repeat**
3   // Repeatedly checks for Unate variables
4   **for** *each* $x_i \in \mathbf{X} \setminus (U_0 \cup U_1)$ **do**
5   **if** *$\widehat{F}$ is positive unate in x_i* // check x_i pure or η_i^+ (Eq 1) SAT ;
6   **then**
7             $\widehat{F} := \widehat{F}[x_i = 1]$, $U_1 = U_1 \cup \{x_i\}$
8   **else if** *$\widehat{F}$ is negative unate in x_i* // $\neg x_i$ pure or η^- (Eq 2)SAT ;
9   **then**
10             $\widehat{F} := \widehat{F}[x_i = 0]$, $U_0 = U_0 \cup \{x_i\}$
11 **until** *F is unchanged* // No Unate variables remaining;
12 Choose an ordering $\preceq$ of $\mathbf{X}$ // Section 6 discusses ordering used;
13 **for** *each $x_i \in \mathbf{X}$ in $\preceq$ order* **do**
14   **if** *$x_i \in U_j$ for $j \in \{0, 1\}$* // *Assume* $x_1 \preceq x_2 \preceq \ldots x_n$;
15   **then**
16         $\psi_i = j$
17   **else**
18   ψ_i is as defined in (Eq 3)
19 **if** *error formula ϵ_{Ψ} is UNSAT* **then**
20   terminate and output Ψ
21 **else**
22   call Phase 2

We now combine all the above ingredients to come up with algorithm BFSS (for *Blazingly Fast Skolem Synthesis*), as shown in Algorithm 1. The algorithm can be divided into three parts. In the first part (lines 2-11), unateness is checked. This is done in two ways: (i) we identify pure literals in F by simply examining the labels of leaves in the DAG representation of F in NNF, and (ii) we check the satisfiability of the formulas η_i^+ and η_i^-, as defined in Eqs. 1 and 2. This requires invoking a SAT solver in the worst-case, and is repeated at most $\mathcal{O}(n^2)$ times until there are no more unate variables. Hence this requires $\mathcal{O}(n^2)$ calls to a SAT solver. Once we have done this, by Proposition 1, the constants 1 or 0 (for positive or negative unate variables respectively) are correct Skolem functions for these variables.

In the second part, we fix an ordering of the remaining output variables according to an experimentally sound heuristic, as described in Sect. 6, and compute candidate Skolem functions for these variables according to Eq. 3. We then check the satisfiability of the error formula ϵ_Ψ to determine if the candidate Skolem functions are indeed correct. If the error formula is found to be unsatisfiable, we know from Theorem 3 that we have the correct Skolem functions, which can therefore be output. This concludes phase 1 of algorithm BFSS. If the error formula is found to be satisfiable, we move to phase 2 of algorithm BFSS – an adaptation of the CEGAR-based technique described in [23], and discussed briefly in Sect. 5. It is not difficult to see that the running time of phase 1 is polynomial in the size of the input, relative to an NP-oracle (SAT solver in practice). This also implies that the Skolem functions generated can be of at most polynomial size. Finally, from Theorem 2 we also obtain that if F satisfies Theorem 2(a), Skolem functions generated in phase 1 are correct. From the above reasoning, we obtain the following properties of phase 1 of BFSS:

Theorem 4. *1. For all unate variables, phase 1 of* BFSS *computes correct Skolem functions.*
2. If $\hat{F}$ is in wDNNF*, phase 1 of* BFSS *computes all Skolem functions correctly.*
3. The running time of phase 1 of BFSS *is polynomial in input size, relative to an* NP*-oracle. Specifically, the algorithm makes $\mathcal{O}(n^2)$ calls to an* NP*-oracle.*
4. The candidate Skolem functions output by phase 1 of BFSS *have size at most polynomial in the size of the input.*

Discussion: We make two crucial and related observations. First, by our hardness results in Sect. 3, we know that the above algorithm cannot solve BFnS for all inputs, unless some well-regarded complexity-theoretic conjectures fail. As a result, we must go to phase 2 on at least some inputs. Surprisingly, our experiments show that this is not necessary in the majority of benchmarks.

The second observation tries to understand why phase 1 works in most cases in practice. While a conclusive explanation isn't easy, we believe Theorem 2 explains the success of phase 1 in several cases. By [15], we know that all Boolean functions have a DNNF (and hence wDNNF) representation, although it may take exponential time to compute this representation. This allows us to define two preprocessing procedures. In the first, we identify cases where we can directly convert to wDNNF and use the Phase 1 algorithm above. And in the second, we use several optimization scripts available in the ABC [26] library to optimize the AIG representation of $\widehat{F}$. For a majority of benchmarks, this appears to yield a representation of $\widehat{F}$ that allows the proof of Theorem 2(a) to go through. For the rest, we apply the Phase 2 algorithm as described below.

Quantitative guarantees of "goodness". Given our theoretical and practical insights of the applicability of phase 1 of BFSS, it would be interesting to measure how much progress we have made in phase 1, even if it does not give the correct Skolem functions. One way to measure this "goodness" is to estimate the number of counterexamples as a fraction of the size of the input space. Specifically, given the error formula, we get an approximate count of the number of models for this formula *projected on the inputs* $\mathbf{Y}$. This can be obtained efficiently in practice with high confidence using state-of-the-art approximate model counters, viz. [13], with complexity in $\mathsf{BPP}^{\mathsf{NP}}$. The approximate count thus obtained, when divided by $2^{|\mathbf{Y}|}$ gives the fraction of input combinations for which the candidate Skolem functions output by phase 1 do not work correctly. We call this the *goodness ratio* of our approximation.

5 Phase 2: Counterexample-Guided Refinement

For phase 2, we can use any off-the-shelf worst-case exponential-time Skolem function generator. However, given that we already have candidate Skolem functions with guarantees on their "goodness", it is natural to use them as starting points for phase 2. Hence, we start off with candidate Skolem functions for all x_i as computed in phase 1, and then update (or refine) them in a counterexample-driven manner. Intuitively, a counterexample is a value of the inputs $\mathbf{Y}$ for which there exists a value of $\mathbf{X}$ that renders $F(\mathbf{X}, \mathbf{Y})$ true, but for which $F(\mathbf{\Psi}, \mathbf{Y})$ evaluates to false. As shown in [23], given a candidate Skolem function vector, every satisfying assignment of the error formula $\varepsilon_{\mathbf{\Psi}}$ gives a counterexample. The refinement step uses this satisfying assignment to update an appropriate subset of the approximate δ_i and γ_i functions computed in phase 1. The entire process is then repeated until no counterexamples can be found. The final updated vector of Skolem functions then gives a solution of the BFnS problem. Note that this idea is not new [3,23]. The only significant enhancement we do over the algorithm in [23] is to use an almost-uniform sampler [12] to efficiently sample the space of counterexamples almost uniformly. This allows us to do refinement with a diverse set of counterexamples, instead of using counterexamples in a corner of the solution space of $\varepsilon_{\mathbf{\Psi}}$ that the SAT solver heuristics zoom down on.

6 Experimental Results

Experimental methodology. Our implementation consists of two parallel pipelines that accept the same input specification but represent them in two different ways. The first pipeline takes the input formula as an AIG and builds an NNF (not necessarily wDNNF) DAG, while the second pipeline builds an ROBDD from the input AIG using dynamic variable reordering (no restrictions on variable order), and then obtains a wDNNF representation from it using the linear-time algorithm described in [15]. Once the NNF/wDNNF representation is built, we use Algorithm 1 in Phase 1 and CEGAR-based synthesis using UniGen [12] to sample counterexamples in Phase 2. We call this ensemble of two pipelines as bfss. We compare bfss with the following algorithms/tools: (*i*) parSyn [3], (*ii*) Cadet [33], (*iii*) RSynth [38], and (*iv*) AbsSynthe-Skolem (based on the BFnS step of AbsSynthe [10]).

Our implementation of bfss uses the ABC [26] library to represent and manipulate Boolean functions. Two different SAT solvers can be used with bfss: ABC's default SAT solver, or UniGen [12] (to give almost-uniformly distributed counterexamples). All our experiments use UniGen.

We consider a total of 504 benchmarks, taken from four different domains: (a) forty-eight *Arithmetic benchmarks* from [17], with varying bit-widths (viz.

32, 64, 128, 256, 512 and 1024) of arithmetic operators, (b) sixty-eight *Disjunctive Decomposition benchmarks* from [3], generated by considering some of the larger sequential circuits in the HWMCC10 benchmark suite, (c) five *Factorization benchmarks*, also from [3], representing factorization of numbers of different bit-widths (8, 10, 12, 14, 16), and (d) three hundred and eighty three *QBFEval benchmarks*, taken from the Prenex 2QBF track of QBFEval 2017 [32][2]. Since different tools accept benchmarks in different formats, each benchmark was converted to both `qdimacs` and `verilog/aiger` formats. All benchmarks and the procedure by which we generated (and converted) them are detailed in [1]. Recall that we use two pipelines for BFSS. We use "balance; rewrite -l; refactor -l; balance; rewrite -l; rewrite -lz; balance; refactor -lz; rewrite -lz; balance" as the ABC script for optimizing the AIG representation of the input specification. We observed that while this results in only 4 benchmarks being in wDNNF in the first pipeline, 219 benchmarks were solved in Phase 1 using this pipeline. This is attributable to specifications being unate in several output variables, and also satisfying the condition of Theorem 2(a) (while not being in wDNNF). In the second pipeline, however, we could represent 230 benchmarks in wDNNF, and all of these were solved in Phase 1.

For each benchmark, the order $\preceq$ (ref. step 12 of Algorithm 1) in which Skolem functions are generated is such that the variable which occurs in the transitive fan-in of the least number of nodes in the AIG representation of the specification is ordered before other variables. This order ($\preceq$) is used for both BFSS and PARSYN. Note that the order $\preceq$ is completely independent of the dynamic variable order used to construct an ROBDD of the input specification in the second pipeline, prior to getting the wDNNF representation.

All experiments were performed on a message-passing cluster, with 20 cores and 64 GB memory per node, each core being a 2.2 GHz Intel Xeon processor. The operating system was Cent OS 6.5. Twenty cores were assigned to each run of PARSYN. For RSYNTH and CADET a single core on the cluster was used, since these tools don't exploit parallel processing. Each pipeline of BFSS was executed on a single node; the computation of candidate functions, building of error formula and refinement of the counterexamples was performed sequentially on 1 thread, and UNIGEN had 19 threads at its disposal (idle during Phase 1).

The maximum time given for execution of any run was 3600 s. The total amount of main memory for any run was restricted to 16GB. The metric used to compare the algorithms was *time taken to synthesize Boolean functions*. The time reported for BFSS is the better of the two times obtained from the alternative pipelines described above. Detailed results from the individual pipelines are available in [2].

Results. Of the 504 benchmarks, 177 benchmarks were not solved by any tool – 6 of these being from arithmetic benchmarks and 171 from QBFEval.

Table 1 gives a summary of the performance of BFSS (considering the combined pipelines) over different benchmarks suites. Of the 504 benchmarks, BFSS

[2] The track contains 384 benchmarks, but we were unsuccessful in converting 1 benchmark to some of the formats required by the various tools.

Table 1. BFSS: Performance summary of combined pipelines

Benchmark domain	Total benchmarks	# Benchmarks solved	Phase 1 solved	Phase 2 started	Solved By phase 2
QBFEval	383	170	159	73	11
Arithmetic	48	35	35	8	0
Disjunctive decomposition	68	68	66	2	2
Factorization	5	5	5	0	0

was successful on 278 benchmarks; of these, 170 are from QBFEval, 68 from Disjunctive Decomposition, 35 from Arithmetic and 5 from Factorization.

Of the 383 benchmarks in the QBFEval suite, we ran BFSS only on 254 since we could not build succinct AIGs for the remaining benchmarks. Of these, 159 *benchmarks were solved by Phase 1 (i.e., 62% of built QBFEval benchmarks)* and 73 proceeded to Phase 2, of which 11 reached completion. On another 11 QBFEval benchmarks Phase 1 timed out. Of the 48 Arithmetic benchmarks, *Phase 1 successfully solved* 35 *(i.e.,* $\sim$ 72%*)* and Phase 2 was started for 8 benchmarks; Phase 1 timed out on 5 benchmarks. Of the 68 Disjunctive Decomposition benchmarks, *Phase 1 successfully solved* 66 *benchmarks (i.e., 97%)*, and Phase 2 was started and reached completion for 2 benchmarks. For the 5 Factorization benchmarks, Phase 1 was successful on all 5 benchmarks.

Recall that the goodness ratio is the ratio of the number of *counterexamples remaining* to the *total size of the input space* after Phase 1. For all benchmarks solved by Phase 1, the goodness ratio is 0. We analyzed the goodness ratio at the beginning of Phase 2 for 83 benchmarks for which Phase 2 started. For 13 benchmarks this ratio was small (< 0.002), and Phase 2 reached completion for these. Of the remaining benchmarks, 34 also had a small goodness ratio (< 0.1), indicating that we were close to the solution at the time of timeout. However, 27 benchmarks in QBFEval had goodness ratio close to > 0.9, indicating that most of the counter-examples were not eliminated by timeout.

We next compare the performance of BFSS with other state-of-art tools. For clarity, since the number of benchmarks in the QBFEval suite is considerably greater, we plot the QBFEval benchmarks separately.

BFSS vs CADET: Of the 504 benchmarks, CADET was successful on 231 benchmarks, of which 24 belonged to Disjunctive Decomposition, 22 to Arithmetic, 1 to Factorization and 184 to QBFEval. Figure 1(a) gives the performance of the two algorithms with respect to time on the QBFEval suite. Here, CADET solved 35 benchmarks that BFSS could not solve, whereas BFSS solved 21 benchmarks that could not be solved by CADET. Figure 1(b) gives the performance of the two algorithms with respect to time on the Arithmetic, Factorization and Disjunctive Decomposition benchmarks. In these categories, there were a total of 62 benchmarks that BFSS solved that CADET could not solve, and there was 1 benchmark that CADET solved but BFSS did not solve. While CADET takes less time on Arithmetic benchmarks and many QBFEval benchmarks, on Disjunctive Decomposition and Factorization, BFSS takes less time.

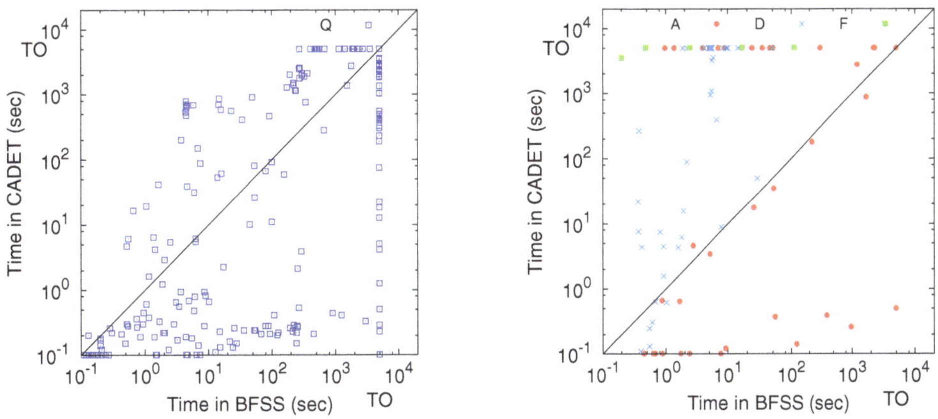

Fig. 1. BFSS vs CADET: Legend: Q: QBFEval, A: Arithmetic, F: Factorization, D: Disjunctive Decomposition. TO: benchmarks for which the corresponding algorithm was unsuccessful.

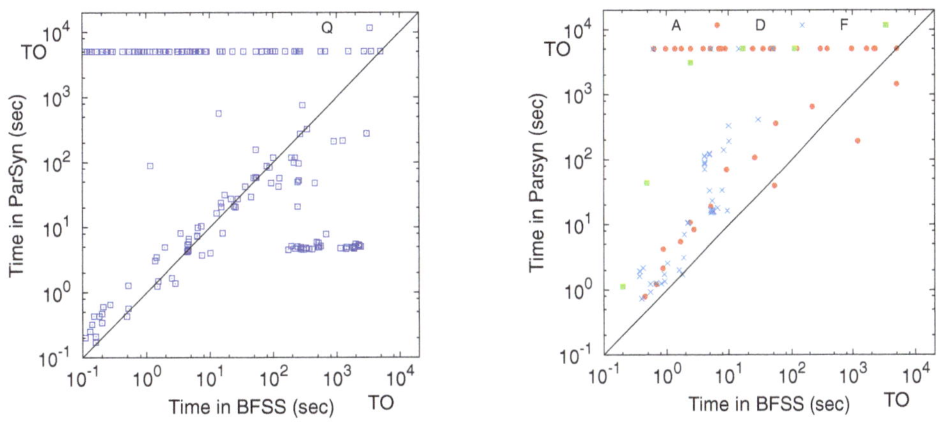

Fig. 2. BFSS vs PARSYN (for legend see Fig. 1)

BFSS vs PARSYN: Fig. 2 shows the comparison of time taken by BFSS and PARSYN. PARSYN was successful on a total of 185 benchmarks, and could solve 1 benchmark which BFSS could not solve. On the other hand, BFSS solved 94 benchmarks that PARSYN could not solve. From Fig. 2, we can see that on most of the Arithmetic, Disjunctive Decomposition and Factorization benchmarks, BFSS takes less time than PARSYN.

BFSS vs RSYNTH: We next compare the performance of BFSS with RSYNTH. As shown in Fig. 3, RSYNTH was successful on 51 benchmarks, with 4 benchmarks that could be solved by RSYNTH but not by BFSS. In contrast, BFSS could solve 231 benchmarks that RSYNTH could not solve! Of the benchmarks that were solved by both solvers, we can see that BFSS took less time on most of them.

BFSS vs ABSSYNTHE-SKOLEM: ABSSYNTHE-SKOLEM was successful on 217 benchmarks, and could solve 31 benchmarks that BFSS could not solve. In contrast, BFSS solved a total of 92 benchmarks that ABSSYNTHE-SKOLEM could not. Figure 4 shows a comparison of running times of BFSS and ABSSYNTHE-SKOLEM.

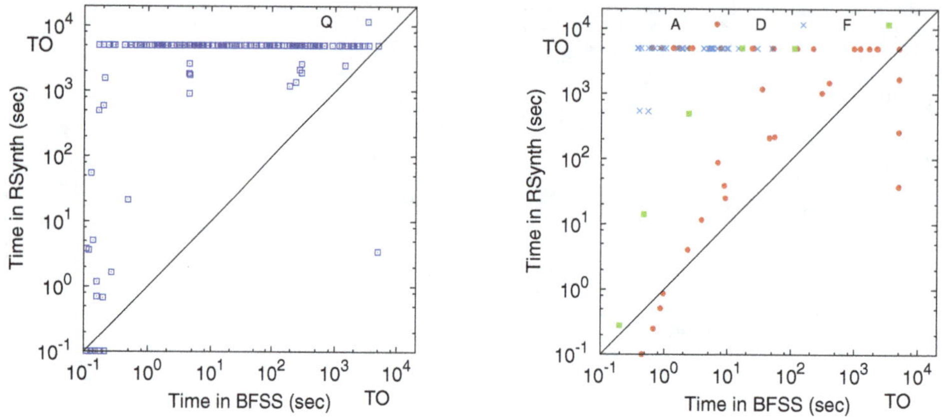

Fig. 3. BFSS vs RSYNTH (for legend see Fig. 1)

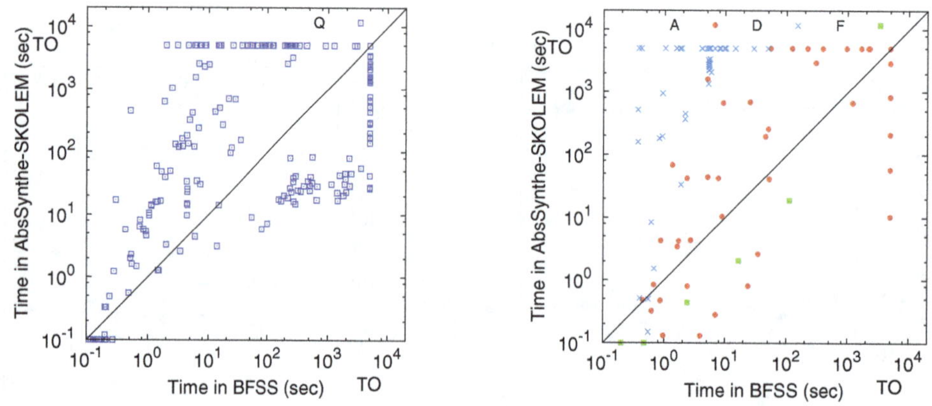

Fig. 4. BFSS vs ABSSYNTHE-SKOLEM (for legend see Fig. 1)

7 Conclusion

In this paper, we showed some complexity-theoretic hardness results for the Boolean functional synthesis problem. We then developed a two-phase approach to solve this problem, where the first phase, which is an efficient algorithm generating poly-sized functions surprisingly succeeds in solving a large number of benchmarks. To explain this, we identified sufficient conditions when phase 1 gives the correct answer. For the remaining benchmarks, we employed the second phase of the algorithm that uses a CEGAR-based approach and builds Skolem functions by exploiting recent advances in SAT solvers/approximate counters. As future work, we wish to explore further improvements in Phase 2, and other structural restrictions on the input that ensure completeness of Phase 1.

Acknowledgements. We are thankful to Ajith John, Kuldeep Meel, Mate Soos, Ocan Sankur, Lucas Martinelli Tabajara and Markus Rabe for useful discussions and for providing us with various software tools used in the experimental comparisons. We also thank the anonymous reviewers for insightful comments.

References

1. Website for CAV 2018 Experiments (2018). https://drive.google.com/drive/folders/0B74xgF9hCly5QXctNFpYR0VnQUU?usp=sharing
2. Akshay, S., Chakraborty, S., Goel, S., Kulal, S., Shah, S.: What's hard for Boolean functional synthesis. arXiv e-prints (2018). https://arxiv.org/abs/1804.05507
3. Akshay, S., Chakraborty, S., John, A.K., Shah, S.: Towards parallel Boolean functional synthesis. In: Legay, A., Margaria, T. (eds.) TACAS 2017. LNCS, vol. 10205, pp. 337–353. Springer, Heidelberg (2017). https://doi.org/10.1007/978-3-662-54577-5_19
4. Alur, R., Madhusudan, P., Nam, W.: Symbolic computational techniques for solving games. STTT **7**(2), 118–128 (2005)
5. Andersson, G., Bjesse, P., Cook, B., Hanna, Z.: A proof engine approach to solving combinational design automation problems. In: Proceedings of the 39th Annual Design Automation Conference, DAC 2002, pp. 725–730. ACM, New York (2002). https://doi.org/10.1145/513918.514101
6. Baader, F.: On the complexity of Boolean unification. Technical report (1999)
7. Balabanov, V., Jiang, J.H.R.: Unified QBF certification and its applications. Form. Methods Syst. Des. **41**(1), 45–65 (2012). https://doi.org/10.1007/s10703-012-0152-6
8. Boole, G.: The Mathematical Analysis of Logic. Philosophical Library (1847). https://books.google.co.in/books?id=zv4YAQAAIAAJ
9. Boudet, A., Jouannaud, J.P., Schmidt-Schauss, M.: Unification in Boolean rings and Abelian groups. J. Symb. Comput. **8**(5), 449–477 (1989). https://doi.org/10.1016/S0747-7171(89)80054-9
10. Brenguier, R., Pérez, G.A., Raskin, J.F., Sankur, O.: Abssynthe: abstract synthesis from succinct safety specifications. In: Proceedings 3rd Workshop on Synthesis (SYNT 2014) Electronic Proceedings in Theoretical Computer Science, vol. 157, pp. 100–116. Open Publishing Association (2014). http://arxiv.org/abs/1407.5961v1
11. Bryant, R.E.: Graph-based algorithms for Boolean function manipulation. IEEE Trans. Comput. **35**(8), 677–691 (1986). https://doi.org/10.1109/TC.1986.1676819
12. Chakraborty, S., Fremont, D.J., Meel, K.S., Seshia, S.A., Vardi, M.Y.: On parallel scalable uniform SAT witness generation. In: Baier, C., Tinelli, C. (eds.) TACAS 2015. LNCS, vol. 9035, pp. 304–319. Springer, Heidelberg (2015). https://doi.org/10.1007/978-3-662-46681-0_25
13. Chakraborty, S., Meel, K.S., Vardi, M.Y.: Algorithmic improvements in approximate counting for probabilistic inference: from linear to logarithmic SAT calls. In: Proceedings of the Twenty-Fifth International Joint Conference on Artificial Intelligence, IJCAI 2016, New York, NY, USA, 9–15 July 2016, pp. 3569–3576 (2016)
14. Chen, Y., Eickmeyer, K., Flum, J.: The exponential time hypothesis and the parameterized clique problem. In: Thilikos, D.M., Woeginger, G.J. (eds.) IPEC 2012. LNCS, vol. 7535, pp. 13–24. Springer, Heidelberg (2012). https://doi.org/10.1007/978-3-642-33293-7_4
15. Darwiche, A.: Decomposable negation normal form. J. ACM **48**(4), 608–647 (2001)
16. Deschamps, J.P.: Parametric solutions of Boolean equations. Discret. Math. **3**(4), 333–342 (1972). https://doi.org/10.1016/0012-365X(72)90090-8
17. Fried, D., Tabajara, L.M., Vardi, M.Y.: BDD-based Boolean functional synthesis. In: Chaudhuri, S., Farzan, A. (eds.) CAV 2016. LNCS, vol. 9780, pp. 402–421. Springer, Cham (2016). https://doi.org/10.1007/978-3-319-41540-6_22

18. Impagliazzo, R., Paturi, R.: On the complexity of k-SAT. J. Comput. Syst. Sci. **62**(2), 367–375 (2001)
19. Jacobs, S., Bloem, R., Brenguier, R., Könighofer, R., Pérez, G.A., Raskin, J., Ryzhyk, L., Sankur, O., Seidl, M., Tentrup, L., Walker, A.: The second reactive synthesis competition (SYNTCOMP 2015). In: Proceedings Fourth Workshop on Synthesis, SYNT 2015, San Francisco, CA, USA, 18th July 2015, pp. 27–57 (2015)
20. Jiang, J.-H.R.: Quantifier elimination via functional composition. In: Bouajjani, A., Maler, O. (eds.) CAV 2009. LNCS, vol. 5643, pp. 383–397. Springer, Heidelberg (2009). https://doi.org/10.1007/978-3-642-02658-4_30
21. Balabanov, V., Jiang, J.-H.R.: Resolution proofs and Skolem functions in QBF evaluation and applications. In: Gopalakrishnan, G., Qadeer, S. (eds.) CAV 2011. LNCS, vol. 6806, pp. 149–164. Springer, Heidelberg (2011). https://doi.org/10.1007/978-3-642-22110-1_12
22. Jo, S., Matsumoto, T., Fujita, M.: Sat-based automatic rectification and debugging of combinational circuits with LUT insertions. In: Proceedings of the 2012 IEEE 21st Asian Test Symposium, ATS 2012, pp. 19–24. IEEE Computer Society (2012)
23. John, A., Shah, S., Chakraborty, S., Trivedi, A., Akshay, S.: Skolem functions for factored formulas. In: FMCAD, pp. 73–80 (2015)
24. Kuehlmann, A., Paruthi, V., Krohm, F., Ganai, M.K.: Robust Boolean reasoning for equivalence checking and functional property verification. IEEE Trans. CAD Integr. Circuits Syst. **21**(12), 1377–1394 (2002). http://dblp.uni-trier.de/db/journals/tcad/tcad21.html#KuehlmannPKG02
25. Kuncak, V., Mayer, M., Piskac, R., Suter, P.: Complete functional synthesis. SIGPLAN Not. **45**(6), 316–329 (2010)
26. Berkeley Logic Synthesis and Verification Group: ABC: A System for Sequential Synthesis and Verification. http://www.eecs.berkeley.edu/~alanmi/abc/
27. Lowenheim, L.: Über die Auflösung von Gleichungen in Logischen Gebietkalkul. Math. Ann. **68**, 169–207 (1910)
28. Macii, E., Odasso, G., Poncino, M.: Comparing different Boolean unification algorithms. In: Proceedings of 32nd Asilomar Conference on Signals, Systems and Computers, pp. 17–29 (2006)
29. Marijn Heule, M.S., Biere, A.: Efficient Extraction of Skolem Functions from QRAT Proofs. In: Formal Methods in Computer-Aided Design, FMCAD 2014, Lausanne, Switzerland, 21–24 October 2014, pp. 107–114 (2014)
30. Martin, U., Nipkow, T.: Boolean unification - the story so far. J. Symb. Comput. **7**(3–4), 275–293 (1989). https://doi.org/10.1016/S0747-7171(89)80013-6
31. Niemetz, A., Preiner, M., Lonsing, F., Seidl, M., Biere, A.: Resolution-based certificate extraction for QBF. In: Cimatti, A., Sebastiani, R. (eds.) SAT 2012. LNCS, vol. 7317, pp. 430–435. Springer, Heidelberg (2012). https://doi.org/10.1007/978-3-642-31612-8_33
32. QBFLib: QBFEval (2017). http://www.qbflib.org/event_page.php?year=2017
33. Rabe, M.N., Seshia, S.A.: Incremental determinization. In: Creignou, N., Le Berre, D. (eds.) SAT 2016. LNCS, vol. 9710, pp. 375–392. Springer, Cham (2016). https://doi.org/10.1007/978-3-319-40970-2_23
34. Rabe, M.N., Tentrup, L.: CAQE: a certifying QBF solver. In: Formal Methods in Computer-Aided Design, FMCAD 2015, Austin, Texas, USA, 27–30 September 2015, pp. 136–143 (2015)
35. Solar-Lezama, A.: Program sketching. STTT **15**(5–6), 475–495 (2013)

36. Solar-Lezama, A., Rabbah, R.M., Bodík, R., Ebcioglu, K.: Programming by sketching for bit-streaming programs. In: Proceedings of the ACM SIGPLAN 2005 Conference on Programming Language Design and Implementation, Chicago, IL, USA, 12–15 June 2005, pp. 281–294 (2005)
37. Srivastava, S., Gulwani, S., Foster, J.S.: Template-based program verification and program synthesis. STTT **15**(5–6), 497–518 (2013)
38. Tabajara, L.M., Vardi, M.Y.: Factored Boolean functional synthesis. In: 2017 Formal Methods in Computer Aided Design, FMCAD 2017, Vienna, Austria, 2–6 October 2017, pp. 124–131 (2017)
39. Trivedi, A.: Techniques in Symbolic Model Checking. Master's thesis, Indian Institute of Technology Bombay, Mumbai, India (2003)
40. Zhu, S., Tabajara, L.M., Li, J., Pu, G., Vardi, M.Y.: Symbolic LTLf synthesis. In: Proceedings of the Twenty-Sixth International Joint Conference on Artificial Intelligence, IJCAI 2017, Melbourne, Australia, 19–25 August 2017, pp. 1362–1369 (2017)

Counterexample Guided Inductive Synthesis Modulo Theories

Alessandro Abate[1], Cristina David[2,3](✉), Pascal Kesseli[3], Daniel Kroening[1,3], and Elizabeth Polgreen[1]

[1] University of Oxford, Oxford, UK
[2] University of Cambridge, Cambridge, UK
cd652@cam.ac.uk
[3] Diffblue Ltd., Oxford, UK

Abstract. Program synthesis is the mechanised construction of software. One of the main difficulties is the efficient exploration of the very large solution space, and tools often require a user-provided syntactic restriction of the search space. We propose a new approach to program synthesis that combines the strengths of a counterexample-guided inductive synthesizer with those of a theory solver, exploring the solution space more efficiently without relying on user guidance. We call this approach CEGIS($\mathcal{T}$), where $\mathcal{T}$ is a first-order theory. In this paper, we focus on one particular challenge for program synthesizers, namely the generation of programs that require non-trivial constants. This is a fundamentally difficult task for state-of-the-art synthesizers. We present two exemplars, one based on Fourier-Motzkin (FM) variable elimination and one based on first-order satisfiability. We demonstrate the practical value of CEGIS($\mathcal{T}$) by automatically synthesizing programs for a set of intricate benchmarks.

1 Introduction

Program synthesis is the problem of finding a program that meets a correctness specification given as a logical formula. This is an active area of research in which substantial progress has been made in recent years.

In full generality, program synthesis is an exceptionally difficult problem, and thus, the research community has explored pragmatic restrictions. One particularly successful direction is *Syntax-Guided Program Synthesis* (SyGuS) [2]. The key idea of SyGuS is that the user supplements the logical specification with a syntactic template for the solution. Leveraging the user's intuition, SyGuS reduces the solution space size substantially, resulting in significant speed-ups.

Unfortunately, it is difficult to provide the syntactic template in many practical applications. A very obvious exemplar of the limits of the syntax-guided approach are programs that require non-trivial constants. In such a scenario, the

Supported by ERC project 280053 (CPROVER) and the H2020 FET OPEN 712689 SC^2. Cristina David is supported by the Royal Society University Research Fellowship UF160079.

H. Chockler and G. Weissenbacher (Eds.): CAV 2018, LNCS 10981, pp. 270–288, 2018.
https://doi.org/10.1007/978-3-319-96145-3_15

syntax-guided approach requires that the user provides the exact value of the constants in the solution.

For illustration, let's consider a user who wants to synthesize a program that rounds up a given 32-bit unsigned number x to the next highest power of two. If we denote the function computed by the program by $f(x)$, then the specification can be written as $x < 2^{31} \Rightarrow f(x) \& (-f(x)) = f(x) \wedge f(x) \geq x \wedge 2x \geq f(x)$. The first conjunct forces $f(x)$ to be a power of two, the other requires it to be the next highest. A possible solution for this is given by the following C program:

```
x=x-1;
x |= x >> 1;
x |= x >> 2;
x |= x >> 4;
x |= x >> 8;
x |= x >> 16;
x=x+1;
```

It is improbable that the user knows that the constants in the solution are exactly 1, 2, 4, 8, 16, and thus, she will be unable to explicitly restrict the solution space. As a result, synthesizers are very likely to enumerate possible combinations of constants, which is highly inefficient.

In this paper we propose a new approach to program synthesis that combines the strengths of a counterexample-guided inductive synthesizer with those of a solver for a first-order theory in order to perform a more efficient exploration of the solution space, without relying on user guidance. Our inspiration for this proposal is DPLL($\mathcal{T}$), which has boosted the performance of solvers for many fragments of quantifier-free first-order logic [16,23]. DPLL($\mathcal{T}$) combines reasoning about the Boolean structure of a formula with reasoning about theory facts to decide satisfiability of a given formula.

In an attempt to generate similar technological advancements in program synthesis, we propose a new algorithm for program synthesis called CounterExample-Guided Inductive Synthesis($\mathcal{T}$), where $\mathcal{T}$ is a given first-order theory for which we have a specialised solver. Similar to its counterpart DPLL($\mathcal{T}$), the CEGIS($\mathcal{T}$) architecture features communication between a synthesizer and a theory solver, which results in a much more efficient exploration of the search space.

While standard CEGIS architectures [19,30] already make use of SMT solvers, the typical role of such a solver is restricted to validating candidate solutions and providing concrete counterexamples that direct subsequent search. By contrast, CEGIS($\mathcal{T}$) allows the theory solver to communicate generalised constraints back to the synthesizer, thus enabling more significant pruning of the search space.

There are instances of more sophisticated collaboration between a program synthesizer and theory solvers. The most obvious such instance is the program synthesizer inside the CVC4 SMT solver [27]. This approach features a very tight coupling between the two components (i.e., the synthesizer and the theory solvers) that takes advantage of the particular strengths of the SMT solver by reformulating the synthesis problem as the problem of refuting a universally quantified formula (SMT solvers are better at refuting universally quantified formulae than at proving them). Conversely, in our approach we maintain a clear separation between the synthesizer and the theory solver while performing comprehensive and well-defined communication between the two components. This enables the flexible combination of CEGIS with a variety of theory solvers, which excel at exploring different solution spaces.

Contributions

- We propose CEGIS($\mathcal{T}$), a program synthesis architecture that facilitates the communication between an inductive synthesizer and a solver for a first-order theory, resulting in an efficient exploration of the search space.
- We present two exemplars of this architecture, one based on Fourier-Motzkin (FM) variable elimination [7] and one using an off-the-shelf SMT solver.
- We have implemented CEGIS($\mathcal{T}$) and compared it against state-of-the-art program synthesizers on benchmarks that require intricate constants in the solution.

2 Preliminaries

2.1 The Program Synthesis Problem

Program synthesis is the task of automatically generating programs that satisfy a given logical specification. A program synthesizer can be viewed as a solver for existential second-order logic. An existential second-order logic formula allows quantification over functions as well as ground terms [28].

The input specification provided to a program synthesizer is of the form $\exists P. \forall \boldsymbol{x}. \sigma(P, \boldsymbol{x})$, where P ranges over functions (where a function is represented by the program computing it), $\boldsymbol{x}$ ranges over ground terms, and σ is a quantifier-free formula.

2.2 CounterExample Guided Inductive Synthesis

CounterExample-Guided Inductive Synthesis (CEGIS) is a popular approach to program synthesis, and is an iterative process. Each iteration performs inductive generalisation based on counterexamples provided by a verification oracle. Essentially, the inductive generalisation uses information about a limited number of inputs to make claims about all the possible inputs in the form of candidate solutions.

The CEGIS framework is illustrated in Fig. 1 and consists of two phases: the synthesis phase and the verification phase. Given the specification of the desired program, σ, the inductive synthesis procedure generates a candidate program P^* that satisfies $\sigma(P^*, \boldsymbol{x})$ for a subset $\boldsymbol{x}_{inputs}$ of all possible inputs. The candidate program P^* is passed to the verification phase, which checks whether

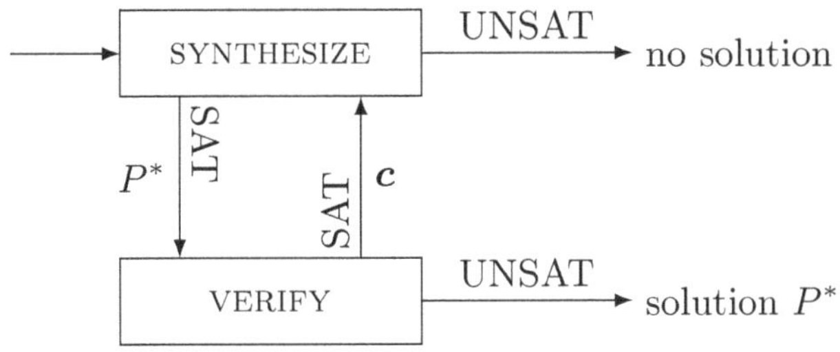

Fig. 1. CEGIS block diagram

it satisfies the specification $\sigma(P^*, \boldsymbol{x})$ for all possible inputs. This is done by checking whether $\neg\sigma(P^*, \boldsymbol{x})$ is unsatisfiable. If so, $\forall x.\neg\sigma(P^*, \boldsymbol{x})$ is valid, and we have successfully synthesized a solution and the algorithm terminates. Otherwise, the verifier produces a counterexample $\boldsymbol{c}$ from the satisfying assignment, which is then added to the set of inputs passed to the synthesizer, and the loop repeats.

The method used in the synthesis and verification blocks varies in different CEGIS implementations; our CEGIS implementation uses Bounded Model Checking [8].

2.3 DPLL($\mathcal{T}$)

DPLL($\mathcal{T}$) is an extension of the DPLL algorithm, used by most propositional SAT solvers, by a theory $\mathcal{T}$. We give a brief overview of DPLL($\mathcal{T}$) and compare DPLL($\mathcal{T}$) with CEGIS($\mathcal{T}$).

Given a formula F from a theory $\mathcal{T}$, a propositional formula F_p is created from F in which the theory atoms are replaced by Boolean variables (the "propositional skeleton"). The standard DPLL algorithm, comprising DECIDE, Boolean Constraint Propagation (BCP), ANALYZE-CONFLICT and BACKTRACK, generates an assignment to the Boolean variables in F_p, as illustrated in Fig. 2. The theory solver then checks whether this assignment is still consistent when the Boolean variables are replaced by their original atoms. If so, a satisfying assignment for F has been found. Otherwise, a constraint over the Boolean variables in F_p is passed back to DECIDE, and the process repeats.

In the very first SMT solvers, a full assignment to the Boolean variables was obtained, and then the theory solver returned only a single counterexample, similar to the implementations of CEGIS that are standard now. Such SMT solvers are prone to enumerating all possible counterexamples, and so the key improvement in DPLL($\mathcal{T}$) was the ability to pass back a more general constraint over the variables in the formula as a counterexample [16]. Furthermore, modern variants of DPLL($\mathcal{T}$) call the theory solver on partial assignments to the variables in F_p. Our proposed, new synthesis algorithm offers equivalents of both of these ideas that have improved DPLL($\mathcal{T}$).

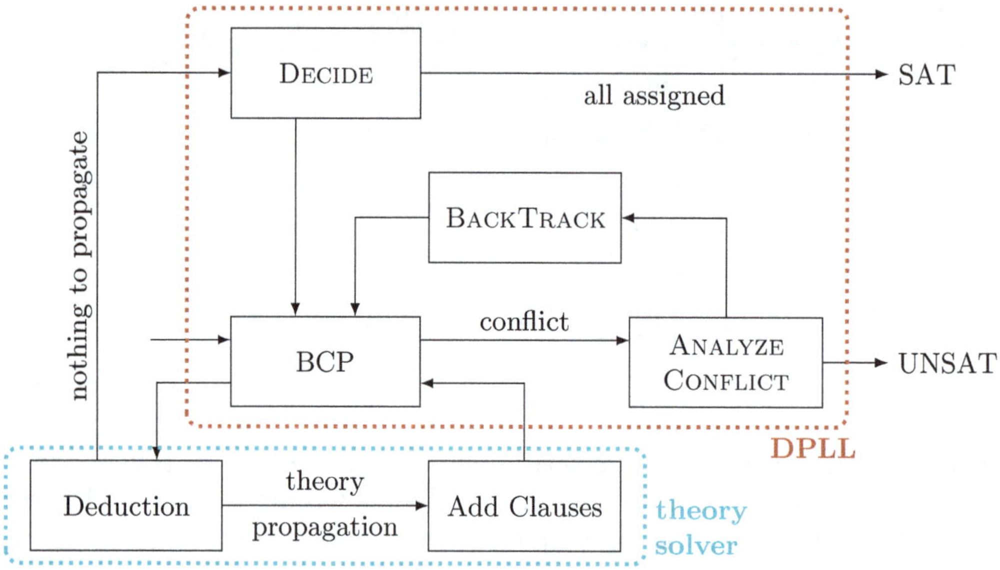

Fig. 2. DPLL($\mathcal{T}$) with theory propagation

3 Motivating Example

In each iteration of a standard CEGIS loop, the communication from the verification phase back to the synthesis phase is restricted to concrete counterexamples. This is particularly detrimental when synthesizing programs that require non-trivial constants. In such a setting, it is typical that a counterexample provided by the verification phase only eliminates a single candidate solution and, consequently, the synthesizer ends up enumerating possible constants.

For illustration, let's consider the trivial problem of synthesizing a function $f(x)$ where $f(x) < 0$ if $x < 334455$ and $f(x) = 0$, otherwise. One possible solution is $f(x) = ite\ (x < 334455) {-1} 0$, where *ite* stands for *if then else*.

In order to make the synthesis task even simpler, we are going to assume that we know a part of this solution, namely we know that it must be of the form $f(x) = ite\ (x < ?)\ {-1}\ 0$, where "?" is a placeholder for the missing constant that we must synthesize. A plausible scenario for a run of CEGIS is presented next: the synthesis phase guesses $f(x) = ite\ (x < 0)\ {-1}\ 0$, for which the verification phase returns $x = 0$ as a counterexample. In the next iteration of the CEGIS loop, the synthesis phase guesses $f(x) = ite(x < 1){-1}\ 0$ (which works for $x = 0$) and the verifier produces $x = 1$ as a counterexample. Following the same pattern, the synthesis phase will enumerate all the candidates

$$f(x) = ite\ (x < 2)\ {-1}\ 0$$
$$\dots$$
$$f(x) = ite\ (x < 334454)\ {-1}\ 0$$

before finding the solution. This is caused by the fact that each of the concrete counterexamples $0, \dots, 334454$ eliminate one candidate only from the solution space. Consequently, we need to propagate more information from the verifier to the synthesis phase in each iteration of the CEGIS loop.

Proving Properties of Programs. Synthesis engines can be used as reasoning engines in program analysers, and constants are important for this application. For illustration, let's consider the very simple program below, which increments a variable x from 0 to 100000 and asserts that its value is less than 100005 on exit from the loop.

```
1 int x=0;
2 while (x<=100000) x++;
3 assert(x<100005);
```

Proving the safety of such a program, i.e., that the assertion at line 3 is not violated in any execution of the program, is a task well-suited for synthesis (the Syntax Guided Synthesis Competition [5] has a track dedicated to synthesizing safety invariants). For this example, a safety invariant is $x < 100002$, which holds on entrance to the loop, is inductive with respect to the loop's body, and implies the assertion on exit from the loop.

While it is very easy for a human to deduce this invariant, the need for a non-trivial constant makes it surprisingly difficult for state-of-the-art synthesizers: both CVC4 (version 1.5) [27] and EUSolver (version 2017-06-15) [3] fail to find a solution in an hour.

4 CEGIS($\mathcal{T}$)

4.1 Overview

In this section, we describe the architecture of CEGIS($\mathcal{T}$), which is obtained by augmenting the standard CEGIS loop with a theory solver. As we are particularly interested in the synthesis of programs with constants, we present CEGIS($\mathcal{T}$) from this particular perspective. In such a setting, CEGIS is responsible for synthesizing program skeletons, whereas the theory solver generates constraints over the literals that denote constants. These constraints are then propagated back to the synthesizer.

In order to explain the main ideas behind CEGIS($\mathcal{T}$) in more detail, we first differentiate between a candidate solution, a candidate solution skeleton, a generalised candidate solution and a final solution.

Definition 1 (Candidate solution). *Using the notation in Sect. 2.2, a program P is a* candidate solution *if $\forall \boldsymbol{x}_{inputs}.\sigma(P, \boldsymbol{x}_{inputs})$ is true for some subset $\boldsymbol{x}_{inputs}$ of all possible $\boldsymbol{x}$.*

Definition 2 (Candidate solution skeleton). *Given a candidate solution P, the* skeleton *of P, denoted by $P[?]$, is obtained by replacing each constant in P with a hole.*

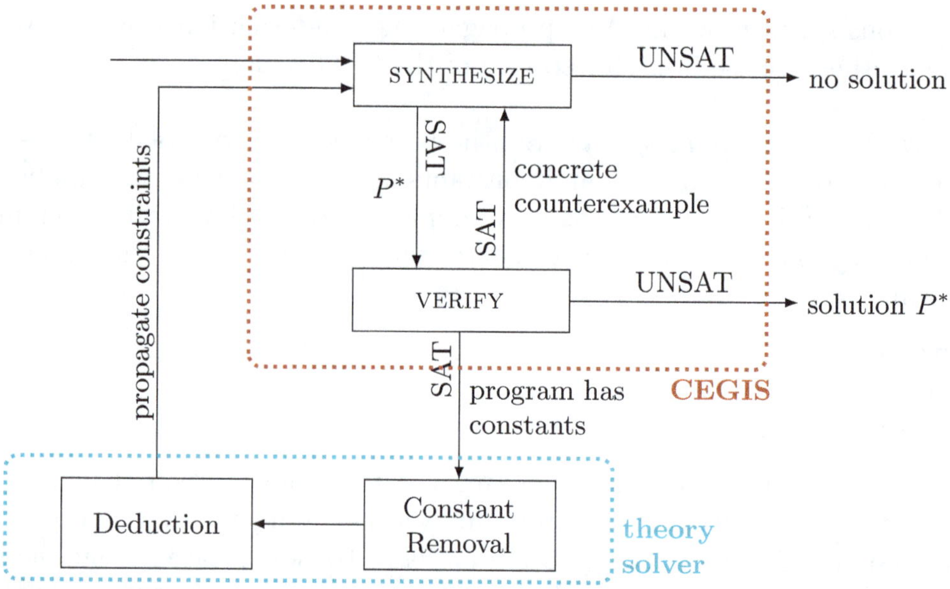

Fig. 3. CEGIS($\mathcal{T}$)

Definition 3 (Generalised candidate solution). *Given a candidate solution skeleton* $P[?]$, *we obtain a* generalised candidate $P[\boldsymbol{v}]$ *by filling each hole in* $P[?]$ *with a distinct symbolic variable, i.e., variable* v_i *will correspond to the i-th hole. Then* $\boldsymbol{v} = [v_1, \ldots, v_n]$, *where n denotes the number of holes in* $P[?]$.

Definition 4 (Final solution). *A candidate solution P is a* final solution *if the formula* $\forall \boldsymbol{x}.\sigma(P, \boldsymbol{x})$ *is valid.*

Example 1 (Candidate solution, candidate solution skeleton, generalised candidate solution, final solution). Given the example in Sect. 3, if $\boldsymbol{x}_{inputs} = \{0\}$, then $f(x) = -2$ is a candidate solution. The corresponding candidate skeleton is $f[?](x) = ?$ and the generalised candidate is $f[v_1](x) = v_1$. A final solution for this example is $f(x) = ite\ (x < 334455)\ {-1}\ 0$.

The communication between the synthesizer and the theory solver in CEGIS($\mathcal{T}$) is illustrated in Fig. 3 and can be described as follows:

- The CEGIS architecture (enclosed in a red rectangle) deduces the candidate solution P^*, which is provided to the theory solver.
- The theory solver (enclosed in a blue rectangle) obtains the skeleton $P^*[?]$ of P^* and generalises it to $P^*[\boldsymbol{v}]$ in the box marked CONSTANT REMOVAL. Subsequently, DEDUCTION attempts to find a constraint over $\boldsymbol{v}$ describing those values for which $P^*[\boldsymbol{v}]$ is a final solution. This constraint is propagated back to CEGIS. Whenever there is no valuation of $\boldsymbol{v}$ for which $P^*[\boldsymbol{v}]$ becomes a final solution, the constraint needs to block the current skeleton $P^*[?]$.

The CEGIS($\mathcal{T}$) algorithm is given as Algorithm 1 and proceeds as follows:

- **CEGIS synthesis phase:** checks the satisfiability of $\forall \boldsymbol{x}_{inputs}. \sigma(P, \boldsymbol{x}_{inputs})$ where $\boldsymbol{x}_{inputs}$ is a subset of all possible $\boldsymbol{x}$ and obtains a candidate solution P^*. If this formula is unsatisfiable, then the synthesis problem has no solution.
- **CEGIS verification phase:** checks whether there exists a concrete counterexample for the current candidate solution by checking the satisfiability of the formula $\neg\sigma(P^*, \boldsymbol{x})$. If the result is UNSAT, then P^* is a final solution to the synthesis problem. If the result is SAT, a concrete counterexample $\boldsymbol{cex}$ can be extracted from the satisfying assignment.
- **Theory solver:** if P^* contains constants, then they are eliminated, resulting in the $P^*[?]$ skeleton, which is afterwards generalised to $P^*[\boldsymbol{v}]$. The goal of the theory solver is to find $\mathcal{T}$-implied literals and communicate them back to the CEGIS part in the form of a constraint, $C(P, P^*, \boldsymbol{v})$. In Algorithm 1, this is done by $Deduction(\sigma, P^*[\boldsymbol{v}])$. The result of $Deduction(\sigma, P^*[\boldsymbol{v}])$ is of the following form: whenever there exists a valuation of $\boldsymbol{v}$ for which the current skeleton $P^*[?]$ is a final solution, $res = true$ and $C(P, P^*, \boldsymbol{v}) = \bigwedge_{i=1 \cdot n} v_i = c_i$, where c_i are constants; otherwise, $res = false$ and $C(P, P^*, \boldsymbol{v})$ needs to block the current skeleton $P^*[?]$, i.e., $C(P, P^*, \boldsymbol{v}) = P[?] \neq P^*[?]$.
- **CEGIS learning phase:** adds new information to the problem specification. If we did not use the theory solver (i.e., the candidate P^* found by the synthesizer did not contain constants or the problem specification was out of the theory solver's scope), then the learning would be limited to adding the concrete counterexample $\boldsymbol{cex}$ obtained from the verification phase to the set $\boldsymbol{x}_{inputs}$. However, if the theory solver is used and returns $res = true$, then the second element in the tuple contains valuations for $\boldsymbol{v}$ such that $P^*[\boldsymbol{v}]$ is a final solution. If $res = false$, then the second element blocks the current skeleton and needs to be added to σ.

4.2 CEGIS($\mathcal{T}$) with a Theory Solver Based on FM Elimination

In this section we describe a theory solver based on FM variable elimination. Other techniques for eliminating existentially quantified variables can be used. For instance, one might use cylindrical algebraic decomposition [9] for specifications with non-linear arithmetic. In our case, whenever the specification σ does not belong to linear arithmetic, the FM theory solver is not called.

As mentioned above, we need to produce a constraint over variables $\boldsymbol{v}$ describing the situation when $P^*[\boldsymbol{v}]$ is a final solution. For this purpose, we consider the formula $\exists \boldsymbol{x}. \neg\sigma(P^*[\boldsymbol{v}], \boldsymbol{x})$, where $\boldsymbol{v}$ is a satisfiability witness if the specification σ admits a counterexample $\boldsymbol{x}$ for P^*. Let $E(\boldsymbol{v})$ be the formula obtained by eliminating $\boldsymbol{x}$ from $\exists \boldsymbol{x}. \neg\sigma(P^*[\boldsymbol{v}], \boldsymbol{x})$. If $\neg E(\boldsymbol{v})$ is satisfiable, any satisfiability witness gives us the necessary valuation for $\boldsymbol{v}$:

$$C(P, P^*, \boldsymbol{v}) = \bigwedge_{i=1 \cdot n} v_i = c_i.$$

Algorithm 1. CEGIS($\mathcal{T}$)

```
function CEGIS(T)(specification σ)
    while true do
        /* CEGIS synthesis phase */
        if ∀x_inputs.σ(P, x_inputs) is UNSAT then return Failure;
        else
            P* = satisfiability witness for ∀x_inputs.σ(P, x_inputs);
            /* CEGIS verification phase */
            if ¬(σ(P*, x)) is UNSAT then return Final solution P*;
            else
                cex = satisfiability witness for ¬(σ(P*, x));
                /* Theory solver */
                if P* contains constants then
                    Obtain P*[?] from P*;
                    Generalise P*[?] to P*[v];
                    (res, C(P, P*, v)) = Deduction(σ, P*[v]);
                end if
            end if
        end if
        /* CEGIS learning phase */
        if res then
            C(P, P*, v) is of the form ⋀_{i=1·n} v_i = c_i.
            return Final solution P*[c];
        else
            σ(P, x) = σ(P, x) ∧ C(P, P*, v);
            x_inputs = x_inputs ∪ {cex};
        end if
    end while
end function
```

If $\neg E(\boldsymbol{v})$ is UNSAT, then the current skeleton $P^*[?]$ needs to be blocked. This reasoning is supported by Lemma 1 and Corollary 1.

Lemma 1. *Let $E(\boldsymbol{v})$ be the formula that is obtained by eliminating $\boldsymbol{x}$ from $\exists \boldsymbol{x}.\neg\sigma(P^*[\boldsymbol{v}], \boldsymbol{x})$. Then, any witness $\boldsymbol{v}^{\#}$ to the satisfiability of $\neg E(\boldsymbol{v})$ gives us a final solution $P^*[\boldsymbol{v}^{\#}]$ to the synthesis problem.*

Proof. From the fact that $E(\boldsymbol{v})$ is obtained by eliminating $\boldsymbol{x}$ from $\exists \boldsymbol{x}.\neg\sigma(P^*[\boldsymbol{v}], \boldsymbol{x})$, we get that $E(\boldsymbol{v})$ is equivalent with $\exists \boldsymbol{x}.\neg\sigma(P^*[\boldsymbol{v}], \boldsymbol{x})$ (we use $\equiv$ to denote equivalence):

$$E(\boldsymbol{v}) \equiv \exists \boldsymbol{x}.\neg\sigma(P^*[\boldsymbol{v}], \boldsymbol{x}).$$

Then:

$$\neg E(\boldsymbol{v}) \equiv \forall \boldsymbol{x}.\sigma(P^*[\boldsymbol{v}], \boldsymbol{x}).$$

Consequently, any $\boldsymbol{v}^{\#}$ satisfying $\neg E(\boldsymbol{v})$ also satisfies $\forall \boldsymbol{x}.\sigma(P^*[\boldsymbol{v}], \boldsymbol{x})$. From $\forall \boldsymbol{x}.\sigma(P^*[\boldsymbol{v}^{\#}], \boldsymbol{x})$ and Definition 4 we get that $P^*[\boldsymbol{v}^{\#}]$ is a final solution.

Corollary 1. *Let $E(v)$ be the formula that is obtained by eliminating $\boldsymbol{x}$ from $\exists \boldsymbol{x}. \neg\sigma(P^*[\boldsymbol{v}], \boldsymbol{x})$. If $\neg E(\boldsymbol{v})$ is unsatisfiable, then the corresponding synthesis problem does not admit a solution for the skeleton $P^*[?]$.*

Proof. Given that $\neg E(\boldsymbol{v}) \equiv \forall \boldsymbol{x}. \sigma(P^*[\boldsymbol{v}], \boldsymbol{x})$, if $\neg E(\boldsymbol{v})$ is unsatisfiable, so is $\forall \boldsymbol{x}. \sigma(P^*[\boldsymbol{v}], \boldsymbol{x})$, meaning that there is no valuation for $\boldsymbol{v}$ such that the specification σ is obeyed for all inputs $\boldsymbol{x}$.

For the current skeleton $P^*[?]$, the constraint $E(\boldsymbol{v})$ generalises the concrete counterexample $\boldsymbol{cex}$ (found during the CEGIS verification phase) in the sense that the instantiation $\boldsymbol{v}^\#$ of $\boldsymbol{v}$ for which $\boldsymbol{cex}$ failed the specification, i.e., $\neg\sigma(P^*[\boldsymbol{v}^\#], \boldsymbol{cex})$, is a satisfiability witness for $E(\boldsymbol{v})$. This is true as $E(\boldsymbol{v}) \equiv \exists \boldsymbol{x}. \neg\sigma(P^*[\boldsymbol{v}], \boldsymbol{x})$, which means that the satisfiability witness $(\boldsymbol{v}^\#, \boldsymbol{cex})$ for $\neg\sigma(P^*[\boldsymbol{v}], \boldsymbol{x})$ projected on $\boldsymbol{v}$ is a satisfiability witness for $E(\boldsymbol{v})$.

Disjunction. The specification σ and the candidate solution may contain disjunctions. However, most theory solvers (and in particular the FM variable elimination [7]) work on conjunctive fragments only. A naïve approach could use case-splitting, i.e., transforming the formula into Disjunctive Normal Form (DNF) and then solving each clause separately. This can result in a number of clauses exponential in the size of the original formula. Instead, we handle disjunction using the Boolean Fourier Motzkin procedure [20,32]. As a result, the constraints we generate may be non-clausal.

Applying CEGIS($\mathcal{T}$) with FM to the Motivational Example. We recall the example in Sect. 3 and apply CEGIS($\mathcal{T}$). The problem is

$$\exists f. \forall x. \, x < 334455 \rightarrow f(x) < 0 \wedge x \geq 334455 \rightarrow f(x) = 0$$

which gives us the following specification:

$$\sigma(f, x) = (x \geq 334455 \vee f(x) < 0) \wedge (x < 334455 \vee f(x) = 0).$$

The first synthesis phase generates the candidate $f^*(x) = 0$ for which the verification phase returns the concrete counterexample $x = 0$. As this candidate contains the constant 0, we generalise it to $f^*[v_1](x) = v_1$, for which we get

$$\sigma(f^*[v_1], x) = (x \geq 334455 \vee v_1 < 0) \wedge (x < 334455 \vee v_1 = 0).$$

Next, we use FM to eliminate x from

$$\exists x. \neg(\sigma(f^*[v_1], x)) = \exists x. (x < 334455 \wedge v_1 \geq 0) \vee (x \geq 334455 \wedge v_1 \neq 0).$$

Note that, given that formula $\neg\sigma(f^*[v_1], x)$ is in DNF, for convenience we directly apply FM to each disjunct and obtain $E(v_1) = v_1 \geq 0 \vee v_1 \neq 0$, which characterises all the values of v_1 for which there exists a counterexample. When negating $E(v_1)$ we get $v_1 < 0 \wedge v_1 = 0$, which is UNSAT. As there is no valuation of

v_1 for which the current f^* is a final solution, the result returned by the theory solver is $(\mathit{false}, f[?] \neq f^*[?])$, which is used to augment the specification. Subsequently, a new CEGIS($\mathcal{T}$) iteration starts. The learning phase has changed the specification σ to

$$\sigma(f, x) = (x \geq 334455 \vee f(x) < 0) \wedge (x < 334455 \vee f(x) = 0) \wedge f[?] \neq ?.$$

This forces the synthesis phase to pick a new candidate solution with a different skeleton. The new candidate solution we get is $f^*(x) = \mathit{ite}\ (x < 100)\ {-3}\ 1$, which works for the previous counterexample $x = 0$. However, the verification phase returns the counterexample $x = 100$. Again, this candidate contains constants which we replace by symbolic variables, obtaining

$$f^*[v_1, v_2, v_3](x) = \mathit{ite}\ (x < v_1)\ v_2\ v_3.$$

Next, we use FM to eliminate x from

$$\begin{aligned}
&\exists x.\neg(\sigma(f^*[v_1, v_2, v_3], x)) = \\
&\exists x.\neg(x \geq 334455 \vee (x < v_1 \rightarrow v_2 < 0 \wedge x \geq v_1 \rightarrow v_3 < 0) \wedge \\
&\qquad x < 334455 \vee (x < v_1 \rightarrow v_2 = 0 \wedge x \geq v_1 \rightarrow v_3 = 0)) = \\
&\exists x.\neg((x \geq 334455 \vee x \geq v_1 \vee v_2 < 0) \wedge (x \geq 334455 \vee x < v_1 \vee v_3 < 0) \wedge \\
&\qquad (x < 334455 \vee x \geq v_1 \vee v_2 = 0) \wedge (x < 334455 \vee x < v_1 \vee v_3 = 0)) = \\
&\quad \exists x.(x < 334455 \wedge x < v_1 \wedge v_2 \geq 0) \vee (x < 334455 \wedge x \geq v_1 \wedge v_3 \geq 0) \vee \\
&\qquad (x \geq 334455 \wedge x < v_1 \wedge v_2 \neq 0) \vee (x \geq 334455 \wedge x \geq v_1 \wedge v_3 \neq 0).
\end{aligned}$$

As we work with integers, we can rewrite $x < 334455$ to $x \leq 334454$ and $x < v_1$ to $x \leq v_1 - 1$. Then, we obtain the following constraint $E(v_1, v_2, v_3)$ (as aforementioned, we applied FM to each disjunct in $\neg\sigma(f^*[v_1, v_2, v_3], x)$)

$$E(v_1, v_2, v_3) = v_2 {\geq} 0 \vee (v_1 \leq 334454 \wedge v_3 \geq 0) \vee (v_1 \geq 334456 \wedge v_2 \neq 0) \vee v_3 \neq 0$$

whose negation is

$$\neg E(v_1, v_2, v_3) = v_2 < 0 \wedge (v_1 > 334454 \vee v_3 < 0) \wedge (v_1 < 334456 \vee v_2 = 0) \wedge v_3 = 0$$

A satisfiability witness is $v_1 = 334455$, $v_2 = -1$ and $v_3 = 0$. Thus, the result returned by the theory solver is $(\mathit{true}, v_1 = 334455 \wedge v_2 = -1 \wedge v_3 = 0)$, which is used by CEGIS to obtain the final solution

$$f^*(x) = \mathit{ite}\ (x < 334455)\ {-1}\ 0\ .$$

4.3 CEGIS($\mathcal{T}$) with an SMT-based Theory Solver

For our second variant of a theory solver, we make use of an off-the-shelf SMT solver that supports quantified first-order formulae. This approach is more generic than the one described in Sect. 4.2, as there are solvers for a broad range of theories.

Recall that our goal is to obtain a constraint $C(P, P^*, \boldsymbol{v})$ that either characterises the valuations of $\boldsymbol{v}$ for which $P^*[\boldsymbol{v}]$ is a final solution or blocks $P^*[?]$ whenever no such valuation exists. Consequently, we use the SMT solver to check the satisfiability of the formula

$$\Phi = \forall \boldsymbol{x}.\, \sigma(P^*[\boldsymbol{v}], \boldsymbol{x}).$$

If Φ is satisfiable, then any satisfiability witness $\boldsymbol{c}$ gives us a valuation for $\boldsymbol{v}$ such that P^* is a final solution: $C(P, P^*, \boldsymbol{v}) = \bigwedge_{i=1 \cdot n} v_i = c_i$. Conversely, if Φ is unsatisfiable then $C(P, P^*, \boldsymbol{v})$ must block the current skeleton $P^*[?]$: $C(P, P^*, \boldsymbol{v}) = P[?] \neq P^*[?]$.

Applying SMT-based CEGIS($\mathcal{T}$) to the Motivational Example. Again, we recall the example in Sect. 3. We will solve it by using SMT-based CEGIS($\mathcal{T}$) for the theory of linear arithmetic. For this purpose, we assume that the synthesis phase finds the same sequence of candidate solutions as in Sect. 3. Namely, the first candidate is $f^*(x) = 0$, which gets generalised to $f^*[v_1](x) = v_1$. Then, the first SMT call is for $\forall x.\, \sigma(v_1, x)$, where

$$\sigma(v_1, x) = (x \geq 334455 \vee v_1 < 0) \wedge (x < 334455 \vee v_1 = 0).$$

The SMT solver returns UNSAT, which means that $C(f, f^*, v_1) = f[?] \neq ?$. The second candidate is $f^*(x) = ite\ (x < 100)\ -3\ 1$, which generalises to $f^*[v_1, v_2, v_3](x) = ite\ (x < v_1)\ v_2\ v_3$. The corresponding call to the SMT solver is for $\forall x.\, \sigma((ite\ (x < v_1)\ v_2\ v_3), x)$, for which we obtain the satisfiability witness $v_1 = 334455$, $v_2 = -1$ and $v_3 = 0$. Then $C(f, f^*, v_1, v_2, v_3) = v_1 = 334455 \wedge v_2 = -1 \wedge v_3 = 0$, which gives us the same final solution we obtained when using FM in Sect. 3.

5 Experimental Evaluation

5.1 Implementation

Incremental Satisfiability Solving. Our implementation of CEGIS may sometimes perform hundreds of loop iterations before finding the correct solution. Recall that the synthesis block of CEGIS is based on Bounded Model Checking (BMC). Ultimately, this BMC module performs calls to a SAT solver. Consequently, we may have hundreds of calls to this SAT solver, which are all very similar (the same base specification with some extra constraints added in each iteration). This makes CEGIS a prime candidate for incremental SAT solving. We implemented incremental solving in the synthesis block of CEGIS.

5.2 Benchmarks

We have selected a set of bitvector benchmarks from the Syntax-Guided Synthesis (SyGuS) competition [4] and a set of benchmarks synthesizing safety invariants and danger invariants for C programs [10]. All benchmarks are written in SyGuS-IF [26], a variant of SMT-LIB2.

Given that the syntactic restrictions (called the *grammar* or the *template*) provided in the SyGuS benchmarks contain all the necessary non-trivial constants, we removed them completely from these benchmarks. Removing just the non-trivial constants and keeping the rest of the grammar (with the only constants being 0 and 1) would have made the problem much more difficult, as the constants would have had to be incrementally constructed by applying the operators available to 0 and 1.

We group the benchmarks into three categories: invariant generation, which covers danger invariants, safety invariants and the class of invariant generation benchmarks from the SyGuS competition; hackers/crypto, which includes benchmarks from hackers-delight and cryptographic circuits; and comparisons, composed of benchmarks that require synthesizing longer programs with comparisons, e.g., finding the maximum value of 10 variables.

5.3 Experimental Setup

We conduct the experimental evaluation on a 12-core 2.40 GHz Intel Xeon E5-2440 with 96 GB of RAM and Linux OS. We use the Linux *times* command to measure CPU time used for each benchmark. The runtime is limited to 600 s per benchmark. We use MiniSat [12] as the SAT solver, and Z3 v4.5.1 [22] as the SMT-solver in CEGIS($\mathcal{T}$) with SMT-based theory solver. The SAT solver could, in principle, be replaced with Z3 to solve benchmarks over a broader range of theories.

We present results for four different configurations of CEGIS:

- CEGIS($\mathcal{T}$)-FM: CEGIS($\mathcal{T}$) with Fourier Motzkin as the theory solver;
- CEGIS($\mathcal{T}$)-SMT: CEGIS($\mathcal{T}$) with Z3 as the theory solver;
- CEGIS: basic CEGIS as described in Sect. 2.2;
- CEGIS-Inc: basic CEGIS with incremental SAT solving.

We compare our results against the latest release of CVC4, version 1.5. As we are interested in running our benchmarks without any syntactic template, the first reason for choosing CVC4 [6] as our comparison point is the fact that it performs well when no such templates are provided. This is illustrated by the fact that it won the Conditional Linear Integer Arithmetic track of the SyGuS competition 2017 [4], one of two tracks where a syntactic template was not used. The other track without syntactic templates is the invariant generation track, in which CVC4 was close second to LoopInvGen [24]. A second reason for picking CVC4 is its overall good performance on all benchmarks, whereas LoopInvGen is a solver specialised to invariant generation.

We also give a row of results for a hypothetical 4-core implementation, as would be allowed in the SyGuS Competition, running 4 configurations in parallel: CEGIS($\mathcal{T}$)-FM, CEGIS($\mathcal{T}$)-SMT, CEGIS, and CEGIS-Inc. A link to the full experimental environment, including scripts to reproduce the results, all benchmarks and the tool, is provided in the footnote as an Open Virtual Appliance (OVA)[1].

[1] www.cprover.org/synthesis.

Table 1. Experimental results – for every set of benchmarks, we give the number of benchmarks solved by each configuration within the timeout and the average time taken per solved benchmark

Configuration	inv		hackers		comparisons		other		total	
	#	s	#	s	#	s	#	s	#	s
CEGIS($\mathcal{T}$)-SMT	33	33.1	4	2.5	3	195.5	16	14.0	56	34.1
CEGIS($\mathcal{T}$)-FM	16	93.1	4	52.8	1	0.06	12	0.7	33	51.8
CEGIS	16	31.3	4	52.0	1	0.03	14	5.3	35	22.4
CEGIS-Inc	16	39.4	5	167.4	1	0.03	14	4.2	36	42.4
Multi-core	33	32.5	5	92.2	3	194.7	16	3.8	57	38.3
CVC4	6	6.5	6	0.002	7	0.006	11	0.003	30	1.3
# benchmarks	48		6		7		19		80	
CVC4 with grammar	4	45.8	0		0		6	2.4	10	19.8
# benchmarks with grammar	8		3		7		16		34	

5.4 Results

The results are given in Table 1. In combination, our CEGIS combination (i.e., CEGIS multi-core) solves 27 more benchmarks than CVC4, but the average time per benchmark is significantly higher.

As expected, both CEGIS($\mathcal{T}$)-SMT and CEGIS($\mathcal{T}$)-FM solve more of the invariant generation benchmarks which require synthesizing arbitrary constants than CVC4. Conversely, CVC4 performs better on benchmarks that require synthesizing long programs with many comparison operations, e.g., finding the maximum value in a series of numbers. CVC4 solves more of the hackers-delight and cryptographic circuit benchmarks, none of which require constants.

Our implementation of basic CEGIS (and consequently of all configurations built on top of this) only increases the length of the synthesized program when no program of a shorter length exists. Thus, it is expensive to synthesize longer programs. However, a benefit of this architecture is that the programs we synthesize are the minimum possible length. Many of the expressions synthesized by CVC4 are very large. This has been noted previously in the Syntax-Guided Synthesis Competition [5], and synthesizing without the syntactic template causes the expressions synthesized to be even longer.

Although CEGIS-Inc is quicker per iteration of the CEGIS loop than basic CEGIS, the average time per benchmark is not significantly better because of the variation in times produced by CEGIS. We hypothesise that the use of incremental solving makes CEGIS-Inc more prone to getting stuck exploring "bad" areas of the solution space than basic CEGIS, and so it requires more iterations than basic CEGIS for some benchmarks. The incremental solving preserves clauses learnt from any conflicts in previous iterations, which means that each SAT solving iteration will begin from exactly the same state as the previous one. The basic implementation doesn't preserve these clauses and so is free to start exploring a new part of the search space each iteration. These effects could be mitigated by running multiple incremental solving instances in parallel.

In order to validate the assumption that CVC4 works better without a template than with one where the non-trivial constants were removed (see Sect. 5.2), we also ran CVC4 on a subset of the benchmarks with a syntactic template comprising the full instruction set we give to CEGIS, plus the constants 0 and 1. Note for some benchmarks it is not possible to add a grammar because the SYGUS-IF language does not allow syntactic templates for benchmarks that use the loop invariant syntax. With a grammar, CVC4 solves fewer of the benchmarks, and takes longer per benchmark. The syntactic template is helpful only in cases where non-trivial constants are needed and the non-trivial constants are contained within the template.

We ran EUSolver on the benchmarks with the syntactic templates, but the bitvector support is incomplete and missing some key operations. As a result EUSolver was unable to solve any benchmarks in the set, and so we have not included the results in the table.

Benefit of Literal Constants. We have investigated how useful the constants in the problem specification are, and have tried a configuration that seeds all constants in the problem specification as hints into the synthesis engine. This proved helpful for basic CEGIS only but not for the CEGIS($\mathcal{T}$) configurations. Our hypothesis is that the latter do not benefit from this because they already have good support for computing constants. We dropped this option in the results presented in this section.

5.5 Threats to Validity

Benchmark Selection: We report an assessment of our approach on a diverse selection of benchmarks. Nevertheless, the set of benchmarks is limited within the scope of this paper, and the performance may not generalise to other benchmarks.

Comparison with State of the Art: CVC4 has not, as far as we are aware, been used for synthesis of bitvector functions without syntactic templates, and so this unanticipated use case may not have been fully tested. We are unable to compare all results to other solvers from the SyGuS Competition because EUSolver and EUPhony do not support synthesizing bitvector programs without a syntactic template, EUSolver's support for bitvectors is incomplete even when used with a template, LoopInvGen and DryadSynth do not support bitvectors, and E3Solver tackles only Programming By Example benchmarks [5].

Choice of Theories: We evaluated the benefits of CEGIS($\mathcal{T}$) in the context of two specific theory instances. While the improvements in our experiments are significant, it is uncertain whether this will generalise to other theories.

6 Related Work

The traditional view of program synthesis is that of synthesis from complete specifications [21]. Such specifications are often unavailable, difficult to write, or expensive to check against using automated verification techniques. This has led to the proposal of inductive synthesis and, more recently, of oracle-based inductive synthesis, in which the complete specification is not available and oracles are queried to choose programs [19].

A well-known application of CEGIS is program sketching [29,31], where the programmer uses a partial program, called a *sketch*, to describe the desired implementation strategy, and leaves the low-level details of the implementation to an automated synthesis procedure. Inspired by sketching, Syntax-Guided Program Synthesis (SyGuS) [2] requires the user to supplement the logical specification provided to the program synthesizer with a syntactic template that constrains the space of solutions. In contrast to SyGuS, our aim is to improve the efficiency of the exploration to the point that user guidance is no longer required.

Another very active area of program synthesis is denoted by component-based approaches [1,13–15,17,18,25]. Such approaches are concerned with assembling programs from a database of existing components and make use of various techniques, from counterexample-guided synthesis [17] to type-directed search with lightweight SMT-based deduction and partial evaluation [14] and Petri-nets [15]. The techniques developed in the current paper are applicable to any component-based synthesis approach that relies on counterexample-guided inductive synthesis.

Heuristics for constant synthesis are presented in [11], where the solution language is parameterised, inducing a lattice of progressively more expressive languages. One of the parameters is word width, which allows synthesizing programs with constants that satisfy the specification for smaller word widths. Subsequently, heuristics extend the program (including the constants) to the required word width. As opposed to this work, CEGIS($\mathcal{T}$) denotes a systematic approach that does not rely on ad-hoc heuristics.

Regarding the use of SMT solvers in program synthesis, they are frequently employed as oracles. By contrast, Reynolds et al. [27] present an efficient encoding able to solve program synthesis constraints directly within an SMT solver. Their approach relies on rephrasing the synthesis constraint as the problem of refuting a universally quantified formula, which can be solved using first-order quantifier instantiation. Conversely, in our approach we maintain a clear separation between the synthesizer and the theory solver, which communicate in a well-defined manner. In Sect. 5, we provide a comprehensive experimental comparison with the synthesizer described in [27].

7 Conclusion

We proposed CEGIS($\mathcal{T}$), a new approach to program synthesis that combines the strengths of a counterexample-guided inductive synthesizer with those of a theory solver to provide a more efficient exploration of the solution space. We discussed two options for the theory solver, one based on FM variable elimination and one relying on an off-the-shelf SMT solver. Our experiments results showed that, although slower than CVC4, CEGIS($\mathcal{T}$) can solve more benchmarks within a reasonable time that require synthesizing arbitrary constants, where CVC4 fails.

References

1. Albarghouthi, A., Gulwani, S., Kincaid, Z.: Recursive program synthesis. In: Sharygina, N., Veith, H. (eds.) CAV 2013. LNCS, vol. 8044, pp. 934–950. Springer, Heidelberg (2013). https://doi.org/10.1007/978-3-642-39799-8_67
2. Alur, R., Bodík, R., Juniwal, G., Martin, M.M.K., Raghothaman, M., Seshia, S.A., Singh, R., Solar-Lezama, A., Torlak, E., Udupa, A.: Syntax-guided synthesis. In: FMCAD, pp. 1–8. IEEE (2013)
3. Alur, R., Černý, P., Radhakrishna, A.: Synthesis through unification. In: Kroening, D., Păsăreanu, C.S. (eds.) CAV 2015. LNCS, vol. 9207, pp. 163–179. Springer, Cham (2015). https://doi.org/10.1007/978-3-319-21668-3_10
4. Alur, R., Fisman, D., Singh, R., Solar-Lezama, A.: SyGuS-Comp 2017: results and analysis. CoRR abs/1711.11438 (2017)
5. Alur, R., Fisman, D., Singh, R., Udupa, A.: Syntax guided synthesis competition (2017). http://sygus.seas.upenn.edu/SyGuS-COMP2017.html
6. Barrett, C., Conway, C.L., Deters, M., Hadarean, L., Jovanović, D., King, T., Reynolds, A., Tinelli, C.: CVC4. In: Gopalakrishnan, G., Qadeer, S. (eds.) CAV 2011. LNCS, vol. 6806, pp. 171–177. Springer, Heidelberg (2011). https://doi.org/10.1007/978-3-642-22110-1_14
7. Bik, A.J.C., Wijshoff, H.A.G.: Implementation of Fourier-Motzkin elimination. Technical report, Rijksuniversiteit Leiden (1994)
8. Clarke, E., Kroening, D., Lerda, F.: A tool for checking ANSI-C programs. In: Jensen, K., Podelski, A. (eds.) TACAS 2004. LNCS, vol. 2988, pp. 168–176. Springer, Heidelberg (2004). https://doi.org/10.1007/978-3-540-24730-2_15
9. Collins, G.E.: Hauptvortrag: quantifier elimination for real closed fields by cylindrical algebraic decompostion. In: Brakhage, H. (ed.) GI-Fachtagung 1975. LNCS, vol. 33, pp. 134–183. Springer, Heidelberg (1975). https://doi.org/10.1007/3-540-07407-4_17
10. David, C., Kesseli, P., Kroening, D., Lewis, M.: Danger invariants. In: Fitzgerald, J., Heitmeyer, C., Gnesi, S., Philippou, A. (eds.) FM 2016. LNCS, vol. 9995, pp. 182–198. Springer, Cham (2016). https://doi.org/10.1007/978-3-319-48989-6_12
11. David, C., Kroening, D., Lewis, M.: Using program synthesis for program analysis. In: Davis, M., Fehnker, A., McIver, A., Voronkov, A. (eds.) LPAR 2015. LNCS, vol. 9450, pp. 483–498. Springer, Heidelberg (2015). https://doi.org/10.1007/978-3-662-48899-7_34
12. Eén, N., Sörensson, N.: An extensible SAT-solver. In: Giunchiglia, E., Tacchella, A. (eds.) SAT 2003. LNCS, vol. 2919, pp. 502–518. Springer, Heidelberg (2004). https://doi.org/10.1007/978-3-540-24605-3_37
13. Feng, Y., Bastani, O., Martins, R., Dillig, I., Anand, S.: Automated synthesis of semantic malware signatures using maximum satisfiability. In: NDSS. The Internet Society (2017)

14. Feng, Y., Martins, R., Geffen, J.V., Dillig, I., Chaudhuri, S.: Component-based synthesis of table consolidation and transformation tasks from examples. In: PLDI, pp. 422–436. ACM (2017)
15. Feng, Y., Martins, R., Wang, Y., Dillig, I., Reps, T.W.: Component-based synthesis for complex APIs. In: POPL, pp. 599–612. ACM (2017)
16. Ganzinger, H., Hagen, G., Nieuwenhuis, R., Oliveras, A., Tinelli, C.: DPLL(T): fast decision procedures. In: Alur, R., Peled, D.A. (eds.) CAV 2004. LNCS, vol. 3114, pp. 175–188. Springer, Heidelberg (2004). https://doi.org/10.1007/978-3-540-27813-9_14
17. Gulwani, S., Jha, S., Tiwari, A., Venkatesan, R.: Synthesis of loop-free programs. In: PLDI, pp. 62–73. ACM (2011)
18. Gulwani, S., Korthikanti, V.A., Tiwari, A.: Synthesizing geometry constructions. In: PLDI, pp. 50–61. ACM (2011)
19. Jha, S., Gulwani, S., Seshia, S.A., Tiwari, A.: Oracle-guided component-based program synthesis. In: ICSE, no. 1, pp. 215–224. ACM (2010)
20. Kroening, D., Strichman, O.: Decision Procedures: An Algorithmic Point of View, 1st edn. Springer, Heidelberg (2008). https://doi.org/10.1007/978-3-540-74105-3
21. Manna, Z., Waldinger, R.: A deductive approach to program synthesis. In: IJCAI. pp. 542–551. William Kaufmann (1979)
22. de Moura, L., Bjørner, N.: Z3: an efficient SMT solver. In: Ramakrishnan, C.R., Rehof, J. (eds.) TACAS 2008. LNCS, vol. 4963, pp. 337–340. Springer, Heidelberg (2008). https://doi.org/10.1007/978-3-540-78800-3_24
23. Nieuwenhuis, R., Oliveras, A., Tinelli, C.: Solving SAT and SAT modulo theories: From an abstract Davis-Putnam-Logemann-Loveland procedure to DPLL(T). J. ACM **53**(6), 937–977 (2006)
24. Padhi, S., Millstein, T.D.: Data-driven loop invariant inference with automatic feature synthesis. CoRR abs/1707.02029 (2017)
25. Perelman, D., Gulwani, S., Grossman, D., Provost, P.: Test-driven synthesis. In: PLDI, pp. 408–418. ACM (2014)
26. Raghothaman, M., Udupa, A.: Language to specify syntax-guided synthesis problems. CoRR abs/1405.5590 (2014)
27. Reynolds, A., Deters, M., Kuncak, V., Tinelli, C., Barrett, C.: Counterexample-guided quantifier instantiation for synthesis in SMT. In: Kroening, D., Păsăreanu, C.S. (eds.) CAV 2015. LNCS, vol. 9207, pp. 198–216. Springer, Cham (2015). https://doi.org/10.1007/978-3-319-21668-3_12
28. Rosen, E.: An existential fragment of second order logic. Arch. Math. Log. **38**(4–5), 217–234 (1999)
29. Solar-Lezama, A.: Program sketching. STTT **15**(5–6), 475–495 (2013)
30. Solar-Lezama, A., Rabbah, R.M., Bodík, R., Ebcioglu, K.: Programming by sketching for bit-streaming programs. In: PLDI, pp. 281–294. ACM (2005)
31. Solar-Lezama, A., Tancau, L., Bodík, R., Seshia, S.A., Saraswat, V.A.: Combinatorial sketching for finite programs. In: ASPLOS, pp. 404–415. ACM (2006)
32. Strichman, O.: On solving Presburger and linear arithmetic with SAT. In: Aagaard, M.D., O'Leary, J.W. (eds.) FMCAD 2002. LNCS, vol. 2517, pp. 160–170. Springer, Heidelberg (2002). https://doi.org/10.1007/3-540-36126-X_10

Synthesizing Reactive Systems from Hyperproperties

Bernd Finkbeiner, Christopher Hahn, Philip Lukert, Marvin Stenger, and Leander Tentrup(✉)

Reactive Systems Group, Saarland University, Saarbrücken, Germany
{finkbeiner,hahn,lukert, stenger,tentrup}@react.uni-saarland.de

Abstract. We study the reactive synthesis problem for hyperproperties given as formulas of the temporal logic HyperLTL. Hyperproperties generalize trace properties, i.e., sets of traces, to *sets of sets* of traces. Typical examples are information-flow policies like noninterference, which stipulate that no sensitive data must leak into the public domain. Such properties cannot be expressed in standard linear or branching-time temporal logics like LTL, CTL, or CTL*. We show that, while the synthesis problem is undecidable for full HyperLTL, it remains decidable for the $\exists^*$, $\exists^*\forall^1$, and the *linear* $\forall^*$ fragments. Beyond these fragments, the synthesis problem immediately becomes undecidable. For universal HyperLTL, we present a semi-decision procedure that constructs implementations and counterexamples up to a given bound. We report encouraging experimental results obtained with a prototype implementation on example specifications with hyperproperties like symmetric responses, secrecy, and information-flow.

1 Introduction

Hyperproperties [5] generalize trace properties in that they not only check the correctness of *individual* computation traces in isolation, but relate *multiple* computation traces to each other. HyperLTL [4] is a logic for expressing temporal hyperproperties, by extending linear-time temporal logic (LTL) with *explicit* quantification over traces. HyperLTL has been used to specify a variety of information-flow and security properties. Examples include classical properties like non-interference and observational determinism, as well as quantitative information-flow properties, symmetries in hardware designs, and formally verified error correcting codes [12]. For example, observational determinism can be expressed as the HyperLTL formula $\forall\pi\forall\pi'. \square(I_\pi = I_{\pi'}) \rightarrow \square(O_\pi = O_{\pi'})$, stating that, for every pair of traces, if the observable inputs are the same, then the observable outputs must be same as well. While the satisfiability [9], model checking [4,12], and runtime verification [1,10] problem for HyperLTL has been studied, the *reactive synthesis* problem of HyperLTL is, so far, still open.

Supported by the European Research Council (ERC) Grant OSARES (No. 683300).

H. Chockler and G. Weissenbacher (Eds.): CAV 2018, LNCS 10981, pp. 289–306, 2018.
https://doi.org/10.1007/978-3-319-96145-3_16

In reactive synthesis, we automatically construct an implementation that is guaranteed to satisfy a given specification. A fundamental difference to verification is that there is no human programmer involved: in verification, the programmer would first produce an implementation, which is then verified against the specification. In synthesis, the implementation is directly constructed from the specification. Because there is no programmer, it is crucial that the specification contains *all* desired properties of the implementation: the synthesized implementation is guaranteed to satisfy the given specification, but nothing is guaranteed beyond that. The added expressive power of HyperLTL over LTL is very attractive for synthesis: with synthesis from hyperproperties, we can guarantee that the implementation does not only accomplish the desired functionality, but is also free of information leaks, is symmetric, is fault-tolerant with respect to transmission errors, etc.

More formally, the reactive synthesis problem asks for a *strategy*, that is a tree branching on environment inputs whose nodes are labeled by the system output. Collecting the inputs and outputs along a branch of the tree, we obtain a trace. If the set of traces collected from the branches of the strategy tree satisfies the specification, we say that the strategy *realizes* the specification. The specification is *realizable* iff there exists a strategy tree that realizes the specification. With LTL specifications, we get trees where the trace on each individual branch satisfies the LTL formula. With HyperLTL, we additionally get trees where the traces between different branches are in a specified relationship. This is dramatically more powerful.

Consider, for example, the well-studied *distributed* version of the reactive synthesis problem, where the system is split into a set of processes, that each only see a subset of the inputs. The distributed synthesis problem for LTL can be expressed as the standard (non-distributed) synthesis problem for HyperLTL, by adding for each process the requirement that the process output is *observationally deterministic* in the process input. HyperLTL synthesis thus subsumes distributed synthesis. The information-flow requirements realized by HyperLTL synthesis can, however, be much more sophisticated than the observational determinism needed for distributed synthesis. Consider, for example, the *dining cryptographers* problem [3]: three cryptographers C_a, C_b, and C_c sit at a table in a restaurant having dinner and either one of cryptographers or, alternatively, the NSA must pay for their meal. Is there a protocol where each cryptographer can find out whether it was a cryptographer who paid or the NSA, but cannot find out which cryptographer paid the bill?

Synthesis from LTL formulas is known to be decidable in doubly exponential time. The fact that the distributed synthesis problem is undecidable [21] immediately eliminates the hope for a similar general result for HyperLTL. However, since LTL is obviously a fragment of HyperLTL, this immediately leads to the question whether the synthesis problem is still decidable for fragments of HyperLTL that are close to LTL but go beyond LTL: when exactly does the synthesis problem become undecidable? From a more practical point of view, the interesting question is whether semi-algorithms for distributed synthesis [7,14], which have been successful in constructing distributed systems from LTL specifications despite the undecidability of the general problem, can be extended to HyperLTL?

In this paper, we answer the first question by studying the $\exists^*$, $\exists^*\forall^1$, and the *linear* $\forall^*$ fragment. We show that the synthesis problem for all three fragments is decidable, and the problem becomes undecidable as soon as we go beyond these fragments. In particular, the synthesis problem for the full $\forall^*$ fragment, which includes observational determinism, is undecidable.

We answer the second question by studying the *bounded* version of the synthesis problem for the $\forall^*$ fragment. In order to detect realizability, we ask whether, for a universal HyperLTL formula φ and a given bound n on the number of states, there exists a representation of the strategy tree as a finite-state machine with no more than n states that satisfies φ. To detect unrealizability, we check whether there exists a counterexample to realizability of bounded size. We show that both checks can be effectively reduced to SMT solving.

Related Work. HyperLTL [4] is a successor of the temporal logic SecLTL [6] used to characterize temporal information-flow. The model-checking [4,12], satisfiability [9], monitoring problem [1,10], and the first-order extension [17] of HyperLTL has been studied before. To the best of the authors knowledge, this is the first work that considers the synthesis problem for temporal hyperproperties. We base our algorithms on well-known synthesis algorithms such as bounded synthesis [14] that itself is an instance of Safraless synthesis [18] for ω-regular languages. Further techniques that we adapt for hyperproperties are lazy synthesis [11] and the bounded unrealizability method [15,16].

Hyperproperties [5] can be seen as a unifying framework for many different properties of interest in multiple distinct areas of research. Information-flow properties in security and privacy research are hyperproperties [4]. HyperLTL subsumes logics that reason over knowledge [4]. Information-flow in distributed systems is another example of hyperproperties, and the HyperLTL realizability problem subsumes both the distributed synthesis problem [13,21] as well as synthesis of fault-tolerant systems [16]. In circuit verification, the semantic independence of circuit output signals on a certain set of inputs, enabling a range of potential optimizations, is a hyperproperty.

2 Preliminaries

HyperLTL. HyperLTL [4] is a temporal logic for specifying hyperproperties. It extends LTL by quantification over trace variables π and a method to link atomic propositions to specific traces. The set of trace variables is $\mathcal{V}$. Formulas in HyperLTL are given by the grammar

$$\varphi ::= \forall \pi .\, \varphi \mid \exists \pi .\, \varphi \mid \psi \ , \text{ and}$$
$$\psi ::= a_\pi \mid \neg\psi \mid \psi \vee \psi \mid \bigcirc \psi \mid \psi \,\mathcal{U}\, \psi \ ,$$

where $a \in \mathrm{AP}$ and $\pi \in \mathcal{V}$. The alphabet of a HyperLTL formula is 2^{AP}. We allow the standard boolean connectives $\wedge$, $\rightarrow$, $\leftrightarrow$ as well as the derived LTL operators release $\varphi \mathcal{R} \psi \equiv \neg(\neg\varphi \mathcal{U} \neg\psi)$, eventually $\Diamond\varphi \equiv true \mathcal{U} \varphi$, globally $\Box\varphi \equiv \neg\Diamond\neg\varphi$, and weak until $\varphi \mathcal{W} \psi \equiv \Box\varphi \vee (\varphi \mathcal{U} \psi)$.

The semantics is given by the satisfaction relation $\vDash_T$ over a set of traces $T \subseteq (2^{\text{AP}})^\omega$. We define an assignment $\Pi : \mathcal{V} \to (2^{\text{AP}})^\omega$ that maps trace variables to traces. $\Pi[i,\infty]$ is the trace assignment that is equal to $\Pi(\pi)[i,\infty]$ for all π and denotes the assignment where the first i items are removed from each trace.

$\Pi \vDash_T a_\pi$ if $a \in \Pi(\pi)[0]$
$\Pi \vDash_T \neg\varphi$ if $\Pi \nvDash_T \varphi$
$\Pi \vDash_T \varphi \vee \psi$ if $\Pi \vDash_T \varphi$ or $\Pi \vDash_T \psi$
$\Pi \vDash_T \bigcirc\varphi$ if $\Pi[1,\infty] \vDash_T \varphi$
$\Pi \vDash_T \varphi \mathcal{U} \psi$ if $\exists i \geq 0.\, \Pi[i,\infty] \vDash_T \psi \wedge \forall 0 \leq j < i.\, \Pi[j,\infty] \vDash_T \varphi$
$\Pi \vDash_T \exists\pi.\, \varphi$ if there is some $t \in T$ such that $\Pi[\pi \mapsto t] \vDash_T \varphi$
$\Pi \vDash_T \forall\pi.\, \varphi$ if for all $t \in T$ holds that $\Pi[\pi \mapsto t] \vDash_T \varphi$

We write $T \vDash \varphi$ for $\{\} \vDash_T \varphi$ where $\{\}$ denotes the empty assignment. Two HyperLTL formulas φ and ψ are equivalent, written $\varphi \equiv \psi$ if they have the same models.

(In)dependence is a common hyperproperty for which we define the following syntactic sugar. Given two disjoint subsets of atomic propositions $C \subseteq \text{AP}$ and $A \subseteq \text{AP}$, we define independence as the following HyperLTL formula

$$D_{A \mapsto C} := \forall\pi\forall\pi'. \left(\bigvee_{a \in A} (a_\pi \nleftrightarrow a_{\pi'}) \right) \mathcal{R} \left(\bigwedge_{c \in C} (c_\pi \leftrightarrow c_{\pi'}) \right) . \tag{1}$$

This guarantees that every proposition $c \in C$ solely depends on propositions A.

Strategies. A *strategy* $f \colon (2^I)^* \to 2^O$ maps sequences of input valuations 2^I to an output valuation 2^O. The behavior of a strategy $f \colon (2^I)^* \to 2^O$ is characterized by an infinite tree that branches by the valuations of I and whose nodes $w \in (2^I)^*$ are labeled with the strategic choice $f(w)$. For an infinite word $w = w_0 w_1 w_2 \cdots \in (2^I)^\omega$, the corresponding labeled path is defined as $(f(\epsilon) \cup w_0)(f(w_0) \cup w_1)(f(w_0 w_1) \cup w_2) \cdots \in (2^{I \cup O})^\omega$. We lift the set containment operator $\in$ to the containment of a labeled path $w = w_0 w_1 w_2 \cdots \in (2^{I \cup O})^\omega$ in a strategy tree induced by $f \colon (2^I)^* \to 2^O$, i.e., $w \in f$ if, and only if, $f(\epsilon) = w_0 \cap O$ and $f((w_0 \cap I) \cdots (w_i \cap I)) = w_{i+1} \cap O$ for all $i \geq 0$. We define the satisfaction of a HyperLTL formula φ (over propositions $I \cup O$) on strategy f, written $f \vDash \varphi$, as $\{w \mid w \in f\} \vDash \varphi$. Thus, a strategy f is a model of φ if the set of labeled paths of f is a model of φ.

3 HyperLTL Synthesis

In this section, we identify fragments of HyperLTL for which the realizability problem is decidable. Our findings are summarized in Table 1.

Definition 1 (HyperLTL Realizability). *A HyperLTL formula φ over atomic propositions $AP = I \dot{\cup} O$ is realizable if there is a strategy $f \colon (2^I)^* \to 2^O$ that satisfies φ.*

Table 1. Summary of decidability results.

$\exists^*$	$\exists^*\forall^1$	$\exists^*\forall^{>1}$	$\forall^*$	$\forall^*\exists^*$	*linear* $\forall^*$
PSPACE-complete	3EXPTIME	undecidable			decidable

We base our investigation on the structure of the quantifier prefix of the HyperLTL formulas. We call a HyperLTL formula φ (quantifier) *alternation-free* if the quantifier prefix consists solely of either universal or existential quantifiers. We denote the corresponding fragments as the (universal) $\forall^*$ and the (existential) $\exists^*$ fragment, respectively. A HyperLTL formula is in the $\exists^*\forall^*$ fragment, if it starts with arbitrarily many existential quantifiers, followed by arbitrarily many universal quantifiers. Respectively for the $\forall^*\exists^*$ fragment. For a given natural number n, we refer to a bounded number of quantifiers with $\forall^n$, respectively $\exists^n$. The $\forall^1$ realizability problem is equivalent to the LTL realizability problem.

$\exists^*$ Fragment. We show that the realizability problem for existential HyperLTL is PSPACE-complete. We reduce the realizability problem to the satisfiability problem for bounded one-alternating $\exists^*\forall^2$HyperLTL [9], i.e., finding a trace set T such that $T \vDash \varphi$.

Lemma 1. *An existential HyperLTL formula φ is realizable if, and only if, $\psi := \varphi \wedge D_{I\mapsto O}$ is satisfiable.*

Proof. Assume $f\colon (2^I)^* \to 2^O$ realizes φ, that is $f \vDash \varphi$. Let $T = \{w \mid w \in f\}$ be the set of traces generated by f. It holds that $T \vDash \varphi$ and $T \vDash D_{I\mapsto O}$. Therefore, ψ is satisfiable. Assume ψ is satisfiable. Let S be a set of traces that satisfies ψ. We construct a strategy $f\colon (2^I)^* \to 2^O$ as

$$f(\sigma) = \begin{cases} w_{|\sigma|} \cap O & \text{if } \sigma \text{ is a prefix of some } w|_I \text{ with } w \in S \text{ , and} \\ \emptyset & \text{otherwise .} \end{cases}$$

where $w|_I$ denotes the trace restricted to I, formally $w_i \cap I$ for all $i \geq 0$. Note that if there are multiple candidates $w \in S$, then $w_{|\sigma|} \cap O$ is the same for all of them because of the required non-determinism $D_{I\mapsto O}$. By construction, all traces in S are contained in f and with $S \vDash \varphi$ it holds that $f \vDash \varphi$ as φ is an existential formula.

Theorem 1. *Realizability of existential HyperLTL specifications is decidable.*

Proof. The formula ψ from Lemma 1 is in the $\exists^*\forall^2$ fragment, for which satisfiability is decidable [9].

Corollary 1. *Realizability of $\exists^*$HyperLTL specifications is* PSPACE*-complete.*

Proof. Given an existential HyperLTL formula, we gave a linear reduction to the satisfiability of the $\exists^*\forall^2$ fragment in Lemma 1. The satisfiability problem for a bounded number of universal quantifiers is in PSPACE [9]. Hardness follows from LTL satisfiability, which is equivalent to the $\exists^1$ fragment.

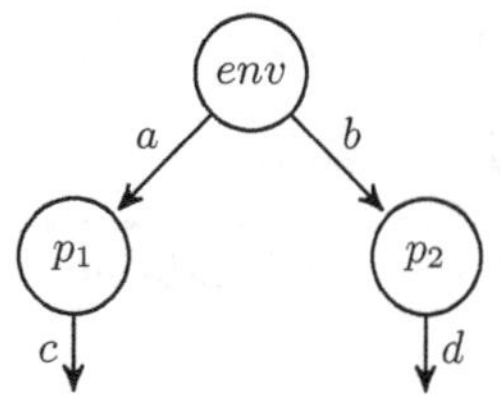

(a) An architecture of two processes that specify process p_1 to produce c from a and p_2 to produce d from b.

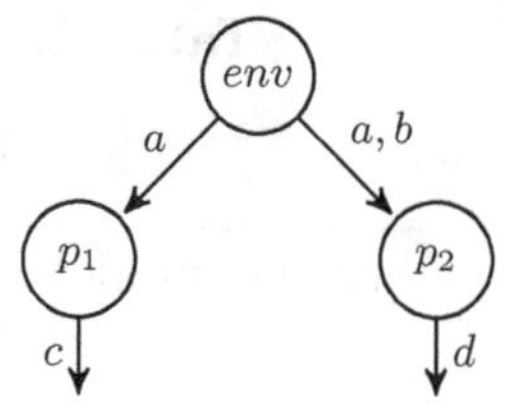

(b) The same architecture as on the left, where only the inputs of process p_2 are changed to a and b.

Fig. 1. Distributed architectures

$\forall^*$ Fragment. In the following, we will use the *distributed synthesis* problem, i.e., the problem whether there is an implementation of processes in a distributed *architecture* that satisfies an LTL formula. Formally, a distributed architecture A is a tuple $\langle P, p_{env}, \mathcal{I}, \mathcal{O}\rangle$ where P is a finite set of processes with distinguished environment process $p_{env} \in P$. The functions $\mathcal{I}\colon P \to 2^{\mathrm{AP}}$ and $\mathcal{O}\colon P \to 2^{\mathrm{AP}}$ define the inputs and outputs of processes. While processes may share the same inputs (in case of broadcasting), the outputs of processes must be pairwise disjoint, i.e., for all $p \neq p' \in P$ it holds that $\mathcal{O}(p) \cap \mathcal{O}(p') = \emptyset$. W.l.o.g. we assume that $\mathcal{I}(p_{env}) = \emptyset$. The distributed synthesis problem for architectures without *information forks* [13] is decidable. Example architectures are depicted in Fig. 1. The architecture in Fig. 1a contains an information fork while the architecture in Fig. 1b does not. Furthermore, the processes in Fig. 1b can be ordered linearly according to the subset relation on the inputs.

Theorem 2. *The synthesis problem for universal HyperLTL is undecidable.*

Proof. In the $\forall^*$ fragment (and thus in the $\exists^*\forall^*$ fragment), we can encode a distributed architecture [13], for which LTL synthesis is undecidable. In particular, we can encode the architecture shown in Fig. 1a. This architecture basically specifies c to depend only on a and analogously d on b. That can be encoded by $D_{\{a\}\mapsto\{c\}}$ and $D_{\{b\}\mapsto\{d\}}$. The LTL synthesis problem for this architecture is already shown to be undecidable [13], i.e., given an LTL formula over $I = \{a, b\}$ and $O = \{c, d\}$, we cannot automatically construct processes p_1 and p_2 that realize the formula.

Linear $\forall^*$ Fragment. For characterizing the linear fragment of HyperLTL, we will present a transformation from a formula with arbitrarily many universal quantifiers to a formula with only one quantifier. This transformation collapses the universal quantifier into a single one and renames the path variables accordingly. For example, $\forall\pi_1\forall\pi_2.\,\Box a_{\pi_1} \vee \Box a_{\pi_2}$ is transformed into an equivalent $\forall^1$ formula $\forall\pi.\,\Box a_\pi \vee \Box a_\pi$. However, this transformation does not always produce equivalent formulas as $\forall\pi_1\forall\pi_2.\,\Box(a_{\pi_1} \leftrightarrow a_{\pi_2})$ is not equivalent to its collapsed form $\forall\pi.\,\Box(a_\pi \leftrightarrow a_\pi)$. Let φ be $\forall\pi_1 \cdots \forall\pi_n.\,\psi$. We define the collapsed formula of φ as $\mathit{collapse}(\varphi) := \forall\pi.\,\psi[\pi_1 \mapsto \pi][\pi_2 \mapsto \pi]\ldots[\pi_n \mapsto \pi]$ where $\psi[\pi_i \mapsto \pi]$ replaces all occurrences of π_i in ψ with π. Although the collapsed term is not always equivalent to the original formula, we can use it as an indicator whether it is possible at all to express a universal formula with only one quantifier as stated in the following lemma.

Lemma 2. *Either $\varphi \equiv \mathit{collapse}(\varphi)$ or φ has no equivalent $\forall^1$ formula.*

Proof. Suppose there is some $\psi \in \forall^1$ with $\psi \equiv \varphi$. We show that $\psi \equiv \mathit{collapse}(\varphi)$. Let T be an arbitrary set of traces. Let $\mathcal{T} = \{\{w\} \mid w \in T\}$. Because $\psi \in \forall^1$, $T \vDash \psi$ is equivalent to $\forall T' \in \mathcal{T}. T' \vDash \psi$, which is by assumption equivalent to $\forall T' \in \mathcal{T}. T' \vDash \varphi$. Now, φ operates on singleton trace sets only. This means that all quantified paths have to be the same, which yields that we can use the same path variable for all of them. So $\forall T' \in \mathcal{T}. T' \vDash \varphi \leftrightarrow T' \vDash \mathit{collapse}(\varphi)$ that is again equivalent to $T \vDash \mathit{collapse}(\varphi)$. Because $\psi \equiv \mathit{collapse}(\varphi)$ and $\psi \equiv \varphi$ it holds that $\varphi \equiv \mathit{collapse}(\varphi)$.

The LTL realizability problem for distributed architectures without information forks [13] are decidable. These architectures are in some way *linear*, i.e., the processes can be ordered such that lower processes always have a subset of the information of upper processes. The linear fragment of universal HyperLTL addresses exactly these architectures.

In the following, we sketch the characterization of the linear fragment of HyperLTL. Given a formula φ, we seek for variable dependencies of the form $D_{J \mapsto \{o\}}$ with $J \subseteq I$ and $o \in O$ in the formula. If the part of the formula φ that relates multiple paths consists only of such constraints $D_{J \mapsto \{o\}}$ with the rest being an LTL property, we can interpret φ as a description of a distributed architecture. If furthermore, the $D_{J_i \mapsto \{o_i\}}$ constraints can be ordered such that $J_i \subseteq J_{i+1}$ for all i, the architecture is linear. There are three steps to check whether φ is in the linear fragment:

1. First, we have to add input-determinism to the formula $\varphi_{det} \coloneqq \varphi \wedge D_{I \mapsto O}$. This preserves realizability as strategies are input-deterministic.
2. Find for each output variable $o_i \in O$ possible sets of variables J_i, o_i depends on, such that $J_i \subseteq J_{i+1}$. To check whether the choice of J's is correct, we test if $\mathit{collapse}(\varphi) \wedge \bigwedge_{o_i \in O} D_{J_i \mapsto \{o_i\}}$ is equivalent to φ_{det}. This equivalence check is decidable as both formulas are in the universal fragment [9].
3. Finally, we construct the corresponding distributed realizability problem with linear architecture. Formally, we define the distributed architecture $A = \langle P, p_{env}, \mathcal{I}, \mathcal{O} \rangle$ with $P = \{p_i \mid o_i \in O\} \cup \{p_{env}\}$, $\mathcal{I}(p_i) = J_i$, $\mathcal{O}(p_i) = \{o_i\}$, and $\mathcal{O}(p_{env}) = I$. The LTL specification for the distributed synthesis problem is $\mathit{collapse}(\varphi)$.

Definition 2 (linear fragment of $\forall^*$). *A formula φ is in the linear fragment of $\forall^*$ iff for all $o_i \in O$ there is a $J_i \subseteq I$ such that $\varphi \wedge D_{I \mapsto O} \equiv \mathit{collapse}(\varphi) \wedge \bigwedge_{o_i \in O} D_{J_i \mapsto \{o_i\}}$ and $J_i \subseteq J_{i+1}$ for all i.*

Note, that each $\forall^1$ formula φ (or φ is collapsible to a $\forall^1$ formula) is in the linear fragment because we can set all $J_i = I$ and additionally $\mathit{collapse}(\varphi) = \varphi$ holds.

As an example of a formula in the linear fragment of $\forall^*$, consider $\varphi = \forall\pi,\pi'.\, D_{\{a\}\mapsto\{c\}} \wedge \square(c_\pi \leftrightarrow d_\pi) \wedge \square(b_\pi \leftrightarrow \bigcirc e_\pi)$ with $I = \{a,b\}$ and $O = \{c,d,e\}$. The corresponding formula asserting input-deterministism is $\varphi_{det} = \varphi \wedge D_{I\mapsto O}$. One possible choice of J's is $\{a,b\}$ for c, $\{a\}$ for d and $\{a,b\}$ for e. Note, that one can use either $\{a,b\}$ or $\{a\}$ for c as $D_{\{a\}\mapsto\{d\}} \wedge (c_\pi \leftrightarrow d_\pi)$ implies $D_{\{a\}\mapsto\{c\}}$. However, the apparent alternative $\{b\}$ for e would yield an undecidable architecture. It holds that φ_{det} and $collapse(\varphi) \wedge D_{\{a,b\}\mapsto\{c\}} \wedge D_{\{a\}\mapsto\{d\}} \wedge D_{\{a,b\}\mapsto\{e\}}$ are equivalent and, thus, that φ is in the linear fragment.

Theorem 3. *The linear fragment of universal HyperLTL is decidable.*

Proof. It holds that $\varphi \equiv collapse(\varphi) \wedge \bigwedge_{o_i\in O} D_{J_i\mapsto\{o_i\}}$ for some J_i's. The LTL distributed realizability problem for $collapse(\varphi)$ in the constructed architecture A is equivalent to the HyperLTL realizability of φ as the architecture A represents exactly the input-determinism represented by formula $\bigwedge_{o_i\in O} D_{J_i\mapsto\{o_i\}}$. The architecture is linear and, thus, the realizability problem is decidable.

$\exists^*\forall^1$ Fragment. In this fragment, we consider arbitrary many existential path quantifier followed by a single universal path quantifier. This fragment turns out to be still decidable. We solve the realizability problem for this fragment by reducing it to a decidable fragment of the distributed realizability problem.

Theorem 4. *Realizability of $\exists^*\forall^1$ HyperLTL specifications is decidable.*

Proof. Let φ be $\exists\pi_1 \ldots \exists\pi_n\forall\pi'.\, \psi$. We reduce the realizability problem of φ to the distributed realizability problem for LTL. For every existential path quantifier π_i, we introduce a copy of the atomic propositions, written a_{π_i} for $a \in \text{AP}$. Intuitively, those select the paths in the strategy tree where the existential path quantifiers are evaluated. Thus, those propositions (1) have to encode an actual path in the strategy tree and (2) may not depend on the branching of the strategy tree. To ensure (1), we add the LTL constraint $\square(I_{\pi_i} = I_{\pi'}) \rightarrow \square(O_{\pi_i} = O_{\pi'})$ that asserts that if the inputs correspond to some path in the strategy tree, the outputs on those paths have to be the same. Property (2) is guaranteed by the distributed architecture, the processes generating the propositions a_{π_i} do not depend on the environment output. The resulting architecture A_φ is $\langle\{p_{env}, p, p'\}, p_{env}, \{p \mapsto \emptyset, p' \mapsto I_{\pi'}\}, \{p_{env} \mapsto I_{\pi'}, p \mapsto \bigcup_{1\leq i\leq n} O_{\pi_i} \cup I_{\pi_i}, p' \mapsto O_{\pi'}\}\rangle$. It is easy to verify that A_φ does not contain an information fork, thus the realizability problem is decidable. The LTL specification θ is $\psi \wedge \bigwedge_{1\leq i\leq n} \square(I_{\pi_i} = I_{\pi'}) \rightarrow \square(O_{\pi_i} = O_{\pi'})$. The implementation of process p' (if it exists) is a model for the HyperLTL formula (process p producing witness for the $\exists$ quantifier). Conversely, a model for φ can be used as an implementation of p'. Thus, the distributed synthesis problem $\langle A_\varphi, \theta\rangle$ has a solution if, and only if, φ is realizable.

$\forall^*\exists^*$ Fragment. The last fragment to consider are formulas in the $\forall^*\exists^*$ fragment. Whereas the $\exists^*\forall^1$ fragment remains decidable, the realizability problem of $\forall^*\exists^*$ turns out to be undecidable even when restricted to only one quantifier of both sorts ($\forall^1\exists^1$).

Theorem 5. *Realizability of* $\forall^*\exists^*$ *HyperLTL is undecidable.*

Proof. The proof is done via reduction from Post's Correspondence Problem (PCP) [22]. The basic idea follows the proof in [9].

4 Bounded Realizability

We propose an algorithm to synthesize strategies from specifications given in universal HyperLTL by searching for finite generators of realizing strategies. We encode this search as a satisfiability problem for a decidable constraint system.

Transition Systems. A *transition system* $\mathcal{S}$ is a tuple $\langle S, s_0, \tau, l\rangle$ where S is a finite set of states, $s_0 \in S$ is the designated initial state, $\tau\colon S \times 2^I \to S$ is the transition function, and $l\colon S \to 2^O$ is the state-labeling or output function. We generalize the transition function to sequences over 2^I by defining $\tau^*\colon (2^I)^* \to S$ recursively as $\tau^*(\epsilon) = s_0$ and $\tau^*(w_0 \cdots w_{n-1}w_n) = \tau(\tau^*(w_0 \cdots w_{n-1}), w_n)$ for $w_0 \cdots w_{n-1}w_n \in (2^I)^+$. A transition system $\mathcal{S}$ *generates* the strategy f if $f(w) = l(\tau^*(w))$ for every $w \in (2^I)^*$. A strategy f is called *finite-state* if there exists a transition system that generates f.

Overview. We first sketch the synthesis procedure and then proceed with a description of the intermediate steps. Let φ be a universal HyperLTL formula $\forall\pi_1 \cdots \forall\pi_n . \psi$. We build the automaton $\mathcal{A}_\psi$ whose language is the set of tuples of traces that satisfy ψ. We then define the acceptance of a transition system $\mathcal{S}$ on $\mathcal{A}_\psi$ by means of the self-composition of $\mathcal{S}$. Lastly, we encode the existence of a transition system accepted by $\mathcal{A}_\psi$ as an SMT constraint system.

Example 1. Throughout this section, we will use the following (simplified) running example. Assume we want to synthesize a system that keeps decisions secret until it is allowed to publish. Thus, our system has three input signals *decision*, indicating whether a decision was made, the secret *value*, and a signal to *publish* results. Furthermore, our system has two outputs, a *high* output *internal* that stores the value of the last decision, and a *low* output *result* that indicates the result. No information about decisions should be inferred until publication. To specify the functionality, we propose the LTL specification

$$\begin{aligned}&\square(\mathit{decision} \to (\mathit{value} \leftrightarrow \bigcirc\, \mathit{internal}))\\ \wedge\ &\square(\neg\mathit{decision} \to (\mathit{internal} \leftrightarrow \bigcirc\, \mathit{internal}))\\ \wedge\ &\square(\mathit{publish} \to \bigcirc(\mathit{internal} \leftrightarrow \mathit{result}))\ . \end{aligned} \tag{2}$$

The solution produced by the LTL synthesis tool BoSy [8], shown in Fig. 2, clearly violates our intention that results should be secret until publish: Whenever a decision is made, the output *result* changes as well.

We formalize the property that no information about the decision can be inferred from *result* until publication as the HyperLTL formula

$$\forall\pi\forall\pi' . (\mathit{publish}_\pi \vee \mathit{publish}_{\pi'})\, \mathcal{R}\, (\mathit{result}_\pi \leftrightarrow \mathit{result}_{\pi'})\ . \tag{3}$$

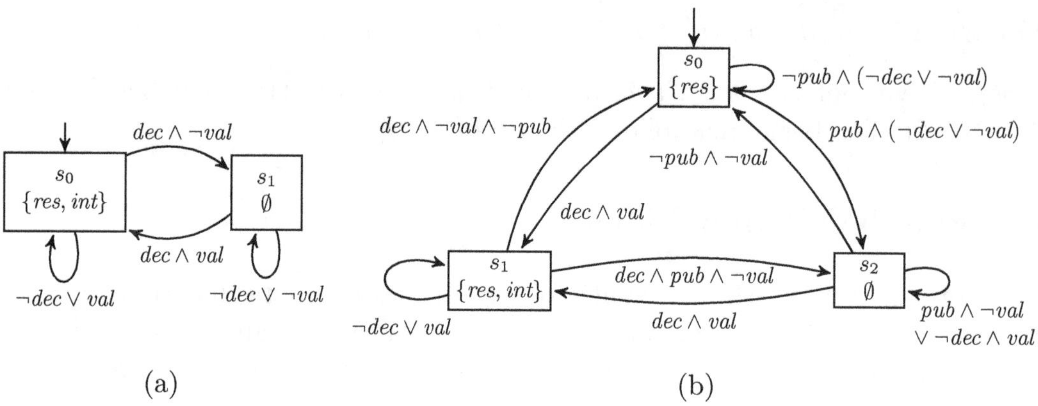

Fig. 2. Synthesized solutions for Example 1.

It asserts that for every pair of traces, the *result* signals have to be the same until (if ever) there is a *publish* signal on either trace. A solution satisfying both, the functional specification and the hyperproperty, is shown in Fig. 2. The system switches states whenever there is a decision with a different value than before and only exposes the decision in case there is a prior publish command.

We proceed with introducing the necessary preliminaries for our algorithm.

Automata. A universal co-Büchi automaton $\mathcal{A}$ over a finite alphabet Σ is a tuple $\langle Q, q_0, \delta, F\rangle$, where Q is a finite set of states, $q_0 \in Q$ is the designated initial state, $\delta : Q \times 2^\Sigma \times Q$ is the transition relation, and $F \subseteq Q$ is the set of rejecting states. Given an infinite word $\sigma = \sigma_0\sigma_1\sigma_2 \cdots \in (2^\Sigma)^\omega$, a run of σ on $\mathcal{A}$ is an infinite path $q_0q_1q_2 \cdots \in Q^\omega$ where for all $i \geq 0$ it holds that $(q_i, \sigma_i, q_{i+1}) \in \delta$. A run is accepting, if it contains only finitely many rejecting states. $\mathcal{A}$ accepts a word σ, if *all* runs of σ on $\mathcal{A}$ are accepting. The language of $\mathcal{A}$, written $\mathcal{L}(\mathcal{A})$, is the set $\{\sigma \in (2^\Sigma)^\omega \mid \mathcal{A} \text{ accepts } \sigma\}$. We represent automata as directed graphs with vertex set Q and a symbolic representation of the transition relation δ as propositional boolean formulas $\mathbb{B}(\Sigma)$. The rejecting states in F are marked by double lines. The automata for the LTL and HyperLTL specifications from Example 1 are depicted in Fig. 3.

Run Graph. The run graph of a transition system $\mathcal{S} = \langle S, s_0, \tau, l\rangle$ on a universal co-Büchi automaton $\mathcal{A} = \langle Q, q_0, \delta, F\rangle$ is a directed graph $\langle V, E\rangle$ where $V = S \times Q$ is the set of vertices and $E \subseteq V \times V$ is the edge relation with

$$((s, q), (s', q')) \in E \text{ iff}$$
$$\exists i \in 2^I . \exists o \in 2^O . (\tau(s, i) = s') \wedge (l(s) = o) \wedge (q, i \cup o, q') \in \delta \ .$$

A run graph is accepting if every path (starting at the initial vertex (s_0, q_0)) has only finitely many visits of rejecting states. To show acceptance, we annotate every reachable node in the run graph with a natural number m, such that any path, starting in the initial state, contains less than m visits of rejecting states. Such an annotation exists if, and only if, the run graph is accepting [14].

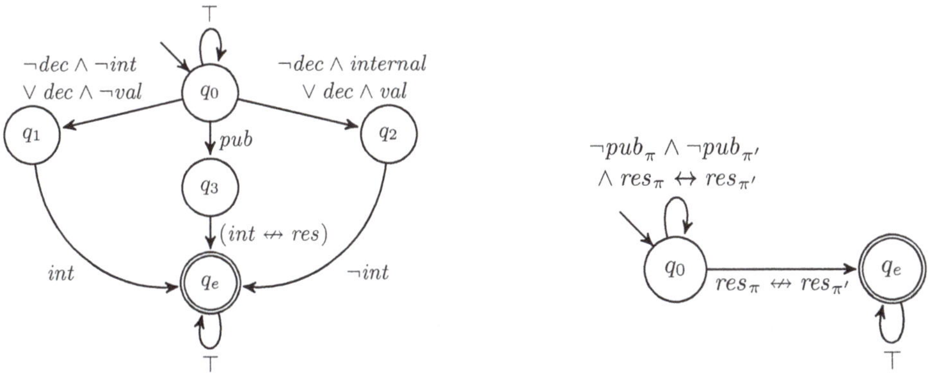

(a) Automaton accepting language defined by LTL formula in (2)

(b) Automaton accepting language defined by HyperLTL formula in (3)

Fig. 3. Universal co-Büchi automata recognizing the languages from Example 1.

Self-composition. The model checking of universal HyperLTL formulas [12] is based on self-composition. Let prj_i be the projection to the i-th element of a tuple. Let *zip* denote the usual function that maps a n-tuple of sequences to a single sequence of n-tuples, for example, $zip([1,2,3],[4,5,6]) = [(1,4),(2,5),(3,6)]$, and let *unzip* denote its inverse. The transition system $\mathcal{S}^n$ is the n-fold self-composition of $\mathcal{S} = \langle S, s_0, \tau, l\rangle$, if $\mathcal{S}^n = \langle S^n, s_0^n, \tau', l^n\rangle$ and for all $s, s' \in S^n$, $\alpha \in (2^I)^n$, and $\beta \in (2^O)^n$ we have that $\tau'(s,\alpha) = s'$ and $l^n(s) = \beta$ iff for all $1 \leq i \leq n$, it hold that $\tau(prj_i(s), prj_i(\alpha)) = prj_i(s')$ and $l(prj_i(s)) = prj_i(\beta)$. If T is the set of traces generated by $\mathcal{S}$, then $\{zip(t_1,\ldots,t_n) \mid t_1,\ldots,t_n \in T\}$ is the set of traces generated by $\mathcal{S}^n$.

We construct the universal co-Büchi automaton $\mathcal{A}_\psi$ such that the language of $\mathcal{A}_\psi$ is the set of words w such that $unzip(w) = \Pi$ and $\Pi \vDash_\emptyset \psi$, i.e., the tuple of traces that satisfy ψ. We get this automaton by dualizing the non-deterministic Büchi automaton for $\neg\psi$ [4], i.e., changing the branching from non-deterministic to universal and the acceptance condition from Büchi to co-Büchi. Hence, $\mathcal{S}$ satisfies a universal HyperLTL formula $\varphi = \forall\pi_1 \ldots \forall\pi_k.\psi$ if the traces generated by self-composition $\mathcal{S}^n$ are a subset of $\mathcal{L}(\mathcal{A}_\psi)$.

Lemma 3. *A transition system $\mathcal{S}$ satisfies the universal HyperLTL formula $\varphi = \forall\pi_1 \cdots \forall\pi_n.\psi$, if the run graph of $\mathcal{S}^n$ and $\mathcal{A}_\psi$ is accepting.*

Synthesis. Let $\mathcal{S} = \langle S, s_0, \tau, l\rangle$ and $\mathcal{A}_\psi = \langle Q, q_0, \delta, F\rangle$. We encode the synthesis problem as an SMT constraint system. Therefore, we use uninterpreted function symbols to encode the transition system and the annotation. For the transition system, those functions are the transition function $\tau : S \times 2^I \to S$ and the labeling function $l : S \to 2^O$. The annotation is split into two parts, a reachability constraint $\lambda^{\mathbb{B}} : S^n \times Q \to \mathbb{B}$ indicating whether a state in the run graph is reachable and a counter $\lambda^{\#} : S^n \times Q \to \mathbb{N}$ that maps every reachable vertex to the maximal number of rejecting states visited by any path starting in the initial vertex. The resulting constraint asserts that there is a transition system with accepting run graph.

$$\forall s, s' \in S^n. \forall q, q' \in Q. \forall i \in (2^I)^n.$$
$$\left(\lambda^{\mathbb{B}}(s,q) \wedge \tau'(s,i) = s' \wedge (q, i \cup l(s), q') \in \delta\right) \rightarrow \lambda^{\mathbb{B}}(s',q') \wedge \lambda^{\#}(s',q') \trianglerighteq \lambda^{\#}(s,q)$$

where $\trianglerighteq$ is $>$ if $q' \in F$ and $\geq$ otherwise.

Theorem 6. *The constraint system is satisfiable with bound b if, and only if, there is a transition system $\mathcal{S}$ of size b that realizes the HyperLTL formula.*

We extract a realizing implementation by asking the satisfiability solver to generate a model for the uninterpreted functions that encode the transition system.

5 Bounded Unrealizability

So far, we focused on the positive case, providing an algorithm for finding small solutions, if they exist. In this section, we shift to the case of detecting if a universal HyperLTL formula is unrealizable. We adapt the definition of counterexamples to realizability for LTL [15] to HyperLTL in the following. Let φ be a universal HyperLTL formula $\forall\pi_1 \cdots \forall\pi_n. \psi$ over inputs I and outputs O, a *counterexample to realizability* is a set of input traces $\mathcal{P} \subseteq (2^I)^\omega$ such that for every strategy $f : (2^I)^* \rightarrow 2^O$ the labeled traces $\mathcal{P}^f \subseteq (2^{I \cup O})^\omega$ satisfy $\neg\varphi = \exists\pi_1 \cdots \exists\pi_n. \neg\psi$.

Proposition 1. *A universal HyperLTL formula $\varphi = \forall\pi_1 \cdots \forall\pi_n. \psi$ is unrealizable if there is a counterexample $\mathcal{P}$ to realizability.*

Proof. For contradiction, we assume φ is realizable by a strategy f. As $\mathcal{P}$ is a counterexample to realizability, we know $\mathcal{P}^f \vDash \exists\pi_1 \cdots \exists\pi_n. \neg\psi$. This means that there exists an assignment $\Pi_\mathcal{P} \in \mathcal{V} \rightarrow \mathcal{P}^f$ with $\Pi_\mathcal{P} \vDash_{\mathcal{P}^f} \neg\psi$. Equivalently $\Pi_\mathcal{P} \nvDash_{\mathcal{P}^f} \psi$. Therefore, not all assignments $\Pi \in \mathcal{V} \rightarrow \mathcal{P}^f$ satisfy $\Pi \vDash_{\mathcal{P}^f} \psi$. Which implies $\mathcal{P}^f \nvDash \forall\pi_1 \cdots \forall\pi_n. \psi = \varphi$. Since φ is universal, we can defer $f \nvDash \varphi$, which concludes the contradiction. Thus, φ is unrealizable.

Despite being independent of strategy trees, there are in many cases finite representations of $\mathcal{P}$. Consider, for example, the unrealizable specification $\varphi_1 = \forall\pi\forall\pi'. \Diamond(i_\pi \leftrightarrow i_{\pi'})$, where the set $\mathcal{P}_1 = \{\emptyset^\omega, \{i\}^\omega\}$ is a counterexample to realizability. As a second example, consider $\varphi_2 = \forall\pi\forall\pi'. \Box(o_\pi \leftrightarrow o_{\pi'}) \wedge \Box(i_\pi \leftrightarrow \bigcirc o_\pi)$ with conflicting requirements on o. $\mathcal{P}_1$ is a counterexample to realizability for φ_2 as well: By choosing a different valuation of i in the first step, the system is forced to either react with different valuations of o (violating first conjunct), or not correctly repeating the initial value of i (violating second conjunct).

There are, however, already linear specifications where the set of counterexample paths is not finite and depends on the strategy tree [16]. For example, the specification $\forall\pi. \Diamond(i_\pi \leftrightarrow o_\pi)$ is unrealizable as the system cannot predict future values of the environment. There is no finite set of traces witnessing this: For every finite set of traces, there is a strategy tree such that $\Diamond(i_\pi \leftrightarrow o_\pi)$ holds on every such trace. On the other hand, there is a simple *counterexample strategy*, that is a strategy that observes output sequences and produces inputs. In this example, the counterexample strategy inverts the outputs given by the system, thus it is guaranteed that $\square(i \nleftrightarrow o)$ for any system strategy.

We combine those two approaches, selecting counterexample paths and using strategic behavior. A k-counterexample strategy for HyperLTL observes k output sequences and produces k inputs, where k is a new parameter ($k \geq n$). The counterexample strategy is winning if (1) either the traces given by the system player do not correspond to a strategy, or (2) the body of the HyperLTL is violated for any n subset of the k traces. Regarding property (1), consider the two traces where the system player produces different outputs initially. Clearly, those two traces cannot be generated by any system strategy since the initial state (root labeling) is fixed.

The search for a k-counterexample strategy can be reduced to LTL synthesis using k-tuple input propositions O^k, k-tuple output propositions I^k, and the specification

$$\neg D_{I^k \mapsto O^k} \vee \bigvee_{P \subseteq \{1,\ldots,k\} \text{ with } |P|=n} \neg\psi[P] \ ,$$

where $\psi[P]$ denotes the replacement of a_{π_i} by the P_ith position of the combined input/output k-tuple.

Theorem 7. *A universal HyperLTL formula $\varphi = \forall\pi_1 \cdots \forall\pi_n. \psi$ is unrealizable if there is a k-counterexample strategy for some $k \geq n$.*

6 Evaluation

We implemented a prototype synthesis tool, called BoSyHyper[1], for universal HyperLTL based on the bounded synthesis algorithm described in Sect. 4. Furthermore, we implemented the search for counterexamples proposed in Sect. 5. Thus, BoSyHyper is able to characterize realizability and unrealizability of universal HyperLTL formulas.

We base our implementation on the LTL synthesis tool BoSy [8]. For efficiency, we split the specifications into two parts, a part containing the linear (LTL) specification, and a part containing the hyperproperty given as HyperLTL formula. Consequently, we build two constraint systems, one using the standard bounded synthesis approach [14] and one using the approach described in Sect. 4. Before solving, those constraints are combined into a single SMT query. This results in a much more concise constraint system compared to the one where the complete specification is interpreted as a HyperLTL formula. For solving the SMT queries, we use the Z3 solver [20]. We continue by describing the benchmarks used in our experiments.

[1] BoSyHyper is available at https://www.react.uni-saarland.de/tools/bosy/.

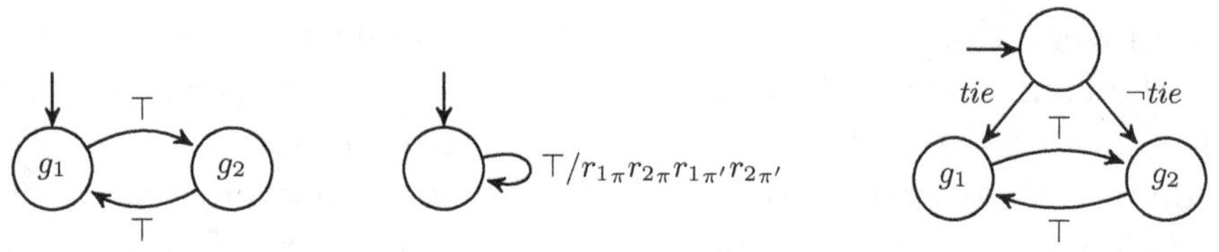

(a) Non-symmetric solution (b) Counterexample to symmetry (c) Symmetry breaking solution

Fig. 4. Synthesized solution of the mutual exclusion protocols.

Symmetric Mutual Exclusion. Our first example demonstrates the ability to specify symmetry in HyperLTL for a simple mutual exclusion protocol. Let r_1 and r_2 be input signals representing mutual exclusive *requests* to a critical section and g_1/g_2 the respective grant to enter the section. Every request should be answered eventually $\square(r_i \rightarrow \diamondsuit g_i)$ for $i \in \{1, 2\}$, but not at the same time $\square\neg(g_1 \wedge g_2)$. The minimal LTL solution is depicted in Fig. 4a. It is well known that no mutex protocol can ensure perfect symmetry [19], thus when adding the symmetry constraint specified by the HyperLTL formula $\forall\pi\forall\pi'. (r_{1\pi} \not\leftrightarrow r_{2\pi'})\, \mathcal{R}\, (g_{1\pi} \leftrightarrow g_{2\pi'})$ the formula becomes unrealizable. Our tool produces the counterexample shown in Fig. 4b. By adding another input signal *tie* that breaks the symmetry in case of simultaneous requests and modifying the symmetry constraint $\forall\pi\forall\pi'. ((r_{1\pi} \not\leftrightarrow r_{2\pi'}) \vee (tie_\pi \not\leftrightarrow \neg tie_{\pi'}))\, \mathcal{R}\, (g_{1\pi} \leftrightarrow g_{2\pi'})$ we obtain the solution depicted in Fig. 4c. We further evaluated the same properties on a version that forbids spurious grants, which are reported in Table 2 with prefix *full*.

Distributed and Fault-Tolerant Systems. In Sect. 3 we presented a reduction of arbitrary distributed architectures to HyperLTL. As an example for our evaluation, consider a setting with two processes, one for *encoding* input signals and one for *decoding*. Both processes can be synthesized simultaneously using a single HyperLTL specification. The (linear) correctness condition states that the decoded signal is always equal to the inputs given to the encoder. Furthermore, the encoder and decoder should solely depend on the inputs and the encoded signal, respectively. Additionally, we can specify desired properties about the encoding like fault-tolerance [16] or Hamming distance of code words [12]. The results are reported in Table 2 where *i*-*j*-*x* means *i* input bits, *j* encoded bits, and *x* represents the property. The property is either tolerance against a single Byzantine signal failure or a guaranteed Hamming distance of code words.

CAP Theorem. The CAP Theorem due to Brewer [2] states that it is impossible to design a distributed system that provides Consistency, Availability, and Partition tolerance (CAP) simultaneously. This example has been considered before [16] to evaluate a technique that could automatically detect unrealizability. However, when we drop either Consistency, Availability, or Partition tolerance, the corresponding instances (AP, CP, and CA) become realizable, which the previous work was not able to prove. We show that our implementation can show both, unrealizability of CAP and realizability of AP, CP, and CA. In contrast to the previous encoding [16] we are not limited to acyclic architectures.

Long-term Information-flow. Previous work on model-checking hyperproperties [12] found that an implementation for the commonly used *I2C* bus protocol could remember input values ad infinitum. For example, it could not be verified that information given to the implementation eventually leaves it, i.e., is forgotten. This is especially unfortunate in high security contexts. We consider a simple bus protocol which is inspired by the widely used *I2C* protocol. Our example protocol has the inputs *send* for initiating a transmission, *in* for the value that should be transferred, and an *ack*nowledgment bit indicating successful transmission. The bus master waits in an *idle* state until a *send* is received. Afterwards, it transmits a header sequence, followed by the value of *in*, waits for an acknowledgement and then indicates *success* or *failure* to the sender before returning to the idle state. We specify the property that the *in*put has no influence on the *data* that is send, which is obviously violated (instance NI1). As a second property, we check that this information leak cannot happen arbitrary long (NI2) for which there is a realizing implementation.

Dining Cryptographers. Recap the dining cryptographers problem introduced earlier. This benchmark is interesting as it contains two types of hyperproperties. First, there is information-flow between the three cryptographers, where some secrets (s_{ab}, s_{ac}, s_{bc}) are shared between pairs of cryptographers. In the formalization, we have 4 entities: three processes describing the 3 cryptographers (out_i) and one process computing the result (p_g), i.e., whether the group has paid or not, from out_i. Second, the final result should only disclose whether one of the cryptographers has paid or the NSA. This can be formalized as a indistinguishability property between different executions. For example, when we compare the two traces π and π' where C_a has paid on π and C_b has paid on π'. Then the outputs of both have to be the same, if their common secret s_{ab} is different on those two traces (while all other secrets s_{ac} and s_{bc} are the same). This ensures that from an outside observer, a flipped output can be either result of a different shared secret or due to the announcement. Lastly, the linear specification asserts that $p_g \leftrightarrow \neg p_{NSA}$.

Results. Table 2 reports on the results of the benchmarks. We distinguish between state-labeled (*Moore*) and transition-labeled (*Mealy*) transition systems. Note that the counterexample strategies use the opposite transition system, i.e., a Mealy system strategy corresponds to a state-labeled (Moore) environment strategy. Typically, Mealy strategies are more compact, i.e., need smaller transition systems and this is confirmed by our experiments. BoSyHyper is able to solve most of the examples, providing realizing implementations or counterexamples. Regrading the unrealizable benchmarks we observe that usually two simultaneously generated paths ($k = 2$) are enough with the exception

Table 2. Results of BoSyHyper on the benchmarks sets described in Sect. 6. They ran on a machine with a dual-core Core i7, 3.3 GHz, and 16 GB memory.

Benchmark	Instance	Result	States		Time[sec.]	
			Moore	Mealy	Moore	Mealy
Symmetric Mutex	non-sym	realizable	2	2	1.4	1.3
	sym	unrealizable ($k = 2$)	1	1	1.9	2.0
	tie	realizable	3	3	1.7	1.6
	full-non-sym	realizable	4	4	1.4	1.4
	full-sym	unrealizable ($k = 2$)	1	1	4.3	6.2
	full-tie	realizable	9	5	1 802.7	5.2
Encoder/Decoder	1-2-hamming-2	realizable	4	1	1.6	1.3
	1-2-fault-tolerant	unrealizable ($k = 2$)	1	-	54.9	-
	1-3-fault-tolerant	realizable	4	1	151.7	1.7
	2-2-hamming-2	unrealizable ($k = 3$)	-	1	-	10.6
	2-3-hamming-2	realizable	16	1	>1 h	1.5
	2-3-hamming-3	unrealizable ($k = 3$)	-	1	-	126.7
CAP Theorem	cap-2-linear	realizable	8	1	7.0	1.3
	cap-2	unrealizable ($k = 2$)	1	-	1 823.9	-
	ca-2	realizable	-	1	-	4.4
	ca-3	realizable	-	1	-	15.0
	cp-2	realizable	1	1	1.8	1.6
	cp-3	realizable	1	1	3.2	10.6
	ap-2	realizable	-	1	-	2.0
	ap-3	realizable	-	1	-	43.4
Bus Protocol	NI1	unrealizable ($k = 2$)	1	1	75.2	69.6
	NI2	realizable	8	8	24.1	33.9
Dining Cryptographers	secrecy	realizable	-	1	-	82.4

of the encoder example. Overall the results are encouraging showing that we can solve a variety of instances with non-trivial information-flow.

7 Conclusion

In this paper, we have considered the reactive realizability problem for specifications given in the temporal logic HyperLTL. We gave a complete characterization of the decidable fragments based on the quantifier prefix and, additionally, identified a decidable fragment in the, in general undecidable, universal fragment of HyperLTL. Furthermore, we presented two algorithms to detect realizable and unrealizable HyperLTL specifications, one based on bounding the system implementation and one based on bounding the number of counterexample paths. Our prototype implementation shows that our approach is able to synthesize systems with complex information-flow properties.

References

1. Agrawal, S., Bonakdarpour, B.: Runtime verification of k-safety hyperproperties in HyperLTL. In: Proceedings of CSF, pp. 239–252. IEEE Computer Society (2016)
2. Brewer, E.A.: Towards robust distributed systems (abstract). In: Proceedings of ACM, p. 7. ACM (2000)
3. Chaum, D.: Security without identification: transaction systems to make big brother obsolete. Commun. ACM **28**(10), 1030–1044 (1985)
4. Clarkson, M.R., Finkbeiner, B., Koleini, M., Micinski, K.K., Rabe, M.N., Sánchez, C.: Temporal logics for hyperproperties. In: Abadi, M., Kremer, S. (eds.) POST 2014. LNCS, vol. 8414, pp. 265–284. Springer, Heidelberg (2014). https://doi.org/10.1007/978-3-642-54792-8_15
5. Clarkson, M.R., Schneider, F.B.: Hyperproperties. J. Comput. Secur. **18**(6), 1157–1210 (2010)
6. Dimitrova, R., Finkbeiner, B., Kovács, M., Rabe, M.N., Seidl, H.: Model checking information flow in reactive systems. In: Kuncak, V., Rybalchenko, A. (eds.) VMCAI 2012. LNCS, vol. 7148, pp. 169–185. Springer, Heidelberg (2012). https://doi.org/10.1007/978-3-642-27940-9_12
7. Faymonville, P., Finkbeiner, B., Rabe, M.N., Tentrup, L.: Encodings of bounded synthesis. In: Legay, A., Margaria, T. (eds.) TACAS 2017. LNCS, vol. 10205, pp. 354–370. Springer, Heidelberg (2017). https://doi.org/10.1007/978-3-662-54577-5_20
8. Faymonville, P., Finkbeiner, B., Tentrup, L.: BoSy: an experimentation framework for bounded synthesis. In: Majumdar, R., Kunčak, V. (eds.) CAV 2017. LNCS, vol. 10427, pp. 325–332. Springer, Cham (2017). https://doi.org/10.1007/978-3-319-63390-9_17
9. Finkbeiner, B., Hahn, C.: Deciding hyperproperties. In: Proceedings of CONCUR. LIPIcs, vol. 59, pp. 13:1–13:14. Schloss Dagstuhl - Leibniz-Zentrum fuer Informatik (2016)
10. Finkbeiner, B., Hahn, C., Stenger, M., Tentrup, L.: Monitoring hyperproperties. In: Lahiri, S., Reger, G. (eds.) RV 2017. LNCS, vol. 10548, pp. 190–207. Springer, Cham (2017). https://doi.org/10.1007/978-3-319-67531-2_12
11. Finkbeiner, B., Jacobs, S.: Lazy synthesis. In: Kuncak, V., Rybalchenko, A. (eds.) VMCAI 2012. LNCS, vol. 7148, pp. 219–234. Springer, Heidelberg (2012). https://doi.org/10.1007/978-3-642-27940-9_15
12. Finkbeiner, B., Rabe, M.N., Sánchez, C.: Algorithms for model checking HyperLTL and HyperCTL*. In: Kroening, D., Păsăreanu, C.S. (eds.) CAV 2015. LNCS, vol. 9206, pp. 30–48. Springer, Cham (2015). https://doi.org/10.1007/978-3-319-21690-4_3
13. Finkbeiner, B., Schewe, S.: Uniform distributed synthesis. In: Proceedings of LICS, pp. 321–330. IEEE Computer Society (2005)
14. Finkbeiner, B., Schewe, S.: Bounded synthesis. STTT **15**(5–6), 519–539 (2013)
15. Finkbeiner, B., Tentrup, L.: Detecting unrealizable specifications of distributed systems. In: Ábrahám, E., Havelund, K. (eds.) TACAS 2014. LNCS, vol. 8413, pp. 78–92. Springer, Heidelberg (2014). https://doi.org/10.1007/978-3-642-54862-8_6
16. Finkbeiner, B., Tentrup, L.: Detecting unrealizability of distributed fault-tolerant systems. Log. Methods Comput. Sci. **11**(3) (2015)
17. Finkbeiner, B., Zimmermann, M.: The first-order logic of hyperproperties. In: Proceedings of STACS. LIPIcs, vol. 66, pp. 30:1–30:14. Schloss Dagstuhl - Leibniz-Zentrum fuer Informatik (2017)

18. Kupferman, O., Vardi, M.Y.: Safraless decision procedures. In: Proceedings of FOCS, pp. 531–542. IEEE Computer Society (2005)
19. Manna, Z., Pnueli, A.: Temporal Verification of Reactive Systems - Safety. Springer, New York (1995). https://doi.org/10.1007/978-1-4612-4222-2
20. de Moura, L., Bjørner, N.: Z3: an efficient SMT solver. In: Ramakrishnan, C.R., Rehof, J. (eds.) TACAS 2008. LNCS, vol. 4963, pp. 337–340. Springer, Heidelberg (2008). https://doi.org/10.1007/978-3-540-78800-3_24
21. Pnueli, A., Rosner, R.: Distributed reactive systems are hard to synthesize. In: Proceedings of FOCS, pp. 746–757. IEEE Computer Society (1990)
22. Post, E.L.: A variant of a recursively unsolvable problem. Bull. Am. Math. Soc. **52**(4), 264–268 (1946)

Reactive Control Improvisation

Daniel J. Fremont[(✉)] and Sanjit A. Seshia

University of California, Berkeley, USA
{dfremont,sseshia}@berkeley.edu

Abstract. Reactive synthesis is a paradigm for automatically building correct-by-construction systems that interact with an unknown or adversarial environment. We study how to do reactive synthesis when part of the specification of the system is that its behavior should be *random*. Randomness can be useful, for example, in a network protocol fuzz tester whose output should be varied, or a planner for a surveillance robot whose route should be unpredictable. However, existing reactive synthesis techniques do not provide a way to ensure random behavior while maintaining functional correctness. Towards this end, we generalize the recently-proposed framework of *control improvisation* (CI) to add reactivity. The resulting framework of *reactive control improvisation* provides a natural way to integrate a randomness requirement with the usual functional specifications of reactive synthesis over a finite window. We theoretically characterize when such problems are realizable, and give a general method for solving them. For specifications given by reachability or safety games or by deterministic finite automata, our method yields a polynomial-time synthesis algorithm. For various other types of specifications including temporal logic formulas, we obtain a polynomial-space algorithm and prove matching PSPACE-hardness results. We show that all of these randomized variants of reactive synthesis are no harder in a complexity-theoretic sense than their non-randomized counterparts.

1 Introduction

Many interesting programs, including protocol handlers, task planners, and concurrent software generally, are *open* systems that interact over time with an external environment. Synthesis of such *reactive systems* requires finding an implementation that satisfies the desired specification no matter what the environment does. This problem, *reactive synthesis*, has a long history (see [7] for a survey). Reactive synthesis from temporal logic specifications [19] has been particularly well-studied and is being increasingly used in applications such as hardware synthesis [3] and robotic task planning [15].

In this paper, we investigate how to synthesize reactive systems with *random behavior*: in fact, systems where *being random in a prescribed way is part of their specification*. This is in contrast to prior work on stochastic games where randomness is used to model uncertain environments or randomized strategies are merely allowed, not required. Solvers for stochastic games may incidentally produce randomized strategies to satisfy a functional specification (and some

H. Chockler and G. Weissenbacher (Eds.): CAV 2018, LNCS 10981, pp. 307–326, 2018.
https://doi.org/10.1007/978-3-319-96145-3_17

types of specification, e.g. multi-objective queries [4], may only be realizable by randomized strategies), but do not provide a general way to *enforce* randomness. Unlike most specifications used in reactive synthesis, our randomness requirement is a property of a system's *distribution* of behaviors, not of an individual behavior. While probabilistic specification languages like PCTL [12] can capture some such properties, the simple and natural randomness requirement we study here cannot be concisely expressed by existing languages (even those as powerful as SGL [2]). Thus, *randomized reactive synthesis* in our sense requires significantly different methods than those previously studied.

However, we argue that this type of synthesis is quite useful, because introducing randomness into the behavior of a system can often be beneficial, enhancing *variety*, *robustness*, and *unpredictability*. Example applications include:

- Synthesizing a black-box fuzz tester for a network service, we want a program that not only conforms to the protocol (perhaps only most of the time) but can generate many different sequences of packets: randomness ensures this.
- Synthesizing a controller for a robot exploring an unknown environment, randomness provides a low-memory way to increase coverage of the space. It can also help to reduce systematic bias in the exploration procedure.
- Synthesizing a controller for a patrolling surveillance robot, introducing randomness in planning makes the robot's future location harder to predict.

Adding randomness to a system in an *ad hoc* way could easily compromise its correctness. This paper shows how a randomness requirement can be integrated *into the synthesis process*, ensuring correctness as well as allowing trade-offs to be explored: how much randomness can be added while staying correct, or how strong can a specification be while admitting a desired amount of randomness?

To formalize randomized reactive synthesis we build on the idea of *control improvisation*, introduced in [6], formalized in [9], and further generalized in [8]. Control improvisation (CI) is the problem of constructing an *improviser*, a probabilistic algorithm which generates finite words subject to three constraints: a *hard constraint* that must always be satisfied, a *soft constraint* that need only be satisfied with some probability, and a *randomness constraint* that no word be generated with probability higher than a given bound. We define *reactive control improvisation* (RCI), where the improviser generates a word incrementally, alternating adding symbols with an adversarial environment. To perform synthesis in a finite window, we encode functional specifications and environment assumptions into the hard constraint, while the soft and randomness constraints allow us to tune how randomness is added to the system. The improviser obtained by solving the RCI problem is then a solution to the original synthesis problem.

The difficulty of solving reactive CI problems depends on the type of specification. We study several types commonly used in reactive synthesis, including reachability games (and variants, e.g. safety games) and formulas in the temporal logics LTL and LDL [5,18]. We also investigate the specification types studied in [8], showing how the complexity of the CI problem changes when adding reactivity. For every type of specification we obtain a randomized synthesis algorithm whose complexity matches that of ordinary reactive synthesis (in a finite window). This suggests that reactive control improvisation should be feasible in applications like robotic task planning where reactive synthesis tools have proved effective.

In summary, the main contributions of this paper are:

- The reactive control improvisation (RCI) problem definition (Sect. 3);
- The notion of *width*, a quantitative generalization of "winning" game positions that measures *how many ways* a player can win from that position (Sect. 4);
- A characterization of when RCI problems are realizable in terms of width, and an explicit construction of an improviser (Sect. 4);
- A general method for constructing efficient improvisation schemes (Sect. 5);
- A polynomial-time improvisation scheme for reachability/safety games and deterministic finite automaton specifications (Sect. 6);
- PSPACE-hardness results for many other specification types including temporal logics, and matching polynomial-space improvisation schemes (Sect. 7).

Finally, Sect. 8 summarizes our results and gives directions for future work.

2 Background

2.1 Notation

Given an alphabet Σ, we write $|w|$ for the length of a finite word $w \in \Sigma^*$, λ for the empty word, Σ^n for the words of length n, and $\Sigma^{\leq n}$ for $\cup_{0 \leq i \leq n} \Sigma^i$, the set of all words of length at most n. We abbreviate deterministic/nondeterministic finite automaton by DFA/NFA, and context-free grammar by CFG. For an instance $\mathcal{X}$ of any such formalism, which we call a *specification*, we write $L(\mathcal{X})$ for the language (subset of Σ^*) it defines (note the distinction between a language and a representation thereof). We view formulas of Linear Temporal Logic (LTL) [18] and Linear Dynamic Logic (LDL) [5] as specifications using their natural semantics on finite words (see [5]).

We use the standard complexity classes #P and PSPACE, and the PSPACE-complete problem *QBF* of determining the truth of a quantified Boolean formula. For background on these classes and problems see for example [1].

Some specifications we use as examples are *reachability games* [16], where players' actions cause transitions in a state space and the goal is to reach a target state. We group these games, *safety games* where the goal is to *avoid* a set of states, and *reach-avoid* games combining reachability and safety goals [20], together as *reachability/safety games* (RSGs). We draw reachability games as graphs in the usual way: squares are adversary-controlled states, and states with a double border are target states.

2.2 Synthesis Games

Reactive control improvisation will be formalized in terms of a 2-player game which is essentially the standard *synthesis game* used in reactive synthesis [7]. However, our formulation is slightly different for compatibility with the definition of control improvisation, so we give a self-contained presentation here.

Fix a finite alphabet Σ. The players of the game will alternate picking symbols from Σ, building up a word. We can then specify the set of winning plays with a language over Σ. To simplify our presentation we assume that players strictly alternate turns and that any symbol from Σ is a legal move. These assumptions can be relaxed in the usual way by modifying the winning set appropriately.

Finite Words: While reactive synthesis is usually considered over infinite words, in this paper we focus on synthesis in a finite window, as it is unclear how best to generalize our randomness requirement to the infinite case. This assumption is not too restrictive, as solutions of bounded length are adequate for many applications. In fuzz testing, for example, we do not want to generate arbitrarily long files or sequences of packets. In robotic planning, we often want a plan that accomplishes a task within a certain amount of time. Furthermore, planning problems with liveness specifications can often be segmented into finite pieces: we do not need an infinite route for a patrolling robot, but can plan within a finite horizon and replan periodically. Replanning may even be *necessary* when environment assumptions become invalid. At any rate, we will see that the bounded case of reactive control improvisation is already highly nontrivial.

As a final simplification, we require that all plays have length exactly $n \in \mathbb{N}$. To allow a range $[m, n]$ we can simply add a new padding symbol to Σ and extend all shorter words to length n, modifying the winning set appropriately.

Definition 2.1. *A* history h *is an element of* $\Sigma^{\leq n}$*, representing the moves of the game played so far. We say the game has* ended *after* h *if* $|h| = n$*; otherwise it is* our turn *after* h *if* $|h|$ *is even, and* the adversary's turn *if* $|h|$ *is odd.*

Definition 2.2. *A* strategy *is a function* $\sigma : \Sigma^{\leq n} \times \Sigma \rightarrow [0, 1]$ *such that for any history* $h \in \Sigma^{\leq n}$ *with* $|h| < n$*,* $\sigma(h, \cdot)$ *is a probability distribution over* Σ*. We write* $x \leftarrow \sigma(h)$ *to indicate that* x *is a symbol randomly drawn from* $\sigma(h, \cdot)$*.*

Since strategies are randomized, fixing strategies for both players does not uniquely determine a play of the game, but defines a *distribution* over plays:

Definition 2.3. *Given a pair of strategies* (σ, τ)*, we can generate a random* play $\pi \in \Sigma^n$ *as follows. Pick* $\pi_0 \leftarrow \sigma(\lambda)$*, then for* i *from* 1 *to* $n - 1$ *pick* $\pi_i \leftarrow \tau(\pi_0 \dots \pi_{i-1})$ *if* i *is odd and* $\pi_i \leftarrow \sigma(\pi_0 \dots \pi_{i-1})$ *otherwise. Finally, put* $\pi = \pi_0 \dots \pi_{n-1}$*. We write* $P_{\sigma,\tau}(\pi)$ *for the probability of obtaining the play* π*. This extends to a* set *of plays* $X \subseteq \Sigma^n$ *in the natural way:* $P_{\sigma,\tau}(X) = \sum_{\pi \in X} P_{\sigma,\tau}(\pi)$*. Finally, the set of* possible *plays is* $\Pi_{\sigma,\tau} = \{\pi \in \Sigma^n \mid P_{\sigma,\tau}(\pi) > 0\}$*.*

The next definition is just the conditional probability of a play given a history, but works for histories with probability zero, simplifying our presentation.

Definition 2.4. *For any history* $h = h_0 \ldots h_{k-1} \in \Sigma^{\leq n}$ *and word* $\rho \in \Sigma^{n-k}$, *we write* $P_{\sigma,\tau}(\rho|h)$ *for the probability that if we assign* $\pi_i = h_i$ *for* $i < k$ *and sample* $\pi_k, \ldots, \pi_{n-1}$ *by the process above, then* $\pi_k \ldots \pi_{n-1} = \rho$.

3 Problem Definition

3.1 Motivating Example

Consider synthesizing a planner for a surveillance drone operating near another, potentially adversarial drone. Discretizing the map into the 7×7 grid in Fig. 1 (ignoring the depicted trajectories for the moment), a route is a word over the four movement directions. Our specification is to visit the 4 circled locations in 30 moves without colliding with the adversary, assuming it cannot move into the 5 highlighted central locations.

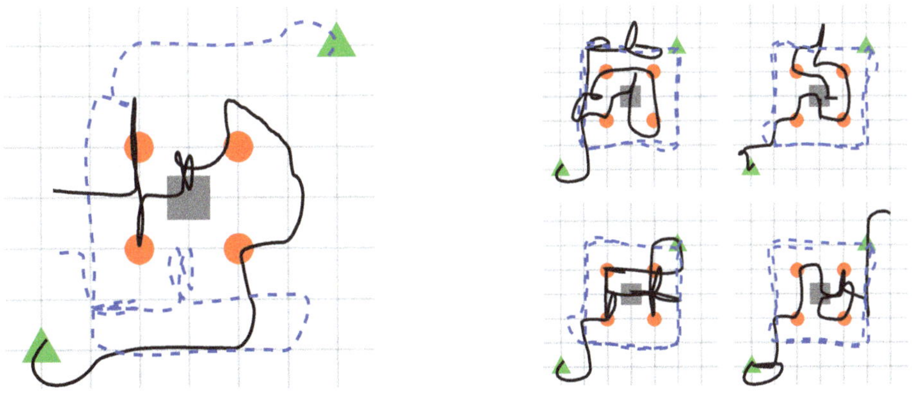

Fig. 1. Improvised trajectories for a patrolling drone (solid) avoiding an adversary (dashed). The adversary may not move into the circles or the square.

Existing reactive synthesis tools can produce a strategy for the patroller ensuring that the specification is always satisfied. However, the strategy may be deterministic, so that in response to a fixed adversary the patroller will always follow the same route. Then it is easy for a third party to predict the route, which could be undesirable, and is in fact unnecessary if there are many other ways the drone can satisfy its specification.

Reactive control improvisation addresses this problem by adding a new type of specification to the *hard constraint* above: a *randomness requirement* stating that no behavior should be generated with probability greater than a threshold ρ. If we set (say) $\rho = 1/5$, then any controller solving the synthesis problem must be able to satisfy the hard constraint in at least 5 different ways, never producing any given behavior more than 20% of the time. Our synthesis algorithm can in fact compute the smallest ρ for which synthesis is possible, yielding a controller that is *maximally-randomized* in that the system's behavior is as close to a uniform distribution as possible.

To allow finer tuning of how randomness is introduced into the controller, our definition also includes a *soft constraint* which need only be satisfied with some probability $1-\epsilon$. This allows us to prefer certain safe behaviors over others. In our drone example, we require that with probability at least 3/4, we do not visit a circled location twice.

These hard, soft, and randomness constraints form an instance of our reactive control improvisation problem. Encoding the hard and soft constraints as DFAs, our algorithm (Sect. 6) produced a controller achieving the smallest realizable $\rho = 2.2 \times 10^{-12}$. We tested the controller using the PX4 autopilot [17] to refine the generated routes into control actions for a drone simulated in Gazebo [14] (videos and code are available online [11]). A selection of resulting trajectories are shown in Fig. 1 (the remainder in Appendix A of the full paper [10]): starting from the triangles, the patroller's path is solid, the adversary's dashed. The left run uses an adversary that moves towards the patroller when possible. The right runs, with a simple adversary moving in a fixed loop, illustrate the randomness of the synthesized controller.

3.2 Reactive Control Improvisation

Our formal notion of randomized reactive synthesis in a finite window is a reactive extension of *control improvisation* [8,9], which captures the three types of constraint (hard, soft, randomness) seen above. We use the notation of [8] for the specifications and languages defining the hard and soft constraints:

Definition 3.1 ([8]). *Given* hard *and* soft *specifications $\mathcal{H}$ and $\mathcal{S}$ of languages over Σ, an* improvisation *is a word $w \in L(\mathcal{H}) \cap \Sigma^n$. It is* admissible *if $w \in L(\mathcal{S})$. The set of all improvisations is denoted I, and admissible improvisations A.*

Running Example. We will use the following simple example throughout the paper: each player may increment (+), decrement (−), or leave unchanged (=) a counter which is initially zero. The alphabet is $\Sigma = \{+, -, =\}$, and we set $n = 4$. The hard specification $\mathcal{H}$ is the DFA in Fig. 2 requiring that the counter stay within $[-2, 2]$. The soft specification $\mathcal{S}$ is a similar DFA requiring that the counter end at a nonnegative value.

Then for example the word ++== is an admissible improvisation, satisfying both hard and soft constraints, and so is in A. The word +−=− on the other hand satisfies $\mathcal{H}$ but not $\mathcal{S}$, so it is in I but not A. Finally, +++− does not satisfy $\mathcal{H}$, so it is not an improvisation at all and is not in I.

A reactive control improvisation problem is defined by $\mathcal{H}$, $\mathcal{S}$, and parameters ϵ and ρ. A solution is then a strategy which ensures that the hard, soft, and randomness constraints hold against every adversary. Formally, following [8,9]:

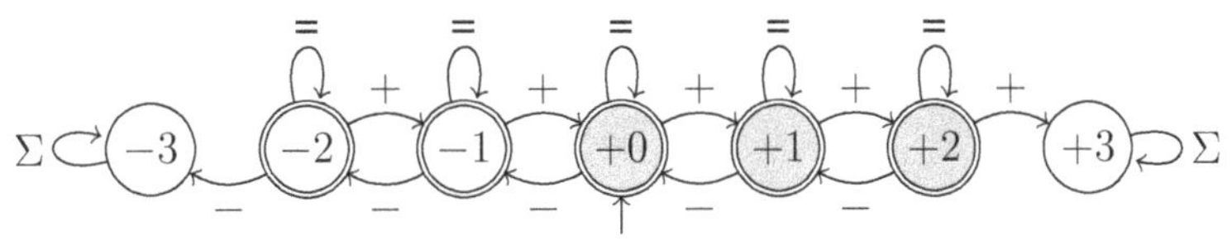

Fig. 2. The hard specification DFA $\mathcal{H}$ in our running example. The soft specification $\mathcal{S}$ is the same but with only the shaded states accepting.

Definition 3.2. *Given an* RCI instance $\mathcal{C} = (\mathcal{H}, \mathcal{S}, n, \epsilon, \rho)$ *with* $\mathcal{H}$, $\mathcal{S}$, *and* n *as above and* $\epsilon, \rho \in [0, 1] \cap \mathbb{Q}$, *a strategy* σ *is an* improvising strategy *if it satisfies the following requirements for every adversary* τ*:*

Hard constraint: $P_{\sigma,\tau}(I) = 1$
Soft constraint: $P_{\sigma,\tau}(A) \geq 1 - \epsilon$
Randomness: $\forall \pi \in I,\ P_{\sigma,\tau}(\pi) \leq \rho$.

If there is an improvising strategy σ, *we say that* $\mathcal{C}$ *is* realizable. *An* improviser *for* $\mathcal{C}$ *is then an expected-finite time probabilistic algorithm implementing such a strategy* σ, *i.e. whose output distribution on input* $h \in \Sigma^{\leq n}$ *is* $\sigma(h, \cdot)$.

Definition 3.3. *Given an RCI instance* $\mathcal{C} = (\mathcal{H}, \mathcal{S}, n, \epsilon, \rho)$, *the* reactive control improvisation *(RCI) problem is to decide whether* $\mathcal{C}$ *is realizable, and if so to generate an improviser for* $\mathcal{C}$.

Running Example. Suppose we set $\epsilon = 1/2$ and $\rho = 1/2$. Let σ be the strategy which picks $+$ or $-$ with equal probability in the first move, and thenceforth picks the action which moves the counter closest to ± 1 respectively. This satisfies the hard constraint, since if the adversary ever moves the counter to ± 2 we immediately move it back. The strategy also satisfies the soft constraint, since with probability 1/2 we set the counter to $+1$ on the first move, and if the adversary moves to 0 we move back to $+1$ and remain nonnegative. Finally, σ also satisfies the randomness constraint, since each choice of first move happens with probability 1/2 and so no play can be generated with higher probability. So σ is an improvising strategy and this RCI instance is realizable.

We will study classes of RCI problems with different types of specifications:

Definition 3.4. *If* HSpec *and* SSpec *are classes of specifications, then the class of RCI instances* $\mathcal{C} = (\mathcal{H}, \mathcal{S}, n, \epsilon, \rho)$ *where* $\mathcal{H} \in$ HSpec *and* $\mathcal{S} \in$ SSpec *is denoted* RCI (HSpec, SSpec). *We use the same notation for the decision problem associated with the class, i.e., given* $\mathcal{C} \in$ RCI (HSpec, SSpec), *decide whether* $\mathcal{C}$ *is realizable. The* size $|\mathcal{C}|$ *of an RCI instance is the total size of the bit representations of its parameters, with* n *represented in unary and* ϵ, ρ *in binary.*

Finally, a *synthesis algorithm* in our context takes a specification in the form of an RCI instance and produces an implementation in the form of an improviser. This corresponds exactly to the notion of an improvisation scheme from [8]:

Definition 3.5 ([8]). *A* polynomial-time improvisation scheme *for a class* $\mathcal{P}$ *of RCI instances is an algorithm* S *with the following properties:*

Correctness: *For any* $\mathcal{C} \in \mathcal{P}$, *if* $\mathcal{C}$ *is realizable then* $S(\mathcal{C})$ *is an improviser for* $\mathcal{C}$, *and otherwise* $S(\mathcal{C}) = \perp$.

Scheme efficiency: *There is a polynomial* $p : \mathbb{R} \to \mathbb{R}$ *such that the runtime of* S *on any* $\mathcal{C} \in \mathcal{P}$ *is at most* $p(|\mathcal{C}|)$.

Improviser efficiency: *There is a polynomial* $q : \mathbb{R} \to \mathbb{R}$ *such that for every* $\mathcal{C} \in \mathcal{P}$, *if* $G = S(\mathcal{C}) \neq \perp$ *then* G *has expected runtime at most* $q(|\mathcal{C}|)$.

The first two requirements simply say that the scheme produces valid improvisers in polynomial time. The third is necessary to ensure that the improvisers themselves are efficient: otherwise, the scheme might for example produce improvisers running in time exponential in the size of the specification.

A main goal of our paper is to determine for which types of specifications there exist polynomial-time improvisation schemes. While we do find such algorithms for important classes of specifications, we will also see that determining the realizability of an RCI instance is often PSPACE-hard. Therefore we also consider *polynomial-space improvisation schemes*, defined as above but replacing time with space.

4 Existence of Improvisers

4.1 Width and Realizability

The most basic question in reactive synthesis is whether a specification is realizable. In *randomized* reactive synthesis, the question is more delicate because the randomness requirement means that it is no longer enough to ensure some property regardless of what the adversary does: there must be *many ways* to do so. Specifically, there must be at least $1/\rho$ improvisations if we are to generate each of them with probability at most ρ. Furthermore, at least this many improvisations must be *possible* given an unknown adversary: even if many exist, the adversary may be able to force us to use only a single one. We introduce a new notion of the size of a set of plays that takes this into account.

Definition 4.1. *The* width *of* $X \subseteq \Sigma^n$ *is* $W(X) = \max_\sigma \min_\tau |X \cap \Pi_{\sigma,\tau}|$.

The width counts how many distinct plays can be generated regardless of what the adversary does. Intuitively, a "narrow" game—one whose set of winning plays has small width—is one in which the adversary can force us to choose among only a few winning plays, while in a "wide" one we always have many safe choices available. Note that *which* particular plays can be generated depends on the adversary: the width only measures *how many* can be generated. For example, $W(X) = 1$ means that a play in X can always be generated, but possibly a different element of X for different adversaries.

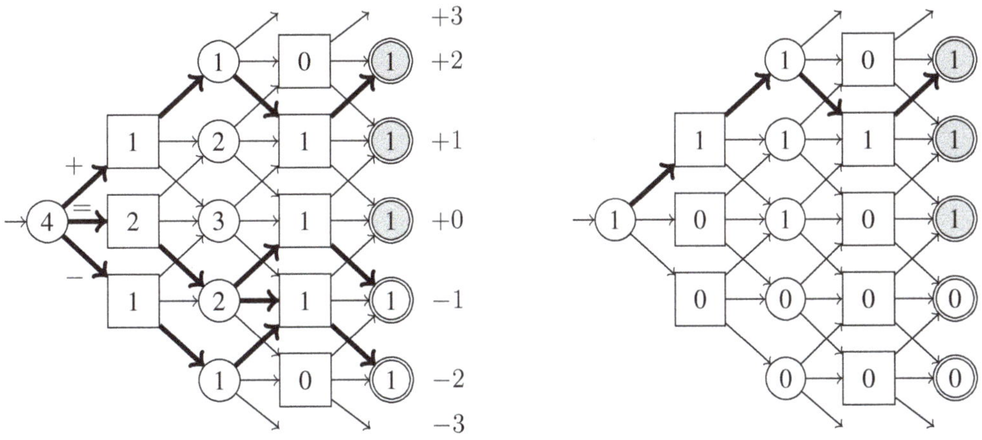

Fig. 3. Synthesis game for our running example. States are labeled with the widths of I (left) and A (right) given a history ending at that state.

Running Example. Figure 3 shows the synthesis game for our running example: paths ending in circled or shaded states are plays in I or A respectively (ignore the state labels for now). At left, the bold arrows show the 4 plays in I possible against the adversary that moves away from 0, and down at 0. This shows $W(I) \leq 4$, and in fact 4 plays are possible against any adversary, so $W(I) = 4$. Similarly, at right we see that $W(A) = 1$.

It will be useful later to have a *relative* version of width that counts how many plays are possible *from a given position*:

Definition 4.2. *Given a set of plays* $X \subseteq \Sigma^n$ *and a history* $h \in \Sigma^{\leq n}$, *the* width *of* X *given* h *is* $W(X|h) = \max_\sigma \min_\tau |\{\pi \mid h\pi \in X \wedge P_{\sigma,\tau}(\pi|h) > 0\}|$.

This is a direct generalization of "winning" positions: if X is the set of winning plays, then $W(X|h)$ counts the number of ways to win from h.

We will often use the following basic properties of $W(X|h)$ without comment (for lack of space this proof and the details of later proof sketches are deferred to Appendix B of the full paper [10]). Note that (3)–(5) provide a recursive way to compute widths that we will use later, and which is illustrated by the state labels in Fig. 3.

Lemma 4.1. *For any set of plays* $X \subseteq \Sigma^n$ *and history* $h \in \Sigma^{\leq n}$:

1. $0 \leq W(X|h) \leq |\Sigma|^{n-|h|}$;
2. $W(X|\lambda) = W(X)$;
3. *if* $|h| = n$, *then* $W(X|h) = \mathbb{1}_{h \in X}$;
4. *if it is our turn after* h, *then* $W(X|h) = \sum_{u \in \Sigma} W(X|hu)$;
5. *if it is the adversary's turn after* h, *then* $W(X|h) = \min_{u \in \Sigma} W(X|hu)$.

Now we can state the realizability conditions, which are simply that I and A have sufficiently large width. In fact, the conditions turn out to be exactly the same as those for non-reactive CI except that width takes the place of size [9].

Theorem 4.1. *The following are equivalent:*

(1) $\mathcal{C}$ is realizable.
(2) $W(I) \geq 1/\rho$ and $W(A) \geq (1-\epsilon)/\rho$.
(3) There is an improviser for $\mathcal{C}$.

Running Example. We saw above that our example was realizable with $\epsilon = \rho = 1/2$, and indeed $4 = W(I) \geq 1/\rho = 2$ and $1 = W(A) \geq (1-\epsilon)/\rho = 1$. However, if we put $\rho = 1/3$ we violate the second inequality and the instance is not realizable: essentially, we need to distribute probability $1 - \epsilon = 1/2$ among plays in A (to satisfy the soft constraint), but since $W(A) = 1$, against some adversaries we can only generate one play in A and would have to give it the whole $1/2$ (violating the randomness requirement).

The difficult part of the Theorem is constructing an improviser when the inequalities (2) hold. Despite the similarity in these conditions to the non-reactive case, the construction is much more involved. We begin with a general overview.

4.2 Improviser Construction: Discussion

Our improviser can be viewed as an extension of the classical random-walk reduction of uniform sampling to counting [21]. In that algorithm (which was used in a similar way for DFA specifications in [8,9]), a uniform distribution over paths in a DAG is obtained by moving to the next vertex with probability proportional to the number of paths originating at it. In our case, which plays are possible depends on the adversary, but the width still tells us *how many* plays are possible. So we could try a random walk using widths as weights: e.g. on the first turn in Fig. 3, picking $+$, $-$, and $=$ with probabilities $1/4$, $2/4$, and $1/4$ respectively. Against the adversary shown in Fig. 3, this would indeed yield a uniform distribution over the four possible plays in I.

However, the soft constraint may require a non-uniform distribution. In the running example with $\epsilon = \rho = 1/2$, we need to generate the single possible play in A with probability $1/2$, not just the uniform probability $1/4$. This is easily fixed by doing the random walk with a *weighted average* of the widths of I and A: specifically, move to position h with probability proportional to $\alpha W(A|h) + \beta(W(I|h) - W(A|h))$. In the example, this would result in plays in A getting probability α and those in $I \setminus A$ getting probability β. Taking α sufficiently large, we can ensure the soft constraint is satisfied.

Unfortunately, this strategy can fail if the adversary makes *more* plays available than the width guarantees. Consider the game on the left of Fig. 4, where $W(I) = 3$ and $W(A) = 2$. This is realizable with $\epsilon = \rho = 1/3$, but no values of α and β yield improvising strategies, essentially because an adversary moving from X to Z breaks the worst-case assumption that the adversary will minimize the number of possible plays by moving to Y. In fact, this instance is realizable but not by any memoryless strategy. To see this, note that all such strategies can be parametrized by the probabilities p and q in Fig. 4. To satisfy the randomness

Fig. 4. Reachability games where a naïve random walk, and all memoryless strategies, fail (left) and where no strategy can optimize either ϵ or ρ against every adversary simultaneously (right).

constraint against the adversary that moves from X to Y, both p and $(1-p)q$ must be at most $1/3$. To satisfy the soft constraint against the adversary that moves from X to Z we must have $pq + (1-p)q \geq 2/3$, so $q \geq 2/3$. But then $(1-p)q \geq (1-1/3)(2/3) = 4/9 > 1/3$, a contradiction.

To fix this problem, our improvising strategy $\hat{\sigma}$ (which we will fully specify in Algorithm 1 below) takes a simplistic approach: it tracks how many plays in A and I are expected to be possible based on their widths, and if more are available it ignores them. For example, entering state Z from X there are 2 ways to produce a play in I, but since $W(I|X) = 1$ we ignore the play in $I \setminus A$. Extra plays in A are similarly ignored by being treated as members of $I \setminus A$. Ignoring unneeded plays may seem wasteful, but the proof of Theorem 4.1 will show that $\hat{\sigma}$ nevertheless achieves the best possible ϵ:

Corollary 4.1. *$\mathcal{C}$ is realizable iff $W(I) \geq 1/\rho$ and $\epsilon \geq \epsilon_{\text{opt}} \equiv \max(1 - \rho W(A), 0)$. Against any adversary, the error probability of Algorithm 1 is at most ϵ_{opt}.*

Thus, if *any* improviser can achieve an error probability ϵ, ours does. We could ask for a stronger property, namely that against each adversary the improviser achieves the smallest possible error probability *for that adversary*. Unfortunately, this is impossible in general. Consider the game on the right in Fig. 4, with $\rho = 1$. Against the adversary which always moves up, we can achieve $\epsilon = 0$ with the strategy that at P moves to Q. We can also achieve $\epsilon = 0$ against the adversary that always moves down, but only with a *different* strategy, namely the one that at P moves to R. So there is no single strategy that achieves the optimal ϵ for every adversary. A similar argument shows that there is also no strategy achieving the smallest possible ρ for every adversary. In essence, optimizing ϵ or ρ in every case would require the strategy to depend on the adversary.

4.3 Improviser Construction: Details

Our improvising strategy, as outlined in the previous section, is shown in Algorithm 1. We first compute α and β, the (maximum) probabilities for generating elements of A and $I \setminus A$ respectively. As in [8], we take α as large as possible given $\alpha \leq \rho$, and determine β from the probability left over (modulo a couple corner cases).

Algorithm 1. the strategy $\hat{\sigma}$

$\alpha \leftarrow \min(\rho, 1/W(A))$ (or 0 instead if $W(A) = 0$)
$\beta \leftarrow (1 - \alpha W(A))/(W(I) - W(A))$ (or 0 instead if $W(I) - W(A) = 0$)
$m^A \leftarrow W(A)$, $m^I \leftarrow W(I)$
$h \leftarrow \lambda$
while the game is not over after h **do**
  if it is our turn after h **then**
    $m_u^A, m_u^I \leftarrow$ PARTITION(m^A, m^I, h) ▷ returns values for each $u \in \Sigma$
    for each $u \in \Sigma$, put $t_u \leftarrow \alpha m_u^A + \beta(m_u^I - m_u^A)$
    pick $u \in \Sigma$ with probability proportional to t_u and append it to h
    $m^A \leftarrow m_u^A$, $m^I \leftarrow m_u^I$
  else
    the adversary picks $u \in \Sigma$ given the history h; append it to h
return h

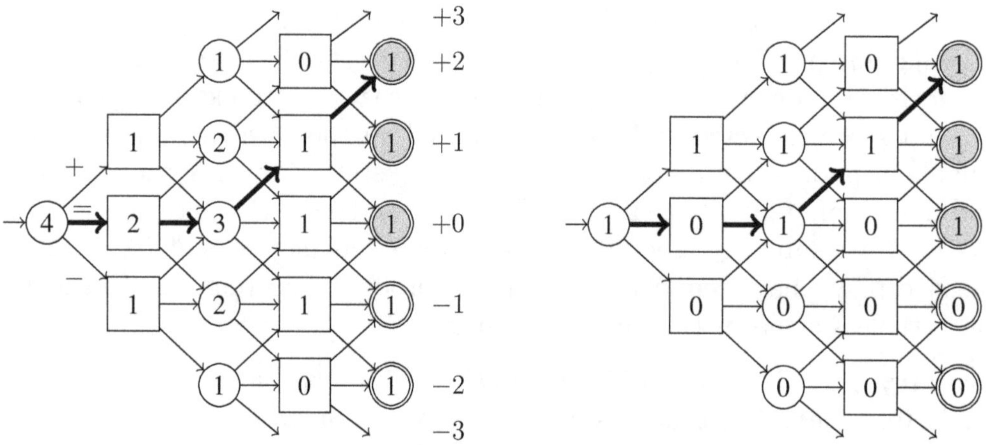

Fig. 5. A run of Algorithm 1, labeling states with corresponding widths of I (left) and A (right).

Next we initialize m^A and m^I, our expectations for how many plays in A and I respectively are still possible to generate. Initially these are given by $W(A)$ and $W(I)$, but as we saw above it is possible for more plays to become available. The function PARTITION handles this, deciding which m^A (resp., m^I) out of the available $W(A|h)$ $(W(I|h))$ plays we will use. The behavior of PARTITION is defined by the following lemma; its proof (in Appendix B [10]) greedily takes the first m^A possible plays in A under some canonical order and the first $m^I - m^A$ of the remaining plays in I.

Lemma 4.2. *If it is our turn after $h \in \Sigma^{\leq n}$, and $m^A, m^I \in \mathbb{Z}$ satisfy $0 \leq m^A \leq m^I \leq W(I|h)$ and $m^A \leq W(A|h)$, there are integer partitions $\sum_{u \in \Sigma} m_u^A$ and $\sum_{u \in \Sigma} m_u^I$ of m^A and m^I respectively such that $0 \leq m_u^A \leq m_u^I \leq W(I|hu)$ and $m_u^A \leq W(A|hu)$ for all $u \in \Sigma$. These are computable in poly-time given oracles for $W(I|\cdot)$ and $W(A|\cdot)$.*

Finally, we perform the random walk, moving from position h to hu with (unnormalized) probability t_u, the weighted average described above.

Running Example. With $\epsilon = \rho = 1/2$, as before $W(A) = 1$ and $W(I) = 4$ so $\alpha = 1/2$ and $\beta = 1/6$. On the first move, m^A and m^I match $W(A|h)$ and $W(I|h)$, so all plays are used and PARTITION returns $(W(A|hu), W(I|hu))$ for each $u \in \Sigma$. Looking up these values in Fig. 5, we see $(m^A_=, m^I_=) = (0, 2)$ and so $t(=) = 2\beta = 1/3$. Similarly $t(+) = \alpha = 1/2$ and $t(-) = \beta = 1/6$. We choose an action according to these weights; suppose $=$, so that we update $m^A \leftarrow 0$ and $m^I \leftarrow 2$, and suppose the adversary responds with $=$. From Fig. 5, $W(A| ==) = 1$ and $W(I| ==) = 3$, whereas $m^A = 0$ and $m^I = 2$. So PARTITION discards a play, say returning $(m^A_u, m^I_u) = (0, 1)$ for $u \in \{+, =\}$ and $(0, 0)$ for $u \in \{-\}$. Then $t(+) = t(=) = \beta = 1/6$ and $t(-) = 0$. So we pick $+$ or $=$ with equal probability, say $+$. If the adversary responds with $+$, we get the play $==++$, shown in bold on Fig. 5. As desired, it satisfies the hard constraint.

The next few lemmas establish that $\hat{\sigma}$ is well-defined and in fact an improvising strategy, allowing us to prove Theorem 4.1. Throughout, we write $m^A(h)$ (resp., $m^I(h)$) for the value of m^A (m^I) at the start of the iteration for history h. We also write $t(h) = \alpha m^A(h) + \beta(m^I(h) - m^A(h))$ (so $t(hu) = t_u$ when we pick u).

Lemma 4.3. *If $W(I) \geq 1/\rho$, then $\hat{\sigma}$ is a well-defined strategy and $P_{\hat{\sigma},\tau}(I) = 1$ for every adversary τ.*

Proof (sketch). An easy induction on h shows the conditions of Lemma 4.2 are always satisfied, and that $t(h)$ is always positive since we never pick a u with $t_u = 0$. So $\sum_u t_u = t(h) > 0$ and $\hat{\sigma}$ is well-defined. Furthermore, $t(h) > 0$ implies $m^I(h) > 0$, so for any $h \in \Pi_{\hat{\sigma},\tau}$ we have $\mathbb{1}_{h \in I} = W(I|h) \geq m^I(h) > 0$ and thus $h \in I$. □

Lemma 4.4. *If $W(I) \geq 1/\rho$, then $P_{\hat{\sigma},\tau}(A) \geq \min(\rho W(A), 1)$ for every τ.*

Proof (sketch). Because of the $\alpha m^A(h)$ term in the weights $t(h)$, the probability of obtaining a play in A starting from h is at least $\alpha m^A(h)/t(h)$ (as can be seen by induction on h in order of decreasing length). Then since $m^A(\lambda) = W(A)$ and $t(\lambda) = 1$ we have $P_{\hat{\sigma},\tau}(A) \geq \alpha W(A) = \min(\rho W(A), 1)$. □

Lemma 4.5. *If $W(I) \geq 1/\rho$, then $P_{\hat{\sigma},\tau}(\pi) \leq \rho$ for every $\pi \in \Sigma^n$ and τ.*

Proof (sketch). If the adversary is deterministic, the weights we use for our random walk yield a distribution where each play π has probability either α or β (depending on whether $m^A(\pi) = 1$ or 0). If the adversary assigns nonzero probability to multiple choices this only decreases the probability of individual plays. Finally, since $W(I) \geq 1/\rho$ we have $\alpha, \beta \leq \rho$. □

Proof (of Theorem 4.1). We use a similar argument to that of [8].

(1)⇒(2) Suppose σ is an improvising strategy, and fix any adversary τ. Then $\rho|\Pi_{\sigma,\tau} \cap I| = \sum_{\pi \in \Pi_{\sigma,\tau} \cap I} \rho \geq \sum_{\pi \in I} P_{\sigma,\tau}(\pi) = P_{\sigma,\tau}(I) = 1$, so $|\Pi_{\sigma,\tau} \cap I| \geq 1/\rho$. Since τ is arbitrary, this implies $W(I) \geq 1/\rho$. Since $A \subseteq I$, we also have $\rho|\Pi_{\sigma,\tau} \cap A| = \sum_{\pi \in \Pi_{\sigma,\tau} \cap A} \rho \geq \sum_{\pi \in A} P_{\sigma,\tau}(\pi) = P_{\sigma,\tau}(A) \geq 1 - \epsilon$, so $|\Pi_{\sigma,\tau} \cap A| \geq (1-\epsilon)/\rho$ and thus $W(A) \geq (1-\epsilon)/\rho$.

(2)⇒(3) By Lemmas 4.3 and 4.5, $\hat{\sigma}$ is well-defined and satisfies the hard and randomness constraints. By Lemma 4.4, $P_{\hat{\sigma},\tau}(A) \geq \min(\rho W(A), 1) \geq 1 - \epsilon$, so $\hat{\sigma}$ also satisfies the soft constraint and thus is an improvising strategy. Its transition probabilities are rational, so it can be implemented by an expected finite-time probabilistic algorithm, which is then an improviser for $\mathcal{C}$.

(3)⇒(1) Immediate. □

Proof (of Corollary 4.1). The inequalities in the statement are equivalent to those of Theorem 4.1 (2). By Lemma 4.4, we have $P_{\hat{\sigma},\tau}(A) \geq \min(\rho W(A), 1)$. So the error probability is at most $1 - \min(\rho W(A), 1) = \epsilon_{\text{opt}}$. □

5 A Generic Improviser

We now use the construction of Sect. 4 to develop a generic improvisation scheme usable with any class of specifications Spec supporting the following operations:

Intersection: Given specs $\mathcal{X}$ and $\mathcal{Y}$, find $\mathcal{Z}$ such that $L(\mathcal{Z}) = L(\mathcal{X}) \cap L(\mathcal{Y})$.

Width Measurement: Given a specification $\mathcal{X}$, a length $n \in \mathbb{N}$ in unary, and a history $h \in \Sigma^{\leq n}$, compute $W(X|h)$ where $X = L(\mathcal{X}) \cap \Sigma^n$.

Efficient algorithms for these operations lead to efficient improvisation schemes:

Theorem 5.1. *If the operations on* Spec *above take polynomial time (resp. space), then* RCI (Spec, Spec) *has a polynomial-time (space) improvisation scheme.*

Proof. Given an instance $\mathcal{C} = (\mathcal{H}, \mathcal{S}, n, \epsilon, \rho)$ in RCI (Spec, Spec), we first apply intersection to $\mathcal{H}$ and $\mathcal{S}$ to obtain $\mathcal{A} \in$ Spec such that $L(\mathcal{A}) \cap \Sigma^n = A$. Since intersection takes polynomial time (space), $\mathcal{A}$ has size polynomial in $|\mathcal{C}|$. Next we use width measurement to compute $W(I) = W(L(\mathcal{H}) \cap \Sigma^n|\lambda)$ and $W(A) = W(L(\mathcal{A}) \cap \Sigma^n|\lambda)$. If these violate the inequalities in Theorem 4.1, then $\mathcal{C}$ is not realizable and we return $\perp$. Otherwise $\mathcal{C}$ is realizable, and $\hat{\sigma}$ above is an improvising strategy. Furthermore, we can construct an expected finite-time probabilistic algorithm implementing $\hat{\sigma}$, using width measurement to instantiate the oracles needed by Lemma 4.2. Determining $m^A(h)$ and $m^I(h)$ takes $O(n)$ invocations of Partition, each of which is poly-time relative to the width measurements. These take time (space) polynomial in $|\mathcal{C}|$, since $\mathcal{H}$ and $\mathcal{A}$ have size polynomial in $|\mathcal{C}|$. As $m^A, m^I \leq |\Sigma|^n$, they have polynomial bitwidth and so the arithmetic required to compute t_u for each $u \in \Sigma$ takes polynomial time. Therefore the total expected runtime (space) of the improviser is polynomial. □

Note that as a byproduct of testing the inequalities in Theorem 4.1, our algorithm can compute the best possible error probability ϵ_{opt} given $\mathcal{H}$, $\mathcal{S}$, and ρ (see Corollary 4.1). Alternatively, given ϵ, we can compute the best possible ρ.

We will see below how to efficiently compute widths for DFAs, so Theorem 5.1 yields a polynomial-time improvisation scheme. If we allow polynomial-*space* schemes, we can use a general technique for width measurement that only requires a very weak assumption on the specifications, namely testability in polynomial space:

Theorem 5.2. RCI (PSA, PSA) *has a polynomial-space improvisation scheme, where* PSA *is the class of polynomial-space decision algorithms.*

Proof (sketch). We apply Theorem 5.1, computing widths recursively using Lemmas 4.1, (3)–(5). As in the PSPACE *QBF* algorithm, the current path in the recursive tree and required auxiliary storage need only polynomial space. □

6 Reachability Games and DFAs

Now we develop a polynomial-time improvisation scheme for RCI instances with DFA specifications. This also provides a scheme for reachability/safety games, whose winning conditions can be straightforwardly encoded as DFAs.

Suppose D is a DFA with states V, accepting states T, and transition function $\delta : V \times \Sigma \to V$. Our scheme is based on the fact that $W(L(D)|h)$ depends only on the state of D reached on input h, allowing these widths to be computed by dynamic programming. Specifically, for all $v \in V$ and $i \in \{0, \dots, n\}$ we define:

$$C(v,i) = \begin{cases} \mathbb{1}_{v \in T} & i = n \\ \min_{u \in \Sigma} C(\delta(v,u), i+1) & i < n \wedge i \text{ odd} \\ \sum_{u \in \Sigma} C(\delta(v,u), i+1) & \text{otherwise.} \end{cases}$$

Running Example. Figure 6 shows the values $C(v,i)$ in rows from $i = n$ downward. For example, $i = 2$ is our turn, so $C(1,2) = C(0,3) + C(1,3) + C(2,3) = 1+1+0 = 2$, while $i = 3$ is the adversary's turn, so $C(-3,3) = \min\{C(-3,4)\} = \min\{0\} = 0$. Note that the values in Fig. 6 agree with the widths $W(I|h)$ shown in Fig. 5.

Lemma 6.1. *For any history $h \in \Sigma^{\leq n}$, writing $X = L(D) \cap \Sigma^n$ we have $W(X|h) = C(D(h), |h|)$, where $D(h)$ is the state reached by running D on h.*

Proof. We prove this by induction on $i = |h|$ in decreasing order. In the base case $i = n$, we have $W(X|h) = \mathbb{1}_{h \in X} = \mathbb{1}_{D(h) \in T} = C(D(h), n)$. Now take any history $h \in \Sigma^{\leq n}$ with $|h| = i < n$. By hypothesis, for any $u \in \Sigma$ we have $W(X|hu) = C(D(hu), i+1)$. If it is our turn after h, then $W(X|h) = \sum_{u \in \Sigma} W(X|hu) = \sum_{u \in \Sigma} C(D(hu), i+1) = C(D(h), i)$ as desired. If instead it is the adversary's turn after h, then $W(X|h) = \min_{u \in \Sigma} W(X|hu) = \min_{u \in \Sigma} C(D(hu), i+1) = C(D(h), i)$ again as desired. So by induction the hypothesis holds for any i. □

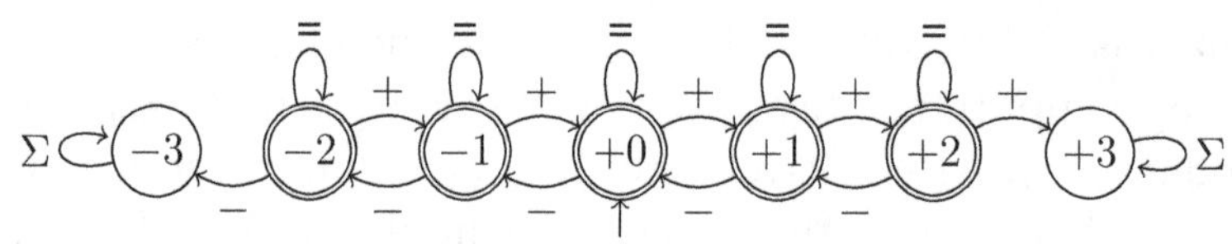

	−3	−2	−1	+0	+1	+2	+3
$i = 4$:	0	1	1	1	1	1	0
$i = 3$:	0	0	1	1	1	0	0
$i = 2$:		1	2	3	2	1	
$i = 1$:			1	2	1		
$i = 0$:				4			

Fig. 6. The hard specification DFA $\mathcal{H}$ in our running example, showing how $W(I|h)$ is computed.

Theorem 6.1. RCI (DFA, DFA) *has a polynomial-time improvisation scheme.*

Proof. We implement Theorem 5.1. Intersection can be done with the standard product construction. For width measurement we compute the quantities $C(v, i)$ by dynamic programming (from $i = n$ down to $i = 0$) and apply Lemma 6.1. □

7 Temporal Logics and Other Specifications

In this section we analyze the complexity of reactive control improvisation for specifications in the popular temporal logics LTL and LDL. We also look at NFA and CFG specifications, previously studied for non-reactive CI [8], to see how their complexities change in the reactive case.

For LTL specifications, reactive control improvisation is PSPACE-hard because this is already true of ordinary reactive synthesis in a finite window (we suspect this has been observed but could not find a proof in the literature).

Theorem 7.1. *Finite-window reactive synthesis for* LTL *is* PSPACE*-hard.*

Proof (sketch). Given a *QBF* $\phi = \exists x \forall y \ldots \chi$, we can view assignments to its variables as traces over a single proposition. In polynomial time we can construct an LTL formula ψ whose models are the satisfying assignments of χ. Then there is a winning strategy to generate a play satisfying ψ iff ϕ is true. □

Corollary 7.1. RCI (LTL, Σ^*) *and* RCI (Σ^*, LTL) *are* PSPACE*-hard.*

This is perhaps disappointing, but is an inevitable consequence of LTL subsuming Boolean formulas. On the other hand, our general polynomial-space scheme applies to LTL and its much more expressive generalization LDL:

Theorem 7.2. RCI (LDL, LDL) *has a polynomial-space improvisation scheme.*

Proof. This follows from Theorem 5.2, since satisfaction of an LDL formula by a finite word can be checked in polynomial time (e.g. by combining dynamic programming on subformulas with a regular expression parser). □

Thus for temporal logics polynomial-time algorithms are unlikely, but adding randomization to reactive synthesis does not increase its complexity.

The same is true for NFA and CFG specifications, where it is again PSPACE-hard to find even a single winning strategy:

Theorem 7.3. *Finite-window reactive synthesis for* NFAs *is* PSPACE*-hard.*

Proof (sketch). Reduce from QBF as in Theorem 7.1, constructing an NFA accepting the satisfying assignments of χ (as done in [13]). □

Corollary 7.2. $\mathrm{RCI}\,(\mathrm{NFA}, \Sigma^*)$ *and* $\mathrm{RCI}\,(\Sigma^*, \mathrm{NFA})$ *are* PSPACE*-hard.*

Theorem 7.4. $\mathrm{RCI}\,(\mathrm{CFG}, \mathrm{CFG})$ *has a polynomial-space improvisation scheme.*

Proof. By Theorem 5.2, since CFG parsing can be done in polynomial time. □

Since NFAs can be converted to CFGs in polynomial time, this completes the picture for the kinds of CI specifications previously studied. In non-reactive CI, DFA specifications admit a polynomial-time improvisation scheme while for NFAs/CFGs the CI problem is #P-equivalent [8]. Adding reactivity, DFA specifications remain polynomial-time while NFAs and CFGs move up to PSPACE.

Table 1. Complexity of the reactive control improvisation problem for various types of hard and soft specifications $\mathcal{H}$, $\mathcal{S}$. Here PSPACE indicates that checking realizability is PSPACE-hard, and that there is a polynomial-space improvisation scheme.

<table>
<tr><th>$\mathcal{H} \backslash \mathcal{S}$</th><th>RSG</th><th>DFA</th><th>NFA</th><th>CFG</th><th>LTL</th><th>LDL</th></tr>
<tr><td>RSG</td><td colspan="2" rowspan="2">poly-time</td><td colspan="4" rowspan="6">PSPACE</td></tr>
<tr><td>DFA</td></tr>
<tr><td>NFA</td><td colspan="2" rowspan="4"></td></tr>
<tr><td>CFG</td></tr>
<tr><td>LTL</td></tr>
<tr><td>LDL</td></tr>
</table>

8 Conclusion

In this paper we introduced *reactive control improvisation* as a framework for modeling reactive synthesis problems where random but controlled behavior is desired. RCI provides a natural way to tune the amount of randomness while ensuring that safety or other constraints remain satisfied. We showed that RCI problems can be efficiently solved in many cases occurring in practice, giving a polynomial-time improvisation scheme for reachability/safety or DFA specifications. We also showed that RCI problems with specifications in LTL or LDL, popularly used in planning, have the PSPACE-hardness typical of bounded games, and gave a matching polynomial-space improvisation scheme. This scheme generalizes to any specification checkable in polynomial space, including NFAs, CFGs, and many more expressive formalisms. Table 1 summarizes these results.

These results show that, at a high level, finding a maximally-randomized strategy using RCI is no harder than finding any winning strategy at all: for specifications yielding games solvable in polynomial time (respectively, space), we gave polynomial-time (space) improvisation schemes. We therefore hope that in applications where ordinary reactive synthesis has proved tractable, our notion of randomized reactive synthesis will also. In particular, we expect our DFA scheme to be quite practical, and are experimenting with applications in robotic planning. On the other hand, our scheme for temporal logic specifications seems unlikely to be useful in practice without further refinement. An interesting direction for future work would be to see if modern solvers for quantified Boolean formulas (QBF) could be leveraged or extended to solve these RCI problems. This could be useful even for DFA specifications, as conjoining many simple properties can lead to exponentially-large automata. Symbolic methods based on constraint solvers would avoid such blow-up.

We are also interested in extending the RCI problem definition to unbounded or infinite words, as typically used in reactive synthesis. These extensions, as well as that to continuous signals, would be useful in robotic planning, cyber-physical system testing, and other applications. However, it is unclear how best to adapt our randomness constraint to settings where the improviser can generate infinitely many words. In such settings the improviser could assign arbitrarily small or even zero probability to every word, rendering the randomness constraint trivial. Even in the bounded case, RCI extensions with more complex randomness constraints than a simple upper bound on individual word probabilities would be worthy of study. One possibility would be to more directly control diversity and/or unpredictability by requiring the distribution of the improviser's output to be close to uniform after transformation by a given function.

Acknowledgements. The authors would like to thank Markus Rabe, Moshe Vardi, and several anonymous reviewers for helpful discussions and comments, and Ankush Desai and Tommaso Dreossi for assistance with the drone simulations. This work is supported in part by the National Science Foundation Graduate Research Fellowship Program under Grant No. DGE-1106400, by NSF grants CCF-1139138 and CNS-1646208, by DARPA under agreement number FA8750-16-C0043, and by TerraSwarm, one of six centers of STARnet, a Semiconductor Research Corporation program sponsored by MARCO and DARPA.

References

1. Arora, S., Barak, B.: Computational Complexity: A Modern Approach. Cambridge University Press, New York (2009)
2. Baier, C., Brázdil, T., Größer, M., Kučera, A.: Stochastic game logic. Acta Inf. **49**(4), 203–224 (2012)

3. Bloem, R., Galler, S., Jobstmann, B., Piterman, N., Pnueli, A., Weiglhofer, M.: Specify, compile, run: hardware from PSL. Electron. Notes Theor. Comput. Sci. **190**, 3–16 (2007). Proceedings of the 6th International Workshop on Compiler Optimization Meets Compiler Verification (COCV 2007). http://www.sciencedirect.com/science/article/pii/S157106610700583X
4. Chen, T., Forejt, V., Kwiatkowska, M., Simaitis, A., Wiltsche, C.: On stochastic games with multiple objectives. In: Chatterjee, K., Sgall, J. (eds.) MFCS 2013. LNCS, vol. 8087, pp. 266–277. Springer, Heidelberg (2013). https://doi.org/10.1007/978-3-642-40313-2_25
5. De Giacomo, G., Vardi, M.Y.: Linear temporal logic and linear dynamic logic on finite traces. In: Proceedings of the 23rd International Joint Conference on Artificial Intelligence. IJCAI 2013, pp. 854–860. AAAI Press (2013). http://dl.acm.org/citation.cfm?id=2540128.2540252
6. Donze, A., Libkind, S., Seshia, S.A., Wessel, D.: Control improvisation with application to music. Technical reports UCB/EECS-2013-183, EECS Department, University of California, Berkeley, Nov 2013. http://www2.eecs.berkeley.edu/Pubs/TechRpts/2013/EECS-2013-183.html
7. Finkbeiner, B.: Synthesis of reactive systems. In: Esparza, J., Grumberg, O., Sickert, S. (eds.) Dependable Software Systems Engineering. NATO Science for Peace and Security Series - D: Information and Communication Security, vol. 45, pp. 72–98. IOS Press, Amsterdam (2016)
8. Fremont, D.J., Donzé, A., Seshia, S.A.: Control improvisation. arXiv preprint (2017)
9. Fremont, D.J., Donzé, A., Seshia, S.A., Wessel, D.: Control improvisation. In: 35th IARCS Annual Conference on Foundations of Software Technology and Theoretical Computer Science (FSTTCS), pp. 463–474 (2015)
10. Fremont, D.J., Seshia, S.A.: Reactive control improvisation. arXiv preprint (2018)
11. Fremont, D.J., Seshia, S.A.: Reactive control improvisation website (2018). https://math.berkeley.edu/~dfremont/reactive.html
12. Hansson, H., Jonsson, B.: A logic for reasoning about time and reliability. Form. Asp. Comput. **6**(5), 512–535 (1994)
13. Kannan, S., Sweedyk, Z., Mahaney, S.: Counting and random generation of strings in regular languages. In: 6th Annual ACM-SIAM Symposium on Discrete Algorithms, pp. 551–557. SIAM (1995)
14. Koenig, N., Howard, A.: Design and use paradigms for Gazebo, an open-source multi-robot simulator. In: 2004 IEEE/RSJ International Conference on Intelligent Robots and Systems (IROS), vol. 3, pp. 2149–2154. IEEE (2004)
15. Kress-Gazit, H., Fainekos, G.E., Pappas, G.J.: Temporal-logic-based reactive mission and motion planning. IEEE Trans. Rob. **25**(6), 1370–1381 (2009)
16. Mazala, R.: Infinite games. In: Grädel, E., Thomas, W., Wilke, T. (eds.) Automata Logics, and Infinite Games. LNCS, vol. 2500, pp. 23–38. Springer, Heidelberg (2002). https://doi.org/10.1007/3-540-36387-4_2
17. Meier, L., Honegger, D., Pollefeys, M.: PX4: a node-based multithreaded open source robotics framework for deeply embedded platforms. In: 2015 IEEE International Conference on Robotics and Automation (ICRA), pp. 6235–6240. IEEE (2015)
18. Pnueli, A.: The temporal logic of programs. In: 18th Annual Symposium on Foundations of Computer Science (FOCS 1977), pp. 46–57. IEEE (1977)
19. Pnueli, A., Rosner, R.: On the synthesis of a reactive module. In: Proceedings of the 16th ACM SIGPLAN-SIGACT Symposium on Principles of Programming

Languages. POPL 1989, pp. 179–190. ACM, New York (1989). http://doi.acm.org/10.1145/75277.75293

20. Tomlin, C., Lygeros, J., Sastry, S.: Computing controllers for nonlinear hybrid systems. In: Vaandrager, F.W., van Schuppen, J.H. (eds.) HSCC 1999. LNCS, vol. 1569, pp. 238–255. Springer, Heidelberg (1999). https://doi.org/10.1007/3-540-48983-5_22
21. Wilf, H.S.: A unified setting for sequencing, ranking, and selection algorithms for combinatorial objects. Adv. Math. **24**(2), 281–291 (1977)

Constraint-Based Synthesis of Coupling Proofs

Aws Albarghouthi[1] and Justin Hsu[2,3](✉)

[1] University of Wisconsin–Madison, Madison, WI, USA
[2] University College London, London, UK
[3] Cornell University, Ithaca, NY, USA
email@justinh.su

Abstract. *Proof by coupling* is a classical technique for proving properties about pairs of randomized algorithms by carefully *relating* (or *coupling*) two probabilistic executions. In this paper, we show how to automatically construct such proofs for probabilistic programs. First, we present *f-coupled postconditions*, an abstraction describing two correlated program executions. Second, we show how properties of f-coupled postconditions can imply various probabilistic properties of the original programs. Third, we demonstrate how to reduce the proof-search problem to a purely logical *synthesis problem* of the form $\exists f.\, \forall X.\, \varphi$, making probabilistic reasoning unnecessary. We develop a prototype implementation to automatically build coupling proofs for probabilistic properties, including uniformity and independence of program expressions.

1 Introduction

In this paper, we aim to automatically synthesize *coupling proofs* for probabilistic programs and properties. Originally designed for proving properties comparing two probabilistic programs—so-called *relational properties*—a coupling proof describes how to correlate two executions of the given programs, simulating both programs with a single probabilistic program. By reasoning about this combined, *coupled* process, we can often give simpler proofs of probabilistic properties for the original pair of programs.

A number of recent works have leveraged this idea to verify relational properties of randomized algorithms, including differential privacy [8,10,12], security of cryptographic protocols [9], convergence of Markov chains [11], robustness of machine learning algorithms [7], and more. Recently, Barthe et al. [6] showed how to reduce certain *non-relational* properties—which describe a single probabilistic program—to relational properties of two programs, by duplicating the original program or by sequentially composing it with itself.

While coupling proofs can simplify reasoning about probabilistic properties, they are not so easy to use; most existing proofs are carried out manually in relational program logics using interactive theorem provers. In a nutshell, the

The full version of this paper is available at https://arxiv.org/abs/1804.04052.

H. Chockler and G. Weissenbacher (Eds.): CAV 2018, LNCS 10981, pp. 327–346, 2018.
https://doi.org/10.1007/978-3-319-96145-3_18

main challenge in a coupling proof is to select a correlation for each pair of corresponding sampling instructions, aiming to induce a particular relation between the outputs of the coupled process; this relation then implies the desired relational property. Just like finding inductive invariants in proofs for deterministic programs, picking suitable couplings in proofs can require substantial ingenuity.

To ease this task, we recently showed how to cast the search for coupling proofs as a program synthesis problem [1], giving a way to automatically find sophisticated proofs of differential privacy previously beyond the reach of automated verification. In the present paper, we build on this idea and present a general technique for constructing coupling proofs, targeting *uniformity* and *probabilistic independence* properties. Both are fundamental properties in the analysis of randomized algorithms, either in their own right or as prerequisites to proving more sophisticated guarantees; uniformity states that a randomized expression takes on all values in a finite range with equal probability, while probabilistic independence states that two probabilistic expressions are somehow uncorrelated—learning the value of one reveals no additional information about the value of the other.

Our techniques are inspired by the automated proofs of differential privacy we considered previously [1], but the present setting raises new technical challenges.

Non-lockstep execution. To prove differential privacy, the behavior of a single program is compared on two related inputs. To take advantage of the identical program structure, previous work restricted attention to *synchronizing* proofs, where the two executions can be analyzed assuming they follow the same control flow path. In contrast, coupling proofs for uniformity and independence often require relating two programs with different shapes, possibly following completely different control flows [6].
To overcome this challenge, we take a different approach. Instead of incrementally finding couplings for corresponding pairs of sampling instructions—requiring the executions to be tightly synchronized—we first lift all sampling instructions to the front of the program and pick a coupling once and for all. The remaining execution of both programs can then be encoded separately, with no need for lockstep synchronization (at least for loop-free programs—looping programs require a more careful treatment).

Richer space of couplings. The heart of a coupling proof is selecting—among multiple possible options—a particular correlation for each pair of random sampling instructions. Random sampling in differentially private programs typically use highly domain-specific distributions, like the Laplace distribution, which support a small number of useful couplings. Our prior work leveraged this feature to encode a collection of primitive couplings into the synthesis system. However, this is no longer possible when programs sample from distributions supporting richer couplings, like the uniform distribution. Since our approach coalesces all sampling instructions at the beginning of the program (more generally, at the head of the loop), we also need to find couplings for products of distributions.

We address this problem in two ways. First, we allow couplings of two sampling instructions to be specified by an injective function f from one range to another. Then, we impose requirements—encoded as standard logical constraints—to ensure that f indeed represents a coupling; we call such couplings *f-couplings.*

More general class of properties. Finally, we consider a broad class of properties rather than just differential privacy. While we focus on uniformity and independence for concreteness, our approach can establish general equalities between products of probabilities, i.e., probabilistic properties of the form

$$\prod_{i=1}^{m} \Pr[e_i \in E_i] = \prod_{j=1}^{n} \Pr[e'_j \in E'_j],$$

where e_i and e'_j are program expressions in the first and second programs respectively, and E_i and E'_j are predicates. As an example, we automatically establish a key step in the proof of Bertrand's Ballot theorem [20].

Paper Outline. After overviewing our technique on a motivating example (Sect. 2), we detail our main contributions.

- **Proof technique:** We introduce *f-coupled postconditions*, a form of postcondition for two probabilistic programs where random sampling instructions in the two programs are correlated by a function f. Using f-coupled postconditions, we present proof rules for establishing uniformity and independence of program variables, fundamental properties in the analysis of randomized algorithms (Sect. 3).
- **Reduction to constraint-based synthesis:** We demonstrate how to automatically find coupling proofs by transforming our proof rules into logical constraints of the form $\exists f.\, \forall X.\, \varphi$—a synthesis problem. A satisfiable constraint shows the existence of a function f—essentially, a compact encoding of a coupling proof—implying the target property (Sect. 4).
- **Extension to looping programs:** We extend our technique to reason about loops, by requiring synchronization at the loop head and finding a coupled invariant (Sect. 5).
- **Implementation and evaluation:** We implement our technique and evaluate it on several case studies, automatically constructing coupling proofs for interesting properties of a variety of algorithms (Sect. 6).

We conclude by comparing our technique with related approaches (Sect. 7).

2 Overview and Illustration

2.1 Introducing f-Couplings

A Simple Example. We begin by illustrating f-couplings over two identical Bernoulli distributions, denoted by the following *probability mass functions*:

$\mu_1(x) = \mu_2(x) = 0.5$ for all $x \in \mathbb{B}$ (where $\mathbb{B} = \{\mathit{true}, \mathit{false}\}$). In other words, the distribution μ_i returns *true* with probability 0.5, and *false* with probability 0.5.

An *f-coupling* for μ_1, μ_2 is a function $f : \mathbb{B} \to \mathbb{B}$ from the domain of the first distribution ($\mathbb{B}$) to the domain of the second (also $\mathbb{B}$); f should be injective and satisfy the *monotonicity property*: $\mu_1(x) \leq \mu_2(f(x))$ for all $x \in \mathbb{B}$. In other words, f relates each element $x \in \mathbb{B}$ with an element $f(x)$ that has an equal or larger probability in μ_2. For example, consider the function $f_\neg$ defined as

$$f_\neg(x) = \neg x.$$

This function relates *true* in μ_1 with *false* in μ_2, and vice versa. Observe that $\mu_1(x) \leqslant \mu_2(f_\neg(x))$ for all $x \in \mathbb{B}$, satisfying the definition of an $f_\neg$-coupling. We write $\mu_1 \leftrightsquigarrow^{f_\neg} \mu_2$ when there is an $f_\neg$-coupling for μ_1 and μ_2.

Using f-Couplings. An f-coupling can imply useful properties about the distributions μ_1 and μ_2. For example, suppose we want to prove that $\mu_1(\mathit{true}) = \mu_2(\mathit{false})$. The fact that there is an $f_\neg$-coupling of μ_1 and μ_2 immediately implies the equality: by the monotonicity property,

$$\mu_1(\mathit{true}) \leqslant \mu_2(f_\neg(\mathit{true})) = \mu_2(\mathit{false})$$
$$\mu_1(\mathit{false}) \leqslant \mu_2(f_\neg(\mathit{false})) = \mu_2(\mathit{true})$$

and therefore $\mu_1(\mathit{true}) = \mu_2(\mathit{false})$. More generally, it suffices to find an f-coupling of μ_1 and μ_2 such that

$$\underbrace{\{(x, f(x)) \mid x \in \mathbb{B}\}}_{\Psi_f} \subseteq \{(z_1, z_2) \mid z_1 = \mathit{true} \iff z_2 = \mathit{false}\},$$

where Ψ_f is induced by f; in particular, the $f_\neg$-coupling satisfies this property.

2.2 Simulating a Fair Coin

Now, let's use f-couplings to prove more interesting properties. Consider the program fairCoin in Fig. 1; the program simulates a fair coin by flipping a possibly biased coin that returns *true* with probability $p \in (0, 1)$, where p is a program parameter. Our goal is to prove that for any p, the output of the program is a uniform distribution—it simulates a fair coin. We consider two separate copies of fairCoin generating distributions μ_1 and μ_2 over the returned value x for the same bias p, and we construct a coupling showing $\mu_1(\mathit{true}) = \mu_2(\mathit{false})$, that is, heads and tails have equal probability.

```
fun fairCoin(p ∈ (0, 1))
  x ← false
  y ← false
  while x = y do
    x ~ bern(p)
    y ~ bern(p)
  return x
```

Fig. 1. Simulating a fair coin using an unfair one

Constructing f-Couplings. At first glance, it is unclear how to construct an f-coupling; unlike the distributions in our simple example, we do not have a concrete description of μ_1 and μ_2 as uniform distributions (indeed, this is what we are trying to establish). The key insight is that we do not need to construct our coupling in one shot. Instead, we can specify a coupling for the concrete, primitive sampling instructions in the body of the loop—which we know sample from $\mathsf{bern}(p)$—and then extend to a f-coupling for the whole loop and μ_1, μ_2.

For each copy of fairCoin, we coalesce the two sampling statements inside the loop into a single sampling statement from the product distribution:

$$x, y \sim \mathsf{bern}(p) \times \mathsf{bern}(p)$$

We have two such joint distributions $\mathsf{bern}(p) \times \mathsf{bern}(p)$ to couple, one from each copy of fairCoin. We use the following function $f_{swap} : \mathbb{B}^2 \to \mathbb{B}^2$:

$$f_{swap}(x, y) = (y, x)$$

which exchanges the values of x and y. Since this is an injective function satisfying the monotonicity property

$$(\mathsf{bern}(p) \times \mathsf{bern}(p))(x, y) \leqslant (\mathsf{bern}(p) \times \mathsf{bern}(p))(f_{swap}(x, y))$$

for all $(x, y) \in \mathbb{B} \times \mathbb{B}$ and $p \in (0, 1)$, we have an f_{swap}-coupling for the two copies of $\mathsf{bern}(p) \times \mathsf{bern}(p)$.

Analyzing the Loop. To extend a f_{body}-coupling on loop bodies to the entire loop, it suffices to check a synchronization condition: the coupling from f_{body} must ensure that the loop guards are equal so the two executions synchronize at the loop head. This holds in our case: every time the first program executes the statement $x, y \sim \mathsf{bern}(p) \times \mathsf{bern}(p)$, we can think of x, y as non-deterministically set to some values (a, b), and the corresponding variables in the second program as set to $f_{swap}(a, b) = (b, a)$. The loop guards in the two programs are equivalent under this choice, since $a = b$ is equivalent to $b = a$, hence we can analyze the loops in lockstep. In general, couplings enable us to relate samples from a pair of probabilistic assignments as if they were selected non-deterministically, often avoiding quantitative reasoning about probabilities.

Our constructed coupling for the loop guarantees that (i) both programs exit the loop at the same time, and (ii) when the two programs exit the loop, x takes opposite values in the two programs. In other words, there is an f_{loop}-coupling of μ_1 and μ_2 for some function f_{loop} such that

$$\Psi_{f_{loop}} \subseteq \{(z_1, z_2) \mid z_1 = \mathit{true} \iff z_2 = \mathit{false}\}, \qquad (1)$$

implying $\mu_1(\mathit{true}) = \mu_2(\mathit{false})$. Since both distributions are output distributions of fairCoin—hence $\mu_1 = \mu_2$—we conclude that fairCoin simulates a fair coin.

Note that our approach does not need to construct f_{loop} concretely—this function may be highly complex. Instead, we only need to show that $\Psi_{f_{loop}}$ (or some over-approximation) lies inside the target relation in Formula 1.

Achieving Automation. Observe that once we have fixed an f_{body}-coupling for the sampling instructions inside the loop body, checking that the f_{loop}-coupling satisfies the conditions for uniformity (Formula 1) is essentially a program verification problem. Therefore, we can cast the problem of constructing a coupling proof as a logical problem of the form $\exists f. \forall X. \varphi$, where f is the f-coupling we need to discover and $\forall X. \varphi$ is a constraint ensuring that (*i*) f indeed represents an f-coupling, and (*ii*) the f-coupling implies uniformity. Thus, we can use established synthesis-verification techniques to solve the resulting constraints (see, e.g., [2,13,27]).

3 A Proof Rule for Coupling Proofs

In this section, we develop a technique for constructing couplings and formalize proof rules for establishing uniformity and independence properties over program variables. We begin with background on probability distributions and couplings.

3.1 Distributions and Couplings

Distributions. A function $\mu : B \to [0,1]$ defines a *distribution* over a countable set B if $\sum_{b \in B} \mu(b) = 1$. We will often write $\mu(A)$ for a subset $A \subseteq B$ to mean $\sum_{x \in A} \mu(x)$. We write $dist(B)$ for the set of all distributions over B.

We will need a few standard constructions on distributions. First, the *support* of a distribution μ is defined as $supp(\mu) = \{b \in B \mid \mu(b) > 0\}$. Second, for a distribution on pairs $\mu \in dist(B_1 \times B_2)$, the first and second *marginals* of μ, denoted $\pi_1(\mu)$ and $\pi_2(\mu)$ respectively, are distributions over B_1 and B_2:

$$\pi_1(\mu)(b_1) \triangleq \sum_{b_2 \in B_2} \mu(b_1, b_2) \qquad \pi_2(\mu)(b_2) \triangleq \sum_{b_1 \in B_1} \mu(b_1, b_2).$$

Couplings. Let $\Psi \subseteq B_1 \times B_2$ be a binary relation. A *Ψ-coupling* for distributions μ_1 and μ_2 over B_1 and B_2 is a distribution $\mu \in dist(B_1 \times B_2)$ with (*i*) $\pi_1(\mu) = \mu_1$ and $\pi_2(\mu) = \mu_2$; and (*ii*) $supp(\mu) \subseteq \Psi$. We write $\mu_1 \leftrightsquigarrow^{\Psi} \mu_2$ when there exists a Ψ-coupling between μ_1 and μ_2.

An important fact is that an injective function $f : B_1 \to B_2$ where $\mu_1(b) \leqslant \mu_2(f(b))$ for all $b \in B_1$ induces a coupling between μ_1 and μ_2; this follows from a general theorem by Strassen [28], see also [23]. We write $\mu_1 \leftrightsquigarrow^{f} \mu_2$ for $\mu_1 \leftrightsquigarrow^{\Psi_f} \mu_2$, where $\Psi_f = \{(b_1, f(b_1)) \mid b_1 \in B_1\}$. The existence of a coupling can imply various useful properties about the two distributions. The following general fact will be the most important for our purposes—couplings can prove equalities between probabilities.

Proposition 1. *Let $E_1 \subseteq B_1$ and $E_2 \subseteq B_2$ be two events, and let $\Psi_= \triangleq \{(b_1, b_2) \mid b_1 \in E_1 \iff b_2 \in E_2\}$. If $\mu_1 \leftrightsquigarrow^{\Psi_=} \mu_2$, then $\mu_1(E_1) = \mu_2(E_2)$.*

3.2 Program Model

Our program model uses an imperative language with probabilistic assignments, where we can draw a random value from primitive distributions. We consider the easier case of loop-free programs first; we consider looping programs in Sect. 5.

Syntax. A (loop-free) program P is defined using the following grammar:

$$\begin{aligned} P \coloneqq\; & V \leftarrow \mathit{exp} && \text{(assignment)} \\ \mid\; & V \sim \mathit{dexp} && \text{(probabilistic assignment)} \\ \mid\; & \texttt{if } \mathit{bexp} \texttt{ then } P \texttt{ else } P && \text{(conditional)} \\ \mid\; & P; P && \text{(sequential composition)} \end{aligned}$$

where V is the set of variables that can appear in P, *exp* is an expression over V, and *bexp* is a Boolean expression over V. A probabilistic assignment samples from a probability distribution defined by expression *dexp*; for instance, *dexp* might be $\mathsf{bern}(p)$, the Bernoulli distribution with probability p of returning *true*. We use $V^I \subseteq V$ to denote the set of input program variables, which are never assigned to. All other variables are assumed to be defined before use.

We make a few simplifying assumptions. First, distribution expressions only mention input variables V^I, e.g., in the example above, $\mathsf{bern}(p)$, we have $p \in V^I$. Also, all programs are in *static single assignment* (SSA) form, where each variable is assigned to only once and are well-typed. These assumptions are relatively minor; they can can be verified using existing tools, or lifted entirely at the cost of slightly more complexity in our encoding.

Semantics. A state s of a program P is a valuation of all of its variables, represented as a map from variables to values, e.g., $s(x)$ is the value of $x \in V$ in s. We extend this mapping to expressions: $s(\mathit{exp})$ is the valuation of *exp* in s, and $s(\mathit{dexp})$ is the probability distribution defined by *dexp* in s.

We use S to denote the set of all possible program states. As is standard [24], we can give a semantics of P as a function $[\![P]\!] : S \to \mathit{dist}(S)$ from states to distributions over states. For an output distribution $\mu = [\![P]\!](s)$, we will abuse notation and write, e.g., $\mu(x = y)$ to denote the probability of the event that the program returns a state s where $s(x = y) = \mathit{true}$.

Self-Composition. We will sometimes need to simulate two separate executions of a program with a single probabilistic program. Given a program P, we use P_i to denote a program identical to P but with all variables *tagged* with the subscript i. We can then define the *self-composition*: given a program P, the program $P_1; P_2$ first executes P_1, and then executes the (separate) copy P_2.

3.3 Coupled Postconditions

We are now ready to present the *f-coupled postcondition*, an operator for approximating the outputs of two coupled programs.

Strongest Postcondition. We begin by defining a standard strongest post-condition operator over single programs, treating probabilistic assignments as no-ops. Given a set of states $Q \subseteq S$, we define post as follows:

$$\begin{aligned}
\mathsf{post}(v \leftarrow exp, Q) &= \{s[v \mapsto s(exp)] \mid s \in Q\}\\
\mathsf{post}(v \sim dexp, Q) &= Q\\
\mathsf{post}(\texttt{if}\ \ bexp\ \ \texttt{then}\ \ P\ \ \texttt{else}\ \ P',\ Q) &= \{s' \mid s \in Q, s' \in \mathsf{post}(P, s), s(bexp) = \mathit{true}\}\\
&\quad \cup \{s' \mid s \in Q, s' \in \mathsf{post}(P', s), s(bexp) = \mathit{false}\}\\
\mathsf{post}(P; P', Q) &= \mathsf{post}(P', \mathsf{post}(P, Q))
\end{aligned}$$

where $s[v \mapsto c]$ is state s with variable v mapped to the value c.

f-Coupled Postcondition. We rewrite programs so that all probabilistic assignments are combined into a single probabilistic assignment to a vector of variables appearing at the beginning of the program, i.e., an assignment of the form $\boldsymbol{v} \sim dexp$ in P and $\boldsymbol{v}' \sim dexp'$ in P', where $\boldsymbol{v}, \boldsymbol{v}'$ are vectors of variables. For instance, we can combine $x \sim \mathsf{bern}(0.5); y \sim \mathsf{bern}(0.5)$ into the single statement $x, y \sim \mathsf{bern}(0.5) \times \mathsf{bern}(0.5)$.

Let B, B' be the domains of $\boldsymbol{v}$ and $\boldsymbol{v}'$, $f : B \to B'$ be a function, and $Q \subseteq S \times S'$ be a set of pairs of input states, where S and S' are the states of P and P', respectively. We define the f-coupled postcondition operator cpost as

$$\begin{aligned}
&\mathsf{cpost}(P, P', Q, f) = \{(\mathsf{post}(P, s), \mathsf{post}(P', s')) \mid (s, s') \in Q'\}\\
&\qquad\qquad \text{where } Q' = \{(s[\boldsymbol{v} \mapsto \boldsymbol{b}], s'[\boldsymbol{v}' \mapsto f(\boldsymbol{b})]) \mid (s, s') \in Q, \boldsymbol{b} \in B\},\\
&\quad \text{assuming that} \quad \forall (s, s') \in Q.\, s(dexp) \leftrightsquigarrow^{f} s'(dexp'). \qquad (2)
\end{aligned}$$

The intuition is that the values drawn from sampling assignments in both programs are coupled using the function f. Note that this operation non-deterministically assigns $\boldsymbol{v}$ from P with some values $\boldsymbol{b}$, and $\boldsymbol{v}'$ with $f(\boldsymbol{b})$. Then, the operation simulates the executions of the two programs. Formula 2 states that there is an f-coupling for every instantiation of the two distributions used in probabilistic assignments in both programs.

Example 1. Consider the simple program P defined as $x \sim \mathsf{bern}(0.5); x = \neg x$ and let $f_\neg(x) = \neg x$. Then, $\mathsf{cpost}(P, P, Q, f_\neg)$ is $\{(s, s') \mid s(x) = \neg s'(x)\}$.

The main soundness theorem shows there is a probabilistic coupling of the output distributions with support contained in the coupled postcondition (we defer all proofs to the full version of this paper).

Theorem 1. *Let programs P and P' be of the form $\boldsymbol{v} \sim dexp; P_D$ and $\boldsymbol{v}' \sim dexp'; P'_D$, for deterministic programs P_D, P'_D. Given a function $f : B \to B'$ satisfying Formula 2, for every $(s, s') \in S \times S'$ we have $[\![P]\!](s) \leftrightsquigarrow^{\Psi} [\![P']\!](s')$, where $\Psi = \mathsf{cpost}(P, P', (s, s'), f)$.*

3.4 Proof Rules for Uniformity and Independence

We are now ready to demonstrate how to establish uniformity and independence of program variables using f-coupled postconditions. We will continue to assume that random sampling commands have been lifted to the front of each program, and that f satisfies Formula 2.

Uniformity. Consider a program P and a variable $v^* \in V$ of finite, non-empty domain B. Let $\mu = [\![P]\!](s)$ for some state $s \in S$. We say that variable v^* is *uniformly distributed* in μ if $\mu(v^* = b) = \frac{1}{|B|}$ for every $b \in B$.

The following theorem connects uniformity with f-coupled postconditions.

Theorem 2 (Uniformity). *Consider a program P with $\boldsymbol{v} \sim dexp$ as its first statement and a designated return variable $v^* \in V$ with domain B. Let $Q = \{(s, s) \mid s \in S\}$ be the input relation. If we have*

$$\exists f.\, \mathsf{cpost}(P, P, Q, f) \subseteq \{(s, s') \in S \times S \mid s(v^*) = b \iff s'(v^*) = b'\}$$

for all $b, b' \in B$, then for any input $s \in S$ the final value of v^* is uniformly distributed over B in $[\![P]\!](s)$.

The intuition is that in the two f-coupled copies of P, the first v^* is equal to b exactly when the second v^* is equal to b'. Hence, the probability of returning b in the first copy and b' in the second copy are the same. Repeating for every pair of values b, b', we conclude that v^* is uniformly distributed.

Example 2. Recall Example 1 and let $b = \mathit{true}$ and $b' = \mathit{false}$. We have

$$\mathsf{cpost}(P, P, Q, f_{\neg}) \subseteq \{(s, s') \in S \times S \mid s(x) = b \iff s'(x) = b'\}.$$

This is sufficient to prove uniformity (the case with $b = b'$ is trivial).

Independence. We now present a proof rule for independence. Consider a program P and two variables $v^*, w^* \in V$ with domains B and B', respectively. Let $\mu = [\![P]\!](s)$ for some state $s \in S$. We say that v^*, w^* are *probabilistically independent* in μ if $\mu(v^* = b \wedge w^* = b') = \mu(v^* = b) \cdot \mu(w^* = b')$ for every $b \in B$ and $b' \in B'$.

The following theorem connects independence with f-coupled postconditions. We will self-compose two tagged copies of P, called P_1 and P_2.

Theorem 3 (Independence). *Assume a program P and define the relation*

$$Q = \{(s, s_1 \oplus s_2) \mid s \in S, s_i \in S_i, s(v) = s_i(v_i), \ \textit{for all} \ v \in V^I\},$$

where $\oplus$ takes the union of two maps with disjoint domains. Fix some $w^*, v^* \in V$ with domains B, B', and assume that for all $b \in B$, $b' \in B'$, there exists a function f such that $\mathsf{cpost}(P, (P_1; P_2), Q, f)$ is contained in

$$\{(s', s'_1 \oplus s'_2) \mid s'(v^*) = b \wedge s'(w^*) = b' \iff s'_1(v^*_1) = b \wedge s'_2(w^*_2) = b'\}.$$

Then, w^*, v^* are independently distributed in $[\![P]\!](s)$ for all inputs $s \in S$.

The idea is that under the coupling, the probability of P returning $v^* = b \wedge w^* = b'$ is the same as the probability of P_1 returning $v^* = b$ and P_2 returning $w^* = b'$, for all values b, b'. Since P_1 and P_2 are two independent executions of P by construction, this establishes independence of v^* and w^*.

4 Constraint-Based Formulation of Proof Rules

In Sect. 3, we formalized the problem of constructing a coupling proof using f-coupled postconditions. We now automatically find such proofs by posing the problem as a constraint, where a solution gives a function f establishing our desired property.

4.1 Generating Logical and Probabilistic Constraints

Logical Encoding. We first encode program executions as formulas in first-order logic, using the following encoding function:

$$\begin{aligned}
\mathsf{enc}(v \leftarrow \mathit{exp}) &\triangleq v = \mathit{exp} \\
\mathsf{enc}(v \sim \mathit{dexp}) &\triangleq \mathit{true} \\
\mathsf{enc}(\texttt{if}\ \ \mathit{bexp}\ \ \texttt{then}\ \ P\ \ \texttt{else}\ \ P') &\triangleq (\mathit{bexp} \Rightarrow \mathsf{enc}(P)) \wedge (\neg \mathit{bexp} \Rightarrow \mathsf{enc}(P')) \\
\mathsf{enc}(P; P') &\triangleq \mathsf{enc}(P) \wedge \mathsf{enc}(P')
\end{aligned}$$

We assume a direct correspondence between expressions in our language and the first-order theory used for our encoding, e.g., linear arithmetic. Note that the encoding disregards probabilistic assignments, encoding them as *true*; this mimics the semantics of our strongest postcondition operator post. Probabilistic assignments will be handled via a separate encoding of f-couplings.

As expected, enc reflects the strongest postcondition post.

Lemma 1. *Let P be a program and let ρ be any assignment of the variables. An assignment ρ' agreeing with ρ on all input variables V^I satisfies the constraint $\mathsf{enc}(P)[\rho'/V]$ precisely when $\mathsf{post}(P, \{\rho\}) = \{\rho'\}$, treating ρ, ρ' as program states.*

Uniformity Constraints. We can encode the conditions in Theorem 2 for showing uniformity as a logical constraint. For a program P and a copy P_1, with first statements $\boldsymbol{v} \sim \mathit{dexp}$ and $\boldsymbol{v}_1 \sim \mathit{dexp}_1$, we define the constraints:

$$\begin{aligned}
&\forall a, a'. \exists f. \forall V, V_1. \\
&\qquad (V^I = V_1^I \wedge \boldsymbol{v}_1 = f(\boldsymbol{v}) \wedge \mathsf{enc}(P) \wedge \mathsf{enc}(P_1)) \qquad (3)\\
&\qquad\qquad \Longrightarrow (v^* = a \iff v_1^* = a') \\
&\qquad V^I = V_1^I \Longrightarrow \mathit{dexp} \leftrightsquigarrow^f \mathit{dexp}_1 \qquad (4)
\end{aligned}$$

Note that this is a second-order formula, as it quantifies over the *uninterpreted function* f. The left side of the implication in Formula 3 encodes an f-coupled execution of P and P_1, starting from equal initial states. The right side of this implication encodes the conditions for uniformity, as in Theorem 2.

Formula 4 ensures that there is an f-coupling between dexp and dexp_1 for any initial state; recall that dexp may mention input variables V^I. The constraint $\mathit{dexp} \leftrightsquigarrow^f \mathit{dexp}_1$ is not a standard logical constraint—intuitively, it is satisfied if $\mathit{dexp} \leftrightsquigarrow^f \mathit{dexp}_1$ holds for some interpretation of f, dexp, and dexp_1.

Example 3. The constraint

$$\exists f.\,\forall p, p'.\, p = p' \Rightarrow \mathsf{bern}(p) \leftrightsquigarrow^{f} \mathsf{bern}(p')$$

holds by setting f to the identity function id, since for any $p = p'$ we have an f-coupling $\mathsf{bern}(p) \leftrightsquigarrow^{\mathrm{id}} \mathsf{bern}(p')$.

Example 4. Consider the program $x \sim \mathsf{bern}(0.5); y = \neg x$. The constraints for uniformity of y are

$$\forall a, a'.\,\exists f.\,\forall V, V_1.(x_1 = f(x) \wedge y = \neg x \wedge y_1 = \neg x_1) \Longrightarrow (y = a \iff y_1 = a')$$
$$\mathsf{bern}(0.5) \leftrightsquigarrow^{f} \mathsf{bern}(0.5).$$

Since there are no input variables, $V^I = V_1^I$ is equivalent to *true*.

Theorem 4 (Uniformity constraints). *Fix a program P and variable $v^* \in V$. Let φ be the uniformity constraints in Formulas 3 and 4. If φ is valid, then v^* is uniformly distributed in $[\![P]\!](s)$ for all $s \in S$.*

Independence Constraints. Similarly, we can characterize independence constraints using the conditions in Theorem 3. After transforming the program $P_1; P_2$ to start with the single probabilistic assignment statement $\boldsymbol{v}_{1,2} \sim dexp_{1,2}$, combining probabilistic assignments in P_1 and P_2, we define the constraints:

$$\begin{aligned}
&\forall a, a'.\exists f.\forall V, V_1, V_2.\\
&\qquad (V^I = V_1^I = V_2^I \wedge \boldsymbol{v}_{1,2} = f(\boldsymbol{v}) \wedge \mathsf{enc}(P) \wedge \mathsf{enc}(P_1; P_2)) && (5)\\
&\qquad\qquad \Longrightarrow (v^* = a \wedge w^* = a' \iff v_1^* = a \wedge w_2^* = a')\\
&\qquad V^I = V_1^I = V_2^I \Longrightarrow dexp \leftrightsquigarrow^{f} dexp_{1,2} && (6)
\end{aligned}$$

Theorem 5 (Independence constraints). *Fix a program P and two variables $v^*, w^* \in V$. Let φ be the independence constraints from Formulas 5 and 6. If φ is valid, then v^*, w^* are independent in $[\![P]\!](s)$ for all $s \in S$.*

4.2 Constraint Transformation

To solve our constraints, we transform our constraints into the form $\exists f.\,\forall X.\,\varphi$, where φ is a first-order formula. Such formulas can be viewed as *synthesis problems*, and are often solvable automatically using standard techniques.

We perform our transformation in two steps. First, we transform our constraint into the form $\exists f.\,\forall X.\,\varphi_p$, where φ_p still contains the coupling constraint. Then, we replace the coupling constraint with a first-order formula by logically encoding primitive distributions as uninterpreted functions.

Quantifier Reordering. Our constraints are of the form $\forall a, a'. \exists f. \forall X. \varphi$. Intuitively, this means that for *every* possible value of a, a', we want *one* function f satisfying $\forall X. \varphi$. We can pull the existential quantifier $\exists f$ to the outermost level by extending the function with additional parameters for a, a', thus defining a different function for every interpretation of a, a'. For the uniformity constraints this transformation yields the following formulas:

$$\exists g. \forall a, a'. \forall V, V_1. \\ (V^I = V_1^I \wedge \boldsymbol{v}_1 = g(a, a', \boldsymbol{v}) \wedge \mathsf{enc}(P) \wedge \mathsf{enc}(P_1)) \\ \implies (v^* = a \iff v_1^* = a') \quad (7)$$

$$V^I = V_1^I \implies \mathit{dexp} \leftrightsquigarrow^{g(a,a',-)} \mathit{dexp}_1 \quad (8)$$

where $g(a, a', -)$ is the function after partially applying g.

Transforming Coupling Constraints. Our next step is to eliminate coupling constraints. To do so, we use the definition of f-coupling, which states that $\mu_1 \leftrightsquigarrow^f \mu_2$ if (i) f is injective and (ii) $\forall x. \mu_1(x) \leqslant \mu_2(f(x))$. The first constraint (injectivity) is straightforward. For the second point (monotonicity), we can encode distribution expressions—which represent functions to reals—as uninterpreted functions, which we then further constrain. For instance, the coupling constraint $\mathsf{bern}(p) \leftrightsquigarrow^f \mathsf{bern}(p')$ can be encoded as

$$\forall x, y. x \neq y \Rightarrow f(x) \neq f(y) \quad \text{(injectivity)}$$
$$\forall x. h(x) \leqslant h'(f(x)) \quad \text{(monotonicity)}$$
$$\forall x. \mathit{ite}(x = \mathit{true}, h(x) = p, h(x) = 1 - p) \quad (\mathsf{bern}(p) \text{ encoding})$$
$$\forall x. \mathit{ite}(x = \mathit{true}, h'(x) = p', h'(x) = 1 - p') \quad (\mathsf{bern}(p') \text{ encoding})$$

where $h, h' : \mathbb{B} \to \mathbb{R}^{\geq 0}$ are uninterpreted functions representing the probability mass functions of $\mathsf{bern}(p)$ and $\mathsf{bern}(p')$; note that the third constraint encodes the distribution $\mathsf{bern}(p)$, which returns *true* with probability p and false with probability $1 - p$, and the fourth constraint encodes $\mathsf{bern}(p')$.

Note that if we cannot encode the definition of the distribution in our first-order theory (e.g., if it requires non-linear constraints), or if we do not have a concrete description of the distribution, we can simply elide the last two constraints and under-constrain h and h'. In Sect. 6 we use this feature to prove properties of a program encoding a Bayesian network, where the primitive distributions are unknown program parameters.

Theorem 6 (Transformation soundness). *Let φ be the constraints generated for some program P. Let φ' be the result of applying the above transformations to φ. If φ' is valid, then φ is valid.*

Constraint Solving. After performing these transformations, we finally arrive at constraints of the form $\exists g. \forall a, a'. \forall V. \varphi$, where φ is a first-order formula. These exactly match constraint-based program synthesis problems. In Sect. 6, we use SMT solvers and enumerative synthesis to handle these constraints.

5 Dealing with Loops

So far, we have only considered loop-free programs. In this section, we our approach to programs with loops.

f-Coupled Postconditions and Loops. We consider programs of the form

$$\mathsf{while}\ \ bexp\ P^b$$

where P^b is a loop-free program that begins with the statement $\boldsymbol{v} \sim dexp$; our technique can also be extended to handle nested loops. We assume all programs terminate with probability 1 for any initial state; there are numerous systems for verifying this basic property automatically (see, e.g., [15–17]). To extend our f-coupled postconditions, we let $\mathsf{cpost}(P, P', Q, f)$ be the smallest set I satisfying:

$$Q \subseteq I \qquad \text{(initiation)}$$
$$\mathsf{cpost}(P^b, P^{b'}, I_{en}, f) \subseteq I \qquad \text{(consecution)}$$
$$I \subseteq \{s(bexp) = s'(bexp') \mid s \in S, s' \in S'\} \qquad \text{(synchronization)}$$

where $I_{en} \triangleq \{(s, s') \in I \mid s(bexp) = true\}$.

Intuitively, the set I is the least inductive invariant for the two coupled programs running with synchronized loops. Theorem 1, which establishes that f-coupled postconditions result in couplings over output distributions, naturally extends to a setting with loops.

Constraint Generation. To prove uniformity, we generate constraints much like the loop-free case except that we capture the invariant I, modeled as a relation over the variables of both programs, using a *Constrained Horn-Clause* (CHC) encoding. As is standard, we use V', V_1' to denote primed copies of program variables denoting their value after executing the body, and we assume that $\mathsf{enc}(P^b)$ encodes a loop-free program as a transition relation from states over V to states over V'.

$$\forall a, a'. \exists f, I. \forall V, V_1, V', V_1'.$$
$$V^I = V_1^I \implies I(V, V_1) \qquad \text{(initiation)}$$
$$I(V, V_1) \wedge bexp \wedge \boldsymbol{v}_1' = f(\boldsymbol{v}') \wedge \mathsf{enc}(P^b) \wedge \mathsf{enc}(P_1^b) \implies I(V', V_1') \qquad \text{(consecution)}$$
$$I(V, V_1) \implies bexp = bexp_1 \qquad \text{(synchronization)}$$
$$I(V, V_1) \implies dexp \leftrightsquigarrow^f dexp_1 \qquad \text{(coupling)}$$
$$I(V, V_1) \wedge \neg bexp \implies (v^* = a \iff v_1^* = a') \qquad \text{(uniformity)}$$

The first three constraints encode the definition of cpost; the last two ensure that f constructs a coupling and that the invariant implies the uniformity condition when the loop terminates. Using the technique presented in Sect. 4.2, we can transform these constraints into the form $\exists f, I. \forall X. \varphi$. That is, in addition to discovering the function f, we need to discover the invariant I.

Proving independence in looping programs poses additional challenges, as directly applying the self-composition construction from Sect. 3 requires relating a single loop with two loops. When the number of loop iterations is deterministic, however, we may simulate two sequentially composed loops with a single loop that interleaves the iterations (known as *synchronized* or *cross* product [4,29]) so that we reduce the synthesis problem to finding a coupling for two loops.

6 Implementation and Evaluation

We now discuss our implementation and five case studies used for evaluation.

```
fun fairCoin(p ∈ (0, 1))
    x ← false
    y ← false
    while x = y do
        x ∼ bern(p)
        y ∼ bern(p)
    return x

fun fairDie
    x ← false
    y ← false
    z ← false
    while x = y = z do
        x ∼ bern(0.5)
        y ∼ bern(0.5)
        z ∼ bern(0.5)
    return (x, y, z)
```

```
fun noisySum(n, p ∈ (0, 1))
    sum ← 0
    for i = 1, ..., n do
        noise[i] ∼ bern(p)
        sum ← sum + noise[i]
    return sum

fun bayes(μ, μ', μ'')
    x ∼ μ
    y ∼ μ'
    z ∼ μ''
    w ← f(x, y)
    w' ← g(y, z)
    return (w, w')
```

```
fun ballot(n)
    tie ← false
    x_A ← 0
    x_B ← 0
    for i = 1, ..., n do
        r ∼ bern(0.5)
        if r = 0 then
            x_A ← x_A + 1
        else
            x_B ← x_B + 1
        if i = 1 then
            first ← r
        if x_A = x_B then
            tie ← true
    return (first, tie)
```

Fig. 2. Case study programs

Implementation. To solve formulas of the form $\exists f.\, \forall X.\, \varphi$, we implemented a simple solver using a *guess-and-check* loop: We iterate through various interpretations of f, insert them into the formula, and check whether the resulting formula is valid. In the simplest case, we are searching for a function f from n-tuples to n-tuples. For instance, in Sect. 2.2, we discovered the function $f(x, y) = (y, x)$. Our implementation is parameterized by a grammar defining an infinite set of interpretations of f, which involves permuting the arguments (as above), conditionals, and other basic operations (e.g., negation for Boolean variables). For checking validity of $\forall X.\, \varphi$ given f, we use the Z3 SMT solver [19] for loop-free programs. For loops, we use an existing constrained-Horn-clause solver based on the MathSAT SMT solver [18].

Benchmarks and Results. As a set of case studies for our approach, we use 5 different programs collected from the literature and presented in Fig. 2. For these programs, we prove uniformity, (conditional) independence properties, and other probabilistic equalities. For instance, we use our implementation to prove a main lemma for the Ballot theorem [20], encoded as the program ballot.

Figure 3 shows the time and number of loop iterations required by our implementation to discover a coupling proof. The small number of iterations and time needed demonstrates the simplicity of the discovered proofs. For instance, the ballot theorem was proved in 3 s and only 4 iterations, while the fairCoin example (illustrated in Sect. 2.2) required only two iterations and 1.4 s. In all cases, the size of the synthesize function f in terms of depth of its AST is no more than 4. We describe these programs and properties in a bit more detail.

Case Studies: Uniformity (fairCoin, fairDie). The first two programs produce uniformly random values. Our approach synthesizes a coupling proof certifying uniformity for both of these programs. The first program fairCoin, which we saw in Sect. 2.2, produces a fair coin flip given access to biased coin flips by repeatedly flipping two coins while they are equal, and returning the result of the first coin as soon as the flips differ. Note that the bias of the coin flip is a program parameter, and not fixed statically. The synthesized coupling swaps the result of the two samples, mapping the values of (x, y) to (y, x).

The second program fairDie gives a different construction for simulating a roll of a fair die given fair coin flips. Three fair coins are repeatedly flipped as long as they are all equal; the returned triple is the binary representation of a number in $\{1, \ldots, 6\}$, the result of the simulated roll. The synthesized coupling is a bijection on triples of booleans $\mathbb{B} \times \mathbb{B} \times \mathbb{B}$; fixing any two possible output triples (b_1, b_2, b_3) and (b'_1, b'_2, b'_3) of distinct booleans, the coupling maps $(b_1, b_2, b_3) \mapsto (b'_1, b'_2, b'_3)$ and vice versa, leaving all other triples unchanged.

Program	Iters.	Time(s)
fairCoin	2	1.4
fairDie	9	6.1
noisySum	4	0.2
bayes	5	0.4
ballot	4	3.0

Fig. 3. Statistics

Case Studies: Independence (noisySum, bayes). In the next two programs, our approach synthesizes coupling proofs of independence and conditional independence of program variables in the output distribution. The first program, noisySum, is a stylized program inspired from privacy-preserving algorithms that sum a series of noisy samples; for giving accuracy guarantees, it is often important to show that the noisy draws are probabilistically independent. We show that any pair of samples are independent.

The second program, bayes, models a simple Bayesian network with three independent variables x, y, z and two dependent variables w and w', computed from (x, y) and (y, z) respectively. We want to show that w and w' are independent conditioned on any value of y; intuitively, w and w' only depend on each other through the value of y, and are independent otherwise. We use a constraint encoding similar to the encoding for showing independence to find a coupling proof of this fact. Note that the distributions μ, μ', μ'' of x, y, z are unknown parameters, and the functions f and g are also uninterpreted. This illustrates the advantage of using a constraint-based technique—we can encode unknown distributions and operations as uninterpreted functions.

Case Studies: Probabilistic Equalities (ballot). As we mentioned in Sect. 1, our approach extends naturally to proving general probabilistic equalities beyond uniformity and independence. To illustrate, we consider a lemma used to prove Bertrand's Ballot theorem [20]. Roughly speaking, this theorem considers counting ballots one-by-one in an election where there are n_A votes cast for candidate A and n_B votes cast for candidate B, where n_A, n_B are parameters. If $n_A > n_B$ (so A is the winner) and votes are counted in a uniformly random order, the Ballot theorem states that the probability that A leads throughout the whole counting process—without any ties—is precisely $(n_A - n_B)/(n_A + n_B)$.

One way of proving this theorem, sometimes called André's reflection principle, is to show that the probability of counting the first vote for A and reaching a tie is equal to the probability of counting the first vote for B and reaching a tie. We simulate the counting process slightly differently—instead of drawing a uniform order to count the votes, our program draws uniform samples for votes—but the original target property is equivalent to the equality

$$\Pr[\mathit{first}_1 = 0 \wedge \mathit{tie}_1 \wedge \psi(x_{A1}, x_{B1})] = \Pr[\mathit{first}_2 = 1 \wedge \mathit{tie}_2 \wedge \psi(x_{A2}, x_{B2})] \quad (9)$$

with $\psi(x_{Ai}, x_{Bi})$ is $x_{Ai} = n_A \wedge x_{Bi} = n_B$. Our approach synthesizes a coupling and loop invariant showing that the coupled post-condition is contained in

$$\{(s_1, s_2) \mid s_1(\mathit{first} = 0 \wedge \mathit{tie} \wedge \psi(x_A, x_B)) \iff s_2(\mathit{first} = 0 \wedge \mathit{tie} \wedge \psi(x_A, x_B))\},$$

giving Formula (9) by Proposition 1 (see Barthe et al. [6] for more details).

7 Related Work

Probabilistic programs have been a long-standing target of formal verification. We compare with two of the most well-developed lines of research: probabilistic model checking and deductive verification via program logics or expectations.

Probabilistic Model Checking. Model checking has proven to be a powerful tool for verifying probabilistic programs, capable of automated proofs for various probabilistic properties (typically encoded in probabilistic temporal logics); there are now numerous mature implementations (see, e.g., [21] or [3, Chap. 10] for more details). In comparison, our approach has the advantage of being fully constraint-based. This gives it a number of unique features: (*i*) it applies to programs with unknown inputs and variables over infinite domains; (*ii*) it applies to programs sampling from distributions with parameters, or even ones sampling from unknown distributions modeled as uninterpreted functions in first-order logic; (*iii*) it applies to distributions over infinite domains; and (*iv*) the generated coupling proofs are compact. At the same time, our approach is specialized to the coupling proof technique and is likely to be more incomplete.

Deductive Verification. Compared to general deductive verification systems for probabilistic programs, like program logics [5,14,22,26] or techniques reasoning by pre-expectations [25], the main benefit of our technique is automation—deductive verification typically requires an interactive theorem prover to manipulate complex probabilistic invariants. In general, the coupling proof method limits reasoning about probabilities and distributions to just the random sampling commands; in the rest of the program, the proof can avoid quantitative reasoning entirely. As a result, our system can work with non-probabilistic invariants and achieve full automation. Our approach also smoothly handles properties involving the probabilities of multiple events, like probabilistic independence, unlike techniques that analyze probabilistic events one-by-one.

Acknowledgements. We thank Samuel Drews, Calvin Smith, and the anonymous reviewers for their helpful comments. Justin Hsu was partially supported by ERC grant #679127 and NSF grant #1637532. Aws Albarghouthi was supported by NSF grants #1566015, #1704117, and #1652140.

References

1. Albarghouthi, A., Hsu, J.: Synthesizing coupling proofs of differential privacy. Proc. ACM Programm. Lang. **2**(POPL), 58:1–58:30 (2018). http://doi.acm.org/10.1145/3158146
2. Alur, R., Bodik, R., Juniwal, G., Martin, M.M., Raghothaman, M., Seshia, S.A., Singh, R., Solar-Lezama, A., Torlak, E., Udupa, A.: Syntax-guided synthesis. In: Formal Methods in Computer-Aided Design (FMCAD), Portland, Oregon, pp. 1–8. IEEE (2013)
3. Baier, C., Katoen, J.P., Larsen, K.G.: Principles of Model Checking. MIT Press, Cambridge (2008)
4. Barthe, G., Crespo, J.M., Kunz, C.: Relational verification using product programs. In: Butler, M., Schulte, W. (eds.) FM 2011. LNCS, vol. 6664, pp. 200–214. Springer, Heidelberg (2011). https://doi.org/10.1007/978-3-642-21437-0_17
5. Barthe, G., Espitau, T., Gaboardi, M., Grégoire, B., Hsu, J., Strub, P.Y.: A program logic for probabilistic programs. In: European Symposium on Programming (ESOP), Thessaloniki, Greece (2018, to appear). https://justinh.su/files/papers/ellora.pdf
6. Barthe, G., Espitau, T., Grégoire, B., Hsu, J., Strub, P.Y.: Proving uniformity and independence by self-composition and coupling. In: International Conference on Logic for Programming, Artificial Intelligence and Reasoning (LPAR), Maun, Botswana. EPiC Series in Computing, vol. 46, pp. 385–403 (2017). https://arxiv.org/abs/1701.06477
7. Barthe, G., Espitau, T., Grégoire, B., Hsu, J., Strub, P.: Proving expected sensitivity of probabilistic programs. Proc. ACM Programm. Lang. **2**(POPL), 57:1–57:29 (2018). http://doi.acm.org/10.1145/3158145
8. Barthe, G., Fong, N., Gaboardi, M., Grégoire, B., Hsu, J., Strub, P.Y.: Advanced probabilistic couplings for differential privacy. In: ACM SIGSAC Conference on Computer and Communications Security (CCS), Vienna, Austria (2016). https://arxiv.org/abs/1606.07143
9. Barthe, G., Fournet, C., Grégoire, B., Strub, P.Y., Swamy, N., Zanella-Béguelin, S.: Probabilistic relational verification for cryptographic implementations. In: ACM SIGPLAN-SIGACT Symposium on Principles of Programming Languages (POPL), San Diego, California, pp. 193–206 (2014). https://research.microsoft.com/en-us/um/people/nswamy/papers/rfstar.pdf
10. Barthe, G., Gaboardi, M., Grégoire, B., Hsu, J., Strub, P.Y.: Proving differential privacy via probabilistic couplings. In: IEEE Symposium on Logic in Computer Science (LICS), New York, pp. 749–758 (2016), http://arxiv.org/abs/1601.05047

11. Barthe, G., Grégoire, B., Hsu, J., Strub, P.Y.: Coupling proofs are probabilistic product programs. In: ACM SIGPLAN-SIGACT Symposium on Principles of Programming Languages (POPL), Paris, France, pp. 161–174 (2017). http://arxiv.org/abs/1607.03455
12. Barthe, G., Köpf, B., Olmedo, F., Zanella-Béguelin, S.: Probabilistic relational reasoning for differential privacy. ACM Trans. Programm. Lang. Syst. **35**(3), 9 (2013). http://software.imdea.org/ bkoepf/papers/toplas13.pdf
13. Beyene, T., Chaudhuri, S., Popeea, C., Rybalchenko, A.: A constraint-based approach to solving games on infinite graphs. In: ACM SIGPLAN-SIGACT Symposium on Principles of Programming Languages (POPL), San Diego, California, pp. 221–233 (2014)
14. Chadha, R., Cruz-Filipe, L., Mateus, P., Sernadas, A.: Reasoning about probabilistic sequential programs. Theor. Comput. Sci. **379**(1), 142–165 (2007)
15. Chatterjee, K., Fu, H., Goharshady, A.K.: Termination analysis of probabilistic programs through Positivstellensatz's. In: Chaudhuri, S., Farzan, A. (eds.) CAV 2016. LNCS, vol. 9779, pp. 3–22. Springer, Cham (2016). https://doi.org/10.1007/978-3-319-41528-4_1
16. Chatterjee, K., Fu, H., Novotný, P., Hasheminezhad, R.: Algorithmic analysis of qualitative and quantitative termination problems for affine probabilistic programs. In: ACM SIGPLAN-SIGACT Symposium on Principles of Programming Languages (POPL), Saint Petersburg, Florida, pp. 327–342 (2016). https://doi.acm.org/10.1145/2837614.2837639
17. Chatterjee, K., Novotný, P., Žikelić, Đ.: Stochastic invariants for probabilistic termination. In: ACM SIGPLAN-SIGACT Symposium on Principles of Programming Languages (POPL), Paris, France, pp. 145–160 (2017). https://doi.acm.org/10.1145/3009837.3009873
18. Cimatti, A., Griggio, A., Schaafsma, B.J., Sebastiani, R.: The MathSAT5 SMT solver. In: Piterman, N., Smolka, S.A. (eds.) TACAS 2013. LNCS, vol. 7795, pp. 93–107. Springer, Heidelberg (2013). https://doi.org/10.1007/978-3-642-36742-7_7
19. de Moura, L., Bjørner, N.: Z3: an efficient SMT solver. In: Ramakrishnan, C.R., Rehof, J. (eds.) TACAS 2008. LNCS, vol. 4963, pp. 337–340. Springer, Heidelberg (2008). https://doi.org/10.1007/978-3-540-78800-3_24
20. Feller, W.: An Introduction to Probability Theory and Its Applications, vol. 1, 3rd edn. Wiley, Hoboken (1968)
21. Forejt, V., Kwiatkowska, M., Norman, G., Parker, D.: Automated verification techniques for probabilistic systems. In: Bernardo, M., Issarny, V. (eds.) SFM 2011. LNCS, vol. 6659, pp. 53–113. Springer, Heidelberg (2011). https://doi.org/10.1007/978-3-642-21455-4_3
22. den Hartog, J.: Probabilistic extensions of semantical models. Ph.D. thesis, Vrije Universiteit Amsterdam (2002)
23. Hsu, J.: Probabilistic Couplings for Probabilistic Reasoning. Ph.D. thesis, University of Pennsylvania (2017). https://arxiv.org/abs/1710.09951
24. Kozen, D.: Semantics of probabilistic programs. J. Comput. Syst. Sci. **22**(3), 328–350 (1981). https://www.sciencedirect.com/science/article/pii/0022000081900362
25. Morgan, C., McIver, A., Seidel, K.: Probabilistic predicate transformers. ACM Trans. Programm. Lang. Syst. **18**(3), 325–353 (1996). dl.acm.org/ft_gateway.cfm?id=229547
26. Rand, R., Zdancewic, S.: VPHL: a verified partial-correctness logic for probabilistic programs. In: Conference on the Mathematical Foundations of Programming Semantics (MFPS), Nijmegen, The Netherlands (2015)

27. Solar-Lezama, A., Tancau, L., Bodík, R., Seshia, S.A., Saraswat, V.A.: Combinatorial sketching for finite programs. In: International Conference on Architectural Support for Programming Langauages and Operating Systems (ASPLOS), San Jose, California, pp. 404–415 (2006). http://doi.acm.org/10.1145/1168857.1168907
28. Strassen, V.: The existence of probability measures with given marginals. Annals Math. Stat. 423–439 (1965). https://projecteuclid.org/euclid.aoms/1177700153
29. Zaks, A., Pnueli, A.: CoVaC: compiler validation by program analysis of the cross-product. In: Cuellar, J., Maibaum, T., Sere, K. (eds.) FM 2008. LNCS, vol. 5014, pp. 35–51. Springer, Heidelberg (2008). https://doi.org/10.1007/978-3-540-68237-0_5

Controller Synthesis Made Real: Reach-Avoid Specifications and Linear Dynamics

Chuchu Fan(✉), Umang Mathur, Sayan Mitra, and Mahesh Viswanathan

University of Illinois at Urbana Champaign, Champaign, IL, USA
{cfan10,umathur3,mitras, vmahesh}@illinois.edu

Abstract. We address the problem of synthesizing provably correct controllers for linear systems with reach-avoid specifications. Our solution uses a combination of an open-loop controller and a tracking controller, thereby reducing the problem to smaller tractable problems. We show that, once a tracking controller is fixed, the reachable states from an initial neighborhood, subject to any disturbance, can be over-approximated by a sequence of ellipsoids, with sizes that are independent of the open-loop controller. Hence, the open-loop controller can be synthesized independently to meet the reach-avoid specification for an initial neighborhood. Exploiting several techniques for tightening the over-approximations, we reduce the open-loop controller synthesis problem to satisfiability over quantifier-free linear real arithmetic. The overall synthesis algorithm, computes a tracking controller, and then iteratively covers the entire initial set to find open-loop controllers for initial neighborhoods. The algorithm is sound and, for a class of robust systems, is also complete. We present RealSyn, a tool implementing this synthesis algorithm, and we show that it scales to several high-dimensional systems with complex reach-avoid specifications.

1 Introduction

The controller synthesis question asks whether an input can be generated for a given system (or a plant) so that it achieves a given specification. Algorithms for answering this question hold the promise of automating controller design. They have the potential to yield high-assurance systems that are correct-by-construction, and even negative answers to the question can convey insights about unrealizability of specifications. This is not a new or a solved problem, but there has been resurgence of interest with the rise of powerful tools and

This work is supported by the grant CCF 1422798 from the National Science Foundation.

H. Chockler and G. Weissenbacher (Eds.): CAV 2018, LNCS 10981, pp. 347–366, 2018.
https://doi.org/10.1007/978-3-319-96145-3_19

compelling applications such as vehicle path planning [11], motion control [10, 23], circuits design [30] and various other engineering areas.

In this paper, we study synthesis for linear, discrete-time, plant models with bounded disturbance—a standard view of control systems [3,17]. We will consider *reach-avoid* specifications which require that starting from any initial state Θ, the controller has to drive the system to a target set G, while avoiding certain unsafe states or obstacles $\mathbf{O}$. *Reach-avoid* specifications arise naturally in many domains such as autonomous and assisted driving, multi-robot coordination, and spacecraft autonomy, and have been studied for linear, nonlinear, as well as stochastic models [7,9,14,18].

Textbook control design methods address specifications like stability, disturbance rejection, asymptotic convergence, but they do not provide formal guarantees about reach-avoid specifications. Another approach is based on *discrete abstraction*, where a discrete, finite-state, symbolic abstraction of the original control system is computed, and a discrete controller is synthesized by solving a two-player game on the abstracted game graph. Theoretically, these methods can be applied to systems with nonlinear dynamics and they can synthesize controllers for a general class of LTL specifications. However, in practice, the discretization step leads to a severe state space explosion for higher dimensional models. Indeed, we did not find any reported evaluation of these tools (see related work) on benchmarks that go beyond 5-dimensional plant models.

In this paper, the controller we synthesize, follows a natural paradigm for designing controllers. The approach is to first design an *open-loop* controller for a single initial state $x_0 \in \Theta$ to meet the reach-avoid specification. This is called the reference trajectory. For the remaining states in the initial set, a *tracking controller* is combined, that drives these other trajectories towards the trajectory starting from x_0.

However, designing such a combined controller can be computationally expensive [32] because of the interdependency between the open-loop controller and the tracking controller. Our secret sauce in making this approach feasible, is to demonstrate that the two controllers can be synthesized in a decoupled way. Our strategy is as follows. We first design a tracking controller using a standard control-theoretical method called LQR (linear quadratic regulator) [5]. The crucial observation that helps decouple the synthesis of the tracking and open-loop controller, is that for such a combined controller, once the tracking controller is fixed, the set of states reached from the initial set is contained within a sequence of ellipsoidal sets [24] centered around the reference trajectory. The size of these ellipsoidal sets is solely dependent on the tracking controller, and is independent of the reference trajectory or the open-loop controller. On the flip side, the open-loop controller and the resulting reference trajectory can be chosen independent of the fixed tracking controller. Based on this, the problem of synthesizing the open-loop controller can be completely decoupled from synthesizing the tracking controller. Our open-loop controller is synthesized by encoding the problem in logic. The straightforward encoding of the synthesis problem results in a $\exists\forall$ formula in the theory of linear arithmetic. Unfortunately, solving large instances of such formulas using current SMT solvers is challenging. To overcome this, we exploit special properties of polytopes and hyper-rectangles, and reduce the original ∃∀-formula into the quantifier-free fragment of linear arithmetic (QF-LRA).

Our overall algorithm (Algorithm 1), after computing an initial tracking controller, iteratively synthesizes open-loop controllers by solving QF-LRA formulas for smaller subsets that cover the initial set. The algorithm will automatically identify the set of initial states for which the combined tracking+open-loop controller is guaranteed to work. Our algorithm is sound (Theorem 1), and for a class of robust linear systems, it is also complete (Theorem 2).

We have implemented the synthesis algorithm in a tool called RealSyn. Any SMT solver can be plugged-in for solving the open-loop problem; we present experimental results with Z3, CVC4 and Yices. We report the performance on 24 benchmark problems (using all three solvers). Results show that our approach scales well for complex models—including a system with 84-dimensional dynamics, another system with 3 vehicles (12-dimensional) trying to reach a common goal while avoiding collision with the obstacles and each other, and yet another system with 10 vehicles (20 dimensional) trying to maintain a platoon. RealSyn usually finds a controller within 10 min with the fastest SMT solver. The closest competing tool, Tulip [13,39], does not return any result even for some of the simpler instances.

Related Work. We briefly review related work on formal controller synthesis according to the plant model type, specifications, and approaches.

Plants and Specifications. In increasing order of generality, the types of plant models that have been considered for controller synthesis are double-integrator models [10], linear dynamical models [20,28,34,38], piecewise affine models [18,40], and nonlinear (possibly switched) models [7,25,31,33]. There is also a line of work on synthesis approaches for stochastic plants (see [1], and the references therein). With the exceptions noted below, most of these papers consider continuous time plant models, unlike our work.

There are three classes of specifications typically used for synthesis. In the order of generality, they are: (1) pure safety or invariance specifications [2,15,33], (2) reach-avoid [7,14,15,18,33], and (3) more general LTL and GR(1) [20,26,39] [16,38,40]. For each of these classes both bounded and unbounded-time variants have been considered.

Synthesis Tools. There is a growing set of controller synthesis algorithms that are available as implemented tools and libraries. This includes tools like CoSyMa [27], Pessoa [30], LTLMop [22,37], Tulip [13,39], SCOTS [31], that rely on the computation of some sort of a discrete (or symbolic) abstraction. Our trial with a 4-dimensional example on Tulip [13,39] did not finish the discretization step in one hour. LTLMop [22,37] handles GR(1) LTL specifications, which are more general than reach-avoid specifications considered in this paper, but it is designed for 2-dimensional robot models working in the Euclidean plane. An alternative synthesis approach generates mode switching sequences for switched system models [19,21,29,35,41] to meet the specifications. This line of work focuses on a finite input space, instead of the infinite input space we are considering in this paper. Abate et al. [2] use a controller template similar to the one considered in this paper for invariant specifications. A counter-example guided inductive synthesis (CEGIS) approach is used to first find a feedback controller for stabilizing the system. Since this feedback controller may not be safe for all initial states of the system, a separate verification step is employed to verify safety, or alternatively find a counter-example. In the latter case, the process is repeated until a valid controller is found. This is different from our approach, where any controller found needs no further verification. Several of the benchmarks are adopted from [2].

2 Preliminaries and Problem Statement

Notation. For a set A and a finite sequence σ in A^*, we denote the tth element of σ by $\sigma[t]$. $\mathbb{R}^n$ is the n-dimensional Euclidean space. Given a vector $x \in \mathbb{R}^n$, $x(i)$ is the ith component of x. We will use boldfaced letters (for example, $\mathbf{x}, \mathbf{d}, \mathbf{u}$, etc.,) to denote a sequence of vectors.

For a vector x, $x^\intercal$ is its transpose. Given an invertible matrix $M \in \mathbb{R}^{n\times n}$, $\|x\|_M \triangleq \sqrt{x^\intercal M^\intercal M x}$ is called the *M-norm* of x. For $M = I$, $\|x\|_M$ is the familiar 2-norm. Alternatively, $\|x\|_M = \|Mx\|_2$. For a matrix A, $A \succ 0$ means A is positive definite. Given two symmetric matrices A and B, $A \preceq B$ means $A - B$ is negative semi-definite. Given a matrix A and an invertible matrix M of the same dimension, there exists an $\alpha \geq 0$ such that $A^\intercal M^\intercal M A \preceq \alpha M^\intercal M$. Intuitively, α is the largest scaling factor that can be achieved by the linear transformation from x to Ax when using M for computing the norm, and can be found as the largest eigenvalue of the symmetric matrix $(MAM^{-1})^\intercal(MAM^{-1})$.

Given a vector $c \in \mathbb{R}^n$, an invertible matrix M, and a scalar value $r \geq 0$, we define $\mathcal{E}_r(c, M) \triangleq \{x \mid \|x - c\|_M \leq r\}$ to be the ellipsoid centered at c with radius r and shape M. $\mathcal{B}_r(c) \triangleq \mathcal{E}_r(c, I)$ is the ball of radius r centered at c. Given two vectors $c, v \in \mathbb{R}^n$, $\mathcal{R}_v(c) \triangleq \{x \mid \wedge_{i=1}^n c(i) - v(i) \leq x(i) \leq c(i) + v(i)\}$ is the rectangle centered at c with the length vector v. For a set $S \subseteq \mathbb{R}^n$, a vector $v \in \mathbb{R}^n$, and a matrix $M \in \mathbb{R}^{n\times n}$ we define $v \oplus S \triangleq \{x + v \mid x \in S\}$ and $M \otimes S \triangleq \{Mx \mid x \in S\}$. We say a set $S \subseteq \mathbb{R}^n$ is a polytope if there is a matrix $A^{m\times n}$ and a vector $b \in \mathbb{R}^m$ such that $S = \{x \mid Ax \leq b\}$, and denote by $vert(S)$ the set of vertices of S.

2.1 Discrete Time Linear Control Systems

An (n, m)-*dimensional discrete-time linear system* $\mathcal{A}$ is a 5-tuple $\langle A, B, \Theta, U, D\rangle$, where (i) $A \in \mathbb{R}^{n\times n}$ is called the *dynamic matrix*, (ii) $B \in \mathbb{R}^{n\times m}$ is called the *input matrix*, (iii) $\Theta \subseteq \mathbb{R}^n$ is a *set of initial states* (iv) $U \subseteq \mathbb{R}^m$ is the *space of inputs*, (v) $D \subseteq \mathbb{R}^n$ is the *space of disturbances*.

A *control sequence* for an (n, m)-dimensional system $\mathcal{A}$ is a (possibly infinite) sequence $\mathbf{u} = \mathbf{u}[0], \mathbf{u}[1], \ldots$, where each $\mathbf{u}[t] \in U$. Similarly, a *disturbance sequence* for $\mathcal{A}$ is a (possibly infinite) sequence $\mathbf{d} = \mathbf{d}[0], \mathbf{d}[1], \ldots$, where each $\mathbf{d}[t] \in D$. Given control $\mathbf{u}$ and disturbance $\mathbf{d}$, and an initial state $\mathbf{x}[0] \in \Theta$, the *execution of* $\mathcal{A}$ is uniquely defined as the (possibly infinite) sequence of states $\mathbf{x} = \mathbf{x}[0], \mathbf{x}[1], \ldots$, where for each $t > 0$,

$$\mathbf{x}[t+1] = A\mathbf{x}[t] + B\mathbf{u}[t] + \mathbf{d}[t]. \tag{1}$$

A *(state feedback) controller* for $\mathcal{A}$ is a function $g : \Theta \times \mathbb{R}^n \to \mathbb{R}^m$, that maps an initial state and a (current) state to an input. That is, given an initial state $x_0 \in \Theta$ and state $x \in \mathbb{R}^n$ at time t, the control input to the plant at time t is:

$$\mathbf{u}[t] = g(x_0, x). \tag{2}$$

This controller is allowed to use the memory of some initial state x_0 (not necessarily the current execution's initial state) for deciding the current state-dependent feedback. Thus, given an initial state $\mathbf{x}[0]$, a disturbance $\mathbf{d}$, and a state feedback controller g, Eqs. (1) and (2) define a unique execution $\mathbf{x}$ of $\mathcal{A}$. A state x is *reachable in t-steps* if there exists an execution $\mathbf{x}$ of $\mathcal{A}$ such that $\mathbf{x}[t] = x$. The set of all reachable states from $S \subseteq \Theta$ in exactly T steps using the controller g is denoted by $\mathsf{Reach}_{\mathcal{A},g}(S, T)$. When $\mathcal{A}$ and g are clear from the context, we write $\mathsf{Reach}(S, T)$.

2.2 Bounded Controller Synthesis Problem

Given a (n, m)-*dimensional discrete-time linear system* $\mathcal{A}$, a sequence $\mathbf{O}$ of *obstacles* or unsafe sets (with $\mathbf{O}[t] \subseteq \mathbb{R}^n$, for each t), a *goal* $G \subseteq \mathbb{R}^n$, and a time bound T, the *bounded time controller synthesis problem* is to find, a state feedback controller g such that for every initial state $\theta \in \Theta$ and disturbance $\mathbf{d} \in D^T$, the unique execution $\mathbf{x}$ of $\mathcal{A}$ with g, starting from $\mathbf{x}[0] = \theta$ satisfies (i) for all $t \leq T$, $\mathbf{u}[t] \in U$, (ii) for all $t \leq T$, $\mathbf{x}[t] \notin \mathbf{O}[t]$, and (iii) $\mathbf{x}[T] \in G$.

For the rest of the paper, we will assume that each of the sets in $\{\mathbf{O}[t]\}_{t \in \mathbb{N}}$, G and U are closed polytopes. Moreover, we assume that the pair (A, B) is controllable [3].

Example. *Consider a mobile robot that needs to reach the green area of an apartment starting from the entrance area, while avoiding the gray areas (Fig. 1). The robot's dynamics is described by a linear model (for example the navigation model from [12]). The obstacle sequence* $\mathbf{O}$ *here is static, that is,* $\mathbf{O}[t] = \mathbf{O}[0]$ *for all* $t \geq 0$*. Both* Θ *and* G *are rectangles. Although these sets are depicted in 2D, the dynamics of the robot may involve a higher dimensional state space.*

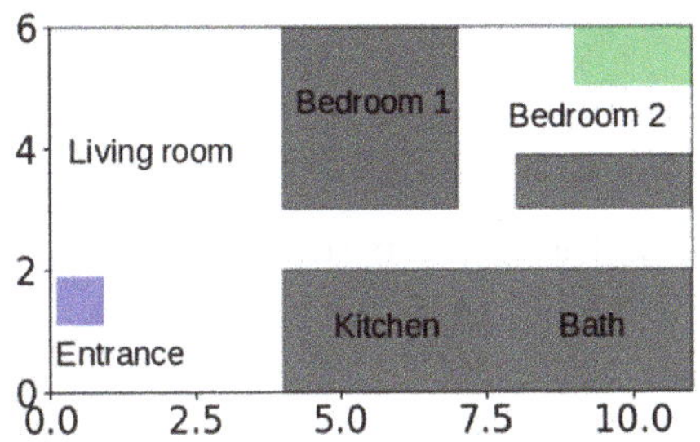

Fig. 1. The settings for controller synthesis of a mobile robot with reach-avoid specification.

In this example, there is no disturbance, but a similar problem can be formulated for an drone flying outdoors, in which case, the disturbance input would model the effect of wind. Time-varying obstacle sets are useful for modeling safety requirements of multi-robot systems.

3 Synthesis Algorithm

3.1 Overview

The controller synthesis problem requires one to find a state feedback controller that ensures that the trajectory starting from any initial state in Θ will meet the reach-avoid specification. Since the set of initial states Θ will typically be an infinite set, this requires the synthesized feedback controller g to have an effective representation. Thus, an "enumerative" representation, where a (separate) *open-loop controller* is constructed for each initial state, is not feasible — by an open-loop controller for initial state $x_0 \in \Theta$, we mean a control sequence $\mathbf{u}$ such that the corresponding execution $\mathbf{x}$ with $\mathbf{x}[0] = x_0$ and 0 disturbance satisfies the reach-avoid constraints. We, therefore, need a useful template that will serve as the representation for the feedback controller.

In control theory, one natural controller design paradigm is to first find a *reference execution* $\mathbf{x}_{\mathsf{ref}}$ which uses an open-loop controller, then add a *tracking controller* which tries to force other executions $\mathbf{x}$ starting from different initial states $\mathbf{x}[0]$ to get close to $\mathbf{x}_{\mathsf{ref}}$ by minimizing the distance between $\mathbf{x}_{\mathsf{ref}}$ and $\mathbf{x}$. This form of controller combining open-loop control with tracking control is also proposed in [32] for reach-avoid specifications. The resulting trajectory under a combination of tracking controller plus reference trajectory can be described by the following system of equations.

$$\begin{aligned} &\mathbf{u}[t] = \mathbf{u}_{\mathsf{ref}}[t] + K(\mathbf{x}[t] - \mathbf{x}_{\mathsf{ref}}[t]), \text{ with} \\ &\mathbf{x}_{\mathsf{ref}}[t+1] = A\mathbf{x}_{\mathsf{ref}}[t] + B\mathbf{u}_{\mathsf{ref}}[t] \end{aligned} \tag{3}$$

The tracking controller is given by the matrix K that determines the additive component of the input based on the difference between the current state and the reference trajectory. Once $\mathbf{x}_{\mathsf{ref}}[0]$ and the open-loop control sequence $\mathbf{u}_{\mathsf{ref}}$ is fixed, the value of $\mathbf{x}_{\mathsf{ref}}[t]$ is determined at each time step $t \in \mathbb{N}$. Therefore, the controller g is uniquely defined by the tuple $\langle K, \mathbf{x}_{\mathsf{ref}}[0], \mathbf{u}_{\mathsf{ref}} \rangle$. We could rewrite the linear system in (3) as an augmented system

$$\begin{bmatrix} \mathbf{x} \\ \mathbf{x}_{\mathsf{ref}} \end{bmatrix} [t+1] = \begin{bmatrix} A+BK & -BK \\ 0 & A \end{bmatrix} \begin{bmatrix} \mathbf{x} \\ \mathbf{x}_{\mathsf{ref}} \end{bmatrix} [t] + \begin{bmatrix} B & 0 \\ 0 & B \end{bmatrix} \begin{bmatrix} \mathbf{u}_{\mathsf{ref}} \\ \mathbf{u}_{\mathsf{ref}} \end{bmatrix} [t], + \begin{bmatrix} \mathbf{d} \\ 0 \end{bmatrix} [t].$$

This can be rewritten as $\hat{\mathbf{x}}[t+1] = \hat{A}\hat{\mathbf{x}}[t] + \hat{B}\hat{\mathbf{u}}[t] + \hat{\mathbf{d}}[t]$. The closed-form solution is $\hat{\mathbf{x}}[t] = \hat{A}^t\hat{\mathbf{x}}[0] + \sum_{i=0}^{t-1} \hat{A}^{t-1-i}(\hat{B}\hat{\mathbf{u}}[i] + \hat{\mathbf{d}}[i])$. To synthesize a controller g of this form, therefore, requires finding $K, \mathbf{x}_{\mathsf{ref}}[0], \mathbf{u}_{\mathsf{ref}}$ such that the closed-form solution meets the reach-avoid specification. This is indeed the approach followed in [32], albeit in the continuous time setting. Observe that in the closed-form solution, $\hat{A}$, $\hat{\mathbf{u}}$, and $\hat{\mathbf{x}}[0]$ all depend on parameters that we need to synthesize. Therefore, solving such constraints involves polynomials whose degrees grow with the time bound. This is very expensive, and unlikely to scale to large dimensions and time bounds.

In this paper, to achieve scalability, we take a slightly different approach than the one where $K, \mathbf{x}_{\mathsf{ref}}[0]$, and $\mathbf{u}_{\mathsf{ref}}$ are simultaneously synthesized. We first synthesize a tracking controller K, *independent* of $\mathbf{x}_{\mathsf{ref}}[0]$ and $\mathbf{u}_{\mathsf{ref}}$, using the standard LQR method. Once K is synthesized, we show that, no matter what $\mathbf{x}_{\mathsf{ref}}[0]$, and $\mathbf{u}_{\mathsf{ref}}$ are, the state of the system at time t starting from x_0 is guaranteed to be contained within an ellipsoid centered at $\mathbf{x}_{\mathsf{ref}}[t]$ and of radius that depends only on K, the initial distance between x_0 and $\mathbf{x}_{\mathsf{ref}}[0]$, time t, and disturbance. Moreover, this radius is only a *linear* function of the initial distance (Lemma 1). Thus, if we can synthesize an open-loop controller $\mathbf{u}_{\mathsf{ref}}$ starting from some state $\mathbf{x}_{\mathsf{ref}}[0]$, such that ellipsoids centered around $\mathbf{x}_{\mathsf{ref}}$ satisfy the reach-avoid specification, we can conclude that the combined controller will work correctly for all initial states in some ball around the initial state $\mathbf{x}_{\mathsf{ref}}[0]$. The radius of the ball around $\mathbf{x}_{\mathsf{ref}}[0]$ for which the controller is guaranteed to work, will depend on the radii of the ellipsoids around $\mathbf{x}_{\mathsf{ref}}$ that satisfy the reach-avoid specification. This decoupled approach to synthesis is the first key idea in our algorithm.

Following the above discussion, crucial to the success of the decoupled approach is to obtain a tight characterization of the radius of the ellipsoid around $\mathbf{x}_{\mathsf{ref}}[t]$ that contains the reach set, as a function of the initial distance — too conservative a bound will imply that the combined controller only works for a tiny set of initial states. The ellipsoid's shape and direction, which is characterized by a coordinate transformation matrix M, also affect the tightness of the over-approximations. We determine the shape and direction of the ellipsoids that give us the tightest over-approximation using an SDP solver (Sect. 3.4).

Synthesizing the tracking controller K, still leaves open the problem of synthesizing an open-loop controller for an initial state $\mathbf{x}_{\mathsf{ref}}[0]$. A straightforward encoding of the problem of synthesizing a open-loop controller, that works for all initial states in some ball around $\mathbf{x}_{\mathsf{ref}}[0]$, results in a $\exists\forall$-formula in the theory of real arithmetic. Unfortunately solving such formulas does not scale to large dimensional systems using current SMT solvers. The next key idea in our algorithm is to simplify these constraints. By exploiting special properties of polytopes and hyper-rectangles, we reduce the original $\exists\forall$-formula into the *quantifier-free* fragment of *linear* real arithmetic (QF-LRA) (Sect. 3.5).

Putting it all together, the overall algorithm (Algorithm 1) works as follows. After computing an initial tracking controller K, coordinate transformation M for optimal ellipsoidal approximation of reach-sets, it synthesizes open-loop controllers for different initial states by solving QF-LRA formulas. After each open-loop controller is synthesized, the algorithm identifies the set of initial states for which the combined tracking+open-loop controller is guaranteed to work, and removes this set from Θ. In each new iteration, it picks a new initial state not covered by previous combined controllers, and the process terminates when all of Θ is covered. Our algorithm is sound (Theorem 1)—whenever a controller is synthesized, it meets the specifications. Further, for robust systems (defined later in the paper), our algorithm is guaranteed to terminate when the system has a combined controller for all initial states (Theorem 2).

3.2 Synthesizing the Tracking Controller K

Given any open-loop controller $\mathbf{u}_{\mathsf{ref}}$ and the corresponding reference execution $\mathbf{x}_{\mathsf{ref}}$, by replacing in Eq. (1) the controller of Eq. (3) we get:

$$\mathbf{x}[t+1] = (A + BK)\mathbf{x}[t] - BK\mathbf{x}_{\mathsf{ref}}[t] + B\mathbf{u}_{\mathsf{ref}}[t] + \mathbf{d}[t]. \tag{4}$$

Subtracting $\mathbf{x}_{\mathsf{ref}}[t+1]$ from both sides, we have that for any execution $\mathbf{x}$ starting from the initial states $\mathbf{x}[0]$ and with disturbance $\mathbf{d}$, the distance between $\mathbf{x}$ and $\mathbf{x}_{\mathsf{ref}}$ changes with time as:

$$\mathbf{x}[t+1] - \mathbf{x}_{\mathsf{ref}}[t+1] = (A + BK)(\mathbf{x}[t] - \mathbf{x}_{\mathsf{ref}}[t]) + \mathbf{d}[t]. \tag{5}$$

With $A_c \triangleq A + BK$, $\mathbf{y}[t] \triangleq \mathbf{x}[t+1] - \mathbf{x}_{\mathsf{ref}}[t+1]$, Eq. (5) becomes $\mathbf{y}[t+1] = A_c\mathbf{y}[t] + d[t]$. We want $\mathbf{x}[t]$ to be as close to $\mathbf{x}_{\mathsf{ref}}[t]$ as possible, which means K should be designed to make $|\mathbf{y}[t]|$ converge to 0. Equivalently, K should be designed as a linear feedback controller such that A_c is stable[1]. Such a matrix K can be computed using classical control theoretic methods. In this work, we compute K as a linear (stable) feedback controller using LQR as stated in the following proposition.

Proposition 1 (LQR). *For linear system $\mathcal{A}$ with (A, B) to be controllable and 0 disturbance, fix any $Q, R \succ 0$ and let $J \triangleq \mathbf{x}^\intercal[T]Q\mathbf{x}[T] + \sum_{i=0}^{T-1}(\mathbf{x}^\intercal[i]Q\mathbf{x}[i] + \mathbf{u}^\intercal[i]R\mathbf{u}[i])$ be the corresponding quadratic cost. Let X be the unique positive definite solution to the discrete-time Algebraic Riccati Equation (ARE): $A^\intercal XA - X - A^\intercal XB(B^\intercal XB + R)^{-1}B^\intercal XA + Q = 0$, and $K \triangleq -(B^\intercal XB + R)^{-1}B^\intercal XA$. Then $A + BK$ is stable, and the corresponding feedback input minimizes J.*

Methods for choosing Q and R are outside the scope of this paper. We fix Q and R to be identity matrices for most examples. Roughly, for a given R, scaling up Q results in a K that makes an execution $\mathbf{x}$ converge faster to the reference execution $\mathbf{x}_{\mathsf{ref}}$.

3.3 Reachset Over-Approximation with Tracking Controller

We present a method for over-approximating the reachable states of the system for a given tracking controller K (computed as in Proposition 1) and an open-loop controller $\mathbf{u}_{\mathsf{ref}}$ (to be computed in Sect. 3.5).

Lemma 1. *Consider any $K \in \mathbb{R}^{m\times n}$, any initial set $S \subseteq \mathcal{E}_{r_0}(\mathbf{x}_{ref}[0], M)$ and disturbance $D \subseteq \mathcal{E}_\delta(0, M)$, where $r_0, \delta \geq 0$ and $M \in \mathbb{R}^{n\times n}$ is invertible.*

For any open-loop controller $\mathbf{u}_{ref}$ and the corresponding reference execution $\mathbf{x}_{ref}$,

$$\mathsf{Reach}(S, t) \subseteq \mathcal{E}_{r_t}(\mathbf{x}_{ref}[t], M), \forall\, t \leq T, \tag{6}$$

where $r_t = \alpha^{\frac{t}{2}} r_0 + \sum_{i=0}^{t-1} \alpha^{\frac{i}{2}}\delta$, and $\alpha \geq 0$ is such that $(A+BK)^\intercal M^\intercal M(A+BK) \preceq \alpha M^\intercal M$.

[1] $A + BK$ has spectral radius $\rho(A + BK) < 1$.

Lemma 1 can be proved using the triangular inequality for the norm of Eq. (5). From Lemma 1, it follows that given a open-loop controller $\mathbf{u}_{\mathsf{ref}}$ and the corresponding reference trajectory $\mathbf{x}_{\mathsf{ref}}$, the reachable states from $S \subseteq \mathcal{E}_{r_0}(\mathbf{x}_{\mathsf{ref}}[0], M)$ at time t can be over-approximated by an ellipsoid centered at $\mathbf{x}_{\mathsf{ref}}[t]$ with size $r_t \triangleq \alpha^{\frac{t}{2}} r_0 + \sum_{i=0}^{t-1} \alpha^{\frac{i}{2}} \delta$. Here M is any invertible matrix that defines the shape of the ellipsoid and it influences the value of α. As the over-approximation (r_t) grows exponentially with t, it makes sense to choose M in a way that makes α small. In next section, we discuss how M and α are chosen to achieve this.

3.4 Shaping Ellipsoids for Tight Over-Approximating Hyper-rectangles

The choice of M and the resulting α may seem like a minor detail, but a bad choice here can doom the rest of the algorithm to be impractical. For example, if we fix M to be the identity matrix I, the resulting value of α may give over-approximations that are too conservative. Even if the actual executions are convergent to $\mathbf{x}_{\mathsf{ref}}$ the resulting over-approximation can exponentially blow up.

We find the smallest exponential convergence/divergence rate (α) by solving for P in the following semi-definite program (SDP):

$$\begin{aligned} \min_{P \succ 0, \alpha \in \mathbb{R}} \quad & \alpha \\ \text{s.t} \quad & (A + BK)^{\intercal} P (A + BK) \preceq \alpha P. \end{aligned} \tag{7}$$

This gives M as the unique matrix such that $P = M^T M$.

In the rest of the paper, the reachset over-approximations will be represented by hyper-rectangles to allow us to efficiently use the existing SMT solvers. That is, the ellipsoids given by Lemma 1 have to be bounded by hyper-rectangles. For any coordinate transformation matrix M, the ellipsoid with unit size $\mathcal{E}_1(0, M) \subseteq \mathcal{R}_v(0)$, with $v(i) = \min_{x \in \mathcal{E}_1(0,M)} x(i)$. This $v(i)$ is also computed by solving an SDP. Similarly, $\mathcal{E}_r(0, M) \subseteq \mathcal{R}_{rv}(0)$. Therefore, from Lemma 1, it follows that $\mathsf{Reach}(S, t) \subseteq \mathcal{R}_{r_t v}(\mathbf{x}_{\mathsf{ref}}[t])$ with $r_t = \alpha^{\frac{t}{2}} r_0 + \sum_{i=0}^{t-1} \alpha^{\frac{i}{2}} \delta$ and v is the size vector of the rectangle bounding $\mathcal{E}_1(0, M)$. These optimization problems for computing M, α, and v have to be solved once per synthesis problem.

Example. *Continuing the previous example. Suppose robot is asked to reach the target set in 20 steps. Figure 2 shows the projection of the reachset on the robot's position with synthesized controller. The curves are the references executions $\mathbf{x}_{ref}$ from 2 initials cover and the rectangles are reachset over-approximations such that every execution of the system starting from each initial cover is guaranteed to be inside the rectangles at each time step.*

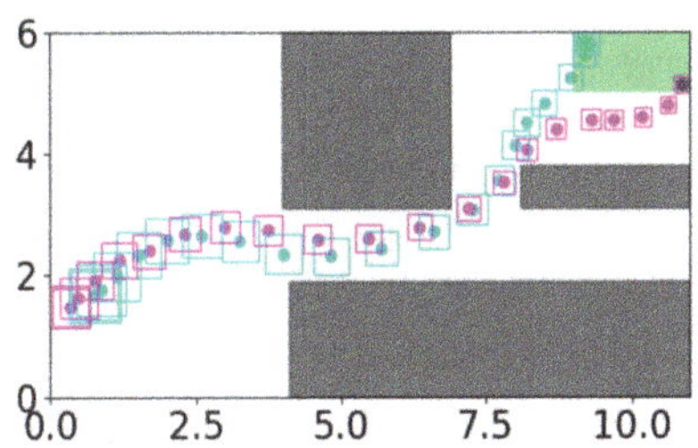

Fig. 2. Robot's position with the synthesized controllers using Algorithm 1.

3.5 Synthesis of Open-Loop Controller

In this section, we will discuss the synthesis of the open-loop controller $\mathbf{u}_{\mathsf{ref}}$ in $\langle K, \mathbf{x}_{\mathsf{ref}}[0], \mathbf{u}_{\mathsf{ref}}\rangle$. From the previous section, we know that given an initial set S, a tracking controller K, and an open-loop controller $\mathbf{u}_{\mathsf{ref}}$, the reachable set (under any disturbance) at time t is over-approximated by $\mathcal{R}_{r_t v}(\mathbf{x}_{\mathsf{ref}}[t])$. Thus, once we fix K and $\mathbf{x}_{\mathsf{ref}}[0]$, the problem of synthesizing a controller reduces to the problem of synthesizing an appropriate $\mathbf{u}_{\mathsf{ref}}$ such that the reachset over-approximations meet the reach-avoid specification. Indeed, for the rest of the presentation, we will assume a fixed K.

For synthesizing $\mathbf{u}_{\mathsf{ref}}$, we would like to formalize the problem in terms of constraints that will allow us to use SMT solvers. In the following, we describe the details of how this problem can be formalized as a quantifier-free first order formula over the theory of reals. We will then lay out specific assumptions and/or simplifications required to reduce the problem to QF-LRA theory, which is implemented efficiently in existing state-of-the-art SMT solvers. Most SMT solvers also provide the functionality of explicit model generation, and the concrete controller values can be read-off from the models generated when the constraints are satisfiable.

Constraints for Synthesizing $\mathbf{u}_{\mathsf{ref}}$. Let us fix an initial state x_0 and a radius r, defining a set of initial states $S = \mathcal{B}_r(x_0)$. The $\mathbf{u}_{\mathsf{ref}}$ synthesis problem can be stated as finding satisfying solutions for the formula $\phi_{\mathsf{synth}}(x_0, r)$.

$$\begin{aligned}\phi_{\mathsf{synth}}(x_0, r) \triangleq\ & \exists \mathbf{u}_{\mathsf{ref}}[0], \mathbf{u}_{\mathsf{ref}}[1], \ldots \mathbf{u}_{\mathsf{ref}}[T-1], \\ & \exists \mathbf{x}_{\mathsf{ref}}[0], \mathbf{x}_{\mathsf{ref}}[1], \ldots \mathbf{x}_{\mathsf{ref}}[T], \\ & \phi_{\mathsf{control}}(\mathbf{u}_{\mathsf{ref}}) \wedge \phi_{\mathsf{execution}}(\mathbf{u}_{\mathsf{ref}}, \mathbf{x}_{\mathsf{ref}}, x_0) \\ & \wedge \phi_{\mathsf{avoid}}(x_0, r, \mathbf{u}_{\mathsf{ref}}, \mathbf{x}_{\mathsf{ref}}) \wedge \phi_{\mathsf{reach}}(x_0, r, \mathbf{u}_{\mathsf{ref}}, \mathbf{x}_{\mathsf{ref}})\end{aligned} \tag{8}$$

where ϕ_{control} constrains the space of inputs, $\phi_{\mathsf{execution}}$ states that the sequence $\mathbf{x}_{\mathsf{ref}}$ is a reference execution following Eq. (3), ϕ_{avoid} specifies the safety constraint, ϕ_{reach} specifies that the system reaches G:

$$\begin{aligned}\phi_{\mathsf{control}}(\mathbf{u}_{\mathsf{ref}}) &\triangleq \bigwedge_{t=0}^{T-1} \mathbf{u}_{\mathsf{ref}}[t] \oplus (K \otimes \mathcal{R}_{r_t v}(0)) \subseteq U \\ \phi_{\mathsf{execution}}(\mathbf{u}_{\mathsf{ref}}, \mathbf{x}_{\mathsf{ref}}, x_0) &\triangleq (\mathbf{x}_{\mathsf{ref}}[0] = x_0) \wedge \bigwedge_{t=0}^{T-1} (\mathbf{x}_{\mathsf{ref}}[t+1] = A\mathbf{x}_{\mathsf{ref}}[t] + B\mathbf{u}_{\mathsf{ref}}[t]) \\ \phi_{\mathsf{avoid}}(x_0, r, \mathbf{u}_{\mathsf{ref}}, \mathbf{x}_{\mathsf{ref}}) &\triangleq \bigwedge_{t=0}^{T} \mathcal{R}_{r_t v}(\mathbf{x}_{\mathsf{ref}}[t]) \cap \mathbf{O}[t] = \varnothing \\ \phi_{\mathsf{reach}}(x_0, r, \mathbf{u}_{\mathsf{ref}}, \mathbf{x}_{\mathsf{ref}}) &\triangleq \mathcal{R}_{r_T v}(\mathbf{x}_{\mathsf{ref}}[T]) \subseteq G.\end{aligned} \tag{9}$$

As discussed in Sect. 3.2, the vector v and the constants $r_0, \ldots, r_T$ are precomputed using the radius r of the initial ball.

We make a few remarks about this formulation. First, each of the formulas $\phi_{\mathsf{control}}, \phi_{\mathsf{avoid}}$ and ϕ_{reach} represent sufficient conditions to check for the existence of $\mathbf{u}_{\mathsf{ref}}$. Second, the constraints stated above belong to the (decidable) theory of reals. However, $\phi_{\mathsf{control}}, \phi_{\mathsf{avoid}}$ and ϕ_{reach}, and thus ϕ_{synth}, are not quantifier free as they use subset and disjointness checks. This is because for sets S, T

expressed as predicates $\varphi_S(\cdot)$ and $\varphi_T(\cdot)$, $S \cap T = \varnothing$ corresponds to the formula $\forall x \cdot \neg(\varphi_S(x) \wedge \varphi_T(x))$ and $S \subseteq T$ (or equivalently $S \cap T^c = \varnothing$) corresponds to the formula $\forall x \cdot \varphi_S(x) \implies \varphi_T(x)$.

Reduction to QF-LRA. Since the sets G and U are bounded polytopes, G^c and U^c can be expressed as finite unions of (possibly unbounded) polytopes. Thus, the subset predicates $\mathbf{u}_{\mathsf{ref}}[t] \oplus (K \otimes \mathcal{R}_{r_t v}(0)) \subseteq U$ in ϕ_{control} and $\mathcal{R}_{r_t v}(\mathbf{x}_{\mathsf{ref}}[t]) \subseteq G$ in ϕ_{reach} can be expressed as a disjunction over finitely many predicates, each expressing the disjointness of two polytopes.

The central idea behind eliminating the universal quantification in the disjointness predicates in ϕ_{avoid} or in the inferred disjointness predicates in ϕ_{reach} and ϕ_{control}, is to find a separating hyperplane that witnesses the disjointness of two polytopes. Let $P_1 = \{x \mid A_1 x \leq b_1\}$ and $P_2 = \{x \mid A_2 x \leq b_2\}$ be two polytopes such that P_1 is closed and bounded. Then, if there is an i for which each vertex v of P_1 satisfies $A_2^{(i)} v > b_2(i)$, we must have that $P_1 \cap P_2 = \varnothing$, where $A_2^{(i)}$ is the ith row vector of the matrix A_2. That is, such a check is sufficient to ensure disjointness. Thus, in the formula ϕ_{avoid}, in order to check if $\mathcal{R}_{r_t v}(\mathbf{x}_{\mathsf{ref}}[t])$ does not intersect with $\mathbf{O}[t]$, we check if there is a face of the polytope $\mathbf{O}[t]$ such that all the vertices of $\mathcal{R}_{r_t v}(\mathbf{x}_{\mathsf{ref}}[t])$ lie on the other side of the face. The same holds for each of the inferred predicates in ϕ_{reach} and ϕ_{control}. Eliminating quantifiers is essential to scale our analysis to large high dimensional systems.

Further, when the set G has a hyper-rectangle representation, the containment check $\mathcal{R}_{r_t v}(\mathbf{x}_{\mathsf{ref}}[T]) \subseteq G$ can directly be encoded as the conjunction of $O(n)$ linear inequalities, stating that for each dimension i, the lower and the upper bounds of $\mathcal{R}_{r_t v}(\mathbf{x}_{\mathsf{ref}}[t])$ in the ith dimension, satisfy $l'_i \leq l_i \leq u_i \leq u'_i$, where l'_i and r'_i represent the bounds for G in the ith dimension. Similarly, when $\mathbf{O}[t]$ has a rectangle representation, we can formulate the emptiness constraint $\mathcal{R}_{r_t v}(\mathbf{x}_{\mathsf{ref}}[t]) \cap \mathbf{O}[t] = \varnothing$ as $\bigvee_{i=1}^{n} (u_i < l'_i \vee l_i > u'_i)$, where l_i and u_i (resp. l'_i and u'_i) are the lower and upper bounds of $\mathcal{R}_{r_t v}(\mathbf{x}_{\mathsf{ref}}[t])$ (resp. $\mathbf{O}[t]$) in the ith dimension. Since such simplifications can exponentially reduce the number of constraints generated, they play a crucial for the scalability.

The constraints for checking emptiness and disjointness, as discussed above, only give rise to linear constraints, do not have the $\forall$ quantification over states, and is a sound transformation of ϕ_{synth} into QF-LRA. In Sect. 3.6 we will see that the reach set over-approximation can be made arbitrarily small when the disturbance is 0 by arbitrarily shrinking the size of the initial cover. Thus, these checks will also turn out to be sufficient to ensure that if there exists a controller, ϕ_{synth} is satisfiable.

Lemma 2. *Let $v \in \mathbb{R}^n$ and $r_0, \ldots, r_T \in \mathbb{R}$ be such that for any execution $\mathbf{x}_{ref}$ starting at x_0, we have $\forall t \leq T \cdot \mathit{Reach}(\mathcal{B}_r(x_0), t) \subseteq \mathcal{R}_{r_t v}(\mathbf{x}_{ref}[t])$. If the formula $\phi_{synth}(x_0, r)$ is satisfiable, then there is a control sequence $\mathbf{u}_{ref}$ such that for every $x \in \mathcal{B}_r(x_0)$ and for every $\mathbf{d} \in \mathcal{D}^T$, the unique execution $\mathbf{x}$ defined by the controller $\langle K, x_0, \mathbf{u}_{ref}\rangle$ and $\mathbf{d}$, starting at x satisfies $\mathbf{x}[T] \in G \wedge \forall t \leq T \cdot \mathbf{x}[t] \notin \mathbf{O}[t]$.*

We remark that a possible alternative for eliminating the $\forall$ quantifier is the use of Farkas' Lemma, but this gives rise to nonlinear constraints[2]. Indeed, in our experimental evaluation, we observed the downside of resorting to Farkas' Lemma in this problem.

3.6 Synthesis Algorithm Putting It All Together

The presentation in Sect. 3.5 describes how to formalize constraints to generate a control sequence that works for a subset of the initial set Θ. The overall synthesis procedure (Algorithm 1), first computes a tracking controller K, then generates open-loop control sequences and reference executions in order to cover the entire set Θ.

Algorithm 1. Algorithm for Synthesizing Combined Controller

Input: $\mathcal{A}, T, \mathbf{O}[0], \ldots, \mathbf{O}[T], G, Q, R$
$r^* \leftarrow \mathsf{diameter}(\Theta)/2$
$K, v, c_1, c_2 \leftarrow$ BLOATPARAMS$(\mathcal{A}, T, Q, R)$
`cover` $\leftarrow \varnothing$
`controllers` $\leftarrow \varnothing$
while $\Theta \not\subseteq$ `cover` **do**
    $\psi_{\mathsf{synth}} \leftarrow$ GETCONSTRAINTS$(\mathcal{A}, T, \mathbf{O}[0], \ldots, \mathbf{O}[T], G, v, c_1, c_2, r^*,$ `cover`$)$
    if CHECKSAT$(\psi_{\mathsf{synth}}) = \mathsf{SAT}$ **then**
        $r, \mathbf{u}_{\mathsf{ref}}, \mathbf{x}_{\mathsf{ref}} \leftarrow$ MODEL(ψ_{synth})
        `cover` $\leftarrow$ `cover` $\cup\, \mathcal{B}_r(\mathbf{x}_{\mathsf{ref}}[0])$
        `controllers` $\leftarrow$ `controllers` $\cup \{ (\langle K, \mathbf{x}_{\mathsf{ref}}[0], \mathbf{u}_{\mathsf{ref}}\rangle, \mathcal{B}_r(\mathbf{x}_{\mathsf{ref}}[0])) \}$
    else
        $r^* \leftarrow r^*/2$
return `controllers`;

The procedure BLOATPARAMS, computes a tracking controller K, a vector v and real valued parameters $\{c_1[t]\}_{t\le T}$, $\{c_2[t]\}_{t\le T}$, for the system $\mathcal{A}$ and time bound T with Q, R for the LQR method. Given any reference execution $\mathbf{x}_{\mathsf{ref}}$ and an initial set $\mathcal{B}_r(\mathbf{x}_{\mathsf{ref}}[0])$, the parameters computed by BLOATPARAMS can be used to over-approximate $\mathsf{Reach}(\mathcal{B}_r(\mathbf{x}_{\mathsf{ref}}[0]), t)$ with the rectangle $\mathcal{R}_{v'}(\mathbf{x}_{\mathsf{ref}}[t])$, where $v' = (c_1[t]r + c_2[t])v$. The computation of these parameters proceeds as follows. Matrix K is determined using LQR (Proposition 1). Now we use Equation (7) to compute the matrix M and the rate of convergence α. Vector v is then computed such that $\mathcal{E}_1(0, M)$ is bounded by $\mathcal{R}_v(0)$. Let $r_{\mathsf{unit}} = \max_{x\in\mathcal{B}_1(0)} \|x\|_M$ and $\delta = \max_{d\in\mathcal{D}} \|d\|_M$. Then we have, $\mathcal{B}_r(x_0) \subseteq \mathcal{E}_{r\cdot r_{\mathsf{unit}}}(x_0, M)$ for any x_0. The constants $c_1[0], \ldots c_1[T]$, $c_2[0], \ldots c_2[T]$ are computed as $c_1[t] = \alpha^{\frac{t}{2}} r_{\mathsf{unit}}$ and $c_2[t] = \sum_{i=0}^{t-1} \alpha^{\frac{i}{2}} \delta$; Sects. 3.2–3.4 establish the correctness guarantees of these

[2] Farkas' Lemma introduces auxiliary variables that get multiplied with existing variables $\mathbf{x}_{\mathsf{ref}}[0], \ldots, \mathbf{x}_{\mathsf{ref}}[T]$, leading to nonlinear constraints.

parameters. Clearly, these computations are independent of any reference executions $\mathbf{x}_{\mathsf{ref}}$ and control sequences $\mathbf{u}_{\mathsf{ref}}$.

The procedure GETCONSTRAINTS constructs the logical formula ψ_{synth} below such that whenever ψ_{synth} holds, we can find an initial radius r, and center x_0 in the set $\Theta \setminus \mathtt{cover}$ and a control sequence $\mathbf{u}_{\mathsf{ref}}$ such that any controlled execution starting from $\mathcal{B}_r(x_0)$ satisfies the reach-avoid requirements.

$$\psi_{\mathsf{synth}} \triangleq \exists x_0 \, \exists r \cdot \Big(x_0 \in \Theta \wedge x_0 \notin \mathtt{cover} \wedge r > r^* \wedge \phi_{\mathsf{synth}}(x_0, r) \Big) \qquad (10)$$

Recall that the constants $r_0, \ldots, r_T$ used in ϕ_{synth} are affine functions of r and thus ψ_{synth} falls in the QF-LRA fragment.

Line 8 checks for the satisfiability of ψ_{synth}. If satisfiable, we extract the model generated to get the radius of the initial ball, the control sequence $\mathbf{u}_{\mathsf{ref}}$ and the reference execution $\mathbf{x}_{\mathsf{ref}}$ in Line 9. The generated controller $\langle K, \mathbf{x}_{\mathsf{ref}}[0], \mathbf{u}_{\mathsf{ref}} \rangle$ is guaranteed to work for the ball $\mathcal{B}_r(\mathbf{x}_{\mathsf{ref}}[0])$, which can be marked *covered* by adding it to the set $\mathtt{cover}$. In order to keep all the constraints linear, one can further underapproximate $\mathcal{B}_r(\mathbf{x}_{\mathsf{ref}}[0])$ with the rectangle $\mathcal{R}_w(\mathbf{x}_{\mathsf{ref}}[0])$, where $w(i) = r/\sqrt{n}$ for each dimension $i \leq n$. If ψ_{synth} is unsatisfiable, then we reduce the minimum radius r^* (Line 13) and continue to look for controllers, until we find that $\Theta \subseteq \mathtt{cover}$.

The set $\mathtt{controllers}$ is the set of pairs $(\langle K, x_0, \mathbf{u}_{\mathsf{ref}} \rangle, S)$, such that the controller $\langle K, x_0, \mathbf{u}_{\mathsf{ref}} \rangle$ drives the set S to meet the desired specification. Each time a new controller is found, it is added to the set $\mathtt{controllers}$ together with the initial set for which it works (Line 11). The following theorem asserts the soundness of Algorithm 1, and it follows from Lemmas 1 and 2.

Theorem 1. *If Algorithm 1 terminates, then the synthesized controller is correct. That is, (a) for each $x \in \Theta$, there is a $(\langle K, x_0, \mathbf{u}_{\mathsf{ref}} \rangle, S) \in \mathtt{controllers}$, such that $x \in S$, and (b) for each $(\langle K, x_0, \mathbf{u}_{\mathsf{ref}} \rangle, S) \in \mathtt{controllers}$, the unique controller $\langle K, x_0, \mathbf{u}_{\mathsf{ref}} \rangle$ is such that for every $x \in S$ and for every $\mathbf{d} \in D^T$, the unique execution defined by $\langle K, x_0, \mathbf{u}_{\mathsf{ref}} \rangle$ and $\mathbf{d}$, starting at x, satisfies the reach-avoid specification.*

Algorithm 1 ensures that, upon termination, every $x \in \Theta$ is covered, i.e., one can construct a combined controller that drives x to G while avoiding $\mathbf{O}$. However it may find multiple controllers for a point $x \in \Theta$. This non-determinism can be easily resolved by picking any controller assigned for x.

Below, we show that, under certain robustness assumptions on the system $\mathcal{A}$, G and the sets $\mathbf{O}$, and in the absence of disturbance Algorithm 1 terminates.

Robustly Controllable Systems. A system $\mathcal{A} = \langle A, B, \Theta, U, D \rangle$ is said to be ε-robustly controllable ($\varepsilon > 0$) with respect to the reach-avoid specification ($\mathbf{O}$, G) and matrix K, if (a) $D = \{0\}$, and (b) for every initial state $\theta \in \Theta$ and for every open loop-controller $\mathbf{u}_{\mathsf{ref}} \in U^T$ such that the unique execution starting from θ using the open-loop controller $\mathbf{u}_{\mathsf{ref}}$ satisfies the reach-avoid specification, then with the controller $\langle K, \theta, \mathbf{u}_{\mathsf{ref}} \rangle$ defined as in Equation (3), $\forall t \leq T, \mathsf{Reach}(\mathcal{B}_\varepsilon(\theta), t) \cap \mathbf{O}[t] = \varnothing$ and $\mathsf{Reach}(\mathcal{B}_\varepsilon(\theta), T) \subseteq G$, i.e., $\forall x \in \mathcal{B}_\varepsilon(\theta)$, the unique trajectory $\mathbf{x}$ defined by the controller $\langle K, \theta, \mathbf{u}_{\mathsf{ref}} \rangle$ starting from x also satisfies the reach avoid specification.

Theorem 2. *Let $\mathcal{A}$ be ε-robust with respect to the reach-avoid specification $(\mathbf{O}, G)$ and K, for some $\varepsilon > 0$. If there is a controller for $\mathcal{A}$ that satisfies the reach-avoid specification, then Algorithm 1 terminates.*

When the system is robust, then (in the absence of any disturbance i.e., $D = \{0\}$), the sizes $r_0, r_1, \ldots, r_T$ of the hyper-rectangles that overapproximate reach-sets go arbitrarily close to 0 as the initial cover converges to a single point (as seen in Lemma 1). Therefore, the over-approximations can be made arbitrarily precise as r^* decreases. Moreover, as r^* approaches 0, Eq. (9) (with simplifications for QF-LRA), also becomes satisfiable whenever there is a controller. The correctness of Theorem 2 follows from both these observations.

4 RealSyn Implementation and Evaluation

4.1 Implementation

We have implemented our synthesis algorithm in a tool called RealSyn. RealSyn is written in Python. For solving Eq. (10) it can interface with any SMT solver through Python APIs. We present experimental results with Z3 (version 4.5.1) [6], Yices (version 2.5.4) [8], and CVC4 (version 1.5) [4]. RealSyn leverages the incremental solving capabilities of these solvers as follows: The constraints ψ_{synth} generated (line 8 in Algorithm 1) can be expressed as $\exists x_0, \exists r \cdot \psi_1 \wedge \psi_2$, where $\psi_1 \triangleq \phi_{\mathsf{synth}}(x_0, r)$ and $\psi_2 \triangleq x_0 \in \Theta \wedge x_0 \notin \mathtt{cover} \wedge r > r^*$. Since the bulk of the formula $\phi_{\mathsf{synth}}(x_0, r)$ is in ψ_1 and it does not change across iterations, we can generate this formula only once, and push it on the context stack of the solvers. The formula ψ_2 is different across iterations, and can be pushed and popped out of the stack as required. This minimizes the time taken for generation of constraints.

4.2 Evaluation

We use 24 benchmark examples[3] to evaluate the performance of RealSyn with three different solvers on a standard laptop with Intel® Core™ i7 processor, 16 GB RAM, running Ubuntu 16.04. The results are reported in Table 1. The results are encouraging and demonstrate the effectiveness of using our approach and the feasibility of scalable controller synthesis for high dimensional systems and complex reach-avoid specifications.

Comparison With Other Tools. We considered other controller synthesis tools for possible comparison with RealSyn. In summary, CoSyMa [27], Pessoa [30], and SCOTS [31] do not explicitly support discrete-time sytems. LTLMop [22,37] is designed to analyze robotic systems in the (2-dimensional)

[3] The examples are available at https://github.com/umangm/realsyn.

Table 1. Controller synthesis using RealSyn and different SMT solvers. An explanation for the * marked entries can be found in Sect. 4.

	Model	n	m	Z3		CVC4		Yices	
				#iter	time(s)	#iter	time(s)	#iter	time(s)
1	1-robot	2	1	9	0.21	1	0.06	7	0.06
2	2-robot	4	2	164	12.62	11	0.31	183	2.26
3	running-example	4	2	N/A	T/O	N/A	T/O	1	319.97
4	1-car dynamic avoid	4	2	9	53.17	1	96.43	12	8.49
5	1-car navigation	4	2	18	7.49	1	3.05	17	6.73
6	2-car navigation	8	4	1	60.14	1	2668.2	1	4.07
7	3-car navigation	12	6	1	733.42	1	481.88	1	741.73
8	4-car platoon	8	4	1	0.37	1	0.21	1	0.15
9	8-car platoon	16	8	1	23.02	1	1.44	1	0.62
10	10-car platoon	20	10	1	459.36	1	20.93	1	7.74
11	Example	3	1	82	2.32	18	0.10	67	0.43
12	Cruise	1	1	1	0.06	1	0.03	1	0.02
13	Motor	2	1	1	0.10	1	0.06	1	0.03
14	Helicopter	3	1	81	2.31	13	0.08	70	0.38
15	Magnetic suspension	2	1	39	0.47	2	0.05	39	0.08
16	Pendulum	2	1	30	0.32	8	0.05	42	0.07
17	Satellite	2	1	40	0.46	5	0.05	32	0.06
18	Suspension	4	1	1	0.17	1	0.11	1	0.09
19	Tape	3	1	1	0.12	1	0.07	1	0.07
20	Inverted pendulum	2	1	39	0.49	2	0.05	39	0.09
21	Magnetic pointer	3	1	44	1.12	12	0.08	134	0.83
22	Helicopter	28	6	N/A (1*)	T/O (650*)	1	651.21	N/A	T/O
23	Building	48	1	1 (1*)	1936.03 (240*)	N/A	T/O	1	552.48
24	Pde	84	1	N/A (1*)	T/O (1800*)	1	8.48	1	8.87

Euclidean plane and thus not suitable for most of our examples. TuLiP [13,39] comes closest to addressing the same class of problems. TuLip relies on discretization of the state space and a receding horizon approach for synthesizing controllers for more general GR(1) specifications. However, we found TuLip succumbs to the state space explosion problem when discretizing the state space, and it did not work on most of our examples. For instance, TuLiP was unable to synthesize a controller for the 2-dimensional system '1-robot' (Table 1), and returned `unrealizable`. On the benchmark '2-robot' ($n = 4$), TuLip did not return any answer within 1 h. We checked these findings with the developers and they concurred that it is typical for TuLip to take hours even for 4-dimensional systems.

Benchmarks. Our benchmarks and their SMT encodings, could be of independent interest to the verification and SMT-community. Examples 1–10 are vehicle motion planning examples we have designed with reach-avoid specifications. Benchmarks 1–2 model robots moving on the Euclidean plane, where each robot is a 2-dimensional system and admits a 1-dimensional input. Starting from some initial region on the plane, the robots are required to reach the common goal area within the given time steps, while avoiding certain obstacles. For '2-robot', the robots are also required to maintain a minimum separation. Benchmarks 3–7 are discrete vehicular models adopted from [12]. Each vehicle is a 4-dimensional system with 2-dimensional input. Benchmark 3 is the system as our running example. Benchmark 4 describes one *ego* vehicle running on a two-lane road, trying to overtake a vehicle in front of it. The second vehicle serves as the obstacle. Benchmarks 5–7 are similar to Benchmark 2 where the vehicles are required to reach a common goal area while avoiding collision with the obstacles and with each other (inspired by a merge). The velocities and accelerations of the vehicles are also constrained in each of these benchmarks.

Benchmarks 8–10 model multiple vehicles trying to form a platoon by maintaining the safe relative distance between consecutive vehicles. The models are adopted (and discretized) from [32]. Each vehicle is a 2-dimensional system with 1-dimensional input. For the 4-car platoon model, the running times reported in Table 1 are much smaller than the time (5 min) reported in [32]. This observation aligns with our analysis in Sect. 3.1.

Benchmarks 11–21 are from [2]. The specification here is that the reach set has to be within a safe rectangle (that is, $G = true$). In [2] each model is discretized using 8 different time steps and here we randomly pick one for each model. In general, the running time of RealSyn is less than those reported in [2] (their reported machine had better configuration). On the other hand, the synthesized controller from [2] considers quantization errors, while our approach does not provide any guarantee for that.

Benchmarks 22–24 are a set of high dimensional examples adopted and discretized from [36]. Similar to previous ones, the only specification is that the reach sets starting from an initial state with the controller should be contained within a safe rectangle.

Synthesis Performance. In Table 1, columns 'n' and 'm' stand for the dimensions of the state space and input space. For each background solver, '#iter' is the number of iterations Algorithm 1 required to synthesize a controller, and 'time' is the respective running times. We specify a time limit of 1 h and report T/O (timeout) for benchmarks that do not finish within this limit. All benchmarks are synthesized for a specification with 10–20 steps.

In general, for low-dimensional systems (for example, in Benchmarks 11–21), each of the solvers finish quickly (in less than 1 s), with CVC4 and Yices outperforming Z3 on most benchmarks. The Yices solver is faster than the other two on most examples. Z3 was the slowest on most, except a few (e.g., Benchmark 3, 6) where CVC4 was much slower. The running time, in general, increases with the increase of the dimensionality but this relationship is far from simple. For example, the 84-dimensional Benchmark 24 was synthesized in less than 9 s by both CVC4 and Yices, possibly because the safety specification is rather simple for this problem.

The three solvers use different techniques for solving QF-LRA formulae with support for incremental solving. The default tactic in Z3 is such that it spends a large chunk of time when a constraint is pushed to the solver stack. In fact, for Benchmark 24, while the other two solvers finish within 9 s, Z3 did not finish pushing the constraints in the solver stack. When we disable incremental solving in Z3, the Benchmarks 22, 23 and 24 finish in about 650, 240 and 1800 s respectively (marked with *). The number of iterations widely vary across solvers, with CVC4 usually finishing in the fewest number of iterations. Despite the larger number of satisfiability queries, Yices manages to finish close to CVC4 on most examples.

5 Conclusion

We proposed a novel technique for synthesizing controllers for systems with discrete time linear dynamics, operating under bounded disturbances,and for reach-avoid specifications. Our approach relies on generating controllers that combine an open loop-controller with a tracking controller, thereby allowing a decoupled approach for synthesizing each component independently. Experimental evaluation using our tool RealSyn demonstrates the value of the approach when analyzing systems with complex dynamics and specifications.

There are several avenues for future work. This includes synthesis of combined controllers for nonlinear dynamical and hybrid systems, and for more general temporal logic specifications. Generating witnesses to show the absence of controllers is also an interesting direction.

References

1. Abate, A., Amin, S., Prandini, M., Lygeros, J., Sastry, S.: Computational approaches to reachability analysis of stochastic hybrid systems. In: Bemporad, A., Bicchi, A., Buttazzo, G. (eds.) HSCC 2007. LNCS, vol. 4416, pp. 4–17. Springer, Heidelberg (2007). https://doi.org/10.1007/978-3-540-71493-4_4
2. Abate, A., et al.: Automated formal synthesis of digital controllers for state-space physical plants. In: Majumdar, R., Kunvcak, V. (eds.) CAV 2017. LNCS, vol. 10426, pp. 462–482. Springer, Cham (2017). https://doi.org/10.1007/978-3-319-63387-9_23
3. Antsaklis, P.J., Michel, A.N.: A Linear Systems Primer, vol. 1. Birkhäuser Boston, Cambridge (2007)
4. Barrett, C., et al.: CVC4. In: Gopalakrishnan, G., Qadeer, S. (eds.) CAV 2011. LNCS, vol. 6806, pp. 171–177. Springer, Heidelberg (2011). https://doi.org/10.1007/978-3-642-22110-1_14
5. Boyd, S., Vandenberghe, L.: Convex Optimization (2004)
6. de Moura, L., Bjorner, N.: Z3: an efficient SMT solver. In: Ramakrishnan, C.R., Rehof, J. (eds.) TACAS 2008. LNCS, vol. 4963, pp. 337–340. Springer, Heidelberg (2008). https://doi.org/10.1007/978-3-540-78800-3_24

7. Ding, J., Tomlin, C.J.: Robust reach-avoid controller synthesis for switched nonlinear systems. In: Proceedings of the 49th IEEE Conference on Decision and Control, CDC 2010, 15–17 December 2010, Atlanta, Georgia, USA, pp. 6481–6486 (2010)
8. Dutertre, B.: Yices 2.2. In: Biere, A., Bloem, R. (eds.) CAV 2014. LNCS, vol. 8559, pp. 737–744. Springer, Cham (2014). https://doi.org/10.1007/978-3-319-08867-9_49
9. Esfahani, P.M., Chatterjee, D., Lygeros, J.: The stochastic reach-avoid problem and set characterization for diffusions. Automatica **70**, 43–56 (2016)
10. Fainekos, G.E., Girard, A., Kress-Gazit, H., Pappas, G.J.: Temporal logic motion planning for dynamic robots. Automatica **45**(2), 343–352 (2009)
11. Fainekos, G.E., Kress-Gazit, H., Pappas, G.J.: Hybrid controllers for path planning: a temporal logic approach. In: 2005 44th IEEE Conference on Decision and Control, and 2005 European Control Conference, CDC-ECC 2005, pp. 4885–4890. IEEE (2005)
12. Fehnker, A., Ivanvcić, F.: Benchmarks for hybrid systems verification. In: Alur, R., Pappas, G.J. (eds.) HSCC 2004. LNCS, vol. 2993, pp. 326–341. Springer, Heidelberg (2004). https://doi.org/10.1007/978-3-540-24743-2_22
13. Filippidis, I., Dathathri, S., Livingston, S.C., Ozay, N., Murray, R.M.: Control design for hybrid systems with tulip: the temporal logic planning toolbox. In: 2016 IEEE Conference on Control Applications, CCA 2016, Buenos Aires, Argentina, 19–22 September 2016, pp. 1030–1041 (2016)
14. Fisac, J.F., Chen, M., Tomlin, C.J., Sastry, S.S.: Reach-avoid problems with time-varying dynamics, targets and constraints. In: Proceedings of the 18th International Conference on Hybrid Systems: Computation and Control, HSCC 2015, Seattle, WA, USA, 14–16 April 2015, pp. 11–20 (2015)
15. Girard, A.: Controller synthesis for safety and reachability via approximate bisimulation. Automatica **48**(5), 947–953 (2012)
16. Gol, E.A., Lazar, M., Belta, C.: Language-guided controller synthesis for linear systems. IEEE Trans. Autom. Control **59**(5), 1163–1176 (2014)
17. Hespanha, J.P.: Linear Systems Theory. Princeton University Press, Princeton (2009)
18. Huang, Z., Wang, Y., Mitra, S., Dullerud, G.E., Chaudhuri, S.: Controller synthesis with inductive proofs for piecewise linear systems: an SMT-based algorithm. In: 54th IEEE Conference on Decision and Control, CDC 2015, Osaka, Japan, 15–18 December 2015, pp. 7434–7439 (2015)
19. Jha, S., Seshia, S.A., Tiwari, A.: Synthesis of optimal switching logic for hybrid systems. In: Proceedings of the 11th International Conference on Embedded Software, EMSOFT 2011, Part of the Seventh Embedded Systems Week, ESWeek 2011, Taipei, Taiwan, 9–14 October 2011, pp. 107–116 (2011)
20. Kloetzer, M., Belta, C.: A fully automated framework for control of linear systems from temporal logic specifications. IEEE Trans. Autom. Control **53**(1), 287–297 (2008)
21. Koo, T.J., Pappas, G.J., Sastry, S.: Mode switching synthesis for reachability specifications. In: Di Benedetto, M.D., Sangiovanni-Vincentelli, A. (eds.) HSCC 2001. LNCS, vol. 2034, pp. 333–346. Springer, Heidelberg (2001). https://doi.org/10.1007/3-540-45351-2_28
22. Kress-Gazit, H., Fainekos, G.E., Pappas, G.J.: Temporal logic based reactive mission and motion planning. IEEE Trans. Robot. **25**(6), 1370–1381 (2009)
23. Kress-Gazit, H., Lahijanian, M., Raman, V.: Synthesis for robots: guarantees and feedback for robot behavior. Ann. Rev. Control Robot. Auton. Syst. **1**(1) (2018)
24. Kurzhanskiy, A.A., Varaiya, P.: Ellipsoidal techniques for reachability analysis of discrete-time linear systems. IEEE Trans. Autom. Control **52**(1), 26–38 (2007)

25. Liu, J., Ozay, N., Topcu, U., Murray, R.M.: Synthesis of reactive switching protocols from temporal logic specifications. IEEE Trans. Autom. Control **58**(7), 1771–1785 (2013)
26. Majumdar, R., Mallik, K., Schmuck, A.-K.: Compositional synthesis of finite state abstractions. CoRR, abs/1612.08515 (2016)
27. Mouelhi, S., Girard, A., Gössler, G.: Cosyma: a tool for controller synthesis using multi-scale abstractions. In: Proceedings of The 16th International Conference on Hybrid Systems: Computation and Control, HSCC 2013, pp. 83–88, New York. ACM (2013)
28. Rami, M.A., Tadeo, F.: Controller synthesis for positive linear systems with bounded controls. IEEE Trans. Circuits Syst. **54–II**(2), 151–155 (2007)
29. Ravanbakhsh, H., Sankaranarayanan, S.: Robust controller synthesis of switched systems using counterexample guided framework. In: Proceedings of the 13th International Conference on Embedded Software, EMSOFT 2016, pp. 8:1–8:10, New York. ACM (2016)
30. Roy, P., Tabuada, P., Majumdar, R.: Pessoa 2.0: a controller synthesis tool for cyber-physical systems. In: Proceedings of the 14th International Conference on Hybrid Systems: Computation and Control, HSCC 2011, pp. 315–316, New York. ACM (2011)
31. Rungger, M, Zamani, M.: SCOTS: a tool for the synthesis of symbolic controllers. In: Proceedings of the 19th International Conference on Hybrid Systems: Computation and Control, HSCC 2016, pp. 99–104, New York. ACM (2016)
32. Schürmann, B., Althoff, M.: Optimal control of sets of solutions to formally guarantee constraints of disturbed linear systems. In: 2017 American Control Conference, ACC 2017, Seattle, WA, USA, 24–26 May 2017, pp. 2522–2529 (2017)
33. Tabuada, P.: Verification and Control of Hybrid Systems - A Symbolic Approach. Springer, Heidelberg (2009). https://doi.org/10.1007/978-1-4419-0224-5
34. Tabuada, P., Pappas, G.J.: Linear time logic control of discrete-time linear systems. IEEE Trans. Autom. Control **51**(12), 1862–1877 (2006)
35. Taly, A., Gulwani, S., Tiwari, A.: Synthesizing switching logic using constraint solving. STTT **13**(6), 519–535 (2011)
36. Tran, H.D., Nguyen, L.V., Johnson, T.T.: Large-scale linear systems from order-reduction. In: ARCH@CPSWeek 2016, 3rd International Workshop on Applied Verification for Continuous and Hybrid Systems, Vienna, Austria, pp. 60–67 (2016)
37. Wong, K.W., Finucane, C., Kress-Gazit, H.: Provably-correct robot control with LTLMoP, OMPL and ROS. In: 2013 IEEE/RSJ International Conference on Intelligent Robots and Systems, Tokyo, Japan, 3–7 November 2013, p. 2073 (2013)
38. Wongpiromsarn, T., Topcu, U., Murray, R.M.: Receding horizon temporal logic planning. IEEE Trans. Autom. Control **57**(11), 2817–2830 (2012)
39. Wongpiromsarn, T., Topcu, U., Ozay, N., Xu, H., Murray, R.M.: TuLiP: a software toolbox for receding horizon temporal logic planning. In: Proceedings of the 14th International Conference on Hybrid Systems: Computation and Control, HSCC 2011, pp. 313–314, New York. ACM (2011)
40. Yordanov, B., Tumova, J., Cerna, I., Barnat, J., Belta, C.: Temporal logic control of discrete-time piecewise affine systems. IEEE Trans. Autom. Control **57**(6), 1491–1504 (2012)
41. Zhao, H., Zhan, N., Kapur, D.: Synthesizing switching controllers for hybrid systems by generating invariants. In: Liu, Z., Woodcock, J., Zhu, H. (eds.) Theories of Programming and Formal Methods. LNCS, vol. 8051, pp. 354–373. Springer, Heidelberg (2013). https://doi.org/10.1007/978-3-642-39698-4_22

Synthesis of Asynchronous Reactive Programs from Temporal Specifications

Suguman Bansal[1(✉)], Kedar S. Namjoshi[2(✉)], and Yaniv Sa'ar[3(✉)]

[1] Rice University, Houston, TX, USA
suguman@rice.edu
[2] Bell Labs, Nokia, Murray Hill, NJ, USA
kedar.namjoshi@nokia-bell-labs.com
[3] Bell Labs, Nokia, Kfar Saba, Israel
yaniv.saar@nokia.bell-labs.com

Abstract. Asynchronous interactions are ubiquitous in computing systems and complicate design and programming. Automatic construction of asynchronous programs from specifications ("synthesis") could ease the difficulty, but known methods are complex, and intractable in practice. This work develops substantially simpler synthesis methods. A direct, exponentially more compact automaton construction is formulated for the reduction of asynchronous to synchronous synthesis. Experiments with a prototype implementation of the new method demonstrate feasibility. Furthermore, it is shown that for several useful classes of temporal properties, automaton-based methods can be avoided altogether and replaced with simpler Boolean constraint solving.

1 Introduction

Modern software and hardware systems harness asynchronous interactions to improve speed, responsiveness, and power consumption: delay-insensitive circuits, networks of sensors, multi-threaded programs and interacting web services are all asynchronous in nature. Various factors contribute to asynchrony, such as unpredictable transmission delays, concurrency, distributed execution, and parallelism. The common result is that each component of a system operates with partial, out-of-date knowledge of the state of the others, which considerably complicates system design and programming. Yet, it is often easier to state the desired behavior of an asynchronous program. We therefore consider the question of automatically constructing (i.e., synthesizing) a correct reactive asynchronous program directly from its temporal specification.

The *asynchronous synthesis problem* was originally formulated by Pnueli and Rosner in 1989 on the heels of their work on synchronous synthesis [31,32]. The task is that of constructing a (finite-state) program which interacts asynchronously with its environment while meeting a temporal specification on the actions at the interface between program and environment. Given a linear temporal specification φ, Pnueli-Rosner show that *asynchronous* synthesis can be

H. Chockler and G. Weissenbacher (Eds.): CAV 2018, LNCS 10981, pp. 367–385, 2018.
https://doi.org/10.1007/978-3-319-96145-3_20

reduced to checking whether a derived specification φ', specifying the required behavior of the scheduler, is *synchronously* synthesizable. That is, an asynchronous program can implement φ iff a synchronous program can implement φ'.

It may then appear straightforward to construct asynchronous programs using one of the many tools that exist for synchronous synthesis. However, the derived formula φ' embeds a nontrivial stutter quantification, which requires a complex intermediate automaton construction; it has not, to the authors' knowledge, ever been implemented. This situation is in stark contrast to that of synchronous synthesis, for which multiple tools and algorithms have been created.

Alternative methods have been proposed for asynchronous synthesis: Finkbeiner and Schewe reduce a bounded form of the problem to a SAT/SMT query [35], and Klein, Piterman and Pnueli show that some GR(1) specifications[1] can be transformed as above to an approximate synchronous GR(1) property [21,22]. These alternatives, however, have drawbacks of their own. The SAT/SMT reduction is exponential in the number of interface (input and output) bits, an important parameter; the GR(1) specifications amenable to transformation are limited and are characterized by semantic conditions that are not easily checked.

This work presents two key simplifications. First, we define a new property, $\mathsf{PR}(\varphi)$ (named in honor of Pnueli-Rosner's pioneering work) which, like φ', is synchronously realizable if, and only if, φ is asynchronously realizable. We then present an automaton construction for $\mathsf{PR}(\varphi)$ that is direct and simpler, and results in an exponentially smaller automaton than the one for φ'. In particular, the automaton for $\mathsf{PR}(\varphi)$ has only at most *twice* the states of the automaton for φ, as opposed to the *exponential blowup* of the state space (in the number of interface bits) incurred in the construction of the automaton for φ'. As almost all synchronous automaton-based synthesis tools use an explicit encoding for automaton states, this reduction is vital in practice.

We show how to implement the transformation PR symbolically (with BDDs), so that interface bits are always represented in symbolic form. One can then apply the modular strategy of Pnueli-Rosner: a symbolic automaton for φ is transformed to a symbolic automaton for $\mathsf{PR}(\varphi)$ (instead of φ'), which is analyzed with a synchronous synthesis tool. We establish that PR is conjunctive and preserves safety[2]. These are important properties, used by tools such as Acacia+ [8] and Unbeast [11] to optimize the synchronous synthesis task. The new construction has been implemented in a prototype tool, BAS, and experiments demonstrate feasibility in practice.

In addition, we establish that for several classes of temporal properties, which are easily characterized by syntax, the automaton-based method can be avoided entirely and replaced with Boolean constraint solving. The constraints are quantified Boolean formulae, with prefix $\exists\forall$ and a kernel that is derived from the original specification. This surprising reduction, which resolves a temporal prob-

[1] The GR(1) ("General Reactivity (1)") subclass has an efficient symbolic procedure for synchronous synthesis, formulated in [28] and implemented in several tools.

[2] I.e., $\mathsf{PR}(\bigwedge_i f_i) = \bigwedge_i \mathsf{PR}(f_i)$, and $\mathsf{PR}(f)$ is a safety property if f is a safety property.

lem with Boolean reasoning, is a consequence of the highly adversarial role of the environment in the asynchronous setting.

These contributions turn a seemingly intractable synthesis task into one that is feasible in practice.

2 Preliminaries

Temporal Specifications. Linear Temporal Logic (LTL) [29] extends propositional logic with temporal operators. LTL formulae are defined as $\varphi ::= \mathsf{True} \mid \mathsf{False} \mid p \mid \neg\varphi \mid \varphi_1 \wedge \varphi_2 \mid X\varphi \mid \varphi_1 U \varphi_2 \mid \Diamond\varphi \mid \Box\varphi \mid \boxminus\varphi$. Here p is a proposition, and X(Next), U (Until), $\Diamond$ (Eventually), $\Box$ (Always), and $\boxminus$(Always in the past) are temporal operators. The LTL semantics is standard, and is in the full version of the paper. For an LTL formula φ, let $\mathcal{L}(\varphi)$ denote the set of words (over subsets of propositions) that satisfy φ.

GR(1) is a useful fragment of LTL, where formulae are of the form $(\Box S_e \wedge \bigwedge_{i=0}^{m} \Box\Diamond P_i) \Rightarrow (\Box S_s \wedge \bigwedge_{i=0}^{n} \Box\Diamond Q_i)$, for propositional formulae S_e, S_s, P_i, Q_i. Typically, the left-hand side of the implication is used to restrict the environment, by requiring safety and liveness assumptions to hold, while the right-hand side is used to define the safety and liveness guarantees required of the system.

LTL specifications can be turned into equivalent Büchi automata, using standard constructions. A Büchi automaton, A, is specified by the tuple $(Q, Q_0, \Sigma, \delta, G)$, where Q is a set of states, $Q_0 \subseteq Q$ defines the initial states, Σ is the alphabet, $\delta \subseteq Q \times \Sigma \times Q$ is the transition relation, and $G \subseteq Q$ defines the "green" (also known as "accepting" or "final") states. A *run* r of the automaton on an infinite word $\sigma = a_0, a_1, \ldots$ over Σ is an infinite sequence $r = q_0, a_0, q_1, a_1, \ldots$ such that q_0 is an initial state, and for each k, (q_k, a_k, q_{k+1}) is in the transition relation. Run r is accepting if a green state appears on it infinitely often; the language of A, denoted $\mathcal{L}(A)$, is the set of words that have an accepting run.

The Asynchronous Synthesis Model. The goal of synthesis is to construct an "open" program M meeting a specification at its interface. In the asynchronous setting, the program M interacts in a fair interleaved manner with its environment E. The fairness restriction requires that E and M are each scheduled infinitely often in all infinite executions. Let $E//M$ denote this composition. The interface between E and M is formed by the variables x and y. Variable x is written by E and is read-only for M, while y is written by M and is read-only for E. One can consider x (resp., y) to represent a vector of variables, i.e., $x = (x_1, \ldots, x_n)$ (resp., $y = (y_1, \ldots, y_m)$) which is read (resp., written) atomically. Many of our results also extend to non-atomic reads and writes, and are discussed in the full version of the paper.

The synthesis task is to construct a program M which satisfies a temporal property $\varphi(x, y)$ over the interface variables in the composition $E//M$, for *any* environment E. The most adversarial environment is the one which sets x to an arbitrary value at each scheduled step, we denote it by $\mathsf{CHAOS}(x)$. The behaviors of the composition $\mathsf{CHAOS}(x)//M$ simulate those of $E//M$ for all E. Hence, it suffices to produce M which satisfies φ in the composition $\mathsf{CHAOS}(x)//M$. One can limit the set of environments through an assumption in the specification.

This leads to the formal definition of an *asynchronous schedule*, given by a pair of functions, $r, w : \mathbb{N} \rightarrow \mathbb{N}$, which represent read and write points, respectively. The initial write point, $w(0) = 0$, and represents the choice of initial value for the variable y. Without loss of generality, the read-write points alternate, i.e., for all $i \geq 0$, $w(i) \leq r(i) < w(i+1)$ and $r(i) < w(i+1) \leq r(i+1)$. A *strict* asynchronous schedule does not allow read and write points to overlap, i.e., the constraints are strengthened to $w(i) < r(i) < w(i+1)$ and $r(i) < w(i+1) < r(i+1)$. A *tight* asynchronous schedule is the strict schedule without any non-read-write gaps, i.e., $r(k) = 2k + 1$ and $w(k) = 2k$, for all k. A *synchronous* schedule is the special non-strict schedule where $r(i) = i$ and $w(i) = i$, for all i.

Let D^v denote the binary domain $\{\mathsf{True}, \mathsf{False}\}$ for a variable v. A program M can be represented semantically as a function $f : (D^x)^* \rightarrow D^y$. For an asynchronous schedule (r, w), a sequence $\sigma = (D^x \times D^y)^\omega$ is said to be an *asynchronous execution of f over (r, w)* if the value of y is changed only at writing points, in a manner that depends only on the values of x at prior reading points. Formally, for all $i \geq 0$, $y_{w(i+1)} = f(x_{r(0)} \dots x_{r(i)})$, and for all j such that $w(i) \leq j < w(i+1)$, $y_j = y_{w(i)}$. The initial value of y is the value it has at point $w(0) = 0$. The set of such sequences is denoted as $\mathsf{asynch}(f)$. Over synchronous schedules, the set of such sequences is denoted by $\mathsf{synch}(f)$. Function f is an asynchronous implementation of φ if all asynchronous executions of f over all possible schedules satisfy φ, i.e., if $\mathsf{asynch}(f) \subseteq \mathcal{L}(\varphi)$.

This formulation agrees with that given by Pnueli and Rosner for strict schedules. For synchronous schedules (and other non-strict schedules), our formulation has a Moore-style semantics – the output depends on strictly earlier inputs – while Pnueli and Rosner formulate a Mealy semantics. A Moore semantics is more appropriate for modeling software programs, where the output variable is part of the state, and fits well with the theoretical constructions that follow.

Definition 1 (Asynchronous LTL Realizability). *Given an LTL property $\varphi(x, y)$ over the input variable x and output variable y, the* asynchronous LTL realizability *problem is to determine whether there is an asynchronous implementation for φ.*

Definition 2 (Asynchronous LTL Synthesis). *Given a realizable LTL-formula φ, the* asynchronous LTL synthesis *problem is to construct an asynchronous implementation of φ.*

Examples. Pnueli and Rosner give a number of interesting specifications. The specification $\square\,(y \equiv Xx)$ ("the current output equals the next input") is satisfiable but not realizable, as any implementation would have to be clairvoyant. On the other hand, the flipped specification $\square\,(x \equiv Xy)$ ("the next output equals the current input") is synchronously realizable by a Moore machine which replays the current input as the next output. The specification $\Diamond\Box x \equiv \Diamond\Box y$ is synchronously realizable by the same machine, but is asynchronously unrealizable, as shown next. Consider two input (x) sequences, under a schedule where reads happen only at odd positions. In both, let x=true at all reading points. Then any program must respond to both inputs with the same output sequence for y. Now suppose that in the first sequence x is false at all non-read positions, while in the second, x is true at all non-read positions. In the first case, the specification forces the output y-sequence to be false infinitely often; in the second, y is forced to be true from some point on, a contradiction.

The negated specification $\Diamond\Box x \not\equiv \Diamond\Box y$ is also asynchronously unrealizable, for the same reason. This "gap" illustrates an intriguing difference from the synchronous case, where either a specification is realizable for the system, or its negation is realizable for the environment. The two halves of the equivalence, i.e., $\Diamond\Box x \Rightarrow \Diamond\Box y$ and $\Diamond\Box y \Rightarrow \Diamond\Box x$ are individually asynchronously realizable, by strategies that fix the output to y=true and to y=false, respectively.

From Asynchronous to Synchronous Synthesis. Pnueli and Rosner reduced asynchronous LTL synthesis to synchronous synthesis of Büchi objectives. Their reduction applied to LTL formulas with a single input and output variable [32]; it was later extended to the non-atomic case [30]. The original Rosner-Pnueli reduction deals exclusively with strict schedules, since they showed that it is sufficient to consider only strict schedules.

Two infinite sequences are said to be *stuttering equivalent* if one sequence can be obtained from the other by a finite duplication ("stretching") of a given state or by deletion ("compressing") of finitely many contiguous identical states retaining at least one of them. The *stuttering quantification* $\exists^{\approx}$ is defined as follows: $\exists^{\approx}x.\varphi$ holds for sequence π if $\exists x.\varphi$ holds for a sequence π' that is stuttering equivalent to π. Pnueli-Rosner showed that an LTL-formula $\varphi(x, y)$ over input x and output y is asynchronously realizable iff a "kernel" formula (this is the precise formula referred to as φ' in the Introduction) $\mathcal{K}(r, w, x, y) = \alpha(r, w) \rightarrow \beta(r, w, x, y)$ over read sequence r, write sequence w, input sequence x and output sequence y is synchronously realizable:

$$\begin{aligned}\alpha(r, w) = \quad & (\neg r \wedge \neg w \,\mathsf{U}\, r) \wedge \Box \neg(r \wedge w) \wedge \Box\, (r \Rightarrow (r \,\mathsf{U}\, (\neg r) \,\mathsf{U}\, w)) \\ & \wedge \Box\, (w \Rightarrow (w \,\mathsf{U}\, (\neg w) \,\mathsf{U}\, r)) \\ \beta(r, w, x, y) = \quad & \varphi(x, y) \wedge \forall a. \Box\, ((y = a) \Rightarrow ((y = a) \,\mathsf{U}\, (\neg w \wedge (y = a) \,\mathsf{U}\, w))) \\ & \wedge \forall^{\approx} x'. (\Box\, (\neg r \Rightarrow \neg r \,\mathsf{U}\, (x = x')) \Rightarrow \varphi(x', y))\end{aligned}$$

Here, α encodes the strict scheduling constraints on read and write points, while β encodes conditions which assure a correct asynchronous execution over (r, w). The $\forall^{\approx}$ quantification, intuitively, quantifies over all adversarial schedules similar to the current (r, w): it requires φ to hold over all sequences obtained from the current sequence σ by stretching or compressing the segments between read and write points, and choosing different values for x on those segments.

3 Symbolic Asynchronous Synthesis

Pnueli and Rosner's procedure for asynchronous synthesis [32] is as follows: first, a Büchi automaton is built for the kernel formula $\neg\mathcal{K}$. This automaton is then determinized and complemented to form a deterministic word automaton for $\mathcal{K}$, which is then re-interpreted as a tree automaton and tested for non-emptiness. The transformations use standard constructions, except for the interpretation of the $\exists^{\approx}$ operator in the formation of the Büchi automaton for $\neg\mathcal{K}$. For a Büchi automaton A, an automaton for $\exists^{\approx}\mathcal{L}(A)$ is constructed in two steps: first applying a "stretching" transformation on A, followed by a "compressing" transformation. Stretching introduces new automaton states of the form (q, a), for each state q of A and each letter a.

When this general construction is applied to the formula $\neg\mathcal{K}$, the alphabet of the automaton A is formed of all possible valuations of the pair of variables (x, y), which has size *exponential* in the number of interface bits. The stretching step introduces a copy of an automaton state for each letter, which results in an exponential blow-up of the state space of the constructed automaton. As all current tools for synchronous synthesis represent automaton states explicitly[3], the exponential blowup introduced by the stuttering quantification is a significant obstacle to implementation.

In Pnueli-Rosner's construction, the determinization and complementation steps are also complex, utilizing Safra's construction. These steps are simplified by the "Safraless" procedure adopted in current tools for synchronous synthesis.

The other major issue with the Pnueli-Rosner construction is that the kernel formula $\mathcal{K}$ introduces the scheduling variables r, w as input variables. However, the actions of a synthesized program should not rely on the values of these variables. Pnueli-Rosner ensure this by checking satisfiability over "canonical" tree models; it is unclear, however, how to realize this effect using a synchronous synthesis tool as a black box.

We define a new property, $\mathsf{PR}(\varphi)$, that differs from $\mathcal{K}$ but, similarly, is synchronously realizable if, and only if, φ is asynchronously realizable. We then present an automaton construction for $\mathsf{PR}(\varphi)$ that bypasses the general construction for $\exists^{\approx}$, avoiding the exponential blowup and resulting in an automaton with *at most twice* the states of the original. Moreover, this construction refers only to x and y, avoiding the second issue as well. We then show that this construction can be implemented fully symbolically.

3.1 Basic Formulations and Properties

As formulated in Sect. 2, an asynchronous execution of f is determined by the schedule (r, w). For a strict schedule, any infinite sequence representing an asynchronous behavior of f over (r, w) may be partitioned into a sequence of *blocks*, as follows. The start of the i'th block is at the i'th writing point, $w(i)$, and it

[3] With one exception. BoSy's DQBF procedure is fully symbolic but does not work as well as the default QBF procedure [12].

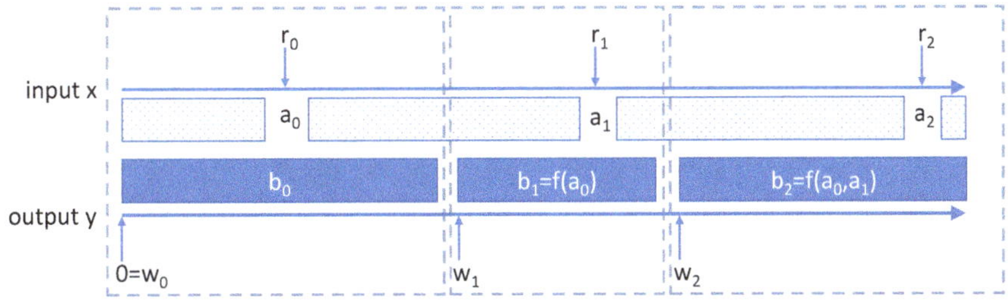

Fig. 1. A strict asynchronous computation for f. Values of x at non-reading points are shown as dotted. The y-value is constant between writing points, illustrated by a solid rectangle. Blocks are shown as dashed rectangles.

ends just before the $i+1$'st writing point, $w(i+1)$. The schedule ensures the i'th block includes the i'th reading point, $r(i)$, associated with the input-output value (x_i, y_i). As the value of y changes only at writing points, y_i is constant in the i'th block. Thus, the i'th block follows the pattern $(\bot, y_i)^*(x_i, y_i)(\bot, y_i)^*$, where $\bot$ denotes an arbitrary choice of x-value. Figure 1 illustrates a strict asynchronous computation and its decomposition into blocks.

Expansions. The set of *expansions* of sequence $\delta = (x_0, y_0)(x_1, y_1)\ldots$ consists of all sequences obtained by simultaneously replacing each (x_i, y_i) in δ by a block with the pattern $(\bot, y_i)^*(x_i, y_i)(\bot, y_i)^*$. Formally, given sequences $\delta = (x_0, y_0)(x_1, y_1)\ldots$ and $\sigma = (\bar{x}_0, \bar{y}_0)(\bar{x}_1, \bar{y}_1)\ldots$, *$\delta$ expands to σ*, denoted as $\delta \,\mathsf{exp}\, \sigma$, if there exists an asynchronous schedule $(\hat{r}, \hat{w})$ for which σ is an execution that is a block pattern of δ, i.e., for all i, $x_i = \bar{x}_{\hat{r}(i)}$ and $y_i = \bar{y}_{\hat{w}(i)}$ and for all j, $\hat{w}(i) \le j < \hat{w}(i+1)$ it is the case that $\bar{y}_j = \bar{y}_{\hat{w}(i)}$. The inverse relation (read as *contracts to*) is denoted by exp^{-1}. Figure 2 shows the synchronous computation that contracts the computation shown in Fig. 1.

Relational Operators. For a relation R, the modal operators $\langle R\rangle$ and $[R]$ are defined as follows. For any set S,

$$u \in \langle R\rangle S = (\exists v : uRv \wedge v \in S) \qquad u \in [R]S = (\forall v : uRv \Rightarrow v \in S)$$

By definition, the operators are negation duals, i.e., $\neg\langle R\rangle(\neg S) = [R](S)$ for any R and any S. For an LTL formula φ and a relation R over infinite sequences, we let $\langle R\rangle\varphi$ abbreviate $\langle R\rangle(\mathcal{L}(\varphi))$, and similarly, let $[R]\varphi$ abbreviate $[R](\mathcal{L}(\varphi))$.

Galois Connections. Given partial orders $(A, \preceq_A)$ and $(B, \preceq_B)$, a pair of functions $g : A \to B$ and $h : B \to A$ form a Galois connection if, for all $a \in A, b \in B$: $g(a) \preceq_B b$ is equivalent to $a \preceq_A h(b)$. From the definitions, it is clear that the operators $(\langle R^{-1}\rangle, [R])$ form a Galois connection over the partial orders defined by the subset relation. I.e., for any sets S and T: $\langle R^{-1}\rangle S \subseteq T$ iff, $S \subseteq [R]T$.

We first establish that the asynchronous executions of f are precisely the synchronous executions of f under an inverse expansion.

Theorem 1. *For an implementation f,* $\mathsf{asynch}(f) = \langle\, \mathsf{exp}^{-1} \rangle \mathsf{synch}(f)$.

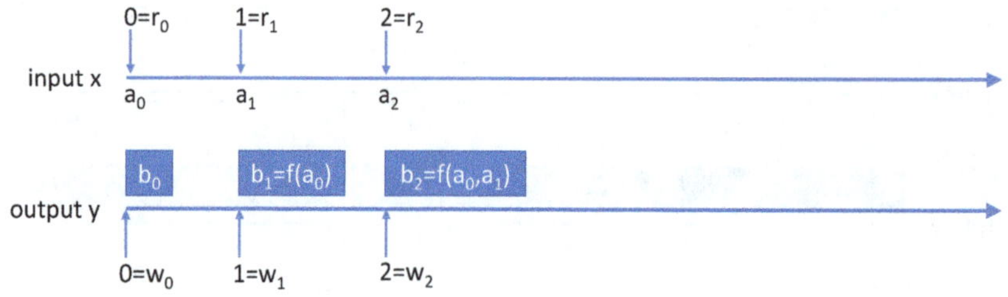

Fig. 2. The contracted synchronous (Moore) computation

Proof. (ping) Let σ be an execution in $\mathsf{asynch}(f)$, generated for some schedule (r, w). For any k, consider the k'th block of σ. This is the set of positions from $w(k)$ to $w(k+1)-1$, which includes the k'th reading point $r(k)$, say with the value (x_k, y_k). Then the block follows the pattern $(\bot, y_k)^*(x_k, y_k)(\bot, y_k)^*$. So σ is an expansion of the sequence $\delta = (x_0, y_0)(x_1, y_1)\ldots$. By the definition of an asynchronous execution, the value $y_{k+1} = f(x_0, \ldots, x_k)$. This is precisely the requirement for δ to be a synchronous execution of f. Hence, we have that there is a δ such that $\delta \,\mathsf{exp}\, \sigma$ and $\delta \in \mathsf{synch}(f)$. Therefore, $\sigma \in \langle\, \mathsf{exp}^{-1} \,\rangle \mathsf{synch}(f)$.

(pong) Let σ be in $\langle\, \mathsf{exp}^{-1} \,\rangle \mathsf{synch}(f)$. By definition, there is a $\mathsf{synch}(f)$ execution $\delta = (x_0, y_0)(x_1, y_1)\ldots$ such that $\delta \,\mathsf{exp}\, \sigma$. As δ is a synchronous execution of f, the value $y_{k+1} = f(x_0, x_1, \ldots, x_k)$, for all k. Then σ is an asynchronous execution of f under the schedule where the k-th reading point is the point that the k'th entry, (x_k, y_k), from δ is mapped to in σ, and the $(k+1)$-th writing point is the first point of the $(k+1)$'st block in the expansion. □

We now use the Galois connection to show how asynchronous synthesis can be reduced to an equivalent synchronous synthesis task. Consider a property φ that must hold asynchronously for an implementation f.

Theorem 2. *Let f be an implementation function, and φ a property. Then* $\mathsf{asynch}(f) \subseteq \mathcal{L}(\varphi)$ *if, and only if,* $\mathsf{synch}(f) \subseteq [\, \mathsf{exp} \,]\varphi$.

Proof. From Theorem 1, $\mathsf{asynch}(f) \subseteq \mathcal{L}(\varphi)$ holds iff $\langle\, \mathsf{exp}^{-1} \,\rangle \mathsf{synch}(f) \subseteq \mathcal{L}(\varphi)$ does. By the Galois connection, this is equivalent to $\mathsf{synch}(f) \subseteq [\, \mathsf{exp} \,]\varphi$. □

3.2 The Pnueli-Rosner Closure

We refer to the property $[\, \mathsf{exp} \,]\varphi$ as the Pnueli-Rosner closure of φ, in honor of their pioneering work on this problem, and denote it by $\mathsf{PR}(\varphi)$. This has interesting mathematical properties, which are useful in practice.

Theorem 3. $\mathsf{PR}(\varphi) = [\, \mathsf{exp} \,]\varphi$ *has the following properties.*

1. *(Closure)* PR *is monotonic and a downward closure, i.e.,* $\mathsf{PR}(\varphi) \subseteq \mathcal{L}(\varphi)$
2. *(Conjunctivity)* PR *is conjunctive, i.e.,* $\mathsf{PR}(\bigwedge_i \varphi_i) = \bigcap_i \mathsf{PR}(\varphi_i)$
3. *(Safety Preservation) If φ is a safety property, so is* $\mathsf{PR}(\varphi)$

The closure property relies on the reflexivity and transitivity of exp, and that $[R]$ is monotonic for every R. Conjunctivity follows from the conjunctivity of $[R]$ for any R. Safety preservation is based on the Alpern-Schneider [4] formulation of safety over infinite words. Proofs are in the full version of the paper.

Conjunctivity is exploited by the tools Acacia+ [8] and Unbeast [11] to optimize the synchronous synthesis procedure. The Unbeast tool also separates out safety from non-safety sub-properties to optimize the synthesis procedure. Thus, if a specification φ has the form $\varphi_1 \wedge \varphi_2$, where φ_1 is a safety property, then $\mathsf{PR}(\varphi) = \mathsf{PR}(\varphi_1) \cap \mathsf{PR}(\varphi_2)$ also denotes the intersection of the safety property $\mathsf{PR}(\varphi_1)$ with another property.

3.3 The Closure Automaton Construction

By negation duality, $\mathsf{PR}(\varphi)$ equals $\neg\langle\,\mathsf{exp}\,\rangle(\neg\varphi)$. We use this property to reduce asynchronous to synchronous synthesis, as follows.

1. Construct a non-deterministic Büchi automaton A for $\neg\varphi$,
2. Transform A to a non-deterministic Büchi automaton B for the negated Pnueli-Rosner closure of φ, i.e., the language of B is $\langle\,\mathsf{exp}\,\rangle\mathcal{L}(A) = \langle\,\mathsf{exp}\,\rangle(\neg\varphi)$,
3. Consider the structure of B as that of a *universal* co-Büchi automaton, which has language $\neg\mathcal{L}(B)$,
4. Synthesize an implementation f in the synchronous model which satisfies $\neg\mathcal{L}(B) = \neg\langle\,\mathsf{exp}\,\rangle\mathcal{L}(A) = \neg\langle\,\mathsf{exp}\,\rangle(\neg\varphi) = [\,\mathsf{exp}\,]\varphi = \mathsf{PR}(\varphi)$.

The new step is the second one, which constructs B from A; the others use standard constructions and tools. This construction is as follows.

- The states and alphabet of B are the states and alphabet of A.
- The transitions of B are determined by a saturation procedure. For every pair of states q, q', and letter (x, y), let $\Pi(q,(x,y),q')$ be the set of paths in A from q to q' where the sequence of letters on the path matches the expansion pattern $(\bot,y)^*(x,y)(\bot,y)^*$. The transition $(q,(x,y),q')$ is in B if, and only if, this set is non-empty,
- If some path in $\Pi(q,(x,y),q')$ passes through a green (accepting) state of A, the transition $(q,(x,y),q')$ in B is colored "green" and that path is assigned as the witness to the transition in B. On the other hand, if none of the paths in $\Pi(q,(x,y),q')$ pass through a green state, this transition is not colored in B, and one of the paths in the set is chosen as the witness for this transition,
- The automaton B inherits the accepting ("green") states of A and it may have, in addition, green transitions introduced as defined above,
- A sequence is accepted by B if there is a run of B on the sequence such that either there are infinitely many green states, or infinitely many green transitions on that run.

We establish that $\mathcal{L}(B) = \langle\,\mathsf{exp}\,\rangle\mathcal{L}(A)$ through the following two lemmas.

Lemma 1. $\langle\,\mathsf{exp}\,\rangle\mathcal{L}(A) \subseteq \mathcal{L}(B)$.

Proof. Let $\delta = (x_0, y_0)(x_1, y_1)\ldots$ be a sequence in $\langle\,\mathsf{exp}\,\rangle\mathcal{L}(A)$. By definition, there exists a sequence σ in $\mathcal{L}(A)$ such that $\delta\,\mathsf{exp}\,\sigma$. The expansion σ follows the pattern $[(\bot, y_0)^*(x_0, y_0)(\bot, y_0)^*][(\bot, y_1)^*(x_1, y_1)(\bot, y_1)^*]\ldots$, where $[\ldots]$ are used merely to indicate the boundaries of a block. An accepting run of A on σ has the form $q_0[(\bot, y_0)^*(x_0, y_0)(\bot, y_0)^*]q_1[(\bot, y_1)^*(x_1, y_1)(\bot, y_1)^*]q_2\ldots$, where the states on the run inside a block have been elided. By the definition of B, the segment $q_0(\bot, y_0)^*(x_0, y_0)(\bot, y_0)^*q_1$ induces a transition from q_0 to q_1 in B on the letter (x_0, y_0). Similarly, the following segment induces a transition from q_1 to q_2 on letter (x_1, y_1), and so forth. These transitions together form a run $q_0(x_0, y_0)q_1(x_1, y_1)q_2\ldots$ of B on δ.

If one of the $\{q_i\}$ is green and appears infinitely often on the run on σ, the induced run on δ is accepting. Otherwise, as the run on σ is accepting, some green state of A occurs in the interior of infinitely many segments of that run. The transitions of B induced by those segments must be green, so the corresponding run on δ has infinitely many green edges, and is accepting for B. □

Lemma 2. $\mathcal{L}(B) \subseteq \langle\,\mathsf{exp}\,\rangle\mathcal{L}(A)$.

Proof. Let δ be accepted by B. We show that there is σ such that $\delta\,\mathsf{exp}\,\sigma$ and σ is accepted by A. Let δ have the form $(x_0, y_0)(x_1, y_1)\ldots$,. Denote the accepting run of B on δ by $r = q_0(x_0, y_0)q_1(x_1, y_1)\ldots$. From the construction of B, the transition from q_0 to q_1 on (x_0, y_0) has an associated witness path through A from q_0 to q_1, which follows the expansion pattern $(\bot, y_0)^*(x_0, y_0)(\bot, y_0)^*$ on its edge labels. Stitching together the witness paths for each transition of r, we obtain both a sequence σ that is an expansion of δ and a run r' of A on σ.

As r is accepting for B, it must enter infinitely often either a green state or a green edge. If it enters a green state infinitely often, that state appears infinitely often on r'. If r enters a green edge infinitely often, the witness path for that edge contains a green state of A, say q; as this path is repeated infinitely often on σ, q appears infinitely often on r'. In either case, a green state of A appears infinitely often on r', which is therefore, an accepting run of A on σ. □

Automaton B can be placed in standard form by converting its green edges to green states as follows, forming a new automaton, $\hat{B}$. Form a green copy of the state space, i.e., for each state q, form a green variant, $G(q)$, which is marked as an accepting state. Set up transitions as follows. If (q, a, q') is an original non-green transition, then (q, a, q') and $(G(q), a, q')$ are new transitions. If (q, a, q') is an original green transition, then $(q, a, G(q'))$ and $(G(q), a, G(q'))$ are new transitions. This at most doubles the size of the automaton. It is straightforward to establish that $\mathcal{L}(B) = \mathcal{L}(\hat{B})$.

3.4 Symbolic Construction

The symbolic construction of $\hat{B}$ closely follows the definitions above. It is easily implemented with BDDs representing predicates on the input and output variables x and y. The crucial step is to use fixpoints to formulate the existence of paths in the set Π used in the definition of B. These definitions are similar to the fixpoint definition of the CTL modality EF. We use $A(q,(x,y),q')$ to denote the predicate on (x,y) describing the transition from q to q' in automaton A.

Fixed Don't-Care Path. Let $\mathsf{EfixedY}(q,y,q')$ hold if there is a path of length 0 or more from q to q' in A where the value of y is fixed. This is the least fixpoint (in Z) of the following implications:

- $(q' = q) \Rightarrow Z(q,y,q')$, and
- $(\exists x, r : A(q,(x,y),r) \wedge Z(r,y,q')) \Rightarrow Z(q,y,q')$

The predicate $A^{\perp}(q,y,r) = (\exists x : A(q,(x,y),r))$ is pre-computed. Then, the least fixpoint is computed iteratively as follows.

$$\mathsf{EfixedY}^0(q,y,q') = (q = q')$$
$$\mathsf{EfixedY}^{i+1}(q,y,q') = \mathsf{EfixedY}^i(q,y,q') \vee (\exists r : A^{\perp}(q,y,r) \wedge \mathsf{EfixedY}^i(r,y,q'))$$

Let predicate $\mathsf{green}_A(r)$ be true for an accepting state r of A. The predicate $\mathsf{Efixedgreen}(q,y,q')$ holds if there is a fixed y-path from q to q' where one of the states on it is green:

$$\mathsf{Efixedgreen}(q,y,q') = (\exists r : \mathsf{EfixedY}(q,y,r) \wedge \mathsf{green}_A(r) \wedge \mathsf{EfixedY}(r,y,q'))$$

Paths and Green Paths. Let $\mathsf{Epath}(q,(x,y),q')$ hold if there is a path following the block pattern $(\perp,y)^*(x,y)(\perp,y)^*$ from q to q' in A. Then,

$$\mathsf{Epath}(q,(x,y),q') = (\exists r, r' : \mathsf{EfixedY}(q,y,r) \wedge A(r,(x,y),r') \wedge \mathsf{EfixedY}(r',y,q'))$$

Similarly, let $\mathsf{Egreenpath}(q,(x,y),q')$ hold if there is a path following the block pattern $(\perp,y)^*(x,y)(\perp,y)^*$ from q to q' in A, with an intermediate green state.

$$\begin{aligned}\mathsf{Egreenpath}(q,(x,y),q') = \\ &(\exists r, r' : \mathsf{Efixedgreen}(q,y,r) \wedge A(r,(x,y),r') \wedge \mathsf{EfixedY}(r',y,q')) \vee \\ &(\exists r, r' : \mathsf{EfixedY}(q,y,r) \wedge A(r,(x,y),r') \wedge \mathsf{Efixedgreen}(r',y,q'))\end{aligned}$$

State Space of $\hat{B}$. The state space of $\hat{B}$ is formed by pairs (q,g), where q is a state of A and g is a Boolean indicating whether it is a new green state. The accepting condition $\mathsf{green}_{\hat{B}}(q,g)$ of $\hat{B}$ is given by $\mathsf{green}_A(q) \vee g$.

Initial States. The initial predicate $I_{\hat{B}}(q,g)$ is $I_A(q) \wedge \neg g$, where $I_A(q)$ is true for initial states of the input automata A.

Transition Relation of $\hat{B}$. The transition relation $\hat{B}((q,g),(x,y),(q',g'))$ is

$$\hat{B}((q,g),(x,y),(q',g')) = \mathsf{Epath}(q,(x,y),q') \wedge (g' \equiv \mathsf{Egreenpath}(q,(x,y),q'))$$

4 Implementation and Experiments

The PR algorithm has been implemented in a framework called BAS (Bounded Asynchronous Synthesis). It uses the LTL-to-automaton converter LTL3BA [3, 6], and follows the modular method, connecting to either of two solvers, BoSy [2, 12] and Acacia+ [1,8] to solve the synchronous realizability of $\mathsf{PR}(\varphi)$. The PR construction is implemented in about 1200 lines of OCaml, using an external BDD library. (The core construction requires only about 400 lines of code.) For an LTL specification φ, the BAS workflow for asynchronous synthesis is as follows:

1. Check whether φ is synchronously realizable; if not, return `UNREALIZABLE`,
2. Construct Büchi automata A for $\neg\varphi$, and $\hat{A}$ for φ,
3. Concurrently
   (a) Construct $\mathsf{PR}(\varphi)$ from A and check whether it is synchronously realizable; if so, return `REALIZABLE` and synthesize the implementation.
   (b) Construct $\mathsf{PR}(\neg\varphi)$ from $\hat{A}$ and check whether it is synchronously realizable for the environment; if so, return `UNREALIZABLE`.

   Upon termination of any, terminate the other execution as well.

The synchronous synthesis tools successively increase a bound until a limit (computed based on automaton structure) is reached. Thus, in theory, only the check in step 3(a) is needed. However, the checks in steps 1 and 3(b) may allow the tool to terminate early (before reaching the limit bound), if a winning strategy for the environment can be discovered.

To evaluate BAS we consider the list of examples presented in Table 1. The reported experiments were performed on a VM configured to have 8 CPU cores at 2.4 GHz, 8 GB RAM, running 64-bit Linux. The running times are reported in milliseconds. For each specification (presented in the second column) we report whether it is asynchronously realizable (third column), the time for the PR construction (our contribution), and the time for checking whether the specification is realizable using BoSy and Acacia+ solvers (resp., fifth and sixth columns).

The first set of examples (Specifications 1–11) list specifications discussed in this paper and in related works. As parameterized example we consider 2 variants of arbiter specifications. The arbiter has n inputs in which clients request permissions, and n outputs in which the clients are granted permissions. In both variants of the arbiter example, no two grants are allowed to be set simultaneously. The first arbiter example (Specification 12) requires that whenever an input request r_i is set, the corresponding output grant g_i must eventually be set. The second variant (Specification 13) also requires that a grant g_i is set only if request r_i is set as well. That is, in order for a client to be granted a permission, its corresponding request must be constantly set. Since the asynchronous case cannot observe the request in between read events, this variant of the arbiter is not realizable. The results are shown for $n = 2, 4, 6$. Note that the only comparable experimental evaluation is given in [18], where they report that asynchronous synthesis of the first arbiter example (Specification 12) takes over 8 h.

Table 1. BAS asynchronous synthesis runtime evaluation (times in milliseconds). We let BoSy run upto 2 h, and Acacia+ upto 1000 iterations. "Na" denotes cases where the executions did not find a winning strategy within these boundaries.

	Specification	Asyn. Realizable?	PR constr.	Asyn. synthesis BoSy	Asyn. synthesis Acacia+
1	$\square\,(x \equiv y)$	False	8	972	30
2	$\lozenge\square x \equiv \lozenge\square y$	False	9	Na	Na
3	$\lozenge\square x \Rightarrow \lozenge\square y$	True	8	899	Na
4	$\lozenge\square y \Rightarrow \lozenge\square x$	True	7	994	Na
5	$(\lozenge\square x \vee \lozenge\square\neg x) \Rightarrow \lozenge\square x \equiv \lozenge\square y$	True	13	1004	Na
6	$\square\,(\neg x \Rightarrow (\neg x)\ \mathsf{U}\ (\neg y)) \Rightarrow \lozenge\square x \equiv \lozenge\square y$	True	10	Na	Na
7	$\square\lozenge\,(x \wedge y) \Rightarrow (\square\lozenge y \wedge \square\lozenge\neg y)$	True	9	1053	30
8	$\square\lozenge\,(x \vee y) \Rightarrow (\square\lozenge y \wedge \square\lozenge\neg y)$	True	9	995	40
9	$\square\lozenge\,(x) \Rightarrow (\square\lozenge y \wedge \square\lozenge\neg y)$	True	8	934	30
10	$\square\,(x \Rightarrow \lozenge y)$	True	8	960	30
11	$\square\,(x \Rightarrow \lozenge y) \wedge \square\,(\neg y\,\mathsf{U}\,x)$	False	10	1058	Na
Variants of parameterized arbiter (results shown are for $n = 2; 4; 6$)					
12	$\bigwedge_{i \neq j} \square\,(\neg g_i \vee \neg g_j) \quad \wedge$ $\bigwedge_{i=1}^{n} \square\,(r_i \Rightarrow \lozenge g_i)$	True	11; 13; 75	854; 1146; 4965	Na; Na; Na
13	$\bigwedge_{i \neq j} \square\,(\neg g_i \vee \neg g_j) \quad \wedge$ $\bigwedge_{i=1}^{n} \square\,(r_i \Rightarrow \lozenge g_i) \wedge \bigwedge_{i=1}^{n} \square\,(g_i \Rightarrow r_i)$	False	17; 3124; 2024K	1129; 362K; Na	Na; Na; Na

The second specification φ is the one discussed in Sect. 2. It is surprisingly difficult to solve. Both φ and its negation are asynchronously unrealizable. Moreover, φ is synchronously realizable. Thus, the early detection tests (steps 1 and 3(b)) failed to discover a winning strategy for the environment; the bounded synthesis tools increase the considered bound monotonically without converging to an answer in a reasonable amount of time. This example highlights the need for better tests for unrealizability. The results in the following section provide simple QBF tests of unrealizability for subclasses of LTL.

5 Efficiently Solvable Subclasses of LTL

The high complexity of direct LTL (synchronous) synthesis has encouraged the search for general procedures that work well in practice, such as Safraless and bounded synthesis [24,35]. Another useful direction has been to identify fragments of LTL with efficient synthesis algorithms [5]. Among the most noteworthy is the GR(1) subclass, for which there is an efficient, symbolic synthesis procedure ([28]). We explore this direction for *asynchronous* synthesis. Surprisingly, we show that synthesis for certain fragments of LTL can be reduced to

Boolean reasoning over properties in QBF. The results cover several types of GR(1) formulae, although the question of a reduction for all of GR(1) is open.

The QBF formulae that arise have the form $\exists y \forall x . p(x, y)$, where x and y are disjoint sets of variables, and p is a propositional formula over x, y. An assignment $y = b$ for which $\forall x . p(x, b)$ holds is called a *witness* to the formula. The first such reduction is for the property $\Box \Diamond P$.

Theorem 4. *$\varphi = \Box \Diamond P$ is asynchronously realizable iff $\exists y \forall x P$ is* True.

Proof. (ping) Let b be a witness to $\exists y \forall x . P$. The function that constantly outputs $y = b$ satisfies φ for any asynchronous schedule.

(pong) Let f be a candidate implementation function and suppose that $\forall y \exists x (\neg P)$ holds. Fix any schedule. For every value $y = b$ that function f outputs at a writing point, there exists an input value $x = a$ such that $\neg P(a, b)$ holds. Thus, the environment, by issuing $x = a$ in the interval from the current writing point (with $y = b$) up to the next one, can ensure that $\neg P$ holds throughout the execution. Thus the specification $\varphi = \Box \Diamond P$ does not hold on this execution. □

The result in Theorem 4 applies to asynchronous synthesis, but does not apply to synchronous synthesis. For example, the property $\Box \Diamond (x \equiv y)$ is asynchronously unrealizable, as $\exists y \forall x (x \equiv y)$ is False. On the other hand, it is synchronously realizable with a Mealy machine that sets y to x at each point.

Theorem 4 extends easily to conjunction and disjunction of $\Box \Diamond$ properties.

Theorem 5. *Specification $\varphi = \bigvee_{i=0}^{m} \Box \Diamond P_i$ is asynchronously realizable iff $\exists y \forall x . (\bigvee_{i=0}^{m} P_i)$ holds. Additionally, specification $\varphi = \bigwedge_{i=0}^{m} \Box \Diamond P_i$ is asynchronously realizable iff for all $i \in \{0, 1 \ldots m\}$, $\exists y \forall x . P_i$ holds.*

Proof. The first claim follows directly from the identity $\bigvee_{i=0}^{m} \Box \Diamond P_i \equiv \Box \Diamond (\bigvee_{i=0}^{m} P_i)$ and Theorem 4.

For the second, for each i, let $y = b_i$ be an assignment such that $\forall x . P_i(x, b_i)$ holds. The function that generates sequence $b_0, b_1, \ldots b_m$, ad infinitum, is an asynchronous implementation of $\bigwedge_{i=0}^{m} \Box \Diamond P_i$. On the other hand, suppose that for some i, $\forall y \exists x \neg P_i$ holds, then following the construction from Theorem 4, one can define an execution where P_i is always False. □

Theorem 6. *$\varphi = \Diamond \Box P$ is asynchronously realizable iff $\exists y \forall x . P$ is* True.

The proof is similar to that for Theorem 4. Theorem 6 also extends to conjunctions and disjunctions of $\Diamond \Box$ properties, by arguments similar to those for Theorem 5. Namely, $\bigwedge_{i=0}^{m} \Diamond \Box P_i$ is asynchronously realizable iff $\exists y \forall x (\bigwedge_{i=0}^{m} P_i)$ is True, and, $\bigvee_{i=0}^{m} \Diamond \Box P_i$ is asynchronously realizable iff for some $i \in \{0, 1, \ldots m\}$, $\exists y \forall x . P_i$ is True. Theorems 4–6 apply to non-atomic reads and writes of multiple input and output variables. Proofs are in the full version of the paper.

We now consider a more general type of GR(1) formula. The *strict semantic* of GR(1) formula $\Box S_e \wedge \Box \Diamond P \Rightarrow \Box S_s \wedge \Box \Diamond Q$ is defined to be $\Box(\boxminus S_e \Rightarrow S_s) \wedge (\Box S_e \wedge \Box \Diamond P \Rightarrow \Box \Diamond Q)$ – i.e., S_s is required to hold so long as S_e has always held in the past; and if S_e holds always and P holds infinitely often, then Q holds infinitely often. This is the interpretation supported by GR(1) synchronous synthesis tools.

Theorem 7. *The strict semantics of GR(1) specification* $\square S_e \wedge \square \lozenge P \Rightarrow \square S_s \wedge \square \lozenge Q$ *is asynchronously realizable iff* $\exists y \forall x.(S_e \Rightarrow (S_s \wedge (P \Rightarrow Q)))$ *is* True.

Proof. (ping) If $y = b$ is a witness to $\exists y \forall x.(S_e \Rightarrow (S_s \wedge (P \Rightarrow Q)))$, let f be a function that always generates b. Suppose S_e holds up to point i, then as $y = b$, regardless of the x-value, S_s holds at point i. This shows that the first part of the specification holds. For the second, suppose that S_e holds always and P is true infinitely often. Then, by choice of $y = b$, $(P \Rightarrow Q)$ holds always, thus Q holds infinitely often as well.

(pong) To prove the other side of the implication, we proceed as in Theorem 4. Let f be a candidate implementation. Fix a schedule, and suppose that $\forall y \exists x.(S_e \wedge (\neg S_s \vee \neg(P \Rightarrow Q)))$ holds. Then for every step of the execution and for every value $y = b$ that function f outputs at a writing point, there exists a value $x = a$ which the environment can choose from that writing point to the next such that $S_e(a, b)$ is true, and one of $S_s(a, b)$ or $(P \Rightarrow Q)(a, b)$ is false at every point in that interval.

On this execution, S_e holds throughout. If S_s is false at some point, this violates the first part of the specification. If not, then $(P \Rightarrow Q)$ must be false everywhere; i.e., at every point P is true but Q is false. Thus, S_e holds everywhere and P holds infinitely often but Q does not hold infinitely often, violating the second part of the specification. □

Theorem 7 applies to atomic reads and writes, showing that asynchronous synthesis of GR(1) specification can be reduced to Boolean reasoning over properties in QBF. For non-atomic reads and writes, safety in asynchronous systems is more nuanced, since there is a delay between the write points of the first and last outputs in each round. This is discussed in the full version of the paper. This proof strategy does not generalize easily to the full GR(1) format, where more than one $\square \lozenge$ property can appear on either side of the implication.

These results establish that the asynchronous synthesis problem for such specifications is easily solvable–more easily than in the synchronous setting, surprisingly avoiding entirely the need for automaton constructions and bounded synthesis. From another, equally valuable, point of view, the results show that such types of specifications may be of limited interest for automated synthesis, as solvable cases have very simple solutions.

6 Conclusions and Related Work

This work tackles the task of asynchronous synthesis from temporal specifications. The main results are a new symbolic automaton construction for general temporal properties, and the reduction of the synthesis question for several classes of specifications to QBF. These are mathematically interesting, being substantial simplifications of prior methods. Moreover, they make it feasible to implement an asynchronous synthesis tool following the modular process suggested by Pnueli and Rosner in 1989, by reducing asynchronous synthesis to a synchronous synthesis question. To the best of our knowledge, this is the first such tool. The prototype, which builds on tools for synchronous synthesis, is able to quickly synthesize asynchronous programs for several interesting properties. There are, undoubtedly, several challenges, one of which is the quick detection of unrealizable specifications.

Our work builds upon several earlier results, which we discuss here. The synthesis question for temporal properties originates from a question posed by Church in the 1950s (see [37]). The problem of synthesizing a synchronous reactive system from a linear temporal specification was formulated and studied by Pnueli and Rosner [31], who gave a solution based on non-emptiness of tree automata. There has been much progress on the synchronous synthesis question since. Key developments include the discovery of efficient symbolic (BDD-based) solutions for the GR(1) class [7,28], the invention of "Safraless" procedures [24], the application of these ideas for bounded synthesis [15,35], and their implementation in a number of tools, e.g. [8,10,11,13,20,34]. These have been applied in many settings (cf. [9,23,25–27]).

The problem of synthesizing asynchronous programs was also formulated and studied by Pnueli and Rosner [32] but has proved to be much more challenging, with only limited progress. The original Pnueli-Rosner constructions are complex and were not implemented. Work by Klein, Piterman and Pnueli, nearly 20 years later [22], shows tractability for some GR(1) specifications. However, the class of specifications that can be so handled is characterized by semantic constraints such as stuttering-closure and memoryless-ness, which are difficult to recognize.

Finkbeiner and Schewe [18,35] present an alternative method, based on bounded synthesis, that applies to all LTL properties: it encodes the existence of a deductive proof for a bounded program into SAT/SMT constraints. However, the encoding represents inputs and outputs explicitly and is, therefore, exponential in the number of input and output bits. The exponential blowup has practical consequences: an asynchronous arbiter specification requires over 8 h to synthesize [18]; the same specification can be synthesized by our method in seconds. (Note, however, that the method in [18] is not specialized to asynchronous synthesis, and this difference may not be solely due to the explicit state representation, as the specification has only 4 bits.) Recent work gives an alternative encoding of synchronous bounded synthesis into QBF constraints, retaining input and output bits in symbolic form [12]. We believe that a similar encoding applies to asynchronous bounded synthesis as well, this is a topic for future work.

Pnueli and Rosner's model of interface communication is not the only choice. Other models for asynchrony could, for instance, be based on CCS/CSP-style rendezvous communication at the interface, or permit shared read-write variables with atomic lock/unlock actions. Petri net game models have also been suggested for distributed synthesis [16]. An orthogonal direction is to weaken the adversarial power of the environment through a probabilistic model which can be used to constrain unlikely, highly adversarial input patterns to have probability 0, thus turning the synthesis problem into one where programs satisfy their specifications with high probability. (The synthesis of multiple processes is known to be undecidable in most cases [17,33].)

In the broader context of fully automatic program synthesis, there are various approaches to the synthesis of single-threaded, terminating programs from formal pre- and post-condition specifications and from examples, using type information and other techniques to prune the search space. (We will not attempt to survey this large field, some examples are [14,19,36].) An intriguing question is to investigate how the techniques developed in these distinct lines of work can be fruitfully combined to aid the development of asynchronous, reactive software.

Acknowledgements. Kedar Namjoshi was supported, in part, by NSF grant CCF-1563393 from the National Science Foundation. We would like to thank Michael Emmi for many helpful discussions during the early stages of this work.

References

1. Acacia+. http://lit2.ulb.ac.be/acaciaplus//
2. BoSy. https://www.react.uni-saarland.de/tools/bosy/
3. LTL3BA. https://sourceforge.net/projects/ltl3ba/
4. Alpern, B., Schneider, F.B.: Defining liveness. Inf. Process. Lett. **21**(4), 181–185 (1985)
5. Alur, R., La Torre, S.: Deterministic generators and games for LTL fragments. ACM Trans. Comput. Log. **5**(1), 1–25 (2004)
6. Babiak, T., Křetínský, M., Řehák, V., Strejček, J.: LTL to Büchi automata translation: fast and more deterministic. In: Flanagan, C., König, B. (eds.) TACAS 2012. LNCS, vol. 7214, pp. 95–109. Springer, Heidelberg (2012). https://doi.org/10.1007/978-3-642-28756-5_8
7. Bloem, R., Jobstmann, B., Piterman, N., Pnueli, A., Sa'ar, Y.: Synthesis of reactive (1) designs. J. Comput. Syst. Sci. **78**(3), 911–938 (2012)
8. Bohy, A., Bruyère, V., Filiot, E., Jin, N., Raskin, J.-F.: Acacia+, a tool for LTL synthesis. In: Madhusudan, P., Seshia, S.A. (eds.) CAV 2012. LNCS, vol. 7358, pp. 652–657. Springer, Heidelberg (2012). https://doi.org/10.1007/978-3-642-31424-7_45
9. D'Ippolito, N., Braberman, V., Piterman, N., Uchitel, S.: Synthesizing nonanomalous event-based controllers for liveness goals. Trans. Softw. Eng. Methodol. **22**(1), 9 (2013)
10. Ehlers, R.: Symbolic bounded synthesis. In: Touili, T., Cook, B., Jackson, P. (eds.) CAV 2010. LNCS, vol. 6174, pp. 365–379. Springer, Heidelberg (2010). https://doi.org/10.1007/978-3-642-14295-6_33
11. Ehlers, R.: Unbeast: symbolic bounded synthesis. In: Abdulla, P.A., Leino, K.R.M. (eds.) TACAS 2011. LNCS, vol. 6605, pp. 272–275. Springer, Heidelberg (2011). https://doi.org/10.1007/978-3-642-19835-9_25
12. Faymonville, P., Finkbeiner, B., Rabe, M.N., Tentrup, L.: Encodings of bounded synthesis. In: Legay, A., Margaria, T. (eds.) TACAS 2017. LNCS, vol. 10205, pp. 354–370. Springer, Heidelberg (2017). https://doi.org/10.1007/978-3-662-54577-5_20
13. Faymonville, P., Finkbeiner, B., Tentrup, L.: BoSy: an experimentation framework for bounded synthesis. In: Majumdar, R., Kunčak, V. (eds.) CAV 2017. LNCS, vol. 10427, pp. 325–332. Springer, Cham (2017). https://doi.org/10.1007/978-3-319-63390-9_17

14. Feng, Y., Martins, R., Wang, Y., Dillig, I., Reps, T.W.: Component-based synthesis for complex APIs. In: Castagna, G., Gordon, A.D. (eds.) Proceedings of the 44th ACM SIGPLAN Symposium on Principles of Programming Languages, POPL 2017, Paris, France, 18–20 January 2017, pp. 599–612. ACM (2017)
15. Filiot, E., Jin, N., Raskin, J.-F.: Compositional algorithms for LTL synthesis. In: Bouajjani, A., Chin, W.-N. (eds.) ATVA 2010. LNCS, vol. 6252, pp. 112–127. Springer, Heidelberg (2010). https://doi.org/10.1007/978-3-642-15643-4_10
16. Finkbeiner, B., Olderog, E.-R.: Petri games: synthesis of distributed systems with causal memory. Inf. Comput. **253**, 181–203 (2017)
17. Finkbeiner, B., Schewe, S.: Uniform distributed synthesis. In: 20th IEEE Symposium on Logic in Computer Science (LICS 2005), 26–29 June 2005, Chicago, IL, USA, Proceedings, pp. 321–330. IEEE Computer Society (2005)
18. Finkbeiner, B., Schewe, S.: Bounded synthesis. STTT **15**(5–6), 519–539 (2013)
19. Frankle, J., Osera, P.M., Walker, D., Zdancewic, S.: Example-directed synthesis: a type-theoretic interpretation. In: Bodík, R., Majumdar, R. (eds.) Proceedings of the 43rd Annual ACM SIGPLAN-SIGACT Symposium on Principles of Programming Languages, POPL 2016, St. Petersburg, FL, USA, 20–22 January 2016, pp. 802–815. ACM (2016)
20. Jobstmann, B., Bloem, R.: Optimizations for LTL synthesis. In: 6th International Conference on Formal Methods in Computer-Aided Design, FMCAD 2006, San Jose, California, USA, 12–16 November 2006, Proceedings, pp. 117–124. IEEE Computer Society (2006)
21. Klein, U.: Topics in Formal Synthesis and Modeling. Ph.D. thesis, New York University (2011)
22. Klein, U., Piterman, N., Pnueli, A.: Effective synthesis of asynchronous systems from GR(1) specifications. In: Kuncak, V., Rybalchenko, A. (eds.) VMCAI 2012. LNCS, vol. 7148, pp. 283–298. Springer, Heidelberg (2012). https://doi.org/10.1007/978-3-642-27940-9_19
23. Kress-Gazit, H., Pappas, G.J.: Automatic synthesis of robot controllers for tasks with locative prepositions. In: International Conference on Robotics and Automation (ICRA), pp. 3215–3220 (2010)
24. Kupferman, O., Vardi, M.Y.: Safraless decision procedures. In: Proceedings of FOCS, pp. 531–540. IEEE (2005)
25. Liu, J., Ozay, N., Topcu, U., Murray, R.M.: Synthesis of reactive switching protocols from temporal logic specifications. IEEE Trans. Autom. Control **58**(7), 1771–1785 (2013)
26. Maoz, S., Sa'ar, Y.: AspectLTL: an aspect language for LTL specifications. In: Borba, P., Chiba, S. (eds.) Proceedings of the 10th International Conference on Aspect-Oriented Software Development, AOSD 2011, Porto de Galinhas, Brazil, 21–25 March 2011, pp. 19–30. ACM (2011)
27. Maoz, S., Sa'ar, Y.: Assume-guarantee scenarios: semantics and synthesis. In: France, R.B., Kazmeier, J., Breu, R., Atkinson, C. (eds.) MODELS 2012. LNCS, vol. 7590, pp. 335–351. Springer, Heidelberg (2012). https://doi.org/10.1007/978-3-642-33666-9_22
28. Piterman, N., Pnueli, A., Sa'ar, Y.: Synthesis of reactive(1) designs. In: Emerson, E.A., Namjoshi, K.S. (eds.) VMCAI 2006. LNCS, vol. 3855, pp. 364–380. Springer, Heidelberg (2005). https://doi.org/10.1007/11609773_24
29. Pnueli, A.: The temporal logic of programs. In: Proceedings of FOCS, pp. 46–57. IEEE (1977)

30. Pnueli, A., Klein, U.: Synthesis of programs from temporal property specifications. In: 2009 7th IEEE/ACM International Conference on Formal Methods and Models for Co-Design, MEMOCODE 2009, pp. 1–7. IEEE (2009)
31. Pnueli, A., Rosner, R.: On the synthesis of a reactive module. In: POPL, pp. 179–190 (1989)
32. Pnueli, A., Rosner, R.: On the synthesis of an asynchronous reactive module. In: Ausiello, G., Dezani-Ciancaglini, M., Della Rocca, S.R. (eds.) ICALP 1989. LNCS, vol. 372, pp. 652–671. Springer, Heidelberg (1989). https://doi.org/10.1007/BFb0035790
33. Pneuli, A., Rosner, R.: Distributed reactive systems are hard to synthesize. In: 31st Annual Symposium on Foundations of Computer Science, St. Louis, Missouri, USA, 22–24 October 1990, vol. II, pp. 746–757. IEEE Computer Society (1990)
34. Pnueli, A., Sa'ar, Y., Zuck, L.D.: JTLV: a framework for developing verification algorithms. In: Touili, T., Cook, B., Jackson, P. (eds.) CAV 2010. LNCS, vol. 6174, pp. 171–174. Springer, Heidelberg (2010). https://doi.org/10.1007/978-3-642-14295-6_18
35. Schewe, S., Finkbeiner, B.: Bounded synthesis. In: Namjoshi, K.S., Yoneda, T., Higashino, T., Okamura, Y. (eds.) ATVA 2007. LNCS, vol. 4762, pp. 474–488. Springer, Heidelberg (2007). https://doi.org/10.1007/978-3-540-75596-8_33
36. Srivastava, S., Gulwani, S., Foster, J.S.: From program verification to program synthesis. In: Hermenegildo, M.V., Palsberg, J. (eds.) Proceedings of the 37th ACM SIGPLAN-SIGACT Symposium on Principles of Programming Languages, POPL 2010, Madrid, Spain, 17–23 January 2010, pp. 313–326. ACM (2010)
37. Thomas, W.: Facets of synthesis: revisiting Church's problem. In: de Alfaro, L. (ed.) FoSSaCS 2009. LNCS, vol. 5504, pp. 1–14. Springer, Heidelberg (2009). https://doi.org/10.1007/978-3-642-00596-1_1

Syntax-Guided Synthesis with Quantitative Syntactic Objectives

Qinheping Hu(✉) and Loris D'Antoni

University of Wisconsin-Madison, Madison, USA
{qhu28,loris}@cs.wisc.edu

Abstract. Automatic program synthesis promises to increase the productivity of programmers and end-users of computing devices by automating tedious and error-prone tasks. Despite the practical successes of program synthesis, we still do not have systematic frameworks to synthesize programs that are "good" according to certain metrics—e.g., produce programs of reasonable sizes or with good runtime—and to understand when synthesis can result in such good programs. In this paper, we propose QSyGuS, a unifying framework for describing syntax-guided synthesis problems with quantitative objectives over the syntax of the synthesized programs. QSyGuS builds on weighted (tree) grammars, a clean and foundational formalism that provides flexible support for different quantitative objectives, useful closure properties, and practical decision procedures. We then present an algorithm for solving QSyGuS. Our algorithm leverages closure properties of weighted grammars to generate intermediate problems that can be solved using non-quantitative SyGuS solvers. Finally, we implement our algorithm in a tool, QuaSi, and evaluate it on 26 quantitative extensions of existing SyGuS benchmarks. QuaSi can synthesize optimal solutions in 15/26 benchmarks with times comparable to those needed to find an arbitrary solution.

1 Introduction

The goal of program synthesis is to find a program in some search space that meets a specification—e.g., a set of examples or a logical formula. Recently, a large family of synthesis problems has been unified into a framework called syntax-guided synthesis (SyGuS). A SyGuS problem is specified by a context-free grammar describing the search space of programs, and a logical formula describing the specification. Many synthesizers now support this format [2] and annually compete in synthesis competitions [4]. Thanks to these competitions, these solvers are now quite mature and are finding wide application [14].

While the logical specification mechanism provided by SyGuS is powerful, it can only capture the functional requirements of the synthesis problem—e.g., the program should perform correctly on a given set of input/output examples. When multiple possible programs can satisfy the specification, SyGuS *does not* provide a way to prefer one to the other—e.g., one cannot ask a solver to return the program with the fewest if-statements. As a consequence, existing synthesis

H. Chockler and G. Weissenbacher (Eds.): CAV 2018, LNCS 10981, pp. 386–403, 2018.
https://doi.org/10.1007/978-3-319-96145-3_21

tools do not provide guarantees about what solution is returned if multiple ones exist. While a few synthesizers have attempted to include some form of specification to express this kind of quantitative intents [7,15,16,19], these approaches are domain-specific, do not apply to SyGuS problems, and do not provide a simple and flexible specification mechanism. The lack of a formal treatment of quantitative requirements stands in the way of designing synthesizers that can take advantage of quantitative objectives to perform more efficient forms of synthesis.

In this paper, we propose QSyGuS, a unifying framework for describing syntax-guided synthesis problems with quantitative objectives over the syntax of the synthesized programs—e.g., find the most likely program with respect to a given probability distribution—and present an algorithm for solving synthesis problems expressed in this framework. We focus on syntactic objectives because they are the most common ones in practical applications of program synthesis. For example, in programming by examples it is desirable to produce small programs with fewer constants because these programs are more likely to generalize to examples outside of the specification [13]. QSyGuS extends SyGuS in two ways. First, in QSyGuS the search space is represented using weighted grammars, which augment context-free grammars with the ability to assign weights to programs. Second, QSyGuS allows the user to specify constraints over the weight of the program, including optimization objectives—e.g., find the program with the fewest if-statements and with the lowest depth.

QSyGuS is a natural, general, and flexible formalism and is grounded in the well-studied theory of weighted grammars. We leverage this theory and design an algorithm for solving QSyGuS problems using closure properties of weighted grammars. Given a QSyGuS problem, our algorithm generates a SyGuS problem that can be delegated to existing SyGuS solvers. The algorithm then iteratively refines the solution returned by the SyGuS solver to find an optimal one by further generating new SyGuS instances using weighted grammar operations. We implement our algorithm in a tool, QuaSi, and evaluate it on 26 quantitative extensions of existing SyGuS benchmarks. QuaSi can synthesize optimal solutions in 15/26 benchmarks with times comparable to those needed to find a solution that does not need to satisfy any quantitative objective.

Contributions. In summary, our contributions are:

- QSyGuS, a formal framework grounded in the theory of weighted grammars that can describe syntax-guided synthesis problems with quantitative objectives over the syntax of the synthesized programs (Sect. 3).
- An algorithm for solving QSyGuS problems that leverages closure properties of weighted grammars and existing SyGuS solvers (Sect. 4).
- QuaSi, a tool for specifying and solving QSyGuS problems that interfaces with existing SyGuS solvers and a comprehensive evaluation of QuaSi, which shows that QuaSi can efficiently solve QSyGuS problems over different types of weights, including additive weights, probabilities, and combinations of multiple weights (Sect. 5).

$$\begin{aligned} \text{Start} ::= \ & \text{Start} + \text{Start}/(\mathbf{0},\mathbf{1}) \\ | \ & \text{if(BExpr) then Start else Start}/(\mathbf{1},\mathbf{0}) \\ | \ & x \mid y \mid 0 \mid 1 \end{aligned} \qquad \begin{aligned} \text{BExpr} ::= \ & \text{Start} > \text{Start} \\ | \ & \neg\text{BExpr} \\ | \ & \text{BExpr} \wedge \text{BExpr} \end{aligned}$$

Fig. 1. Weighted grammar that assigns weight $(w_1, w_2) \in \mathsf{Nat} \times \mathsf{Nat}$ to a program where w_1 is the number of if-statements and w_2 is the number of plus-statements.

2 Illustrative Example

In this section, we illustrate the main components of our framework using an example. We start with a Syntax-Guided Synthesis (SyGuS) problem in which no quantitative objective is provided. We recall that the goal of a SyGuS problem is to synthesize a function f of a given type that is accepted by a context-free grammar G, and such that $\forall x.\phi(f, x)$ holds (for a given Boolean constraint ϕ).

The following SyGuS problem asks to synthesize a function that is accepted by the following grammar and that computes the max of two numbers.

$$\begin{aligned} \text{Start} ::= & \text{Start} + \text{Start} \mid \text{if(BExpr) then Start else Start} \mid x \mid y \mid 0 \mid 1 \\ \text{BExpr} ::= & \text{Start} > \text{Start} \mid \neg\text{BExpr} \mid \text{BExpr} \wedge \text{BExpr} \end{aligned}$$

The semantic constraint is given by the following formula.

$$\psi(f) \stackrel{\text{def}}{=} \forall x, y.f(x, y) \geq x \wedge f(x, y) \geq y \wedge (f(x, y) = x \vee f(x, y) = y)$$

The following three programs are semantically equivalent, but syntactically different solutions.

$$\begin{aligned} max_1(x, y) &= \text{if}(x > y) \text{ then } x \text{ else } y \\ max_2(x, y) &= \text{if}(x > y) \text{ then } (x + 0) \text{ else } (y + 0) \\ max_3(x, y) &= \text{if}(x > y) \text{ then } x \text{ else } (\text{if}(y > x) \text{ then } y \text{ else } x) \end{aligned}$$

All solutions are correct, but the user might, for example, prefer the smallest one. However, SyGuS does not provide ways to specify this quantitative intent.

Adding Weights. In our formalism, QSyGuS, we augment context-free grammars to assign weights to programs in the search space. Concretely, we adopt weighted grammars [10], a well-studied formalism with many desirable properties. In a weighted grammar, each production is assigned a weight. For example, the weighted grammar shown in Fig. 1 extends the one from the previous SyGuS example to assign to each program p a pair of weights (w_1, w_2) where w_1 is the number of if-statements and w_2 is the number of plus operators in p. In this case, the weights are pairs of integers and the weight of a grammar derivation is the pairwise sum of all the weights of the productions involved in the derivation—e.g., the sum of (w_1, w_2) and (w'_1, w'_2) is $(w_1 + w'_1, w_2 + w'_2)$. In the figure, we write $/(w_1, w_2)$ to assign weight (w'_1, w'_2) to a production. We omit the weight for productions with cost $(0, 0)$. The functions max_1, max_2 and max_3 have weights $(1, 0)$, $(1, 2)$, and $(2, 0)$ respectively.

Adding and Solving Quantitative Objectives. Once we have a way to assign weights to programs, QSyGuS allows the user to specify quantitative objectives over the weights of the productions—e.g., only allow solutions with fewer than 4 if-statements. In our example, we could require the solution to be minimal with respect to the number of if-statements, i.e., minimize the first component of the paired weight. With these constraints both max_1 and max_2 would be considered optimal solutions because there exists no solution with 0 if-statements. If we require the solution to also be minimal with respect to the second component of the paired weight, max_1 will be *a possible* optimal solution.

Our tool QuaSi can automatically discover solutions in both these cases. Let's consider the last minimization objective. In this case, QuaSi first uses existing SyGuS solvers to synthesize an initial solution using the non-weighted version of the grammar. Let's say that the returned solution is, for example, max_3 of weight $(2, 0)$. QuaSi uses this solution to build a new SyGuS instance that only accepts programs with at most one if-statement. Solving this SyGuS problem can, for example, result in the program max_2 of weight $(1, 2)$, which will require our solver to build yet another SyGuS instance. This approach is repeated and if it terminates, an optimal program is found.

3 SyGuS with Quantitative Objectives

In this section, we introduce our framework for defining syntax-guided synthesis problems with quantitative objectives over the syntax of the synthesized programs. We first provide preliminary definitions for notions such as semirings (Sect. 3.1) and weighted tree grammars (Sect. 3.2), and then use these notions to augment SyGuS problems with quantitative objectives (Sect. 3.3).

3.1 Weights over Semirings

We now define the universe of weights we will assign to programs. In general, weights are defined using monoids—i.e., sets equipped with an addition operator—but when a grammar is nondeterministic—i.e., it can produce the same term using multiple derivations—the same term might be assigned multiple weights. Hence, we choose to use semirings. Since we also care about optimization objectives, we assume all our semirings are equipped with a partial order.

Definition 1 (Semiring). *A (ordered)* semiring *is a pair* $(\boldsymbol{S}, \preceq)$ *where (i)* $\boldsymbol{S} = (S, \oplus, \otimes, 0, 1)$ *is an algebra consisting of a commutative monoid* $(S, \oplus, 0)$ *and a monoid* $(S, \otimes, 1)$ *such that* $\otimes$ *distributes over* $\oplus$*,* $0 \neq 1$*, and, for every* $x \in S$*,* $x \otimes 0 = 0$*, (ii)* $\preceq \subset S \times S$ *is a partial order over* S*.*

We often use the word semiring to refer to just the algebra $\mathbf{S}$.

Example 1. In this paper, we focus on semirings with the following algebras.

Boolean $\mathsf{Bool} = (\mathbb{B}, \vee, \wedge, 0, 1)$. This semiring only contains the values *true* and *false* and is used to represent non-quantitative problems.

Tropical $\mathsf{Trop} = (\mathbb{Z} \cup \{\infty\}, \min, +, \infty, 0)$. This semiring is the most common one and is used to assign additive weights—e.g., term sizes and term depth. In this case, we typically consider the order $\preceq \stackrel{\text{def}}{=} \leq$.

Probabilistic $\mathsf{Prob} = ([0, 1], +, \cdot, 0, 1)$. This semiring is used to assign probabilities to terms in a grammar. □

In our framework, we allow synthesis problems to have multiple objectives. Hence, we define a product operation to compose semirings. Intuitively, the following operation composes algebras of semirings to create a pair and applies the operation of each algebra to the corresponding projections of the pair. Similarly, two orders can be composed to create an order over pairs of elements. We propose two such compositions, one which assigns equal weights to the two orders and one which prefers one order over the other (Sorted).

Definition 2 (Products). *Given two algebras $\boldsymbol{S}_1 = (S_1, \oplus_1, \otimes_1, 0_1, 1_1)$ and $\boldsymbol{S}_2 = (S_2, \oplus_2, \otimes_2, 0_2, 1_2)$, the* product algebra *is the tuple $\boldsymbol{S}_1 \times_{\boldsymbol{S}} \boldsymbol{S}_2 = (S_1 \times S_2, \oplus, \otimes, (0_1, 0_2), (1_1, 1_2))$ such that for every $x_1, x_2 \in S_1$ and $y_1, y_2 \in S_2$, we have $(x_1, y_1) \oplus (x_2, y_2) \stackrel{\text{def}}{=} (x_1 \oplus_1 x_2, y_1 \oplus_2 y_2)$ and $(x_1, y_1) \otimes (x_2, y_2) \stackrel{\text{def}}{=} (x_1 \otimes_1 x_2, y_1 \otimes_2 y_2)$.*

Given two partial orders $\preceq_1 \subset S_1 \times S_1$ and $\preceq_2 \subset S_2 \times S_2$, the Pareto product *of the two orders is defined as the partial order $\preceq_p = \text{PAR}(\preceq_1, \preceq_2) \subseteq (S_1 \times S_2) \times (S_1 \times S_2)$ such that, for every $x_1, x_2 \in S_1$ and $y_1, y_2 \in S_2$, we have $(x_1, y_1) \preceq_p (x_2, y_2)$ iff $x_1 \preceq_1 x_2$ and $y_1 \preceq_2 y_2$.*

Given two partial orders $\preceq_1 \subset S_1 \times S_1$ and $\preceq_2 \subset S_2 \times S_2$, the Sorted product *of the two orders is defined as the partial order $\preceq_s = \text{SORT}(\preceq_1, \preceq_2) \subseteq (S_1 \times S_2) \times (S_1 \times S_2)$ such that, for every $x_1, x_2 \in S_1$ and $y_1, y_2 \in S_2$, we have $(x_1, y_1) \preceq_s (x_2, y_2)$ iff $x_1 \preceq_1 x_2$ or ($x_1 = x_2$ and $y_1 \preceq_2 y_2$).*

Example 2. The weights in the grammar in Fig. 1 are from the product semiring $\mathsf{Trop} \times_{\mathsf{S}} \mathsf{Trop}$. When using the Pareto partial orders, we have, for example, $(1, 0) \preceq (2, 0)$ and $(1, 0) \preceq (1, 2)$, but $(1, 2)$ is incomparable to $(2, 0)$. When using the Sorted product, we have, for example, $(1, 0) \preceq (1, 2) \preceq (2, 0)$. □

3.2 Weighted Tree Grammars

Since SyGuS defines search spaces using context-free grammars, we propose to extend this formalism with weights to assign costs to terms in the grammar. We focus our attention on a restricted class of context-free grammars called regular tree grammars—i.e., grammars generating regular tree languages—because, to our knowledge, the benchmarks appearing in the SyGuS competition [3] and in practical applications of SyGuS operate over tree grammars. Moreover, it was recently shown that SyGuS problems that are undecidable for context-free grammars become decidable with weighted tree grammars [8].

Trees A *ranked alphabet* is a tuple (Σ, rk_Σ) where Σ is a finite set of symbol and $rk_\Sigma : \Sigma \to \mathbb{N}$ associates a rank to each symbol. For every $m \geq 0$, the set of all symbols in Σ with rank m is denoted by $\Sigma^{(m)}$. In our examples, a ranked alphabet is specified by showing the set Σ and attaching the respective rank to every symbol as superscript—e.g., $\Sigma = \{+^{(2)}, c^{(0)}\}$. We use T_Σ to denote the set of all (ranked) trees over Σ—i.e., T_Σ is the smallest set such that (i) $\Sigma^{(0)} \subseteq T_\Sigma$, (ii) if $\sigma \in \Sigma^{(k)}$ and $t_1, \ldots, t_k \in T_\Sigma$, then $\sigma(t_1, \cdots, t_k) \in T_\Sigma$. In the following we assume a fixed ranked alphabet (Σ, rk_Σ).

Weighted Tree Grammars. Tree grammars are similar to word grammars but they generate ranked trees instead of words. Weighted tree grammars augment tree grammars by assigning weights from a semiring to trees. They do so by associating weights to productions in the grammar. Weighted grammars can, for example, compute the height of a tree, the number of occurrences of some node in the tree, or the probability of a tree with respect to some distribution In the following, we assume a fixed semiring $(\mathbf{S}, \preceq)$ where $\mathbf{S} = (S, \oplus, \otimes, 0, 1)$.

Definition 3 (Weighted Tree Grammar). *A weighted tree grammar (WTG) is a tuple $G = (N, Z, P, \mu)$, where N is a set of non-terminal symbols with arity 0, Z is an axiom with $Z \in N$, P is a set of production rules of the form $A \to \beta$ where $A \in N$ is a non-terminal and β is a tree of $T(\Sigma \cup N)$, and $\mu : P \to S$ is a function assigning to each production a weight from the semiring.*

We can now define the semantics of a WTG as a function $\mathrm{W}_G : T_\Sigma \mapsto S$, which assigns weights to trees. Intuitively, the weight of a tree is $\oplus$-sum of the weight of every possible derivation of that tree in a grammar and the weight of a derivation is the $\otimes$-product of the weights of the productions appearing in the derivation. We use $MS(\beta) = \langle X_1, \ldots, X_k \rangle$ to denote the multi-set of all nonterminals appearing in β and $\beta[t_1/X_1, \ldots, t_k/X_k]$ to denote the result of simultaneously substituting each X_i with t_i in β. Given a derivation $p = A \to \beta$ such that $MS(\beta) = \langle X_1, \ldots, X_k \rangle$, we assume that p is a symbol of arity k. A derivation d starting at non-terminal X is a tree of productions $d \in T(P)$ representing one possible way to derive a tree starting from X. The derivation has to be such that: (i) the root of d is a production of the form $X \to \beta$, (ii) for every node $p = A \to \beta$ in d, if $MS(\beta) = \langle X_1, \ldots, X_k \rangle$, then, for every $1 \leq i \leq k$, the i-th child of p is a production $X_i \to \beta_i$. Given a derivation d with root $p = X \to \beta$, such that $MS(\beta) = \langle X_1, \ldots, X_k \rangle$ and p has children subtrees $d_1, \ldots, d_k$, the tree generated by d is recursively defined as $tree(d) = \beta[tree(d_1)/X_1, \ldots, tree(d_k)/X_k]$. We use $\mathrm{DER}(X, t)$ to denote the set of all derivations d starting at X, such that $tree(d) = t$. The weight $\mathrm{DW}(d)$ of a derivation d is the $\otimes$-product of the weights of the productions appearing in the derivation. Finally, the weight of a tree t is the $\oplus$-sum of the weights of all the derivations of t from the initial nonterminal $\mathrm{W}_G(t) = \bigoplus_{d \in \mathrm{DER}(Z,t)} \mathrm{DW}(d)$. A weighted tree grammar is *unambiguous* iff, for every $t \in T_\Sigma$, there exists at most one derivation—i.e., $|\mathrm{DER}(Z, t)| \leq 1$.

Weighted tree grammars generalize weighted tree automata. In particular, a *weighted tree automaton* (WTA) is a WTG in which every production is of the form $A \to \sigma(T_1, \ldots, T_n)$, where $A \in N$, each $T_i \in N$, and $\sigma \in \Sigma^{(n)}$. Finally, a *tree automaton* (TA) is a WTA over the Boolean semiring—i.e., the TA accepts all trees with some derivations yielding *true*. Similarly, a *tree grammar* (TG) is a WTG over the Boolean semiring. Given a TA (resp. TG) G, we use $L(G)$ to denote the set of trees accepted by G—i.e., $L(G) = \{t \mid \mathrm{w}_G(t) = true\}$.

Example 3. The weighted grammar in Fig. 1 operates over the semiring $\mathsf{Trop} \times \mathsf{Trop}$, $N = \{\text{Start}, \text{BExpr}\}$, $Z = \text{Start}$, P contains 9 productions, and μ assigns non-zero weights to two of them. □

Aside from being a natural formalism for assigning weights to trees, TGs and WTGs enjoy properties that make them a good choice for our model. First, WTGs (resp. TGs) are equi-expressive to WTAs (resp. TAs) and have logic characterizations [9–11]. Due to this reason, tree grammars are closed under Boolean operations and enjoy decidable equivalence [9]. Second, WTGs enjoy many closure and decidability properties—e.g., given two WTGs G_1 and G_2, we can compute the grammars $G_1 \oplus G_2$ and $G_1 \otimes G_2$ such that, for every f, $\mathrm{w}_{G_1 \oplus G_2}(f) = \mathrm{w}_{G_1}(f) \oplus \mathrm{w}_{G_2}(f)$ and $\mathrm{w}_{G_1 \otimes G_2}(f) = \mathrm{w}_{G_1}(f) \otimes \mathrm{w}_{G_2}(f)$. This operation is convenient for building grammars over product semirings.

3.3 QSyGuS

In this section, we formally define QSyGuS, which extends SyGuS with quantitative objectives. In SyGuS a problem is specified with respect to a background theory T—e.g., linear arithmetic—and the goal is to synthesize a function f that satisfies two constraints provided by the user. The first constraint describes a *functional semantic property* that f should satisfy and is given as a predicate $\psi(f) \stackrel{\text{def}}{=} \forall x.\phi(f, x)$. The second constraint limits the *search space* S of f and is given as a set of expressions specified by a context-free grammar G defining a subset of all the terms in T. A solution to the SyGuS problem is an expression e in S such that the formula $\psi(e)$ is valid.

We augment such a framework in two ways. First, we replace context free grammars with WTGs, which we use to assign weights (from a given semiring) to terms. Second, we augment the problem formulation with constraints over the weight of the synthesized program—i.e., only consider programs of weight greater than 2—and optimization objectives over the same weight—i.e., find the solution of minimal weight. Weight constraints range over the grammar

$$WC := WC \wedge WC \mid WC \vee WC \mid \neg WC \mid w \preceq s \mid s \preceq w \mid w \prec s \mid s \prec w,$$

where w is a special variable and s is an element of the semiring under consideration. Given a constraint $\omega \in WC$, we write $\omega(t)$ to denote the term obtained by replacing w with t in ω.

Definition 4 (QSyGuS). *A* QSyGuS *problem is a tuple* $(T, (\boldsymbol{S}, \preceq), \psi(f), G, \omega, \text{OPT})$ *where:*

- T *is a background theory.*
- $(\boldsymbol{S}, \preceq)$ *is an ordered semiring defining the set of weights and their operations.*

Algorithm 1. QSyGuS synthesis algorithm

```
1: procedure QSyGuS-solve(T, S, ψ, G, ω, opt)
2:     G′ ← ReduceGrammar(G, ω)                 ▷ extract grammar satisfying ω
3:     f* ← SyGuS(T, ψ, G′)                     ▷ solve corresponding SyGuS problem
4:     if opt = false then return f*
5:     while true do
6:         G′ ← ReduceGrammar(G′, w ≺ w_G(f*))
7:         f ← SyGuS(T, ψ, G′)                  ▷ Try to find better solution
8:         if f = ⊥ then return f*              ▷ Return the optimal solution
9:         f* ← f
```

- *G is a weighted tree grammar with weights over the semiring $\boldsymbol{S}$ and that only contains terms in T—i.e., $L(G) \subseteq T$.*
- *$\psi(f) \stackrel{\text{def}}{=} \forall x.\phi(f, x)$ is a Boolean formula constraining the semantic behavior of the synthesized program f.*
- *$\omega \in WC$ is a set of constraints over the weight w of the synthesized program.*
- opt *is a Boolean denoting whether the solution has to have minimal weight with respect to $\preceq$.*

A solution to the QSyGuS *problem is a term e such that $e \in L(G)$, $\psi(e)$ is true, and $\omega(\mathrm{W}_G(e))$ is true. If* opt *is true, we also require that there is no g that satisfies the previous conditions and such that $\omega(\mathrm{W}_G(g)) \prec \omega(\mathrm{W}_G(e))$.*

A SyGuS problem is a QSyGuS problem without weight constraints—i.e., $\omega \equiv true$ and opt $= false$. We denote such problems just as triples $(T, \psi(f), G)$.

Example 4. Consider the QSyGuS problem described in Sect. 2. We already described all the components but ω and opt in the rest of this section. In this example, $\omega = true$ and opt $= true$ because we want to synthesize the solution with minimal weight.

4 Solving QSyGuS Problems via Grammar Reduction

In this section, we present an algorithm for solving QSyGuS problems (Algorithm 1), which works as follows. First, given a QSyGuS problem, we construct (under certain assumptions) a SyGuS problem for which the solution is guaranteed to satisfy the weight constraints ω (line 2) and use existing SyGuS solvers to find a solution to such a problem (line 3). If the QSyGuS problem requires minimization, our algorithm produces a new SyGuS instance to search for a solution that is better than the previously found one and tries to solve it (lines 6-7). This procedure is repeated until an optimal solution is found (line 8).

4.1 From QSyGuS to SyGuS

The first step of our algorithm is to construct a SyGuS problem characterizing exactly all the solutions of the QSyGuS problem that satisfy the weight constraints. Given a QSyGuS problem $P = (T, (\mathbf{S}, \preceq), \psi(f), G, \omega, \text{OPT})$, we construct a SyGuS problem $P' = (T, \psi(f), G')$ such that a function g is a solution to the SyGuS problem P' iff g is a solution of $P = (T, (\mathbf{S}, \preceq), \psi(f), G, \omega, false)$, where the optimization constraint has been dropped. We denote the grammar reduction operation as $G' \leftarrow \text{ReduceGrammar}(G, \omega)$.

Base case. First we show how to solve the problem when ω is an atomic formula—i.e. of the form $w \preceq s$, $s \preceq w$, $w \prec s$, or $s \prec w$. We start by showing how to solve the problem for $w \preceq s$ as the construction is identical for the other constraints.

Concretely, we are given a WTG $G = (N, Z, P, \mu)$ and we want to construct a TG $G_{\preceq s} = (N', Z', P')$ such that $t \in L(G_{\preceq s})$ iff $\text{w}_G(t) \preceq s$. In general, it is not possible to perform this construction for arbitrary semirings and grammars. We first present our algorithm and then describe sufficient conditions under which we can ensure termination and correctness.

The idea behind our construction is to introduce new nonterminals in the grammar $G_{\preceq s}$ to keep track of the weight of the trees that can be produced from those nonterminals. For example, a nonterminal pair (X, s') will derive all trees derivable from X using a single derivation of weight s'. Therefore, the set of nonterminals N' is a subset of $N \times S$ (plus an initial nonterminal Z'), where S is the universe of the WTG's semiring. We construct our set of nonterminals N' starting from the leaf productions of G and then recursively explore other productions. At the same time we generate the set of productions P'. Formally, N' and P' are the smallest sets such that the following conditions hold.

1. $Z' \in N'$ (the initial nonterminal).
2. For every production $p \in P$ such that $p = (A \to \beta)$ and $\beta \in T_\Sigma$—i.e., p is a leaf—and $\mu(p) \preceq s$, then $(A, \mu(p)) \in N'$ and $((A, \mu(p)) \to \beta) \in P'$. If $A = Z$, then $Z' \to (A, \mu(p)) \in P'$.
3. For every production $p \in P$ such that $p = (A \to \beta)$, $MS(\beta) = \langle X_1, \ldots, X_k \rangle$, $(X_1, s_1), \ldots, (X_k, s_k) \in N'$ (for some values $s_i \in S$), and $\mu(p) \otimes s_1 \otimes \ldots \otimes s_k = s'$, $s' \preceq s$, then $(A, s') \in N'$, and $((A, s') \to \beta[(X_1, s_1)/X_1, \ldots, (X_k, s_k)/X_k]) \in P'$. If $A = Z$, then $Z' \to (A, s') \in P'$.

Example 5. We illustrate our construction using the grammar in Fig. 1 . Assume the weight constraint is $w \preceq (1, 0)$ and the partial order is built using a Pareto product—i.e., we accept terms with 1 or less if-statements and no plus-statements. Our construction yields the following grammar.

Z' ::=(Start,1,0) | (Start,0,0)
(Start,1,0) ::=if((BExpr,0,0)) then (Start,0,0) else (Start,0,0) | x | y | 0 | 1
(Start,0,0) ::=x | y | 0 | 1
(BExpr,0,0) ::=(Start,0,0) > (Start,0,0) | ¬(BExpr,0,0) | (BExpr,0,0) ∧ (BExpr,0,0)

□

The construction of $G_{\preceq s}$ only terminates for certain semirings and grammars, and only guarantees that individual derivations yield the correct weight—i.e., it does not account for the $\oplus$-sum of multiple derivations.

Example 6. The following WTG over Prob is ambiguous and, if we apply the grammar reduction algorithm for $\omega := w \preceq 0.6$, the resulting grammar will be empty. However, the tree $1+1$ has weight $0.9 \not\preceq 0.6$ $(0.9 \geq 0.6)$.

$$\begin{array}{ll}\text{Start} ::= \text{Start} + \text{Start}/0.5 & \text{Expr} ::= \text{Expr} + \text{Expr}/0.4 \\ \quad |x \mid 0 \mid 1 \mid \text{Expr} & \quad |x \mid 0 \mid 1\end{array}$$ □

We now identify sufficient conditions under which the construction of $G_{\preceq s}$ terminates and is sound. In particular, we start by restricting our attention to unambiguous WTGs, which are the common ones in practice. We use $\text{WEIGHTS}(G) = \{s \mid p \in P \wedge \mu(p) = s\}$ to denote the set of weights used by G and $M_{\mathbf{S},G} = (S', \otimes, 1)$ to denote the submonoid of $\mathbf{S}$ generated by $\text{WEIGHTS}(G)$—i.e., the set of all weights we can generate using $\otimes$ and $\text{WEIGHTS}(G)$.

Theorem 1. *Given an unambiguous WTG G over a semiring $\mathbf{S}$ such that $M_{\mathbf{S},G} = (S', \otimes, 1)$, and a weight $s \in S$, the construction of $G_{\preceq s}$ terminates if the set $\{s' \mid s' \preceq s \wedge w \in S'\}$ is finite. Moreover, if the set of weights $\text{WEIGHTS}(G)$ is monotonically increasing with respect to $\preceq$—i.e. for every $s \in S$ and $s' \in \text{WEIGHTS}(G)$, $s \preceq s \otimes s'$—then $L(G_{\preceq s})$ contains exactly every tree t such that $\text{W}_G(t) \preceq s$.*

The theorem above also holds for other atomic constraints $w \prec s$, $s \preceq w$, or $s \prec w$ (for these last two, the direction of the monotonicity is reversed). Moreover, in certain cases, even if the construction may not terminate for, let's say $s \preceq w$, it might terminate for the negated constraint $w \prec s$. In such a case, we can use the closure properties of regular tree grammars/automata to construct the reduced grammar for $s \preceq w$ as $G_{\preceq w} = \text{INTERSECT}(G, \text{COMPLEMENT}(G_{\succ w}))$. The same idea can be applied to all atomic constraints.

In practice, the restriction of Theorem 1 holds for grammars that operate over the Boolean and probabilistic semirings, and the tropical semiring only with positive weights. Theorem 1 never holds when $\mathbf{S}$ is the tropical semiring and the grammar contains negative weights. In general, one cannot construct the constrained grammar in this case. However, it is easy to modify our algorithm to work with grammars that do not contain loops—i.e., derivations from a nonterminal to a tree containing the same nonterminal—with negative weights.

Intuitively, when the grammar contains no negative loops, we can find a constant SH such that any intermediate derivation with weight greater than $s+SH$ will never result in tree with weight smaller than s. We use this idea to modify the construction of $G^{\mathsf{Trop}}_{\leq s}$—i.e., $G_{\leq s}$ for Trop—as follows. First, this constant is bounded by ck^{n+1} where c is the absolute value of the smallest negative weight in the grammar, k is the largest number of nonterminals appearing in one grammar production, and $n = |N|$ is the number of nonterminals. Second, in steps 2 and 3 of the construction, a new nonterminal and the corresponding productions are produced if $\mu(p) \leq s + |SH|$ (previously $\mu(p) \leq s$). However, if $A = Z$ in steps 2 and 3, we add a new production $Z' \rightarrow (A, s')$ only if $s' \preceq s$.

We now show when this construction terminates and return correct values. Since the tropical semiring combines multiple runs using the min operator, we can *drop* the requirement that the grammar has to be unambiguous.

Theorem 2. *Given a WTG G over Trop and a weight $s \in \mathbb{Z}$, the construction of $G^{\mathsf{Trop}}_{\leq s}$ terminates if G contains no loop with cumulative negative weight. Moreover, $G^{\mathsf{Trop}}_{\leq s}$ contains exactly every tree t such that $\mathrm{w}_G(t) \leq s$.*

Composing semirings. We next discuss how Theorem 1 relates to product semirings. Given a grammar $G = (N, Z, P, \mu)$ over a semiring $\mathbf{S}_1 \times_{\mathbf{S}} \mathbf{S}_2$, we use $G^{\mathbf{S}_i}$ to denote the grammar (N, Z, P, μ_i) in which the weight function outputs the corresponding projected weight—i.e., if $\mu(p) = (s_1, s_2)$, then $\mu_i(p) = s_i$.

Let's first consider the case where the product semiring uses a Pareto partial order. In this case, if Theorem 1 holds for each grammar $G^{\mathbf{S}_i}$ and $w_i \preceq_i s_i$, then it holds for G and $(w_1, w_2) \preceq_p (s_1, s_2)$. However, the other direction is not true. Theorem 3 proves this intuition and states that, in some sense, solving Pareto partial orders is easier than solving the individual partial orders.

Theorem 3. *Given an unambiguous WTG G over the semiring $\boldsymbol{S} = \boldsymbol{S}_1 \times_S \boldsymbol{S}_2$ with Pareto partial order $\preceq_p = \mathrm{PAR}(\preceq_1, \preceq_2)$ and a weight $s = (s_1, s_2) \in S$, if the constructions $G^{\boldsymbol{S}_1}_{\preceq_1 s_1}$ and $G^{\boldsymbol{S}_2}_{\preceq_2 s_2}$ terminate, then the construction of $G_{\preceq s}$ terminates.*

When we move to Sorted partial order we cannot get an analogous theorem: if Theorem 1 holds for each grammar $G^{\mathbf{S}_i}$ and $w_i \preceq_i s_i$, then it does not necessary hold for G and $(w_1, w_2) \preceq_s (s_1, s_2)$. In particular, if the semiring $\mathbf{S}_2$ is infinite and there exists an $s_1' \prec s_1$, there will be infinitely many elements $(s_1', \_) \prec (s_1, s_2)$. Using this observation, we devise a modified algorithm for reducing grammars with sorted objectives. First, we compute the grammars $G^{\mathbf{S}_1}_{\prec_1 s_1}$, $G^{\mathbf{S}_1}_{= s_1}$, and $G^{\mathbf{S}_2}_{\prec_2 s_2}$. Second, we use WTG closure properties to compute $G_{\preceq_s}(s_1, s_2)$ as the union of $G^{\mathbf{S}_1}_{\prec_1 s_1}$ and $\mathrm{INTERSECT}(G^{\mathbf{S}_1}_{= s_1}, G^{\mathbf{S}_2}_{\prec_2 s_2})$.

General formulas. We can now inductively construct the grammar accepting only terms satisfying all constraints in ω. We again use the fact that tree grammars are closed under Boolean operations to compute intersections and unions and correctly characterize all conjunctions and unions appearing in the formulas.

4.2 Finding an Optimal Solution

If our QSyGuS problem does not require minimization—i.e., OPT $= \mathit{false}$—the technique presented in Sect. 4.1 can be used to generate an equivalent SyGuS problem $P' = (T, \psi(f), G')$, which can be solved using off-the-shelf SyGuS solvers. In this section, we show how to extend this technique to handle minimization objectives. Our idea is to use SyGuS solvers to find a non-optimal solution for P' and then iteratively refine our grammar G' to search for a better solution. This loop is illustrated in Algorithm 1 (lines 5-9). Given the initial solution f^* to P' such that $\mathrm{w}_G(f^*) = s$, we can construct a new grammar $G_{\prec s}$ and look for a solution with lower weight. If the SyGuS solver we use is sound—it can find a solution if it exists—and complete—it can detect if a solution does not exist—Algorithm 1 terminates with an optimal solution.

In general, the above conditions are too strict and in practice this implies that the algorithm will often not terminate. However, if the SyGuS solver is sound, the Algorithm 1 will eventually find the optimal solution, but it will not be able to prove that no smaller one exists. In our experiments, we will show that this approach can yield better solutions than those given by vanilla SyGuS solvers even when Algorithm 1 does not terminate.

5 Implementation and Evaluation

First, We extended the SyGuS format with new syntax for expressing QSyGuS problems. Our format supports all semirings presented in Sect. 3.1 as well as additional ones. The format also allows creating tuples of semirings using the product operation described in Sect. 3.1. We augment the original SyGuS syntax to support weights on grammar productions. Weight constraints are added using an SMT-like syntax.

Second, we implemented Algorithm 1 in a tool called QuaSi. QuaSi already interfaces with three SyGuS solvers: CVC4 [6], ESolver [4], and EUSolver [5]. QuaSi supports all the semirings allowed in our format and implements a library for tree automata/grammars and weighted tree automata/grammars operations, as well as several optimizations we did not discuss in the paper. In particular, QuaSi often uses simple grammar reduction techniques to simplify the generated grammars, remove unnecessary productions, and consolidate equivalent ones.

We evaluate QuaSi through the following questions (experiments performed on an Intel Core i7 4.00 GHz CPU with 32 GB/RAM).

Q1 Can QuaSi solve quantitative variants of real SyGuS benchmarks? (Sect. 5.1)
Q2 What is the overhead of synthesizing optimal solutions? (Sect. 5.2)
Q3 How do multiple iterations of Algorithm 1 affect the solution's weight? (Sect. 5.3)
Q4 Can QuaSi solve QSyGuS problems with multiple objectives? (Sect. 5.4)

Benchmarks. We perform our evaluation on 26 quantitative extensions of existing SyGuS competition benchmarks taken from 4 SyGuS benchmark tracks [4]: Hackers Delight, Integers, ICFP and Bitvector. 18 of our benchmarks only use a minimization objective over a single semiring (Table 1), while 8 use a minimization objective (Pareto or Sorted) over a product semiring (Table 2). We select SyGuS benchmarks using the following criteria: (*i*) the benchmark can be solved by either CVC4 [6] or ESolver [4], and (*ii*) the solution is not optimal according to some reasonable metric—e.g., size or number of if statements.

5.1 Effectiveness of QSyGuS Solver

We evaluate the effectiveness of QuaSi on the 18 single-minimization-objective benchmarks. For each benchmark, we run QuaSi using either CVC4 or ESolver as the backend SyGuS solver (we also evaluated QuaSi using EUSolver [5], but, due to its poor performance, we do not report the results). The results are shown in Table 1. The timeout for each iteration of Algorithm 1 is 10 min.

With CVC4, QuaSi terminates with an optimal solution in 9/18 benchmarks, taking less than 5 s (avg: 0.7 s) to solve each sub-problem. In 3 of these cases, the initial solution is already optimal and the second iteration is used to prove optimality. With ESolver, QuaSi terminates with an optimal solution in 8/18 benchmarks, taking less than 7 s (avg: 0.9 s) to solve each sub-problem. In 1 cases, it can find a better solution than the original one, but it cannot prove that the solution is optimal. Overall, by combining solvers, QuaSi can find a better solution than the original SyGuS solution given by one of the two solvers in 9/18 benchmarks. QuaSi cannot improve the initial solution of the linear integer arithmetic benchmarks (`array_search` and `LinExpr_eq1ex`).

Both solvers timeout on large grammars. The grammars in Table 1 are 1 to 2 order of magnitude larger than those in existing SyGuS benchmarks (avg: 224 vs 13 rules) and existing solvers have not yet been optimized for this parameter. In some cases, the solver times out for intermediate grammars that do not contain a solution, but that generate infinitely many terms. In general, existing SyGuS solvers cannot prove unsatisfiability for these types of problems. To answer **Q1**, QuaSi can **solve quantitative variants of 10/18 real SyGuS benchmarks**.

Table 1. Performance of QuaSi. **Time** shows the sequence of times taken to solve individual iterations of Algorithm 1. **Largest** is the size of the largest SyGuS sub-problem. **Grammar Size** is the number of rules in the original grammar.

	Problem	CVC4		ESolver		Grammar
		Time [sec]	Largest	Time [sec]	Largest	Size
Trop	`max_ite(2,3)`	0.1+0.1	42	0.1	42	13
	`max_ite(2,15)`	0.1+0.1	239	0.3	239	13
	`max_ite(3,15)`	0.1+0.1+0.1	238	OOM	238	13
	`max_ite(10,15)`	0.5+0.5+0.9	226	OOM	226	13
	`parity_not`	0.1+TO	301	26.9+TO	43	6
	`max3_ite`	0.1+TO	31	OOM	–	14
	`array_search_3`	0.1+TO	135	TO	–	15
	`array_search_5`	0.1+TO	108	TO	–	16
	`hackers_5`	0.1+0.1	27	0.1+0.1+0.1	35	13
	`hackers_7`	0.1+0.3	35	0.1+0.1+0.2	41	13
	`hackers_17`	0.1+0.7	41	2.8+3.0+1.0	62	13
	`hackers_19`	0.2+TO	174	TO	–	13
	`icfp_7`	0.2+TO	146	TO	–	11
	`LinExpr_eq1ex`	0.7+TO	1717	TO	–	14
Prob	`hackers_2_prob`	0.6+4.1+0.1	95	0.8+0.1+0.2	154	13
	`hackers_5_prob`	0.1+0.9+0.1	96	0.1+0.2+0.1	154	13
	`hackers_7_prob`	0.1+TO	162	0.1+0.1+0.2	212	13
	`hackers_17_prob`	0.1+TO	187	3.4+6.5+OOM	291	13

5.2 Solving Time for Different Iterations

In this section, we evaluate the time required by each iteration of Algorithm 1. Figure 2 shows the ratio of time taken by each iteration with respect to the initial non-quantitative SyGuS solving time. Some of the iterations shown in Fig. 1 do not appear in Fig. 2 since they resulted in no solution—i.e., the initial solution was minimal. CVC4 is typically slower in subsequent iterations and can take up to 10 times the original solving time, while ESolver has comparable runtime to the initial run and is often faster. These numbers are largely due to how the two solvers work: CVC4 is optimized to solve problems where the grammar imposes no restrictions on the structure of the solution, while ESolver performs enumerative search and takes advantage of more restrictive grammars.

One interesting point is the `parity_not` benchmark. ESolver takes 26.9 s to find an initial solution. But, with a weight constraint $w < 11$, an solution can be found in 2.2 s. CVC4 can find the initial solution with weight 11 in 0.1 s but cannot solve the next iteration. We tried using different solvers in different iterations of our algorithm and, in fact, found that, if we use CVC4 to find an initial solution and then ESolver in subsequent iterations with restricted grammars we can fully solve this benchmark in a total of 2.3 s which is much better than the time taken by a single solver. To answer **Q2**, with appropriate choices of solvers **the overhead of synthesizing optimal solutions is minimal**.

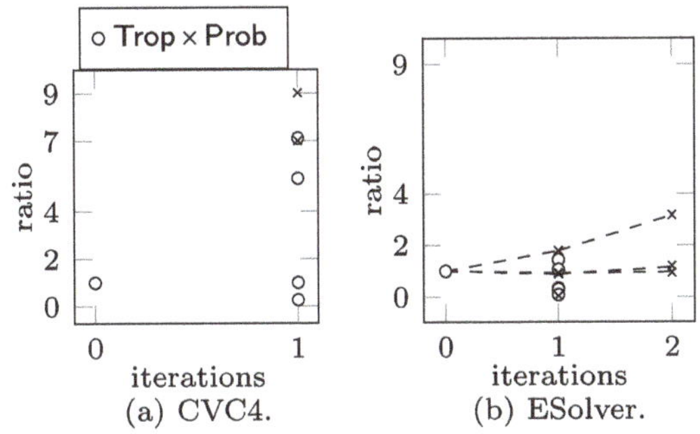

Fig. 2. Solving time across iterations

5.3 Solution Weight Across Iterations

In this section, we present how the weight of the synthesized solutions change across each iteration of Algorithm 1. Figure 3 shows the percentage of weight of solutions synthesized at each iteration with respect to the weight of the initial SyGuS solution. The result shows that we can improve the solutions of CVC4 by 15–25% in one iteration, and the solutions of ESolver by 20–50% when taking one iteration and 50–60% when taking two. The Prob benchmarks, which require two iterations, can be improved more when using ESolver because ESolver tends to synthesize small terms whose probability may also be small. To answer **Q3**, QuaSi can **improve the weights of SyGuS solutions by 20–60%**.

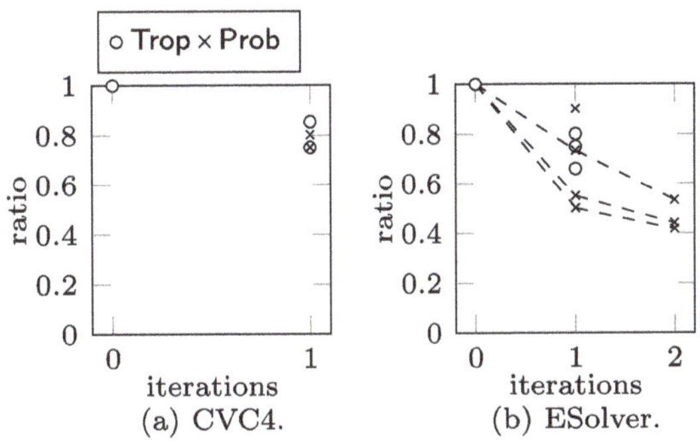

Fig. 3. Solution weight across iterations.

5.4 Multi-objective Optimization

In this section, we evaluate the effectiveness of QuaSi on the 8 benchmarks involving two minimization objectives. The benchmarks consists of two families, 4 for sorted optimization and 4 for Pareto optimization. The sorted optimization benchmarks ask to minimize first the number of occurrences of specified operator (`bvand` in `hacks` and `ite` in `array_search`) and then the size of the solution. The Pareto optimization benchmarks have the same objectives as sorted optimization but here we are synthesizing a Pareto optimal solution instead of sorted optimal one. The results are shown in Table 2. We do not present the results using CVC4 because it cannot solve any of the benchmarks.

The `array_search` times out since it is already hard on a single objective. For the `hackers_5` benchmarks, the initial solution is already optimized for the first objective, so the problem degenerates to the single-objective optimization problem. For the `hackers_7` and `hackers_17`, we present the weights of the intermediate solutions we can see that Pareto and Sorted optimizations yield different solutions. To answer **Q4**, QuaSi can **solve problems with multiple objectives** when the same problems are feasible with a single objective.

Table 2. Performance of QuaSi on multi-objective benchmarks. **Weight** denotes the sequence of weights explored during minimization.

	Problem	Time [sec]	Weight	Largest	Size
Trop × Trop	`array_search_sorted`	TO	-	-	15
	`hackers_5_sorted`	0.1+0.1+01	$(0,3) \rightarrow (0,2)$	31	13
	`hackers_7_sorted`	0.1+0.3+0.1	$(1,4) \rightarrow (0,5) \rightarrow (0,3)$	72	13
	`hackers_17_sorted`	0.1+156.1+TO	$(2,5) \rightarrow (1,4) \rightarrow (0,6)$	97	13
	`array_search_pareto`	TO	-	-	15
	`hackers_5_pareto`	0.1+0.1+01	$(0,3) \rightarrow (0,2)$	31	13
	`hackers_7_pareto`	0.1+0.3+0.1	$(1,4) \rightarrow (1,3) \rightarrow (0,3)$	74	13
	`hackers_17_pareto`	0.1+9.1+0.1	$(2,5) \rightarrow (2,4) \rightarrow (1,4)$	54	13

6 Related Work

Qualitative Synthesis. Existing program synthesizers fall in three categories: (*i*) enumeration solvers, which typically output the smallest program [1], (*ii*) symbolic solvers, which reduce the synthesis problem to a constraint solving problem and output whatever program is produced by the constraint solver [21], (*iii*) probabilistic synthesizers, which randomly search the space for a solution and are typically unpredictable [18]. Since the introduction of the SyGuS format [2], these techniques have been used to build several SyGuS solvers that have competed in SyGuS competitions [4]. The most effective ones, which are used in this paper are ESolver a2nd EUSolver [1] (enumeration), and CVC4 [6] (symbolic).

Quantitative synthesis. Domain-specific synthesizers typically employ hard-coded ranking functions that guide the search towards a "preferable" program [17], but these functions are typically hard to write and are decoupled from the functional specification. Unlike QSyGuS, these synthesizers allow arbitrary ranking functions to be expressed in general purpose languages, but typically only support limited grammars for synthesis. Moreover, in many practical applications the ranking functions are very simple. For example, the popular spreadsheet formula synthesizer FlashFill [12] uses a ranking function to prefer small programs with few constants. This type of objective is expressible in our framework.

The Sketch synthesizer supports optimization objectives over variables in sketched programs [20]. This work differs from ours in that sketches are a different specification mechanism from SyGuS. In Sketch the search space is encoded as a program with holes to facilitate synthesis by constraint solving. Translating SyGuS problems into sketches is non-trivial and results in poor performance.

The work closest to ours is Synapse [7], which combines sketching with an approach similar to ours. For the same reasons as for Sketch, Synapse differs from our work because it proposes a different search space mechanisms. However, there are a few analogies between our work and Synapse that are worth explaining in detail. Synapse supports syntactic cost functions that are defined using a decidable theory, and separately from the sketch search space. Synthesis is done using an iterative search where sketches—i.e., set of partial programs with holes—of increasing sizes are given to the synthesizer. At the high level, the intermediate sketches are related to our notion of reduced grammars—i.e., they accept solution of weight less than a given constant. However, while our algorithm generates reduced grammars automatically for a well-defined family of semirings, Synapse requires the user to provide a function for generating the intermediate sketches. Moreover, since Synapse requires cost functions that are defined using a decidable theory, it would not support certain families of costs QSyGuS supports—e.g., the probabilistic semiring.

Koukoutos et al. [15] have proposed the use of probabilistic tree grammars to guide the search of enumerative synthesizers on applications outside of SyGuS. Their algorithm enumerates all terms accepted by the grammar in decreasing probability using a variant of the search algorithm A^* and requires the grammar to not contain transitions of weight 1 to avoid getting stuck. Probabilistic tree grammars are a special case of QSyGuS and our algorithm does not impose limitations of what weights can appear in the grammar. Moreover, our algorithm does not require implementing a new solver when changing the cost semiring.

7 Conclusion

We presented QSyGuS, a general framework for defining and solving SyGuS problems in the presence of quantitative objectives over the syntax of the programs. QSyGuS is (*i*) *natural*: requires minimal modification to the SyGuS format, (*ii*) *general*: it supports complex but practical types of weights, (*iii*) *formal*: it is grounded in the theory of weighted tree grammars, (*iv*) *effective*: our tool QuaSi can solve quantitative variations of existing SyGuS benchmarks with little overhead. In the future, we plan to extend our framework to handle probabilistic objectives and quantitative objectives over the semantics of the program—e.g., synthesize programs that satisfy most of the specification.

Acknowledgements. The authors were supported by National Science Foundation Grants CCF-1637516, CCF-1704117 and a Google Research Award.

References

1. ESolver. https://github.com/abhishekudupa/sygus-comp14
2. Alur, R., Bodik, R., Juniwal, G., Martin, M.M., Raghothaman, M., Seshia, S.A., Singh, R., Solar-Lezama, A., Torlak, E., Udupa, A.: Syntax-guided synthesis. In: 2013 Formal Methods in Computer-Aided Design (FMCAD), pp. 1–8. IEEE (2013)
3. Alur, R., Fisman, D., Singh, R., Solar-Lezama, A.: Results and analysis of SyGuS-comp 2015. arXiv preprint arXiv:1602.01170 (2016)
4. Alur, R., Fisman, D., Singh, R., Solar-Lezama, A.: Sygus-comp 2016: results and analysis. arXiv preprint arXiv:1611.07627 (2016)
5. Alur, R., Radhakrishna, A., Udupa, A.: Scaling enumerative program synthesis via divide and conquer. In: Legay, A., Margaria, T. (eds.) TACAS 2017. LNCS, vol. 10205, pp. 319–336. Springer, Heidelberg (2017). https://doi.org/10.1007/978-3-662-54577-5_18
6. Barrett, C., et al.: CVC4. In: Gopalakrishnan, G., Qadeer, S. (eds.) CAV 2011. LNCS, vol. 6806, pp. 171–177. Springer, Heidelberg (2011). https://doi.org/10.1007/978-3-642-22110-1_14
7. Bornholt, J., Torlak, E., Grossman, D., Ceze, L.: Optimizing synthesis with metasketches. In: Proceedings of the 43rd Annual ACM SIGPLAN-SIGACT Symposium on Principles of Programming Languages, POPL 2016, pp. 775–788. ACM, New York (2016)
8. Caulfield, B., Rabe, M.N., Seshia, S.A., Tripakis, S.: What's decidable about syntax-guided synthesis? CoRR abs/1510.08393 (2015)
9. Comon, H., Dauchet, M., Gilleron, R., Löding, C., Jacquemard, F., Lugiez, D., Tison, S., Tommasi, M.: Tree automata techniques and applications (2007). http://www.grappa.univ-lille3.fr/tata. Accessed 12 Oct 2007
10. Droste, M., Kuich, W., Vogler, H.: Handbook of Weighted Automata, 1st edn. Springer, Heidelberg (2009). https://doi.org/10.1007/978-3-642-01492-5
11. Droste, M., Vogler, H.: Weighted tree automata and weighted logics. Theor. Comput. Sci. **366**(3), 228–247 (2006). Automata and Formal Languages
12. Gulwani, S.: Automating string processing in spreadsheets using input-output examples. In: Proceedings of the 38th ACM SIGPLAN-SIGACT Symposium on Principles of Programming Languages, POPL 2011, 26–28 January 2011, Austin, TX, USA, pp. 317–330 (2011)
13. Gulwani, S.: Programming by examples: applications, algorithms, and ambiguity resolution. In: Olivetti, N., Tiwari, A. (eds.) IJCAR 2016. LNCS (LNAI), vol. 9706, pp. 9–14. Springer, Cham (2016). https://doi.org/10.1007/978-3-319-40229-1_2
14. Hu, Q., D'Antoni, L.: Automatic program inversion using symbolic transducers. In: Proceedings of the 38th ACM SIGPLAN Conference on Programming Language Design and Implementation, PLDI 2017, 18–23 June 2017, Barcelona, Spain, pp. 376–389 (2017)

15. Koukoutos, M., Raghothaman, M., Kneuss, E., Kuncak, V.: On repair with probabilistic attribute grammars. CoRR abs/1707.04148 (2017)
16. Ngo, V.C., Dehesa-Azuara, M., Fredrikson, M., Hoffmann, J.: Verifying and synthesizing constant-resource implementations with types. In: 2017 IEEE Symposium on Security and Privacy (SP), pp. 710–728, May 2017
17. Polozov, O., Gulwani, S.: Flashmeta: a framework for inductive program synthesis. In: Proceedings of the 2015 ACM SIGPLAN International Conference on Object-Oriented Programming, Systems, Languages, and Applications, OOPSLA 2015, part of SPLASH 2015, 25–30 October 2015, Pittsburgh, PA, USA, pp. 107–126 (2015)
18. Schkufza, E., Sharma, R., Aiken, A.: Stochastic program optimization. Commun. ACM **59**(2), 114–122 (2016)
19. Singh, R., Gulwani, S.: Predicting a correct program in programming by example. In: Kroening, D., Păsăreanu, C.S. (eds.) CAV 2015. LNCS, vol. 9206, pp. 398–414. Springer, Cham (2015). https://doi.org/10.1007/978-3-319-21690-4_23
20. Singh, R., Gulwani, S., Solar-Lezama, A.: Automated feedback generation for introductory programming assignments. In: Proceedings of PLDI 2013, pp. 15–26. ACM, New York (2013)
21. Solar-Lezama, A.: Program sketching. Int. J. Softw. Tools Technol. Transf. **15**(5), 475–495 (2013)

Learning

Learning Abstractions for Program Synthesis

Xinyu Wang[1(✉)], Greg Anderson[1(✉)], Isil Dillig[1(✉)], and K. L. McMillan[2(✉)]

[1] University of Texas, Austin, USA
{xwang,ganderso,isil}@cs.utexas.edu
[2] Microsoft Research, Redmond, USA
kenmcmil@microsoft.com

Abstract. Many example-guided program synthesis techniques use *abstractions* to prune the search space. While abstraction-based synthesis has proven to be very powerful, a domain expert needs to provide a suitable abstract domain, together with the abstract transformers of each DSL construct. However, coming up with useful abstractions can be non-trivial, as it requires both domain expertise and knowledge about the synthesizer. In this paper, we propose a new technique for learning abstractions that are useful for instantiating a general synthesis framework in a new domain. Given a DSL and a small set of training problems, our method uses *tree interpolation* to infer reusable predicate templates that speed up synthesis in a given domain. Our method also learns suitable abstract transformers by solving a certain kind of second-order constraint solving problem in a data-driven way. We have implemented the proposed method in a tool called ATLAS and evaluate it in the context of the BLAZE meta-synthesizer. Our evaluation shows that (a) ATLAS can learn useful abstract domains and transformers from few training problems, and (b) the abstractions learned by ATLAS allow BLAZE to achieve significantly better results compared to manually-crafted abstractions.

1 Introduction

Program synthesis is a powerful technique for automatically generating programs from high-level specifications, such as input-output examples. Due to its myriad use cases across a wide range of application domains (e.g., spreadsheet automation [1–3], data science [4–6], cryptography [7,8], improving programming productivity [9–11]), program synthesis has received widespread attention from the research community in recent years.

Because program synthesis is, in essence, a very difficult search problem, many recent solutions prune the search space by utilizing *program abstractions* [4,12–16]. For example, state-of-the-art synthesis tools, such as BLAZE [14], MORPHEUS [4] and Scythe [16], symbolically execute (partial) programs over some abstract domain and reject those programs whose abstract behavior is inconsistent with the given specification. Because many programs share the same behavior in terms of their abstract semantics, the use of abstractions allows these synthesis tools to significantly reduce the search space.

H. Chockler and G. Weissenbacher (Eds.): CAV 2018, LNCS 10981, pp. 407–426, 2018.
https://doi.org/10.1007/978-3-319-96145-3_22

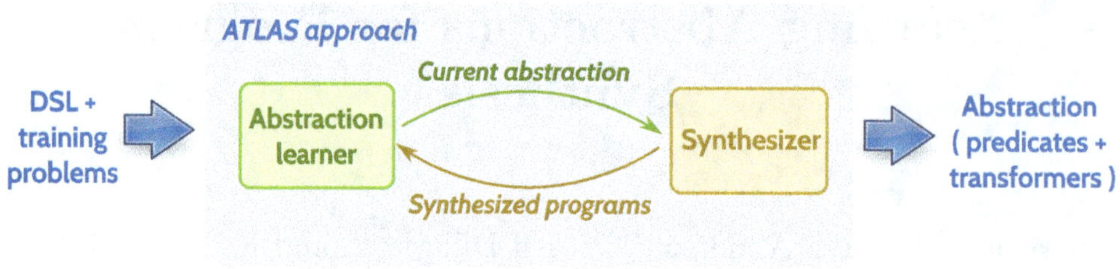

Fig. 1. Schematic overview of our approach.

While the abstraction-guided synthesis paradigm has proven to be quite powerful, a down-side of such techniques is that they require a domain expert to manually come up with a suitable abstract domain and write abstract transformers for each DSL construct. For instance, the BLAZE synthesis framework [14] expects a domain expert to manually specify a universe of predicate templates, together with sound abstract transformers for every DSL construct. Unfortunately, this process is not only time-consuming but also requires significant insight about the application domain as well as the internal workings of the synthesizer.

In this paper, we propose a novel technique for automatically learning domain-specific abstractions that are useful for instantiating an example-guided synthesis framework in a new domain. Given a DSL and a training set of synthesis problems (i.e., input-output examples), our method learns a useful abstract domain in the form of predicate templates and infers sound abstract transformers for each DSL construct. In addition to eliminating the significant manual effort required from a domain expert, the abstractions learned by our method often outperform manually-crafted ones in terms of their benefit to synthesizer performance.

The workflow of our approach, henceforth called ATLAS[1], is shown schematically in Fig. 1. Since ATLAS is meant to be used as an *off-line* training step for a general-purpose programming-by-example (PBE) system, it takes as input a DSL as well as a set of synthesis problems $\mathcal{E}$ that can be used for training purposes. Given these inputs, our method enters a refinement loop where an *Abstraction Learner* component discovers a sequence of increasingly precise abstract domains $\mathcal{A}_1, \cdot\cdot, \mathcal{A}_n$, and their corresponding abstract transformers $\mathcal{T}_1, \cdot\cdot, \mathcal{T}_n$, in order to help the *Abstraction-Guided Synthesizer* (AGS) solve all training problems. While the AGS can reject many incorrect solutions using an abstract domain $\mathcal{A}_i$, it might still return some incorrect solutions due to the insufficiency of $\mathcal{A}_i$. Thus, whenever the AGS returns an incorrect solution to any training problem, the Abstraction Learner discovers a more precise abstract domain and automatically synthesizes the corresponding abstract transformers. Upon termination of the algorithm, the final abstract domain $\mathcal{A}_n$ and transformers $\mathcal{T}_n$ are sufficient for the AGS to correctly solve *all* training problems. Furthermore, because our method learns *general* abstractions in the form of

[1] ATLAS stands for AuTomated Learning of AbStractions.

predicate templates, the learned abstractions are expected to be useful for solving many *other* synthesis problems beyond those in the training set.

From a technical perspective, the Abstraction Learner uses two key ideas, namely *tree interpolation* and *data-driven constraint solving*, for learning useful abstract domains and transformers respectively. Specifically, given an incorrect program $\mathcal{P}$ that cannot be refuted by the AGS using the current abstract domain $\mathcal{A}_i$, the Abstraction Learner generates a tree interpolant $\mathcal{I}_i$ that serves as a proof of $\mathcal{P}$'s incorrectness and constructs a new abstract domain $\mathcal{A}_{i+1}$ by extracting templates from the predicates used in $\mathcal{I}_i$. The Abstraction Learner also synthesizes the corresponding abstract transformers for $\mathcal{A}_{i+1}$ by setting up a *second-order constraint solving* problem where the goal is to find the unknown relationship between symbolic constants used in the predicate templates. Our method solves this problem in a data-driven way by sampling input-output examples for DSL operators and ultimately reduces the transformer learning problem to solving a system of linear equations.

We have implemented these ideas in a tool called Atlas and evaluate it in the context of the Blaze program synthesis framework [14]. Our evaluation shows that the proposed technique eliminates the manual effort involved in designing useful abstractions. More surprisingly, our evaluation also shows that the abstractions generated by Atlas outperform manually-crafted ones in terms of the performance of the Blaze synthesizer in two different application domains.

To summarize, this paper makes the following key contributions:

- We describe a method for learning abstractions (domains/transformers) that are useful for instantiating program synthesis frameworks in new domains.
- We show how tree interpolation can be used for learning abstract domains (i.e., predicate templates) from a few training problems.
- We describe a method for automatically synthesizing transformers for a given abstract domain under certain assumptions. Our method is guaranteed to find the unique best transformer if one exists.
- We implement our method in a tool called Atlas and experimentally evaluate it in the context of the Blaze synthesis framework. Our results demonstrate that the abstractions discovered by Atlas outperform manually-written ones used for evaluating Blaze in two application domains.

2 Illustrative Example

Suppose that we wish to use the Blaze meta-synthesizer to automate the class of string transformations considered by FlashFill [1] and BlinkFill [17]. In the original version of the Blaze framework [14], a domain expert needs to come up with a universe of suitable predicate templates as well as abstract transformers for each DSL construct. We will now illustrate how Atlas automates this process, given a suitable DSL and its semantics (e.g., the one used in [17]).

In order to use Atlas, one needs to provide a set of synthesis problems $\mathcal{E}$ (i.e., input-output examples) that will be used in the training process. Specifically, let us consider the three synthesis problems given below:

$$\mathcal{E} = \left\{ \begin{array}{l} \mathcal{E}_1 : \{ \text{“}\texttt{CAV}\text{”} \mapsto \text{“}\texttt{CAV2018}\text{”}, \text{“}\texttt{SAS}\text{”} \mapsto \text{“}\texttt{SAS2018}\text{”}, \text{“}\texttt{FSE}\text{”} \mapsto \text{“}\texttt{FSE2018}\text{”} \}, \\ \mathcal{E}_2 : \{ \text{“}\texttt{510.220.5586}\text{”} \mapsto \text{“}\texttt{510-220-5586}\text{”} \}, \\ \mathcal{E}_3 : \left\{ \begin{array}{l} \text{“}\texttt{\textbackslash Company\textbackslash Code\textbackslash index.html}\text{”} \mapsto \text{“}\texttt{\textbackslash Company\textbackslash Code\textbackslash}\text{”}, \\ \text{“}\texttt{\textbackslash Company\textbackslash Docs\textbackslash Spec\textbackslash specs.html}\text{”} \mapsto \text{“}\texttt{\textbackslash Company\textbackslash Docs\textbackslash Spec\textbackslash}\text{”} \end{array} \right\} \end{array} \right\}.$$

In order to construct the abstract domain $\mathcal{A}$ and transformers $\mathcal{T}$, Atlas starts with the trivial abstract domain $\mathcal{A}_0 = \{\top\}$ and transformers $\mathcal{T}_0$, defined as $[\![F(\top, \cdot\cdot, \top)]\!]^\sharp = \top$ for each DSL construct F. Using this abstraction, Atlas invokes Blaze to find a program $\mathcal{P}_0$ that satisfies specification $\mathcal{E}_1$ under the current abstraction $(\mathcal{A}_0, \mathcal{T}_0)$. However, since the program $\mathcal{P}_0$ returned by Blaze is incorrect with respect to the concrete semantics, Atlas tries to find a more precise abstraction that allows Blaze to succeed.

Towards this goal, Atlas enters a refinement loop that culminates in the discovery of the abstract domain $\mathcal{A}_1 = \{\top, \mathit{len}(\boxed{\alpha}) = \mathtt{c}, \mathit{len}(\boxed{\alpha}) \neq \mathtt{c}\}$, where α denotes a variable and $\mathtt{c}$ is an integer constant. In other words, $\mathcal{A}_1$ tracks equality and inequality constraints on the length of strings. After learning these predicate templates, Atlas also synthesizes the corresponding abstract transformers $\mathcal{T}_1$. In particular, for each DSL construct, Atlas learns one abstract transformer for each combination of predicate templates used in $\mathcal{A}_1$. For instance, for the `Concat` operator which returns the concatenation y of two strings x_1, x_2, Atlas synthesizes the following abstract transformers, where $\star$ denotes any predicate:

$$\mathcal{T}_1 = \left\{ \begin{array}{r} [\![\texttt{Concat}(\top, \star)]\!]^\sharp = \top \\ [\![\texttt{Concat}(\star, \top)]\!]^\sharp = \top \\ [\![\texttt{Concat}\big(\mathit{len}(x_1) \neq \mathtt{c}_1, \mathit{len}(x_2) \neq \mathtt{c}_2\big)]\!]^\sharp = \top \\ [\![\texttt{Concat}\big(\mathit{len}(x_1) = \mathtt{c}_1, \mathit{len}(x_2) = \mathtt{c}_2\big)]\!]^\sharp = \big(\mathit{len}(y) = \mathtt{c}_1 + \mathtt{c}_2\big) \\ [\![\texttt{Concat}\big(\mathit{len}(x_1) = \mathtt{c}_1, \mathit{len}(x_2) \neq \mathtt{c}_2\big)]\!]^\sharp = \big(\mathit{len}(y) \neq \mathtt{c}_1 + \mathtt{c}_2\big) \\ [\![\texttt{Concat}\big(\mathit{len}(x_1) \neq \mathtt{c}_1, \mathit{len}(x_2) = \mathtt{c}_2\big)]\!]^\sharp = \big(\mathit{len}(y) \neq \mathtt{c}_1 + \mathtt{c}_2\big) \end{array} \right\}.$$

Since the AGS can successfully solve $\mathcal{E}_1$ using $(\mathcal{A}_1, \mathcal{T}_1)$, Atlas now moves on to the next training problem.

For synthesis problem $\mathcal{E}_2$, the current abstraction $(\mathcal{A}_1, \mathcal{T}_1)$ is *not* sufficient for Blaze to discover the correct program. After processing $\mathcal{E}_2$, Atlas refines the abstract domain to the following set of predicate templates:

$$\mathcal{A}_2 = \{ \top, \mathit{len}(\boxed{\alpha}) = \mathtt{c}, \mathit{len}(\boxed{\alpha}) \neq \mathtt{c}, \mathit{charAt}(\boxed{\alpha}, \mathtt{i}) = \mathtt{c}, \mathit{charAt}(\boxed{\alpha}, \mathtt{i}) \neq \mathtt{c} \}.$$

Observe that Atlas has discovered two additional predicate templates that track positions of characters in the string. Atlas also learns the corresponding abstract transformers $\mathcal{T}_2$ for $\mathcal{A}_2$.

Moving on to the final training problem $\mathcal{E}_3$, Blaze can already successfully solve it using $(\mathcal{A}_2, \mathcal{T}_2)$; thus, Atlas terminates with this abstraction.

3 Overall Abstraction Learning Algorithm

Our top-level algorithm for learning abstractions, called LearnAbstractions, is shown in Fig. 2. The algorithm takes two inputs, namely a domain-specific

1: **procedure** LEARNABSTRACTIONS($\mathcal{L}, \boldsymbol{\mathcal{E}}$)
  input: Domain-specific language $\mathcal{L}$ and a set of training problems $\boldsymbol{\mathcal{E}}$.
  output: Abstract domain $\mathcal{A}$ and transformers $\mathcal{T}$.
2: $\quad \mathcal{A} \leftarrow \{ \top \}$; ▷ Initialization.
3: $\quad \mathcal{T} \leftarrow \{ [\![F(\top, \cdot\cdot, \top)]\!]^\sharp = \top \mid F \in \mathsf{Constructs}(\mathcal{L}) \}$;
4: $\quad$ **for** $i \leftarrow 1, \cdot\cdot, |\boldsymbol{\mathcal{E}}|$ **do**
5: $\quad\quad$ **while** true **do** ▷ Refinement loop.
6: $\quad\quad\quad \mathcal{P} \leftarrow \mathsf{Synthesize}(\mathcal{L}, \mathcal{E}_i, \mathcal{A}, \mathcal{T})$; ▷ Invoke AGS.
7: $\quad\quad\quad$ **if** $\mathcal{P} = null$ **then break**;
8: $\quad\quad\quad$ **if** $\mathsf{IsCorrect}(\mathcal{P}, \mathcal{E}_i)$ **then break**;
9: $\quad\quad\quad \mathcal{A} \leftarrow \mathcal{A} \cup$ LEARNABSTRACTDOMAIN($\mathcal{P}, \mathcal{E}_i$);
10: $\quad\quad\quad \mathcal{T} \leftarrow$ LEARNTRANSFORMERS($\mathcal{L}, \mathcal{A}$);
11: $\quad$ **return** $(\mathcal{A}, \mathcal{T})$;

Fig. 2. Overall learning algorithm. Constructs gives the DSL constructs in $\mathcal{L}$.

language $\mathcal{L}$ (both syntax and semantics) as well as a set of training problems $\boldsymbol{\mathcal{E}}$, where each problem is specified as a *set* of input-output examples $\mathcal{E}_i$. The output of our algorithm is a pair $(\mathcal{A}, \mathcal{T})$, where $\mathcal{A}$ is an abstract domain represented by a set of predicate templates and $\mathcal{T}$ is the corresponding abstract transformers.

At a high-level, the LEARNABSTRACTIONS procedure starts with the most imprecise abstraction (just consisting of $\top$) and incrementally improves the precision of the abstract domain $\mathcal{A}$ whenever the AGS fails to synthesize the correct program using $\mathcal{A}$. Specifically, the outer loop (lines 4–10) considers each training instance $\mathcal{E}_i$ and performs a fixed-point computation (lines 5–10) that terminates when the current abstract domain $\mathcal{A}$ is good enough to solve problem $\mathcal{E}_i$. Thus, upon termination, the learned abstract domain $\mathcal{A}$ is sufficiently precise for the AGS to solve all training problems $\boldsymbol{\mathcal{E}}$.

Specifically, in order to find an abstraction that is sufficient for solving $\mathcal{E}_i$, our algorithm invokes the AGS with the current abstract domain $\mathcal{A}$ and corresponding transformers $\mathcal{T}$ (line 6). We assume that Synthesize returns a program $\mathcal{P}$ that is consistent with $\mathcal{E}_i$ under abstraction $(\mathcal{A}, \mathcal{T})$. That is, symbolically executing $\mathcal{P}$ (according to $\mathcal{T}$) on inputs $\mathcal{E}_i^{in}$ yields abstract values φ that are consistent with the outputs $\mathcal{E}_i^{out}$ (i.e., $\forall j.\ \mathcal{E}_{ij}^{out} \in \gamma(\varphi_j)$). However, while $\mathcal{P}$ is guaranteed to be consistent with $\mathcal{E}_i$ under the abstract semantics, it may not satisfy $\mathcal{E}_i$ under the concrete semantics. We refer to such a program $\mathcal{P}$ as *spurious*.

Thus, whenever the call to IsCorrect fails at line 8, we invoke the LEARNABSTRACTDOMAIN procedure (line 9) to learn additional predicate templates that are later added to $\mathcal{A}$. Since the refinement of $\mathcal{A}$ necessitates the synthesis of new transformers, we then call LEARNTRANSFORMERS (line 10) to learn a new $\mathcal{T}$. The new abstraction is guaranteed to rule out the spurious program $\mathcal{P}$ as long as there is a unique best transformer of each DSL construct for domain $\mathcal{A}$.

4 Learning Abstract Domain Using Tree Interpolation

In this section, we present the LEARNABSTRACTDOMAIN procedure: Given a spurious program $\mathcal{P}$ and a synthesis problem $\mathcal{E}$ that $\mathcal{P}$ does not solve, our goal is to find new predicate templates $\mathcal{A}'$ to add to the abstract domain $\mathcal{A}$ such that the Abstraction-Guided Synthesizer no longer returns $\mathcal{P}$ as a valid solution to the synthesis problem $\mathcal{E}$. Our key insight is that we can mine for such useful predicate templates by constructing a *tree interpolation* problem. In what follows, we first review tree interpolants (based on [18]) and then explain how we use this concept to find useful predicate templates.

Definition 1 (Tree interpolation problem). *A tree interpolation problem $T = (V, r, P, L)$ is a directed labeled tree, where V is a finite set of nodes, $r \in V$ is the root, $P : (V \backslash \{r\}) \mapsto V$ is a function that maps children nodes to their parents, and $L : V \mapsto \mathbb{F}$ is a labeling function that maps nodes to formulas from a set $\mathbb{F}$ of first-order formulas such that $\bigwedge_{v \in V} L(v)$ is unsatisfiable.*

In other words, a tree interpolation problem is defined by a tree T where each node is labeled with a formula and the conjunction of these formulas is unsatisfiable. In what follows, we write $Desc(v)$ to denote the set of all descendants of node v, including v itself, and we write $NonDesc(v)$ to denote all nodes other than those in $Desc(v)$ (i.e., $V \backslash Desc(v)$). Also, given a set of nodes V', we write $L(V')$ to denote the set of all formulas labeling nodes in V'.

Given a tree interpolation problem T, a *tree interpolant* $\mathcal{I}$ is an annotation from every node in V to a formula such that the label of the root node is *false* and the label of an internal node v is entailed by the conjunction of annotations of its children nodes. More formally, a tree interpolant is defined as follows:

Definition 2 (Tree interpolant). *Given a tree interpolation problem $T = (V, r, P, L)$, a tree interpolant for T is a function $\mathcal{I} : V \mapsto \mathbb{F}$ that satisfies the following conditions:*

1. $\mathcal{I}(r) = \text{false}$;
2. *For each* $v \in V$: $\Big(\big(\bigwedge_{P(c_i)=v} \mathcal{I}(c_i) \big) \wedge L(v) \Big) \Rightarrow \mathcal{I}(v)$;
3. *For each* $v \in V$: $Vars\big(\mathcal{I}(v)\big) \subseteq Vars\big(L(Desc(v))\big) \bigcap Vars\big(L(NonDesc(v))\big)$.

Intuitively, the first condition ensures that $\mathcal{I}$ establishes the unsatisfiability of formulas in T, and the second condition states that $\mathcal{I}$ is a valid annotation. As standard in Craig interpolation [19,20], the third condition stipulates a "shared vocabulary" condition by ensuring that the annotation at each node v refers to the common variables between the descendants and non-descendants of v.

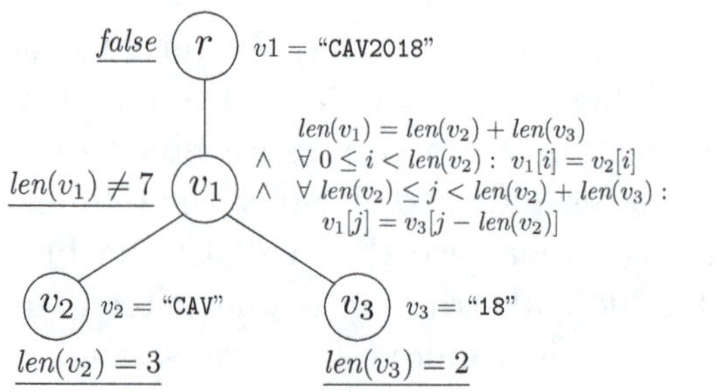

Fig. 3. A tree interpolation problem and a tree interpolant (underlined).

1: **procedure** LEARNABSTRACTDOMAIN($\mathcal{P}, \mathcal{E}$)
  input: Program $\mathcal{P}$ that does not solve problem $\mathcal{E}$ (set of examples).
  output: Set of predicate templates $\mathcal{A}'$.
2: $\mathcal{A}' \leftarrow \emptyset$;
3: **for each** $(e_{in}, e_{out}) \in \mathcal{E}$ **do**
4: **if** $[\![\mathcal{P}]\!]e_{in} \neq e_{out}$ **then**
5: $T \leftarrow$ CONSTRUCTTREE($\mathcal{P}, e_{in}, e_{out}$);
6: $\mathcal{I} \leftarrow$ FindTreeItp(T);
7: **for each** $v \in$ Nodes(T)$\backslash\{r\}$ **do**
8: $\mathcal{A}' \leftarrow \mathcal{A}' \cup \{\mathsf{MakeSymbolic}(\mathcal{I}(v))\}$;
9: **return** $\mathcal{A}'$;

Fig. 4. Algorithm for learning abstract domain using tree interpolation.

Example 1. Consider the tree interpolation problem $T = (V, r, P, L)$ in Fig. 3, where $L(v)$ is shown to the right of each node v. A tree interpolant $\mathcal{I}$ for this problem maps each node to the corresponding underlined formula. For instance, we have $\mathcal{I}(v_1) = (len(v_1) \neq 7)$. It is easy to confirm that $\mathcal{I}$ is a valid interpolant according to Definition 2.

To see how tree interpolation is useful for learning predicates, suppose that the spurious program $\mathcal{P}$ is represented as an abstract syntax tree (AST), where each non-leaf node is labeled with the axiomatic semantics of the corresponding DSL construct. Now, since $\mathcal{P}$ does not satisfy the given input-output example (e_{in}, e_{out}), we are able to use this information to construct a labeled tree where the conjunction of labels is unsatisfiable. Our key idea is to mine useful predicate templates from the formulas used in the resulting tree interpolant.

With this intuition in mind, let us consider the LEARNABSTRACTDOMAIN procedure shown in Fig. 4: The algorithm uses a procedure called CONSTRUCTTREE to generate a tree interpolation problem T for each input-output example (e_{in}, e_{out})[2] that program $\mathcal{P}$ does not satisfy (line 5). Specifically, letting Π denote the AST representation of $\mathcal{P}$, we construct $T = (V, r, P, L)$ as follows:

- V consists of all AST nodes in Π as well as a "dummy" node d.
- The root r of T is the dummy node d.
- P is a function that maps children AST nodes to their parents and maps the root AST node to the dummy node d.
- L maps each node $v \in V$ to a formula as follows:

$$L(v) = \begin{cases} v' = e_{out} & v \text{ is the dummy root node with child } v'. \\ v = e_{in} & v \text{ is a leaf representing program input } e_{in}. \\ v = c & v \text{ is a leaf representing constant } c. \\ \phi_F[\boldsymbol{v}'/\boldsymbol{x}, v/y] & v \text{ represents DSL operator } F \text{ with axiomatic semantics} \\ & \phi_F(\boldsymbol{x}, y) \text{ and } \boldsymbol{v}' \text{ represents children of } v. \end{cases}$$

[2] Without loss of generality, we assume that programs take a single input x, as we can always represent multiple inputs as a list.

Essentially, the ConstructTree procedure labels any leaf node representing the program input with the input example e_{in} and the root node with the output example e_{out}. All other internal nodes are labeled with the axiomatic semantics of the corresponding DSL operator (modulo renaming).[3] Observe that the formula $\bigwedge_{v \in V} L(v)$ is guaranteed to be unsatisfiable since $\mathcal{P}$ does not satisfy the I/O example (e_{in}, e_{out}); thus, we can obtain a tree interpolant for T.

Example 2. Consider program $\mathcal{P}$: $\texttt{Concat}(x, \text{“18”})$ which concatenates constant string “18” to input x. Figure 3 shows the result of invoking ConstructTree for $\mathcal{P}$ and input-output example (“CAV”, “CAV2018”). As mentioned in Example 1, the tree interpolant $\mathcal{I}$ for this problem is indicated with the underlined formulas.

Since the tree interpolant $\mathcal{I}$ effectively establishes the incorrectness of program $\mathcal{P}$, the predicates used in $\mathcal{I}$ serve as useful abstract values that the synthesizer (AGS) should consider during the synthesis task. Towards this goal, the LearnAbstractDomain algorithm iterates over each predicate used in $\mathcal{I}$ (lines 7–8 in Fig. 4) and converts it to a suitable template by replacing the constants and variables used in $\mathcal{I}(v)$ with symbolic names (or “holes”). Because the original predicates used in $\mathcal{I}$ may be too specific for the current input-output example, extracting templates from the interpolant allows our method to learn reusable abstract domains.

Example 3. Given the tree interpolant $\mathcal{I}$ from Example 1, LearnAbstractDomain extracts two predicate templates, namely, $len(\boxed{\alpha}) = \mathsf{c}$ and $len(\boxed{\alpha}) \neq \mathsf{c}$.

5 Synthesis of Abstract Transformers

In this section, we turn our attention to the LearnTransformers procedure for synthesizing abstract transformers $\mathcal{T}$ for a given abstract domain $\mathcal{A}$. Following presentation in prior work [14], we consider abstract transformers that are described using equations of the following form:

$$[\![F(\chi_1(x_1, \boldsymbol{c}_1), \cdot\cdot, \chi_n(x_n, \boldsymbol{c}_n))]\!]^\sharp = \bigwedge_{1 \leq j \leq m} \chi'_j(y, \boldsymbol{f}_j(\boldsymbol{c})) \tag{1}$$

Here, F is a DSL construct, χ_i, χ'_j are predicate templates[4], x_i is the i'th input of F, y is F's output, $\boldsymbol{c}_1, \cdot\cdot, \boldsymbol{c}_n$ are vectors of *symbolic* constants, and $\boldsymbol{f}_j$ denotes a vector of *affine functions* over $\boldsymbol{c} = \boldsymbol{c}_1, \cdot\cdot, \boldsymbol{c}_n$. Intuitively, given concrete predicates describing the inputs to F, the transformer returns concrete predicates describing the output. Given such a transformer τ, let $\mathsf{Outputs}(\tau)$ be the set of pairs $(\chi'_j, \boldsymbol{f}_j)$ in Eq. 1.

---

[3] Here, we assume access to the DSL's axiomatic semantics. If this is not the case (i.e., we are only given the DSL's operational semantics), we can still annotate each node as $v = c$ where c denotes the output of the partial program rooted at node v when executed on e_{in}. However, this may affect the quality of the resulting interpolant.

[4] We assume that $\chi'_1, \cdot\cdot, \chi'_m$ are distinct.

1: **procedure** LEARNTRANSFORMERS($\mathcal{L}, \mathcal{A}$)
  input: DSL $\mathcal{L}$ and abstract domain $\mathcal{A}$.
  output: A set of transformers $\mathcal{T}$ for constructs in $\mathcal{L}$ and abstract domain $\mathcal{A}$.
2: **for each** $F \in \mathsf{Constructs}(\mathcal{L})$ **do**
3: **for** $(\chi_1, \cdots, \chi_n) \in \mathcal{A}^n$ **do**
4: $\varphi \leftarrow \top$; ▷ φ is output of transformer.
5: **for** $\chi'_j \in \mathcal{A}$ **do**
6: $E \leftarrow$ GENERATEEXAMPLES($\phi_F, \chi'_j, \chi_1, \cdots, \chi_n$);
7: $\boldsymbol{f}_j \leftarrow \mathsf{Solve}(E)$;
8: **if** $\boldsymbol{f}_j \neq \textit{null} \wedge \mathsf{Valid}(\Lambda[\boldsymbol{f}_j])$ **then** $\varphi \leftarrow (\varphi \wedge \chi'_j(y, \boldsymbol{f}_j(\boldsymbol{c}_1, \cdots, \boldsymbol{c}_n)))$
9: $\mathcal{T} \leftarrow \mathcal{T} \cup \{[\![F(\chi_1(x_1, \boldsymbol{c}_1), \cdots, \chi_n(x_n, \boldsymbol{c}_n))]\!]^\sharp = \varphi\}$;
10: **return** $\mathcal{T}$;

Fig. 5. Algorithm for synthesizing abstract transformers. ϕ_F at line 6 denotes the axiomatic semantics of DSL construct F. Formula Λ at line 8 refers to Eq. 5.

We define the soundness of a transformer τ for DSL operator F with respect to F's axiomatic semantics ϕ_F. In particular, we say that the abstract transformer from Eq. 1 is *sound* if the following implication is valid:

$$\Big(\phi_F(\boldsymbol{x}, y) \wedge \bigwedge_{1 \leq i \leq n} \chi_i(x_i, \boldsymbol{c}_i)\Big) \Rightarrow \bigwedge_{1 \leq j \leq m} \chi'_j(y, \boldsymbol{f}_j(\boldsymbol{c})) \tag{2}$$

That is, the transformer for F is sound if the (symbolic) output predicate is indeed implied by the (symbolic) input predicates according to F's semantics.

Our key observation is that the problem of learning sound transformers can be reduced to solving the following *second-order constraint solving* problem:

$$\exists \boldsymbol{f}.\ \forall \boldsymbol{V}.\Big(\big(\phi_F(\boldsymbol{x}, y) \wedge \bigwedge_{1 \leq i \leq n} \chi_i(x_i, \boldsymbol{c}_i)\big) \Rightarrow \bigwedge_{1 \leq j \leq m} \chi'_j(y, \boldsymbol{f}_j(\boldsymbol{c}))\Big) \tag{3}$$

where $\boldsymbol{f} = \boldsymbol{f}_1, \cdots, \boldsymbol{f}_m$ and $\boldsymbol{V}$ includes all variables and functions from Eq. 2 other than $\boldsymbol{f}$. In other words, the goal of this constraint solving problem is to find interpretations of the unknown functions $\boldsymbol{f}$ that make Eq. 2 valid. Our key insight is to solve this problem in a *data-driven* way by exploiting the fact that each unknown function $f_{j,k}$ is affine.

Towards this goal, we first express each affine function $f_{j,k}(\boldsymbol{c})$ as follows:

$$f_{j,k}(\boldsymbol{c}) = p_{j,k,1} \cdot c_1 + \cdots + p_{j,k,|\boldsymbol{c}|} \cdot c_{|\boldsymbol{c}|} + p_{j,k,|\boldsymbol{c}|+1}$$

where each $p_{j,k,l}$ corresponds to an unknown integer constant that we would like to learn. Now, arranging the coefficients of functions $f_{j,1}, \cdots, f_{j,|\boldsymbol{f}_j|}$ in $\boldsymbol{f}_j$ into a $|\boldsymbol{f}_j| \times (|\boldsymbol{c}| + 1)$ matrix P_j, we can represent $\boldsymbol{f}_j(\boldsymbol{c})$ in the following way:

$$\boldsymbol{f}_j(\boldsymbol{c})^\intercal = \underbrace{\begin{bmatrix} f_{j,1}(\boldsymbol{c}) \\ \cdot\cdot \\ f_{j,|\boldsymbol{f}_j|}(\boldsymbol{c}) \end{bmatrix}}_{\boldsymbol{c}_j'^\intercal} = \underbrace{\begin{bmatrix} p_{j,1,1} & \cdot\cdot & p_{j,1,|\boldsymbol{c}|+1} \\ \cdot\cdot & & \cdot\cdot \\ p_{j,|\boldsymbol{f}_j|,1} & \cdot\cdot & p_{j,|\boldsymbol{f}_j|,|\boldsymbol{c}|+1} \end{bmatrix}}_{P_j} \underbrace{\begin{bmatrix} c_1 \\ \cdot\cdot \\ c_{|\boldsymbol{c}|} \\ 1 \end{bmatrix}}_{\boldsymbol{c}^\dagger} \tag{4}$$

where $\boldsymbol{c}^\dagger$ is $\boldsymbol{c}^\intercal$ appended with the constant 1.

Given this representation, it is easy to see that the problem of synthesizing the unknown functions $\boldsymbol{f}_1, \cdot\cdot, \boldsymbol{f}_m$ from Eq. 2 boils down to finding the unknown matrices $P_1, \cdot\cdot, P_m$ such that each P_j makes the following implication valid:

$$\Lambda \equiv \Big(\big((\boldsymbol{c}_j'^\intercal = P_j \boldsymbol{c}^\dagger) \wedge \phi_F(\boldsymbol{x}, y) \wedge \bigwedge_{1 \le i \le n} \chi_i(x_i, \boldsymbol{c}_i)\big) \Rightarrow \chi_j'(y, \boldsymbol{c}_j')\Big) \tag{5}$$

Our key idea is to infer these unknown matrices $P_1, \cdot\cdot, P_m$ in a data-driven way by generating input-output examples of the form $[i_1, \cdot\cdot, i_{|\boldsymbol{c}|}] \mapsto [o_1, \cdot\cdot, o_{|\boldsymbol{f}_j|}]$ for each $\boldsymbol{f}_j$. In other words, $\boldsymbol{i}$ and $\boldsymbol{o}$ correspond to instantiations of $\boldsymbol{c}$ and $\boldsymbol{f}_j(\boldsymbol{c})$ respectively. Given sufficiently many such examples for every $\boldsymbol{f}_j$, we can then reduce the problem of learning each unknown matrix P_j to the problem of solving a system of linear equations.

Based on this intuition, the LearnTransformers procedure from Fig. 5 describes our algorithm for learning abstract transformers $\mathcal{T}$ for a given abstract domain $\mathcal{A}$. At a high-level, our algorithm synthesizes one abstract transformer for each DSL construct F and n argument predicate templates $\chi_1, \cdot\cdot, \chi_n$. In particular, given F and $\chi_1, \cdot\cdot, \chi_n$, the algorithm constructs the "return value" of the transformer as:

$$\varphi = \bigwedge_{1 \le j \le m} \chi_j'(y, \boldsymbol{f}_j(\boldsymbol{c}))$$

where $\boldsymbol{f}_j$ is the inferred affine function for each predicate template χ_j'.

The key part of our LearnTransformers procedure is the inner loop (lines 5–8) for inferring each of these $\boldsymbol{f}_j$'s. Specifically, given an output predicate template χ_j', our algorithm first generates a set of input-output examples E of the form $[p_1, \cdot\cdot, p_n] \mapsto p_0$ such that $[\![F(p_1, \cdot\cdot, p_n)]\!]^\sharp = p_0$ is a sound (albeit overly specific) transformer. Essentially, each p_i is a concrete instantiation of a predicate template, so the examples E generated at line 6 of the algorithm can be viewed as sound input-output examples for the general symbolic transformer given in Eq. 1. (We will describe the GenerateExamples procedure in Sect. 5.1).

Once we generate these examples E, the next step of the algorithm is to learn the unknown coefficients of matrix P_j from Eq. 5 by solving a system of linear equations (line 7). Specifically, observe that we can use each input-output example $[p_1, \cdot\cdot, p_n] \mapsto p_0$ in E to construct one row of Eq. 4. In particular, we can directly extract $\boldsymbol{c} = \boldsymbol{c}_1, \cdot\cdot, \boldsymbol{c}_n$ from $p_1, \cdot\cdot, p_n$ and the corresponding value of $\boldsymbol{f}_j(\boldsymbol{c})$ from p_0. Since we have one instantiation of Eq. 4 for each of the input-output examples in E, the problem of inferring matrix P_j now reduces to solving a system of linear equations of the form $AP_j^T = B$ where A is a $|E| \times (|\boldsymbol{c}| + 1)$ (input) matrix and B is a $|E| \times |\boldsymbol{f}_j|$ (output) matrix. Thus, a solution to the

1: **procedure** GenerateExamples($\phi_F, \chi_0, \cdot\cdot, \chi_n$)

input: Semantics ϕ_F of operator F and templates $\chi_0, \cdot\cdot, \chi_n$ for output and inputs.
output: A set of valid input-output examples E for DSL construct F.

2: $E \leftarrow \emptyset$;
3: **while** $\neg\mathsf{FullRank}(E)$ **do**
4: Draw $(s_1, \cdot\cdot, s_n)$ randomly from distribution R_F over $\mathsf{Domain}(F)$;
5: $s_0 \leftarrow [\![F(s_1, \cdot\cdot, s_n)]\!]$;
6: $(A_0, \cdot\cdot, A_n) \leftarrow \mathsf{Abstract}(s_0, \chi_0, \cdot\cdot, s_n, \chi_n)$;
7: **for each** $(p_0, \cdot\cdot, p_n) \in A_0 \times \cdot\cdot \times A_n$ **do**
8: **if** $\mathsf{Valid}\big(\bigwedge_{1 \leq i \leq n} p_i \wedge \phi_F \Rightarrow p_0\big)$ **then** $E \leftarrow E \cup \big\{[p_1, \cdot\cdot, p_n] \mapsto p_0\big\}$;
9: **return** E;

Fig. 6. Example generation for learning abstract transformers.

equation $AP_j^T = B$ generated from E corresponds to a candidate solution for matrix P_j, which in turn uniquely defines $\boldsymbol{f}_j$.

Observe that the call to Solve at line 7 may return *null* if no affine function exists. Furthermore, any *non-null* $\boldsymbol{f}_j$ returned by Solve is just a *candidate* solution and may not satisfy Eq. 5. For example, this situation can arise if we do not have sufficiently many examples in E and end up discovering an affine function that is "over-fitted" to the examples. Thus, the validity check at line 8 of the algorithm ensures that the learned transformers are actually sound.

5.1 Example Generation

In our discussion so far, we assumed an oracle that is capable of generating valid input-output examples for a given transformer. We now explain our GenerateExamples procedure from Fig. 6 that essentially implements this oracle. In a nutshell, the goal of GenerateExamples is to synthesize input-output examples of the form $[p_1, \cdot\cdot, p_n] \mapsto p_0$ such that $[\![F(p_1, \cdot\cdot, p_n)]\!]^\sharp = p_0$ is sound where each p_i is a concrete predicate (rather than symbolic).

Going into more detail, GenerateExamples takes as input the semantics ϕ_F of DSL construct F for which we want to learn a transformer for as well as the input predicate templates $\chi_1, \cdot\cdot, \chi_n$ and output predicate template χ_0 that are supposed to be used in the transformer. For any example $[p_1, \cdot\cdot, p_n] \mapsto p_0$ synthesized by GenerateExamples, each concrete predicate p_i is an instantiation of the predicate template χ_i where the symbolic constants used in χ_i are substituted with *concrete* values.

Conceptually, the GenerateExamples algorithm proceeds as follows: First, it generates *concrete* input-output examples $[s_1, \cdot\cdot, s_n] \mapsto s_0$ by evaluating F on randomly-generated inputs $s_1, \cdot\cdot, s_n$ (lines 4–5). Now, for each concrete I/O example $[s_1, \cdot\cdot, s_n] \mapsto s_0$, we generate a set of *abstract* I/O examples of the form $[p_1, \cdot\cdot, p_n] \mapsto p_0$ (line 6). Specifically, we assume that the return value $(A_0, \cdot\cdot, A_n)$ of Abstract at line 6 satisfies the following properties for every $p_i \in A_i$:

- p_i is an instantiation of template χ_i.
- p_i is a sound over-approximation of s_i (i.e., $s_i \in \gamma(p_i)$).
- For any other p'_i satisfying the above two conditions, p'_i is not logically stronger than p_i.

In other words, we assume that Abstract returns a set of "best" sound abstractions of $(s_0, \cdot\cdot, s_n)$ under predicate templates $(\chi_0, \cdot\cdot, \chi_n)$.

Next, given abstractions $(A_0, \cdot\cdot, A_n)$ for $(s_0, \cdot\cdot, s_n)$, we consider each candidate abstract example of the form $[p_1, \cdot\cdot, p_n] \mapsto p_0$ where $p_i \in A_i$. Even though each p_i is a sound abstraction of s_i, the example $[p_1, \cdot\cdot, p_n] \mapsto p_0$ may not be valid according to the semantics of operator F. Thus, the validity check at line 8 ensures that each example added to E is in fact valid.

Example 4. Given abstract domain $\mathcal{A} = \{len(\boxed{\alpha}) = \mathsf{c}\}$, suppose we want to learn an abstract transformer τ for the Concat operator of the following form:

$$[\![\texttt{Concat}\big(len(x_1) = \mathsf{c}_1, len(x_2) = \mathsf{c}_2\big)]\!]^\sharp = \big(len(y) = f([\mathsf{c}_1, \mathsf{c}_2])\big)$$

We learn the affine function f used in the transformer by first generating a set E of I/O examples for f (line 6 in LEARNTRANSFORMERS). In particular, GENERATEEXAMPLES generates concrete input values for Concat at random and obtains the corresponding output values by executing Concat on the input values. For instance, it may generate $s_1 =$ "*abc*" and $s_2 =$ "*de*" as inputs, and obtain $s_0 =$ "*abcde*" as output. Then, it abstracts these values under the given templates. In this case, we have an abstract example with $p_1 = \big(len(x_1) = 3\big)$, $p_2 = \big(len(x_2) = 2\big)$ and $p_0 = \big(len(y) = 5\big)$. Since $[p_1, p_2] \mapsto p_0$ is a valid example, it is added in E (line 8 in GENERATEEXAMPLES). At this point, E is not yet full rank, so the algorithm keeps generating more examples. Suppose it generates two more valid examples $\big(len(x_1) = 1, len(x_2) = 4\big) \mapsto \big(len(y) = 5\big)$ and $\big(len(x_1) = 6, len(x_2) = 4\big) \mapsto \big(len(y) = 10\big)$. Now E is full rank, so LEARNTRANSFORMERS computes f by solving the following system of linear equations:

$$\begin{bmatrix} 3\ 2\ 1 \\ 1\ 4\ 1 \\ 6\ 4\ 1 \end{bmatrix} P^T = \begin{bmatrix} 5 \\ 5 \\ 10 \end{bmatrix} \xRightarrow{\textsf{Solve}} P = [1\ 1\ 0]$$

Here, P corresponds to the function $f([\mathsf{c}_1, \mathsf{c}_2]) = \mathsf{c}_1 + \mathsf{c}_2$, and this function defines the sound transformer: $[\![\texttt{Concat}\big(len(x_1) = \mathsf{c}_1, len(x_2) = \mathsf{c}_2\big)]\!]^\sharp = \big(len(y) = \mathsf{c}_1 + \mathsf{c}_2\big)$ which is added to $\mathcal{T}$ at line 9 in LEARNTRANSFORMERS.

6 Soundness and Completeness

In this section we present theorems stating some of the soundness, completeness, and termination guarantees of our approach. All proofs can be found in the extended version of this paper [21].

Theorem 1 (Soundness of LEARNTRANSFORMERS). *Let $\mathcal{T}$ be the set of transformers returned by* LEARNTRANSFORMERS. *Then, every $\tau \in \mathcal{T}$ is sound according to Eq. 2.*

The remaining theorems are predicated on the assumptions that for each DSL construct F and input predicate templates $\chi_1, \cdot\cdot, \chi_n$ (i) there exists a unique best abstract transformer and (ii) the strongest transformer expressible in Eq. 2 is logically equivalent to the unique best transformer. Thus, before stating these theorems, we first state what we mean by a *unique best abstract transformer.*

Definition 3 (Unique best function). *Consider a family of transformers of the shape* $[\![F(\chi_1(x_1, \boldsymbol{c}_1), \cdot\cdot, \chi_n(x_n, \boldsymbol{c}_n))]\!]^\sharp = \chi'(y, \star)$. *We say that* $\boldsymbol{f}$ *is the unique best function for* $(F, \chi_1, \cdot\cdot, \chi_n, \chi')$ *if (a) replacing* $\star$ *with* $\boldsymbol{f}$ *yields a sound transformer, and (b) replacing* $\star$ *with any other* $\boldsymbol{f}'$ *yields a transformer that is either unsound or strictly worse (i.e.,* $\chi'(y, \boldsymbol{f}) \Rightarrow \chi'(y, \boldsymbol{f}')$ *and* $\chi'(y, \boldsymbol{f}') \not\Rightarrow \chi'(y, \boldsymbol{f})$*).*

We now define unique best transformer in terms of unique best function:

Definition 4 (Unique best transformer). *Let* F *be a DSL construct and let* $(\chi_1, \cdot\cdot, \chi_n) \in \mathcal{A}^n$ *be the input templates for* F. *We say that the abstract transformer* τ *is a unique best transformer for* $F, \chi_1, \cdot\cdot, \chi_n$ *if (a)* τ *is sound, and (b) for any predicate template* $\chi \in \mathcal{A}$, *we have* $(\chi, \boldsymbol{f}) \in \mathsf{Outputs}(\tau)$ *if and only if* $\boldsymbol{f}$ *is a unique best function for* $(F, \chi_1, \cdot\cdot, \chi_n, \chi)$ *for some affine* $\boldsymbol{f}$.

Definition 5 (Complete sampling oracle). *Let* F *be a construct,* $\mathcal{A}$ *an abstract domain, and* R_F *a probability distribution over* $\text{Domain}(F)$ *with finite support* S. *Futher, for any input predicate templates* $\chi_1, \cdot\cdot, \chi_n$ *and output predicate template* χ_0 *in* $\mathcal{A}$ *admitting a unique best function* $\boldsymbol{f}$, *let* $C(\chi_0, \cdot\cdot, \chi_n)$ *be the set of tuples* $(c_0, \cdot\cdot, c_n)$ *such that* $(\chi_0(y, c_0), \chi_1(x_1, c_1), \cdot\cdot, \chi_n(x_n, c_n)) \in A_0 \times \cdot\cdot \times A_n$ *and* $c_0 = \boldsymbol{f}(c_1, \cdot\cdot, c_n)$, *where* $A_0 \times \cdot\cdot \times A_n = \text{Abstract}(s_0, \chi_0, \cdot\cdot, s_n, \chi_n)$ *and* $(s_1, \cdot\cdot, s_n) \in S$ *and* $s_0 = [\![F(s_1, \cdot\cdot, s_n)]\!]$. *The distribution* R_F *is a* complete sampling oracle *if* $C(\chi_0, \cdot\cdot, \chi_n)$ *has full rank for all* $\chi_0, \cdot\cdot, \chi_n$.

The following theorem states that LearnTransformers is guaranteed to synthesize the best transformer if a unique one exists:

Theorem 2 (Completeness of LearnTransformers). *Given an abstract domain* $\mathcal{A}$ *and a complete sampling oracle* R_F *for* $\mathcal{A}$, LearnTransformers *terminates. Further, let* $\mathcal{T}$ *be the set of transformers returned and let* τ *be the unique best transformer for DSL construct* F *and input predicate templates* $\chi_1, \cdot\cdot, \chi_n \in \mathcal{A}^n$. *Then we have* $\tau \in \mathcal{T}$.

Using this completeness (modulo unique best transformer) result, we can now state the termination guarantees of our LearnAbstractions algorithm:

Theorem 3 (Termination of LearnAbstractions). *Given a complete sampling oracle* R_F *for every abstract domain and the unique best transformer assumption, if there exists a solution for every problem* $\mathcal{E}_i \in \boldsymbol{\mathcal{E}}$, *then* LearnAbstractions *terminates.*

7 Implementation and Evaluation

We have implemented the proposed method as a new tool called ATLAS, which is written in Java. ATLAS takes as input a set of training problems, an Abstraction-Guided Synthesizer (AGS), and a DSL and returns an abstract domain (in the form of predicate templates) and the corresponding transformers. Internally, ATLAS uses the Z3 theorem prover [22] to compute tree interpolants and the JLinAlg linear algebra library [23] to solve linear equations.

To assess the usefulness of ATLAS, we conduct an experimental evaluation in which our goal is to answer the following two questions:

1. How does ATLAS perform during training? That is, how many training problems does it require and how long does training take?
2. How useful are the abstractions learned by ATLAS in the context of synthesis?

7.1 Abstraction Learning

To answer our first question, we use ATLAS to automatically learn abstractions for two application domains: (i) string manipulations and (ii) matrix transformations. We provide ATLAS with the DSLs used in [14] and employ BLAZE as the underlying Abstraction-Guided Synthesizer. Axiomatic semantics for each DSL construct were given in the theory of equality with uninterpreted functions.

Training Set Information. For the string domain, our training set consists of exactly the four problems used as motivating examples in the BlinkFill paper [17]. Specifically, each training problem consists of 4–6 examples that demonstrate the desired string transformation. For the matrix domain, our training set consists of four (randomly selected) synthesis problems taken from online forums. Since almost all online posts contain a single input-output example, each training problem includes one example illustrating the desired matrix transformation.

Main Results. Our main results are summarized in Fig. 7. The main take-away message is that ATLAS can learn abstractions quite efficiently and does not require a large training set. For example, ATLAS learns 5 predicate templates and 30 abstract transformers for the string domain in a total of 10.2 s. Interestingly, ATLAS does not need all the training problems to infer these four predicates and converges to the final abstraction after just processing the first training instance. Furthermore, for the first training instance, it takes ATLAS 4 iterations in the learning loop (lines 5–10 from Fig. 2) before it converges to the final abstraction. Since this abstraction is sufficient, it takes just one iteration for each following training problem to synthesize a correct program.

Looking at the right side of Fig. 7, we also observe similar results for the matrix domain. In particular, ATLAS learns 10 predicate templates and 59 abstract transformers in a total of 22.5 s. Furthermore, ATLAS converges to the final abstract domain after processing the first three problems[5] and the number of iterations for each training instance is also quite small (ranging from 1 to 3).

[5] The learned abstractions can be found in the extended version of this paper [21].

	$\lvert\mathcal{A}\rvert$	$\lvert\mathcal{T}\rvert$	Iters.	Running time (sec)			
				T_{AGS}	$T_{\mathcal{A}}$	$T_{\mathcal{T}}$	T_{total}
$\mathcal{E}_1$	5	30	4	0.6	0.2	0.2	1.0
$\mathcal{E}_2$	5	30	1	4.9	0	0	4.9
$\mathcal{E}_3$	5	30	1	0.2	0	0	0.2
$\mathcal{E}_4$	5	30	1	4.1	0	0	4.1
Total	5	30	7	9.8	0.2	0.2	**10.2**

String domain

	$\lvert\mathcal{A}\rvert$	$\lvert\mathcal{T}\rvert$	Iters.	Running time (sec)			
				T_{AGS}	$T_{\mathcal{A}}$	$T_{\mathcal{T}}$	T_{total}
$\mathcal{E}_1$	8	45	3	2.9	0.7	0.5	4.1
$\mathcal{E}_2$	8	45	1	2.8	0	0	2.8
$\mathcal{E}_3$	10	59	2	0.5	0.3	0.2	1.0
$\mathcal{E}_4$	10	59	1	14.6	0	0	14.6
Total	10	59	7	20.8	1.0	0.7	**22.5**

Matrix domain

Fig. 7. Training results. $\lvert\mathcal{A}\rvert, \lvert\mathcal{T}\rvert$, Iters denote the number of predicate templates, abstract transformers, and iterations taken per training instance (lines 5–10 from Fig. 2), respectively. $T_{\text{AGS}}, T_{\mathcal{A}}, T_{\mathcal{T}}$ denote the times for invoking the synthesizer (AGS), learning the abstract domain, and learning the abstract transformers, respectively. T_{total} shows the total training time in seconds.

	Original BLAZE† benchmarks				Additional benchmarks				All benchmarks		
	#Solved		Running time improvement		#Solved		Running time improvement		Time (sec)	Running time improvement	
	BLAZE*	BLAZE†	max.	avg.	BLAZE*	BLAZE†	max.	avg.	avg.	max.	avg.
String	**93**	91	15.7×	2.1×	**40**	40	56×	22.3×	**2.8**	**56**×	**8.3**×
Matrix	**39**	39	6.1×	3.1×	**20**	19	83×	21.5×	**5.0**	**83**×	**9.2**×

Fig. 8. Improvement of BLAZE* over BLAZE† on string and matrix benchmarks.

7.2 Evaluating the Usefulness of Learned Abstractions

To answer our second question, we integrated the abstractions synthesized by ATLAS into the BLAZE meta-synthesizer. In the remainder of this section, we refer to all instantiations of BLAZE using the ATLAS-generated abstractions as BLAZE*. To assess how useful the automatically generated abstractions are, we compare BLAZE* against BLAZE†, which refers to the manually-constructed instantiations of BLAZE described in [14].

Benchmark Information. For the string domain, our benchmark suite consists of (1) *all* 108 string transformation benchmarks that were used to evaluate BLAZE† and (2) 40 additional challenging problems that are collected from online forums which involve manipulating file paths, URLs, etc. The number of examples for each benchmark ranges from 1 to 400, with a median of 7 examples. For the matrix domain, our benchmark set includes (1) *all* 39 matrix transformation benchmarks in the BLAZE† benchmark suite and (2) 20 additional challenging problems collected from online forums. *We emphasize that the set of benchmarks used for evaluating* BLAZE* *are completely* disjoint *from the set of synthesis problems used for training* ATLAS.

Experimental Setup. We evaluate BLAZE* and BLAZE† using the same DSLs from the BLAZE paper [14]. For each benchmark, we provide the same set of input-output examples to BLAZE* and BLAZE†, and use a time limit of 20 min per synthesis task.

Main Results. Our main evaluation results are summarized in Fig. 8. The key observation is that BLAZE* consistently improves upon BLAZE† for both string and matrix transformations. In particular, BLAZE* not only solves more benchmarks than BLAZE† for both domains, but also achieves about an order of magnitude speed-up on average for the common benchmarks that both tools can solve. Specifically, for the string domain, BLAZE* solves 133 (out of 148) benchmarks within an average of 2.8 s and achieves an average 8.3$\times$ speed-up over BLAZE†. For the matrix domain, we also observe a very similar result where BLAZE* leads to an overall speed-up of 9.2$\times$ on average.

In summary, this experiment confirms that the abstractions discovered by ATLAS are indeed useful and that they outperform manually-crafted abstractions despite eliminating human effort.

8 Related Work

To our knowledge, this paper is the first one to automatically learn abstract domains and transformers that are useful for program synthesis. We also believe it is the first to apply interpolation to program synthesis, although interpolation has been used to synthesize other artifacts such as circuits [24] and strategies for infinite games [25]. In what follows, we briefly survey existing work related to program synthesis, abstraction learning, and abstract transformer computations.

Program Synthesis. Our work is intended to complement example-guided program synthesis techniques that utilize program abstractions to prune the search space [4,14–16]. For example, SIMPL [15] uses abstract interpretation to speed up search-based synthesis and applies this technique to the generation of imperative programs for introductory programming assignments. Similarly, SCYTHE [16] and MORPHEUS [4] perform enumeration over program sketches and use abstractions to reject sketches that do not have any valid completion. Somewhat different from these techniques, BLAZE constructs a finite tree automaton that accepts all programs whose behavior is consistent with the specification according to the DSL's abstract semantics. We believe that the method described in this paper can be useful to all such abstraction-guided synthesizers.

Abstraction Refinement. In verification, as opposed to synthesis, there have been many works that use Craig interpolants to refine abstractions [20,26,27]. Typically, these techniques generalize the interpolants to abstract domains by extracting a vocabulary of predicates, but they do not generalize by adding parameters to form templates. In our case, this is essential because interpolants derived from fixed input values are too specific to be directly useful. Moreover, we *reuse* the resulting abstractions for subsequent synthesis problems. In verification, this would be analogous to re-using an abstraction from one property or program to the next. It is conceivable that template-based generalization could be applied in verification to facilitate such reuse.

Abstract Transformers. Many verification techniques use logical abstract domains [28–32]. Some of these, following Yorsh, *et al.* [33] use sampling with a decision procedure to evaluate the abstract transformer [34]. Interpolation has also been used to compile efficient symbolic abstract transformers [35]. However, these techniques are restricted to finite domains or domains of finite height to allow convergence. Here, we use infinite parameterized domains to obtain better generalization; hence, the abstract transformer computation is more challenging. Nonetheless, the approach might also be applicable in verification.

9 Limitations

While this paper takes a first step towards automatically inferring useful abstractions for synthesis, our proposed method has the following limitations:

Shapes of Transformers. Following prior work [14], our algorithm assumes that abstract transformers have the shape given in Eq. 1. We additionally assume that constants $\boldsymbol{c}$ used in predicate templates are numeric values and that functions in Eq. 1 are affine. This assumption holds in several domains considered in prior work [4, 14] and allows us to develop an efficient learning algorithm that reduces the problem to solving a system of linear equations.

DSL Semantics. Our method requires the DSL designer to provide the DSL's logical semantics. We believe that giving logical semantics is much easier than coming up with useful abstractions, as it does not require insights about the internal workings of the synthesizer. Furthermore, our technique could, in principle, also work without logical specifications although the learned abstract domain may not be as effective (see Footnote 3 in Sect. 4) and the synthesized transformers would not be provably sound.

UBT Assumption. Our completeness and termination theorems are predicated on the *unique best transformer (UBT)* assumption. While this assumption holds in our evaluation, it may not hold in general. However, as mentioned in Sect. 6, we can always guarantee termination by including the concrete predicates used in the interpolant $\mathcal{I}$ in addition to the symbolic templates extracted from $\mathcal{I}$.

10 Conclusion

We proposed a new technique for automatically instantiating abstraction-guided synthesis frameworks in new domains. Given a DSL and a few training problems, our method automatically discovers a useful abstract domain and the corresponding transformers for each DSL construct. From a technical perspective, our method uses tree interpolation to extract reusable templates from failed synthesis attempts and automatically synthesizes unique best transformers if they exist. We have incorporated the proposed approach into the Blaze meta-synthesizer and show that the abstractions discovered by Atlas are very useful.

While we have applied the proposed technique to program synthesis, we believe that some of the ideas introduced here are more broadly applicable. For instance, the idea of extracting reusable predicate templates from interpolants and synthesizing transformers in a data-driven way could also be useful in the context of program verification.

References

1. Gulwani, S.: Automating string processing in spreadsheets using input-output examples. In: Proceedings of the 38th Annual ACM SIGPLAN-SIGACT Symposium on Principles of Programming Languages, POPL, pp. 317–330. ACM (2011)
2. Singh, R., Gulwani, S.: Transforming spreadsheet data types using examples. In: Proceedings of the 43rd Annual ACM SIGPLAN-SIGACT Symposium on Principles of Programming Languages, POPL, pp. 343–356. ACM (2016)
3. Wang, X., Gulwani, S., Singh, R.: FIDEX: filtering spreadsheet data using examples. In: OOPSLA, pp. 195–213. ACM (2016)
4. Feng, Y., Martins, R., Van Geffen, J., Dillig, I., Chaudhuri, S.: Component-based synthesis of table consolidation and transformation tasks from examples. In: PLDI, pp. 422–436. ACM (2017)
5. Wang, X., Dillig, I., Singh, R.: Synthesis of data completion scripts using finite tree automata. Proc. ACM Program. Lang. **1**(OOPSLA), 62:1–62:26 (2017)
6. Yaghmazadeh, N., Wang, X., Dillig, I.: Automated migration of hierarchical data to relational tables using programming-by-example. In: Proceedings of the VLDB Endowment (2018)
7. Gascón, A., Tiwari, A., Carmer, B., Mathur, U.: Look for the proof to find the program: decorated-component-based program synthesis. In: Majumdar, R., Kunčak, V. (eds.) CAV 2017. LNCS, vol. 10427, pp. 86–103. Springer, Cham (2017). https://doi.org/10.1007/978-3-319-63390-9_5
8. Tiwari, A., Gascón, A., Dutertre, B.: Program synthesis using dual interpretation. In: Felty, A.P., Middeldorp, A. (eds.) CADE 2015. LNCS (LNAI), vol. 9195, pp. 482–497. Springer, Cham (2015). https://doi.org/10.1007/978-3-319-21401-6_33
9. Feng, Y., Martins, R., Wang, Y., Dillig, I., Reps, T.W.: Component-based synthesis for complex APIs. In: POPL, vol. 52, pp. 599–612. ACM (2017)
10. Gvero, T., Kuncak, V., Kuraj, I., Piskac, R.: Complete completion using types and weights. In: Proceedings of the 34th ACM SIGPLAN Conference on Programming Language Design and Implementation, PLDI, pp. 27–38. ACM (2013)
11. Mandelin, D., Xu, L., Bodík, R., Kimelman, D.: Jungloid mining: helping to navigate the API jungle. In: Proceedings of the 26th ACM SIGPLAN Conference on Programming Language Design and Implementation, PLDI, pp. 48–61. ACM (2005)
12. Feser, J.K., Chaudhuri, S., Dillig, I.: Synthesizing data structure transformations from input-output examples. In: Proceedings of the 36th ACM SIGPLAN Conference on Programming Language Design and Implementation, PLDI, pp. 229–239. ACM (2015)

13. Polikarpova, N., Kuraj, I., Solar-Lezama, A.: Program synthesis from polymorphic refinement types. In: Proceedings of the 37th ACM SIGPLAN Conference on Programming Language Design and Implementation, PLDI, pp. 522–538. ACM (2016)
14. Wang, X., Dillig, I., Singh, R.: Program synthesis using abstraction refinement, vol. 2, pp. 63:1–63:30. ACM (2017)
15. So, S., Oh, H.: Synthesizing imperative programs from examples guided by static analysis. In: Ranzato, F. (ed.) SAS 2017. LNCS, vol. 10422, pp. 364–381. Springer, Cham (2017). https://doi.org/10.1007/978-3-319-66706-5_18
16. Wang, C., Cheung, A., Bodik, R.: Synthesizing highly expressive SQL queries from input-output examples. In: Proceedings of the 38th ACM SIGPLAN Conference on Programming Language Design and Implementation, PLDI, pp. 452–466. ACM (2017)
17. Singh, R.: BlinkFill: semi-supervised programming by example for syntactic string transformations. Proc. VLDB Endow. **9**(10), 816–827 (2016)
18. Blanc, R., Gupta, A., Kovács, L., Kragl, B.: Tree interpolation in vampire. In: McMillan, K., Middeldorp, A., Voronkov, A. (eds.) LPAR 2013. LNCS, vol. 8312, pp. 173–181. Springer, Heidelberg (2013). https://doi.org/10.1007/978-3-642-45221-5_13
19. McMillan, K.L.: Applications of craig interpolants in model checking. In: Halbwachs, N., Zuck, L.D. (eds.) TACAS 2005. LNCS, vol. 3440, pp. 1–12. Springer, Heidelberg (2005). https://doi.org/10.1007/978-3-540-31980-1_1
20. McMillan, K.L.: Interpolation and SAT-based model checking. In: Hunt, W.A., Somenzi, F. (eds.) CAV 2003. LNCS, vol. 2725, pp. 1–13. Springer, Heidelberg (2003). https://doi.org/10.1007/978-3-540-45069-6_1
21. Wang, X., Dillig, I., Singh, R.: Learning Abstractions for Program Synthesis. arXiv preprint arXiv:1804.04152 (2018)
22. Z3. https://github.com/Z3Prover/z3
23. Keilhauer, A., Levy, S., Lochbihler, A., Ökmen, S., Thimm, G., Würzebesser, C.: JLinAlg: a java-library for linear algebra without rounding errors. Technical report (2003–2010). http://jlinalg.sourceforge.net/
24. Bloem, R., Egly, U., Klampfl, P., Könighofer, R., Lonsing, F.: Sat-based methods for circuit synthesis. In: Formal Methods in Computer-Aided Design, FMCAD 2014, 21–24 October 2014, Lausanne, Switzerland, pp. 31–34. IEEE (2014)
25. Farzan, A., Kincaid, Z.: Strategy synthesis for linear arithmetic games. Proc. ACM Program. Lang. **2**(POPL), 61 (2017)
26. Beyer, D., Henzinger, T.A., Jhala, R., Majumdar, R.: The software model checker BLAST. Int. J. Softw. Tools Technol. Transf. **9**(5–6), 505–525 (2007)
27. Albarghouthi, A., Li, Y., Gurfinkel, A., Chechik, M.: Ufo: a framework for abstraction- and interpolation-based software verification. In: Madhusudan, P., Seshia, S.A. (eds.) CAV 2012. LNCS, vol. 7358, pp. 672–678. Springer, Heidelberg (2012). https://doi.org/10.1007/978-3-642-31424-7_48
28. Lev-Ami, T., Manevich, R., Sagiv, M.: TVLA: a system for generating abstract interpreters. In: Jacquart, R. (ed.) Building the Information Society. IIFIP, vol. 156, pp. 367–375. Springer, Boston, MA (2004). https://doi.org/10.1007/978-1-4020-8157-6_28
29. Lev-Ami, T., Sagiv, M.: TVLA: a system for implementing static analyses. In: Palsberg, J. (ed.) SAS 2000. LNCS, vol. 1824, pp. 280–301. Springer, Heidelberg (2000). https://doi.org/10.1007/978-3-540-45099-3_15

30. Pnueli, A., Ruah, S., Zuck, L.: Automatic deductive verification with invisible invariants. In: Margaria, T., Yi, W. (eds.) TACAS 2001. LNCS, vol. 2031, pp. 82–97. Springer, Heidelberg (2001). https://doi.org/10.1007/3-540-45319-9_7
31. Lahiri, S.K., Bryant, R.E.: Constructing quantified invariants via predicate abstraction. In: Steffen, B., Levi, G. (eds.) VMCAI 2004. LNCS, vol. 2937, pp. 267–281. Springer, Heidelberg (2004)
32. Reps, T., Thakur, A.: Automating abstract interpretation. In: Jobstmann, B., Leino, K.R.M. (eds.) VMCAI 2016. LNCS, vol. 9583, pp. 3–40. Springer, Heidelberg (2016). https://doi.org/10.1007/978-3-662-49122-5_1
33. Reps, T., Sagiv, M., Yorsh, G.: Symbolic implementation of the best transformer. In: Steffen, B., Levi, G. (eds.) VMCAI 2004. LNCS, vol. 2937, pp. 252–266. Springer, Heidelberg (2004)
34. Thakur, A., Reps, T.: A method for symbolic computation of abstract operations. In: Madhusudan, P., Seshia, S.A. (eds.) CAV 2012. LNCS, vol. 7358, pp. 174–192. Springer, Heidelberg (2012). https://doi.org/10.1007/978-3-642-31424-7_17
35. Jhala, R., McMillan, K.L.: Interpolant-based transition relation approximation. In: Etessami, K., Rajamani, S.K. (eds.) CAV 2005. LNCS, vol. 3576, pp. 39–51. Springer, Heidelberg (2005). https://doi.org/10.1007/11513988_6

The Learnability of Symbolic Automata

George Argyros[1(✉)] and Loris D'Antoni[2]

[1] Columbia University, New York, NY, USA
argyros@cs.columbia.edu
[2] University of Wisconsin-Madison, Madison, WI, USA
loris@cs.wisc.edu

Abstract. Symbolic automata (s-FAs) allow transitions to carry predicates over rich alphabet theories, such as linear arithmetic, and therefore extend classic automata to operate over infinite alphabets, such as the set of rational numbers. In this paper, we study the problem of the learnability of symbolic automata. First, we present MAT^*, a novel L^*-style algorithm for learning symbolic automata using membership and equivalence queries, which treats the predicates appearing on transitions as their own learnable entities. The main novelty of MAT^* is that it can take as input an algorithm Λ for learning predicates in the underlying alphabet theory and it uses Λ to infer the predicates appearing on the transitions in the target automaton. Using this idea, MAT^* is able to learn automata operating over alphabets theories in which predicates are efficiently learnable using membership and equivalence queries. Furthermore, we prove that a necessary condition for efficient learnability of an s-FA is that predicates in the underlying algebra are also efficiently learnable using queries and thus settling the learnability of a large class of s-FA instances. We implement MAT^* in an open-source library and show that it can efficiently learn automata that cannot be learned using existing algorithms and significantly outperforms existing automata learning algorithms over large alphabets.

1 Introduction

In 1987, Dana Angluin showed that finite automata *can be learned* in polynomial time using membership and equivalence queries [3]. In this learning model, often referred to as a *minimally adequate teacher* (MAT), the teacher can answer (i) whether a given string belongs to the target language being learned and (ii) whether a certain automaton is correct and accepts the target language, and provide a counterexample if the automaton is incorrect. Following this result, her L^* algorithm has been studied extensively [16,17], it has been extended to several variants of finite automata [4,12,20] and has found many applications in program analysis [2,6,7] and program synthesis [25].

Recent work [6,11] developed algorithms which can efficiently learn s-FAs over certain alphabet theories. These algorithms operate using an underlying predicate learning algorithm which can learn partitions of the domain using

H. Chockler and G. Weissenbacher (Eds.): CAV 2018, LNCS 10981, pp. 427–445, 2018.
https://doi.org/10.1007/978-3-319-96145-3_23

predicates from counterexamples. While such results give sufficient conditions under which s-FAs can be efficiently learned, they do not provide any necessary conditions. More precisely, the following question remains open:

For what alphabet theories can s-FAs be efficiently learned?

In this paper, we make significant progress towards answering this question by providing new sufficient and necessary conditions for efficiently learning symbolic automata. More specifically, we present MAT^*, a new algorithm for learning s-FAs using membership and equivalence queries. The main novelty of MAT^* is that it can accept as input a MAT learning algorithm Λ for predicates in the underlying alphabet theory. Afterwards, MAT^* spawns instances of Λ to infer each transition in the target s-FA and efficiently answers membership and equivalence queries performed by Λ using the s-FA membership and equivalence oracles. The predicate learning algorithms do not need to learn entire partitions but individual predicates and therefore, MAT^* greatly simplifies the design of learning algorithms for s-FAs by allowing one to reuse existing learning algorithms for the underlying alphabet theory. Moreover, MAT^* allows the underlying predicate learning algorithms to perform *both* membership and equivalence queries, thus extending the class of efficiently learnable s-FAs to MAT-learnable alphabet theories—e.g., bit-vector predicates expressed as BDDs.

Furthermore, we show that a necessary condition for efficiently learning a symbolic automaton over a Boolean algebra is that the individual predicates in the algebra also have to be efficiently learnable. Moreover, we provide a characterization of the instances which are not efficiently learnable by our algorithm and conjecture that such instances are not learnable by any efficient algorithm.

We implement MAT^* in the open-source `symbolicautomata` library [1] and evaluate it on 15 regular-expression benchmarks, 1,500 s-FA benchmarks over bit-vector alphabets, and 18 synthetic benchmarks over infinite alphabets. Our results show that MAT^* can efficiently learn automata over different alphabet theories, some of which cannot be learned using existing algorithms. Moreover, for large finite alphabets, MAT^* significantly outperforms existing automata learning algorithms.

Contributions. In summary, our contributions are:

- MAT^*, the first algorithm for learning symbolic automata that operate over MAT-learnable alphabet theories—i.e., in which predicates can be learned using only membership and equivalence queries (Sect. 3).
- A soundness result for MAT^* and new necessary and sufficient conditions for the learnability of symbolic automata. Moreover, a characterization of the remaining class for which the learnability is not settled (Sect. 4).
- A modular implementation of MAT^* in an existing open-source library together with a comprehensive evaluation on existing and new automata-learning benchmarks (Sect. 6).

2 Background

2.1 Boolean Algebras and Symbolic Automata

In symbolic automata, transitions carry predicates over a decidable Boolean algebra. An *effective Boolean algebra* $\mathcal{A}$ is a tuple $(\mathfrak{D}, \Psi, [\![\_]\!], \bot, \top, \vee, \wedge, \neg)$ where $\mathfrak{D}$ is a set of *domain elements*; Ψ is a set of *predicates* closed under the Boolean connectives, with $\bot, \top \in \Psi$; $[\![\_]\!] : \Psi \to 2^{\mathfrak{D}}$ is a *denotation function* such that (i) $[\![\bot]\!] = \emptyset$, (ii) $[\![\top]\!] = \mathfrak{D}$, and (iii) for all $\varphi, \psi \in \Psi$, $[\![\varphi \vee \psi]\!] = [\![\varphi]\!] \cup [\![\psi]\!]$, $[\![\varphi \wedge \psi]\!] = [\![\varphi]\!] \cap [\![\psi]\!]$, and $[\![\neg\varphi]\!] = \mathfrak{D} \setminus [\![\varphi]\!]$.

Example 1 (Equality Algebra). The *equality algebra* for an arbitrary set $\mathfrak{D}$ has predicates formed from Boolean combinations of formulas of the form $\lambda c.\, c = a$ where $a \in \mathfrak{D}$. Formally, Ψ is generated from the Boolean closure of $\Psi_0 = \{\varphi_a \mid a \in \mathfrak{D}\} \cup \{\bot, \top\}$ where for all $a \in \mathfrak{D}$, $[\![\varphi_a]\!] = \{a\}$. Examples of predicates in this algebra include $\lambda c.\, c = 5 \vee c = 10$ and $\lambda c.\, \neg(c = 0)$.

Definition 1 (Symbolic Finite Automata). *A symbolic finite automaton (s-FA) M is a tuple $(\mathcal{A}, Q, q_{init}, F, \Delta)$ where $\mathcal{A}$ is an effective Boolean algebra, called the* alphabet*; Q is a finite set of states; $q_{init} \in Q$ is the* initial state*; $F \subseteq Q$ is the set of* final states*; and $\Delta \subseteq Q \times \Psi_{\mathcal{A}} \times Q$ is the* transition relation *consisting of a finite set of* moves *or* transitions.

Characters are elements of $\mathfrak{D}_{\mathcal{A}}$, and *words* or *strings* are finite sequences of characters, or elements of $\mathfrak{D}_{\mathcal{A}}^*$. The empty word of length 0 is denoted by ϵ. A move $\rho = (q_1, \varphi, q_2) \in \Delta$, also denoted by $q_1 \xrightarrow{\varphi} q_2$, is a transition from the *source* state q_1 to the *target* state q_2, where φ is the *guard* or *predicate* of the move. For a state $q \in Q$, we denote by $\mathtt{guard}(q)$ the set of guards for all moves from q. For a character $a \in \mathfrak{D}_{\mathcal{A}}$, an *a-move* of M, denoted $q_1 \xrightarrow{a} q_2$ is a move $q_1 \xrightarrow{\varphi} q_2$ such that $a \in [\![\varphi]\!]$.

An s-FA M is *deterministic* if, for all transitions $(q, \varphi_1, q_1), (q, \varphi_2, q_2) \in \Delta$, $q_1 \neq q_2 \to [\![\varphi_1 \wedge \varphi_2]\!] = \emptyset$—i.e., for each state q and character a there is at most one a-move out of q. An s-FA M is *complete* if, for all $q \in Q$, $[\![\bigvee_{(q,\varphi_i,q_i)\in\Delta} \varphi_i]\!] = \mathfrak{D}$—i.e., for each state q and character a there exists an a-move out of q. Throughout the paper we assume all s-FAs are deterministic and complete, since determinization and completion are always possible [10]. Given an s-FA $M = (\mathcal{A}, Q, q_{\text{init}}, F, \Delta)$ and a state $q \in Q$, we say a word $w = a_1 a_2 \cdots a_k$ is *accepted at state* q if, for $1 \leq i \leq k$, there exist moves $q_{i-1} \xrightarrow{a_i} q_i$ such that $q_{\text{init}} = q$ and $q_k \in F$.

For a deterministic s-FA M and a word w, we denote by $M_q[w]$ the state reached in M by w when starting at state q. When q is omitted we assume that execution starts at q_{init}. For a word $w = a_1 \cdots a_k$, we use $w[i..] = a_i \cdots a_k, w[..i] = a_1 \cdots a_i, w[i] = a_i$ to denote the suffix starting from the i-th position, the prefix up to the i-th position and the character at the i-th position respectively. We use $\mathbb{B} = \{\mathbf{T}, \mathbf{F}\}$ to denote the Boolean domain. A word w is called an *access string* for state $q \in Q$ if $M[w] = q$. For two states $q, p \in Q$, a word w is called a distinguishing string, if exactly one of $M_q[w]$ and $M_p[w]$ is final.

2.2 Learning Model

In this paper, we follow the notation from [17]. A concept is a Boolean function $c : \mathfrak{D} \to \mathbb{B}$. A concept class $\mathcal{C}$ is a set of concepts which is represented using representation class $\mathcal{R}$. By representation class we denote a fixed function from strings to concepts in $\mathcal{C}$. For example, regular expressions, DFAs and NFAs are different representation classes for the concept class of regular languages.

The learning model under which all learning algorithms in this paper operate is called *exact learning from membership and equivalence queries* or learning using a Minimal Adequate Teacher (MAT), and was originally introduced by Angluin [3]. In this model, to learn an unknown concept $c \in \mathcal{C}$, a learning algorithm has access to two types of queries:

Membership Query: In a membership query $\mathcal{O}(x)$, the input is $x \in \mathfrak{D}$ and the query returns the value $c(x)$ of the concept on given input x—i.e., **T** if x belongs to the concept and **F** otherwise.

Equivalence Query: In an equivalence query $\mathcal{E}(H)$, the input given is a hypothesis (or model) H. The query returns **T** if for every $x \in \mathfrak{D}$, $H(x) = c(x)$. Otherwise, an input $w \in \mathfrak{D}$ is returned such that $H(w) \neq c(w)$.

An algorithm is a learning algorithm for a concept class $\mathcal{C}$ if, for any $c \in \mathcal{C}$, the algorithm terminates with a correct model for c after making a finite number of membership and equivalence queries. In this paper, we will say that a learning algorithm is *efficient* for a concept class $\mathcal{C}$ if it learns any concept $c \in \mathcal{C}$ using a polynomial number of queries on the size of the representation of the target concept in $\mathcal{R}$ and the length of the longest counterexample provided to the algorithm.

An effective Boolean algebra $\mathcal{A} = (\mathfrak{D}, \Psi, [\![\_]\!], \bot, \top, \vee, \wedge, \neg)$ naturally defines the concept class $2^{\mathfrak{D}}$ with representations in Ψ of predicates over the domain $\mathfrak{D}$. We will say that an algorithm is a learning algorithm for the algebra $\mathcal{A}$ to denote a learning algorithm that can efficiently learn predicates from the representation class Ψ.

3 The MAT^* Algorithm

Our learning algorithm, MAT^*, can be viewed as a symbolic version of the TTT algorithm for learning DFAs [16], but without discriminator finalization. The learning algorithm accepts as input a membership oracle $\mathcal{O}$, an equivalence oracle $\mathcal{E}$ as well as a learning algorithm Λ for the underlying Boolean algebra used in the target s-FA $\mathcal{M}$. The algorithm uses a classification tree [17] to generate a partition of $\mathfrak{D}^*$ into equivalence classes which represent the states in the target s-FA. Once a tree is obtained, we can use it to determine, for any word $w \in \mathfrak{D}^*$, the state accessed by w in $\mathcal{M}$—i.e., what state the automaton reaches when reading the word w. Then, we build an s-FA model $\mathcal{H}$, using the algebra learning algorithm Λ to create models for each transition guard and utilizing the classification tree in order to implement a membership oracle for Λ. Once a

Algorithm 1. s-FA-LEARN($\mathcal{O}, \mathcal{E}, \Lambda$) // s-FA Learning algorithm

Require: $\mathcal{O}$: membership oracle, $\mathcal{E}$: equivalence oracle, Λ: algebra learning algorithm.
  $T \leftarrow$ InitializeClassificationTree($\mathcal{O}$)
  $S_\Lambda \leftarrow$ InitializeGuardLearners(T, Λ)
  $\mathcal{H} \leftarrow$ GetSFAModel($T, S_\Lambda, \mathcal{O}$)
  while $\mathcal{E}(\mathcal{H}) \neq \mathbf{T}$ **do**
    $w \leftarrow$ GetCounterexample($\mathcal{H}$)
    $T, S_\Lambda \leftarrow$ ProcessCounterexample($T, S_\Lambda, w, \mathcal{O}$)
    $\mathcal{H} \leftarrow$ GetSFAModel($T, S_\Lambda, \mathcal{O}$)
  return H

model is generated, we check for equivalence and, given a counterexample, we either update the classification tree with a new state and a corresponding distinguishing string, or propagate the counterexample into one of the instances of the algebra learning algorithm Λ. The structure of MAT^* is shown in Algorithm 1. In the rest of the section, we use the s-FA in Fig. 1 as a running example for our algorithm.

3.1 The Classification Tree

The main data structure used by our learning algorithm is the classification tree (CT) [17]. The classification tree is a tree data structure used to store the access and distinguishing strings for the target s-FA so that all internal nodes of the tree are labelled using a distinguishing string while all leafs are labeled using access strings.

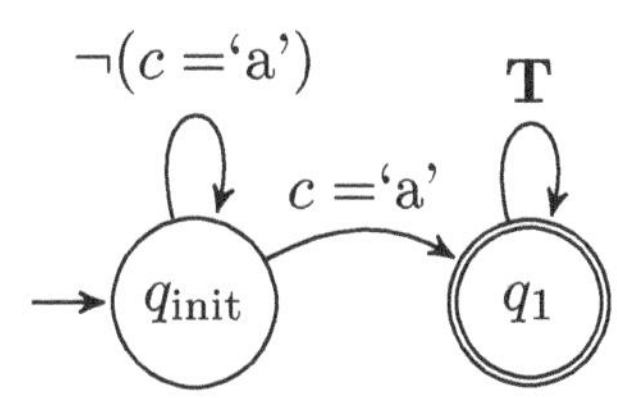

Fig. 1. An s-FA over equality algebra.

Definition 2. *A classification tree $T = (V, L, E)$ is a binary tree such that:*

- $V \subset \Sigma^*$ *is the set of nodes.*
- $L \subset V$ *is the set of leafs.*
- $E \subset V \times V \times \mathbb{B}$ *is the transition relation. For $(v, u, b) \in E$, we say that v is the parent of u and furthermore, if $b = \boldsymbol{T}$ (resp. $b = \boldsymbol{F}$) we say that u is the* **T***-child (resp.* **F***-child).*

Intuitively, given any internal node $v \in V$, any leaf l_T reached by following the **T**-child of v can be distinguished from any leaf l_F reached by the **F**-child using v. In other words, the membership queries for $l_T v$ and $l_F v$ produce different results—i.e., $\mathcal{O}(l_T v) \neq \mathcal{O}(l_F v)$.

Tree Initialization. To initialize the CT data structure, we use a membership query on the empty word ϵ. Then, we create a CT with two nodes, a root node labeled with ϵ and one child also labeled with ϵ. The child of the root is either a **T**-child or **F**-child, according to the result of the $\mathcal{O}(\epsilon)$ query.

The `sift` *Operation.* The main operation performed using the classification tree is an operation called `sift` which allows one to determine, for any input word s,

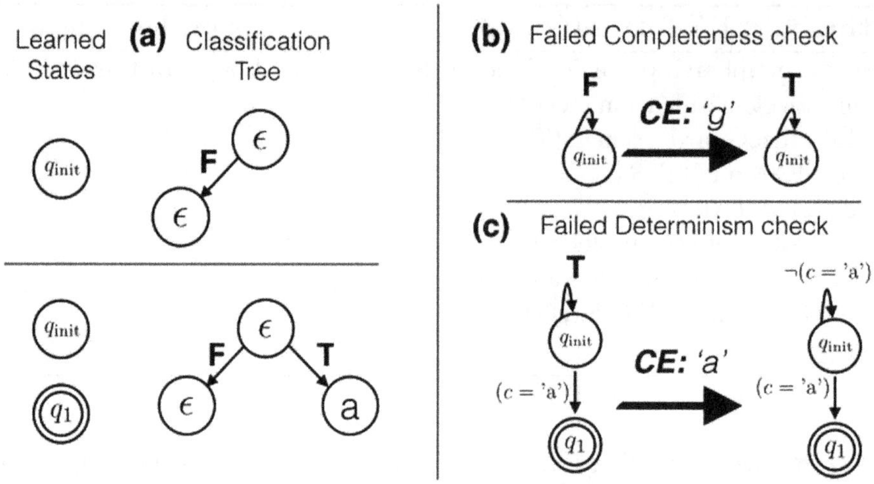

Fig. 2. (left) Classification tree and corresponding learned states for our running example. (right) Two different instances of failed partition verification checks that occured during learning and their respective updates on the given counterexamples (CE).

the state reached by s in the target s-FA. The $\texttt{sift}(s)$ operation performs the following steps:

1. Set the current node to be the root node of the tree and let w be the label at the root. Perform a membership query on the word sw.
2. Let $b = \mathcal{O}(sw)$. Select the b-child of the current node and repeat step 2 until a leaf is reached.
3. Once a leaf is reached, return the access string with which the leaf is labelled.

Note that, until both children of the root node are added, we will have inputs that may not end up in any leaf node. In these cases our `sift` operation will return $\bot$ and MAT^* will add the queried input as a new leaf in the tree.

Once a classification tree is obtained, we use it to simulate a membership oracle for the underlying algebra learning algorithm Λ. This oracle is then used to infer models for the transitions and eventually construct an s-FA model. In Fig. 2 we show the classification tree and the corresponding states learned by the MAT^* algorithm during the execution on our running example from Fig. 1.

3.2 Building an s-FA Model

Assume we are given a classification tree $T = (V, L, E)$. Our next task is to use the tree along with the underlying algebra learning algorithm Λ to produce an s-FA model. The main idea is to spawn an instance of the Λ algorithm for each potential transition and then use the classification tree to answer membership queries posed by each Λ instance. Initially, we define an s-FA $\mathcal{H} = (\mathcal{A}, Q_\mathcal{H}, q_\epsilon, F_\mathcal{H}, \Delta_\mathcal{H})$, where $Q_\mathcal{H} = \{q_s \mid s \in L\}$—i.e. we create one state for each leaf of the classification tree T. Finally, for any $q \in Q_\mathcal{H}$, we have that $q \in F_\mathcal{H}$ if and only if $\mathcal{O}(q) = \mathbf{T}$. Next, we will show how to build the transition relation for $\mathcal{H}$. As mentioned above, our construction is based on the idea of spawning instances of Λ for each potential transition of the s-FA and then using the classification tree to decide, for each character, if the character satisfies the guard of the potential transition thus answering membership queries performed by the underlying algebra learner.

Guard Inference. To infer the set of guards in the transition relation $\Delta_{\mathcal{H}}$, we spawn, for each pair of states $(q_u, q_v) \in Q_{\mathcal{H}} \times Q_{\mathcal{H}}$, an instance $\Lambda^{(q_u,q_v)}$ of the algebra learning algorithm. We answer membership queries to $\Lambda^{(q_u,q_v)}$ as follows. Let $\alpha \in \mathfrak{D}$ be a symbol queried by $\Lambda^{(q_u,q_v)}$. Then, we return **T** as the answer to $\mathcal{O}(\alpha)$ if $\texttt{sift}(u\alpha) = v$ and **F** otherwise. Once $\Lambda^{(q_u,q_v)}$ submits an equivalence query $\mathcal{E}(\phi)$ using a model ϕ, we suspend the execution of the algorithm and add the transition (q_u, ϕ, q_v) in $\Delta_{\mathcal{H}}$.

Partition Verification. Once all algebra learners have submitted a model through an equivalence query, we have a complete transition relation $\Delta_{\mathcal{H}}$. However, at this point there is no guarantee that for each state q the outgoing transitions from q form a partition of the domain $\mathfrak{D}$. Therefore, it may be the case that our s-FA model $\mathcal{H}$ is in fact non-deterministic and, moreover, that certain symbols do not satisfy any guard. Using such a model in an equivalence query would result in an *improper* learning algorithm and potential problems in the counterexample processing algorithm in Sect. 3.3. To mitigate this issue we perform the following checks:

Determinism check: For each state $q_s \in Q_{\mathcal{H}}$ and each pair of moves $(q_s, \phi_1, q_u), (q_s, \phi_2, q_v) \in \Delta_{\mathcal{H}}$, we verify that $[\![\phi_1 \wedge \phi_2]\!] = \emptyset$. Assume that a character α is found such that $\alpha \in [\![\phi_1 \wedge \phi_2]\!]$ and let $m = \texttt{sift}(s\alpha)$. Then, it must be the case that the guard of the transition $q_s \to q_m$ must satisfy α. Therefore, we check if $m = u$ and $m = v$ and provide α as a counterexample to $\Lambda^{(q_s,q_u)}$ and $\Lambda^{(q_s,q_v)}$ respectively if the corresponding check fails.

Completeness check: For each state $q_u \in Q_{\mathcal{H}}$ let $S = \{\phi \mid (q, \phi, p) \in \Delta_{\mathcal{H}}\}$. We check that $[\![\bigvee_{\phi \in S} \phi]\!] = \mathfrak{D}$. If a symbol $h \notin [\![\bigvee_{\phi \in S} \phi]\!]$ is found then, let $v = \texttt{sift}(uh)$. Following the same reasoning as above, we provide h as a counterexample to $\Lambda^{(q_u,q_v)}$.

These checks are iterated for each state until no more counterexamples are found. In Fig. 2 we demonstrate instances of failed determinism and completeness checks while learning our running example from Fig. 1 along with the corresponding updates on the predicates. For details regarding the equality algebra learner, see Sect. 5.

Optimizing the Number of Algebra Learning Instances. Note that in the description above, MAT^* spawns one instance of Λ for each possible transition between states in $\mathcal{H}$. To reduce the number of spawned algebra learning instances, we perform the following optimization: For each state q_s we initially spawn a single algebra learning instance $\Lambda^{(q_s,?)}$. Let α be the first symbol queried by $\Lambda^{(q_s,?)}$ and let $u = \texttt{sift}(s\alpha)$. We return $\top$ as a query answer for α to $\Lambda^{(q_s,?)}$ and set the target state for the instance to q_u, i.e. we convert the algebra learning instance to $\Lambda^{(q_s,q_u)}$. Afterwards, we keep a set $R = \{q_v \mid v = \texttt{sift}(s\beta)\}$ for all $\beta \in \mathfrak{D}$ queried by the different algebra learning instances and generate new instances only for states $q_v \in R$ for which the guards are not yet inferred. Using this optimization, the total number of generated algebra learning instances never exceeds the number of transitions in the target s-FA.

3.3 Processing Counterexamples

For counterexample processing, we adapt the algorithm used in [6] in the setting of MAT^* . In a nutshell, our algorithm works similarly to the classic Rivest-Schapire algorithm [23] and the TTT algorithm [16] for learning DFAs, where a binary search is performed to locate the index in the counterexample where the executions of the model automaton and the target one diverge. However, once this breakpoint index is found, our algorithm performs further analysis to determine if the divergence is caused by an undiscovered state in our model automaton or because the guard predicate that consumes the breakpoint index character is incorrect.

Error Localization. Let w be a counterexample for a model $\mathcal{H}$ generated as described above. For each index $i \in [0..|w|]$, let $q_u = \mathcal{H}[w[..i]]$ be the state accessed by $w[..i]$ in $\mathcal{H}$ and let $\gamma_i = uw[i+1..]$. In other words, γ_i is obtained by first running w in $\mathcal{H}$ for i steps and then, concatenating the access string for the state reached in $\mathcal{H}$ with the word $w[i+1..]$. Note that, because initially the model $\mathcal{H}$ and the target s-FA start at the same state accessed by ϵ, the two machines are synchronized and therefore, $\mathcal{O}(\gamma_0) = \mathcal{O}(w)$. Moreover, since w is a counterexample, we have that $\mathcal{O}(\gamma_{|w|}) \neq \mathcal{O}(w)$. It follows that, there exists an index j, which we will refer to as *breakpoint*, for which $\mathcal{O}(\gamma_j) \neq \mathcal{O}(\gamma_{j+1})$. The counterexample processing algorithm uses a binary search on the index j to find such a breakpoint. For more information on the correctness of this method we refer the reader to [6,23].

Breakpoint Analysis. Once we find an index j such that $\mathcal{O}(\gamma_j) \neq \mathcal{O}(\gamma_{j+1})$ we can conclude that the transition taken in $\mathcal{H}$ from $\mathcal{H}[w[..j]]$ with the symbol $w[j+1]$ is incorrect. In traditional algorithms for learning DFAs, the sole reason for having an incorrect transition would be that the transition is actually directed to a yet undiscovered state in the target automaton. However, in the symbolic setting we have to explore two different possibilities. Let $q_u = \mathcal{H}[w[..j]]$ be the state accessed in $\mathcal{H}$ by $w[..j]$, $q_v = \texttt{sift}(uw[j+1])$ be the result of sifting $uw[j+1]$ in the classification tree and consider the transition $(q_u, \phi, q_v) \in \Delta_{\mathcal{H}}$. We use the guard ϕ to determine if the counterexample was caused by an invalid predicate guard or an undiscovered state in the target s-FA.

Case 1. Incorrect guard. Assume that $w[j+1] \notin [\![\phi]\!]$. Note that, ϕ was generated as a model by $\Lambda^{(q_u,q_v)}$ and therefore, a membership query from $\Lambda^{(q_u,q_v)}$ for a character α returns $\mathbf{T}$ if $\texttt{sift}(u\alpha) = v$. Moreover, we have that $\texttt{sift}(uw[j+1]) = v$. Therefore, if $w[j+1] \notin [\![\phi]\!]$, then $w[j+1]$ is a counterexample for the learning instance $\Lambda^{(q_u,q_v)}$ which produced ϕ. We proceed to supply $\Lambda^{(q_u,q_v)}$ with

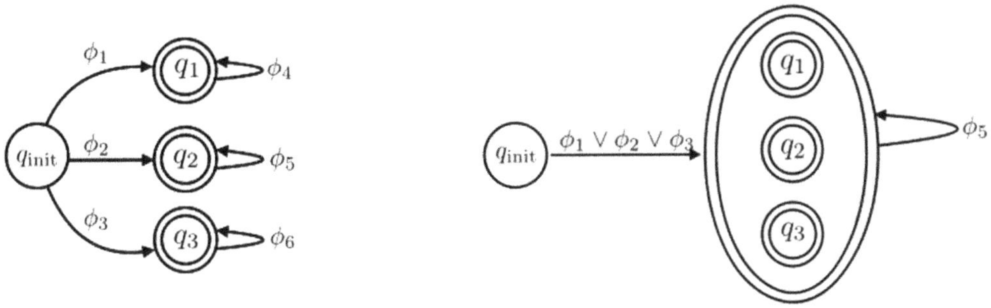

Fig. 3. (left) A minimal s-FA. (right) The s-FA corresponding to the classification tree of MAT^* with access strings for q_{init} and q_2 and a single distinguishing string ϵ.

the counterexample $w[j+1]$, update the corresponding guard and continue to generate a new s-FA model.

Case 2. Undiscovered state. Assume $w[j+1] \in [\![\phi]\!]$. It follows that ϕ is behaving as expected on the symbol $w[j+1]$ based on the current classification tree. We conclude that the state accessed by $w[..j+1]$ is in fact an undiscovered state in the target s-FA which we have to distinguish from the previously discovered states. Therefore, we proceed to add a new leaf in the tree to access this state. More specifically, we replace the leaf labelled with v with a sub-tree consisting of three nodes: the root is the word $w[j+1..]$, which is the distinguishing string for the states accessed by v and $uw[j+1]$. The **T**-child and **F**-child of this node are labelled with the words v and $uw[j]$ based on the results of $\mathcal{O}(v)$ and $\mathcal{O}(uw[j+1])$.

Finally, we have to take care of one last point: Once we add another state in the classification tree, certain queries that were previously directed to v may be directed to $uw[j]$ once we sift them down in the tree. This change implies that certain previous queries performed by algebra learning instances $\Lambda^{(q_s,q_v)}$ may be given invalid results and therefore, we can no longer guarantee correctness of the generated predicates. To solve this problem, we terminate all instances $\Lambda^{(q_s,q_v)}$ for all $q_s \in Q_{\mathcal{H}}$ and replace them with fresh instances of the algebra learning algorithm.

4 Correctness and Completeness of MAT^*

Given a learning algorithm Λ, we use $\mathcal{C}_{\text{m}}^{\Lambda}(n)$ to denote the number of membership queries and $\mathcal{C}_{\text{e}}^{\Lambda}(n)$ to denote the number of equivalence queries performed by Λ for a target concept with representation size n. In our analysis we will also use the following definitions:

Definition 3. *Let $\mathcal{M} = (\mathcal{A}, Q, q_0, F, \Delta)$ over a Boolean algebra $\mathcal{A}$ and let $S \subseteq \Psi_{\mathcal{A}}$. Then, we define:*

- *The maximum size of the union of predicates in S as $\mathcal{U}(S) \stackrel{def}{=} \max_{\Phi \subseteq S} |\bigvee_{\phi \in \Phi} \phi|$.*

– *The maximum guard union size for* $\mathcal{M}$ *as* $\mathcal{B}(\mathcal{M}) \stackrel{def}{=} \max_{q \in Q} \mathcal{U}(\textit{guard}(q))$.

The value $\mathcal{B}(\mathcal{M})$ denotes the maximum size that a predicate guard may take in any intermediate hypothesis produced by MAT^* during the learning process. Contrary to traditional L^*-style algorithms, the size of the intermediate hypothesis produced by MAT^* may fluctuate as we demonstrate in the following example.

Example 2. Consider the s-FA in the left side of Fig. 3. When we execute the MAT^* algorithm in this s-FA, and after an access string for q_2 is added to the classification tree, the tree will correspond to the s-FA shown on the right, in which the transition from q_{init} is taken over the union of the individual transitions in the target. Certain sequences of answers to equivalence queries can force MAT^* to first learn a correct model of $\phi_1 \vee \phi_2 \vee \phi_3$ before revealing a new state in the target s-FA.

We now state the correctness and query complexity of our algorithm.

Theorem 1. *Let* $\mathcal{M} = (\mathcal{A}, Q, q_0, F, \Delta)$ *be an s-FA,* Λ *be a learning algorithm* $\mathcal{A}$ *and let* $k = \mathcal{B}(\mathcal{M})$. *Then,* MAT^* *will learn* $\mathcal{M}$ *using* Λ *with* $O(|Q|^2|\Delta|\mathcal{C}_m^{\Lambda}(k) + |Q|^2|\Delta|\mathcal{C}_{\text{e}}^{\Lambda}(k)\log m)$ *membership and* $O(|Q||\Delta|\mathcal{C}_{\text{e}}^{\Lambda}(k))$ *equivalence queries, where* m *is the length of the longest counterexample given to* MAT^*.

Proof. First, we note that our counterexample processing algorithm only splits a leaf if there exists a valid distinguishing condition separating the two newly generated leafs. Therefore, the number of leafs in the discrimination tree is always at most $|Q|$. Next, note that each counterexample is processed using a binary search with complexity $O(\log m)$ to detect the breakpoint and, afterwards, either a new state is added or a counterexample is dispatched to the corresponding algebra learner.

Each classification tree $T = (V, L, E)$ defines a partition over $\mathfrak{D}^*$ and, therefore, an s-FA $\mathcal{H}_T$. In the worst case, MAT^* will learn $\mathcal{H}_T$ exactly before a new state in the target s-FA is revealed through an equivalence query. Since $\mathcal{H}_T$ is the result of merging states in the target s-FA, we conclude that the size of each predicate in $\mathcal{H}_T$ is at most k. It follows that, for each classification tree T, we can get at most $|\Delta_{\mathcal{H}_T}|\mathcal{C}_{\text{e}}^{\Lambda}(k)$ counterexamples until a new state is uncovered on the target s-FA. Note here, that our counterexample processing algorithm ensures that each counterexample will be either a valid counterexample for a predicate guard in $\mathcal{H}_T$ or it will uncover a new state. For each membership query performed by an underlying algebra learner, we have to sift a string in the classification tree which requires at most $|Q|$ membership queries. Therefore, the total number of membership queries performed for each candidate model $\mathcal{H}$ is bounded by $O(|\Delta|(|Q|\mathcal{C}_{\text{m}}^{\Lambda}(k) + \mathcal{C}_{\text{e}}^{\Lambda}(k)\log m)$ where m is the size of the longest counterexample so far. The number of equivalence queries is bounded by $O(|\Delta|\mathcal{C}_{\text{e}}^{\Lambda}(k))$. When a new state is uncovered, we assume that, in the worst case, all the algebra learners will be restarted (this is an overestimation) and therefore, the same process will be repeated at most $|Q|$ times giving us the stated bounds.

Note that the bounds on the number of queries stated in Theorem 1 are based on the worst-case assumption that we may have to restart *all* guard learning instances each time we discover a new state. In practice, we expect these bounds to be closer $O(|\Delta|\mathcal{C}_{\mathrm{m}}^{\Lambda}(k)+(|\Delta|\mathcal{C}_{\mathrm{e}}^{\Lambda}(k)+|Q|)\log m)$ membership and $O(|\Delta|\mathcal{C}_{\mathrm{e}}^{\Lambda}(k)+|Q|)$ equivalence queries.

Minimality of Learned s-FA. Since the MAT^* will only add a new state in the s-FA if a distinguishing sequence is found it follows that the total number of states in the s-FA is minimal. Moreover, MAT^* will not modify in any way the predicates returned by the underlying algebra learning instances. Therefore, if the size of the predicates returned by the Λ instances is minimal, MAT^* will maintain their minimality.

The following theorem shows that it is indeed not possible to learn s-FAs over a Boolean algebra that is not itself learnable.

Theorem 2. *Let $\Lambda^{s\text{-}FA}$ be an efficient learning algorithm for the algebra of s-FAs over a Boolean algebra $\mathcal{A}$. Then, the Boolean algebra $\mathcal{A}$ is efficiently learnable.*

Which s-FAs Are Efficiently Learnable? Theorem 2 shows that efficient learnability of an s-FA requires efficient learnability of the underlying algebra. Moreover, from Theorem 1 it follows that efficiently learnability using MAT^* depends on the following property of the underlying algebra:

Corollary 1. *Let $\mathcal{A}$ be an efficiently learnable Boolean algebra and consider the class $\mathcal{R}_{\mathcal{A}}^{s\text{-}FA}$ of s-FAs over $\mathcal{A}$. Then, $\mathcal{R}_{\mathcal{A}}^{s\text{-}FA}$ is efficiently learnable using MAT^* if and only if, for any set $S \subseteq \Psi_{\mathcal{A}}$ such that for any distinct $\phi, \psi \in S \implies [\![\phi \wedge \psi]\!] = \emptyset$, we have that $\mathcal{U}(S) = \mathtt{poly}(|S|, \max_{\phi \in S} |\phi|)$.*

At this point we would like to point out that the above condition arises due to the fact that MAT^* is a congruence-based algorithm which successively computes hypothesis automata based on refining a set of access and distinguishing strings which is a common characteristic among all L^*-based algorithms. Therefore, this limitation of MAT^* is expected to be shared by any other algorithm in the same family. Given the fact that after three decades of research, L^*-based algorithms are the only known, provably efficient algorithms for learning DFAs (and subsequently s-FAs), we expect that expanding the class of learnable s-FAs is a very challenging task.

5 Learnable Boolean Algebras

We will now describe a number of interesting effective Boolean algebras which are efficiently learnable using membership and equivalence queries.

Boolean Algebras Over Finite Domains. Let $\mathcal{A}$ be any Boolean Algebra over a finite domain $\mathfrak{D}$. Then, any predicate $\phi \in \Psi$ can be learned using $|\mathfrak{D}|$ membership queries. More specifically, the learning algorithm constructs a predicate ϕ

accepting all elements in $\mathfrak{D}$ for which the membership queries return true as $\phi = \{c \mid c \in \mathfrak{D} \wedge \mathcal{O}(c) = \mathbf{T}\}$. Plugging this algebra learning algorithm into our algorithm, we get the TTT learning algorithm for DFAs without discriminator finalization [16]. This simple example demonstrates that algorithms for DFAs can be viewed as special cases of our s-FA learning algorithm for finite domains.

Equality Algebra. Consider the equality algebra defined in Example 1. Predicates in this algebra of size $|\phi| = k$ can be learned using $2k$ equivalence queries and no membership queries. Initially, the algorithm outputs the empty set $\bot$ as a hypothesis. In any subsequent step, the algorithm keeps a list of the counterexamples obtained so far in two sets $P, N \subseteq \mathfrak{D}$ such that P holds all the positive examples received so far and N holds all the negative examples. Afterwards, the algorithm finds the smallest hypothesis consistent with the counterexamples given. This hypothesis can be found efficiently as follows:

1. If $|P| > |N|$ then, $\phi = \lambda c. \neg(\bigvee_{d \in N} c = d)$.
2. If $|P| \leq |N|$ then, $\phi = \lambda c. (\bigvee_{d \in P} c = d)$.

It can be easily shown that the algorithm will find a correct hypothesis after at most $2k$ equivalence queries.

Other Algebras. The following Boolean algebras can be efficiently learned using membership and equivalence queries. All these algebras also have approximate fingerprints [3], which means that they are not learnable by equivalence queries alone. Thus, s-FAs over these algebras are not efficiently learnable by previous s-FA learning algorithms [6,11].

BDD algebra. The algebra of ordered binary decision diagrams (OBDDs) is efficiently learnable using a variant of the L* algorithm [22].

Tree automata algebra. Deterministic finite tree automata form an algebra which is also learnable using membership and equivalence queries [13].

s-FA algebra. s-FAs themselves form an effective Boolean algebra and therefore, s-FAs over s-FAs over learnable algebras are also learnable.

6 Evaluation

We have implemented MAT^* in the open-source `symbolicautomata` library [1], as well as the learning algorithms for boolean algebras over finite domains, equality algebras and BDD algebras as discussed in Sect. 5. Our implementation is fully modular: Once an algebra learning algorithm is defined in our library, it can be seamlessly plugged in as a guard learning algorithm for s-FAs. Since MAT^* is also an algebra learning algorithm, this allows us to easily learn automata over automata. All experiments were ran in a Macbook air with an 1.8 GHz Intel Core i5 and 8 GiB of memory. The goal of our evaluation is to answer the following research questions:

Q1: How does MAT^* perform on automata over large finite alphabets? (Subsect. 6.1)

Table 1. Evaluation of MAT^* on regular expressions.

ID	$\|Q\|$	$\|\Delta\|$	Memb	Equiv	R-CE	GU	D-CE	C-CE
RE.1	11	35	653	17	19	25	106	78
RE.2	24	113	7203	66	45	87	565	479
RE.3	11	15	483	11	16	16	59	45
RE.4	18	40	1745	17	33	32	188	164
RE.5	25	55	3180	22	48	45	244	211
RE.6	52	155	43737	588	104	640	3102	2953
RE.7	179	658	66477	1486	91	1398	7748	6540
RE.8	115	175	929261	299	206	390	28606	28354
RE.9	144	369	844213	699	261	817	30485	30135
RE.10	175	551	3228102	5346	286	5457	172180	170483
RE.11	6	9	3409	281	14	289	723	710
RE.12	10	14	1367	88	8	86	314	291
RE.13	29	46	20903	743	49	764	2637	2550
RE.14	8	13	5949	365	24	381	854	836
RE.15	8	15	661	82	2	76	228	198

Q2: How does MAT^* perform on automata over algebras that require both membership and equivalence queries? (Subsect. 6.2)

Q3: How does the size of predicates affect the performance of MAT^*? (Subsect. 6.3)

6.1 Equality Algebra Learning

In this experiment, we use MAT^* to learn s-FAs obtained from 15 regular expressions drawn from 3 domains: (1) Regular expressions used in web application sanitization frameworks such as in the CodeIgniter framework, (2) Regular expressions drawn from popular web application firewall ModSecurity and finally (3) Regular expressions from [18]. For this set of experiments we utilize as alphabet the entire UTF-16 (2^{16} characters) and used the equality algebra to represent predicates. Since the alphabet is finite, we also tried learning the same automata using TTT [16], the most efficient algorithm for learning finite automata over finite alphabets.

Results. Table 1 presents the results of MAT^*. The **Memb** and **Equiv** columns present the number of distinct membership and equivalence queries respectively. The **R-CE** column shows how many times a counterexample was reused, while the **GU** column shows the number of counterexamples that were used to update an underlying predicate (as opposed to adding a new state in the s-FA). Finally, **D-CE** shows the number of counterexamples provided to an underlying algebra learner due to failed determinism checks, while **C-CE** shows the number of counterexamples due to failed completeness checks. Note that these counterexamples did not require invoking the equivalence oracle.

Given the large alphabet sizes, TTT runs out of memory on all our benchmarks. This is not surprising since the number of queries required by TTT just to construct the *correct* model for a DFA with $128 = 2^7$ states is at least $|\Sigma||Q|\log|Q| = 2^{16} * 2^7 * 7 \approx 2^{26}$. We point out that a corresponding lower bound of $\Omega(|Q|\log|Q||\Sigma|)$ exists for the number of queries any DFA algorithm may perform and therefore, the size of the alphabet provides a fundamental limitation for any such algorithm.

Analysis. First, we observe that the performance of the algorithm is not always monotone in the number of states or transitions of the s-FA. For example, RE.10 requires more than 10x more membership and equivalence queries than RE.7 despite the fact that both the number of states and transitions of RE.10 are smaller. In this case, RE.10 has fewer transitions, but they contain predicates that are harder to learn—e.g., large character classes. Second, the completeness check and the corresponding counterexamples are not only useful to ensure that the generated guards form a partition but also to restore predicates after new states are discovered. Recall that, once we discover (split) a new state, a number of learning instances is discarded. Usually, the newly created learning instances will simply output $\bot$ as the initial hypothesis. At this point, completeness counterexamples are used to update the newly created hypothesis accordingly and thus save the MAT^* from having to rerun a large number of equivalence queries. Finally, we point out that the equality algebra learner made no special assumptions on the structure of the predicates such as recognizing character classes which are used in regular expressions and others. We expect that providing such heuristics can greatly improve the performance MAT^* in these benchmarks.

6.2 BDD Algebra Learning

In this experiment, we use MAT^* to learn s-FAs over a BDD algebra. We run MAT^* on 1,500 automata obtained by transforming Linear Temporal Logic over finite traces into s-FAs [9]. The formulas have 4 atomic propositions and the height in each BDD used by the s-FAs is four. To learn the underlying BDDs we use MAT^* with the learning algorithm for algebras over finite domains (see Sect. 5) since ordered BDDs can be seen as s-FAs over $\mathfrak{D} = \{0, 1\}$.

Figure 4 shows the number of membership (top left) and equivalence (top right) queries performed by MAT^* for s-FAs with different number of states. For this s-FAs, MAT^* is highly efficient with respect to both the number of membership and equivalence queries, scaling linearly with the number of states. Moreover, we note that the size of the set of transitions $|\Delta|$ does not drastically affect the overall performance of the algorithm. This is in agreement with the results presented in the previous section, where we argued that the difficulty of the underlying predicates and not their number is the primary factor affecting performance.

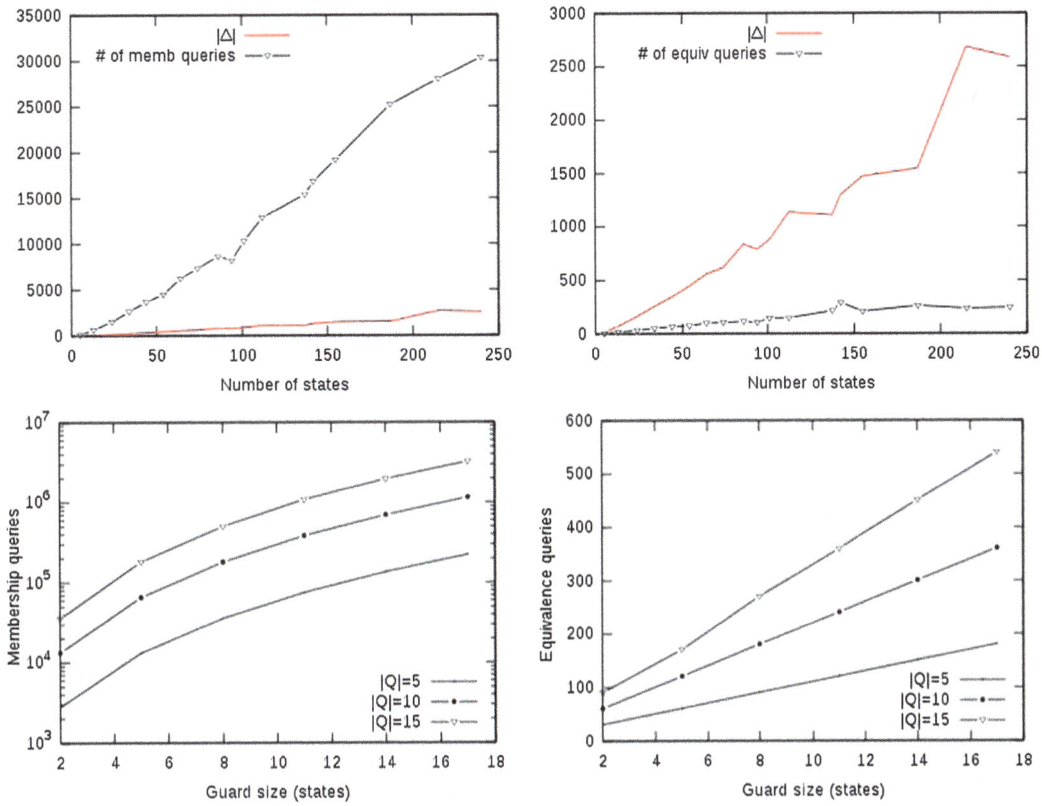

Fig. 4. (Top) Evaluation of MAT^* on s-FAs over a BDD algebra. (Bottom) Evaluation of MAT^* on s-FAs over an s-FA algebra. For an s-FA $\mathcal{M}_{m,n}$, the x-axis denotes the values of n. Different lines correspond to different values of m.

6.3 s-FA Algebra Learning

In this experiment, we use MAT^* to learn 18 s-FAs over s-FAs, which accept strings of strings. We evaluate the scalability of our algorithms when the difficulty of learning the underlying predicates increases. The possible internal s-FAs, which we will use as predicates, operate over the equality algebra and are denoted as I_k (where $2 \leq k \leq 17$). Each s-FA I_k accepts exactly one word $a \cdots a$ of length k and has $k+1$ states and $2k+1$ transitions. The external s-FAs are denoted as $\mathcal{M}_{m,n}$ (where $m \in \{5, 10, 15\}$ and $2 \leq n \leq 17$). Each s-FA $\mathcal{M}_{m,n}$ accepts exactly one word $s \cdots s$ of length m where each s is accepted by I_n.

Analysis. For simplicity, let's assume that we have the s-FA $\mathcal{M}_{n,n}$. Consider a membership query performed by one of the underlying algebra learning instances. Answering the membership query requires sifting a sequence in the classification tree of height at most n which requires $O(n)$ membership queries. Therefore, the number of membership queries required to learn each individual predicate is increased by a factor of $O(n)$. Moreover, for each equivalence query performed by an algebra learning instance, the s-FA learning algorithm has to pinpoint the counterexample to the specific algebra learning instance, a process which requires $\log m$ membership queries, where m is the length of the counterexample.

Therefore, we conclude that each underlying guard with n states will require a number of membership queries which is of the order of $O(n^3)$ at the worst and $O(n^2 \log n)$ queries at the best (since the CT has height $\Omega(\log n)$), ignoring the queries required for counterexample processing.

Figure 4 shows the number of membership (bottom left) and equivalence (bottom right) queries, which verify the theoretical analysis presented in the previous paragraph. Indeed, we see that in terms of membership queries, we have a very sharp increase in the number of membership queries which is in fact about quadratic in the number of states in the underlying guards. On the other hand, equivalence queries are not affected so drastically, and only increase linearly.

7 Related Work

Learning Finite Automata. The L* algorithm proposed by Dana Angluin [3] was the first to introduce the notion of minimally adequate teacher—i.e., learning using membership and equivalence queries—and was also the first for learning finite automata in polynomial time. Following Angluin's result, L* has been studied extensively [16,17], it has been extended to many other models—e.g., to nondeterministic automata [12] alternating automata [4]—and has found many applications in program analysis [2,5–7,24] and program synthesis [25]. Since finite automata only operate over finite alphabets, all the automata that can be learned using variants of L*, can also be learned using MAT^*.

Learning Symbolic Automata. The problem of scaling L^* to large alphabets was initially studied outside the setting of s-FAs using alphabet abstractions [14,15]. The first algorithm for symbolic automata over ordered alphabets was proposed in [20] but the algorithm assumes that the counterexamples provided to the learning algorithm are of minimal length. Argyros et al. [6] proposed the first algorithm for learning symbolic automata in the standard MAT model and also described the algorithm to distinguish counterexamples leading to new states from counterexamples due to invalid predicates which we adapt in MAT^* . Drews and D'Antoni [11] proposed a symbolic extension to the L^*algorithm, gave a general definition of learnability and demonstrated more learnable algebras such as union and product algebras. The algorithms in [6,11,19] are all extensions of L^* and assume the existence of an underlying learning algorithm capable of learning partitions of the domain from counterexamples. MAT^* does not require that the predicate learning algorithms are able to learn partitions, thus allowing to easily plug existing learning algorithms for Boolean algebras. Moreover, MAT^* allows the underlying algebra learning algorithms to perform both equivalence and membership queries, a capability not present in any previous work, thus expanding the class of s-FAs which can be efficiently learned.

Learning Other Models. Argyros et al. [6] and Botincan et al. [7] presented algorithms for learning restricted families of symbolic transducers—i.e., symbolic automata with outputs. Other algorithms can learn nominal [21] and register automata [8]. In these models, the alphabet is infinite but not structured (i.e., it does not form a Boolean algebra) and characters at different positions can be compared using binary relations.

Acknowledgements. The authors would like to thank the anonymous reviewers for their valuable comments. Loris D'Antoni was supported by National Science Foundation Grants CCF-1637516, CCF-1704117 and a Google Research Award. George Argyros was supported by the Office of Naval Research (ONR) through contract N00014-12-1-0166.

References

1. lorisdanto/symbolicautomata: Library for symbolic automata and symbolic visibly pushdown automata. https://github.com/lorisdanto/symbolicautomata/. Accessed 29 Jan 2018
2. Alur, R., Černý, P., Madhusudan, P., Nam, W.: Synthesis of interface specifications for java classes. SIGPLAN Not. **40**(1), 98–109 (2005)
3. Angluin, D.: Learning regular sets from queries and counterexamples. Inf. Comput. **75**(2), 87–106 (1987)
4. Angluin, D., Eisenstat, S., Fisman, D.: Learning regular languages via alternating automata. In: Proceedings of the 24th International Conference on Artificial Intelligence, IJCAI 2015, pp. 3308–3314. AAAI Press (2015)
5. Argyros, G., Stais, I., Jana, S., Keromytis, A.D., Kiayias, A.: SFADiff: automated evasion attacks and fingerprinting using black-box differential automata learning. In: Proceedings of the 2016 ACM SIGSAC Conference on Computer and Communications Security, pp. 1690–1701. ACM (2016)
6. Argyros, G., Stais, I., Kiayias, A., Keromytis, A.D.: Back in black: towards formal, black box analysis of sanitizers and filters. In: IEEE Symposium on Security and Privacy, SP 2016, 22–26 May 2016, San Jose, CA, USA, pp. 91–109 (2016)
7. Botincan, M., Babic, D.: Sigma*: symbolic learning of input-output specifications. In: The 40th Annual ACM SIGPLAN-SIGACT Symposium on Principles of Programming Languages, POPL 2013, 23–25 January 2013, Rome, Italy, pp. 443–456 (2013)
8. Cassel, S., Howar, F., Jonsson, B., Steffen, B.: Active learning for extended finite state machines. Formal Aspects Comput. **28**(2), 233–263 (2016)
9. D'Antoni, L., Kincaid, Z., Wang, F.: A symbolic decision procedure for symbolic alternating finite automata. arXiv preprint arXiv:1610.01722 (2016)
10. D'Antoni, L., Veanes, M.: The power of symbolic automata and transducers. In: Majumdar, R., Kunčak, V. (eds.) CAV 2017. LNCS, vol. 10426, pp. 47–67. Springer, Cham (2017). https://doi.org/10.1007/978-3-319-63387-9_3
11. Drews, S., D'Antoni, L.: Learning symbolic automata. In: Legay, A., Margaria, T. (eds.) TACAS 2017. LNCS, vol. 10205, pp. 173–189. Springer, Heidelberg (2017). https://doi.org/10.1007/978-3-662-54577-5_10
12. García, P., de Parga, M.V., Álvarez, G.I., Ruiz, J.: Learning regular languages using nondeterministic finite automata. In: Ibarra, O.H., Ravikumar, B. (eds.) CIAA 2008. LNCS, vol. 5148, pp. 92–101. Springer, Heidelberg (2008). https://doi.org/10.1007/978-3-540-70844-5_10

13. Habrard, A., Oncina, J.: Learning multiplicity tree automata. In: Sakakibara, Y., Kobayashi, S., Sato, K., Nishino, T., Tomita, E. (eds.) ICGI 2006. LNCS (LNAI), vol. 4201, pp. 268–280. Springer, Heidelberg (2006). https://doi.org/10.1007/11872436_22
14. Howar, F., Steffen, B., Merten, M.: Automata learning with automated alphabet abstraction refinement. In: Jhala, R., Schmidt, D. (eds.) VMCAI 2011. LNCS, vol. 6538, pp. 263–277. Springer, Heidelberg (2011). https://doi.org/10.1007/978-3-642-18275-4_19
15. Isberner, M., Howar, F., Steffen, B.: Inferring automata with state-local alphabet abstractions. In: Brat, G., Rungta, N., Venet, A. (eds.) NFM 2013. LNCS, vol. 7871, pp. 124–138. Springer, Heidelberg (2013). https://doi.org/10.1007/978-3-642-38088-4_9
16. Isberner, M., Howar, F., Steffen, B.: The TTT algorithm: a redundancy-free approach to active automata learning. In: Bonakdarpour, B., Smolka, S.A. (eds.) RV 2014. LNCS, vol. 8734, pp. 307–322. Springer, Cham (2014). https://doi.org/10.1007/978-3-319-11164-3_26
17. Kearns, M.J., Vazirani, U.V.: An Introduction to Computational Learning Theory. MIT Press, Cambridge (1994)
18. Li, N., Xie, T., Tillmann, N., de Halleux, J., Schulte, W.: Reggae: automated test generation for programs using complex regular expressions. In: 2009 24th IEEE/ACM International Conference on Automated Software Engineering. ASE 2009, pp. 515–519. IEEE (2009)
19. Maler, O., Mens, I.-E.: A generic algorithm for learning symbolic automata from membership queries. In: Aceto, L., et al. (eds.) Models, Algorithms, Logics and Tools. LNCS, vol. 10460, pp. 146–169. Springer, Cham (2017). https://doi.org/10.1007/978-3-319-63121-9_8
20. Mens, I., Maler, O.: Learning regular languages over large ordered alphabets. Log. Methods Comput. Sci. **11**(3) (2015)
21. Moerman, J., Sammartino, M., Silva, A., Klin, B., Szynwelski, M.: Learning nominal automata. In: Proceedings of the 44th ACM SIGPLAN-SIGACT Symposium on Principles of Programming Languages (POPL) (2017)
22. Nakamura, A.: An efficient query learning algorithm for ordered binary decision diagrams. Inf. Comput. **201**(2), 178–198 (2005)
23. Rivest, R.L., Schapire, R.E.: Inference of finite automata using homing sequences. Inf. Comput. **103**(2), 299–347 (1993)
24. Sivakorn, S., Argyros, G., Pei, K., Keromytis, A.D., Jana, S.: HVLearn: automated black-box analysis of hostname verification in SSL/TLS implementations. In: 2017 IEEE Symposium on Security and Privacy (SP), pp. 521–538. IEEE (2017)
25. Yuan, Y., Alur, R., Loo, B.T.: NetEgg: programming network policies by examples. In: Proceedings of the 13th ACM Workshop on Hot Topics in Networks, HotNets-XIII, pp. 20:1–20:7. ACM, New York (2014)

Runtime Verification, Hybrid and Timed Systems

Reachable Set Over-Approximation for Nonlinear Systems Using Piecewise Barrier Tubes

Hui Kong[1(✉)], Ezio Bartocci[2], and Thomas A. Henzinger[1]

[1] IST Austria, Klosterneuburg, Austria
hui.kong@ist.ac.at
[2] TU Wien, Vienna, Austria

Abstract. We address the problem of analyzing the reachable set of a polynomial nonlinear continuous system by over-approximating the flowpipe of its dynamics. The common approach to tackle this problem is to perform a numerical integration over a given time horizon based on Taylor expansion and interval arithmetic. However, this method results to be very conservative when there is a large difference in speed between trajectories as time progresses. In this paper, we propose to use combinations of barrier functions, which we call piecewise barrier tube (PBT), to over-approximate flowpipe. The basic idea of PBT is that for each segment of a flowpipe, a coarse box which is big enough to contain the segment is constructed using sampled simulation and then in the box we compute by linear programming a set of barrier functions (called barrier tube or BT for short) which work together to form a tube surrounding the flowpipe. The benefit of using PBT is that (1) BT is independent of time and hence can avoid being stretched and deformed by time; and (2) a small number of BTs can form a tight over-approximation for the flowpipe, which means that the computation required to decide whether the BTs intersect the unsafe set can be reduced significantly. We implemented a prototype called PBTS in C++. Experiments on some benchmark systems show that our approach is effective.

1 Introduction

Hybrid systems [17] are widely used to model dynamical systems which exhibit both discrete and continuous behaviors. The reachability analysis of hybrid systems has been a challenging problem over the last few decades. The hard core of this problem lies in dealing with the continuous behavior of systems that are described by ordinary differential equations (ODEs). Although there are currently several quite efficient and scalable approaches for reachability analysis of linear systems [8–10,14,16,19,20,26,34], nonlinear ODEs are much harder

This research was supported by the Austrian Science Fund (FWF) under grants S11402-N23, S11405-N23 (RiSE/SHiNE) and Z211-N23 (Wittgenstein Award).

H. Chockler and G. Weissenbacher (Eds.): CAV 2018, LNCS 10981, pp. 449–467, 2018.
https://doi.org/10.1007/978-3-319-96145-3_24

to handle and the current approaches can be characterized into the following groups.

Invariant Generation [18,21,22,27,28,36,37,39]. An invariant I for a system S is a set such that any trajectory of S originating from I never escapes from I. Therefore, finding an invariant I such that the initial set $I_0 \subseteq I$ and the unsafe set $U \cap I = \emptyset$ indicates the safety of the system. In this way, there is no need to compute the flowpipe. The main problem with invariant generation is that it is hard to define a set of high quality constraints which can be solved efficiently.

Abstraction and Hybridization [2,11,24,31,35]. The basic idea of the abstraction-based approach is first constructing a linear model which over-approximates the original nonlinear dynamics and then applying techniques for linear systems to the abstraction model. However, how to construct an abstraction with the fewest discrete states and sufficiently high accuracy is still a challenging issue.

Satisfiability Modulo Theory (SMT) Over Reals [6,7,23]. This approach encodes the reachability problem for nonlinear systems as first-order logic formulas over the real numbers. These formulas can be solved using for example $\delta-$complete decision procedures that overcome the theoretical limits in nonlinear theories over the reals, by choosing a desired precision δ. An SMT implementing such procedures can return either *unsat* if the reachability problem is unsatisfiable or δ-sat if the problem is satisfiable given the chosen precision. The δ-sat verdict does not guarantee that the dynamics of the system will reach a particular region. It may happens that by increasing the precision the problem would result *unsat*. In general the limit of this approach is that it does not provide as a result a complete and comprehensive description of the reachability set.

Bounded Time Flowpipe Computation [1,3–5,25,32]. The common technique to compute a bounded flowpipe is based on interval method or Taylor model. Interval-based approach is quite efficient even for high dimensional systems [29], but it suffers the wrapping effect of intervals and can quickly accumulate over-approximation errors. In contrast, the Taylor-model-based approach is more precise in that it uses a vector of polynomials plus a vector of small intervals to symbolically represent the flowpipe. However, for the purpose of safety verification or reachability analysis, the Taylor model has to be further over-approximated by intervals, which may bring back the wrapping effect. In particular, the wrapping effect can explode easily when the flowpipe segment over a time interval is stretched drastically due to a large difference in speed between individual trajectories. This case is demonstrated by the following example.

Example 1 (Running example). Consider the 2D system [30] described by $\dot{x} = y$ and $\dot{y} = x^2$. Let the initial set X_0 be a line segment $x \in [1.0, 1.0]$ and $y \in [-1.05, -0.95]$, Fig. 1a shows the simulation result on three points in X_0 over time interval $[0, 6.6]$. The reachable set at $t = 6.6$ s is a smooth curve connecting the end points of the three trajectories. As can be seen, the trajectory originating from the top is left far behind the one originating from the bottom, which means that the tiny initial line segment is being stretched into a huge curve very quickly,

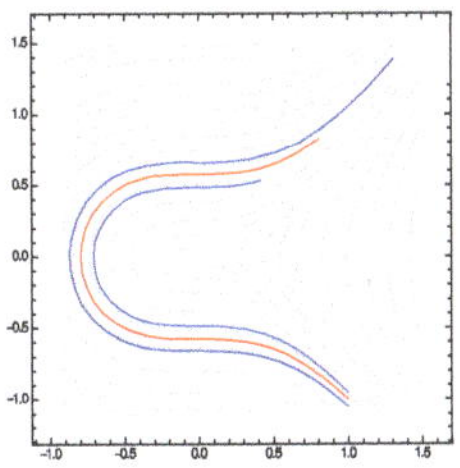

(a)

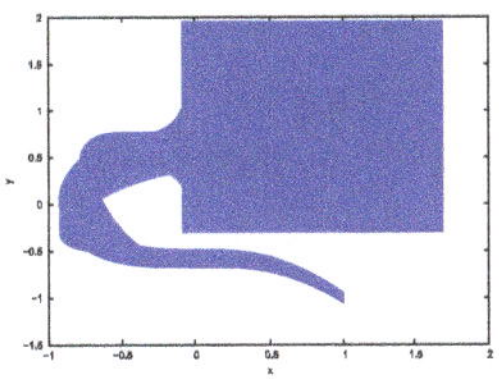

(b)

Fig. 1. (a) Simulation for Example 1 showing flowpipe segment being extremely stretched and deformed, (b) Interval over-approximation of the Taylor model computed by *Flow** [3].

while the width of the flowpipe is actually converging to 0. As a result, the interval over-approximation of this huge curve can be extremely conservative even if its Taylor model representation is precise, and reducing the time step size is not helpful. To prove this point, we computed with *Flow** [3] a Taylor model series for the time horizon of 6.6 s which consists of 13200 Taylor models. Figure 1b shows the interval approximation of the Taylor model series, which apparently starts exploding.

In this paper, we propose to use piecewise barrier tubes (PBTs) to over-approximate flowpipes of polynomial nonlinear systems, which can avoid the issue caused by the excessive stretching of a flowpipe segment. The idea of PBT is inspired from barrier certificate [22,33]. A barrier certificate $B(\boldsymbol{x})$ is a real-valued function such that (1) $B(\boldsymbol{x}) \geq 0$ for all $\boldsymbol{x}$ in the initial set X_0; (2) $B(\boldsymbol{x}) < 0$ for all $\boldsymbol{x}$ in the unsafe set X_U; (3) no trajectory can escape from $\{\boldsymbol{x} \in \mathbb{R}^n \mid B(\boldsymbol{x}) \geq 0\}$ through the boundary $\{\boldsymbol{x} \in \mathbb{R}^n \mid B(\boldsymbol{x}) = 0\}$. A sufficient condition for this constraint is that the Lie derivative of $B(\boldsymbol{x})$ w.r.t the dynamics $\dot{\boldsymbol{x}} = \boldsymbol{f}$ is positive all over the invariant region, i.e., $\mathcal{L}_{\boldsymbol{f}} B(\boldsymbol{x}) > 0$, which means that all the trajectories must move in the increasing direction of the level sets of $B(\boldsymbol{x})$.

Barrier certificates can be used to verify safety properties without computing the flowpipe explicitly. The essential idea is to use the zero level set of $B(\boldsymbol{x})$ as a barrier to separate the flowpipe from the unsafe set. Moreover, if the unsafe set is very close to the boundary of the flowpipe, the barrier has to fit the shape of the flowpipe to make sure that all components of the constraint are satisfied. However, the zero level set of a polynomial of fixed degree may not have the power to mimic the shape of the flowpipe, which means that there may exist no solution for the above constraints even if the system is safe. This problem might be addressed using piecewise barrier certificate, i.e., cutting the flowpipe into small pieces so that every piece is straight enough to have a barrier certificate of simple form. Unfortunately, this is infeasible because we know nothing about the flowpipe locally. Therefore, we have to find another way to proceed.

Instead of computing a single barrier certificate, we propose to compute barrier tubes to piecewise over-approximate the flowpipe. Concretely, in the beginning, we first construct a containing box, called **enclosure**, for the initial set using interval approach [29] and simulation, then, using linear programming, we compute a group of barrier functions which work together to form a tight tube (called barrier tube) around the flowpipe. Similarly, taking the intersection of the barrier tube and the boundary of the box as the new initial set, we repeat the previous operations to obtain successive barrier tubes step by step. The key point here is how to compute a group of tightly enclosing barriers around the flowpipe without a constraint on the unsafe set inside the box. Our basic idea is to construct a group of auxiliary state sets U around the flowpipe and then, for each $U_i \in U$, we compute a barrier certificate between U_i and the flowpipe. If a barrier certificate is found, we expand U_i towards the flowpipe iteratively until no more barrier certificate can be found; otherwise, we shrink U_i away from the flowpipe until a barrier certificate is found. Since the auxiliary sets are distributed around the flowpipe, so is the barrier tube. The benefit of such piecewise barrier tubes is that they are time independent, and hence can avoid the issue of stretched flowpipe segments caused by speed differences between trajectories. Moreover, usually a small number of BTs can form a tight over-approximation of the flowpipe, which means that less computation is needed to decide the intersection of PBT and the unsafe set.

The main contributions of this paper are as follows:

1. We transform the constraint-solving problem for barrier certificates into a linear programming problem using Handelman representation [15];
2. We introduce PBT to over-approximate the flowpipe of nonlinear systems, thus dealing with flowpipes independent of time and hence avoiding the error explosion caused by stretched flowpipe segments;
3. We implement a prototype in C++ to compute PTB automatically and we show the effectiveness of our approach by providing a comparison with the state-of-the-art tools for reachability analysis of polynomial nonlinear systems such as *CORA* [1] and *Flow** [3].

The paper is organized as follows. Section 2 is devoted to the preliminaries. Section 3 shows how to compute barrier certificates using Handelman representation, while in Sect. 4 we present a method to compute Piecewise Barrier Tubes. Section 5 provides our experimental results and we conclude in Sect. 6.

2 Preliminaries

In this section, we recall some concepts used throughout the paper. We first clarify some notation conventions. If not specified otherwise, we use boldface lower case letters to denote vectors, we use $\mathbb{R}$ for the real number field and $\mathbb{N}$ for the set of natural numbers, and we consider multivariate polynomials in $\mathbb{R}[\boldsymbol{x}]$, where the components of $\boldsymbol{x}$ act as indeterminates. In addition, for all the polynomials $B(\boldsymbol{u}, \boldsymbol{x})$, we denote by $\boldsymbol{u}$ the vector composed of all the u_i and denote by $\boldsymbol{x}$ the vector composed of all the remaining variables x_i that occur in the polynomial. We use $\mathbb{R}_{\geq 0}$ and $\mathbb{R}_{>0}$ to denote the domain of nonnegative real number and positive real number respectively.

Let $P \subseteq \mathbb{R}^n$ be a convex and compact polyhedron with non-empty interior, bounded by linear polynomials $p_1, \cdots, p_m \in \mathbb{R}[\boldsymbol{x}]$. Without lose of generality, we may assume $P = \{\boldsymbol{x} \in \mathbb{R}^n \mid p_i(\boldsymbol{x}) \geq 0, i = 1, \cdots, m\}$.

Next, we present the notation of the Lie derivative, which is widely used in the discipline of differential geometry. Let $\boldsymbol{f} : \mathbb{R}^n \to \mathbb{R}^n$ be a continuous vector field such that $\dot{x}_i = f_i(\boldsymbol{x})$ where $\dot{x}_i$ is the time derivative of $x_i(t)$.

Definition 1 (Lie derivative). *For a given polynomial $p \in \mathbb{R}[\boldsymbol{x}]$ over $\boldsymbol{x} = (x_1, \ldots, x_n)$ and a continuous system $\dot{\boldsymbol{x}} = \boldsymbol{f}$, where $\boldsymbol{f} = (f_1, \ldots, f_n)$, the **Lie derivative** of $p \in \mathbb{R}[x]$ along $\boldsymbol{f}$ of order k is defined as follows.*

$$\mathcal{L}_{\boldsymbol{f}}^k p \stackrel{def}{=} \begin{cases} p, & k = 0 \\ \sum_{i=1}^n \frac{\partial \mathcal{L}_{\boldsymbol{f}}^{k-1} p}{\partial x_i} \cdot f_i, & k \geq 1 \end{cases}$$

Essentially, the k-th order Lie derivative of p is the k-th derivative of p w.r.t. time, i.e., reflects the change of p over time. We write $\mathcal{L}_{\boldsymbol{f}} p$ for $\mathcal{L}_{\boldsymbol{f}}^1 p$.

In this paper, we focus on semialgebraic nonlinear systems, which are defined as follows.

Definition 2 (Semialgebraic system). *A **semialgebraic system** is a triple $M \stackrel{def}{=} \langle X, \boldsymbol{f}, X_0, I \rangle$, where*

1. *$X \subseteq \mathbb{R}^n$ is the state space of the system M,*
2. *$\boldsymbol{f} \in \mathbb{R}[\boldsymbol{x}]^n$ is locally Lipschitz continuous vector function,*
3. *$X_0 \subseteq X$ is the initial set, which is semialgebraic [40],*
4. *I is the invariant of the system.*

The local Lipschitz continuity guarantees the existence and uniqueness of the differential equation $\dot{\boldsymbol{x}} = \boldsymbol{f}$ locally. A trajectory of a semialgebraic system is defined as follows.

Definition 3 (Trajectory). *Given a semialgebraic system M, a **trajectory** originating from a point $\boldsymbol{x}_0 \in X_0$ to time $T > 0$ is a continuous and differentiable function $\boldsymbol{\zeta}(\boldsymbol{x}_0, t) : [0, T) \to \mathbb{R}^n$ such that (1) $\boldsymbol{\zeta}(\boldsymbol{x}_0, 0) = \boldsymbol{x}_0$, and (2) $\forall \tau \in [0, T)$: $\frac{d\boldsymbol{\zeta}}{dt}\big|_{t=\tau} = \boldsymbol{f}(\boldsymbol{\zeta}(\boldsymbol{x}_0, \tau))$. T is assumed to be within the maximal interval of existence of the solution from $\boldsymbol{x}_0$.*

For ease of readability, we also use $\zeta(t)$ for $\zeta(\boldsymbol{x}_0, t)$. In addition, we use $Flow_{\boldsymbol{f}}(X_0)$ to denote the flowpipe of initial set X_0, i.e.,

$$Flow_{\boldsymbol{f}}(X_0) \stackrel{\text{def}}{=} \{\boldsymbol{\zeta}(\boldsymbol{x}_0, t) \mid \boldsymbol{x}_0 \in X_0, t \in \mathbb{R}_{\geq}, \dot{\boldsymbol{\zeta}} = \boldsymbol{f}(\boldsymbol{\zeta})\} \tag{1}$$

Definition 4 (Safety). *Given an unsafe set $X_U \subseteq X$, a semialgebraic system $M = \langle X, \boldsymbol{f}, X_0, I \rangle$ is said to be **safe** if no trajectory $\boldsymbol{\zeta}(\boldsymbol{x}_0, t)$ of M satisfies that $\exists \tau \in \mathbb{R}_{\geq 0} : \boldsymbol{x}(\tau) \in X_U$, where $\boldsymbol{x}_0 \in X_0$.*

3 Computing Barrier Certificates

Given a semialgebraic system M, a barrier certificate is a real-valued function $B(\boldsymbol{x})$ such that (1) $B(\boldsymbol{x}) \geq 0$ for all $\boldsymbol{x}$ in the initial set; (2) $B(\boldsymbol{x}) < 0$ for all $\boldsymbol{x}$ in the unsafe set; (3) no trajectory can escape from the region of $B(\boldsymbol{x}) \geq 0$. Then, the hyper-surface $\{\boldsymbol{x} \in \mathbb{R}^n \mid B(\boldsymbol{x}) = 0\}$ forms a barrier separating the flowpipe from the unsafe set. To compute such a barrier certificate, the most common approach is template based constraint solving, i.e., firstly figure out a sufficient condition for the above condition and then, set up a template polynomial $B(\boldsymbol{u}, \boldsymbol{x})$ of fixed degree, and finally solve the constraint on $\boldsymbol{u}$ derived from the sufficient condition on $B(\boldsymbol{u}, \boldsymbol{x})$. There are a couple of sufficient conditions available for this purpose [13,22,27]. In order to have an efficient constraint solving method, we adopt the following condition [33].

Theorem 1. *Given a semialgebraic system M, let X_0 and U be the initial set and the unsafe set respectively, the system is guaranteed to be safe if there exists a real-valued function $B(\boldsymbol{x})$ such that*

$$\forall \boldsymbol{x} \in X_0 : B(\boldsymbol{x}) > 0 \tag{2}$$

$$\forall \boldsymbol{x} \in I : \mathcal{L}_f B > 0 \tag{3}$$

$$\forall \boldsymbol{x} \in X_U : B(\boldsymbol{x}) < 0 \tag{4}$$

In Theorem 1, the condition (3) means that all the trajectories of the system always point in the increasing direction of the level sets of $B(\boldsymbol{x})$ in the region I. Therefore, no trajectory starting from the initial set would cross the zero level set. The benefit of this condition is that it can be solved more efficiently than other existing conditions [13,22] although it is relatively conservative. The most widely used approach is to transform the constraint-solving problem into a sum-of-squares (*SOS*) programming problem [33], which can be solved in polynomial time. However, a serious problem with *SOS* programming based approach is that automatic generation of polynomial templates is very hard to perform. We now show an example to demonstrate the reason. For simplicity, we assume that the initial set, the unsafe set and the invariant are defined by the polynomial inequalities $X_0(\boldsymbol{x}) \geq 0$, $X_U(\boldsymbol{x}) \geq 0$ and $I(\boldsymbol{x}) \geq 0$ respectively, then the *SOS* relaxation of Theorem 1 is that the following polynomials are all *SOS*

$$B(\boldsymbol{x}) - \mu_1(\boldsymbol{x})X_0(\boldsymbol{x}) + \epsilon_1 \tag{5}$$

$$\mathcal{L}_f B - \mu_2(\boldsymbol{x})I(\boldsymbol{x}) + \epsilon_2 \tag{6}$$

$$-B(\boldsymbol{x}) - \mu_3(\boldsymbol{x})X_U(\boldsymbol{x}) + \epsilon_3 \tag{7}$$

where $\mu_i(\boldsymbol{x}), i = 1, \cdots, 3$ are *SOS* polynomials as well and $\epsilon_i > 0, i = 1, \cdots, 3$. Suppose the degrees of $X_0(\boldsymbol{x})$, $I(\boldsymbol{x})$ and $X_U(\boldsymbol{x})$ are all odd numbers. Then, the degree of the template for $B(\boldsymbol{x})$ must be an odd number too. The reason is that, if $deg(B)$ is an even number, in order for the first and third polynomials to be *SOS* polynomials, $deg(B)$ must be greater than both $deg(\mu_3 X_U)$ and $deg(\mu_1 X_0)$, which are odd numbers. However, since the first and third condition contain $B(\boldsymbol{x})$

and $-B(\boldsymbol{x})$ respectively, their leading monomials must have the opposite sign, which means that they cannot be *SOS* polynomial simultaneously. Moreover, the degrees of the templates for the auxiliary polynomials $\mu_1(\boldsymbol{x}), \mu_3(\boldsymbol{x})$ must also be chosen properly so that $deg(\mu_1 X_0) = deg(\mu_3 X_U) = deg(B)$, because only in this way the leading monomials (which has an odd degree) of (5) and (7) have the chance to be resolved so that the resultant polynomial can be a *SOS*. Similarly, in order to make the second polynomial a *SOS* as well, one has to choose an appropriate degree for $\mu_2(\boldsymbol{x})$ according to the degree of $\mathcal{L}_f B$ and $I(\boldsymbol{x})$. As a result, the tangled constraints on the relevant template polynomials reduce the power of *SOS* programming significantly.

Due to the above reason, inspired by the work [38], we use Handelman representation to relax Theorem 1. We assume that the initial set X_0, the unsafe set X_U and the invariant I are all convex and compact polyhedra, i.e., $X_0 = \{\boldsymbol{x} \in \mathbb{R}^n \mid p_1(\boldsymbol{x}) \geq 0, \cdots, p_{m_1}(\boldsymbol{x}) \geq 0\}$, $I = \{\boldsymbol{x} \in \mathbb{R}^n \mid q_1(\boldsymbol{x}) \geq 0, \cdots, q_{m_2}(\boldsymbol{x}) \geq 0\}$ and $X_U = \{\boldsymbol{x} \in \mathbb{R}^n \mid r_1(\boldsymbol{x}) \geq 0, \cdots, r_{m_3}(\boldsymbol{x}) \geq 0\}$, where $p_i(\boldsymbol{x}), q_j(\boldsymbol{x}), r_k(\boldsymbol{x})$ are linear polynomials. Then, we have the following theorem.

Theorem 2. *Given a semialgebraic system M, let X_0, X_U and I be defined as above, the system is guaranteed to be safe if there exists a real-valued polynomial function $B(\boldsymbol{x})$ such that*

$$B(\boldsymbol{x}) \equiv \sum_{|\alpha| \leq M_1} \lambda_\alpha p_1^{\alpha_1} \cdots p_{m_1}^{\alpha_{m_1}} + \epsilon_1 \tag{8}$$

$$\mathcal{L}_f B \equiv \sum_{|\beta| \leq M_2} \lambda_\beta q_1^{\beta_1} \cdots q_{m_2}^{\beta_{m_2}} + \epsilon_2 \tag{9}$$

$$-B(\boldsymbol{x}) \equiv \sum_{|\gamma| \leq M_3} \lambda_\gamma r_1^{\gamma_1} \cdots r_{m_3}^{\gamma_{m_3}} + \epsilon_3 \tag{10}$$

where $\lambda_\alpha, \lambda_\beta, \lambda_\gamma \in \mathbb{R}_{\geq 0}$, $\epsilon_i \in \mathbb{R}_{>0}$ and $M_i \in \mathbb{N}, i = 1, \cdots, 3$.

Theorem 2 provides us with an alternative to *SOS* programming to find barrier certificate $B(\boldsymbol{x})$ by transforming it into a linear programming problem. The basic idea is that we first set up a template $B(\boldsymbol{u}, \boldsymbol{x})$ of fixed degree as well as the appropriate $M_i, i = 1, \cdots, 3$ that make the both sides of the three identities (8)–(10) have the same degree. Since (8)–(10) are identities, the coefficients of the corresponding monomials on both sides must be identical as well. Thus, we derive a system S of linear equations and inequalities over $\boldsymbol{u}, \lambda_\alpha, \lambda_\beta, \lambda_\gamma$. Now, finding a barrier certificate is just to find a feasible solution for S, which can be solved by linear programming. Compared to *SOS* programming based approach, this approach is more flexible in choosing the polynomial template as well as other parameters. We consider now a linear system to show how it works.

Example 2. Given a 2D system defined by $\dot{x} = 2x + 3y, \dot{y} = -4x + 2y$, let $X_0 = \{(x, y) \in \mathbb{R}^2 \mid p_1 = x + 100 \geq 0, p_2 = -90 - x \geq 0, p_3 = y + 45 \geq 0, p_4 = -40 - y \geq 0\}$, $I = \{(x, y) \in \mathbb{R}^2 \mid q_1 = x + 110 \geq 0, q_2 = -80 - x \geq 0, q_3 = y + 45 \geq 0, q_4 = -20 - y \geq 0\}$ and $X_U = \{(x, y) \in \mathbb{R}^2 \mid r_1 = x + 98 \geq 0, r_2 =$

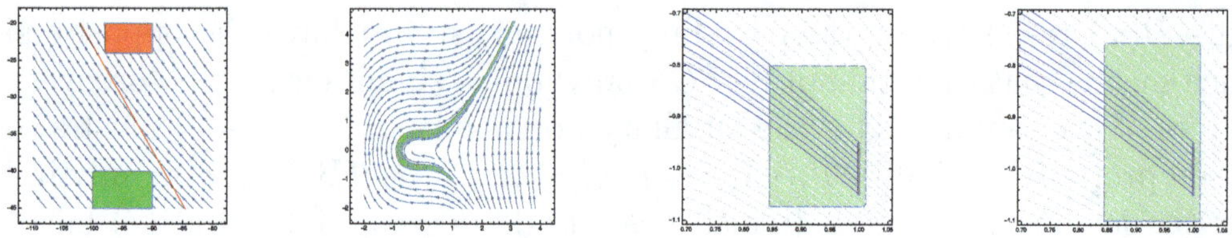

Fig. 2. (a) Linear barrier certificate (straight red line) for Example 2. Rectangle in green: initial set, rectangle in red: unsafe set. (b) PBT for the running Example 5, consisting of 45 BTs. (c) Enclosure (before bloating) for flowpipe of Example 3 (green shadow region). (d) Enclosure (after bloating) for flowpipe of Example 3. (Color figure online)

$-90-x \geq 0, r_3 = y+24 \geq 0, r_4 = -20-y \geq 0\}$. Assume $B(\boldsymbol{u}, \boldsymbol{x}) = u_1+u_2x+u_3y$, $M_i = \epsilon_i = 1$ for $i = 1, \cdots, 3$, then we obtain the following polynomial identities according to Theorem 2

$$u_1 + u_2x + u_3y - \sum_{i=1}^{4} \lambda_{1i}p_i - \epsilon_1 \equiv 0$$

$$u_2(2x + 3y) + u_3(-4x + 2y) - \sum_{j=1}^{4} \lambda_{2j}q_j - \epsilon_2 \equiv 0$$

$$-(u_1 + u_2x + u_3y) - \sum_{k=1}^{4} \lambda_{3k}r_k - \epsilon_3 \equiv 0$$

where $\lambda_{ij} \geq 0$ for $i = 1, \cdots, 3$, $j = 1, \cdots, 4$. By collecting the coefficients of x, y in the above polynomials, we obtain a system S of linear polynomial equations and inequalities over u_i, λ_{jk}. By solving S using linear programming, we obtain a feasible solution and Fig. 2a shows the computed linear barrier certificate. Note that, for the aforementioned reason, it is impossible to find a linear barrier certificate using *SOS* programming for this example.

4 Piecewise Barrier Tubes

In this section, we introduce how to construct PBTs for nonlinear polynomial systems. The basic idea of constructing PBT is that, for each segment of the flowpipe, an enclosure box is first constructed and then, a BT is constructed to form a tighter over-approximation for the flowpipe segment inside the box.

4.1 Constructing an Enclosure Box

Given an initial set, the first task is to construct an enclosure box for the initial set and the following segment of the flowpipe. As pointed out in Sect. 1, one principle to construct an enclosure box is to simplify the shape of the flowpipe segment, or in other words, to approximately bound the twisting of trajectories by some θ in the box, where the *twisting* of a trajectory is defined as follows.

Definition 5 (Twisting of a trajectory). *Let M be a continuous system and $\zeta(t)$ be a trajectory of M. Then, $\zeta(t)$ is said to have a twisting of θ on the time interval $I = [T_1, T_2]$, written as $\xi_I(\zeta)$, if it satisfies that $\xi_I(\zeta) = \theta$, where* $\xi_I(\zeta) \stackrel{def}{=} \sup_{t_1,t_2 \in I} \arccos\left(\frac{\langle \dot{\zeta}(t_1), \dot{\zeta}(t_2)\rangle}{\|\zeta(t_1)\|\|\zeta(t_2)\|}\right)$.

The basic idea to construct an enclosure box is depicted in Algorithm 1.

Algorithm 1. Algorithm to construct an enclosure box

---

input : M: dynamics of the system; n: dimension of system; X_O: initial set
θ_1: twisting of simulation; d: maximum distance of simulation;
output: E: an enclosure box containing X_O; P: plane where flowpipe exits ;
G: range of intersection of $Flow_f(X_O)$ with plane P by simulation

sample a set S_0 of points from X_O;
select a point $\boldsymbol{x}_0 \in S_0$;
find a time step size ΔT_0 by (θ, d)-bounded simulation for $\boldsymbol{x}_0$;
$\Delta T \longleftarrow \Delta T_0$;
while $\Delta T > \epsilon$ **do**
  $[found, \mathsf{E}] \longleftarrow$ find an enclosure box by interval arithmetic using ΔT;
  if *found* **then**
    do a simulation for all $\boldsymbol{x}_i \in S_0$, select the plane P which intersects with the most of simulations; generate G;
    bloat E s.t $Flow_f(X_O)$ gets out of E only through the facet in P;
    break;
  else
    $\Delta T \longleftarrow 1/2 * \Delta T$;

Remark 1. In Algorithm 1, we use interval arithmetic [29] and simulation to construct an enclosure box E for a given initial set and its following flowpipe segment. Meanwhile, we obtain a coarse range of the intersection of the flowpipe and the boundary of the enclosure, which helps to accelerate the construction of barrier tube. To be simple, the enclosure is constructed in a way such that the flowpipe gets out of the box through a single facet. Given an initial set X_O, we first sample a set S_0 of points from X_O for simulation. Then, we select a point $\boldsymbol{x}_0$ from S_0 and do (θ, d)-simulation on $\boldsymbol{x}_0$ to obtain a time step ΔT. A (θ, d)-simulation is a simulation that stops either when the twisting of the simulation reaches θ or when the distance between x_0 and the end point reaches d. On the one hand, by using a small θ, we aim to achieve a straight flowpipe segment. On the other hand, by specifying a maximal distance d, we make sure that the simulation can stop for a long and straight flowpipe. At each iteration of the *while* loop in line 5, we first try to construct an enclosure box by interval arithmetic over ΔT. If such an enclosure box is created, we then perform a simulation (see line 8) for all the points in S_0 to find out the plane P of facet which intersects with the most of the simulations. The idea behind line 9 is that in order to better over-approximate the intersection of the flowpipe with the boundary of the box using intervals, we push the other planes outwards to make P the only plane where the flowpipe get out of the box. Certainly, simply by simulation we cannot guarantee that the flowpipe does not intersect the other facets. Therefore, we have the following theorem for the decision.

Theorem 3. *Given a semialgebraic system M and an initial set X_0, a box E is an enclosure of X_0 and F_i is a facet of E. Then, $(Flow_f(X_0) \cap E) \cap F_i = \emptyset$ if there exists a barrier certificate $B_i(\boldsymbol{x})$ for X_0 and F_i inside E.*

Remark 2. According to the definition of barrier certificate, the proof of Theorem 3 is straightforward, which is ignored here. Therefore, to make sure that the flowpipe does not intersect the facet F_i, we only need to find a barrier certificate, which can be done using the approach presented in Sect. 3. Moreover, if no barrier certificate can be found, we further bloat the facet. Next, we still use the running Example 1 to demonstrate the process of constructing an enclosure.

Example 3 (running example). Consider the system in Example 1 and the initial set $x = 1.0, -1.05 \leq y \leq -0.95$, let the bounding twisting of simulation be $\theta = \pi/18$, then the time step size we computed for interval evaluation is $\Delta T = 0.2947$. The corresponding enclosure computed by interval arithmetic is shown in Fig. 2c. Furthermore, by simulation, we know that the flowpipe can reach both left facet and top facet. Therefore, we have two options to bloat the facet: bloat the left facet to make the flowpipe intersects the top facet only or bloat the top facet to make the flowpipe intersects left facet only. In this example, we choose the latter option and the bloated enclosure is shown in Fig. 2d. In this way, we can over-approximate the intersection of the flowpipe and the facet by intervals if we can obtain its boundary on every side. This can be achieved by finding barrier tube.

4.2 Compute a Barrier Tube Inside a Box

An important fact about the flowpipe of continuous system is that it tends to be straight if it is short enough, given that the initial set is straight as well (otherwise, we can split it). Suppose there is a small box E around a straight flowpipe, it will be easy to compute a barrier certificate for a given initial set and unsafe set inside E. A barrier tube for the flowpipe in E is a group of barrier certificates which form a tube around a flowpipe inside E. Formally,

Definition 6 (Barrier Tube). *Given a semialgebraic system M, a box E and an initial set $X_0 \subseteq E$, a barrier tube is a set of real-valued functions $BT = \{B_i(\boldsymbol{x}), i = 1, \cdots, m\}$ such that for all $B_i(\boldsymbol{x}) \in BT$: (1) $\forall \boldsymbol{x} \in X_0 : B_i(\boldsymbol{x}) > 0$ and, (2) $\forall \boldsymbol{x} \in E : \mathcal{L}_f B_i > 0$.*

According to Definition 6, a barrier tube BT is defined by a set of real-valued functions and every function inequality $B_i(\boldsymbol{x}) > 0$ is an invariant of M in E and so do their conjunction. The property of a barrier tube BT is formally described in the following theorem.

Theorem 4. *Given a semialgebraic system M, a box E and an initial set $X_0 \subseteq E$, let $BT = \{B_i(\boldsymbol{x}) : i = 1, \cdots, m\}$ be a barrier tube of M and $\Omega = \{\boldsymbol{x} \in \mathbb{R}^n \mid \bigwedge B_i(\boldsymbol{x}) > 0, B_i \in BT\}$, then $Flow_{\boldsymbol{f}}(X_0) \cap E \subseteq \Omega \cap E$.*

Remark 3. Theorem 4 states that an arbitrary barrier tube is able to form an over-approximation for the reach pipe in the box E. Compared to a single barrier certificate, multiple barrier certificates could over-approximate the flowpipe more precisely. However, since there is no constraint on unsafe sets in Definition 6, a barrier tube satisfying the definition could be very conservative. In order to obtain an accurate approximation for the flowpipe, we choose to create additional auxiliary constraints.

Auxiliary Unsafe Set (AUS). To obtain an accurate barrier tube, there are two main questions to be answered: (1) How many barrier certificates are needed? and (2) How do we control their positions to make the tube well-shaped to better over-approximate the flowpipe? The answer for the first question is quite simple: the more, the better. This will be explained later on. For the second question, the answer is to construct a group of properly distributed auxiliary state sets (AUSs). Each set of the AUSs is used as an unsafe set U_i for the system and then we compute a barrier certificate B_i for U_i according to Theorem 2. Since the zero level set of B_i serves as a barrier between the flowpipe and U_i, the space where a barrier could appear is fully determined by the position of U_i. Roughly speaking, when U_i is far away from the flowpipe, the space for a barrier to exist is wide as well. Correspondingly, the barrier certificate found would usually locate far away from the flowpipe as well. Certainly, as U_i gets closer to the flowpipe, the space for barrier certificates also contracts towards the flowpipe accordingly. Therefore, by expanding U_i towards the flowpipe, we can get more precise over-approximations for the flowpipe.

Why Multiple AUS? Although the accuracy of the barrier certificate over-approximation can be improved by expanding the AUS towards the flowpipe, the capability of a single barrier certificate is very limited because it can erect a barrier which only matches a single profile of the flow pipe. However, if we have a set U of AUSs which are distributed evenly around the flowpipe and there is a barrier certificate B_i for each $U_i \in U$, these barrier certificates would be able to over-approximate the flowpipe from a number of profiles. Therefore, increasing the number of AUSs can increase the quality of the over-approximation as well. Furthermore, if all these auxiliary sets are connected, all the barriers would form a tube surrounding the flowpipe. Therefore, if we can create a series of boxes piecewise covering the flowpipe and then construct a barrier tube for every piece of the flowpipe, we obtain an over-approximation for the flowpipe by PBT.

Based on the above idea, we provide Algorithm 2 to compute barrier tube.

Algorithm 2. Algorithm to compute barrier tube

input : M: dynamics of the system; X_O: Initial set;
E: interval enclosure of initial set;
G: interval approx. of $(\partial \mathsf{E} \cap Flow_f(X_O))$ by simulation;
P: plane where flowpipe exits from box;
D: candidate degree list for template polynomial;
ϵ: difference in size between AUS (auxiliary unsafe set)
output: BT: barrier tube; X_0': interval over-approximation of $(\mathsf{BT} \cap E)$

1 **foreach** G_{ij}: *an facet of* G **do**
2   *found* $\longleftarrow$ *false* ;
3   **foreach** $d \in D$ **do**
4   AUS $\longleftarrow$ `CreateAUS`(G, P, G_{ij});
5   **while** *true* **do**
6   [*found*, B_{ij}] $\longleftarrow$ `ComputeBarrierCert`(X_O, E, AUS, d) ;
7   **if** *found* **then** AUS′ $\longleftarrow$ `Expand` (AUS);
8   **else** AUS′ $\longleftarrow$ `Contract` (AUS) ;
9   **if** `Diff`(AUS′, AUS) $\leq \epsilon$ **then** break;
10   **else** AUS' $\longleftarrow$ AUS;
11   **if** *found* **then** BT $\longleftarrow$ `Push`(BT, B_{ij}); break;
12   **else** return FAIL;
13 return SUCCEED;

Remark 4. In Algorithm 2, for an n-dimensional flowpipe segment, we aim to build a barrier tube composed of $2(n-1)$ barrier certificates, which means we need to construct $2(n-1)$ `AUS`s. According to Algorithm 1, we know that the plane `P` is the only exit of the flowpipe from the enclosure `E` and `G` is roughly the region where they intersect. Let F^G be the facet of `E` that contains `G`, then for every facet F^G_{ij} of F^G, we can take an $(n-1)$-dimensional rectangle between F^G_{ij} and G_{ij} as an `AUS`, where G_{ij} is the facet of G adjacent to F^{ij}_G. Therefore, enumerating all the facets of G in line 1 would produce $2(n-1)$ positions for `AUS`. The loop in line 3 is attempting to find a polynomial barrier certificate of different degrees in D. In the while loop 5, we iteratively compute the best barrier certificate by adjusting the width of `AUS` through binary search until the difference in width between two successive `AUS`s is less than the specified threshold ϵ.

Example 4 (Running example). Consider the initial set and the enclosure computed in Example 3, we use Algorithm 2 to compute a barrier tube. The initial set is $X_O = [1.0, 1.0] \times [-1.05, -0.95]$ and the enclosure of X_O is $E = [0.84, 1.01] \times [-1.1, -0.75]$, $G = [0.84, 0.84] \times [-0.91, -0.80]$, the plane P is $x = 0.84$, $D = \{2\}$ and $\epsilon = 0.001$. The barrier tube consists of two barrier certificates. As shown in Fig. 3, each of the barrier certificates is derived from an `AUS` (red line segment) which is located respectively on the bottom-left and top-left boundary of E.

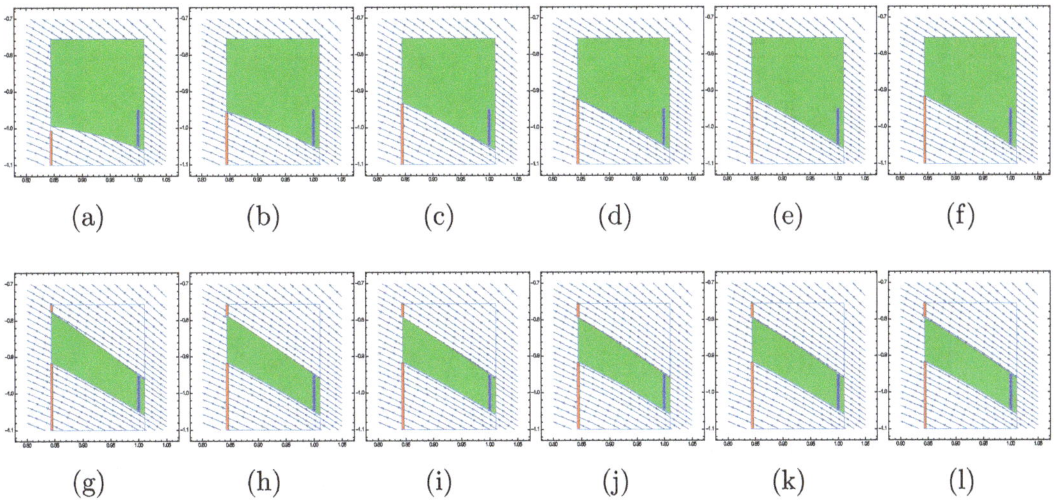

Fig. 3. Computing process of BT for Example 4. Blue line segment: initial set, red line segment: AUS. Figure a–l show how intermediate barrier certificates changed with the width of the AUSs and Fig. 1 shows the final BT (shadow region in green). (Color figure online)

4.3 Compute Piecewise Barrier Tube

During the computation of a barrier tube by Algorithm 2, we create a series of AUSs around the flowpipe, which build up a rectangular enclosure for the intersection of the flowpipe and the facet of the enclosure box. As a result, such a rectangular enclosure can be taken as an initial set for the following flowpipe segment and then Algorithm 2 can be applied repeatedly to compute a PBT. The basic procedure to compute PBT is presented in Algorithm 3.

Remark 5. In Algorithm 3, initially a box that contains the initial set X_0 is constructed using Algorithm 1. The loop in line 2 consists of 3 major parts: (1) In lines 3–6, a barrier tube BT is firstly computed using Algorithm 2. The **while** loop keeps shrinking the box until a barrier tube is found; (2) In line 8, the initial set X_0 is updated for the next box; (3) In line 9, a new box is constructed to contain X_0 and the process is repeated.

Example 5 (Running example). Let us consider again the running example. We set the length of PBT to 45 and the PBT we obtained is shown in Fig. 2b. Compared to the interval over-approximation of the Taylor model obtained using *Flow**, the computed PBT consists of a significantly reduced number of segments and is more precise for the absence of stretching.

Safety Verification Based on PBT. The idea of safety verification based on PBT is straightforward. Given an unsafe set X_U, for each intermediate initial set X_0 and the corresponding enclosure box E, we first check whether $X_U \cap E = \emptyset$. If not empty, we would further find a barrier certificate between X_U and the flowpipe of X_0 inside E. If empty or barrier found, we continue to compute

Algorithm 3. Algorithm to compute PBT

```
input : M: dynamics of the system; X_0: Initial set;
        N: length of piecewise barrier tube
output: PBT: piecewise barrier tube
E ← construct an initial box containing X_0;
for i ← 1 to N do
    [Found, BT] ← findBarrierTube (E,X_0) ;
    while not Found do
        E ← Shrink (E) ;
        [Found, BT] ← findBarrierTube (E,X_0) ;
    if Found then
        X_0 ← OverApprox(BT ∩ Facet(E)) ;
        E ← construct the next box containing X_0;
```

Table 1. Model definitions

Model	Dynamics	Initial set X_0	Time horizon (TH)
Controller 2D	$\dot{x} = xy + y^3 + 2$	$x \in [29.9, 30.1]$	0.0125
	$\dot{y} = x^2 + 2x - 3y$	$y \in [-38, -36]$	
Van der Pol	$\dot{x} = y$	$x \in [1, 1.5]$	6.74
Oscillator	$\dot{y} = y - x - x^2 y$	$y \in [2.0, 2.45]$	
Lotka-Volterra	$\dot{x} = x(1.5 - y)$	$x \in [4.5, 5.2]$	3.2
	$\dot{y} = -y(3 - x)$	$y \in [1.8, 2.2]$	
	$\dot{x} = 10(y - x)$	$x \in [1.79, 1.81]$	0.51
Controller 3D	$\dot{y} = x^3$	$y \in [1.0, 1.1]$	
	$\dot{z} = xy - 2.667z$	$y \in [0.5, 0.6]$	

longer PBT. The refinement of PBT computation can be achieved by using smaller E and higher d for template polynomial.

5 Implementation and Experiments

We have implemented the proposed approach as a C++ prototype called Piecewise Barrier Tube Solver (*PBTS*), choosing *Gurobi* [12] as our internal linear programming solver. We have also performed some experiments on a benchmark of four nonlinear polynomial dynamical systems (described in Table 1) to compare the efficiency and the effectiveness of our approach w.r.t. other tools. Our experiments were performed on a desktop computer with a 3.6 GHz *Intel Core i7-7700* 8 Core CPU and 32 GB memory. The results are presented in Table 2.

Remark 6. There are a number of outstanding tools for flowpipe computation [1,3–5]. Since our approach is to perform flowpipe computation for polynomial

Table 2. Tool Comparison on Nonlinear Systems. #var: number of variables; T: computing time; NFS: number of flowpipe segments; DEG: candidate degrees for template polynomial (only for *PBTS*); TH: time horizon for flowpipe (only for *Flow** and *CORA*). FAIL: failed to terminate under 30 min.

		PBTS				Flow*		CORA	
Model	#var	T	NFS	DEG	TH	T	NFS	T	NFS
Controller 2D	2	5.62	46	2	0.0125	22.17	6250	FAIL	-
Van der Pol	2	13.38	110	2,3	6.74	15.28	337	212.51	12523
Lotka-Volterra	2	6.65	30	3,4	3.2	10.59	3200	35.84	2903
Controller 3D	3	83.65	15	4	0.51	11.61	5100	65.18	6767

nonlinear systems, we pick two of the most relevant state-of-the-art tools for comparison: *CORA* [1] and *Flow** [3]. Note that a big difference between our approach and the other two approaches is that *PBTS* is time-independent, which means that we cannot compare PBTS with *CORA* or *Flow** over the exactly same time horizon. To be fair enough, for *Flow** and *CORA*, we have used the same time horizon for the flowpipe computation, while we have computed a slightly longer flowpipe using *PBTS*. To guide the reader, we have also used different plotting colors to visualize the difference between the flowpipes obtained from the three different tools.

Evaluation. As pointed out in Sect. 1, a common problem with the bounded-time integration based approaches is that the flowpipe segment of a dynamics system can be extremely stretched with time so that the interval over-approximation of the flowpipe segment is very conservative and usually the solver has to stop prematurely due to the error explosion. This fact can be found easily from the figures Fig. 4, 5, 6 and 7. In particular, for *Controller 2D*, *Flow** can give quite nice result in the beginning but started producing an exploding flowpipe very quickly (Note that *Flow** offers options to produce better plotting which however is expensive and was not used for safety verification. *CORA* even failed to give a result after over 30 min of running). This phenomenon reappeared with both *Flow** and *CORA* for *Controller 3D*. Notice that most of the time horizons used in the experiment are basically the time limits that *Flow** and *CORA* can reach, i.e., a slightly larger value for the time horizon would cause the solvers to fail. In comparison, our tool has no such problem and can survive a much longer flowpipe before exploding or even without exploding as shown in Fig. 4a.

Another important factor of the approaches is the efficiency. As is shown in Table 2, our approach is more efficient on the first three examples but slower on the last example than the other two tools. The reason for this phenomenon is that the degree d of the template polynomial used in the last example is higher than the others and increasing d led to an increase in the number of decision variables in the linear constraint. This suggests that using smaller d on shorter flowpipe segment would be better. In addition, we can also see in Table 2 that the number of the flowpipe segments produced by *PBTS* is much fewer than that

(a) PBTS (b) Flow*

Fig. 4. Flowpipe for Controller 2D.

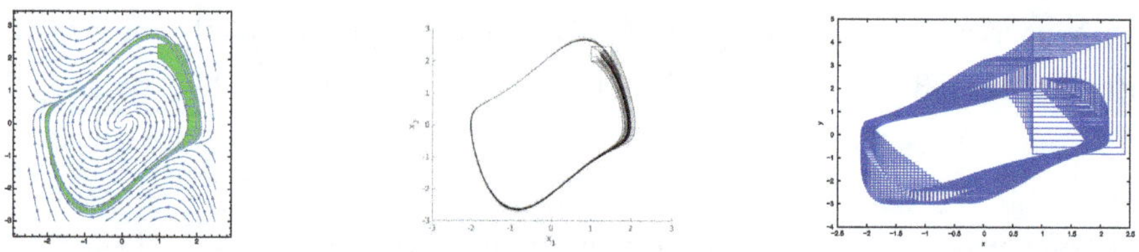

(a) PBTS (b) CORA (c) Flow*

Fig. 5. Flowpipe for Van der Pol Oscillator.

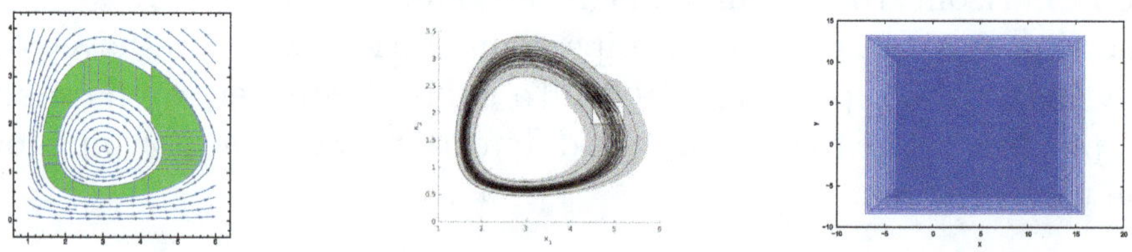

(a) PBTS (b) CORA (c) Flow*

Fig. 6. Flowpipe for Lotka-Volterra.

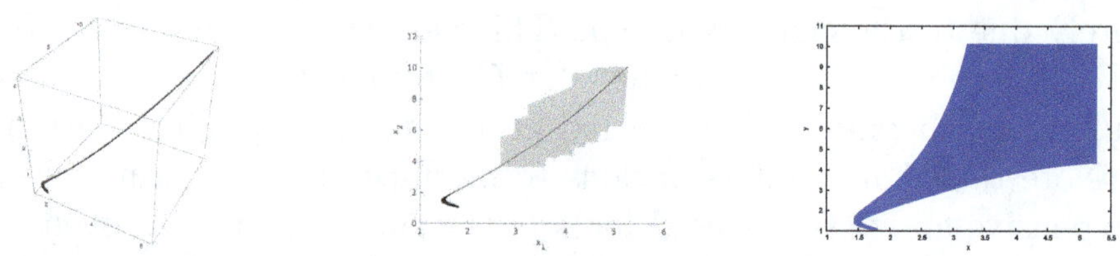

(a) PBTS (b) CORA (projection) (c) Flow* (projection)

Fig. 7. Flowpipe (projection) for Controller 3D.

produced by *Flow** and *CORA*. In this respect, *PBTS* would be more efficient on safety verification.

6 Conclusion

We have presented PBTS, a novel approach to over-approximate flowpipes of nonlinear systems with polynomial dynamics. The benefit of using BTs is that they are time-independent and hence cannot be stretched or deformed by time.

Moreover, this approach only results in a small number of BTs which are sufficient to form a tight over-approximation for the flowpipe, hence the safety verification with PBT can be very efficient.

References

1. Althoff, M., Grebenyuk, D.: Implementation of interval arithmetic in CORA 2016. In: Proceedings of ARCH@CPSWeek 2016: The 3rd International Workshop on Applied Verification for Continuous and Hybrid Systems, EPiC Series in Computing, vol. 43, pp. 91–105. EasyChair (2017)
2. Asarin, E., Dang, T., Girard, A.: Hybridization methods for the analysis of nonlinear systems. Acta Inform. **43**(7), 451–476 (2007)
3. Chen, X., Ábrahám, E., Sankaranarayanan, S.: Flow*: an analyzer for non-linear hybrid systems. In: Sharygina, N., Veith, H. (eds.) CAV 2013. LNCS, vol. 8044, pp. 258–263. Springer, Heidelberg (2013). https://doi.org/10.1007/978-3-642-39799-8_18
4. Dang, T., Le Guernic, C., Maler, O.: Computing reachable states for nonlinear biological models. In: Degano, P., Gorrieri, R. (eds.) CMSB 2009. LNCS, vol. 5688, pp. 126–141. Springer, Heidelberg (2009). https://doi.org/10.1007/978-3-642-03845-7_9
5. Duggirala, P.S., Mitra, S., Viswanathan, M., Potok, M.: C2E2: a verification tool for stateflow models. In: Baier, C., Tinelli, C. (eds.) TACAS 2015. LNCS, vol. 9035, pp. 68–82. Springer, Heidelberg (2015). https://doi.org/10.1007/978-3-662-46681-0_5
6. Fränzle, M., Herde, C.: HySAT: an efficient proof engine for bounded model checking of hybrid systems. Form. Methods Syst. Des. **30**(3), 179–198 (2007)
7. Fränzle, M., Herde, C., Teige, T., Ratschan, S., Schubert, T.: Efficient solving of large non-linear arithmetic constraint systems with complex boolean structure. JSAT **1**(3–4), 209–236 (2007)
8. Frehse, G., et al.: SpaceEx: scalable verification of hybrid systems. In: Gopalakrishnan, G., Qadeer, S. (eds.) CAV 2011. LNCS, vol. 6806, pp. 379–395. Springer, Heidelberg (2011). https://doi.org/10.1007/978-3-642-22110-1_30
9. Girard, A.: Reachability of uncertain linear systems using zonotopes. In: Morari, M., Thiele, L. (eds.) HSCC 2005. LNCS, vol. 3414, pp. 291–305. Springer, Heidelberg (2005). https://doi.org/10.1007/978-3-540-31954-2_19
10. Girard, A., Le Guernic, C.: Efficient reachability analysis for linear systems using support functions. In: Proceedings of IFAC World Congress, vol. 41, no. 2, pp. 8966–8971 (2008)
11. Grosu, R., et al.: From cardiac cells to genetic regulatory networks. In: Gopalakrishnan, G., Qadeer, S. (eds.) CAV 2011. LNCS, vol. 6806, pp. 396–411. Springer, Heidelberg (2011). https://doi.org/10.1007/978-3-642-22110-1_31
12. Gu, Z., Rothberg, E., Bixby, R.: Gurobi optimizer reference manual (2017). http://www.gurobi.com/documentation/7.5/refman/refman.html
13. Gulwani, S., Tiwari, A.: Constraint-based approach for analysis of hybrid systems. In: Gupta, A., Malik, S. (eds.) CAV 2008. LNCS, vol. 5123, pp. 190–203. Springer, Heidelberg (2008). https://doi.org/10.1007/978-3-540-70545-1_18
14. Gurung, A., Ray, R., Bartocci, E., Bogomolov, S., Grosu, R.: Parallel reachability analysis of hybrid systems in xspeed. Int. J. Softw. Tools Technol. Transf. (2018)

15. Handelman, D.: Representing polynomials by positive linear functions on compact convex polyhedra. Pac. J. Math. **132**(1), 35–62 (1988)
16. Hartmanns, A., Hermanns, H.: The modest toolset: an integrated environment for quantitative modelling and verification. In: Ábrahám, E., Havelund, K. (eds.) TACAS 2014. LNCS, vol. 8413, pp. 593–598. Springer, Heidelberg (2014). https://doi.org/10.1007/978-3-642-54862-8_51
17. Henzinger, T.A.: The theory of hybrid automata. In: Proceedings of IEEE Symposium on Logic in Computer Science, pp. 278–292 (1996)
18. Huang, Z., Fan, C., Mereacre, A., Mitra, S., Kwiatkowska, M.: Invariant verification of nonlinear hybrid automata networks of cardiac cells. In: Biere, A., Bloem, R. (eds.) CAV 2014. LNCS, vol. 8559, pp. 373–390. Springer, Cham (2014). https://doi.org/10.1007/978-3-319-08867-9_25
19. Jiang, Y., Yang, Y., Liu, H., Kong, H., Gu, M., Sun, J., Sha, L.: From stateflow simulation to verified implementation: a verification approach and a real-time train controller design. In: 2016 IEEE Real-Time and Embedded Technology and Applications Symposium (RTAS), pp. 1–11. IEEE (2016)
20. Jiang, Y., Zhang, H., Li, Z., Deng, Y., Song, X., Ming, G., Sun, J.: Design and optimization of multiclocked embedded systems using formal techniques. IEEE Trans. Ind. Electron. **62**(2), 1270–1278 (2015)
21. Kong, H., Bogomolov, S., Schilling, C., Jiang, Y., Henzinger, T.A.: Safety verification of nonlinear hybrid systems based on invariant clusters. In: Proceedings of HSCC 2017: The 20th International Conference on Hybrid Systems: Computation and Control, pp. 163–172. ACM (2017)
22. Kong, H., He, F., Song, X., Hung, W.N.N., Gu, M.: Exponential-condition-based barrier certificate generation for safety verification of hybrid systems. In: Sharygina, N., Veith, H. (eds.) CAV 2013. LNCS, vol. 8044, pp. 242–257. Springer, Heidelberg (2013). https://doi.org/10.1007/978-3-642-39799-8_17
23. Kong, S., Gao, S., Chen, W., Clarke, E.: dReach: δ-reachability analysis for hybrid systems. In: Baier, C., Tinelli, C. (eds.) TACAS 2015. LNCS, vol. 9035, pp. 200–205. Springer, Heidelberg (2015). https://doi.org/10.1007/978-3-662-46681-0_15
24. Krilavicius, T.: Hybrid techniques for hybrid systems. Ph.D. thesis, University of Twente, Enschede, Netherlands (2006)
25. Lal, R., Prabhakar, P.: Bounded error flowpipe computation of parameterized linear systems. In: Proceedings of EMSOFT 2015: The International Conference on Embedded Software, pp. 237–246. IEEE (2015)
26. Le Guernic, C., Girard, A.: Reachability analysis of hybrid systems using support functions. In: Bouajjani, A., Maler, O. (eds.) CAV 2009. LNCS, vol. 5643, pp. 540–554. Springer, Heidelberg (2009). https://doi.org/10.1007/978-3-642-02658-4_40
27. Liu, J., Zhan, N., Zhao, H.: Computing semi-algebraic invariants for polynomial dynamical systems. In: Proceedings of EMSOFT 2011: The 11th International Conference on Embedded Software, pp. 97–106. ACM (2011)
28. Matringe, N., Moura, A.V., Rebiha, R.: Generating invariants for non-linear hybrid systems by linear algebraic methods. In: Cousot, R., Martel, M. (eds.) SAS 2010. LNCS, vol. 6337, pp. 373–389. Springer, Heidelberg (2010). https://doi.org/10.1007/978-3-642-15769-1_23
29. Nedialkov, N.S.: Interval tools for ODEs and DAEs. In: Proceedings of SCAN 2006: The 12th GAMM - IMACS International Symposium on Scientific Computing, Computer Arithmetic and Validated Numerics, p. 4. IEEE (2006)
30. Neher, M., Jackson, K.R., Nedialkov, N.S.: On Taylor model based integration of ODEs. SIAM J. Numer. Anal. **45**(1), 236–262 (2007)

31. Prabhakar, P., Soto, M.G.: Hybridization for stability analysis of switched linear systems. In: Proceedings of HSCC 2016: The 19th International Conference on Hybrid Systems: Computation and Control, pp. 71–80. ACM (2016)
32. Prabhakar, P., Viswanathan, M.: A dynamic algorithm for approximate flow computations. In: Proceedings of HSSC 2011: The 14th International Conference on Hybrid Systems: Computation and Control, pp. 133–142. ACM (2011)
33. Prajna, S., Jadbabaie, A.: Safety verification of hybrid systems using barrier certificates. In: Alur, R., Pappas, G.J. (eds.) HSCC 2004. LNCS, vol. 2993, pp. 477–492. Springer, Heidelberg (2004). https://doi.org/10.1007/978-3-540-24743-2_32
34. Ray, R., et al.: XSpeed: accelerating reachability analysis on multi-core processors. In: Piterman, N. (ed.) HVC 2015. LNCS, vol. 9434, pp. 3–18. Springer, Cham (2015). https://doi.org/10.1007/978-3-319-26287-1_1
35. Roohi, N., Prabhakar, P., Viswanathan, M.: Hybridization based CEGAR for hybrid automata with affine dynamics. In: Chechik, M., Raskin, J.-F. (eds.) TACAS 2016. LNCS, vol. 9636, pp. 752–769. Springer, Heidelberg (2016). https://doi.org/10.1007/978-3-662-49674-9_48
36. Sankaranarayanan, S.: Automatic invariant generation for hybrid systems using ideal fixed points. In: Proceedings of HSCC 2010: The 13th ACM International Conference on Hybrid Systems: Computation and Control, pp. 221–230. ACM (2010)
37. Sankaranarayanan, S., Sipma, H.B., Manna, Z.: Constructing invariants for hybrid systems. In: Alur, R., Pappas, G.J. (eds.) HSCC 2004. LNCS, vol. 2993, pp. 539–554. Springer, Heidelberg (2004). https://doi.org/10.1007/978-3-540-24743-2_36
38. Sankaranarayanan, S., Chen, X., et al.: Lyapunov function synthesis using handelman representations. In: IFAC Proceedings Volumes, vol. 46, no. 23, pp. 576–581 (2013)
39. Sogokon, A., Ghorbal, K., Jackson, P.B., Platzer, A.: A method for invariant generation for polynomial continuous systems. In: Jobstmann, B., Leino, K.R.M. (eds.) VMCAI 2016. LNCS, vol. 9583, pp. 268–288. Springer, Heidelberg (2016). https://doi.org/10.1007/978-3-662-49122-5_13
40. Stengle, G.: A nullstellensatz and a positivstellensatz in semialgebraic geometry. Math. Ann. **207**(2), 87–97 (1974)

Space-Time Interpolants

Goran Frehse[1], Mirco Giacobbe[2(✉)], and Thomas A. Henzinger[2]

[1] Univ. Grenoble Alpes, CNRS, Grenoble INP, VERIMAG, Grenoble, France
[2] IST Austria, Klosterneuburg, Austria
mgiacobbe@ist.ac.at

Abstract. Reachability analysis is difficult for hybrid automata with affine differential equations, because the reach set needs to be approximated. Promising abstraction techniques usually employ interval methods or template polyhedra. Interval methods account for dense time and guarantee soundness, and there are interval-based tools that overapproximate affine flowpipes. But interval methods impose bounded and rigid shapes, which make refinement expensive and fixpoint detection difficult. Template polyhedra, on the other hand, can be adapted flexibly and can be unbounded, but sound template refinement for unbounded reachability analysis has been implemented only for systems with piecewise constant dynamics. We capitalize on the advantages of both techniques, combining interval arithmetic and template polyhedra, using the former to abstract time and the latter to abstract space. During a CEGAR loop, whenever a spurious error trajectory is found, we compute additional space constraints and split time intervals, and use these *space-time interpolants* to eliminate the counterexample. Space-time interpolation offers a lazy, flexible framework for increasing precision while guaranteeing soundness, both for error avoidance and fixpoint detection. To the best of out knowledge, this is the first abstraction refinement scheme for the reachability analysis over *unbounded* and *dense* time of affine hybrid systems, which is both *sound* and *automatic*. We demonstrate the effectiveness of our algorithm with several benchmark examples, which cannot be handled by other tools.

1 Introduction

Formal verification techniques can be used to either provide rigorous guarantees about the behaviors of a critical system, or detect instances of violating behavior if such behaviors are possible. Formal verification has become widely used in the design of software and digital hardware, but has yet to show a similar success for physical and cyber-physical systems. One of the reasons for this is a scarcity of suitable algorithmic verification tools, such as model checkers, which are formally sound, precise, and scale reasonably well. In this paper, we propose a novel verification algorithm that meets these criteria for systems with piecewise affine dynamics. The performance of the approach is illustrated experimentally on a number of benchmarks. Since systems with affine dynamics have been studied before, we first describe why the available methods and tools do not handle this

H. Chockler and G. Weissenbacher (Eds.): CAV 2018, LNCS 10981, pp. 468–486, 2018.
https://doi.org/10.1007/978-3-319-96145-3_25

class of systems sufficiently well, and then describe our approach and its core contributions.

Previous Approaches. The algorithmic verification of systems with continuous or discrete-continuous (hybrid) dynamics is a hard problem both in theory and practice. For piecewise constant dynamics (PCD), the continuous successor states (a.k.a. flow pipe) can be computed exactly, and the complexity is exponential in the number of variables [17,19]. While in principle, any dynamics can be approximated arbitrarily well by PCD systems using an approach called hybridization [20], this requires partitioning of the state space, which often leads to prohibitive computational costs. For piecewise affine dynamics (PWA), one-step successors can be computed approximately using complex set representations. However, all published approaches suffer either from a possibly exponential increase in the complexity of the set representation, or from a possibly exponential increase in the approximation error as the considered time interval increases; this will be argued in detail in Sect. 4.

In addition to these theoretical obstacles, we note the following practical obstacles for the available tools and their performance in experiments. The only available model checkers that are (i) *sound* (i.e., they compute provable dense-time overapproximations), (ii) *unbounded* (i.e., they overapproximate the flow-pipe for an infinite time horizon), and (iii) *arbitrarily precise* (i.e., they support precision refinement) are, with one exception, limited to PCD systems, namely, HyTech [18], PHAVer [13], and Lyse [7]. The tool Ariadne [6] can deal with affine dynamics and is sound, unbounded, and precise. However, Ariadne discretizes the reachable state space with a rectangular grid. This invariably leads to an exponential complexity in terms of the number of variables. Other tools that are applicable to PWA systems do not meet our criteria in that they are either not formally sound (e.g., CORA [2], SpaceEx [15]), not arbitrarily precise because of templates or particular data structures (e.g., SpaceEx, Flow* [8], CORA), or limited to bounded model checking (e.g., dReach [24], Flow*). All the above tools exhibit fatal limitations in scalability or precision on standard PWA benchmarks; they typically work only on well-chosen examples. Note that while these tools do not meet the criteria we advance in this paper, they of course have strengths in other areas handling nonlinear and nondeterministic dynamics.

Our Approach. We view iterative abstraction refinement as critical for soundness and precision management, and fixpoint detection as critical for evaluating unbounded properties. We implement, for the first time, a CEGAR (counterexample-guided abstraction refinement) scheme in combination with a fixpoint detection criterion for PWA systems. Our abstraction refinement scheme manages complexity and precision trade-offs in a flexible way by decoupling time from space: the dense timeline is partitioned into a sequence of intervals that are refined individually and lazily, by splitting intervals, to achieve the necessary precision and detect fixpoints; state sets are overapproximated using template polyhedra that are also refined individually and lazily, by adding normal directions to templates; and both refinement processes are interleaved for optimal results, while maintaining soundness with each step. A similar approach was recently proposed for the limited class of PCA systems [7]; this paper can be seen as an extension of the approach to the class of piecewise affine dynamics.

With each iteration of the CEGAR loop, a spurious counterexample is removed by computing a proof of infeasibility in terms of a sequence of linear constraints in space and interval constraints in time, which we call a sequence of *space-time interpolants*. We use linear programming to construct a suitable sequence of space-time intervals and check for fixpoints. If a fixpoint check fails, we increase the time horizon by adding new intervals. The separation of time from space gives us the flexibility to explore different refinement strategies. Fine-tuning the iteration of space refinement (adding template directions), time refinement (splitting intervals), and fixpoint checking (adding intervals), we find that it is generally best to prefer fewer time intervals over fewer space constraints. Based on performance evaluation, we even expand individual intervals time when this is possible without sacrificing the necessary precision for removing a counterexample.

2 Motivating Example

The ordinary differential equation over the variables x and y

$$\begin{aligned}\dot{x} &= 0.1x - y + 1.8 \\ \dot{y} &= x + 0.1y - 2.2\end{aligned} \tag{1}$$

moves counterclockwise around the point $(2, 2)$ in an outward spiral. We center a box B (of side 0.92) on the same point and place a diagonal segment S close to the bottom right corner of B, without touching it (between $(2, 1)$ and $(3.5, 2)$; see Fig. 1). Then, we consider the problem of proving that every trajectory starting from any point in S never hits B. This is a time-unbounded reachability problem for a hybrid automaton with piecewise affine dynamics and two control modes. The first mode has the dynamics above (Eq. 1) and S as initial region. It has a transition to a second mode, which in its turn has B as invariant. The second mode is a bad mode, which all trajectories indeed avoid.

We tackle the reachability problem by abstraction refinement. In particular, we aim at automatically constructing an enclosure for the flowpipe—i.e., for the set of trajectories from S—which (i) avoids the bad state B and (ii) covers the continuous timeline up to infinity. Figure 1 shows three abstractions that result from different strategies for refining an initial space partition (i.e., template) and time partition (i.e., sequence of time intervals). All three refinement schemes start by enclosing S with an initial template polyhedron P, and then transforming P into a sequence of abstract flowpipe sections $\text{intflow}^{[\underline{t},\overline{t}]}(P)$, one for each interval $[\underline{t}, \overline{t}]$ of an initial partitioning of the unbounded timeline. The computation of new flowpipe sections stops when a fixpoint is reached,—i.e., we reach a time threshold t^* whose flowpipe section closes a cycle with $\text{intflow}^{t^*}(P) \subseteq P$, sufficient condition for any further flowpipe section to be contained within the union of previously computed sections.

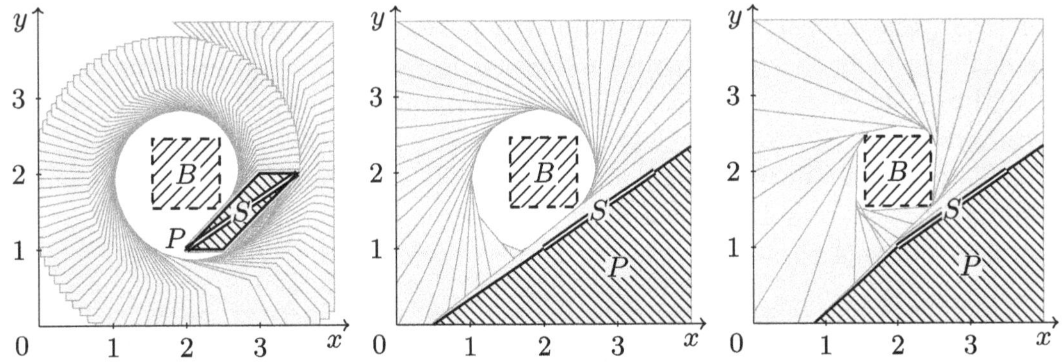

Time refinement only
(a)

Uniform-time interpolation
(b)

Ada tive-time interpolation
(c)

Fig. 1. Comparison of abstraction refinement methods for the ODE in Eq. 1, the segment S as initial region, and the box B as bad region. The polyhedron P is the template polyhedron of S, and the gray polyhedra are the flowpipe sections $\text{intflow}^{[\underline{t},\overline{t}]}(P)$.

Refinement scheme (a) sticks to a fixed octagonal template P—i.e., to the normals of a regular octagon—and iteratively halves all time intervals until every flowpipe section avoids the bad set B. This is achieved at interval width $1/64$, but the computation does not terminate because no fixpoint is reached. Refinement scheme (b) splits time similarly but also computes a different, more accurate template for every iteration: first, an interval $[\underline{t},\overline{t}]$ is halved until it admits a halfspace interpolant —i.e., a halfspace H that $S \subseteq H$ and $\text{intflow}^{[\underline{t},\overline{t}]}(H) \cap B = \emptyset$; then, a maximal set of linearly independent directions is chosen as template from the normals of the obtained halfspaces. Refinement scheme (b) succeeds at interval width $1/16$ to avoid B and reach a fixpoint; the latter at time 6.25, with $\text{intflow}^{6.25}(P) \subseteq P$. Refinement scheme (c) modifies (b) by optimizing the refinement of the time partition: instead of halving time intervals, the maximal intervals which admit halfspace interpolants are chosen. This scheme produces a nonuniform time partitioning with an average interval width of about $1/8$, discovers five template directions, and finds a fixpoint in fewer steps.

Each iteration of the abstraction refinement loop consists of first abstracting the initial region into a template polyhedron, second solving the differential equation into a sequence of interval matrices, and finally transforming the template polyhedron using each of the interval matrices. We represent each transformation symbolically, by means of its support function. Then, we verify (i) the separation between every support function and the bad region, and (ii) the containment of any support function in the initial template polyhedron. The separation problem amounts to solving one LP, and the inclusion problem amounts to solving an LP in each template direction. If the separation fails, then we independently bisect each time that does not admit halfspace interpolants and expand each that does, until all are proven separated. Together, these halfspace interpolants form an infeasibility proof for the counterexample: a space-time interpolant. We forward the resulting new time intervals and halfspaces to the abstraction generator, and repeat, using the refined partitioning and the augmented template. If the inclusion fails, then we increase the time horizon by some amount Δ, and repeat. Once we succeed with both separation and inclusion, the system is proved safe.

This example shows the advantage of lazily refining *both* the space partitioning (i.e., the template) by adding directions, and the time partitioning, by splitting intervals.

3 Hybrid Automata with Piecewise Affine Dynamics

A hybrid automaton with piecewise affine dynamics consists of an n-dimensional vector x of real-valued variables and a finite directed multigraph (V, E), the control graph. We call it the control graph, the vertices $v \in V$ the control modes, and the edges $e \in E$ the control switches. We decorate each mode $v \in V$ with an initial condition $Z_v \subseteq \mathbb{R}^n$, a nonnegative invariant condition $I_v \subseteq \mathbb{R}^n_{\geq 0}$, and a flow condition given by the system of ordinary differential equations

$$\dot{x} = A_v x + b_v. \tag{2}$$

We decorate each switch $e \in E$ with a guard condition $G_e \subseteq \mathbb{R}^n$ and an update condition given the difference equations $x := R_e x + s_e$. All constraints I, G, and Z are conjuctions of rational linear inequalities, A and R are constant matrices, and b and s constant vectors of rational coefficients. In this paper, whenever an indexing of modes and switches is clear from the context, we index the respective constraints and transformations similarly, e.g., we abbreviate A_{v_i} with A_i.

A trajectory is a possibly infinite sequence of states $(v, x) \in V \times \mathbb{R}^n$ repeatedly interleaved first by a switching time $t \in \mathbb{R}_{\geq 0}$ and then by a switch $e \in E$

$$(v_0, x_0)t_0(v_0, y_0)e_0(v_1, x_1)t_1(v_1, y_1)e_1 \ldots \tag{3}$$

for which there exists a sequence of solutions $\psi_0, \psi_1, \ldots : \mathbb{R} \to \mathbb{R}_n$ such that $\psi_i(0) = x_i$, $\psi_i(t_i) = y_i$ and they satisfy (i) the invariant conditions $\psi_i(t) \in I_i$ and (ii) the flow conditions $\dot{\psi}_i(t) = A_i \psi_i(t) + b_i$, for all $t \in [0, t_i]$. Moreover, $x_0 \in Z_0$, every switch e_i has source v_i, destination v_{i+1}, and the respective states satisfy (i) the guard condition $y_i \in G_i$ and (ii) the update $x_{i+1} = R_i y_i + s_i$. The maximal set of its trajectories is the semantics of the hybrid automaton, which is safe if none of them contains a special bad mode.

Every hybrid automaton with affine dynamics can be transformed into an equivalent hybrid automaton with linear dynamics, i.e., the special case where $b = 0$ on every mode. We obtain such transformation by adding one extra variable y, rewriting the flow of every mode into $\dot{x} = Ax + by$, and forcing y to be always equal to 1, i.e., invariant $y = 1$ and flow $\dot{y} = 0$ on every mode and update $y' = y$ on every switch. For this reason, in the following sections we discuss w.l.o.g. the reachability analysis of hybrid automata with linear dynamics.

4 Time Abstraction Using Interval Arithmetic

We abstract the reach set of the hybrid automaton with a union of convex polyhedra. In particular, we abstract the states that are reachable in a mode using a finite sequence of images of the initial region over a *time partitioning*, until a completeness threshold is reached. Thereafter, we compute the *template polyhedron* of each of the images that can take a switch. Then, we repeat in the destination mode and we continue until a fixpoint is found.

Precisely, a time partitioning T is a (possibly infinite) set of disjoint closed time intervals whose union is a single (possibly open) interval. For a finite set of directions $D \subseteq \mathbb{R}^n$, the D-polyhedron of a closed convex set X is the tightest polyhedral enclosure whose facets normals are in D. In the following, we associate every mode v to a template D_v and a time partitioning T_v of the time axis $\mathbb{R}_{\geq 0}$, we employ interval arithmetic for abstracting the continuous dynamics (Sect. 4.1), and on top of it we develop a procedure for hybrid dynamics (Sect. 4.2).

4.1 Continuous Dynamics

We consider w.l.o.g. a mode with ODE reduced to the linear form $\dot{x} = A_v x$, invariant I_v, and a given time interval $[\underline{t}, \overline{t}]$. Every linear ODE $\dot{x} = Ax$ has the unique solution

$$\psi(t) = \exp(At)\psi(0). \tag{4}$$

It follows (see also [16]) that the set of states reachable in v after exactly t time units from an initial region X is

$$\text{flow}_v^t(X) \stackrel{\text{def}}{=} \exp(A_v t)X \cap \bigcap_{0 \leq \tau \leq t} \exp(A_v(t-\tau))I_v, \tag{5}$$

Then, the flowpipe section over the time interval $[\underline{t}, \overline{t}]$ is

$$\text{flow}_v^{[\underline{t},\overline{t}]}(X) \stackrel{\text{def}}{=} \cup\{\text{flow}_v^t(X) \mid t \in [\underline{t}, \overline{t}]\}. \tag{6}$$

We note three straightforward but consequential properties of the reach set: (i) The accuracy of any convex abstraction depends on the size of the time interval: While $\text{flow}_v^t(X)$ is convex for convex X, this is generally not the case for $\text{flow}_v^{[\underline{t},\overline{t}]}(X)$. (ii) We can prune the time interval whenever we detect that the reach set no longer overlaps with the invariant: If for any $t^* \geq 0$, $\text{flow}_v^{t^*}(X) = \emptyset$, then for all $\overline{t} \geq t^*$, $\text{flow}_v^{\overline{t}}(X) = \emptyset$ and $\text{flow}_v^{[\underline{t},\overline{t}]}(X) = \text{flow}_v^{[\underline{t},t^*]}(X)$. (iii) We can prune the time interval whenever we detect containment in the initial states: If $\text{flow}_v^{t^*}(X) \subseteq X$, then $\text{flow}_v^{[\underline{t},\infty]}(X) = \text{flow}_v^{[\underline{t},t^*]}(X)$.

For given A and t, the matrix $\exp(At)$ can be computed with arbitrary, but only finite, accuracy. We resolve this problem by computing a rational interval matrix $[\underline{M}, \overline{M}]$, which we denote $\text{intexp}(A, \underline{t}, \overline{t})$, such that for all $t \in [\underline{t}, \overline{t}]$ we have element-wise that

$$\exp(At) \in \text{intexp}(A, \underline{t}, \overline{t}). \tag{7}$$

This interval matrix can be derived efficiently with a variety of methods [25], e.g., using a guaranteed ODE solver or using interval arithmetic. The width of the interval matrix can be made arbitrarily small at the price of increasing the number of computations and the size of the representation of the rational numbers. In our approach, we do not rely in a fixed accuracy of the interval matrix. Instead, we require that the accuracy increases as the width of the time interval goes to zero. That way, we don't need to introduce an extra parameter. To ensure progress in our refinement loop, we require that the interval matrix decreases monotonically when we split the time interval. Formally, if $[\underline{t},\overline{t}] \subseteq [\underline{u},\overline{u}]$ we require the element-wise inclusion $\text{intexp}(A,\underline{t},\overline{t}) \subseteq \text{intexp}(A,\underline{u},\overline{u})$. This can be ensured by intersecting the interval matrices with the original interval matrix after time splitting.

While the mapping with interval matrices is in general not convex [29], we can simplify the problem by assuming that all points of X are in the positive orthant. As long as X is bounded from below, this condition can be satisfied by inducing an appropriate coordinate change. Under the assumption that $X \subseteq \mathbb{R}^n_{\geq 0}$,

$$[\underline{M},\overline{M}](X) = \{y \in \mathbb{R}^n \mid \underline{M}x \leq y \leq \overline{M}x \text{ and } x \in X\}. \tag{8}$$

Combining the above results, we obtain a convex abstraction of the flowpipe over a time interval as

$$\text{intflow}_v^{[\underline{t},\overline{t}]}(X) \stackrel{\text{def}}{=} \text{intexp}(A,\underline{t},\overline{t})X \cap I_v. \tag{9}$$

The abstraction is conservative in the sense that $\text{flow}_v^{[\underline{t},\overline{t}]}(X) \subseteq \text{intflow}_v^{[\underline{t},\overline{t}]}(X)$. On the other hand, the longer is the time interval, the coarser is the abstraction. For this reason, we construct an abstraction of the flowpipe in terms of a union of convex approximations over a time partitioning. The abstract flowpipe over the time partitioning T is

$$\text{intflow}_v^T(X) \stackrel{\text{def}}{=} \cup\{\text{intflow}_v^{[\underline{t},\overline{t}]}(X) \mid [\underline{t},\overline{t}] \in T\}. \tag{10}$$

Again, this is conservative w.r.t. the concrete flowpipe, i.e., for all time partitionings T it holds that $\text{flow}_v^{\cup T}(X) \subseteq \text{intflow}_v^T(X)$. Moreover, it is conservative w.r.t. any refinement of T, i.e., the time partitioning U refines T if $\cup U = \cup T$ and $\forall[\underline{u},\overline{u}] \in U\colon \exists[\underline{t},\overline{t}] \in T\colon [\underline{u},\overline{u}] \subseteq [\underline{t},\overline{t}]$, then $\text{intflow}_v^U(X) \subseteq \text{intflow}_v^T(X)$.

4.2 Hybrid Dynamics

We embed the flowpipe abstraction routine into a reachability algorithm that accounts for the switching induced by the hybrid automaton. The discrete post operator is the image of a set $Y \subseteq \mathbb{R}^n$ through a switch $e \in E$

$$\text{jump}_e(Y) \stackrel{\text{def}}{=} R_e(Y \cap G_e) \oplus \{s_e\}. \tag{11}$$

We explore the hybrid automaton constructing a set of abstract trajectories, namely sequences abstract states interleaved by time intervals and switches

$$(v_0,X_0)[\underline{t}_0,\overline{t}_0](v_0,Y_0)e_0(v_1,X_1)[\underline{t}_1,\overline{t}_1](v_1,Y_1)e_1\ldots \tag{12}$$

```
input : Template {D_v} and partitioning {T_v} indexed by V
output: Optionally an abstract trajectory (counterexample)
foreach v ∈ V with nonempty Z_v do
    push (v, Z_v)[0, Δ] into the stack W;
    add the D_v-polyhedron of Z_v to P_v;
while W is not empty do
    pop ...(v, X)[t̲, t̄] from W;
    P ← D_v-polyhedron of X;
    if v is bad and P ∩ I_v is nonempty then                // check counterexample
        return ...(v, X);
    foreach t* ∈ {t̲ + δ, t̲ + 2δ, ..., t̄} do                // find completeness threshold
        if intflow_v^{t*}(P) ⊆ P_v then break;
    if t* = t̄ and intflow_v^{t̄}(P) ⊄ P_v then              // otherwise extend time horizon
        push ...(v, X)[t̄, t̄ + Δ] into W;
    foreach [u̲, ū] ∈ T_v and [u̲, ū] ∩ [t̲, t*] ≠ ∅ do       // construct flowpipe
        Y ← intflow_v^{[u̲,ū]}(P);
        foreach e ∈ E with source v and destination v' do
            X' ← jump_e(Y);
            if X' ⊆ P_{v'} then continue;
            push ...(v, X)[u̲, ū](v, Y)e(v', X')[0, Δ] into W;
            add the D_{v'}-polyhedron of X' to P_{v'};
```

Algorithm 1. Reachability procedure.

where $X_0, Y_0, \dots \subseteq \mathbb{R}^n$ are nonempty sets of states that comply with template $\{D_v\}$ and partitioning $\{T_v\}$ in the following sense. First, $X_0 = Z_0$ and $X_{i+1} = \text{jump}_i(Y_i)$ for all $i \geq 0$. Second, $Y_i = \text{intflow}_i^{[\underline{t}_i, \overline{t}_i]}(P_i)$ for all $i \geq 0$, where P_i is the D_i-polyhedron of X_i and $[\underline{t}_i, \overline{t}_i] \in T_i$. The maximal set of abstract trajectories, the abstract semantics induced by $\{D_v\}$ and $\{T_v\}$, overapproximates the concrete semantics in the sense that every concrete trajectory (see Eq. 3) has an abstract trajectory that subsumes it, i.e., modes and switches match, $x_i \in X_i$, $t_i \in [\underline{t}_i, \overline{t}_i]$, and $y_i \in Y_i$, for all $i \geq 0$.

Computing the abstraction involves several difficulties. First, the trajectories might be not finitary. Indeed, this is unsolvable in theory, because the reachability problem is undecidable [21]. Second, the post operators are hard to compute. In particular, obtaining the sets X and Y in terms of conjunctions of linear inequalities in $\mathbb{R}^n$ requires eliminating quantifiers. In Algorithm 1, we present a procedure (which does not necessarily terminate) for tackling the first problem. In the next section, we show how to tackle the second using support functions.

We employ Algorithm 1 to explore the tree of abstract trajectories. We store in the stack W the leaves to process $\dots(v, X)$, followed by a candidate interval $[\underline{t}, \overline{t}]$. For each leaf, we retrieve P, the template polyhedron of X. If it leads to a bad mode, we return, otherwise we search for a completeness threshold t^* between $\underline{t}$ excluded and $\overline{t}$, checking for inclusion in the union of visited polyhedra P_v. In case of failure, we extend the time horizon of Δ and push the next candidate to the stack. Then, we partition the time between $\underline{t}$ and t^*, construct the flowpipe, and process switching. Upon each successful switch, we augment $P_{v'}$ with the $D_{v'}$-polyhedron of the switching region X', avoiding to store redundant polyhedra. Notably, the latter operation is efficient because all polyhedra comply with the same template. For the same reason, we obtain efficient inclusion checks, which we implement by first computing the template polyhedron of the left hand side, and then comparing the constant terms of the respective linear inequalities.

In conclusion, this reachability procedure that takes a template $\{D_v\}$ and a partitioning $\{T_v\}$ and constructs a tree of reachable sets of states X and Y. It manipulates them through the post operators and overapproximate them into template polyhedra. In the next section, we discuss how to efficiently represent X and Y, so to efficiently compute their template polyhedra. In Sect. 6 we discuss how to discover appropriate $\{D_v\}$ and $\{T_v\}$, so to eliminate spurious counterexamples.

5 Space Abstraction Using Support Functions

Abstracting away time left us with the task of representing the state space of the hybrid automaton, namely the space of its variable valuations. Such sets consists of polyhedra emerging from operations such as intersections, Minkowski sums, and linear maps with simple or interval matrices. In this section, we discuss how to represent precisely all sets emerging from any of these operations by means of their support functions (Sect. 5.1) and then how to abstract them into template polyhedra (Sect. 5.2). In the next section, we discuss how to refine the abstraction.

5.1 Support Functions

The support function of a closed convex set $X \subseteq \mathbb{R}^n$ in direction $d \in \mathbb{R}^n$ consists of the maximizer scalar product of d over X

$$\rho_X(d) = \sup\{d^\mathsf{T} x \mid x \in X\}, \tag{13}$$

and, indeed, uniquely represents any closed convex set [28]. Classic work on the verification of hybrid automata with affine dynamic have posed a framework for the construction of support functions from basic set operations, but under the assumption of unboundedness and nonemptiness of the represented set, and with approximated intersection [16]. Indeed, if the set is empty then its support function is $-\infty$, while if it is unbounded an d points toward a direction of recession is $+\infty$, making the framework end up into undefined values. Such conditions turn out to be limiting in our context, first because we find desirable to represent unbounded sets so to accelerate the convergence to a fixpoint of the abstraction procedure, but most importantly because when encoding support functions for long abstract trajectories we might be not aware whether its concretization is infeasible. Checking this is a crucial element of a counterexample-guided abstraction refinement routine.

Recent work on the verification of hybrid automata with constant dynamics, i.e., with flows defined by constraints on the derivative only, provides us with a generalization of the classic support function framework which relaxes away the assumptions of boundedness and nonemptiness and yields precise intersection [7]. The framework encodes combinations of convex sets of states into LP (linear programs) which enjoy strong duality with their support function. Similarly, we encode the support function in direction d of any set X into the LP

$$\begin{aligned} &\text{minimize } c^{\mathsf{T}}\lambda \\ &\text{subject to } A\lambda = Bd, \end{aligned} \tag{14}$$

over the nonnegative vector of variables λ. The LP is dual to $\rho_X(d)$, which is to say that if the LP is infeasible then X is unbounded in direction d, and if the LP is unbounded then X is the empty set. Moreover, if the LP has bounded solution so does $\rho_X(d)$ and the solutions coincide.

The construction is inductive on operations between sets. For the base case, we recall that from duality of linear programming the support function of a polyhedron given by a system of inequalities $Px \leq q$ is dual to the LP over $\lambda \geq 0$

$$\begin{aligned} &\text{minimize } q^{\mathsf{T}}\lambda \\ &\text{subject to } P^{\mathsf{T}}\lambda = d. \end{aligned} \tag{15}$$

Then, inductively, we assume that for the set $X \subseteq \mathbb{R}^n$ we are given an LP with the coefficients A_X, B_X, and c_X, and similarly for the set $Y \subseteq \mathbb{R}^n$. For the support functions of $X \oplus Y$, MX, and $X \cap Y$ we respectively construct the following LP over the nonnegative vectors of variables λ, μ, α, and β:

$$\begin{aligned} &\text{minimize } c_X^{\mathsf{T}}\lambda + c_Y^{\mathsf{T}}\mu \\ &\text{subject to } A_X\lambda = B_X d \text{ and } A_Y\mu = B_Y d, \end{aligned} \tag{16}$$

$$\begin{aligned} &\text{minimize } c_X^{\mathsf{T}}\lambda \\ &\text{subject to } A_X\lambda = B_X M^T d, \text{ and} \end{aligned} \tag{17}$$

$$\begin{aligned} &\text{minimize } c_X^{\mathsf{T}}\lambda + c_Y^{\mathsf{T}}\mu \\ &\text{subject to } A_X\lambda - B_X(\alpha - \beta) = 0 \text{ and} \\ &\qquad\qquad A_Y\mu + B_Y(\alpha - \beta) = B_Y d. \end{aligned} \tag{18}$$

Such construction follows as a special case of [7], which we extend with the support function of a map through an interval matrix.

The time abstraction of Sect. 4 additionally requires us to represent the map of sets of states through interval matrices. Precisely, we are given convex set of nonnegative values $X \subseteq \mathbb{R}^n_{\geq 0}$, the coefficients for the respective LP, an interval matrix $[\underline{M}, \overline{M}] \subseteq \mathbb{R}^{n \times n}$, and we aim at computing the support function of all values in X mapped by all matrices in $[\underline{M}, \overline{M}]$. To this end, we define the LP

$$\begin{aligned} &\text{minimize } c_X^{\mathsf{T}}\lambda \\ &\text{subject to } A_X\lambda + B_X(\underline{M}^{\mathsf{T}}\mu - \overline{M}^{\mathsf{T}}\nu) = 0 \text{ and} \\ &\qquad\qquad -\mu + \nu = d, \end{aligned} \tag{19}$$

over the vectors λ, μ, and ν of nonnegative variables. This linear program corresponds to the the dual of the interval matrix map in Eq. 8.

5.2 Computing Template Polyhedra

We represent all space abstractions X and Y in our procedure by their support functions. In particular, whenever set operations are applied, instead of solving the operation by removing quantifiers, we construct an LP. We delay solving it until we need to compute a template polyhedron. In that case, we compute the D-polyhedron of the set X by computing its support function in each of the directions in D, and constructing the intersection of halfspaces $\cap\{d^\mathsf{T} x \leq \rho_X(d) \mid d \in D\}$.

6 Abstraction Refinement Using Space-Time Interpolants

The reachability analysis of hybrid automata by means of the combination of interval arithmetic and support functions presented in Sects. 4 and 5 builds an overapproximation of the system dynamics. It is always sound for safety, but it may produce spurious counterexamples, due to an inherent lack of precision of the time abstraction and the polyhedral approximation. The level of precision is given by two factors, namely the choice of time partitioning and the choice of template directions, excluding the parameters for approximation of the exponential function, which we assume constant (see Sect. 4.1). In the following, we present a procedure to extract infeasibility proofs from spurious counterexamples. We produce them in the form of time partitions and bounding polyhedra, which we call space-time interpolants. Space-time interpolants can then be used to properly refine time partitioning and template directions.

Consider the bounded path $v_0, e_0, v_1, e_1, \ldots, v_k, e_k, v_{k+1}$ over the control graph and a sequence of dwell time intervals $[\underline{t}_0, \overline{t}_0], [\underline{t}_1, \overline{t}_1], \ldots, [\underline{t}_k, \overline{t}_k]$ emerging from an abstract trajectory. We aim at extracting a sequence $X_0, X_1, \ldots, X_{k+1}$ of (possibly nonconvex) polyhedra and a sequence $T_0, T_1, \ldots, T_k$ of refinements of the respective dwell times such that $Z_0 \subseteq X_0$, $\text{jump}_0 \circ \text{intflow}_0^{T_0}(X_0) \subseteq X_1$, $\ldots$, $\text{jump}_k \circ \text{intflow}_k^{T_k}(X_k) \subseteq X_{k+1}$, and $X_{k+1} \cap I_{k+1}$ is empty. In other words, we want every X_{i+1} to contain all states that can enter mode v_{i+1} after dwelling on v_i between $\underline{t}_i$ and $\overline{t}_i$ time, and the last to be separated from the invariant of mode v_{k+1}. Containment is to hold inductively, namely X_{i+1} has to contain what is reachable from X_i, and the time refinements T are to be chosen in such a way that containment holds in the abstraction. Then, we call the sequence $X_0, T_0, X_1, T_1, \ldots, X_k, T_k, X_{k+1}$ a sequence of space-time interpolants for the path and the dwell times above.

We compute a sequence of space-time interpolants by alternating multiple strategies. First, for the given sequence of dwell times, we attempt to extract a sequence of halfspace interpolants using linear programming (Sect. 6.1). In case of failure, we iteratively partition the dwell times in sets of smaller intervals, separating nonswitching from switching times and until every combination of intervals along the path admits halfspace interpolants (Sect. 6.2). We accumulate all halfspaces to form a sequence of unions of convex polyhedra that, together with the obtained time partitionings, will form a valid sequence of space-time interpolants. Finally, we refine the abstraction using the time partitionings and the outwards pointing directions of all computed halfspaces, in order to eliminate the spurious counterexample (Sect. 6.3).

6.1 Halfspace Interpolation

Halfspace interpolants are the special case of space-time interpolants where every polyhedron in the sequence is defined by a single linear inequality [1]. Indeed, they are the simplest kind of space-time interpolants, and, for the same reason, the ones that best generalize the reachable states along the path. Unfortunately, not all paths admit halfspace interpolants, but, if one such sequence exists, then it can be extrapolated from the solution of a linear program.

Consider a path $v_0, e_0, \dots, v_{k+1}$ with the respective dwell times $[\underline{t}_0, \overline{t}_0], \dots, [\underline{t}_k, \overline{t}_k]$. A sequence of halfspace interpolants consists of a sequence of sets $H_0, \dots, H_{k+1}$ among either any halfspace, or the empty set, or the universe, such that $Z_0 \subseteq H_0$, $\text{jump}_0 \circ \text{intflow}_0^{[\underline{t}_0, \overline{t}_0]}(H_0) \subseteq H_1, \dots, \text{jump}_k \circ \text{intflow}_k^{[\underline{t}_k, \overline{t}_k]}(H_k) \subseteq H_{k+1}$, and $H_{k+1} \cap I_{k+1}$ is empty. In contrast with general space-time interpolants, every time partition consists of a single time interval and therefore the support function of every post operator $\text{jump} \circ \text{intflow}^{[\underline{t}, \overline{t}]}$ can be encoded into a single LP (see Sect. 5). We exploit the encoding for extracting halfspace interpolants, similarly to a recent interpolation technique for PCD systems [7].

We encode the support function in direction d of the closure of the image of the post operators along the path, i.e., the set $\text{jump}_k \circ \text{intflow}_k^{[\underline{t}_k, \overline{t}_k]} \circ \dots \circ \text{jump}_0 \circ \text{intflow}_0^{[\underline{t}_0, \overline{t}_0]}(Z_0)$, intersected with the invariant I_{k+1}. We obtain the following LP over the free vectors $\alpha_0, \dots, \alpha_{k+1}$ and the nonnegative vectors $\beta, \delta_0, \dots, \delta_k, \gamma_0, \dots, \gamma_{k+1}, \mu_0, \dots, \mu_k$, and $\nu_0, \dots, \nu_k$:

$$\begin{array}{lll} \text{minimize} & q_{Z_0}^\mathsf{T}\beta + \sum_{i=0}^{k}(q_{I_i}^\mathsf{T}\gamma_i + q_{G_i}^\mathsf{T}\delta_i + s_i^\mathsf{T}\alpha_{i+1}) + q_{I_{k+1}}^\mathsf{T}\gamma_{k+1} & \\ \text{subject to} & P_{Z_0}^\mathsf{T}\beta = \alpha_0, & \\ & \underline{M}_i^\mathsf{T}\mu_i - \overline{M}_i^\mathsf{T}\nu_i = -\alpha_i & \text{for each } i \in [0..k], \\ & -\mu_i + \nu_i + P_{I_i}^\mathsf{T}\gamma_i + P_{G_i}^\mathsf{T}\delta_i = R_i^\mathsf{T}\alpha_{i+1} & \text{for each } i \in [0..k], \\ & P_{I_{k+1}}^\mathsf{T}\gamma_{k+1} = -\alpha_{k+1} + d, & \end{array} \tag{20}$$

where every system of inequalities $Px \le q$ corresponds to the constraints of the respective init, guard, or invariant, every $R_i x + s_i$ is an update equation, and every interval matrix $[\overline{M}_i, \underline{M}_i] = \text{intexp}(A_i, \underline{t}_i, \overline{t}_i)$. In general, one can check whether the closure is contained in a halfspace $a^\mathsf{T}x \le b$ by setting the direction to its linear term $d = a$ and checking whether the objective function can equal its constant term b. In particular, we check for emptiness, which we pose as checking inclusion in $0x \le -1$. Therefore, we set $d = 0$ and the objective function to equal -1. Upon affirmative answer, from the solution $\alpha_0^\star, \alpha_1^\star, \dots, \nu_k^\star$ we obtain a valid sequence of halfspace interpolants whose i-th linear term is given by $\alpha_i^\star$ and i-th constant term is given by $q_{Z_0}^\mathsf{T}\beta^\star + \sum_{j=0}^{i-1}(q_{I_j}^\mathsf{T}\gamma_j^\star + q_{G_j}^\mathsf{T}\delta_j^\star + s_j^\mathsf{T}\alpha_{j+1}^\star)$.

input : sequence of intervals $[\underline{u}_0, \overline{u}_0], \ldots, [\underline{u}_j, \overline{u}_j]$
output: set of intervals

$b \leftarrow \underline{u}_j$;
while $b < \overline{u}_j$ **do**
  $a \leftarrow b$;
  $b \leftarrow b + \varepsilon$;
  $c \leftarrow \overline{u}_j$;
  if $[\underline{u}_0, \overline{u}_0], \ldots, [\underline{u}_{j-1}, \overline{u}_{j-1}], [a, b]$ *does not admit halfspace interpolants* **then**
    continue;
  if $[\underline{u}_0, \overline{u}_0], \ldots, [\underline{u}_{j-1}, \overline{u}_{j-1}], [a, c]$ *admits halfspace interpolants* **then**
    push $[a, c]$ to the output;
    return;
  while $c - b > \varepsilon$ **do**
    if $[\underline{u}_0, \overline{u}_0], \ldots, [\underline{u}_{j-1}, \overline{u}_{j-1}], [a, \varepsilon\lfloor \frac{b+c}{2\varepsilon} \rfloor]$ *admits halfspace interpolants* **then**
      $b \leftarrow \varepsilon\lfloor \frac{b+c}{2\varepsilon} \rfloor$;
    else
      $c \leftarrow \varepsilon\lfloor \frac{b+c}{2\varepsilon} \rfloor$;
  push $[a, b]$ to the output;

Algorithm 2. Nonswitching time partitioning.

6.2 Time Partitioning

Halfspace interpolation attempts to compute a sequence of enclosures that are convex for a sequence of sets that are not necessarily convex. Specifically, it requires each halfspace to enclose the set of solutions of a linear differential equation, which is nonconvex, by enclosing its convex overapproximation along a whole time interval. As a result, large time intervals produce large overapproximations, on which halfspace interpolation might be impossible. Likewise, shorter intervals produce tighter overapproximations, which are more likely to admit halfspace interpolants. In this section, we exploit such observation to enable interpolation over large time intervals. In particular, we properly partition the time into smaller subintervals and we treat each of them as a halfspace interpolation problem. Later, we combine the results to refine the abstraction.

Time partitioning is a delicate task in the whole abstraction refinement loop. In fact, while template refinement affects linearly the performance of the abstractor, partitioning time intervals that can switch induces branching in the search, possibly leading to an exponential blowup. For this reason, we partition time by narrowing down the switching time, for incremental precision, until no more is left. In particular, we use Algorithm 2 to compute a set N of maximal intervals that admit halfspace interpolants, by enlarging or narrowing them of ε amounts. We embed this procedure in Algorithm 3 which, along the sequence, excludes the time in N, constructing a set of intervals S that overapproximate the switching time. In particular, we construct the set with the widest possible intervals that are disjoint from N. Algorithm 3 succeeds when no more intervals are left, otherwise we half ε and reapply it to the sequences that are left to process.

input : sequence of intervals $[\underline{t}_0, \overline{t}_0], \ldots, [\underline{t}_k, \overline{t}_k]$
output: set of sequences of intervals

push $[\underline{t}_0, \overline{t}_0]$ to the queue Q;
while Q *is not empty* **do**
  pop $[\underline{u}_0, \overline{u}_0], \ldots, [\underline{u}_j, \overline{u}_j]$ from Q;
  $N \leftarrow$ nonswitching time partitioning of $[\underline{u}_0, \overline{u}_0], \ldots, [\underline{u}_j, \overline{u}_j]$;
  foreach $[\underline{a}, \overline{a}] \in N$ **do**
    push $[\underline{u}_0, \overline{u}_0], \ldots, [\underline{u}_{j-1}, \overline{u}_{j-1}], [\underline{a}, \overline{a}]$ to the output;
  if $j = k$ **then**
    assert $[\underline{u}_j, \overline{u}_j] \setminus \cup N = \emptyset$;
    continue;
  $S \leftarrow$ choose set of intervals that cover $[\underline{u}_j, \overline{u}_j] \setminus \cup N$;
  foreach $[\underline{b}, \overline{b}] \in S$ **do**
    push $[\underline{u}_0, \overline{u}_0], \ldots, [\underline{u}_{j-1}, \overline{u}_{j-1}], [\underline{b}, \overline{b}], [\underline{t}_{j+1}, \overline{t}_{j+1}]$ to Q;

Algorithm 3. Dwell time partitioning.

6.3 Abstraction Refinement

The procedures above construct sequences of time intervals $[\underline{u}_0, \overline{u}_0], \ldots, [\underline{u}_j, \overline{u}_j]$ that are included in $[\underline{t}_0, \overline{t}_0], \ldots, [\underline{t}_k, \overline{t}_k]$ and that, with the respective halfspace interpolants, this constitutes a proof of infeasibility for the counterexample. Yet, it does not form a sequence of space-time interpolants $X_0, T_0, \ldots, X_{k+1}$. We form each partitioning T_i by splitting $[\underline{t}_i, \overline{t}_i]$ in such a way each element of T_i is either contained in $[\underline{u}_i, \overline{u}_i]$ or disjoint from it, for all intervals $[\underline{u}_i, \overline{u}_i]$. Then, we refine the partitioning of mode v_i similarly. Each polyhedron X_i is a union of convex polyhedra, each of which is the intersection of all halfspaces H_i corresponding to some sequence $[\underline{u}_0, \overline{u}_0], \ldots, [\underline{u}_i, \overline{u}_i]$. Nevertheless, to refine the abstraction we do not need to construct X_i, but just to take the outward point directions of all H_i and add them to the template of v_i.

7 Experimental Evaluation

We implemented our method in C++ using GMP and Eigen for multiple precision linear algebra, Arb for interval arithmetic, and PPL for linear programming [5,23]. In particular, all libraries we are using are meant to provide guaranteed solutions, as well as our implementation. We evaluate it on several instances of a *filtered oscillator* and a *rod reactor*, which are both parametric in the number of variables, and the latter in the number of modes too [15,35]. We record several statistics from every execution of our tool: the number #cex of counterexamples found during the CEGAR loop, the number #dir of linearly independent directions and the average width of the time partitionings extracted from all space-time interpolants. Moreover, we independently measure three times. First, the time spent in finding counterexamples, namely the total time taken by inconclusive abstractions which returned a spurious counterexample. Second, the refinement time, that is the total time consumed by computing space-time interpolants. Finally, the verification time, that is the time spend in the last abstraction of the CEGAR loop, which terminates with a fixpoint proving the system safe. We compare the outcome and the performance of our tool against Ariadne which, to the best of our knowledge, is the only verification tool available that is numerically sound and time-unbounded [11].

Table 1. Statistics for the benchmark examples (oot when > 1000 s).

	# vars	# modes	# cex	# dirs	avg. width	cex. time	ref. time	ver. time	tot. time	Ariadne
filtosc_1st_ord	3	4	7	13	0.55	0.57	0.96	0.13	**1.66**	27.56
filtosc_2nd_ord	4	4	7	15	0.55	0.83	1.78	0.20	**2.81**	150.7
filtosc_3rd_ord	5	4	7	16	0.55	1.28	4.65	0.32	**6.25**	oot
filtosc_4th_ord	6	4	7	18	0.55	1.53	11.39	0.37	**13.29**	oot
filtosc_5th_ord	7	4	7	19	0.55	2.61	26.60	0.70	**29.37**	-
filtosc_6th_ord	8	4	7	18	0.55	4.56	101.8	1.29	**107.7**	-
filtosc_7th_ord	9	4	7	18	0.55	4.36	109.9	1.13	**114.6**	-
filtosc_8th_ord	10	4	7	17	0.55	5.92	150.9	1.54	**158.4**	-
filtosc_9th_ord	11	4	7	16	0.55	6.49	383.1	1.83	**391.3**	-
filtosc_10th_ord	12	4	7	17	0.55	12.84	428.87	3.73	**445.4**	-
filtosc_11th_ord	13	4	7	17	0.55	15.10	525.2	4.38	**544.6**	-
reactor_1_rod	2	4	11	3	0.11	5.24	10.64	1.59	**17.47**	oot
reactor_2_rods	3	5	9	7	0.79	5.68	5.36	2.33	**13.37**	oot
reactor_3_rods	4	6	12	13	1.07	14.46	13.94	13.13	**41.53**	-
reactor_4_rods	5	7	15	29	1.67	45.50	42.47	111.5	**199.9**	-
reactor_5_rods	6	8	16	31	1.81	73.77	27.36	696.46	**797.5**	-

The filtered oscillator is hybrid automaton with four modes that smoothens a signal x into a signal z. It has $k+2$ variables and a system of $k+2$ affine ODE, where k is the order of the filter. Table 1 shows the results, for a scaling of k up to the 11-th order. The first observation is that the CEGAR loop behaves quite similarly on all scalings: number of counterexamples, number of directions, and time partitionings are almost identical. On the other hand, the computation times show a growth, particularly in the refinement phase which dominates over abstraction and verification. This suggests us that our procedure exploits efficiently the symmetries of the benchmark. In particular, time partitioning seems unaffected. What affects the performance is linear programming, whose size depends on the number of variables of the system.

The rod reactor consists of a heating reactor tank and k rods each of which cools the tank for some amount of time, excluding each other. The hybrid automaton has one variable x for the temperature, k clock variables, one heating mode, one error mode, and k cooling modes. If the temperature reaches a critical threshold and no rod can intervene, it goes into an error. For this benchmark, we start with a simple template, the interval around x, and we discover further directions. Table 1 highlights two fundamental differences with the previous benchmark. First, the average width grows with the model size. This is because the heating mode requires finer time partitioning than the cooling modes. The cooling modes increase with the number of rods, and so does the average width over all time partitions. Second, while with the filtered oscillator the difficulty laid at interpolation, for the rod reactor interpolation is rather easy as well as finding counterexamples. Most of the time is spent in the verification phase, where all fixpoint checks must be concluded, without being interrupted by a counterexample. This shows the advantage of our lazy approach, which first processes the counterexamples and finally proves the fixpoint.

Our method outperforms Ariadne on all benchmarks. On the other hand, tools like Flow* and SpaceEx can be dramatically faster [9]. For instance, they analyze `filtosc_8th_ord` in resp. 9.1 s and 0.36 s (time horizon of 4 and jump depth of 10). This is hardly surprising, as our method has primarily been designed to comply with soundness and time-unboundedness, and pays the price for that.

8 Related Work

There is a rich literature on CEGAR approaches for hybrid automata, either abstracting to a purely discrete system [3, 10, 27, 33, 34] or to a hybrid automaton with simpler dynamics [22, 30]. Both categories exploit the principle that the verification step is easier to carry out in the abstract domain. The abstraction entails a considerable loss of precision that can only be counteracted by increasing the number of abstract states. This leads to a state explosion that severely limits the applicability of such approaches. In contrast, our approach allows us to increase the precision by adding template directions, which does not increase the number of abstract states. The only case where we incur additional abstract states is when partitioning the time domain. This is a direct consequence of the nonconvexity of flowpipes of affine systems, and therefore seems to be unavoidable when using convex sets in abstractions. In [26], the abstraction consists of removing selected ODE entirely. This reduces the complexity, but does not achieve any fine-tuning between accuracy and complexity. Template reachability has been shown to be very effective in both scaling up reachability tasks to more efficient successor computations [15, 31, 32] and achieving termination even over unbounded time horizons [12]. The drawback of templates is the lack of accuracy, which may lead to an approximation error that accumulates excessively. Efforts to dynamically refine templates have so far not scaled well for affine dynamics [14]. A single-step refinement was proposed in [4], but as was illustrated in [7], the refinement needs to be inductive in order to exclude counterexamples in a CEGAR scheme.

9 Conclusion

We have developed an abstraction refinement scheme that combines the efficiency and scalability of template reachability with just enough precision to exclude all detected paths to the bad states. At each iteration of the refinement loop, only one template direction is added per mode and time-step. This does not increase the number of abstract states. Additional abstract states are only introduced when required by the nonconvexity of flowpipes of affine systems, a problem that we consider unavoidable. In contrast, existing CEGAR approaches for hybrid automata tend to suffer from state explosion, since refining the abstraction immediately requires additional abstract states. As our experiments confirm, our approach results in templates over very low complexity and terminates with an unbounded proof of safety after a relatively small number of iterations. Further research is required to extend this work to nondeterministic and nonlinear dynamics.

Acknowledgments. We thank Luca Geretti for helping us setting up Ariadne. This research was supported in part by the Austrian Science Fund (FWF) under grants S11402-N23 (RiSE/SHiNE) and Z211-N23 (Wittgenstein Award), by the European Commission under grant 643921 (UnCoVerCPS).

References

1. Albarghouthi, A., McMillan, K.L.: Beautiful interpolants. In: Sharygina, N., Veith, H. (eds.) CAV 2013. LNCS, vol. 8044, pp. 313–329. Springer, Heidelberg (2013). https://doi.org/10.1007/978-3-642-39799-8_22
2. Althoff, M.: An introduction to CORA 2015. In: Frehse, G., Althoff, M. (eds.) ARCH14-15. 1st and 2nd International Workshop on Applied veRification for Continuous and Hybrid Systems. EPiC Series in Computer Science, vol. 34, pp. 120–151. EasyChair (2015)
3. Alur, R., Dang, T., Ivančić, F.: Counterexample-guided predicate abstraction of hybrid systems. Theor. Comput. Sci. **354**(2), 250–271 (2006)
4. Asarin, E., Dang, T., Maler, O., Testylier, R.: Using redundant constraints for refinement. In: Bouajjani, A., Chin, W.-N. (eds.) ATVA 2010. LNCS, vol. 6252, pp. 37–51. Springer, Heidelberg (2010). https://doi.org/10.1007/978-3-642-15643-4_5
5. Bagnara, R., Hill, P.M., Zaffanella, E.: The Parma Polyhedra Library: toward a complete set of numerical abstractions for the analysis and verification of hardware and software systems. Sci. Comput. Program. **72**(1–2), 3–21 (2008)
6. Benvenuti, L., Bresolin, D., Collins, P., Ferrari, A., Geretti, L., Villa, T.: Assume-guarantee verification of nonlinear hybrid systems with Ariadne. Int. J. Robust Nonlinear Control **24**(4), 699–724 (2014)
7. Bogomolov, S., Frehse, G., Giacobbe, M., Henzinger, T.A.: Counterexample-guided refinement of template polyhedra. In: Legay, A., Margaria, T. (eds.) TACAS 2017. LNCS, vol. 10205, pp. 589–606. Springer, Heidelberg (2017). https://doi.org/10.1007/978-3-662-54577-5_34
8. Chen, X., Ábrahám, E., Sankaranarayanan, S.: Taylor model flowpipe construction for non-linear hybrid systems. In: RTSS 2012, pp. 183–192 (2012)
9. Chen, X., Schupp, S., Makhlouf, I.B., Ábrahám, E., Frehse, G., Kowalewski, S.: A benchmark suite for hybrid systems reachability analysis. In: Havelund, K., Holzmann, G., Joshi, R. (eds.) NFM 2015. LNCS, vol. 9058, pp. 408–414. Springer, Cham (2015). https://doi.org/10.1007/978-3-319-17524-9_29
10. Clarke, E., Fehnker, A., Han, Z., Krogh, B., Ouaknine, J., Stursberg, O., Theobald, M.: Abstraction and counterexample-guided refinement in model checking of hybrid systems. Int. J. Found. Comput. Sci. **14**(04), 583–604 (2003)
11. Collins, P., Bresolin, D., Geretti, L., Villa, T.: Computing the evolution of hybrid systems using rigorous function calculus. In: Proceedings of the 4th IFAC Conference on Analysis and Design of Hybrid Systems (ADHS12), Eindhoven, The Netherlands, pp. 284–290, June 2012

12. Dang, T., Gawlitza, T.M.: Template-based unbounded time verification of affine hybrid automata. In: Yang, H. (ed.) APLAS 2011. LNCS, vol. 7078, pp. 34–49. Springer, Heidelberg (2011). https://doi.org/10.1007/978-3-642-25318-8_6
13. Frehse, G.: PHAVer: algorithmic verification of hybrid systems past HyTech. STTT **10**(3), 263–279 (2008)
14. Frehse, G., Bogomolov, S., Greitschus, M., Strump, T., Podelski, A.: Eliminating spurious transitions in reachability with support functions. In: Proceedings of the 18th International Conference on Hybrid Systems: Computation and Control, pp. 149–158. ACM (2015)
15. Frehse, G., Le Guernic, C., Donzé, A., Cotton, S., Ray, R., Lebeltel, O., Ripado, R., Girard, A., Dang, T., Maler, O.: SpaceEx: scalable verification of hybrid systems. In: Gopalakrishnan, G., Qadeer, S. (eds.) CAV 2011. LNCS, vol. 6806, pp. 379–395. Springer, Heidelberg (2011). https://doi.org/10.1007/978-3-642-22110-1_30
16. Le Guernic, C., Girard, A.: Reachability analysis of hybrid systems using support functions. In: Bouajjani, A., Maler, O. (eds.) CAV 2009. LNCS, vol. 5643, pp. 540–554. Springer, Heidelberg (2009). https://doi.org/10.1007/978-3-642-02658-4_40
17. Halbwachs, N., Proy, Y.-E., Raymond, P.: Verification of linear hybrid systems by means of convex approximations. In: Le Charlier, B. (ed.) SAS 1994. LNCS, vol. 864, pp. 223–237. Springer, Heidelberg (1994). https://doi.org/10.1007/3-540-58485-4_43
18. Henzinger, T., Ho, P.H., Wong-Toi, H.: HyTech: a model checker for hybrid systems. Softw. Tools Technol. Transf. **1**, 110–122 (1997)
19. Henzinger, T.A.: The theory of hybrid automata. In: Inan, M.K., Kurshan, R.P. (eds.) Verification of Digital and Hybrid Systems, vol. 170, pp. 265–292. Springer, Heidelberg (2000). https://doi.org/10.1007/978-3-642-59615-5_13
20. Henzinger, T.A., Ho, P.H., Wong-Toi, H.: Algorithmic analysis of nonlinear hybrid systems. IEEE Trans. Autom. Control **43**, 540–554 (1998)
21. Henzinger, T.A., Kopke, P.W., Puri, A., Varaiya, P.: What's decidable about hybrid automata? In: Proceedings of the Twenty-Seventh Annual ACM Symposium on Theory of Computing, 29 May–1 June 1995, Las Vegas, Nevada, USA, pp. 373–382 (1995)
22. Jha, S.K., Krogh, B.H., Weimer, J.E., Clarke, E.M.: Reachability for linear hybrid automata using iterative relaxation abstraction. In: Bemporad, A., Bicchi, A., Buttazzo, G. (eds.) HSCC 2007. LNCS, vol. 4416, pp. 287–300. Springer, Heidelberg (2007). https://doi.org/10.1007/978-3-540-71493-4_24
23. Johansson, F.: Arb: efficient arbitrary-precision midpoint-radius interval arithmetic. IEEE Trans. Comput. **66**, 1281–1292 (2017)
24. Kong, S., Gao, S., Chen, W., Clarke, E.: dReach: δ-reachability analysis for hybrid systems. In: Baier, C., Tinelli, C. (eds.) TACAS 2015. LNCS, vol. 9035, pp. 200–205. Springer, Heidelberg (2015). https://doi.org/10.1007/978-3-662-46681-0_15
25. Moler, C., Van Loan, C.: Nineteen dubious ways to compute the exponential of a matrix, twenty-five years later. SIAM Rev. **45**(1), 3–49 (2003)
26. Nellen, J., Ábrahám, E., Wolters, B.: A CEGAR tool for the reachability analysis of PLC-controlled plants using hybrid automata. In: Bouabana-Tebibel, T., Rubin, S.H. (eds.) Formalisms for Reuse and Systems Integration. AISC, vol. 346, pp. 55–78. Springer, Cham (2015). https://doi.org/10.1007/978-3-319-16577-6_3
27. Ratschan, S., She, Z.: Safety verification of hybrid systems by constraint propagation-based abstraction refinement. ACM Trans. Embed. Comput. Syst. (TECS) **6**(1), 8 (2007)

28. Rockafellar, R.T.: Convex Analysis. Princeton University Press, Princeton (1970)
29. Rohn, J.: Systems of linear interval equations. Linear Algebra Appl. **126**, 39–78 (1989)
30. Roohi, N., Prabhakar, P., Viswanathan, M.: Hybridization based CEGAR for hybrid automata with affine dynamics. In: Chechik, M., Raskin, J.-F. (eds.) TACAS 2016. LNCS, vol. 9636, pp. 752–769. Springer, Heidelberg (2016). https://doi.org/10.1007/978-3-662-49674-9_48
31. Sankaranarayanan, S., Dang, T., Ivančić, F.: Symbolic model checking of hybrid systems using template polyhedra. In: Ramakrishnan, C.R., Rehof, J. (eds.) TACAS 2008. LNCS, vol. 4963, pp. 188–202. Springer, Heidelberg (2008). https://doi.org/10.1007/978-3-540-78800-3_14
32. Sankaranarayanan, S., Sipma, H.B., Manna, Z.: Scalable analysis of linear systems using mathematical programming. In: Cousot, R. (ed.) VMCAI 2005. LNCS, vol. 3385, pp. 25–41. Springer, Heidelberg (2005). https://doi.org/10.1007/978-3-540-30579-8_2
33. Segelken, M.: Abstraction and counterexample-guided construction of ω-automata for model checking of step-discrete linear hybrid models. In: Damm, W., Hermanns, H. (eds.) CAV 2007. LNCS, vol. 4590, pp. 433–448. Springer, Heidelberg (2007). https://doi.org/10.1007/978-3-540-73368-3_46
34. Sorea, M.: Lazy approximation for dense real-time systems. In: Lakhnech, Y., Yovine, S. (eds.) FORMATS/FTRTFT-2004. LNCS, vol. 3253, pp. 363–378. Springer, Heidelberg (2004). https://doi.org/10.1007/978-3-540-30206-3_25
35. Vaandrager, F.: Hybrid systems. Images of SMC Research, pp. 305–316 (1996)

Monitoring Weak Consistency

Michael Emmi[1(✉)] and Constantin Enea[2]

[1] SRI International, New York, NY, USA
michael.emmi@sri.com
[2] IRIF, Univ. Paris Diderot and CRNS, Paris, France
cenea@irif.fr

Abstract. High-performance implementations of distributed and multicore shared objects often guarantee only the weak consistency of their concurrent operations, foregoing the de-facto yet performance-restrictive consistency criterion of linearizability. While such weak consistency is often vital for achieving performance requirements, practical automation for checking weak-consistency is lacking. In principle, algorithmically checking the consistency of executions according to various weak-consistency criteria is hard: in addition to the enumeration of linearizations of an execution's operations, such criteria generally demand the enumeration of possible visibility relations among the linearized operations; a priori, both enumerations are exponential.

In this work we identify an optimization to weak-consistency checking: rather than enumerating every possible visibility relation, it suffices to consider only the *minimal* visibility relations which adhere to the various constraints of the given criterion, for a significant class of consistency criteria. We demonstrate the soundness of this optimization, and describe an associated minimal-visibility consistency checking algorithm. Empirically, we show that our algorithm significantly outperforms the baseline weak-consistency checking algorithm, which naïvely enumerates all visibilities, and adds only modest overhead to the baseline linearizability checking algorithm, which does not enumerate visibilities.

Keywords: Linearizability · Consistency · Runtime verification

1 Introduction

Programming software applications that can deal with multiple clients at the same time, and possibly, with clients that connect at different sites in a network, relies on optimized concurrent or distributed objects which encapsulate lock-free shared memory access or message passing protocols into high-level abstract data types. Given the potentially-enormous amount of software that relies on

This work is supported in part by the European Research Council (ERC) under the European Union's Horizon 2020 research and innovation programme (grant agreement No 678177).

H. Chockler and G. Weissenbacher (Eds.): CAV 2018, LNCS 10981, pp. 487–506, 2018.
https://doi.org/10.1007/978-3-319-96145-3_26

these objects, it is important to maintain precise specifications and ensure that implementations adhere to their specifications.

One of the standard correctness criteria used in this context is linearizability (or strong consistency) [22], which ensures that the results of concurrently-executed invocations match the results of some serial execution of those same invocations. Ensuring such a criterion in a distributed context (when data is replicated at different sites in a network) is practically infeasible or even impossible [17,19]. Therefore, various weak consistency criteria have been proposed like eventual consistency [23,36], "session guarantees" like read-my-writes or monotonic-reads [35], causal consistency [25,28], etc.

An axiomatic framework for formalizing such criteria has been proposed by Burckhardt et al. [9,11]. Essentially, this extends the linearizability-based specification methodology with a dynamic *visibility* relation among operations, in addition to the standard dynamic *happens-before* and *linearization* relations. Permitting weaker visibility relations models outcomes in which an operation may not observe the effects of concurrent operations that are linearized before it.

In this work, we propose an online monitoring algorithm that checks whether an execution of a concurrent (or distributed) object satisfies a consistency model defined in this axiomatic framework. This algorithm constructs a linearization and visibility relation satisfying the axioms of the consistency model gradually as the execution extends with more operations. It is possible that the linearization and visibility constructed until some point in time are invalidated as more operations get executed, which requires the algorithm to backtrack and search for different candidates. This exponential blow-up is unavoidable since even the problem of checking linearizability is NP-hard in general [18].

The main difficulty in devising such an algorithm is coming up with efficient strategies for enumerating linearizations and visibility relations which minimize the number of candidates needed to be explored and the number of times the algorithm has to backtrack. We build on previous works that propose such strategies for enumerating linearizations [29,38] in the context of linearizability checking. Roughly, the linearizations are extended iteratively by appending operations which are minimal in the happens-before order (among non-linearized operations). The choice of the minimal operations to append varies from one approach to the other. Our work focuses on combining such strategies with an efficient enumeration of visibility relations which are compatible with a given linearization.

Rather than specializing our results to one single consistency model, we consider a general class of consistency models from Burckhardt et al.'s axiomatic framework [9,11] in which the visibility relation among operations is constrained to be contained in the linearization relation. That class includes, for instance, time-stamp based models employed in distributed object implementations, in which time stamps serve to resolve conflicts by effectively linearizing concurrent operations. We show that within this class of consistency models, it is *not* necessary to enumerate the set of all possible visibility relations (included in the linearization) in order to check consistency of an execution. More precisely, we develop an algorithm for enumerating visibility relations that traverses operations in linearization order and chooses for each operation o, a *minimal* set of operations visible to o that conforms to the consistency axioms (up to the linearization prefix that includes o). In general there may exist multiple such minimal sets of operations, and each of them must be explored. When the visibility relation cannot be extended, the algorithm needs to backtrack and choose different minimal visibility sets for previous operations. However, when all the minimal candidates have been explored, the algorithm can soundly report that the execution is not consistent, without resorting to the exploration of non-minimal visibility relations.

Besides demonstrating the soundness of minimal-visibility consistency checking, we also demonstrate its empirical impact by applying our algorithm to concurrent traces of Java concurrent data structures. We find that our algorithm consistently outperforms the baseline naïve approach to enumerating visibilities, which considers also non-minimal visibility relations. Furthermore, we demonstrate that minimal-visibility checking adds only modest overhead (roughly 2×) to the baseline linearizability checking algorithm, which does not enumerate visibilities. This suggests that small sets of minimal visibilities typically suffice in practice, and that the additional exponential enumeration of visibilities, atop the exponential enumeration of linearizations, may be avoidable in practice. Our implementation and experiments are open source, and publicly available on GitHub.[1]

In summary, this work makes the following contributions:

- we develop a new *minimal-visibility* consistency-checking algorithm for Burckhardt et al.'s axiomatic consistency framework [9,11];
- we demonstrate the soundness of minimal-visibility consistency checking; and
- we demonstrate an empirical evaluation comparing minimal-visibility consistency checking with the state-of-the-art consistency-checking algorithms.

To the best of our knowledge, our algorithm is the first completely automatic algorithm for checking weak-consistency of arbitrary abstract data type implementations which avoids the naïve enumeration of all possible visibility relations.

The rest of this paper is organized as follows. Section 2 elaborates a formalization of Burckhardt et al.'s axiomatic consistency framework [9,11], and Sect. 3 develops a formal argument to the soundness of considering only minimal visibility relations. Section 4 describes our overall consistency checking algorithms, and Sect. 5 describes our implementation and empirical evaluation. Section 6 describes related work, and finally Sect. 7 concludes.

2 Weak Consistency

We describe a formal model for concurrent (distributed) object implementations. Clients interact with an object by making *invocations* from a set $\mathbb{I}$ and receiving

[1] https://github.com/michael-emmi/violat/releases/tag/cav-2018-submission.

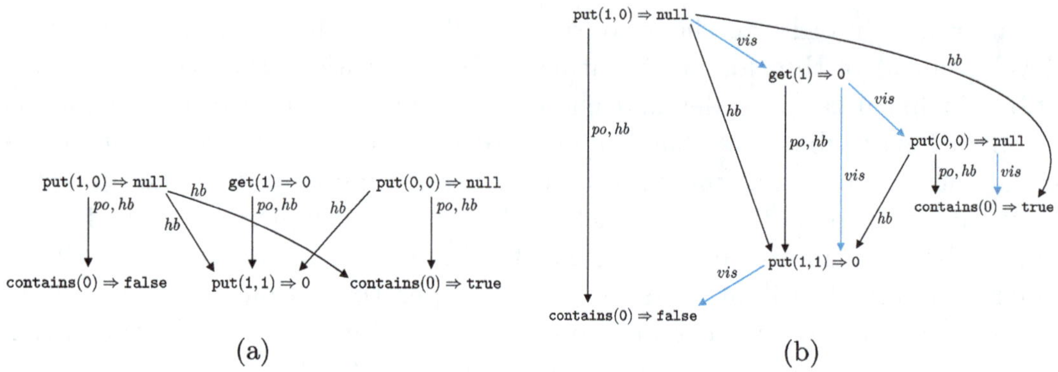

Fig. 1. A history h and an abstract execution containing h.

returns from a set $\mathbb{R}$ (parameters of invocations, if any, are part of the invocation name). An *operation* is an invocation $i \in I$ paired with a return $r \in R$; we denote such an operation by $i \Rightarrow r$. We denote individual operations by o. The invocation, resp., the return, in an operation o is denoted by $inv(o)$, resp., $ret(o)$.

The interaction between a client and an object is represented by a *history* $\langle po, hb\rangle$ over a set of operations O which consists of

- a *program (order) po* which is a partial order on O, and
- a *happens-before (order) hb* which is a partial order on O.

The program order is enforced by the client, e.g., by invoking a set of operations within the same thread or process, while the happens-before order represents the order in which the operations finished, i.e., $(o_1, o_2) \in hb$ iff operation o_1 finished before o_2 started. We assume that the program order is included in the happens-before order.

Example 1. Let us consider a key-value map ADT containing operations of the form `put(key, value)` ⇒ `old`, which insert key-value pairs and return previously-mapped values for the given keys, `remove(key)` ⇒ `value`, which remove key mappings and return previously-mapped values, `contains(value)` ⇒ `true/false`, which test whether values are currently mapped, and `get(key)` ⇒ `value`, which return currently-mapped values for the given keys. Figure 1(a) pictures a history h where edges denote the program order *po* and happens-before *hb*. Such a history can be obtained by a client with three threads each making two invocations (the invocations within the same thread are aligned vertically).

The axiomatic specifications of concurrent objects we consider are based on the following abstract representation of executions: an *abstract execution* over operations O is a tuple $\langle po, hb, lin, vis\rangle$ that consists of a history $\langle po, hb\rangle$ over O,

- a *linearization (order) lin*[2] which is a total order on O, and
- a *visibility (relation) vis* which is an acyclic relation on O.

[2] The linearization is also called *arbitration* in previous works, e.g., [9].

Intuitively, the visibility relation represents the inter-thread communication, how effects of operations are visible to other threads, while the linearization order models the "conflict resolution policy", how the effects of concurrent operations are ordered when they become visible to other threads.

We say that an operation o_1 such that $\langle o_1, o_2 \rangle \in vis$ is *visible* to o_2, and that o_2 *sees* o_1. Also, the set of operations visible to o_2 is called the *visibility set* of o_2. The extensions of *inv* and *ret* to partial orders on O are defined component-wise as usual.

Example 2. Figure 1(b) pictures an abstract execution containing the history in Fig. 1(a). The visibility relation is defined by the edges labeled *vis* together with their transitive closure. The linearization order is defined by the order in which operations are written (from top to bottom).

A consistency criterion for concurrent objects is defined by a set of axioms over the relations in an abstract execution. These axioms relate abstract executions to a sequential semantics of the operations, which is defined by a function $Spec : \mathbb{I}^* \times \mathbb{I} \to \mathbb{R}$ that determines the return value of an invocation given the sequence of invocations previously executed on the object[3].

Example 3. The sequential semantics of the key-value map ADT considered in Example 1 is defined as expected. For instance, the return value of `put(key, value)` after a sequence of invocations σ is the value `null` if σ contains no invocation `put(key, ...)`, or `old` if `put(key, old)` is the last invocation of the form `put(key, ...)` in σ.

The *domain* $\text{dom}(R)$ of a relation R is the set of elements x such that $\langle x, y \rangle \in R$ for some y; the *codomain* $\text{codom}(R)$ is the set of elements y such that $\langle x, y \rangle \in R$ for some x. By an abuse of notation, if x is an individual element, $x \in R$ denotes the fact that $x \in \text{dom}(R) \cup \text{codom}(R)$. The *(left) composition* $R_1 \circ R_2$ of two binary relations R_1 and R_2 is the set of pairs $\langle x, z \rangle$ such that $\langle x, y \rangle \in R_1$ and $\langle y, z \rangle \in R_2$ for some y. We denote the identity binary relation $\{\langle x, x \rangle : x \in X\}$ on a set X by $[X]$, and we write $[x]$ to denote $[\{x\}]$.

Return-value consistency [9], a variant of eventual consistency without liveness guarantees, states that the return r of every operation $i \Rightarrow r$ can be obtained from a sequential execution of i that follows the invocations visible to o (in the linearization order). This constraint will be formalized as an axiom called Ret. The visibility relation can be chosen arbitrarily. Standard "session guarantees" can be described in the same framework by adding constraints on the visibility relation: for instance, *read my writes*, i.e., operations previously executed in the same thread remain visible, can be stated as $\mathsf{vis} \supseteq \mathsf{po}$ and *monotonic reads*, i.e., the set of visible operations to some thread grows monotonically over time, can

[3] Previous works have considered more general, concurrent semantics for operations. We restrict ourselves to sequential semantics in order to simplify the exposition. Our results extend easily to the general case.

$$\begin{aligned} \phi &::= \mathsf{Ret} \mid ord \\ ord &::= qrel \supseteq rel \\ qrel &::= \mathsf{lin} \mid \mathsf{vis} \\ rel &::= qrel \mid \mathsf{po} \mid \mathsf{hb} \mid rel \circ rel \end{aligned}$$

Fig. 2. The grammar of consistency axioms.

$\langle po, hb, lin, vis \rangle \models \mathsf{Ret}$ iff
$\quad \forall o. ret(o) = Spec(inv(ctxt(lin, vis, o)), inv(o))$

$\langle po, hb, lin, vis \rangle \models ord$ iff
$\quad ord[po/\mathsf{po}][hb/\mathsf{hb}][lin/\mathsf{lin}][vis/\mathsf{vis}]$ is valid

Fig. 3. Consistency axiom satisfaction for abstract executions. The satisfaction relation $\models$ is implicitly parameterized by a sequential semantics *Spec* which we consider fixed.

be stated as $\mathsf{vis} \supseteq \mathsf{vis} \circ \mathsf{po}$. Then, a version of causal consistency [7,9], called *causal convergence*, is defined by the following set of axioms:

$$\mathsf{vis} \supseteq \mathsf{vis} \circ \mathsf{vis} \quad \mathsf{vis} \supseteq \mathsf{po} \quad \mathsf{lin} \supseteq \mathsf{vis} \quad \mathsf{Ret}$$

which state that the visibility relation is transitive, it includes program order, and it is included in the linearization order. Finally, *linearizability* is defined by the set of axioms $\mathsf{lin} \supseteq \mathsf{hb}$, $\mathsf{vis} = \mathsf{lin}$, and Ret.

To state our results in a general context that concerns multiple consistency criteria defined in the literature (including the ones mentioned above) and variations there of, we consider a language of *consistency axioms* ϕ defined by the grammar in Fig. 2. A *consistency model* Φ is a set $\{\phi_1, \phi_2, \ldots\}$ of consistency axioms.

In the following, we assume that every consistency model is stronger than return-value consistency, and also, that the linearization order is consistent with the visibility and happens-before relations. The assumptions concerning the linearization order correspond to the fact that for instance, concurrent operations are ordered using timestamps that correspond to real-time. Formally, we assume that every consistency model contains the axioms

$$\Phi_0 = \{\mathsf{Ret}, \mathsf{lin} \supseteq \mathsf{vis}, \mathsf{lin} \supseteq \mathsf{hb}\}.$$

Figure 3 defines the precise semantics of consistency axioms on abstract executions: the *context* of an operation o according to a linearization *lin* and visibility *vis*, denoted $ctxt(lin, vis, o)$ is the restriction $([O_o] \circ lin \circ [O_o])$ of *lin* to the operations $O_o = \mathrm{dom}(vis \circ [o])$ visible to o. For instance, for the abstract execution in Fig. 1(b), $ctxt(lin, vis, \mathtt{contains}(0) \Rightarrow \mathtt{false})$ is the sequence of operations $\mathtt{put}(1,0) \Rightarrow \mathtt{null}; \mathtt{get}(1) \Rightarrow 0; \mathtt{put}(1,1) \Rightarrow 0$.

We extend this semantics to consistency models as $e \models \Phi$ iff $e \models \phi$ for all $\phi \in \Phi$ and to histories as:

$$\langle po, hb \rangle \models \Phi \ \text{ iff } \ \exists lin, vis.\ \langle po, hb, lin, vis \rangle \models \Phi$$

Example 4. The abstract execution in Fig. 1(b) satisfies causal convergence: the visibility relation is transitive, it includes program order, and it is consistent with the linearization order. Moreover, the axiom Ret is also satisfied.

For instance, the invocation $\texttt{contains}(0)$ returns exactly $\texttt{false}$ when executed after $\texttt{put}(1,0);\texttt{get}(1);\texttt{put}(1,1)$. Similarly, it returns $\texttt{true}$ when executed after $\texttt{put}(1,0);\texttt{get}(1);\texttt{put}(0,0)$.

3 Minimal Visibility Extensions

Checking whether a given history satisfies a consistency model is intractable in general. This essentially follows from the fact that checking linearizability is NP-hard in general [18]. While the main issue in checking linearizability is enumerating the exponentially many linearizations, checking weaker criteria like causal convergence requires also an enumeration of the exponentially many visibility relations (included in a given linearization). We prove in this section that it is enough to enumerate only *minimal* visibility relations (w.r.t. set inclusion), included in a given linearization, in order to conclude whether a given history and linearization satisfy a consistency model.

A *linearized history* $\sigma = \langle po, hb, lin\rangle$ consists of a history and a linearization lin such that $lin \supseteq hb$. The extension of $\models$ to linearized histories is defined as:

$$\langle po, hb, lin\rangle \models \Phi \text{ iff } \exists vis.\ \langle po, hb, lin, vis\rangle \models \Phi$$

The i-th element of a sequence s is denoted by $s[i]$ and the prefix of s of length i is denoted by s_i. The projection of a linearized history $\sigma = \langle po, hb, lin\rangle$ to a prefix lin_i of lin is denoted by σ_i. Formally, $O_i = \text{dom}(lin_i) \cup \text{codom}(lin_i)$ and $\sigma_i = \langle po \cap (O_i \times O_i), hb \cap (O_i \times O_i), lin_i\rangle$.

For a linearized history $\langle po, hb, lin\rangle$ and a consistency model Φ, a visibility relation vis_i on operations from a prefix lin_i of lin is called *Φ-extensible* when there exists a visibility relation $vis \supseteq vis_i$ such that $\langle po, hb, lin, vis\rangle \models \Phi$. The relation vis is called a *Φ-extension of vis_i up to lin*. By extrapolation, a Φ-extension of vis_i *up to lin_j* is a visibility relation vis_j such that $\langle \sigma_j, vis_j\rangle \models \Phi$, for any $i < j$. Such an extension is called *minimal* when for every other Φ-extension vis'_j of vis_i up to lin_j, we have that $vis'_j \not\subseteq vis_j$.

Example 5. Consider again the abstract execution in Fig. 1(b). Ignoring the edges labeled by vis, it becomes a linearized history σ. The prefix σ_2 contains just the two operations $\texttt{put}(1,0) \Rightarrow \texttt{null}$ and $\texttt{get}(1) \Rightarrow 0$. For causal convergence, the visibility relation $vis_2 = \{\langle \texttt{put}(1,0) \Rightarrow \texttt{null}, \texttt{get}(1) \Rightarrow 0\rangle\}$ on operations of σ_2 is extensible, as witnessed by the visibility relation defined for the rest of the operations in this execution. The visibility relation

$$\begin{aligned} vis_3 = \{&\langle \texttt{put}(1,0) \Rightarrow \texttt{null}, \texttt{get}(1) \Rightarrow 0\rangle, \langle \texttt{put}(1,0) \Rightarrow \texttt{null}, \texttt{put}(0,0) \Rightarrow \texttt{null}\rangle, \\ &\langle \texttt{get}(1) \Rightarrow 0, \texttt{put}(0,0) \Rightarrow \texttt{null}\rangle\} \end{aligned}$$

is an extension of vis_2 up to lin_3, and contains the operations in σ_2 together with $\texttt{put}(0,0) \Rightarrow \texttt{null}$. Note that this extension is *not* minimal. A minimal extension would be exactly equal to vis_2 since, intuitively, $\texttt{put}(0,0) \Rightarrow \texttt{null}$ is not required to observe operations on keys other than 0.

The next lemma shows that minimizing the visibility sets of operations in a linearization prefix, while preserving the truth of the axioms on that prefix, doesn't exclude visibility choices for future operations (occurring beyond that prefix). In more precise terms, the Φ-extensibility status is not affected by choosing smaller visibility sets for operations in a linearization prefix. For instance, since the visibility vis_3 in Example 5 is extensible (for causal convergence), the smaller visibility relation in which $\texttt{put}(0,0) \Rightarrow \texttt{null}$ doesn't see any operation, is also extensible. This result relies on the specific form of the axioms, which ensure that smaller visibility sets impose fewer constraints on the visibility sets of future operations. For instance, the axiom $vis \supseteq vis \circ vis$ enforces that vis contains $\{\langle o, o_2\rangle : \langle o, o_1\rangle \in vis\}$ whenever a pair $\langle o_1, o_2\rangle$ is added to vis. Minimizing the visibility set of o_1 will minimize the set of operations that *must* be seen by o_2, thus making the choice of the operations visible to o_2 more liberal.

Lemma 1. *For every linearized history σ and consistency model Φ, if*

$$\langle \sigma_i, vis_i\rangle \models \Phi, \qquad vis_i \textit{ is } \Phi\textit{-extensible}, \qquad \langle \sigma_i, vis'_i\rangle \models \Phi, \qquad \textit{and } vis'_i \subseteq vis_i,$$

then vis'_i is Φ-extensible.

Proof (Sketch). We show that the Φ-extension vis of vis_i up to lin can be transformed to a Φ-extension of vis'_i up to lin by simply removing the pairs of operations in $vis_i \setminus vis'_i$. Let vis' be this visibility relation and Φ a consistency model. We prove that $\langle po, hb, lin, vis'\rangle \models \Phi$ by considering the different types of axioms defined in Fig. 2.

Suppose that Φ contains an axiom of the form $\mathsf{vis} \supseteq rel$ (according to the notations in Fig. 2). We have that $vis'_i \supseteq (rel[po/\mathsf{po}][hb/\mathsf{hb}][lin/\mathsf{lin}][vis'/\mathsf{vis}]) \circ [O_i]$ by the hypothesis (from $\langle \sigma_i, vis'_i\rangle \models \Phi$). Then, $vis'_i \subseteq vis_i$ implies that

$$\begin{aligned}&(rel[po/\mathsf{po}][hb/\mathsf{hb}][lin/\mathsf{lin}][vis/\mathsf{vis}]) \circ [O \setminus O_i]\\ &\supseteq (rel[po/\mathsf{po}][hb/\mathsf{hb}][lin/\mathsf{lin}][vis'/\mathsf{vis}]) \circ [O \setminus O_i]\end{aligned}$$

which together with $vis' \circ [O \setminus O_i] = vis \circ [O \setminus O_i]$ (the visibility relations vis and vis' are the same for operations which are not included in the prefix lin_i) implies that

$$vis' \circ [O \setminus O_i] \supseteq (rel[po/\mathsf{po}][hb/\mathsf{hb}][lin/\mathsf{lin}][vis'/\mathsf{vis}]) \circ [O \setminus O_i].$$

Therefore, $\langle po, hb, lin, vis'\rangle \models \mathsf{vis} \supseteq rel$.

The axiom Ret relates the return value of each operation o in σ to the set of operations visible to o. This relation is insensitive to the set of operations seen by an operation before o in the linearization order. Therefore, $\langle po, hb, lin, vis'\rangle \models$ Ret is an immediate consequence of $\langle \sigma_i, vis'_i\rangle \models$ Ret and the fact that vis and vis' are the same for operations which are not included in the prefix lin_i.

The axioms of the form $\mathsf{lin} \supseteq rel$ (according to the notations in Fig. 2) are straightforward implications of $\mathsf{lin} \supseteq \mathsf{hb}$ and $\mathsf{lin} \supseteq \mathsf{vis}$, which are assumed to be included in any consistency model. They hold for any linearized history. □

The main result of this section shows that a visibility enumeration strategy that considers operations in the linearization order and computes minimal extensions iteratively, possibly backtracking to another choice of minimal extension if necessary, is complete in general (it finds a visibility relation satisfying the consistency axioms Φ iff the input linearized history satisfies Φ). Backtracking is necessary since in general, there may exist multiple minimal extensions and all of them should be explored. For a given linearized history σ and visibility relation *vis* on operations of σ, $vis_i = vis \circ [O_i]$ denotes the restriction of *vis* to operations from the prefix lin_i.

Theorem 1. *For every linearized history σ and consistency model Φ, $\sigma \models \Phi$ iff there exists a visibility relation vis such that*

$$\textit{for every } i,\ vis_{i+1} \textit{ is a minimal } \Phi\textit{-extension of } vis_i \textit{ up to } lin_{i+1}.$$

Proof. (Sketch) Let σ be a linearized history such that $\sigma \models \Phi$. Therefore, there exists a visibility relation *vis* such that $\langle \sigma, vis \rangle \models \Phi$. We prove by induction that there exists a visibility relation vis' satisfying the claim of the theorem. Assume that there exists a Φ-extensible visibility relation vis^j on operations in lin_j which satisfies the claim of the theorem for every $i < j$ (we take $vis^0 = vis$). Let vis^{j+1} be a minimal visibility relation on operations in lin_{j+1} such that $vis^{j+1} \circ [O_j] = vis^j \circ [O_j]$ and $(\sigma_{j+1}, vis^{j+1}) \models \Phi$ (such a set exists because vis^j is Φ-extensible). By Lemma 1, vis^{j+1} is Φ-extensible. Also, vis^{j+1} satisfies the claim of the theorem for every $i < j + 1$. The reverse direction is trivial. □

Example 6. In the context of the abstract execution in Fig. 1(b), the visibility relation defined by removing the *vis* edge ending in $\texttt{put}(0,0) \Rightarrow \texttt{null}$, and adding the transitive closure, satisfies the requirements in Theorem 1.

4 Efficient Monitoring of Consistency Models

We describe an algorithm for checking whether a given history satisfies a consistency model, which combines linearization enumeration strategies proposed in [29,38] with the visibility enumeration strategy proposed in Sect. 3.

The algorithm is defined by the procedure `checkConsistency` listed in Fig. 4. This recursive procedure searches for extensions of the input linearization and visibility (initially, `checkConsistency` will be called with $lin = vis = \emptyset$) which witness that the input history h satisfies Φ. It assumes that the inputs *lin* and *vis* satisfy the axioms of the consistency model Φ when the input history is projected on the linearized operations (the operations in *lin*). This projection is denoted by h_{lin}. Formally, the precondition of this procedure is that $\langle h_{lin}, lin, vis \rangle \models \Phi$.

The extensions of *lin* and *vis* are built in successive steps. At each step, the linearization is extended according to the procedure `linExtensions` and the visibility according to the procedure `visExtensions`.

The abstract implementation of `linExtensions`, presented in Fig. 4, chooses a set of *non-linearized* operations O which are *minimal* among non-linearized

```
proc checkConsistency(h,Φ,lin,vis) {
  if (isComplete(h,lin)) then
    return true;
  forall lin' of linExtensions(h,lin) do
    forall vis' of visExtensions(h,lin',vis) do
      if checkConsistency(h,Φ,lin',vis') then
        return true;
  return false;
}
```

```
proc linExtensions(h,lin) {
  let O = minimals(h,lin);
  forall O' of subsets(O)
   forall seq of linearizations(O')
    let lin' = append(lin,seq);
    yield lin';
}
```

```
proc visExtensions(h,lin,vis){
  forall vis' a minimal Φ-extension
               of vis up to lin
    yield vis';
}
```

Fig. 4. Checking consistency of a history. The procedures `linExtensions`, resp., `visExtensions` return the set of linearizations, resp., visibilities, produced by the instruction `yield`.

operations w.r.t. happens-before, i.e., returned by `minimals`(h, lin), and appends any linearization of the operations in O to the input linearization lin. Formally, $O \subseteq \{o : o \notin lin \text{ and } \forall o'.\ o' \notin lin \Rightarrow \neg o' \prec o\}$, where $\prec$ denotes the happens-before relation. The fact that the operations in O are minimal among non-linearized operations ensures that the returned linearizations are consistent with the happens-before order.

Two linearization enumeration strategies proposed in the literature can be seen as instances of `linExtensions`. The strategy in [38] corresponds to the case where O contains exactly one minimal operation. For instance, for the history in Fig. 1(a), this strategy will start by picking a minimal element in the happens-before relation, say `put`$(1, 0) \Rightarrow$ `null`, then, a minimal operation among the rest, say `get`$(1) \Rightarrow 0$, and so on.

The strategy proposed in [29] is slightly more involved (and according to experimental results, more efficient), but it relies on a presentation of histories h as sequences of call and return actions (an operation spanning the time interval between its call and return action). The happens-before order is extracted as usual: an operation o_1 happens before an operation o_2 if its return occurs before the call of o_2. This strategy defines O as the first non-linearized operation o that returned in h together with a set of non-linearized operations O' that are concurrent with o (i.e., are not ordered after o in the happens-before order). The operation o is linearized last in the returned extensions. For instance, consider the history h in Fig. 5 represented as a sequence of call/return actions (small boxes at the begin, resp., end, of an interval denote call actions, resp., return actions). The first linearization extension (when $lin = \emptyset$) includes `put`$(1, 0) \Rightarrow$ `null` (the first operation to return) after some sequence of operations concurrent with it, for

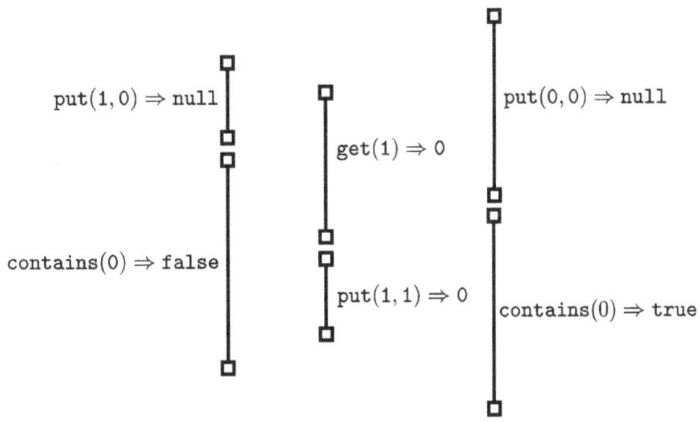

Fig. 5. The history h in Fig. 1 presented as a sequence of call/return actions.

instance the empty sequence. Next, the current linearization $\texttt{put}(1, 0) \Rightarrow \texttt{null}$ can be extended by adding $\texttt{put}(0, 0) \Rightarrow \texttt{null}$ (the first operation to return, if we exclude $\texttt{put}(1, 0) \Rightarrow \texttt{null}$ which is already linearized) and possibly $\texttt{get}(1) \Rightarrow 0$ before it. Suppose that we choose $\texttt{put}(1, 0) \Rightarrow \texttt{null}; \texttt{get}(1) \Rightarrow 0; \texttt{put}(0, 0) \Rightarrow \texttt{null}$. Then, the extension will include $\texttt{put}(1, 1) \Rightarrow 0$ and possibly $\texttt{contains}(0) \Rightarrow \texttt{true}$ or $\texttt{contains}(0) \Rightarrow \texttt{false}$, and so on. Compared to the previous strategy, an extension step can add multiple operations.

The extensions of the visibility relation (returned by `visExtensions`) are minimal Φ-extensions of *vis* up to the input linearization. They can be constructed iteratively by considering the newly linearized operations one by one and each time compute a minimal extension of the visibility. For instance, the linearization construction explained in the previous paragraph can be expanded with a visibility enumeration as follows:

- $lin = \texttt{put}(1, 0) \Rightarrow \texttt{null}$: the minimal visibility is $vis_1 = \emptyset$,
- $lin = \texttt{put}(1, 0) \Rightarrow \texttt{null}; \texttt{get}(1) \Rightarrow 0; \texttt{put}(0, 0) \Rightarrow \texttt{null}$: the minimal visibility is $vis_2 = \{\langle \texttt{put}(1, 0) \Rightarrow \texttt{null}, \texttt{get}(1) \Rightarrow 0 \rangle\}$, and so on.

The procedure `checkConsistency` backtracks to a different extension when the current one cannot be completed to include all the operations in the input history (checked by the recursive call). The correctness of the algorithm is stated in the following theorem.

Theorem 2. $\texttt{checkConsistency}(h, \Phi, \emptyset, \emptyset)$ *returns true iff* $h \models \Phi$.

5 Empirical Results

While our minimal-visibility consistency checking algorithm is applicable to a wide class of distributed and multicore shared object implementations, here we demonstrate its efficacy on histories recorded from executions of Java Development Kit (JDK) Standard Edition concurrent data structures. Recent work demonstrates that JDK concurrent data structures regularly admit non-atomic behaviors, often by design [14]; these weakly-consistent behaviors span many methods of the `java.util.concurrent` package, including the ConcurrentHashMap, ConcurrentSkipListMap, ConcurrentSkipListSet, ConcurrentLinkedQueue, and the ConcurrentLinkedDeque, for instance, including the contains method described in Example 3.

We extracted 4,000 randomly-sampled histories from approximately 8,000 observed over approximately 1,000,000 executions in stress testing 20 randomly-generated client programs of the ConcurrentSkipListMap with up to 15 invocations across up to 3 threads. In each program, the given number of threads invokes its share of randomly-generated methods with randomly-generated values. We consider random generation superior to collecting programs *in the wild*, since found client programs can mask inconsistencies by restricting method argument values, or by being agnostic to inconsistent return values. Furthermore, automated generation gives us the ability to evaluate our algorithm on unbiased sample sets, and avoid any technical problems in the collection of programs; it also allows us to test method combinations which might not appear in publicly-available examples.

We subject each client program to 1 s of stress testing[4] to record histories. The return value of each invocation is stored in a different thread-local variable which is read at the end of the execution. Recording the happens-before order between invocations without affecting implementation behavior significantly (e.g., without influencing the memory orderings between shared-memory accesses) is challenging. For instance, we found the use of high-precision timers to be unsuitable, since the response-time of `System.nanoTime` calls is much higher than calls to the implementations under test; invoking such timers between each invocation of implementation methods would prevent implementation methods from overlapping in time, and thus hide any possible inconsistent behaviors. Similarly, the use of atomic operations and volatile variables would impose additional synchronization constraints and prevent many weak-memory reorderings.

Essentially, our solution is to introduce a shared variable per thread storing its program counter – in our context, the program counter stores the number of call and return events thus far executed. A thread's program counter is read by every other thread before and after each invocation. Figure 6 demonstrates a simplified version[5] of our encoding for a program with two threads each invoking two methods. The program counter variables `pc0` and `pc1` are not declared volatile, which, in principle, provides stronger guarantees concerning the derived happens-before relation; such declarations would interfere with implementation weak-memory effects. The program counter values read by each thread allows

[4] For stress testing we leverage OpenJDK's JCStress tool: http://openjdk.java.net/projects/code-tools/jcstress/.

[5] In our actual implementation, each program-counter access is encapsulated within a method call in order to avoid compiler reordering between the reads of other threads' counters and the increment of one's own. While the Java memory model does not guarantee that such encapsulation will prevent reordering, we found this solution to be adequate on Oracle's Java SE runtime version 9. Our actual implementation also wraps invocations in try-catch blocks to deal with exceptions.

```
int pc0 = 0, pc1 = 0;
ConcurrentHashMap obj = new ConcurrentHashMap();
```

```
void thread0() {
  Object r0, r1;
  int pcs[][] = new int[4][1];
  int n = 0;

  // first invocation
  pcs[n][0] = pc1; n++; pc0++;
  r0 = obj.elements();
  pcs[n][0] = pc1; n++; pc0++;

  // second invocation
  pcs[n][0] = pc1; n++; pc0++;
  r1 = obj.put(1,0);
  pcs[n][0] = pc1; n++; pc0++;

  // store the values of r0, r1, pcs
  ...
}
```

```
void thread1() {
  Object r0, r1;
  int pcs[][] = new int[4][1];
  int n = 0;

  // first invocation
  pcs[n][0] = pc0; n++; pc1++;
  r0 = obj.remove(1);
  pcs[n][0] = pc0; n++; pc1++;

  // second invocation
  pcs[n][0] = pc0; n++; pc1++;
  r1 = obj.put(0,1);
  pcs[n][0] = pc0; n++; pc1++;

  // store the values of r0, r1, pcs
  ...
}
```

Fig. 6. Our encoding for recording ConcurrentHashMap histories. Each thread's program counter is read before and after other threads' invocations, and incremented subsequent to each such read. The two-dimensional `pcs`[n][m] array stores n program counter values for m neighboring threads.

us to extract a happens-before order between invocations which is *sound* in the sense that the actual happens-before may order more operations, but not fewer – assuming that shared-memory accesses satisfy at least the total-store order (TSO) semantics in which writes are guaranteed to be performed according to program order. For instance, when $\mathsf{pcs}[0][0] > 2$ in the second thread (`thread1`), the first invocation in the other thread (`thread0`) happens-before the first invocation in this thread. Otherwise, if $\mathsf{pcs}[0][0] < 2$, then the two invocations are overlapping in time. The latter may not be true in the real happens-before due to the delay in incrementing and reading the program counter variables. Although some loss of precision is possible, we are unaware of other methods for tracking happens-before which avoid significant interference with the implementation under test.

Based on the encoding described above, we generate histories as sequences of call and return actions which serve as input to our consistency checking algorithms. For simplicity, we have considered just two consistency models, linearizability and a weak consistency model defined by $\{\mathsf{Ret}, \mathsf{lin} \supseteq \mathsf{vis}, \mathsf{lin} \supseteq \mathsf{hb}, \mathsf{vis} \supseteq \mathsf{hb}\}$ – see Sect. 2. We consider linearizability in order to measure the overhead of checking weak consistency due to visibility enumeration; the second model is simply the easiest weak-consistency model to support with our implementation; the choice among possible weak-consistency models appears fairly arbitrary, since the enumeration of visibility relations is common to all.

We consider several measurements, the results of which are listed in Figs. 7 and 8; all times are measured in milliseconds on logarithmic scale on a 2.7 GHz Intel Core i5 MacBook Pro with Oracle–s Java SE runtime version 9; and

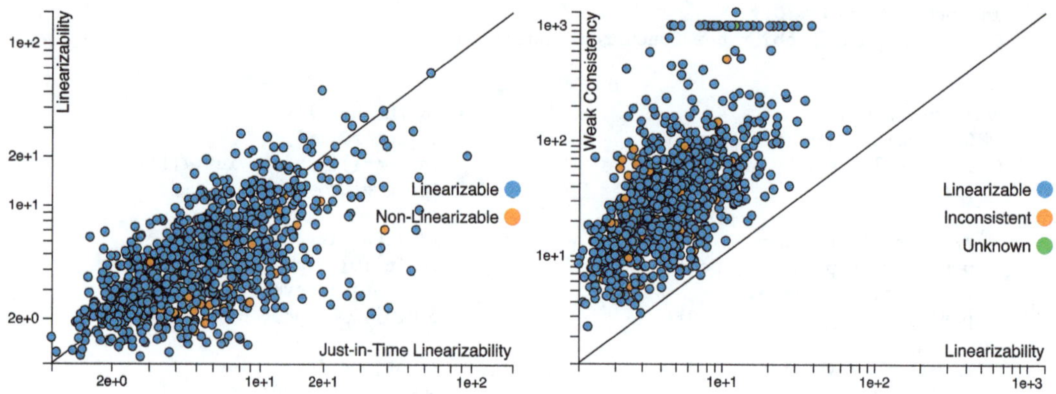

Fig. 7. Empirical comparison of (left) standard linearizability checking versus just-in-time linearizability checking on concurrent traces of Java data structures; and (right) weak-consistency checking versus standard linearizability checking. Each point reflects the time in milliseconds for checking a given trace.

timeouts are set to 1000 ms. We note that while accurate and *recording* of operation timings within an execution without interference is challenging, timing the *validation* of each recorded history, which we report here, is accomplished accurately, without interference, by computing the clock difference just before and after validation.

Our first measurements establish the baseline linearizability and weak-consistency checking algorithms. On the left side of Fig. 7 we consider the time required to check linearizability for each history by our own implementations of Wing and Gong's standard enumerative approach [38], along with Lowe's "just-in-time linearizability" algorithm [29] – see Sect. 4. We resolve the nondeterminism in these algorithms (e.g., in choosing which pending operation to attempt linearizing first) arbitrarily (e.g., first called), finding no clear winner: each algorithm performs better on some histories. Since these subtleties are outside the scope of our work, we avoid further investigation and choose Wing and Gong's algorithm as our baseline linearizability-checking algorithm.

Our second measurement exposes the overhead of enumerating visibility relations for checking weak consistency. On the right side of Fig. 7 we consider the time required to check weak consistency of a given history versus the time required to check its linearizability.[6] We observe an overhead of approximately 10× due to visibility enumeration and validation. Our naïve implementation enumerates candidate visibilities in size-decreasing order since we expect visibility-loss to be the exception rather than the rule; for instance, atomic operations observe all linearized-before operations. We omit the analogous comparison between weak-consistency checking and just-in-time linearizability checking to avoid redundancy, since the just-in-time optimization is a seemingly-insignificant factor in our experiments: the results are nearly identical.

---

[6] Due to a benign error in the decoding of results of stress testing, we observe one single point on which the two algorithms conflict – labeled by "Unknown.".

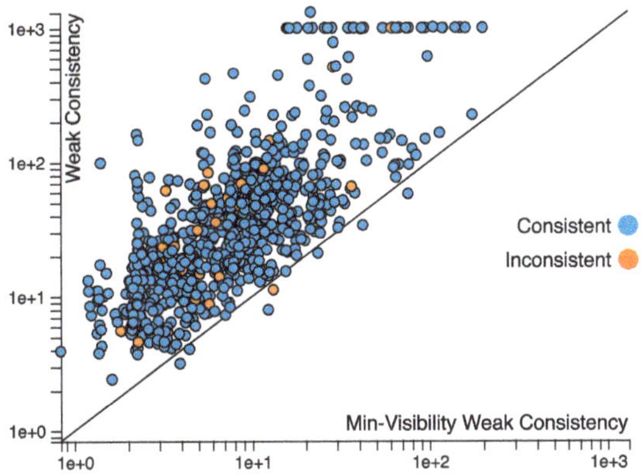

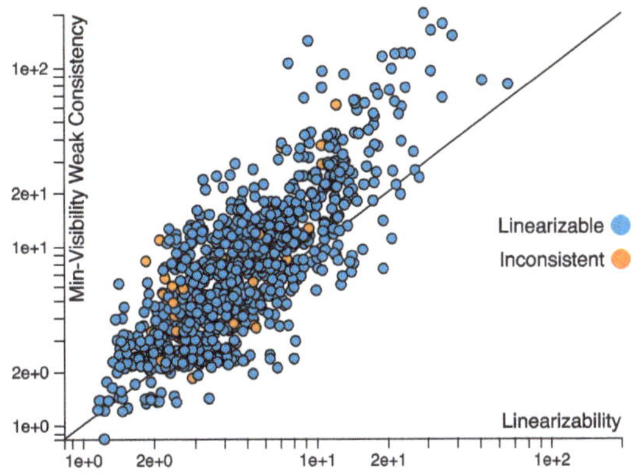

Fig. 8. Empirical comparison of (left) standard weak-consistency checking versus minimal-visibility weak-consistency checking on concurrent traces of Java data structures; and (right) the latter versus standard linearizability checking. Each point reflects the time in milliseconds for checking a given trace.

Our third measurement demonstrates the impact of our minimal-visibility consistency checking optimization. On the left side of Fig. 8 we consider the time required to check weak consistency without and with our optimization. The difference is dramatic, with our optimized algorithm consistently outperforming, sometimes up to multiple orders of magnitude: the leftmost 1000 ms timeout of the naïve algorithm is matched by a roughly 18 ms positive identification. Finally, our fourth measurement, on the right side of Fig. 8, demonstrates that the overhead of our minimal-visibility checking algorithm over linearizability checking is quite modest: we observe roughly a 2× overhead, compared with the observed 10× overhead without optimization.

While our experiments clearly demonstrate the efficacy of our minimal-visibility consistency checking algorithm, we will continue to evaluate this optimization across a wide range of concurrent objects, consistency models, and client programs, e.g., including many more concurrent threads. While we do expect the performance of linearizability- and weak-consistency checking to vary with thread count, we expect the performance gains of minimal-visibility consistency checking to continue to hold.

6 Related Work

Herlihy and Wing [22] described linearizability, which is the standard consistency criterion for shared-memory concurrent objects. Motivated by replication-based distributed systems, Burckhardt et al. [9,11] describe a more general axiomatic framework for specifying weaker consistencies like eventual consistency [36] and causal consistency [2]. Our weak consistency checking algorithm applies to consistency models described in this framework.

While several static techniques have been developed to prove linearizability [1,4,6,12,13,21,22,24,26,27,30–34,37,39], few have addressed dynamic techniques such as testing and runtime verification. The works in [29,38] describe monitors for checking linearizability that construct linearizations of a given history incrementally, in an online fashion. Line-Up [10] performs systematic concurrency testing via schedule enumeration, and offline linearizability checking via linearization enumeration. Our weak consistency checking algorithm combines these approaches with an efficient enumeration of visibility relations. The works in [15,16] propose a symbolic enumeration of linearizations based on a SAT solver. Although more efficient in practice, this approach applies only to certain ADTs. In this work, we propose a generic approach that assumes no constraints on the sequential semantics of the concurrent objects.

Bouajjani et al. [7] consider the problem of verifying causal consistency. They propose an algorithm for checking whether a given execution satisfies causal consistency, but only for the key-value map ADT with simple `put` and `get` operations. Our work proposes a generic algorithm that can deal with various weak consistency criteria and ADTs.

From the complexity standpoint, Gibbons and Korach [18] showed that monitoring even the single-value register type for linearizability is NP-hard. Alur et al. [3] showed that checking linearizability of all executions of a given implementation is in EXPSPACE when the number of concurrent operations is bounded, and then Hamza [20] established EXPSPACE-completeness. Bouajjani et al. [5] showed that the problem becomes undecidable once the number of concurrent operations is unbounded. Also, Bouajjani et al. [7,8] investigate various ADTs for which the problems of checking eventual and causal consistency are decidable.

7 Conclusion

We have developed the first completely-automatic algorithm for checking weak consistency of arbitrary concurrent object implementations which avoids the naïve enumeration of all possible visibility relations. While methodologies for constructing reliable yet weakly-consistent implementations are relatively immature, we believe that such implementations will continue to be important for the development of distributed and multicore software systems. Likewise, automation for testing and verifying such implementations is, and will increasingly be, important. Besides improving state-of-the-art verification algorithms, our results represent an important step for future research which may find other ways to exploit the soundness of considering only minimal visibilities, on which our optimized algorithm relies.

References

1. Abdulla, P.A., Haziza, F., Holík, L., Jonsson, B., Rezine, A.: An integrated specification and verification technique for highly concurrent data structures. In: Piterman, N., Smolka, S.A. (eds.) TACAS 2013. LNCS, vol. 7795, pp. 324–338. Springer, Heidelberg (2013). https://doi.org/10.1007/978-3-642-36742-7_23
2. Ahamad, M., Neiger, G., Burns, J.E., Kohli, P., Hutto, P.W.: Causal memory: definitions, implementation, and programming. Distrib. Comput. **9**(1), 37–49 (1995). https://doi.org/10.1007/BF01784241

3. Alur, R., McMillan, K.L., Peled, D.A.: Model-checking of correctness conditions for concurrent objects. Inf. Comput. **160**(1–2), 167–188 (2000). https://doi.org/10.1006/inco.1999.2847
4. Amit, D., Rinetzky, N., Reps, T., Sagiv, M., Yahav, E.: Comparison under abstraction for verifying linearizability. In: Damm, W., Hermanns, H. (eds.) CAV 2007. LNCS, vol. 4590, pp. 477–490. Springer, Heidelberg (2007). https://doi.org/10.1007/978-3-540-73368-3_49
5. Bouajjani, A., Emmi, M., Enea, C., Hamza, J.: Verifying concurrent programs against sequential specifications. In: Felleisen, M., Gardner, P. (eds.) ESOP 2013. LNCS, vol. 7792, pp. 290–309. Springer, Heidelberg (2013). https://doi.org/10.1007/978-3-642-37036-6_17
6. Bouajjani, A., Emmi, M., Enea, C., Hamza, J.: Tractable refinement checking for concurrent objects. In: Rajamani, S.K., Walker, D. (eds.) Proceedings of the 42nd Annual ACM SIGPLAN-SIGACT Symposium on Principles of Programming Languages, POPL 2015, 15–17 January 2015, Mumbai, India, pp. 651–662. ACM (2015). https://doi.org/10.1145/2676726.2677002
7. Bouajjani, A., Enea, C., Guerraoui, R., Hamza, J.: On verifying causal consistency. In: Castagna, G., Gordon, A.D. (eds.) Proceedings of the 44th ACM SIGPLAN Symposium on Principles of Programming Languages, POPL 2017, 18–20 January 2017, Paris, France, pp. 626–638. ACM (2017). http://dl.acm.org/citation.cfm?id=3009888
8. Bouajjani, A., Enea, C., Hamza, J.: Verifying eventual consistency of optimistic replication systems. In: Jagannathan, S., Sewell, P. (eds.) The 41st Annual ACM SIGPLAN-SIGACT Symposium on Principles of Programming Languages, POPL 2014, 20–21 January 2014, San Diego, CA, USA, pp. 285–296. ACM (2014). https://doi.org/10.1145/2535838.2535877
9. Burckhardt, S.: Principles of eventual consistency. Found. Trends Program. Lang. **1**(1–2), 1–150 (2014). https://doi.org/10.1561/2500000011
10. Burckhardt, S., Dern, C., Musuvathi, M., Tan, R.: Line-up: a complete and automatic linearizability checker. In: Zorn, B.G., Aiken, A. (eds.) Proceedings of the 2010 ACM SIGPLAN Conference on Programming Language Design and Implementation, PLDI 2010, 5–10 June 2010, Toronto, Ontario, Canada, pp. 330–340. ACM (2010). https://doi.org/10.1145/1806596.1806634
11. Burckhardt, S., Gotsman, A., Yang, H., Zawirski, M.: Replicated data types: specification, verification, optimality. In: Jagannathan, S., Sewell, P. (eds.) The 41st Annual ACM SIGPLAN-SIGACT Symposium on Principles of Programming Languages, POPL 2014, 20–21 January 2014, San Diego, CA, USA, pp. 271–284. ACM (2014). https://doi.org/10.1145/2535838.2535848
12. Dodds, M., Haas, A., Kirsch, C.M.: A scalable, correct time-stamped stack. In: Rajamani, S.K., Walker, D. (eds.) Proceedings of the 42nd Annual ACM SIGPLAN-SIGACT Symposium on Principles of Programming Languages, POPL 2015, 15–17 January 2015, Mumbai, India, pp. 233–246. ACM (2015). https://doi.org/10.1145/2676726.2676963
13. Drăgoi, C., Gupta, A., Henzinger, T.A.: Automatic linearizability proofs of concurrent objects with cooperating updates. In: Sharygina, N., Veith, H. (eds.) CAV 2013. LNCS, vol. 8044, pp. 174–190. Springer, Heidelberg (2013). https://doi.org/10.1007/978-3-642-39799-8_11
14. Emmi, M., Enea, C.: Exposing non-atomic methods of concurrent objects. CoRR abs/1706.09305 (2017). http://arxiv.org/abs/1706.09305

15. Emmi, M., Enea, C.: Sound, complete, and tractable linearizability monitoring for concurrent collections. PACMPL **2**(POPL), 25:1–25:27 (2018). https://doi.org/10.1145/3158113
16. Emmi, M., Enea, C., Hamza, J.: Monitoring refinement via symbolic reasoning. In: Grove, D., Blackburn, S. (eds.) Proceedings of the 36th ACM SIGPLAN Conference on Programming Language Design and Implementation, 15–17 June 2015, Portland, OR, USA, pp. 260–269. ACM (2015). https://doi.org/10.1145/2737924.2737983
17. Fischer, M.J., Lynch, N.A., Paterson, M.: Impossibility of distributed consensus with one faulty process. J. ACM **32**(2), 374–382 (1985). https://doi.org/10.1145/3149.214121
18. Gibbons, P.B., Korach, E.: Testing shared memories. SIAM J. Comput. **26**(4), 1208–1244 (1997). https://doi.org/10.1137/S0097539794279614
19. Gilbert, S., Lynch, N.A.: Brewer's conjecture and the feasibility of consistent, available, partition-tolerant web services. SIGACT News **33**(2), 51–59 (2002). https://doi.org/10.1145/564585.564601
20. Hamza, J.: On the complexity of linearizability. In: Bouajjani, A., Fauconnier, H. (eds.) NETYS 2015. LNCS, vol. 9466, pp. 308–321. Springer, Cham (2015). https://doi.org/10.1007/978-3-319-26850-7_21
21. Henzinger, T.A., Sezgin, A., Vafeiadis, V.: Aspect-oriented linearizability proofs. In: D'Argenio, P.R., Melgratti, H. (eds.) CONCUR 2013. LNCS, vol. 8052, pp. 242–256. Springer, Heidelberg (2013). https://doi.org/10.1007/978-3-642-40184-8_18
22. Herlihy, M., Wing, J.M.: Linearizability: a correctness condition for concurrent objects. ACM Trans. Program. Lang. Syst. **12**(3), 463–492 (1990). https://doi.org/10.1145/78969.78972
23. Kawell Jr., L., Beckhardt, S., Halvorsen, T., Ozzie, R., Greif, I.: Replicated document management in a group communication system. In: Proceedings of the 1988 ACM Conference on Computer-Supported Cooperative Work, p. 395. CSCW 1988. ACM, New York (1988). https://doi.org/10.1145/62266.1024798
24. Khyzha, A., Gotsman, A., Parkinson, M.: A generic logic for proving linearizability. In: Fitzgerald, J., Heitmeyer, C., Gnesi, S., Philippou, A. (eds.) FM 2016. LNCS, vol. 9995, pp. 426–443. Springer, Cham (2016). https://doi.org/10.1007/978-3-319-48989-6_26
25. Lamport, L.: Time, clocks, and the ordering of events in a distributed system. Commun. ACM **21**(7), 558–565 (1978). https://doi.org/10.1145/359545.359563
26. Liang, H., Feng, X.: Modular verification of linearizability with non-fixed linearization points. In: Boehm, H., Flanagan, C. (eds.) ACM SIGPLAN Conference on Programming Language Design and Implementation, PLDI 2013, 16–19 June 2013, Seattle, WA, USA, pp. 459–470. ACM (2013). https://doi.org/10.1145/2462156.2462189
27. Liu, Y., Chen, W., Liu, Y.A., Sun, J.: Model checking linearizability via refinement. In: Cavalcanti, A., Dams, D.R. (eds.) FM 2009. LNCS, vol. 5850, pp. 321–337. Springer, Heidelberg (2009). https://doi.org/10.1007/978-3-642-05089-3_21
28. Lloyd, W., Freedman, M.J., Kaminsky, M., Andersen, D.G.: Don't settle for eventual: scalable causal consistency for wide-area storage with COPS. In: Wobber, T., Druschel, P. (eds.) Proceedings of the 23rd ACM Symposium on Operating Systems Principles 2011, SOSP 2011, 23–26 October 2011, Cascais, Portugal, pp. 401–416. ACM (2011). https://doi.org/10.1145/2043556.2043593
29. Lowe, G.: Testing for linearizability. Concurr. Comput.: Pract. Exp. **29**(4) (2017). https://doi.org/10.1002/cpe.3928

30. O'Hearn, P.W., Rinetzky, N., Vechev, M.T., Yahav, E., Yorsh, G.: Verifying linearizability with hindsight. In: Richa, A.W., Guerraoui, R. (eds.) Proceedings of the 29th Annual ACM Symposium on Principles of Distributed Computing, PODC 2010, 25–28 July 2010, Zurich, Switzerland, pp. 85–94. ACM (2010). https://doi.org/10.1145/1835698.1835722
31. Schellhorn, G., Wehrheim, H., Derrick, J.: How to prove algorithms linearisable. In: Madhusudan, P., Seshia, S.A. (eds.) CAV 2012. LNCS, vol. 7358, pp. 243–259. Springer, Heidelberg (2012). https://doi.org/10.1007/978-3-642-31424-7_21
32. Sergey, I., Nanevski, A., Banerjee, A.: Mechanized verification of fine-grained concurrent programs. In: Grove, D., Blackburn, S. (eds.) Proceedings of the 36th ACM SIGPLAN Conference on Programming Language Design and Implementation, 15–17 June 2015, Portland, OR, USA, pp. 77–87. ACM (2015). https://doi.org/10.1145/2737924.2737964
33. Sergey, I., Nanevski, A., Banerjee, A.: Specifying and verifying concurrent algorithms with histories and subjectivity. In: Vitek, J. (ed.) ESOP 2015. LNCS, vol. 9032, pp. 333–358. Springer, Heidelberg (2015). https://doi.org/10.1007/978-3-662-46669-8_14
34. Shacham, O., Bronson, N.G., Aiken, A., Sagiv, M., Vechev, M.T., Yahav, E.: Testing atomicity of composed concurrent operations. In: Lopes, C.V., Fisher, K. (eds.) Proceedings of the 26th Annual ACM SIGPLAN Conference on Object-Oriented Programming, Systems, Languages, and Applications, OOPSLA 2011, part of SPLASH 2011, 22–27 October 2011, Portland, OR, USA, pp. 51–64. ACM (2011). https://doi.org/10.1145/2048066.2048073
35. Terry, D.B., Demers, A.J., Petersen, K., Spreitzer, M.J., Theimer, M.M., Welch, B.B.: Session guarantees for weakly consistent replicated data. In: Proceedings of the Third International Conference on on Parallel and Distributed Information Systems, PDIS 1994, pp. 140–150. IEEE Computer Society Press, Los Alamitos (1994). http://dl.acm.org/citation.cfm?id=381992.383631
36. Terry, D.B., Theimer, M., Petersen, K., Demers, A.J., Spreitzer, M., Hauser, C.: Managing update conflicts in bayou, a weakly connected replicated storage system. In: Jones, M.B. (ed.) Proceedings of the Fifteenth ACM Symposium on Operating System Principles, SOSP 1995, 3–6 December 1995, Copper Mountain Resort, Colorado, USA, pp. 172–183. ACM (1995). https://doi.org/10.1145/224056.224070
37. Vafeiadis, V.: Automatically proving linearizability. In: Touili, T., Cook, B., Jackson, P. (eds.) CAV 2010. LNCS, vol. 6174, pp. 450–464. Springer, Heidelberg (2010). https://doi.org/10.1007/978-3-642-14295-6_40
38. Wing, J.M., Gong, C.: Testing and verifying concurrent objects. J. Parallel Distrib. Comput. **17**(1–2), 164–182 (1993). https://doi.org/10.1006/jpdc.1993.1015
39. Zhang, S.J.: Scalable automatic linearizability checking. In: Taylor, R.N., Gall, H.C., Medvidovic, N. (eds.) Proceedings of the 33rd International Conference on Software Engineering, ICSE 2011, 21–28 May 2011, Waikiki, Honolulu, HI, USA, pp. 1185–1187. ACM (2011). https://doi.org/10.1145/1985793.1986037

Monitoring CTMCs by Multi-clock Timed Automata

Yijun Feng[1], Joost-Pieter Katoen[2(✉)], Haokun Li[1(✉)], Bican Xia[1(✉)], and Naijun Zhan[3,4(✉)]

[1] LMAM and School of Mathematical Sciences, Peking University, Beijing, China
ker@protonmail.ch, xbc@math.pku.edu.cn

[2] RWTH Aachen University, Aachen, Germany
katoen@cs.rwth-aachen.de

[3] State Key Laboratory of Computer Science, Institute of Software, Chinese Academy of Sciences, Beijing, China
znj@ios.ac.cn

[4] University of Chinese Academy of Sciences, Beijing, China

Abstract. This paper presents a numerical algorithm to verify continuous-time Markov chains (CTMCs) against multi-clock deterministic timed automata (DTA). These DTA allow for specifying properties that cannot be expressed in CSL, the logic for CTMCs used by state-of-the-art probabilistic model checkers. The core problem is to compute the probability of timed runs by the CTMC $\mathcal{C}$ that are accepted by the DTA $\mathcal{A}$. These likelihoods equal reachability probabilities in an embedded piecewise deterministic Markov process (EPDP) obtained as product of $\mathcal{C}$ and $\mathcal{A}$'s region automaton. This paper provides a numerical algorithm to efficiently solve the PDEs describing these reachability probabilities. The key insight is to solve an ordinary differential equation (ODE) that exploits the specific characteristics of the product EPDP. We provide the numerical precision of our algorithm and present experimental results with a prototypical implementation.

1 Introduction

Continuous-time Markov chains (CTMCs) [17] are ubiquitous. They are used to model safety-critical systems like communicating networks and power management systems, are key to performance and dependability analysis, and naturally describe chemical reaction networks. The algorithmic verification of CTMCs has received quite some attention. Aziz *et al.* [3] proved that verifying CTMCs against CSL (Continuous Stochastic Logic) is decidable. CSL is a probabilistic and timed branching-time logic that allows for expressing properties like "is the probability of a given chemical reaction within 50 time units at least 10^{-3}?". Baier *et al.* [5] gave efficient numerical algorithms for CSL model checking that nowadays provide the basis of CTMC model checking in PRISM [23], MRMC [22] and Storm [15], as well as GreatSPN [2]. Extensions of CSL to cascaded timed-until operators [27], conditional probabilities [19], and (simple) timed regular expressions [4] have been considered.

H. Chockler and G. Weissenbacher (Eds.): CAV 2018, LNCS 10981, pp. 507–526, 2018.
https://doi.org/10.1007/978-3-319-96145-3_27

This paper considers the verification of CTMCs against *linear-time* real-time properties. These include relevant properties in the design of a gas burner [28], like "the probability that the duration of leaking is more than one twentieth over an interval with a length more than 20 s is less than 10^{-6}". Such real-time properties can be conveniently expressed by deterministic timed automata (DTA) [1]. The core problem in the verification of CTMC $\mathcal{C}$ against DTA $\mathcal{A}$ is to compute the probability of $\mathcal{C}$'s timed runs that are accepted by $\mathcal{A}$, i.e. $\Pr(\mathcal{C} \models \mathcal{A})$. Chen *et al.* [10,11] showed that this quantity equals the reachability probability in a piecewise deterministic Markov process (PDP) [14]. This PDP is obtained by taking the product of CTMC $\mathcal{C}$ and the region automaton of $\mathcal{A}$. Computing reachability probabilities in PDPs is a challenge.

Practical implementations of verifying CTMCs against DTA specifications are rare. Barbot *et al.* [7] showed that for *single-clock* DTA, the PDP is in fact a Markov regenerative process. (This observation is also at the heart of model-checking CSL^{TA} [16].) This implies that for single-clock DTA, off-the-shelf CSL model-checking algorithms can be employed resulting in an efficient procedure [7]. Mikeev *et al.* [24] generalised these ideas to infinite-state CTMCs obtained from stoichiometric equations, whereas Chen *et al.* [12] showed the theory to generalize verifying single-clock DTA to continuous-time Markov decision processes.

Multi-clock DTA are however much harder to handle. The characterisation of PDP reachability probabilities as the unique solution of a set of partial differential equations (PDEs) [10,11] does not give insight into an efficient computational procedure. With the notable exception of [25], verifying PDPs has not been considered. Fu [18] provided an algorithm to approximate the probabilities using finite difference methods and gave an error bound. This method hampers scalability and therefore was never implemented. The same holds for model-checking using other linear-time real-time formalisms such as MTL and timed automata [9], linear duration invariants [8], and probabilistic duration calculus [13]. All these multi-clock approaches suffer from scalability issues due to the low efficiency of solving PDEs and/or integral equations on which they heavily depend.

This paper presents a numerical technique to approximate the reachability probability in the product PDP. The DTA $\mathcal{A}$ is approximated by DTA $\mathcal{A}[t_f]$ which extends $\mathcal{A}$ with an additional clock that is never reset and that needs to be at most t_f when accepting. By increasing the time-bound t_f, DTA $\mathcal{A}[t_f]$ approximates $\mathcal{A}$ arbitrarily closely. We show that the set of PDPs characterizing the reachability probability in the embedded PDP of $\mathcal{C}$ and $\mathcal{A}[t_f]$ can be reduced to solving an ordinary differential equation (ODE). The specific characteristics of the product EPDP, in particular the fact that all clocks run at the same pace, are key to obtain these ODEs. Our numerical algorithm to solve the ODEs is based on computing the approximations in a backward manner using t_f and the sum of all clocks. The complexity of the resulting procedure is linear in the EPDP size, and exponential in $\lceil \frac{t_f}{\delta} \rceil$ where δ is the discretization step size. We show the approximations converges to the real solution of the ODEs at a linear speed of δ. Using a prototypical tool implementation we present some results on a number of case studies such as robot navigation with varying number of clocks in their specification. The experimental results show promising results for checking CTMCs against multi-clock DTA.

Organization of the Paper. Section 2 introduces basic notions including CTMCs, DTA, and PDPs. Section 3 presents the product of a CTMC and the region graph of a DTA and shows this is an embedded PDP. Section 4 derives the PDE (fixing some flaw in [10]), the reduction to the set of ODEs and presents the numerical algorithm to solve these ODEs. Section 5 presents the experimental results and Sect. 6 concludes.

2 Preliminaries

In this section, we introduce some basic notions which will be used later.

A probability space is denoted by a triple $(\Omega, \mathcal{F}, Pr)$, where Ω is a set of samples, $\mathcal{F}$ is a σ-algebra over Ω, and $Pr : \mathcal{F} \to [0,1]$ is a probability measure on $\mathcal{F}$ with $Pr(\Omega) = 1$. Let $\mathbb{P}_r(\Omega)$ denote the set of all probability measures over Ω. For a random variable X on the probability space, its expectation is denoted by $\mathbb{E}(X)$.

2.1 Continuous-Time Markov Chain (CTMC)

Definition 1 (CTMC). *A CTMC is a tuple $\mathcal{C} = (S, \mathbf{P}, \alpha, AP, L, E)$, where*

- *S is a finite set of states;*
- *$\mathbf{P}$: $S \times S \to [0,1]$ is the transition probability function, which is identified with the matrix $\mathbf{P} \in [0,1]^{|S|\times|S|}$ such that $\sum_{t\in S} \mathbf{P}(s,t) = 1$, for all $s \in S$;*
- *$\alpha \in \mathbb{P}_r(S)$ is the initial distribution;*
- *AP is a finite set of atomic propositions;*
- *$L : S \to 2^{AP}$ is a labeling function; and*
- *$E : S \to \mathbb{R}_{>0}$ is the exit rate function.*

We denote by $s \xrightarrow{t} s'$ a transition from state s to state s' after residing in state s for t time units. The probability of the occurrence of this transition within t time units is $\mathbf{P}(s,s') \int_0^t E(s) \exp^{-E(s)x}\, dx$, where $\int_0^t E(s) \exp^{-E(s)x}\, dx$ stands for the probability to leave state s in t time units, and $\mathbf{P}(s,s')$ for the probability to select the transition to s' from all transitions outgoing from s. A state s is called *absorbing* if $\mathbf{P}(s,s) = 1$. Given a CTMC $\mathcal{C}$, removing the exit rate function E results in a discrete-time Markov chain (DMTC), which is called *embedded* DTMC of $\mathcal{C}$. A CTMC $\mathcal{C}$ is called *irreducible* if there exists a unique stationary distribution α, such that $\alpha(s) > 0$ for all $s \in S$, and *weakly irreducible* if $\alpha(s)$ may be zero for some $s \in S$.

Definition 2 (CTMC Path). *Let $\mathcal{C}$ be a CTMC, a path ρ of $\mathcal{C}$ starting form s_0 with length n is a sequence $\rho = s_0 \xrightarrow{t_0} s_1 \xrightarrow{t_1} \dots \xrightarrow{t_{n-1}} s_n \in S \times (\mathbb{R}_{>0} \times S)^n$. The* *set of paths in* $\mathcal{C}$ *with length* n *is denoted by* $Path_n^{\mathcal{C}}$*; the set of all finite paths of* $\mathcal{C}$ *is* $Path_{fin}^{\mathcal{C}} = \cup_n Path_n^{\mathcal{C}}$ *and the set of infinite paths of* $\mathcal{C}$ *is* $Path_{inf}^{\mathcal{C}} = (S \times \mathbb{R}_{>0})^{\omega}$*. We use* $Path^{\mathcal{C}} = Path_{fin}^{\mathcal{C}} \cup Path_{inf}^{\mathcal{C}}$ *to denote all paths in* $\mathcal{C}$*. As a convention,* ε *stands for the empty path.*

Note that we assume the time to exit a state is strictly greater than 0. For an infinite path ρ, we use *Pref*(ρ) to denote the set of its finite prefixes. For a (finite or infinite) path ρ with prefix $s_0 \xrightarrow{t_0} s_1 \xrightarrow{t_1} \ldots$, the trace of the path is the sequence of states *trace*$(\rho) = s_0 s_1 \ldots$. Let $\rho(n) = s_n$ be the n-th state in the path and $\rho[n] = t_n$ be the corresponding exit time for s_n. For a finite path $\rho = s_0 \xrightarrow{t_0} s_1 \xrightarrow{t_1} \ldots \xrightarrow{t_{n-1}} s_n$, we use $T(\rho) = \sum_{i=0}^{n-1} t_i$ to denote the total time spent on this path if $n \geq 1$, otherwise $T(\rho) = 0$. For a time $t \leq T(\rho)$, $\rho(0 \ldots t)$ denotes the prefix of ρ within t time units, i.e., $s_0 \xrightarrow{t_0} s_1 \xrightarrow{t_1} \ldots \xrightarrow{t_{m-1}} s_m$ if there exists some $m \leq n$ with $\sum_{i=0}^{m-1} \rho[m] \leq t \wedge \sum_{i=0}^{m} \rho[m] > t$, otherwise ε.

A basic cylinder set $C(s_0, I_0, \cdots, I_{n-1}, s_n)$ consists of all paths $\rho \in Path^{\mathcal{C}}$ such that $\rho(i) = s_i$ for $0 \leq i \leq n$, and $\rho[i] \in I_i$ for $0 \leq i < n$. Then the σ−algebra $\mathcal{F}_{s_0}(\mathcal{C})$ associated with CTMC $\mathcal{C}$ and initial state s_0 is the smallest σ−algebra that contains all cylinder sets $C(s_0, I_0, \cdots, I_{n-1}, s_n)$ with $\alpha(s_0) > 0$, and $\mathbf{P}(s_i, s_{i+1}) > 0$, for $1 \leq i \leq n$, and $I_0, \ldots, I_{n-1}$ are non-empty intervals in $\mathbb{R}_{\geq 0}$. There is a unique probability measure $Pr^{\mathcal{C}}$ on the σ−algebra $\mathcal{F}_{s_0}(\mathcal{C})$, by which the probability for a cylinder set is given by

$$Pr^{\mathcal{C}}(C(s_0, I_0, \cdots, I_n, s_n)) = \alpha(s_0) \cdot \prod_{i=1}^{n} \int_{I_i} E(s_{i-1}) \exp^{-E(s_{i-1})x} dx \cdot \mathbf{P}(s_{i-1}, s_i)$$

Example 1. An example of CTMC is shown in Fig. 1, with $AP = \{a, b, c\}$ and initial state s_0. The exit rate r_i, $i = 0, 1, 2, 3$ and transition probability are shown in the figure.

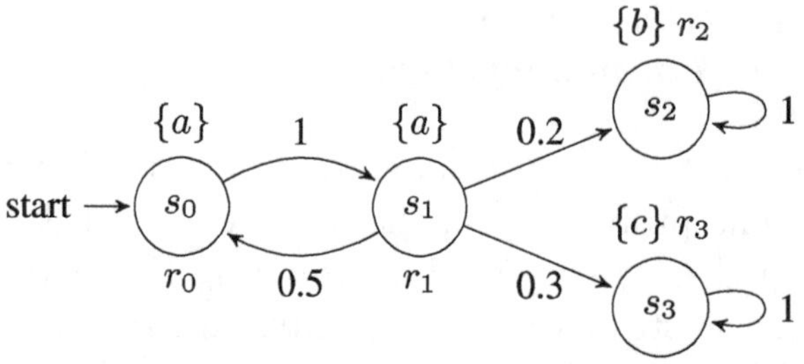

Fig. 1. An example of CTMC

2.2 Deterministic Timed Automaton (DTA)

A timed automaton is a finite state graph equipped with a finite set of non-negative real-valued clock variables, or clocks for short. Clocks can only be reset to zero, or proceed with rate 1 as time progresses independently. Let $\mathcal{X} = \{x_1, \ldots, x_n\}$ be a set of clocks. $\eta(x) : \mathcal{X} \to \mathbb{R}_{\geq 0}$ is a $\mathcal{X}$-valuation which records the amount of time since its last reset. Let $Val(\mathcal{A})$ be the set of all clock valuations of $\mathcal{A}$. For a subset $X \subseteq \mathcal{X}$, the reset of X, denoted as $\eta[X := 0]$, is the valuation η' such that $\eta'(x) = 0, \forall x \in X$, and $\eta'(x) = \eta(x)$, otherwise. For $d \in \mathbb{R}_{>0}$, $(\eta + d)(x) = \eta(x) + d$ for any clock $x \in \mathcal{X}$.

A clock constraint over $\mathcal{X}$ is a formula with the following form

$$g := x < c \mid x \leq c \mid x > c \mid x \geq c \mid x - y \geq c \mid g \wedge g,$$

where x, y are clocks, $c \in \mathbb{N}$. Let $Con(\mathcal{X})$ denote the set of clock constraints over $\mathcal{X}$. A valuation η satisfies a guard g, denoted as $\eta \models g$, iff $\eta(x) \bowtie c$ when g is $x \bowtie c$, where $\bowtie \in \{<, \leq, >, \geq\}$; and $\eta \models g_1$ and $\eta \models g_2$ iff $g = g_1 \wedge g_2$.

Definition 3 (DTA). *A DTA is a tuple* $\mathcal{A} = (\Sigma, \mathcal{X}, Q, q_0, Q_F, \hookrightarrow)$, *where*

- Σ *is a finite set of actions;*
- $\mathcal{X}$ *is a finite set of clocks;*
- Q *is a finite set of locations;*
- $q_0 \in Q$ *is the initial location;*
- $Q_F \subseteq Q$ *is the set of accepting locations;*
- $\hookrightarrow \in (Q \backslash Q_F) \times \Sigma \times Con(\mathcal{X}) \times 2^{\mathcal{X}} \times Q$ *is the transition relation, satisfying if* $q \xhookrightarrow{a,g,X} q'$ *and* $q \xhookrightarrow{a,g',X'} q''$ *with* $q' \neq q''$ *then* $g \cap g' = \emptyset$.

Each transition relation, or edge, $q \hookrightarrow q'$ in $\mathcal{A}$ is endowed with (a, g, X), where $a \in \Sigma$ is an action, $g \in Con(\mathcal{X})$ is the guard of the transition, and $X \subseteq \mathcal{X}$ is a set of clocks, which should be reset to 0 after the transition. An intuitive interpretation of the transition is that $\mathcal{A}$ can move from q to q' by taking action a and resetting all clocks in X to be 0 only if g is satisfied. There are no outgoing transitions from any accepting location in Q_F.

A finite timed path of $\mathcal{A}$ is of the form $\theta = q_0 \xhookrightarrow{a_0,t_0} q_1 \xhookrightarrow{a_1,t_1} \ldots \xhookrightarrow{a_{n-1},t_{n-1}} q_n$, where $t_i \geq 0$, for $i = 0, \ldots, n-1$. Moreover, there exists a sequence of transitions $q_j \xhookrightarrow{a_j,g_j,X_j} q_{j+1}$, for $0 \leq j \leq n-1$, such that $\eta_0 = \mathbf{0}$, $\eta_j + t_j \models g_j$ and $\eta_{j+1} = \eta_j[X_j := 0]$, where η_k denotes the clock valuation when entering q_k. θ is said to be *accepted by* $\mathcal{A}$ if there exists a state $q_i \in Q_F$ for some $0 \leq i \leq n$. As normal, it is assumed all DTA are non-Zeno [6], that is any circular transition sequence takes nonzero dwelling time.

A region is a set of valuations, usually represented by a set of clock constraints. Let $Reg(\mathcal{X})$ be the set of regions over $\mathcal{X}$. Given $\Theta, \Theta' \in Reg(\mathcal{X})$, Θ' is called a *successor* of Θ if for all $\eta \models \Theta$, there exists $t > 0$ such that $\eta + t \models \Theta'$ and $\forall t' < t, \eta + t' \models \Theta \vee \Theta'$. A region Θ satisfies a guard g, denoted as $\Theta \models g$, iff $\forall \eta \models \Theta$ implies $\eta \models g$. The reset operation on a region Θ is defined as $\Theta[X := 0] = \{\eta[X := 0] \mid \eta \models \Theta\}$. Then the region graph, viewed as a quotient transition system related to clock equivalence [6] can be defined as follows:

Definition 4 (Region Graph). *The region graph for DTA* $\mathcal{A} = (\Sigma, \mathcal{X}, Q, q_0, Q_F, \hookrightarrow)$ *is a tuple* $\mathcal{G}(\mathcal{A}) = (\Sigma, \mathcal{X}, \overline{Q}, \overline{q_0}, \overline{Q_F}, \mapsto)$, *where*

- $\overline{Q} = Q \times Reg(\mathcal{X})$ *is the set of states;*
- $\overline{q_0} = (q_0, \mathbf{0}) \in \overline{Q}$ *is the initial state;*
- $\overline{Q_F} \subseteq Q_F \times Reg(\mathcal{X})$ *is the set of final states;*
- $\mapsto \subseteq \overline{Q} \times ((\Sigma \times 2^{\mathcal{X}}) \cup \{\lambda\}) \times \overline{Q}$ *is the transition relation satisfying*
  - $(q, \Theta) \overset{\lambda}{\mapsto} (q, \Theta')$ *if* Θ' *is a successor of* Θ*;*
  - $(q, \Theta) \xmapsto{a,X} (q', \Theta'')$ *if there exists* $g \in Con(\mathcal{X})$ *and transition* $q \xhookrightarrow{a,g,X} q'$ *such that* $\Theta \models g$ *and* $\Theta'' = \Theta[X := 0]$.

Example 2 (Adapted from [10]). Figure 2 presents an example of DTA and Fig. 3 gives its region graph, in which double circle and double rectangle stand for final states, respectively.

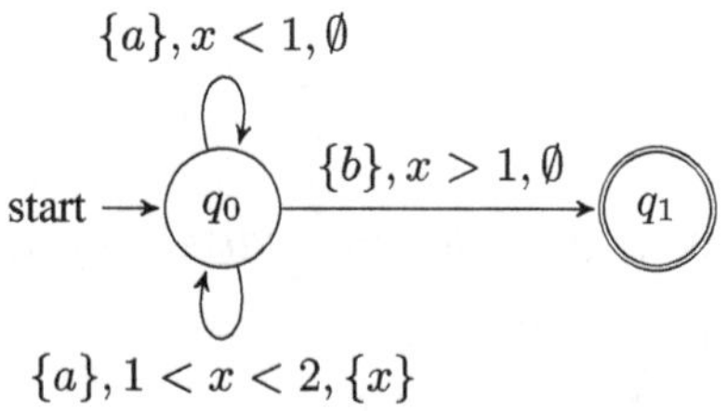

Fig. 2. A DTA $\mathcal{A}$

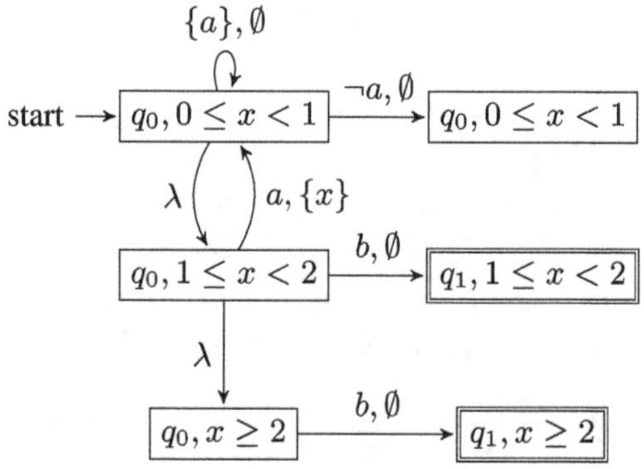

Fig. 3. The region graph of $\mathcal{A}$

2.3 Piecewise-Deterministic Markov Process (PDP)

Piecewise-deterministic Markov Processes (PDPs for short) [14] cover a wide range of stochastic models in which the randomness appears as discrete events at fixed or random times, whose evolution is deterministically governed by an ODE system between these times. A PDP consists of a mixture of deterministic motion and random jumps between a finite set of locations. During staying in a location, a PDP evolves deterministically following a flow function, which is a solution to an ODE system. A PDP can jump between locations either randomly, in which case the residence time of a location is governed by an exponential distribution, or when the location invariant is violated. The successor state of the jump follows a probability measure depending on the current state. A PDP is right-continuous and has the strong Markov property [14].

Definition 5 (PDP [14]). *A PDP is a tuple* $\mathcal{Q} = (Z, \mathcal{X}, Inv, \phi, \Lambda, \mu)$ *with*

- Z *is a finite set of locations;*
- $\mathcal{X}$ *is a finite set of variables;*
- $Inv : Z \to 2^{\mathbb{R}^{|\mathcal{X}|}}$ *is an invariant function;*

- $\phi : Z \times \mathbb{R}^{|\mathcal{X}|} \times \mathbb{R}_{\geq 0} \to \mathbb{R}^{|\mathcal{X}|}$, *is a flow function, which is a solution of a system of ODEs with Lipschitz continuous vector fields;*
- $\Lambda : \mathbb{S} \to \mathbb{R}_{>0}$ *is an exit rate function;*
- $\overline{\mathbb{S}} \to \mathbb{P}_r(\mathbb{S})$, *is the transition probability function, where* $\mathbb{S} = \{\xi := (z, \eta) \mid z \in Z, \eta \models Inv(z)\}$ *is the state space for* $\mathcal{Q}$, $\overline{\mathbb{S}}$ *is the closure of* $\mathbb{S}$, $\mathbb{S}^o = \{(z, \eta) \mid z \in Z, \eta \models Inv(z)^o\}$ *is the interior of* $\mathbb{S}$, *in which* $Inv(z)^o$ *stands for the interior of* $Inv(z)$, *and* $\partial\mathbb{S} = \cup_{z \in Z}\{z\} \times \partial Inv(z)$ *is the boundary of* $\mathbb{S}$, *in which* $\partial Inv(z) = \overline{Inv(z)} \backslash Inv^o$ *and* $\overline{Inv(z)}$ *is the closure of* $Inv(z)$.

For any $\xi = (z, \eta) \in \mathbb{S}$, there is an $\delta(\xi) > 0$ such that $\Lambda(z, \phi(z, \eta, t))$ is integrable on $[0, \delta(\xi))$. $\mu(\xi)(A)$ is measurable for any $A \in \mathcal{F}(\mathbb{S})$, where $\mathcal{F}(\mathbb{S})$ is the smallest $\sigma-$algebra generated by $\{\bigcup_{z \in Z} z \times A_z | A_z \in \mathcal{F}(Inv(z))\}$ and $\mu(\xi)(\{\xi\}) = 0$.

There are two ways to take transitions between locations in PDP $\mathcal{Q}$. A PDP $\mathcal{Q}$ is allowed to stay in a current location z only if $Inv(z)$ is satisfied. During its residence, the valuation η evolves time-dependently according to the flow function. Let $\xi \oplus t = (z, \phi(z, \eta, t))$ be the successor state of $\xi = (z, \eta)$ after residing t time units in z. Thus, $\mathcal{Q}$ is piecewise-deterministic since its behavior is determined by the flow function ϕ in each location. In a state $\xi = (z, \eta)$ with $\eta \models Inv(z)^o$, the PDP $\mathcal{Q}$ can either evolve to a state $\xi' = \xi \oplus t$ by delaying t time units, or take a Markovian jump to $\xi'' = (z'', \eta'') \in \mathbb{S}$ with probability $\mu(\xi)(\{\xi''\})$. When $\eta \models \partial Inv(z)$, $\mathcal{Q}$ is forced to take a boundary jump to $\xi'' = (z'', \eta'') \in \mathbb{S}$ with probability $\mu(\xi)(\{\xi''\})$.

3 Reduction to the Reachability Probability of EPDP

As proved in [10], model-checking of a given CTMC $\mathcal{C}$ against a linear real-time property expressed by a DTA $\mathcal{A}$, i.e., determining $Pr(\mathcal{C} \models \mathcal{A})$, can be reduced to computing the reachability probability of the product of $\mathcal{C}$ and $\mathcal{G}(\mathcal{A})$. This can be further reduced to computing the reachability probability of the embedded PDP (EPDP) of the product. But how to efficiently compute the reachability probability of the EPDP still remains challenging, as existing approaches [7,10, 16] can only handle DTA with one clock. We will attack this challenge in this paper. For self-containedness, we reformulate the reduction reported in [10] in this section.

A path $\rho = s_0 \xrightarrow{t_0} s_1 \xrightarrow{t_1} \ldots$ of CTMC $\mathcal{C}$ is accepted by DTA $\mathcal{A}$ if $\hat{\rho} = q_0 \xhookrightarrow{L(s_0),t_0} q_1 \xhookrightarrow{L(s_1),t_1} \cdots \xhookrightarrow{L(s_{n-1}),t_{n-1}} q_n$ induced by some ρ's prefix is an accepting path of $\mathcal{A}$. Then $Pr(\mathcal{C} \models \mathcal{A}) = Pr\{\rho \in Path^{\mathcal{C}} \mid \rho \text{ is accepted by } \mathcal{A}\}$.

Definition 6 (Product Region Graph [7]**).** *The product of CTMC* $\mathcal{C} = (S, \mathbf{P}, \alpha, AP, L, E)$ *and the region graph of DTA* $\mathcal{G}(\mathcal{A}) = (\Sigma, \mathcal{X}, \overline{Q}, \overline{q_0}, \overline{Q_F}, \mapsto)$, *denoted by* $\mathcal{C} \otimes \mathcal{G}(\mathcal{A})$, *is a tuple* $(\mathcal{X}, V, \alpha', V_F, \rightharpoonup, \Lambda)$, *where*

- $V = S \times \overline{Q}$ *is the state space;*
- $\alpha'(s, \overline{q_0}) = \alpha(s)$ *is the initial distribution;*
- $V_F = S \times \overline{Q_F}$ *is the set of accepting states;*
- $\rightharpoonup \subseteq V \times (([0, 1] \times 2^{\mathcal{X}}) \cup \{\lambda\}) \times V$ *is the smallest relation satisfying*

- $(s, \overline{q}) \xrightarrow{\lambda} (s, \overline{q'})$ *(called* delay transition*), if* $\overline{q} \overset{\lambda}{\mapsto} \overline{q'}$;
- $(s, \overline{q}) \overset{p,X}{\longmapsto} (s'', \overline{q''})$ *(called* Markovian transition*), if* $\mathbf{P}(s, s'') = p, p > 0$ *and* $\overline{q} \overset{L(s),X}{\longmapsto} \overline{q''}$;

– $\Lambda : V \to \mathbb{R}_{>0}$ *is the exit rate function, where*

$$\Lambda(s, \overline{q}) = \begin{cases} E(s) & \text{if there exists a Markovian transition from } (s, \overline{q}) \\ 0 & \text{otherwise} \end{cases}$$

Remark 1. Note that the definition of region graph here is slightly different from the usual one in the sense that Markovian transitions starting from a boundary do not contribute to the reachability probability. Therefore we can merge the boundary into its unique delay successor.

Example 3 (Adapted from [10]*).* Figure 4 shows the product region graph of CTMC $\mathcal{C}$ in Example 1 and DTA $\mathcal{A}$ in Example 2. The graph can be split into three subgraphs in a column-wise manner, where all transitions within a subgraph are probabilistic, all transitions evolve to the next subgraph are delay transitions, and transitions with reset lead to a state in the first subgraph. For conciseness, the location v_9 stands for all nodes that may be reached by a Markovian transition yet cannot reach an accepting node.

Proposition 1 ([10]). *For CTMC* $\mathcal{C}$ *and DTA* $\mathcal{A}$, $Pr(\mathcal{C} \models \mathcal{A})$ *is measurable and*

$$Pr(\mathcal{C} \models \mathcal{A}) = Pr^{\mathcal{C} \otimes \mathcal{G}(\mathcal{A})}\{Path^{\mathcal{C} \otimes \mathcal{G}(\mathcal{A})}(\Diamond \overline{Q_F})\}.$$

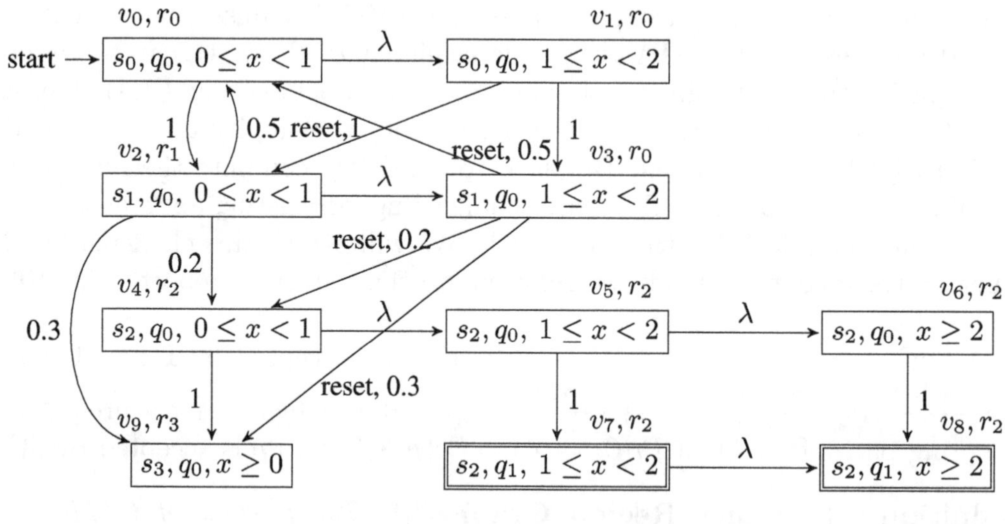

Fig. 4. Product region graph $\mathcal{C} \otimes \mathcal{G}(\mathcal{A})$ of CTMC $\mathcal{C}$ in Example 1 and DTA $\mathcal{A}$ in Example 2

When treated as a stochastic process, $\mathcal{C} \otimes \mathcal{G}(\mathcal{A})$ can be interpreted as a PDP. In this way, computing the reachability probability of Q_F in $\mathcal{C} \otimes \mathcal{G}(\mathcal{A})$ can be reduced to computing the time-unbounded reachability probability in the EPDP of $\mathcal{C} \otimes \mathcal{G}(\mathcal{A})$.

Definition 7 (EPDP, [7]). *Given $\mathcal{C} \otimes \mathcal{G}(\mathcal{A}) = (\mathcal{X}, V, \alpha', V_F, \rightharpoonup, \Lambda)$, the EPDP $\mathcal{Q}^{\mathcal{C}\otimes\mathcal{A}}$ is a tuple $(\mathcal{X}, V, Inv, \phi, \Lambda, \mu)$ where for any $v = (s, (q, \Theta)) \in V$*

- $Inv(v) = \Theta$, $\mathbb{S} = \{(v, \boldsymbol{\eta}) \mid v \in V, \boldsymbol{\eta} \models Inv(v)\}$ *is the state space;*
- $\phi(v, \boldsymbol{\eta}, t) = \boldsymbol{\eta} + t$ *for* $\boldsymbol{\eta} \models Inv(v)$*;*
- $\Lambda(v, \eta) = \Lambda(v)$ *is the exit rate of* (v, η)*;*
- Boundary jump: *for each delay transition* $v \xrightharpoonup{\lambda} v'$ *in* $\mathcal{C} \otimes \mathcal{G}(\mathcal{A})$, $\mu(\xi, \{\xi'\}) = 1$ *whenever* $\xi = (v, \boldsymbol{\eta})$, $\xi' = (v', \boldsymbol{\eta})$ *and* $\boldsymbol{\eta} \models \partial Inv(v)$*;*
- Markovian transition jump: *for each Markovian transition* $v \xrightharpoonup{p,X} v''$ *in* $\mathcal{C} \otimes \mathcal{G}(\mathcal{A})$, $\mu(\xi, \{\xi''\}) = p$ *whenever* $\xi = (v, \boldsymbol{\eta})$, $\boldsymbol{\eta} \models Inv(v)$ *and* $\xi'' = (v'', \boldsymbol{\eta}[X := 0])$.

The flow function here describes that all clocks increase with a uniform rate (i.e., $\dot{x_1} = 1, \ldots, \dot{x_n} = 1$, or simply $\dot{\mathcal{X}} = 1$) at all locations. The original reachability problem is then reduced to the reachability probability of the set $\{(v, \boldsymbol{\eta}) \mid v \in V_F, \boldsymbol{\eta} \models Inv(v)\}$, given the initial state $(v_0, \mathbf{0})$ and the EPDP $\mathcal{Q}^{\mathcal{C}\otimes\mathcal{A}}$. Let $Pr_v^{\mathcal{Q}^{\mathcal{C}\otimes\mathcal{A}}}(\boldsymbol{\eta})$ stand for the probability to reach the final states $(V_F \times *)$ from $(v, \boldsymbol{\eta})$ in $\mathcal{Q}^{\mathcal{C}\otimes\mathcal{A}}$. Thus, $Pr_v^{\mathcal{Q}^{\mathcal{C}\otimes\mathcal{A}}}(\boldsymbol{\eta})$ can be computed recursively by

$$Pr_v^{\mathcal{Q}^{\mathcal{C}\otimes\mathcal{A}}}(\boldsymbol{\eta}) = \begin{cases} Pr_{v,\lambda}^{\mathcal{Q}^{\mathcal{C}\otimes\mathcal{A}}}(\boldsymbol{\eta}) + \sum_{v \xrightharpoonup{p,X} v'} Pr_{v,v'}^{\mathcal{Q}^{\mathcal{C}\otimes\mathcal{A}}}(\boldsymbol{\eta}) & \text{if } v \notin V_F \\ 1, & v \in V_F \wedge \boldsymbol{\eta} \models Inv(v) \\ 0, & \text{otherwise.} \end{cases} \quad (1)$$

Let $t_z^*(v, \boldsymbol{\eta})$ denote the minimal time for $\mathcal{Q}^{\mathcal{C}\otimes\mathcal{A}}$ to reach $\partial Inv(v)$ from $(v, \boldsymbol{\eta})$. More precisely,

$$t_z^*(v, \boldsymbol{\eta}) = \inf\{t \mid \phi(v, \boldsymbol{\eta}, t) \models Inv(v)\}.$$

$Pr_{v,\lambda}^{\mathcal{Q}^{\mathcal{C}\otimes\mathcal{A}}}(\boldsymbol{\eta})$ is the probability from (v, η) with a delay and then a forced jump to $(v', \eta + t_z^*(v, \boldsymbol{\eta}))$, onwards evolves to an accepting state, which can be recursively computed by

$$Pr_{v,\lambda}^{\mathcal{Q}^{\mathcal{C}\otimes\mathcal{A}}}(\boldsymbol{\eta}) = exp(-\Lambda(v) t_z^*(v, \boldsymbol{\eta})) \cdot Pr_{v'}^{\mathcal{Q}^{\mathcal{C}\otimes\mathcal{A}}}(\boldsymbol{\eta} + t_z^*(v, \boldsymbol{\eta})).$$

$Pr_{v,v'}^{\mathcal{Q}^{\mathcal{C}\otimes\mathcal{A}}}(\boldsymbol{\eta})$ is the probability that a Markovian transition $v \xrightharpoonup{p,X} v'$ happens within $t_z^*(v, \boldsymbol{\eta})$ time units, onwards involves to an accepted state, which can be recursively computed by

$$Pr_{v,v'}^{\mathcal{Q}^{\mathcal{C}\otimes\mathcal{A}}}(\boldsymbol{\eta}) = \int_0^{t_z^*(v,\eta)} p \cdot \Lambda(v) \exp(-\Lambda(v)s) \cdot Pr_{v'}^{\mathcal{Q}^{\mathcal{C}\otimes\mathcal{A}}}(\boldsymbol{\eta} + s[X := 0])\, ds.$$

$Pr(\mathcal{C} \models \mathcal{A})$ is reduced to compute $Pr_{v_0}^{\mathcal{Q}^{\mathcal{C}\otimes\mathcal{A}}}(\mathbf{0})$, equivalent to computing the least fixed point of the Eq. (1). That is,

Theorem 1. [10] *For CTMC $\mathcal{C}$ and DTA $\mathcal{A}$, $Pr(\mathcal{C} \models \mathcal{A}) = Pr^{\mathcal{C}\otimes\mathcal{A}}\{Path^{\mathcal{C}\otimes\mathcal{A}}(\Diamond \overline{Q_F})\}$ is the least fixed point of (1).*

Remark 2. Generally, it is difficult to solve a recursive equation like (1). As an alternative, we discuss the augmented EPDP of $\mathcal{Q}^{\mathcal{C}\otimes\mathcal{A}}$ by replacing $\mathcal{A}$ with a bounded DTA resulting from $\mathcal{A}$. As a consequence, using the extended generator of the augmented EPDP, we can induce a partial differential equation (PDE) whose solution is the reachability probability. We will elaborate the idea in the subsequent section.

4 Approximating the Reachability Probability of EPDP

In this section, we present a numerical method to approximate $Pr_{v_0}^{\mathcal{Q}^{\mathcal{C}\otimes\mathcal{A}}}(\mathbf{0})$, as we discussed previously that exactly computing is impossible, at least too expensive, in general. We will first introduce the basic idea of our approach in detail, then discuss its time complexity and convergence property. A key point is that our approach exploits the observation that the flow function of $\mathcal{Q}^{\mathcal{C}\otimes\mathcal{A}}$ is linear, only related to time t, and remains the same at all locations. This enables to reduce computing $Pr_{v_0}^{\mathcal{Q}^{\mathcal{C}\otimes\mathcal{A}}}(\mathbf{0})$ to solving an ODE system.

4.1 Reduction to a PDE System

In this subsection, we first show that $Pr_{v_0}^{\mathcal{Q}^{\mathcal{C}\otimes\mathcal{A}}}(\mathbf{0})$ can be approximated by that of the EPDP of $\mathcal{C}$ and a bounded DTA derived from $\mathcal{A}$, i.e., the length of all its paths is bounded. Then show that the latter can be reduced to solving a PDE system.

Given a DTA $\mathcal{A}$, we construct a bounded DTA $\mathcal{A}[t_f]$ by introducing a new clock y, adding a timing constraint $y < t_f$ to the guard of each transition of $\mathcal{A}$ ingoing to an accepting state in Q_F, and never resetting y, where $t_f \in \mathbb{N}$ is a parameter. So, the length of all accepting paths of $\mathcal{A}[t_f]$ is time-bounded by t_f. Obviously, $Path^{\mathcal{C}}(\mathcal{A}[t_f])$ is a subset of $Path^{\mathcal{C}}(\mathcal{A})$. As $Pr(\mathcal{C} \models \mathcal{A})$ is measurable and $\mathcal{Q}^{\mathcal{C}\otimes\mathcal{A}}$ is Borel right continuous, we have the following proposition.

Proposition 2. *Given a CTMC $\mathcal{C}$, a DTA $\mathcal{A}$, and $t_f \in \mathbb{N}$,*

$$\lim_{t_f\to\infty} Pr(\mathcal{C} \models \mathcal{A}[t_f]) = Pr(\mathcal{C} \models \mathcal{A}). \tag{2}$$

Moreover, if $\mathcal{C}$ is weakly irreducible or satisfies some conditions (please refer to Chap. 4 of [26] for details), then there exist positive constants $K, K_0 \in \mathbb{R}_{\geq 0}$ such that

$$Pr(\mathcal{C} \models \mathcal{A}) - Pr(\mathcal{C} \models \mathcal{A}[t_f]) \leq K \exp\{-K_0 t_f\}. \tag{3}$$

Remark 3. (2) was first observed in [7], thereof the authors pointed out the feasibility of using a bounded system to approximate the original unbounded system in order to simplify a verification obligation. (3) further indicates that such approximation is exponentially convergent w.r.t. $-t_f$ if the CTMC is weakly irreducible.

For a path starting in a state $(v, \boldsymbol{\eta})$ at time y, we use $Path^{y}_{(v,\boldsymbol{\eta})}[t]$ to denote the set of its locations at time t, and $\hbar_v(y, \boldsymbol{\eta}) = Pr(Path^{y}_{(v,\boldsymbol{\eta})}[t_f] \in V_F) = \mathbb{E}(\mathbf{1}_{Path^{y}_{(v,\boldsymbol{\eta})}[t_f]\in V_F})$ as the probability of a path reaching V_F within t_f time units, where $\mathbf{1}_{Path^{y}_{(v,\boldsymbol{\eta})}[t_f]\in V_F}$ is the indicator function of $Path^{y}_{(v,\boldsymbol{\eta})}[t_f] \in V_F$. Then, $\hbar_{v_0}(0, \mathbf{0}) = Pr(\mathcal{C} \models \mathcal{A}[t_f])$ is the probability to reach the set of accepting states from the initial state $(0, \mathbf{0})$, which satisfies the following system of PDEs.

Theorem 2. *Given a CTMC $\mathcal{C}$, a bounded DTA $\mathcal{A}[t_f]$, and the EPDP $\mathcal{Q}^{\mathcal{C}\otimes\mathcal{G}(\mathcal{A}[t_f])} = (\mathcal{X}, V, Inv, \phi, \Lambda, \mu)$, $\hbar_{v_0}(0, \mathbf{0})$ is the unique solution of the following system of PDEs:*

$$\frac{\partial \hbar_v(y, \boldsymbol{\eta})}{\partial y} + \sum_{i=1}^{|\mathcal{X}|} \frac{\partial \hbar_v(y, \boldsymbol{\eta})}{\partial \boldsymbol{\eta}^{(i)}} + \Lambda(v) \cdot \sum_{v \xrightarrow{p,X} v'} p \cdot (\hbar_{v'}(y, \boldsymbol{\eta}[X := 0]) - \hbar_v(y, \boldsymbol{\eta})) = 0, \quad (4)$$

where $v \in V \backslash V_F, \boldsymbol{\eta} \models Inv(v), \boldsymbol{\eta}^{(i)}$ is the i-th clock variable and $y \in [0, t_f)$. The boundary conditions are:

(i) $\hbar_v(y, \boldsymbol{\eta}) = \hbar_{v'}(y, \boldsymbol{\eta})$, for every $\boldsymbol{\eta} \models \partial Inv(v)$ and transition $v \xrightarrow{\lambda} v'$;
(ii) $\hbar_v(y, \boldsymbol{\eta}) = 1$, for every vertex $v \in V_F$, $\boldsymbol{\eta} \models Inv(v)$, and $y \in [0, t_f)$;
(iii) $\hbar_v(t_f, \boldsymbol{\eta}) = 0$, for every vertex $v \in V \backslash V_F$ and $\boldsymbol{\eta} \models Inv(v) \cup \partial Inv(v)$.

Remark 4. Note that the PDE system (4) in Theorem 2 is different from the one presented in [10] for reducing $Pr^{\mathcal{Q}^{\mathcal{C}\otimes\mathcal{A}}}_{v_0}(\mathbf{0})$. In particular, the boundary condition in [10] has been corrected here.

4.2 Reduction to an ODE System

There are several classical methods to solve PDEs. *Finite element method*, which is a numerical technique for solving PDEs as well as integral equations, is a prominent one, of which different versions have been established to solve different PDEs with specific properties. Other numerical methods include finite difference method and finite volume method and so on, the reader is referred to [20,21] for details. Thanks to the special form of the Eq. (4), we are able to obtain a numerical solution in a more efficient way.

The fact that the flow function (which is the solution to the ODE system$\bigwedge_{x\in\mathcal{X}} \dot{x} = 1 \wedge \dot{y} = 1$) is the same at all locations of the EPDP $\mathcal{Q}^{\mathcal{C}\otimes\mathcal{A}[t_f]}$ suggests that the partial derivatives of $\boldsymbol{\eta}$ and y in the left side of (4) evolve with the same pace. Thus, we can view all clocks as an array, and reformulate (4) as

$$\left[\frac{\partial \hbar_v(y, \boldsymbol{\eta})}{\partial y}, \frac{\partial \hbar_v(y, \boldsymbol{\eta})}{\partial \boldsymbol{\eta}^{(1)}}, \ldots, \frac{\partial \hbar_v(y, \boldsymbol{\eta})}{\partial \boldsymbol{\eta}^{(|\mathcal{X}|)}}\right] \bullet \mathbf{1} + \Lambda(v) \cdot \sum_{v \xrightarrow{p,X} v'} p \cdot (\hbar_{v'}(y, \boldsymbol{\eta}[X := 0]) - \hbar_v(y, \boldsymbol{\eta})) = 0, \quad (5)$$

where $\bullet$ stands for the inner product of two vectors of the same dimension, e.g., $(a_1, \ldots, a_n) \bullet (b_1, \ldots, b_n) = \sum_{i=1}^{n} a_i b_i$, and $\mathbf{1}$ for the vector $\overbrace{(1, \ldots, 1)}^{n \text{ times}}$.

By Theorem 2, there exist v_0, y_0 and η_0 such that $v_0 \in V_F$, $y_0 = t_f$, and $\boldsymbol{\eta}_0 \models \mathit{Inv}(v) \vee \partial \mathit{Inv}(v)$. Besides, by the definition of $\mathcal{Q}^{\mathcal{C} \otimes \mathcal{A}[t_f]}$, it follows $\frac{\partial z}{\partial t} = 1$, which implies $dz = dt$, for any $z \in \{y\} \cup \mathcal{X}$. Hence, we can simplify (5) as the following ODE system:

$$\frac{d\hbar_v((y_0, \boldsymbol{\eta}_0) + t)}{dt} + \Lambda(v) \cdot \sum_{v \xrightarrow{p,X} v'} p \cdot (\hbar_{v'}((y_0, \boldsymbol{\eta}_0) + t)[X := 0]) - \hbar_v(y_0, \boldsymbol{\eta}_0)) = 0, \quad (6)$$

with the initial condition $v_0 \in V_F$, $y_0 = t_f$, and $\boldsymbol{\eta}_0 \models \mathit{Inv}(v) \vee \partial \mathit{Inv}(v)$, where $v \in V \backslash V_F$. Note that we compute the reachability probability by (6) backwards.

4.3 Numerical Solution

Since $\hbar_v((y_0, \boldsymbol{\eta}_0) + t)$ satisfies an ODE equation, we can apply a discretization method to (6) and obtain an approximation efficiently. To this end, the remaining obstacle is how to deal with the reset part $\hbar_{v'}(y_0 + t, (\boldsymbol{\eta}_0 + t)[X := 0])$. Notice that $X \neq \emptyset \Rightarrow \mathrm{sum}((\boldsymbol{\eta}_0 + t)[X := 0]) + (t_f - y_0 - t)) < \mathrm{sum}(\boldsymbol{\eta}_0 + t) + (t_f - t_0 - t)$, where $\mathrm{sum}(\boldsymbol{\eta}) = \sum_{x \in \mathcal{X}} \boldsymbol{\eta}(x)$. So we just need to solve the ODE system starting from $(t_f, \boldsymbol{\eta}_0)$ using the descending order over $\mathrm{sum}(\boldsymbol{\eta})$ in a backward manner. In this way, all of the reset values needed for the current iteration have been computed in the previous iterations. Therefore for each iteration, the derivation is fixed and easy to calculate.

We denote by δ the length of discretization step, the number of total discretization steps is $\lceil \frac{t_f}{\delta} \rceil \in \mathbb{N}$. An approximate solution to (4) can be computed efficiently by the following algorithm.

Line 4 in Algorithm 1 computes a numerical solution to (6) on $[t_f - t, t_f]$ by discretizing $\frac{d\hbar_v((y_0, \boldsymbol{\eta}_0)+t)}{dt}$ with $\frac{1}{\delta}(\hbar_v((y_0, \boldsymbol{\eta}_0) + (t + \delta)) - \hbar_v((y_0, \boldsymbol{\eta}_0) + t))$. A pictorial illustration to Algorithm 1 for the two-dimensional setting is shown in Fig. 5. The blue polyhedron covers all the points we need to calculate. The algorithm starts from $(0, 0, t_f)$, where $\mathrm{sum}(\boldsymbol{\eta}) = x_1 + x_2 = 0$. Then $\mathrm{sum}(\boldsymbol{\eta})$ is incremented until $2t_f$ in a stepwise manner. For each fixed $\mathrm{sum}(\boldsymbol{\eta})$, for example $\mathrm{sum}(\boldsymbol{\eta}) = t_f$, the algorithm calculates all discrete points in the gray plane following the direction $(-1, -1, -1)$, and finally reaches the two reset lines. The red line reaching the origin provides the final result.

Algorithm 1. Finding numerical solution to (4)

Input: $\mathcal{C} \otimes \mathcal{G}(\mathcal{A})$, the region graph of the product of CTMC $\mathcal{C}$ and DTA $\mathcal{A}$; t_f, the time bound
Output: A numerical solution for $\hbar_{v_0}(0, \mathbf{0})$, an approximation of $Pr(\mathcal{C} \models \mathcal{A}[t_f])$

```
for n ← 0 to |X| · t_f by δ do
    for each η in {η' | sum(η') = n ∧ ∀i ∈ {1, ..., |X|} 0 ≤ η^(i) ≤ t_f} do
        for t from 0 down to − min(t_f, η) do
            Compute numerical solution to (6) with (y_0, η_0) = (t_f, η) on [t_f − t, t_f]
        end for
    end for
end for
return numerical solution for ħ_{v_0}(0, 0)
```

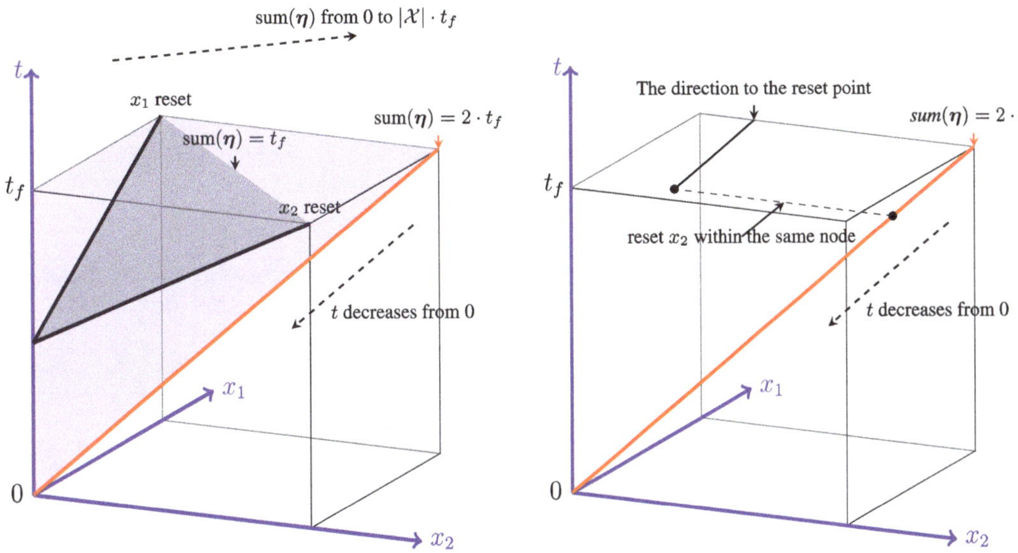

Fig. 5. Illustrating Algorithm 1 (left) and Algorithm 2 (right) for the 2-dimensional setting (Color figure online)

Example 4. Consider the product $\mathcal{C} \otimes \mathcal{G}(\mathcal{A})$ shown in Example 3 (in page 8). For state v_3 in which clock x is 1 and y is arbitrary, the corresponding PDE is

$$\frac{\partial \hbar_{v_3}(y,1)}{\partial y} + \frac{\partial \hbar_{v_3}(y,1)}{\partial x} + r_0[0.5 \cdot \hbar_{v_0}(y,0) + 0.2 \cdot \hbar_{v_4}(y,0) + 0.4 \cdot \hbar_{v_9}(y,0) - \hbar_{v_3}(y,0)] = 0.$$

Since $\text{sum}(y, 0) = y < y + 1 = \text{sum}(y, 1)$, the value for $\hbar_{v_0}(y, 0)$, $\hbar_{v_4}(y, 0)$ and $\hbar_{v_3}(y, 0)$ have been calculated in the previous iterations, thus the value for $\hbar_{v_3}(y, 1)$ can be computed.

To optimize Algorithm 1 for multi-clock objects, we exploit the idea of "lazy computation". In Algorithm 1, in order to determine the reset part for (6), we calculate all discretized points generated by all ODEs. The efficiency is influenced since the amount of ODEs is quite large (the same as the number of states in product automaton). However in Algorithm 2, we only compute the reset part that we need for computing $\hbar_{v_0}(0, \mathbf{0})$. If we meet a reset part $\hbar_v(y, \boldsymbol{\eta}[X := 0])$ which has not been decided yet, we suspend the equation we are computing now and switch to compute the equation leading to the undecided point following the direction of $(-1, \ldots, -1)$. The algorithm terminates since the number of points it computes is no more than that of Algorithm 1. A pseudo-code is described in Algorithm 2.

Algorithm 2. The lazy computation to find numerical solution to (4)

```
Input: C ⊗ G(A), the region graph of the product of CTMC C and DTA A; t_f, the time bound
Output: A numerical solution for ħ_v0(0, 0), an approximation of Pr(C ⊨ A[t_f])
Procedure dhv(y, η) //Computing numerical solution for (y, η)
  for t from 0 down to −min(t_f, η) by δ do
    for v ∈ V do
      Check if η satisfies initial and boundary condition from Theorem 2
      for each Markovian transition v --p,X--> v' do
        up = (−t − δ) · 1 + ((t + δ) · 1)[X := 0]
        if reset exists and η[X := 0] + up is undecided then
          call dhv(t_f, η[X := 0] + up)
        end if
        comput h_v
      end for
    end for
    execute λ−transition according to Theorem 2
    compute ħ_v((y_0, η_0) + t) by equation (6)
  end for
  mark η decided
End Procedure
  Call dhv(v_0, t_f, (t_f))
  return numerical solution for ħ_v0(0, 0)
```

4.4 Complexity Analysis

Let $|S|$ be the number of the states of the CTMC, and n the number of the clocks of the DTA. The worst-case time complexity of Algorithms 1 and 2 lies in $\mathcal{O}(|V| \cdot \lceil \frac{t_f}{\delta} \rceil^{(n+1)})$, where $|V|$ is the number of the equations in (4), i.e., the number of the locations in the product region graph, that are not accepting. The number of states in the region graph of the DTA is bounded by $n! \cdot 2^{n-1} \cdot \prod_{x \in \mathcal{X}}(c_x + 1)$, denoted by C_b, where c_x is the maximum constant occurring in the guards that constrain x. Note that C_b differs from the bound given in [1], since the boundaries of a region do not matter in our setting and hence can be merged into the region. Thus, the number of states in the product region graph, as well as the number of PDE equations in Theorem 2, is at most $C_b \cdot |S|$. So the total complexity is $\mathcal{O}(C_b \cdot |S| \cdot \lceil \frac{t_f}{\delta} \rceil^{(n+1)})$.

Let $\hbar_{v,n}(y_0, \boldsymbol{\eta}_0)$ denote the numerical solution to ODE (6) with $t = -n\delta$, and $\Lambda_{max} = \max\{\Lambda(v_i) \mid 0 \leq i \leq |S|\}$. Let $N = \lceil \frac{t_f}{\delta} \rceil$. By Proposition 2, $\lim_{t_f \to +\infty} \hbar_v(0, \mathbf{0}) = Pr(\mathcal{C} \models \mathcal{A})$ and $\hbar_v(0, \mathbf{0})$ is monotonically increasing for t_f. In the following proposition, for simplicity of discussion, we assume t_f equal to $N\delta$. Then, the error caused by discretization can be estimated as follows:

Proposition 3. *For $N \in \mathbb{N}^+$ and $\delta = \frac{t_f}{N}$,*

$$|\hbar_{v_0,N}(t_f, t_f \cdot \mathbf{1}) - \hbar_{v_0}(0, \mathbf{0})| = \mathcal{O}(\delta)$$

For function $f(\delta)$, f is of the magnitude $\mathcal{O}(\delta)$ if $\overline{\lim_{\delta \to 0}} \left|\frac{f(\delta)}{\delta}\right| = C$, where C is a constant. From Proposition 3, if we view $\Lambda_{\max}$ and t_f as constants, then the error is $\mathcal{O}(\delta)$ to the step length δ. By Proposition 2, the numerical solution generated by Algorithm 1 converges to the reachability probability of $\mathcal{C} \otimes \mathcal{A}$, and the error can be as small as we expect if we decrease the size of discretization δ, and increase the time bound t_f.

5 Experimental Results

We implemented a prototype including Algorithms 1 and 2 in C and a tool taking a CTMC $\mathcal{C}$ and a DTA $\mathcal{A}$ as input and generating a .c file to store their product in Python, which is used as an input to Algorithms 1 and 2. The first two examples (Examples 5 and 6) come from [10] to show the feasibility of our tool. The last case study is an example of robot navigation from [7]. In order to demonstrate the scalability of our approach, we revise the example with different real-time requirements, which require DTA with different number of clocks. The examples are executed in Linux 16.04 LTS with Intel(R) Core(TM) i7-4710HQ 2.50 GHz CPU and 16 G RAM. The column "time" reports the running time for Algorithm 1, and "time (lazy)" reports the running time for Algorithm 2. All time is counted in seconds.

Example 5. Consider Example 3 with $r_i = 1$, $i = 0, \ldots 3$ and $\delta = 0.01$, experimental result is shown in Table 1. The relevant error when $t_f = 30$ and $t_f = 40$ is 5×10^{-7}.

Table 1. The experimental results for Examples 5 and 6

t_f	Example 5			Example 6		
	$\hbar_{v_0}(0, \mathbf{0})$	time	time (lazy)	$\hbar_{v_0}(0, \mathbf{0})$	time	time (lazy)
20	0.110791	0.8070	0.7232	0.999999	0.1685	0.0002
30	0.110792	1.7246	1.6260	0.999999	0.3453	0.0003
40	0.110792	3.0344	2.8760	0.999999	0.6265	0.0003

Example 6. Consider the reachability probability for the product of a CTMC and a DTA as shown in Fig. 6. A part of its region graph is shown in Fig. 7. Set $r_0 = r_1 = 1$, $\delta = 0.1$, the experimental result is given in Table 1. The relevant error when $t_f = 30$ and $t_f = 40$ is 1×10^{-7}. Note that even for this simple example, none of existing tools can handle it.

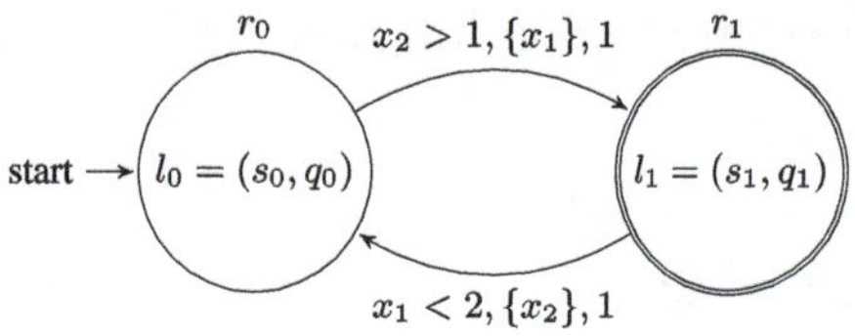

Fig. 6. The product automaton of Example 6

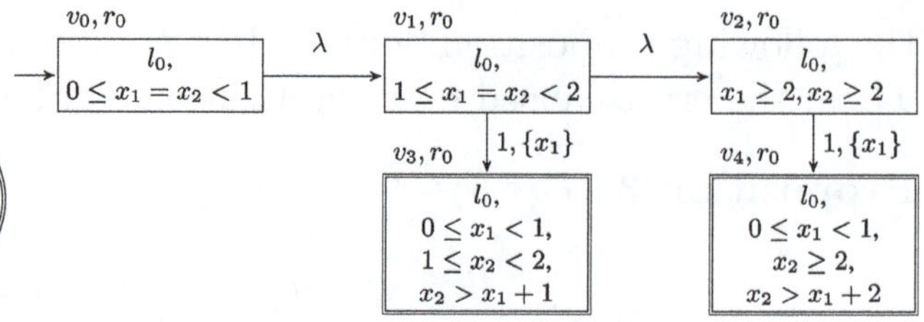

Fig. 7. The reachable product region graph of Fig. 6.

Example 7. Consider a robot moves on a $N \times N$ grid as shown in Fig. 8 (adapted from [7]). It can move up, down, left and right. For each possible direction, the robot moves with the same probability. The cells are grouped with A, B, C and D. We consider the following real-time constraints:

P_1: The robot is allowed to stay in adjacent C-cells for at most T_1 time units, and D-cells for at most T_2 time units;

P_2: The total time of the robot continuously resides in adjacent C-cell and D-cell is no more than T_3 time units, with $T_1 \le T_3$ and $T_2 \le T_3$;

P_3: The total time of the robot continuously resides in adjacent A-cell and C-cell is no more than T_4 time units, with $T_1 \le T_4$.

In this example, we are verifying whether the CTMC satisfies (i) P_1; (ii) $P_1 \wedge P_2$; (iii) $P_1 \wedge P_2 \wedge P_3$. Obviously, P_1 can be expressed by a DTA with one clock, see Fig. 9; to express $P_1 \wedge P_2$, a DTA with two clocks is necessary, see Fig. 10; to express $P_1 \wedge P_2 \wedge P_3$, A DTA with three clocks is necessary, see Fig. 11.

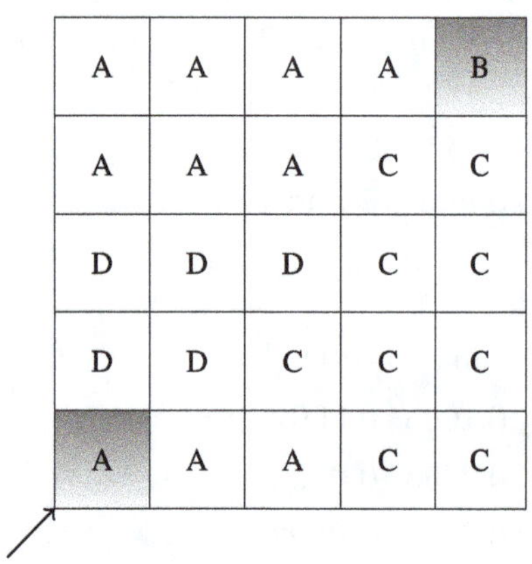

Fig. 8. An example grid

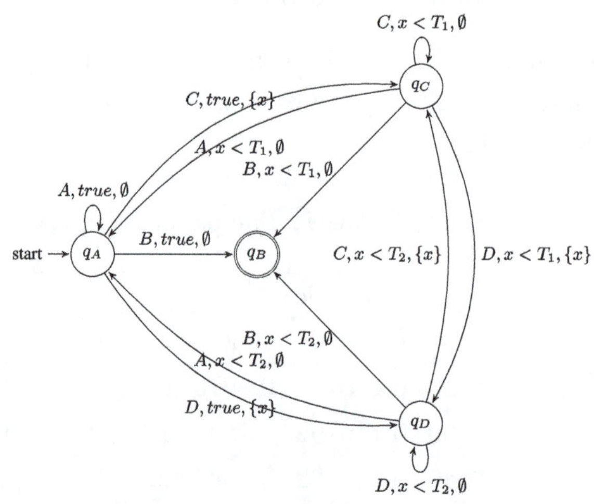

Fig. 9. A DTA with one clock for P_1

The experimental results are summarized in Table 2. The relevant error of $t_f = 20$ and $t_f = 21$ is smaller than 10^{-2}. As can be seen, the running time of our approach heavily depends on the number of clocks. Compared with the

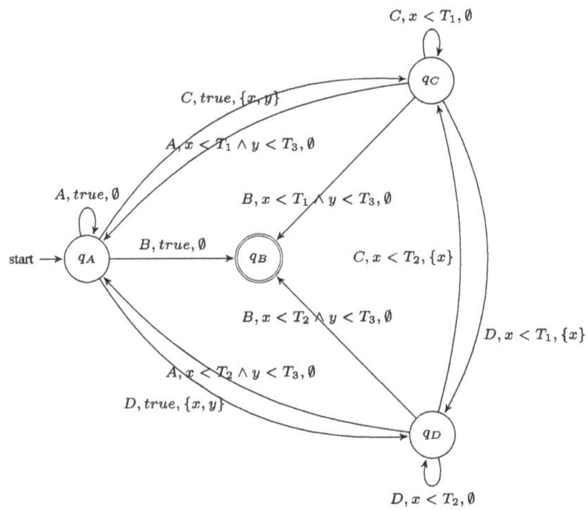

Fig. 10. A DTA with two clocks for $P_1 \wedge P_2$

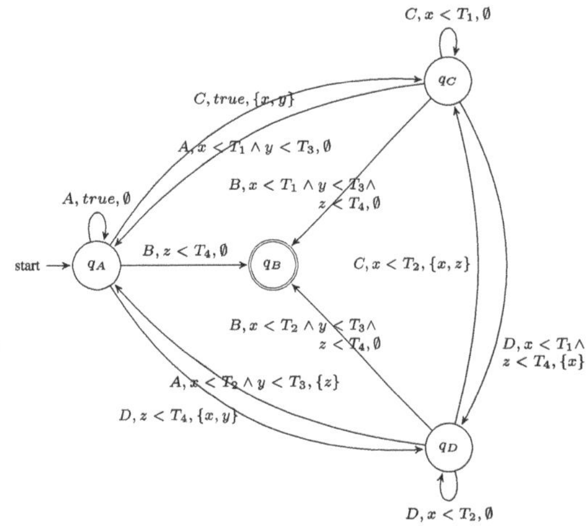

Fig. 11. A DTA with three clocks for $P_1 \wedge P_2 \wedge P_3$

Table 2. Experimental results for the robot example with $\delta = 0.1$, running time longer than 2700 s is denoted by 'TO' (timeout), the column "#(P)" counts the number of states in the product automaton $\mathcal{C} \otimes \mathcal{G}(\mathcal{A})$, "time([7])" is the running time of prototype in [7] when precision = 0.01, $T_1 = T_2 = 3$, $T_3 = 5$, $T_4 = 7$

		One clock				Two clocks			Three clocks		
N	t_f	#(P)	time	time (lazy)	time([7])	#(P)	time	time (lazy)	#(P)	time	time (lazy)
4	10	39	0.027	0.027	0.011	139	2.583	1.746	733	525.7	141.4
	15		0.049	0.043			7.117	3.445		TO	257.35
	20		0.070	0.071			12.88	5.49		TO	583.76
10	10	232	0.167	0.164	0.087	968	39.41	25.92	5134	TO	1039.7
	15		0.278	0.278			108.48	53.28		TO	TO
	20		0.417	0.421			226.56	89.50		TO	TO
20	10	940	1.142	0.909	1.23	4000	250.1	180.7		TO	TO
	15		1.65	1.54			672.8	375.6		TO	TO
	20		2.54	2.41			1326.8	616.1		TO	TO
30	10	2125	2.38	2.45	6.84	9120	812.9	380.5		TO	TO
	15		4.45	5.42			2058.1	770.8		TO	TO
	20		7.45	7.28			TO	1283.4		TO	TO
40	10	3820	5.62	6.52	20.31	16395	1484.3	759.8		TO	TO
	15		11.97	11.02			TO	1619.9		TO	TO
	20		15.26	16.17			TO	2661.3		TO	TO

results reported in [7] for the case of one clock in this case study (when the precision is set to be 10^{-2}), our result is as fast as theirs, but their tool cannot handle the cases of multiple clocks. In contrast, our approach can handle DTA with multiple clocks as indicated in the verification of P_2 and P_3. Algorithm 2 is much more faster than Algorithm 1 when the number of clocks grows up. To the best of our knowledge, this is the first prototypical tool verifying CTMCs against multi-clock DTA.

6 Concluding Remarks

In this paper, we present a practical approach to verify CTMCs against DTA objectives. First, the desired probability can be reduced to the reachability probability of the product region graph in the form of PDPs. Then we use the augmented PDP to approximate the reachability probability, in which the reachability probability coincides with the solution to a PDE system at the starting point. We further propose a numerical solution to the PDE system by reduction it to a ODE system. The experimental results indicate the efficiency and scalability compared with existing work, as it can handle DTA with multiple clocks.

As a future work, it deserves to investigate whether our approach also works in the verification of CTMCs against more complicated real-time properties, either expressed by timed automata and MTL as considered in [9], or by linear duration invariants as considered in [8].

Acknowledgements. This research is partly funded by the Sino-German Center for Research Promotion as part of the project CAP (GZ 1023), from Yijun Feng, Haokun Li and Bican Xia is partly funded by NSFC under grant No. 61732001 and 61532019, from Joost-Pieter Katoen is partly funded by the DFG Research Training Group 2236 UnRAVeL, from Naijun Zhan is funded partly by NSFC under grant No. 61625206 and 61732001, by "973 Program" under grant No. 2014CB340701 and by the CAS/SAFEA International Partnership Program for Creative Research Teams.

References

1. Alur, R., Dill, D.L.: A theory of timed automata. Theoret. Comput. Sci. **126**(2), 183–235 (1994)
2. Amparore, E.G., Beccuti, M., Donatelli, S.: (Stochastic) model checking in GreatSPN. In: Ciardo, G., Kindler, E. (eds.) PETRI NETS 2014. LNCS, vol. 8489, pp. 354–363. Springer, Cham (2014). https://doi.org/10.1007/978-3-319-07734-5_19
3. Aziz, A., Sanwal, K., Singhal, V., Brayton, R.: Model-checking continous-time Markov chains. ACM Trans. Comput. Log. **1**(1), 162–170 (2000)
4. Baier, C., Cloth, L., Haverkort, B.R., Kuntz, M., Siegle, M.: Model checking Markov chains with actions and state labels. IEEE Trans. Softw. Eng. **33**(4), 209–224 (2007)
5. Baier, C., Haverkort, B., Hermanns, H., Katoen, J.-P.: Model-checking algorithms for continuous-time Markov chains. IEEE Trans. Softw. Eng. **29**(6), 524–541 (2003)
6. Baier, C., Katoen, J.-P.: Principles of Model Checking. MIT Press, Cambridge (2008)
7. Barbot, B., Chen, T., Han, T., Katoen, J.-P., Mereacre, A.: Efficient CTMC model checking of linear real-time objectives. In: Abdulla, P.A., Leino, K.R.M. (eds.) TACAS 2011. LNCS, vol. 6605, pp. 128–142. Springer, Heidelberg (2011). https://doi.org/10.1007/978-3-642-19835-9_12

8. Chen, T., Diciolla, M., Kwiatkowska, M., Mereacre, A.: Verification of linear duration properties over continuous-time Markov chains. ACM Trans. Comput. Log. **14**(4), 33 (2013)
9. Chen, T., Diciolla, M., Kwiatkowska, M., Mereacre, A.: Time-bounded verification of CTMCs against real-time specifications. In: Fahrenberg, U., Tripakis, S. (eds.) FORMATS 2011. LNCS, vol. 6919, pp. 26–42. Springer, Heidelberg (2011). https://doi.org/10.1007/978-3-642-24310-3_4
10. Chen, T., Han, T., Katoen, J.-P., Mereacre, A.: Quantitative model checking of continuous-time Markov chains against timed automata specifications. In: LICS, pp. 309–318 (2009)
11. Chen, T., Han, T., Katoen, J., Mereacre, A.: Model checking of continuous-time Markov chains against timed automata specifications. Log. Methods Comput. Sci. **7**(1) (2011)
12. Chen, T., Han, T., Katoen, J.-P., Mereacre, A.: Observing continuous-time MDPs by 1-clock timed automata. In: Delzanno, G., Potapov, I. (eds.) RP 2011. LNCS, vol. 6945, pp. 2–25. Springer, Heidelberg (2011). https://doi.org/10.1007/978-3-642-24288-5_2
13. Dang, V.H., Zhou, C.: Probabilistic duration calculus for continuous time. Formal Aspects Comput. **11**(1), 21–44 (1999)
14. Davis, M.H.: Markov Models and Optimization, vol. 49. CRC Press, Boca Raton (1993)
15. Dehnert, C., Junges, S., Katoen, J.-P., Volk, M.: A Storm is coming: a modern probabilistic model checker. In: Majumdar, R., Kunčak, V. (eds.) CAV 2017. LNCS, vol. 10427, pp. 592–600. Springer, Cham (2017). https://doi.org/10.1007/978-3-319-63390-9_31
16. Donatelli, S., Haddad, S., Sproston, J.: Model checking timed and stochastic properties with $\mathrm{CSL}^{\mathit{TA}}$. IEEE Trans. Softw. Eng. **35**(2), 224–240 (2009)
17. Feller, W.: An Introduction to Probability Theory and Its Applications, vol. 3. Wiley, New York (1968)
18. Fu, H.: Approximating acceptance probabilities of CTMC-paths on multi-clock deterministic timed automata. In: HSCC, pp. 323–332. ACM (2013)
19. Gao, Y., Xu, M., Zhan, N., Zhang, L.: Model checking conditional CSL for continuous-time Markov chains. Inf. Process. Lett. **113**(1–2), 44–50 (2013)
20. Grossmann, C., Roos, H.-G., Stynes, M.: Numerical Treatment of Partial Differential Equations, vol. 154. Springer, Heidelberg (2007)
21. Johnson, C.: Numerical Solution of Partial Differential Equations by the Finite Element Method. Courier Corporation, Chelmsford (2012)
22. Katoen, J.-P., Zapreev, I.S., Hahn, E.M., Hermanns, H., Jansen, D.N.: The ins and outs of the probabilistic model checker MRMC. Perform. Eval. **68**(2), 90–104 (2011)
23. Kwiatkowska, M., Norman, G., Parker, D.: PRISM 4.0: verification of probabilistic real-time systems. In: Gopalakrishnan, G., Qadeer, S. (eds.) CAV 2011. LNCS, vol. 6806, pp. 585–591. Springer, Heidelberg (2011). https://doi.org/10.1007/978-3-642-22110-1_47
24. Mikeev, L., Neuhäußer, M.R., Spieler, D., Wolf, V.: On-the-fly verification and optimization of DTA-properties for large Markov chains. Formal Methods Syst. Des. **43**(2), 313–337 (2013)
25. Wisniewski, R., Sloth, C., Bujorianu, M.L., Piterman, N.: Safety verification of piecewise-deterministic Markov processes. In: HSCC, pp. 257–266. ACM (2016)

26. Yin, G.G., Zhang, Q.: Continuous-Time Markov Chains and Applications: A Two-Time-Scale Approach, vol. 37. Springer, New York (2012). https://doi.org/10.1007/978-1-4614-4346-9
27. Zhang, L., Jansen, D.N., Nielson, F., Hermanns, H.: Efficient CSL model checking using stratification. Log. Methods Comput. Sci. **8**(2:17), 1–18 (2012)
28. Zhou, C., Hoare, C.A.R., Ravn, A.P.: A calculus of durations. Inf. Process. Lett. **40**(5), 269–276 (1991)

Start Pruning When Time Gets Urgent: Partial Order Reduction for Timed Systems

Frederik M. Bønneland, Peter Gjøl Jensen, Kim Guldstrand Larsen, Marco Muñiz, and Jiří Srba(✉)

Department of Computer Science, Aalborg University, Aalborg, Denmark
{frederikb,pgj,kgl,muniz,srba}@cs.aau.dk

Abstract. Partial order reduction for timed systems is a challenging topic due to the dependencies among events induced by time acting as a global synchronization mechanism. So far, there has only been a limited success in finding practically applicable solutions yielding significant state space reductions. We suggest a working and efficient method to facilitate stubborn set reduction for timed systems with urgent behaviour. We first describe the framework in the general setting of timed labelled transition systems and then instantiate it to the case of timed-arc Petri nets. The basic idea is that we can employ classical untimed partial order reduction techniques as long as urgent behaviour is enforced. Our solution is implemented in the model checker TAPAAL and the feature is now broadly available to the users of the tool. By a series of larger case studies, we document the benefits of our method and its applicability to real-world scenarios.

1 Introduction

Partial order reduction techniques for untimed systems, introduced by Godefroid, Peled, and Valmari in the nineties (see e.g. [6]), have since long proved successful in combating the notorious state space explosion problem. For *timed* systems, the success of partial order reduction has been significantly challenged by the strong dependencies between events caused by time as a global synchronizer. Only recently—and moreover in combination with *approximate* abstraction techniques—stubborn set techniques have demonstrated a true reduction potential for systems modelled by timed automata [23].

We pursue an orthogonal solution to the current partial order approaches for timed systems and, based on a stubborn set reduction [28,39], we target a general class of timed systems with *urgent behaviour*. In a modular modelling approach for timed systems, urgency is needed to realistically model behaviour in a component that should be unobservable to other components [36]. Examples of such instantaneously evolving behaviours include, among others, cases like behaviour detection in a part of a sensor (whose duration is assumed to be

H. Chockler and G. Weissenbacher (Eds.): CAV 2018, LNCS 10981, pp. 527–546, 2018.
https://doi.org/10.1007/978-3-319-96145-3_28

negligible) or handling of release and completion of periodic tasks in a real-time operating system. We observe that focusing on the urgent part of the behaviour of a timed system allows us to exploit the full range of partial order reduction techniques already validated for untimed systems. This leads to an exact and broadly applicable reduction technique, which we shall demonstrate on a series of industrial case studies showing significant space and time reduction. In order to highlight the generality of the approach, we first describe our reduction technique in the setting of timed labelled transition systems. We shall then instantiate it to timed-arc Petri nets and implement and experimentally validate it in the model checker TAPAAL [19].

Let us now briefly introduce the model of timed-arc Peri nets and explain our reduction ideas. In timed-arc Petri nets, each token is associated with a nonnegative integer representing its age and input arcs to transitions contain intervals, restricting the ages of tokens available for transition firing (if an interval is missing, we assume the default interval $[0, \infty]$ that accepts all token ages). In Fig. 1a we present a simple monitoring system modelled as a timed-arc Petri net. The system consists of two identical sensors where sensor i, $i \in \{1, 2\}$, is represented by the places b_i and m_i, and the transitions s_i and r_i. Once a token of age 0 is placed into the place b_i, the sensor gets started by executing the transition s_i and moving the token from place b_i to m_i where the monitoring process starts. As the place b_i has an associated age invariant ≤ 0, meaning that all tokens in b_i must be of age at most 0, no time delay is allowed and the firing of s_i becomes urgent. In the monitoring place m_i we have to delay one time unit before the transition r_i reporting the reading of the sensor becomes enabled. Due to the age invariant ≤ 1 in the place m_i, we cannot wait longer than one time unit, after which r_i becomes also urgent.

The places c_1, c_2 and c_3 together with the transitions i_1, i_2 and t are used to control the initialization of the sensors. At the execution start, only the transition i_1 is enabled and because it is an urgent transition (denoted by the white circle), no delay is initially possible and i_1 must be fired immediately while removing the token of age 0 from c_1 and placing a new token of age 0 into c_2. At the same time, the first sensor gets started as i_1 also places a fresh token of age 0 into b_1. Now the control part of the net can decide to fire without any delay the transition i_2 and start the second sensor, or it can delay one unit of time after which i_2 becomes urgent due to the age invariant ≤ 1 as the token in c_2 is now of age 1. If i_2 is fired now, it will place a fresh token of age 0 into b_2. However, the token that is moved from c_2 to c_3 by the pair of transport arcs with the diamond-shaped arrow tips preserves its age 1, so now we have to wait precisely one more time unit before t becomes enabled. Moreover, before t can be fired, the places m_1 and m_2 must be empty as otherwise the firing of t is disabled due to inhibitor arcs with circle-shaped arrow tips.

In Fig. 1b we represent the reachable state space of the simple monitoring system where markings are represented using the notation like $c_3 : 1 + b_2 : 2$ that stands for one token of age 1 in place c_3 and one token of age 2 in place b_2. The dashed boxes represent the markings that can be avoided during the state space exploration when we apply our partial order reduction method for checking if

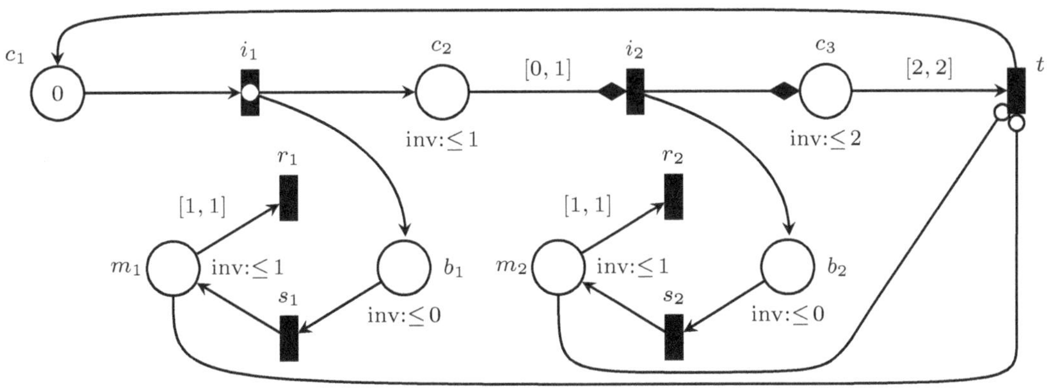

(a) TAPN model of a simple monitoring system

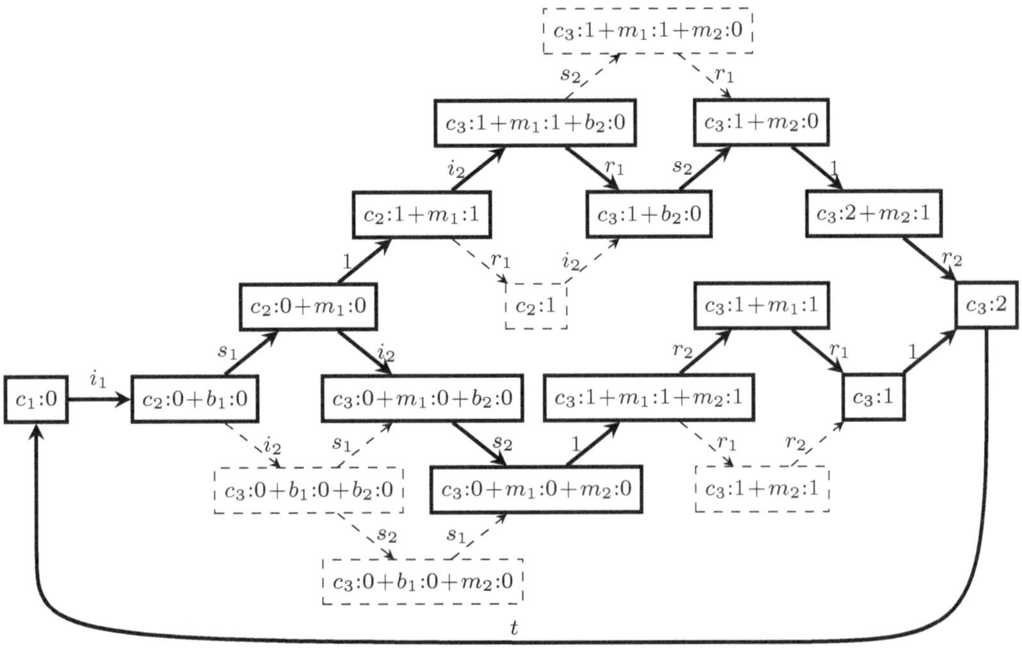

(b) Reachable state space generated by the net in Figure 1a

Fig. 1. Simple monitoring system

the termination transition t can become enabled from the initial marking. We can see that the partial order reduction is applied such that it preserves at least one path to all configurations where our goal is reached (transition t is enabled) and where time is not urgent anymore (i.e. to the configurations that allow the delay of 1 time unit). The basic idea of our approach is to apply the stubborn set reduction on the commutative diamonds where time is not allowed to elapse.

Related Work. Our stubborn set reduction is based on the work of Valmari et al. [28,39]. We formulate their stubborn set method in the abstract framework of labelled transition systems with time and add further axioms for time elapsing in order to guarantee preservation of the reachability properties.

For Petri nets, Yoneda and Schlingloff [41] apply a partial order reduction to one-safe time Petri nets, however, as claimed in [38], the method is mainly suitable for small to medium models due to a computational overhead, confirmed also in [29]. The experimental evaluation in [41] shows only one selected example. Sloan and Buy [38] try to improve on the efficiency of the method, at the expense of considering only a rather limited model of *simple time Petri nets* where each transition has a statically assigned duration. Lilius [29] suggests to instead use alternative semantics of timed Petri nets to remove the issues related to the global nature of time, allowing him to apply directly the untimed partial order approaches. However, the semantics is nonstandard and no experiments are reported. Another approach is by Virbitskaite and Pokozy [40], who apply a partial order method on the *region graph* of bounded time Petri nets. Region graphs are in general not an efficient method for state space representation and the method is demonstrated only on a small buffer example with no further experimental validation. Recently, partial order techniques were suggested by André et al. for parametric time Petri nets [5], however, the approach is working only for safe and acyclic nets. Boucheneb and Barkaoui [12–14] discuss a partial order reduction technique for timed Petri nets based on *contracted state class graphs* and present a few examples on a prototype implementation (the authors do not refer to any publicly available tool). Their method is different from ours as it aims at adding timing constrains to the independence relation, but it does not exploit urgent behaviour. Moreover, the models of time Petri nets and timed-arc Petri nets are, even on the simplest nets, incomparable due to the different way to modelling time.

The fact that we are still lacking a practically applicable method for the time Petri net model is documented by a missing implementation of the technique in leading tools for time Petri net model checking like TINA [9] and Romeo [22]. We are not aware of any work on partial order reduction technique for the class of timed-arc Petri nets that we consider in this paper. This is likely because this class of nets provides even more complex timing behaviour, as we consider unbounded nets where each token carries its timing information (and needs a separate clock to remember the timing), while in time Petri nets timing is associated only to a priory fixed number of transitions in the net.

In the setting of timed automata [3], early work on partial order reduction includes Bengtsson et al. [8] and Minea [32] where they introduce the notion of local as well as global clocks but provide no experimental evaluation. Dams et al. [18] introduce the notion of *covering* in order to generalize dependencies but also here no empirical evaluation is provided. Lugiez, Niebert et al. [30,34] study the notion of *event zones* (capturing time-durations between events) and use it to implement Mazurkiewicz-trace reductions. Salah et al. [37] introduce and implement an exact method based on merging zones resulting from different interleavings. The method achieves performance comparable with the approximate convex-hull abstraction which is by now superseded by the exact LU-abstraction [7]. Most recently, Hansen et al. [23] introduce a variant of stubborn sets for reducing an *abstracted zone graph*, thus in general offering overapproximate analysis. Our technique is orthogonal to the other approaches mentioned above; not only is the model different but also the application of our reduction gives exact results and is based on new reduction ideas. Finally, the idea of applying partial order reduction for independent events that happen at the same time appeared also in [15] where the authors, however, use a static method that declares actions as independent only if they do not communicate, do not emit signals and do not access any shared variables. Our realization of the method to the case of timed-arc Petri nets applies a dynamic (on-the-fly) reduction, while executing a detailed timing analysis that allows us to declare more transitions as independent—sometimes even in the case when they share resources.

2 Partial Order Reduction for Timed Systems

We shall now describe the general idea of our partial order reduction technique (based on stubborn sets [28,39]) in terms of timed transition systems. We consider real-time delays in the rest of this section, as these results are not specific only to discrete time semantics. Let A be a given set of actions such that $A \cap \mathbb{R}_{\geq 0} = \emptyset$ where $\mathbb{R}_{\geq 0}$ stands for the set of nonnegative real numbers.

Definition 1 (Timed Transition System). *A* timed transition system *is a tuple $(S, s_0, \rightarrow)$ where S is a set of states, $s_0 \in S$ is the initial state, and $\rightarrow \subseteq S \times (A \cup \mathbb{R}_{\geq 0}) \times S$ is the transition relation.*

If $(s, \alpha, s') \in \rightarrow$ we write $s \xrightarrow{\alpha} s'$. We implicitly assume that if $s \xrightarrow{0} s'$ then $s = s'$, i.e. zero time delays do not change the current state. The set of *enabled actions* at a state $s \in S$ is defined as $\mathsf{En}(s) \stackrel{\mathsf{def}}{=} \{a \in A \mid \exists s' \in S.\ s \xrightarrow{a} s'\}$. Given a sequence of actions $w = \alpha_1\alpha_2\alpha_3 \ldots \alpha_n \in (A \cup \mathbb{R}_{\geq 0})^*$ we write $s \xrightarrow{w} s'$ iff $s \xrightarrow{\alpha_1} \ldots \xrightarrow{\alpha_n} s'$. If there is a sequence w of length n such that $s \xrightarrow{w} s'$, we also write $s \rightarrow^n s'$. Finally, let $\rightarrow^*$ be the reflexive and transitive closure of the relation $\rightarrow$ such that $s \rightarrow s'$ iff there is $\alpha \in \mathbb{R}_{\geq 0} \cup A$ and $s \xrightarrow{\alpha} s'$.

For the rest of this section, we assume a fixed transition system $(S, s_0, \rightarrow)$ and a set of goal states $G \subseteq S$. The *reachability problem*, given a timed transition system $(S, s_0, \rightarrow)$ and a set of goal states G, is to decide whether there is $s' \in G$ such that $s_0 \rightarrow^* s'$.

We now develop the theoretical foundations of stubborn sets for timed transition systems. A state $s \in S$ is *zero time* if time can not elapse at s. We denote the zero time property of a state s by the predicate $\mathsf{zt}(s)$ and define it as $\mathsf{zt}(s)$ iff for all $s' \in S$ and all $d \in \mathbb{R}_{\geq 0}$ if $s \xrightarrow{d} s'$ then $d = 0$. A *reduction* of a timed transition system is a function $\mathsf{St} : S \rightarrow 2^A$. A reduction defines a reduced transition relation $\underset{\mathsf{St}}{\rightarrow} \subseteq \rightarrow$ such that $s \underset{\mathsf{St}}{\xrightarrow{\alpha}} s'$ iff $s \xrightarrow{\alpha} s'$ and $\alpha \in \mathsf{St}(s) \cup \mathbb{R}_{\geq 0}$. For a given state $s \in S$ we define $\overline{\mathsf{St}(s)} \stackrel{\mathsf{def}}{=} A \setminus \mathsf{St}(s)$ as the set of all actions that are not in $\mathsf{St}(s)$.

Definition 2 (Reachability Conditions). *A reduction* St *on a timed transition system $(S, s_0, \rightarrow)$ is* reachability preserving *if it satisfies the following four conditions.*

$(\mathcal{Z})$ $\forall s \in S.\ \neg \mathsf{zt}(s) \implies \mathsf{En}(s) \subseteq \mathsf{St}(s)$
$(\mathcal{D})$ $\forall s, s' \in S.\ \forall w \in \overline{\mathsf{St}(s)}^*.\ \mathsf{zt}(s) \wedge s \xrightarrow{w} s' \implies \mathsf{zt}(s')$
$(\mathcal{R})$ $\forall s, s' \in S.\ \forall w \in \overline{\mathsf{St}(s)}^*.\ \mathsf{zt}(s) \wedge s \xrightarrow{w} s' \wedge s \notin G \implies s' \notin G$
$(\mathcal{W})$ $\forall s, s' \in S.\ \forall w \in \overline{\mathsf{St}(s)}^*.\ \forall a \in \mathsf{St}(s).\ \mathsf{zt}(s) \wedge s \xrightarrow{wa} s' \implies s \xrightarrow{aw} s'$

Condition $\mathcal{Z}$ declares that in a state where a delay is possible, all enabled actions become stubborn actions. Condition $\mathcal{D}$ guarantees that in order to enable a time delay from a state where delaying is not allowed, a stubborn action must be executed. Similarly, Condition $\mathcal{R}$ requires that a stubborn action must be executed before a goal state can be reached from a non-goal state. Finally, Condition $\mathcal{W}$ allows us to commute stubborn actions with non-stubborn actions. The following theorem shows that reachability preserving reductions generate pruned transition systems where the reachability of goal states is preserved.

Theorem 1 (Shortest-Distance Reachability Preservation). *Let* St *be a reachability preserving reduction satisfying* $\mathcal{Z}$, $\mathcal{D}$, $\mathcal{R}$ *and* $\mathcal{W}$. *Let* $s \in S$. *If* $s \rightarrow^n s'$ *for some* $s' \in G$ *then also* $s \underset{\mathsf{St}}{\longrightarrow}^m s''$ *for some* $s'' \in G$ *where* $m \leq n$.

Proof. We proceed by induction on n. *Base step.* If $n = 0$, then $s = s'$ and $m = n = 0$. *Inductive step.* Let $s_0 \xrightarrow{\alpha_0} s_1 \xrightarrow{\alpha_1} \dots \xrightarrow{\alpha_n} s_{n+1}$ where $s_0 \notin G$ and $s_{n+1} \in G$. Without loss of generality we assume that for all i, $0 \leq i \leq n$, we have $\alpha_i \neq 0$ (otherwise we can simply skip these 0-delay actions and get a shorter sequence). We have two cases. Case $\neg\mathsf{zt}(s_0)$: by condition $\mathcal{Z}$ we have $\mathsf{En}(s_0) \subseteq \mathsf{St}(s_0)$ and by the definition of $\underset{\mathsf{St}}{\longrightarrow}$ we have $s_0 \underset{\mathsf{St}}{\xrightarrow{\alpha_0}} s_1$ since $\alpha_0 \in \mathsf{En}(s_0) \cup \mathbb{R}_{\geq 0}$. By the induction hypothesis we have $s_1 \underset{\mathsf{St}}{\longrightarrow}^m s''$ with $s'' \in G$ and $m \leq n$ and $m + 1 \leq n + 1$. Case $\mathsf{zt}(s_0)$: let $w = \alpha_0\alpha_1 \dots \alpha_n$ and α_i be such that $\alpha_i \in \mathsf{St}(s_0)$ and for all $k < i$ holds that $\alpha_k \notin \mathsf{St}(s_0)$, i.e. α_i is the first stubborn action in w. Such an α_i has to exist otherwise $s_{n+1} \notin G$ due to condition $\mathcal{R}$. Because of condition $\mathcal{D}$ we get $\mathsf{zt}(s_k)$ for all k, $0 \leq k < i$, otherwise α_i cannot be the first stubborn action in w. We can split w as $w = u\alpha_i v$ with $u \in \overline{\mathsf{St}(s_0)}^*$. Since all states in the path to s_i are zero time, by $\mathcal{W}$ we can swap α_i as $s_0 \xrightarrow{\alpha_i} s_1' \xrightarrow{u} s_i \xrightarrow{v} s'$ with $|uv| = n$. Since $\alpha_i \in \mathsf{St}(s_0)$ we get $s_0 \underset{\mathsf{St}}{\xrightarrow{\alpha_i}} s_1'$ and by the induction hypothesis we have $s_1' \underset{\mathsf{St}}{\longrightarrow}^m s''$ where $s'' \in G$, $m \leq n$, and $m + 1 \leq n + 1$. □

3 Timed-Arc Petri Nets

We shall now define the model of timed-arc Petri nets (as informally described in the introduction) together with a reachability logic and a few technical lemmas needed later on. Let $\mathbb{N}_0 = \mathbb{N} \cup \{0\}$ and $\mathbb{N}_0^\infty = \mathbb{N}_0 \cup \{\infty\}$. We define the set of *well-formed closed time intervals* as $\mathcal{I} \overset{\text{def}}{=} \{[a, b] \mid a \in \mathbb{N}_0, b \in \mathbb{N}_0^\infty, a \leq b\}$ and its subset $\mathcal{I}^{\text{inv}} \overset{\text{def}}{=} \{[0, b] \mid b \in \mathbb{N}_0^\infty\}$ used in age invariants.

Definition 3 (Timed-Arc Petri Net). *A timed-arc Petri net (TAPN) is a 9-tuple* $N = (P, T, T_{urg}, IA, OA, g, w, Type, I)$ *where*

- P *is a finite set of* places,
- T *is a finite set of* transitions *such that* $P \cap T = \emptyset$,
- $T_{urg} \subseteq T$ *is the set of* urgent transitions,
- $IA \subseteq P \times T$ *is a finite set of* input arcs,
- $OA \subseteq T \times P$ *is a finite set of* output arcs,
- $g : IA \to \mathcal{I}$ *is a* time constraint function *assigning guards (time intervals) to input arcs s.t.*
  - *if* $(p, t) \in IA$ *and* $t \in T_{urg}$ *then* $g((p, t)) = [0, \infty]$,
- $w : IA \cup OA \to \mathbb{N}$ *is a function assigning* weights *to input and output arcs,*
- $Type : IA \cup OA \to \textbf{Types}$ *is a* type function *assigning a type to all arcs where* $\textbf{Types} = \{Normal, Inhib\} \cup \{Transport_j \mid j \in \mathbb{N}\}$ *such that*
  - *if* $Type(z) = Inhib$ *then* $z \in IA$ *and* $g(z) = [0, \infty]$,
  - *if* $Type((p, t)) = Transport_j$ *for some* $(p, t) \in IA$ *then there is exactly one* $(t, p') \in OA$ *such that* $Type((t, p')) = Transport_j$,
  - *if* $Type((t, p')) = Transport_j$ *for some* $(t, p') \in OA$ *then there is exactly one* $(p, t) \in IA$ *such that* $Type((p, t)) = Transport_j$,
  - *if* $Type((p, t)) = Transport_j = Type((t, p'))$ *then* $w((p, t)) = w((t, p'))$,
- $I : P \to \mathcal{I}^{inv}$ *is a function assigning* age invariants *to places.*

Note that for transport arcs we assume that they come in pairs (for each type $Transport_j$) and that their weights match. Also for inhibitor arcs and for input arcs to urgent transitions, we require that the guards are $[0, \infty]$.

Before we give the formal semantics of the model, let us fix some notation. Let $N = (P, T, T_{urg}, IA, OA, g, w, Type, I)$ be a TAPN. We denote by ${}^{\bullet}x \stackrel{\text{def}}{=} \{y \in P \cup T \mid (y, x) \in IA \cup OA,\ Type((y, x)) \neq Inhib\}$ the preset of a transition or a place x. Similarly, the postset is defined as $x^{\bullet} \stackrel{\text{def}}{=} \{y \in P \cup T \mid (x, y) \in (IA \cup OA)\}$. We denote by ${}^{\circ}t \stackrel{\text{def}}{=} \{p \in P \mid (p, t) \in IA \wedge Type((p, t)) = Inhib\}$ the inhibitor preset of a transition t. The inhibitor postset of a place p is defined as $p^{\circ} \stackrel{\text{def}}{=} \{t \in T \mid (p, t) \in IA \wedge Type((p, t)) = Inhib\}$. Let $\mathcal{B}(\mathbb{R}^{\geq 0})$ be the set of all finite multisets over $\mathbb{R}^{\geq 0}$. A *marking* M on N is a function $M : P \longrightarrow \mathcal{B}(\mathbb{R}^{\geq 0})$ where for every place $p \in P$ and every token $x \in M(p)$ we have $x \in I(p)$, in other words all tokens have to satisfy the age invariants. The set of all markings in a net N is denoted by $\mathcal{M}(N)$.

We write (p, x) to denote a token at a place p with the age $x \in \mathbb{R}^{\geq 0}$. Then $M = \{(p_1, x_1), (p_2, x_2), \ldots, (p_n, x_n)\}$ is a multiset representing a marking M with n tokens of ages x_i in places p_i. We define the size of a marking as $|M| = \sum_{p \in P} |M(p)|$ where $|M(p)|$ is the number of tokens located in the place p. A marked TAPN (N, M_0) is a TAPN N together with an initial marking M_0 with all tokens of age 0.

Definition 4 (Enabledness). *Let* $N = (P, T, T_{urg}, IA, OA, g, w, Type, I)$ *be a TAPN. We say that a transition* $t \in T$ *is* enabled *in a marking* M *by the multisets of tokens* $In = \{(p, x_p^1), (p, x_p^2), \ldots, (p, x_p^{w((p,t))}) \mid p \in {}^{\bullet}t\} \subseteq M$ *and* $Out = \{(p', x_{p'}^1), (p', x_{p'}^2), \ldots, (p', x_{p'}^{w((t,p'))}) \mid p' \in t^{\bullet}\}$ *if*

- *for all input arcs except the inhibitor arcs, the tokens from In satisfy the age guards of the arcs, i.e.*

$$\forall p \in {}^\bullet t.\ x_p^i \in g((p,t)) \textit{ for } 1 \leq i \leq w((p,t))$$

- *for any inhibitor arc pointing from a place p to the transition t, the number of tokens in p is smaller than the weight of the arc, i.e.*

$$\forall (p,t) \in IA. Type((p,t)) = Inhib \Rightarrow |M(p)| < w((p,t))$$

- *for all input arcs and output arcs which constitute a transport arc, the age of the input token must be equal to the age of the output token and satisfy the invariant of the output place, i.e.*

$$\forall (p,t) \in IA. \forall (t,p') \in OA. Type((p,t)) = Type((t,p')) = Transport_j$$
$$\Rightarrow \left(x_p^i = x_{p'}^i \wedge x_{p'}^i \in I(p')\right) \textit{ for } 1 \leq i \leq w((p,t))$$

- *for all normal output arcs, the age of the output token is* 0, *i.e.*

$$\forall (t,p') \in OA. Type((t,p')) = Normal \Rightarrow x_{p'}^i = 0 \textit{ for } 1 \leq i \leq w((t,p')).$$

A given marked TAPN (N, M_0) defines a timed transition system $T(N) \stackrel{\text{def}}{=} (\mathcal{M}(N), M_0, \rightarrow)$ where the states are markings and the transitions are as follows.

- If $t \in T$ is enabled in a marking M by the multisets of tokens In and Out then t can *fire* and produce the marking $M' = (M \setminus In) \uplus Out$ where $\uplus$ is the multiset sum operator and $\setminus$ is the multiset difference operator; we write $M \xrightarrow{t} M'$ for this action transition.
- A time *delay* $d \in \mathbb{N}_0$ is allowed in M if
  - $(x + d) \in I(p)$ for all $p \in P$ and all $x \in M(p)$, i.e. by delaying d time units no token violates any of the age invariants, and
  - if $M \xrightarrow{t} M'$ for some $t \in T_{urg}$ then $d = 0$, i.e. enabled urgent transitions disallow time passing.

  By delaying d time units in M we reach the marking M' defined as $M'(p) = \{x + d \mid x \in M(p)\}$ for all $p \in P$; we write $M \xrightarrow{d} M'$ for this delay transition.

Note that the semantics above defines the discrete-time semantics as the delays are restricted to nonnegative integers. It is well known that for timed-arc Petri nets with nonstrict intervals, the marking reachability problem on discrete and continuous time nets coincide [31]. This is, however, not the case for more complex properties like liveness that can be expressed in the CTL logic (for counter examples that can be expressed in CTL see e.g. [25]).

3.1 Reachability Logic and Interesting Sets of Transitions

We now describe a logic for expressing the properties of markings based on the number of tokens in places and transition enabledness, inspired by the logic

Table 1. Interesting transitions of φ (assuming $M \not\models \varphi$, otherwise $A_M(\varphi) = \emptyset$)

Formula φ	$A_M(\varphi)$	$A_M(\neg\varphi)$
deadlock	$({}^\bullet t)^\bullet \cup {}^\bullet({}^\circ t)$ for some $t \in \mathsf{En}(M)$	$\emptyset$
t	${}^\bullet p$ for some $p \in {}^\bullet t$ where $M(p) < w((p,t))$ or $p^\bullet$ for some $p \in {}^\circ t$ where $M(p) \geq w((p,t))$	$({}^\bullet t)^\bullet \cup {}^\bullet({}^\circ t)$
$e_1 < e_2$	$decr_M(e_1) \cup incr_M(e_2)$	$A_M(e_1 \geq e_2)$
$e_1 \leq e_2$	$decr_M(e_1) \cup incr_M(e_2)$	$A_M(e_1 > e_2)$
$e_1 > e_2$	$incr_M(e_1) \cup decr_M(e_2)$	$A_M(e_1 \leq e_2)$
$e_1 \geq e_2$	$incr_M(e_1) \cup decr_M(e_2)$	$A_M(e_1 < e_2)$
$e_1 = e_2$	$decr_M(e_1) \cup incr_M(e_2)$ if $eval_M(e_1) > eval_M(e_2)$ $incr_M(e_1) \cup decr_M(e_2)$ if $eval_M(e_1) < eval_M(e_2)$	$A_M(e_1 \neq e_2)$
$e_1 \neq e_2$	$incr_M(e_1) \cup decr_M(e_1) \cup incr_M(e_2) \cup decr_M(e_2)$	$A_M(e_1 = e_2)$
$\varphi_1 \wedge \varphi_2$	$A_M(\varphi_i)$ for some $i \in \{1,2\}$ where $M \not\models \varphi_i$	$A_M(\neg\varphi_1 \vee \neg\varphi_2)$
$\varphi_1 \vee \varphi_2$	$A_M(\varphi_1) \cup A_M(\varphi_2)$	$A_M(\neg\varphi_1 \wedge \neg\varphi_2)$

Table 2. Increasing and decreasing transitions of expression e

Expression e	$incr_M(e)$	$decr_M(e)$
c	$\emptyset$	$\emptyset$
p	${}^\bullet p$	$p^\bullet$
$e_1 + e_2$	$incr_M(e_1) \cup incr_M(e_2)$	$decr_M(e_1) \cup decr_M(e_2)$
$e_1 - e_2$	$incr_M(e_1) \cup decr_M(e_2)$	$decr_M(e_1) \cup incr_M(e_2)$
$e_1 * e_2$	$incr_M(e_1) \cup decr_M(e_1) \cup incr_M(e_2) \cup decr_M(e_2)$	$incr_M(e_1) \cup decr_M(e_1) \cup incr_M(e_2) \cup decr_M(e_2)$

used in the Model Checking Contest (MCC) Property Language [27]. Let $N = (P, T, T_{urg}, IA, OA, g, w, Type, I)$ be a TAPN. The formulae of the logic are given by the abstract syntax:
$\varphi ::= \ deadlock \,|\, t \,|\, e_1 \bowtie e_2 \,|\, \varphi_1 \wedge \varphi_2 \,|\, \varphi_1 \vee \varphi_2 \,|\, \neg\varphi$
$e ::= \ c \,|\, p \,|\, e_1 \oplus e_2$
where $t \in T$, $\bowtie \in \{<, \leq, =, \neq, >, \geq\}$, $c \in \mathbb{Z}$, $p \in P$, and $\oplus \in \{+, -, *\}$. Let Φ be the set of all such formulae and let E_N be the set of arithmetic expressions over the net N. The semantics of φ in a marking $M \in \mathcal{M}(N)$ is given by

$$\begin{array}{ll} M \models deadlock & \text{if } \mathsf{En}(M) = \emptyset \\ M \models t & \text{if } t \in \mathsf{En}(M) \\ M \models e_1 \bowtie e_2 & \text{if } eval_M(e_1) \bowtie eval_M(e_2) \end{array}$$

assuming a standard semantics for Boolean operators and where the semantics of arithmetic expressions in a marking M is as follows: $eval_M(c) = c$, $eval_M(p) = |M(p)|$, and $eval_M(e_1 \oplus e_2) = eval_M(e_1) \oplus eval_M(e_2)$.

Let φ be a formula. We are interested in the question, whether we can reach from the initial marking some of the goal markings from $G_\varphi = \{M \in \mathcal{M}(N) \mid M \models \varphi\}$. In order to guide the reduction such that transitions that lead to the goal markings are included in the generated stubborn set, we define the notion of *interesting transitions* for a marking M relative to φ, and we let $A_M(\varphi) \subseteq T$ denote the set of interesting transitions. Formally, we shall require that whenever $M \xrightarrow{w} M'$ via a sequence of transitions $w = t_1 t_2 \dots t_n \in T^*$ where $M \notin G_\varphi$ and $M' \in G_\varphi$, then there must exist i, $1 \leq i \leq n$, such that $t_i \in A_M(\varphi)$.

Table 1 gives a possible definition of $A_M(\varphi)$. Let us remark that the definition is at several places nondeterministic, allowing for a variety of sets of interesting transitions. Table 1 uses the functions $incr_M : E_N \to 2^T$ and $decr_M : E_N \to 2^T$ defined in Table 2. These functions take as input an expression e, and return all transitions that can possibly, when fired, increase resp. decrease the evaluation of e. The following lemma formally states the required property of the functions $incr_M$ and $decr_M$.

Lemma 1. *Let $N = (P, T, T_{urg}, IA, OA, g, w, Type, I)$ be a TAPN and $M \in \mathcal{M}(N)$ a marking. Let $e \in E_N$ and let $M \xrightarrow{w} M'$ where $w = t_1 t_2 \dots t_n \in T^*$.*

- *If $eval_M(e) < eval_{M'}(e)$ then there is i, $1 \leq i \leq n$, such that $t_i \in incr_M(e)$.*
- *If $eval_M(e) > eval_{M'}(e)$ then there is i, $1 \leq i \leq n$, such that $t_i \in decr_M(e)$.*

We finish this section with the main technical lemma, showing that at least one interesting transition must be fired before we can reach a marking satisfying a given reachability formula.

Lemma 2. *Let $N = (P, T, T_{urg}, IA, OA, g, w, Type, I)$ be a TAPN, let $M \in \mathcal{M}(N)$ be its marking and let $\varphi \in \Phi$ be a given formula. If $M \not\models \varphi$ and $M \xrightarrow{w} M'$ where $w \in \overline{A_M(\varphi)}^*$ then $M' \not\models \varphi$.*

4 Partial Order Reductions for TAPN

We are now ready to state the main theorem that provides sufficient syntax-driven conditions for a reduction in order to guarantee preservation of reachability. Let $N = (P, T, T_{urg}, IA, OA, g, w, Type, I)$ be a TAPN, let $M \in \mathcal{M}(N)$ be a marking of N, and let $\varphi \in \Phi$ be a formula. We recall that $A_M(\varphi)$ is the set of interesting transitions as defined earlier.

Theorem 2 (Reachability Preserving Closure). *Let St be a reduction such that for all $M \in \mathcal{M}(N)$ it satisfies the following conditions.*

1 If $\neg \mathsf{zt}(M)$ then $\mathsf{En}(M) \subseteq \mathsf{St}(M)$.
2 If $\mathsf{zt}(M)$ then $A_M(\varphi) \subseteq \mathsf{St}(M)$.
3 If $\mathsf{zt}(M)$ then either
(a) there is $t \in T_{urg} \cap \mathsf{En}(M) \cap \mathsf{St}(M)$ where ${}^\bullet({}^\circ t) \subseteq \mathsf{St}(M)$, or
(b) there is $p \in P$ where $I(p) = [a, b]$ and $b \in M(p)$ such that $t \in \mathsf{St}(M)$ for every $t \in p^\bullet$ where $b \in g((p, t))$.

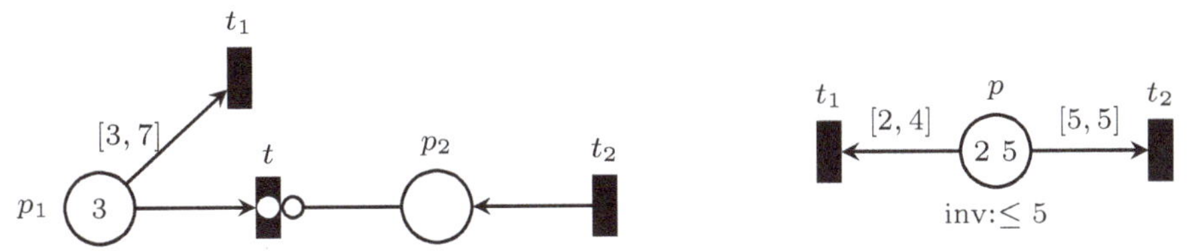

(a) Transitions t_1 and t_2 can disable resp. inhibit the urgent transition t

(b) Transition t_2 can remove the token of age 5 from p

Fig. 2. Cases for Condition 3

4 *For all* $t \in \mathsf{St}(M) \setminus \mathsf{En}(M)$ *either*
  (a) *there is* $p \in {}^\bullet t$ *such that* $|\{x \in M(p) \mid x \in g((p,t))\}| < w((p,t))$ *and*
    – $t' \in \mathsf{St}(M)$ *for all* $t' \in {}^\bullet p$ *where there is* $p' \in {}^\bullet t'$ *with* $Type((t',p)) = Type((p',t')) = Transport_j$ *and where* $g((p',t')) \cap g((p,t)) \neq \emptyset$, *and*
    – *if* $0 \in g((p,t))$ *then also* ${}^\bullet p \subseteq \mathsf{St}(M)$, *or*
  (b) *there is* $p \in {}^\circ t$ *where* $|M(p)| \geq w((p,t))$ *such that*
    – $t' \in \mathsf{St}(M)$ *for all* $t' \in p^\bullet$ *where* $M(p) \cap g((p,t')) \neq \emptyset$.

5 *For all* $t \in \mathsf{St}(M) \cap \mathsf{En}(M)$ *we have*
  (a) $t' \in \mathsf{St}(M)$ *for every* $t' \in p^\bullet$ *where* $p \in {}^\bullet t$ *and* $g((p,t)) \cap g((p,t')) \neq \emptyset$, *and*
  (b) $(t^\bullet)^\circ \subseteq \mathsf{St}(M)$.

Then St *satisfies* $\mathcal{Z}$, $\mathcal{D}$, $\mathcal{R}$, *and* $\mathcal{W}$.

Let us now briefly discuss the conditions of Theorem 2. Clearly, Condition 1 ensures that if time can elapse, we include all enabled transitions into the stubborn set and Condition 2 guarantees that all interesting transitions (those that can potentially make the reachability proposition true) are included as well.

Condition 3 makes sure that if time elapsing is disabled then any transition that can possibly enable time elapsing will be added to the stubborn set. There are two situations how time progress can be disabled. Either, there is an urgent enabled transition, like the transition t in Fig. 2a. Since t_2 can add a token to p_2 and by that inhibit t, Condition 3a makes sure that t_2 is added into the stubborn set in order to satisfy $\mathcal{D}$. As t_1 can remove the token of age 3 from p_1 and hence disable t, we must add t_1 to the stubborn set too (guaranteed by Condition 5a). The other situation when time gets stopped is when a place with an age invariant contains a token that disallows time passing, like in Fig. 2b where time is disabled because the place p has a token of age 5, which is the maximum possible age of tokens in p due to the age invariant. Since t_2 can remove the token of age 5 from p, we include it to the stubborn set due to Condition 3b. On the other hand t_1 does not have to be included in the stubborn set as its firing cannot remove the token of age 5 from p.

Condition 4 makes sure that an disabled stubborn transition can never be enabled by a non-stubborn transition. There are two reasons why a transition is disabled. Either, as in Fig. 3a where t is disabled, there is an insufficient number of tokens of appropriate age to fire the transition. In this case, Condition 4a

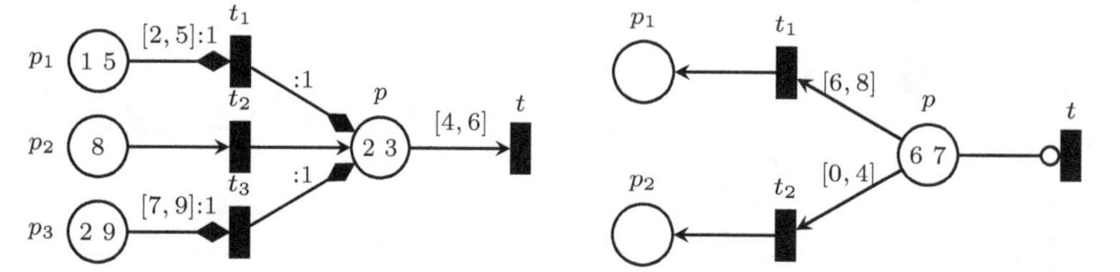

(a) Transition t_1 can transport well-aged tokens into p and enable t

(b) Transition t_1 can enable t by removing tokens from p

Fig. 3. Cases for Condition 4

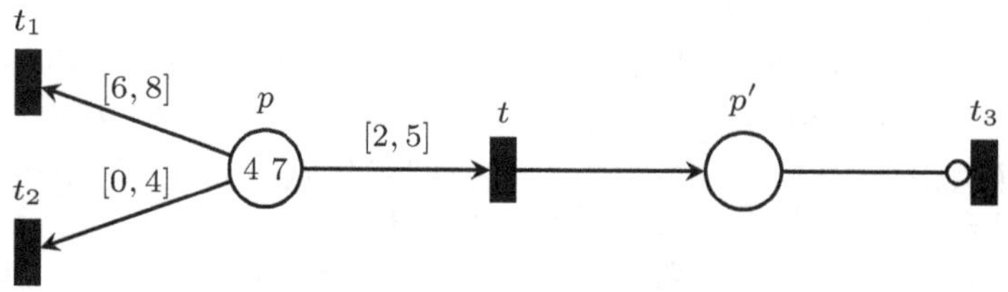

(a) Stubborn transition t can disable both t_2 and t_3

Fig. 4. Cases for Condition 5

makes sure that transitions that can add tokens of a suitable age via transport arcs are included in the stubborn set. This is the case for the transition t_1 in our example, as $[2, 5]$ has a nonempty intersection with $[4, 6]$. On the other hand, t_3 does not have to be added. As the transition t_2 only adds fresh tokens of age 0 to p via normal arcs, there is no need to add t_2 into the stubborn set either. The other reason for a transition to be disabled is due to inhibitor arcs, as shown on the transition t in Fig. 3b. Condition 4b makes sure that t_1 is added to the stubborn set, as it can enable t (the interval $[6, 8]$ has a nonempty intersection with the tokens of age 6 and 7 in the place p). As this is not the case for t_2, this transition can be left out from the stubborn set.

Finally, Condition 5 guarantees that enabled stubborn transitions can never disable any non-stubborn transitions. For an illustration, take a look at Fig. 4a and assume that t is an enabled stubborn transition. Firing of t can remove the token of age 4 from p and disable t_2, hence t_2 must become stubborn by Condition 5a in order to satisfy $\mathcal{W}$. On the other hand, the intervals $[6, 8]$ and $[2, 5]$ have empty intersection, so there is no need to declare t_1 as a stubborn transition. Moreover, firing of t can also disable the transition t_3 due to the inhibitor arc, so we must add t_3 to the stubborn set by Condition 5b.

The conditions of Theorem 2 can be turned into an iterative saturation algorithm for the construction of stubborn sets as shown in Algorithm 1. When running this algorithm for the net in our running example, we can reduce the state space exploration for fireability of the transition t as depicted in Fig. 1b. Our last theorem states that the algorithm returns stubborn subsets of enabled

Algorithm 1. Construction of a reachability preserving stubborn set

```
input  : N = (P, T, T_urg, IA, OA, g, w, Type, I), M ∈ 𝓜(N), φ ∈ Φ
output : St(M) ∩ En(M)
if ¬zt(M) then
    return En(M);
X := ∅; Y := A_M(φ);
if T_urg ∩ En(M) ≠ ∅ then
    pick any t ∈ T_urg ∩ En(M);
    if t ∉ Y then
        Y := Y ∪ {t};
    Y := Y ∪ •(°t);
else
    pick any p ∈ P where I(p) = [a, b] and b ∈ M(p)
    forall t ∈ p• do
        if b ∈ g((p, t)) then
            Y := Y ∪ {t};
while Y ≠ ∅ do
    pick any t ∈ Y;
    if t ∉ En(M) then
        if ∃p ∈ •t. |{x ∈ M(p) | x ∈ g((p, t))}| < w((p, t)) then
            pick any such p;
            forall t' ∈ •p \ X do
                forall p' ∈ •t' do
                    if Type((t', p)) = Type((p', t')) =
                    Transport_j ∧ g((p', t')) ∩ g((p, t)) ≠ ∅ then
                        Y := Y ∪ {t'};
            if 0 ∈ g((p, t)) then
                Y := Y ∪ (•p \ X);
        else
            pick any p ∈ °t s.t. |M(p)| ≥ w((p, t));
            forall t' ∈ p• \ X do
                if M(p) ∩ g((p, t')) ≠ ∅ then
                    Y := Y ∪ {t'};
    else
        forall p ∈ •t do
            Y := Y ∪ ({t' ∈ p• | g((p, t)) ∩ g((p, t')) ≠ ∅} \ X);
        Y := Y ∪ ((t•)° \ X);
    Y := Y \ {t};
    X := X ∪ {t};
return X ∩ En(M);
```

transitions that satisfy the four conditions of Theorem 1 and hence we preserve the reachability property as well as the minimum path to some reachable goal.

Theorem 3. *Algorithm 1 terminates and returns* $\mathsf{St}(M) \cap \mathsf{En}(M)$ *for some reduction* St *that satisfies* $\mathcal{Z}$, $\mathcal{D}$, $\mathcal{R}$, *and* $\mathcal{W}$.

5 Implementation and Experiments

We implemented our partial order method in C++ and integrated it within the model checker TAPAAL [19] and its discrete time engine `verifydtapn` [4,11]. We evaluate our partial order reduction on a wide range of case studies.

PatientMonitoring. The patient monitoring system [17] models a medical system that through sensors periodically scans patient's vital functions, making sure that abnormal situations are detected and reported within given deadlines. The timed-arc Petri net model was described in [17] for two sensors monitoring patient's pulse rate and oxygen saturation level. We scale the case study by adding additional sensors. *BloodTransfusion.* This case study models a larger blood transfusion workflow [16], the benchmarking case study of the little-JIL language. The timed-arc Petri net model was described in [10] and we verify that the workflow is free of deadlocks (unless all sub-workflows correctly terminate). The problem is scaled by the number of patients receiving a blood transfusion. *FireAlarm.* This case study uses a modified (due to trade secrets) fire alarm system owned by a German company [20,21]. It models a four-channel round-robin frequency-hopping transmission scheduling in order to ensure a reliable communication between a number of wireless sensors (by which the case study is scaled) and a central control unit. The protocol is based on time-division multiple access (TDMA) channel access and we verify that for a given frequency-jammer, it takes never more than three cycles before a fire alarm is communicated to the central unit. *BAwPC.* Business Activity with Participant Completion (BAwPC) is a web-service coordination protocol from WS-BA specification [33] that ensures a consistent agreement on the outcome of long-running distributed applications. In [26] it was shown that the protocol is flawed and a correct, enhanced variant was suggested. We model check this enhanced protocol and scale it by the capacity of the communication buffer. *Fischer.* Here we consider a classical Fischer's protocol for ensuring mutual exclusion for a number of timed processes. The timed-arc Petri net model is taken from [2] and it is scaled by the number of processes. *LynchShavit.* This is another timed-based mutual exclusion algorithm by Lynch and Shavit, with the timed-arc Petri net model taken from [1] and scaled by the number of processes. *MPEG2.* This case study describes the workflow of the MPEG-2 video encoding algorithm run on a multicore processor (the timed-arc Petri net model was published in [35]) and we verify the maximum duration of the workflow. The model is scaled by the number of B frames in the IB^{n}P frame sequence. *AlternatingBit.* This is a classical case study of alternating bit protocol, based on the timed-arc Petri net model given in [24]. The purpose of the protocol is to ensure a safe communication between a sender and a receiver over an unreliable medium. Messages are time-stamped in order to compensate

Table 3. Experiments with and without partial order reduction (POR)

	Time (seconds)		Markings ×1000		Reduction	
Model	NORMAL	POR	NORMAL	POR	%Time	%Markings
PatientMonitoring 3	5.88	0.35	333	28	94	92
PatientMonitoring 4	22.06	0.48	1001	36	98	96
PatientMonitoring 5	80.76	0.65	3031	44	99	99
PatientMonitoring 6	305.72	0.85	9248	54	100	99
PatientMonitoring 7	5516.93	5.75	130172	318	100	100
BloodTransfusion 2	0.32	0.41	48	43	−28	11
BloodTransfusion 3	7.88	6.45	792	546	18	31
BloodTransfusion 4	225.18	109.30	14904	7564	51	49
BloodTransfusion 5	5256.01	1611.14	248312	94395	69	62
FireAlarm 10	28.95	14.17	796	498	51	37
FireAlarm 12	116.97	17.51	1726	526	85	70
FireAlarm 14	598.89	21.65	5367	554	96	90
FireAlarm 16	5029.25	29.48	19845	582	99	97
FireAlarm 18	27981.90	34.55	77675	610	100	99
FireAlarm 20	154495.29	41.47	308914	638	100	100
FireAlarm 80	>2 days	602.71	–	1522	–	–
FireAlarm 125	>2 days	1957.00	–	2260	–	–
BAwPC 2	0.21	0.41	19	16	−95	15
BAwPC 4	3.45	4.04	193	125	−17	35
BAwPC 6	23.01	17.08	900	452	26	50
BAwPC 8	73.73	39.29	2294	952	47	58
BAwPC 10	135.62	60.66	3819	1412	55	63
BAwPC 12	173.09	73.53	4736	1665	58	65
Fischer-9	3.24	2.37	281	233	27	17
Fischer-11	12.68	8.73	923	738	31	20
Fischer-13	42.52	28.53	2628	2041	33	22
Fischer-15	121.31	77.50	6700	5066	36	24
Fischer-17	313.69	198.36	15622	11536	37	26
Fischer-19	748.52	456.30	33843	24469	39	28
Fischer-21	1622.69	985.07	68934	48904	39	29
LynchShavit 9	3.98	3.31	282	234	17	17
LynchShavit 11	15.73	12.19	925	740	23	20
LynchShavit 13	51.08	37.97	2631	2043	26	22
LynchShavit 15	146.63	103.63	6703	5069	29	24
LynchShavit 17	384.52	258.09	15626	11540	33	26
LynchShavit 19	907.60	597.68	33848	24474	34	28
LynchShavit 21	2011.58	1307.72	68940	48910	35	29
MPEG2 3	13.17	15.43	2188	2187	−17	0
MPEG2 4	109.62	125.45	15190	15180	−14	0
MPEG2 5	755.54	840.84	87568	87478	−11	0
MPEG2 6	4463.19	5092.58	435023	434354	−14	0
AlternatingBit 20	9.17	9.51	617	617	−4	0
AlternatingBit 30	48.20	49.13	2804	2804	−2	0
AlternatingBit 40	161.18	162.94	8382	8382	−1	0
AlternatingBit 50	408.34	408.86	19781	19781	0	0

(via retransmission) for the possibility of losing messages. The case study is scaled by the maximum number of messages in transfer.

All experiments were run on AMD Opteron 6376 Processors with 500 GB memory. In Table 3 we compare the time to verify a model without (NORMAL) and with (POR) partial order reduction, the number of explored markings (in thousands) and the percentage of time and memory reduction. We can observe clear benefits of our technique on PatientMonitoring, BloodTransfusion and FireAlarm where we are both exponentially faster and explore only a fraction of all reachable markings. For example in FireAlarm, we are able to verify its correctness for all 125 sensors, as it is required by the German company [21]. This would be clearly unfeasible without the use of partial order reduction.

In BAwPC, we can notice that for the smallest instances, there is some computation overhead from computing the stubborn sets, however, it clearly pays off for the larger instances where the percentages of reduced state space are closely followed by the percentages of the verification times and in fact improve with the larger instances. Fischer and LynchShavit case studies demonstrate that even moderate reductions of the state space imply considerable reduction in the running time and computing the stubborn sets is well worth the extra effort.

MPEG2 is an example of a model that allows only negligible reduction of the state space size, and where we observe an actual slowdown in the running time due to the computation of the stubborn sets. Nevertheless, the overhead stays constant in the range of about 15%, even for increasing instance sizes. Finally, AlternatingBit protocol does not allow for any reduction of the state space (even though it contains age invariants) but the overhead in the running time is negligible.

We observed similar performance of our technique also for the cases where the reachability property does not hold and a counter example can be generated.

6 Conclusion

We suggested a simple, yet powerful and application-ready partial order reduction for timed systems. The reduction comes into effect as soon as the timed system enters an urgent configuration where time cannot elapse until a nonempty sequence of transitions gets executed. The method is implemented and fully integrated, including GUI support, into the open-source tool TAPAAL. We demonstrated its practical applicability on several case studies and conclude that computing the stubborn sets causes only a minimal overhead while providing large benefits for reducing the state space in numerous models. The method is not specific to stubborn reduction technique only and it preserves the shortest execution sequences. Moreover, once the time gets urgent, other classical (untimed) partial order approaches should be applicable too. Our method was instantiated to (unbounded) timed-arc Petri nets with discrete time semantics, however, we claim that the technique allows for general application to other modelling formalisms like timed automata and timed Petri nets, as well as an extension to continuous time. We are currently working on adapting the theory and providing an efficient implementation for UPPAAL-style timed automata with continuous time semantics.

Acknowledgements. We thank Mads Johannsen for his help with the GUI support for partial order reduction. The work was funded by the center IDEA4CPS, Innovation Fund Denmark center DiCyPS and ERC Advanced Grant LASSO. The last author is partially affiliated with FI MU in Brno.

References

1. Abdulla, P., Deneux, J., Mahata, P., Nylén, A.: Using forward reachability analysis for verification of timed Petri nets. Nord. J. Comput. **14**, 1–42 (2007)
2. Abdulla, P.A., Nylén, A.: Timed Petri nets and BQOs. In: Colom, J.-M., Koutny, M. (eds.) ICATPN 2001. LNCS, vol. 2075, pp. 53–70. Springer, Heidelberg (2001). https://doi.org/10.1007/3-540-45740-2_5
3. Alur, R., Dill, D.L.: A theory of timed automata. Theor. Comput. Sci. **126**(2), 183–235 (1994)
4. Andersen, M., Gatten Larsen, H., Srba, J., Grund Sørensen, M., Haahr Taankvist, J.: Verification of liveness properties on closed timed-arc Petri nets. In: Kučera, A., Henzinger, T.A., Nešetřil, J., Vojnar, T., Antoš, D. (eds.) MEMICS 2012. LNCS, vol. 7721, pp. 69–81. Springer, Heidelberg (2013). https://doi.org/10.1007/978-3-642-36046-6_8
5. André, E., Chatain, T., Rodríguez, C.: Preserving partial-order runs in parametric time Petri nets. ACM Trans. Embed. Comput. Syst. **16**(2), 43:1–43:26 (2017)
6. Baier, C., Katoen, J.-P.: Principles of Model Checking. The MIT Press, Cambridge (2008)
7. Behrmann, G., Bouyer, P., Larsen, K.G., Pelánek, R.: Lower and upper bounds in zone-based abstractions of timed automata. STTT **8**(3), 204–215 (2006)
8. Bengtsson, J., Jonsson, B., Lilius, J., Yi, W.: Partial order reductions for timed systems. In: Sangiorgi, D., de Simone, R. (eds.) CONCUR 1998. LNCS, vol. 1466, pp. 485–500. Springer, Heidelberg (1998). https://doi.org/10.1007/BFb0055643
9. Berthomieu, B., Vernadat, F.: Time Petri nets analysis with TINA. In: Third International Conference on Quantitative Evaluation of Systems, pp. 123–124. IEEE Computer Society (2006)
10. Bertolini, C., Liu, Z., Srba, J.: Verification of timed healthcare workflows using component timed-arc Petri nets. In: Weber, J., Perseil, I. (eds.) FHIES 2012. LNCS, vol. 7789, pp. 19–36. Springer, Heidelberg (2013). https://doi.org/10.1007/978-3-642-39088-3_2
11. Viesmose Birch, S., Stig Jacobsen, T., Jon Jensen, J., Moesgaard, C., Nørgaard Samuelsen, N., Srba, J.: Interval abstraction refinement for model checking of timed-arc Petri nets. In: Legay, A., Bozga, M. (eds.) FORMATS 2014. LNCS, vol. 8711, pp. 237–251. Springer, Cham (2014). https://doi.org/10.1007/978-3-319-10512-3_17
12. Boucheneb, H., Barkaoui, K.: Reducing interleaving semantics redundancy in reachability analysis of time Petri nets. ACM Trans. Embed. Comput. Syst. **12**(1), 7:1–7:24 (2013)
13. Boucheneb, H., Barkaoui, K.: Stubborn sets for time Petri nets. ACM Trans. Embed. Comput. Syst. **14**(1), 11:1–11:25 (2015)

14. Boucheneb, H., Barkaoui, K.: Delay-dependent partial order reduction technique for real time systems. Real-Time Syst. **54**, 278–306 (2017)
15. Bozga, M., Graf, S., Ober, I., Ober, I., Sifakis, J.: The IF toolset. In: Bernardo, M., Corradini, F. (eds.) SFM-RT 2004. LNCS, vol. 3185, pp. 237–267. Springer, Heidelberg (2004). https://doi.org/10.1007/978-3-540-30080-9_8
16. Christov, S., Avrunin, G., Clarke, A., Osterweil, L., Henneman, E.: A benchmark for evaluating software engineering techniques for improving medical processes. In: SEHC 2010, pp. 50–56. ACM (2010)
17. Cicirelli, F., Furfaro, A., Nigro, L.: Model checking time-dependent system specifications using time stream Petri nets and UPPAAL. Appl. Math. Comput. **218**(16), 8160–8186 (2012)
18. Dams, D., Gerth, R., Knaack, B., Kuiper, R.: Partial-order reduction techniques for real-time model checking. Form. Asp. Comput. **10**(5–6), 469–482 (1998)
19. David, A., Jacobsen, L., Jacobsen, M., Jørgensen, K.Y., Møller, M.H., Srba, J.: TAPAAL 2.0: integrated development environment for timed-arc Petri nets. In: Flanagan, C., König, B. (eds.) TACAS 2012. LNCS, vol. 7214, pp. 492–497. Springer, Heidelberg (2012). https://doi.org/10.1007/978-3-642-28756-5_36
20. Feo-Arenis, S., Westphal, B., Dietsch, D., Muñiz, M., Andisha, A.S.: The wireless fire alarm system: ensuring conformance to industrial standards through formal verification. In: Jones, C., Pihlajasaari, P., Sun, J. (eds.) FM 2014. LNCS, vol. 8442, pp. 658–672. Springer, Cham (2014). https://doi.org/10.1007/978-3-319-06410-9_44
21. Feo-Arenis, S., Westphal, B., Dietsch, D., Muñiz, M., Andisha, S., Podelski, A.: Ready for testing: ensuring conformance to industrial standards through formal verification. Form. Asp. Comput. **28**(3), 499–527 (2016)
22. Gardey, G., Lime, D., Magnin, M., Roux, O.H.: Romeo: a tool for analyzing time Petri nets. In: Etessami, K., Rajamani, S.K. (eds.) CAV 2005. LNCS, vol. 3576, pp. 418–423. Springer, Heidelberg (2005). https://doi.org/10.1007/11513988_41
23. Hansen, H., Lin, S.-W., Liu, Y., Nguyen, T.K., Sun, J.: Diamonds are a girl's best friend: partial order reduction for timed automata with abstractions. In: Biere, A., Bloem, R. (eds.) CAV 2014. LNCS, vol. 8559, pp. 391–406. Springer, Cham (2014). https://doi.org/10.1007/978-3-319-08867-9_26
24. Jacobsen, L., Jacobsen, M., Møller, M.H., Srba, J.: Verification of timed-arc Petri Nets. In: Černá, I., Gyimóthy, T., Hromkovič, J., Jefferey, K., Královič, R., Vukolić, M., Wolf, S. (eds.) SOFSEM 2011. LNCS, vol. 6543, pp. 46–72. Springer, Heidelberg (2011). https://doi.org/10.1007/978-3-642-18381-2_4
25. Jensen, P., Larsen, K., Srba, J.: Discrete and continuous strategies for timed-arc Petri net games. Int. J. Softw. Tools Technol. Transf. (STTT), 1–18 (2017, to appear). Online since September 2017
26. Marques Jr., A., Ravn, A., Srba, J., Vighio, S.: Model-checking web services business activity protocols. Int. J. Softw. Tools Technol. Transf. (STTT) **15**(2), 125–147 (2012)
27. Kordon, F., Garavel, H., Hillah, L.M., Hulin-Hubard, F., Chiardo, G., Hamez, A., Jezequel, L., Miner, A., Meijer, J., Paviot-Adet, E., Racordon, D., Rodriguez, C., Rohr, C., Srba, J., Thierry-Mieg, Y., Trịnh, G., Wolf, K.: Complete Results for the 2016 Edition of the Model Checking Contest, June 2016. http://mcc.lip6.fr/2016/results.php
28. Kristensen, L.M., Schmidt, K., Valmari, A.: Question-guided stubborn set methods for state properties. Form. Methods Syst. Des. **29**(3), 215–251 (2006)
29. Lilius, J.: Efficient state space search for time Petri nets. Electron. Notes Theo. Comput. Sci. **18**, 113–133 (1998). MFCS 1998 Workshop on Concurrency

30. Lugiez, D., Niebert, P., Zennou, S.: A partial order semantics approach to the clock explosion problem of timed automata. Theor. Comput. Sci. **345**(1), 27–59 (2005)
31. Mateo, J., Srba, J., Sørensen, M.: Soundness of timed-arc workflow nets in discrete and continuous-time semantics. Fundam. Inform. **140**(1), 89–121 (2015)
32. Minea, M.: Partial order reduction for model checking of timed automata. In: Baeten, J.C.M., Mauw, S. (eds.) CONCUR 1999. LNCS, vol. 1664, pp. 431–446. Springer, Heidelberg (1999). https://doi.org/10.1007/3-540-48320-9_30
33. Newcomer, E., Robinson, I.: Web services business activity (WS-businessactivity) version 1.2 (2009). http://docs.oasis-open.org/ws-tx/wstx-wsba-1.2-spec-os/wstx-wsba-1.2-spec-os.html
34. Niebert, P., Qu, H.: Adding invariants to event zone automata. In: Asarin, E., Bouyer, P. (eds.) FORMATS 2006. LNCS, vol. 4202, pp. 290–305. Springer, Heidelberg (2006). https://doi.org/10.1007/11867340_21
35. Pelayo, F., Cuartero, F., Valero, V., Macia, H., Pelayo, M.: Applying timed-arc Petri nets to improve the performance of the MPEG-2 encoding algorithm. In: 10th International Multimedia Modelling Conference, pp. 49–56. IEEE Computer Society (2004)
36. Perin, M., Faure, J.: Coupling timed plant and controller models with urgent transitions without introducing deadlocks. In: 17th International Conference on Emerging Technologies and Factory Automation (ETFA 2012), pp. 1–9. IEEE (2012)
37. Salah, R.B., Bozga, M., Maler, O.: On interleaving in timed automata. In: Baier, C., Hermanns, H. (eds.) CONCUR 2006. LNCS, vol. 4137, pp. 465–476. Springer, Heidelberg (2006). https://doi.org/10.1007/11817949_31
38. Sloan, R.H., Buy, U.: Stubborn sets for real-time Petri nets. Form. Methods Syst. Des. **11**(1), 23–40 (1997)
39. Valmari, A., Hansen, H.: Stubborn set intuition explained. In: Koutny, M., Kleijn, J., Penczek, W. (eds.) Transactions on Petri Nets and Other Models of Concurrency XII. LNCS, vol. 10470, pp. 140–165. Springer, Heidelberg (2017). https://doi.org/10.1007/978-3-662-55862-1_7
40. Virbitskaite, I., Pokozy, E.: A partial order method for the verification of time Petri nets. In: Ciobanu, G., Păun, G. (eds.) FCT 1999. LNCS, vol. 1684, pp. 547–558. Springer, Heidelberg (1999). https://doi.org/10.1007/3-540-48321-7_46
41. Yoneda, T., Schlingloff, B.-H.: Efficient verification of parallel real-time systems. Form. Methods Syst. Des. **11**(2), 187–215 (1997)

A Counting Semantics for Monitoring LTL Specifications over Finite Traces

Ezio Bartocci[1(✉)], Roderick Bloem[2], Dejan Nickovic[3], and Franz Roeck[2]

[1] TU Wien, Vienna, Austria
ezio.bartocci@tuwien.ac.at
[2] Graz University of Technology, Graz, Austria
[3] Austrian Institute of Technology GmbH, Vienna, Austria

Abstract. We consider the problem of monitoring a Linear Time Logic (LTL) specification that is defined on infinite paths, over finite traces. For example, we may need to draw a verdict on whether the system satisfies or violates the property "p holds infinitely often." The problem is that there is always a continuation of a finite trace that satisfies the property and a different continuation that violates it.

We propose a two-step approach to address this problem. First, we introduce a counting semantics that computes the number of steps to witness the satisfaction or violation of a formula for each position in the trace. Second, we use this information to make a prediction on inconclusive suffixes. In particular, we consider a *good* suffix to be one that is shorter than the longest witness for a satisfaction, and a *bad* suffix to be shorter than or equal to the longest witness for a violation. Based on this assumption, we provide a verdict assessing whether a continuation of the execution on the same system will presumably satisfy or violate the property.

1 Introduction

Alice is a verification engineer and she is presented with a new exciting and complex design. The requirements document coming with the design already incorporates functional requirements formalized in Linear Temporal Logic (LTL) [13]. The design contains features that are very challenging for exhaustive verification and her favorite model checking tool does not terminate in reasonable time.

This work was partially supported by the European Union (IMMORTAL project, grant no. 644905), the Austrian FWF (National Research Network RiSE/SHiNE S11405-N23 and S11406-N23), the SeCludE project (funded by UnivPM) and the ENABLE-S3 project that has received funding from the ECSEL Joint Undertaking under Grant Agreement no. 692455. This Joint Undertaking receives support from the European Unions HORIZON 2020 research and innovation programme and Austria, Denmark, Germany, Finland, Czech Republic, Italy, Spain, Portugal, Poland, Ireland, Belgium, France, Netherlands, United Kingdom, Slovakia, Norway.

H. Chockler and G. Weissenbacher (Eds.): CAV 2018, LNCS 10981, pp. 547–564, 2018.
https://doi.org/10.1007/978-3-319-96145-3_29

Runtime Verification. Alice decides to tackle this problem using runtime verification (RV) [3], a light, yet rigorous verification method. RV drops the exhaustiveness of model checking and analyzes individual traces generated by the system. Thus, it scales much better to the industrial-size designs. RV enables automatic generation of monitors from formalized requirements and thus provides a systematic way to check if the system traces satisfy (violate) the specification.

Motivating Example. In particular, Alice considers the following specification:

$$\psi \equiv \mathsf{G}(\mathsf{request} \rightarrow \mathsf{F}\,\mathsf{grant})$$

This LTL formula specifies that every request coming from the environment must be granted by the design in some finite (but unbounded) future. Alice realizes that she is trying to check a *liveness* property over a set of *finite* traces. She looks closer at the executions and identifies the two interesting examples trace τ_1 and trace τ_2, depicted in Table 1.

Table 1. Unbounded response property example.

trace	time	1	2	3	4	5	6	7
τ_1	request	$\top$	–	–	$\top$	–	–	–
	grant	–	–	$\top$	–	–	–	–
τ_2	request	$\top$	–	–	$\top$	–	–	$\top$
	grant	–	–	$\top$	–	–	$\top$	–

We use "–" instead of "$\perp$" to improve the trace readability.

The monitoring tool reports that both τ_1 and τ_2 presumably violate the unbounded response property. This verdict is against Alice's intuition. The evaluation of trace τ_1 seems right to her – the request at Cycle 1 is followed by a grant at Cycle 3, however the request at Cycle 4 is never granted during that execution. There are good reasons to suspect a bug in the design. Then she looks at τ_2 and observes that after every request the grant is given exactly after 2 cycles. It is true that the last request at Cycle 7 is not followed by a grant, but this seems to happen because the execution ends at that cycle – the past trace observations give reason to think that this request would be followed by a grant in cycle 9 if the execution was continued. Thus, Alice is not satisfied by the second verdict.

Alice looks closer at the way that the LTL property is evaluated over finite traces. She finds out that temporal operators are given *strength* – *eventually* and *until* are declared as *strong* operators, while *always* and *weak until* are defined to be *weak* [9]. A strong temporal operator requires all outstanding obligations to be met before the end of the trace. In contrast, a weak temporal operator must not witness any outstanding obligation violation before the end of the trace. Under this interpretation, both τ_1 and τ_2 violate the unbounded response property.

Alice explores another popular approach to evaluate future temporal properties over finite traces – the 3-valued semantics for LTL [4]. In this setting, the Boolean set of verdicts is extended with a third unknown (or maybe) value. A finite trace satisfies (violates) the 3-valued LTL formula if and only if all the infinite extensions of the trace satisfy (violate) the same LTL formula under its classical interpretation. In all other cases, we say that the satisfaction of the formula by the trace is unknown. Alice applies the 3-valued interpretation of LTL on the traces τ_1 and τ_2 to evaluate the unbounded response property. In both situations, she ends up with the unknown verdict. Once again, this is not what she expects and it does not meet her intuition about the satisfaction of the formula by the observed traces.

Alice desires a semantics that evaluates LTL properties on finite traces by taking previous observations into account.

Contributions. In this paper, we study the problem of LTL evaluation over finite traces encountered by Alice and propose a solution. We introduce a new counting semantics for LTL that takes into account the intuition illustrated by the example from Table 1. This semantics computes for every position of a trace two values – the distances to the nearest satisfaction and violation of the co-safety, respectively safety, part of the specification. We use this quantitative information to make *predictions* about the (infinite) suffixes of the finite observations. We infer from these values the maximum time that we expect for a future obligation to be fulfilled. We compare it to the value that we have for an open obligation at the end of the trace. If the latter is greater (smaller) than the expected maximum value, we have a good indication of a *presumed violation (satisfaction)* that we report to the user. In particular, our approach will indicate that τ_1 is likely to violate the specification and should be further inspected. In contrast, it will evaluate that τ_2 most likely satisfies the unbounded response property.

Organization of the Paper. The rest of the paper is organized as follows. We discuss the related work in Sect. 2 and we provide the preliminaries in Sect. 3. In Sect. 4 we present our new counting semantics for LTL and we show how to make *predictions* about (infinite) suffixes of the finite observations. Section 5 shows the application of our approach to some examples. Finally in Sect. 6 we draw our conclusions.

2 Related Work

The finitary interpretation of LTL was first considered in [11], where the authors propose to enrich the logic with the *weak* next operator that is dual to the (strong) next operator defined on infinite traces. While the strong next requires the existence of a next state, the weak next trivially evaluates to true at the end of the trace. In [9], the authors propose a more semantic approach with *weak* and *strong* views for evaluating future obligations at the end of the trace. In essence the empty word satisfies (violates) every formula according to the weak (strong) view. These two approaches result in the violation of the specification ψ by both traces τ_1 and τ_2.

The authors in [4] propose a 3-valued finitary LTL interpretation of LTL, in which the set {true, false} of verdicts is extended with a third inconclusive verdict. According to the 3-valued LTL, a finite trace satisfies (violates) a specification iff all its infinite extensions satisfy (violate) the same property under the classical LTL interpretation. Otherwise, it evaluates to inconclusive. The main disadvantage of the 3-valued semantics is the dominance of the inconclusive verdict in the evaluation of many interesting LTL formulas. In fact, both τ_1 and τ_2 from Table 1 evaluate to inconclusive against the unbounded response specification ψ.

In [5], the authors combine the weak and strong operators with the 3-valued semantics to refine the inconclusive with {presumably true, presumably false}. The strength of the remaining future obligation dictates the presumable verdict. The authors in [12] propose a finitary semantics for each of the LTL (safety, liveness, persistence and recurrence) hierarchy classes that asymptotically converges to the infinite traces semantics of the logic. In these two works, the specification ψ also evaluates to the same verdict for both the traces τ_1 and τ_2.

To summarize, none of the related work handles the unbounded response example from Table 1 in a satisfactory manner. This is due to the fact that these approaches decide about the verdict based on the specification and its remaining future obligations at the end of the trace. In contrast, we propose an approach in which the past observations within the trace are used to predict the future and derive the appropriate verdict. In particular, the application of our semantics for the evaluation of ψ over τ_1 and τ_2 results in presumably true and presumably false verdicts.

In [17], the authors propose another predictive semantics for LTL. In essence, this work assumes that at every point in time the monitor is able to precisely predict a segment of the trace that it has not observed yet and produce its outcome accordingly. In order to ensure such predictive power, this approach requires a white-box setting in which instrumentation and some form of static analysis of the systems are needed in order to foresee in advance the upcoming observations. This is in contrast to our work, in which the monitor remains a passive participant and predicts its verdict only based on the past observations.

In a different research thread [15], the authors introduce the notion of *monitorable* specifications that can be positively or negatively determined by a finite trace. The monitorability of LTL is further studied in [6,14]. This classification of specifications is orthogonal to our work. We focus on providing a sensible evaluation to all LTL properties, including the non-monitorable ones (e.g., $\mathsf{GF}\,p$).

We also mention the recent work on statistical model checking for LTL [8]. In this work, the authors assume a gray-box setting, where the system-under-test (SUT) is a Markov chain with the known minimum transition probability. This is in contrast to our work, in which we passively observe existing finite traces generated by the SUT, i.e., we have a blackbox setting.

In [1], the authors propose extending LTL with a discounting operator and study the properties of the augmented logic. The LTL specification formalism is extended with path-accumulation assertions in [7]. These LTL extensions are motivated by the need for a more quantitative and refined analysis of the systems. In our work, the motivation for the counting semantics is quite different. We use the quantitative information that we collect during the execution of the trace to predict the future behavior of the system and thus improve the quality of the monitoring verdict.

3 Preliminaries

We first introduce *traces* and Linear Temporal Logic (LTL) that we interpret over 3-valued semantics.

Definition 1 (Trace). *Let P a finite set of* propositions *and let $\Pi = 2^P$. A (finite or infinite)* trace *π is a sequence $\pi_1, \pi_2, \ldots \in \Pi^* \cup \Pi^\omega$. We denote by $|\pi| \in \mathbb{N} \cup \{\infty\}$ the* length *of π. We denote by $\pi \cdot \pi'$ the concatenation of $\pi \in \Pi^*$ and $\pi' \in \Pi^* \cup \Pi^\omega$.*

Definition 2 (Linear Temporal Logic). *In this paper, we consider linear temporal logic (LTL) and we define its syntax by the grammar:*

$$\phi := p \mid \neg\phi \mid \phi_1 \vee \phi_2 \mid \mathsf{X}\,\phi \mid \phi_1\,\mathsf{U}\,\phi_2,$$

where $p \in P$. We denote by Φ the set of all LTL formulas.

From the basic definition we can derive other standard Boolean and temporal operators as follows:

$$\top = p \vee \neg p,\ \ \bot = \neg\top,\ \ \phi \wedge \psi = \neg(\neg\phi \vee \neg\psi),\ \ \mathsf{F}\,\phi = \top\,\mathsf{U}\,\phi,\ \ \mathsf{G}\,\phi = \neg\,\mathsf{F}\,\neg\phi$$

Let $\pi \in \Pi^\omega$ be an infinite trace and ϕ an LTL formula. The satisfaction relation $(\pi, i) \models \phi$ is defined inductively as follows

$$\begin{array}{ll}
(\pi, i) \models p & \text{iff } p \in \pi_i, \\
(\pi, i) \models \neg\phi & \text{iff } (\pi, i) \not\models \phi, \\
(\pi, i) \models \phi_1 \vee \phi_2 & \text{iff } (\pi, i) \models \phi_1 \text{ or } (\pi, i) \models \phi_2, \\
(\pi, i) \models \mathsf{X}\,\phi & \text{iff } (\pi, i+1) \models \phi, \\
(\pi, i) \models \phi_1\,\mathsf{U}\,\phi_2 & \text{iff } \exists j \geq i \text{ s.t. } (\pi, j) \models \phi_2 \text{ and } \forall i \leq k < j, (\pi, k) \models \phi_1.
\end{array}$$

We now recall the 3-valued semantics from [4]. We denote by $[\pi \models_3 \phi]$ the evaluation of ϕ with respect to the trace $\pi \in \Pi^*$ that yields a value in $\{\top, \bot, ?\}$.

$$[\pi \models_3 \phi] = \begin{cases} \top & \forall \pi' \in \Pi^\omega, \pi \cdot \pi' \models \phi, \\ \bot & \forall \pi' \in \Pi^\omega, \pi \cdot \pi' \not\models \phi, \\ ? & \text{otherwise.} \end{cases}$$

We now restrict LTL to a fragment without explicit $\top$ and $\bot$ symbols and with the explicit F operator that we add to the syntax. We provide an alternative 3-valued semantics for this fragment, denoted by $\mu_\pi(\phi, i)$ where $i \in \mathbb{N}_{>0}$ indicates a position in or outside the trace. We assume the order $\bot <? < \top$, and extend the Boolean operations to the 3-valued domain with the rules $\neg_3\top = \bot$, $\neg_3\bot = \top$ and $\neg_3? =?$ and $\phi_1 \vee_3 \phi_2 = max(\phi_1, \phi_2)$. We define the semantics inductively as follows:

$$\begin{array}{lll}
\mu_\pi(p,i) & = & \begin{cases} \top & \text{if } i \leq |\pi| \text{ and } p \in \pi_i, \\ \bot & \text{else if } i \leq |\pi| \text{ and } p \notin \pi_i, \\ ? & \text{otherwise,} \end{cases} \\
\mu_\pi(\neg\phi,i) & = & \neg_3 \mu_\pi(\phi,i), \\
\mu_\pi(\phi_1 \vee \phi_2,i) & = & \mu_\pi(\phi_1,i) \vee_3 \mu_\pi(\phi_2,i), \\
\mu_\pi(\mathsf{X}\,\phi,i) & = & \mu_\pi(\phi,i+1), \\
\mu_\pi(\mathsf{F}\,\phi,i) & = & \begin{cases} \mu_\pi(\phi,i) \vee_3 \mu_\pi(\mathsf{XF}\,\phi,i) & \text{if } i \leq |\pi|, \\ \mu_\pi(\phi,i) & \text{if } i > |\pi|, \end{cases} \\
\mu_\pi(\phi_1 \,\mathsf{U}\, \phi_2,i) & = & \begin{cases} \mu_\pi(\phi_2,i) \vee_3 (\mu_\pi(\phi_1,i) \wedge_3 \mu_\pi(\mathsf{X}(\phi_1 \,\mathsf{U}\, \phi_2),i)) & \text{if } i \leq |\pi|, \\ \mu_\pi(\phi_2,i) & \text{if } i > |\pi|. \end{cases}
\end{array}$$

We note that the adapted semantics allows evaluating a finite trace in polynomial time, in contrast to $[\pi \models_3 \phi]$, which requires a PSPACE-complete algorithm. This improvement in complexity comes at a price – the adapted semantics cannot semantically characterize tautologies and contradiction. We have for example that $\mu_\pi(p \vee \neg p, 1)$ for the empty word evaluates to ?, despite the fact that $p \vee \neg p$ is semantically equivalent to $\top$. The novel semantics that we introduce in the following sections make the same tradeoff.

In the following lemma, we relate the two three-valued semantics.

Lemma 3. *Given an LTL formula and a trace* $\pi \in \Pi^*$, $|\pi| \neq 0$, *we have that*

$$\mu_\pi(\phi,1) = \top \Rightarrow [\pi \models_3 \phi] = \top,$$
$$\mu_\pi(\phi,1) = \bot \Rightarrow [\pi \models_3 \phi] = \bot.$$

Proof. These two statements can be proven by induction on the structure of the LTL formula (see Appendix A.1 in [2]). $[\pi \models_3 \phi] = \;? \Rightarrow \mu_\pi(\phi,1) = \;?$ is the consequence of the first two.

4 Counting Finitary Semantics for LTL

In this section, we introduce the counting semantics for LTL. We first provide necessary definitions in Sect. 4.1, we present the new semantics in Sect. 4.2 and finally propose a predictive mapping that transforms the counting semantics into a qualitative 5-valued verdict in Sect. 4.3.

4.1 Definitions

Let $\mathbb{N}_+ = \mathbb{N}_0 \cup \{\infty, -\}$ be the set of *natural* numbers (incl. 0) extended with the two special symbols ∞ (infinite) and $-$ (impossible) such that $\forall n \in \mathbb{N}_0$, we define $n < \infty < -$. We define the addition $\oplus$ of two elements $a, b \in \mathbb{N}_+$ as follows.

Definition 4 (Operator $\oplus$). *We define the binary operator $\oplus : \mathbb{N}_+ \times \mathbb{N}_+ \rightarrow \mathbb{N}_+$ s. t. for $a \oplus b$ with $a, b \in \mathbb{N}_+$ we have $a + b$ if $a, b \in \mathbb{N}_0$ and $\max\{a, b\}$ otherwise.*

We denote by (s, f) a pair of two extended numbers $s, f \in \mathbb{N}_+$. In Definition 5, we introduce several operations on pairs: (1) the *swap* between the two values ($\sim$), (2) the increment by 1 of both values ($\oplus 1$), (3) the *minmax* binary operation ($\sqcup$) that gives the pair consisting of the minimum first value and the maximum second value, and (4) the *maxmin* binary operation ($\sqcap$) that is symmetric to ($\sqcup$).

Definition 7 introduces the counting semantics for LTL that for a finite trace π and LTL formula ϕ gives a pair $(s, f) \in \mathbb{N}_+ \times \mathbb{N}_+$. We call s and f *satisfaction* and *violation witness counts*, respectively. Intuitively, the s (f) value denotes the minimal number of additional steps that is needed to witness the satisfaction (violation) of the formula. The value ∞ is used to denote that the property can be satisfied (violated) only in an infinite number of steps, while $-$ means the property cannot be satisfied (violated) by any continuation of the trace.

Definition 5 (Operations $\sim$, $\oplus 1$, $\sqcup$, $\sqcap$). *Given two pairs $(s, f) \in \mathbb{N}_+ \times \mathbb{N}_+$ and $(s', f') \in \mathbb{N}_+ \times \mathbb{N}_+$, we have:*

$$\begin{aligned} \sim (s, f) &= (f, s), \\ (s, f) \oplus 1 &= (s \oplus 1, f \oplus 1), \\ (s, f) \sqcup (s', f') &= (\min(s, s'), \max(f, f')), \\ (s, f) \sqcap (s', f') &= (\max(s, s'), \min(f, f')). \end{aligned}$$

Example 6. Given the pairs $(0, 0)$, $(\infty, 1)$ and $(7, -)$ we have the following:

$$\begin{aligned} \sim (0,0) &= (0,0), & \sim (\infty,1) &= (1,\infty), \\ (0,0) \oplus 1 &= (1,1), & (\infty,1) \oplus 1 &= (\infty,2), \\ (0,0) \sqcup (\infty,1) &= (0,1), & (\infty,1) \sqcup (7,-) &= (7,-), \\ (0,0) \sqcap (\infty,1) &= (\infty,0), & (\infty,1) \sqcap (7,-) &= (\infty,1). \end{aligned}$$

Remark. Note that $\mathbb{N}_+ \times \mathbb{N}_+$ forms a lattice where $(s, f) \trianglelefteq (s', f')$ when $s \geq s'$ and $f \leq f'$ with join $\sqcup$ and meet $\sqcap$. Intuitively, larger values are closer to true.

4.2 Semantics

We now present our finitary semantics.

Definition 7 (Counting finitary semantics). *Let $\pi \in \Pi^*$ be a finite trace, $i \in \mathbb{N}_{>0}$ be a position in or outside the trace and $\phi \in \Phi$ be an LTL formula. We define the counting finitary semantics of LTL as the function $d_\pi : \Phi \times \Pi^* \times \mathbb{N}_{>0} \rightarrow \mathbb{N}_+ \times \mathbb{N}_+$ such that:*

$$\begin{aligned}
d_\pi(p,i) &= \begin{cases} (0,-) & \textit{if } i \le |\pi| \wedge p \in \pi_i, \\ (-,0) & \textit{if } i \le |\pi| \wedge p \notin \pi_i, \\ (0,0) & \textit{if } i > |\pi|, \end{cases} \\
d_\pi(\neg\phi,i) &= \sim d_\pi(\phi,i), \\
d_\pi(\phi_1 \vee \phi_2,i) &= d_\pi(\phi_1,i) \sqcup d_\pi(\phi_2,i), \\
d_\pi(\mathsf{X}\,\phi,i) &= d_\pi(\phi,i+1) \oplus 1, \\
d_\pi(\phi\,\mathsf{U}\,\psi,i) &= \begin{cases} d_\pi(\psi,i) \sqcup \left(d_\pi(\phi,i) \sqcap d_\pi(\mathsf{X}(\phi\,\mathsf{U}\,\psi),i)\right) & \textit{if } i \le |\pi|, \\ d_\pi(\psi,i) \sqcup \left(d_\pi(\phi,i) \sqcap (-,\infty)\right) & \textit{if } i > |\pi|, \end{cases} \\
d_\pi(\mathsf{F}\,\phi,i) &= \begin{cases} d_\pi(\phi,i) \sqcup d_\pi(\mathsf{XF}\,\phi,i) & \textit{if } i \le |\pi|, \\ d_\pi(\phi,i) \sqcup (-,\infty) & \textit{if } i > |\pi|. \end{cases}
\end{aligned}$$

We now provide some motivations behind the above definitions.

Proposition. A proposition is either evaluated before or after the end of the trace. If it is evaluated before the end of the trace and the proposition holds, the satisfaction and violations witness counts are trivially 0 and $-$, respectively. In the case that the proposition does not hold, we have the symmetric witness counts. Finally, we take an optimistic view in case of evaluating a proposition after the end of the trace: The trace can be extended to a trace with i steps s.t. either p holds or p does not hold.

Negation. Negating a formula simply swaps the witness counts. If we witness the satisfaction of ϕ in n steps, we witness the violation of $\neg\phi$ in n steps, and vice versa.

Disjunction. We take the shorter satisfaction witness count, because the satisfaction of one subformula is enough to satisfy the property. And we take the longer violation witness count, because both subformulas need to be violated to violate the property.

Next. The next operator naturally increases the witness counts by one step.

Eventually. We use the rewriting rule $\mathsf{F}\,\phi \equiv \phi \vee \mathsf{XF}\,\phi$ to define the semantics of the eventually operator. When evaluating the formula after the end of the trace, we replace the remaining obligation $(\mathsf{XF}\,\phi)$ by $(-,\infty)$. Thus, $\mathsf{F}\,\phi$ evaluated on the empty word is satisfied by a suffix that satisfies ϕ, and it is violated only by infinite suffixes.

Until. We use the same principle for defining the until semantics that we used for the eventually operator. We use the rewriting rule $\phi\,\mathsf{U}\,\psi \equiv \psi \vee (\phi \wedge \mathsf{X}(\phi\,\mathsf{U}\,\psi))$. On the empty word, $\phi\,\mathsf{U}\,\psi$ is satisfied (in the shortest way) by a suffix that satisfies ψ, and it is violated by a suffix that violates both ϕ and ψ.

Example 8. We refer to our motivating example from Table 1 and evaluate the trace τ_2 with respect to the specification ψ. We present the outcome in Table 2. We see that every proposition evaluates to $(0,-)$ when true. The satisfaction of a proposition that holds at time i is immediately witnessed and it cannot be violated by any suffix. Similarly, a proposition evaluates to $(-,0)$ when false. The valuations of $\mathsf{F}\,g$ count the number of steps to positions in which g holds. For instance, the first time at which g holds is $i = 3$, hence $\mathsf{F}\,g$ evaluates to

$(2,-)$ at time 1, $(1,-)$ at time 2 and $(0,-)$ at time 3. We also note that $\mathsf{F}\,g$ evaluates to $(0,\infty)$ at the end of the trace – it could be immediately satisfied with the continuation of the trace with g that holds, but could be violated only by an infinite suffix in which g never holds. We finally observe that $\mathsf{G}(r \rightarrow \mathsf{F}\,g)$ evaluates to (∞,∞) at all positions – the property can be both satisfied and violated only with infinite suffixes.

Table 2. Unbounded response property example: $d_\pi(\phi, i)$ with the trace $\pi = \tau_2$.

	1	2	3	4	5	6	7	EOT
r	$\top$	$-$	$-$	$\top$	$-$	$-$	$\top$	
g	$-$	$-$	$\top$	$-$	$-$	$\top$	$-$	
$d_\pi(r,i)$	$(0,-)$	$(-,0)$	$(-,0)$	$(0,-)$	$(-,0)$	$(-,0)$	$(0,-)$	(0,0)
$d_\pi(g,i)$	$(-,0)$	$(-,0)$	$(0,-)$	$(-,0)$	$(-,0)$	$(0,-)$	$(-,0)$	(0,0)
$d_\pi(\neg r,i)$	$(-,0)$	$(0,-)$	$(0,-)$	$(-,0)$	$(0,-)$	$(0,-)$	$(-,0)$	(0,0)
$d_\pi(\mathsf{F}\,g,i)$	$(2,-)$	$(1,-)$	$(0,-)$	$(2,-)$	$(1,-)$	$(0,-)$	$(1,\infty)$	$(0,\infty)$
$d_\pi(r \rightarrow \mathsf{F}\,g,i)$	$(2,-)$	$(0,-)$	$(0,-)$	$(2,-)$	$(0,-)$	$(0,-)$	$(1,\infty)$	$(0,\infty)$
$d_\pi(\mathsf{G}(r \rightarrow \mathsf{F}\,g),i)$	(∞,∞)	(∞,∞)	(∞,∞)	(∞,∞)	(∞,∞)	(∞,∞)	(∞,∞)	(∞,∞)

We use "$-$" instead of "$\bot$" in the traces r and g to improve the readability.

Not all pairs $(s,f) \in \mathbb{N}_+ \times \mathbb{N}_+$ are possible according to the counting semantics. We present the possible pairs in Lemma 9.

Lemma 9. *Let $\pi \in \Pi^*$ be a finite trace, ϕ an LTL formula and $i \in \mathbb{N}_0$ an index. We have that $d_\pi(\phi,i)$ is of the form $(a,-)$, $(-,a)$, (b_1,b_2), (b_1,∞), (∞,b_2) or (∞,∞), where $a \leq |\pi| - i$ and $b_j > |\pi| - i$ for $j \in \{1,2\}$.*

Proof. The proof can be obtained using structural induction on the LTL formula (see Appendix A.2 in [2]).

Finally, we relate our counting semantics to the three valued semantics in Lemma 10.

Lemma 10. *Given an LTL formula and a trace $\pi \in \Pi^*$ where $i \in \mathbb{N}_{>0}$ is an index and ϕ is an LTL formula, we have that*

$$\begin{aligned}
d_\pi(\phi,i) = (a,-) &\leftrightarrow \mu_\pi(\phi,i) = \top, \\
&\quad \text{and } \nexists x < a\,.\,\pi' = \pi_i \cdot \pi_{i+1} \cdot \ldots \pi_{i+x}, \mu_{\pi'}(\phi,1) = \top \\
d_\pi(\phi,i) = (-,a) &\leftrightarrow \mu_\pi(\phi,i) = \bot, \\
&\quad \text{and } \nexists x < a\,.\,\pi' = \pi_i \cdot \pi_{i+1} \cdot \ldots \pi_{i+x}, \mu_{\pi'}(\phi,1) = \bot \\
d_\pi(\phi,i) = (b_1,b_2) &\leftrightarrow \mu_\pi(\phi,i) = ?,
\end{aligned}$$

where $a \leq |\pi| - i$ and b_j is either ∞ or $b_j > |\pi| - i$ for $j \in \{1,2\}$.

Intuitively, Lemma 10 holds because we only introduce the symbol "$-$" within the trace when a satisfaction (violation) is observed. And the values of a pair only propagate into the past (and never into the future).

4.3 Evaluation

We now propose a mapping that predicts a qualitative verdict from our counting semantics. We adopt a 5-valued set consisting of true ($\top$), presumably true ($\top_P$), inconclusive (?), presumably false ($\bot_P$) and false ($\bot$) verdicts. We define the following order over these five values: $\bot < \bot_P < ? < \top_P < \top$. We equip this 5-valued domain with the negation ($\neg$) and disjunction ($\vee$) operations, letting $\neg\top = \bot$, $\neg\top_P = \bot_P$, $\neg? = ?$, $\neg\bot_P = \top_P$, $\neg\bot = \top$ and $\phi_1 \vee \phi_2 = \max\{\phi_1, \phi_2\}$. We define other Boolean operators such as conjunction by the usual logical equivalences ($\phi_1 \wedge \phi_2 = \neg(\neg\phi_1 \vee \neg\phi_2)$, etc.).

We evaluate a property on a trace to $\top$ ($\bot$) when the satisfaction (violation) can be fully determined from the trace, following the definition of the three-valued semantics μ. Intuitively, this takes care of the case in which the safety (co-safety) part of a formula has been violated (satisfied), at least for properties that are intentionally safe (intentionally co-safe, resp.) [10].

Whenever the truth value is not determined, we distinguish whether $d_\pi(\phi, i)$ indicates the possibility for a satisfaction, respective violation, in finite time or not. For possible satisfactions, respective violations, in finite time we make a prediction on whether past observations support the believe that the trace is going to satisfy or violate the property. If the predictions are not inconclusive and not contradicting, then we evaluate the trace to the (presumable) truth value $\top_P$ or$\bot_P$. If we cannot make a prediction to a truth value, we compute the truth value recursively based on the operator in the formula and the truth values of the subformulas (with temporal operators unrolled).

We use the predicate pred_π to give the prediction based on the observed witnesses for satisfaction. The predicate $\text{pred}_\pi(\phi, i)$ becomes ? when no witness for satisfaction exists in the past. When there exists a witness that requires at least the same amount of additional steps as the trace under evaluation then the predicate evaluates to $\top$. If all the existing witnesses (and at least one exists) are shorter than the current trace, then the predicate evaluates to $\bot$. For a prediction on the violation we make a prediction on the satisfaction of $d_\pi(\neg\phi, i)$, i.e., we compute $\text{pred}_\pi(\neg\phi, i)$.

Definition 11 (Prediction predicate). *Let s, f denote natural numbers and let $s_\pi(\phi, i), f_\pi(\phi, i) \in \mathbb{N}_+$ such that $d_\pi(\phi, i) = \big(s_\pi(\phi, i), f_\pi(\phi, i)\big)$. We define the 3-valued predicate pred_π as*

$$\text{pred}_\pi(\phi, i) = \begin{cases} \top & \text{if } \exists j < i \,.\, d_\pi(\phi, j) = (s', -) \text{ and } s_\pi(\phi, i) \leq s', \\ ? & \text{if } \nexists j < i \,.\, d_\pi(\phi, j) = (s', -), \\ \bot & \text{if } \exists j < i \,.\, d_\pi(\phi, j) = (s', -) \text{ and }, \\ & \quad s_\pi(\phi, i) > \max_{0 \leq j < i}\{s' \mid d_\pi(\phi, j) = (s', -)\}, \end{cases}$$

For the evaluation we consider a case split among the possible combinations of values in the pairs.

Definition 12 (Predictive evaluation). *We define the* predictive evaluation *function* $e_\pi(\phi, i)$, *with* $a \leq |\pi| - i$ *and* $b_j > |\pi| - i$ *for* $j \in \{1, 2\}$ *and* $a, b_j \in \mathbb{N}_0$, *for the different cases of* $d_\pi(\phi, i)$:

$d_\pi(\phi, i)$		$e_\pi(\phi, i)$
$(a, -)$		$\top$
(b_1, b_2)	*if* $pred_\pi(\phi, i) > pred_\pi(\neg\phi, i)$	$\top_P$
	if $pred_\pi(\phi, i) = pred_\pi(\neg\phi, i)$	$r_\pi(\phi, i)$
	if $pred_\pi(\phi, i) < pred_\pi(\neg\phi, i)$	$\bot_P$
(b_1, ∞)	*if* $pred_\pi(\phi, i) = \top$	$\top_P$
	if $pred_\pi(\phi, i) = ?$	$r_\pi(\phi, i)$
	if $pred_\pi(\phi, i) = \bot$	$\bot_P$
(∞, b_1)		$e_\pi(\neg\phi, i)$
(∞, ∞)		$r_\pi(\phi, i)$
$(-, a)$		$\bot$

where $r_\pi(\phi, i)$ is an auxiliary function defined inductively as follows:

$$r_\pi(p, i) = ?$$
$$r_\pi(\neg\phi, i) = \neg e_\pi(\phi, i)$$
$$r_\pi(\phi_1 \vee \phi_2, i) = e_\pi(\phi_1, i) \vee e_\pi(\phi_2, i)$$
$$r_\pi(\mathsf{X}^n\, \phi, i) = e_\pi(\phi, i + n)$$
$$r_\pi(\mathsf{F}\, \phi, i) = \begin{cases} e_\pi(\phi, i) \vee r_\pi(\mathsf{X}\,\mathsf{F}\, \phi, i) & \text{if } i \leq |\pi| \\ e_\pi(\phi, i) & \text{if } i > |\pi| \end{cases}$$
$$r_\pi(\phi_1\, \mathsf{U}\, \phi_2, i) = \begin{cases} e_\pi(\phi_2, i) \vee (e_\pi(\phi_2, i) \wedge e_\pi(\mathsf{X}(\phi_1\, \mathsf{U}\, \phi_2), i) & \text{if } i \leq |\pi| \\ e_\pi(\phi_2, i) & \text{if } i > |\pi| \end{cases}$$

The predictive evaluation function is symmetric. Hence, $e_\pi(\phi, i) = \neg e_\pi(\neg\phi, i)$ holds.

Example 13. The outcome of evaluating τ_2 from Table 1 is shown in Table 3. Subformula $r \rightarrow \mathsf{F}\, g$ is predicted to be $\top_P$ at $i = 7$ because there exists a longer witness for satisfaction in the past (e.g., at $i = 1$). Thus, the trace evaluates to $\top_P$, as expected.

In Fig. 1 we visualize the evaluation of a pair $d_\pi(\phi, i) = (s, f)$ for a fixed ϕ and a fixed position i. On the x-axis is the witness count s for a satisfaction and on the y-axis is the witness count f for a violation. For a value s, respectively f, that is smaller than the length of the suffix starting at position i (with the other value of the pair always being $-$), the evaluation is either $\top$ or $\bot$. Otherwise the evaluation depends on the values s_{max} and f_{max}. These two values

Table 3. Unbounded response property example with $\pi = \tau_2$.

	1	2	3	4	5	6	7	EOT
r	$\top$	$-$	$-$	$\top$	$-$	$-$	$\top$	
g	$-$	$-$	$\top$	$-$	$-$	$\top$	$-$	
$d_\pi(r,i)$	$(0,-)$	$(-,0)$	$(-,0)$	$(0,-)$	$(-,0)$	$(-,0)$	$(0,-)$	(0,0)
$e_\pi(r,i)$	$\top$	$\bot$	$\bot$	$\top$	$\bot$	$\bot$	$\top$	?
$d_\pi(g,i)$	$(-,0)$	$(-,0)$	$(0,-)$	$(-,0)$	$(-,0)$	$(0,-)$	$(-,0)$	(0,0)
$e_\pi(g,i)$	$\bot$	$\bot$	$\top$	$\bot$	$\bot$	$\top$	$\bot$	?
$d_\pi(\mathsf{F}\,g,i)$	$(2,-)$	$(1,-)$	$(0,-)$	$(2,-)$	$(1,-)$	$(0,-)$	$(1,\infty)$	$(0,\infty)$
$e_\pi(\mathsf{F}\,g,i)$	$\top$	$\top$	$\top$	$\top$	$\top$	$\top$	$\top_P$	$\top_P$
$d_\pi(r\rightarrow \mathsf{F}\,g,i)$	$(2,-)$	$(0,-)$	$(0,-)$	$(2,-)$	$(0,-)$	$(0,-)$	$(1,\infty)$	$(0,\infty)$
$e_\pi(r\rightarrow \mathsf{F}\,g,i)$	$\top$	$\top$	$\top$	$\top$	$\top$	$\top$	$\top_P$	$\top_P$
$d_\pi(\mathsf{G}(r\rightarrow \mathsf{F}\,g),i)$	(∞,∞)	(∞,∞)	(∞,∞)	(∞,∞)	(∞,∞)	(∞,∞)	(∞,∞)	(∞,∞)
$e_\pi(\mathsf{G}(r\rightarrow \mathsf{F}\,g),i)$	$\top_P$	$\top_P$	$\top_P$	$\top_P$	$\top_P$	$\top_P$	$\top_P$	$\top_P$

We use "$-$" instead of "$\bot$" in the traces r and g to improve the readability.

represent the largest witness counts for a satisfaction and a violation in the past, i.e., for positions smaller than i in the trace. Based on the prediction function $\text{pred}_\pi(\phi,i)$ the evaluation becomes $\top_P$, ? or $\bot_P$, where ? indicates that the auxiliary function $r_\pi(\phi,i)$ has to be applied. Starting at an arbitrary point in the diagram and moving to the right increases the witness count for a satisfaction while the witness count for a violation remains constant. Thus, moving to the right makes the pair "more false". The same holds when keeping the witness count for a satisfaction constant and moving up in the diagram as this decrease the witness count for a violation. Analogously, moving down and/or left makes the pair "more true" as the witness count for a violation gets larger and/or the witness count for a satisfaction gets smaller.

Our 5-valued predictive evaluation refines the 3-valued LTL semantics.

Theorem 14. *Let ϕ be an LTL formula, $\pi \in \Pi^*$ and $i \in \mathbb{N}_{>0}$. We have*

$$\mu_\pi(\phi,i) = \top \leftrightarrow e_\pi(\phi,i) = \top,$$
$$\mu_\pi(\phi,i) = \bot \leftrightarrow e_\pi(\phi,i) = \bot,$$
$$\mu_\pi(\phi,i) = ? \leftrightarrow e_\pi(\phi,i) \in \{\top_P, \bot_P, ?\}.$$

Theorem 14 holds, because the evaluation to $\top$ and $\bot$ is simply the mapping of a pair that contains the symbol "$-$", which we have shown in Lemma 10.

Remember that $\mathbb{N}_+ \times \mathbb{N}_+$ is partially ordered by $\trianglelefteq$. We now show that having a trace that is "more true" than another is correctly reflected in our finitary semantics. To define "more true", we first need the polarity of a proposition in an LTL formula.

Example 15. Note that g has positive polarity in $\phi = \mathsf{G}(r \rightarrow \mathsf{F}\,g)$. If we define τ_2' to be as τ_2, except that $g \in \tau_2'(i)$ for $i \in \{1,\ldots,6\}$, we have $e_{\tau_2'}(\phi,i) = \bot_P$, whereas $e_{\tau_2}(\phi,i) = \top_P$.

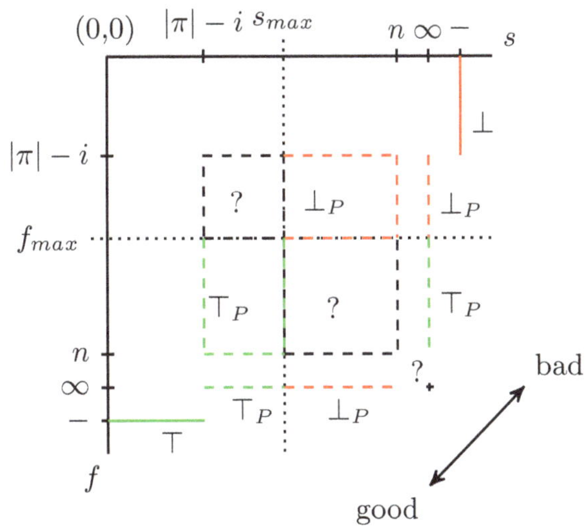

Fig. 1. Lattice for (s, f) with ϕ and $i < |\pi|$ fixed.

Definition 16 (Polarity). *Let $\#\neg$ be the number of negation operators on a specific path in the parse tree of ϕ starting at the root. We define the polarity as the function pol(p) with proposition p in an LTL formula ϕ as follows:*

$$pol(p) = \begin{cases} pos, & \text{if } \#\neg \text{ on all paths to a leaf with proposition } p \text{ is even,} \\ neg, & \text{if } \#\neg \text{ on all paths to a leaf with proposition } p \text{ is odd,} \\ mixed, & \text{otherwise.} \end{cases}$$

With the polarity defined, we now define the constraints for a trace to be "more true" with respect to an LTL formula ϕ.

Definition 17 ($\pi \sqsubseteq_\phi \pi'$). *Given two traces π and π' of equal length and an LTL formula ϕ over proposition p, we define that $\pi \sqsubseteq_\phi \pi'$ iff*

$$\begin{aligned} \forall i \forall p \,.\, pol(p) = mixed &\Rightarrow p \in \pi_i \leftrightarrow p \in \pi'_i \text{ and} \\ pol(p) = pos &\Rightarrow p \in \pi_i \rightarrow p \in \pi'_i \text{ and} \\ pol(p) = neg &\Rightarrow p \in \pi_i \leftarrow p \in \pi'_i. \end{aligned}$$

Whenever one trace is "more true" than another, this is correctly reflected in our finitary semantics.

Theorem 18. *For two traces π and π' of equal length and an LTL formula ϕ over proposition p, we have that*

$$\pi \sqsubseteq_\phi \pi' \Rightarrow d_{\pi'}(\phi, 1) \trianglelefteq d_\pi(\phi, 1).$$

Therefore, we have for $\pi \sqsubseteq_\phi \pi'$ that

$$\begin{aligned} e_\pi(\phi, 1) = \top &\Rightarrow e_{\pi'}(\phi, 1) = \top, \text{ and} \\ e_\pi(\phi, 1) = \bot &\Leftarrow e_{\pi'}(\phi, 1) = \bot. \end{aligned}$$

Theorem 18 holds, because we have that replacing an arbitrary observed value in π by one with positive polarity in π' always results with $d_\pi(\phi, 1) = (s, f)$ and $d_{\pi'}(\phi, 1) = (s', f')$ in $s' \leq s$ and $f' \geq f$, as with $\pi \sqsubseteq_\phi \pi'$ we have that π' witnesses a satisfaction of ϕ not later than π and π' also witness a violation of ϕ not earlier than π.

Table 4. Making a system "more true".

ϕ	π	$d_\pi(\phi, 1)$	$e_\pi(\phi, 1)$
p	$-$	$(-, 0)$	$\bot$
	$\top$	$(0, -)$	$\top$
$p \wedge \mathsf{X}\,\mathsf{F}\,p$	$- - -$	$(-, 0)$	$\bot$
	$\top - -$	$(3, \infty)$	$\bot_P$
$\mathsf{G}\,p$	$-\top\top$	$(-, 0)$	$\bot$
	$\top\top\top$	$(\infty, 3)$	$\top_P$
$\mathsf{F}\,p$	$- - -$	$(3, \infty)$	$\bot_P$
	$\top - -$	$(0, -)$	$\top$

ϕ	π	$d_\pi(\phi, 1)$	$e_\pi(\phi, 1)$
$\mathsf{F}\,\mathsf{G}\,p$	$\top - \top - \top$	(∞, ∞)	$\bot_P$
	$\top - \top\top\top$	(∞, ∞)	$\top_P$
$\mathsf{G}\,\mathsf{F}\,p$	$- - \top - -$	(∞, ∞)	$\top_P$
	$\top - \top - -$	(∞, ∞)	$\bot_P$
$p \vee \mathsf{X}\,\mathsf{G}\,p$	$-\top\top$	$(\infty, 3)$	$\top_P$
	$\top\top\top$	$(0, -)$	$\top$

In Table 4 we give examples to illustrate the transition of one evaluation to another one. Note that it is possible to change from $\top_P$ to $\bot_P$. However, this is only the predicated truth value that becomes "worse", because we have strengthened the prefix on which the prediction is based on, the values of $d_\pi(\phi, i)$ do not change and remain the same is such a case.

5 Examples

We demonstrate the strengths and weaknesses of our approach on the examples of LTL specifications and traces shown in Table 5. We fully develop these examples in Appendix B in [2].

Table 5. Examples of LTL specifications and traces

Specifications	Traces	
$\psi_1 \equiv \mathsf{F}\,\mathsf{X}\,g$	$\pi_1 : g : \bot\bot\bot\bot$	$\pi_5 : r : \bot\top\top\top\top\bot\top\top$
$\psi_2 \equiv \mathsf{G}\,\mathsf{X}\,g$	$\pi_2 : g : \top\top\top\top$	$g : \bot\top\bot\bot\bot\bot\top\bot$
$\psi_3 \equiv \mathsf{G}(r \rightarrow \mathsf{F}\,g)$	$\pi_3 : r : \bot\top\bot\bot\top\bot$	$\pi_6 : g : \top\top\bot\bot\top\top\bot\bot\top\top\bot\bot\top$
$\psi_4 \equiv \bigwedge_{i \in \{1,2\}} \mathsf{G}(r_i \rightarrow \mathsf{F}\,g_i)$	$g : \bot\bot\top\bot\bot\bot$	$\pi_7 : g : \top\top\bot\bot\top\top\bot\bot\top\top\top\top\top$
$\psi_5 \equiv \mathsf{G}((\mathsf{X}\,r)\,\mathsf{U}\,(\mathsf{X}\,\mathsf{X}\,g))$	$\pi_4 : r_1 : \top\bot\top\bot\top\bot\top$	$\pi_8 : r : \top\top\top\top\bot\bot$
$\psi_6 \equiv \mathsf{F}\,\mathsf{G}\,g \vee \mathsf{F}\,\mathsf{G}\,\neg g$	$g_1 : \bot\top\bot\top\bot\top\bot$	$g : \top\bot\top\bot\top\bot$
$\psi_7 \equiv \mathsf{G}(\mathsf{F}\,r \vee \mathsf{F}\,g)$	$r_2 : \bot\top\bot\top\bot\top\bot$	
$\psi_8 \equiv \mathsf{G}\,\mathsf{F}(r \vee g)$	$g_2 : \top\bot\top\bot\top\bot\top$	
$\psi_9 \equiv \mathsf{G}\,\mathsf{F}\,r \vee \mathsf{G}\,\mathsf{F}\,g$		

Table 6 summarizes the evaluation of our examples. The first and the second column denote the evaluated specification and trace. We use these examples to compare LTL with counting semantics (c-LTL) presented in this paper, to the other two popular finitary LTL interpretations, the 3-valued LTL semantics [4] (3-LTL) and LTL on trucated paths [9] (t-LTL). We recall that in t-LTL there is a distinction between a weak and a strong next operator. We denote by t-LTL-s (t-LTL-w) the specifications from our examples in which X is interpreted as the strong (weak) next operator and assume that we always give a strong interpretation to U and F and a weak interpretation to G.

Table 6. Comparison of different verdicts with different semantics

Spec.	Trace	c-LTL	3-LTL	t-LTL-s	t-LTL-w
ψ_1	π_1	$\bot_P$	?	$\bot$	$\top$
ψ_2	π_2	$\top_P$	?	$\bot$	$\top$
ψ_3	π_3	$\bot_P$	?	$\bot$	$\bot$
ψ_4	π_4	$\top_P$	?	$\bot$	$\bot$
ψ_5	π_5	$\top_P$	?	$\bot$	$\top$

Spec.	Trace	c-LTL	3-LTL	t-LTL-s	t-LTL-w
ψ_6	π_6	$\bot_P$	?	$\top$	$\top$
ψ_6	π_7	$\top_P$	?	$\top$	$\top$
ψ_7	π_8	$\bot_P$	?	$\bot$	$\bot$
ψ_8	π_8	$\bot_P$	?	$\bot$	$\bot$
ψ_9	π_8	$\top_P$	?	$\bot$	$\bot$

There are two immediate observations that we can make regarding the results presented in Table 6. First, the 3-valued LTL gives for all the examples an *inconclusive* verdict, a feedback that after all has little value to a verification engineer. The second observation is that the verdicts from c-LTL and t-LTL can differ quite a lot, which is not very surprising given the different strategies to interpret the unseen future. We now further comment on these examples, explaining in more details the results and highlighting the intuitive outcomes of c-LTL for a large class of interesting LTL specifications.

Effect of Nested Next. We evaluate with ψ_1 and ψ_2 the effect of nesting X in an F and an G formula, respectively. We make a prediction on Xg at the end of the trace before evaluating F and G. As a consequence, we find that (ψ_1, π_1) evaluates to presumably false, while (ψ_2, π_2) evaluates to presumably true. In t-LTL, this class of specification is very sensitive to the weak/strong interpretation of next, as we can see from the verdicts.

Request/Grants. We evaluate the request/grant property ψ_3 from the motivating example on the trace π_3. We observe that r at cycle 2 is followed by g at cycle 3, while r at cycle 5 is not followed by g at cycle 6. Hence, (ψ_3, π_3) evaluates to presumably false.

Concurrent Request/Grants. We evaluate the specification ψ_4 against the trace π_4. In this example r_1 is triggered at even time stamps and r_2 is triggered at odd time stamps. Every request is granted in one cycle. It follows that regardless of the time when the trace ends, there is one request that is not granted yet. We note that ψ_4 is a conjunction of two basic request/grant properties and we make independent predictions for each conjunct. Every basic request/grant property is evaluated to presumably true, hence (ψ_4, π_4) evaluates to presumably true. At this point, we note that in t-LTL, every request that is not granted by the end of the trace results in the property violation, regardless of the past observations.

Until. We use the specification ψ_5 and the trace π_5 to evaluate the effect of U on the predictions. The specification requires that $\mathsf{X}\,r$ continuously holds until $\mathsf{X}\,\mathsf{X}\,g$ becomes true. We can see that in π_5 $\mathsf{X}\,r$ is witnessed at cycles $1-4$, while $\mathsf{X}\,\mathsf{X}\,g$ is witnessed at cycle 5. We can also see that $\mathsf{X}\,r$ is again witnessed from cycle 6 until the end of the trace at cycle 8. As a consequence, (ψ_5, π_5) is evaluated to presumably true.

Stabilization. The specification ψ_6 says that the value of g has to eventually stabilize to either true or false. We evaluate the formula on two traces π_6 and π_7. In the trace π_6, g alternates between true and false every two cycles and becomes true in the last cycle. Hence, there is no sufficiently long witness of trace stabilization (ψ_6, π_6) evaluates to presumably false. In the trace π_7, g also alternates between true and false every two cycles, but in the last four cycles g remains continuously true. As a consequence, (ψ_6, π_7) evaluates to presumably true. This example also illustrates the importance of when the trace truncation occurs. If both π_6 and π_7 were truncated at cycle 5, both (ψ_6, π_6) and (ψ_6, π_7) would evaluate to presumably false. We note that ψ_6 is satisfied by all traces in t-LTL.

Sub-formula Domination. The specification ψ_7 exposes a weakness of our approach. It requires that in every cycle, either r or g is witnessed in some unbounded future. With our approach, (ψ_7, π_8) evaluates to presumably false. This is against our intuition because we have observed that g becomes regularly true very second time step. However, in this example our prediction for $\mathsf{F}\,r$ dominates over the prediction for $\mathsf{F}\,g$, leading to the unexpected presumably false verdict. On the other hand, t-LTL interpretation of the same specification is dependent only on the last value of r and g.

Semantically Equivalent Formulas. We now demonstrate that our approach may give different answers for semantically equivalent formulas. For instance, both ψ_8 and ψ_9 are semantically equivalent to ψ_7. We have that (ψ_8, π_8) evaluates to presumably false, while (ψ_9, π_8) evaluates to presumably true. We note that t-LTL verdicts are stable for semantically different formulas.

6 Conclusion

We have presented a novel finitary semantics for LTL that uses the history of satisfaction and violation in a finite trace to predict whether the co-safety and safety aspects of a formula will be satisfied in the extension of the trace to an infinite one. We claim that the semantics closely follow human intuition when predicting the truth value of a trace. The presented examples (incl. non-monitorable LTL properties) illustrate our approach and support this claim.

Our definition of the semantics is trace-based, but it is easily extended to take an entire database of traces into account, which may make the approach more precise. Our approach currently uses a very simple form of learning to predict the future. We would like to consider more sophisticated statistical methods to make better predictions. In particular, we plan to apply nonparametric statistical methods (i.e., the Wilcoxon signed-rank test [16]), in combination with our counting semantics, to identify and quantify the traces that are outliers.

References

1. Almagor, S., Boker, U., Kupferman, O.: Discounting in LTL. In: Ábrahám, E., Havelund, K. (eds.) TACAS 2014. LNCS, vol. 8413, pp. 424–439. Springer, Heidelberg (2014). https://doi.org/10.1007/978-3-642-54862-8_37
2. Bartocci, E., Bloem, R., Nickovic, D., Roeck, F.: A counting semantics for monitoring LTL specifications over finite traces. CoRR, abs/1804.03237 (2018)
3. Bartocci, E., Falcone, Y. (eds.): Lectures on Runtime Verification. LNCS, vol. 10457. Springer, Cham (2018). https://doi.org/10.1007/978-3-319-75632-5
4. Bauer, A., Leucker, M., Schallhart, C.: Monitoring of real-time properties. In: Arun-Kumar, S., Garg, N. (eds.) FSTTCS 2006. LNCS, vol. 4337, pp. 260–272. Springer, Heidelberg (2006). https://doi.org/10.1007/11944836_25
5. Bauer, A., Leucker, M., Schallhart, C.: The good, the bad, and the ugly, but how ugly is ugly? In: Sokolsky, O., Taşıran, S. (eds.) RV 2007. LNCS, vol. 4839, pp. 126–138. Springer, Heidelberg (2007). https://doi.org/10.1007/978-3-540-77395-5_11
6. Bauer, A., Leucker, M., Schallhart, C.: Runtime verification for LTL and TLTL. ACM Trans. Softw. Eng. Methodol. **20**(4), 14:1–14:64 (2011)
7. Boker, U., Chatterjee, K., Henzinger, T.A., Kupferman, O.: Temporal specifications with accumulative values. ACM Trans. Comput. Logic **15**(4), 27:1–27:25 (2014)
8. Daca, P., Henzinger, T.A., Křetínský, J., Petrov, T.: Faster statistical model checking for unbounded temporal properties. In: Chechik, M., Raskin, J.-F. (eds.) TACAS 2016. LNCS, vol. 9636, pp. 112–129. Springer, Heidelberg (2016). https://doi.org/10.1007/978-3-662-49674-9_7
9. Eisner, C., Fisman, D., Havlicek, J., Lustig, Y., McIsaac, A., Van Campenhout, D.: Reasoning with temporal logic on truncated paths. In: Hunt, W.A., Somenzi, F. (eds.) CAV 2003. LNCS, vol. 2725, pp. 27–39. Springer, Heidelberg (2003). https://doi.org/10.1007/978-3-540-45069-6_3
10. Kupferman, O., Vardi, M.Y.: Model checking of safety properties. Form. Methods Syst. Des. **19**(3), 291–314 (2001)
11. Manna, Z., Pnueli, A.: The Temporal Logic of Reactive and Concurrent Systems - Specification. Springer, Heidelberg (1992). https://doi.org/10.1007/978-1-4612-0931-7
12. Morgenstern, A., Gesell, M., Schneider, K.: An asymptotically correct finite path semantics for LTL. In: Bjørner, N., Voronkov, A. (eds.) LPAR 2012. LNCS, vol.

7180, pp. 304–319. Springer, Heidelberg (2012). https://doi.org/10.1007/978-3-642-28717-6_24
13. Pnueli, A.: The temporal logic of programs. In: 18th Annual Symposium on Foundations of Computer Science, Providence, Rhode Island, USA, 31 October–1 November 1977, pp. 46–57 (1977)
14. Pnueli, A., Zaks, A.: PSL model checking and run-time verification via testers. In: Misra, J., Nipkow, T., Sekerinski, E. (eds.) FM 2006. LNCS, vol. 4085, pp. 573–586. Springer, Heidelberg (2006). https://doi.org/10.1007/11813040_38
15. Viswanathan, M., Kim, M.: Foundations for the run-time monitoring of reactive systems – fundamentals of the MaC language. In: Liu, Z., Araki, K. (eds.) ICTAC 2004. LNCS, vol. 3407, pp. 543–556. Springer, Heidelberg (2005). https://doi.org/10.1007/978-3-540-31862-0_38
16. Wilcoxon, F.: Individual comparisons by ranking methods. Biom. Bull. **1**(6), 80–83 (1945)
17. Zhang, X., Leucker, M., Dong, W.: Runtime verification with predictive semantics. In: Goodloe, A.E., Person, S. (eds.) NFM 2012. LNCS, vol. 7226, pp. 418–432. Springer, Heidelberg (2012). https://doi.org/10.1007/978-3-642-28891-3_37

Tools

Rabinizer 4: From LTL to Your Favourite Deterministic Automaton

Jan Křetínský(✉), Tobias Meggendorfer, Salomon Sickert, and Christopher Ziegler

Technical University of Munich, Munich, Germany
jan.kretinsky@gmail.com, {meggendo,sickert}@in.tum.de

Abstract. We present Rabinizer 4, a tool set for translating formulae of linear temporal logic to different types of deterministic ω-automata. The tool set implements and optimizes several recent constructions, including the first implementation translating the frequency extension of LTL. Further, we provide a distribution of PRISM that links Rabinizer and offers model checking procedures for probabilistic systems that are not in the official PRISM distribution. Finally, we evaluate the performance and in cases with any previous implementations we show enhancements both in terms of the size of the automata and the computational time, due to algorithmic as well as implementation improvements.

1 Introduction

Automata-theoretic approach [VW86] is a key technique for verification and synthesis of systems with linear-time specifications, such as formulae of linear temporal logic (LTL) [Pnu77]. It proceeds in two steps: first, the formula is translated into a corresponding automaton; second, the product of the system and the automaton is further analyzed. The size of the automaton is important as it directly affects the size of the product and thus largely also the analysis time, particularly for deterministic automata and probabilistic model checking in a very direct proportion. For verification of non-deterministic systems, mostly non-deterministic Büchi automata (NBA) are used [EH00,SB00,GO01,GL02, BKŘS12,DLLF+16] since they are typically very small and easy to produce.

Probabilistic LTL model checking cannot profit directly from NBA. Even the qualitative question, whether a formula holds with probability 0 or 1, requires automata with at least a restricted form of determinism. The prime example are the limit-deterministic (also called semi-deterministic) Büchi automata (LDBA) [CY88] and the generalized LDBA (LDGBA). However, for the general quantitative questions, where the probability of satisfaction is computed, general limit-determinism is not sufficient. Instead, deterministic Rabin automata (DRA) have

This work has been partially supported by the Czech Science Foundation grant No. P202/12/G061 and the German Research Foundation (DFG) project KR 4890/1-1 "Verified Model Checkers" (317422601). A part of the frequency extension has been implemented within Google Summer of Code 2016.

H. Chockler and G. Weissenbacher (Eds.): CAV 2018, LNCS 10981, pp. 567–577, 2018.
https://doi.org/10.1007/978-3-319-96145-3_30

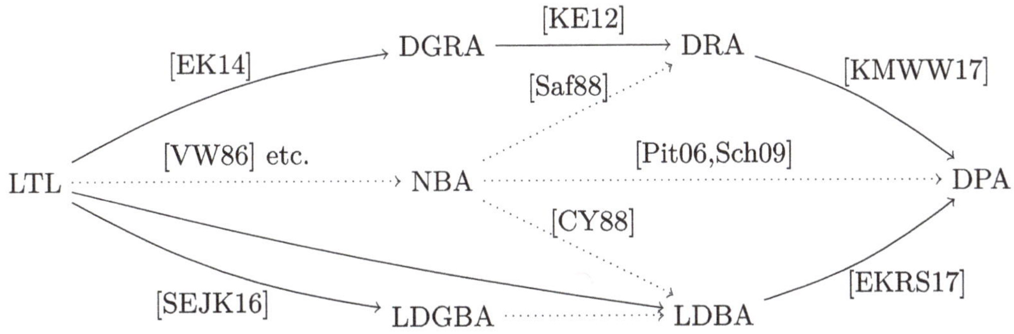

Fig. 1. LTL translations to different types of automata. Translations implemented in Rabinizer 4 are indicated with a solid line. The traditional approaches are depicted as dotted arrows. The determinization of NBA to DRA is implemented in ltl2dstar [Kle], to LDBA in Seminator [BDK+17] and to (mostly) DPA in spot [DLLF+16].

been mostly used [KNP11] and recently also deterministic generalized Rabin automata (DGRA) [CGK13]. In principle, all standard types of deterministic automata are applicable here except for deterministic Büchi automata (DBA), which are not as expressive as LTL. However, other types of automata, such as deterministic Muller and deterministic parity automata (DPA) are typically larger than DGRA in terms of acceptance condition or the state space, respectively.[1] Recently, several approaches with specific LDBA were proved applicable to the quantitative setting [HLS+15, SEJK16] and competitive with DGRA. Besides, model checking MDP against LTL properties involving frequency operators [BDL12] also allows for an automata-theoretic approach, via deterministic generalized Rabin mean-payoff automata (DGRMA) [FKK15].

LTL synthesis can also be solved using the automata-theoretic approach. Although DRA and DGRA transformed into games can be used here, the algorithms for the resulting Rabin games [PP06] are not very efficient in practice. In contrast, DPA may be larger, but in this setting they are the automata of choice due to the good practical performance of parity-game solvers [FL09, ML16, JBB+17].

Types of Translations. The translations of LTL to NBA, e.g., [VW86], are typically *"semantic"* in the sense that each state is given by a set of logical formulae and the language of the state can be captured in terms of semantics of these formulae. In contrast, the determinization of Safra [Saf88] or its improvements [Pit06, Sch09, TD14, FL15] are not "semantic" in the sense that they ignore the structure and produce trees as the new states that, however, lack the logical interpretation. As a result, if we apply Safra's determinization on semantically created NBA, we obtain DRA that lack the structure and, moreover, are unnecessarily large since the construction cannot utilize the original structure. In contrast, the

[1] Note that every DGRA can be written as a Muller automaton on the same state space with an exponentially-sized acceptance condition, and DPA are a special case of DRA and thus DGRA.

recent works [KE12,KLG13,EK14,KV15,SEJK16,EKRS17,MS17,KV17] provide "semantic" constructions, often producing smaller automata. Furthermore, various transformations such as degeneralization [KE12], index appearance record [KMWW17] or determinization of limit-deterministic automata [EKRS17] preserve the semantic description, allowing for further optimizations of the resulting automata.

Our Contribution. While all previous versions of Rabinizer [GKE12,KLG13, KK14] featured only the translation LTL→DGRA→DRA, Rabinizer 4 now implements all the translations depicted by the solid arrows in Fig. 1. It improves all these translations, both algorithmically and implementation-wise, and moreover, features the first implementation of the translation of a frequency extension of LTL [FKK15].

Further, in order to utilize the resulting automata for verification, we provide our own distribution[2] of the PRISM model checker [KNP11], which allows for model checking MDP against LTL using not only DRA and DGRA, but also using LDBA and against frequency LTL using DGRMA. Finally, the tool can turn the produced DPA into parity games between the players with input and output variables. Therefore, when linked to parity-game solvers, Rabinizer 4 can be also used for LTL synthesis.

Rabinizer 4 is freely available at http://rabinizer.model.in.tum.de together with an on-line demo, visualization, usage instructions and examples.

2 Functionality

We recall that the previous version Rabinizer 3 has the following functionality:

- It translates LTL formulae into equivalent DGRA or DRA.
- It is linked to PRISM, allowing for probabilistic verification using DGRA (previously PRISM could only use DRA).

2.1 Translations

Rabinizer 4 inputs formulae of LTL and outputs automata in the standard HOA format [BBD+15], which is used, e.g., as the input format in PRISM. Automata in the HOA format can be directly visualized, displaying the "semantic" description of the states. Rabinizer 4 features the following command-line tools for the respective translations depicted as the solid arrows in Fig. 1:

ltl2dgra and **ltl2dra** correspond to the original functionality of Rabinizer 3, i.e., they translate LTL (now with the extended syntax, including all common temporal operators) to DGRA and DRA [EK14], respectively.

[2] Merging these features into the public release of PRISM as well as linking the new version of Rabinizer is subject to current collaboration with the authors of PRISM.

ltl2ldgba and **ltl2ldba** translate LTL to LDGBA using the construction of [SEJK16] and to LDBA, respectively. The latter is our modification of the former, which produces smaller automata than chaining the former with the standard degeneralization.

ltl2dpa translates LTL to DPA using two modes:

- The default mode uses the translation to LDBA, followed by a LDBA-to-DPA determinization [EKRS17] specially tailored to LDBA with the "semantic" labelling of states, avoiding additional exponential blow-up of the resulting automaton.
- The alternative mode uses the translation to DRA, followed by our improvement of the index appearance record of [KMWW17].

fltl2dgrma translates the frequency extension of $\text{LTL}_{\setminus \mathbf{GU}}$, i.e. $\text{LTL}_{\setminus \mathbf{GU}}$ [KLG13] with $\mathbf{G}^{\sim\rho}$ operator[3], to DGRMA using the construction of [FKK15].

2.2 Verification and Synthesis

The resulting automata can be used for model checking probabilistic systems and for LTL synthesis. To this end, we provide our own distribution of the probabilistic model checker PRISM as well as a procedure transforming automata into games to be solved.

Model checking: PRISM distribution. For model checking Markov chains and Markov decision processes, PRISM [KNP11] uses DRA and recently also more efficient DGRA [CGK13, KK14]. Our distribution, which links Rabinizer, additionally features model checking using the LDBA [SEJK16, SK16] that are created by our **ltl2ldba**.
Further, the distribution provides an implementation of frequency $\text{LTL}_{\setminus \mathbf{GU}}$ model checking, using DGRMA. To the best of our knowledge, there are no other implemented procedures for logics with frequency. Here, techniques of linear programming for multi-dimensional mean-payoff satisfaction [CKK15] and the model-checking procedure of [FKK15] are implemented and applied.

Synthesis: Games. The automata-theoretic approach to LTL synthesis requires to transform the LTL formula into a game of the input and output players. We provide this transformer and thus an end-to-end LTL synthesis solution, provided a respective game solver is linked. Since current solutions to Rabin games are not very efficient we implemented a transformation of DPA into parity games and a serialization to the format of PG Solver [FL09]. Due to the explicit serialization, we foresee the main use in quick prototyping.

[3] The *frequential globally* construct [BDL12, BMM14] $\mathbf{G}^{\sim\rho}\varphi$ with $\sim \in \{\geq, >, \leq, <\}, \rho \in [0,1]$ intuitively means that the fraction of positions satisfying φ satisfies $\sim\rho$. Formally, the fraction on an infinite run is defined using the long-run average [BMM14].

3 Optimizations, Implementation, and Evaluation

Compared to the theoretical constructions and previous implementations, there are numerous improvements, heuristics, and engineering enhancements. We evaluate the improvements both in terms of the size of the resulting automaton as well as the running time. When comparing with respect to the original Rabinizer functionality, we compare our implementation **ltl2dgra** to the previous version Rabinizer 3.1, which is already a significantly faster [EKS16] re-implementation of the official release Rabinizer 3 [KK14]. All of the benchmarks have been executed on a host with i7-4700MQ CPU (4x2.4 GHz), running Linux 4.9.0-5-amd64 and the Oracle JRE 9.0.4+11 JVM. Due to the start-up time of JVM, all times below 2 s are denoted by <2 and not specified more precisely. All experiments were given a time-out of 900 s and mem-out of 4GB, denoted by −.

Algorithmic improvements and heuristics for each of the translations:

ltl2dgra and **ltl2dra.** These translations create a master automaton monitoring the satisfaction of the given formula and a dedicated slave automaton for each subformula of the form $\mathbf{G}\psi$ [EK14]. We (i) simplify several classes of slaves and (ii) "suspend" (in the spirit of [BBDL+13]) some so that they appear in the final product only in some states. The effect on the size of the state space is illustrated in Table 1 on a nested formula. Further, (iii) the acceptance condition is considered separately for each strongly connected component (SCC) and then combined. On a concrete example of Table 2, the automaton for $i = 8$ has 31 atomic propositions, whereas the number of atomic propositions relevant in each component of the master automaton is constant, which we utilize and thus improve performance on this family both in terms of size and time.

ltl2ldba. This translation is based on breakpoints for subformulae of the form $\mathbf{G}\psi$. We provide a heuristic that avoids breakpoints when ψ is a safety or co-safety subformula, see Table 3.
Besides, we add an option to generate a non-deterministic initial component for the LDBA instead of a deterministic one. Although the LDBA is then no more suitable for quantitative probabilistic model checking, it still is for qualitative model checking. At the same time, it can be much smaller, see Table 4 which shows a significant improvement on the particular formula.

ltl2dpa. Both modes inherit the improvements of the respective **ltl2ldba** and **ltl2dgra** translations. Further, since complementing DPA is trivial, we can run in parallel both the translation of the input formula and of its negation, returning the smaller of the two results. Finally, we introduce several heuristics to optimize the treatment of safety subformulae of the input formula.

dra2dpa. The index appearance record of [KMWW17] keeps track of a permutation (ordering) of Rabin pairs. To do so, all ties between pairs have to be resolved. In our implementation, we keep a pre-order instead, where irrelevant ties are not resolved. Consequently, it cannot happen that an irrelevant tie is resolved in two different ways like in [KMWW17], thus effectively merging such states.

Table 1. Effect of simplifications and suspension for **ltl2dgra** on the formulae $\psi_i = \mathbf{G}\phi_i$ where $\phi_1 = a_1, \phi(i) = (a_i\mathbf{U}(\mathbf{X}\phi_{i-1}))$, and $\psi'_i = \mathbf{G}\phi'_i$ where $\phi'_1 = a_1$, $\phi'_1 = (\phi'_{i-1}\mathbf{U}(\mathbf{X}^i a_i)$, displaying execution time in seconds/#states.

	ψ_2	ψ_3	ψ_4	ψ_5	ψ_6
Rabinizer 3.1 [EKS16]	<2/4	<2/16	<2/73	3/332	60/1463
ltl2dgra	<2/3	<2/7	<2/35	3/199	13/1155
	ψ'_2	ψ'_3	ψ'_4	ψ'_5	ψ'_6
Rabinizer 3.1 [EKS16]	<2/4	<2/16	2/104	128/670	–
ltl2dgra	<2/3	<2/10	<2/38	7/175	239/1330

Table 2. Effect of computing acceptance sets per SCC on formulae $\psi_1 = x_1 \wedge \phi_1$, $\psi_2 = (x_1 \wedge \phi_1) \vee (\neg x_1 \wedge \phi_2)$, $\psi_3 = (x_1 \wedge x_2 \wedge \phi_1) \vee (\neg x_1 \wedge x_2 \wedge \phi_2) \vee (x_1 \wedge \neg x_2 \wedge \phi_3), \ldots,$ where $\phi_i = \mathbf{XG}((a_i\mathbf{U}b_i) \vee (c_i\mathbf{U}d_i))$, displaying execution time in seconds/#acceptance sets.

	ψ_1	ψ_2	ψ_3	ψ_4	ψ_5	...	ψ_8
Rabinizer 3.1 [EKS16]	<2/2	<2/7	<2/19	–	–		–
ltl2dgra	<2/1	<2/1	<2/1	<2/1	<2/1		<2/1

Table 3. Effect of break-point elimination for **ltl2ldba** on safety formulae $s(n, m) = \bigwedge_{i=1}^{n} \mathbf{G}(a_i \vee \mathbf{X}^m b_i)$ and for **ltl2ldgba** on liveness formulae $l(n, m) = \bigwedge_{i=1}^{n} \mathbf{GF}(a_i \wedge \mathbf{X}^m b_i)$, displaying #states (#Büchi conditions)

	$s(1,3)$	$s(2,3)$	$s(3,3)$	$s(4,3)$	$s(1,4)$	$s(2,4)$	$s(3,4)$	$s(4,4)$
[SEJK16]	20 (1)	400 (2)	$8 \cdot 10^3$(3)	$16 \cdot 10^4$(4)	48 (1)	2304 (2)	110592 (3)	–
ltl2ldba	8 (1)	64 (1)	512 (1)	4096 (1)	16 (1)	256 (1)	4096 (1)	65536 (1)
	$l(1,1)$	$l(2,1)$	$l(3,1)$	$l(4,1)$	$l(1,4)$	$l(2,4)$	$l(3,4)$	$l(4,4)$
[SEJK16]	3 (1)	9 (2)	27 (3)	81 (4)	10 (1)	100 (2)	10^3 (3)	10^4 (4)
ltl2ldgba	3 (1)	5 (2)	9 (3)	17 (4)	3 (1)	5 (2)	9 (3)	17 (4)

Table 4. Effect of non-determinism of the initial component for **ltl2ldba** on formulae $f(i) = \mathbf{F}(a \wedge \mathbf{X}^i\mathbf{G}b)$, displaying #states (#Büchi conditions)

	$f(1)$	$f(2)$	$f(3)$	$f(4)$	$f(5)$	$f(6)$
[SEJK16]	4 (1)	6 (1)	10 (1)	18 (1)	34 (1)	66 (1)
ltl2ldba	2 (1)	3 (1)	4 (1)	5 (1)	6 (1)	7 (1)

Table 5. Comparison of the average performance with the previous version of Rabinizer. The statistics are taken over a set of 200 standard formulae [KMS18] used, e.g., in [BKS13,EKS16], run in a batch mode for both tools to eliminate the effect of the JVM start-up overhead.

Tool	Avg # states	Avg # acc. sets	Avg runtime
Rabinizer 3.1 [EKS16]	6.3	6.7	0.23
ltl2dgra	6.2	4.4	0.12

Implementation. The main performance bottleneck of the older implementations is that explicit data structures for the transition system are not efficient for larger alphabets. To this end, Rabinizer 3.1 provided symbolic (BDD) representation of states and edge labels. On the top, Rabinizer 4 represents the transition function symbolically, too.

Besides, there are further engineering improvements on issues such as storing the acceptance condition only as a local edge labelling, caching, data-structure overheads, SCC-based divide-and-conquer constructions, or the introduction of parallelization for batch inputs.

Average Performance Evaluation. We have already illustrated the improvements on several hand-crafted families of formulae. In Tables 1 and 2 we have even seen the respective running-time speed-ups. As the basis for the overall evaluation of the improvements, we use some established datasets from literature, see [KMS18], altogether two hundred formulae. The results in Table 5 indicate that the performance improved also on average among the more realistic formulae.

4 Conclusion

We have presented Rabinizer 4, a tool set to translate LTL to various deterministic automata and to use them in probabilistic model checking and in synthesis. The tool set extends the previous functionality of Rabinizer, improves on previous translations, and also gives the very first implementations of frequency LTL translation as well as model checking. Finally, the tool set is also more user-friendly due to richer input syntax, its connection to PRISM and PG Solver, and the on-line version with direct visualization, which can be found at http://rabinizer.model.in.tum.de.

References

[BBD+15] Babiak, T., et al.: The hanoi omega-automata format. In: Kroening, D., Păsăreanu, C.S. (eds.) CAV 2015. LNCS, vol. 9206, pp. 479–486. Springer, Cham (2015). https://doi.org/10.1007/978-3-319-21690-4_31

[BBDL+13] Babiak, T., Badie, T., Duret-Lutz, A., Křetínský, M., Strejček, J.: Compositional approach to suspension and other improvements to LTL translation. In: Bartocci, E., Ramakrishnan, C.R. (eds.) SPIN 2013. LNCS, vol. 7976, pp. 81–98. Springer, Heidelberg (2013). https://doi.org/10.1007/978-3-642-39176-7_6

[BDK+17] Blahoudek, F., Duret-Lutz, A., Klokočka, M., Křetínský, M., Strejček, J.: Seminator: a tool for semi-determinization of omega-automata. In: LPAR, pp. 356–367 (2017)

[BDL12] Bollig, B., Decker, N., Leucker, M.: Frequency linear-time temporal logic. In: TASE, pp. 85–92 (2012)

[BKŘS12] Babiak, T., Křetínský, M., Řehák, V., Strejček, J.: LTL to Büchi automata translation: fast and more deterministic. In: Flanagan, C., König, B. (eds.) TACAS 2012. LNCS, vol. 7214, pp. 95–109. Springer, Heidelberg (2012). https://doi.org/10.1007/978-3-642-28756-5_8

[BKS13] Blahoudek, F., Křetínský, M., Strejček, J.: Comparison of LTL to deterministic rabin automata translators. In: McMillan, K., Middeldorp, A., Voronkov, A. (eds.) LPAR 2013. LNCS, vol. 8312, pp. 164–172. Springer, Heidelberg (2013). https://doi.org/10.1007/978-3-642-45221-5_12

[BMM14] Bouyer, P., Markey, N., Matteplackel, R.M.: Averaging in LTL. In: Baldan, P., Gorla, D. (eds.) CONCUR 2014. LNCS, vol. 8704, pp. 266–280. Springer, Heidelberg (2014). https://doi.org/10.1007/978-3-662-44584-6_19

[CGK13] Chatterjee, K., Gaiser, A., Křetínský, J.: Automata with generalized rabin pairs for probabilistic model checking and LTL synthesis. In: Sharygina, N., Veith, H. (eds.) CAV 2013. LNCS, vol. 8044, pp. 559–575. Springer, Heidelberg (2013). https://doi.org/10.1007/978-3-642-39799-8_37

[CKK15] Chatterjee, K., Komárková, Z., Křetínský, J.: Unifying two views on multiple mean-payoff objectives in Markov decision processes. In: LICS, pp. 244–256 (2015)

[CY88] Courcoubetis, C., Yannakakis, M.: Verifying temporal properties of finite-state probabilistic programs. In: FOCS, pp. 338–345 (1988)

[DLLF+16] Duret-Lutz, A., Lewkowicz, A., Fauchille, A., Michaud, T., Renault, É., Xu, L.: Spot 2.0 — a framework for LTL and ω-automata manipulation. In: Artho, C., Legay, A., Peled, D. (eds.) ATVA 2016. LNCS, vol. 9938, pp. 122–129. Springer, Cham (2016). https://doi.org/10.1007/978-3-319-46520-3_8

[EH00] Etessami, K., Holzmann, G.J.: Optimizing Büchi automata. In: Palamidessi, C. (ed.) CONCUR 2000. LNCS, vol. 1877, pp. 153–168. Springer, Heidelberg (2000). https://doi.org/10.1007/3-540-44618-4_13

[EK14] Esparza, J., Křetínský, J.: From LTL to deterministic automata: a safraless compositional approach. In: Biere, A., Bloem, R. (eds.) CAV 2014. LNCS, vol. 8559, pp. 192–208. Springer, Cham (2014). https://doi.org/10.1007/978-3-319-08867-9_13

[EKRS17] Esparza, J., Křetínský, J., Raskin, J.-F., Sickert, S.: From LTL and limit-deterministic Büchi automata to deterministic parity automata. In: Legay, A., Margaria, T. (eds.) TACAS 2017. LNCS, vol. 10205, pp. 426–442. Springer, Heidelberg (2017). https://doi.org/10.1007/978-3-662-54577-5_25

[EKS16] Esparza, J., Kretínský, J., Sickert, S.: From LTL to deterministic automata - a safraless compositional approach. Formal Methods Syst. Des. **49**(3), 219–271 (2016)

[FKK15] Forejt, V., Krčál, J., Křetínský, J.: Controller synthesis for MDPs and frequency LTL\GU. In: LPAR, pp. 162–177 (2015)

[FL09] Friedmann, O., Lange, M.: Solving parity games in practice. In: Liu, Z., Ravn, A.P. (eds.) ATVA 2009. LNCS, vol. 5799, pp. 182–196. Springer, Heidelberg (2009). https://doi.org/10.1007/978-3-642-04761-9_15

[FL15] Fisman, D., Lustig, Y.: A modular approach for büchi determinization. In: CONCUR, pp. 368–382 (2015)

[GKE12] Gaiser, A., Křetínský, J., Esparza, J.: Rabinizer: small deterministic automata for LTL(**F**,**G**). In: Chakraborty, S., Mukund, M. (eds.) ATVA 2012. LNCS, pp. 72–76. Springer, Heidelberg (2012). https://doi.org/10.1007/978-3-642-33386-6_7

[GL02] Giannakopoulou, D., Lerda, F.: From states to transitions: improving translation of LTL formulae to Büchi automata. In: Peled, D.A., Vardi, M.Y. (eds.) FORTE 2002. LNCS, vol. 2529, pp. 308–326. Springer, Heidelberg (2002). https://doi.org/10.1007/3-540-36135-9_20

[GO01] Gastin, P., Oddoux, D.: Fast LTL to Büchi automata translation. In: Berry, G., Comon, H., Finkel, A. (eds.) CAV 2001. LNCS, vol. 2102, pp. 53–65. Springer, Heidelberg (2001). https://doi.org/10.1007/3-540-44585-4_6. http://www.lsv.ens-cachan.fr/ gastin/ltl2ba/

[HLS+15] Hahn, E.M., Li, G., Schewe, S., Turrini, A., Zhang, L.: Lazy probabilistic model checking without determinisation. In: CONCUR. LIPIcs, vol. 42, pp. 354–367 (2015)

[JBB+17] Jacobs, S., Basset, N., Bloem, R., Brenguier, R., Colange, M., Faymonville, P., Finkbeiner, B., Khalimov, A., Klein, F., Michaud, T., Pérez, G.A., Raskin, J.-F., Sankur, O., Tentrup, L.: The 4th reactive synthesis competition (SYNTCOMP 2017): benchmarks, participants & results. CoRR, abs/1711.11439 (2017)

[KE12] Křetínský, J., Esparza, J.: Deterministic automata for the (F,G)-fragment of LTL. In: Madhusudan, P., Seshia, S.A. (eds.) CAV 2012. LNCS, vol. 7358, pp. 7–22. Springer, Heidelberg (2012). https://doi.org/10.1007/978-3-642-31424-7_7

[KK14] Komárková, Z., Křetínský, J.: Rabinizer 3: safraless translation of LTL to small deterministic automata. In: Cassez, F., Raskin, J.-F. (eds.) ATVA 2014. LNCS, vol. 8837, pp. 235–241. Springer, Cham (2014). https://doi.org/10.1007/978-3-319-11936-6_17

[Kle] Klein, J.: ltl2dstar - LTL to deterministic Streett and Rabin automata. http://www.ltl2dstar.de/

[KLG13] Křetínský, J., Garza, R.L.: Rabinizer 2: Small Deterministic Automata for LTL\GU. In: Van Hung, D., Ogawa, M. (eds.) ATVA 2013. LNCS, vol. 8172, pp. 446–450. Springer, Cham (2013). https://doi.org/10.1007/978-3-319-02444-8_32

[KMS18] Křetínský, J., Meggendorfer, T., Sickert, S.: LTL store: repository of LTL formulae from literature and case studies. CoRR, abs/1807.03296 (2018)

[KMWW17] Křetínský, J., Meggendorfer, T., Waldmann, C., Weininger, M.: Index appearance record for transforming rabin automata into parity automata. In: Legay, A., Margaria, T. (eds.) TACAS 2017. LNCS, vol. 10205, pp. 443–460. Springer, Heidelberg (2017). https://doi.org/10.1007/978-3-662-54577-5_26

[KNP11] Kwiatkowska, M., Norman, G., Parker, D.: PRISM 4.0: verification of probabilistic real-time systems. In: Gopalakrishnan, G., Qadeer, S. (eds.) CAV 2011. LNCS, vol. 6806, pp. 585–591. Springer, Heidelberg (2011). https://doi.org/10.1007/978-3-642-22110-1_47

[KV15] Kini, D., Viswanathan, M.: Limit deterministic and probabilistic automata for LTL\GU. In: Baier, C., Tinelli, C. (eds.) TACAS 2015. LNCS, vol. 9035, pp. 628–642. Springer, Heidelberg (2015). https://doi.org/10.1007/978-3-662-46681-0_57

[KV17] Kini, D., Viswanathan, M.: Optimal translation of LTL to limit deterministic automata. In: Legay, A., Margaria, T. (eds.) TACAS 2017. LNCS, vol. 10206, pp. 113–129. Springer, Heidelberg (2017). https://doi.org/10.1007/978-3-662-54580-5_7

[ML16] Meyer, P.J., Luttenberger, M.: Solving mean-payoff games on the GPU. In: Artho, C., Legay, A., Peled, D. (eds.) ATVA 2016. LNCS, vol. 9938, pp. 262–267. Springer, Cham (2016). https://doi.org/10.1007/978-3-319-46520-3_17

[MS17] Müller, D., Sickert, S.: LTL to deterministic Emerson-Lei automata. In: GandALF, pp. 180–194 (2017)

[Pit06] Piterman, N.: From nondeterministic Büchi and Streett automata to deterministic parity automata. In: LICS, pp. 255–264 (2006)

[Pnu77] Pnueli, A.: The temporal logic of programs. In: FOCS, pp. 46–57 (1977)

[PP06] Piterman, N., Pnueli, A.: Faster solutions of Rabin and Streett games. In: LICS, pp. 275–284 (2006)

[Saf88] Safra, S.: On the complexity of omega-automata. In: FOCS, pp. 319–327 (1988)

[SB00] Somenzi, F., Bloem, R.: Efficient Büchi automata from LTL formulae. In: Emerson, E.A., Sistla, A.P. (eds.) CAV 2000. LNCS, vol. 1855, pp. 248–263. Springer, Heidelberg (2000). https://doi.org/10.1007/10722167_21

[Sch09] Schewe, S.: Tighter bounds for the determinisation of Büchi automata. In: de Alfaro, L. (ed.) FoSSaCS 2009. LNCS, vol. 5504, pp. 167–181. Springer, Heidelberg (2009). https://doi.org/10.1007/978-3-642-00596-1_13

[SEJK16] Sickert, S., Esparza, J., Jaax, S., Křetínský, J.: Limit-deterministic Büchi automata for linear temporal logic. In: Chaudhuri, S., Farzan, A. (eds.) CAV 2016. LNCS, vol. 9780, pp. 312–332. Springer, Cham (2016). https://doi.org/10.1007/978-3-319-41540-6_17

[SK16] Sickert, S., Křetínský, J.: MoChiBA: probabilistic LTL model checking using limit-deterministic Büchi automata. In: Artho, C., Legay, A., Peled, D. (eds.) ATVA 2016. LNCS, vol. 9938, pp. 130–137. Springer, Cham (2016). https://doi.org/10.1007/978-3-319-46520-3_9

[TD14] Tian, C., Duan, Z.: Buchi determinization made tighter. Technical report abs/1404.1436, arXiv.org (2014)

[VW86] Vardi, M.Y., Wolper, P.: An automata-theoretic approach to automatic program verification (preliminary report). In: LICS, pp. 332–344 (1986)

Strix: Explicit Reactive Synthesis Strikes Back!

Philipp J. Meyer, Salomon Sickert(✉), and Michael Luttenberger

Technical University of Munich, Munich, Germany
{meyerphi,sickert,luttenbe}@in.tum.de

Abstract. STRIX is a new tool for reactive LTL synthesis combining a direct translation of LTL formulas into deterministic parity automata (DPA) and an efficient, multi-threaded explicit state solver for parity games. In brief, STRIX (1) decomposes the given formula into simpler formulas, (2) translates these on-the-fly into DPAs based on the queries of the parity game solver, (3) composes the DPAs into a parity game, and at the same time already solves the intermediate games using strategy iteration, and (4) finally translates the winning strategy, if it exists, into a Mealy machine or an AIGER circuit with optional minimization using external tools. We experimentally demonstrate the applicability of our approach by a comparison with PARTY, BOSY, and LTLSYNT using the SYNTCOMP2017 benchmarks. In these experiments, our prototype can compete with BOSY and LTLSYNT with only PARTY performing slightly better. In particular, our prototype successfully synthesizes the full and unmodified LTL specification of the AMBA protocol for $n = 2$ masters.

1 Introduction

Reactive synthesis refers to the problem of finding for a formal specification of an input-output relation, in our case a *linear temporal logic (LTL)*, a matching implementation [22], e.g. a *Mealy machine* or an *and-inverter-graph (AIG)*. Since the automata-theoretic approach to synthesis involves the construction of a potentially double exponentially sized automaton (in the length of the specification) [13], most existing tools focus on symbolic and bounded methods in order to combat the state-space explosion [5,9,11,18]. A beneficial side effect of these approaches is that they tend to yield succinct implementations.

In contrast to these approaches, we present a prototype implementation of an LTL synthesis tool which follows the automata theoretic approach using parity games as an intermediate step. STRIX[1] uses the LTL-to-DPA translation

This work was partially funded and supported by the German Research Foundation (DFG) projects "Game-based Synthesis for Industrial Automation" (253384115) and "Verified Model Checkers" (317422601).

[1] https://strix.model.in.tum.de/

H. Chockler and G. Weissenbacher (Eds.): CAV 2018, LNCS 10981, pp. 578–586, 2018.
https://doi.org/10.1007/978-3-319-96145-3_31

presented in [10,23] and the multi-threaded explicit-state parity game solver presented in [14,20]: First, the given formula is decomposed into much simpler requirements, often resulting in a large number of safety and co-safety conditions and only a few requiring Büchi or parity acceptance conditions, which is comparable to the approach of [5,21]. These requirements are then translated on-the-fly into automata, keeping the invariant that the parity game solver can easily compose the actual parity game. Further, by querying only for states that are actually required for deciding the winner, the implementation avoids unnecessary work.

The parity game solver is based on the *strategy iteration* of [19] which iteratively improves non-deterministic strategies, i.e. strategies that can allow several actions for a given state as long as they all are guaranteed to lead to the specified system behaviour. When translating the winning strategy into a Mealy automaton or an AIG this non-determinism can be used similarly to "don't cares" when minimizing boolean circuits. Strategy iteration offers us two additional advantages, first, we can directly take advantage of multi-core systems; second, we can reuse the winning strategies which have been computed for the intermediate arenas.

Related Work and Experimental Evaluation. From the tools submitted to SYNTCOMP2017, LTLSYNT [15] is closest to our approach: it also combines an LTL-to-DPA-translation with an explicit-state parity game solver, but it does not intertwine the two steps, instead it uses a different approach for the translation leading to one monolithic DPA which is then turned in a parity game. In contrast, the two best performing tools from SYNTCOMP2017, BoSy and Party, use bounded synthesis, by reduction either to SAT, SMT, or safety games.

In order to give a realistic estimation of how our tool would have faired at SYNTCOMP2017 (TLSF/LTL track), we tried to re-create the benchmark environment of SYNTCOMP2017 as close as possible on our hardware: in its current state, our tool would have been ranked below Party, but before LTLSYNT and BoSy. Due to time and resource constraints, we could only do an in-depth comparison with the current version of LTLSYNT; in particular we used the TLSF specification of the complete[2] AMBA protocol for $n = 2$ as a benchmark. We refer to Sect. 3 for details on the benchmarking procedure.

2 Design and Implementation

Strix is implemented in Java and C++. It supports LTL and TLSF [16] (only the reduced *basic* variant) as input languages, while the latter one is preferred, since it contains more information about the specification. We describe the main steps of the tool in the following paragraphs with examples given in Fig. 1.

[2] i.e. no decomposition in masters and clients or structural properties were used.

Splitting and Translation. As a preprocessing step the specification is split into syntactic (co)safety and (co)Büchi formulas, and one remaining general LTL formula. These are then translated into the simplest deterministic automaton class using the constructions of [10,23]. To speed up the process these automata are constructed on-the-fly, i.e., states are created only if requested by later stages. Furthermore, since DPAs can be easily complemented, the implementation translates the formula and its negation and chooses the faster obtained one.

$$\varphi = \underbrace{\mathbf{G}(\neg g_0 \vee \neg g_1)}_{\psi_1} \wedge \underbrace{\mathbf{G}(r_0 \rightarrow \mathbf{F} g_0)}_{\psi_2} \wedge \underbrace{\mathbf{G}(r_1 \rightarrow \mathbf{F} g_1)}_{\psi_3} \quad I = \{r_0, r_1\} \quad O = \{g_0, g_1\}$$

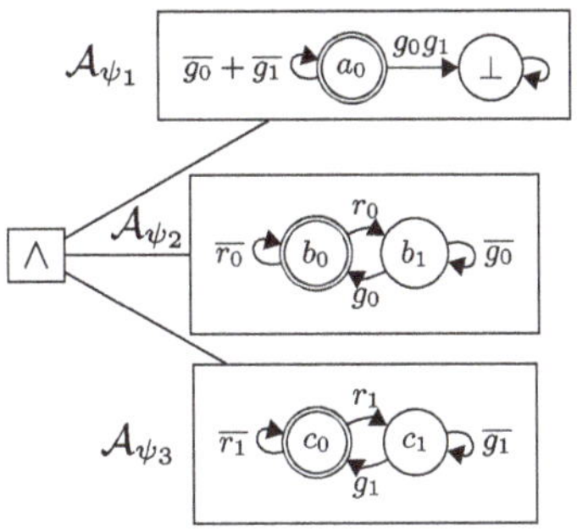

Splitted specification with one safety and two Büchi automata.

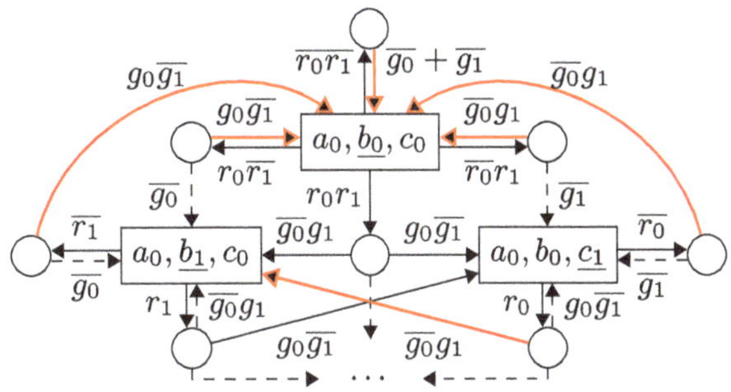

Partial min-even parity arena. Red thick edges have parity 0 and thin black edges parity 1.

Fig. 1. Synthesis of a simple arbiter with two clients. Here, a winning strategy is already obtained on the partial arena: always take any of the non-dashed edges.

Arena Construction. Here we construct one product automaton and combine the various acceptance conditions into a single parity acceptance condition: for this, we use the idea underlying the last-appearance-record construction, known from the translation of Muller to parity games, to directly obtain a parity game again.

Parity Game Solving. The parity game solver runs in parallel to the arena construction on the partially constructed game in order to guide the translation process, with the possibility for early termination when a winning strategy for the system player is found. It uses strategy iteration that supports non-deterministic strategies [19] from which we can benefit in several ways: First, in the translation process, the current strategy stays valid when adding nodes to the arena and thus can be used as initial strategy when solving the extended arena. Second, the non-deterministic strategies allow us to later heuristically select actions of the strategy that minimize the generated controller and to identify irrelevant output signals (similar to "don't care"-cells in Karnaugh maps). Finally, the strategy iteration can easily take advantage of multi-core architectures [14,20].

Controller Generation and Minimization. From the non-deterministic strategy we obtain an incompletely specified Mealy machine and optionally pass it to the external SAT-based minimizer MeMin [1] for Mealy machines and extract a more compact description.

AIGER Circuit Generation and Minimization. We translate the minimized Mealy machine with the tool Speculoos[3] into an AIGER circuit. In parallel, we also construct an AIGER circuit out of the non-minimized Mealy machine, since this can sometimes result in smaller circuits. The two AIGER circuits are then further compressed using ABC [6], and the smaller one is returned.

3 Experimental Evaluation

We evaluate Strix on the TLFS/LTL-track benchmark of the syntcomp2017 competition, which consists of 177 realizable and 67 unrealizable temporal logic synthesis specifications [15]. The experiment was run on a server with an Intel E5-2630 v4 clocked at 2.2 GHz (boost disabled). To mimic syntcomp2017 we imposed a limit of 8 threads for parallelization, a memory limit of 32 GB and a timeout of one hour for each specification. Every specification for that a tool correctly decides realizability within these limits is counted as solved for the category **Realizability**, and every specification for that it can additionally produce an AIGER circuit that is successfully verified is counted as solved for the category **Synthesis**. For this we verified the circuits with an additional time limit of one hour using the nuXmv model checker [7] with the `check_ltlspec` and `check_ltlspec_klive` routines in parallel.

We compared Strix with ltlsynt in the latest available release (version 2.5) at time of writing. This version differs from the one used during syntcomp2017 as it contains several improvements, but also performs worse in a few cases and exhibits erroneous behaviour: for **Realizability**, it produced one wrong answer, and for **Synthesis**, it failed in 72 cases to produce AIGER circuits due to a program error.

Additionally, we compare our results with the best configuration of the top tools competing in syntcomp2017: Party (portfolio), ltlsynt and BoSy (spot). Due to the difficulty of recreating the syntcomp2017 hardware setup[4], we compiled the results for these tools in Table 1 from the syntcomp2017 webpage[5] combining them with our results.

[3] https://github.com/romainbrenguier/Speculoos

[4] syntcomp2017 was run on an Intel E3-1271 v3 (4 cores/8 threads) at 3.6 GHz with 32 GB of RAM available for the tools. As stated above, we imposed the same constraints regarding timeout, maximal number of threads, and memory limit; but the Intel E3-1271 v3 runs at 3.6 GHz (with boost 4.0 GHz), while the Intel E5-2630 v4 used by us runs at only 2.2 GHz (boost disabled) resulting in a lower per-thread-performance (potentially 30% slower); on the other hand our system has a larger cache and a theoretically much higher memory bandwidth from up to 68.3 GB/s compared to 25.6 GB/s (for random reads, as in the case of dynamically generated parity games, these numbers are much closer). It seems therefore likely that for some benchmark-tool combinations our system is faster while for others it is slower.

[5] http://syntcomp.cs.uni-saarland.de/syntcomp2017/experiments/

The **Quality** rating compares the size of the solutions according to the SYNTCOMP2017 formula, where a tool gets $2 - \log_{10} \frac{n+1}{r+1}$ quality points for each verified solution of size n for a specification with reference size r. We now move on to a detailed discussion of the results and their interpretation.

Table 1. Results for STRIX compared with LTLSYNT and selected results from SYNTCOMP2017 on the TLSF/LTL-track benchmark and on noteable instances. We mark timeouts by TIME, memouts by MEM, and errors by ERR.

		Our system		SYNTCOMP2017		
		STRIX	LTLSYNT (2.5)	PARTY	LTLSYNT	BOSY
Solved	**Realizability**	214	204	224	195	181
	Synthesis	197	123	203	182	181
	Quality	330	136	308	180	298
	Avg. Quality	1.68	1.10	1.52	0.99	1.64
Time (s) Realizability	full_arbiter_7	11.34	MEM	8.77	MEM	TIME
	prioritized_arbiter_7	58.53	TIME	372.95	TIME	TIME
	round_robin_arbiter_6	8.45	158.33	TIME	733.92	TIME
	ltl2dba_E_10	6.79	324.84	TIME	TIME	TIME
	ltl2dba_Q_8	2.13	346.12	TIME	TIME	TIME
Size (AIG)	amba_..._encode_12	89	ERR	1040	3251	369
	full_arbiter_5	531	ERR	2257	7393	TIME
	full_arbiter_6	626	ERR	7603	26678	TIME
	ltl2dba_E_4	7	406	243	406	TIME
	ltl2dba_E_6	11	3952	1955	3952	TIME

Realizability. We were able to correctly decide realizability for 163 and unrealizability for 51 specifications, resulting in 214 solved instances. We solve five instances that were previously unsolved in SYNTCOMP2017.

Synthesis. We produced AIGER circuits for 148 of the realizable specifications. In 15 cases, we only constructed a Mealy machine, but the subsequent steps (MEMIN for minimization or SPECULOOS for circuit generation) reached the time or memory limit. We were able to verify correctness for 146 of the circuits, reaching the model checking time limit in two case. Together with the 51 specifications for which we determined unrealizability, this results in 197 solved instances.

Quality. We produced 36 solutions that are smaller than any solution during SYNTCOMP2017. The most significant reductions are for the AMBA encoder and the full arbiter, with reductions of over 75%, and for `ltl2dba_E_4` and `ltl2dba_E_6`, where we produce indeed the smallest implementation there is.

3.1 Effects of Minimization

We could reduce the size of the Mealy machine in 80 cases, and on average by 45%. However the data showed that this did not always reduce the size of the generated AIGER circuit: in 13 cases (most notably for several arbiter specifications) the size of the circuit generated from the Mealy machine actually increased when applying minimization (on average by 190%), while it decreased in 62 cases (on average by 55%).

We conjecture that the structure of the product-arena is sometimes amenable to compact representation in an AIGER circuit, while after the (SAT-based) minimization this is lost. In these cases the SAT/SMT-based bounded synthesis tools such as BoSy and Party also have difficulties producing a small solution, if any at all.

3.2 Synthesis of Complete AMBA AHB Arbiter

To test maturity and scalability of our tool, we synthesized the AMBA AHB arbiter [2], a common case study for reactive synthesis. We used the parameterized specification from [17] for $n = 2$ masters, which was also part of SYNT-COMP2016, but was left unsolved by any tool. With a memory limit of 128 GB, we could decide realizability within 26 min and produce a Mealy machine with 83 states after minimization. While specialised GR(1) solvers [2,4,12] or decompositional approaches [3] are able to synthesize the specification in a matter of minutes, to the best of our knowledge we are the first full LTL synthesis tool that can handle the complete non-decomposed specification in a reasonable amount of time. For comparison, ltlsynt (2.5) needs more than 2.5 days on our system and produces a Mealy machine with 340 states.

3.3 Discussion

The ltlsynt tool is part of Spot [8], which uses a Safra-style determinization procedure for NBAs. Conceptually, it also uses DPAs and a parity game solver as a decision procedure. However, as shown in [10] the produced automata tend to be larger compared to our translation, which probably results in the lower quality score. Our approach has similar performance and scales better on certain cases. The instances where ltlsynt performs better than Strix are specifications that we cannot split efficiently and the DPA construction becomes the bottleneck.

Bounded synthesis approaches (BoSy, Party) tend to produce smaller Mealy machines and to be able to handle larger alphabets. However, they fail when the minimal machine implementing the desired property is large, even if there is a compact implementation as a circuit. In our approach, we can often solve these cases and still regain compactness of the implementation through minimization afterwards. The strength of the Party portfolio is the combination of traditional bounded synthesis and a novel approach by reduction to safety games, which results in a large number of solved instances, but reduces the avg. quality score.

Future Work. Strix combines Java (LTL simplification and automata translations) and C++ (parity game construction and solving). We believe that a pure C++ implementation will further improve the overall runtime and reduce the memory footprint. Next, there are several algorithmic questions we want to investigate going forward, especially expanding parallelization of the tool. Furthermore, we want to reduce the dependency on external tools for circuit generation in order to be able to fine-tune this step better. Especially replacing Speculoos is important, since it turned out that it was unable to handle complex transition systems.

References

1. Abel, A., Reineke, J.: MeMin: SAT-based exact minimization of incompletely specified mealy machines. In: Proceedings of the IEEE/ACM International Conference on Computer-Aided Design, ICCAD 2015, Austin, TX, USA, 2–6 November 2015, pp. 94–101 (2015). https://doi.org/10.1109/ICCAD.2015.7372555
2. Bloem, R., Galler, S.J., Jobstmann, B., Piterman, N., Pnueli, A., Weiglhofer, M.: Specify, compile, run: hardware from PSL. Electr. Notes Theor. Comput. Sci. **190**(4), 3–16 (2007). https://doi.org/10.1016/j.entcs.2007.09.004
3. Bloem, R., Jacobs, S., Khalimov, A.: Parameterized synthesis case study: AMBA AHB. In: Proceedings of the 3rd Workshop on Synthesis, SYNT 2014, Vienna, Austria, 23–24 July 2014, pp. 68–83 (2014). https://doi.org/10.4204/EPTCS.157.9
4. Bloem, R., Jobstmann, B., Piterman, N., Pnueli, A., Sa'ar, Y.: Synthesis of reactive(1) designs. J. Comput. Syst. Sci. **78**(3), 911–938 (2012). https://doi.org/10.1016/j.jcss.2011.08.007
5. Bohy, A., Bruyère, V., Filiot, E., Jin, N., Raskin, J.-F.: Acacia+, a tool for LTL synthesis. In: Madhusudan, P., Seshia, S.A. (eds.) CAV 2012. LNCS, vol. 7358, pp. 652–657. Springer, Heidelberg (2012). https://doi.org/10.1007/978-3-642-31424-7_45
6. Brayton, R., Mishchenko, A.: ABC: an academic industrial-strength verification tool. In: Touili, T., Cook, B., Jackson, P. (eds.) CAV 2010. LNCS, vol. 6174, pp. 24–40. Springer, Heidelberg (2010). https://doi.org/10.1007/978-3-642-14295-6_5
7. Cavada, R., et al.: The nuXmv symbolic model checker. In: Biere, A., Bloem, R. (eds.) CAV 2014. LNCS, vol. 8559, pp. 334–342. Springer, Cham (2014). https://doi.org/10.1007/978-3-319-08867-9_22
8. Duret-Lutz, A., Lewkowicz, A., Fauchille, A., Michaud, T., Renault, É., Xu, L.: Spot 2.0 — a framework for LTL and ω-automata manipulation. In: Artho, C., Legay, A., Peled, D. (eds.) ATVA 2016. LNCS, vol. 9938, pp. 122–129. Springer, Cham (2016). https://doi.org/10.1007/978-3-319-46520-3_8
9. Ehlers, R.: Unbeast: symbolic bounded synthesis. In: Abdulla, P.A., Leino, K.R.M. (eds.) TACAS 2011. LNCS, vol. 6605, pp. 272–275. Springer, Heidelberg (2011). https://doi.org/10.1007/978-3-642-19835-9_25
10. Esparza, J., Křetínský, J., Raskin, J.-F., Sickert, S.: From LTL and limit-deterministic Büchi automata to deterministic parity automata. In: Legay, A., Margaria, T. (eds.) TACAS 2017. LNCS, vol. 10205, pp. 426–442. Springer, Heidelberg (2017). https://doi.org/10.1007/978-3-662-54577-5_25

11. Faymonville, P., Finkbeiner, B., Tentrup, L.: BoSy: an experimentation framework for bounded synthesis. In: Majumdar, R., Kunčak, V. (eds.) CAV 2017. LNCS, vol. 10427, pp. 325–332. Springer, Cham (2017). https://doi.org/10.1007/978-3-319-63390-9_17
12. Godhal, Y., Chatterjee, K., Henzinger, T.A.: Synthesis of AMBA AHB from formal specification: a case study. STTT **15**(5–6), 585–601 (2013). https://doi.org/10.1007/s10009-011-0207-9
13. Grädel, E., Thomas, W., Wilke, T. (eds.): Automata Logics, and Infinite Games: A Guide to Current Research. LNCS, vol. 2500. Springer, Heidelberg (2002). https://doi.org/10.1007/3-540-36387-4
14. Hoffmann, P., Luttenberger, M.: Solving parity games on the GPU. In: Van Hung, D., Ogawa, M. (eds.) ATVA 2013. LNCS, vol. 8172, pp. 455–459. Springer, Cham (2013). https://doi.org/10.1007/978-3-319-02444-8_34
15. Jacobs, S., Basset, N., Bloem, R., Brenguier, R., Colange, M., Faymonville, P., Finkbeiner, B., Khalimov, A., Klein, F., Michaud, T., Pérez, G.A., Raskin, J., Sankur, O., Tentrup, L.: The 4th reactive synthesis competition (SYNTCOMP 2017): benchmarks, participants and results. arXiv:1711.11439 [cs.LO] (2017)
16. Jacobs, S., Klein, F., Schirmer, S.: A high-level LTL synthesis format: TLSF v1.1. In: Proceedings of the Fifth Workshop on Synthesis, SYNT@CAV 2016, Toronto, Canada, 17–18 July 2016, pp. 112–132 (2016). https://doi.org/10.4204/EPTCS.229.10
17. Jobstmann, B.: Applications and optimizations for LTL synthesis. Ph.D. thesis, Graz University of Technology (2007)
18. Khalimov, A., Jacobs, S., Bloem, R.: PARTY parameterized synthesis of token rings. In: Sharygina, N., Veith, H. (eds.) CAV 2013. LNCS, vol. 8044, pp. 928–933. Springer, Heidelberg (2013). https://doi.org/10.1007/978-3-642-39799-8_66
19. Luttenberger, M.: Strategy iteration using non-deterministic strategies for solving parity games. arXiv:0806.2923 [cs.GT] (2008)
20. Meyer, P.J., Luttenberger, M.: Solving mean-payoff games on the GPU. In: Artho, C., Legay, A., Peled, D. (eds.) ATVA 2016. LNCS, vol. 9938, pp. 262–267. Springer, Cham (2016). https://doi.org/10.1007/978-3-319-46520-3_17
21. Morgenstern, A., Schneider, K.: Exploiting the temporal logic hierarchy and the non-confluence property for efficient LTL synthesis. In: Proceedings of the First Symposium on Games, Automata, Logic, and Formal Verification, GANDALF 2010, Minori (Amalfi Coast), Italy, 17–18 June 2010, pp. 89–102 (2010). https://doi.org/10.4204/EPTCS.25.11
22. Pnueli, A., Rosner, R.: On the synthesis of a reactive module. In: Proceedings of the 16th ACM SIGPLAN-SIGACT Symposium on Principles of Programming Languages, POPL 1989, pp. 179–190. ACM, New York (1989). https://doi.org/10.1145/75277.75293
23. Sickert, S., Esparza, J., Jaax, S., Křetínský, J.: Limit-deterministic Büchi automata for linear temporal logic. In: Chaudhuri, S., Farzan, A. (eds.) CAV 2016. LNCS, vol. 9780, pp. 312–332. Springer, Cham (2016). https://doi.org/10.1007/978-3-319-41540-6_17

Btor2 , BtorMC and Boolector 3.0

Aina Niemetz[1,2](✉), Mathias Preiner[1,2], Clifford Wolf[3], and Armin Biere[1]

[1] Johannes Kepler University Linz, Linz, Austria
[2] Stanford University, Stanford, USA
niemetz@cs.stanford.edu
[3] Symbiotic EDA, Vienna, Austria

Abstract. We describe Btor2, a word-level model checking format for capturing models of hardware and potentially software in a bit-precise manner. This simple, line-based and easy to parse format can be seen as a sorted extension of the word-level format Btor. It uses design principles from the bit-level format Aiger and follows semantics of the Smt-Lib logics of bit-vectors with arrays. This intermediate format can be used in various verification flows and is perfectly suited to establish a word-level model checking competition. It is supported by our new open source model checker BtorMC, which is built on top of version 3.0 of our SMT solver Boolector. We further provide new word-level benchmarks on which these open source tools are evaluated.

Our format Btor2 generalizes and extends the Btor [5] format, which can be seen as a word-level generalization of the initial version of the bit-level format Aiger [2]. Btor is a format for quantifier-free formulas over bit-vectors and arrays with Smt-Lib [1] semantics but also provides sequential extensions for specifying word-level model checking problems with registers and memories. In contrast to Btor, which is tailored towards bit-vectors and one-dimensional bit-vector arrays, Btor2 has explicit sort declarations. It further allows to explicitly initialize registers and memories (instead of implicit initialization in Btor) and extends the set of sequential features with witnesses, invariant and fairness constraints, and liveness properties. All of these are word-level variants lifted from corresponding features in the latest Aiger format [4], the input format of the hardware model checking competition (HWMCC) [3,6] since 2011. We provide an open source Btor2 tool suite, which includes a generic parser, random simulator and witness checker. We further implemented a reference bounded model checker BtorMC on top of our SMT solver Boolector. We consider Btor2 as an ideal candidate to establish a word-level hardware model checking competition.

1 Format Description

The syntax of Btor2 is shown in Fig. 1. The sort keyword is used to define arbitrary bit-vector and array sorts. This not only allows to specify multi-dimensional

Supported by Austrian Science Fund (FWF) under NFN Grant S11408-N23 (RiSE).

H. Chockler and G. Weissenbacher (Eds.): CAV 2018, LNCS 10981, pp. 587–595, 2018.
https://doi.org/10.1007/978-3-319-96145-3_32

```
⟨num⟩      ::= positive unsigned integer (greater than zero)
⟨uint⟩     ::= unsigned integer (including zero)
⟨string⟩   ::= sequence of whitespace and printable characters without '\n'
⟨symbol⟩   ::= sequence of printable characters without '\n'
⟨comment⟩  ::= ';' ⟨string⟩
⟨nid⟩      ::= ⟨num⟩
⟨sid⟩      ::= ⟨num⟩
⟨const⟩    ::= 'const' ⟨sid⟩ [0-1]+
⟨constd⟩   ::= 'constd' ⟨sid⟩ ['-']⟨uint⟩
⟨consth⟩   ::= 'consth' ⟨sid⟩ [0-9a-fA-F]+
⟨input⟩    ::= ( 'input' | 'one' | 'ones' | 'zero' ) ⟨sid⟩ | ⟨const⟩ | ⟨constd⟩ | ⟨consth⟩
⟨state⟩    ::= 'state' ⟨sid⟩
⟨bitvec⟩   ::= 'bitvec' ⟨num⟩
⟨array⟩    ::= 'array' ⟨sid⟩ ⟨sid⟩
⟨node⟩     ::= ⟨sid⟩ 'sort' ( ⟨array⟩ | ⟨bitvec⟩ )
             | ⟨nid⟩ ( ⟨input⟩ | ⟨state⟩ )
             | ⟨nid⟩ ⟨opidx⟩ ⟨sid⟩ ⟨nid⟩ ⟨uint⟩ [⟨uint⟩]
             | ⟨nid⟩ ⟨op⟩ ⟨sid⟩ ⟨nid⟩ [⟨nid⟩ [⟨nid⟩]]
             | ⟨nid⟩ ( 'init' | 'next' ) ⟨sid⟩ ⟨nid⟩ ⟨nid⟩
             | ⟨nid⟩ ( 'bad' | 'constraint' | 'fair' | 'output' ) ⟨nid⟩
             | ⟨nid⟩ 'justice' ⟨num⟩ ( ⟨nid⟩ )+
⟨line⟩     ::= ⟨comment⟩ | ⟨node⟩ [ ⟨symbol⟩ ] [ ⟨comment⟩ ]
⟨btor⟩     ::= ( ⟨line⟩'\n' )+
```

Fig. 1. Syntax of BTOR2. Non-terminals ⟨opidx⟩ and ⟨op⟩ are indexed and non-indexed operators as defined in Table 1 (sequential part in red). (Color figure online)

arrays but can be extended to support (uninterpreted) functions, floating points and other sorts. As a consequence, BTOR2 is not backwards compatible with BTOR. For clarity, in Fig. 1 we distinguish between node (line) identifiers ⟨nid⟩ and sort identifiers ⟨sid⟩, and do not allow an identifier to occur in both sets. Introducing sorts renders type specific keywords such as var, array and acond from BTOR obsolete. Instead, BTOR2 uses the keyword input to declare bit-vector and array variables of a given sort. Bit-vector constants are created as in BTOR with the keywords const[dh], one, ones and zero.

Bit-vector and array operators as supported by BTOR2 and their respective sorts are shown in Table 1. We use $\mathcal{B}^n$ for a bit-vector sort of width n, and $\mathcal{I}$ and $\mathcal{E}$ for the index and element sorts of an array sort $\mathcal{A}^{\mathcal{I}\rightarrow\mathcal{E}}$. Note that some bit-vector operators can be interpreted as *signed* or *unsigned*. In signed context, as in SMT-LIB, bit-vectors are represented in two's complement.

2 Sequential Extension

As shown in Fig. 1, the sequential extension of BTOR2 introduces a state keyword, which allows to specify registers and memories. In contrast to BTOR, where registers are implicitly zero-initialized and memories are uninitialized, BTOR2 provides a keyword init to explicitly define initialization functions for states. This enables us to also model partial initialization. For example, initializing a memory with a bit-vector constant zero, zero-initializes the whole memory, whereas

Table 1. Operators supported by BTOR2, where $\mathcal{B}^n$ represents a bit-vector sort of size n and $\mathcal{A}^{\mathcal{I}\rightarrow\mathcal{E}}$ represents an array sort with index sort $\mathcal{I}$ and element sort $\mathcal{E}$.

indexed		
[su]ext w	(un)signed extension	$\mathcal{B}^n \rightarrow \mathcal{B}^{n+w}$
slice u l	extraction, $n > u \geq l$	$\mathcal{B}^n \rightarrow \mathcal{B}^{u-l+1}$
unary		
not	bit-wise	$\mathcal{B}^n \rightarrow \mathcal{B}^n$
inc, dec, neg	arithmetic	$\mathcal{B}^n \rightarrow \mathcal{B}^n$
redand, redor, redxor	reduction	$\mathcal{B}^n \rightarrow \mathcal{B}^1$
binary		
iff, implies	Boolean	$\mathcal{B}^1 \times \mathcal{B}^1 \rightarrow \mathcal{B}^1$
eq, neq	(dis)equality	$\mathcal{S} \times \mathcal{S} \rightarrow \mathcal{B}^1$
[su]gt, [su]gte, [su]lt, [su]lte	(un)signed inequality	$\mathcal{B}^n \times \mathcal{B}^n \rightarrow \mathcal{B}^1$
and, nand, nor, or, xnor, xor	bit-wise	$\mathcal{B}^n \times \mathcal{B}^n \rightarrow \mathcal{B}^n$
rol, ror, sll, sra, srl	rotate, shift	$\mathcal{B}^n \times \mathcal{B}^n \rightarrow \mathcal{B}^n$
add, mul, [su]div, smod, [su]rem, sub	arithmetic	$\mathcal{B}^n \times \mathcal{B}^n \rightarrow \mathcal{B}^n$
[su]addo, [su]divo, [su]mulo, [su]subo	overflow	$\mathcal{B}^n \times \mathcal{B}^n \rightarrow \mathcal{B}^1$
concat	concatenation	$\mathcal{B}^n \times \mathcal{B}^m \rightarrow \mathcal{B}^{n+m}$
read	array read	$\mathcal{A}^{\mathcal{I}\rightarrow\mathcal{E}} \times \mathcal{I} \rightarrow \mathcal{E}$
ternary		
ite	conditional	$\mathcal{B}^1 \times \mathcal{B}^n \times \mathcal{B}^n \rightarrow \mathcal{B}^n$
write	array write	$\mathcal{A}^{\mathcal{I}\rightarrow\mathcal{E}} \times \mathcal{I} \times \mathcal{E} \rightarrow \mathcal{A}^{\mathcal{I}\rightarrow\mathcal{E}}$

partially initializing a register can be achieved by applying a bit-mask to an uninitialized register.

Transition functions for both registers and memories are defined with the next keyword. It takes the current and next states as arguments. A state variable without associated next function is treated as a *primary* input, i.e., it has the same behaviour as inputs defined via keyword input. Note that BTOR provides a next keyword for registers and an anext keyword for memories. Using sorts in BTOR2 avoids such sort specific keyword variants.

As in the latest version of AIGER [4], BTOR2 supports bad state properties, which are essentially negations of safety properties. Multiple properties can be specified by simply adding multiple bad state properties. Invariant constraints can be introduced via the constraint keyword and are assumed to hold globally. A witness for a bad state property is an initialized finite path, which reaches (actually, contains) a bad state and satisfies all invariant constraints.

Again as in AIGER [4], keywords fair and justice allow to specify (global) fairness constraints and (negations of) liveness properties. Each *justice* property consists of a set of Büchi conditions. A witness for a justice property is an infinite initialized path on which all Büchi conditions and all global fairness constraints are satisfied infinitely often. In addition, all global invariant constraints have to hold. The justice keyword takes a number (the number of Büchi conditions) and an arbitrary number of nodes (the Büchi conditions) as arguments.

3 Witness Format

The syntax of the BTOR2 witness format is shown in Fig. 2. A BTOR2 witness consists of a sequence of valid input assignments grouped by (time) frames. It starts with 'sat' followed by a list of properties that are satisfied by the witness. A property is identified by a prefix 'b' (for **b**ad) and 'j' (for **j**ustice) followed by a number i, which ranges over the number of defined *bad* and *justice* properties starting from 0. For example, 'b0 j0' refers to the first bad and first justice property in the order as they occur in the BTOR2 input. The list of properties is followed by a sequence of $k+1$ frames at time $t \in \{0, \dots, k\}$. A *frame* is divided into a state and input part. The *state* part starts with '#t' and is mandatory for the first frame ($t = 0$) and optional for later frames ($t > 0$). It contains state assignments at time t. The *input* part starts with '@t' and consists of input assignments of the transition from time t to $t + 1$. If states are uninitialized (no init), their initial assignment is required to be specified in frame '#0'. The state part is usually omitted for $t > 0$ since state assignments can be computed from states and inputs at time $t - 1$. While don't care inputs can be omitted, our witness checker assumes that they are zero. Input and state assignments use the same numbering scheme as properties, i.e., states and inputs are numbered separately in the order they are defined, starting from 0. For example, 0 in frame '#t' (or '@t') refers to the first state (or input) as defined in the BTOR2 input. For justice properties we assume the witness to be lasso shaped, i.e., the next state, which can be computed from the last state and inputs at time k, is identical to one of the previous states at time $t = 0 \dots k$. As in AIGER, a BTOR2 witness is terminated with '.' on a separate line.

```
⟨binary-string⟩      ::= [0-1]+
⟨bv-assignment⟩      ::= ⟨binary-string⟩
⟨array-assignment⟩   ::= '[' ⟨binary-string⟩ ']' ⟨binary-string⟩
⟨assignment⟩         ::= ⟨uint⟩ ( ⟨bv-assignment⟩ | ⟨array-assignment⟩ ) [⟨symbol⟩]
⟨model⟩              ::= ( ⟨comment⟩'\n' | ⟨assignment⟩'\n' )+
⟨state part⟩         ::= '#' ⟨uint⟩ '\n' ⟨model⟩
⟨input part⟩         ::= '@' ⟨uint⟩ '\n' ⟨model⟩
⟨frame⟩              ::= [ ⟨state part⟩ ] ⟨input part⟩
⟨prop⟩               ::= ( 'b' | 'j' )⟨uint⟩
⟨header⟩             ::= 'sat\n' ( ⟨prop⟩ )+ '\n'
⟨witness⟩            ::= ( ⟨comment⟩'\n' )+ | ⟨header⟩ ( ⟨frame⟩ )+ '.'
```

Fig. 2. BTOR2 model and witness format syntax (sequential part in red). (Color figure online)

Figure 3 illustrates a simple C program (left), the corresponding BTOR2 model with the negation of the assertion as a bad property (center), and a

```c
#include <assert.h>
#include <stdio.h>
#include <stdlib.h>
#include <stdbool.h>
static bool read_bool () {
  int ch = getc (stdin);
  if (ch == '0') return false;
  if (ch == '1') return true;
  exit (0);
}
int main () {
  bool turn;              // input
  unsigned a = 0, b = 0; // states
  for (;;) {
    turn = read_bool ();
    assert (!(a == 3 && b == 3));
    if (turn) a = a + 1;
    else      b = b + 1;
  }
}
```

```
1 sort bitvec 1
2 sort bitvec 32
3 input 1 turn
4 state 2 a
5 state 2 b
6 zero 2
7 init 2 4 6
8 init 2 5 6
9 one 2
10 add 2 4 9
11 add 2 5 9
12 ite 2 3 4 10
13 ite 2 -3 5 11
14 next 2 4 12
15 next 2 5 13
16 constd 2 3
17 eq 1 4 16
18 eq 1 5 16
19 and 1 17 18
20 bad 19
```

```
sat
b0
#0
@0
0 1 turn@0
@1
0 0 turn@1
@2
0 0 turn@2
@3
0 0 turn@3
@4
0 1 turn@4
@5
0 1 turn@5
@6
0 0 turn@6
```

Fig. 3. Example C program with corresponding BTOR2 model and witness.

BTOR2 witness for the violated property (right). The BTOR2 model defines one bad property (`a == 3 && b == 3`), which is satisfied in frame 6. The corresponding witness identifies this property as bad property '`b0`' (first bad property defined in the model). All states are initialized, hence '#0' is empty, and '`@0`' to '`@6`' indicate the assignments of input 0 (`turn`, the first input defined in the model) in frames 0 to 6, e.g., `turn` $= 1$ at $t = 0$, `turn` $= 0$ at $t = 1$ and so on. In frame 6, both states `a` and `b` reach value 3, and therefore property '`b0`' is satisfied.

4 Tools

We provide a generic stand-alone parser for BTOR2, which features basic type checking and consists of approx. 1,500 lines of C code. We implemented a reference bounded model checker BtorMC, which currently supports checking safety (aka. bad state) properties for models with registers and memories and produces witnesses for satisfiable properties. Unrolling the model is performed by symbolic simulation, i.e., symbolic substitution of current state expressions into next state functions, and incremental SMT solving. We also implemented a simulator for randomly simulating BTOR2 models. It further supports checking BTOR2 witnesses. The model checker is tightly integrated into our SMT solver Boolector [18], an award-winning SMT solver for the theory of fixed-size bit-vectors with arrays and uninterpreted functions. Since the last major version [18], we extended Boolector with several new features. Most notably, Boolector 3.0 now comes with support for quantified bit-vectors [24] and two different local search strategies for quantifier-free bit-vector formulas that don't rely on but can be combined with bit-blasting [19,21,22]. It further provides support for BTOR2. In contrast to previous versions of Boolector, Boolector 3.0 and all BTOR2 tools are released under the MIT open source license and the source code is hosted on GitHub[1].

5 Experiments

We collected ten real-world (System)Verilog designs with safety properties from various open source projects [11,26–28]. The majority of these designs include memories. We used the open synthesis suite Yosys [29] to synthesize these designs into BTOR2 and SMT-LIB. For BTOR2, Yosys directly generates the models from a circuit description. For SMT-LIB, since the language does not support describing model checking problems, we used Yosys in combination with Yosys-SMTBMC to produce unrolled (incremental) problems.

We compared BtorMC against the most recent versions of Boolector (3.0) and Yices [10] (2.5.4), the two best solvers of the QF_ABV division of the SMT competition 2017. The BTOR2 models serve as input for BtorMC, and the incremental SMT-LIB benchmarks serve as input for Boolector and Yices. All benchmarks, synthesis scripts, generated files, log files and the source code of our tools for this evaluation are available at http://fmv.jku.at/cav18-btor2.

The results in Table 2 show that our flow using BTOR2 as intermediate format is competetive with simple unrolling. Note that our model checker BtorMC issues incremental calls to Boolector. However, in Boolector, sophisticated word-level rewriting is currently disabled in incremental mode. We expect a major performance boost by fully supporting incremental word-level preprocessing.

Table 2. BtorMC/BTOR2 vs. unrolled SMT-LIB with a time limit of 3600 s, where k is the bound and #bad is the number of bad properties.

Benchmark	k	#bad	BtorMC time[s]	Boolector time[s]	Yices time[s]
picorv32-check	30	23	**4.8**	18.9	10.8
picorv32-pcregs	20	3	**63.0**	293.0	TO
ponylink-slaveTXlen-sat	230	1	305.5	406.8	**145.6**
ponylink-slaveTXlen-unsat	231	1	183.8	131.4	**71.4**
VexRiscv-regch0-15	17	2	**9.6**	48.3	12.2
VexRiscv-regch0-20	22	2	528.8	**520.7**	2232.2
VexRiscv-regch0-30	32	2	TO	TO	TO
zipcpu-busdelay	100	50	**157.0**	287.0	181.2
zipcpu-pfcache	100	39	**17.4**	19.9	32.5
zipcpu-zipmmu	30	57	86.0	412.9	**46.5**

[1] https://github.com/boolector.

6 Conclusion

We propose BTOR2, a new word-level model-checking and witness format. For this format we provide a generic parser implementation, a simulator that also checks witnesses, and a reference bounded model checker BtorMC, which is tightly integrated with our SMT solver Boolector. These open source tools are evaluated on new real-world benchmarks, which we synthesized from open source hardware (System) Verilog models into BTOR2 and SMT-LIB with Yosys. The tool Verilog2SMV [14] translates Verilog into model-checking problems in several formats, including nuXmv [7] and BTOR. However, its translation to BTOR is incomplete and development discontinued.

We plan to provide a translator from BTOR2 into SALLY [25], and VMT [8], which are both extensions of SMT-LIB to model symbolic transition systems. It might also be interesting to translate incremental SMT-LIB benchmarks and horn clause models (as handled by, e.g., μZ [13]) into BTOR2 and vice versa. We hope other compilers and model checkers such as SAL [9], EBMC [15] and ABC [12,16] will provide support to produce and read BTOR2 models. We want to extend the format to other logics, in particular to support lambdas as in [23]. There is also a need for fuzzing [20] and delta-debugging tools [17].

Last but not least, we want to use this format to bootstrap a word-level model checking competition, which of course needs more benchmarks.

References

1. Barrett, C., Fontaine, P., Tinelli, C.: The SMT-LIB Standard: Version 2.6. Technical report, Department of Computer Science, The University of Iowa (2017). www.SMT-LIB.org
2. Biere, A.: The AIGER And-Inverter Graph (AIG) format version 20071012. Technical report, FMV Reports Series, Institute for Formal Models and Verification, Johannes Kepler University, Altenbergerstr 69, 4040 Linz, Austria (2007)
3. Biere, A., van Dijk, T., Heljanko, K.: Hardware model checking competition 2017. In: Stewart, D., Weissenbacher, G. (eds.) 2017 Formal Methods in Computer Aided Design, FMCAD 2017, Vienna, Austria, 2–6 October 2017, p. 9. IEEE (2017). https://doi.org/10.23919/FMCAD.2017.8102233
4. Biere, A., Heljanko, K., Wieringa, S.: AIGER 1.9 and beyond. Technical report, FMV Reports Series, Institute for Formal Models and Verification, Johannes Kepler University, Altenbergerstr 69, 4040 Linz, Austria (2011)
5. Brummayer, R., Biere, A., Lonsing, F.: BTOR: bit-precise modelling of word-level problems for model checking. In: Proceedings of the Joint Workshops of the 6th International Workshop on Satisfiability Modulo Theories and 1st International Workshop on Bit-Precise Reasoning, SMT 2008/BPR 2008, pp. 33–38. ACM, New York, USA (2008). http://doi.acm.org/10.1145/1512464.1512472
6. Cabodi, G., Loiacono, C., Palena, M., Pasini, P., Patti, D., Quer, S., Vendraminetto, D., Biere, A., Heljanko, K.: Hardware model checking competition 2014: an analysis and comparison of solvers and benchmarks. J. Satisf. Boolean Model. Comput. **9**, 135–172 (2014). Published 2016

7. Cavada, R., et al.: The NUXMV symbolic model checker. In: Biere, A., Bloem, R. (eds.) CAV 2014. LNCS, vol. 8559, pp. 334–342. Springer, Cham (2014). https://doi.org/10.1007/978-3-319-08867-9_22
8. Cimatti, A., Roveri, M., Griggio, A., Irfan, A.: Verification modulo theories. http://es.fbk.eu/projects/vmt-lib/
9. De Moura, L., Owre, S., Shankar, N.: The SAL language manual. Technical report CSL-01-01, Computer Science Laboratory, SRI International, Menlo Park (2003)
10. Dutertre, B.: Yices 2.2. In: Biere, A., Bloem, R. (eds.) CAV 2014. LNCS, vol. 8559, pp. 737–744. Springer, Cham (2014). https://doi.org/10.1007/978-3-319-08867-9_49
11. Gisselquist, D.: ZipCPU. https://github.com/ZipCPU/zipcpu
12. Ho, Y., Mishchenko, A., Brayton, R.K.: Property directed reachability with word-level abstraction. In: FMCAD, pp. 132–139. IEEE (2017)
13. Hoder, K., Bjørner, N., de Moura, L.: μZ - an efficient engine for fixed points with constraints. In: Gopalakrishnan, G., Qadeer, S. (eds.) CAV 2011. LNCS, vol. 6806, pp. 457–462. Springer, Heidelberg (2011). https://doi.org/10.1007/978-3-642-22110-1_36
14. Irfan, A., Cimatti, A., Griggio, A., Roveri, M., Sebastiani, R.: Verilog2SMV: a tool for word-level verification. In: DATE, pp. 1156–1159. IEEE (2016)
15. Kroening, D.: Computing over-approximations with bounded model checking. Electr. Notes Theor. Comput. Sci. **144**(1), 79–92 (2006)
16. Long, J., Ray, S., Sterin, B., Mishchenko, A., Brayton, R.K.: Enhancing ABC for stabilization verification of systemverilog/VHDL models. In: Proceedings of the CEUR Workshop DIFTS@FMCAD, vol. 832. CEUR-WS.org (2011)
17. Niemetz, A., Biere, A.: ddSMT: a delta debugger for the SMT-LIB v2 format. In: Bruttomesso, R., Griggio, A. (eds.) Proceedings of the 11th International Workshop on Satisfiability Modulo Theories, SMT 2013, Affiliated with the 16th International Conference on Theory and Applications of Satisfiability Testing, SAT 2013, Helsinki, Finland, 8–9 July 2013, pp. 36–45 (2013)
18. Niemetz, A., Preiner, M., Biere, A.: Boolector 2.0. JSAT **9**, 53–58 (2015)
19. Niemetz, A., Preiner, M., Biere, A.: Precise and complete propagation based local search for satisfiability modulo theories. In: Chaudhuri, S., Farzan, A. (eds.) CAV 2016. LNCS, vol. 9779, pp. 199–217. Springer, Cham (2016). https://doi.org/10.1007/978-3-319-41528-4_11
20. Niemetz, A., Preiner, M., Biere, A.: Model-based API testing for SMT solvers. In: Brain, M., Hadarean, L. (eds.) Proceedings of the 15th International Workshop on Satisfiability Modulo Theories, SMT 2017, Affiliated with the 29th International Conference on Computer Aided Verification, CAV 2017, Heidelberg, Germany, 24–28 July 2017, p. 10 (2017)
21. Niemetz, A., Preiner, M., Biere, A.: Propagation based local search for bit-precise reasoning. Formal Methods Syst. Des. **51**(3), 608–636 (2017). https://doi.org/10.1007/s10703-017-0295-6
22. Niemetz, A., Preiner, M., Biere, A., Fröhlich, A.: Improving local search for bit-vector logics in SMT with path propagation. In: Proceedings of the Fourth International Workshop on Design and Implementation of Formal Tools and Systems, Austin, USA, 26–27 September 2015, pp. 1–10 (2015)
23. Preiner, M., Niemetz, A., Biere, A.: Lemmas on demand for lambdas. In: Proceedings of the CEUR Workshop DIFTS@FMCAD, vol. 1130. CEUR-WS.org (2013)
24. Preiner, M., Niemetz, A., Biere, A.: Counterexample-guided model synthesis. In: Legay, A., Margaria, T. (eds.) TACAS 2017. LNCS, vol. 10205, pp. 264–280. Springer, Heidelberg (2017). https://doi.org/10.1007/978-3-662-54577-5_15

25. SRI International's Computer Science Laboratory: Sally - a model checker for infinite-state systems. https://github.com/SRI-CSL/sally
26. Wolf, C.: PicoRV32. https://github.com/cliffordwolf/picorv32
27. Wolf, C.: PonyLink. https://github.com/cliffordwolf/PonyLink
28. Wolf, C.: riscv-formal. https://github.com/cliffordwolf/riscv-formal
29. Wolf, C.: Yosys. https://github.com/YosysHQ/yosys

Nagini: A Static Verifier for Python

Marco Eilers(✉) and Peter Müller

Department of Computer Science, ETH Zurich, Zurich, Switzerland
{marco.eilers,peter.mueller}@inf.ethz.ch

Abstract. We present Nagini, an automated, modular verifier for statically-typed, concurrent Python 3 programs, built on the Viper verification infrastructure. Combining established concepts with new ideas, Nagini can verify memory safety, functional properties, termination, deadlock freedom, and input/output behavior. Our experiments show that Nagini is able to verify non-trivial properties of real-world Python code.

1 Introduction

Dynamic languages have become widely used because of their expressiveness and ease of use. The Python language in particular is popular in domains like teaching, prototyping, and more recently data science. Python's lack of safety guarantees can be problematic when, as is increasingly the case, it is used for critical applications with high correctness demands. The Python community has reacted to this trend by integrating type annotations and optional static type checking into the language [20]. However, there is currently virtually no tool support for reasoning about Python programs beyond type safety.

We present Nagini, a sound verifier for statically-typed, concurrent Python programs. Nagini can prove memory safety, data race freedom, and user-supplied assertions. Nagini performs *modular* verification, which is important for verification to scale and to be able to verify libraries, and *automates* the verification process for programs annotated with specifications.

Nagini builds on many techniques established in existing tools: (1) Like VeriFast [10] and other tools [4,19,22], it uses separation logic style permissions [16] in order to locally reason about concurrent programs. (2) Like .NET Code Contracts [7], it uses a contract library to enable users to write code-level specifications. (3) Like many verification tools [2,6,11,13], it verifies programs by encoding the program and its specification into an intermediate verification language [1,8], namely Viper [14], for which automatic verifiers already exist.

Nagini combines these techniques with new ideas in order to verify advanced properties and handle the dynamic aspects of Python. In particular, Nagini implements a comprehensive system for verifying finite blocking [5] and input/output behavior [18], and builds on Mypy [12] to verify safety while also supporting important dynamic language features. Nagini is intended for verifying substantial, real-world code, and is currently used to verify the Python

H. Chockler and G. Weissenbacher (Eds.): CAV 2018, LNCS 10981, pp. 596–603, 2018.
https://doi.org/10.1007/978-3-319-96145-3_33

implementation of the SCION internet architecture [3]. To our knowledge, it is the first tool to enable automatic verification of Python code. Existing tools for JavaScript [21,24] also target a dynamic language, but focus on faithfully modeling JavaScript's complex semantics rather than practical verification of high-level properties.

Due to its wide range of verifiable properties, Nagini has applications in many domains: In addition to memory safety, programmers can choose to prove that a server implementation will stay responsive, that data science code has desired functional properties, or that algorithms terminate and preserve certain invariants, for example in a teaching context. Nagini is open-source and available online[1], and can be used from the popular PyCharm IDE via a prototype plugin.

In this paper, we describe Nagini's supported Python subset and specification language, give an overview of its implementation and the encoding from Python to Viper, and provide an experimental evaluation of Nagini on real-world code.

2 Language and Specifications

Python Subset: Nagini requires input programs to comply to the static, nominal type system defined in PEP 484 [20] as implemented in the Mypy type checker [12], which requires type annotations for function parameters and return types, but can normally infer types of local variables. Nagini fully supports the non-gradual part of Mypy's type system, including generics and union types.

The Python subset accepted by Mypy and Nagini can accommodate most real Python programs, potentially via some workarounds like using union types instead of structural typing. While our subset is statically typed, it includes many features and potential pitfalls not found in static languages, such as dynamic addition and removal fields from objects. Some other features like reflection and dynamic code generation are not supported.

Where compromises are necessary, Nagini aims for modularity, performance, and completeness for features typically found in user code over general support for all language features. As an example, Nagini works with a simplified model of Python's object attribute lookup behavior: A simple attribute access in Python leads to the invocation of several "magic" methods, which, if modelled correctly, would result in an overhead that would likely make automatic verification intractable. Nagini exploits the fact that these methods are mostly used to implement decorators, metaclasses, and system libraries, but rarely in user code. It assumes the default behavior of those methods, and implements direct support for frequently-used decorators and metaclasses that change their behavior. Importantly, Nagini flags an error if verified programs override these methods or are otherwise outside the supported subset, and is therefore sound.

Specification Language: Nagini includes a library of specification functions similar to .NET Code Contracts [7] to express pre- and postconditions, loop invariants, and other assertions. Calls to these functions are interpreted as specifications by Nagini, but can be automatically removed before execution. Users can

[1] https://github.com/marcoeilers/nagini.

```
1   from nagini_contracts.contracts import *
2   from typing import List
3   import db
4
5   class Ticket:
6       def __init__(self, show: int, row: int, seat: int) -> None:
7           self.show_id = show
8           self.row, self.seat = row, seat
9           Fold(self.state())
10          Ensures(self.state() and MayCreate(self, 'discount_code'))
11
12      @Predicate
13      def state(self) -> bool:
14          return Acc(self.show_id) and Acc(self.row) and Acc(self.seat)
15
16  def order_tickets(num: int, show_id: int, code: str=None) -> List[Ticket]:
17      Requires(num > 0)
18      Exsures(SoldoutException, True)
19      seats = db.get_seats(show_id, num)
20      res = []  # type: List[Ticket]
21      for row, seat in seats:
22          Invariant(list_pred(res))
23          Invariant(Forall(res, lambda t: t.state() and
24                                Implies(code is not None, Acc(t.discount_code))))
25          Invariant(MustTerminate(len(seats) - len(res)))
26          ticket = Ticket(show_id, row, seat)
27          if code:
28              ticket.discount_code = code
29          res.append(ticket)
30      return res
```

Fig. 1. Example program demonstrating Nagini's specification language. Contract functions are highlighted in italics. Note that functional specifications and postconditions are largely omitted to highlight the different specification constructs.

annotate Mypy-style type stub files for external libraries with specifications; the program will then be verified assuming they are correct. A detailed explanation of the specification language can be found in Nagini's Wiki[2].

An example of an annotated program is shown in Fig. 1. The first two lines import the contract library and Python's library for type annotations. Pre- and postconditions are declared via calls to the contract functions Requires and Ensures in lines 17 and 10, respectively. The arguments of these functions are interpreted as assertions, which can be side-effect free boolean Python expressions or calls to other contract functions. Similarly, loops must be annotated with invariants (line 22), and special *exceptional* postconditions specify which exceptions a method may raise, and what postconditions must hold in this case. The Exsures annotation in line 18 states that a SoldoutException may be raised and makes no guarantees in this case. The invariant MustTerminate in line 25 specifies that the loop terminates; the argument represents a ranking function [5].

Like the underlying Viper language, Nagini uses Implicit Dynamic Frames (IDF) [23], a variation of separation logic [16], to achieve framing and allow local reasoning in the presence of concurrency. IDF establishes a system of *permissions* for heap locations that roughly corresponds to separation logic's points-to predicates. Methods may only read or write heap locations they currently hold a permission for, and can specify which permissions they require from and give

[2] https://github.com/marcoeilers/nagini/wiki.

back to their caller in their pre- and postconditions. Since there is only ever a single permission per heap location, holding a permission guarantees that neither other threads nor called methods can modify the respective location.

In Nagini, a permission is created when a field is assigned to for the first time; e.g., when executing line 9, the __init__ method will have permission to three fields. Permission assertions are expressed using the Acc function (line 14). Assertions can be abstracted over using predicates [17], declared in Nagini by using annotated functions (line 12). In the example, the constructor of Ticket bundles all available permissions in the predicate state using the ghost statement Fold in line 9 and subsequently returns this predicate to its caller via its postcondition.

In addition, Nagini offers a second kind of permission that allows *creating* a field that does not currently exist, but cannot be used for reading (since that would cause a runtime error). Constructors implicitly get this kind of permission for every field mentioned in a class; in the example, such a permissions is returned to the caller (line 10) and used in line 28. The loop invariant contains the permission to modify the res list using one of several built-in predicates for Python's standard data types (line 22) as well as permissions to the fields of all objects in the list (line 23). This kind of *quantified permission* [15], corresponding to separation logic's iterated separating conjunction, is one of two supported ways to express permissions over unbounded numbers of heap locations.

Other contract functions allow specifying, e.g., I/O behavior, and some have variations for advanced users, e.g., the Forall function can take trigger expressions to specify when the underlying SMT solver should instantiate the quantifier.

Verified properties: Nagini verifies some safety properties by default: Verified programs will not raise runtime errors or undeclared exceptions. The permission system guarantees that verified code is memory safe and free of data races. Nagini also verifies some properties that Mypy only checks optimistically, e.g., that referenced names are defined before they are used. As an example, if the Ticket class were defined after the order_tickets function, Nagini would not allow calls to the function *before* the class definition, because of the call in line 26.

Beyond this, Nagini can verify (1) functional properties, (2) input/output properties, i.e., which I/O operations may or must occur, using a generalization of the method by Penninckx et al. [18], and (3) finite blocking [5], i.e., that no thread blocks indefinitely when trying to acquire a lock or join another thread, which includes deadlock freedom and termination. Verification is modular in the sense that adding code to a program only requires verifying the added parts; any code that verified before is guaranteed to still verify. Top level statements are an exception and have to be reverified when any part of the program changes, since Python's import mechanism is inherently non-modular.

3 Implementation

Nagini's verification workflow is depicted in Fig. 2. After parsing, Nagini invokes the Mypy type checker on the input and rejects the program if errors are found.

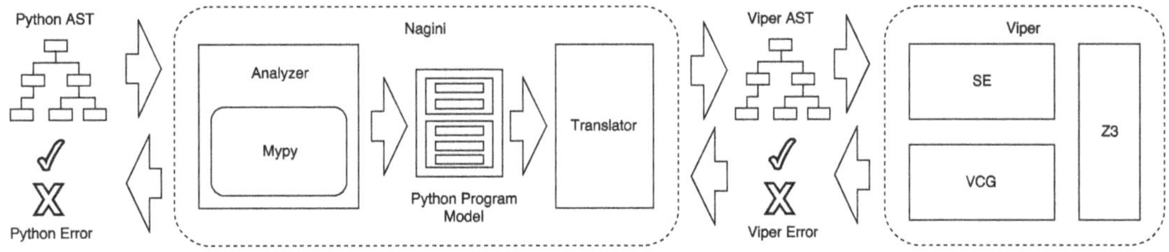

Fig. 2. Nagini verification workflow.

It then analyzes the input program and extracts structural information into an internal model, which is then encoded into a Viper program. The program is verified using one of the two Viper backends, based on either symbolic execution (SE) or verification condition generation (VCG), respectively. Any resulting Viper-level error messages are mapped back to a Python-level error.

Encoding: Nagini encodes Python programs into Viper programs that verify only if the original program was correct. At the top level, Viper programs consist of *methods*, whose bodies contain imperative code, side-effect free *functions*, and the aforementioned *predicates*, as well as *domains*, which can be used to declare and axiomatize custom data types. The structure of a created Viper program roughly follows the structure of the Python program: Each function in the Python program corresponds to either a method, a function, or a predicate in the Viper program, depending on its annotation. Additional Viper methods are generated to check proof obligations like behavioral subtyping and to model the execution of all top level statements.

Nagini maintains various kinds of ghost state, e.g., for verifying finite blocking and to represent which names are currently defined. It models Python's type system using a Viper domain axiomatized to reflect subtype relations. Nagini desugars complex Python language constructs into simple ones that exist in Viper, but subtle language differences often require additional effort in the encoding. As an example, Viper distinguishes references from primitive values whereas Python does not, requiring boxing and unboxing operations in the encoding.

Tool interaction: Nagini is invoked on an annotated Python file, and verifies this file and all (transitive) imports without user interaction. It then outputs either a success message or Python-level error messages that indicate type or verification errors, use of unsupported features, or invalid specifications, along with the source location. As an example, removing the Fold statement in line 9 of Fig. 1 yields the error message "Postcondition of __init__ might not hold. There might be insufficient permission to access self.state(). (example.py@10.16)".

4 Evaluation

In addition to having a comprehensive test suite of over 12,500 lines of code, we have evaluated Nagini on a set of examples containing (parts of) implemen-

	Example	LOC / Spec.	Viper LOC	SF	FC	FB	IO	T_{Seq}	T_{Par}
1	rosetta/quicksort	31 / 10	635	✓	-	✓	-	8.48	8.31
2	interactivepython/bst	145 / 65	947	✓	✓	-	-	57.44	41.80
3	keon/knapsack	33 / 10	864	✓	-	-	-	19.39	14.49
4	wikipedia/duck_typing	19 / 0	486	✓	-	-	-	1.82	1.92
5	scion/path_store	207 / 94	2133	✗	-	-	-	51.37	35.26
6	example	40 / 19	736	✓	-	✓	-	6.11	5.91
7	verifast/brackets_checker	143 / 82	1081	✓	✓	✓	✓	7.66	6.63
8	verifast/putchar_with_buffer	139 / 88	865	✓	-	✓	✓	4.74	4.29
9	chalice2viper/watchdog	66 / 22	769	✓	-	✓	-	3.66	3.41
10	parkinson/recell	46 / 25	561	✓	✓	-	-	2.09	2.07

Fig. 3. Experiments. For each example, we list the lines of code (excluding whitespace and comments), the number of those lines that are used for specifications, the length of the resulting Viper program, properties (SF = safety, FC = functional correctness, FB = finite blocking, IO = input/output behavior) that could be verified (✓), could not be verified (✗) or were not attempted (-), and the verification times with Viper's SE backend, sequential and parallelized, in seconds.

tations of standard algorithms from the internet[3], the example from Fig. 1, a class from the SCION implementation, as well as examples from other verifiers translated to Python. Figure 3 shows the examples and which properties were verified; the functional property we proved for the binary search tree implementation is that it maintains a sorted tree. The examples cover language features like inheritance (example 10), comprehensions (3), dynamic field addition (6), operator overloading (3), union types (4), threads and locks (9), as well as specification constructs like quantified permissions (6) and predicate families (10). Nagini correctly finds an error in the SCION example and successfully verifies all other examples.

The runtimes shown in Fig. 3 were measured by averaging over ten runs on a Lenovo Thinkpad T450s running Ubuntu 16.04, Python 3.5 and OpenJDK 8 on a warmed-up JVM. They show that Nagini can effectively verify non-trivial properties of real-life Python programs in reasonable time. Due to modular verification, parts of a program can be verified independently and in parallel (which Nagini does by default), so that larger programs will not inherently lead to performance problems. This is demonstrated by the speedup achieved via parallelization on the two larger examples; for the smaller ones, verification time is dominated by a single complex method. Additionally, the annotation overhead is well within the range of other verification tools [9].

Acknowledgements. Thanks to Vytautas Astrauskas, Samuel Hitz, and Fábio Pakk Selmi-Dei for their contributions to Nagini. We gratefully acknowledge support from the Zurich Information Security and Privacy Center (ZISC).

---

[3] We chose examples that do not make use of dynamic features or external libraries from rosettacode.org, interactivepython.org and github.com/keon/algorithms.

References

1. Barnett, M., Chang, B.-Y.E., DeLine, R., Jacobs, B., Leino, K.R.M.: Boogie: a modular reusable verifier for object-oriented programs. In: de Boer, F.S., Bonsangue, M.M., Graf, S., de Roever, W.-P. (eds.) FMCO 2005. LNCS, vol. 4111, pp. 364–387. Springer, Heidelberg (2006). https://doi.org/10.1007/11804192_17
2. Barnett, M., Fähndrich, M., Leino, K.R.M., Müller, P., Schulte, W., Venter, H.: Specification and verification: the Spec# experience. Commun. ACM **54**(6), 81–91 (2011)
3. Barrera, D., Chuat, L., Perrig, A., Reischuk, R.M., Szalachowski, P.: The scion internet architecture. Commun. ACM **60**(6), 56–65 (2017)
4. Berdine, J., Calcagno, C., O'Hearn, P.W.: Smallfoot: modular automatic assertion checking with separation logic. In: de Boer, F.S., Bonsangue, M.M., Graf, S., de Roever, W.-P. (eds.) FMCO 2005. LNCS, vol. 4111, pp. 115–137. Springer, Heidelberg (2006). https://doi.org/10.1007/11804192_6
5. Boström, P., Müller, P.: Modular verification of finite blocking in non-terminating programs. In: Boyland, J.T. (ed.) European Conference on Object-Oriented Programming (ECOOP). LIPIcs, vol. 37, pp. 639–663. Schloss Dagstuhl (2015)
6. Dahlweid, M., Moskal, M., Santen, T., Tobies, S., Schulte, W.: VCC: contract-based modular verification of concurrent C. In: 2009 31st International Conference on Software Engineering - Companion Volume, pp. 429–430, May 2009
7. Fähndrich, M., Barnett, M., Logozzo, F.: Code contracts (2008). http://research.microsoft.com/contracts
8. Filliâtre, J.-C., Paskevich, A.: Why3—where programs meet provers. In: Felleisen, M., Gardner, P. (eds.) ESOP 2013. LNCS, vol. 7792, pp. 125–128. Springer, Heidelberg (2013). https://doi.org/10.1007/978-3-642-37036-6_8
9. Hawblitzel, C., Howell, J., Lorch, J.R., Narayan, A., Parno, B., Zhang, D., Zill, B.: Ironclad apps: end-to-end security via automated full-system verification. In: 11th USENIX Symposium on Operating Systems Design and Implementation, OSDI 2014, Broomfield, CO, USA, 6–8 October 2014, pp. 165–181 (2014)
10. Jacobs, B., Smans, J., Philippaerts, P., Vogels, F., Penninckx, W., Piessens, F.: VeriFast: a powerful, sound, predictable, fast verifier for C and Java. In: Bobaru, M., Havelund, K., Holzmann, G.J., Joshi, R. (eds.) NFM 2011. LNCS, vol. 6617, pp. 41–55. Springer, Heidelberg (2011). https://doi.org/10.1007/978-3-642-20398-5_4
11. Kirchner, F., Kosmatov, N., Prevosto, V., Signoles, J., Yakobowski, B.: Frama-C: a software analysis perspective. Formal Aspects Comput. **27**(3), 573–609 (2015)
12. Lehtosalo, J., et al.: Mypy - optional static typing for python (2017). http://mypy-lang.org
13. Leino, K.R.M.: Dafny: an automatic program verifier for functional correctness. In: Clarke, E.M., Voronkov, A. (eds.) LPAR 2010. LNCS (LNAI), vol. 6355, pp. 348–370. Springer, Heidelberg (2010). https://doi.org/10.1007/978-3-642-17511-4_20
14. Müller, P., Schwerhoff, M., Summers, A.J.: Viper: a verification infrastructure for permission-based reasoning. In: Jobstmann, B., Leino, K.R.M. (eds.) VMCAI 2016. LNCS, vol. 9583, pp. 41–62. Springer, Heidelberg (2016). https://doi.org/10.1007/978-3-662-49122-5_2
15. Müller, P., Schwerhoff, M., Summers, A.J.: Automatic verification of iterated separating conjunctions using symbolic execution. In: Chaudhuri, S., Farzan, A. (eds.) CAV 2016. LNCS, vol. 9779, pp. 405–425. Springer, Cham (2016). https://doi.org/10.1007/978-3-319-41528-4_22

16. O'Hearn, P., Reynolds, J., Yang, H.: Local reasoning about programs that alter data structures. In: Fribourg, L. (ed.) CSL 2001. LNCS, vol. 2142, pp. 1–19. Springer, Heidelberg (2001). https://doi.org/10.1007/3-540-44802-0_1
17. Parkinson, M., Bierman, G.: Separation logic and abstraction. In: Proceedings of the 32nd ACM SIGPLAN-SIGACT Symposium on Principles of Programming Languages, POPL 2005, pp. 247–258. ACM, New York (2005)
18. Penninckx, W., Jacobs, B., Piessens, F.: Sound, modular and compositional verification of the input/output behavior of programs. In: Vitek, J. (ed.) ESOP 2015. LNCS, vol. 9032, pp. 158–182. Springer, Heidelberg (2015). https://doi.org/10.1007/978-3-662-46669-8_7
19. Piskac, R., Wies, T., Zufferey, D.: GRASShopper: complete heap verification with mixed specifications. In: Ábrahám, E., Havelund, K. (eds.) TACAS 2014. LNCS, vol. 8413, pp. 124–139. Springer, Heidelberg (2014). https://doi.org/10.1007/978-3-642-54862-8_9
20. van Rossum, G., Lehtosalo, J., Langa, Ł.: Type Hints (2014). https://www.python.org/dev/peps/pep-0484/
21. Santos, J.F., Maksimovic, P., Naudziuniene, D., Wood, T., Gardner, P.: JaVert: JavaScript verification toolchain. PACMPL **2**(POPL), 50:1–50:33 (2018)
22. Smans, J., Jacobs, B., Piessens, F.: VeriCool: an automatic verifier for a concurrent object-oriented language. In: Barthe, G., de Boer, F.S. (eds.) FMOODS 2008. LNCS, vol. 5051, pp. 220–239. Springer, Heidelberg (2008). https://doi.org/10.1007/978-3-540-68863-1_14
23. Smans, J., Jacobs, B., Piessens, F.: Implicit dynamic frames. ACM Trans. Program. Lang. Syst. **34**(1), 2:1–2:58 (May 2012)
24. Stefanescu, A., Park, D., Yuwen, S., Li, Y., Rosu, G.: Semantics-based program verifiers for all languages. In: Proceedings of the 2016 ACM SIGPLAN International Conference on Object-Oriented Programming, Systems, Languages, and Applications, OOPSLA 2016, Part of SPLASH 2016, Amsterdam, The Netherlands, 30 October–4 November 2016, pp. 74–91 (2016)

PEREGRINE: A Tool for the Analysis of Population Protocols

Michael Blondin, Javier Esparza, and Stefan Jaax(✉)

Technische Universität München, Munich, Germany
{blondimi,esparza,jaax}@in.tum.de

Abstract. We introduce PEREGRINE, the first tool for the analysis and parameterized verification of population protocols. Population protocols are a model of computation very much studied by the distributed computing community, in which mobile anonymous agents interact stochastically to achieve a common task. PEREGRINE allows users to design protocols, to simulate them both manually and automatically, to gather statistics of properties such as convergence speed, and to verify correctness automatically. This paper describes the features of PEREGRINE and their implementation.

Keywords: Population protocols · Distributed computing
Parameterized verification · Simulation

1 Introduction

Population protocols [1,3,4] are a model of distributed computing in which replicated, mobile agents with limited computational power interact stochastically to achieve a common task. They provide a simple and elegant formalism to model, e.g., networks of passively mobile sensors [1,5], trust propagation [13], evolutionary dynamics [14], and chemical systems, under the name chemical reaction networks [12,16,19].

Population protocols are parameterized: the number of agents does not change during the execution of the protocol, but is *a priori* unbounded. A protocol is correct if it behaves correctly for all of its infinitely many initial configurations. For this reason, it is challenging to design correct and efficient protocols.

In this paper we introduce PEREGRINE[1], the first tool for the parameterized analysis of population protocols. PEREGRINE is intended for use by researchers in distributed computing and systems biology. It allows the user to specify protocols either through an editor or as simple scripts, and to analyze them via a

M. Blondin was supported by the Fonds de recherche du Québec – Nature et technologies (FRQNT).

[1] PEREGRINE can be found at https://peregrine.model.in.tum.de.

H. Chockler and G. Weissenbacher (Eds.): CAV 2018, LNCS 10981, pp. 604–611, 2018.
https://doi.org/10.1007/978-3-319-96145-3_34

graphical interface. The analysis features of PEREGRINE include manual step-by-step simulation; automatic sampling; statistics generation of average convergence speed; detection of incorrect executions through simulation; and formal verification of correctness. The first four features are supported for all protocols, while verification is supported for silent protocols, a large subclass of protocols [6]. Verification is performed automatically over *all* of the infinitely many initial configurations using the recent approach of [6] for solving the so-called well-specification problem.

Related Work. The problem of automatically verifying that a population protocol conforms to its specification for *one fixed initial configuration* has been considered in [10,11,17,20]. In [10], *ad hoc* search algorithms are used. In [11,17], the authors show how to model the problem in the probabilistic model checker PRISM, and under certain conditions in SPIN. In [20], the problem is modeled with the PAT toolkit for model checking under fairness assumptions. All these tools increase our confidence in the correctness of a protocol. However, compared to PEREGRINE, they are not visual tools, they do not offer simulation capabilities, and they can only verify the correctness of a protocol for a finite number of initial configurations, with typically a small number of agents. PEREGRINE proves correctness for all of the infinitely many initial configurations, with an arbitrarily large number of agents.

As mentioned in the introduction, population protocols are isomorphic to chemical reaction networks (CRNs), a popular model in natural computing. Cardelli et al. have recently developed model checking techniques and analysis algorithms for *stochastic* CRNs [7–9]. The problems studied therein are incomparable to the parameterized questions addressed by PEREGRINE.

The verification algorithm of PEREGRINE is based on [6], where a novel approach for the parameterized verification of silent population protocols has been presented. The command-line tool of [6] only offers support for proving correctness, with no functionality for visualization or simulation. Further, contrary to PEREGRINE, the tool cannot produce counterexamples when correctness fails.

2 Population Protocols

We introduce population protocols through a simple example and then briefly formalize the model. We refer the reader to [4] for a more thorough but still intuitive presentation. Suppose anonymous and mobile agents wish to take a majority vote. Intuitively, *anonymous* means that agents have no identity, and *mobile* that agents are "wandering around", and can only interact whenever they bump into each other. In order to vote, all agents conduct the following protocol. Each agent is in one out of four states $\{Y, N, y, n\}$. Initially all agents are in the states Y or N, corresponding to how they want to vote (states y, n are auxiliary states). Agents repeatedly interact pairwise according to the following rules:

$$a\colon YN \mapsto yn \qquad b\colon Yn \mapsto Yy \qquad c\colon Ny \mapsto Nn \qquad d\colon yn \mapsto yy$$

For example, if the population initially has two agents of opinion "yes" and one agent of opinion "no", then a possible execution is:

$$\{\!\!\{\underline{Y}, Y, \underline{N}\}\!\!\} \xrightarrow{a} \{\!\!\{y, \underline{Y}, \underline{n}\}\!\!\} \xrightarrow{b} \{\!\!\{y, Y, y\}\!\!\}, \tag{1}$$

where e.g. $\{\!\!\{Y, Y, N\}\!\!\}$ denotes the multiset with two agents in state Y and one agent in state N.

The goal of every population protocol is to ensure that the agents eventually reach a lasting consensus, i.e., a multiset in which (1) either all agents are in "yes"-states, or all agents are in "no"-states, and (2) further interactions do not destroy the consensus. On top of this universal specification, each protocol has an individual goal, determining which initial configurations should reach the "yes" and the "no" lasting consensus. In the majority protocol above, the agents should reach a "yes"-consensus iff 50% or more agents vote "yes".

Execution (1) above leads to a lasting "yes"-consensus; further, the consensus is the right one, since 2 out of 3 agents voted "yes". In fact, assuming agents interact uniformly and independently at random, the above protocol is correct: executions almost surely reach a correct lasting consensus.

More formally, a population protocol is a tuple (Q, T, I, O) where Q is a finite set of *states*, $T \subseteq Q^2 \times Q^2$ is a set of *transitions*, $I \subseteq Q$ are the *initial states* and $O\colon Q \to \{0, 1\}$ is the *output mapping*. A *configuration* is a non-empty multiset over Q, an *initial configuration* is a non-empty multiset over I, and a configuration is *terminal* if it cannot be altered by any transition. A configuration is in a *consensus* if all of its states map to the same output under O.

An *execution* is a finite or infinite sequence $C_0 \xrightarrow{t_1} C_1 \xrightarrow{t_2} \cdots$ such that C_i is obtained from applying transition t_i to C_{i-1}. A *fair execution* is either a finite execution that reaches a terminal configuration, or an infinite execution such that if $\{i \in \mathbb{N} : C_i \xrightarrow{*} D\}$ is infinite, then $\{i \in \mathbb{N} : C_i = D\}$ is infinite for any configuration D. In other words, fairness ensures that a configuration cannot be avoided forever if it is reachable infinitely often. Fairness is an abstraction of the random interactions occurring within a population. A configuration C is in a *lasting consensus* if every execution from C only leads to configurations of the same consensus.

If for every initial configuration C, all fair executions from C lead to a lasting consensus $\varphi(C) \in \{0, 1\}$, then we say that the protocol *computes* the predicate φ. For example, the above majority protocol with $O(Y) = O(y) = 1$ and $O(N) = O(n) = 0$ computes the predicate $C[Y] \geq C[N]$, where $C[x]$ denotes the number of occurrences of state x in C. A protocol does not necessarily compute a predicate. For example, if we alter the majority protocol by removing transition d, then $\{\!\!\{Y, N\}\!\!\} \xrightarrow{a} \{\!\!\{y, n\}\!\!\}$ is a fair execution, but $\{\!\!\{y, n\}\!\!\}$ is not in a consensus. In other words, transition d acts as a tie-breaker which allows to reach the consensus configuration $\{\!\!\{y, y\}\!\!\}$. A protocol that computes a predicate is said to be *well-specified*. It is well-known that well-specified population protocols compute precisely the predicates definable in Presburger arithmetic [3]. On top of different *majority protocols* for the predicate $C[x] \geq C[y]$, the literature contains, e.g., different families of so-called *flock-of-birds protocols* for the predicates $C[x] \geq c$, where c is an integer constant, and families of *threshold protocols* for the predicates $a_1 \cdot C[x_1] + \cdots + a_n \cdot C[x_n] \geq c$, where $a_1, \ldots, a_n, c$ are integer constants and $x_1, \ldots, x_n$ are initial states.

3 Analyzing Population Protocols

PEREGRINE is a web tool with a JavaScript frontend and a Haskell backend. The backend makes use of the SMT solver Z3 [15] to test satisfiability of Presburger arithmetic formulas. The user has access to four main features through the graphical frontend. We present these features in the remainder of the section.

Protocol Description. PEREGRINE offers a description language for both single protocols and families of protocols depending on some parameters. Single protocols are described either through a graphical editor or as simple Python scripts. Families of protocols (called parametric protocols) can only be specified as scripts, but PEREGRINE assists the user by generating a code skeleton.

Simulation. Population protocols can be simulated through a graphical player depicted in Fig. 1. The user can pick an initial configuration and simulate the protocol by either manual selection of interactions, or by letting a scheduler pick interactions uniformly at random. The simulator keeps a history of the execution which can be rewound at any time, making it easy to experiment with the different behaviours of a protocol. Configurations can be displayed in two ways: either as explicit populations, as illustrated in Fig. 1, or as bar charts of the states count, more convenient for large populations.

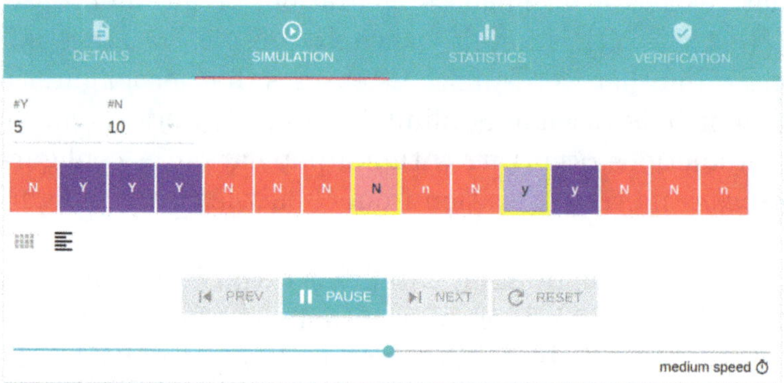

Fig. 1. Simulation of the majority protocol from the initial configuration $\wr 5 \cdot Y, 10 \cdot N \wr$.

Statistics. PEREGRINE can generate statistics from batch simulations. The user provides four parameters: $s_{\min}, s_{\max}, m$ and n. PEREGRINE generates n random executions as follows. For each execution, a number s is picked uniformly at random from $[s_{\min}, s_{\max}]$, and an initial configuration of size s is then picked uniformly at random. Each step of an execution is picked uniformly at random among enabled interactions. If no terminal configuration is reached within m steps, then the simulation halts. In the end, n executions of length at most m are gathered. PEREGRINE classifies the generated executions according to their consensus, and computes statistics on the convergence speed (see the next two paragraphs). The results can be visualized in different ways, and the raw data can be exported as a JSON file.

Consensus. For each random execution, PEREGRINE checks whether the last configuration of an execution is in a consensus and, if so, whether the consensus corresponds to the expected output of the protocol. PEREGRINE reports which percentage of the executions reach a consensus, and whether the consensus is correct and/or lasting. In normal mode, PEREGRINE only classifies an execution as lasting consensus if it ends in a terminal configuration. In the *increased accuracy* mode, if the execution ends in a configuration C of consensus $b \in \{0, 1\}$, then the model checker LoLA [18] is used to determine whether there exists a configuration C' such that $C \xrightarrow{*} C'$ and C' is not of consensus b. If it is not the case, then PEREGRINE concludes that C is in a lasting consensus. PEREGRINE plots the percentage of executions in each category as a function of the population size, as illustrated on the left of Fig. 2.

Average Convergence Speed. PEREGRINE also provides statistics on the convergence speed of a protocol. Let $C_0 \xrightarrow{t_1} C_1 \xrightarrow{t_2} \cdots \xrightarrow{t_\ell} C_\ell$ be an execution such that C_ℓ is in a consensus $b \in \{0, 1\}$. The *number of steps to convergence* of the execution is defined as 0 if all configurations are of consensus b, and otherwise as $i+1$, where i is the largest index such that C_i is not in consensus b. For each population size, PEREGRINE computes the average number of steps to convergence of all consensus executions of that population size, and plots the information as illustrated on the right of Fig. 2.

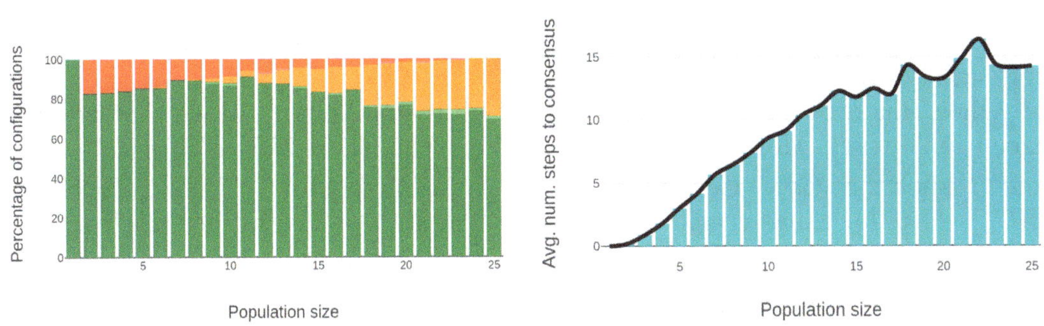

Fig. 2. Statistics for 5000 random executions of the approximate majority protocol of [2], of length at most 40, from initial configurations of size at most 25. The left plot shows the percentage of executions reaching a consensus (dark green: lasting correct, light green: correct, light red: incorrect, dark red: lasting incorrect) and no consensus (orange). In this example the occurrences of light red are negligible. The right plot shows the average number of steps to convergence. (Color figure online)

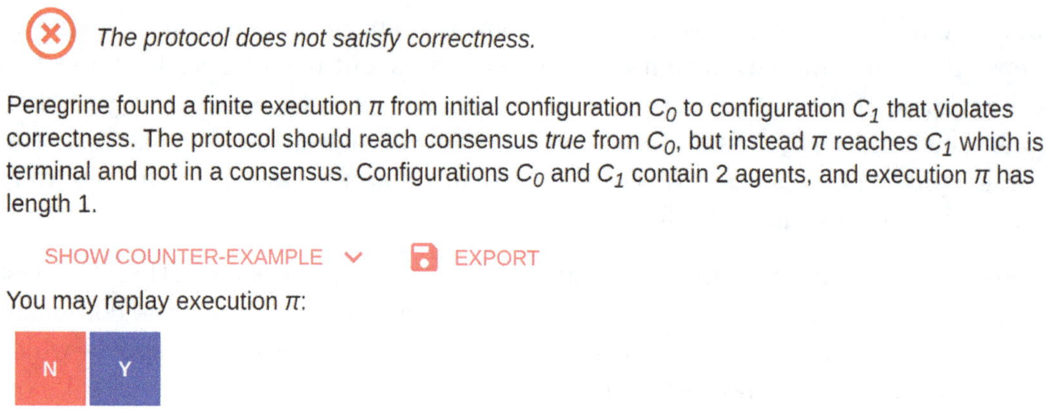

Fig. 3. Verification of the majority protocol of Sect. 2 without transition d: $yn \mapsto yy$.

Verification. PEREGRINE can automatically verify that a population protocol computes a given predicate. Predicates can be specified by the user in quantifier-free Presburger arithmetic extended with the family of predicates $\{x \equiv y \pmod{c}\}_{c \geq 2}$, which is equivalent to Presburger arithmetic. For example, for the majority protocol of Sect. 2, the user simply specifies `C[Y] >= C[N]`.

PEREGRINE implements the approach of [6] to verify correctness of protocols which are silent. A protocol is said to be *silent* if from every initial configuration, every fair execution leads to a terminal configuration. The majority protocol of Sect. 2 and most existing protocols from the literature are silent [6]. We briefly describe the approach of [6] and how it is integrated into PEREGRINE.

Suppose we are given a population protocol $\mathcal{P}$ and we wish to determine whether it computes a predicate φ. The procedure first tries to prove that $\mathcal{P}$ is silent. This is done by verifying a more restricted condition called *layered termination*. Verifying the latter property reduces to testing satisfiability of a Presburger arithmetic formula. If this formula holds, then the protocol is silent, otherwise no conclusion is derived. However, essentially all existing silent protocols satisfy layered termination [6].

Once $\mathcal{P}$ is proven to be silent, the procedure attempts to prove that no "bad execution" exists. More precisely, it checks whether there exist configurations C_0 and C_1 such that $C_0 \xrightarrow{*} C_1$, C_0 is initial, C_1 is terminal, and C_1 is not in consensus $\varphi(C_0) \in \{0, 1\}$. Since reachability is not definable in Presburger arithmetic, a Presburger-definable over-approximation $\dashrightarrow^{*}$ of reachability, borrowed from Petri net theory, is used instead. We obtain the following formula $\Phi_{\text{bad-exec}}$:

$$\exists C_0, C_1 \colon C_0 \dashrightarrow^{*} C_1 \wedge \bigwedge_{q \notin I} C_0[q] = 0 \wedge \bigwedge_{t \in T} \text{succ}(C_1, t) \subseteq \{C_1\} \wedge \bigvee_{q \in C_1} (O(q) = \neg\varphi(C_0)).$$

If $\Phi_{\text{bad-exec}}$ is unsatisfiable, then $\mathcal{P}$ is correct. Otherwise, no conclusion is reached, and $\Phi_{\text{bad-exec}}$ is iteratively strengthened by enriching the over-approximation $\dashrightarrow^{*}$. Whenever $\Phi_{\text{bad-exec}}$ is satisfied by (C_0, C_1), PEREGRINE calls the model-checker LOLA to test whether C_1 is indeed reachable from C_0. If so, then PEREGRINE reports $\mathcal{P}$ to be incorrect, and generates a counter-example execution, which can be replayed or exported as a JSON file (see Fig. 3).

Currently PEREGRINE can verify protocols with up to a hundred states and a few thousands transitions. The bottleneck is the size of the constraint system. Due to lack of space, we refer the reader to [6] for detailed experimental results.

References

1. Angluin, D., Aspnes, J., Diamadi, Z., Fischer, M.J., Peralta, R.: Computation in networks of passively mobile finite-state sensors. In: Proceedings of the 23rd Annual ACM Symposium on Principles of Distributed Computing (PODC), pp. 290–299 (2004). https://doi.org/10.1145/1011767.1011810
2. Angluin, D., Aspnes, J., Eisenstat, D.: A simple population protocol for fast robust approximate majority. Distrib. Comput. **21**(2), 87–102 (2008). https://doi.org/10.1007/s00446-008-0059-z
3. Angluin, D., Aspnes, J., Eisenstat, D., Ruppert, E.: The computational power of population protocols. Distrib. Comput. **20**(4), 279–304 (2007). https://doi.org/10.1007/s00446-007-0040-2
4. Aspnes, J., Ruppert, E.: An introduction to population protocols. In: Garbinato, B., Miranda, H., Rodrigues, L. (eds.) Middleware for Network Eccentric and Mobile Applications, pp. 97–120. Springer, Heidelberg (2009). https://doi.org/10.1007/978-3-540-89707-1_5
5. Beauquier, J., Blanchard, P., Burman, J., Delaët, S.: Tight complexity analysis of population protocols with cover times - the ZebraNet example. Theor. Comput. Sci. **512**, 15–27 (2013). https://doi.org/10.1016/j.tcs.2012.10.032
6. Blondin, M., Esparza, J., Jaax, S., Meyer, P.J.: Towards efficient verification of population protocols. In: Proceedings of the 36th ACM Symposium on Principles of Distributed Computing (PODC), pp. 423–430 (2017). https://doi.org/10.1145/3087801.3087816
7. Cardelli, L., Češka, M., Fränzle, M., Kwiatkowska, M., Laurenti, L., Paoletti, N., Whitby, M.: Syntax-guided optimal synthesis for chemical reaction networks. In: Majumdar, R., Kunčak, V. (eds.) CAV 2017. LNCS, vol. 10427, pp. 375–395. Springer, Cham (2017). https://doi.org/10.1007/978-3-319-63390-9_20
8. Cardelli, L., Kwiatkowska, M., Laurenti, L.: Stochastic analysis of chemical reaction networks using linear noise approximation. Biosystems **149**, 26–33 (2016). https://doi.org/10.1016/j.biosystems.2016.09.004
9. Cardelli, L., Tribastone, M., Tschaikowski, M., Vandin, A.: Syntactic Markovian bisimulation for chemical reaction networks. In: Aceto, L., et al. (eds.) Models, Algorithms, Logics and Tools. LNCS, vol. 10460, pp. 466–483. Springer, Cham (2017). https://doi.org/10.1007/978-3-319-63121-9_23
10. Chatzigiannakis, I., Michail, O., Spirakis, P.G.: Algorithmic verification of population protocols. In: Dolev, S., Cobb, J., Fischer, M., Yung, M. (eds.) SSS 2010. LNCS, vol. 6366, pp. 221–235. Springer, Heidelberg (2010). https://doi.org/10.1007/978-3-642-16023-3_19
11. Clément, J., Delporte-Gallet, C., Fauconnier, H., Sighireanu, M.: Guidelines for the verification of population protocols. In: ICDCS, pp. 215–224. IEEE Computer Society (2011). https://doi.org/10.1109/ICDCS.2011.36
12. Cummings, R., Doty, D., Soloveichik, D.: Probability 1 computation with chemical reaction networks. Nat. Comput. **15**(2), 245–261 (2016). https://doi.org/10.1007/s11047-015-9501-x

13. Diamadi, Z., Fischer, M.J.: A simple game for the study of trust in distributed systems. Wuhan Univ. J. Nat. Sci. **6**(1), 72–82 (2001). https://doi.org/10.1007/BF03160228
14. Moran, P.A.P.: Random processes in genetics. Math. Proc. Cambridge Philos. Soc. **54**(1), 60–71 (1958). https://doi.org/10.1017/S0305004100033193
15. de Moura, L., Bjørner, N.: Z3: an efficient SMT solver. In: Ramakrishnan, C.R., Rehof, J. (eds.) TACAS 2008. LNCS, vol. 4963, pp. 337–340. Springer, Heidelberg (2008). https://doi.org/10.1007/978-3-540-78800-3_24. z3 is available at https://github.com/Z3Prover/z3
16. Navlakha, S., Bar-Joseph, Z.: Distributed information processing in biological and computational systems. Commun. ACM **58**(1), 94–102 (2014). https://doi.org/10.1145/2678280
17. Pang, J., Luo, Z., Deng, Y.: On automatic verification of self-stabilizing population protocols. In: Proceedings of the 2nd IEEE/IFIP International Symposium on Theoretical Aspects of Software Engineering (TASE), pp. 185–192 (2008). https://doi.org/10.1109/TASE.2008.8
18. Schmidt, K.: LoLA a low level analyser. In: Nielsen, M., Simpson, D. (eds.) ICATPN 2000. LNCS, vol. 1825, pp. 465–474. Springer, Heidelberg (2000). https://doi.org/10.1007/3-540-44988-4_27. LoLA is available at http://service-technology.org/lola/
19. Soloveichik, D., Cook, M., Winfree, E., Bruck, J.: Computation with finite stochastic chemical reaction networks. Nat. Comput. **7**(4), 615–633 (2008). https://doi.org/10.1007/s11047-008-9067-y
20. Sun, J., Liu, Y., Dong, J.S., Pang, J.: PAT: towards flexible verification under fairness. In: Bouajjani, A., Maler, O. (eds.) CAV 2009. LNCS, vol. 5643, pp. 709–714. Springer, Heidelberg (2009). https://doi.org/10.1007/978-3-642-02658-4_59

ADAC: Automated Design of Approximate Circuits

Milan Češka(✉), Jiří Matyáš, Vojtech Mrazek, Lukas Sekanina, Zdenek Vasicek, and Tomáš Vojnar

Faculty of Information Technology, IT4Innovations Centre of Excellence, Brno University of Technology, Brno, Czech Republic
ceskam@fit.vutbr.cz

Abstract. Approximate circuits with relaxed requirements on functional correctness play an important role in the development of resource-efficient computer systems. Designing approximate circuits is a very complex and time-demanding process trying to find optimal trade-offs between the approximation error and resource savings. In this paper, we present ADAC—a novel framework for automated design of approximate arithmetic circuits. ADAC integrates in a unique way efficient simulation and formal methods for approximate equivalence checking into a search-based circuit optimisation. To make ADAC easily accessible, it is implemented as a module of the ABC tool: a state-of-the-art system for circuit synthesis and verification. Within several hours, ADAC is able to construct high-quality Pareto sets of complex circuits (including even 32-bit multipliers), providing useful trade-offs between the resource consumption and the error that is formally guaranteed. This demonstrates outstanding performance and scalability compared with other existing approaches.

1 Introduction

In the recent years, reduction of power consumption of computer systems and mobile devices has become one of the biggest challenges in the computer industry. *Approximate computing* has been established as a new research field aiming at reducing system resource demands (and, in particular, power demands) by relaxing the requirement that all computations are always performed correctly. Approximate computing exploits the fact that many applications, including image and multimedia processing, signal processing, data mining, machine learning, neural networks, and scientific computations, are *error resilient*, i.e.

This work was supported by the IT4Innovations excellence in science project No. LQ1602.

H. Chockler and G. Weissenbacher (Eds.): CAV 2018, LNCS 10981, pp. 612–620, 2018.
https://doi.org/10.1007/978-3-319-96145-3_35

produce acceptable results even though the underlying computations are performed with a certain error. Therefore, the error can be used as a design metric and traded for chip area, power consumption, or runtime. Chippa et al. [7] claims that almost 80% of runtime is spent in procedures that could be approximated.

Approximate computing can be conducted at different system levels with arithmetic circuit approximation being one of the most popular as such circuits are frequently used in the core computations. In our work, we focus on functional approximation where the original circuit is replaced by a less complex one which exhibits some errors but improves non-functional circuit parameters such as power consumption or chip area. Circuit approximation can be formulated as an optimisation problem where the error and non-functional circuit parameters are conflicting design objectives. Designing complex approximate circuits is a time-demanding and error-prone process. Moreover, its automation is challenging too since the design space including candidate solutions is huge and checking that a candidate solution has the required error is itself a computationally demanding task, especially if formal guarantees on the error have to be ensured.

In this tool paper, we present *ADAC*[1]—a novel framework for automated design of approximate circuits. The framework implements a design loop including (i) a *generator* of candidate solutions employing genetic search algorithms, (ii) an *evaluator* estimating non-functional parameters of a candidate solution, and (iii) a *verifier* checking that the candidate solution does not exceed the permissible error. ADAC is integrated as a new module into the ABC tool—a state-of-the-art and widely used system for circuit synthesis and verification [1]. The framework takes as the inputs:

- a golden combinational circuit in Verilog implementing the correct functionality,
- an error metric (such as the worst-case error, mean error, Hamming distance, etc.),
- a threshold on the error metric representing the maximal permissible error,
- a time limit on the overall design process, and
- a file specifying sizes of gates available to the design process.

With these inputs, ADAC searches for an approximate circuit satisfying the error threshold and having the minimal estimated chip area. Previous works [3,14,20,22] confirmed that the chip area is a good optimization objective as it highly correlates with power consumption, which is a crucial target in approximate computing.

The results of [21] clearly demonstrate that search algorithms based on *Cartesian Genetic Programming* (CGP) [12] are well capable of generating high-quality approximate circuits. For complex circuits, however, a high number of candidate solutions has to be generated and evaluated, which significantly limits the scalability of the design process. Our framework implements several approaches for error evaluation suitable for different error metrics and application domains. They include both *SAT and BDD-based techniques* for

[1] https://github.com/imatyas/ADAC.

approximate equivalence checking providing *formal error guarantees* as well as a *bit-parallel circuit simulation* utilising the computing power of modern processors. We also implement a novel search strategy that drives the search towards *promptly verifiable approximate circuits*, which significantly accelerates the design process in many cases [3]. As such, the framework offers a unique integration of techniques based on simulation, formal reasoning, and evolutionary circuit optimisation. Our extensive experimental evaluation demonstrates that ADAC offers outstanding performance and scalability compared with existing methods and tools and paves a way towards an automated design process of complex provably-correct circuit approximations.

2 Architecture and Implementation

The ADAC framework has a modular architecture illustrated in Fig. 1.

The setup phase is responsible mainly for preparing a chromosome representation of the golden circuit. The circuit is given in a high-level Verilog format, which is first translated to a gate-level representation using the tool Yosys [25], and then the chromosome representation is obtained using our V2CH script. The setup phase is also responsible for generating a configuration file controlling the main design loop. It is generated from the user inputs and optional parameters for CGP and search strategies.

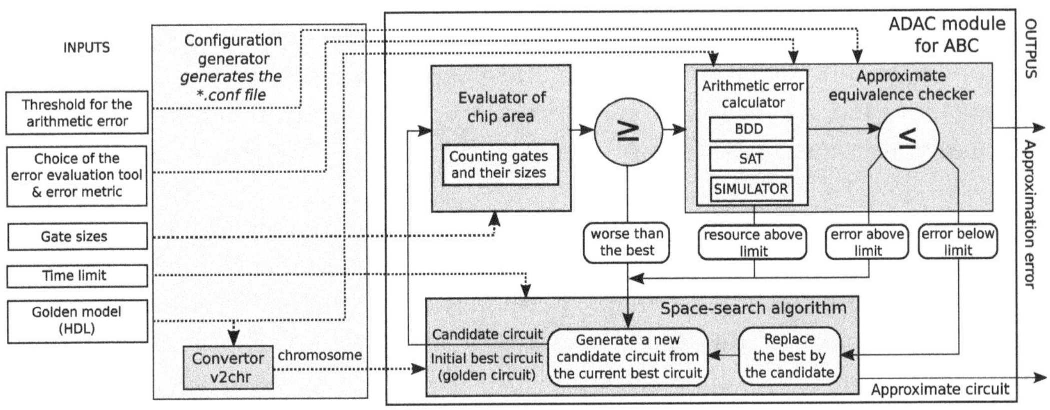

Fig. 1. A scheme of the ADAC architecture.

The design loop consists of three components: (i) a generator of candidate designs, (ii) an evaluator of non-functional parameters of the candidate circuit (currently estimating the chip area), and (iii) a verifier evaluating the candidate error. The chip area and the error form a basis of the *fitness function*, whose value is minimised via our search strategy. In particular, the fitness is infinity if the circuit error exceeds the given threshold, and the chip area otherwise. In the future, we plan to support a more general specification of the fitness. As an additional feature, ADAC can also quantify the difference (in the given metric) between two given circuits.

The real values of non-functional parameters, such as the chip area or the power-delay product (PDP), depend on the target technology, and the synthesis of an optimal implementation of the given circuit using the target technology is highly time-consuming. Therefore, our design loop currently uses the *chip area* as the sole non-functional parameter. The chip area is estimated as the sum of the sizes of the gates of the circuit, which are given as one of the inputs of ADAC. The chip area is typically a good estimate of the power consumption [3, 14, 20, 22]. The output of ADAC (in the gate-level Verilog format) can be passed to industrial circuit design tools to obtain accurate circuit parameters for the target technology. In our experiments, we report PDP for the 45 nm technology synthesised by the Synopsys Design Compiler [19].

We now briefly describe the candidate circuit generator and three methods for error evaluation that are currently supported in ADAC.

The *candidate circuit generator* is based on CGP where a candidate solution is encoded as a chromosome describing an oriented acyclic graph, given as a 2-dimensional array of 2-input nodes. Every node is numbered and is encoded by 3 integers where the first two numbers denote the inputs and the third represents the function of the node. New candidate circuits are obtained using a mutation operator that performs random changes in the chromosome. The mutations can either modify the node interconnection or functionality. The area of candidate circuits is reduced by making some nodes unreachable (such nodes, however, are removed only at the very end, and so they can still be mutated and even become reachable again). The candidates are evaluated, and the one with the best one is used in the next iteration of the design loop. The whole loop starts with the golden circuit and iteratively generates approximate solutions with better fitness values until a termination criterion (typically a given time limit) is met. Optionally, user can provide approximate circuit satisfying the threshold on the error as a seed to start with.

The *bit-parallel circuit simulation* supports all common error metrics, including the worst-case error (WCE), the mean error, the error rate representing the number of inputs leading to an incorrect output, and the Hamming distance. It utilises the power of modern processors by simulating the circuit on multiple inputs vectors (e.g. 64 inputs for 64-bit processors) in a single pass through the circuit [24]. However, despite the parallel processing that significantly accelerates the simulation, for circuits with arguments of larger bit-widths (beyond 12 bits), it is not feasible to simulate the circuits on all possible inputs, and so statistical guarantees on the approximation error are provided only.

The *BDD-based evaluation* also supports all common error metrics, and, unlike simulation, it is able to provide formal error guarantees for circuits with larger input bit-widths. For the purpose of the evaluation, the original correct circuit and its approximation are interconnected into an auxiliary circuit called a *miter* such that the error can be deduced from its output (e.g. to compute the error rate, the outputs of the golden and candidate circuits are subtracted, and the result is compared with 0). The miter is encoded as a BDD on which the circuit error is evaluated using BDD operations [22, 23]. However, this technique does not scale well with the complexity of the circuits in terms of the number of their gates as the resulting BDD representation becomes prohibitively huge. Hence, this approach works well for large adders and similar circuits, but, it fails, e.g., for multipliers beyond 12-bits.

The *SAT-based evaluation* currently supports WCE only, but it provides formal guarantees and a superior performance to the BDD-based technique. ADAC implements a novel miter construction based on subtracting the output of the golden and approximate circuit, followed by a comparison with the error threshold [3]. The construction is optimised for SAT-based evaluation by avoiding long XOR chains known to cause poor performance of state-of-the-art SAT solvers [5, 9]. This allows us to exploit the ABC engine `iprove`, designed originally for miter-based exact circuit equivalence checking, to quickly evaluate WCE.

The final ingredient of the design process is the *search strategy*. Apart from the standard evolutionary strategies based solely on the fitness function, ADAC also implements a novel verifiability-driven approach [3] combined with the SAT-based evaluation.

The *verifiability-driven search strategy* uses a limit L on the resources available to the underlying SAT decision procedure. The limit effectively controls the time the SAT solver can use. We require that every improving candidate has to be verifiable using the resource limit L. Therefore the strategy drives the search towards candidates that improve the fitness and can be promptly evaluated. As the result, we can evaluate in the given time a much larger set of candidate circuits. Our experiments indicate that this strategy often leads to a higher number of improving solutions and thus finds circuits having a smaller chip area meeting the permissible error. On the other hand, it can happen that, for a limit L, no improving sequence exists, while it exists for a slightly greater resource limit. We are currently implementing auto-adaptive techniques that should automatically select the adequate resource limit for the given circuit.

Integration to the ABC Tool. To make ADAC easily accessible, it is implemented as a new module for the ABC tool. ABC allows us to support an important subset of the Verilog specification and implementation language. We also utilize ABC to translate the circuits among different intermediate representations used for constructing miters. As mentioned before, we employ the `iprove` engine in our SAT-based method for evaluating the WCE. Note that `iprove` uses MiniSat [18] as the SAT solver. Despite the fact that ABC supports a BDD-based circuit representation and manipulation, we implemented our own BDD component (based on the BuDDy library [2]) that is tailored for evolutionary circuit approximation.

Extensibility. Due to its modular architecture, ADAC can be easily extended. Apart from the extensions mentioned above, we are working on a new component for error evaluation based on SAT counting methods (e.g. #SAT [4]) that could offer formal guarantees and a better scalability for the mean error and error-rate metrics, and on new candidate circuit generators counter-examples produced during the verification of candidate circuits. In a long term perspective, we plan to generalise the underlying methods and support also design of approximate sequential circuits.

3 Evaluation, Related Works, and Applications

We first compare the performance of the different methods of circuit error evaluation supported in ADAC. For that, we use results from adder approximation obtained from 10 runs, each for 5 min. The table in Fig. 2 shows average runtimes of a single error evaluation using the bit-parallel simulation, the BDD-based approach, and the SAT-based approach. The reported speedups are with respect to the simulation. We can see that the simulation provides the best performance for small bit-widths only, but it does not scale well The SAT-based method offers the best scalability and dominates for larger circuits, but it supports the WCE evaluation only. The BDD-based method, like simulation, supports all metrics and significantly outperforms the simulation for larger circuits. Note that, for more complex circuits such as multipliers, we would observe similar results with a worse relative performance of the BDD-based approach.

There indeed exist also other known methods for computing approximation errors for arithmetic circuits, including methods based on BDDs [6] or a SAT-based miter solution [5]. Comparing to ADAC, these methods are less scalable, which is demonstrated by the fact that they have been used for approximating multipliers limited to 8-bit operands and adders limited to 16-bit operands only. Apart from that, there are efficient methods for *exact* equivalence checking based on algebraic computations [8,16]. However, they are so far not known for approximate equivalence checking.

	Bit-width of the arguments		
	w = 6	w = 10	w = 14
Simulation	**210μs**	76 ms	31.23 s
BDD ϵ_{wce}	350 μs	12 ms	0.38 s
speedup	0.59×	6.04×	80.74×
BDD ϵ_{me}	370 μs	**13ms**	**0.79s**
speedup	0.59×	5.72×	38.94×
SAT ϵ_{wce}	920 μs	**1.4ms**	**1.7ms**
speedup	0.23×	53.7×	18468×

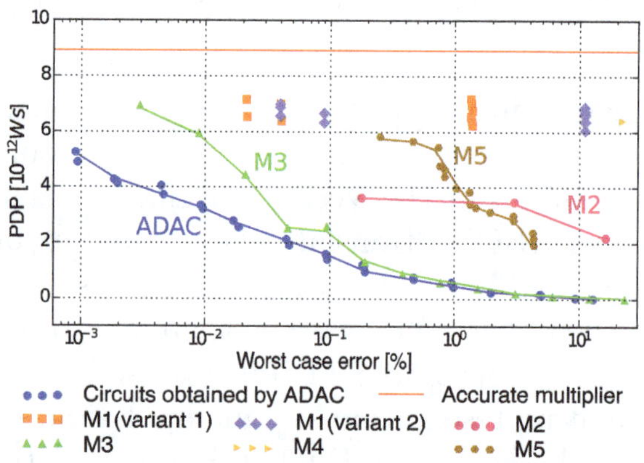

Fig. 2. (Left) Performance of error evaluation methods for adders. (Right) A comparison of 16-bit approximate multipliers designed by ADAC vs. the best known solutions.

Next, we compare the quality of approximate circuits obtained using ADAC with circuits that appeared in the literature. We consider 16-bit multipliers since existing approaches are not able to handle larger and more complex circuits. The different points in Fig. 2 correspond to circuits with different trade-offs between WCE in % and the power-delay product (PDP[2]), which is a key non-functional circuit characteristic. These circuits were obtained using various existing approaches including: (M1) configurable circuits from the lpACLib library [17], (M2) the bit-significance-driven logic compression [15], (M3) the bit-width truncation [10], (M4) compositional techniques [11], and (M5) circuits from the EvoApproxLib library [13]. We can see that just the bit-width truncation can provide a quality of results comparable with ADAC (in terms of the PDP reduction for the given WCE), but for large target errors (20% WCE or more) only. For small target errors, ADAC clearly dominates.

Note that, for each target WCE, we performed 30 independent runs of CGP to obtain statistically significant results. For each run, ADAC was executed for 2 h on an Intel Xeon X5670 2.4 GHz processor using a single core. Also note that the individual runs are independent and thus can be easily parallelised.

Further, Fig. 3 presents approximate multipliers up to 32 bits obtained by ADAC. It shows Pareto fronts representing circuits with different compromises between WCE in % and PDP, and demonstrates that ADAC goes beyond capabilities of existing methods and tools. For each target WCE, ADAC was executed for 4 hours in the case of the 24-bit instances and for 6 hours in the case of the larger instances. Note that a 32-bit exact multiplier requires over 6,300 gates, and, to the best of our knowledge, ADAC is the first tool that is able to approximate such complex circuits with formal error guarantees.

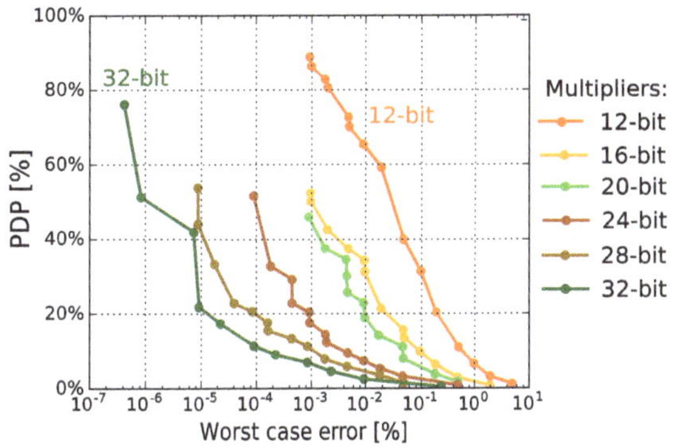

Fig. 3. Approximate multipliers designed by ADAC. 100% refers to PDP of the accurate circuits for the given bit-width.

Besides the approaches mentioned above, there also exist general-purpose methods, such as SALSA [14] or SASIMI [15], approximating circuits independently of their structure. We were unable to perform a direct comparison with them due to their implementation is not available, but based on the published results, ADAC is able to provide a significantly better scalability.

Practical Impacts. The following list briefly characterises several resource-aware applications that build on approximate circuits. The circuits were obtained using prototype implementations of the above mentioned approaches that are now integrated in ADAC.

Approximate multipliers for convolutional neural networks [14]. In such networks, millions of multiplications have to be performed. The usage of application-specific approximate multipliers led to 90% savings in terms of power consumption of the data path for a negligible drop in classification accuracy.

[2] PDP characterises both the speed and energy efficiency of the circuit.

Approximate Adders and Subtractors for a Discrete Convolutional Transformation [22]. These adders and subtractors were designed to reduce the power consumption in video compression for the High Efficiency Video Coding (HEVC) standard. They show better quality/power trade-offs than implementations available in the literature. For example, a 25% power reduction for the same error was obtained in comparison with a recent highly-optimised implementation.

Approximate Adders and Multipliers for Image Processing [20]. These circuits were used in the development of efficient hardware implementations of filters and edge detectors. A 50% reduction was observed in the number of look-up tables used in a field programmable gate array for a negligible drop in the image visual quality.

References

1. Brayton, R., Mishchenko, A.: ABC: an academic industrial-strength verification tool. In: Touili, T., Cook, B., Jackson, P. (eds.) CAV 2010. LNCS, vol. 6174, pp. 24–40. Springer, Heidelberg (2010). https://doi.org/10.1007/978-3-642-14295-6_5
2. BuDDy: A BDD package, January 2018. http://buddy.sourceforge.net/manual/main.html
3. Češka, M., Matyáš, J., Mrazek, V., Sekanina, L., Vasicek, Z., Vojnar, T.: Approximating complex arithmetic circuits with formal error guarantees: 32-bit multipliers accomplished. In: Proceedings of the ICCAD 2017, pp. 416–423. IEEE (2017)
4. Chakraborty, S., Meel, K.S., Mistry, R., Vardi, M.Y.: Approximate probabilistic inference via word-level counting. In: Proceedings of the AAAI 2016, pp. 3218–3224. AAAI Press (2016)
5. Chandrasekharan, A., Soeken, M., Große, D., Drechsler, R.: Precise error determination of approximated components in sequential circuits with model checking. In: Proceedings of the DAC 2016, pp. 129:1–129:6. ACM (2016)
6. Chandrasekharan, A., Soeken, M., et al.: Approximation-aware rewriting of AIGs for error tolerant applications. In: Proceedings of the ICCAD 2016, pp. 83:1–83:8. ACM (2016)
7. Chippa, V.K., Chakradhar, S.T., Roy, K., Raghunathan, A.: Analysis and characterization of inherent application resilience for approximate computing. In: Proceedings of the DAC 2013, pp. 1–9. IEEE (2013)
8. Ciesielski, M., Yu, C., Brown, W., Liu, D., Rossi, A.: Verification of gate-level arithmetic circuits by function extraction. In: Proceedings of the DAC 2015. ACM (2015)
9. Han, C.-S., Jiang, J.-H.R.: When boolean satisfiability meets gaussian elimination in a simplex way. In: Madhusudan, P., Seshia, S.A. (eds.) CAV 2012. LNCS, vol. 7358, pp. 410–426. Springer, Heidelberg (2012). https://doi.org/10.1007/978-3-642-31424-7_31
10. Jiang, H., Liu, C., Liu, L., Lombardi, F., Han, J.: A review, classification, and comparative evaluation of approximate arithmetic circuits. J. Emerg. Technol. Comput. Syst. **13**(4), 60:1–60:34 (2017)
11. Kulkarni, P., Gupta, P., Ercegovac, M.D.: Trading accuracy for power in a multiplier architecture. J. Low Power Electron. **7**(4), 490–501 (2011)
12. Miller, J.F.: Cartesian Genetic Programming. Springer, Berlin (2011). https://doi.org/10.1007/978-3-642-17310-3

13. Mrazek, V., Hrbacek, R., et al.: EvoApprox8B: library of approximate adders and multipliers for circuit design and benchmarking of approximation methods. In: Proceedings of the DATE 2017, pp. 258–261. EDAA (2017)
14. Mrazek, V., Sarwar, S.S., Sekanina, L., Vasicek, Z., Roy, K.: Design of power-efficient approximate multipliers for approximate artificial neural networks. In: Proceedings of the ICCAD 2016, pp. 81:1–81:7. ACM (2016)
15. Qiqieh, I., Shafik, R., et al.: Energy-efficient approximate multiplier design using bit significance-driven logic compression. In: Proceedings of the DATE 2017. EDAA (2017)
16. Sayed-Ahmed, A., Große, D., et al.: Formal verification of integer multipliers by combining Gröbner basis with logic reduction. In: Proceedings of the DATE 2016, pp. 1048–1053. IEEE (2016)
17. Shafique, M., Ahmad, W., et al.: A low latency generic accuracy configurable adder. In: Proceedings of the DAC 2015, pp. 86:1–86:6. ACM (2015)
18. Sorensson, N., Een, N.: MiniSat v1.13 – a sat solver with conflict-clause minimization. SAT 2005, no. 53, pp. 1–2 (2005)
19. Synopsys design compiler, January 2018. https://www.synopsys.com/
20. Vasicek, Z., Mrazek, V., Sekanina, L.: Evolutionary functional approximation of circuits implemented into FPGAs. In: Proceedings of the SSCI 2016, pp. 1–8. IEEE (2016)
21. Vasicek, Z., Sekanina, L.: Evolutionary approach to approximate digital circuits design. Trans. Evol. Comput. **19**(3), 432–444 (2015)
22. Vasicek, Z., Mrazek, V., Sekanina, L.: Towards low power approximate DCT architecture for HEVC standard. In: Proceedings of the DATE 2017, pp. 1576–1581. EDAA (2017)
23. Vasicek, Z., Sekanina, L.: Evolutionary design of complex approximate combinational circuits. Genet. Program Evolvable Mach. **17**(2), 169–192 (2016)
24. Vašíček, Z., Slaný, K.: Efficient phenotype evaluation in cartesian genetic programming. In: Moraglio, A., Silva, S., Krawiec, K., Machado, P., Cotta, C. (eds.) EuroGP 2012. LNCS, vol. 7244, pp. 266–278. Springer, Heidelberg (2012). https://doi.org/10.1007/978-3-642-29139-5_23
25. Wolf, C.: Yosys open synthesis suite, January 2018. http://www.clifford.at/yosys/

Probabilistic Systems

Value Iteration for Simple Stochastic Games: Stopping Criterion and Learning Algorithm

Edon Kelmendi, Julia Krämer, Jan Křetínský[✉], and Maximilian Weininger

Technical University of Munich, Munich, Germany
jan.kretinsky@tum.de

Abstract. Simple stochastic games can be solved by value iteration (VI), which yields a sequence of under-approximations of the value of the game. This sequence is guaranteed to converge to the value only in the limit. Since no stopping criterion is known, this technique does not provide any guarantees on its results. We provide the first stopping criterion for VI on simple stochastic games. It is achieved by additionally computing a convergent sequence of *over-approximations* of the value, relying on an analysis of the game graph. Consequently, VI becomes an anytime algorithm returning the approximation of the value and the current error bound. As another consequence, we can provide a simulation-based asynchronous VI algorithm, which yields the same guarantees, but without necessarily exploring the whole game graph.

1 Introduction

Simple Stochastic Game. (SG) [Con92] is a zero-sum two-player game played on a graph by Maximizer and Minimizer, who choose actions in their respective vertices (also called states). Each action is associated with a probability distribution determining the next state to move to. The objective of Maximizer is to maximize the probability of reaching a given target state; the objective of Minimizer is the opposite.

Stochastic games constitute a fundamental problem for several reasons. From the theoretical point of view, the complexity of this problem[1] is known to be in **UP** $\cap$ **coUP** [HK66], but no polynomial-time algorithm is known. Further,

This research was funded in part by the German Excellence Initiative and the European Union Seventh Framework Programme under grant agreement No. 291763 for TUM – IAS, the Studienstiftung des deutschen Volkes project "Formal methods for analysis of attack-defence diagrams", the Czech Science Foundation grant No. 18-11193S, TUM IGSSE Grant 10.06 (PARSEC), and the German Research Foundation (DFG) project KR 4890/2-1 "Statistical Unbounded Verification".

[1] Formally, the problem is to decide, for a given $p \in [0, 1]$ whether Maximizer has a strategy ensuring probability at least p to reach the target.

H. Chockler and G. Weissenbacher (Eds.): CAV 2018, LNCS 10981, pp. 623–642, 2018.
https://doi.org/10.1007/978-3-319-96145-3_36

several other important problems can be reduced to SG, for instance parity games, mean-payoff games, discounted-payoff games and their stochastic extensions [CF11]. The task of solving SG is also polynomial-time equivalent to solving perfect information Shapley, Everett and Gillette games [AM09]. Besides, the problem is practically relevant in verification and synthesis. SG can model reactive systems, with players corresponding to the controller of the system and to its environment, where quantified uncertainty is explicitly modelled. This is useful in many application domains, ranging from smart energy management [CFK+13a] to autonomous urban driving [CKSW13], robot motion planning [LaV00] to self-adaptive systems [CMG14]; for various recent case studies, see e.g. [SK16]. Finally, since Markov decision processes (MDP) [Put14] are a special case with only one player, SG can serve as abstractions of large MDP [KKNP10].

Solution Techniques. There are several classes of algorithms for solving SG, most importantly strategy iteration (SI) algorithms [HK66] and value iteration (VI) algorithms [Con92]. Since the repetitive evaluation of strategies in SI is often slow in practice, VI is usually preferred, similarly to the special case of MDPs [KM17]. For instance, the most used probabilistic model checker PRISM [KNP11] and its branch PRISM-Games [CFK+13a] use VI for MDP and SG as the default option, respectively. However, while SI is in principle a precise method, VI is an approximative method, which converges only in the limit. Unfortunately, there is no known stopping criterion for VI applied to SG. Consequently, there are no guarantees on the results returned in finite time. Therefore, current tools stop when the difference between the two most recent approximations is low, and thus may return arbitrarily imprecise results [HM17].

Value Iteration with Guarantees. In the special case of MDP, in order to obtain bounds on the imprecision of the result, one can employ a *bounded* variant of VI [MLG05,BCC+14] (also called *interval iteration* [HM17]). Here one computes not only an under-approximation, but also an over-approximation of the actual value as follows. On the one hand, iterative computation of the least fixpoint of Bellman equations yields an under-approximating sequence converging to the value. On the other hand, iterative computation of the greatest fixpoint yields an over-approximation, which, however, does not converge to the value. Moreover, it often results in the trivial bound of 1. A solution suggested for MDPs [BCC+14,HM17] is to modify the underlying graph, namely to collapse end components. In the resulting MDP there is only one fixpoint, thus the least and greatest fixpoint coincide and both approximating sequences converge to the actual value. In contrast, for general SG no procedure where the greatest fixpoint converges to the value is known. In this paper we provide one, yielding a stopping criterion. We show that the pre-processing approach of collapsing is not applicable in general and provide a solution on the original graph. We also characterize SG where the fixpoints coincide and no processing is needed. The main technical challenge is that states in an end component in SG can have different values, in contrast to the case of MDP.

Practical Efficiency Using Guarantees. We further utilize the obtained guarantees to practically improve our algorithm. Similar to the MDP case [BCC+14], the quantification of the error allows for ignoring parts of the state space, and thus a speed up without jeopardizing the correctness of the result. Indeed, we provide a technique where some states are not explored and processed at all, but their potential effect is still taken into account The information is further used to decide the states to be explored next and to be analyzed in more detail. To this end, simulations and learning are used as tools. While for MDP this idea has already demonstrated speed ups in orders of magnitude [BCC+14, ACD+17], this paper provides the first technique of this kind for SG. **Our contribution** is summarized as follows

- We introduce a VI algorithm yielding both under- and over-approximation sequences, both of which converge to the value of the game. Thus we present the first stopping criterion for VI on SG and the first anytime algorithm with guaranteed precision. We also characterize when a simpler solution is sufficient.
- We provide a learning-based algorithm, which preserves the guarantees, but is in some cases more efficient since it avoids exploring the whole state space.
- We evaluate the running times of the algorithms experimentally, concluding that obtaining guarantees requires an overhead that is either negligible or mitigated by the learning-based approach.

Related Work. The works closest to ours are the following. As mentioned above, [BCC+14, HM17] describe the solution to the special case of MDP. While [BCC+14] also provides a learning-based algorithm, [HM17] discusses the convergence rate and the exact solution. The basic algorithm of [HM17] is implemented in PRISM [BKL+17] and the learning approach of [BCC+14] in STORM [DJKV17a]. The extension for SG where the interleaving of players is severely limited (every end component belongs to one player only) is discussed in [Ujm15].

Further, in the area of probabilistic planning, bounded real-time dynamic programming [MLG05] is related to our learning-based approach. However, it is limited to the setting of stopping MDP where the target sink or the non-target sink is reached almost surely under any pair of strategies and thus the fixpoints coincide. Our algorithm works for general SG, not only for stopping ones, without any blowup.

For SG, the tools implementing the standard SI and/or VI algorithms are PRISM-games [CFK+13a], GAVS+ [CKLB11] and GIST [CHJR10]. The latter two are, however, neither maintained nor accessible via the links provided in their publications any more.

Apart from fundamental algorithms to solve SG, there are various practically efficient heuristics that, however, provide none or weak guarantees, often based on some form of learning [BT00, LL08, WT16, TT16, AY17, BBS08]. Finally, the only currently available way to obtain any guarantees through VI is to perform γ^2 iterations and then round to the nearest multiple of $1/\gamma$, yielding the value of the game with precision $1/\gamma$ [CH08]; here γ cannot be freely chosen, but it is a fixed number, exponential in the number of states and the used probability denominators. However, since the precision cannot be chosen and the number of iterations is always exponential, this approach is infeasible even for small games.

Organization of the Paper. Section 2 introduces the basic notions and revises value iteration. Section 3 explains the idea of our approach on an example. Section 4 provides a full technical treatment of the method as well as the learning-based variation. Section 5 discusses experimental results and Sect. 6 concludes. The appendix (available in [KKKW18]) gives technical details on the pseudocode as well as the conducted experiments and provides more extensive proofs to the theorems and lemmata; in this paper, there are only proof sketches and ideas.

2 Preliminaries

2.1 Basic Definitions

A probability distribution on a finite set X is a mapping $\delta : X \to [0,1]$, such that $\sum_{x \in X} \delta(x) = 1$. The set of all probability distributions on X is denoted by $\mathcal{D}(X)$. Now we define stochastic games, in literature often referred as simple stochastic games or stochastic two-player games with a reachability objective.

Definition 1 (SG). *A* stochastic game (SG) *is a tuple* $(S, S_\Box, S_\bigcirc, \mathsf{s}_0, \mathsf{A}, \mathsf{Av}, \delta, \mathtt{1}, \mathtt{0})$*, where S is a finite set of* states *partitioned into the sets $S_\Box$ and $S_\bigcirc$ of states of the player* Maximizer *and* Minimizer*, respectively,* $\mathsf{s}_0, \mathtt{1}, \mathtt{0} \in S$ *is the* initial *state,* target *state, and* sink *state, respectively,* A *is a finite set of* actions*,* $\mathsf{Av} : S \to 2^{\mathsf{A}}$ *assigns to every state a set of* available *actions, and* $\delta : S \times \mathsf{A} \to \mathcal{D}(S)$ *is a* transition function *that given a state* s *and an action* $\mathsf{a} \in \mathsf{Av}(\mathsf{s})$ *yields a probability distribution over* successor *states.*

A Markov decision process (MDP) *is a special case of SG where* $S_\bigcirc = \emptyset$.

We assume that SGs are non-blocking, so for all states s we have $\mathsf{Av}(\mathsf{s}) \neq \emptyset$. Further, $\mathtt{1}$ and $\mathtt{0}$ only have one action and it is a self-loop with probability 1. Additionally, we can assume that the SG is preprocessed so that all states with no path to $\mathtt{1}$ are merged with $\mathtt{0}$.

For a state s and an available action $\mathsf{a} \in \mathsf{Av}(\mathsf{s})$, we denote the set of successors by $\mathsf{Post}(\mathsf{s}, \mathsf{a}) := \{\mathsf{s}' \mid \delta(\mathsf{s}, \mathsf{a}, \mathsf{s}') > 0\}$. Finally, for any set of states $T \subseteq S$, we use $T_\Box$ and $T_\bigcirc$ to denote the states in T that belong to Maximizer and Minimizer, whose states are drawn in the figures as $\Box$ and $\bigcirc$, respectively.

The semantics of SG is given in the usual way by means of strategies and the induced Markov chain and the respective probability space, as follows. An *infinite path* ρ is an infinite sequence $\rho = \mathsf{s}_0\mathsf{a}_0\mathsf{s}_1\mathsf{a}_1 \cdots \in (S \times \mathsf{A})^\omega$, such that for every $i \in \mathbb{N}$, $\mathsf{a}_i \in \mathsf{Av}(\mathsf{s}_i)$ and $\mathsf{s}_{i+1} \in \mathsf{Post}(\mathsf{s}_i, \mathsf{a}_i)$. *Finite paths* are defined analogously as elements of $(S \times \mathsf{A})^* \times S$. Since this paper deals with the reachability objective, we can restrict our attention to memoryless strategies, which are optimal for this objective. We still allow randomizing strategies, because they are needed for the learning-based algorithm later on. A *strategy* of Maximizer or Minimizer is a function $\sigma : S_\Box \to \mathcal{D}(\mathsf{A})$ or $S_\bigcirc \to \mathcal{D}(\mathsf{A})$, respectively, such that $\sigma(\mathsf{s}) \in \mathcal{D}(\mathsf{Av}(\mathsf{s}))$

for all s. We call a strategy *deterministic* if it maps to Dirac distributions only. Note that there are finitely many deterministic strategies. A pair (σ, τ) of strategies of Maximizer and Minimizer induces a Markov chain $\mathsf{G}^{\sigma,\tau}$ where the transition probabilities are defined as $\delta(\mathsf{s},\mathsf{s}') = \sum_{\mathsf{a}\in\mathsf{Av}(\mathsf{s})} \sigma(\mathsf{s},\mathsf{a}) \cdot \delta(\mathsf{s},\mathsf{a},\mathsf{s}')$ for states of Maximizer and analogously for states of Minimizer, with σ replaced by τ. The Markov chain induces a unique probability distribution $\mathbb{P}_{\mathsf{s}}^{\sigma,\tau}$ over measurable sets of infinite paths [BK08, Chap. 10].

We write $\Diamond \mathfrak{1} := \{\rho \mid \exists i \in \mathbb{N}.\ \rho(i) = \mathfrak{1}\}$ to denote the (measurable) set of all paths which eventually reach $\mathfrak{1}$. For each $\mathsf{s} \in S$, we define the *value* in s as

$$\mathsf{V}(\mathsf{s}) := \sup_{\sigma} \inf_{\tau} \mathbb{P}_{s}^{\sigma,\tau}(\Diamond \mathfrak{1}) = \inf_{\tau} \sup_{\sigma} \mathbb{P}_{s}^{\sigma,\tau}(\Diamond \mathfrak{1}),$$

where the equality follows from [Mar75]. We are interested not only in $\mathsf{V}(\mathsf{s}_0)$, but also its ε-approximations and the corresponding (ε-)optimal strategies for both players.

Now we recall a fundamental tool for analysis of MDP called end components. We introduce the following notation. Given a set of states $T \subseteq S$, a state $\mathsf{s} \in T$ and an action $\mathsf{a} \in \mathsf{Av}(\mathsf{s})$, we say that $(\mathsf{s},\mathsf{a})\,\mathrm{exits}\,T$ if $\mathsf{Post}(\mathsf{s},\mathsf{a}) \not\subseteq T$. We define an end component of a SG as the end component of the underlying MDP with both players unified.

Definition 2 (EC). *A non-empty set $T \subseteq S$ of states is an* end component (EC) *if there is a non-empty set $B \subseteq \bigcup_{\mathsf{s}\in T} \mathsf{Av}(s)$ of actions such that*

1. *for each $\mathsf{s} \in T, \mathsf{a} \in B \cap \mathsf{Av}(\mathsf{s})$ we do* not *have $(\mathsf{s},\mathsf{a})\,\mathrm{exits}\,T$,*
2. *for each $\mathsf{s},\mathsf{s}' \in T$ there is a finite path $\mathsf{w} = \mathsf{s}\mathsf{a}_0 \ldots \mathsf{a}_n\mathsf{s}' \in (T \times B)^* \times T$, i.e. the path stays inside T and only uses actions in B.*

Intuitively, ECs correspond to bottom strongly connected components of the Markov chains induced by possible strategies, so for some pair of strategies all possible paths starting in the EC remain there. An end component T is a *maximal end component (MEC)* if there is no other end component T' such that $T \subseteq T'$. Given an SG G, the set of its MECs is denoted by $\mathsf{MEC}(\mathsf{G})$ and can be computed in polynomial time [CY95].

2.2 (Bounded) Value Iteration

The value function V satisfies the following system of equations, which is referred to as the *Bellman equations*:

$$\mathsf{V}(\mathsf{s}) = \begin{cases} \max_{\mathsf{a}\in\mathsf{Av}(\mathsf{s})} \mathsf{V}(\mathsf{s},\mathsf{a}) & \text{if } \mathsf{s} \in S_{\Box} \\ \min_{\mathsf{a}\in\mathsf{Av}(\mathsf{s})} \mathsf{V}(\mathsf{s},\mathsf{a}) & \text{if } \mathsf{s} \in S_{\bigcirc} \\ 1 & \text{if } \mathsf{s} = \mathfrak{1} \\ 0 & \text{if } \mathsf{s} = \mathfrak{0} \end{cases} \tag{1}$$

where[2]

$$\mathsf{V}(\mathsf{s},\mathsf{a}) := \sum_{s' \in S} \delta(\mathsf{s},\mathsf{a},\mathsf{s}') \cdot \mathsf{V}(\mathsf{s}') \tag{2}$$

Moreover, V is the *least* solution to the Bellman equations, see e.g. [CH08]. To compute the value of V for all states in an SG, one can thus utilize the iterative approximation method *value iteration (VI)* as follows. We start with a lower bound function $\mathsf{L}_0 \colon S \to [0,1]$ such that $\mathsf{L}_0(\mathtt{1}) = 1$ and, for all other $\mathsf{s} \in S$, $\mathsf{L}_0(\mathsf{s}) = 0$. Then we repetitively apply Bellman updates (3) and (4)

$$\mathsf{L}_n(\mathsf{s},\mathsf{a}) := \sum_{s' \in S} \delta(\mathsf{s},\mathsf{a},\mathsf{s}') \cdot \mathsf{L}_{n-1}(\mathsf{s}') \tag{3}$$

$$\mathsf{L}_n(\mathsf{s}) := \begin{cases} \max_{\mathsf{a} \in \mathsf{Av}(\mathsf{s})} \mathsf{L}_n(\mathsf{s},\mathsf{a}) & \text{if } \mathsf{s} \in S_\Box \\ \min_{\mathsf{a} \in \mathsf{Av}(\mathsf{s})} \mathsf{L}_n(\mathsf{s},\mathsf{a}) & \text{if } \mathsf{s} \in S_\bigcirc \end{cases} \tag{4}$$

until convergence. Note that convergence may happen only in the limit even for such a simple game as in Fig. 1 on the left. The sequence is monotonic, at all times a *lower* bound on V, i.e. $\mathsf{L}_i(\mathsf{s}) \leq \mathsf{V}(\mathsf{s})$ for all $\mathsf{s} \in S$, and the least fixpoint satisfies $\mathsf{L}^* := \lim_{n \to \infty} \mathsf{L}_n = \mathsf{V}$.

Unfortunately, there is no known stopping criterion, i.e. no guarantees how close the current under-approximation is to the value [HM17]. The current tools stop when the difference between two successive approximations is smaller than a certain threshold, which can lead to arbitrarily wrong results [HM17].

For the special case of MDP, it has been suggested to also compute the greatest fixpoint [MLG05] and thus an *upper* bound as follows. The function $\mathsf{G} : S \to [0,1]$ is initialized for all states $\mathsf{s} \in S$ as $\mathsf{G}_0(\mathsf{s}) = 1$ except for $\mathsf{G}_0(\mathtt{0}) = 0$. Then we repetitively apply updates (3) and (4), where L is replaced by G. The resulting sequence G_n is monotonic, provides an upper bound on V and the greatest fixpoint $\mathsf{G}^* := \lim_n \mathsf{G}_n$ is the greatest solution to the Bellman equations on $[0,1]^S$.

This approach is called *bounded value iteration (BVI)* (or *bounded real-time dynamic programming (BRTDP)* [MLG05, BCC+14] or *interval iteration* [HM17]). If $\mathsf{L}^* = \mathsf{G}^*$ then they are both equal to V and we say that *BVI converges*. BVI is guaranteed to converge in MDP if the only ECs are those of $\mathtt{1}$ and $\mathtt{0}$ [BCC+14]. Otherwise, if there are non-trivial ECs they have to be "collapsed"[3]. Computing the greatest fixpoint on the modified MDP results in another sequence U_i of upper bounds on V, converging to $\mathsf{U}^* := \lim_n \mathsf{U}_n$. Then BVI converges even for general MDPs, $\mathsf{U}^* = \mathsf{V}$ [BCC+14], when transformed this way. The next section illustrates this difficulty and the solution through collapsing on an example.

---

[2] Throughout the paper, for any function $f : S \to [0,1]$ we overload the notation and also write $f(\mathsf{s},\mathsf{a})$ meaning $\sum_{s' \in S} \delta(\mathsf{s},\mathsf{a},\mathsf{s}') \cdot f(\mathsf{s}')$.

[3] All states of an EC are merged into one, all leaving actions are preserved and all other actions are discarded. For more detail see [KKKW18, Appendix A.1].

In summary, all versions of BVI discussed so far and later on in the paper follow the pattern of Algorithm 1. In the naive version, UPDATE just performs the Bellman update on L and U according to Eqs. (3) and (4).[4] For a general MDP, U does not converge to V, but to G^*, and thus the termination criterion may never be met if $\mathsf{G}^*(\mathsf{s}_0)-\mathsf{V}(\mathsf{s}_0) > 0$. If the ECs are collapsed in pre-processing then U converges to V.

For the general case of SG, the collapsing approach fails and this paper provides another version of BVI where U converges to V, based on a more detailed structural analysis of the game.

Algorithm 1. Bounded value iteration algorithm

```
procedure BVI(precision ϵ > 0)
    for s ∈ S do            \* Initialization * \
        L(s) = 0            \* Lower bound * \
        U(s) = 1            \* Upper bound * \
    L(1) = 1                \* Value of sinks is determined a priori * \
    U(0) = 0
    repeat
        UPDATE(L, U)                 \* Bellman updates or their modification * \
    until U(s0) − L(s0) < ϵ          \* Guaranteed error bound * \
```

3 Example

In this section, we illustrate the issues preventing BVI convergence and our solution on a few examples. Recall that G is the sequence converging to the greatest solution of the Bellman equations, while U is in general any sequence over-approximating V that one or another BVI algorithm suggests.

Firstly, we illustrate the issue that arises already for the special case of MDP. Consider the MPD of Fig. 1 on the left. Although $\mathsf{V}(\mathsf{s}) = \mathsf{V}(\mathsf{t}) = 0.5$, we have $\mathsf{G}_i(\mathsf{s}) = \mathsf{G}_i(\mathsf{t}) = 1$ for all i. Indeed, the upper bound for t is always updated as the maximum of $\mathsf{G}_i(\mathsf{t},\mathsf{c})$ and $\mathsf{G}_i(\mathsf{t},\mathsf{b})$. Although $\mathsf{G}_i(\mathsf{t},\mathsf{c})$ decreases over time, $\mathsf{G}_i(\mathsf{t},\mathsf{b})$ remains the same, namely equal to $\mathsf{G}_i(\mathsf{s})$, which in turn remains equal to $\mathsf{G}_i(\mathsf{s},\mathsf{a}) = \mathsf{G}_i(\mathsf{t})$. This cyclic dependency lets both s and t remain in an "illusion" that the value of the other one is 1.

The solution for MDP is to remove this cyclic dependency by collapsing all MECs into singletons and removing the resulting purely self-looping actions. Figure 1 in the middle shows the MDP after collapsing the EC $\{\mathsf{s},\mathsf{t}\}$. This turns the MDP into a stopping one, where $\mathtt{1}$ or $\mathtt{0}$ is under any strategy reached with probability 1. In such MDP, there is a unique solution to the Bellman equations. Therefore, the greatest fixpoint is equal to the least one and thus to V.

[4] For the straightforward pseudocode, see [KKKW18, Appendix A.2].

Secondly, we illustrate the issues that additionally arise for general SG. It turns out that the collapsing approach can be extended only to games where all states of each EC belong to one player only [Ujm15]. In this case, both Maximizer's and Minimizer's ECs are collapsed the same way as in MDP.

However, when both players are present in an EC, then collapsing may not solve the issue. Consider the SG of Fig. 2. Here α and β represent the values of the respective actions.[5] There are three cases:

First, let $\alpha < \beta$. If the bounds converge to these values we eventually observe $\mathsf{G}_i(q, e) < \mathsf{L}_i(r, f)$ and learn the induced inequality. Since p is a Minimizer's state it will never pick the action leading to the greater value of β. Therefore, we can safely merge p and q, and remove the action leading to r, as shown in the second subfigure.

Second, if $\alpha > \beta$, p and r can be merged in an analogous way, as shown in the third subfigure.

Third, if $\alpha = \beta$, both previous solutions as well as collapsing all three states as in the fourth subfigure is possible. However, since the approximants may only converge to α and β in the limit, we may not know in finite time which of these cases applies and thus cannot decide for any of the collapses.

Consequently, the approach of collapsing is not applicable in general. In order to ensure BVI convergence, we suggest a different method, which we call *deflating*. It does not involve changing the state space, but rather decreasing the upper bound U_i to the least value that is currently provable (and thus still correct). To this end, we analyze the exiting actions, i.e. with successors outside of the EC, for the following reason. If the play stays in the EC forever, the target is never reached and Minimizer wins. Therefore, Maximizer needs to pick some exiting action to avoid staying in the EC.

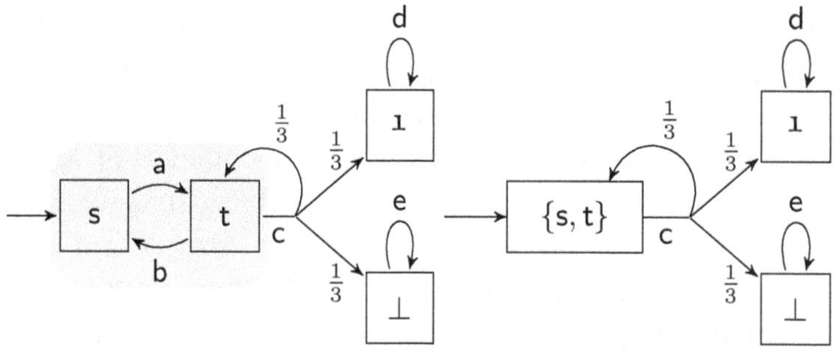

i	$\mathsf{L}_i(\{\mathsf{s},\mathsf{t}\})$	$\mathsf{G}_i(\{\mathsf{s},\mathsf{t}\})$
0	0	1
1	$\frac{1}{3}$	$\frac{2}{3}$
2	$\frac{4}{9}$	$\frac{5}{9}$
3	$\frac{13}{27}$	$\frac{14}{27}$

Fig. 1. Left: An MDP (as special case of SG) where BVI does not converge due to the grayed EC. Middle: The same MDP where the EC is collapsed, making BVI converge. Right: The approximations illustrating the convergence of the MDP in the middle.

[5] Precisely, we consider them to stand for a probabilistic branching with probability α (or β) to 1 and with the remaining probability to 0. To avoid clutter in the figure, we omit this branching and depict only the value.

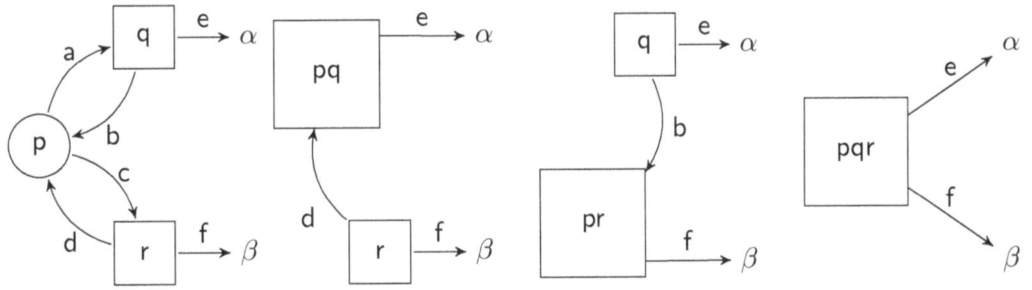

Fig. 2. Left: Collapsing ECs in SG may lead to incorrect results. The Greek letters on the leaving arrows denote the values of the exiting actions. Right three figures: Correct collapsing in different cases, depending on the relationship of α and β. In contrast to MDP, some actions of the EC exiting the collapsed part have to be removed.

For the EC with the states s and t in Fig. 1, the only exiting action is c. In this example, since c is the only exiting action, $\mathsf{U}_i(\mathsf{t}, \mathsf{c})$ is the highest possible upper bound that the EC can achieve. Thus, by decreasing the upper bound of all states in the EC to that number[6], we still have a safe upper bound. Moreover, with this modification BVI converges in this example, intuitively because now the upper bound of t depends on action c as it should.

For the example in Fig. 2, it is correct to decrease the upper bound to the maximal exiting one, i.e. $\max\{\hat{\alpha}, \hat{\beta}\}$, where $\hat{\alpha} := \mathsf{U}_i(\mathsf{a}), \hat{\beta} := \mathsf{U}_i(\mathsf{b})$ are the current approximations of α and of β. However, this itself does not ensure BVI convergence. Indeed, if for instance $\hat{\alpha} < \hat{\beta}$ then deflating all states to $\hat{\beta}$ is not tight enough, as values of p and q can even be bounded by $\hat{\alpha}$. In fact, we have to find a certain sub-EC that corresponds to $\hat{\alpha}$, in this case $\{\mathsf{p}, \mathsf{q}\}$ and set all its upper bounds to $\hat{\alpha}$. We define and compute these sub-ECs in the next section.

In summary, the general structure of our convergent BVI algorithm is to produce the sequence U by application of Bellman updates and occasionally find the relevant sub-ECs and deflate them. The main technical challenge is that states in an EC in SG can have different values, in contrast to the case of MDP.

4 Convergent Over-Approximation

In Sect. 4.1, we characterize SGs where Bellman equations have more solutions. Based on the analysis, subsequent sections show how to alter the procedure computing the sequence G_i over-approximating V so that the resulting tighter sequence U_i still over-approximates V, but also converges to V. This ensures that thus modified BVI converges. Section 4.4 presents the learning-based variant of our BVI.

[6] We choose the name "deflating" to evoke decreasing the overly high "pressure" in the EC until it equalizes with the actual "pressure" outside.

4.1 Bloated End Components Cause Non-convergence

As we have seen in the example of Fig. 2, BVI generally does not converge due to ECs with a particular structure of the exiting actions. The analysis of ECs relies on the extremal values that can be achieved by exiting actions (in the example, α and β). Given the value function V or just its current over-approximation U_i, we define the most profitable exiting action for Maximizer (denoted by $\square$) and Minimizer (denoted by $\bigcirc$) as follows.

Definition 3 **(bestExit).** *Given a set of states $T \subseteq S$ and a function $f : S \to [0,1]$ (see footnote 2), the f-value of the best T-exiting action of Maximizer and Minimizer, respectively, is defined as*

$$\mathsf{bestExit}_f^{\square}(T) = \max_{\substack{\mathsf{s} \in T_{\square} \\ (\mathsf{s},\mathsf{a}) \text{ exits } T}} f(\mathsf{s},\mathsf{a})$$

$$\mathsf{bestExit}_f^{\bigcirc}(T) = \min_{\substack{\mathsf{s} \in T_{\bigcirc} \\ (\mathsf{s},\mathsf{a}) \text{ exits } T}} f(\mathsf{s},\mathsf{a})$$

with the convention that $\max_{\emptyset} = 0$ *and* $\min_{\emptyset} = 1$.

Example 1. In the example of Fig. 2 on the left with $T = \{\mathsf{p},\mathsf{q},\mathsf{r}\}$ and $\alpha < \beta$, we have $\mathsf{bestExit}_{\mathsf{V}}^{\square}(T) = \beta$, $\mathsf{bestExit}_{\mathsf{V}}^{\bigcirc}(T) = 1$. It is due to $\beta < 1$ that BVI does not converge here. We generalize this in the following lemma. △

Lemma 1. *Let T be an EC. For every m satisfying $\mathsf{bestExit}_{\mathsf{V}}^{\square}(T) \leq m \leq \mathsf{bestExit}_{\mathsf{V}}^{\bigcirc}(T)$, there is a solution $f : S \to [0,1]$ to the Bellman equations, which on T is constant and equal to m.*

Proof (Idea). Intuitively, such a constant m is a solution to the Bellman equations on T for the following reasons. As both players prefer getting m to exiting and getting "only" the values of their respective bestExit, they both choose to stay in the EC (and the extrema in the Bellman equations are realized on non-exiting actions). On the one hand, Maximizer (Bellman equations with max) is hoping for the promised m, which is however not backed up by any actions actually exiting towards the target. On the other hand, Minimizer (Bellman equations with min) does not realize that staying forever results in her optimal value 0 instead of m. □

Corollary 1. *If $\mathsf{bestExit}_{\mathsf{V}}^{\bigcirc}(T) > \mathsf{bestExit}_{\mathsf{V}}^{\square}(T)$ for some EC T, then $\mathsf{G}^* \neq \mathsf{V}$.*

Proof. Since there are m_1, m_2 such that $\mathsf{bestExit}_{\mathsf{V}}^{\square}(T) < m_1 < m_2 < \mathsf{bestExit}_{\mathsf{V}}^{\bigcirc}(T)$, by Lemma 1 there are two different solutions to the Bellman equations. In particular, $\mathsf{G}^* > \mathsf{L}^* = \mathsf{V}$, and BVI does not converge. □

In accordance with our intuition that ECs satisfying the above inequality should be deflated, we call them bloated.

Definition 4 (BEC). *An EC* T *is called a* bloated end component (BEC), *if* $\mathsf{bestExit}_{\mathsf{V}}^{\bigcirc}(T) > \mathsf{bestExit}_{\mathsf{V}}^{\square}(T)$.

Example 2. In the example of Fig. 2 on the left with $\alpha < \beta$, the ECs $\{\mathsf{p}, \mathsf{q}\}$ and $\{\mathsf{p}, \mathsf{q}, \mathsf{r}\}$ are BECs. △

Example 3. If an EC T has no exiting actions of Minimizer (or no Minimizer's states at all, as in an MDP), then $\mathsf{bestExit}_{\mathsf{V}}^{\bigcirc}(T) = 1$ (the case with $\min_{\emptyset}$). Hence all numbers between $\mathsf{bestExit}_{\mathsf{V}}^{\square}(T)$ and 1 are a solution to the Bellman equations and $\mathsf{G}^*(s) = 1$ for all states $s \in T$.

Analogously, if Maximizer does not have any exiting action in T, then it holds that $\mathsf{bestExit}_{\mathsf{V}}^{\square}(T) = 0$ (the case with $\max_{\emptyset}$), T is a BEC and all numbers between 0 and $\mathsf{bestExit}_{\mathsf{V}}^{\bigcirc}(T)$ are a solution to the Bellman equations.

Note that in MDP all ECs belong to one player, namely Maximizer. Consequently, all ECs are BECs except for ECs where Maximizer has an exiting action with value 1; all other ECs thus have to be collapsed (or deflated) to ensure BVI convergence in MDPs. Interestingly, all non-trivial ECs in MDPs are a problem, while in SGs through the presence of the other player some ECs can converge, namely if both players want to exit (See e.g. [KKKW18, Appendix A.3]). △

We show that BECs are indeed the only obstacle for BVI convergence.

Theorem 1. *If the SG contains no BECs except for* $\{\mathsf{0}\}$ *and* $\{\mathsf{1}\}$, *then* $\mathsf{G}^* = \mathsf{V}$.

Proof (Sketch). Assume, towards a contradiction, that there is some state s with a positive difference $\mathsf{G}^*(\mathsf{s}) - \mathsf{V}(\mathsf{s}) > 0$. Consider the set D of states with the maximal difference. D can be shown to be an EC. Since it is not a BEC there has to be an action exiting D and realizing the optimum in that state. Consequently, this action also has the maximal difference, and all its successors, too. Since some of the successors are outside of D, we get a contradiction with the maximality of D. □

In Sect. 4.2, we show how to eliminate BECs by collapsing their "core" parts, called below MSECs (maximal simple end components). Since MSECs can only be identified with enough information about V, Sect. 4.3 shows how to avoid direct *a priori* collapsing and instead dynamically deflate candidates for MSECs in a conservative way.

4.2 Static MSEC Decomposition

Now we turn our attention to SG with BECs. Intuitively, since in a BEC all Minimizer's exiting actions have a higher value than what Maximizer can achieve, Minimizer does not want to use any of his own exiting actions and prefers staying in the EC (or steering Maximizer towards his worse exiting actions). Consequently, only Maximizer wants to take an exiting action. In the MDP case he can pick any desirable one. Indeed, he can wait until he reaches a state where it is available. As a result, in MDP all states of an EC have the *same value* and can all be collapsed into one state. In the SG case, he may be restricted by Minimizer's behaviour or even not given any chance to exit the EC at all. As a result, a BEC may contain several parts (below denoted MSECs), each with different value, intuitively corresponding to different exits. Thus instead of MECs, we have to decompose into finer MSECs and only collapse these.

Definition 5 (*Simple EC*). *An EC T is called* simple (SEC), *if for all* $\mathsf{s} \in T$ *we have* $\mathsf{V}(\mathsf{s}) = \mathsf{bestExit}^{\square}_{\mathsf{V}}(T)$.

A SEC C is maximal (MSEC) *if there is no SEC C' such that $C \subsetneq C'$.*

Intuitively, an EC is simple, if Minimizer cannot keep Maximizer away from his bestExit. Independently of Minimizer's decisions, Maximizer can reach the bestExit almost surely, unless Minimizer decides to leave, in which case Maximizer could achieve an even higher value.

Example 4. Assume $\alpha < \beta$ in the example of Fig. 2. Then $\{\mathsf{p}, \mathsf{q}\}$ is a SEC and an MSEC. Further observe that action c is sub-optimal for Minimizer and removing it does not affect the value of any state, but simplifies the graph structure. Namely, it destructs the whole EC into several (here only one) SECs and some non-EC states (here r). △

Algorithm 2, called FIND_MSEC, shows how to compute MSECs. It returns the set of all MSECs if called with parameter V. However, later we also call this function with other parameters $f : S \to [0, 1]$. The idea of the algorithm is the following. The set X consists of Minimizer's sub-optimal actions, leading to a higher value. As such they cannot be a part of any SEC and thus should be ignored when identifying SECs. (The previous example illustrates that ignoring X is indeed safe as it does not change the value of the game.) We denote the game G where the available actions Av are changed to the new available actions Av' (ignoring the Minimizer's sub-optimal ones) as $\mathsf{G}_{[\mathsf{Av}/\mathsf{Av}']}$. Once removed, Minimizer has no choices to affect the value and thus each EC is simple.

Algorithm 2. FIND_MSEC

1: **function** FIND_MSEC($f : S \to [0, 1]$)
2: $\quad X \leftarrow \{(\mathsf{s}, \{\mathsf{a} \in \mathsf{Av}(\mathsf{s}) \mid f(\mathsf{s}, \mathsf{a}) > f(\mathsf{s})\}) \mid \mathsf{s} \in S_{\bigcirc}\}$
3: $\quad \mathsf{Av}' \leftarrow \mathsf{Av} \setminus X$ * Minimizer's f-suboptimal actions removed * \
4: $\quad$ **return** $\mathsf{MEC}(\mathsf{G}_{[\mathsf{Av}/\mathsf{Av}']})$ * $\mathsf{MEC}(\mathsf{G}_{[\mathsf{Av}/\mathsf{Av}']})$ are MSECs of the original G * \

Lemma 2 (Correctness of Algorithm 2). $T \in \mathsf{FIND\_MSEC}(\mathsf{V})$ *if and only if T is a MSEC.*

Proof (Sketch). "If": As T is an MSEC, all states in T have the value $\mathsf{bestExit}^{\square}_{\mathsf{V}}(T)$, and hence also all actions that stay inside T have this value. Thus, no action that stays in T is removed by Line 3 and it is still a MEC in the modified game.

"Only if": If $T \in \mathsf{FIND\_MSEC}(\mathsf{V})$, then T is a MEC of the game where the suboptimal available actions (those in X) of Minimizer have been removed. Hence for all $\mathsf{s} \in T : \mathsf{V}(\mathsf{s}) = \mathsf{bestExit}^{\Box}_{\mathsf{V}}(T)$, because intuitively Minimizer has no possibility to influence the value any further, since all actions that could do so were in X and have been removed. Since T is a MEC in the modified game, it certainly is an EC in the original game. Hence T is a SEC. The inclusion maximality follows from the fact that we compute MECs in the modified game. Thus T is an MSEC. □

Remark 1 (Algorithm with an oracle). In Sect. 3, we have seen that collapsing MECs does not ensure BVI convergence. Collapsing does not preserve the values, since in BECs we would be collapsing states with different values. Hence we want to collapse only MSECs, where the values are the same. If, moreover, we remove X in such a collapsed SG, then there are no (non-sink) ECs and BVI converges on this SG to the original value.

The difficulty with this algorithm is that it requires an oracle to compare values, for instance a sufficiently precise approximation of V. Consequently, we cannot pre-compute the MSECs, but have to find them while running BVI. Moreover, since the approximations converge only in the limit we may never be able to conclude on simplicity of some ECs. For instance, if $\alpha = \beta$ in Fig. 2, and if the approximations converge at different speeds, then Algorithm 2 always outputs only a part of the EC, although the whole EC on $\{\mathsf{p}, \mathsf{q}, \mathsf{r}\}$ is simple.

In MDPs, all ECs are simple, because there is no second player to be resolved and all states in an EC have the same value. Thus for MDPs it suffices to collapse all MECs, in contrast to SG.

4.3 Dynamic MSEC Decomposition

Since MSECs cannot be identified from approximants of V for sure, we refrain from collapsing[7] and instead only decrease the over-approximation in the corresponding way. We call the method *deflating*, by which we mean decreasing the upper bound of all states in an EC to its $\mathsf{bestExit}^{\Box}_{\mathsf{U}}$, see Algorithm 3. The procedure $\mathsf{DEFLATE}$ (called on the current upper bound U_i) decreases this upper bound to the minimum possible value according to the current approximation and thus prevents states from only depending on each other, as in SECs. Intuitively, it gradually approximates SECs and performs the corresponding adjustments, but does not commit to any of the approximations.

Algorithm 3. DEFLATE

```
1: function DEFLATE(EC T, f : S → [0,1])
2:     for s ∈ T do
3:         f(s) ← min(f(s), bestExit□_f(T))      \* Decrease the upper bound * \
4:     return f
```

[7] Our subsequent method can be combined with local collapsing whenever the lower and upper bounds on V are conclusive.

Lemma 3 (DEFLATE is sound). *For any* $f : S \to [0,1]$ *such that* $f \geq \mathsf{V}$ *and any EC* T, $\mathsf{DEFLATE}(T, f) \geq \mathsf{V}$.

This allows us to define our BVI algorithm as the naive BVI with only the additional lines 3–4, see Algorithm 4.

Algorithm 4. UPDATE procedure for bounded value iteration on SG

1: **procedure** UPDATE($\mathsf{L} : S \to [0,1]$, $\mathsf{U} : S \to [0,1]$)
2: $\quad$ L, U get updated according to Eq. (3) and (4) $\quad$ * Bellman updates * \
3: $\quad$ **for** $T \in \mathsf{FIND\_MSEC}(\mathsf{L})$ **do** $\quad$ * Use lower bound to find ECs * \
4: $\quad\quad$ $\mathsf{U} \leftarrow \mathsf{DEFLATE}(T, \mathsf{U})$ $\quad$ * and deflate the upper bound there * \

Theorem 2 (Soundness and completeness). *Algorithm 1 (calling Algorithm 4) produces monotonic sequences* L *under- and* U *over-approximating* V, *and terminates.*

Proof (Sketch). The crux is to show that U converges to V. We assume towards a contradiction, that there exists a state s with $\lim_{n\to\infty} \mathsf{U}_n(\mathsf{s}) - \mathsf{V}(\mathsf{s}) > 0$. Then there exists a nonempty set of states X where the difference between $\lim_{n\to\infty} \mathsf{U}_n$ and V is maximal. If the upper bound of states in X depends on states outside of X, this yields a contradiction, because then the difference between upper bound and value would decrease in the next Bellman update. So X must be an EC where all states depend on each other. However, if that is the case, calling DEFLATE decreases the upper bound to something depending on the states outside of X, thus also yielding a contradiction. □

Summary of Our Approach:

1. We cannot collapse MECs, because we cannot collapse BECs with non-constant values.
2. If we remove X (the sub-optimal actions of Minimizer) we can collapse MECs (now actually MSECs with constant values).
3. Since we know neither X nor SECs we gradually deflate SEC approximations.

4.4 Learning-Based Algorithm

Asynchronous value iteration selects in each round a subset $T \subseteq S$ of states and performs the Bellman update in that round only on T. Consequently, it may speed up computation if "important" states are selected. However, using the standard VI it is even more difficult to determine the current error bound. Moreover, if some states are not selected infinitely often the lower bound may not even converge.

In the setting of bounded value iteration, the current error bound is known for each state and thus convergence can easily be enforced. This gave rise to asynchronous VI, such as BRTDP (bounded real time dynamic programing) in the setting of stopping MDPs [MLG05], where the states are selected as those that appear on a simulation run. Very similar is the adaptation for general MDP [BCC+14]. In order to simulate a run, the transition probabilities determine how to resolve the probabilistic choice. In order to resolve the non-deterministic choice of Maximizer, the "most promising action" is taken, i.e., with the highest U. This choice is derived from a reinforcement algorithm called delayed Q-learning and ensures convergence while practically performing well [BCC+14].

In this section, we harvest our convergence results and BVI algorithm for SG, which allow us to trivially extend the asynchronous learning-based approach of BRTDP to SGs. On the one hand, the only difference to the MDP algorithm is how to resolve the choice for Minimizer. Since the situation is dual, we again pick the "most promising action", in this case with the lowest L. On the other hand, the only difference to Algorithm 1 calling Algorithm 4 is that the Bellman updates of U and L are performed on the states of the simulation run only, see lines 2–3 of Algorithm 5.

Algorithm 5. Update procedure for the learning/BRTDP version of BVI on SG

1: **procedure** UPDATE($\mathsf{L} : S \to [0,1]$, $\mathsf{U} : S \to [0,1]$)
2: $\quad \rho \leftarrow$ path $\mathsf{s}_0, \mathsf{s}_1, \ldots, \mathsf{s}_\ell$ of length $\ell \leq k$, obtained by simulation where the successor of s is s' with probability $\delta(\mathsf{s}, \mathsf{a}, \mathsf{s}')$ and a is sampled randomly from $\arg\max_{\mathsf{a}} \mathsf{U}(\mathsf{s}, \mathsf{a})$ and $\arg\min_{\mathsf{a}} \mathsf{L}(\mathsf{s}, \mathsf{a})$ for $\mathsf{s} \in S_\square$ and $\mathsf{s} \in S_\bigcirc$, respectively
3: $\quad \mathsf{L}, \mathsf{U}$ get updated by Eq. (3) and (4) on states $\mathsf{s}_\ell, \mathsf{s}_{\ell-1}, \ldots, \mathsf{s}_0$ * all $\mathsf{s} \in \rho$ * \
4: $\quad$ **for** $T \in$ FIND_MSEC(L) **do**
5: $\quad\quad$ DEFLATE(T, U)

If $\mathtt{1}$ or $\mathtt{0}$ is reached in a simulation, we can terminate it. It can happen that the simulation cycles in an EC. To that end, we have a bound k on the maximum number of steps. The choice of k is discussed in detail in [BCC+14] and we use $2 \cdot |S|$ to guarantee the possibility of reaching sinks as well as exploring new states. If the simulation cycles in an EC, the subsequent call of DEFLATE ensures that next time there is a positive probability to exit this EC. Further details can be found in [KKKW18, Appendix A.4].

5 Experimental Results

We implemented both our algorithms as an extension of PRISM-games [CFK+13a], a branch of PRISM [KNP11] that allows for modelling SGs, utilizing previous work of [BCC+14, Ujm15] for MDP and SG with single-player ECs. We tested the implementation on the SGs from the PRISM-games case studies [gam] that have reachability properties and one additional model from [CKJ12] that was also used in [Ujm15]. We compared the results with both the explicit and the hybrid engine of PRISM-games, but since the models are small both of them performed similar and we only display the results of the hybrid engine in Table 1.

Furthermore we ran experiments on MDPs from the PRISM benchmark suite [KNP12]. We compared our results there to the hybrid and explicit engine of PRISM, the interval iteration implemented in PRISM [HM17], the hybrid engine of STORM [DJKV17a] and the BRTDP implementation of [BCC+14].

Recall that the aim of the paper is not to provide a faster VI algorithm, but rather the first guaranteed one. Consequently, the aim of the experiments is not to show any speed ups, but to experimentally estimate the overhead needed for computing the guarantees.

For information on the technical details of the experiments, all the models and the tables for the experiments on MDPs we refer to [KKKW18, Appendix B]. Note that although some of the SG models are parametrized they could only be scaled by manually changing the model file, which complicates extensive benchmarking.

Although our approaches compute the additional upper bound to give the convergence guarantees, for each of the experiments one of our algorithms performed similar to PRISM-games. Table 1 shows this result for three of the four SG models in the benchmarking set. On the fourth model, PRISM's pre-computations already solve the problem and hence it cannot be used to compare the approaches. For completeness, the results are displayed in [KKKW18, Appendix B.5].

Table 1. Experimental results for the experiments on SGs. The left two columns denote the model and the given parameters, if present. Columns 3 to 5 display the verification time in seconds for each of the solvers, namely PRISM-games (referred as PRISM), our BVI algorithm (BVI) and our learning-based algorithm (BRTDP). The next two columns compare the number of states that BRTDP explored (#States_B) to the total number of states in the model. The rightmost column shows the number of MSECs in the model.

Model	Parameters	PRISM	BVI	BRTDP	#States_B	#States	#MSECs
mdsm	prop = 1	8	8	17	767	62,245	1
	prop = 2	4	4	29	407	62,245	1
cdmsn		2	2	3	1,212	1,240	1
cloud	N = 5	3	7	15	1,302	8,842	4,421
	N = 6	6	59	4	570	34,954	17,477

Whenever there are few MSECs, as in mdsm and cdmsn, BVI performs like PRISM-games, because only little time is used for deflating. Apparently the additional upper bound computation takes very little time in comparison to the other tasks (e.g. parsing, generating the model, pre-computation) and does not slow down the verification significantly. For cloud, BVI is slower than PRISM-games, because there are thousands of MSECs and deflating them takes over 80% of the time. This comes from the fact that we need to compute the expensive end component decomposition for each deflating step. BRTDP performs well for cloud, because in this model, as well as generally often if there are many MECs [BCC+14], only a small part of the state space is relevant for convergence. For the other models, BRTDP is slower than the deterministic approaches, because the models are so small that it is faster to first construct them completely than to explore them by simulation.

Our more extensive experiments on MDPs compare the guaranteed approaches based on collapsing (i.e. learning-based from [BCC+14] and deterministic from [HM17]) to our guaranteed approaches based on deflating (so BRTDP and BVI). Since both learning-based approaches as well as both deterministic approaches perform similarly (see Table 2 in [KKKW18, Appendix B]), we conclude that collapsing and deflating are both useful for practical purposes, while the latter is also applicable to SGs. Furthermore we compared the usual unguaranteed value iteration of PRISM's explicit engine to BVI and saw that our guaranteed approach did not take significantly more time in most cases. This strengthens the point that the overhead for the computation of the guarantees is negligible.

6 Conclusions

We have provided the first stopping criterion for value iteration on simple stochastic games and an anytime algorithm with bounds on the current error (guarantees on the precision of the result). The main technical challenge was that states in end components in SG can have different values, in contrast to the case of MDP. We have shown that collapsing is in general not possible, but we utilized the analysis to obtain the procedure of *deflating*, a solution on the original graph. Besides, whenever a SEC is identified for sure it can be collapsed and the two techniques of collapsing and deflating can thus be combined.

The experiments indicate that the price to pay for the overhead to compute the error bound is often negligible. For each of the available models, at least one of our two implementations has performed similar to or better than the standard approach that yields no guarantees. Further, the obtained guarantees open the door to (e.g. learning-based) heuristics which treat only a part of the state space and can thus potentially lead to huge improvements. Surprisingly, already our straightforward adaptation of such an algorithm for MDP to SG yields interesting results, palliating the overhead of our non-learning method, despite the most naive implementation of deflating. Future work could reveal whether other heuristics or more efficient implementation can lead to huge savings as in the case of MDP [BCC+14].

References

[ACD+17] Ashok, P., Chatterjee, K., Daca, P., Křetínský, J., Meggendorfer, T.: Value iteration for long-run average reward in Markov decision processes. In: Majumdar, R., Kunčak, V. (eds.) CAV 2017. LNCS, vol. 10426, pp. 201–221. Springer, Cham (2017). https://doi.org/10.1007/978-3-319-63387-9_10

[AM09] Andersson, D., Miltersen, P.B.: The complexity of solving stochastic games on graphs. In: Dong, Y., Du, D.-Z., Ibarra, O. (eds.) ISAAC 2009. LNCS, vol. 5878, pp. 112–121. Springer, Heidelberg (2009). https://doi.org/10.1007/978-3-642-10631-6_13

[AY17] Arslan, G., Yüksel, S.: Decentralized Q-learning for stochastic teams and games. IEEE Trans. Autom. Control **62**(4), 1545–1558 (2017)

[BBS08] Busoniu, L., Babuska, R., De Schutter, B.: A comprehensive survey of multiagent reinforcement learning. IEEE Trans. Syst. Man Cybern. Part C **38**(2), 156–172 (2008)

[BCC+14] Brázdil, T., Chatterjee, K., Chmelík, M., Forejt, V., Křetínský, J., Kwiatkowska, M., Parker, D., Ujma, M.: Verification of Markov decision processes using learning algorithms. In: Cassez, F., Raskin, J.-F. (eds.) ATVA 2014. LNCS, vol. 8837, pp. 98–114. Springer, Cham (2014). https://doi.org/10.1007/978-3-319-11936-6_8

[BK08] Baier, C., Katoen, J.-P.: Principles of Model Checking (2008)

[BKL+17] Baier, C., Klein, J., Leuschner, L., Parker, D., Wunderlich, S.: Ensuring the reliability of your model checker: interval iteration for Markov decision processes. In: Majumdar, R., Kunčak, V. (eds.) CAV 2017. LNCS, vol. 10426, pp. 160–180. Springer, Cham (2017). https://doi.org/10.1007/978-3-319-63387-9_8

[BT00] Brafman, R.I., Tennenholtz, M.: A near-optimal polynomial time algorithm for learning in certain classes of stochastic games. Artif. Intell. **121**(1–2), 31–47 (2000)

[CF11] Chatterjee, K., Fijalkow, N.: A reduction from parity games to simple stochastic games. In: GandALF, pp. 74–86 (2011)

[CFK+13a] Chen, T., Forejt, V., Kwiatkowska, M., Parker, D., Simaitis, A.: PRISM-games: a model checker for stochastic multi-player games. In: Piterman, N., Smolka, S.A. (eds.) TACAS 2013. LNCS, vol. 7795, pp. 185–191. Springer, Heidelberg (2013). https://doi.org/10.1007/978-3-642-36742-7_13

[CH08] Chatterjee, K., Henzinger, T.A.: Value iteration. In: Grumberg, O., Veith, H. (eds.) 25 Years of Model Checking. LNCS, vol. 5000, pp. 107–138. Springer, Heidelberg (2008). https://doi.org/10.1007/978-3-540-69850-0_7

[CHJR10] Chatterjee, K., Henzinger, T.A., Jobstmann, B., Radhakrishna, A.: GIST: a solver for probabilistic games. In: Touili, T., Cook, B., Jackson, P. (eds.) CAV 2010. LNCS, vol. 6174, pp. 665–669. Springer, Heidelberg (2010). https://doi.org/10.1007/978-3-642-14295-6_57

[CKJ12] Calinescu, R., Kikuchi, S., Johnson, K.: Compositional reverification of probabilistic safety properties for large-scale complex IT systems. In: Calinescu, R., Garlan, D. (eds.) Monterey Workshop 2012. LNCS, vol. 7539, pp. 303–329. Springer, Heidelberg (2012). https://doi.org/10.1007/978-3-642-34059-8_16

[CKLB11] Cheng, C.-H., Knoll, A., Luttenberger, M., Buckl, C.: GAVS+: an open platform for the research of algorithmic game solving. In: Abdulla, P.A., Leino, K.R.M. (eds.) TACAS 2011. LNCS, vol. 6605, pp. 258–261. Springer, Heidelberg (2011). https://doi.org/10.1007/978-3-642-19835-9_22

[CKSW13] Chen, T., Kwiatkowska, M., Simaitis, A., Wiltsche, C.: Synthesis for multi-objective stochastic games: an application to autonomous urban driving. In: Joshi, K., Siegle, M., Stoelinga, M., D'Argenio, P.R. (eds.) QEST 2013. LNCS, vol. 8054, pp. 322–337. Springer, Heidelberg (2013). https://doi.org/10.1007/978-3-642-40196-1_28

[CMG14] Cámara, J., Moreno, G.A., Garlan, D.: Stochastic game analysis and latency awareness for proactive self-adaptation. In: 9th International Symposium on Software Engineering for Adaptive and Self-Managing Systems, SEAMS 2014, Proceedings, Hyderabad, India, 2–3 June 2014, pp. 155–164 (2014)

[Con92] Condon, A.: The complexity of stochastic games. Inf. Comput. **96**(2), 203–224 (1992)

[CY95] Courcoubetis, C., Yannakakis, M.: The complexity of probabilistic verification. J. ACM **42**(4), 857–907 (1995)

[DJKV17a] Dehnert, C., Junges, S., Katoen, J.-P., Volk, M.: A Storm is coming: a modern probabilistic model checker. In: Majumdar, R., Kunčak, V. (eds.) CAV 2017. LNCS, vol. 10427, pp. 592–600. Springer, Cham (2017). https://doi.org/10.1007/978-3-319-63390-9_31

[gam] PRISM-games Case Studies. prismmodelchecker.org/games/casestudies.php. Accessed 18 Sept 2017

[HK66] Hoffman, A.J., Karp, R.M.: On nonterminating stochastic games. Manag. Sci. **12**(5), 359–370 (1966)

[HM17] Haddad, S., Monmege, B.: Interval iteration algorithm for MDPs and IMDPs. Theor. Comput. Sci. **735**, 111–131 (2018). https://doi.org/10.1016/j.tcs.2016.12.003

[KKKW18] Kelmendi, E., Krämer, J., Křetínský, J., Weininger, M.: Value iteration for simple stochastic games: stopping criterion and learning algorithm. Technical report abs/1804.04901, arXiv.org (2018)

[KKNP10] Kattenbelt, M., Kwiatkowska, M.Z., Norman, G., Parker, D.: A game-based abstraction-refinement framework for Markov decision processes. Formal Methods Syst. Des. **36**(3), 246–280 (2010)

[KM17] Křetínský, J., Meggendorfer, T.: Efficient strategy iteration for mean payoff in Markov decision processes. In: D'Souza, D., Narayan Kumar, K. (eds.) ATVA 2017. LNCS, vol. 10482, pp. 380–399. Springer, Cham (2017). https://doi.org/10.1007/978-3-319-68167-2_25

[KNP11] Kwiatkowska, M., Norman, G., Parker, D.: PRISM 4.0: verification of probabilistic real-time systems. In: Gopalakrishnan, G., Qadeer, S. (eds.) CAV 2011. LNCS, vol. 6806, pp. 585–591. Springer, Heidelberg (2011). https://doi.org/10.1007/978-3-642-22110-1_47

[KNP12] Kwiatkowska, M., Norman, G., Parker, D.: The prism benchmark suite. In: 9th International Conference on Quantitative Evaluation of Systems (QEST 2012), pp. 203–204. IEEE (2012)

[LaV00] LaValle, S.M.: Robot motion planning: a game-theoretic foundation. Algorithmica **26**(3–4), 430–465 (2000)

[LL08] Li, J., Liu, W.: A novel heuristic Q-learning algorithm for solving stochastic games. In: IJCNN, pp. 1135–1144 (2008)

[Mar75] Martin, D.A.: Borel determinacy. Ann. Math. **102**, 363–371 (1975)

[MLG05] Mcmahan, H.B., Likhachev, M., Gordon, G.J.: Bounded real-time dynamic programming: RTDP with monotone upper bounds and performance guarantees. In: ICML 2005, pp. 569–576 (2005)

[Put14] Puterman, M.L.: Markov Decision Processes: Discrete Stochastic Dynamic Programming. Wiley, Hoboken (2014)

[SK16] Svorenová, M., Kwiatkowska, M.: Quantitative verification and strategy synthesis for stochastic games. Eur. J. Control **30**, 15–30 (2016)

[TT16] Tcheukam, A., Tembine, H.: One swarm per queen: a particle swarm learning for stochastic games. In: SASO, pp. 144–145 (2016)

[Ujm15] Ujma, M.: On verification and controller synthesis for probabilistic systems at runtime. Ph.D. thesis, Wolfson College, Oxford (2015)

[WT16] Wen, M., Topcu, U.: Probably approximately correct learning in stochastic games with temporal logic specifications. In: IJCAI, pp. 3630–3636 (2016)

Sound Value Iteration

Tim Quatmann(✉) and Joost-Pieter Katoen

RWTH Aachen University, Aachen, Germany
tim.quatmann@cs.rwth-aachen.de

Abstract. Computing reachability probabilities is at the heart of probabilistic model checking. All model checkers compute these probabilities in an iterative fashion using value iteration. This technique approximates a fixed point from below by determining reachability probabilities for an increasing number of steps. To avoid results that are significantly off, variants have recently been proposed that converge from both below and above. These procedures require starting values for both sides. We present an alternative that does not require the a priori computation of starting vectors and that converges faster on many benchmarks. The crux of our technique is to give tight and safe bounds—whose computation is cheap—on the reachability probabilities. Lifting this technique to expected rewards is trivial for both Markov chains and MDPs. Experimental results on a large set of benchmarks show its scalability and efficiency.

1 Introduction

Markov decision processes (MDPs) [1,2] have their roots in operations research and stochastic control theory. They are frequently used for stochastic and dynamic optimization problems and are widely applicable in, e.g., stochastic scheduling and robotics. MDPs are also a natural model in randomized distributed computing where coin flips by the individual processes are mixed with non-determinism arising from interleaving the processes' behaviors. The central problem for MDPs is to find a policy that determines what action to take in the light of what is known about the system at the time of choice. The typical aim is to optimize a given objective, such as minimizing the expected cost until a given number of repairs, maximizing the probability of being operational for 1,000 steps, or minimizing the probability to reach a "bad" state.

Probabilistic model checking [3,4] provides a scalable alternative to tackle these MDP problems, see the recent surveys [5,6]. The central computational issue in MDP model checking is to solve a system of linear inequalities. In absence of non-determinism—the MDP being a Markov Chain (MC)—a linear equation system is obtained. After appropriate pre-computations, such as determining the states for which no policy exists that eventually reaches the goal state, the (in)equation system has a unique solution that coincides with the extremal value

This work is partially supported by the Sino-German Center project CAP (GZ 1023).

H. Chockler and G. Weissenbacher (Eds.): CAV 2018, LNCS 10981, pp. 643–661, 2018.
https://doi.org/10.1007/978-3-319-96145-3_37

that is sought for. Possible solution techniques to compute such solutions include policy iteration, linear programming, and value iteration. Modern probabilistic model checkers such as `PRISM` [7] and `Storm` [8] use value iteration by default. This approximates a fixed point from below by determining the probabilities to reach a target state within k steps in the k-th iteration. The iteration is typically stopped if the difference between the value vectors of two successive (or vectors that are further apart) is below the desired accuracy ε.

This procedure however can provide results that are significantly off, as the iteration is stopped prematurely, e.g., since the probability mass in the MDP only changes slightly in a series of computational steps due to a "slow" movement. This problem is not new; similar problems, e.g., occur in iterative approaches to compute long-run averages [9] and transient measures [10] and pop up in statistical model checking to decide when to stop simulating for unbounded reachability properties [11]. As recently was shown, this phenomenon does not only occur for hypothetical cases but affects practical benchmarks of MDP model checking too [12]. To remedy this, Haddad and Monmege [13] proposed to iteratively approximate the (unique) fixed point from both below and above; a natural termination criterion is to halt the computation once the two approximations differ less than $2{\cdot}\varepsilon$. This scheme requires two starting vectors, one for each approximation. For reachability probabilities, the conservative values zero and one can be used. For expected rewards, it is non-trivial to find an appropriate upper bound—how to "guess" an adequate upper bound to the expected reward to reach a goal state? Baier *et al.* [12] recently provided an algorithm to solve this issue.

This paper takes an alternative perspective to obtaining a sound variant of value iteration. *Our approach does not require the a priori computation of starting vectors and converges faster on many benchmarks.* The crux of our technique is to give tight and safe bounds—whose computation is cheap and that are obtained during the course of value iteration—on the reachability probabilities. The approach is simple and can be lifted straightforwardly to expected rewards. The central idea is to split the desired probability for reaching a target state into the sum of

(i) the probability for reaching a target state *within* k steps and
(ii) the probability for reaching a target state *only after* k steps.

We obtain (i) via k iterations of (standard) value iteration. A second instance of value iteration computes the probability that a target state is still reachable after k steps. We show that from this information safe lower and upper bounds for (ii) can be derived. We illustrate that the same idea can be applied to expected rewards, topological value iteration [14], and Gauss-Seidel value iteration. We also discuss in detail its extension to MDPs and provide extensive experimental evaluation using our implementation in the model checker `Storm` [8]. Our experiments show that on many practical benchmarks we need significantly fewer iterations, yielding a speed-up of about 20% on average. More importantly though, is the conceptual simplicity of our approach.

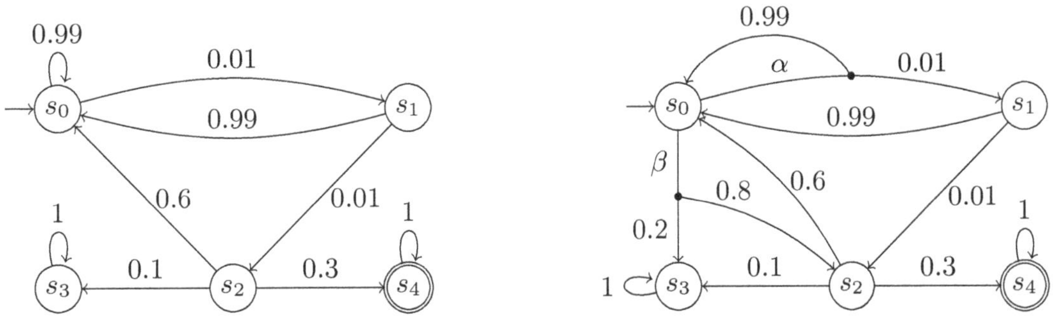

(a) A sample MC $\mathcal{D}$. (b) A sample MDP $\mathcal{M}$.

Fig. 1. Example models.

2 Preliminaries

For a finite set S and vector $x \in \mathbb{R}^{|S|}$, let $x[s] \in \mathbb{R}$ denote the entry of x that corresponds to $s \in S$. Let $S' \subseteq S$ and $a \in \mathbb{R}$. We write $x[S'] = a$ to denote that $x[s] = a$ for all $s \in S'$. Given $x, y \in \mathbb{R}^{|S|}$, $x \leq y$ holds iff $x[s] \leq y[s]$ holds for all $s \in S$. For a function $f\colon \mathbb{R}^{|S|} \to \mathbb{R}^{|S|}$ and $k \geq 0$ we write f^k for the function obtained by applying f k times, i.e., $f^0(x) = x$ and $f^k(x) = f(f^{k-1}(x))$ if $k > 0$.

2.1 Probabilistic Models and Measures

We briefly present probabilistic models and their properties. More details can be found in, e.g., [15].

Definition 1 (Probabilistic Models). *A* Markov Decision Process (MDP) *is a tuple* $\mathcal{M} = (S, \mathit{Act}, \mathbf{P}, s_I, \rho)$, *where*

- S *is a finite set of states,* Act *is a finite set of actions,* s_I *is the initial state,*
- $\mathbf{P}\colon S \times \mathit{Act} \times S \to [0,1]$ *is a transition probability function satisfying* $\sum_{s' \in S} \mathbf{P}(s, \alpha, s') \in \{0, 1\}$ *for all* $s \in S, \alpha \in \mathit{Act}$, *and*
- $\rho\colon S \times \mathit{Act} \to \mathbb{R}$ *is a reward function.*

$\mathcal{M}$ *is a* Markov Chain (MC) *if* $|\mathit{Act}| = 1$.

Example 1. Figure 1 shows an example MC and an example MDP.

We often simplify notations for MCs by omitting the (unique) action. For an MDP $\mathcal{M} = (S, \mathit{Act}, \mathbf{P}, s_I, \rho)$, the set of *enabled actions* of state $s \in S$ is given by $\mathit{Act}(s) = \{\alpha \in \mathit{Act} \mid \sum_{s' \in S} \mathbf{P}(s, \alpha, s') = 1\}$. We assume that $\mathit{Act}(s) \neq \emptyset$ for each $s \in S$. Intuitively, upon performing action α at state s reward $\rho(s, \alpha)$ is collected and with probability $\mathbf{P}(s, \alpha, s')$ we move to $s' \in S$. Notice that rewards can be positive or negative.

A state $s \in S$ is called *absorbing* if $\mathbf{P}(s, \alpha, s) = 1$ for every $\alpha \in \mathit{Act}(s)$. A *path* of $\mathcal{M}$ is an infinite alternating sequence $\pi = s_0 \alpha_0 s_1 \alpha_1 \dots$ where $s_i \in S$, $\alpha_i \in$

$Act(s_i)$, and $\mathbf{P}(s_i, \alpha_i, s_{i+1}) > 0$ for all $i \geq 0$. The set of paths of $\mathcal{M}$ is denoted by $Paths^{\mathcal{M}}$. The set of paths that start at $s \in S$ is given by $Paths^{\mathcal{M},s}$. A *finite path* $\hat{\pi} = s_0\alpha_0 \dots \alpha_{n-1}s_n$ is a finite prefix of a path ending with $last(\hat{\pi}) = s_n \in S$. $|\hat{\pi}| = n$ is the length of $\hat{\pi}$, $Paths_{fin}^{\mathcal{M}}$ is the set of finite paths of $\mathcal{M}$, and $Paths_{fin}^{\mathcal{M},s}$ is the set of finite paths that start at state $s \in S$. We consider LTL-like notations for sets of paths. For $k \in \mathbb{N} \cup \{\infty\}$ and $G, H \subseteq S$ let

$$H\,\mathcal{U}^{\leq k}\,G = \{s_0\alpha_0 s_1 \dots \in Paths^{\mathcal{M},s_I} \mid s_0, \dots, s_{j-1} \in H,\ s_j \in G \text{ for some } j \leq k\}$$

denote the set of paths that, starting from the initial state s_I, only visit states in H until after at most k steps a state in G is reached. Sets $H\,\mathcal{U}^{>k}\,G$ and $H\,\mathcal{U}^{=k}\,G$ are defined similarly. We use the shorthands $\lozenge^{\leq k}G := S\,\mathcal{U}^{\leq k}\,G$, $\lozenge G := \lozenge^{\leq \infty}G$, and $\square^{\leq k}G := Paths^{\mathcal{M},s_I} \setminus \lozenge^{\leq k}(S \setminus G)$.

A *(deterministic) scheduler* for $\mathcal{M}$ is a function $\sigma\colon Paths_{fin}^{\mathcal{M}} \to Act$ such that $\sigma(\hat{\pi}) \in Act(last(\hat{\pi}))$ for all $\hat{\pi} \in Paths_{fin}^{\mathcal{M}}$. The set of (deterministic) schedulers for $\mathcal{M}$ is $\mathfrak{S}^{\mathcal{M}}$. $\sigma \in \mathfrak{S}^{\mathcal{M}}$ is called *positional* if $\sigma(\hat{\pi})$ only depends on the last state of $\hat{\pi}$, i.e., for all $\hat{\pi}, \hat{\pi}' \in Paths_{fin}^{\mathcal{M}}$ we have $last(\hat{\pi}) = last(\hat{\pi}')$ implies $\sigma(\hat{\pi}) = \sigma(\hat{\pi}')$. For MDP $\mathcal{M}$ and scheduler $\sigma \in \mathfrak{S}^{\mathcal{M}}$ the *probability measure* over finite paths is given by $\Pr_{fin}^{\mathcal{M},\sigma}\colon Paths_{fin}^{\mathcal{M},s_I} \to [0,1]$ with $\Pr_{fin}^{\mathcal{M},\sigma}(s_0 \dots s_n) = \prod_{i=0}^{n-1} \mathbf{P}(s_i, \sigma(s_0 \dots s_i), s_{i+1})$. The probability measure $\Pr^{\mathcal{M},\sigma}$ over measurable sets of infinite paths is obtained via a standard cylinder set construction [15].

Definition 2 (Reachability Probability). *The* reachability probability *of MDP $\mathcal{M} = (S, Act, \mathbf{P}, s_I, \rho)$, $G \subseteq S$, and $\sigma \in \mathfrak{S}^{\mathcal{M}}$ is given by* $\Pr^{\mathcal{M},\sigma}(\lozenge G)$.

For $k \in \mathbb{N} \cup \{\infty\}$, the function $\blacklozenge^{\leq k}G\colon \lozenge G \to \mathbb{R}$ yields the k-bounded reachability reward of a path $\pi = s_0\alpha_0 s_1 \dots \in \lozenge G$. We set $\blacklozenge^{\leq k}G(\pi) = \sum_{i=0}^{j-1} \rho(s_i, \alpha_i)$, where $j = \min(\{i \geq 0 \mid s_i \in G\} \cup \{k\})$. We write $\blacklozenge G$ instead of $\blacklozenge^{\leq \infty}G$.

Definition 3 (Expected Reward). *The* expected (reachability) reward *of MDP $\mathcal{M} = (S, Act, \mathbf{P}, s_I, \rho)$, $G \subseteq S$, and $\sigma \in \mathfrak{S}^{\mathcal{M}}$ with $\Pr^{\mathcal{M},\sigma}(\lozenge G) = 1$ is given by the expectation $\mathbb{E}^{\mathcal{M},\sigma}(\blacklozenge G) = \int_{\pi \in \lozenge G} \blacklozenge G(\pi)\, \mathrm{d}\Pr^{\mathcal{M},\sigma}(\pi)$.*

We write $\Pr_s^{\mathcal{M},\sigma}$ and $\mathbb{E}_s^{\mathcal{M},\sigma}$ for the probability measure and expectation obtained by changing the initial state of $\mathcal{M}$ to $s \in S$. If $\mathcal{M}$ is a Markov chain, there is only a single scheduler. In this case we may omit the superscript σ from $\Pr^{\mathcal{M},\sigma}$ and $\mathbb{E}^{\mathcal{M},\sigma}$. We also omit the superscript $\mathcal{M}$ if it is clear from the context. The maximal reachability probability of $\mathcal{M}$ and G is given by $\Pr^{\max}(\lozenge G) = \max_{\sigma \in \mathfrak{S}^{\mathcal{M}}} \Pr^{\sigma}(\lozenge G)$. There is a a positional scheduler that attains this maximum [16]. The same holds for minimal reachability probabilities and maximal or minimal expected rewards.

Example 2. Consider the MDP $\mathcal{M}$ from Fig. 1(b). We are interested in the maximal probability to reach state s_4 given by $\Pr^{\max}(\lozenge\{s_4\})$. Since s_4 is not reachable from s_3 we have $\Pr_{s_3}^{\max}(\lozenge\{s_4\}) = 0$. Intuitively, choosing action β at state s_0 makes reaching s_3 more likely, which should be avoided in order to maximize the probability to reach s_4. We therefore assume a scheduler σ that always chooses action α at state s_0. Starting from the initial state s_0, we then eventually take the transition from s_2 to s_3 or the transition from s_2 to s_4 with probability one. The resulting probability to reach s_4 is given by $\mathrm{Pr}^{\max}(\lozenge\{s_4\}) = \mathrm{Pr}^{\sigma}(\lozenge\{s_4\}) = 0.3/(0.1 + 0.3) = 0.75$.

2.2 Probabilistic Model Checking via Interval Iteration

In the following we present approaches to compute reachability probabilities and expected rewards. We consider approximative computations. Exact computations are handled in e.g. [17,18] For the sake of clarity, we focus on reachability probabilities and sketch how the techniques can be lifted to expected rewards.

Reachability Probabilities. We fix an MDP $\mathcal{M} = (S, \mathit{Act}, \mathbf{P}, s_I, \rho)$, a set of goal states $G \subseteq S$, and a precision parameter $\varepsilon > 0$.

Problem 1. Compute an ε-approximation of the maximal reachability probability $\mathrm{Pr}^{\max}(\lozenge G)$, i.e., compute a value $r \in [0, 1]$ with $|r - \mathrm{Pr}^{\max}(\lozenge G)| < \varepsilon$.

We briefly sketch how to compute such a value r via *interval iteration* [12,13,19]. The computation for minimal reachability probabilities is analogous.

W.l.o.g. it is assumed that the states in G are absorbing. Using graph algorithms, we compute $S_0 = \{s \in S \mid \mathrm{Pr}^{\max}_s(\lozenge G) = 0\}$ and partition the state space of $\mathcal{M}$ into $S = S_0 \uplus G \uplus S_?$ with $S_? = S \setminus (G \cup S_0)$. If $s_I \in S_0$ or $s_I \in G$, the probability $\mathrm{Pr}^{\max}(\lozenge G)$ is 0 or 1, respectively. From now on we assume $s_I \in S_?$.

We say that $\mathcal{M}$ is *contracting* with respect to $S' \subseteq S$ if $\mathrm{Pr}^{\sigma}_s(\lozenge S') = 1$ for all $s \in S$ and for all $\sigma \in \mathfrak{S}^{\mathcal{M}}$. We assume that $\mathcal{M}$ is contracting with respect to $G \cup S_0$. Otherwise, we apply a transformation on the so-called *end components*[1] of $\mathcal{M}$, yielding a contracting MDP $\mathcal{M}'$ with the same maximal reachability probability as $\mathcal{M}$. Roughly, this transformation replaces each end component of $\mathcal{M}$ with a single state whose enabled actions coincide with the actions that previously lead outside of the end component. This step is detailed in [13,19].

We have $x^*[s] = \mathrm{Pr}^{\max}_s(\lozenge G)$ for $s \in S$ and the unique fixpoint x^* of the function $f\colon \mathbb{R}^{|S|} \to \mathbb{R}^{|S|}$ with $f(x)[S_0] = 0$, $f(x)[G] = 1$, and

$$f(x)[s] = \max_{\alpha \in \mathit{Act}(s)} \sum_{s' \in S} \mathbf{P}(s, \alpha, s') \cdot x[s']$$

for $s \in S_?$. Hence, computing $\mathrm{Pr}^{\max}(\lozenge G)$ reduces to finding the fixpoint of f.

A popular technique for this purpose is the *value iteration* algorithm [1]. Given a starting vector $x \in \mathbb{R}^{|S|}$ with $x[S_0] = 0$ and $x[G] = 1$, standard value iteration computes $f^k(x)$ for increasing k until $\max_{s \in S} |f^k(x)[s] - f^{k-1}(x)[s]| < \varepsilon$ holds for a predefined precision $\varepsilon > 0$. As pointed out in, e.g., [13], there is no

[1] Intuitively, an end component is a set of states $S' \subseteq S$ such that there is a scheduler inducing that from any $s \in S'$ exactly the states in S' are visited infinitely often.

guarantee on the preciseness of the result $r = f^k(x)[s_I]$, i.e., standard value iteration does not give any evidence on the error $|r - \mathrm{Pr}^{\max}(\lozenge G)|$. The intuitive reason is that value iteration only approximates the fixpoint x^* from one side, yielding no indication on the distance between the current result and x^*.

Example 3. Consider the MDP $\mathcal{M}$ from Fig. 1(b). We invoked standard value iteration in PRISM [7] and Storm [8] to compute the reachability probability $\mathrm{Pr}^{\max}(\lozenge\{s_4\})$. Recall from Example 2 that the correct solution is 0.75. With (absolute) precision $\varepsilon = 10^{-6}$ both model checkers returned 0.7248. Notice that the user can improve the precision by considering, e.g., $\varepsilon = 10^{-8}$ which yields 0.7497. However, there is no guarantee on the preciseness of a given result.

The *interval iteration* algorithm [12,13,19] addresses the impreciseness of value iteration. The idea is to approach the fixpoint x^* from below and from above. The first step is to find starting vectors $x_\ell, x_u \in \mathbb{R}^{|S|}$ satisfying $x_\ell[S_0] = x_u[S_0] = 0$, $x_\ell[G] = x_u[G] = 1$, and $x_\ell \leq x^* \leq x_u$. As the entries of x^* are probabilities, it is always valid to set $x_\ell[S_?] = 0$ and $x_u[S_?] = 1$. We have $f^k(x_\ell) \leq x^* \leq f^k(x_u)$ for any $k \geq 0$. Interval iteration computes $f^k(x_\ell)$ and $f^k(x_u)$ for increasing k until $\max_{s\in S} |f^k(x_\ell)[s] - f^k(x_u)[s]| < 2\varepsilon$. For the result $r = 1/2 \cdot (f^k(x_\ell)[s_I] + f^k(x_u)[s_I])$ we obtain that $|r - \mathrm{Pr}^{\max}(\lozenge G)| < \varepsilon$, i.e., we get a sound approximation of the maximal reachability probability.

Example 4. We invoked interval iteration in PRISM and Storm to compute the reachability probability $\mathrm{Pr}^{\max}(\lozenge\{s_4\})$ for the MDP $\mathcal{M}$ from Fig. 1(b). Both implementations correctly yield an ε-approximation of $\mathrm{Pr}^{\max}(\lozenge\{s_4\})$, where we considered $\varepsilon = 10^{-6}$. However, both PRISM and Storm required roughly 300,000 iterations for convergence.

Expected Rewards. Whereas [13,19] only consider reachability probabilities, [12] extends interval iteration to compute expected rewards. Let $\mathcal{M}$ be an MDP and G be a set of absorbing states such that $\mathcal{M}$ is contracting with respect to G.

Problem 2. Compute an ε-approximation of the maximal expected reachability reward $\mathbb{E}^{\max}(\blacklozenge G)$, i.e., compute a value $r \in \mathbb{R}$ with $|r - \mathbb{E}^{\max}(\blacklozenge G)| < \varepsilon$.

We have $x^*[s] = \mathbb{E}_s^{\max}(\blacklozenge G)$ for the unique fixpoint x^* of $g\colon \mathbb{R}^{|S|} \to \mathbb{R}^{|S|}$ with

$$g(x)[G] = 0 \ \text{ and } \ g(x)[s] = \max_{\alpha \in Act(s)} \rho(s,\alpha) + \sum_{s' \in S} \mathbf{P}(s,\alpha,s') \cdot x[s']$$

for $s \notin G$. As for reachability probabilities, interval iteration can be applied to approximate this fixpoint. The crux lies in finding appropriate starting vectors $x_\ell, x_u \in \mathbb{R}^{|S|}$ guaranteeing $x_\ell \leq x^* \leq x_u$. To this end, [12] describe graph based algorithms that give an upper bound on the expected number of times each individual state $s \in S \setminus G$ is visited. This then yields an approximation of the expected amount of reward collected at the various states.

3 Sound Value Iteration for MCs

We present an algorithm for computing reachability probabilities and expected rewards as in Problems 1 and 2. The algorithm is an alternative to the interval iteration approach [12,20] but (i) does not require an a priori computation of starting vectors $x_\ell, x_u \in \mathbb{R}^{|S|}$ and (ii) converges faster on many practical benchmarks as shown in Sect. 5. For the sake of simplicity, we first restrict to computing reachability probabilities on MCs.

In the following, let $\mathcal{D} = (S, \mathbf{P}, s_I, \rho)$ be an MC, $G \subseteq S$ be a set of absorbing goal states and $\varepsilon > 0$ be a precision parameter. We consider the partition $S = S_0 \uplus G \uplus S_?$ as in Sect. 2.2. The following theorem captures the key insight of our algorithm.

Theorem 1. *For MC $\mathcal{D}$ let G and $S_?$ be as above and $k \geq 0$ with $\Pr_s(\Box^{\leq k} S_?) < 1$ for all $s \in S_?$. We have*

$$\Pr(\Diamond^{\leq k} G) + \Pr(\Box^{\leq k} S_?) \cdot \min_{s \in S_?} \frac{\Pr_s(\Diamond^{\leq k} G)}{1 - \Pr_s(\Box^{\leq k} S_?)}$$
$$\leq \Pr(\Diamond G) \leq \Pr(\Diamond^{\leq k} G) + \Pr(\Box^{\leq k} S_?) \cdot \max_{s \in S_?} \frac{\Pr_s(\Diamond^{\leq k} G)}{1 - \Pr_s(\Box^{\leq k} S_?)}.$$

Theorem 1 allows us to approximate $\Pr(\Diamond G)$ by computing for increasing $k \in \mathbb{N}$

- $\Pr(\Diamond^{\leq k} G)$, the probability to reach a state in G within k steps, and
- $\Pr(\Box^{\leq k} S_?)$, the probability to stay in $S_?$ during the first k steps.

This can be realized via a value-iteration based procedure. The obtained bounds on $\Pr(\Diamond G)$ can be tightened arbitrarily since $\Pr(\Box^{\leq k} S_?)$ approaches 0 for increasing k. In the following, we address the correctness of Theorem 1, describe the details of our algorithm, and indicate how the results can be lifted to expected rewards.

3.1 Approximating Reachability Probabilities

To approximate the reachability probability $\Pr(\Diamond G)$, we consider the step bounded reachability probability $\Pr(\Diamond^{\leq k} G)$ for $k \geq 0$ and provide a lower and an upper bound for the 'missing' probability $\Pr(\Diamond G) - \Pr(\Diamond^{\leq k} G)$. Note that $\Diamond G$ is the disjoint union of the paths that reach G *within* k steps (given by $\Diamond^{\leq k} G$) and the paths that reach G only *after* k steps (given by $S_? \, \mathcal{U}^{>k} \, G$).

Lemma 1. *For any $k \geq 0$ we have* $\Pr(\Diamond G) = \Pr(\Diamond^{\leq k} G) + \Pr(S_? \, \mathcal{U}^{>k} \, G)$.

A path $\pi \in S_? \, \mathcal{U}^{>k} \, G$ reaches some state $s \in S_?$ after *exactly* k steps. This yields the partition $S_? \, \mathcal{U}^{>k} \, G = \biguplus_{s \in S_?} (S_? \, \mathcal{U}^{=k} \{s\} \cap \Diamond G)$. It follows that

$$\Pr(S_? \, \mathcal{U}^{>k} \, G) = \sum_{s \in S_?} \Pr(S_? \, \mathcal{U}^{=k} \, \{s\}) \cdot \Pr_s(\Diamond G).$$

Consider $\ell, u \in [0,1]$ with $\ell \leq \Pr_s(\lozenge G) \leq u$ for all $s \in S_?$, i.e., ℓ and u are lower and upper bounds for the reachability probabilities within $S_?$. We have

$$\sum_{s \in S_?} \Pr(S_? \mathcal{U}^{=k} \{s\}) \cdot \Pr_s(\lozenge G) \leq \sum_{s \in S_?} \Pr(S_? \mathcal{U}^{=k} \{s\}) \cdot u = \Pr(\square^{\leq k} S_?) \cdot u.$$

We can argue similar for the lower bound ℓ. With *Lemma* 1 we get the following.

Proposition 1. *For MC $\mathcal{D}$ with G, $S_?$, ℓ, u as above and any $k \geq 0$ we have*

$$\Pr(\lozenge^{\leq k} G) + \Pr(\square^{\leq k} S_?) \cdot \ell \leq \Pr(\lozenge G) \leq \Pr(\lozenge^{\leq k} G) + \Pr(\square^{\leq k} S_?) \cdot u.$$

Remark 1. The bounds for $\Pr(\lozenge G)$ given by Proposition 1 are similar to the bounds obtained after performing k iterations of interval iteration with starting vectors $x_\ell, x_u \in \mathbb{R}^{|S|}$, where $x_\ell[S_?] = \ell$ and $x_u[S_?] = u$.

We now discuss how the bounds ℓ and u can be obtained from the step bounded probabilities $\Pr_s(\lozenge^{\leq k} G)$ and $\Pr_s(\square^{\leq k} S_?)$ for $s \in S_?$. We focus on the upper bound u. The reasoning for the lower bound ℓ is similar.

Let $s_{\max} \in S_?$ be a state with maximal reachability probability, that is $s_{\max} \in \arg\max_{s \in S_?} \Pr_s(\lozenge G)$. From Proposition 1 we get

$$\Pr_{s_{\max}}(\lozenge G) \leq \Pr_{s_{\max}}(\lozenge^{\leq k} G) + \Pr_{s_{\max}}(\square^{\leq k} S_?) \cdot \Pr_{s_{\max}}(\lozenge G).$$

We solve the inequality for $\Pr_{s_{\max}}(\lozenge G)$ (assuming $\Pr_s(\square^{\leq k} S_?) < 1$ for all $s \in S_?$):

$$\Pr_{s_{\max}}(\lozenge G) \leq \frac{\Pr_{s_{\max}}(\lozenge^{\leq k} G)}{1 - \Pr_{s_{\max}}(\square^{\leq k} S_?)} \leq \max_{s \in S_?} \frac{\Pr_s(\lozenge^{\leq k} G)}{1 - \Pr_s(\square^{\leq k} S_?)}.$$

Proposition 2. *For MC $\mathcal{D}$ let G and $S_?$ be as above and $k \geq 0$ such that $\Pr_s(\square^{\leq k} S_?) < 1$ for all $s \in S_?$. For every $\hat{s} \in S_?$ we have*

$$\min_{s \in S_?} \frac{\Pr_s(\lozenge^{\leq k} G)}{1 - \Pr_s(\square^{\leq k} S_?)} \leq \Pr_{\hat{s}}(\lozenge G) \leq \max_{s \in S_?} \frac{\Pr_s(\lozenge^{\leq k} G)}{1 - \Pr_s(\square^{\leq k} S_?)}.$$

Theorem 1 is a direct consequence of Propositions 1 and 2.

3.2 Extending the Value Iteration Approach

Recall the standard value iteration algorithm for approximating $\Pr(\lozenge G)$ as discussed in Sect. 2.2. The function $f \colon \mathbb{R}^{|S|} \to \mathbb{R}^{|S|}$ for MCs simplifies to $f(x)[S_0] = 0$, $f(x)[G] = 1$, and $f(x)[s] = \sum_{s' \in S} \mathbf{P}(s, s') \cdot x[s']$ for $s \in S_?$. We can compute the k-step bounded reachability probability at every state $s \in S$

Input : MC $\mathcal{D} = (S, \mathbf{P}, s_I, \rho)$, absorbing states $G \subseteq S$, precision $\varepsilon > 0$
Output : $r \in \mathbb{R}$ with $|r - \Pr(\Diamond G)| < \varepsilon$

$S_? \leftarrow S \setminus (\{s \in S \mid \Pr_s(\Diamond G) = 0\} \cup G)$
initialize $x_0, y_0 \in \mathbb{R}^{|S|}$ with $x_0[G] = 1$, $x_0[S \setminus G] = 0$, $y_0[S_?] = 1$, $y_0[S \setminus S_?] = 0$
$\ell_0 \leftarrow -\infty$; $u_0 \leftarrow +\infty$
$k \leftarrow 0$
repeat
  $k \leftarrow k + 1$
  $x_k \leftarrow f(x_{k-1})$; $y_k \leftarrow h(y_{k-1})$
  if $y_k[s] < 1$ for all $s \in S_?$ **then**
    $\ell_k \leftarrow \max(\ell_{k-1}, \min_{s \in S_?} \frac{x_k[s]}{1 - y_k[s]})$; $u_k \leftarrow \min(u_{k-1}, \max_{s \in S_?} \frac{x_k[s]}{1 - y_k[s]})$
until $y_k[s_I] \cdot (u_k - \ell_k) < 2 \cdot \varepsilon$
return $x_k[s_I] + y_k[s_I] \cdot \frac{\ell_k + u_k}{2}$

Algorithm 1: Sound value iteration for MCs.

by performing k iterations of value iteration [15, Remark 10.104]. More precisely, when applying f k times on starting vector $x \in \mathbb{R}^{|S|}$ with $x[G] = 1$ and $x[S \setminus G] = 0$ we get $\Pr_s(\Diamond^{\leq k} G) = f^k(x)[s]$. The probabilities $\Pr_s(\Box^{\leq k} S_?)$ for $s \in S$ can be computed similarly. Let $h \colon \mathbb{R}^{|S|} \to \mathbb{R}^{|S|}$ with $h(y)[S \setminus S_?] = 0$ and $h(y)[s] = \sum_{s' \in S} \mathbf{P}(s, s') \cdot y[s']$ for $s \in S_?$. For starting vector $y \in \mathbb{R}^{|S|}$ with $y[S_?] = 1$ and $y[S \setminus S_?] = 0$ we get $\Pr_s(\Box^{\leq k} S_?) = h^k(y)[s]$.

Algorithm 1 depicts our approach. It maintains vectors $x_k, y_k \in \mathbb{R}^{|S|}$ which, after k iterations of the loop, store the k-step bounded probabilities $\Pr_s(\Diamond^{\leq k} G)$ and $\Pr_s(\Box^{\leq k} S_?)$, respectively. Additionally, the algorithm considers lower bounds ℓ_k and upper bounds u_k such that the following invariant holds.

Lemma 2. *After executing the loop of Algorithm 1 k times we have for all $s \in S_?$ that $x_k[s] = \Pr_s(\Diamond^{\leq k} G)$, $y_k[s] = \Pr_s(\Box^{\leq k} S_?)$, and $\ell_k \leq \Pr_s(\Diamond G) \leq u_k$.*

The correctness of the algorithm follows from Theorem 1. Termination is guaranteed since $\Pr(\Diamond(S_0 \cup G)) = 1$ and therefore $\lim_{k \to \infty} \Pr(\Box^{\leq k} S_?) = \Pr(\Box S_?) = 0$.

Theorem 2. *Algorithm 1 terminates for any MC $\mathcal{D}$, goal states G, and precision $\varepsilon > 0$. The returned value r satisfies $|r - \Pr(\Diamond G)| < \varepsilon$.*

Example 5. We apply Algorithm 1 for the MC in Fig. 1(a) and the set of goal states $G = \{s_4\}$. We have $S_? = \{s_0, s_1, s_2\}$. After $k = 3$ iterations it holds that

$$x_3[s_0] = 0.00003 \quad x_3[s_1] = 0.003 \quad x_3[s_2] = 0.3$$
$$y_3[s_0] = 0.99996 \quad y_3[s_1] = 0.996 \quad y_3[s_2] = 0.6$$

Hence, $\frac{x_3[s]}{1 - y_3[s]} = \frac{3}{4} = 0.75$ for all $s \in S_?$. We get $\ell_3 = u_3 = 0.75$. The algorithm converges for any $\varepsilon > 0$ and returns the correct solution $x_3[s_0] + y_3[s_0] \cdot 0.75 = 0.75$.

3.3 Sound Value Iteration for Expected Rewards

We lift our approach to expected rewards in a straightforward manner. Let $G \subseteq S$ be a set of absorbing goal states of MC $\mathcal{D}$ such that $\Pr(\lozenge G) = 1$. Further let $S_? = S \setminus G$. For $k \geq 0$ we observe that the expected reward $\mathbb{E}(\blacklozenge G)$ can be split into the expected reward collected within k steps and the expected reward collected only after k steps, i.e., $\mathbb{E}(\blacklozenge G) = \mathbb{E}(\blacklozenge^{\leq k} G) + \sum_{s \in S_?} \Pr(S_? \, \mathcal{U}^{=k} \{s\}) \cdot \mathbb{E}_s(\blacklozenge G)$. Following a similar reasoning as in Sect. 3.1 we can show the following.

Theorem 3. *For MC $\mathcal{D}$ let G and $S_?$ be as before and $k \geq 0$ such that $\Pr_s(\Box^{\leq k} S_?) < 1$ for all $s \in S_?$. We have*

$$\mathbb{E}(\blacklozenge^{\leq k} G) + \Pr(\Box^{\leq k} S_?) \cdot \min_{s \in S_?} \frac{\mathbb{E}_s(\blacklozenge^{\leq k} G)}{1 - \Pr_s(\Box^{\leq k} S_?)}$$

$$\leq \mathbb{E}(\blacklozenge G) \leq \mathbb{E}(\blacklozenge^{\leq k} G) + \Pr(\Box^{\leq k} S_?) \cdot \max_{s \in S_?} \frac{\mathbb{E}_s(\blacklozenge^{\leq k} G)}{1 - \Pr_s(\Box^{\leq k} S_?)}.$$

Recall the function $g \colon \mathbb{R}^{|S|} \to \mathbb{R}^{|S|}$ from Sect. 2.2, given by $g(x)[G] = 0$ and $g(x)[s] = \rho(s) + \sum_{s' \in S} \mathbf{P}(s, s') \cdot x[s']$ for $s \in S_?$. For $s \in S$ and $x \in \mathbb{R}^{|S|}$ with $x[S] = 0$ we have $\mathbb{E}_s(\blacklozenge^{\leq k} G) = g^k(x)[s]$. We modify Algorithm 1 such that it considers function g instead of function f. Then, the returned value r satisfies $|r - \mathbb{E}(\blacklozenge G)| < \varepsilon$.

3.4 Optimizations

Algorithm 1 can make use of *initial bounds* $\ell_0, u_0 \in \mathbb{R}$ with $\ell_0 \leq \Pr_s(\lozenge G) \leq u_0$ for all $s \in S_?$. Such bounds could be derived, e.g., from domain knowledge or during preprocessing [12]. The algorithm always chooses the largest available lower bound for ℓ_k and the lowest available upper bound for u_k, respectively. If Algorithm 1 and interval iteration are initialized with the same bounds, Algorithm 1 always requires as most as many iterations compared to interval iteration (cf. Remark 1).

Gauss-Seidel value iteration [1,12] is an optimization for standard value iteration and interval iteration that potentially leads to faster convergence. When computing $f(x)[s]$ for $s \in S_?$, the idea is to consider already computed results $f(x)[s']$ from the current iteration. Formally, let $\prec \subseteq S \times S$ be some strict total ordering of the states. Gauss-Seidel value iteration considers instead of function f the function $f_\prec \colon \mathbb{R}^{|S|} \to \mathbb{R}^{|S|}$ with $f_\prec[S_0] = 0$, $f_\prec[G] = 1$, and

$$f_\prec(x)[s] = \sum_{s' \prec s} \mathbf{P}(s, s') \cdot f_\prec(x)[s'] + \sum_{s' \not\prec s} \mathbf{P}(s, s') \cdot x[s'].$$

Values $f_\prec(x)[s]$ for $s \in S$ are computed in the order defined by $\prec$. This idea can also be applied to our approach. To this end, we replace f by $f_\prec$ and h by $h_\prec$, where $h_\prec$ is defined similarly. More details are given in [21].

Topological value iteration [14] employs the graphical structure of the MC $\mathcal{D}$. The idea is to decompose the states S of $\mathcal{D}$ into strongly connected components[2]

[2] $S' \subseteq S$ is a connected component if s can be reached from s' for all $s, s' \in S'$. S' is a strongly connected component if no superset of S' is a connected component.

(SCCs) that are analyzed individually. The procedure can improve the runtime of classical value iteration since for a single iteration only the values for the current SCC have to be updated. A topological variant of interval iteration is introduced in [12]. Given these results, sound value iteration can be extended similarly.

4 Sound Value Iteration for MDPs

We extend sound value iteration to compute reachability probabilities in MDPs. Assume an MDP $\mathcal{M} = (S, Act, \mathbf{P}, s_I, \rho)$ and a set of absorbing goal states G. For simplicity, we focus on maximal reachability probabilities, i.e., we compute $\Pr^{\max}(\lozenge G)$. Minimal reachability probabilities and expected rewards are analogous. As in Sect. 2.2 we consider the partition $S = S_0 \uplus G \uplus S_?$ such that $\mathcal{M}$ is contracting with respect to $G \cup S_0$.

4.1 Approximating Maximal Reachability Probabilities

We argue that our results for MCs also hold for MDPs under a given scheduler $\sigma \in \mathfrak{S}^{\mathcal{M}}$. Let $k \geq 0$ such that $\Pr_s^\sigma(\Box^{\leq k} S_?) < 1$ for all $s \in S_?$. Following the reasoning as in Sect. 3.1 we get

$$\Pr^\sigma(\lozenge^{\leq k} G) + \Pr^\sigma(\Box^{\leq k} S_?) \cdot \min_{s \in S_?} \frac{\Pr_s^\sigma(\lozenge^{\leq k} G)}{1 - \Pr_s^\sigma(\Box^{\leq k} S_?)} \leq \Pr^\sigma(\lozenge G) \leq \Pr^{\max}(\lozenge G).$$

Next, assume an upper bound $u \in \mathbb{R}$ with $\Pr_s^{\max}(\lozenge G) \leq u$ for all $s \in S_?$. For a scheduler $\sigma_{\max} \in \mathfrak{S}^{\mathcal{M}}$ that attains the maximal reachability probability, i.e., $\sigma_{\max} \in \arg\max_{\sigma \in \mathfrak{S}^{\mathcal{M}}} \Pr^\sigma(\lozenge \mathrm{G})$ it holds that

$$\begin{aligned}\Pr^{\max}(\lozenge G) = \Pr^{\sigma_{\max}}(\lozenge G) &\leq \Pr^{\sigma_{\max}}(\lozenge^{\leq k} G) + \Pr^{\sigma_{\max}}(\Box^{\leq k} S_?) \cdot u \\ &\leq \max_{\sigma \in \mathfrak{S}^{\mathcal{M}}} \big(\Pr^\sigma(\lozenge^{\leq k} G) + \Pr^\sigma(\Box^{\leq k} S_?) \cdot u\big).\end{aligned}$$

We obtain the following theorem which is the basis of our algorithm.

Theorem 4. *For MDP $\mathcal{M}$ let G, $S_?$, and u be as above. Assume $\sigma \in \mathfrak{S}^{\mathcal{M}}$ and $k \geq 0$ such that $\sigma \in \arg\max_{\sigma' \in \mathfrak{S}^{\mathcal{M}}} \Pr^{\sigma'}(\lozenge^{\leq k} \mathrm{G}) + \Pr^{\sigma'}(\Box^{\leq k} \mathrm{S}_?) \cdot \mathrm{u}$ and $\Pr_s^\sigma(\Box^{\leq k} S_?) < 1$ for all $s \in S_?$. We have*

$$\begin{aligned}&\Pr^\sigma(\lozenge^{\leq k} G) + \Pr^\sigma(\Box^{\leq k} S_?) \cdot \min_{s \in S_?} \frac{\Pr_s^\sigma(\lozenge^{\leq k} G)}{1 - \Pr_s^\sigma(\Box^{\leq k} S_?)} \\ \leq &\Pr^{\max}(\lozenge G) \leq \Pr^\sigma(\lozenge^{\leq k} G) + \Pr^\sigma(\Box^{\leq k} S_?) \cdot u.\end{aligned}$$

Similar to the results for MCs it also holds that $\Pr^{\max}(\lozenge G) \leq \max_{\sigma \in \mathfrak{S}^{\mathcal{M}}} \hat{u}_k^\sigma$ with

$$\hat{u}_k^\sigma := \Pr^\sigma(\lozenge^{\leq k} G) + \Pr^\sigma(\Box^{\leq k} S_?) \cdot \max_{s \in S_?} \frac{\Pr_s^\sigma(\lozenge^{\leq k} G)}{1 - \Pr_s^\sigma(\Box^{\leq k} S_?)}.$$

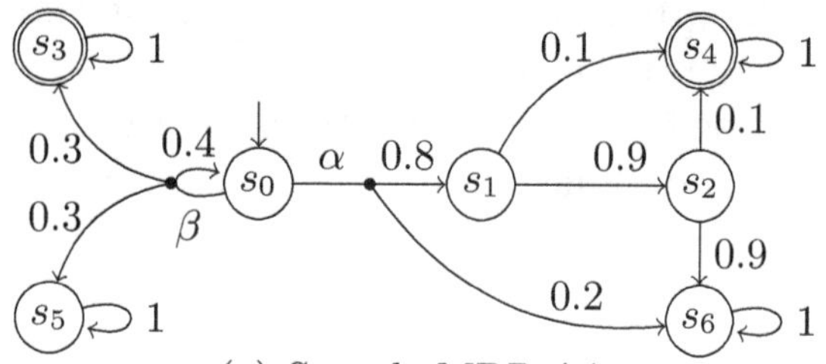

(a) Sample MDP $\mathcal{M}$.

	$\Pr^{\sigma_\alpha}_{s_0}$	$\Pr^{\sigma_{\beta\alpha}}_{s_0}$	$\Pr^{\sigma_{\beta\beta}}_{s_0}$	$\Pr^{\sigma}_{s_1}$	$\Pr^{\sigma}_{s_2}$
$\lozenge^{\leq 1} G$	0	0.3	0.3	0.1	0.1
$\Box^{\leq 1} S_?$	0.8	0.4	0.4	0.9	0
$\lozenge^{\leq 2} G$	0.1	0.3	0.42	0.1	0.1
$\Box^{\leq 2} S_?$	0.72	0.32	0.16	0	0

(b) Step bounded probabilities for $\mathcal{M}$.

Fig. 2. Example MDP with corresponding step bounded probabilities.

However, this upper bound can not trivially be embedded in a value iteration based procedure. Intuitively, in order to compute the upper bound for iteration k, one can not necessarily build on the results for iteration $k-1$.

Example 6. Consider the MDP $\mathcal{M}$ given in Fig. 2(a). Let $G = \{s_3, s_4\}$ be the set of goal states. We therefore have $S_? = \{s_0, s_1, s_2\}$. In Fig. 2(b) we list step bounded probabilities with respect to the possible schedulers, where σ_α, $\sigma_{\beta\alpha}$, and $\sigma_{\beta\beta}$ refer to schedulers with $\sigma_\alpha(s_0) = \alpha$ and for $\gamma \in \{\alpha, \beta\}$, $\sigma_{\beta\gamma}(s_0) = \beta$ and $\sigma_{\beta\gamma}(s_0 \beta s_0) = \gamma$. Notice that the probability measures $\Pr^\sigma_{s_1}$ and $\Pr^\sigma_{s_2}$ are independent of the considered scheduler σ. For step bounds $k \in \{1, 2\}$ we get

- $\max_{\sigma \in \mathfrak{S}^{\mathcal{M}}} \hat{u}^\sigma_1 = \hat{u}^{\sigma_\alpha}_1 = 0 + 0.8 \cdot \max(0, 1, 0) = 0.8$ and
- $\max_{\sigma \in \mathfrak{S}^{\mathcal{M}}} \hat{u}^\sigma_2 = \hat{u}^{\sigma_{\beta\beta}}_2 = 0.42 + 0.16 \cdot \max(0.5, 0.19, 1) = 0.5$.

4.2 Extending the Value Iteration Approach

The idea of our algorithm is to compute the bounds for $\Pr^{\max}(\lozenge G)$ as in Theorem 4 for increasing $k \geq 0$. Algorithm 2 outlines the procedure. Similar to Algorithm 1 for MCs, vectors $x_k, y_k \in \mathbb{R}^{|S|}$ store the step bounded probabilities $\Pr^{\sigma_k}_s(\lozenge^{\leq k} G)$ and $\Pr^{\sigma_k}_s(\Box^{\leq k} S_?)$ for any $s \in S$. In addition, schedulers σ_k and upper bounds $u_k \geq \max_{s \in S_?} \Pr^{\max}_s(\lozenge G)$ are computed in a way that Theorem 4 is applicable.

Lemma 3. *After executing k iterations of Algorithm 2 we have for all $s \in S_?$ that $x_k[s] = \Pr^{\sigma_k}_s(\lozenge^{\leq k} G)$, $y_k[s] = \Pr^{\sigma_k}_s(\Box^{\leq k} S_?)$, and $\ell_k \leq \Pr^{\max}_s(\lozenge G) \leq u_k$, where $\sigma_k \in \arg\max_{\sigma \in \mathfrak{S}^{\mathcal{M}}} \Pr^\sigma_s(\lozenge^{\leq k} G) + \Pr^\sigma_s(\Box^{\leq k} S_?) \cdot u_k$.*

The lemma holds for $k = 0$ as x_0, y_0, and u_0 are initialized accordingly. For $k > 0$ we assume that the claim holds after $k-1$ iterations, i.e., for x_{k-1}, y_{k-1}, u_{k-1} and scheduler σ_{k-1}. The results of the kth iteration are obtained as follows.

The function *findAction* illustrated in Algorithm 3 determines the choices of a scheduler $\sigma_k \in \arg\max_{\sigma \in \mathfrak{S}^{\mathcal{M}}} \Pr^\sigma_s(\lozenge^{\leq k} G) + \Pr^\sigma_s(\Box^{\leq k} S_?) \cdot u_{k-1}$ for $s \in S_?$. The idea is to consider at state s an action $\sigma_k(s) = \alpha \in Act(s)$ that maximizes

$$\Pr^{\sigma_k}_s(\lozenge^{\leq k} G) + \Pr^{\sigma_k}_s(\Box^{\leq k} S_?) \cdot u_{k-1} = \sum_{s' \in S} \mathbf{P}(s, \alpha, s') \cdot (x_{k-1}[s'] + y_{k-1}[s'] \cdot u_{k-1}).$$

Input : MDP $\mathcal{M} = (S, Act, \mathbf{P}, s_I, \rho)$, absorbing states $G \subseteq S$, precision $\varepsilon > 0$
Output : $r \in \mathbb{R}$ with $|r - \mathrm{Pr}^{\max}(\lozenge G)| < \varepsilon$

1 $S_0 \leftarrow \{s \in S \mid \mathrm{Pr}_s^{\max}(\lozenge G) = 0\}$
2 assert that $\mathcal{M}$ is contracting with respect to $G \cup S_0$
3 $S_? \leftarrow S \setminus (S_0 \cup G)$
4 initialize $x_0, y_0 \in \mathbb{R}^{|S|}$ with $x_0[G] = 1$, $x_0[S \setminus G] = 0$, $y_0[S_?] = 1$, $y_0[S \setminus S_?] = 0$
5 $\ell_0 \leftarrow -\infty$; $u_0 \leftarrow +\infty$; $d_0 \leftarrow -\infty$
6 $k \leftarrow 0$
7 **repeat**
8 $\quad k \leftarrow k + 1$
9 $\quad$ initialize $x_k, y_k \in \mathbb{R}^{|S|}$ with $x_k[G] = 1$, $x_k[S_0] = 0$, $y_k[S \setminus S_?] = 0$
10 $\quad d_k \leftarrow d_{k-1}$
11 $\quad$ **foreach** $s \in S_?$ **do**
12 $\quad\quad \alpha \leftarrow \mathit{findAction}(x_{k-1}, y_{k-1}, s, u_{k-1})$
13 $\quad\quad d_k \leftarrow \max(d_k, \mathit{decisionValue}(x_{k-1}, y_{k-1}, s, \alpha))$
14 $\quad\quad x_k[s] \leftarrow \sum_{s' \in S} \mathbf{P}(s, \alpha, s') \cdot x_{k-1}[s']$
15 $\quad\quad y_k[s] \leftarrow \sum_{s' \in S} \mathbf{P}(s, \alpha, s') \cdot y_{k-1}[s']$
16 $\quad$ **if** $y_k[s] < 1$ for all $s \in S_?$ **then**
17 $\quad\quad \ell_k \leftarrow \max(\ell_{k-1}, \min_{s \in S_?} \frac{x_k[s]}{1 - y_k[s]})$
18 $\quad\quad u_k \leftarrow \min(u_{k-1}, \max(d_k, \max_{, \in S_?} \frac{x_k[s]}{1 - y_k[s]}))$
19 **until** $y_k[s_I] \cdot (u_k - \ell_k) < 2 \cdot \varepsilon$
20 **return** $x_k[s_I] + y_k[s_I] \cdot \frac{\ell_k + u_k}{2}$

Algorithm 2: Sound value iteration for MDPs

For the case where no real upper bound is known (i.e., $u_{k-1} = \infty$) we implicitly assume a sufficiently large value for u_{k-1} such that $\mathrm{Pr}_s^{\sigma}(\lozenge^{\leq k} G)$ becomes negligible. Upon leaving state s, σ_k mimics σ_{k-1}, i.e., we set $\sigma_k(s\alpha s_1 \alpha_1 \ldots s_n) = \sigma_{k-1}(s_1 \alpha_1 \ldots s_n)$. After executing Line 15 of Algorithm 2 we have $x_k[s] = \mathrm{Pr}_s^{\sigma_k}(\lozenge^{\leq k} G)$ and $y_k[s] = \mathrm{Pr}_s^{\sigma_k}(\square^{\leq k} S_?)$.

It remains to derive an upper bound u_k. To ensure that Lemma 3 holds we require (i) $u_k \geq \max_{s \in S_?} \mathrm{Pr}_s^{\max}(\lozenge G)$ and (ii) $u_k \in U_k$, where

$$U_k = \{u \in \mathbb{R} \mid \sigma_k \in \arg\max_{\sigma \in \mathfrak{S}^{\mathcal{M}}} \mathrm{Pr}_s^{\sigma}(\lozenge^{\leq k} G) + \mathrm{Pr}_s^{\sigma}(\square^{\leq k} S_?) \cdot u \text{ for all } s \in S_?\}.$$

Intuitively, the set $U_k \subseteq \mathbb{R}$ consists of all possible upper bounds u for which σ_k is still optimal. $U_k \subseteq$ is convex as it can be represented as a conjunction of inequalities with $U_0 = \mathbb{R}$ and $u \in U_k$ if and only if $u \in U_{k-1}$ and for all $s \in S_?$ with $\sigma_k(s) = \alpha$ and for all $\beta \in Act(s) \setminus \{\alpha\}$

$$\sum_{s' \in S} \mathbf{P}(s, \alpha, s') \cdot (x_{k-1}[s'] + y_{k-1}[s'] \cdot u) \geq \sum_{s' \in S} \mathbf{P}(s, \beta, s') \cdot (x_{k-1}[s'] + y_{k-1}[s'] \cdot u).$$

The algorithm maintains the so-called *decision value* d_k which corresponds to the minimum of U_k (or $-\infty$ if the minimum does not exist). Algorithm 4 outlines the

```
function findAction(x, y, s, u)
    if u ≠ ∞ then
        return α ∈ argmax_{α∈Act(s)} Σ_{s'∈S} P(s, α, s') · (x[s'] + y[s'] · u)
    else
        return α ∈ argmax_{α∈Act(s)} Σ_{s'∈S} P(s, α, s') · (y[s'])
```

Algorithm 3: Computation of optimal action.

```
function decisionValue(x, y, s, α)
    d ← −∞
    foreach β ∈ Act(s) \ {α} do
        y_Δ ← Σ_{s'∈S} (P(s, α, s') − P(s, β, s')) · y[s']
        if y_Δ > 0 then
            x_Δ ← Σ_{s'∈S} (P(s, β, s') − P(s, α, s')) · x[s']
            d ← max(d, x_Δ/y_Δ)
    return d
```

Algorithm 4: Computation of decision value.

procedure to obtain the decision value at a given state. Our algorithm ensures that u_k is only set to a value in $[d_k, u_{k-1}] \subseteq U_k$.

Lemma 4. *After executing Line 18 of Algorithm 2:* $u_k \geq \max_{s \in S_?} \mathrm{Pr}_s^{\max}(\Diamond G)$.

To show that u_k is a valid upper bound, let $s_{\max} \in \arg\max_{\mathrm{s} \in \mathrm{S}_?} \mathrm{Pr}_{\mathrm{s}}^{\max}(\Diamond \mathrm{G})$ and $u^* = \mathrm{Pr}_{s_{\max}}^{\max}(\Diamond G)$. From Theorem 4, $u_{k-1} \geq u^*$, and $u_{k-1} \in U_k$ we get

$$u^* \leq \max_{\sigma \in \mathfrak{S}^{\mathcal{M}}} \mathrm{Pr}_{s_{\max}}^{\sigma}(\Diamond^{\leq k} G) + \mathrm{Pr}_{s_{\max}}^{\sigma}(\Box^{\leq k} S_?) \cdot u_{k-1}$$
$$= \mathrm{Pr}_{s_{\max}}^{\sigma_k}(\Diamond^{\leq k} G) + \mathrm{Pr}_{s_{\max}}^{\sigma_k}(\Box^{\leq k} S_?) \cdot u_{k-1} = x_k[s_{\max}] + y_k[s_{\max}] \cdot u_{k-1}$$

which yields a new upper bound $x_k[s_{\max}] + y_k[s_{\max}] \cdot u_{k-1} \geq u^*$. We repeat this scheme as follows. Let $v_0 := u_{k-1}$ and for $i > 0$ let $v_i := x_k[s_{\max}] + y_k[s_{\max}] \cdot v_{i-1}$. We can show that $v_{i-1} \in U_k$ implies $v_i \geq u^*$. Assuming $y_k[s_{\max}] < 1$, the sequence $v_0, v_1, v_2, \ldots$ converges to $v_\infty := \lim_{i \to \infty} v_i = \frac{x_k[s_{\max}]}{1 - y_k[s_{\max}]}$. We distinguish three cases to show that $u_k = \min(u_{k-1}, \max(d_k, \max_{s \in S_?} \frac{x_k[s]}{1 - y_k[s]})) \geq u^*$.

- If $v_\infty > u_{k-1}$, then also $\max_{s \in S_?} \frac{x_k[s]}{1 - y_k[s]} > u_{k-1}$. Hence $u_k = u_{k-1} \geq u^*$.
- If $d_k \leq v_\infty \leq u_{k-1}$, we can show that $v_i \leq v_{i-1}$. It follows that for all $i > 0$, $v_{i-1} \in U_k$, implying $v_i \geq u^*$. Thus we get $u_k = \max_{s \in S_?} \frac{x_k[s]}{1 - y_k[s]} \geq v_\infty \geq u^*$.
- If $v_\infty < d_k$ then there is an $i \geq 0$ with $v_i \geq d_k$ and $u^* \leq v_{i+1} < d_k$. It follows that $u_k = d_k \geq u^*$.

Example 7. Reconsider the MDP $\mathcal{M}$ from Fig. 2(a) and goal states $G = \{s_3, s_4\}$. The maximal reachability probability is attained for a scheduler that always chooses β at state s_0, which results in $\Pr^{\max}(\lozenge G) = 0.5$. We now illustrate how Algorithm 2 approximates this value by sketching the first two iterations. For the first iteration *findAction* yields action α at s_0. We obtain:

$$x_1[s_0] = 0,\ x_1[s_1] = 0.1,\ x_1[s_2] = 0.1,\ y_1[s_0] = 0.8,\ y_1[s_1] = 0.9,\ y_1[s_2] = 0,$$
$$d_1 = 0.3/(0.8 - 0.4) = 0.75,\ \ell_1 = \min(0, 1, 0) = 0,\ u_1 = \max(0.75, 0, 1, 0) = 1.$$

In the second iteration *findAction* yields again α for s_0 and we get:

$$x_2[s_0] = 0.08,\ x_2[s_1] = 0.19,\ x_2[s_2] = 0.1,\ y_2[s_0] = 0.72,\ y_2[s_1] = 0,\ y_2[s_2] = 0,$$
$$d_2 = 0.75,\ \ell_2 = \min(0.29, 0.19, 0.1) = 0.1,\ u_2 = \max(0.75, 0.29, 0.19, 0.1) = 0.75.$$

Due to the decision value we do not set the upper bound u_2 to $0.29 < \Pr^{\max}(\lozenge G)$.

Theorem 5. *Algorithm 2 terminates for any MDP $\mathcal{M}$, goal states G and precision $\varepsilon > 0$. The returned value r satisfies $|r - \Pr^{\max}(\lozenge G)| \leq \varepsilon$.*

The correctness of the algorithm follows from Theorem 4 and Lemma 3. Termination follows since $\mathcal{M}$ is contracting with respect to $S_0 \cup G$, implying $\lim_{k\to\infty} \Pr^{\sigma}(\square^{\leq k} S_?) = 0$. The optimizations for Algorithm 1 mentioned in Sect. 3.4 can be applied to Algorithm 2 as well.

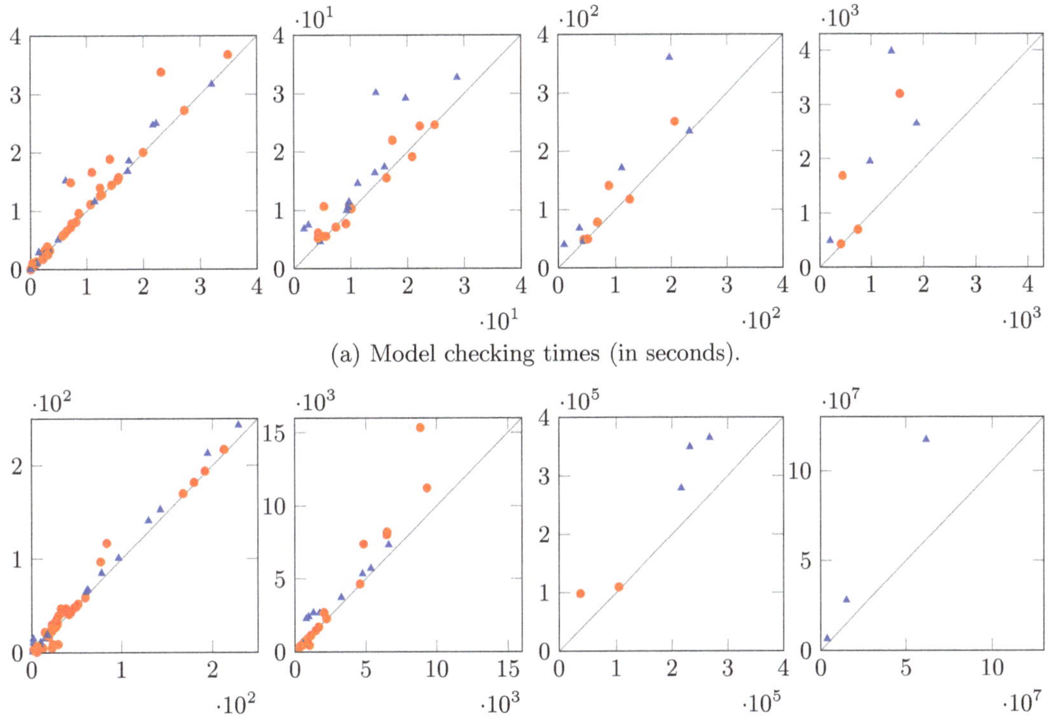

(a) Model checking times (in seconds).

(b) Required iterations.

Fig. 3. Comparison of sound value iteration (x-axis) and interval iteration (y-axis).

5 Experimental Evaluation

Implementation. We implemented sound value iteration for MCs and MDPs into the model checker `Storm` [8]. The implementation computes reachability probabilities and expected rewards using explicit data structures such as sparse matrices and vectors. Moreover, Multi-objective model checking is supported, where we straightforwardly extend the value iteration-based approach of [22] to sound value iteration. We also implemented the optimizations given in Sect. 3.4.

The implementation is available at www.stormchecker.org.

Experimental Results. We considered a wide range of case studies including

- all MCs, MDPs, and CTMCs from the `PRISM` benchmark suite [23],
- several case studies from the `PRISM` website www.prismmodelchecker.org,
- Markov automata accompanying `IMCA` [24], and
- multi-objective MDPs considered in [22].

In total, 130 model and property instances were considered. For CTMCs and Markov automata we computed (untimed) reachability probabilities or expected rewards on the underlying MC and the underlying MDP, respectively. In all experiments the precision parameter was given by $\varepsilon = 10^{-6}$.

We compare sound value iteration (SVI) with interval iteration (II) as presented in [12,13]. We consider the Gauss-Seidel variant of the approaches and compute initial bounds ℓ_0 and u_0 as in [12]. For a better comparison we consider the implementation of II in `Storm`. [21] gives a comparison with the implementation of II in `PRISM`. The experiments were run on a single core (2GHz) of an HP BL685C G7 with 192GB of available memory. However, almost all experiments required less than 4GB. We measured model checking times and required iterations. All logfiles and considered benchmarks are available at [25].

Figure 3(a) depicts the model checking times for SVI (x-axis) and II (y-axis). For better readability, the benchmarks are divided into four plots with different scales. Triangles (▲) and circles (●) indicate MC and MDP benchmarks, respectively. Similarly, Fig. 3(b) shows the required iterations of the approaches. We observe that SVI converged faster and required fewer iterations for almost all MCs and MDPs. SVI performed particularly well on the challenging instances where many iterations are required. Similar observations were made when comparing the topological variants of SVI and II. Both approaches were still competitive if no a priori bounds are given to SVI. More details are given in [21].

Figure 4 indicates the model checking times of SVI and II as well as their topological variants. For reference, we also consider standard (unsound) value iteration (VI). The x-axis depicts the number of instances that have been solved by the corresponding approach within the time limit indicated on the y-axis. Hence, a point (x, y) means that for x instances the model checking time was less or equal than y. We observe that the topological variant of SVI yielded the best run times among all sound approaches and even competes with (unsound) VI.

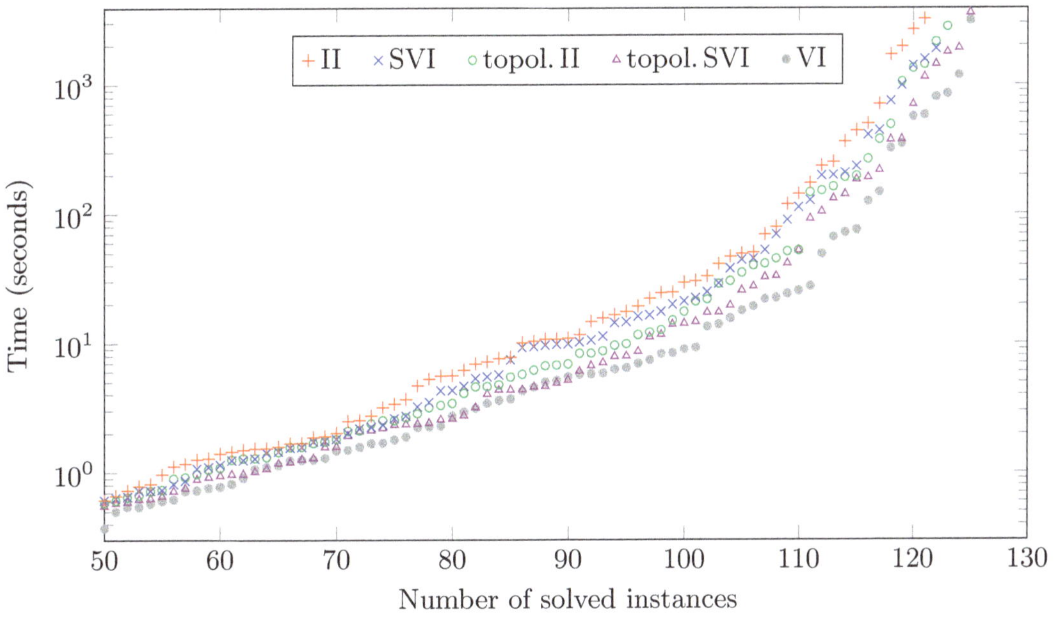

Fig. 4. Runtime comparison between different approaches.

6 Conclusion

In this paper we presented a sound variant of the value iteration algorithm which safely approximates reachability probabilities and expected rewards in MCs and MDPs. Experiments on a large set of benchmarks indicate that our approach is a reasonable alternative to the recently proposed interval iteration algorithm.

References

1. Puterman, M.L.: Markov Decision Processes: Discrete Stochastic Dynamic Programming. Wiley, Hoboken (1994)
2. Feinberg, E.A., Shwartz, A.: Handbook of Markov Decision Processes: Methods and Applications. Kluwer, Dordrecht (2002)
3. Katoen, J.P.: The probabilistic model checking landscape. In: LICS, pp. 31–45. ACM (2016)
4. Baier, C.: Probabilistic model checking. In: Dependable Software Systems Engineering. NATO Science for Peace and Security Series - D: Information and Communication Security, vol. 45, pp. 1–23. IOS Press (2016)
5. Etessami, K.: Analysis of probabilistic processes and automata theory. In: Handbook of Automata Theory. European Mathematical Society (2016, to appear)
6. Baier, C., de Alfaro, L., Forejt, V., Kwiatkowska, M.: Probabilistic model checking. In: Clarke, E., Henzinger, T., Veith, H., Bloem, R. (eds.) Handbook of Model Checking, pp. 963–999. Springer, Cham (2018)
7. Kwiatkowska, M., Norman, G., Parker, D.: PRISM 4.0: verification of probabilistic real-time systems. In: Gopalakrishnan, G., Qadeer, S. (eds.) CAV 2011. LNCS, vol. 6806, pp. 585–591. Springer, Heidelberg (2011). https://doi.org/10.1007/978-3-642-22110-1_47

8. Dehnert, C., Junges, S., Katoen, J.-P., Volk, M.: A STORM is coming: a modern probabilistic model checker. In: Majumdar, R., Kunčak, V. (eds.) CAV 2017. LNCS, vol. 10427, pp. 592–600. Springer, Cham (2017). https://doi.org/10.1007/978-3-319-63390-9_31
9. Katoen, J., Zapreev, I.S.: Safe on-the-fly steady-state detection for time-bounded reachability. In: QEST, pp. 301–310. IEEE Computer Society (2006)
10. Malhotra, M.: A computationally efficient technique for transient analysis of repairable markovian systems. Perform. Eval. **24**(4), 311–331 (1996)
11. Daca, P., Henzinger, T.A., Kretínský, J., Petrov, T.: Faster statistical model checking for unbounded temporal properties. ACM Trans. Comput. Log. **18**(2), 12:1–12:25 (2017)
12. Baier, C., Klein, J., Leuschner, L., Parker, D., Wunderlich, S.: Ensuring the reliability of your model checker: interval iteration for markov decision processes. In: Majumdar, R., Kunčak, V. (eds.) CAV 2017. LNCS, vol. 10426, pp. 160–180. Springer, Cham (2017). https://doi.org/10.1007/978-3-319-63387-9_8
13. Haddad, S., Monmege, B.: Interval iteration algorithm for MDPs and IMDPs. Theor. Comput. Sci. **735**, 111–131 (2017)
14. Dai, P., Weld, D.S., Goldsmith, J.: Topological value iteration algorithms. J. Artif. Intell. Res. **42**, 181–209 (2011)
15. Baier, C., Katoen, J.P.: Principles of Model Checking. The MIT Press, Cambridge (2008)
16. Bertsekas, D.P., Tsitsiklis, J.N.: An analysis of stochastic shortest path problems. Math. Oper. Res. **16**(3), 580–595 (1991)
17. Giro, S.: Efficient computation of exact solutions for quantitative model checking. In: QAPL. EPTCS, vol. 85, pp. 17–32 (2012)
18. Bauer, M.S., Mathur, U., Chadha, R., Sistla, A.P., Viswanathan, M.: Exact quantitative probabilistic model checking through rational search. In: FMCAD, pp. 92–99. IEEE (2017)
19. Brázdil, T., et al.: Verification of Markov decision processes using learning algorithms. In: Cassez, F., Raskin, J.-F. (eds.) ATVA 2014. LNCS, vol. 8837, pp. 98–114. Springer, Cham (2014). https://doi.org/10.1007/978-3-319-11936-6_8
20. Haddad, S., Monmege, B.: Reachability in MDPs: refining convergence of value iteration. In: Ouaknine, J., Potapov, I., Worrell, J. (eds.) RP 2014. LNCS, vol. 8762, pp. 125–137. Springer, Cham (2014). https://doi.org/10.1007/978-3-319-11439-2_10
21. Quatmann, T., Katoen, J.P.: Sound value iteration. Technical report, CoRR abs/1804.05001 (2018)
22. Forejt, V., Kwiatkowska, M., Parker, D.: Pareto curves for probabilistic model checking. In: Chakraborty, S., Mukund, M. (eds.) ATVA 2012. LNCS, pp. 317–332. Springer, Heidelberg (2012). https://doi.org/10.1007/978-3-642-33386-6_25
23. Kwiatkowska, M., Norman, G., Parker, D.: The PRISM benchmark suite. In: Proceedings of QEST, pp. 203–204. IEEE CS (2012)
24. Guck, D., Timmer, M., Hatefi, H., Ruijters, E., Stoelinga, M.: Modelling and analysis of markov reward automata. In: Cassez, F., Raskin, J.-F. (eds.) ATVA 2014. LNCS, vol. 8837, pp. 168–184. Springer, Cham (2014). https://doi.org/10.1007/978-3-319-11936-6_13
25. Quatmann, T., Katoen, J.P.: Experimental Results for Sound Value Iteration. figshare (2018). https://doi.org/10.6084/m9.figshare.6139052

Safety-Aware Apprenticeship Learning

Weichao Zhou and Wenchao Li(✉)

Department of Electrical and Computer Engineering, Boston University, Boston, USA
{zwc662,wenchao}@bu.edu

Abstract. Apprenticeship learning (AL) is a kind of Learning from Demonstration techniques where the reward function of a Markov Decision Process (MDP) is unknown to the learning agent and the agent has to derive a good policy by observing an expert's demonstrations. In this paper, we study the problem of how to make AL algorithms inherently safe while still meeting its learning objective. We consider a setting where the unknown reward function is assumed to be a linear combination of a set of state features, and the safety property is specified in Probabilistic Computation Tree Logic (PCTL). By embedding probabilistic model checking inside AL, we propose a novel *counterexample-guided* approach that can ensure safety while retaining performance of the learnt policy. We demonstrate the effectiveness of our approach on several challenging AL scenarios where safety is essential.

1 Introduction

The rapid progress of artificial intelligence (AI) comes with a growing concern over its safety when deployed in real-life systems and situations. As highlighted in [3], if the objective function of an AI agent is wrongly specified, then maximizing that objective function may lead to harmful results. In addition, the objective function or the training data may focus only on accomplishing a specific task and ignore other aspects, such as safety constraints, of the environment. In this paper, we propose a novel framework that combines explicit safety specification with learning from data. We consider safety specification expressed in Probabilistic Computation Tree Logic (PCTL) and show how probabilistic model checking can be used to ensure safety and retain performance of a learning algorithm known as *apprenticeship learning* (AL).

We consider the formulation of apprenticeship learning by Abbeel and Ng [1]. The concept of AL is closely related to *reinforcement learning* (RL) where an agent learns what actions to take in an environment (known as a policy) by maximizing some notion of long-term reward. In AL, however, the agent is not given the reward function, but instead has to first estimate it from a set of expert demonstrations via a technique called *inverse reinforcement learning* [18]. The formulation assumes that the reward function is expressible as a linear combination of *known state features*. An expert demonstrates the task by maximizing this reward function and the agent tries to derive a policy that can match the feature expectations of the expert's demonstrations. Apprenticeship learning can also be

H. Chockler and G. Weissenbacher (Eds.): CAV 2018, LNCS 10981, pp. 662–680, 2018.
https://doi.org/10.1007/978-3-319-96145-3_38

viewed as an instance of the class of techniques known as Learning from Demonstration (LfD). One issue with LfD is that *the expert often can only demonstrate how the task works but not how the task may fail.* This is because failure may cause irrecoverable damages to the system such as crashing a vehicle. In general, the lack of "negative examples" can cause a heavy bias in how the learning agent constructs the reward estimate. In fact, *even if all the demonstrations are safe, the agent may still end up learning an unsafe policy.*

The key idea of this paper is to incorporate formal verification in apprenticeship learning. We are inspired by the line of work on formal inductive synthesis [10] and counterexample-guided inductive synthesis [22]. Our approach is also similar in spirit to the recent work on safety-constrained reinforcement learning [11]. However, our approach uses the results of model checking in a novel way. We consider safety specification expressed in probabilistic computation tree logic (PCTL). We employ a verification-in-the-loop approach by embedding PCTL model checking as a safety checking mechanism inside the learning phase of AL. In particular, when a learnt policy does not satisfy the PCTL formula, we leverage counterexamples generated by the model checker to steer the policy search in AL. In essence, counterexample generation can be viewed as supplementing negative examples for the learner. Thus, the learner will try to find a policy that not only imitates the expert's demonstrations but also stays away from the failure scenarios as captured by the counterexamples.

In summary, we make the following contributions in this paper.

- We propose a novel framework for incorporating formal safety guarantees in Learning from Demonstration.
- We develop a novel algorithm called CounterExample Guided Apprenticeship Learning (CEGAL) that combines probabilistic model checking with the optimization-based approach of apprenticeship learning.
- We demonstrate that our approach can guarantee safety for a set of case studies and attain performance comparable to that of using apprenticeship learning alone.

The rest of the paper is organized as follows. Section 2 reviews background information on apprenticeship learning and PCTL model checking. Section 3 defines the safety-aware apprenticeship learning problem and gives an overview of our approach. Section 4 illustrates the counterexample-guided learning framework. Section 5 describes the proposed algorithm in detail. Section 6 presents a set of experimental results demonstrating the effectiveness of our approach. Section 7 discusses related work. Section 8 concludes and offers future directions.

2 Preliminaries

2.1 Markov Decision Process and Discrete-Time Markov Chain

Markov Decision Process (MDP) is a tuple $M = (S, A, T, \gamma, s_0, R)$, where S is a finite set of states; A is a set of actions; $T : S \times A \times S \rightarrow [0, 1]$ is a transition function describing the probability of transitioning from one state $s \in S$ to another state by taking action $a \in A$ in state s; $R : S \to \mathbb{R}$ is a reward function which maps each state $s \in S$ to a real number indicating the reward of being in state s; $s_0 \in S$ is the initial state; $\gamma \in [0, 1)$ is a discount factor which describes how future rewards attenuate when a sequence of transitions is made. A deterministic and stationary (or memoryless) policy $\pi : S \to A$ for an MDP M is a mapping from states to actions, i.e. the policy deterministically selects what action to take solely based on the current state. In this paper, we restrict ourselves to deterministic and stationary policy. A policy π for an MDP M induces a Discrete-Time Markov Chain (DTMC) $M_\pi = (S, T_\pi, s_0)$, where $T_\pi : S \times S \to [0, 1]$ is the probability of transitioning from a state s to another state in one step. A trajectory $\tau = s_0 \xrightarrow{T_\pi(s_0,s_1)>0} s_1 \xrightarrow{T_\pi(s_1,s_2)>0} s_2, \ldots,$ is a sequence of states where $s_i \in S$. The accumulated reward of τ is $\sum\limits_{i=0}^{\infty} \gamma^i R(s_i)$. The value function $V_\pi : S \to \mathbb{R}$ measures the expectation of accumulated reward $E[\sum\limits_{i=0}^{\infty} \gamma^i R(s_i)]$ starting from a state s and following policy π. An *optimal policy* π for MDP M is a policy that maximizes the value function [4].

2.2 Apprenticeship Learning via Inverse Reinforcement Learning

Inverse reinforcement learning (IRL) aims at recovering the reward function R of $M \backslash R = (S, A, T, \gamma, s_0)$ from a set of m trajectories $\Gamma_E = \{\tau_0, \tau_1, \ldots, \tau_{m-1}\}$ demonstrated by an expert. *Apprenticeship learning (AL)* [1] assumes that the reward function is a linear combination of state features, i.e. $R(s) = \omega^T f(s)$ where $f : S \to [0,\ 1]^k$ is a vector of known features over states S and $\omega \in \mathbb{R}^k$ is an unknown weight vector that satisfies $||\omega||_2 \leq 1$. The expected features of a policy π are the expected values of the cumulative discounted state features $f(s)$ by following π on M, i.e. $\mu_\pi = E[\sum_{t=0}^{\infty} \gamma^t f(s_t)|\pi]$. Let μ_E denote the expected features of the unknown expert's policy π_E. μ_E can be approximated by the expected features of expert's m demonstrated trajectories $\hat{\mu}_E = \frac{1}{m} \sum\limits_{\tau \in \Gamma_E} \sum\limits_{t=0}^{\infty} \gamma^t f(s_t)$ if m is large enough. With a slight abuse of notations, we use μ_Γ to also denote the expected features of a set of paths Γ. Given an error bound ϵ, a policy π^* is defined to be *ϵ-close* to π_E if its expected features μ_{π^*} satisfies $||\mu_E - \mu_{\pi^*}||_2 \leq \epsilon$. The expected features of a policy can be calculated by using Monte Carlo method, value iteration or linear programming [1,4].

The algorithm proposed by Abbeel and Ng [1] starts with a random policy π_0 and its expected features μ_{π_0}. Assuming that in iteration i, a set of i candidate policies $\Pi = \{\pi_0, \pi_1, \ldots, \pi_{i-1}\}$ and their corresponding expected features $\{\mu_\pi | \pi \in \Pi\}$ have been found, the algorithm solves the following optimization problem.

$$\delta = \max_{\omega} \min_{\pi \in \Pi} \ \omega^T(\hat{\mu}_E - \mu_\pi) \qquad s.t.\ ||\omega||_2 \leq 1 \tag{1}$$

The optimal ω is used to find the corresponding optimal policy π_i and the expected features μ_{π_i}. If $\delta \leq \epsilon$, then the algorithm terminates and π_i is produced as the output. Otherwise, μ_{π_i} is added to the set of features for the candidate policy set Π and the algorithm continues to the next iteration.

2.3 PCTL Model Checking

Probabilistic model checking can be used to verify properties of a stochastic system such as "is the probability that the agent reaches the unsafe area within 10 steps smaller than 5%?". *Probabilistic Computation Tree Logic* (PCTL) [7] allows for probabilistic quantification of properties. The syntax of PCTL includes state formulas and path formulas [13]. A state formula ϕ asserts property of a single state $s \in S$ whereas a path formula ψ asserts property of a trajectory.

$$\phi ::= \ true \mid l_i \mid \neg\phi_i \mid \phi_i \wedge \phi_j \mid P_{\bowtie p^*}[\psi] \tag{2}$$

$$\psi ::= \ \mathbf{X}\phi \mid \phi_1 \mathbf{U}^{\leq k}\phi_2 \mid \phi_1 \mathbf{U} \phi_2 \tag{3}$$

where l_i is atomic proposition and ϕ_i, ϕ_j are state formulas; $\bowtie \in \{\leq, \geq, <, >\}$; $P_{\bowtie p^*}[\psi]$ means that the probability of generating a trajectory that satisfies formula ψ is $\bowtie p^*$. $\mathbf{X}\phi$ asserts that the next state after initial state in the trajectory satisfies ϕ; $\phi_1\, \mathbf{U}^{\leq k}\, \phi_2$ asserts that ϕ_2 is satisfied in at most k transitions and all preceding states satisfy ϕ_1; $\phi_1\, \mathbf{U}\, \phi_2$ asserts that ϕ_2 will be eventually satisfied and all preceding states satisfy ϕ_1. The semantics of PCTL is defined by a satisfaction relation $\models$ as follows.

$$s \models true \ \text{ iff state } s \in S \tag{4}$$

$$s \models \ \phi \ \text{ iff state s satisfies the state formula } \phi \tag{5}$$

$$\tau \models \ \psi \ \text{ iff trajectory } \tau \text{ satisfies the path formula } \psi. \tag{6}$$

Additionally, $\models_{min}$ denotes the minimal satisfaction relation [6] between τ and ψ. Defining $pref(\tau)$ as the set of all prefixes of trajectory τ including τ itself, then $\tau \models_{min} \psi$ iff $(\tau \models \psi) \wedge (\forall \tau' \in pref(\tau) \backslash \tau, \tau' \not\models \psi)$. For instance, if $\psi = \phi_1\, \mathbf{U}^{\leq k}\, \phi_2$, then for any finite trajectory $\tau \models_{min} \phi_1 \mathbf{U}^{\leq k} \phi_2$, only the final state in τ satisfies ϕ_2. Let $P(\tau)$ be the probability of transitioning along a trajectory τ and let Γ_ψ be the set of all finite trajectories that satisfy $\tau \models_{min} \psi$, the value of PCTL property ψ is defined as $P_{=?|s_0}[\psi] = \sum\limits_{\tau \in \Gamma_\psi} P(\tau)$. For a DTMC M_π and a state formula $\phi = P_{\leq p^*}[\psi]$, $M_\pi \models \phi$ iff $P_{=?|s_0}[\psi] \leq p^*$.

A *counterexample* of ϕ is a set $cex \subseteq \Gamma_\psi$ that satisfies $\sum\limits_{\tau \in cex} P(\tau) > p^*$. Let $\mathbb{P}(\Gamma) = \sum\limits_{\tau \in \Gamma} P(\tau)$ be the sum of probabilities of all trajectories in a set Γ. Let $CEX_\phi \subseteq 2^{\Gamma_\psi}$ be the set of all counterexamples for a formula ϕ such that $(\forall cex \in CEX_\phi, \mathbb{P}(cex) > p^*)$ and $(\forall \Gamma \in 2^{\Gamma_\psi} \backslash CEX_\phi, \mathbb{P}(\Gamma) \leq p^*)$. A *minimal counterexample* is a set $cex \in CEX_\phi$ such that $\forall cex' \in CEX_\phi, |cex| \leq |cex'|$. By converting DTMC M_π into a weighted directed graph, counterexample can be found by solving a k-shortest paths (KSP) problem or a hop-constrained KSP (HKSP) problem [6]. Alternatively, counterexamples can be found by using Satisfiability Modulo Theory solving or mixed integer linear programming to determine the minimal critical subsystems that capture the counterexamples in M_π [23].

A policy can also be synthesized by solving the objective $\underset{\pi}{min}\ P_{=?}[\psi]$ for an MDP M. This problem can be solved by linear programming or policy iteration (and value iteration for step-bounded reachability) [14].

3 Problem Formulation and Overview

Suppose there are some unsafe states in an $MDP\backslash RM = (S, A, T, \gamma, s_0)$. A safety issue in apprenticeship learning means that an agent following the learnt policy would have a higher probability of entering those unsafe states than it should. There are multiple reasons that can give rise to this issue. First, it is possible that the expert policy π_E itself has a high probability of reaching the unsafe states. Second, human experts often tend to perform only successful demonstrations that do not highlight the unwanted situations [21]. This *lack of negative examples* in the training set can cause the learning agent to be unaware of the existence of those unsafe states.

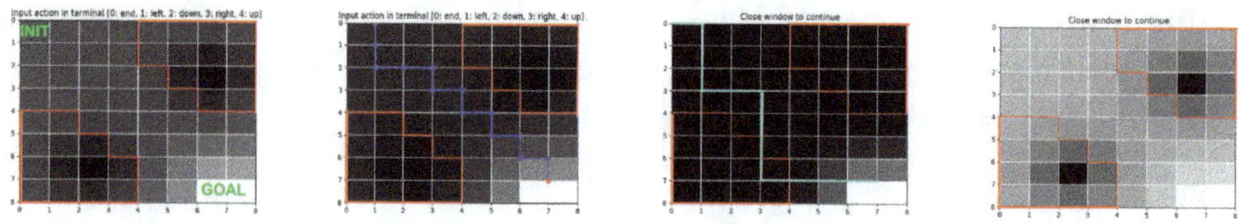

(a) (b) (c) (d)

Fig. 1. The 8×8 grid-world. (a) Lighter grid cells have higher rewards than the darker ones. The two black grid cells have the lowest rewards, while the two white ones have the highest rewards. The grid cells enclosed by red lines are considered *unsafe*. (b) The blue line is an example trajectory demonstrated by the expert. (c) Only the goal states are assigned high rewards and there is little difference between the unsafe states and their nearby states. As a result, the learnt policy has a high probability of passing through the unsafe states as indicated by the cyan line. (d) $p^* = 20\%$. The learnt policy is optimal to a reward function that correctly assigns low rewards to the unsafe states. (Color figure online)

We use a 8×8 grid-world navigation example as shown in Fig. 1 to illustrate this problem. An agent starts from the upper-left corner and moves from cell to cell until it reaches the lower-right corner. The 'unsafe' cells are enclosed by the red lines. These represent regions that the agent should avoid. In each step, the agent can choose to stay in current cell or move to an adjacent cell but with 20% chance of moving randomly instead of following its decision. The goal area, the unsafe area and the reward mapping for all states are shown in Fig. 1(a). For each state $s \in S$, its feature vector consists of 4 radial basis feature functions with respect to the squared Euclidean distances between s and the 4 states with the highest or lowest rewards as shown in Fig. 1(a). In addition, a specification

Φ formalized in PCTL is used to capture the safety requirement. In (7), p^* is the required upper bound of the probability of reaching an unsafe state within $t = 64$ steps.

$$\Phi ::= P_{\leq p^*}[\texttt{true}\ \mathbf{U}^{\leq t}\ \texttt{unsafe}] \tag{7}$$

Let π_E be the optimal policy under the reward map shown in Fig. 1(a). The probability of entering an unsafe region within 64 steps by following π_E is 24.6%. Now consider the scenario where the expert performs a number of demonstrations by following π_E. *All demonstrated trajectories in this case successfully reach the goal areas without ever passing through any of the unsafe regions.* Figure 1(b) shows a representative trajectory (in blue) among 10, 000 such demonstrated trajectories. The resulting reward map by running the AL algorithm on these 10,000 demonstrations is shown in Fig. 1(c). Observe that only the goal area has been learnt whereas the agent is oblivious to the unsafe regions (treating them in the same way as other dark cells). In fact, the probability of reaching an unsafe state within 64 steps with this policy turns out to be 82.6% (thus violating the safety requirement by a large margin). To make matters worse, the value of p^* may be decided or revised after a policy has been learnt. In those cases, even the original expert policy π_E may be unsafe, e.g., when $p^* = 20\%$. Thus, we need to adapt the original AL algorithm so that it will take into account of such safety requirement. Figure 1(d) shows the resulting reward map learned using our proposed algorithm (to be described in detail later) for $p^* = 20\%$. It clearly matches well with the color differentiation in the original reward map and captures both the goal states and the unsafe regions. This policy has an unsafe probability of 19.0%. We are now ready to state our problem.

Definition 1. ***The safety-aware apprenticeship learning (SafeAL) problem*** *is, given an MDP\R, a set of m trajectories $\{\tau_0, \tau_1, \ldots, \tau_{m-1}\}$ demonstrated by an expert, and a specification Φ, to learn a policy π that satisfies Φ and is ϵ-close to the expert policy π_E.*

Remark 1. We note that a solution may not always exist for the SafeAL problem. While the decision problem of checking whether a solution exists is of theoretical interest, in this paper, we focus on tackling the problem of finding a policy π that satisfies a PCTL formula Φ (if Φ is satisfiable) and whose performance is as close to that of the expert's as possible, i.e. we relax the condition on μ_π being ϵ-close to μ_E.

4 A Framework for Safety-Aware Learning

In this section, we describe a general framework for safety-aware learning. This novel framework utilizes information from both the expert demonstrations and a verifier. The proposed framework is illustrated in Fig. 2. Similar to the *counterexample-guided inductive synthesis* (CEGIS) paradigm [22], our framework consists of a *verifier* and a *learner*. The verifier checks if a candidate policy satisfies the safety specification Φ. In case Φ is not satisfied, the verifier generates a counterexample for Φ. The main difference from CEGIS is that our framework considers not only functional correctness, e.g., safety, but also performance (as captured by the learning objective). Starting from an initial policy π_0, each time the learner learns a new policy, the verifier checks if the specification is satisfied. If true, then this policy is added to the candidate set, otherwise the verifier will generate a (minimal) counterexample and add it to the counterexample set. During the learning phase, the learner uses both the counterexample set and candidate set to find a policy that is close to the (unknown) expert policy and far away from the counterexamples. The goal is to find a policy that is ϵ-close to the expert policy and satisfies the specification. For the grid-world example introduced in Sect. 3, when $p^* = 5\%$ (thus presenting a stricter safety requirement compared to the expert policy π_E), our approach produces a policy with only 4.2% of reaching an unsafe state within 64 steps (with the correspondingly inferred reward mapping shown in Fig. 1(d)).

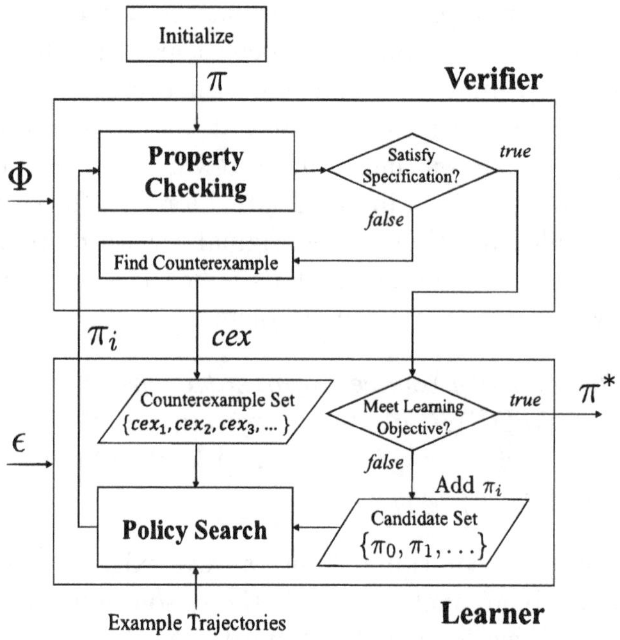

Fig. 2. Our safety-aware learning framework. Given an initial policy π_0, a specification Φ and a learning objective (as captured by ϵ), the framework iterates between a *verifier* and a *learner* to search for a policy π^* that satisfies both Φ and ϵ. One invariant that this framework maintains is that all the π_i's in the candidate policy set satisfy Φ.

Learning from a (minimal) counterexample cex_π of a policy π is similar to learning from expert demonstrations. The basic principle of the AL algorithm proposed in [1] is to find a weight vector ω under which the expected reward of π_E maximally outperforms any mixture of the policies in the candidate policy set $\Pi = \{\pi_0, \pi_1, \pi_2, \ldots\}$. Thus, ω can be viewed as the normal vector of the hyperplane $\omega^T(\mu - \mu_E) = 0$ that has the maximal distance to the convex hull of the set $\{\mu_\pi \mid \pi \in \Pi\}$ as illustrated in the 2D feature space in Fig. 3(a). It can be shown

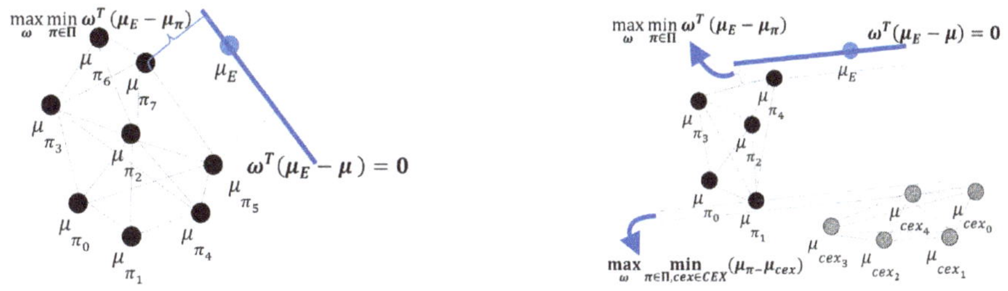

(a) (b)

Fig. 3. (a) Learn from expert. (b) Learn from both expert demonstrations and counterexamples.

that $\omega^T \mu_\pi \geq \omega^T \mu_{\pi'}$ for all previously found π's. Intuitively, this helps to move the candidate μ_π closer to μ_E. Similarly, we can apply the same max-margin separation principle to maximize the distance between the candidate policies and the counterexamples (in the μ space). Let $CEX = \{cex_0, cex_1, cex_2, ...\}$ denote the set of counterexamples of the policies that do not satisfy the specification Φ. Maximizing the distance between the convex hulls of the sets $\{\mu_{cex} | cex \in CEX\}$ and $\{\mu_\pi \mid \pi \in \Pi\}$ is equivalent to maximizing the distance between the parallel supporting hyperplanes of the two convex hulls as shown in Fig. 3(b). The corresponding optimization function is given in Eq. (8).

$$\delta = \max_{\omega} \min_{\pi \in \Pi, cex \in CEX} \omega^T(\mu_\pi - \mu_{cex}) \qquad s.t. \ ||\omega||_2 \leq 1 \tag{8}$$

To attain good performance similar to that of the expert, we still want to learn from μ_E. Thus, the overall problem can be formulated as a multi-objective optimization problem that combines (1) and (8) into (9).

$$\max_{\omega} \min_{\pi \in \Pi, \tilde{\pi} \in \Pi, cex \in CEX} (\omega^T(\mu_E - \mu_\pi), \ \omega^T(\mu_{\tilde{\pi}} - \mu_{cex})) \qquad s.t. \ ||\omega||_2 \leq 1 \tag{9}$$

5 Counterexample-Guided Apprenticeship Learning

In this section, we introduce the CounterExample Guided Apprenticeship Learning (CEGAL) algorithm to solve the SafeAL problem. It can be viewed as a special case of the safety-aware learning framework described in the previous section. In addition to combining policy verification, counterexample generation and AL, our approach uses an adaptive weighting scheme to weight the separation from μ_E with the separation from μ_{cex}.

$$\max_{\omega} \min_{\pi \in \Pi_S, \tilde{\pi} \in \Pi_S, cex \in CEX} \omega^T(k(\mu_E - \mu_\pi) + (1-k)(\mu_{\tilde{\pi}} - \mu_{cex})) \tag{10}$$

$$\begin{aligned} s.t. \ & ||\omega||_2 \leq 1, \ k \in [0, 1] \\ & \omega^T(\mu_E - \mu_\pi) \leq \omega^T(\mu_E - \mu_{\pi'}), \ \forall \pi' \in \Pi_S \\ & \omega^T(\mu_{\tilde{\pi}} - \mu_{cex}) \leq \omega^T(\mu_{\tilde{\pi}'} - \mu_{cex'}), \ \forall \tilde{\pi}' \in \Pi_S, \forall cex' \in CEX \end{aligned}$$

In essence, we take a weighted-sum approach for solving the multi-objective optimization problem (9). Assuming that $\Pi_S = \{\pi_1, \pi_2, \pi_3, \ldots\}$ is a set of candidate policies that all satisfy Φ, $CEX = \{cex_1, cex_2, cex_3, \ldots\}$ is a set of counterexamples. We introduce a parameter k and change (9) into a weighted sum optimization problem (10). Note that π and $\tilde{\pi}$ can be different. The optimal ω solved from (10) can be used to generate a new policy π_ω by using algorithms such as policy iteration. We use a probabilistic model checker, such as PRISM [13], to check if π_ω satisfies Φ. If it does, then it will be added to Π_S. Otherwise, a counterexample generator, such as COMICS [9], is used to generate a (minimal) counterexample cex_{π_ω}, which will be added to CEX.

Algorithm 1. Counterexample-Guided Apprenticeship Learning (CEGAL)

Input:
  $M \leftarrow$ A partially known $MDP \backslash R$; $f \leftarrow$ A vector of feature functions
  $\mu_E \leftarrow$ The expected features of expert trajectories $\{\tau_0, \tau_1, \ldots, \tau_m\}$
  $\Phi \leftarrow$ Specification; $\epsilon \leftarrow$ Error bound for the expected features;
  $\sigma, \alpha \in (0, 1) \leftarrow$ Error bound σ and step length α for the parameter k;
Initialization:
  If $||\mu_E - \mu_{\pi_0}||_2 \leq \epsilon$, **then return** π_0 ▷ π_0 is the **initial safe policy**
  $\Pi_S \leftarrow \{\pi_0\}$, $CEX \leftarrow \emptyset$ ▷ Initialize candidate and counterexample set
  $inf \leftarrow 0, sup \leftarrow 1, k \leftarrow sup$ ▷ Initialize multi-optimization parameter k
  $\pi_1 \leftarrow$ Policy learnt from μ_E via apprenticeship learning
Iteration i $(i \geq 1)$:
  Verifier:
    status $\leftarrow Model\_Checker(M, \pi_i, \Phi)$
    If status = SAT, **then go to Learner**
    If status = UNSAT
      $cex_{\pi_i} \leftarrow Counterexample\_Generator(M, \pi_i, \Phi)$
      Add cex_{π_i} to CEX and solve $\mu_{cex_{\pi_i}}$, **go to Learner**
  Learner:
    If status = SAT
      If $||\mu_E - \mu_{\pi_i}||_2 \leq \epsilon$, **then return** $\pi^* \leftarrow \pi_i$
        ▷ Terminate. π_i is ϵ-close to π_E
      Add π_i to Π_S, $inf \leftarrow k, k \leftarrow sup$ ▷ Update Π_S, inf and reset k
    If status = UNSAT
      If $|k - inf| \leq \sigma$, **then return** $\pi^* \leftarrow \underset{\pi \in \Pi_S}{argmin} ||\mu_E - \mu_\pi||_2$
        ▷ Terminate. k is too close to its lower bound.
      $k \leftarrow \alpha \cdot inf + (1 - \alpha)k$ ▷ Decrease k to learn for safety
    $\omega_{i+1} \leftarrow \underset{\omega}{argmax} \underset{\pi \in \Pi_S, \tilde{\pi} \in \Pi_S, cex \in CEX}{\min} \omega^T(k(\mu_E - \mu_\pi) + (1-k)(\mu_{\tilde{\pi}} - \mu_{cex}))$
  ▷ Note that the multi-objective optimization function recovers AL when $k = 1$
    $\pi_{i+1}, \mu_{\pi_{i+1}} \leftarrow$ Compute the optimal policy π_{i+1} and its expected features $\mu_{\pi_{i+1}}$ for the MDP M with reward $R(s) = \omega_{i+1}^T f(s)$
  Go to next iteration

Algorithm 1 describes CEGAL in detail. With a constant $sup = 1$ and a variable $inf \in [0, sup]$ for the upper and lower bounds respectively, the learner determines the value of k within $[inf, sup]$ in each iteration depending on the outcome of the verifier and uses k in solving (10) in line 27. Like most nonlinear optimization algorithms, this algorithm requires an initial guess, which is an initial safe policy π_0 to make Π_S nonempty. A good initial candidate would be the maximally safe policy for example obtained using PRISM-games [15]. Without loss of generality, we assume this policy satisfies Φ. Suppose in iteration i, an intermediate policy π_i learnt by the learner in iteration $i-1$ is verified to satisfy Φ, then we increase inf to $inf = k$ and reset k to $k = sup$ as shown in line 22. If π_i does not satisfy Φ, then we reduce k to $k = \alpha \cdot inf + (1-\alpha)k$ as shown in line 26 where $\alpha \in (0, 1)$ is a step length parameter. If $|k - inf| \leq \sigma$ and π_i still does not satisfy Φ, the algorithm chooses from Π_S a best safe policy π^* which has the smallest margin to π_E as shown in line 24. If π_i satisfies Φ and is ϵ-close to π_E, the algorithm outputs π_i as show in line 19. For the occasions when π_i satisfies Φ and $inf = sup = k = 1$, solving (10) is equivalent to solving (1) as in the original AL algorithm.

Remark 2. The initial policy π_0 does not have to be maximally safe, although such a policy can be used to verify if Φ is satisfiable at all. Naively safe policies often suffice for obtaining a safe and performant output at the end. Such a policy can be obtained easily in many settings, e.g., in the grid-world example one safe policy is simply staying in the initial cell. In both cases, π_0 typically has very low performance since satisfying Φ is the only requirement for it.

Theorem 1. *Given an initial policy π_0 that satisfies Φ, Algorithm 1 is guaranteed to output a policy π^*, such that (1) π^* satisfies Φ, and (2) the performance of π^* is at least as good as that of π_0 when compared to π_E, i.e. $\|\mu_E - \mu_{\pi^*}\|_2 \leq \|\mu_E - \mu_{\pi_0}\|_2$.*

Proof Sketch. The first part of the guarantee can be proven by case splitting. Algorithm 1 outputs π^* either when π^* satisfies Φ and is ϵ-close to π_E, or when $|k - inf| \leq \sigma$ in some iteration. In the first case, π^* clearly satisfies Φ. In the second case, π^* is selected from the set Π_S which contains all the policies that have been found to satisfy Φ so far, so π^* satisfies Φ. For the second part of the guarantee, the initial policy π_0 is the final output π^* if π_0 satisfies Φ and is ϵ-close to π_E. Otherwise, π_0 is added to Π_S if it satisfies Φ. During the iteration, if $|k - inf| \leq \sigma$ in some iteration, then the final output is $\pi^* = \underset{\pi \in \Pi_S}{argmin} \|\mu_E - \mu_\pi\|_2$, so it must satisfy $\|\mu_E - \mu_{\pi^*}\|_2 \leq \|\mu_E - \mu_{\pi_0}\|_2$. If a learnt policy π^* satisfies Φ and is ϵ-close to π_E, then Algorithm 1 outputs π^* without adding it to Π_S. Obviously $\|\mu_E - \mu_\pi\|_2 > \epsilon, \forall \pi \in \Pi_S$, so $\|\mu_E - \mu_{\pi^*}\|_2 \leq \|\mu_E - \mu_{\pi_0}\|_2$.

Discussion. In the worst case, CEGAL will return the initial safe policy. However, this can be because a policy that simultaneously satisfies Φ and is ϵ-close to the expert's demonstrations does not exist. Comparing to AL which offers no safety guarantee and finding the maximally safe policy which has very poor performance, CEGAL provides a principled way of guaranteeing safety while retaining performance.

Convergence. Algorithm 1 is guaranteed to terminate. Let inf_t be the tth assigned value of inf. After inf_t is given, k is decreased from $k_0 = sup$ iteratively by $k_i = \alpha \cdot inf_t + (1-\alpha)k_{i-1}$ until either $|k_i - inf_t| \leq \sigma$ in line 24 or a new safe policy is found in line 18. The update of k satisfies the following equality.

$$\frac{|k_{i+1} - inf_t|}{|k_i - inf_t|} = \frac{\alpha \cdot inf_t + (1-\alpha)k_i - inf_t}{k_i - inf_t} = 1 - \alpha \tag{11}$$

Thus, it takes no more than $1 + \log_{1-\alpha} \frac{\sigma}{sup - inf_t}$ iterations for either the algorithm to terminate in line 24 or a new safe policy to be found in line 18. If a new safe policy is found in line 18, inf will be assigned in line 22 by the current value of k as $inf_{t+1} = k$ which obviously satisfies $inf_{t+1} - inf_t \geq (1-\alpha)\sigma$. After the assignment of inf_{t+1}, the iterative update of k resumes. Since $sup - inf_t \leq 1$, the following inequality holds.

$$\frac{|inf_{t+1} - sup|}{|inf_t - sup|} \leq \frac{sup - inf_t - (1-\alpha)\sigma}{sup - inf_t} \leq 1 - (1-\alpha)\sigma \tag{12}$$

Obviously, starting from an initial $inf = inf_0 < sup$, with the alternating update of inf and k, inf will keep getting close to sup unless the algorithm terminates as in line 24 or a safe policy ϵ-close to π_E is found as in line 19. The extreme case is that finally $inf = sup$ after no more than $\frac{sup - inf_0}{(1-\alpha)\sigma}$ updates on inf. Then, the problem becomes AL. Therefore, the worst case of this algorithm can have two phases. In the first phase, inf increases from $inf = 0$ to $inf = sup$. Between each two consecutive updates $(t, t+1)$ on inf, there are no more than $\log_{1-\alpha} \frac{(1-\alpha)\sigma}{sup - inf_t}$ updates on k before inf is increased from inf_t to inf_{t+1}. Overall, this phase takes no more than

$$\sum_{0 \leq i < \frac{sup - inf_0}{(1-\alpha)\sigma}} \log_{1-\alpha} \frac{(1-\alpha)\sigma}{sup - inf_0 - i \cdot (1-\alpha)\sigma} = \sum_{0 \leq i < \frac{1}{(1-\alpha)\sigma}} \log_{1-\alpha} \frac{(1-\alpha)\sigma}{1 - i \cdot (1-\alpha)\sigma} \tag{13}$$

iterations to reduce the multi-objective optimization problem to original apprenticeship learning and then the second phase begins. Since $k = sup$, the iteration will stop immediately when an unsafe policy is learnt as in line 24. This phase will not take more iterations than original AL algorithm does to converge and the convergence result of AL is given in [1].

In each iteration, the algorithm first solves a second-order cone programming (SOCP) problem (10) to learn a policy. SOCP problems can be solved in polynomial time by interior-point (IP) methods [12]. PCTL model checking for DTMCs can be solved in time linear in the size of the formula and polynomial in the size of the state space [7]. Counterexample generation can be done either by enumerating paths using the k-shortest path algorithm or determining a critical subsystem using either a SMT formulation or mixed integer linear programming (MILP) [23]. For the k-shortest path-based algorithm, it can be computationally expensive sometimes to enumerate a large amount of paths (i.e. a large k) when p^* is large. This can be alleviated by using a smaller p^* during calculation, which is equivalent to considering only paths that have high probabilities.

6 Experiments

We evaluate our algorithm on three case studies: (1) grid-world, (2) cart-pole, and (3) mountain-car. The cart-pole environment[1] and the mountain-car environment[2] are obtained from OpenAI Gym. All experiments are carried out on a quad-core i7-7700K processor running at 3.6 GHz with 16 GB of memory. Our prototype tool was implemented in Python[3]. The parameters are $\gamma = 0.99, \epsilon = 10, \sigma = 10^{-5}, \alpha = 0.5$ and the maximum number of iterations is 50. For the OpenAI-gym experiments, in each step, the agent sends an action to the OpenAI environment and the environment returns an observation and a reward (0 or 1). We show that our algorithm can guarantee safety while retaining the performance of the learnt policy compared with using AL alone.

6.1 Grid World

We first evaluate the scalability of our tool using the grid-world example. Table 1 shows the average runtime (per iteration) for the individual components of our tool as the size of the grid-world increases. The first and second columns indicate the size of the grid world and the resulting state space. The third column shows the average runtime that policy iteration takes to compute an optimal policy π for a known reward function. The forth column indicates the average runtime that policy iteration takes to compute the expected features μ for a known policy. The fifth column indicates the average runtime of verifying the PCTL formula using PRISM. The last column indicates the average runtime that generating a counterexample using COMICS.

Table 1. Average runtime per iteration in seconds.

Size	Num. of states	Compute π	Compute μ	MC	Cex
8×8	64	0.02	0.02	1.39	0.014
16×16	256	0.05	0.05	1.43	0.014
32×32	1024	0.07	0.08	3.12	0.035
64×64	4096	6.52	25.88	22.877	1.59

6.2 Cart-Pole from OpenAI Gym

In the cart-pole environment as shown in Fig. 4(a), the goal is to keep the pole on a cart from falling over as long as possible by moving the cart either to the left or to the right in each time step. The maximum step length is $t = 200$. The

[1] https://github.com/openai/gym/wiki/CartPole-v0.
[2] https://github.com/openai/gym/wiki/MountainCar-v0.
[3] https://github.com/zwc662/CAV2018.

position, velocity and angle of the cart and the pole are continuous values and observable, but the actual dynamics of the system are unknown[4].

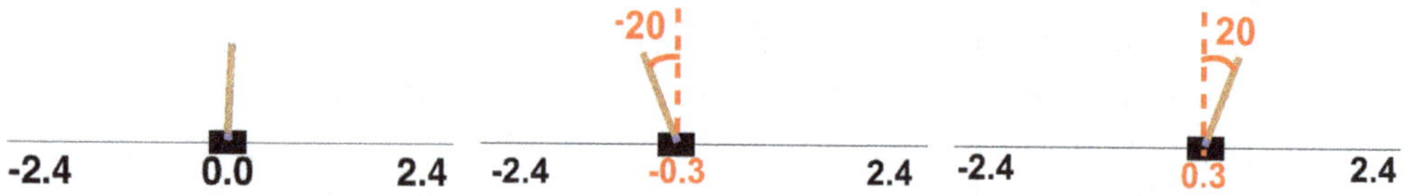

(a) (b) (c)

Fig. 4. (a) The cart-pole environment. (b) The cart is at −0.3 and pole angle is −20°. (c) The cart is at 0.3 and pole angle is 20°.

A maneuver is deemed *unsafe* if the pole angle is larger than ±20° while the cart's horizontal position is more than ±0.3 as shown in Fig. 4(b) and (c). We formalize the safety requirement in PCTL as (14).

$$\Phi ::= P_{\leq p^*}[\mathit{true}\ \mathbf{U}^{\leq t}\ (\mathit{angle} \leq -20^\circ \wedge \mathit{position} \leq -0.3) \vee (\mathit{angle} \geq 20^\circ \wedge \mathit{position} \geq 0.3)] \quad (14)$$

Table 2. In the cart-pole environment, *higher* average steps mean better performance. The safest policy is synthesized using PRISM-games.

	MC Result	Avg. Steps	Num. of Iters
AL	49.1%	165	2
Safest Policy	0.0%	8	N.A.
$p^* = 30\%$	17.2%	121	10
$p^* = 25\%$	9.3%	136	14
$p^* = 20\%$	17.2%	122	10
$p^* = 15\%$	6.9%	118	22
$p^* = 10\%$	7.2%	136	22
$p^* = 5\%$	0.04%	83	50

We used 2000 demonstrations for which the pole is held upright without violating any of the safety conditions for all 200 steps in each demonstration. The safest policy synthesized by PRISM-games is used as the initial safe policy. We also compare the different policies learned by CEGAL for different safety threshold p^*s. In Table 2, the policies are compared in terms of model checking results

[4] The MDP is built from sampled data. The feature vector in each state contains 30 radial basis functions which depend on the squared Euclidean distances between current state and other 30 states which are uniformly distributed in the state space.

('MC Result') on the PCTL property in (14) using the constructed MDP, the average steps ('Avg. Steps') that a policy (executed in the OpenAI environment) can hold across 5000 rounds (the higher the better), and the number of iterations ('Num. of Iters') it takes for the algorithm to terminate (either converge to an ϵ-close policy, or terminate due to σ, or terminate after 50 iterations). The policy in the first row is the result of using AL alone, which has the best performance but also a 49.1% probability of violating the safety requirement. The safest policy as shown in the second row is always safe has almost no performance at all. This policy simply letts the pole fall and thus does not risk moving the cart out of the range $[-0.3, 0.3]$. On the other hand, it is clear that the policies learnt using CEGAL always satisfy the safety requirement. From $p^* = 30\%$ to 10%, the performance of the learnt policy is comparable to that of the AL policy. However, when the safety threshold becomes very low, e.g., $p^* = 5\%$, the performance of the learnt policy drops significantly. This reflects the phenomenon that the tighter the safety condition is the less room for the agent to maneuver to achieve a good performance.

6.3 Mountain-Car from OpenAI Gym

Our third experiment uses the mountain-car environment from OpenAI Gym. As shown in Fig. 5(a), a car starts from the bottom of the valley and tries to reach the mountaintop on the right as quickly as possible. In each time step the car can perform one of the three actions, accelerating to the left, coasting, and accelerating to the right. The agent fails if the step length reaches the maximum ($t = 66$). The velocity and position of the car are continuous values and observable while the exact dynamics are unknown[5]. In this game setting, the car cannot reach the right mountaintop by simply accelerating to the right. It has to accumulate momentum first by moving back and forth in the valley. The safety rules we enforce are shown in Fig. 5(b). They correspond to speed limits when the car is close to the left mountaintop or to the right mountaintop (in case it is a cliff on the other side of the mountaintop). Similar to the previous experiments, we considered 2000 expert demonstrations for which all of them successfully reach the right mountaintop without violating any of the safety conditions. The average number of steps for the expert to drive the car to the right mountaintop is 40. We formalize the safety requirement in PCTL as (15).

$$\begin{aligned}\Phi ::= \; & P_{\leq p^*}[\mathit{true}\ \mathbf{U}^{\leq t}\ (\mathit{speed} \leq -0.04 \wedge \mathit{position} \leq -1.1) \\ & \vee(\mathit{speed} \geq 0.04 \wedge \mathit{position} \geq 0.5)] \qquad (15)\end{aligned}$$

We compare the different policies using the same set of categories as in the cart-pole example. The numbers are averaged over 5000 runs. As shown in the

[5] The MDP is built from sampled data. The feature vector for each state contains 2 exponential functions and 18 radial basis functions which respectively depend on the squared Euclidean distances between the current state and other 18 states which are uniformly distributed in the state space.

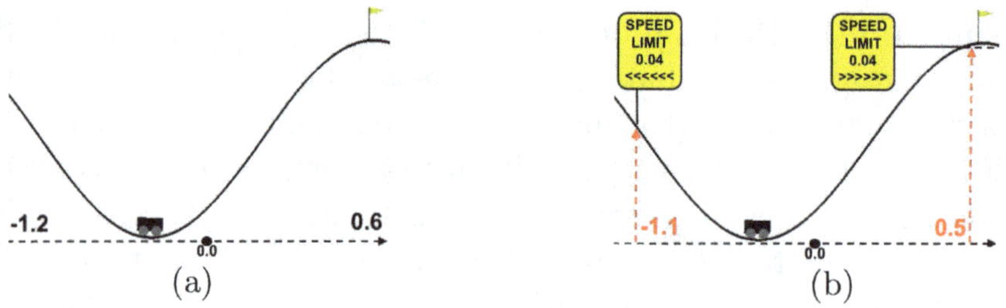

Fig. 5. (a) The original mountain-car environment. (b) The mountain-car environment with traffic rules: when the distance from the car to the left edge or the right edge is shorter than 0.1, the speed of the car should be lower than 0.04.

first row, the policy learnt via AL[6] has the highest probability of going over the speed limits. We observed that this policy made the car speed up all the way to the left mountaintop to maximize its potential energy. The safest policy corresponds to simply staying in the bottom of the valley. The policies learnt via CEGAL for safety threshold p^* ranging from 60% to 50% not only have lower probability of violating the speed limits but also achieve comparable performance. As the safety threshold p^* decreases further, the agent becomes more conservative and it takes more time for the car to finish the task. For $p^* = 20\%$, the agent never succeeds in reaching the top within 66 steps (Table 3).

Table 3. In the mountain-car environment, *lower* average steps mean better performance. The safest policy is synthesized via PRISM-games.

	MC Result	Avg. steps	Num. of Iters
Policy Learnt via AL	69.2%	54	50
Safest Policy	0.0%	*Fail*	N.A.
$p^* = 60\%$	43.4%	57	9
$p^* = 50\%$	47.2%	55	17
$p^* = 40\%$	29.3%	61	26
$p^* = 30\%$	18.9%	64	17
$p^* = 20\%$	4.9%	*Fail*	40

7 Related Work

A taxonomy of AI safety problems is given in [3] where the issues of misspecified objective or reward and insufficient or poorly curated training data are highlighted. There have been several attempts to address these issues from different angles. The problem of *safe exploration* is studied in [8,17]. In particular, the latter work proposes to add a safety constraint, which is evaluated by amount

6 AL did not converge to an ϵ-close policy in 50 iterations in this case.

of damage, to the optimization problem so that the optimal policy can maximize the return without violating the limit on the expected damage. An obvious shortcoming of this approach is that actual failures will have to occur to properly assess damage.

Formal methods have been applied to the problem of AI safety. In [5], the authors propose to combine machine learning and reachability analysis for dynamical models to achieve high performance and guarantee safety. In this work, we focus on probabilistic models which are natural in many modern machine learning methods. In [20], the authors propose to use formal specification to synthesize a control policy for reinforcement learning. They consider formal specifications captured in Linear Temporal Logic, whereas we consider PCTL which matches better with the underlying probabilistic model. Recently, the problem of *safe reinforcement learning* was explored in [2] where a monitor (called shield) is used to enforce temporal logic properties either during the learning phase or execution phase of the reinforcement learning algorithm. The shield provides a list of safe actions each time the agent makes a decision so that the temporal property is preserved. In [11], the authors also propose an approach for controller synthesis in reinforcement learning. In this case, an SMT-solver is used to find a scheduler (policy) for the synchronous product of an MDP and a DTMC so that it satisfies both a probabilistic reachability property and an expected cost property. Another approach that leverages PCTL model checking is proposed in [16]. A so-called abstract Markov decision process (AMDP) model of the environment is first built and PCTL model checking is then used to check the satisfiability of safety specification. Our work is similar to these in spirit in the application of formal methods. However, while the concept of AL is closely related to reinforcement learning, an agent in the AL paradigm needs to learn a policy from demonstrations without knowing the reward function a priori.

A distinguishing characteristic of our method is the tight integration of formal verification with learning from data (apprenticeship learning in particular). Among imitation or apprenticeship learning methods, margin based algorithms [1,18,19] try to maximize the margin between the expert's policy and all learnt policies until the one with the smallest margin is produced. The apprenticeship learning algorithm proposed by Abbeel and Ng [1] was largely motivated by the support vector machine (SVM) in that features of expert demonstration is maximally separately from all features of all other candidate policies. Our algorithm makes use of this observation when using counterexamples to steer the policy search process. Recently, the idea of learning from failed demonstrations started to emerge. In [21], the authors propose an IRL algorithm that can learn from both successful and failed demonstrations. It is done by reformulating maximum entropy algorithm in [24] to find a policy that maximally deviates from the failed demonstrations while approaching the successful ones as much as possible. However, this entropy-based method requires obtaining many failed demonstrations and can be very costly in practice.

Finally, our approach is inspired by the work on formal inductive synthesis [10] and counterexample-guided inductive synthesis (CEGIS) [22]. These frameworks typically combine a constraint-based synthesizer with a verification oracle. In each iteration, the agent refines her hypothesis (i.e. generates a new candidate solution) based on counterexamples provided by the oracle. Our approach can be viewed as an extension of CEGIS where the objective is not just functional correctness but also meeting certain learning criteria.

8 Conclusion and Future Work

We propose a counterexample-guided approach for combining probabilistic model checking with apprenticeship learning to ensure safety of the apprenticehsip learning outcome. Our approach makes novel use of counterexamples to steer the policy search process by reformulating the feature matching problem into a multi-objective optimization problem that additionally takes safety into account. Our experiments indicate that the proposed approach can guarantee safety and retain performance for a set of benchmarks including examples drawn from OpenAI Gym. In the future, we would like to explore other imitation or apprenticeship learning algorithms and extend our techniques to those settings.

Acknowledgement. This work is funded in part by the DARPA BRASS program under agreement number FA8750-16-C-0043 and NSF grant CCF-1646497.

References

1. Abbeel, P., Ng, A.Y.: Apprenticeship learning via inverse reinforcement learning. In: Proceedings of the Twenty-First International Conference on Machine Learning, ICML 2004, p. 1. ACM, New York (2004)
2. Alshiekh, M., Bloem, R., Ehlers, R., Könighofer, B., Niekum, S., Topcu, U.: Safe reinforcement learning via shielding. CoRR, abs/1708.08611 (2017)
3. Amodei, D., Olah, C., Steinhardt, J., Christiano, P., Schulman, J., Mané, D.: Concrete problems in AI safety. CoRR, abs/1606.06565 (2016)
4. Bellman, R.: A Markovian decision process. Indiana Univ. Math. J. **6**, 15 (1957)
5. Gillulay, J.H., Tomlin, C.J.: Guaranteed safe online learning of a bounded system. In: 2011 IEEE/RSJ International Conference on Intelligent Robots and Systems (IROS), pp. 2979–2984. IEEE (2011)
6. Han, T., Katoen, J.P., Berteun, D.: Counterexample generation in probabilistic model checking. IEEE Trans. Softw. Eng. **35**(2), 241–257 (2009)
7. Hansson, H., Jonsson, B.: A logic for reasoning about time and reliability. Formal Aspects Comput. **6**(5), 512–535 (1994)
8. Held, D., McCarthy, Z., Zhang, M., Shentu, F., Abbeel, P.: Probabilistically safe policy transfer. CoRR, abs/1705.05394 (2017)
9. Jansen, N., Ábrahám, E., Scheffler, M., Volk, M., Vorpahl, A., Wimmer, R., Katoen, J., Becker, B.: The COMICS tool - computing minimal counterexamples for discrete-time Markov chains. CoRR, abs/1206.0603 (2012)
10. Jha, S., Seshia, S.A.: A theory of formal synthesis via inductive learning. Acta Informatica **54**(7), 693–726 (2017)

11. Junges, S., Jansen, N., Dehnert, C., Topcu, U., Katoen, J.-P.: Safety-constrained reinforcement learning for MDPs. In: Chechik, M., Raskin, J.-F. (eds.) TACAS 2016. LNCS, vol. 9636, pp. 130–146. Springer, Heidelberg (2016). https://doi.org/10.1007/978-3-662-49674-9_8
12. Kuo, Y.-J., Mittelmann, H.D.: Interior point methods for second-order cone programming and or applications. Comput. Optim. Appl. **28**(3), 255–285 (2004)
13. Kwiatkowska, M., Norman, G., Parker, D.: PRISM: probabilistic symbolic model checker. In: Field, T., Harrison, P.G., Bradley, J., Harder, U. (eds.) TOOLS 2002. LNCS, vol. 2324, pp. 200–204. Springer, Heidelberg (2002). https://doi.org/10.1007/3-540-46029-2_13
14. Kwiatkowska, M., Parker, D.: Automated verification and strategy synthesis for probabilistic systems. In: Van Hung, D., Ogawa, M. (eds.) ATVA 2013. LNCS, vol. 8172, pp. 5–22. Springer, Cham (2013). https://doi.org/10.1007/978-3-319-02444-8_2
15. Kwiatkowska, M., Parker, D., Wiltsche, C.: PRISM-games: verification and strategy synthesis for stochastic multi-player games with multiple objectives. Int. J. Softw. Tools Technol. Transfer **20**, 195–210 (2017)
16. Mason, G.R., Calinescu, R.C., Kudenko, D., Banks, A.: Assured reinforcement learning for safety-critical applications. In: Doctoral Consortium at the 10th International Conference on Agents and Artificial Intelligence. SciTePress (2017)
17. Moldovan, T.M., Abbeel, P.: Safe exploration in Markov decision processes. arXiv preprint arXiv:1205.4810 (2012)
18. Ng, A.Y., Russell, S.J.: Algorithms for inverse reinforcement learning. In: Proceedings of the Seventeenth International Conference on Machine Learning, ICML 2000, pp. 663–670. Morgan Kaufmann Publishers Inc., San Francisco (2000)
19. Ratliff, N.D., Bagnell, J.A., Zinkevich, M.A.: Maximum margin planning. In: Proceedings of the 23rd International Conference on Machine Learning, ICML 2006, pp. 729–736. ACM, New York (2006)
20. Sadigh, D., Kim, E.S., Coogan, S., Sastry, S.S., Seshia, S.A.: A learning based approach to control synthesis of Markov decision processes for linear temporal logic specifications. CoRR, abs/1409.5486 (2014)
21. Shiarlis, K., Messias, J., Whiteson, S.: Inverse reinforcement learning from failure. In: Proceedings of the 2016 International Conference on Autonomous Agents and Multiagent Systems, pp. 1060–1068. International Foundation for Autonomous Agents and Multiagent Systems (2016)
22. Solar-Lezama, A., Tancau, L., Bodik, R., Seshia, S., Saraswat, V.: Combinatorial sketching for finite programs. SIGOPS Oper. Syst. Rev. **40**(5), 404–415 (2006)
23. Wimmer, R., Jansen, N., Ábrahám, E., Becker, B., Katoen, J.-P.: Minimal critical subsystems for discrete-time Markov models. In: Flanagan, C., König, B. (eds.) TACAS 2012. LNCS, vol. 7214, pp. 299–314. Springer, Heidelberg (2012). https://doi.org/10.1007/978-3-642-28756-5_21
24. Ziebart, B.D., Maas, A., Bagnell, J.A., Dey, A.K.: Maximum entropy inverse reinforcement learning. In: Proceedings of the 23rd National Conference on Artificial Intelligence, AAAI 2008, vol. 3, pp. 1433–1438. AAAI Press (2008)

Deciding Probabilistic Bisimilarity Distance One for Labelled Markov Chains

Qiyi Tang(✉) and Franck van Breugel

DisCoVeri Group, York University, Toronto, Canada
{qiyitang,franck}@eecs.yorku.ca

Abstract. Probabilistic bisimilarity is an equivalence relation that captures which states of a labelled Markov chain behave the same. Since this behavioural equivalence only identifies states that transition to states that behave exactly the same with exactly the same probability, this notion of equivalence is not robust. Probabilistic bisimilarity distances provide a quantitative generalization of probabilistic bisimilarity. The distance of states captures the similarity of their behaviour. The smaller the distance, the more alike the states behave. In particular, states are probabilistic bisimilar if and only if their distance is zero. This quantitative notion is robust in that small changes in the transition probabilities result in small changes in the distances.

During the last decade, several algorithms have been proposed to approximate and compute the probabilistic bisimilarity distances. The main result of this paper is an algorithm that decides distance one in $O(n^2 + m^2)$, where n is the number of states and m is the number of transitions of the labelled Markov chain. The algorithm is the key new ingredient of our algorithm to compute the distances. The state of the art algorithm can compute distances for labelled Markov chains up to 150 states. For one such labelled Markov chain, that algorithm takes more than 49 h. In contrast, our new algorithm only takes 13 ms. Furthermore, our algorithm can compute distances for labelled Markov chains with more than 10,000 states in less than 50 min.

Keywords: Labelled Markov chain · Probabilistic bisimilarity
Probabilistic bisimilarity distance

1 Introduction

A *behavioural equivalence* captures which states of a model give rise to the same behaviour. Bisimilarity, due to Milner [22] and Park [25], is one of the best known behavioural equivalences. Verifying that an implementation satisfies a specification boils down to checking that the model of the implementation gives rise to the same behaviour as the model of the specification, that is, the models are behavioural equivalent (see [1, Chap. 3]).

In this paper, we focus on models of probabilistic systems. These models can capture randomized algorithms, probabilistic protocols, biological systems and

H. Chockler and G. Weissenbacher (Eds.): CAV 2018, LNCS 10981, pp. 681–699, 2018.
https://doi.org/10.1007/978-3-319-96145-3_39

many other systems in which probabilities play a central role. In particular, we consider *labelled Markov chains*, that is, Markov chains the states of which are labelled.

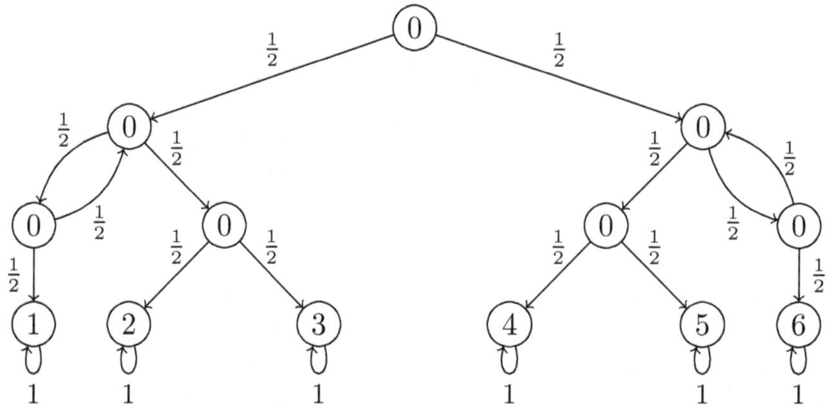

The above example shows how the behaviour of rolling a die can be mimicked by flipping a coin, an example due to Knuth and Yao [19]. Six of the states are labelled with the values of a die and the other states are labelled zero. In this example, we are interested in the labels representing the value of a die. As the reader can easily verify, the states with these labels are each reached with probability $\frac{1}{6}$ from the initial, top most, state. In general, labels are used to identify particular states that have properties of interest. As a consequence, states with different labels are not behaviourally equivalent.

Probabilistic bisimilarity, due to Larsen and Skou [21], is a key behavioural equivalence for labelled Markov chains. As shown by Katoen et al. [16], minimizing a labelled Markov chain by identifying those states that are probabilistic bisimilar speeds up model checking. Probabilistic bisimilarity only identifies those states that behave exactly the same with exactly the same probability. If, for example, we replace the fair coin in the above example with a biased one, then none of the states labelled with zero in the original model with the fair coin are behaviourally equivalent to any of the states labelled with zero in the model with the biased coin. Behavioural equivalences like probabilistic bisimilarity rely on the transition probabilities and, as a result, are sensitive to minor changes of those probabilities. That is, such behavioural equivalences are not robust, as first observed by Giacalone et al. [12].

The *probabilistic bisimilarity distances* that we study in this paper were first defined by Desharnais et al. in [11]. Each pair of states of a labelled Markov chain is assigned a distance, a real number in the unit interval $[0, 1]$. This distance captures the similarity of the behaviour of the states. The smaller the distance, the more alike the states behave. In particular, states have distance zero if and only if they are probabilistic bisimilar. This provides a quantitative generalization of probabilistic bisimilarity that is robust in that small changes in the transition probabilities give rise to small changes in the distances. For example, we can model a biased die by using a biased coin instead of a fair coin in the above example. Let us assume that the odds of heads of the biased coin, that is, going to the left, is $\frac{51}{100}$. A state labelled zero in the model of the fair die has a *non-trivial* distance, that is, a distance greater than zero and smaller than one, to the corresponding state in the model of the biased die. For example, the initial states have distance about 0.036. We refer the reader to [7] for a more detailed discussion of a similar example.

As we already mentioned earlier, behavioural equivalences can be used to verify that an implementation satisfies a specification. Similarly, the distances can be used to check how similar an implementation is to a specification. We also mentioned that probabilistic bisimilarity can be used to speed up model checking. The distances can be used in a similar way, by identifying those states that behave almost the same, that is, have a small distance (see [3,23,26]).

We focus in this paper on computing the probabilistic bisimilarity distances. In particular, we present a *decision procedure* for *distance one*. That is, we compute the set of pairs of states that have distance one. Recall that distance one is the maximal distance and, therefore, captures that states behave very differently. States with different labels have distance one. However, also states with the same label can have distance one, as the next example illustrates.

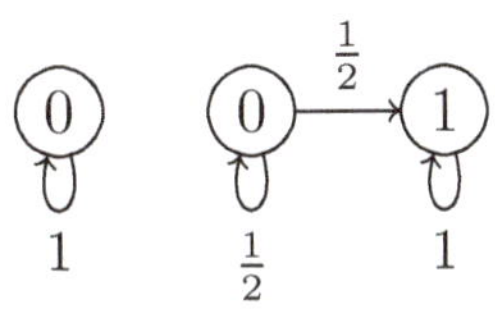

Instead of computing the set of state pairs that have distance one, we compute the complement, that is, the set of state pairs with distance smaller than one. Obviously, the set of state pairs with distance zero is included in this set. First, we decide distance zero. As we mentioned earlier, distance zero coincides with probabilistic bisimilarity. The first decision procedure for probabilistic bisimilarity was provided by Baier [4]. More efficient decision procedures were subsequently proposed by Derisavi et al. [10] and also by Valmari and Franceschinis [30]. The latter two both run in $O(m \log n)$, where n and m are the number of states and transitions of the labelled Markov chain. Subsequently, we use a traversal of a directed graph derived from the labelled Markov chain. This traversal takes $O(n^2 + m^2)$.

The decision procedures for distance zero and one can be used to compute or approximate probabilistic bisimilarity distances as indicated below.

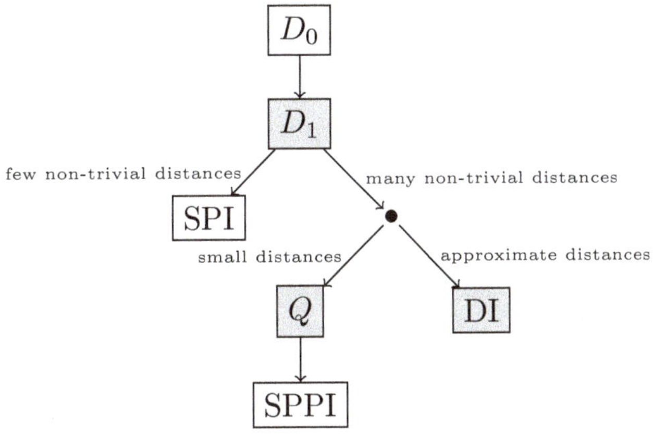

Once we have computed the sets D_0 and D_1 of state pairs that have distance zero or one, we can easily compute the number of state pairs with non-trivial distances. If the number of non-trivial distances is small, then we can use the *simple policy iteration* (SPI) algorithm due to Bacci et al. [2] to compute those distances. Otherwise, we can either compute all distances smaller than a chosen $\varepsilon > 0$ or we can approximate the distances up to some chosen accuracy $\alpha > 0$. In the former case, we first compute a query set Q of state pairs that contains all state pairs the distances of which are at most ε. Subsequently, we apply the *simple partial policy iteration* (SPPI) algorithm due to Bacci et al. [2] to compute the distances for all state pairs in Q. In the latter case, we start with a pair of distance functions, one being a lower-bound and the other being an upper-bound of the probabilistic bisimilarity distances, and iteratively improve the accuracy of those until they are α close. We call this new approximation algorithm *distance iteration* (DI) as it is similar in spirit to Bellman's value iteration [5].

Chen et al. [8] presented an algorithm to compute the distances by means of Khachiyan's ellipsoid method [17]. Though the algorithm is polynomial time, in practice it is not as efficient as the policy iteration algorithms (see the examples in [28, Sect. 8]). The state of the art algorithm to compute the probabilistic bisimilarity distances consists of two components: D_0 and SPI. To compare this algorithm with our new algorithm consisting of the components D_0, D_1 and SPI, we implemented all the components in Java and ran both implementations on several labelled Markov chains. These labelled Markov chains model randomized algorithms and probabilistic protocols that are part of the distribution of probabilistic model checkers such as PRISM [20]. Whereas the original state of the art algorithm can handle labelled Markov chains with up to 150 states, our new algorithm can handle more than 10,000 states. Furthermore, for one such labelled Markov chain with 150 states, the original algorithm takes more than 49 h, whereas our new algorithm takes only 13 ms. Also, the new algorithm consisting of the components D_0, D_1, Q and SPPI to compute only small distances along with the new algorithm consisting of the components D_0, D_1 and DI to approximate the distances give rise to even less execution times for a number of the labelled Markov chains.

The main contributions of this paper are

- a polynomial decision procedure for distance one,
- an algorithm to compute the probabilistic bisimilarity distances,
- an algorithm to compute those probabilistic bisimilarity distances smaller than some given $\varepsilon > 0$, and
- an approximation algorithm to compute the probabilistic bisimilarity distances up to some given accuracy $\alpha > 0$.

Furthermore, by means of experiments we have shown that these three new algorithms are very effective, improving significantly on the state of the art.

2 Labelled Markov Chains and Probabilistic Bisimilarity Distances

We start by reviewing the model of interest, labelled Markov chains, its most well known behavioural equivalence, probabilistic bisimilarity due to Larsen and Skou [21], and the probabilistic bisimilarity pseudometric due to Desharnais et al. [11]. We denote the set of rational probability distributions on a set S by $\mathrm{Distr}(S)$. For $\mu \in \mathrm{Distr}(S)$, its support is defined by $\mathrm{support}(\mu) = \{ s \in S \mid \mu(s) > 0 \}$. Instead of $S \times S$, we often write S^2.

Definition 1. *A labelled Markov chain is a tuple $\langle S, L, \tau, \ell \rangle$ consisting of*

- *a nonempty finite set S of states,*
- *a nonempty finite set L of labels,*
- *a transition function $\tau : S \to \mathrm{Distr}(S)$, and*
- *a labelling function $\ell : S \to L$.*

For the remainder of this section, we fix such a labelled Markov chain $\langle S, L, \tau, \ell \rangle$.

Definition 2. *Let μ, $\nu \in \mathrm{Distr}(S)$. The set $\Omega(\mu, \nu)$ of couplings of μ and ν is defined by*

$$\Omega(\mu,\nu) = \left\{ \omega \in \mathrm{Distr}(S^2) \;\middle|\; \begin{array}{l} \forall s \in S : \sum_{t \in S} \omega(s,t) = \mu(s) \wedge \\ \forall t \in S : \sum_{s \in S} \omega(s,t) = \nu(t) \end{array} \right\}.$$

Note that $\omega \in \Omega(\mu, \nu)$ is a joint probability distribution with marginals μ and ν. The following proposition will be used to prove Proposition 5.

Proposition 1. *For all μ, $\nu \in \mathrm{Distr}(S)$ and $X \subseteq S^2$,*

$$\forall \omega \in \Omega(\mu,\nu) : \mathrm{support}(\omega) \subseteq X \textit{ if and only if } \mathrm{support}(\mu) \times \mathrm{support}(\nu) \subseteq X.$$

Definition 3. *An equivalence relation $R \subseteq S^2$ is a probabilistic bisimulation if for all $(s,t) \in R$, $\ell(s) = \ell(t)$ and there exists $\omega \in \Omega(\tau(s), \tau(t))$ such that $\mathrm{support}(\omega) \subseteq R$. Probabilistic bisimilarity, denoted $\sim$, is the largest probabilistic bisimulation.*

The probabilistic bisimilarity pseudometric of Desharnais et al. [11] maps each pair of states of a labelled Markov chain to a distance, an element of the unit interval $[0,1]$. Hence, the pseudometric is a function from S^2 to $[0,1]$, that is, an element of $[0,1]^{S^2}$. As we will discuss below, it can be defined as a fixed point of the following function.

Definition 4. *The function $\Delta : [0,1]^{S^2} \to [0,1]^{S^2}$ is defined by*

$$\Delta(d)(s,t) = \begin{cases} 1 & \textit{if } \ell(s) \neq \ell(t) \\ \displaystyle\min_{\omega \in \Omega(\tau(s),\tau(t))} \sum_{u,v \in S} \omega(u,v)\, d(u,v) & \textit{otherwise} \end{cases}$$

Since a concave function on a convex polytope attains its minimum (see [18, p. 260]), the above minimum exists. We will use this fact in Proposition 4, one of the key technical results in this paper. We endow the set $[0,1]^{S^2}$ of functions from S^2 to $[0,1]$ with the following partial order: $d \sqsubseteq e$ if $d(s,t) \leq e(s,t)$ for all s, $t \in S$. The set $[0,1]^{S^2}$ together with the order $\sqsubseteq$ form a complete lattice (see [9, Chap. 2]). The function Δ is monotone (see [6, Sect. 3]). According to the Knaster-Tarski fixed point theorem [29, Theorem 1], a monotone function on a complete lattice has a least fixed point. Hence, Δ has a least fixed point, which we denote by $\boldsymbol{\mu}(\Delta)$. This fixed point assigns to each pair of states their probabilistic bisimilarity distance.

Given that $\boldsymbol{\mu}(\Delta)$ captures the probabilistic bisimilarity distances, we define the following sets.

$$D_0 = \{(s,t) \in S^2 \mid \boldsymbol{\mu}(\Delta)(s,t) = 0\}$$
$$D_1 = \{(s,t) \in S^2 \mid \boldsymbol{\mu}(\Delta)(s,t) = 1\}$$

The probabilistic bisimilarity pseudometric $\boldsymbol{\mu}(\Delta)$ provides a quantitative generalization of probabilistic bisimilarity as captured by the following result by Desharnais et al. [11, Theorem 1].

Theorem 1. $D_0 = \{\, (s,t) \in S^2 \mid s \sim t \,\}$.

3 Distance One

We concluded the previous section with the characterization of D_0 as the set of state pairs that are probabilistic bisimilar. In this section we present a characterization of D_1 as a fixed point of the function introduced in Definition 5.

Let us consider the case that the probabilistic bisimilarity distance of states s and t is one, that is, $\boldsymbol{\mu}(\Delta)(s,t) = 1$. Then $\Delta(\boldsymbol{\mu}(\Delta))(s,t) = 1$. From the definition of Δ, we can conclude that either $\ell(s) \neq \ell(t)$, or for all couplings $\omega \in \Omega(\tau(s),\tau(t))$ we have $\text{support}(\omega) \subseteq D_1$.

We partition the set S^2 of state pairs into

$$S^2_0 = \{(s,t) \in S^2 \mid s \sim t\}$$
$$S^2_1 = \{(s,t) \in S^2 \mid \ell(s) \neq \ell(t)\}$$
$$S^2_? = S^2 \setminus (S^2_0 \cup S^2_1)$$

Hence, if $\boldsymbol{\mu}(\Delta)(s,t) = 1$, then either $(s,t) \in S^2_1$, or $(s,t) \in S^2_?$ and for all couplings $\omega \in \Omega(\tau(s),\tau(t))$ we have $\text{support}(\omega) \subseteq D_1$. This leads us to the following function.

Definition 5. *The function* $\Gamma : 2^{S^2} \to 2^{S^2}$ *is defined by*

$$\Gamma(X) = S^2_1 \cup \{\, (s,t) \in S^2_? \mid \forall \omega \in \Omega(\tau(s),\tau(t)) : \text{support}(\omega) \subseteq X \,\}.$$

Proposition 2. *The function* Γ *is monotone.*

Since the set 2^{S^2} of subsets of S^2 endowed with the order $\subseteq$ is a complete lattice (see [9, Example 2.6(2)]) and the function Γ is monotone, we can conclude from the Knaster-Tarski fixed point theorem that Γ has a greatest fixed point, which we denote by $\boldsymbol{\nu}(\Gamma)$. Next, we show that D_1 is a fixed point of Γ.

Proposition 3. $D_1 = \Gamma(D_1)$.

Since we have already seen that D_1 is a fixed point of Γ, we have that $D_1 \subseteq \boldsymbol{\nu}(\Gamma)$. To conclude that D_1 is the greatest fixed point of Γ, it remains to show that $\boldsymbol{\nu}(\Gamma) \subseteq D_1$, which is equivalent to the following.

Proposition 4. $\boldsymbol{\nu}(\Gamma) \setminus D_1 = \emptyset$.

Proof. Towards a contradiction, assume that $\boldsymbol{\nu}(\Gamma) \setminus D_1 \neq \emptyset$. Let

$$m = \min\{\boldsymbol{\mu}(\Delta)(s,t) \mid (s,t) \in \boldsymbol{\nu}(\Gamma) \setminus D_1\}$$
$$M = \{(s,t) \in \boldsymbol{\nu}(\Gamma) \setminus D_1 \mid \boldsymbol{\mu}(\Delta)(s,t) = m\}$$

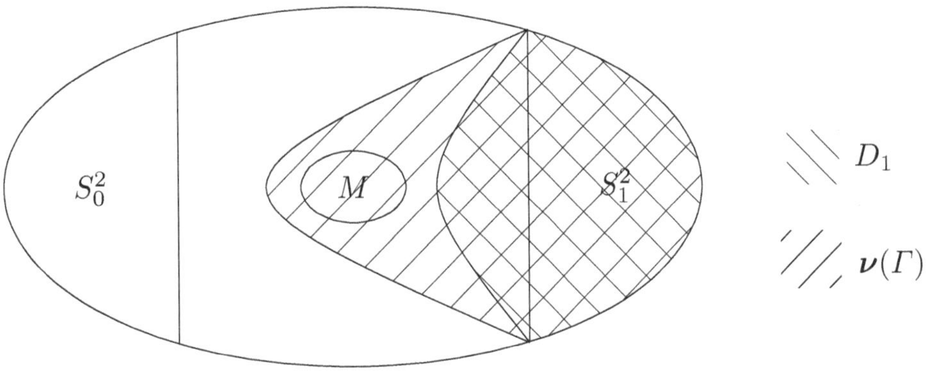

Since $\boldsymbol{\nu}(\Gamma) \setminus D_1 \neq \emptyset$, we have that $M \neq \emptyset$. Furthermore,

$$M \subseteq \boldsymbol{\nu}(\Gamma) \setminus D_1. \tag{1}$$

Since $\boldsymbol{\nu}(\Gamma) \setminus D_1 \subseteq \boldsymbol{\nu}(\Gamma)$, we have

$$M \subseteq \boldsymbol{\nu}(\Gamma) = \Gamma(\boldsymbol{\nu}(\Gamma)) \subseteq S_1^2 \cup S_?^2. \tag{2}$$

For all $(s,t) \in M$,

$$\begin{aligned} &(s,t) \in \boldsymbol{\nu}(\Gamma) \wedge (s,t) \notin D_1 \quad [(1)] \\ &\Rightarrow (s,t) \in \Gamma(\boldsymbol{\nu}(\Gamma)) \wedge (s,t) \notin S_1^2 \\ &\Rightarrow \forall \omega \in \Omega(\tau(s),\tau(t)) : \text{support}(\omega) \subseteq \boldsymbol{\nu}(\Gamma). \end{aligned} \tag{3}$$

For each $(s,t) \in M$, let

$$\omega_{s,t} = \underset{\omega \in \Omega(\tau(s),\tau(t))}{\text{argmin}} \sum_{u,v \in S} \omega(u,v)\, \boldsymbol{\mu}(\Delta)(u,v). \tag{4}$$

We distinguish the following two cases.

– Assume that there exists $(s,t) \in M$ such that $\text{support}(\omega_{s,t}) \cap D_1 \neq \emptyset$. Let

$$p = \sum_{(u,v) \in \boldsymbol{\nu}(\Gamma) \cap D_1} \omega_{s,t}(u,v).$$

By (3), we have that $\text{support}(\omega_{s,t}) \subseteq \boldsymbol{\nu}(\Gamma)$. Since $\text{support}(\omega_{s,t}) \cap D_1 \neq \emptyset$ by assumption, we can conclude that $p > 0$. Again using the fact that $\text{support}(\omega_{s,t}) \subseteq \boldsymbol{\nu}(\Gamma)$, we have that

$$\sum_{(u,v) \in \boldsymbol{\nu}(\Gamma) \setminus D_1} \omega_{s,t}(u,v) = 1 - p. \tag{5}$$

Furthermore,

$$\begin{aligned}
m &= \boldsymbol{\mu}(\Delta)(s,t) \\
&= \Delta(\boldsymbol{\mu}(\Delta))(s,t) \\
&= \min_{\omega \in \Omega(\tau(s),\tau(t))} \sum_{u,v \in S} \omega(u,v)\, \boldsymbol{\mu}(\Delta)(u,v) \\
&= \sum_{u,v \in S} \omega_{s,t}(u,v)\, \boldsymbol{\mu}(\Delta)(u,v) \quad [(4)] \\
&= \sum_{(u,v) \in \boldsymbol{\nu}(\Gamma)} \omega_{s,t}(u,v)\, \boldsymbol{\mu}(\Delta)(u,v) \quad [(3)] \\
&= \sum_{(u,v) \in \boldsymbol{\nu}(\Gamma) \cap D_1} \omega_{s,t}(u,v)\, \boldsymbol{\mu}(\Delta)(u,v) + \sum_{(u,v) \in \boldsymbol{\nu}(\Gamma) \setminus D_1} \omega_{s,t}(u,v)\, \boldsymbol{\mu}(\Delta)(u,v) \\
&= p + \sum_{(u,v) \in \boldsymbol{\nu}(\Gamma) \setminus D_1} \omega_{s,t}(u,v)\, \boldsymbol{\mu}(\Delta)(u,v) \\
&\geq p + (1-p)m.
\end{aligned}$$

The last step follows from (5) and the fact that $\boldsymbol{\mu}(\Delta)(u,v) \geq m$ for all $(u,v) \in \boldsymbol{\nu}(\Gamma) \setminus D_1$. From the facts that $p > 0$ and $m \geq p + (1-p)m$ we can conclude that $m \geq 1$. This contradicts (1).

– Otherwise, $\text{support}(\omega_{s,t}) \cap D_1 = \emptyset$ for all $(s,t) \in M$. Next, we will show that M is a probabilistic bisimulation under this assumption. From the fact that M is a probabilistic bisimulation, we can conclude from Theorem 1 that $\boldsymbol{\mu}(\Delta)(s,t) = 0$ for all $(s,t) \in M$. Hence, since $M \neq \emptyset$ we have that $M \cap S_0^2 \neq \emptyset$ which contradicts (2).

  Next, we prove that M is a probabilistic bisimulation. Let $(s,t) \in M$. Since $M \subseteq \boldsymbol{\nu}(\Gamma) \setminus D_1$ by (1), we have that $(s,t) \notin D_1$ and, hence, $\Delta(\boldsymbol{\mu}(\Delta))(s,t) = \boldsymbol{\mu}(\Delta)(s,t) < 1$. From the definition of Δ, we can conclude that $\ell(s) = \ell(t)$. Since

$$\begin{aligned}
m &= \boldsymbol{\mu}(\Delta)(s,t) \\
&= \sum_{(u,v) \in \boldsymbol{\nu}(\Gamma) \setminus D_1} \omega_{s,t}(u,v)\, \boldsymbol{\mu}(\Delta)(u,v) \quad [\text{as above}]
\end{aligned}$$

and $\mu(\Delta)(u,v) \geq m$ for all $(u,v) \in \nu(\Gamma) \setminus D_1$, we can conclude that $\mu(\Delta)(u,v) = m$ for all $(u,v) \in \text{support}(\omega_{s,t})$. Hence, $\text{support}(\omega_{s,t}) \subseteq M$. Therefore, M is a probabilistic bisimulation. □

Theorem 2. $D_1 = \nu(\Gamma)$.

Proof. Immediate consequence of Proposition 3 and 4. □

We have shown that D_1 can be characterized as the greatest fixed point of Γ. Next, we will show that D_1 can be decided in polynomial time.

Theorem 3. *Distance one can be decided in* $O(n^2 + m^2)$.

Proof. As we will show in Theorem 5, distance smaller than one can be decided in $O(n^2 + m^2)$. Hence, distance one can be decided in $O(n^2 + m^2)$ as well. □

4 Distance Smaller Than One

To compute the set of state pairs which have distance one, we can first compute the set of state pairs which have distance less than one. The latter set we denote by $D_{<1}$. We can then obtain D_1 by taking the complement of $D_{<1}$. As we will discuss below, $D_{<1}$ can be characterized as the least fixed point of the following function.

Definition 6. *The function* $\daleth : 2^{S^2} \to 2^{S^2}$ *is defined by*

$$\daleth(X) = S^2 \setminus \Gamma(S^2 \setminus X).$$

The next theorem follows from Theorem 2.

Theorem 4. $D_{<1} = \mu(\daleth)$.

Next, we show that the computation of $D_{<1}$ can be formulated as a reachability problem on a directed graph which is induced by the labelled Markov chain. Thus, we can use standard search algorithms, for example, breadth-first search, on the induced graph.

Next, we present the graph induced by the labelled Markov chain.

Definition 7. *The directed graph* $G = (V, E)$ *is defined by*

$$\begin{aligned} V &= S_0^2 \cup S_?^2 \\ E &= \{ \langle (u,v), (s,t) \rangle \mid \tau(s)(u) > 0 \wedge \tau(t)(v) > 0 \} \end{aligned}$$

We are left to show that in the graph G defined above, a vertex (s,t) is reachable from some vertex in S_0^2 if and only if the state pair (s,t) in the labelled Markov chain has distance less than one.

As we have discussed earlier, if a state pair (s,t) has distance one, either s and t have different labels, or for all couplings $\omega \in \Omega(\tau(s), \tau(t))$ we have that $\text{support}(\omega) \subseteq D_1$. To avoid the universal quantification over couplings, we will use Proposition 1 in the proof of following proposition.

Proposition 5. $\mu(\daleth) = \{ (s,t) \mid (s,t) \textit{ is reachable from some } (u,v) \in S_0^2 \}$.

Theorem 5. *Distance smaller than one can be decided in* $O(n^2 + m^2)$.

Proof. Distance smaller than one can be decided as follows.

1. Decide distance zero.
2. Breadth-first search of G, with the queue initially containing the pairs of states that have distance zero.

By Theorem 4 and Proposition 5, we have that s and t have distance smaller than one if and only if (s,t) is reachable in the directed graph G from some (u,v) such that u and v have distance zero. These reachable state pairs can be computed using breadth-first search, with the queue initially containing S_0^2.

Distance zero, that is, probabilistic bisimilarity, can be decided in $O(m \log n)$ as shown by Derisavi et al. in [10]. The directed graph G has n^2 vertices and m^2 edges. Hence, breadth-first search takes $O(n^2 + m^2)$. □

5 Number of Non-trivial Distances

As we have already discussed earlier, distance zero captures that states behave exactly the same, that is, they are probabilistic bisimilar, and distance one indicates that states behave very differently. The remaining distances, that is, those greater than zero and smaller than one, we call non-trivial. Being able to determine quickly the number of non-trivial distances of a labelled Markov chain allows us to decide whether computing all these non-trivial distances (using some policy iteration algorithm) is feasible.

To determine the number of non-trivial distances of a labelled Markov chain, we use the following algorithm.

1. Decide distance zero.
2. Decide distance one.

As first proved by Baier [4], distance zero, that is, probabilistic bisimilarity, can be decided in polynomial time. As we proved in Theorem 3, distance one can be decided in polynomial time as well. Hence, we can compute the number of non-trivial distances in polynomial time.

To decide distance zero, we implemented the algorithm to decide probabilistic bisimilarity due to Derisavi et al. [10] in Java. We also implemented our algorithm to decide distance one, described in the proof of Theorems 3 and 5.

We applied our implementation to labelled Markov chains that model randomized algorithms and probabilistic protocols. These labelled Markov chains have been obtained from the verification tool PRISM [20]. We compute the number of non-trivial distances for two models: the randomized self-stabilising algorithm due to Herman [14] and the bounded retransmission protocol by Helmink et al. [13].

For the randomized self-stabilising algorithm, the size of the labelled Markov chain grows exponentially in the numbers of processes, N. The results for the randomized self-stabilising algorithm are shown in the table below. As we can see from the table, for systems up to 128 states, the algorithm runs for less than a second. For the system with 512 states, the algorithm terminates within seven minutes. For the case $N = 3$, there are only 12 non-trivial distances. The size is so small that we can easily compute all the non-trivial distances. Section 6 will use the simple policy iteration algorithm as the next step to compute them. The same applies to the case $N = 5$. For $N = 7$ or 9, the number of non-trivial distances is around 11,000 and 200,000, respectively. This makes computing all of them infeasible. Thus, instead of computing all of them, we need to find alternative ways to handle systems with a large number of non-trivial distances. We will discuss two alternative ways in Sects. 7 and 8. Moreover, in this example, as $|D_1| = |S_1^2|$, we know that all the state pairs with distance one are those that have different labels.

N	$\|S\|$	$D_0 + D_1$	Non-trivial	$\|D_0\|$	$\|D_1\|$	$\|S_1^2\|$
3	8	1.00 ms	12	38	14	14
5	32	6.06 ms	280	304	440	440
7	128	0.77 s	11,032	2,160	3,192	3,192
9	512	378.42 s	230,712	13,648	17,784	17,784

In the bounded retransmission protocol, there are two parameters: N denotes the number of chunks and M the maximum allowed number of retransmissions of each chunk. The results are shown in the table below. The algorithm can handle systems up to 3,526 states within 11 min. In this example, there are no non-trivial distances. As a consequence, deciding distance zero and one suffices to compute all the distances in this case.

N	M	S	$D_0 + D_1$	$\|D_0\|$	$\|D_1\|$	$\|S_1^2\|$
16	2	677	3.0 s	456,977	1,352	1,352
16	3	886	8.6 s	783,226	1,770	1,770
16	4	1,095	17.5 s	1,196,837	2,188	2,188
16	5	1,304	22.8 s	1,697,810	2,606	2,606
32	2	1,349	24.7 s	1,817,105	2,696	2,696
32	3	1,766	69.7 s	3,115,226	3,530	3,530
32	4	2,183	141.0 s	4,761,125	4,364	4,364
32	5	2,600	208.6 s	6,754,802	5,198	5,198
64	2	2,693	235.2 s	7,246,865	5,384	5,384
64	3	3,526	616.4 s	12,425,626	7,050	7,050

6 All Distances

To compute all distances of a labelled Markov chain, we augment the existing state of the art algorithm, which is based on algorithms due to Derisavi et al. [10] (step 1) and Bacci et al. [2] (step 3), by incorporating our decision procedure (step 2) as follows.

1. Decide distance zero.
2. Decide distance one.
3. Simple policy iteration.

Given that we not only decide distance zero, but also distance one, before running simple policy iteration, the correctness of the simple policy iteration algorithm in the augmented setting needs an adjusted proof.

As we already discussed in the previous section, step 1 and 2 are polynomial time. However, step 3 may take at least exponential time in the worst case, as we have shown in [27]. Hence, the overall algorithm is exponential time.

The first example we consider here is the synchronous leader election protocol of Itai and Rodeh [15] which is taken from PRISM. The protocol takes the number of processors, N, and a constant K as parameters. We compare the running time of our new algorithm with the state of the art algorithm, that combines algorithms due to Derisavi et al. and due to Bacci et al. The results are shown in the table below. In this protocol, the number of non-trivial distances is zero. Thus, our new algorithm terminates without running step 3 which is the simple policy iteration algorithm. On the other hand, the original simple policy iteration algorithm computes the distances of all the elements in the set $D_1 \setminus S_1^2$, the size of which is huge as can be seen from the last two columns of the table.

N	K	$\lvert S\rvert$	$D_0 + \text{SPI}$	$D_0 + D_1 + \text{SPI}$	Speed-up	$\lvert D_0\rvert$	$\lvert D_1\rvert$	$\lvert S_1^2\rvert$
3	2	26	4 s	1 ms	4,281	122	554	50
3	4	147	49 h	13 ms	13,800,000	7,419	14,190	292
3	6	459	-	214 ms	-	88,671	122,010	916
3	8	1,059	-	3 s	-	508,851	612,630	2,116
4	2	61	812 s	3 ms	305,000	459	3, 262	120
4	4	812	-	388 ms	-	145,780	513,564	1,622
4	6	3,962	-	82 s	-	4,350,292	11,347,152	7,922
4	8	12,400	-	2,971 s	-	46, 198,188	107,561,812	24,798
5	2	141	-	6 ms	-	2,399	17,482	280
5	4	4,244	-	33 s	-	3,318,662	14,692,874	8,486
6	2	335	-	25 ms	-	14,327	97,898	668

The simple policy iteration algorithm can only handle a limited number of states. For the labelled Markov chain with 26 states ($N = 3$ and $K = 2$) the simple policy iteration algorithm takes four seconds, while our new algorithm takes one millisecond. The speed-up is more than 4,000 times. For the labelled Markov chain with 61 states ($N = 4$ and $K = 2$), the simple policy iteration algorithm runs in 812 s, while our new algorithm takes three milliseconds. The speed-up of the new algorithm is 30,000 times. The biggest system the simple policy iteration algorithm can handle is the one with 147 states ($N = 3$ and $K = 4$) and it takes more than 49 h. In contrast, our new algorithm terminates within 13 ms. That makes the new algorithm seven orders of magnitude faster than the state of the art algorithm. This example also shows that the new algorithm can handle systems with at least 12,400 states.

In the second example, we model two dies, one using a fair coin and the other one using a biased coin. The goal is to compute the probabilistic bisimilarity distance between these two dies. An implementation of the die algorithm is part of PRISM. The resulting labelled Markov chain has 20 states.

As there are only 30 non-trivial distances, we run the simple policy iteration algorithm as step 3. The new algorithm is about 46 times faster than the original algorithm.

$\|S\|$	D_0+SPI	$D_0 + D_1 +$SPI	Speed-up	Non-trivial	$\|D_0\|$	$\|D_1\|$	$\|S_1^2\|$
20	5.55 s	0.12 s	46.25	30	20	350	198

7 Small Distances

As we have discussed in Sect. 5, for systems of which the number of non-trivial distances is so large that computing all of them is infeasible, we have to find alternative ways. In practice, as we only identify the state pairs with small distances, we can cut down the number of non-trivial distances by only computing those with small distances.

To compute the non-trivial distances smaller than a positive number, ε, we use the following algorithm.

1. Decide distance zero.
2. Decide distance one.
3. Compute the query set

$$Q = \{\, (s,t) \in S^2 \setminus (D_0 \cup D_1) \mid \Delta(d)(s,t) \leq \varepsilon \,\}$$

where

$$d(s,t) = \begin{cases} 1 \text{ if } (s,t) \in D_1 \\ 0 \text{ otherwise} \end{cases}$$

4. Simple partial policy iteration for Q.

The first two steps remain the same. In step 3, we compute a query set Q that contains all state pairs with distances no greater than ε, as shown in Proposition 6. In step 4, we use this set as the query set to run the simple partial policy iteration algorithm by Bacci et al. [2].

Proposition 6. *Let d be the distance function defined in step 3. For all $(s,t) \in S^2 \setminus (D_0 \cup D_1)$, if $\boldsymbol{\mu}(\Delta)(s,t) \leq \varepsilon$, then $\Delta(d)(s,t) \leq \varepsilon$.*

Given that we not only decide distance zero, but also distance one, before running simple partial policy iteration, the correctness of the simple partial policy iteration algorithm in the augmented setting needs an adjusted proof.

As we have seen before, step 1 and 2 take polynomial time. In step 3, computing $\Delta(d)$ corresponds to solving a minimum cost network flow problem. Such a problem can be solved in polynomial time using, for example, Orlin's network simplex algorithm [24]. As we have shown in [28], step 4 takes at least exponential time in the worst case. Therefore, the overall algorithm is exponential time.

We consider the randomized quicksort algorithm, an implementation of which is part of jpf-probabilistic [31]. The input of the algorithm is the list to be sorted. The list of size 6 gives rise to a labelled Markov chain with 82 states. We compare the running time of the new algorithm for small distances ($D_0 + D_1 + Q$ + SPPI) to the original algorithm (D_0 + SPI) and the new algorithm presented in Sect. 6 ($D_0 + D_1$ + SPI). The original algorithm (D_0 + SPI) takes about 14 h, the new algorithm which incorporates the decision procedure of distance one takes less than 7 h. For $\varepsilon = 0.1$, the new algorithm for small distances takes 57 min. This makes it about 7 times faster than the algorithm presented in Sect. 6 and about 15 times faster than the original simple policy iteration algorithm. For $\varepsilon = 0.01$, the new algorithm for small distances takes even less time, namely 41 min. As can be seen in the table below, the total number of non-trivial distances is 2,300. The simple partial policy iteration algorithm starts with the query set Q but may have to compute the distances of other state pairs as well. The total number of state pairs considered by the simple partial policy iteration algorithm can be found in the column labelled Total.

ε	$D_0 + D_1 + Q$ + SPPI	$\lvert Q \rvert$	Total	Non-trivial
0.1	57 min	96	1,002	2,300
0.01	41 min	84	842	2,300

8 Approximation Algorithm

We propose another solution to deal with a large number of non-trivial distances by approximating the distances rather than computing the exact values. To approximate the distances such that the approximate values differ from the exact ones by at most α, a positive number, we use the following algorithm.

1. Decide distance zero.
2. Decide distance one.

3. $l(s,t) = \begin{cases} 1 \text{ if } (s,t) \in D_1 \\ 0 \text{ otherwise} \end{cases}$

$u(s,t) = \begin{cases} 0 \text{ if } (s,t) \in D_0 \\ 1 \text{ otherwise} \end{cases}$

```
repeat
  for each (s,t) ∈ S² \ (D₀ ∪ D₁)
    if l(s,t) ≠ u(s,t)
      l(s,t) = Δ(l)(s,t)
      u(s,t) = Δ(u)(s,t)
until ||l − u|| ≤ α
```

Again, the first two steps remain the same. Step 3 contains the new approximation algorithm called *distance iteration* (DI). In this step, we define two distance functions, a lower-bound l and an upper-bound u. We repeatedly apply Δ to these two functions until the difference of the non-trivial distances in these two functions is smaller than the threshold α. For each state pair we end up with an interval of at most size α in which their distance lies. To prove the algorithm correct, we modify the function Δ defining the probabilistic bisimilarity distances slightly as follows.

Definition 8. *The function* $\Delta_0 : [0,1]^{S^2} \to [0,1]^{S^2}$ *is defined by*

$$\Delta_0(d)(s,t) = \begin{cases} 0 & \text{if } (s,t) \in D_0 \\ \Delta(d)(s,t) & \text{otherwise} \end{cases}$$

Some properties of Δ_0, which are key to the correctness proof of the above algorithm, are collected in the following theorem.

Theorem 6.

(a) The function Δ_0 *is monotone.*
(b) The function Δ_0 *is nonexpansive.*
(c) $\boldsymbol{\mu}(\Delta_0) = \boldsymbol{\mu}(\Delta)$.
(d) $\boldsymbol{\mu}(\Delta_0) = \boldsymbol{\nu}(\Delta_0)$.
(e) $\boldsymbol{\mu}(\Delta_0) = \sup_{m \in \mathbb{N}} \Delta_0^m(d_0)$, *where* $d_0(s,t) = 0$ *for all* $s,t \in S$.
(f) $\boldsymbol{\nu}(\Delta_0) = \inf_{n \in \mathbb{N}} \Delta_0^n(d_1)$, *where* $d_1(s,t) = 1$ *for all* $s,t \in S$.

Let us use randomized quicksort introduced in Sect. 7 and the randomized self-stabilising algorithm due to Herman [14] introduced in Sect. 5 as examples. Recall that for the randomized self-stabilising algorithm, when $N = 7$, the number of non-trivial distances is 11,032, which we are not able to handle using the simple policy iteration algorithm. We apply the approximation algorithm to this model and the randomized quicksort example with 82 states and present the results below. The accuracy α is set to be 0.01.

The approximation algorithm for randomized quicksort runs for about 14 min, which is about 3 to 4 times faster than the algorithm for small distances in Sect. 7. For the randomized self-stabilising algorithm with 128 states, the approximation algorithm terminates in about 54 h. Although the number of non-trivial distances for the randomized self-stabilising algorithm is about 5 times of that of the randomized quicksort, the running time is more than 200 times slower. It is unknown whether this approximation algorithm has exponential running time.

Model	$\lvert S\rvert$	Non-trivial	$D_0 + D_1$+DI
Randomized quicksort	82	2,300	14 min
Randomized self-stabilising algorithm	128	11,032	54 h

9 Conclusion

In this paper, we have presented a decision procedure for probabilistic bisimilarity distance one. This decision procedure provides the basis for three new algorithms to compute and approximate the probabilistic bisimilarity distances of a labelled Markov chain. The first algorithm decides distance zero, then decides distance one, and finally uses simple policy iteration to compute the remaining distances. As shown experimentally, this new algorithm significantly improves the state of the art algorithm that only decides distance zero and then uses simple policy iteration. The second algorithm computes all probabilistic bisimilarity distances that are smaller than some given upper bound, by deciding distance zero, deciding distance one, computing a query set, and running simple partial policy iteration for that query set. This second algorithm can handle labelled Markov chains that have considerably more non-trivial distances than our first algorithm. The third algorithm approximates the probabilistic bisimilarity distances up to a given accuracy, deciding distance zero, deciding distance one and running distance iteration. Also this third algorithm can handle labelled Markov chains that have considerably more non-trivial distances than our first algorithm. Whereas we know that the first two algorithms take at least exponential time in the worst case, the analysis of the running time of the third algorithm has not yet been determined. Moreover, if we are only interested in the probabilistic bisimilarity distances for a few state pairs, with pre-computation of distance zero and one we can exclude the state pairs with trivial distances. We can add the remaining state pairs to a query set and run simple partial policy iteration to get the distances. Alternatively, we can modify the distance iteration algorithm to approximate the distances for the predefined state pairs. The details of these new algorithms will be studied in the future.

Acknowledgements. The authors would like to thank Daniela Petrisan, Eric Ruppert and Dana Scott for discussions related to this research. The authors are also grateful to the referees for their constructive feedback.

References

1. Aceto, L., Ingolfsdottir, A., Larsen, K., Srba, J.: Reactive Systems: Modelling, Specification and Verification. Cambridge University Press, Cambridge (2003)
2. Bacci, G., Bacci, G., Larsen, K.G., Mardare, R.: On-the-fly exact computation of bisimilarity distances. In: Piterman, N., Smolka, S.A. (eds.) TACAS 2013. LNCS, vol. 7795, pp. 1–15. Springer, Heidelberg (2013). https://doi.org/10.1007/978-3-642-36742-7_1
3. Bacci, G., Bacci, G., Larsen, K.G., Mardare, R.: On the metric-based approximate minimization of Markov chains. In: Chatzigiannakis, I., Indyk, P., Kuhn, F., Muscholl, A. (eds.) Proceedings of the 44th International Colloquium on Automata, Languages, and Programming, Warsaw, Poland, July 2017. Leibniz International Proceedings in Informatics, vol. 80, pp. 104:1–104:14. Schloss Dagstuhl - Leibniz-Zentrum für Informatik (2017)
4. Baier, C.: Polynomial time algorithms for testing probabilistic bisimulation and simulation. In: Alur, R., Henzinger, T.A. (eds.) CAV 1996. LNCS, vol. 1102, pp. 50–61. Springer, Heidelberg (1996). https://doi.org/10.1007/3-540-61474-5_57
5. Bellman, R.: A Markovian decision process. J. Math. Mech. **6**(5), 679–684 (1957)
6. van Breugel, F.: On behavioural pseudometrics and closure ordinals. Inf. Process. Lett. **112**(18), 715–718 (2012)
7. van Breugel, F.: Probabilistic bisimilarity distances. ACM SIGLOG News **4**(4), 33–51 (2017)
8. Chen, D., van Breugel, F., Worrell, J.: On the complexity of computing probabilistic bisimilarity. In: Birkedal, L. (ed.) FoSSaCS 2012. LNCS, vol. 7213, pp. 437–451. Springer, Heidelberg (2012). https://doi.org/10.1007/978-3-642-28729-9_29
9. Davey, B., Priestley, H.: Introduction to Lattices and Order. Cambridge University Press, Cambridge (2002)
10. Derisavi, S., Hermanns, H., Sanders, W.: Optimal state-space lumping in Markov chains. In. Process. Lett. **87**(6), 309–315 (2003)
11. Desharnais, J., Gupta, V., Jagadeesan, R., Panangaden, P.: Metrics for labeled Markov systems. In: Baeten, J.C.M., Mauw, S. (eds.) CONCUR 1999. LNCS, vol. 1664, pp. 258–273. Springer, Heidelberg (1999). https://doi.org/10.1007/3-540-48320-9_19
12. Giacalone, A., Jou, C.-C., Smolka, S.: Algebraic reasoning for probabilistic concurrent systems. In: Proceedings of the IFIP WG 2.2/2.3 Working Conference on Programming Concepts and Methods, Sea of Gallilee, Israel, April 1990, pp. 443–458. North-Holland (1990)
13. Helmink, L., Sellink, M.P.A., Vaandrager, F.W.: Proof-checking a data link protocol. In: Barendregt, H., Nipkow, T. (eds.) TYPES 1993. LNCS, vol. 806, pp. 127–165. Springer, Heidelberg (1994). https://doi.org/10.1007/3-540-58085-9_75
14. Herman, T.: Probabilistic self-stabilization. Inf. Process. Lett. **35**(2), 63–67 (1990)
15. Itai, A., Rodeh, M.: Symmetry breaking in distributed networks. Inf. Comput. **88**(1), 60–87 (1990)
16. Katoen, J.-P., Kemna, T., Zapreev, I., Jansen, D.N.: Bisimulation minimisation mostly speeds up probabilistic model checking. In: Grumberg, O., Huth, M. (eds.) TACAS 2007. LNCS, vol. 4424, pp. 87–101. Springer, Heidelberg (2007). https://doi.org/10.1007/978-3-540-71209-1_9
17. Khachiyan, L.: A polynomial algorithm in linear programming. Sov. Math. Dokl. **20**(1), 191–194 (1979)

18. Klee, V., Witzgall, C.: Facets and vertices of transportation polytopes. In: Dantzig, G., Veinott, A. (eds.) Proceedings of 5th Summer Seminar on the Mathematis of the Decision Sciences, Stanford, CA, USA, July/August 1967. Lectures in Applied Mathematics, vol. 11, pp. 257–282. AMS (1967)
19. Knuth, D., Yao, A.: The complexity of nonuniform random number generation. In: Traub, J. (ed.) Proceedings of a Symposium on New Directions and Recent Results in Algorithms and Complexity, Pittsburgh, PA, USA, April 1976, pp. 375–428. Academic Press (1976)
20. Kwiatkowska, M., Norman, G., Parker, D.: PRISM 4.0: verification of probabilistic real-time systems. In: Gopalakrishnan, G., Qadeer, S. (eds.) CAV 2011. LNCS, vol. 6806, pp. 585–591. Springer, Heidelberg (2011). https://doi.org/10.1007/978-3-642-22110-1_47
21. Larsen, K., Skou, A.: Bisimulation through probabilistic testing. In: Proceedings of the 16th Annual ACM Symposium on Principles of Programming Languages, Austin, TX, USA, January 1989, pp. 344–352. ACM (1989)
22. Milner, R. (ed.): A Calculus of Communicating Systems. LNCS, vol. 92. Springer, Heidelberg (1980). https://doi.org/10.1007/3-540-10235-3
23. Murthy, A., et al.: Approximate bisimulations for sodium channel dynamics. In: Gilbert, D., Heiner, M. (eds.) CMSB 2012. LNCS, pp. 267–287. Springer, Heidelberg (2012). https://doi.org/10.1007/978-3-642-33636-2_16
24. Orlin, J.: A polynomial time primal network simplex algorithm for minimum cost flows. Math. Program. **78**(2), 109–129 (1997)
25. Park, D.: Concurrency and automata on infinite sequences. In: Deussen, P. (ed.) GI-TCS 1981. LNCS, vol. 104, pp. 167–183. Springer, Heidelberg (1981). https://doi.org/10.1007/BFb0017309
26. Sen, P., Deshpande, A., Getoor, L.: Bisimulation-based approximate lifted inference. In: Bilmes, J., Ng, A. (eds.) Proceedings of the 25th Conference on Uncertainty in Artificial Intelligence, Montreal, QC, Canada, pp. 496–505. AUAI Press (2009)
27. Tang, Q., van Breugel, F.: Computing probabilistic bisimilarity distances via policy iteration. In: Desharnais, J., Jagadeesan, R. (eds.) Proceedings of the 27th International Conference on Concurrency Theory, Quebec City, QC, Canada, August 2016. Leibniz International Proceedings in Informatics, vol. 59, pp. 22:1–22:15. Schloss Dagstuhl - Leibniz-Zentrum für Informatik (2016)
28. Tang, Q., van Breugel, F.: Algorithms to compute probabilistic bisimilarity distances for labelled Markov chains. In: Meyer, R., Nestmann, U. (eds.) Proceedings of the 28th International Conference on Concurrency Theory, Berlin, Germany, September 2017. Leibniz International Proceedings in Informatics, vol. 85, pp. 27:1–27:16. Schloss Dagstuhl - Leibniz-Zentrum für Informatik (2017)
29. Tarski, A.: A lattice-theoretic fixed point theorem and its applications. Pac. J. Math. **5**(2), 285–309 (1955)
30. Valmari, A., Franceschinis, G.: Simple $O(m \log n)$ time Markov chain lumping. In: Esparza, J., Majumdar, R. (eds.) TACAS 2010. LNCS, vol. 6015, pp. 38–52. Springer, Heidelberg (2010). https://doi.org/10.1007/978-3-642-12002-2_4
31. Zhang, X., van Breugel, F.: Model checking randomized algorithms with Java PathFinder. In: Proceedings of the 7th International Conference on the Quantitative Evaluation of Systems, Williamsburg, VA, USA, September 2010, pp. 157–158. IEEE (2010)

Author Index

www.ingramcontent.com/pod-product-compliance
Lightning Source LLC
LaVergne TN
LVHW062151200926
848484LV00007B/1900
* 9 7 8 1 0 1 3 2 7 0 9 9 4 *